Lecture Notes in Computer Sc

Commenced Publication in 1973
Founding and Former Series Editors:
Gerhard Goos, Juris Hartmanis, and Jan van Leeuwen

Advanced Research in Computing and Software Science

Subline of Lectures Notes in Computer Science

Maciej Koutny Irek Ulidowski (Eds.)

CONCUR 2012 – Concurrency Theory

23rd International Conference, CONCUR 2012
Newcastle upon Tyne, UK, September 4-7, 2012
Proceedings

Springer

Volume Editors

Maciej Koutny
Newcastle University
School of Computing Science
Claremont Tower
Claremont Road
Newcastle upon Tyne, NE1 7RU, UK
E-mail: maciej.koutny@ncl.ac.uk

Irek Ulidowski
University of Leicester
Department of Computer Science
Computer Science Building
University Road
Leicester, LE1 7RH, UK
E-mail: i.ulidowski@mcs.le.ac.uk

ISSN 0302-9743
e-ISSN 1611-3349
ISBN 978-3-642-32939-5
e-ISBN 978-3-642-32940-1
DOI 10.1007/978-3-642-32940-1
Springer Heidelberg Dordrecht London New York

Library of Congress Control Number: 2012945070

CR Subject Classification (1998): F.3, D.2.4, D.2, D.3, C.2.4, C.2, H.4

LNCS Sublibrary: SL 1 – Theoretical Computer Science and General Issues

Typesetting: Camera-ready by author, data conversion by Scientific Publishing Services, Chennai, India

Printed on acid-free paper

Springer is part of Springer Science+Business Media (www.springer.com)

Preface

This volume contains the proceedings of the 23rd International Conference on Concurrency Theory (CONCUR 2012) held in Newcastle upon Tyne, UK, during September 4–7, 2012. The aim of the CONCUR conference series is to bring together researchers, developers and students in order to advance the theory of concurrency and to promote its applications.

This edition of the conference was an official event of The Alan Turing Year, a centenary celebration of the life and work of Alan Turing. To mark this special occasion, the conference programme included two invited talks on the historical context of his work and on its relevance to the current developments in the field of concurrency theory, presented by Brian Randell (Newcastle University) and Jos Baeten (CWI), respectively. The conference programme was further greatly enhanced by the invited talks by Gordon Plotkin (University of Edinburgh) and Peter Sewell (University of Cambridge).

CONCUR 2012 attracted 97 submissions, and we would like to thank everyone who submitted. Each submission was reviewed by at least three reviewers who provided detailed evaluations as well as constructive comments and recommendations. After careful reviewing and extensive discussions, the Programme Committee decided to accept 35 papers for presentation at the conference. We would like to thank the Programme Committee members and all the additional reviewers for their truly professional work and strong commitment to the success of CONCUR 2012. We are also grateful to the authors for taking into account the comments and suggestions provided by the referees during the preparation of the final versions of their papers.

The conference was organised jointly with the 22nd International Workshop on Power and Timing Modeling, Optimization and Simulation (PATMOS 2012) and the 7th Symposium on Trustworthy Global Computing (TGC 2012). In addition, CONCUR included eight satellite workshops:

- Combined 19th International Workshop on Expressiveness in Concurrency and 9th Workshop on Structural Operational Semantics (EXPRESS/SOS), organised by Bas Luttik and Michel Reniers
- 4th Workshop on Games for Design, Verification and Synthesis (GASICS), organised by Kim G. Larsen, Nicolas Markey, Jean-François Raskin, and Wolfgang Thomas
- First International Workshop on Hybrid Systems and Biology (HSB), organised by Luca Bortolussi
- Workshop on Trustworthy Cyber-Physical Systems (TCPS), organised by John Fitzgerald, Terrence Mak, Alexander Romanovsky, and Alex Yakovlev
- Young Researchers Workshop on Concurrency Theory (YR-CONCUR), organised by Benedikt Bollig

- 11th International Workshop on Foundations of Coordination Languages and Self-Adaptive Systems (FOCLASA), organised by Natallia Kokash, and António Ravara
- 6th Workshop on Membrane Computing and Biologically Inspired Process Calculi (MeCBIC), organised by Bogdan Aman, and Gabriel Ciobanu
- Trends in Concurrency Theory (TRENDS), organised by Jos Baeten, and Bas Luttik

We would like to thank everyone who contributed to the organisation of CONCUR 2012, especially the workshop organisation chairs Jason Steggles and Emilio Tuosto, and the workshop organisers. Furthermore, we thank Microsoft Research Cambridge, Formal Methods Europe, the School of Computing Science and Centre for Software Reliability of Newcastle University, and the Department of Computer Science of the University of Leicester for their financial support.

We are also grateful to Andrei Voronkov for the conference software system EasyChair, which was extremely helpful for the Programme Committee discussions and the production of the proceedings.

June 2012

Maciej Koutny
Irek Ulidowski

Organisation

Steering Committee

Roberto Amadio	Université Paris Diderot, France
Jos Baeten	CWI Amsterdam, The Netherlands
Eike Best	Universität Oldenburg, Germany
Kim Larsen	Aalborg University, Denmark
Ugo Montanari	Università di Pisa, Italy
Scott Smolka	SUNY, Stony Brook University, USA

Programme Committee

Luca Aceto	Reykjavik University, Iceland
Eike Best	Universität Oldenburg, Germany
Roberto Bruni	Università di Pisa, Italy
Tomáš Brázdil	Masaryk University, Czech Republic
Luis Caires	Universidade Nova de Lisboa, Portugal
Luca Cardelli	Microsoft Research, UK
Gabriel Ciobanu	Romanian Academy, Romania
Pedro R. D'Argenio	Universidad Nacional de Córdoba, Argentina
Philippe Darondeau	INRIA, France
Luca De Alfaro	University of California, Santa Cruz, USA
Rocco De Nicola	IMT Lucca, Italy
Wan Fokkink	Vrije Universiteit Amsterdam, The Netherlands
Paul Gastin	ENS Cachan, France
Keijo Heljanko	Aalto University, Finland
Jane Hillston	University of Edinburgh, UK
Jetty Kleijn	Leiden University, The Netherlands
Maciej Koutny	Newcastle University, UK
Barbara König	Universität Duisburg-Essen, Germany
Cosimo Laneve	University of Bologna, Italy
Gavin Lowe	University of Oxford, UK
Mohammadreza Mousavi	Eindhoven University of Technology, The Netherlands
Uwe Nestmann	Technische Universität Berlin, Germany
Catuscia Palamidessi	Ecole Polytechnique, France
Wojciech Penczek	IPI PAN and University of Podlasie, Poland
Iain Phillips	Imperial College London, UK
Shaz Qadeer	Microsoft Research, USA
Jean-François Raskin	Université Libre de Bruxelles, Belgium

Philippe Schnoebelen	LSV - CNRS and ENS Cachan, France
Irek Ulidowski	University of Leicester, UK
Franck Van Breugel	York University, Canada
Rob Van Glabbeek	NICTA, Australia
Björn Victor	Uppsala University, Sweden
Shoji Yuen	Nagoya University, Japan

Conference Co-chairs

Maciej Koutny	Newcastle University, UK
Irek Ulidowski	University of Leicester, UK

Workshop Co-chairs

Jason Steggles	Newcastle University, UK
Emilio Tuosto	University of Leicester, UK

Organising Committee

Joan Atkinson	Newcastle University, UK
Denise Carr	Newcastle University, UK
Roy Crole	University of Leicester, UK
Victor Khomenko	Newcastle University, UK
Delong Shang	Newcastle University, UK
Claire Smith	Newcastle University, UK
Jason Steggles	Newcastle University, UK
Emilio Tuosto	University of Leicester, UK
Irek Ulidowski	University of Leicester, UK
Alexandre Yakovlev	Newcastle University, UK

Additional Reviewers

Agrigoroaiei, Oana
Akshay, S.
Aldini, Alessandro
Alglave, Jade
Aman, Bogdan
Babiak, Tomas
Badouel, Eric
Bartoletti, Massimo
Berdine, Josh
Berger, Martin
Bernardi, Giovanni
Bernardo, Marco
Berwanger, Dietmar
Bettini, Lorenzo
Birgisson, Arnar
Blume, Christoph
Bollig, Benedikt
Bonchi, Filippo
Bono, Viviana
Borgstrom, Johannes
Bradley, Jeremy
Bravetti, Mario

Bruggink, Harrie Jan Sander
Bulling, Nils
Carayol, Arnaud
Chatzikokolakis, Konstantinos
Chen, Xiwen
Cheney, James
Cimini, Matteo
Coppo, Mario
Costa Seco, João
Cyriac, Aiswarya
Czerwiński, Wojciech
De Boer, Frank
Demangeon, Romain
Deng, Yuxin
Dias, Ricardo
Dingel, Juergen
Doyen, Laurent
Dubrovin, Jori
Emmi, Michael
Esik, Zoltan
Ferreira, Carla
Ferrer Fioriti, Luis María
Finkel, Alain
Fleischhack, Hans
Forejt, Vojtech
Fournet, Cedric
Fu, Yuxi
Furusawa, Hitoshi
Gan, Xiang
Ganty, Pierre
Garg, Deepak
Gay, Simon
Gazda, Maciej
Gebler, Daniel
Geeraerts, Gilles
Giachino, Elena
Gibson-Robinson, Thomas
Giro, Sergio
Golas, Ulrike
Goltz, Ursula
Gorrieri, Roberto
Gotsman, Alexey
Grossman, Dan
Hahn, Ernst Moritz
Haller, Philipp
Harju, Tero
Hasuo, Ichiro
Helouet, Loic
Hermida, Claudio
Heunen, Chris
Hicks, Michael
Hildebrandt, Thomas
Hirschkoff, Daniel
Hirschowitz, Tom
Holik, Lukas
Honsell, Furio
Hoogeboom, Hendrik Jan
Horne, Ross
Huisman, Marieke
Hym, Samuel
Hüttel, Hans
Imai, Keigoi
Jacobs, Bart
Jancar, Petr
Janicki, Ryszard
Kerstan, Henning
Khomenko, Victor
Kiefer, Stefan
Klaedtke, Felix
Knapik, Michał
Knight, Sophia
Koutavas, Vasileios
Krcal, Jan
Kretinsky, Jan
Kucera, Antonin
Kuznetsov, Petr
Kähkönen, Kari
Köpf, Boris
Küfner, Philipp
Křetinský, Jan
Křetinský, Mojmír
Laarman, Alfons
Labella, Anna
Lammich, Peter
Lanese, Ivan
Lange, Julien
Laroussinie, Francois
Lasota, Sławomir
Launiainen, Tuomas
Lding, Christof

Lee, Matías D.
Liang, Hongjin
Lluch Lafuente, Alberto
Lodaya, Kamal
Long, Huan
Loreti, Michele
Luttik, Bas
Mardare, Radu
Markey, Nicolas
Mayr, Richard
Meski, Artur
Meyer, Roland
Mikučionis, Marius
Monmege, Benjamin
Monniaux, David
Morvan, Christophe
Mukund, Madhavan
Nakata, Akio
Neuhäußer, Martin R.
Norman, Gethin
Obdrzalek, Jan
Ogawa, Mizuhito
Olesen, Mads Chr.
Ouaknine, Joel
Padovani, Luca
Panangaden, Prakash
Parker, David
Pashalidis, Andreas
Peters, Kirstin
Pinna, G. Michele
Pérez, Jorge A.
Półrola, Agata
Randour, Mickael
Rehak, Vojtech
Ridge, Tom
Roscoe, Bill
Ruppert, Eric
Sack, Joshua
Sarkar, Susmit
Sawa, Zdenek
Schmitz, Sylvain
Seki, Hiroyuki
Serre, Olivier
Sokolova, Ana
Sproston, Jeremy
Steffen, Martin
Steggles, Jason
Stevens, Perdita
Stirling, Colin
Strejcek, Jan
Stückrath, Jan
Sutre, Grégoire
Swamy, Nikhil
Sznajder, Nathalie
Szreter, Maciej
Talupur, Murali
Tanabe, Yoshinori
Tarasyuk, Igor
Toninho, Bernardo
Tuosto, Emilio
Turon, Aaron
Van Bakel, Steffen
Vandin, Andrea
Varghese, Thomas M.
Vicary, Jamie
Vogler, Walter
Vytiniotis, Dimitrios
Weber, Tjark
Wieringa, Siert
Wilkeit, Elke
Willemse, Tim
Winkowski, Józef
Winskel, Glynn
Worrell, James
Zanella Béguelin, Santiago
Zantema, Hans
Zavattaro, Gianluigi
Zeitoun, Marc
Zielonka, Wiesław
Zufferey, Damien

Table of Contents

Invited Talks

Reachability Analysis

Qualitative and Timed Systems

Behavioural Equivalences

Temporal Logics

Session Types

Abstraction

Mobility and Space in Process Algebras

Stochastic Systems

Probabilistic Systems

Petri Nets and Non-sequential Semantics

Verification

Decidability

Turing Meets Milner

Jos C.M. Baeten[1,2], Bas Luttik[2,3], and Paul van Tilburg[2]

[1] Centrum Wiskunde & Informatica (CWI),
P.O. Box 94079, 1090 GB Amsterdam, The Netherlands
[2] Division of Computer Science, Eindhoven University of Technology,
P.O. Box 513, 5600 MB Eindhoven, The Netherlands
[3] Department of Computer Science, Vrije Universiteit Amsterdam,
De Boelelaan 1081a, 1081 HV Amsterdam, The Netherlands
{j.c.m.baeten,s.p.luttik,p.j.a.v.tilburg}@tue.nl

Abstract. We enhance the notion of a computation of the classical theory of computing with the notion of interaction from concurrency theory. In this way, we enhance a Turing machine as a model of computation to a Reactive Turing Machine that is an abstract model of a computer as it is used nowadays, always interacting with the user and the world.

1 Introduction

What is a computation? This is a central question in the theory of computing, dating back to the work of Alan Turing in 1936 [24]. The classical answer is that a computation is given by a Turing machine, with the input given on its tape at the beginning, after which a deterministic sequence of steps takes place, leaving the output on the tape at the end. A computable function is a function of which the transformation of input to output can be computed by a Turing machine.

A Turing machine can serve in this way as a basic model of a computation, but cannot serve as a basic model of a computer. Well, it could up to the advent of the terminal in the 1970s. Before that, input was given as a stack of punch cards at the start, and output of a computation appeared as a printout later. The terminal made direct interaction with the computer possible. Nowadays, a computer is interacting continuously, with the user at the click of a mouse or with many other computers all over the world through the Internet.

An execution of a computer is thus not just a series of steps of a computation, but also involves interaction. It cannot be modeled as a function, and has inherent nondeterminism. In this paper, we make the notion of an execution precise, and compare this to the notion of a computation. To illustrate the difference between a computation and an execution, we can say that a Turing machine cannot fly an airplane, but a computer can. An automatic pilot cannot know all weather conditions en route beforehand, but can react to changing conditions run-time.

Computability theory is firmly grounded in automata theory and formal language theory. It progresses from the study of finite automata to pushdown automata and Turing machines. Of these different classes of automata, it studies

M. Koutny and I. Ulidowski (Eds.): CONCUR 2012, LNCS 7454, pp. 1–20, 2012.

the languages, the sets of strings, induced by them. We can view a language as an equivalence class of automata (under language equivalence).

The notion of interaction has been studied extensively in concurrency theory and process theory exemplified by the work of Robin Milner [17]. Milner has played a central role in the development of concurrency theory. He proposed a powerful parallel composition operator that is used to compose systems in parallel, including their interaction [19]. The semantics of concurrency theory is mostly given in terms of transition systems, which are almost like automata. However, there are important differences.

First of all, a notion of final state, of termination, is often missing in concurrency theory. The idea is that concurrency theory often deals with so-called *reactive systems*, which need not terminate but are always on, reacting to stimuli from the environment. As a result, termination is often neglected in concurrency theory, but is nevertheless an important ingredient, as shown and fully worked out in [1]. Using this presentation of concurrency theory as a starting point, we obtain a full correspondence with automata theory: a finite transition system is exactly a finite automaton. On the other hand, we stress that we fully incorporate the reactive systems approach of concurrency theory: non-terminating behaviour is also relevant behaviour, which is taken into account.

A second difference between automata theory and concurrency theory is that transition systems need not be finite. Still, studying the subclass of finite transition systems yields useful insights for the extension to pushdown automata and Turing machines.

The third and main difference between automata theory and concurrency theory is that language equivalence is too coarse to capture a notion of interaction. Looking at an automaton as a language acceptor, acceptance of a string represents a particular computation of the automaton, and the language is the set of all its computations. The language-theoretic interpretation abstracts from the moments of choice within an automaton. For instance, it does not distinguish between, on the one hand, the automaton that first accepts an a and subsequently chooses between accepting a b or a c, and, on the other hand, the automaton that starts with a choice between accepting ab and accepting ac. As a consequence, the language-theoretic interpretation is only suitable under the assumption that an automaton is a stand-alone computational device; it is unsuitable if some form of interaction of the automaton with its environment (user, other automata running in parallel, etc.) may influence the course of computation.

Therefore, other notions of equivalence are studied in concurrency theory, capturing more of the branching structure of an automaton. Prominent among these is bisimulation equivalence [21]. When silent steps are taken into account, the preferred variant is *branching bisimilarity*, arguably preserving all relevant moments of choice in a system [15]. Moreover, it is important to keep track of possible divergencies as advocated in the work on CSP [16].

In this paper we study the notion of a computation, taking interaction into account. We define, next to the notion of a computable function, the notion of an executable process. An executable process is a behaviour that can be exhibited by a computer (interacting with its environment). An executable process is a divergence-preserving branching bisimulation equivalence class of transition systems defined by a Reactive Turing Machine. A Reactive Turing Machine is an adaptation of the classical Turing Machine that can properly deal with ubiquitous interaction. Leading up to the definition of the Reactive Turing Machine, we reconsider some of the standard results from automata theory when automata are considered modulo *divergence-preserving branching bisimilarity* instead of language equivalence.

There have been attempts before to add a notion of interaction to computability theory, see e.g. [12,10,11]. These attempts do not take full advantage of the results of concurrency theory. We find that interaction is still not given the status it deserves; in all the formalisations of interaction machines we could find, the notion of interaction itself is still very implicit. It is added as an asymmetric notion (e.g., by allowing an algorithm to query its environment, or by assuming that the environment periodically writes a write-only input tape and reads a read-only output tape of a Turing machine). The focus remains completely on the computational aspect, and interaction is included as a second-class citizen, only to the extent that it may have a benificial effect on computational power.

This paper is an update of [7] with results from [23], [8] and [6].

In Section 2 we briefly review the process theory we use. In Section 3 we consider *finite-state processes*, defined as divergence-preserving branching bisimulation equivalence classes of finite labeled transition systems (finite automata). The section illustrates the correspondence between finite automata and linear recursive specifications that can be thought of as the process-theoretic counterpart of regular grammars.

In Section 4 we consider *pushdown processes*, defined as divergence-preserving branching bisimulation equivalence classes of labeled transition systems associated with pushdown automata. We investigate the correspondence between pushdown processes and processes definable by sequential recursive specifications, which can be thought of as the process-theoretic counterpart of context-free grammars. We show this correspondence is not optimal, and define a new grammar that fits better, based on the universality of the stack process.

In Section 5 we define *executable processes*, defined as divergence-preserving branching bisimulation equivalence classes of labeled transition systems associated with Reactive Turing Machines. We highlight the relationship of computable functions and executable processes, laying the foundations of executability theory alongside computability theory. We define a new grammar for executable processes, based on the universality of the queue process.

2 Process Theory

In this section we briefly recap the basic definitions of the process algebra TCP^*_τ (Theory of Communicating Processes with silent step and iteration). This process algebra has a rich syntax, allowing to express all key ingredients of concurrency theory and includes a full incorporation of regular expressions. It also has a rich theory, fully worked out in [1].

Syntax. We presuppose a finite *action alphabet* $\mathcal{A}$, and a countably infinite set of *names* $\mathcal{N}$. The actions in $\mathcal{A}$ denote the basic events that a process may perform. We furthermore presuppose a finite *data alphabet* $\mathcal{D}$, a finite set $\mathcal{C}$ of *channels*, and assume that $\mathcal{A}$ includes special actions $c?d$, $c!d$, $c!?d$ ($d \in \mathcal{D}$, $c \in \mathcal{C}$), which, intuitively, denote the events that datum d is received, sent, or communicated along channel c.

Let $\mathcal{N}'$ be a finite subset of $\mathcal{N}$. The set of *process expressions* $\mathcal{P}$ over $\mathcal{A}$ and $\mathcal{N}'$ is generated by the following grammar:

$$p ::= \mathbf{0} \mid \mathbf{1} \mid a.p \mid \tau.p \mid p \cdot p \mid p^* \mid p+p \mid p \parallel p \mid \partial_c(p) \mid \tau_c(p) \mid N \\ (a \in \mathcal{A}, N \in \mathcal{N}', c \in \mathcal{C}) \ .$$

Let us briefly comment on the operators in this syntax. The constant $\mathbf{0}$ denotes inaction or *deadlock*, the unsuccessfully terminated process. It can be thought of as the automaton with one initial state that is not final and has no transitions. The constant $\mathbf{1}$ denotes the successfully terminated process. It can be thought of as the automaton with one initial state that is final, without transitions. For each action $a \in \mathcal{A}$ there is a unary operator $a.$ denoting action prefix; the process denoted by $a.p$ can do an a-transition to the process denoted by p. The τ-transitions of a process will, in the semantics below, be treated as unobservable, and as such they are the process-theoretic counterparts of the so-called λ- or ϵ-transitions in the theory of automata and formal languages. We write $\mathcal{A}_\tau$ for $\mathcal{A} \cup \{\tau\}$. The binary operator $\cdot$ denotes *sequential composition*. The unary operator * is iteration or *Kleene star*. The binary operator $+$ denotes *alternative composition* or *choice*. The binary operator $\parallel$ denotes *parallel composition*; actions of both arguments are interleaved, and in addition a communication $c!?d$ of a datum d on channel c can take place if one argument can do an input action $c?d$ that matches an output action $c!d$ of the other component. The unary operator $\partial_c(p)$ encapsulates the process p in such a way that all input actions $c?d$ and output actions $c!d$ are blocked (for all data) so that communication is enforced. Finally, the unary operator $\tau_c(p)$ denotes abstraction from communication over channel c in p by renaming all communications $c!?d$ to τ-transitions.

Let $\mathcal{N}'$ be a finite subset of $\mathcal{N}$, used to define processes by means of (recursive) equations. A *recursive specification* E over $\mathcal{N}'$ is a set of equations of the form $N \stackrel{\text{def}}{=} p$ with as left-hand side a name N and as right-hand side a process expression p. It is required that a recursive specification E contains, for every $N \in \mathcal{N}'$, precisely one equation with N as left-hand side.

One way to formalize our operational intuitions for the syntactic constructions of TCP^*_τ, is to associate with every process expression a labeled transition system.

Definition 1 (Labeled Transition System). *A labeled transition system L is defined as a four-tuple $(\mathcal{S}, \rightarrow, \uparrow, \downarrow)$ where:*

1. *$\mathcal{S}$ is a set of states,*
2. *$\rightarrow \subseteq \mathcal{S} \times \mathcal{A}_\tau \times \mathcal{S}$ is an $\mathcal{A}_\tau$-labeled* transition relation *on $\mathcal{S}$,*

3. $\uparrow \in \mathcal{S}$ *is the* initial *state,*
4. $\downarrow \subseteq \mathcal{S}$ *is the set of* final *states.*

If $(s, a, t) \in \rightarrow$, *we write* $s \xrightarrow{a} t$. *If* s *is a final state, i.e.,* $s \in \downarrow$, *we write* $s\downarrow$.

A labeled transition system with a finite set of states is exactly a finite (non-deterministic) automaton.

We use Structural Operational Semantics [22] to associate a transition relation with process expressions: we let $\rightarrow$ be the $\mathcal{A}_\tau$-labeled transition relation induced on the set of process expressions $\mathcal{P}$ by the operational rules in Table 1. Note that the operational rules presuppose a recursive specification E.

Table 1. Operational rules for TCP^*_τ and a recursive specification E (a ranges over $\mathcal{A}_\tau$, d ranges over $\mathcal{D}$, and c ranges over $\mathcal{C}$)

$$\frac{}{\mathbf{1}\downarrow} \qquad \frac{}{p^*\downarrow} \qquad \frac{}{a.p \xrightarrow{a} p}$$

$$\frac{p \xrightarrow{a} p'}{(p+q) \xrightarrow{a} p'} \qquad \frac{q \xrightarrow{a} q'}{(p+q) \xrightarrow{a} q'} \qquad \frac{p\downarrow}{(p+q)\downarrow} \qquad \frac{q\downarrow}{(p+q)\downarrow}$$

$$\frac{p \xrightarrow{a} p'}{p \cdot q \xrightarrow{a} p' \cdot q} \qquad \frac{p\downarrow \quad q \xrightarrow{a} q'}{p \cdot q \xrightarrow{a} q'} \qquad \frac{p\downarrow \quad q\downarrow}{p \cdot q\downarrow} \qquad \frac{p \xrightarrow{a} p'}{p^* \xrightarrow{a} p' \cdot p^*}$$

$$\frac{p \xrightarrow{a} p'}{p \parallel q \xrightarrow{a} p' \parallel q} \qquad \frac{q \xrightarrow{a} q'}{p \parallel q \xrightarrow{a} p \parallel q'} \qquad \frac{p\downarrow \quad q\downarrow}{p \parallel q\downarrow}$$

$$\frac{p \xrightarrow{c!d} p' \quad q \xrightarrow{c?d} q'}{p \parallel q \xrightarrow{c!?d} p' \parallel q'} \qquad \frac{p \xrightarrow{c?d} p' \quad q \xrightarrow{c!d} q'}{p \parallel q \xrightarrow{c!?d} p' \parallel q'}$$

$$\frac{p \xrightarrow{a} p' \quad a \neq c?d, c!d}{\partial_c(p) \xrightarrow{a} \partial_c(p')} \qquad \frac{p\downarrow}{\partial_c(p)\downarrow}$$

$$\frac{p \xrightarrow{c!?d} p'}{\tau_c(p) \xrightarrow{\tau} \tau_c(p')} \qquad \frac{p \xrightarrow{a} p' \quad a \neq c!?d}{\tau_c(p) \xrightarrow{a} \tau_c(p')} \qquad \frac{p\downarrow}{\tau_c(p)\downarrow}$$

$$\frac{p \xrightarrow{a} p' \quad (N \stackrel{\mathrm{def}}{=} p) \in E}{N \xrightarrow{a} p'} \qquad \frac{p\downarrow \quad (N \stackrel{\mathrm{def}}{=} p) \in E}{N\downarrow}$$

Let $\rightarrow$ be an $\mathcal{A}_\tau$-labeled transition relation on a set $\mathcal{S}$ of states. For $s, s' \in \mathcal{S}$ and $w \in \mathcal{A}^*$ we write $s \overset{w}{\twoheadrightarrow} s'$ if there exist states $s_0, \ldots, s_n \in \mathcal{S}$ and actions $a_1, \ldots, a_n \in \mathcal{A}_\tau$ such that $s = s_0 \xrightarrow{a_1} \cdots \xrightarrow{a_n} s_n = s'$ and w is obtained from $a_1 \cdots a_n$ by omitting all occurrences of τ. ε denotes the empty word. We say a state $t \in \mathcal{S}$ is *reachable* from a state $s \in \mathcal{S}$ if there exists $w \in \mathcal{A}^*$ such that $s \stackrel{w}{\twoheadrightarrow} t$.

Definition 2. *Let E be a recursive specification and let p be a process expression. We define the labeled transition system $\mathcal{T}_E(p) = (\mathcal{S}_p, \rightarrow_p, \uparrow_p, \downarrow_p)$ associated with p and E as follows:*

1. *the set of states $\mathcal{S}_p$ consists of all process expressions reachable from p;*
2. *the transition relation $\rightarrow_p$ is the restriction to $\mathcal{S}_p$ of the transition relation $\rightarrow$ defined on all process expressions by the operational rules in Table 1, i.e., $\rightarrow_p = \rightarrow \cap (\mathcal{S}_p \times \mathcal{A}_\tau \times \mathcal{S}_p)$.*
3. *the process expression p is the initial state, i.e. $\uparrow_p = p$; and*
4. *the set of final states consists of all process expressions $q \in \mathcal{S}_p$ such that $q\downarrow$, i.e., $\downarrow_p = \downarrow \cap \mathcal{S}_p$.*

If we start out from a process expression not containing a name, then the transition system defined by this construction is finite and so is a finite automaton.

Given the set of (possibly infinite) labeled transition systems, we can divide out different equivalence relations on this set. Dividing out language equivalence throws away too much information, as the moments where choices are made are totally lost, and behavior that does not lead to a final state is ignored. An equivalence relation that keeps all relevant information, and has many good properties, is branching bisimulation as proposed by van Glabbeek and Weijland [15]. For motivations to use branching bisimulation as the preferred notion of equivalence, see [13]. Moreover, by taking divergence into account, as advocated e.g. in [16], most of our results do not depend on fairness assumptions. Divergence-preserving branching bisimulation is called branching bisimulation with explicit divergence in [15].

Let $\rightarrow$ be an $\mathcal{A}_\tau$-labeled transition relation, and let $a \in \mathcal{A}_\tau$; we write $s \xrightarrow{(a)} t$ if $s \xrightarrow{a} t$ or $a = \tau$ and $s = t$.

Definition 3 (Divergence-preserving branching bisimilarity). *Let $L_1 = (\mathcal{S}_1, \rightarrow_1, \uparrow_1, \downarrow_1)$ and $L_2 = (\mathcal{S}_2, \rightarrow_2, \uparrow_2, \downarrow_2)$ be labeled transition systems. A* branching bisimulation *from L_1 to L_2 is a binary relation $\mathcal{R} \subseteq \mathcal{S}_1 \times \mathcal{S}_2$ such that $\uparrow_1 \mathcal{R} \uparrow_2$ and, for all states s_1 and s_2, $s_1 \mathcal{R} s_2$ implies*

1. *if $s_1 \xrightarrow{a}_1 s_1'$, then there exist $s_2', s_2'' \in \mathcal{S}_2$ such that $s_2 \stackrel{\varepsilon}{\twoheadrightarrow}_2 s_2'' \xrightarrow{(a)}_2 s_2'$, $s_1 \mathcal{R} s_2''$ and $s_1' \mathcal{R} s_2'$;*
2. *if $s_2 \xrightarrow{a}_2 s_2'$, then there exist $s_1', s_1'' \in \mathcal{S}_1$ such that $s_1 \stackrel{\varepsilon}{\twoheadrightarrow}_1 s_1'' \xrightarrow{(a)}_1 s_1'$, $s_1'' \mathcal{R} s_2$ and $s_1' \mathcal{R} s_2'$;*
3. *if $s_1\downarrow_1$, then there exists s_2' such that $s_2 \stackrel{\varepsilon}{\twoheadrightarrow}_2 s_2'$ and $s_2'\downarrow_2$; and*
4. *if $s_2\downarrow_2$, then there exists s_1' such that $s_1 \stackrel{\varepsilon}{\twoheadrightarrow}_1 s_1'$ and $s_1'\downarrow_1$.*

The labeled transition systems L_1 and L_2 are branching bisimilar *(notation: $L_1 \leftrightarrows_b L_2$) if there exists a branching bisimulation from L_1 to L_2.*

A branching bisimulation $\mathcal{R}$ from L_1 to L_2 is divergence-preserving *if for all states s_1, s_2, $s_1 \mathcal{R} s_2$ implies*

5. *if there exists an infinite sequence* $s_{1,0}, s_{1,1}, s_{1,2}, \ldots$ *such that* $s_1 = s_{1,0}$, $s_{1,i} \xrightarrow{\tau}_1 s_{1,i+1}$ *and* $s_{1,i} \mathcal{R} s_2$ *for all natural numbers* i, *then there exists a state* $s_2{}'$ *such that* $s_2 \xrightarrow{\varepsilon}\!\!\!\!\rightarrow_2 s_2{}'$ *with at least one step and* $s_{1,i} \mathcal{R} s_2{}'$ *for some natural number* i; *and*
6. *if there exists an infinite sequence* $s_{2,0}, s_{2,1}, s_{2,2}, \ldots$ *such that* $s_2 = s_{2,0}$, $s_{2,i} \xrightarrow{\tau}_2 s_{2,i+1}$ *and* $s_1 \mathcal{R} s_{2,i}$ *for all natural numbers* i, *then there exists a state* $s_1{}'$ *such that* $s_1 \xrightarrow{\varepsilon}\!\!\!\!\rightarrow_1 s_1{}'$ *with at least one step and* $s_1{}' \mathcal{R} s_{2,i}$ *for some natural number* i.

Labeled transition systems L_1 *and* L_2 *are* divergence-preserving branching bisimilar *(notation:* $L_1 \leftrightarrow_b^\Delta L_2$*) if there exists a divergence-preserving branching bisimulation from* L_1 *to* L_2.

(Divergence-preserving) branching bisimilarity is an equivalence relation on labeled transition systems [9,14]. A branching bisimulation from a transition system to itself is called a branching bisimulation *on* this transition system. Each transition system has a maximal branching bisimulation, identifying as many states as possible, found as the union of all possible branching bisimulations. Dividing out this maximal branching bisimulation, we get the quotient of the transition system w.r.t. the maximal branching bisimulation. We define the *branching degree* of a state as the cardinality of the set of outgoing edges of its equivalence class in the maximal divergence-preserving branching bisimulation.

A transition system has *finite branching* if all states have a finite branching degree. We say a transition system has *bounded branching* if there exists a natural number $n \geq 0$ such that every state has a branching degree of at most n. Divergence-preserving branching bisimulations respect branching degrees.

3 Regular Processes

A computer with a fixed-size, finite memory is a finite-state system, which can be modeled as a finite automaton. Automata theory starts with the notion of a finite automaton. As nondeterminism is relevant and basic in concurrency theory, we look at a nondeterministic finite automaton. A nondeterministic finite automaton is exactly a finite labeled transition system (see Definition 1).

Two examples of finite automata are given in Figure 1.

A finite automaton $M = (\mathcal{S}, \rightarrow, \uparrow, \downarrow)$ is *deterministic* if, for all states $s, t_1, t_2 \in \mathcal{S}$ and for all actions $a \in \mathcal{A}$, $s \xrightarrow{a} t_1$ and $s \xrightarrow{a} t_2$ implies $t_1 = t_2$, and if $s \xrightarrow{\tau} t_1$, then not $s \xrightarrow{a} t_2$.

The upper automaton in Figure 1 is nondeterministic and has an unreachable c-transition. The lower automaton is deterministic and does not have unreachable transitions.

In the theory of automata and formal languages, finite automata are considered as language acceptors.

Definition 4 (Language equivalence). *The* language $\mathcal{L}(L)$ *accepted by a labeled transition system* $L = (\mathcal{S}, \rightarrow, \uparrow, \downarrow)$ *is defined as*

$$\mathcal{L}(L) = \{w \in \mathcal{A}^* \mid \exists s \in \downarrow \text{ such that } \uparrow \xrightarrow{w}\!\!\!\!\rightarrow s\} .$$

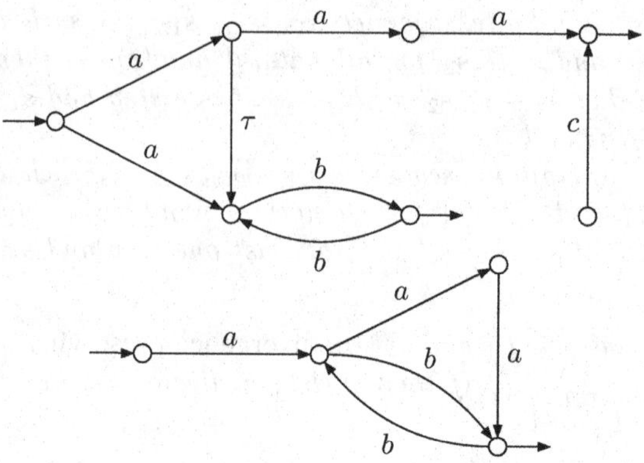

Fig. 1. Two examples of finite automata

Labeled transition systems L_1 *and* L_2 *are* language equivalent *(notation:* $L_1 \equiv L_2$*) if* $\mathcal{L}(L_1) = \mathcal{L}(L_2)$.

The language of both automata in Figure 1 is $\{aaa\} \cup \{ab^{2n-1} \mid n \geq 1\}$; the automata are language equivalent.

A language $L \subseteq \mathcal{A}^*$ accepted by a finite automaton is called a *regular language.* A *regular process* is a divergence-preserving branching bisimilarity class of labeled transition systems that contains a finite automaton.

A standard result in automata theory is that every silent step τ and all nondeterminism can be removed from a finite automaton. These results are no longer valid when we consider finite automata modulo branching bisimulation. Not every regular process has a representation as a finite automaton without τ-transitions, and not every regular process has a representation as a deterministic finite automaton. In fact, it can be proved that there does not exist a finite automaton without τ-transitions that is branching bisimilar with the upper finite automaton in Figure 1. Nor does there exist a deterministic finite automaton branching bisimilar with the upper finite automaton in Figure 1.

Regular expressions. A *regular expression* is a process expression using only the first 7 items in the definition of process syntax above, that is, it does not contain parallel composition, encapsulation, abstraction or recursion. Not every regular process is given by a regular expression, see [18,2]. We show a simple example in Figure 2 of a finite transition system that is not bisimilar to any transition system that can be associated with a regular expression.

However, if we can also use parallel composition and encapsulation, then we can find an expression for every finite automaton, see [5]. Abstraction and recursion are not needed for this result. We can illustrate this with the finite automaton in Figure 2. Then, we can define the following expressions for states s, t:

$$s = (ts?b.(st!a.\mathbf{1} + \mathbf{1}))^*, \qquad t = (st?a.(ts!b.\mathbf{1} + \mathbf{1}))^* \ .$$

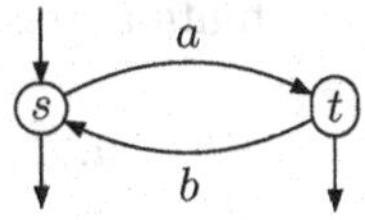

Fig. 2. Not bisimilar to a regular expression

The expressions give the possibilities to enter a state, followed by the possibilities to leave a state, and then iterate. With s and t as defined just now, the automaton associated, according to the operational rules, to the expression

$$\partial_{st,ts}(((st!a.\mathbf{1} + \mathbf{1}) \cdot s) \parallel \mathbf{1} \cdot t)$$

is isomorphic (and hence also divergence-preserving branching bisimilar) to the finite automaton in Figure 2 (replacing label a by $st!?a$ and label b by $ts!?b$).

Regular grammars. In the theory of automata and formal languages, the notion of *grammar* is used as a syntactic mechanism to describe languages. The corresponding mechanism in concurrency theory is the notion of recursive specification.

If we use only the syntax elements $\mathbf{0}$, $\mathbf{1}$, N ($N \in \mathcal{N}'$), $a.\_$ ($a \in \mathcal{A}_\tau$) and $\_+\_$ of the definition above, then we get so-called *linear* recursive specifications. That is, in a linear recursive specification, we do not use sequential composition, parallel composition, encapsulation and abstraction.

Every linear recursive specification, according to the operational rules, generates a finite automaton, and conversely, every finite automaton can be specified, up to isomorphism, by a linear recursive specification. We illustrate the construction with an example.

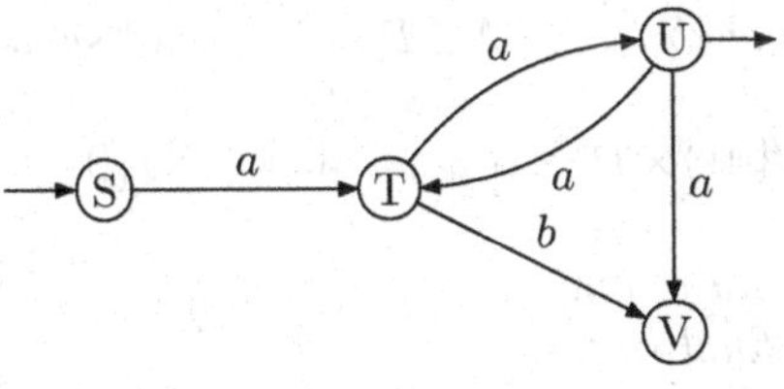

Fig. 3. Example automaton

Consider the automaton depicted in Figure 3. Note that we have labeled each state of the automaton with a unique name; we are going to define a recursive specification E over the finite set of names thus associated with the states of the automaton. We define each of the names with an equation, in such a way that the labeled transition system $\mathcal{T}_E(S)$ generated by the operational semantics in Table 1 is isomorphic (so certainly divergence-preserving branching bisimilar) with the automaton in Figure 3.

The recursive specification for the finite automaton in Figure 3 is:

$$S \stackrel{\text{def}}{=} a.T, \qquad T \stackrel{\text{def}}{=} a.U + b.V, \qquad U \stackrel{\text{def}}{=} a.V + \mathbf{1}, \qquad V \stackrel{\text{def}}{=} \mathbf{0}.$$

This result can be viewed as the process-theoretic counterpart of the result from the theory of automata and formal languages that states that every language accepted by a finite automaton is generated by a so-called *right-linear* grammar. There is no reasonable process-theoretic counterpart of the similar result in the theory of automata and formal languages that every language accepted by a finite automaton is generated by a *left-linear* grammar. If we use *action postfix* instead of action prefix, then on the one hand not every finite automaton can be specified, and on the other hand, by means of a simple recursive equation we can specify an infinite transition system (see [3]).

We conclude that the classes of processes defined by right-linear and left-linear grammars do not coincide.

4 Pushdown and Context-Free Processes

As an intermediate between the notions of finite automaton and Turing machine, the theory of automata and formal languages treats the notion of pushdown automaton, which is a finite automaton with a stack as memory. Several definitions of the notion appear in the literature, which are all equivalent in the sense that they accept the same languages.

Definition 5 (Pushdown automaton). *A* pushdown automaton M *is defined as a sixtuple* $(\mathcal{S}, \mathcal{A}, \mathcal{D}, \rightarrow, \uparrow, \downarrow)$ *where:*

1. $\mathcal{S}$ *a finite set of states,*
2. $\mathcal{A}$ *is a finite action alphabet,*
3. $\mathcal{D}$ *is a finite data alphabet, and* $\emptyset \notin \mathcal{D}$ *is a special symbol denoting an empty stack,*
4. $\rightarrow \subseteq \mathcal{S} \times \mathcal{A}_\tau \times (\mathcal{D} \cup \{\emptyset\}) \times \mathcal{D}^* \times \mathcal{S}$ *is an* $\mathcal{A}_\tau \times (\mathcal{D} \cup \{\emptyset\}) \times \mathcal{D}^*$*-labeled transition relation on* $\mathcal{S}$,
5. $\uparrow \in \mathcal{S}$ *is the initial state, and*
6. $\downarrow \subseteq \mathcal{S}$ *is the set of final states.*

If $(s, a, d, \delta, t) \in \rightarrow$, *we write* $s \xrightarrow{a[d/\delta]} t$.

The pair of a state together with particular stack contents will be referred to as the *configuration* of a pushdown automaton. Intuitively, a transition $s \xrightarrow{a[d/\delta]} t$ (with $a \in \mathcal{A}$) means that the automaton, when it is in a configuration consisting of a state s and a stack with the datum d on top, can execute a, replace d by the string δ and move to state t. Likewise, writing $s \xrightarrow{a[\emptyset/\delta]} t$ means that the automaton, when it is in state s and the stack is empty, can consume input symbol a, put the string δ on the stack, and move to state t. Transitions of the form $s \xrightarrow{\tau[d/\delta]} t$ or $s \xrightarrow{\tau[\emptyset/\delta]} t$ do not entail the consumption of an input symbol, but just modify the stack contents.

When considering a pushdown automaton as a language acceptor, it is generally assumed that it starts in its initial state with an empty stack. A computation consists of repeatedly consuming input symbols (or just modifying stack contents without consuming input symbols). When it comes to determining whether or not to accept an input string there are two approaches: "acceptance by final state" (FS) and "acceptance by empty stack" (ES). The first approach accepts a string if the pushdown automaton can move to a configuration with a final state by consuming the string, ignoring the contents of the stack in this configuration. The second approach accepts the string if the pushdown automaton can move to a configuration with an empty stack, ignoring whether the state of this configuration is final or not. These approaches are equivalent from a language-theoretic point of view, but not from a process-theoretic point of view. We also have a third approach in which a configuration is terminating if it consists of a terminating state *and* an empty stack (FSES). We note that, from a process-theoretic point of view, the ES and FSES approaches lead to the same notion of pushdown process, whereas the FS approach leads to a different notion. We choose the FS approach here, as this gives us more flexibility, allows us to define more pushdown processes. For further details, see [3,23].

Definition 6. *Let $M = (\mathcal{S}, \mathcal{A}, \mathcal{D}, \rightarrow, \uparrow, \downarrow)$ be a pushdown automaton. The labeled transition system $\mathcal{T}(M)$ associated with M is defined as follows:*

1. *the set of states of $\mathcal{T}(M)$ is $\mathcal{S} \times \mathcal{D}^*$;*
2. *the transition relation of $\mathcal{T}(M)$ satisfies*
   (a) $(s, d\zeta) \xrightarrow{a} (t, \delta\zeta)$ *iff* $s \xrightarrow{a[d/\delta]} t$ *for all* $s, t \in \mathcal{S}$, $a \in \mathcal{A}_\tau$, $d \in \mathcal{D}$, $\delta, \zeta \in \mathcal{D}^*$, *and*
   (b) $(s, \varepsilon) \xrightarrow{a} (t, \delta)$ *iff* $s \xrightarrow{a[\emptyset/\delta]} t$;
3. *the initial state of $\mathcal{T}(M)$ is $(\uparrow, \varepsilon)$; and*
4. *the set of final states is $\{(s, \zeta) \mid s\downarrow, \zeta \in \mathcal{D}^*\}$.*

This definition now gives us the notions of pushdown language and pushdown process: a *pushdown language* is the language of the transition system associated with a pushdown automaton, and a *pushdown process* is a divergence-preserving branching bisimilarity class of labeled transition systems containing a labeled transition system associated with a pushdown automaton.

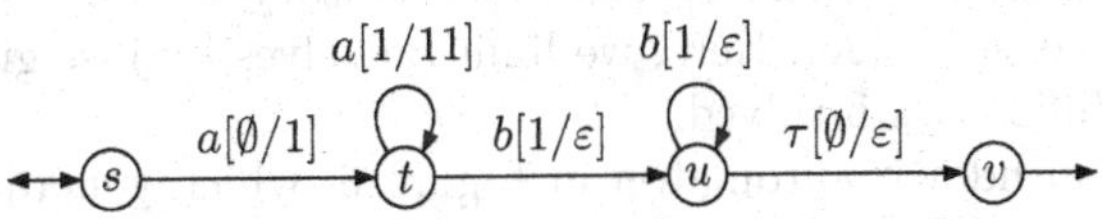

Fig. 4. Example pushdown automaton

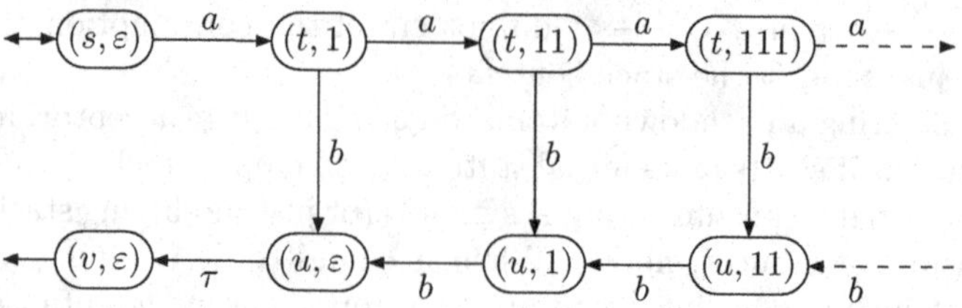

Fig. 5. A pushdown process

As an example, the pushdown automaton in Figure 4 defines the infinite transition system in Figure 5, that accepts the language $\{a^n b^n \mid n \geq 0\}$.

Context-free grammars. We shall now consider the process-theoretic version of the standard result in the theory of automata and formal languages that the set of pushdown languages coincides with the set of languages generated by context-free grammars. As the process-theoretic counterparts of context-free grammars we shall consider so-called *sequential* recursive specifications in which only the constructions $\mathbf{0}$, $\mathbf{1}$, N ($N \in \mathcal{N}'$), $a.\_$ ($a \in \mathcal{A}_\tau$), $\_ \cdot \_$ and $\_ + \_$ occur, so adding sequential composition to linear recursive specifications.

Sequential recursive specifications can be used to specify pushdown processes. To give an example, the process expression X defined in the sequential recursive specification

$$X \stackrel{\text{def}}{=} \mathbf{1} + a.X \cdot b.\mathbf{1}$$

has a labeled transition system that is divergence-preserving branching bisimilar to the one in Figure 5, which is associated with the pushdown automaton in Figure 4.

The notion of a sequential recursive specification naturally corresponds with with the notion of context-free grammar: for every pushdown automaton there exists a sequential recursive specification such that their transition systems are language equivalent, and, vice versa, for every sequential recursive specification there exists a pushdown automaton such that their transition systems are language equivalent. A similar result with language equivalence replaced by divergence-preserving branching bisimilarity does not hold. There are pushdown processes that are not recursively definable by a sequential recursive specification, and also there are sequential recursive specifications that define non-pushdown processes. Extra restrictions are necessary in order to retrieve the desired equivalence, see [3,23]. Here, we limit ourselves by just giving examples illustrating the difficulties involved.

Consider the pushdown automaton in Figure 6, which generates the transition system shown in Figure 7 (omitting the τ-step, this preserves divergence-preserving branching bisimilarity). In [20], Moller proved that this transition system cannot be defined with a BPA recursive specification, where BPA is the restriction of sequential recursive specifications by omitting the τ-prefix and the

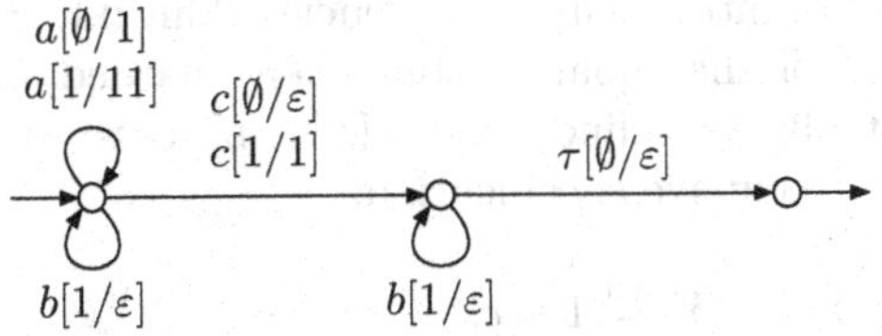

Fig. 6. Pushdown automaton that does not have a sequential recursive specification

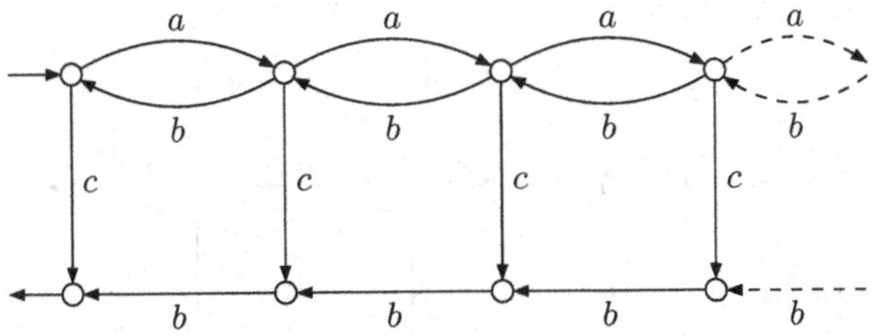

Fig. 7. Transition system of automaton of Figure 6

constant $\mathbf{0}$ and by disallowing $\mathbf{1}$ to occur as a summand in a nontrivial alternative composition. Moller's proof can be modified to show that the transition system is not definable with a sequential recursive specification either. We conclude that not every pushdown process is definable with a sequential recursive specification.

Another example of a pushdown automaton that does not have a sequential recursive specification is the stack itself, used as memory in the definition of a pushdown automaton. The stack can be modeled as a pushdown process, in fact (as we will see shortly) it can be considered the prototypical pushdown process. Given a finite nonempty data set $\mathcal{D}$, the stack St^{io} has an input channel i over which it can receive elements of $\mathcal{D}$ and an output channel o over which it can signal that it is empty, and send elements of $\mathcal{D}$. The stack process is given by a pushdown automaton with one state $\uparrow$ (which is both initial and final) and transitions $\uparrow \xrightarrow{i?d[\emptyset/d]} \uparrow$, $\uparrow \xrightarrow{i?d[e/de]} \uparrow$, and $\uparrow \xrightarrow{o!\emptyset[\emptyset/\varepsilon]} \uparrow$, $\uparrow \xrightarrow{o!d[d/\varepsilon]} \uparrow$ for all $d, e \in \mathcal{D}$. As the transition system generated by this pushdown automaton has infinitely many final states that are not branching bisimilar (as we are using FS termination), it can be shown there is no sequential recursive specification for it. If we allow termination only when the stack is empty, then we can find the following sequential recursive specification:

$$S \stackrel{\text{def}}{=} \mathbf{1} + o!\emptyset.\mathbf{1} + \sum_{d \in \mathcal{D}} i?d.T \cdot o!d.S \qquad T \stackrel{\text{def}}{=} \mathbf{1} + \sum_{d \in \mathcal{D}} i?d.T \cdot o!d.T.$$

Conversely, not every sequential recursive specification defines a pushdown process. To give an example, the sequential recursive equation $X \stackrel{\text{def}}{=} X \cdot a.\mathbf{1}$ generates an infinitely branching transition system, which can only be given a pushdown automaton at the cost of introducing divergencies. This infinite branching is due to the unguardedness of the equation, but even guarded sequential recursive specifications do not always define a pushdown process. To give an example, consider the following recursive specification:

$$X \stackrel{\text{def}}{=} a.X \cdot Y + b.\mathbf{1}, \qquad Y \stackrel{\text{def}}{=} \mathbf{1} + c.\mathbf{1}.$$

The labeled transition system associated with X, which is depicted in Figure 8, has finite but unbounded branching. We claim this cannot be a pushdown process.

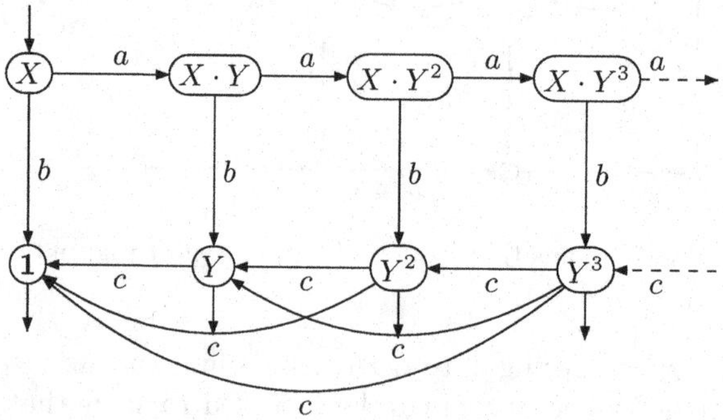

Fig. 8. Process with unbounded branching

Because of these difficulties with the correspondence between pushdown processes and sequential recursive specifications, we consider another type of grammar for pushdown processes. This type of grammar includes a specification for the stack process St^{io} defined above (that can terminate irrespective of the contents) as a standard component. We present a specification for it in our full process theory, only sequential composition and iteration are not used (see [23,6])

We start out from the observation that an unbounded stack can be seen as a buffer of capacity one (for the top of the stack) communicating with a copy of the unbounded stack. An unbounded stack with input port i and output port o is equal to a regular *Top* process with external input i, internal input j, external output o, internal output p, communicating with an unbounded stack with input port j and output port p. See Figure 9.

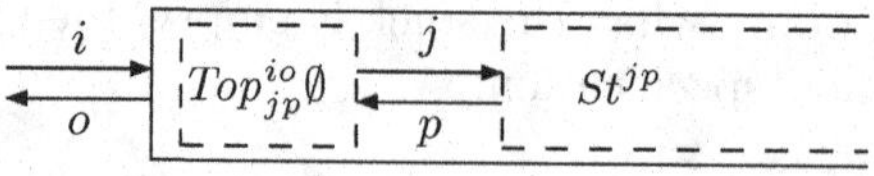

Fig. 9. Intuition for specification of always terminating stack

In a formula, we want to achieve

$$St^{io} \leftrightarrow^{\Delta}_{b} \tau_{jp}(\partial_{jp}(Top^{io}_{jp}\emptyset \parallel St^{jp})).$$

In turn, the stack with input j and output p will satisfy

$$St^{jp} \leftrightarrow^{\Delta}_{b} \tau_{io}(\partial_{io}(Top^{jp}_{io}\emptyset \parallel St^{io})).$$

We do this by the following specification E_{St} over names St^{io} and St^{jp}, with auxiliary variables $Top^{io}_{jp}\emptyset$, $Top^{jp}_{io}\emptyset$ and $Top^{io}_{jp}d$, $Top^{jp}_{io}d$ for every $d \in \mathcal{D}$:

$$St^{io} \stackrel{\text{def}}{=} \mathbf{1} + o!\emptyset.St^{io} + \sum_{d\in\mathcal{D}} i?d.\tau_{jp}(\partial_{jp}(Top^{io}_{jp}d \parallel St^{jp}))$$

$$St^{jp} \stackrel{\text{def}}{=} \mathbf{1} + p!\emptyset.St^{jp} + \sum_{d\in\mathcal{D}} j?d.\tau_{io}(\partial_{io}(Top^{jp}_{io}d \parallel St^{io}))$$

$$Top^{io}_{jp}\emptyset \stackrel{\text{def}}{=} \mathbf{1} + o!\emptyset.Top^{io}_{jp}\emptyset + \sum_{d\in\mathcal{D}} i?d.Top^{io}_{jp}d$$

$$Top^{jp}_{io}\emptyset \stackrel{\text{def}}{=} \mathbf{1} + p!\emptyset.Top^{jp}_{io}\emptyset + \sum_{d\in\mathcal{D}} j?d.Top^{jp}_{io}d$$

$$Top^{io}_{jp}d \stackrel{\text{def}}{=} \mathbf{1} + o!d.(p?\emptyset.Top^{io}_{jp}\emptyset + \sum_{e\in\mathcal{D}} p?e.Top^{io}_{jp}e) + \sum_{f\in\mathcal{D}} i?f.j!d.Top^{io}_{jp}f$$

$$Top^{jp}_{io}d \stackrel{\text{def}}{=} \mathbf{1} + p!d.(o?\emptyset.Top^{jp}_{io}\emptyset + \sum_{e\in\mathcal{D}} o?e.Top^{jp}_{io}e) + \sum_{f\in\mathcal{D}} j?f.i!d.Top^{jp}_{io}f$$

The last two equations occur for every $d \in \mathcal{D}$. Notice that the subspecification of the *Top* processes define these as regular processes.

On the basis of this specification, the divergence-preserving branching bisimilarities above are straightforward to prove.

The stack process can be used to make the interaction between control and memory in a pushdown automaton explicit [19,4]. This is illustrated by the following theorem, stating that every pushdown process is equal to a regular process interacting with a stack.

Theorem 1. *For every pushdown automaton M there exists a regular process expression p and a linear recursive specification E, and for every regular process expression p and linear recursive specification E there exists a pushdown automaton M such that*

$$\mathcal{T}(M) \leftrightarrow_b \mathcal{T}_{E\cup E_{St}}(\tau_{i,o}(\partial_{i,o}(p \parallel St^{io}))) .$$

5 Computable Processes

We proceed to give a definition of a Turing machine that can interact. The classical definition of a Turing machine uses the memory tape to hold the input string at system start up. Staying true to the principle that all interaction with the device should be modeled explicitly, we do not want to fix the input string beforehand, but want to be able to input symbols one at a time.

Definition 7 (Reactive Turing Machine). *A* Reactive Turing Machine *M is defined as a six-tuple $(\mathcal{S}, \mathcal{A}, \mathcal{D}, \rightarrow, \uparrow, \downarrow)$ where:*

1. $\mathcal{S}$ *is a finite set of states,*
2. $\mathcal{A}$ *is a finite action alphabet,* $\mathcal{A}_\tau$ *also includes the silent step* τ,
3. $\mathcal{D}$ *is a finite data alphabet, we add a special symbol* $\Box$ *standing for a blank and put* $\mathcal{D}_\Box = \mathcal{D} \cup \{\Box\}$,
4. $\rightarrow \subseteq \mathcal{S} \times \mathcal{A}_\tau \times \mathcal{D}_\Box \times \mathcal{D}_\Box \times \{L, R\} \times \mathcal{S}$ *is a finite set of* transitions *or* steps,
5. $\uparrow \in \mathcal{S}$ *is the initial state,*
6. $\downarrow \subseteq \mathcal{S}$ *is the set of final states.*

If $(s, a, d, e, M, t) \in \rightarrow$, we write $s \xrightarrow{a[d/e]M} t$, and this means that the machine, when it is in state s and reading symbol d on the tape, will execute input action a, change the symbol on the tape to e, will move one step left if $M = L$ and right if $M = R$ and thereby move to state t. It is also possible that d and/or e is $\Box$: if d is $\Box$, then, intuitively, the reading head is looking at an empty cell on the tape and writes e; if e is $\Box$ (and d is not), then d is erased, leaving an empty cell. At the start of a Turing machine computation, we will assume the Turing machine is in the initial state, and that the memory tape is empty (only contains blanks). The action alphabet $\mathcal{A}$ is used for input and output actions, and τ-labeled steps are internal steps (steps of a classical Turing machine).

By looking at all possible executions, we can define the transition system of a Turing machine. The states of this transition system are the configurations of the Reactive Turing Machine, consisting of a state, the current tape contents, and the position of the read/write head. We represent the tape contents by an element of $\mathcal{D}_\Box^*$, replacing exactly one occurrence of a type symbol d by a marked symbol $\bar{d}$, indicating that the read/write head is on that symbol. We denote by $\bar{\mathcal{D}_\Box} = \{\bar{d} \mid d \in \mathcal{D}_\Box\}$ the set of marked tape symbols; a *tape instance* is a sequence $\delta \in (\mathcal{D}_\Box \cup \bar{\mathcal{D}_\Box})$ such that δ contains exactly one element of $\bar{\mathcal{D}_\Box}$.

A tape instance thus is a finite sequence of symbols that represents the contents of a two-way infinite tape. We do not distinguish between tape instances that are equal modulo the addition or removal of extra occurrences of a blank at the left or right extremes of the sequence. The set of configurations of a Reactive Turing Machine now consists of pairs of a state and a tape instance. In order to concisely describe the semantics of a Reactive Turing Machine in terms of transition systems on configurations, we use some additional notation.

If $\delta \in \mathcal{D}_\Box$, then δ^- is the tape instance obtained by placing the marker on the right-most symbol of δ if this exists, and is $\bar{\Box}$ otherwise. Likewise, ${}^-\delta$ is the tape instance obtained by placing the marker on the left-most symbol of δ if this exists, and is $\bar{\Box}$ otherwise.

Definition 8. *Let* $M = (\mathcal{S}, \mathcal{A}, \mathcal{D}, \rightarrow, \uparrow, \downarrow)$ *be a Reactive Turing Machine. The* labeled transition system *of* M, $\mathcal{T}(M)$, *is defined as follows:*

1. *The set of states is the set of configurations* $\{(s, \delta) \mid s \in \mathcal{S}, \delta$ *a tape instance*$\}$.
2. *The transition relation* $\rightarrow$ *is the least relation satisfying, for all* $a \in \mathcal{A}_\tau, d, e \in \mathcal{D}_\Box, \delta, \zeta \in \mathcal{D}_\Box^*$:
   - $(s, \delta\bar{d}\zeta) \xrightarrow{a} (t, \delta^- e\zeta)$ *iff* $s \xrightarrow{a[d/e]L} t$,
   - $(s, \delta\bar{d}\zeta) \xrightarrow{a} (t, \delta e{}^-\zeta)$ *iff* $s \xrightarrow{a[d/e]R} t$.

3. The initial state is $(\uparrow, \bar{\Box})$*;*
4. $(s, \delta)\downarrow$ *iff* $s\downarrow$.

Now we define an *executable process* as the divergence-preserving branching bisimulation equivalence class of a transition system of a Reactive Turing Machine.

As an example of a Reactive Turing Machine, we define the (first-in first-out) queue over a data set $\mathcal{D}$. It has the initial and final state at the head of the queue. There, output of the value at the head can be given, after which one move to the left occurs. If an input comes, then the position travels to the left until a free position is reached, where the value input is stored, after which the position travels to the right until the head is reached again. We show the Turing machine in Figure 10 in case $\mathcal{D} = \{0, 1\}$. A label containing an n, like $\tau[n/n]L$ means there are two labels $\tau[0/0]L$ and $\tau[1/1]L$.

The queue process is an executable process, but not a pushdown process.

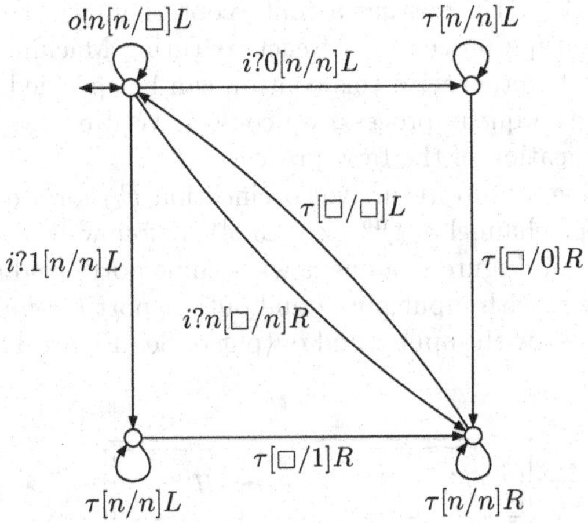

Fig. 10. Reactive Turing Machine for the FIFO queue

A transition system is *computable* if it is finitely branching and there is a coding of the states such that the set of final states is decidable, and for each state, the set of its outgoing transitions can be computed. The following results are in [8]. First of all, it is easy to see that the transition system defined by a Reactive Turing Machine is computable.

Theorem 2. *Every boundedly branching computable transition system is executable.*

Theorem 3. *The parallel composition of two executable transition systems is again executable.*

Theorem 4. *For each n, Reactive Turing Machine exists, that is universal for all Reactive Turing Machines that have a transition system with branching degree bounded by n.*

A truly universal Reactive Turing Machine can only be achieved at the cost of introducing divergencies.

As in the case of the pushdown automaton, we can make the interaction between the finite control and the memory explicit, and turn this into a recursive specification.

Theorem 5. *For every Reactive Turing Machine M there exists a regular process expression p and a linear recursive specification E such that*

$$\mathcal{T}(M) \leftrightarrow_b^\Delta \mathcal{T}_{E \cup E_Q}(\tau_{i,o}(\partial_{i,o}(p \parallel Q^{io}))) \ .$$

In this theorem, we use the queue process as defined above, and its specification E_Q to be defined next. By putting a finite control in parallel with a queue, we can simulate the tape process of a Reactive Turing Machine. The control of the Turing machine together with this control, can be specified as a finite-state process. Instead of the queue process, we could have used two stacks, or have given a direct specification of the tape process.

We finish by giving a finite recursive specification E_Q for a queue with input channel i and output channel o, Q^{io} (see [23,6]). It follows the same pattern as the one for the stack in Figure 9: a queue with input port i and output port o is the same as the queue with input port i and output port ℓ communicating with a regular *head* process with input ℓ and output o. See Figure 11.

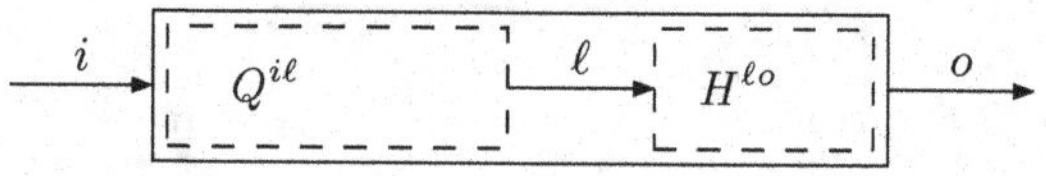

Fig. 11. Intuition for specification of always terminating queue

In a formula, we want to achieve

$$Q^{io} \leftrightarrow_b^\Delta \tau_\ell(\partial_\ell(Q^{i\ell} \parallel H^{\ell o})).$$

In turn, the queue with input i and output ℓ will satisfy

$$Q^{i\ell} \leftrightarrow_b^\Delta \tau_o(\partial_o(Q^{io} \parallel H^{o\ell})).$$

We do this by the following specification over names Q^{io} and $Q^{i\ell}$, with auxiliary variables $H^{\ell o}$ and $H^{o\ell}$, where the *Head* processes are just always terminating one place buffers:

$$Q^{io} \stackrel{\text{def}}{=} \mathbf{1} + \sum_{d\in\mathcal{D}} i?d.\tau_\ell(\partial_\ell(Q^{i\ell} \parallel (\mathbf{1} + o!d.H^{\ell o})))$$

$$Q^{i\ell} \stackrel{\text{def}}{=} \mathbf{1} + \sum_{d\in\mathcal{D}} i?d.\tau_o(\partial_o(Q^{io} \parallel (\mathbf{1} + \ell!d.H^{o\ell})))$$

$$H^{\ell o} \stackrel{\text{def}}{=} \mathbf{1} + \sum_{e\in\mathcal{D}} \ell?e.(\mathbf{1} + o!e.H^{\ell o})$$

$$H^{o\ell} \stackrel{\text{def}}{=} \mathbf{1} + \sum_{e\in\mathcal{D}} o?e.(\mathbf{1} + \ell!e.H^{o\ell}).$$

Now, the theorem above implies that recursive specifications over our syntax (even omitting sequential composition and iteration) constitute a grammar for all executable processes. The queue is shown to be a prototypical executable process.

6 Conclusion

We discussed in this paper the notion of an execution, that enhances a computation by taking interaction into account. We did this by marrying computability theory, moving up from finite automata through pushdown automata to Turing machines, with concurrency theory, not using language equivalence but divergence-preserving branching bisimilarity on automata.

Every undergraduate curriculum in computer science contains a course on automata theory and formal languages. On the other hand, an introduction to concurrency theory is usually not given in the undergraduate program. Both theories as basic models of computation are part of the foundations of computer science. Automata theory and formal languages provide a model of computation where interaction is not taken into account, so a computer is considered as a stand-alone device executing batch processes. On the other hand, concurrency theory provides a model of computation where interaction is taken into account. Concurrency theory is sometimes called the theory of reactive processes.

Both theories can be integrated into one course in the undergraduate curriculum, providing students with the foundation of computing, see [6]. This paper provides a glimpse of what happens to the Chomsky hierarchy in a concurrency setting, taking a labeled transition system as a central notion, and dividing out bisimulation semantics on such transition systems.

References

1. Baeten, J.C.M., Basten, T., Reniers, M.A.: Process Algebra (Equational Theories of Communicating Processes). Cambridge Tracts in Theoretical Computer Science, vol. 50. Cambridge University Press (2009)
2. Baeten, J.C.M., Corradini, F., Grabmayer, C.A.: A characterization of regular expressions under bisimulation. Journal of the ACM 54(2), 6.1–6.28 (2007)

3. Baeten, J.C.M., Cuijpers, P.J.L., Luttik, B., van Tilburg, P.J.A.: A Process-Theoretic Look at Automata. In: Arbab, F., Sirjani, M. (eds.) FSEN 2009. LNCS, vol. 5961, pp. 1–33. Springer, Heidelberg (2010)
4. Baeten, J.C.M., Cuijpers, P.J.L., van Tilburg, P.J.A.: A Context-Free Process as a Pushdown Automaton. In: van Breugel, F., Chechik, M. (eds.) CONCUR 2008. LNCS, vol. 5201, pp. 98–113. Springer, Heidelberg (2008)
5. Baeten, J., Luttik, B., Muller, T., van Tilburg, P.: Expressiveness modulo bisimilarity of regular expressions with parallel composition (extended abstract). In: Fröschle, S., Valencia, F.D. (eds.) Proceedings EXPRESS 2010. EPTCS, vol. 41, pp. 1–15 (2010)
6. Baeten, J.C.M.: Models of Computation: Automata, Formal Languages and Communicating Processes. Technische Universiteit Eindhoven (2011), Syllabus 2IT15
7. Baeten, J.C.M., Luttik, B., van Tilburg, P.: Computations and Interaction. In: Natarajan, R., Ojo, A. (eds.) ICDCIT 2011. LNCS, vol. 6536, pp. 35–54. Springer, Heidelberg (2011)
8. Baeten, J.C.M., Luttik, B., van Tilburg, P.: Reactive Turing Machines. In: Owe, O., Steffen, M., Telle, J.A. (eds.) FCT 2011. LNCS, vol. 6914, pp. 348–359. Springer, Heidelberg (2011)
9. Basten, T.: Branching bisimilarity is an equivalence indeed! Information Processing Letters 58(3), 141–147 (1996)
10. Blass, A., Gurevich, Y.: Ordinary interactive small-step algorithms, ii. ACM Trans. Comput. Log. 8(3) (2007)
11. Blass, A., Gurevich, Y.: Ordinary interactive small-step algorithms, iii. ACM Trans. Comput. Log. 8(3) (2007)
12. Blass, A., Gurevich, Y., Rosenzweig, D., Rossman, B.: Interactive small-step algorithms i: Axiomatization. Logical Methods in Computer Science 3(4) (2007)
13. van Glabbeek, R.J.: What is Branching Time Semantics and why to use it? Bulletin of the EATCS 53, 190–198 (1994)
14. van Glabbeek, R.J., Luttik, B., Trčka, N.: Branching bisimilarity with explicit divergence. Fundamenta Informaticae 93(4), 371–392 (2009)
15. van Glabbeek, R.J., Weijland, W.P.: Branching time and abstraction in bisimulation semantics. Journal of the ACM 43(3), 555–600 (1996)
16. Hoare, C.A.R.: Communicating Sequential Processes. Prentice Hall (1985)
17. Milner, R.: A Calculus of Communicating Systems. LNCS, vol. 92. Springer (1980)
18. Milner, R.: A complete inference system for a class of regular behaviours. Journal of Comput. System Sci. 28(3), 439–466 (1984)
19. Milner, R.: Elements of interaction. Communications of the ACM 36(1), 78–89 (1993)
20. Moller, F.: Infinite Results. In: Montanari, U., Sassone, V. (eds.) CONCUR 1996. LNCS, vol. 1119, pp. 195–216. Springer, Heidelberg (1996)
21. Park, D.M.R.: Concurrency and Automata on Infinite Sequences. In: Deussen, P. (ed.) GI-TCS 1981. LNCS, vol. 104, pp. 167–183. Springer, Heidelberg (1981)
22. Plotkin, G.D.: A structural approach to operational semantics. J. Log. Algebr. Program. 60-61, 17–139 (2004)
23. van Tilburg, P.J.A.: From Computability to Executability (A Process-Theoretic View on Automata Theory). PhD thesis, Eindhoven University of Technology (2011)
24. Turing, A.M.: On computable numbers, with an application to the entscheidungsproblem. Proceedings of the London Mathematical Society 42(2), 230–265 (1936)

Concurrency and the Algebraic Theory of Effects
(Abstract)

Gordon D. Plotkin

LFCS, School of Informatics, University of Edinburgh
gdp@inf.ed.ac.uk

The algebraic theory of effects [7,8,4] continues Moggi's monadic approach to effects [5,6,1] by concentrating on a particular class of monads: the *algebraic* ones, that is, the free algebra monads of given equational theories. The operations of such equational theories can be thought of as *effect constructors*, as it is they that give rise to effects. Examples include exceptions (when the theory is that of a set of constants with no axioms), nondeterminism (when the theory could be that of a semilattice, for nondeterminism, with a zero, for deadlock), and action (when the theory could be a set of unary operations with no axioms).

Two natural, apparently unrelated, questions arise: how can exception handlers and how can concurrency combinators be incorporated into this picture? For the first, in previous work with Pretnar [9], we showed how free algebras give rise to a natural notion of computation handling, generalising Benton and Kennedy's exception handling construct. The idea is that the action of a unary deconstructor on a computation (identified as an element of a free algebra) is the application to it of a homomorphism, with the homomorphism being obtained via the universal characterisation of the free algebra. This can be thought of as an account of *unary effect deconstructors.*

In general, such unary deconstructors can be defined using parameters, and simultaneously defined unary deconstructors are also possible. The more complex definitions are reduced to the simple homomorphic ones by using homomorphisms to power and product algebras. This is entirely analogous to treatments of (simultaneous) primitive recursion on natural numbers, or of structural recursion on lists.

For the second, turning to, for example, CCS, the evident theory, at least for strong bisimulation, is that of nondeterminism plus action. Then restriction and relabelling are straightforwardly dealt with as unary deconstructors. However the concurrency combinator is naturally thought of as a *binary* deconstructor and the question arises as to how, if at all, one might understand it, and similar binary operators, in terms of homomorphisms. This question was already posed in [9] in the cases of the CCS concurrency and the Unix pipe combinators. In addition, a treatment of CSP in terms of constructors and deconstructors was given in [10], but again still leaving open the question of how to treat concurrency.

Following an idea found in the ACP literature [2], concurrency combinators can generally be split into a sum of left and right combinators, according to which of their arguments' actions occur first. This leads to a natural simultaneous recursive definition of the left and right combinators, with a symmetry

M. Koutny and I. Ulidowski (Eds.): CONCUR 2012, LNCS 7454, pp. 21–22, 2012.

between recursion variables and parameters; however the definition is not in the form required for unary deconstructors. We give a general theory of such binary deconstructors, in which solutions to the equations are found by breaking the symmetry and defining unary deconstructors with higher-order parameters.[1] The theory applies to CCS and other process calculi, as well as to shared memory parallelism. In this way we demonstrate a possibility: that the monadic approach, which has always included (algebraic) monads for interaction and for shared variable parallelism—see [1,3,4]—can be fruitfully integrated with the world of concurrency.

References

1. Benton, N., Hughes, J., Moggi, E.: Monads and Effects. In: Barthe, G., Dybjer, P., Pinto, L., Saraiva, J. (eds.) APPSEM 2000. LNCS, vol. 2395, pp. 42–122. Springer, Heidelberg (2002)
2. Bergstra, J.A., Klop, J.W.: Algebra of communicating processes with abstraction. Theor. Comput. Sci. 37, 77–121 (1985)
3. Cenciarelli, P., Moggi, E.: A syntactic approach to modularity in denotational semantics. In: Proc. 5th. Biennial Meeting on Category Theory and Computer Science. CWI Technical report (1993)
4. Hyland, M., Plotkin, G., Power, J.: Combining effects: sum and tensor. Theor. Comput. Science 357(1-3), 70–99 (2006)
5. Moggi, E.: Computational lambda-calculus and monads. In: Proc. 4th. LICS, pp. 14–23. IEEE Press (1989)
6. Moggi, E.: Notions of computation and monads. Inf. and Comp. 93(1), 55–92 (1991)
7. Plotkin, G., Power, J.: Notions of Computation Determine Monads. In: Nielsen, M., Engberg, U. (eds.) FOSSACS 2002. LNCS, vol. 2303, pp. 342–356. Springer, Heidelberg (2002)
8. Plotkin, G., Power, J.: Algebraic operations and generic effects. Appl. Categor. Struct. 11(1), 69–94 (2003)
9. Plotkin, G., Pretnar, M.: Handlers of Algebraic Effects. In: Castagna, G. (ed.) ESOP 2009. LNCS, vol. 5502, pp. 80–94. Springer, Heidelberg (2009)
10. van Glabbeek, R., Plotkin, G.: On CSP and the algebraic theory of effects. In: Jones, C.B., Roscoe, A.W., Wood, K.R. (eds.) Reflections on the work of C.A.R. Hoare, pp. 333–370. Springer (2010)

[1] The idea was also found independently by both Alex Simpson and Paul Levy.

A Turing Enigma

Brian Randell

School of Computing Science
Newcastle University
Newcastle upon Tyne, NE1 7RU
United Kingdom
Brian.Randell@ncl.ac.uk

Abstract. I describe my investigations into the highly-secret role that Alan Turing played during World War II, after his pre-war theoretical work on computability and the concept of a universal machine, in the development of the world's first electronic computers. These investigations resulted in my obtaining and publishing, in 1972, some limited information about Turing's contributions to the work on code-breaking machines at Bletchley Park, the fore-runner of the UK Government Communications Headquarters (GCHQ). Some years later I was able to obtain permission to compile and publish the first officially-authorised account of the work, led by T.H. (Tommy) Flowers at the Post Office Dollis Hill Research Station, on the construction of a series of special purpose electronic computers for Bletchley Park, computers that made a vital contribution to the Allied war effort.

Keywords: Alan Turing, Tommy Flowers, Enigma, Colossus, Bletchley Park.

1 Introduction

There are many who are far better equipped than I am to speak of the various aspects of the late great Alan Turing's scientific career that are of direct technical relevance to the CONCUR community. Instead, at the conference organisers' request, in this year in which the hundredth anniversary of his birth is being celebrated, I am going to tell you of a historical investigation that I undertook some forty years ago into the then complete mystery of what Alan Turing had worked on, in great secrecy, during World War II.

In about 1971 my growing interest in the history of computing led to my assembling, with a view to publishing in book form, a representative set of papers and reports documenting the many fascinating inventions and projects that eventually culminated in the development of the "modern" electronic computer,

I took Charles Babbage's work as my main starting point, and decided on a cut-off date of 1949, when the first practical stored program electronic computer became operational. So I planned on including material on ENIAC, EDVAC, the Manchester "Baby" machine, and the Cambridge EDSAC, but decided to leave coverage of all the many subsequent machines to other would-be computer historians.

I circulated a list of my planned set of documents to a number of colleagues for comment – one of the responses I received queried the absence of Alan Turing from my list. My excuse was that, to the best of my knowledge, Turing's work on computers at

M. Koutny and I. Ulidowski (Eds.): CONCUR 2012, LNCS 7454, pp. 23–36, 2012.

the National Physical Laboratory (NPL) had post-dated Manchester's and Cambridge's successful efforts, and that his pre-war work on computability, in which he described what we now call a Turing Machine, was purely theoretical, and so fell outside the chosen scope of my collection.

I had first become interested in computers in 1956 in my last year at Imperial College. There weren't many books on computers at that time – one was *Faster than Thought* [1]. My 1955 copy of this book was probably my first source of knowledge about both Babbage and Turing, and indeed about the work of the various early UK computer projects, though soon afterwards I had learned much more about Babbage, and his collaboration with Lady Lovelace, from the excellent Dover paperback *Charles Babbage and his Calculating Engines* [13]. In Bowden I had read:

> "The basic concepts and abstract principles of computation by a machine were formulated by Dr. A.M. Turing, F.R.S. in a paper read before the London Mathematical Society in 1936, but work on such machines in Britain was delayed by the war. In 1945, however, an examination of the problems was made at the National Physical Laboratory by Mr. J.R. Womersley, then Superintendent of the Mathematics Division of the Laboratory. He was joined by Dr. Turing and a small staff of specialists ... "

However, piqued by the query about my having omitted Turing from my envisaged collection, I set out to try to find out more about Turing's work during the interval 1936-1945. I obtained a copy of the 1959 biography by his mother, Mrs Sara Turing [26], to find that its only indication of what her son had done during World War II was the following:

> " ... immediately on the declaration of war he was taken on as a Temporary Civil Servant in the Foreign Office, in the Department of Communications ... At first even his whereabouts were kept secret, but later it was divulged that he was working at Bletchley Park, Bletchley. No hint was ever given of the nature of his secret work, nor has it ever been revealed."

In fact by this time I had learned somehow that his wartime work had related to codebreaking, though neither I nor any of my colleagues were familiar with the name Bletchley Park. On rechecking my copy of David Kahn's magnificent tome *The Codebreakers* [10] I found Kahn's statement that Bletchley Park was what the Foreign Office "euphemistically called its Department of Communications", i.e. was the centre of Britain's wartime code-breaking efforts. However Kahn gave little information about what was done at Bletchley Park, and made no mention of Turing.

At about this stage I came across the following statement by Lord Halsbury [6]:

> "One of the most important events in the evolution of the modern computer was a meeting of two minds which cross-fertilised one another at a critical epoch in the technological development which they exploited. I refer of course to the meeting of the late Doctors Turing and von Neumann during the war, and all that came thereof ... "

I wrote to Lord Halsbury, who in 1949 was Managing Director of the National Research Development Corporation, the UK government body that had provided financial support to several of the early UK computer projects. Unfortunately he could not recollect the source of his information, his response (quoted in [16]) to my query being:

> "I am afraid I cannot tell you more about the meeting between Turing and von Neumann except that they met and sparked one another off. Each had, as it were, half the picture in his head and the two halves came together during the course of their meeting. I believe both were working on the mathematics of the atomic bomb project."

Inquiries of those of Turing's colleagues who were still at NPL produced little, but Donald Davies, who was then Superintendent of the Division of Computing Science at NPL, arranged for me to visit Mrs Turing. She was very helpful and furnished me with several further leads, but was not really able to add much to the very brief, and unspecific, comments in her book.

Various other leads proved fruitless, and my enthusiasm for the search was beginning to wane. I eventually had the opportunity to inspect a copy of Turing's report giving detailed plans for the ACE [25]. This proved to postdate, and even contain a reference to, von Neumann's *First Draft of a Report on the EDVAC* [14] so I did not examine it as carefully as I later realised I should have. However, I did note that Turing's report alluded to the fact that he had obtained much experience of electronic circuits.

2 Secret Wartime Computers

But then my investigation took a dramatic turn.

I had written to a number of people, seeking to understand more fully whether and if so how Turing had contributed to the initial development of practical stored program computers. One of my enquiries — to Donald Michie — elicited the following response (quoted in [16]) :

> "I believe that Lord Halsbury is right about the von Neumann-Turing meeting ... . The implication of Newman's obituary notice, as you quote it[1], is quite misleading; but it depends a bit on what one means by: a 'computer'. If we restrict this to mean a stored-program digital machine, then Newman's implication is fair, because no-one conceived this device (apart from Babbage) until Eckert and Mauchly (sometimes attributed to von Neumann). But if one just means high-speed electronic digital computers, then Turing among others was thoroughly familiar during the war with such equipment, which predated ENIAC (itself not a stored-program machine) by a matter of years."

---

[1] The obituary notice for Turing [15], written by Professor M.H.A. Newman, who was associated with the post-war computer developments at Manchester University, stated that:

> "At the end of the war many circumstances combined to turn his attention to the new automatic computing machines. They were in principle realisations of the 'universal machine' which he had described in the 1937 paper for the purpose of a logical argument, though their designers did not yet know of Turing's work."

I then found that there had in fact already been several (rather obscure) references in the open literature to the work at Bletchley Park with which Turing was associated, of which the most startling was a paper by I.J. (Jack) Good [5]. This gave a listing of successive generations of general purpose computers, including:

> "Cryptanalytic (British): classified, electronic, calculated complicated Boolean functions involving up to about 100 symbols, binary circuitry, electronic clock, plugged and switched programs, punched paper tape for data input, typewriter output, pulse repetition frequency 10^5, about 1000 gas-filled tubes; 1943 (M.H.A. Newman, D. Michie, I.J. Good and M. Flowers. Newman was inspired by his knowledge of Turing's 1936 paper)." [(Tommy) Flowers' initials were in fact "T.H."]

Furthermore Good's paper went on to claim that there was a causal chain leading from Turing's 1936 paper [24] through the wartime cryptanalytic machine, to the first Manchester computers, although it states that the main influence was from von Neumann's plans for the IAS machine (at Princeton University's Institute for Advanced Study).

Further details of Turing's role, and the war-time code-breaking machines, were provided in a letter I received from Tommy Flowers (quoted in [16]):

> "In our war-time association, Turing and others provided the requirements for machines which were top secret and have never been declassified. What I can say about them is that they were electronic (which at that time was unique and anticipated the ENIAC), with electromechanical input and output. They were digital machines with wired programs. Wires on tags were used for semi-permanent memories, and thermionic valve bi-stable circuits for temporary memory. For one purpose we did in fact provide for variable programming by means of lever keys which controlled gates which could be connected in series and parallel as required, but of course the scope of the programming was very limited. The value of the work I am sure to engineers like myself and possibly to mathematicians like Alan Turing, was that we acquired a new understanding of and familiarity with logical switching and processing because of the enhanced possibilities brought about by electronic technologies which we ourselves developed. Thus when stored program computers became known to us we were able to go right ahead with their development. It was lack of funds which finally stopped us, not lack of know-how."

Another person whom I had contacted in an effort to check the story of the Turing/von Neumann meeting was Dr S. Frankel, who had known von Neumann whilst working at Los Alamos. Although unable to help in this matter, he provided further evidence of the influence of Turing's pre-war work (quoted in [16]):

> "I know that in or about 1943 or '44 von Neumann was well aware of the fundamental importance of Turing's paper of 1936 'On computable numbers ... ' which describes in principle the 'Universal Computer' of which every modern computer (perhaps not ENIAC as first completed but certainly all later ones) is a realization. Von Neumann introduced me to that paper and at his urging I studied it with care."

By now I realised that I was onto a very big story indeed, and that I had been very wrong to omit Turing's name from the list of pioneers whose work should be covered in my planned collection of documents on the origins of digital computers.

I prepared a confidential draft account of my investigation, which I sent to each of the people who I had quoted, for their comments and to obtain permission to publish what they had told me, and in the hope that my draft might prompt yet further revelations. This hope was fulfilled, when in response Donald Michie amplified his comments considerably. The information (quoted more fully in [16]) that he provided included:

> "Turing was not directly involved in the design of the Bletchley electronic machines, although he was in touch with what was going on. He was, however, concerned in the design of electromagnetic devices used for another cryptanalytic purpose; the Post Office engineer responsible for the hardware side of this work was Bill Chandler … First machines: The 'Heath Robinson' was designed by Wynn Williams … at the Telecommunications Research Establishment at Malvern, and installed in 1942/1943. All machines, whether 'Robinsons' or 'Colossi', were entirely automatic in operation, once started. They could only be stopped manually! Two five-channel paper tape loops, typically of more than 1000 characters length, were driven by pulley-drive (aluminium pulleys) at 2000 characters/sec. A rigid shaft, with two sprocket wheels, engaged the sprocket-holes of the two tapes, keeping the two in alignment. Second crop: The 'Colossi' were commissioned from the Post Office, and the first installation was made in December 1943 (the Mark 1). This was so successful that by great exertions the first of three more orders (for a Mark 2 version) was installed before D-day (June 6th 1944). The project was under the direction of T.H. Flowers, and on Flowers' promotion, A.W.M. Coombs took over the responsibility of coordinating the work. The design was jointly done by Flowers, Coombs, S.W. Broadbent and Chandler … There was only one pulley-driven tape, the data tape. Any pre-set patterns which were to be stepped through these data were generated internally from stored component-patterns. These components were stored as ring registers made of thyrotrons and could be set manually by plug-in pins. The data tape was driven at 5000 characters/sec, but (for the Mark 2) by a combination of parallel operations with short-term memory an effective speed of 25,000/sec was obtained … The total number of Colossi installed and on order was about a dozen by the end of the war, of which about 10 had actually been installed."

So now the names of these still-secret machines had become known to me, and it had become possible for me to attempt to assess the Colossi with respect to the modern digital computer. It seemed clear that their arithmetical, as opposed to logical, capabilities were minimal, involving only counting, rather than general addition or other operations. They did, however, have a certain amount of electronic storage, as well as paper-tape 'backing storage'. Although fully automatic, even to the extent of providing printed output, they were very much special purpose machines, but within their field of specialization the facilities provided by plug-boards and banks of switches afforded a considerable degree of flexibility, by at least a rudimentary form of programming. There seemed, however, no question of the Colossi being stored program computers, and the exact sequence of developments, and patterns of influence, that led to the first post-war British stored program computer projects remained very unclear.

At about this stage in my investigation I decided "nothing ventured nothing gained" and wrote directly to Mr Edward Heath, the Prime Minister, urging that the UK Government declassify Britain's wartime electronic computer developments. In January 1972 my request was regretfully denied but Mr Heath assured me that a detailed report on the project would be commissioned, though it would have to remain classified. (His reply to me was for some time the only unclassified official document I knew of that in effect admitted that Britain had built an electronic computer during World War II!)

The classified official history that the Prime Minister had commissioned following my request was, it turns out, compiled by one of the engineers involved with Colossus, Don Horwood [8]. Tony Sale recently described Horwood's report as having been "absolutely essential" to him when he set out in 1993 to recreate the Colossus [22].

3 The Stored Program Concept

The earliest suggestion that instructions be stored in the main computer memory, that I knew of, was contained in von Neumann's famous EDVAC report [14]. This describes the various purposes for which memory capacity was needed — intermediate results, instructions, tables of numerical constants — ending:

> "The device requires a considerable memory. While it appeared that various parts of this memory have to perform functions which differ somewhat in their nature and considerably in their purpose, it is nevertheless tempting to treat the entire memory as one organ, and to have its parts even as interchangeable as possible for the various functions enumerated above."

On the other hand, a later report by Eckert and Mauchly [4] claims that in early 1944, prior to von Neumann's association with the EDVAC project, they had designed a "magnetic calculating machine" in which the program would "be stored in exactly the same sort of memory device as that used for numbers".

These accounts imply that the idea of storing the program in the same memory as that used for numerical values arose from considerations of efficient resource utilization, and the need to fetch and decode instructions at a speed commensurate with that of the basic computer operations. The question of who first had the idea of, and an understanding of the fundamental importance of, the full stored program concept, that is of an extensive addressable internal memory, used for both instructions and numerical qualities, together with the ability to program the modification of stored instructions, has been for years a very vexed one. In particular there is no consensus regarding the relative contributions of Eckert, Mauchly, von Neumann and Goldstine – a controversy that I did not wish to enter into.

What was indisputable was that the various papers and reports emanating from the EDVAC group, from 1945 onwards, were a source of inspiration to computer designers in many different countries, and played a vital part in the rapid development of the modern computer. But Alan Turing's role remained obscure.

The initial major goals of my investigation, which were to check out the story of a decisive wartime meeting of von Neumann and Turing, and to establish whether Turing had played a direct role in the development of the stored program computer concept, had not been achieved. Instead, and perhaps more importantly, I had to my own surprise by this stage accumulated evidence that in 1943, two to three years before ENIAC, which hitherto had been generally accepted as having been the world's first electronic digital computer, became operational, a group of people directed by M.H.A. Newman and T.H. Flowers, and with which Alan Turing was associated, had built a working special purpose electronic digital computer, the Colossus.

I had established that this computer was developed at the Post Office's Dollis Hill Research Station, and installed at Bletchley Park. The Colossus, and its successors, were in at least a limited sense 'program-controlled'. Moreover, there were believable claims that Turing's classic pre-war paper on computability, a paper which is usually regarded as being of 'merely' theoretical importance, was a direct influence on the British machine's designers, and also on von Neumann, at a time when he was becoming involved in American computer developments.

Having obtained permission from all my informants to use the information that they had provided to me, I and Donald Michie were keen that a summary of my investigation [16] be placed in the public domain. The vehicle we chose was his *1972 Machine Intelligence Workshop*, the proceedings of which were published by Edinburgh University Press.

Afterwards, I managed to persuade Donald to contribute a two page summary of my findings, and thus at last some coverage of Turing, to my collection of historical computer documents – a collection that was published in 1973 by Springer-Verlag as *The Origins of Digital Computers: Selected Papers* [17].

4 Ultra Revelations

There things rested, and it seemed possible that it might be a long time before anything more would become public about Bletchley Park, Alan Turing's work there, or the Colossus Project.

But then in spring 1974 the official ban on any reference to Ultra, a code name for information obtained at Bletchley Park from decrypted German message traffic, was relaxed somewhat, and Frederick Winterbotham's book *The Ultra Secret* [27] was published. This was the "story of how, during World War II, the highest form of intelligence, obtained from the 'breaking' of the supposedly 'unbreakable' German machine cyphers, was 'processed' and distributed with complete security to President Roosevelt, Winston Churchill, and all the principal Chiefs of Staff and commanders in the field throughout the war". The book caused a sensation, and brought Bletchley Park, the Enigma cipher machine, and the impact on the war of the breaking of wartime Enigma traffic, to the general public's attention in a very big way.

The book's one reference to computers came in the statement, "It is no longer a secret that the backroom boys of Bletchley used the new science of electronics to help them ... I am not of the computer age nor do I attempt to understand them, but early in 1940 I was ushered with great solemnity into the shrine where stood a bronze coloured face, like some Eastern Goddess who was destined to become, the oracle of Bletchley". No mention was made of Alan Turing, or any of the others who I had learned were involved with Bletchley's code-breaking machines.

A further, even more sensational, book *Bodyguard of Lies* [3] then revealed more about how the Germans had been using Enigma cipher machines, and gave some information about the work of first the Polish cryptanalysts, and then of Turing and others at Bletchley Park on a machine called the "Bombe" that was devised for breaking Enigma codes. However it made no mention of computers and referred to electronics only in connection with radar and radio; its main topic was the immense impact of all this work on the Allies' conduct of the war.

Emboldened by what seemed to be a rather significant change in Government policy concerning discussion of Bletchley Park's activities, I made some enquiries as to whether another request to declassify the Colossus Project might now have a chance of being treated favourably. I was strongly urged not to write to the Prime Minister again – apparently my earlier request had caused considerable waves on both sides of the Atlantic. Instead, on the advice of David Kahn, I wrote on 4 Nov 1974 to Sir Leonard Hooper, who David Kahn described as being the former head of GCHQ, and who was by then an Under Secretary in the Cabinet Office, I believe with the title Co-ordinator for Intelligence and Security. After a brief exchange of correspondence, in a letter from Sir Leonard dated 22 May 1975 I received the welcome news that "approval had been given for the release of some information about the equipment", and that it was proposed to release some wartime photographs of Colossus to the Public Record Office. I was invited to come to London for discussions at the Cabinet Office. This visit occurred on 2 July 1975.

When I arrived, somewhat nervously, in the Cabinet Office building I was escorted to a panelled room where I met Sir Leonard Hooper, his personal assistant, and a Dr Ralph Benjamin. (I do not recall whether it was then, or later, that I learned that Dr Benjamin was GCHQ Chief Scientist.) I was shown the photographs, and we discussed in detail the wording of the explanatory document.

And then I was told that the Government were willing to facilitate my interviewing the people who had led the Colossus Project, after they had been briefed as to just what topics they were allowed to discuss with me. This was with a view to my being allowed to write a history of the project, providing that I would submit my account for approval prior to publication. Needless to say I agreed.

The photographs and explanatory document were made available at the Public Record Office (now The National Archives) on the 25th October 1975, and I had the pleasure of sending a letter (now on display in the Turing Exhibition at Bletchley Park) to Mrs Turing, informing her that "the Government have recently made an official release of information which contains an explicit recognition of the importance of your son's work to the development of the modern computer".

During the period October-December 1975 I interviewed the leading Colossus designers: Tommy Flowers (twice), Bill Chandler, Sidney Broadhurst, and Allen 'Doc' Coombs. I found all four of them to be delightful individuals, immensely impressive, and amazingly modest about their achievements. All were unfailingly pleasant and helpful as they tried to recollect happenings at Dollis Hill and Bletchley Park. I had the further pleasure of interviewing Max Newman and Donald Michie, and David Kahn kindly interviewed Jack Good for me at his home in Roanoke, Virginia. I also corresponded, in some cases quite intensively, with all these interviewees, and with a considerable number of other people, including several of the Americans who had been stationed at Bletchley Park.

Each interview was tape-recorded, and I had the tapes transcribed in full. The people I interviewed and corresponded with were being asked to recall happenings of thirty or so years earlier, and to do so without any opportunity of inspecting original files and documents. Secrecy considerations had been paramount and had given rise to a rigid compartmentalisation of activities. Few had any detailed knowledge of the work of people outside their own small group. Many of them had made conscious efforts to try and forget about their wartime work.

Piecing together all the information I thus obtained, and even establishing a reasonably accurate chronology, was therefore very difficult. I was greatly aided in this task by the advice I'd read in Kenneth May's magnificent *Bibliography and Research Manual on the History of Mathematics* [12]. For example, the techniques that he described for creating and using a set of correlated card indexes greatly helped me in sorting out a major chronological confusion amongst my interviewees concerning the development of the Robinson machines.

What became clear from my discussions with the Colossus designers was that their interactions with Turing had mainly occurred on projects that preceded Colossus. My investigation led me to summarize their and other's attitude to him as follows (quoted from [18]):

> "Turing, clearly, was viewed with considerable awe by most of his colleagues at Bletchley because of his evident intellect and the great originality and importance of his contributions, and by many with considerable discomfort because his personality was so outlandish. Many people found him incomprehensible, perhaps being intimidated by his reputation but more likely being put off by his character and mannerisms. But all of the Post Office engineers who worked with him say that they found him very easy to understand — Broadhurst characterised him as 'a born teacher — he could put any obscure point very well'. Their respect for him was immense, though as Chandler said 'the least said about him as an engineer the better'. This point is echoed by Michie who said 'he was intrigued by devices of every kind, whether abstract or concrete – his friends thought it would be better if he kept to the abstract devices but that didn't deter him'."

I submitted the draft of my paper on Colossus to Dr Benjamin on 12 April 1976. Subsequent correspondence and discussions with Dr Benjamin and Mr Horwood led to my incorporating a number of relatively small changes into the paper and its abstract, the main effect of which was to remove any explicit indication that the projects I was describing were in fact related to code-breaking. I was merely allowed to say that "The nature of the work that was undertaken at Bletchley Park during World War II is still officially secret but statements have been appearing in published works in recent years which strongly suggest that it included an important part of the British Government's cryptologic effort". This, and the fact I was allowed to retain references to books such as The Ultra Secret and Bodyguard of Lies, however meant that readers would be left in little doubt as to what Turing and his colleagues had been engaged in, and the purpose of the Robinson and Colossus machines.

5 The Outing of Colossus

The cleared paper was then submitted to the *International Conference on the History of Computing*, which was held in Los Alamos in June 1976. (No attempt is made to detail the contents of this 21,000-word paper here!)

Doc Coombs and his wife were planning to be on vacation in the States at about the time of the conference, so to my delight he suggested that he accompany me to the conference and I arranged for him to participate. It is fair to say that my presentation created a sensation – how could it not, given the material I had been allowed to gather?

I have recently found that Bob Bemer has reported[2] his impressions of the event:

> "I was there at a very dramatic moment of the invitational International Research Conference on the History of Computing, in Los Alamos ... Among the many that I conversed with was a medium-sized Englishman named Dr. A.W.M. Coombs, who was so excited about something that he was literally bouncing up and down. Not being bashful I asked (and he didn't mind) about the cause of his excitement, and he replied 'You'll know tomorrow morning – you'll know'. Saturday morning we regathered in the Auditorium of the Physics Division. I sat third row from the front, a couple seats in from the right, to get a good view of all the famous attendees. To my left in the same row, three empty seats intervening, was the bouncy Englishman, all smiles and laughter. In front of him, two seats to his left, was Professor Konrad Zuse ... In the fifth row, again to the left, was Dr. John Mauchly, of ENIAC fame. On stage came Prof. Brian Randell, asking if anyone had ever wondered what Alan Turing had done during World War II? He then showed slides of a place called Bletchley Park, home base of the British cryptographic services during that period. After a while he showed us a slide of a lune-shaped aperture device he had found in a drawer whilst rummaging around there[3]. Turned out it was part of a 5000-character-per-second (!) paper tape reader. From there he went on to tell the story of Colossus, the world's really first electronic computer ... I looked at Mauchly, who had thought up until that moment that he was involved in inventing the world's first electronic computer. I have heard the expression

[2] `http://www.bobbemer.com/COLOSSUS.HTM` (checked 14 May 2012).

[3] In fact it was one of the Colossus team that found this aperture device, which is now on show with some other small Colossus artefacts at Newcastle University.

many times about jaws dropping, but I had really never seen it happen before. And Zuse – with a facial expression that could have been anguish. I'll never know whether it was national, in that Germany lost the war in part because he was not permitted to build his electronic computer, or if it was professional, in that he could have taken first honors in the design of the world's most marvelous tool. But my English friend was the man doing the day-to-day running of Colossus. I saw then why he was so terribly excited. Just imagine the relief of a man who, a third of a century later, could at last answer his children on 'What did you do in the war, Daddy?'."

The conference organisers hurriedly organised an additional evening session, at which Doc Coombs and I fielded a barrage of questions from a packed audience. Doc Coombs' role at this session became that of adding detail to some of the events that my paper described rather guardedly, and mine became at least in part that of endeavouring to make sure that his splendidly ebullient character did not lead him to too many indiscretions. (Tommy Flowers had beforehand warned me that "in his natural exuberance [Doc Coombs] is likely to give away too much for the Foreign Office and you should be careful not to provoke him!")

My paper was promptly published and circulated widely as a Newcastle University Computing Laboratory Technical Report [18] - the proceedings of the Los Alamos conference did not appear until four years later [20]. In addition, a summary version of my paper, including all the Colossus photographs, was published in the *New Scientist* in February 1977 [19], after I had also cleared this with the authorities. This version was afterwards included in the third and final edition of my book *The Origins of Digital Computers* [21] in place of the earlier two-page account by Michie.

Some time in early 1976, I believe, I became aware that BBC Television were planning the *Secret War* series, and that the sixth, and originally last, episode (entitled *Still Secret*) was going to be about Enigma. I met with the producer of this episode, Dominic Flessati, told him — very guardedly — about the Colossus, and showed him the Colossus photographs, at which he became very excited.

The result of this meeting was that Flessati revised his plans for the sixth episode in *The Secret War* series, so as to cover Colossus as well as Enigma. The BBC brought their formidable research resources to bear on the making of this episode. The Enigma section of the episode gave extensive details of the work of the Polish cryptanalysts who originally broke Enigma, how the Enigma worked, and how Bletchley Park made use of a large number of machines, the so-called "bombes", designed by Alan Turing and Gordon Welchman to break Enigma traffic on an industrial scale. It also took the Colossus story on somewhat further than I had managed. For the Colossus section of *Still Secret* they interviewed Tommy Flowers, Gordon Welchman, Max Newman, and Jack Good, mainly on camera, and filmed a number of scenes at Dollis Hill and Bletchley Park, as well as showing the official Colossus photographs.

Whereas I had had to be very guarded in my paper regarding the purpose of the Colossus, *Still Secret* made it abundantly clear that Colossus was used to help break high-level German messages sent in a telegraphic code, via a machine that it said was called a Geheimschreiber ("secret writer"). However the machine that it described, and whose workings it showed, was a teleprinter-based device made by Siemens & Halske.

It was in fact a number of years before this inaccurate identification of the target of the Colossus project was corrected and it became known that the Colossus was in fact used to help break teleprinter messages that were enciphered using a separate ciphering device (the SZ40/42 made by Lorenz AG) to which an ordinary teleprinter was connected, rather than an enciphering teleprinter.

6 The Aftermath

The TV series was very successful when it was broadcast in early 1977. Undoubtedly it, and the accompanying book [9] by the overall editor of the series, did much to bring Bletchley Park, Alan Turing, the Enigma and the Colossus to public attention, though it was some years before there was a general awareness that Colossus was not used against Enigma, and one still occasionally sees confusion over this point.

My original query, concerning the story of a wartime meeting between Turing and von Neumann at which the seeds of the modern computer were planted remained — and remains — unanswered. The present general consensus, with which I tend to agree, dismisses this as a legend. However I should mention that after my account was published one senior US computer scientist, well-connected with the relevant authorities there, did hint to me rather strongly that it would be worth my continuing my quest! But nothing ever came of this, I'm afraid.

I did feel that my investigations had cleared up some of the more important misconceptions and misattributions regarding the stored program computer concept, not least exactly what the concept involved. However, my investigation of Turing's postwar work at NPL did not match the thoroughness with which Carpenter & Doran [2] analyzed his 1945 design for ACE. Their comparison of the fully-developed stored program facilities that Turing proposed in 1945 for the ACE against the rather rudimentary ones in the EDVAC report that slightly predated it [14], and which he cited, indicate to me that I really should have included at least some of Turing's 1945 Report, in my collection of selected papers.

There was one very amusing aftermath, as far as I was concerned, of my involvement with the BBC television programme. I had been asked by Domenic Flessati to tell him the next time I would be in London after the TV series had been broadcast, so that we could have a celebratory dinner. This I did, and we met on the front steps of Bush House, where he introduced me to Sue Bennett, his researcher for *Still Secret*, in the following terms "Miss Bennett, I'd like you to meet Professor Randell, the 'Deep Throat' of the *Secret War* series." I'm rarely left speechless, but this was one of the occasions!

One final happening in 1977 needs to be mentioned – the conferment on Tommy Flowers of an Honorary Doctorate by Newcastle University, an event that was reported prominently by The Times the next day [23]. I take great pride in the fact that I played a role in arranging this very belated public recognition for his tremendous achievement.

7 Concluding Remarks

By way of a Conclusion, one further Newcastle-related incident is worth reporting. At my invitation Professor Harry Hinsley, a Bletchley Park veteran and senior author of the multi-volume official history *British Intelligence in the Second World War* [7], gave a Public Lecture at Newcastle University, soon after the first volume was published in 1979. His lecture was on the subject of the impact of Bletchley Park's activities on the war. One of the questions he received after his lecture was "If this work was so significant, why didn't it shorten the War?" His reply was short and to the point: "It did, by about two years!"

As I indicated earlier, the request that I devote this lecture to my investigation into Turing's wartime work was motivated by the overall relevance of his career to the CONCUR community. Interestingly, there is a link between my 1970s historical investigation and my own most recent computer science research, which in fact is directly related to your topic of concurrency. This research concerns a new formalism, based on occurrence nets, for representing the activity of a complex evolving system [11]. One of the potential applications of this research is to the design of software for supporting large-scale crime and accident investigations.

I have in this lecture described the problems that I had in piecing together a coherent account of the work at Bletchley Park from a large amount of fragmentary evidence, e.g. even the basic problem of establishing an overall chronology of events. I have mentioned that I had been greatly helped in overcoming these problems by the use of Kenneth May's card index system. I now realise how much more useful to me might have been the sort of (criminal) investigation support system that is now one focus of my current research – but that is another story, for another time.

References

1. Bowden, B.V.: Faster Than Thought, Pitman, London (1953)
2. Carpenter, B., Doran, R.: The other Turing machine. Comp. J. 20(3), 269–279 (1977)
3. Cave Brown, A.: Bodyguard of Lies: The vital role of deceptive strategy in World War II. Harper and Row, New York (1975)
4. Eckert, J.: Disclosure of a magnetic calculating machine. Tech. rep. (1945) (unpublished typescript); reprinted in: Eckert, J.P.: The ENIAC. In: A History of Computing in the Twentieth Century, pp. 525–539. Academic Press, New York (1980)
5. Good, I.: Some future social repercussions of computors. Int. J. of Environmental Studies 1(1), 67–79 (1970)
6. Halsbury, L.: Ten years of computer development. Comp. J. 1, 153–159 (1959)
7. Hinsley, F., Thomas, E., Ransom, C., Knight, R.: British Intelligence in the Second World War (5 vols.). Her Majesty's Stationery Office, London (1979-1990)
8. Horwood, D.: A technical description of Colossus I. Tech. Rep. Report P/0921/8103/16, Government Code and Cypher School (August 1973), National Archives HW 25/24
9. Johnson, B.: The Secret War. British Broadcasting Corporation, London (1978)
10. Kahn, D.: The Codebreakers. MacMillan, New York (1967)
11. Koutny, M., Randell, B.: Structured occurrence nets: A formalism for aiding system failure prevention and analysis techniques. Fundamenta Informaticae 97(1-2), 41–91 (2009)
12. May, K.: Bibliography and Research Manual on the History of Mathematics. University of Toronto Press (1973)
13. Morrison, P., Morrison, E.: Charles Babbage and his Calculating Engines. Dover Publications Inc., New York (1961)

14. von Neumann, J.: First draft of a report on the EDVAC. contract no. w-670-ord-4926. Tech. rep., Moore School of Electrical Engineering. University of Pennsylvania, Philadelphia, PA (1945); extracts reprinted in: Randell, B.(ed.) Origins of Digital Computers: Selected Papers. Springer (1973)
15. Newman, M.: Alan Mathison Turing 1912-1954. Biographical Memoirs of Fellows of the Royal Society 1, 253–263 (1955)
16. Randell, B.: On Alan Turing and the origins of digital computers. In: Meltzer, B., Michie, D. (eds.) Machine Intelligence, vol. 7, pp. 3–20. Edinburgh Univ. Press (1972)
17. Randell, B.: The Origins of Digital Computers: Selected Papers. Springer, Heidelberg (1973)
18. Randell, B.: The Colossus. Tech. Rep. 90, Computing Laboratory (1976)
19. Randell, B.: Colossus: Godfather of the computer. New Scientist 73(1038), 346–348 (1977); reprinted in: Randell, B.(ed.) Origins of Digital Computers: Selected Papers, 3rd edn. Springer (1982)
20. Randell, B.: The Colossus. In: Metropolis, N., Howlett, J., Rota, G. (eds.) A History of Computing in the Twentieth Century, pp. 47–92. Academic Press, New York (1980); Proceedings of the 1976 Los Alamos Conference on the History of Computing
21. Randell, B.: The Origins of Digital Computers: Selected Papers, 3rd edn. Springer, Heidelberg (1982)
22. Swade, D.: Pre-electronic Computing. In: Jones, C.B., Lloyd, J.L. (eds.) Festschrift Randell. LNCS, vol. 6875, pp. 58–83. Springer, Heidelberg (2011)
23. Times: Computer pioneer: Mr. Thomas Flowers. The Times, p.16 (May 14,1977), Gale CS270237870
24. Turing, A.M.: On computable numbers, with an application to the Entscheidungsproblem. Proc. London Math. Soc. s2 42, 230–267 (1936)
25. Turing, A.M.: Proposals for the development in the Mathematics Division of an Automatic Computing Engine (ACE). Tech. Rep. Report E882, National Physical Laboratory (1945); reprinted with foreword by: Davies, D.W.: NPL Report Comm. Sci. 57 (April 1972)
26. Turing, S.: Alan M. Turing. W. Heffer and Sons, Cambridge (1959)
27. Winterbotham, F.: The Ultra Secret. Weidenfeld and Nicolson, London (1974)

False Concurrency and Strange-but-True Machines (Abstract)

Peter Sewell

University of Cambridge

Concurrency theory and real-world multiprocessors have developed in parallel for the last 50 years, from their beginnings in the mid 1960s. Both have been very productive: concurrency theory has given us a host of models, calculi, and proof techniques, while engineered multiprocessors are now ubiquitous, from 2–8 core smartphones and laptops through to servers with 1024 or more hardware threads. But the fields have scarcely communicated, and the shared-memory interaction primitives offered by those mainstream multiprocessors are very different from the theoretical models that have been heavily studied.

My colleagues and I have been working at this interface: establishing rigorous and accurate concurrency semantics for multiprocessors (x86 [1,2], IBM POWER [3,8], and ARM) and for the C11 and C++11 programming languages [4], and reasoning about them, developing the CompCertTSO verified compiler from a concurrent C-like language to x86 [5,6], verified compilation schemes from C/C++11 to POWER/ARM [7,8], and verified concurrent algorithms and optimisations [9,10]. The models and reasoning principles are new, but we draw on the toolbox established in the theoretical world. In this talk I will highlight a few examples of this work.

For more details, see `http://www.cl.cam.ac.uk/users/pes20/weakmemory`.

Acknowledgments. This work has been supported by funding from EPSRC grants EP/F036345, EP/H005633, and EP/H027351, ANR project ParSec (ANR-06-SETIN-010), ANR grant WMC (ANR-11-JS02-011), and INRIA associated team MM.

References

1. Owens, S., Sarkar, S., Sewell, P.: A Better x86 Memory Model: x86-TSO. In: Berghofer, S., Nipkow, T., Urban, C., Wenzel, M. (eds.) TPHOLs 2009. LNCS, vol. 5674, pp. 391–407. Springer, Heidelberg (2009)
2. Sewell, P., Sarkar, S., Owens, S., Zappa Nardelli, F., Myreen, M.O.: x86-TSO: A rigorous and usable programmer's model for x86 multiprocessors. Communications of the ACM 53(7), 89–97 (2010) (Research Highlights)
3. Sarkar, S., Sewell, P., Alglave, J., Maranget, L., Williams, D.: Understanding POWER multiprocessors. In: Proc. PLDI (2011)
4. Batty, M., Owens, S., Sarkar, S., Sewell, P., Weber, T.: Mathematizing C++ concurrency. In: Proc. POPL (2011)

M. Koutny and I. Ulidowski (Eds.): CONCUR 2012, LNCS 7454, pp. 37–38, 2012.

5. Ševčík, J., Vafeiadis, V., Zappa Nardelli, F., Jagannathan, S., Sewell, P.: Relaxed-memory concurrency and verified compilation. In: Proc. POPL (2011)
6. Vafeiadis, V., Zappa Nardelli, F.: Verifying Fence Elimination Optimisations. In: Yahav, E. (ed.) Static Analysis. LNCS, vol. 6887, pp. 146–162. Springer, Heidelberg (2011)
7. Batty, M., Memarian, K., Owens, S., Sarkar, S., Sewell, P.: Clarifying and Compiling C/C++ Concurrency: from C++11 to POWER. In: Proc. POPL (2012)
8. Sarkar, S., Memarian, K., Owens, S., Batty, M., Sewell, P., Maranget, L., Alglave, J., Williams, D.: Synchronising C/C++ and POWER. In: Proc. PLDI (2012)
9. Owens, S.: Reasoning about the Implementation of Concurrency Abstractions on x86-TSO. In: D'Hondt, T. (ed.) ECOOP 2010. LNCS, vol. 6183, pp. 478–503. Springer, Heidelberg (2010)
10. Ševčík, J.: Safe optimisations for shared-memory concurrent programs. In: Proc. PLDI (2011)

Concurrent Games on VASS with Inhibition*

Béatrice Bérard[1], Serge Haddad[2], Mathieu Sassolas[3], and Nathalie Sznajder[1]

[1] Université Pierre & Marie Curie, LIP6/MoVe, CNRS UMR 7606, Paris, France
{Beatrice.Berard,Nathalie.Sznajder}@lip6.fr
[2] ENS Cachan, LSV, CNRS UMR 8643 & INRIA, Cachan, France
Serge.Haddad@lsv.ens-cachan.fr
[3] Département d'Informatique, Université Libre de Bruxelles, Bruxelles, Belgium
mathieu.sassolas@ulb.ac.be

Abstract. We propose to study concurrent games on a new extension of Vector Addition Systems with States, where inhibition conditions are added for modeling purposes. Games are a well-suited framework to solve control problems, and concurrent semantics reflect realistic situations where the environment can always produce a move before the controller, although it is never required to do so. This is in contrast with previous works, which focused mainly on turn-based semantics. Moreover, we consider asymmetric games, where environment and controller do not have the same capabilities, although they both have restricted power. In this setting, we investigate reachability and safety objectives, which are not dual to each other anymore, and we prove that (i) reachability games are undecidable for finite targets, (ii) they are 2-EXPTIME-complete for upward-closed targets and (iii) safety games are co-NP-complete for finite, upward-closed and semi-linear targets. Moreover, for the decidable cases, we build a finite representation of the corresponding controllers.

1 Introduction

Context. Games on infinite structures, and their relation to control theory, have been largely studied in the last ten years [1], [16], [17], [11], [12], [19], [18], [5], [7]. Given a plant in an environment and a specification, controllability asks if there exists a controller such that the controlled plant satisfies the specification. When the answer is positive, the synthesis problem requires to build a controller. This problem can be expressed as a game with two players, environment and controller, and the question becomes the existence (and construction) of a controller strategy to win the game.

In this context, various parameters come into play. The underlying models can be continuous or discrete transition systems, the latter being those considered here. The game semantics can be turn-based or concurrent, with identical or

* Work partially supported by projects CoChaT (DIGITEO-2009-27HD), ImpRo (ANR-2010-BLAN-0317), ERC Starting Grant inVEST (279499) and the European Union Seventh Framework Programme [FP7/2007-2013] under grant agreement 257462 HYCON2 NOE.

M. Koutny and I. Ulidowski (Eds.): CONCUR 2012, LNCS 7454, pp. 39–52, 2012.

asymmetrical rules for the two players, with or without the ability to waive a move, and so on. Finally, different winning objectives can be considered: from basic reachability or avoidance objectives (w.r.t. some target set S of system configurations) to general LTL specifications [19,18,3]. In addition, the target set S can be specified in several ways: a finite set, an upward-closed set (with respect to some ordering), a set of (bounded) linear constraints, a semi-linear set, etc.

Related Work. In [12,11], the underlying models are Symbolic Transition Systems or Assignment Program Models with turn-based semantics and avoidance objectives, for which controllability is undecidable. Abstract interpretation techniques are proposed to compute over-approximations of the subset of unsafe states [12] and decidability results are obtained for particular cases, among them Petri nets with upward-closed targets [11]. In [1,16,17], the authors introduce monotonic game structures, which also include Petri nets. The games are turn-based and symmetrical, with safety, reachability and parity objectives for finite and upward-closed target sets. While the problems are still undecidable, the authors investigate subclasses like B-game structures [16,17] or B-downward closed games [1] (where A and B are the two players), thus breaking the symmetry, and they establish decidability results for these games.

Vector Addition Systems with States (VASS) were also used as a model for control and two-player games. A possibly infinitely branching extension of VASS is studied in [5], again with a turn-based symmetrical game, reachability objectives, and a target set containing configurations where one of the counters is null. Decidability is obtained in this case, with an EXPSPACE upper bound, while adding the selection of control states again brings undecidability. Among other results, the complexity bound mentioned above is improved in [7] in the more general framework of Energy and Mean-Payoff games, which is another way of dealing with VASS with specific targets corresponding to minimal or mean values for the counters.

Contribution. In this work, we consider another extension of VASS, called VASSI, obtained by adding inhibition conditions, which correspond to inhibitor arcs in Petri nets (as is done in [3] with boundedness constraints). This feature is useful for modeling purposes: for instance, consider the cooling system of a plant, where temperature can increase when the water level is below some threshold. This can be described by an environment's transition with inhibition conditions (see Fig. 1 in Section 2).

Concerning semantics, we consider concurrent and asymmetric games: we argue that such games are more realistic than turn-based symmetric games in the context of controllability problems, since usually the environment can always produce a move, whatever the controller is willing to do. Along the same line, no player is forced to play. Moreover, environment and controller do not have the same capabilities. They both have restricted power but in an asymmetrical way. Our model is described in Section 2.

Note that in this setting, safety and reachability are not dual objectives with respect to the two players. Also, contrary to [1,16,17], the games are not monotonic anymore. We prove in Section 3 that reachability games are undecidable for finite target sets (hence also for semi-linear sets) and 2EXPTIME-complete for upward-closed targets. On the other hand, we establish in Section 4 that safety games are co-NP-complete for semi-linear targets, as well as finite and upward-closed sets (see summary in Table 1). For decidable games, we also provide finite representations of controllers, the one for safety games implementing a most permissive strategy. Detailed proofs can be found in [2].

Table 1. Summary of results

Objective/Target	Finite	Semi-linear	Upward-closed
Reachability	Undecidable $\Longrightarrow$	Undecidable	2-EXPTIME-complete
Safety	co-NP-complete	co-NP-complete	co-NP-complete

2 Games on VASS with Inhibition Conditions

We denote by A^* (resp. A^ω) the set of finite (resp. infinite) sequences of elements of a set A, with ε the empty sequence, and $|w|$ the length of $w \in A^*$. A finite sequence u is a *prefix* of w, if there is a sequence v such that $uv = w$. We write $A^+ = A^* \setminus \{\varepsilon\}$ and $A^\infty = A^* \cup A^\omega$. The set of all subsets of A is denoted by $\mathcal{P}(A)$ and $\uplus$ denotes the disjoint union of subsets.

We write $\mathbb{Z}$ (resp. $\mathbb{N}$) for the set of integers (resp. nonnegative integers). For $n \in \mathbb{N}$, let $[n]$ denote the set $\{1, \ldots, n\}$. For a vector $v = (v_j)_{j \in [n]} \in \mathbb{Z}^n$ and for $i \in [n]$, let $v(i) = v_i$ be the ith component of v and $v[i] = (v_j)_{j \in [i]}$ be the projection of v onto its first i components. The vector with all components equal to 0 is denoted by $\mathbf{0}$. Given $v_1, v_2 \in \mathbb{N}^n$, operations are defined componentwise: $v_1 \geq v_2$ if $v_1(i) \geq v_2(i)$ for all $i \in [n]$, and $v_1 + v_2$ is defined by $(v_1 + v_2)(i) = v_1(i) + v_2(i)$ for all $i \in [n]$.

We extend the definition of Vector Addition System with States to include inhibition conditions.

Definition 1 (Vector Addition Systems with States and Inhibition conditions). *A* Vector Addition System with States and Inhibition conditions *(VASSI) is a tuple $\mathcal{V} = (Q, n, T, \alpha, \beta, \delta, Inh)$ where*

- *Q is a finite set of states,*
- *$n \in \mathbb{N}$ is the number of counters (called the dimension),*
- *T is the set of transitions, $\alpha, \beta : T \to Q$ associate respectively with each $t \in T$, its source and target states,*
- *$\delta : T \to \mathbb{Z}^n$ is the displacement function,*
- *and $Inh : T \to (\mathbb{N} \setminus \{0\} \cup \{\infty\})^n$ is the inhibition function.*

A *configuration* of a VASSI $\mathcal{V} = (Q, n, T, \alpha, \beta, \delta, Inh)$ is a pair $c = (q, m) \in \mathcal{C} = Q \times \mathbb{N}^n$. The semantics of $\mathcal{V}$ is given by the transition system $\mathcal{T}_\mathcal{V} = (\mathcal{C}, \rightarrow)$, where $\rightarrow \subseteq \mathcal{C} \times \mathcal{C}$ is the transition relation defined by $(q, m) \rightarrow (q', m')$ if and only if there is a transition $t \in T$ such that $\alpha(t) = q$, $\beta(t) = q'$, $m < Inh(t)$ and $m' = m + \delta(t)$; note that since $m' \in \mathbb{N}^n$, $m + \delta(t) \geq \mathbf{0}$. In such a case, we say that t is *fireable* in (q, m) and we may also write the transition as $(q, m) \xrightarrow{t} (q', m')$.

A *run* of $\mathcal{T}_\mathcal{V}$ (or, equivalently, of $\mathcal{V}$) is a sequence of configurations $\rho = c_0 c_1 \cdots \in \mathcal{C}^\infty$ such that $c_i \rightarrow c_{i+1}$ for all $0 \leq i < |\rho|$.

Given $c, c' \in \mathcal{C}$ two configurations, we say that c' is *reachable* from c if there is a finite run $c_0 c_1 \ldots c_k$ of $\mathcal{V}$ with $c = c_0$ and $c' = c_k$. Like above, we may also write $c \xrightarrow{\tau} c'$, indicating the corresponding sequence of transitions $\tau = t_1 t_2 \ldots t_k$, which forms what we call a *fireable path* in the underlying graph (Q, T).

Our games are played by two players (environment and controller) on a subclass of VASSI, where the set of transitions is partitioned into controllable and uncontrollable transitions, with the additional constraint that uncontrollable transitions can only increase the values of the counters (as in [16,17]) and controllable transitions cannot be inhibited:

Definition 2 (Asymmetric VASSI). *An* Asymmetric VASSI *(shortly AVASSI) is a VASSI where the set of transitions is partitioned into two subsets: $T = T_c \uplus T_u$, and such that $\delta(T_u) \subseteq \mathbb{N}^n$ and $Inh(T_c) = \{(\infty)^n\}$.*

If we consider that environment sends events to the system through a unidirectional channel, the counters can represent the number of environment events the system is *aware of* that have not been handled yet (actual content of events is abstracted away). The system does not necessarily observe all the events in the channel (due to delay of transmission from a sensor for instance), hence it cannot test the value 0 of the counter (which corresponds to the fact that the transition cannot be inhibited).

To illustrate this definition, we give another example where our model is appropriate: the case of a (simple) cooling system is depicted by the AVASSI in Fig. 1, where the three counters represent respectively the amount of water in a tank, the temperature, and the cost associated with pumping water into the tank. A transition of the controller is represented by a solid line and labeled by a column vector corresponding to the displacement function δ. A transition of the environment is represented by a dotted line and labeled by two column vectors corresponding to the displacement function δ and the inhibition function Inh. When the pump is *on*, the controller can add water into the tank. The environment can increase the global cost. When the pump is *off*, the controller can choose to empty the tank. In both cases, when the water gets below some threshold x, cooling is prevented, which is described by an environment's transition with inhibition condition that increases the temperature counter. Of course, this toy example could be made more realistic.

Strategies. Given an AVASSI $\mathcal{V}$, a *strategy* for the controller is a mapping $f : \mathcal{C}^+ \rightarrow 2^{T_c}$ that gives the subset of fireable transitions of T_c permitted after a sequence of configurations. A strategy f is *memoryless* if $f(\rho_1 \cdot c) = f(\rho_2 \cdot c)$,

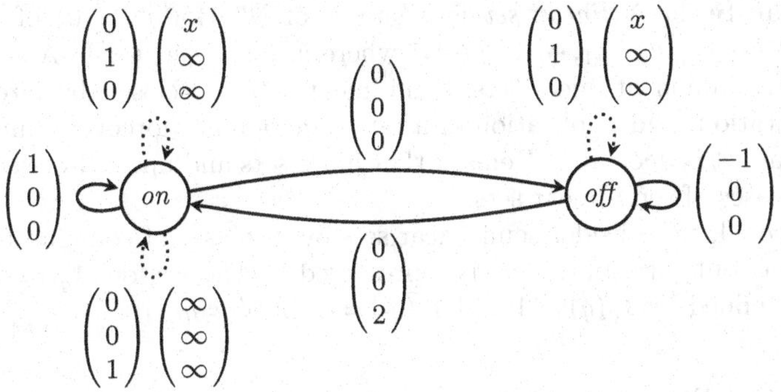

Fig. 1. Cooling system as an AVASSI. Solid edges belong to the controller while dotted edges belong to the environment.

for all $\rho_1, \rho_2 \in \mathcal{C}^*$, $c \in \mathcal{C}$. In this case, we may simply define it as a mapping $f : \mathcal{C} \to 2^{T_c}$.

Outcome of a Strategy. Given an AVASSI $\mathcal{V}$ and a strategy $f : \mathcal{C}^+ \to 2^{T_c}$, a run $\rho = c_0c_1 \cdots \in \mathcal{C}^\infty$ is *f-consistent* (and also called an *f-run*) if, at each step, either a transition permitted by the strategy has been fired, or the environment has played instead, *i.e.* for all $0 < i < |\rho|$, there exists a transition $t \in f(c_0 \dots c_{i-1}) \cup T_u$ such that $c_{i-1} \xrightarrow{t} c_i$.

An f-run ρ is *f-maximal* if it is infinite or such that $f(\rho) = \emptyset$. Given a configuration $c \in \mathcal{C}$, we define *Outcome*$(f, \mathcal{V}, c)$ as the set of f-maximal f-runs of $\mathcal{V}$ that start in c.

Winning Condition and Winning Strategies. Given a AVASSI $\mathcal{V}$, a *winning condition* is a set of sequences $W \subseteq \mathcal{C}^\infty$. A run is *winning* if it belongs to W and a strategy f is *winning* from configuration $c \in \mathcal{C}$ for W if *Outcome*$(f, \mathcal{V}, c) \subseteq W$.

Control Problem. The control problem for AVASSI can be expressed as follows: given an AVASSI $\mathcal{V}$, an initial configuration $c_0 \in \mathcal{C}$, and a winning condition W, does there exist a winning strategy for the controller for W from c_0? We consider in this work two variants of winning conditions: given a AVASSI, and a set of configurations $S \subseteq \mathcal{C}$ (the *target*),

- a *reachability objective* is defined by $W = \mathcal{C}^* \cdot S \cdot \mathcal{C}^\infty$,
- a *safety objective* is defined by $W = (\mathcal{C} \setminus S)^\infty$.

In the rest of the paper, we call these problems respectively *reachability game* and *safety game* and we consider three types of targets: finite sets, upward-closed sets, and semi-linear sets of configurations.

Upward-Closed Sets. Let $(A, \preceq)$ be an ordered set. A subset $S \subseteq A$ is *upward-closed* if for all $a_1 \in S$ and $a_2 \in A$, if $a_1 \preceq a_2$, then $a_2 \in S$. Such a set can be represented by a finite set of minimal elements.

In this work, we consider upward-closed sets of configurations with respect to the covering order on configurations of an AVASSI: (q_1, m_1) *covers* (q_2, m_2), written $(q_1, m_1) \succeq (q_2, m_2)$, if $q_1 = q_2$ and $m_1 \geq m_2$.

Semi-linear Sets. A *linear set* is a subset of $\mathbb{N}^n$ (for $n > 0$) of the form $\{v + k_1u_1 + \cdots + k_pu_p \mid k_1, \cdots, k_p \in \mathbb{N}\}$ where $v, u_1, \cdots, u_p \in \mathbb{N}^n$. A *semi-linear set* is a finite union of linear-sets. Semi-linear sets are closed by intersection, complementation, and application of a linear mapping. Moreover, emptiness of a semi-linear set is decidable. Remark that finite sets and upward-closed sets are particular cases of semi-linear sets.

In the sequel, we consider semi-linear sets over the set of configurations seen as $\mathbb{N}^{Q \uplus [n]}$: a configuration (q, m) is represented by the vector $(\mathbf{1}_q, m)$, with $\mathbf{1}_q$ the vector defined by $\mathbf{1}_q(q) = 1$ and $\mathbf{1}_q(q') = 0$ for $q' \neq q$.

3 Reachability Games

Finite Targets. In the simplest case where the target is a finite set of configurations, reachability games are undecidable.

Theorem 3. *Reachability games are undecidable on AVASSI for finite targets.*

Proof (Sketch). The proof works by reduction of the halting problem for a two-counter machine. The goal of this game is then to reach a state *end* with the two counters equal to 0. As usual, the instruction not readily implementable on VASS (hence on AVASSI) is the conditional instruction that compares the value of a counter with 0. In our encoding, this choice is made by the environment: first, a widget allows the controller to reach the winning configuration when the environment tries to block the game. Moreover, when the counter is greater than 0, the environment is prevented from firing the transition mimicking the fact that the counter is empty, due to inhibition condition. Then, the only case where the environment can deviate from the actual simulation of the machine is when the counter is empty. If (and only if) it cheats, another widget allows the controller to reach the winning configuration. □

A direct consequence of this result is that the control problem for reachability objective with semi-linear targets is also undecidable.

Upward-Closed Targets. We now consider the case of upward-closed targets:

Theorem 4. *Reachability games on AVASSI with upward-closed targets are 2-EXPTIME-complete.*

Before giving the proof of Theorem 4, we establish in Proposition 5 (reminiscent of [15]) an upper bound on the "size" of the optimal winning strategy, when it exists. By "size", we mean the depth of the tree of possible configurations encountered while playing according to this strategy, where branches stop growing as soon as they reach a winning configuration.

In this section, we say that a run is a min-winning f-run if it is winning while none of its prefixes is. It is sufficient to consider only those runs, since any suffix starting from a configuration covering the target is irrelevant to the winning condition.

Let an input consist of an AVASSI $\mathcal{V} = (Q, n, T, \alpha, \beta, \delta, Inh)$, with an initial configuration $c_0 \in \mathcal{C}$, and an upward-closed set as target, given by the finite set of its minimal elements $B = \{b_1, \ldots, b_m\}$. We denote by $\mathcal{K}$ the size of this input, i.e., the space needed to describe $\mathcal{V}$, c_0 and B. We define $\delta_{\max} = 1 + \max_{t \in T; i \in [n]}(|\delta(t)(i)|)$ and $Inh_{\max} = 1 + \max_{t \in T; i \in [n]}\{Inh(t)(i) \mid Inh(t)(i) < \infty\}$.

Proposition 5. *For an AVASSI $\mathcal{V}$ and an upward-closed target described by $B = \{b_1, \ldots, b_m\}$, there is a winning strategy for the reachability game if and only if there is a winning strategy f such that all the min-winning f-runs have length less than or equal to $2^{\mathcal{K}^{\mathcal{K}+1}}$.*

Proof. We proceed inductively on the AVASSI obtained by projecting onto the p first counters and removing transitions of the environment that contained inhibition conditions on the omitted counters. Formally for $p \leq n$, let $\mathcal{V}_p = (Q, p, T_p, \alpha_p, \beta_p, \delta_p, Inh_p)$, where $T_p = T_c \uplus \{t \in T_u \mid Inh(t)(i) = \infty, \text{ for all } p < i \leq n\}$, α_p and β_p are the functions α and β restricted on T_p, and δ_p and Inh_p are respectively the functions δ and Inh restricted to T_p and projected onto the first p dimensions. We set $\mathcal{C}_p = Q \times \mathbb{N}^p$. We say that a run (resp. strategy) is p-winning if it is winning in $\mathcal{V}_p$ for the projection of B (minimal elements of the target) on the first p components. In particular, n-winning means winning.

A run $\rho_p = c_1 \ldots c_k \in \mathcal{C}_p^+$ of $\mathcal{V}_p$ is *p-covering* if it is a minimal p-winning run: c_k covers $b[p]$ for some $b \in B$ and for all $i < k$, for all $b \in B$, c_i does not cover $b[p]$. Note that any p-winning run starts with a p-covering run.

Given $c \in \mathcal{C}_p$ and $f : \mathcal{C}_p^+ \to 2^{T_c}$ a strategy, we define $\text{size}(f, p, c) = \max\{|\sigma| \mid \sigma \text{ is a prefix of } \rho, \rho \in \mathit{Outcome}(f, \mathcal{V}_p, c) \text{ and } \sigma \text{ is } p\text{-covering}\}$ if f is p-winning from c, and $\text{size}(f, p, c) = \infty$ otherwise. From a configuration c, a strategy f reaches the target (in $\mathcal{V}_p$) in at most $\text{size}(f, p, c)$ steps (which can be infinite if the strategy f is not p-winning).

A strategy f is *(p, c)-optimal* if $\text{size}(f, p, c) \leq \text{size}(f', p, c)$ for any strategy $f' : \mathcal{C}_p^+ \to 2^{T_c}$. We denote by $f_{p,c}$ a (p, c)-optimal strategy. Note that since the objective here is reachability, $f_{p,c}$ can be assumed memoryless. If it is not, it is possible to define another (p, c)-optimal strategy that is memoryless in the following way: if $f_{p,c}$ is winning, for all $d \in \mathcal{C}$, we let $f'_{p,c}(d) = f_{p,c}(\sigma d)$ where σd is one of the longest $f_{p,c}$-run having not covered the target yet. If $f_{p,c}$ is not winning, we let $f'_{p,c}(d) = f_{p,c}(\sigma d)$ for some $f_{p,c}$-run σ.

We now assume that there exists a winning strategy from the initial configuration. In the rest of this proof, we therefore consider only configurations for which there exists a winning strategy: $\mathcal{C}_p^{\text{w}} = \{c \in \mathcal{C}_p \mid \exists f, \ p\text{-winning from } c\}$. Let

$$\ell(p) = \max\{\text{size}(f_{p,c}, p, c) \mid c \in \mathcal{C}_p^{\text{w}}, \ f_{p,c} \text{ is a } p\text{-winning strategy from } c\}$$

be the maximal number of steps required to win in $\mathcal{V}_p$ with an optimal winning strategy.

begin
  $\mathcal{C}$:= the set of configurations with counters bounded by $c_0 + \delta_{\max} \cdot L$;
  $\mathcal{C}_A, \mathcal{C}_E$:= copies of $\mathcal{C}$; $\forall c \in \mathcal{C}$, c_A (resp. c_E) is the copy of c in $\mathcal{C}_A$ (resp. $\mathcal{C}_E$);
  mark(c):= false for each c in $\mathcal{C}_A \uplus \mathcal{C}_E$;
  If $c_A \in \mathcal{C}_A$, $succ(c_A)$:= successors of c in $\mathcal{C}_A$ by transitions of T_u and $c_E \in \mathcal{C}_E$;
  If $c_E \in \mathcal{C}_E$, $succ(c_E)$:= successors of c in $\mathcal{C}_A$ by transitions of T_c;
  forall the *configurations c in $\mathcal{C}_A \uplus \mathcal{C}_E$* **do**
    if *$c \succcurlyeq b$ for some $b \in B$* **then** mark(c):= true;
  while *not* end **do**
    end:= true;
    forall the $c \in \mathcal{C}_A$ **do**
      if *all $c' \in succ(c)$ such that* mark(c')=true **then** mark(c):=true; end:=false;
    forall the $c \in \mathcal{C}_E$ **do**
      if *there is $c' \in succ(c)$ such that* mark(c')=true **then** mark(c):=true; end:=false;
  return mark($c_{0,A}$);

Algorithm 1. Guessing a winning strategy

In order to bound $\ell(n)$, we compute by induction on $p \leq n$ an upper bound for $\ell(p)$. To do so, we use the fact that $\ell(0) \leq |Q|$ and $\ell(p+1) \leq (2^{\mathcal{K}})^{p+2} \cdot (\ell(p)+1)^{p+1} + \ell(p)$ (this can be done by induction on p). This recurrence relation can now be used in order to bound $\ell(n)$. Let g be the function defined by $g(0) = 2^{\mathcal{K}}$ and $g(p+1) = g(p)^{2p+4}$. We show by recurrence that $\ell(p) \leq g(p)$ for all p. The case $p = 0$ is trivial. Now assume the inequality holds for p. By the previous recurrence relation, we have:

$$\begin{aligned}\ell(p+1) \leq (2^{\mathcal{K}})^{p+2} \cdot (\ell(p)+1)^{p+1} + \ell(p) &\leq (2^{\mathcal{K}})^{p+2} \cdot (g(p)+1)^{p+1} + g(p)\\ &\leq (2^{\mathcal{K}})^{p+2} \cdot g(p)^{p+2} \qquad \text{(since } g(p) \geq p+2)\\ &\leq g(p)^{p+2} \cdot g(p)^{p+2} \leq g(p)^{2p+4}\end{aligned}$$

Hence: $\ell(p+1) \leq g(p+1)$.
On the other hand, one can show that $g(p) = 2^{\mathcal{K} \cdot 2^p \cdot (p+1)!}$. Therefore

$$L = \ell(n) \leq g(n) \leq 2^{\mathcal{K} \cdot 2^n \cdot (n+1)!} \leq 2^{\mathcal{K} \cdot n^{n+1}} \leq 2^{\mathcal{K} \cdot \mathcal{K}^{\mathcal{K}}} \leq 2^{\mathcal{K}^{\mathcal{K}+1}}.$$ □

Proof (Theorem 4). Having a bound $L = 2^{\mathcal{K}^{\mathcal{K}+1}}$ on the size of the optimal strategy gives us the decision procedure described by Algorithm 1, which runs in doubly exponential time.

We now prove the lower bound. As in [8], we reduce the following problem: given an alternating counter machine of size N, does it have a halting computation in which the value of each counter is bounded by 2^{2^N}? This problem is AEXPSPACE-hard, hence 2-EXPTIME-hard [6]. Given such an alternating counter machine, we build an AVASSI with an upward-closed target for which

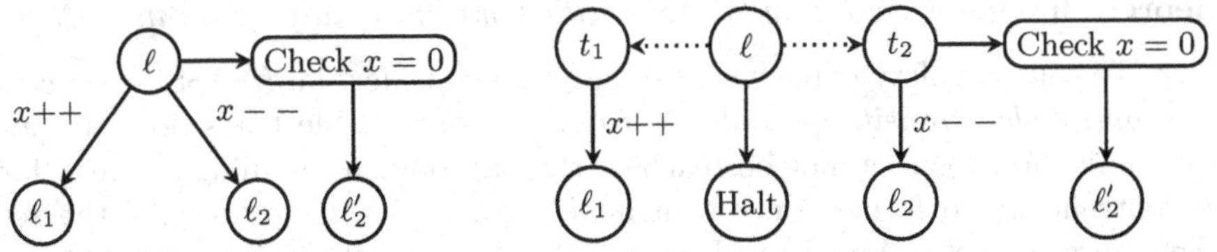

(a) Case of an existential state. (b) Case of a universal state.

Fig. 2. Simulation of a state ℓ of the machine with available transitions t_1: $x{+}{+}$ **goto** ℓ_1 and t_2: **if** $x = 0$ **then** $x - -$ **goto** ℓ_2 **else goto** ℓ'_2. Two cases corresponding to whether ℓ is an existential state or a universal one.

there is a winning strategy if and only if there is a 2^{2^N}-bounded halting computation in the counter machine. We know from Lipton [13] that a 2^{2^N}-bounded counter machine of size N can be simulated by a Petri net of size $O(N^2)$. This construction is easily adapted to our case.

The VASS hence built (in which the set of states contains the set of states of the counter machine) can be turned into an AVASSI in the following way: to each existential state of the counter machine corresponds a state of the AVASSI from which all the outgoing transitions are controllable (and simulate the instructions available from this state in the machine). To each universal state of the counter machine corresponds a state of the AVASSI from which all the outgoing transitions are uncontrollable and lead to intermediate states simulating the instructions. An additional controllable transition to a winning state forces the environment to play. From each intermediate state, there is a single transition, which is controllable, leaving no choice to the controller. This transition simulates the instruction[1]. The target is the set of configurations in an halting state. An example of this simulation in the case of existential and universal states are depicted Fig. 2. □

Observe that an alternate proof for deciding reachability games with upward-closed targets can be performed using the classical construction of *controllable predecessors*. In this case, it can be shown that if a set of configurations is upward-closed, then so is the set of its controllable predecessors. Since the covering order is a well-quasi-ordering, this construction terminates, but this does not provide a complexity upper bound. However, using this alternate construction gives a finite representation of a controller. We do not detail it here as it is standard.

4 Safety Games

In this section, we prove the co-NP-completeness of safety games with semi-linear, finite and upward-closed targets, and we give the construction of the most permissive strategy. We first establish:

[1] The environment cannot decrement vectors: it cannot perform the instruction itself.

Theorem 6. *Safety games on AVASSI with semi-linear targets are in co-NP.*

Proof. To solve a safety game with target S, we consider the AVASSI *restricted to uncontrollable transitions.* Indeed, if only uncontrollable transitions are allowed, and the target cannot be reached, then an obvious winning strategy for the controller is to forbid every controllable transition. Conversely, if the set of configurations S to avoid can be reached by using only uncontrollable transition, there can be no winning strategy for the controller: any run obtained by firing only uncontrollable transitions is an f-run, for any strategy f. Let $Target = \bigcup_{i\in I} \{m_i^* + \sum_{u\in U_i} y_u \cdot u \mid y_u \in \mathbb{N}\}$ be the semi-linear target and let $\mathcal{V}$ be an AVASSI restricted to uncontrollable transitions.

We first introduce some additional notations. Transition t is said *enabled* in configuration $c = (q,m)$ if it is *not inhibited* by m, *i.e.* $m < Inh(t)$. The set of transitions enabled in (q,m) is denoted by $En(q,m)$; we also use the notation $En(m)$ since q is not relevant here. A path $\tau = t_1 \cdots t_k$ in (Q,T) is fireable from configuration $c = (q,m)$ iff for all $j \in [k]$, $t_j \in En(m + \sum_{i=1}^{j-1} \delta(t_i))$. We define the *flow* vector $Flow(t) \in \{-1,0,1\}^Q$ ranging over Q as follows: (i) for $q \in Q \setminus \{\alpha(t), \beta(t)\}$, $Flow(t)(q) = 0$; (ii) if $\alpha(t) = \beta(t)$, then $Flow(t)(\alpha(t)) = 0$; (iii) if $\alpha(t) \neq \beta(t)$, then $Flow(t)(\alpha(t)) = -1$ and $Flow(t)(\beta(t)) = 1$.

The decision procedure described by Algorithm 2 proceeds as follows.

- It (non deterministically) builds a linear system $\mathcal{S}$ with two sets of variables: X, the number of occurrences of some transitions in a sequence τ, and Y, the coefficients of a linear set U of *Target*.
- It guesses a small potential solution of this system (in case of non emptiness) as in [14, Chap. 13][2] and returns true if it is an actual solution.

The sequence τ (which is not built) is of the form $\tau = \tau_1 t_1 \tau_2 \dots t_k \tau_{k+1}$ with $k \leq |T|$. The algorithm guesses the following items: k, $\{t_i\}_{1\leq i\leq k}$, connected subgraphs $\{(Q_i, T_i)\}_{1\leq i\leq k+1}$ of (Q,T) such that T_i is exactly the set of transitions fired in τ_i and finally a linear subset U of *Target*. The set of variables is $X = \{x_{i,t} \mid 1 \leq i \leq k+1 \wedge t \in T_i\}$ and $Y = \{y_u \mid u \in U\}$. The system $\mathcal{S}$ checks if there is a fireable sequence τ whose Parikh vector is $\sum_{i=1}^{k} \mathbf{1}_{t_i} + \sum_{i=1}^{k+1} \sum_{t\in T_i} x_{i,t} \mathbf{1}_t$ and whose final marking belongs to U.

Complexity. The construction of the set of transitions appearing in the solution is done in polynomial time, and the number of variables created is at most $|T|(|T|+1)$. The coefficients of $\mathcal{S}$ are either coefficients of $\delta(t)$ or the integers occurring in U. Hence the size of the system is polynomial. Furthermore, the bound on the small solution provided in [14, Chap. 13] has a polynomial representation in the size of the system. Therefore in our case, this solution can be guessed and checked in polynomial time w.r.t. the input of the safety problem.

Soundness. Assume the algorithm returns true and consider the corresponding solution. For $1 \leq i \leq k+1$, since transitions in T_i form a connected subgraph

[2] If the integer system $AX = B$, with A an (m,n) matrix, has a feasible solution, then it has a feasible solution with coefficients bounded by $n \times (ma)^{2m+4}$, where a is greater than the maximal absolute value of all coefficients of A and B.

begin
  Choose $k \leq |T|$; Choose $q \in Q$;
  $\beta(t_0) := q_0$ *(t_0 is a fictitious transition)*;
  $\alpha(t_{k+1}) := q$ *(t_{k+1} is a fictitious transition)*;
  $X = \emptyset$; $i := 1$;
  while $i \leq k+1$ **do**
    if $i \leq k$ **then** choose $t_i \in T$;
    Choose (Q_i, T_i) a connected subgraph containing $\beta(t_{i-1})$ and $\alpha(t_i)$;
    $X := X \cup \{x_{i,t} \mid t \in T_i\}$;
    if $i \leq k$ **then** $T'_i := T_i \cup \{t_i\}$ **else** $T'_i := T_i$;
    $i := i+1$;
  Choose a linear set $U = \left(m^* + \sum_{u \in U} y_u \cdot u\right) \in \mathit{Target}$;
  Define the linear system $\mathcal{S}$;

$$\mathcal{S} := \begin{cases} \forall x \in X, x \geq 1 \wedge \\ \forall 1 \leq i \leq k+1, \mathbf{1}_{\beta(t_{i-1})} + \sum_{t \in T_i} x_{i,t} \mathit{Flow}(t) = \mathbf{1}_{\alpha(t_i)} & (*) \\ \forall 1 \leq i \leq k+1, \forall t \in T'_i, \\ m_0 + \sum_{j \leq i} \sum_{t \in T_j} x_{j,t} \delta(t) + \sum_{j<i} \delta(t_i) < \mathit{Inh}(t) & (**) \\ m_0 + \sum_{i=1}^{k+1} \sum_{t \in T_i} x_{i,t} \cdot \delta(t) + \sum_{i=1}^{k} \delta(t_i) = m^* + \sum_{u \in U} y_u \cdot u & (***) \end{cases}$$

  Choose *small* values for $(x_{i,t})_{i \leq k+1, t \in T}$ and $(y_u)_{u \in U}$;
  return *whether* $(x_{i,t})_{i \leq k+1, t \in T}, (y_u)_{u \in U}$ *is a solution for* $\mathcal{S}$

Algorithm 2. Guessing a Parikh vector for a firing sequence to an offending configuration

(when the underlying graph is seen as an undirected one), condition $(*)$ of $\mathcal{S}$ is an Euler condition ensuring that one can derive a path τ_i from $\beta(t_{i-1})$ to $\alpha(t_i)$ in which every transition $t \in T_i$ appears exactly $x_{i,t}$ times. Let us denote m_i the marking reached after the sequence $\tau_1 t_1 \ldots \tau_i$. Condition $(**)$ ensures that transitions of T'_i are enabled in m_i, thus they are also enabled in any previous marking occurring along the sequence (since the marking does not decrease after a transition firing). Thus by recurrence, $\tau_1 t_1 \ldots \tau_{k+1}$ is a firing sequence. At last condition $(***)$ ensures that marking $m_{k+1} \in U \subseteq \mathit{Target}$.

Completeness. Let $c_0 \xrightarrow{t_1} \cdots c_{k-1} \xrightarrow{t_k} \cdots$ be a fireable sequence of transitions from c_0, and let I_{Inh} be the subset of indices of those transition occurrences that actually disable other transitions: $j \in I_{Inh}$ if and only if $En(c_j) \subsetneq En(c_{j-1})$. In the worst case, each transition firing with index in I_{Inh} inhibits exactly one other transition. Then, there cannot be more elements in I_{Inh} than the total number of transitions: $|I_{Inh}| \leq |T|$.

Now, assume there is a reachable configuration $m_f = m^* + \sum_{u \in U} \beta_u \cdot u$ in some linear subset $U \subset \mathit{Target}$. Let $\tau_1 t_1 \cdots \tau_k t_k \tau_{k+1}$ be the sequence of transitions leading to this configuration, where the transitions t_i are exactly the ones inducing a modification in the set of enabled transitions. By the above observation, $k \leq |T|$. Let T_i be the transitions occurring in τ_i. Since the enabled transitions are unchanged during the firing of τ_i, transitions T_i for $i \leq k$ (resp. $i = k+1$) are still enabled before the firing of t_i (resp. in m_f). So denoting by

$\sum_{t \in T_i} \alpha_{i,t} \mathbf{1}_t$ the Parikh vector of τ_i, the $\alpha_{i,t}$'s and the β_u's are a solution of the corresponding system $\mathcal{S}$. Using the results of [14, Chap. 13], the algorithm will then find a *small* solution of $\mathcal{S}$.

Summarizing the results, the problem of existence of a winning strategy to ensure a safety objective is in co-NP. □

In general, the set of reachable markings of a Petri Net (and therefore configurations of a VASS) is not semi-linear [10]. However, it was shown to be the case for some restricted models [9,4]. If one determinizes Algorithm 2 and one sets for *Target* all the possible markings, one obtains:

Theorem 7. *Let $\mathcal{V} = (Q, n, T, \alpha, \beta, \delta, Inh)$ be a VASSI s.t. $\delta(T) \subseteq \mathbb{N}^n$. Then its set of reachable configurations is effectively semi-linear.*

By a reduction from 3-SAT, we also obtain the following result.

Theorem 8. *Safety games on AVASSI with finite targets or upward-closed targets are co-NP-hard even with $|Q| = 1$.*

Proof (Sketch). The idea behind the construction is to associate a counter with each literal (a variable or its negation). By deciding to increment a literal or its negation, the environment choses a valuation of variables. Then it can mark clauses as satisfied (through a counter per clause) only when they agree with the chosen valuation. The goal (for the environment) is to reach (or cover) the configuration where all clauses are marked, hence when the whole formula is *true*. □

Corollary 9. *Safety games on AVASSI with finite, upward-closed or semi-linear targets are co-NP-complete.*

Construction of the Most Permissive Strategy. We show now how to build off-line the most permissive strategy.

Theorem 10. *The most permissive strategy for safety games on AVASSI with semi-linear targets can be represented by a finite-state machine.*

Proof. If we determinize again Algorithm 2 and take the (finite) union on all linear sets $U \in Target$ of all possible systems of equations obtained, we get the set of configurations from which the system cannot avoid the target and deduce that this set is semi-linear. These configurations happen to be exactly the ones the strategy should avoid.

One can then compute, for a given controllable transition t, the set of configurations from which this transition is allowed. Let $Pre_{Forbid}(t) = \{(q, m) \in \mathcal{C} \mid \exists (q', m') \in Forbid, q = q' - Flow(t), m = m' - \delta(t)\}$. Since *Forbid* is semi-linear and the image of a semi-linear by an affine application is still semi-linear, we get that $Pre_{Forbid}(t)$ is semi-linear, for any controllable transition t. Then, the set of configurations from which t is allowed is given by $\mathcal{C} \setminus Pre_{Forbid}(t)$, which is still semi-linear. □

5 Conclusion

We solve reachability and safety games with concurrent semantics for an extension of VASS with inhibition conditions, for finite, upward-closed and semi-linear targets. When the reachability games are decidable, the procedures are elementary. For safety games, which are co-NP-complete, the procedure allows to construct the most permissive strategy. Future work includes studying more complex winning objectives, *e.g.*, parity games. Another direction could concern games on continuous models, like timed extensions of Petri nets.

References

1. Abdulla, P.A., Bouajjani, A., d'Orso, J.: Monotonic and downward closed games. J. Log. Comput. 18(1), 153–169 (2008)
2. Bérard, B., Haddad, S., Sassolas, M., Sznajder, N.: Concurrent games on VASS with inhibition. Technical Report LSV-12-10, LSV, ENS Cachan (2012)
3. Bollue, K., Slaats, M., Abraham, E., Thomas, W., Abel, D.: Synthesis of Behavioral Controllers for DES: Increasing Efficiency. In: WODES 2010, IFAC (2010)
4. Bouziane, Z., Finkel, A.: Cyclic petri net reachability sets are semi-linear effectively constructible. Electr. Notes Theor. Comput. Sci. 9, 15–24 (1997)
5. Brázdil, T., Jančar, P., Kučera, A.: Reachability Games on Extended Vector Addition Systems with States. In: Abramsky, S., Gavoille, C., Kirchner, C., Meyer auf der Heide, F., Spirakis, P.G. (eds.) ICALP 2010, Part II. LNCS, vol. 6199, pp. 478–489. Springer, Heidelberg (2010)
6. Chandra, A.K., Kozen, D., Stockmeyer, L.J.: Alternation J. ACM 28(1), 114–133 (1981)
7. Chatterjee, K., Doyen, L., Henzinger, T.A., Raskin, J.F.: Generalized mean-payoff and energy games. In: Lodaya, K., Mahajan, M. (eds.) FSTTCS 2010. LIPIcs, Schloss Dagstuhl - Leibniz-Zentrum für Informatik, vol. 8, pp. 505–516 (2010)
8. Demri, S., Jurdziński, M., Lachish, O., Lazić, R.: The covering and boundedness problems for branching vector addition systems. In: Proc. of the 29th Conference on Foundations of Software Technology and Theoretical Computer Science (FSTTCS 2009). Leibniz International Proceedings in Informatics, Leibniz-Zentrum für Informatik, vol. 4, pp. 181–192 (December 2009)
9. Esparza, J.: Petri nets, commutative context-free grammars, and basic parallel processes. Fundam. Inform. 31(1), 13–25 (1997)
10. Hopcroft, J.E., Pansiot, J.J.: On the reachability problem for 5-dimensional vector addition systems. Theor. Comput. Sci. 8, 135–159 (1979)
11. Kumar, R., Garg, V.: On computation of state avoidance control for infinite state systems in assignment program framework. IEEE Trans. Autom. Sci. Eng. 2(1), 87–91 (2005)
12. Le Gall, T., Jeannet, B., Marchand, H.: Supervisory Control of Infinite Symbolic Systems using Abstract Interpretation. In: CDC 2005, pp. 31–35. IEEE Press (2005)
13. Lipton, R.: The reachability problem requires exponential space. Technical Report 62, Dept. of Computer Science. Yale University (1976)
14. Papadimitriou, C.H., Steiglitz, K.: Combinatorial Optimization: algorithms and complexity. Prentice-Hall (1982)

15. Rackoff, C.: The covering and boundedness problems for vector addition systems. Theor. Comput. Sci. 6, 223–231 (1978)
16. Raskin, J.F., Samuelides, M., Van Begin, L.: Petri games are monotonic but difficult to decide. Technical Report 508, Université Libre de Bruxelles (2003)
17. Raskin, J.F., Samuelides, M., Van Begin, L.: Games for counting abstractions. Electr. Notes Theor. Comput. Sci. 128(6), 69–85 (2005)
18. Serre, O.: Parity Games Played on Transition Graphs of One-Counter Processes. In: Aceto, L., Ingólfsdóttir, A. (eds.) FOSSACS 2006. LNCS, vol. 3921, pp. 337–351. Springer, Heidelberg (2006)
19. Sreenivas, R.S.: Some observations on supervisory policies that enforce liveness in partially controlled free-choice petri nets. Math. Comp. Simul. 70(5-6), 266–274 (2006)

Reachability Problem for Weak Multi-Pushdown Automata

Wojciech Czerwiński, Piotr Hofman, and Sławomir Lasota*

Institute of Informatics, University of Warsaw
{wczerwin,sl}@mimuw.edu.pl

Abstract. This paper is about reachability analysis in a restricted subclass of multi-pushdown automata: we assume that the control states of an automaton are partially ordered, and all transitions of an automaton go downwards with respect to the order. We prove decidability of the reachability problem, and computability of the backward reachability set. As the main contribution, we identify relevant subclasses where the reachability problem becomes NP-complete. This matches the complexity of the same problem for communication-free vector addition systems (known also as commutative context-free graphs), a special case of stateless multi-pushdown automata.

1 Introduction

This paper is about reachability analysis of *multi-pushdown systems*, i.e., systems with a global control state and multiple stacks. The motivation for our work is twofold. On one side, a practical motivation coming from context-bounded analysis of recursive concurrent programs [23, 20, 3]. On the other side, a theoretical motivation coming from partially-commutative context-free grammars, developed recently in [11–13].

Context bounded analysis. Multi-pushdown systems may be used as an abstract model of concurrent programs with recursive procedures. As multi-pushdown systems are a Turing-complete model of computation, they are only applicable for verification under further tractable restrictions. One remarkably successful restriction is imposing a bound on the number of context switches; between consecutive context switches, the system may only perform operations on one stack (local operations). In [23], the context-bounded reachability has been shown decidable, by reduction to reachability of ordinary pushdown systems [5]. This line of research, with applications in formal verification, has been continued successfully, e.g., in [6, 20, 3].

Weak control states. As our starting point we observe that if the number of context switches is bounded, one may safely assume that the control state space is *weak*, in the sense that there is a partial order on control states such that transitions go only downwards with respect to the order. Indeed, the local state space of every thread may be eliminated using a stack, and the global control state essentially enumerates context

* The first author acknowledges a partial support by the Polish MNiSW grant N N206 568640. The other authors acknowledge a partial support by the Polish MNiSW grant N N206 567840.

M. Koutny and I. Ulidowski (Eds.): CONCUR 2012, LNCS 7454, pp. 53–68, 2012.

switches. Roughly speaking, the model investigated in this paper extends the above one with respect to operations allowed between two context switches, namely, we do not restrict these operations to one stack only. Thus, if k is the number of stacks, we assume that transitions of a system are of the following form:

$$q,\ \mathrm{X} \xrightarrow{a} q',\ \alpha_1, \ldots, \alpha_k, \tag{1}$$

to mean that in state q, symbol X is popped from one of the stacks, and sequences of symbols $\alpha_1, \ldots, \alpha_k$, respectively, are pushed on stacks. Wlog. one may assume that the symbols of different stacks are different.

Partially-commutative context-free grammars. A special case of the model investigated in this paper is *stateless* multi-pushdown systems. This is still a quite expressible model that subsumes, among the others, context-free graphs (so called Basic Process Algebra [8]) and communication-free Petri nets (so called Basic Parallel Processes [8]). In the stateless case, transitions (1) may be understood as productions of a grammar, with the nonterminal symbols on the right-hand side (stack symbols) subject to a commutativity law. More precisely, for any two symbols X and Y from different stacks, we impose the commutativity law

$$\mathrm{XY} = \mathrm{YX}.$$

One easily observes that this is a special case of *independence relation* over nonterminal symbols, as defined in trace theory [14][1]. In multi-pushdown systems, the *dependency relation* (complement of independence relation) is always transitive. A general theory of context-free grammars modulo dependency relation that is not necessarily transitive, has been studied recently in [13]; complexity of bisimulation equivalence checking has been investigated in [11, 12]. The present paper complements these results by focusing on reachability analysis.

Contributions. This paper contains two main results. First, we prove decidability of reachability for weak multi-pushdown automata. Our argument is based on a suitable well order on the set of configurations, that strongly depends on the assumption that the control states are weak.

Second, we identify additional restrictions under which the problem is NP-complete; one such restriction is stateless multi-pushdown systems. Our result subsumes (and gives a simpler algorithm for) the case of communication-free Petri nets; reachability thereof is NP-complete as shown in [15]. The last result is similar to NP-completeness of the word problem for partially-commutative context-free grammars [16], where one asks if the given input word is accepted. The reachability question is more difficult to answer, as an input word is not given in advance. In fact the main technical difficulty is to show existence of a polynomial witness for reachability.

As further results, we investigate forward and backward reachability sets, and prove that the backward reachability set of a regular set of configurations is regular and computable, while the forward reachability set needs not be regular in general. Finally,

[1] Note however that the independence is imposed on nonterminal symbols, and not on input letters, as usually in trace theory.

we identify the decidability border for reachability of weak multi-pushdown systems. Roughly speaking, the problem becomes undecidable when one asks about reachability of a given regular set of configurations, instead of a single configuration.

The standard techniques useful for analysis of pushdown systems, such as pumping or the automaton-based approach of [5], do not extend to the multi-pushdown setting. This is why the proofs of our results are based on new insights. The NP-membership proofs are, roughly speaking, based on polynomial witnesses obtained by careful elimination of 'irrelevant' transitions. On the other hand, the decidability results are based on a suitable well order on configurations.

Related research. Multi-pushdown systems are a fundamental model of recursive multi-threaded programs. This is why different instantiations of the multi-pushdown paradigm have been appearing in the literature recently, most often in the context of formal verification. We only mention here a few relevant positions we are aware of, without claiming completeness. All the papers cited below bring some restricted decidability results for reachability or model checking.

Most often, a model has global control states, subject to some restriction. For instance, the author of [1] assumes that the stacks are ordered, and pop operation can only be performed on the first nonempty stack. Another example is the model introduced in [7] and then further investigated e.g. in [6, 2, 4], that allows for unbounded creation of new stacks; on the other hand, operations on each stack are local, thus no communication between threads is allowed.

Another possible approach is to replace global state space with some communication mechanism between threads. Some successful results on analysis of multi-threaded programs communicating via locks, in a restricted way, has been reported in [18, 17, 9].

In [21] the algorithm for reachability over PA [8] graphs has been provided. The PA class is a generalization of both BPA and BPP that allows, similarly like multi-pushdown systems, both for sequential and interleaved behavior. Finally, in [19] the reachability problem has been shown decidable for Process Rewrite Systems [22] extended with weak control states.

Outline. In the following Section 2 we define the model we work with. Then in Section 3 we state all our results. In the remaining sections we provide proofs of some of the results. The other proofs are omitted due to space limitation.

2 Multi-pushdown Automata

A multi-pushdown automaton (MPDA) is like a single-pushdown one. In a single step one symbol is popped from one of stacks[2], and a number of symbols are pushed on the stacks. Assume there is k stacks. A transition of an automaton is thus of the form:

$$q,\ \mathrm{X} \xrightarrow{a} q',\ \alpha_1, \ldots, \alpha_k, \tag{2}$$

[2] If we allowed for popping from more than one stack at a time, the model would clearly become Turing-complete, even with 1 state only.

to mean that when an automaton reads a in state q, it pops X from one of the stacks, pushes the sequence of symbols α_i on the ith stack, for $i = 1 \dots k$, and goes to state q'. We allow for silent transitions with $a = \varepsilon$. Observe that wlog. one may assume that stack alphabets are disjoint.

Formally, the ingredients of a MPDA are: a finite set of states Q, the number of stacks k, pairwise-disjoint finite stack alphabets $\mathsf{S}_1 \dots \mathsf{S}_k$, an input alphabet A, and a finite set of transition rules:

$$\longrightarrow \subseteq \mathsf{Q} \times (\bigcup_{i \leq k} \mathsf{S}_i) \times (\mathsf{A} \cup \{\varepsilon\}) \times \mathsf{Q} \times {\mathsf{S}_1}^* \times \dots \times {\mathsf{S}_k}^* \tag{3}$$

written as in (2). A configuration of a MPDA is a tuple $\langle q, \beta_1, \dots, \beta_k \rangle \in \mathsf{Q} \times {\mathsf{S}_1}^* \times \dots \times {\mathsf{S}_k}^*$. The transition rules (2) induce the transition relation over all configurations in a standard way:

$$\frac{q, \mathrm{X} \xrightarrow{a} q', \alpha_1, \dots, \alpha_k \qquad \mathrm{X} \in \mathsf{S}_i \qquad \beta_i = \mathrm{X}\beta}{\langle q, \beta_1, \dots \beta_i \dots, \beta_k \rangle \xrightarrow{a} \langle q', \alpha_1\beta_1, \dots \alpha_i\beta \dots, \alpha_k\beta_k \rangle}$$

thus defining the configuration graph of a MPDA. For a configuration $\langle q, \alpha_1, \dots, \alpha_k \rangle$, its *size* is defined as the sum of lengths of the words α_i, $i \leq k$. The same applies to a right-hand side of any transition rule $q\,\mathrm{X} \xrightarrow{a} q'\,\alpha_1 \dots \alpha_k$.

An MPDA is *stateless* if there is just one state (or equivalently no states). Transition rules of an automaton are then of the form:

$$\mathrm{X} \xrightarrow{a} \alpha_1, \dots, \alpha_k \tag{4}$$

and configurations are of the form $\langle \beta_1, \dots, \beta_k \rangle$.

A less severe restriction on control states is the following one. We say that an automaton is *weak* if there is a partial order $\leq$ on its states such that every transition (2) satisfies $q' \leq q$. Clearly, every stateless automaton is weak.

Remark 1. Note that stateless one-stack automata are essentially context-free grammars in Greibach normal form. Thus the configuration graphs are precisely context-free graphs, called also BPA graphs [22, 8]. Another special case is many stacks with singleton alphabets. The stacks are thus essentially counters without zero tests. In this subclass, stateless automata corresponds to communication-free Petri nets [15], called also BPP [10], or commutative context-free graphs [12]. The BPA and BPP classes are members of the Process Rewrite Systems hierarchy of [22] that contains, among the others, pushdown systems and unrestricted Petri nets.

Example 1. Assuming a distinguished initial state and acceptance by all stacks empty, weak MPDAs can recognize non-context-free languages. For instance, the language

$$\{a^n b^n c^n : n \geq 0\} \tag{5}$$

is recognized by an automaton described below. The automaton has two states q_1, q_2 and two stacks. The alphabets of the stacks are $\{\mathrm{X}, \mathrm{B}, \mathrm{D}\}$ and $\{\mathrm{C}\}$, respectively. The starting configuration is $(q_1, \mathrm{XD}, \varepsilon)$. Besides the transition rules, we also present the automaton in a diagram, using *push* and *pop* operations with natural meaning.

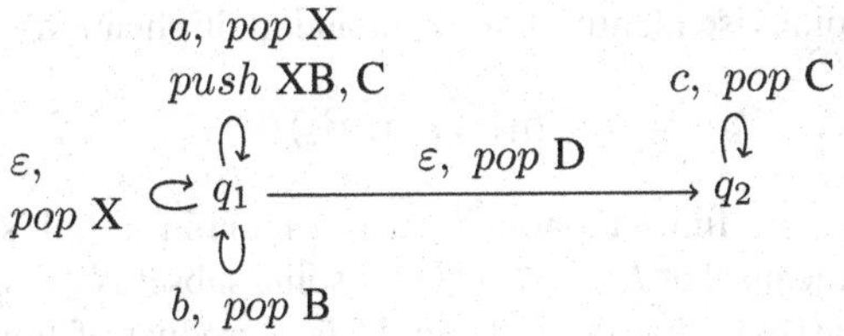

$$
\begin{aligned}
q_1, \mathrm{X} &\xrightarrow{a} q_1, \mathrm{XB}, \mathrm{C}\\
q_1, \mathrm{X} &\xrightarrow{\varepsilon} q_1, \varepsilon, \varepsilon\\
q_1, \mathrm{B} &\xrightarrow{b} q_1, \varepsilon, \varepsilon\\
q_1, \mathrm{D} &\xrightarrow{\varepsilon} q_2, \varepsilon, \varepsilon\\
q_2, \mathrm{C} &\xrightarrow{c} q_2, \varepsilon, \varepsilon
\end{aligned}
$$

The automaton is weak and uses ε-transitions, which may be however easily eliminated. Acceptance by empty stacks may be easily simulated using acceptance by states. The language (5) is not recognized by a stateless automaton, as shown in [13].

Example 2. Non-context-free languages are recognized even by stateless MPDAs with singleton stack alphabets. The class of languages recognized by this subclass is called *commutative context-free* languages [16], see also [13]. One example is the commutative closure of the language of the previous example: the set of all words with the same number of occurrences of a, b and c.

In the sequel we do not care about initial states nor about acceptance condition, as we will focus on the configuration graph of an automaton. Furthermore, as we only consider reachability problem, the labeling of transitions with input alphabet letters will be irrelevant, thus we write $\longrightarrow$ instead of $\xrightarrow{a}$ from now on.

Using a standard terminology, we say that a MPDA is *normed* if for any state q and any configuration $\langle q, \alpha_1, \ldots, \alpha_k \rangle$, there is a path to the empty configuration

$$\langle q, \alpha_1, \ldots, \alpha_k \rangle \longrightarrow \ldots \longrightarrow \langle p, \varepsilon, \ldots, \varepsilon \rangle$$

for whatever state p. In general, whenever a MPDA is not assumed to be normed we call it *unnormed* for clarity. Note that in all examples above the automata were normed. In fact normedness is not a restriction as far as languages are considered. In the sequel we will however analyze the configuration graphs, and then normedness will play a role.

Further, we say that a MPDA is *strongly normed* if for any state q and any configuration $\langle q, \alpha_1, \ldots, \alpha_k \rangle$, there is a path to the empty configuration

$$\langle q, \alpha_1, \ldots, \alpha_k \rangle \longrightarrow \ldots \longrightarrow \langle q, \varepsilon, \ldots, \varepsilon \rangle$$

containing only transitions that do not change state. Intuitively, whatever is the state q we start in, any top-most symbol X in any stack may „disappear". For stateless automata, strong normedness is the same as normedness.

3 Reachability

Regular Sets. We will consider various reachability problems in the configuration graph of a given MPDA. Therefore, we need a finite way of describing infinite sets of configurations. A standard approach is to consider *regular* sets. Below we adapt this approach to the multi-stack scenario we deal with.

Consider the configurations of a stateless MPDA, $\mathsf{S} = \mathsf{S}_1{}^* \times \ldots \times \mathsf{S}_\mathsf{k}{}^*$. There is a natural monoid structure in S, with pointwise identity $\langle \varepsilon, \ldots, \varepsilon \rangle$ and multiplication

$$\langle \alpha_1, \ldots, \alpha_k \rangle \cdot \langle \beta_1, \ldots, \beta_k \rangle = \langle \alpha_1 \beta_1, \ldots, \alpha_k \beta_k \rangle.$$

Call a subset $L \subseteq \mathsf{S}$ *regular* if there is a finite monoid M and a monoid morphism $\gamma : \mathsf{S} \to M$ that *recognizes* L, which means that $L = \gamma^{-1}(N)$ for some subset $N \subseteq M$. Without loss of generality one may assume that the monoid M is a product of finite monoids $M = M_1 \times \ldots \times M_k$, and that

$$\gamma = \gamma_1 \times \ldots \times \gamma_k \quad \text{where} \quad \gamma_i : \mathsf{S}_\mathsf{i}{}^* \to M_i \text{ for } i = 1 \ldots k.$$

Thus we may use an equivalent but more compact representation of regular sets, based on automata: a regular set L is given by a tuple of (nondeterministic) finite automata $\mathcal{B}_1 \ldots \mathcal{B}_k$ over alphabets $\mathsf{S}_1 \ldots \mathsf{S}_\mathsf{k}$, respectively, together with a set

$$F \subseteq Q_1 \times \ldots \times Q_k$$

of accepting tuples of states, where Q_i denotes the state space of automaton $\mathcal{B}_i$.

Unless stated otherwise, in the sequel we always use such representations of regular sets of configurations. If there are more than one state, we assume a representation for every state. In particular, when saying "polynomial wrt. L", for a regular language L, we mean polynomial wrt. the sum of sizes of automata representing L.

Remark 2. Clearly, the cardinality of the set F of accepting tuples may be exponential wrt. the cardinalities of state spaces of automata $\mathcal{B}_i$. However, complexities we derive in the sequel will never depend on cardinality of F.

Example 3. Assume that there are two stacks. An example of properties we can define is: „odd number of elements on the first stack and symbol A on the top of the second stack, or an even number of the elements on the first stack and the odd number of elements on the second stack". On the other hand, "all stacks have equal size" is not a regular property according to our definition.

Remark 3. We have deliberately chosen a notion of regularity of languages of *tuples* of words. Another possible approach could be to consider regular languages of words, over the product alphabet $(\mathsf{S}_1 \cup \bot) \times \ldots \times (\mathsf{S}_\mathsf{k} \cup \bot)$, where the additional symbol $\bot$ is necessary for padding. This would yield a larger class, for instance the last language from Example 3 would be regular. The price to pay would be however undecidability of the reachability problems. The undecidability will be discussed below.

Reachability. In this paper we consider the following reachability problem:

INPUT: a MPDA $\mathcal{A}$ and two regular sets of configurations $L, K \subseteq \mathsf{S}$.
QUESTION: is there a path in the configuration graph from L to K?

We will write $L \rightsquigarrow_{\mathcal{A}} K$ if a path from L to K exists in the automaton $\mathcal{A}$. The sets L and K we call *source* and *target* sets, respectively. We will distinguish special cases, when either L or K or both the sets are singletons, thus obtaining four different variants of reachability altogether. For brevity we will use symbol '*1*' for a singleton, and symbol 'REG' for a regular set, and speak of *1*$\rightsquigarrow$REG *reachability* (when L is a singleton), REG$\rightsquigarrow$REG *reachability* (the unrestricted case), and likewise for REG$\rightsquigarrow$*1* and *1*$\rightsquigarrow$*1*.

Before stating the results, we note that all the problems we consider here are NP-hard:

Lemma 1. *The 1$\rightsquigarrow$1 reachability is NP-hard for strongly normed stateless MPDAs, even if all stack alphabets are singletons.*

The above fact follows immediately from NP-completeness of the reachability problem for communication-free Petri nets, see [15] for details.

Results. In presence of states, the 1$\rightsquigarrow$1 reachability problem is obviously undecidable, because the model is Turing powerful. Undecidability holds even for normed MPDAs. We will thus consider only stateless or weak MPDAs from now on.

We start by observing that out of four combinations of the reachability problem, it is sufficient to consider only two, namely the REG$\rightsquigarrow$1 and REG$\rightsquigarrow$REG cases. Indeed, as far as complexity is concerned, we observe the following collapse:

$$1 \rightsquigarrow 1 = \text{REG} \rightsquigarrow 1 \qquad\qquad 1 \rightsquigarrow \text{REG} = \text{REG} \rightsquigarrow \text{REG} \tag{6}$$

independently of a restriction on automata. The first equality follows from our first result:

Lemma 2. *Suppose $\mathcal{A}$ is a weak MPDA. Let L be a regular set of configurations of $\mathcal{A}$ and let t be a configuration of $\mathcal{A}$. Then*

$$L \rightsquigarrow_{\mathcal{A}} t \implies s \rightsquigarrow_{\mathcal{A}} t \text{ for some } s \in L \text{ of size polynomial wrt. } \mathcal{A}, L \text{ and } t.$$

Indeed, the reduction from REG$\rightsquigarrow$1 to 1$\rightsquigarrow$1 is by nondeterministic guessing a source configuration of polynomial size.

The second equality (6) will follow from our results listed below.

Before stating the remaining results, we summarize all of them in the following table. We distinguish cases, corresponding to strongly normed/normed/unnormed case and stateless/weak case. Each entry of the table contains the complexity of REG$\rightsquigarrow$REG reachability problem. Additionally, the complexity of REG$\rightsquigarrow$1 reachability problem is given in cases it is different from the complexity of REG$\rightsquigarrow$REG reachability.

For clarity, we do not distinguish stateless strongly normed case from stateless normed one, as these two cases obviously coincide.

[REG$\rightsquigarrow$1] REG$\rightsquigarrow$REG	strongly normed	normed	unnormed
stateless	NP-compl. (Thm. 2)		[NP-compl. (Thm. 3)] undecidable (Thm. 1)
weak	NP-compl. (Thm. 2)	[decidable] undecidable (Thm. 1)	[decidable (Thm. 4)] undecidable

Now we discuss the results in detail. We first observe an apparent decidability frontier witnessed by stateless unnormed MPDAs and weak normed MPDAs:

Theorem 1. *The 1$\rightsquigarrow$*REG *reachability is undecidable for stateless unnormed MPDAs and for weak normed MPDAs.*

The proof is by reduction of the nonemptiness of intersection of context-free languages and uses three stacks. The case of two stacks remains open.

Thus lack of strong normedness combined with a regular target set yields undecidability in case of stateless automata. Surprisingly, restricting additionally:

- either the automaton to be strongly normed,
- or the target set to a singleton,

makes a dramatical difference for complexity of the problem, as summarized in Theorems 2, 3 and 4 below. In the first theorem we only assume strong normedness:

Theorem 2. *The* REG$\rightsquigarrow$REG *reachability is NP-complete for strongly normed weak MPDAs.*

Theorem 2 is the main result of this paper. It is proved by showing that reachability is always witnessed by a polynomial witness, obtained by careful elimination of 'irrelevant' transitions.

In the following two theorems we do not assume strong normedness, thus according to Theorem 1 we have to restrict target set to singleton. Under such a restriction, we are able to prove NP-completeness only in the class of stateless MPDA, while for all weak MPDA we merely state decidability:

Theorem 3. *The* REG$\rightsquigarrow$*1 reachability is NP-complete for stateless unnormed MPDAs.*

Theorem 4. *The* REG$\rightsquigarrow$*1 reachability is decidable for weak unnormed MPDAs.*

Theorem 3 is shown similarly to Theorem 2, while the proof of Theorem 4 is based on a well order, the point-wise extension of a variant of Higman ordering.

Open Questions. Except for two entries in the summarizing table above, we know the exact complexity of the reachability problem. The important open question that remains is the actual complexity of 1$\rightsquigarrow$1 reachability for (normed and unnormed) weak MPDAs. Another interesting question is whether undecidability carries over to automata with two stacks only.

Reachability Set. Now we consider the problem of computing the whole reachability set. For a given automaton $\mathcal{A}$, and a set L of configurations, we consider forward and backward reachability sets of L, defined as:

$$\{s : L \rightsquigarrow_{\mathcal{A}} s\} \quad \text{and} \quad \{s : s \rightsquigarrow_{\mathcal{A}} L\},$$

respectively. It turns out that the backward reachability set may be computed under the strong normedness assumption.

Theorem 5. *For weak strongly normed MPDAs, the backward reachability set of a regular set is an effectively computable regular set.*

Roughly speaking, we show that the backward reachability set is upward closed with respect to the point-wise extension of a suitable variant of Higman ordering.

On the other hand, the forward reachability set needs not be regular, even in the case of strongly normed stateless automata, as shown in the following example.

Example 4. Consider a stateless automaton with two stacks, over alphabets $\{A, X\}$ and $\{B\}$, and the following transition rules:

$$X \longrightarrow XA,\ B \qquad X \rightarrow \varepsilon,\ \varepsilon \qquad A \rightarrow \varepsilon,\ \varepsilon \qquad B \rightarrow \varepsilon,\ \varepsilon.$$

The set of configurations reachable from the configuration (X, ε) is not regular:

$$\{(A^i, B^j) : i, j \in \mathbb{N}\} \ \cup\ \{(XA^k, B^l) : k \geq l\}.$$

Relaxed Regularity. The relaxed definition of regularity, as discusses in Remark 3, makes the reachability problem intractable in all cases. The following theorem is shown by reduction from the Post Correspondence Problem:

Theorem 6. *The* $1 \rightsquigarrow$REG *reachability is undecidable for stateless strongly normed MPDAs, under the relaxed notion of regularity.*

Furthermore, the backward reachability set of a relaxed regular set is not necessarily regular, even in stateless strongly normed MPDAs. The illustrating example is omitted due to space limitation.

4 Proof of Lemma 2

Consider a MPDA $\mathcal{A}$ and a regular set L of configurations of $\mathcal{A}$. Let $s \in L$ be source configuration and let t be an arbitrary target configuration. Suppose $s \rightsquigarrow_{\mathcal{A}} t$. We will show that the size of s may be reduced, while preserving membership in L. The crucial but simple idea of the proof will rely on an analysis of *relevance* of symbol occurrences, to be defined below.

Symbol occurrences. Suppose that there is a path π from s to t, consisting of consecutive transitions $s \longrightarrow s_1 \longrightarrow s_2 \ldots \longrightarrow s_n = t$. We will consider all individual occurrences of symbols that appear in the configurations. For instance, in the following exemplary sequence of two-stack configurations

$$\langle q, AA, C\rangle \longrightarrow \langle q, BBA, DC\rangle \longrightarrow \langle q, ABBA, DC\rangle \tag{7}$$

there are altogether 14 *symbol occurrences*: 3 in the first configuration, 5 in the second one and 6 in the third one.

Recall that every transition $s_i \longrightarrow s_{i+1}$ is induced by some transition rule $X \longrightarrow \alpha$ of the automaton. Then there is a distinguished occurrence of symbol X in s_i that is involved in the transition. In the sequel we use the term *symbol occurrence involved in a transition.*

Precisely one occurrence of symbol in s_i is involved in the transition $s_i \longrightarrow s_{i+1}$; for every other occurrence of a symbol in s_i there is a *corresponding* occurrence of the same symbol in s_{i+1}. (Note that we always make a difference between corresponding symbol occurrences from different configurations.) All remaining occurrences of symbols in s_{i+1} are created by the transition; we call these occurrences *fresh.*

We define the *descendant* relation as follows. All fresh symbol occurrences in s_{i+1} are descendants of the symbol occurrence in s_i involved in the transition $s_i \longrightarrow s_{i+1}$. Moreover, a symbol occurrence in s_{i+1} corresponding to a symbol occurrence in s_i is its descendant too. We will use term *descendant* for the reflexive-transitive closure of the relation defined above and the term *ancestor* for its inverse relation. In particular, every symbol occurrence in t is descendant of a unique symbol occurrence in s. The descendant relation is a forest, i.e., a disjoint union of trees.

Example 5. As an example, consider again the sequence of transitions (7), with symbol occurrences identified by subscripts 1 . . . 14:

$$\langle q, \mathrm{A}_1\mathrm{A}_2, \mathrm{C}_3\rangle \longrightarrow \langle q, \mathrm{B}_4\mathrm{B}_5\mathrm{A}_6, \mathrm{D}_7\mathrm{C}_8\rangle \longrightarrow \langle q, \mathrm{A}_9\mathrm{B}_{10}\mathrm{B}_{11}\mathrm{A}_{12}, \mathrm{D}_{13}\mathrm{C}_{14}\rangle \quad (8)$$

Say the transitions are induced by the following two transition rules:

$$q,\ \mathrm{A} \longrightarrow q,\ \mathrm{BB},\ \mathrm{D} \qquad\qquad q,\ \mathrm{D} \longrightarrow q,\ \mathrm{A},\ \mathrm{D}$$

The descendant relation can be presented as the following forest:

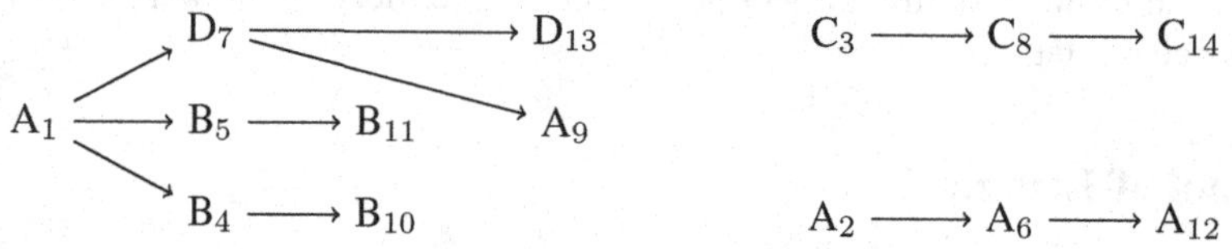

The symbol occurrences involved in the two transitions (8) are A_1 in the first configuration and D_7 in the second one. The fresh symbol occurrences are B_4, B_5 and D_7 in the second configuration, and A_9 and D_{13} in the third one.

Relevant symbol occurrences. As the automaton $\mathcal{A}$ is weak, the number of transitions in π that change state is bounded by the number of states of $\mathcal{A}$. All remaining transitions in π do not change state.

Consider all the occurrences of all symbols in all configurations along the path π, including configurations s and t themselves. A symbol occurrence is called *relevant* if some of its descendants:

- belongs to the target configuration t; or
- is involved in some transition in π that changes state.

Otherwise, a symbol occurrences is *irrelevant.* In particular, all symbol occurrences in t are relevant. Referring back to our example, all symbol occurrences appearing in (8) are relevant.

Note that if t is not the empty configuration then every configuration in π contains at least one relevant symbol occurrence. On the other side, in every configuration, the number of relevant occurrences is always bounded by the sum of the size of t and the number of states of $\mathcal{A}$.

Small source configuration. So prepared, we are ready to prove that there is a configuration $s' \in L$ of polynomial size with $s' \rightsquigarrow_{\mathcal{A}} t$. We will rely on the following claim:

Lemma 3. *For any configuration s' obtained from s by removing some irrelevant symbol occurrences, it holds $s' \rightsquigarrow_{\mathcal{A}} t$.*

The lemma follows from the following two observations: (1) all the transitions in π involving symbol occurrences remaining in s' and their descendants may be re-done; (2) the resulting configuration will be exactly t, as only irrelevant symbol occurrences have been removed from s.

Recall that the language L is represented by a tuple $\mathcal{B}_1 \ldots \mathcal{B}_k$ of deterministic finite automata, one automaton per stack. Consider the content of a fixed ith stack in s, say $w \in \mathsf{A}_i^*$. Let n be the number of states of $\mathcal{B}_i$. The run of the automaton $\mathcal{B}_i$ over w labels every position of w by some state. We will use a standard pumping argument to argue that every block of consecutive irrelevant symbol occurrences in s may be reduced in length to at most n. Indeed, upon every repetition of a state of $\mathcal{B}_i$, the word w may be shortened by removing the induced infix, while preserving membership in L. By repeating the pumping argument for all blocks of consecutive irrelevant symbol occurrences in all stacks in s, one obtains a configuration s', still belonging to L, of quadratic size. By Lemma 3 we know that $s' \rightsquigarrow t$, as required.

5 Proof of Theorem 2

NP-hardness follows from Lemma 1. The proof of membership in NP relies on the following two core lemmas:

Lemma 4. *The 1$\rightsquigarrow$1 reachability problem is in NP for strongly normed weak MPDAs.*

Lemma 5. *Let $\mathcal{A}$ be a strongly normed weak MPDA and let L, K be regular sets of configurations. If $L \rightsquigarrow K$ then $s \rightsquigarrow t$ for some $s \in L$ and $t \in K$ of size polynomial wrt. the sizes of $\mathcal{A}$, L and K.*

The two lemmas easily yield a decision procedure for REG$\rightsquigarrow$REG reachability: guess configurations $s \in L$ and $t \in K$ of size bounded by a polynomial deduced from the proof of Lemma 5, and then apply the procedure of Lemma 4 to check if $s \rightsquigarrow t$.

The rest of this section is devoted to the part of the proof of Lemma 4. The remaining part of the proof, together with the proof of Lemma 5, are omitted.

5.1 Proof of Lemma 4

Consider a MPDA $\mathcal{A}$ and two configurations s and t. We will define a nondeterministic polynomial-time decision procedure for $s \rightsquigarrow_{\mathcal{A}} t$.

Stateless assumption. For simplicity, we assume that both s and t have the same control state. Thus we can treat transitions that lead from s to t as stateless transitions. At the very end of the proof, we will discuss how to generalize it to the general case of strongly normed weak MPDAs.

Polynomial witness. Our aim is to show that if there is a path from s to t then there is a path of polynomial length. So stated, the above claim may not be verbally true, even in the case of context-free graphs, as witnessed by the following simple example.

$$\mathrm{X}_1 \longrightarrow \mathrm{X}_2\mathrm{X}_2 \qquad \mathrm{X}_2 \longrightarrow \mathrm{X}_3\mathrm{X}_3 \qquad \ldots \qquad \mathrm{X}_{n-1} \longrightarrow \mathrm{X}_n\mathrm{X}_n \qquad \mathrm{X}_n \longrightarrow \varepsilon \tag{9}$$

The example scales with respect to n, and thus the shortest path from the configuration X_1 to X_n is of exponential length. As a conclusion, one must use some subtle analysis in order to be able to reduce the length of a witness of existence of the path as required. Note that X_1 is relevant and thus can not be simply omitted.

Proof idea. As a first step towards a polynomial bound on the witness of the path from s to t, we will modify the notion of transition. Intuitively speaking, our aim is to consider exclusively relevant symbol occurrences.

By a *subword* we mean any subsequence of a given word. For instance, $aaccbc$ is a subword of $aacabbcbcbc$. Further, by a subtransition of $\mathrm{X} \longrightarrow \alpha_1 \ldots \alpha_k$ we mean any $\mathrm{X} \longrightarrow \beta_1 \ldots \beta_k$ such that the following conditions hold:

- *subword*: β_i is a subword of α_i, for all $i \in \{1 \ldots k\}$; and
- *nonemptiness*: $\beta_1 \ldots \beta_k \neq \varepsilon$, i.e., at least one of words β_i is nonempty.

Note that relying on the notion of relevance one easily deduces that whenever there is a sequence of transitions from s to t, then there is also sequence of *subtransitions*. Indeed, it is sufficient to remove irrelevant symbol occurrences in all transitions along the path from s to t.

Clearly, the converse implication is not true in general. For instance, if we add symbols X_0, A and the transition $\mathrm{X}_0 \longrightarrow \mathrm{X}_1\mathrm{A}$ to the example (9), there is a sequence of subtransitions from the configuration X_0 to X_n. Our aim now it to modify the notion of subtransition in such a way that the converse implication does hold as well, i.e., that existence of a sequence of subtransitions implies existence of a sequence of transitions. This requires certain amount of boring book-keeping, as defined in detail below.

Marked subtransitions. We will need an additional copy of every stack alphabet A_i, denoted by $\bar{\mathsf{A}}_i$, for $i = 1 \ldots k$. Thus for every $a \in \mathsf{A}_i$ there is a corresponding marked symbol $\bar{a} \in \bar{\mathsf{A}}_i$. Formally, let the ith stack alphabet be $\mathsf{A}_i \cup \bar{\mathsf{A}}_i$.

A *marked subword* of a word $w \in \mathsf{A}_i^*$ is any word in $(\mathsf{A}_i \cup \bar{\mathsf{A}}_i)^*$ that may be obtained from w by the following *marking procedure*:

- color arbitrary occurrences in w (the idea is to color irrelevant symbol occurrences),
- mark every occurrence that is followed by any colored occurrence,
- and finally remove colored occurrences.

For instance, according to the coloring $a\mathbf{ac}a\mathbf{bb}c\mathbf{b}cbc$, a marked subword of $aacabbcbcbc$ is $\bar{a}\bar{a}\bar{c}cbc$.

Recall that a word $w \in \mathsf{A}_i^*$ represents a content of the ith stack, with the left-most symbol being the top-most. Intuitively, the idea behind the notion of marked subword is to keep track of removed occurrences that are covered by other symbols on the stack.

A notion of *marked subtransition* is a natural adaptation of the notion of subtransition. Compared to subtransitions, there are two differences: 'subword' is replaced with 'marked subword'; and whenever the left-side symbol is marked, then it may only put marked symbols on its stack. Formally, a marked subtransition of $\mathsf{X} \longrightarrow \alpha_1 \dots \alpha_k$ is any $\mathsf{X} \longrightarrow \beta_1 \dots \beta_k$ such that the following conditions hold:

- *subword*: β_i is a marked subword of α_i, for all $i \in \{1 \dots k\}$;
- *nonemptiness*: $\beta_1 \dots \beta_k \neq \varepsilon$, i.e., at least one of words β_i is nonempty; and
- *marking inheritance*: if $X \in \bar{\mathsf{A}}_i$ is marked then all symbols in β_i are marked.

Note that there are exponentially many different marked subtransitions, but each one is of polynomial size. Finally, note that every subtransition is obtained from some transition by the marking procedure as above, applied to every stack separately.

By the nonemptiness assumption on marked subtransitions we obtain a simple but crucial observation:

Lemma 6. *Along a sequence of marked subtransitions, the size of configuration can not decrease.*

A *marked subconfiguration* of a configuration $\langle \alpha_1, \dots, \alpha_k \rangle$ is any tuple $\langle \beta_1, \dots, \beta_k \rangle$ such that β_i is a marked subword of α_i for all $i \in \{1 \dots k\}$.

Lemma 7. *For two configurations s and t, the following conditions are equivalent:*

(1) there is a sequence of transitions from s to t,
(2) there is a sequence of marked subtransitions from u to t, for some marked subconfiguration u of s.

Proof. The implication from (1) to (2) follows immediately. The sequence of marked subtransitions is obtained by application of the marking procedure to all transitions. For every transition, color in the marking procedure precisely those symbol occurrences that are irrelevant.

Now we show the implication from (2) to (1). The proof uses strong normedness.

Assume a sequence π of marked subtransitions from u to t, for some marked subconfiguration u of s. Recall that each subtransition in π has its original transition of $\mathcal{A}$. We claim that there is a sequence of transitions from s to t, that contains the original transitions of all the marked subtransitions appearing in π, and *canceling sequences*

$$q\,\mathsf{X} \longrightarrow \dots \longrightarrow \langle q, \varepsilon, \dots, \varepsilon \rangle \tag{10}$$

for some stack symbols X, existing due to strong normedness assumption.

The sequence of transitions from s to t is constructed by reversing the marking procedure. For the ease of presentation, beside letters from A_i, we will also use colored letters.

Start with the configuration s, and choose any coloring of symbol occurrences in s that induces u as the outcome of the marking procedure. Then consecutively apply the following rule:

- If the top-most symbol X on some stack is colored, apply a canceling sequence for X.
- Otherwise, apply the original transition of the next subtransition from π, using again some coloring that could have been used in the marking procedure.

For correctness, we need to show that all colored occurrences of symbols are eventually canceled out, as this guarantees that the final configuration is precisely t.

Let's inspect π. As no symbol in t is marked, every marked symbol occurrence eventually disappears as a result of firing of some subtransition. Recall that marking of a symbol $\bar{X}$ disappears only if the subtransition pushes nothing on the stack of $\bar{X}$. As a consequence, every colored symbol occurrence will eventually appear on the top of its stack. Thus the canceling sequence for X will be eventually applied. □

Lemma 8. *For two configurations u and v, if there is a sequence of marked subtransitions from u to v, then there is such a sequence of polynomial length wrt. the sizes of u, v and $\mathcal{A}$.*

This is the last lemma needed for NP-membership. Its proof is omitted.

Decision procedure. Now we drop the stateless assumption. Note that the notion of marked subconfiguration and marked subtransition may be easily adapted to transitions that change state. We do not impose however the nonemptiness condition on transitions that change state, which is in accordance with the intuition that irrelevant symbol occurrences are removed in the marking procedure. Using Lemmas 6, 7 and 8 we will define the nondeterministic decision procedure for strongly normed weak MPDAs.

Let the two given configurations s and t have control states q and p, respectively. In the first step, the algorithm guesses a number of marked subconfigurations $t_1 \dots t_{n-1}$, where n is not greater than the number of states of $\mathcal{A}$, and marked subtransitions that change state:

$$t_1 \longrightarrow s_1 \qquad t_2 \longrightarrow s_2 \qquad \dots \qquad t_{n-1} \longrightarrow s_{n-1}$$

such that s_i and t_{i+1} have the same control states for $i \in \{0 \dots n-1\}$. For convenience, we write s_0 instead of s and t_n instead of t. In particular, we assume that the control state of t_1 is q, and the control state of s_{n-1} is p. Relying on Lemma 6, it is sufficient to consider configurations of sizes satisfying the following inequalities:

$$\text{size}(s_i) \leq \text{size}(t_{i+1}) \qquad \text{for } i \in \{1 \dots n-1\}. \tag{11}$$

In the second phase, the algorithm guesses, for $i \in \{0 \dots n-1\}$, a sequence of subtransitions from s_i to t_{i+1} of length bounded by polynomial derived from the proof of Lemma 8; and checks that the respective sequences of subtransitions lead from s_i to t_{i+1}, as required by Lemma 7. □

Acknowledgements. We are grateful to anonymous reviewers for careful reading and many valuable comments.

References

1. Atig, M.F.: From Multi to Single Stack Automata. In: Gastin, P., Laroussinie, F. (eds.) CONCUR 2010. LNCS, vol. 6269, pp. 117–131. Springer, Heidelberg (2010)
2. Atig, M.F., Bouajjani, A.: On the Reachability Problem for Dynamic Networks of Concurrent Pushdown Systems. In: Bournez, O., Potapov, I. (eds.) RP 2009. LNCS, vol. 5797, pp. 1–2. Springer, Heidelberg (2009)
3. Atig, M.F., Bouajjani, A., Qadeer, S.: Context-bounded analysis for concurrent programs with dynamic creation of threads. Logical Methods in Computer Science 7(4) (2011)
4. Bouajjani, A., Emmi, M.: Analysis of recursively parallel programs. In: POPL, pp. 203–214 (2012)
5. Bouajjani, A., Esparza, J., Maler, O.: Reachability Analysis of Pushdown Automata: Application to Model-Checking. In: Mazurkiewicz, A., Winkowski, J. (eds.) CONCUR 1997. LNCS, vol. 1243, pp. 135–150. Springer, Heidelberg (1997)
6. Bouajjani, A., Esparza, J., Schwoon, S., Strejcek, J.: Reachability analysis of multithreaded software with asynchronous communication. In: Software Verification: Infinite-State Model Checking and Static Program Analysis (2006)
7. Bouajjani, A., Müller-Olm, M., Touili, T.: Regular Symbolic Analysis of Dynamic Networks of Pushdown Systems. In: Abadi, M., de Alfaro, L. (eds.) CONCUR 2005. LNCS, vol. 3653, pp. 473–487. Springer, Heidelberg (2005)
8. Burkart, O., Caucal, D., Moller, F., Steffen, B.: Verification of infinite structures. In: Handbook of Process Algebra, pp. 545–623. Elsevier (2001)
9. Chadha, R., Madhusudan, P., Viswanathan, M.: Reachability under Contextual Locking. In: Flanagan, C., König, B. (eds.) TACAS 2012. LNCS, vol. 7214, pp. 437–450. Springer, Heidelberg (2012)
10. Christensen, S.: Decidability and Decomposition in process algebras. PhD thesis, Dept. of Computer Science. University of Edinburgh, UK (1993)
11. Czerwiński, W., Fröschle, S., Lasota, S.: Partially-Commutative Context-Free Processes. In: Bravetti, M., Zavattaro, G. (eds.) CONCUR 2009. LNCS, vol. 5710, pp. 259–273. Springer, Heidelberg (2009)
12. Czerwiński, W., Fröschle, S., Lasota, S.: Partially-commutative context-free processes: expressibility and tractability. Information and Computation 209, 782–798 (2011)
13. Czerwiński, W., Lasota, S.: Partially-commutative context-free languages (submitted, 2012)
14. Diekert, V., Rozenberg, G.: The book of traces. World Scientific (1995)
15. Esparza, J.: Petri nets, commutative context-free grammars, and basic parallel processes. Fundam. Inform. 31(1), 13–25 (1997)
16. Huynh, D.T.: Commutative grammars: The complexity of uniform word problems. Information and Control 57(1), 21–39 (1983)
17. Kahlon, V.: Reasoning about Threads with Bounded Lock Chains. In: Katoen, J.-P., König, B. (eds.) CONCUR 2011. LNCS, vol. 6901, pp. 450–465. Springer, Heidelberg (2011)
18. Kahlon, V., Ivančić, F., Gupta, A.: Reasoning About Threads Communicating via Locks. In: Etessami, K., Rajamani, S.K. (eds.) CAV 2005. LNCS, vol. 3576, pp. 505–518. Springer, Heidelberg (2005)

19. Kretínský, M., Rehák, V., Strejcek, J.: Reachability is decidable for weakly extended process rewrite systems. Inf. Comput. 207(6), 671–680 (2009)
20. Lal, A., Reps, T.W.: Reducing concurrent analysis under a context bound to sequential analysis. Formal Methods in System Design 35(1), 73–97 (2009)
21. Lugiez, D., Schnoebelen, P.: The regular viewpoint on PA-processes. Theor. Comput. Sci. 274(1-2), 89–115 (2002)
22. Mayr, R.: Process rewrite systems. Inf. Comput. 156(1-2), 264–286 (2000)
23. Qadeer, S., Rehof, J.: Context-Bounded Model Checking of Concurrent Software. In: Halbwachs, N., Zuck, L.D. (eds.) TACAS 2005. LNCS, vol. 3440, pp. 93–107. Springer, Heidelberg (2005)

Reachability and Termination Analysis of Concurrent Quantum Programs

Nengkun Yu and Mingsheng Ying

Tsinghua University, China
University of Technology, Sydney, Australia
nengkunyu@gmail.com, Mingsheng.Ying@uts.edu.au

Abstract. We introduce a Markov chain model of concurrent quantum programs. This model is a quantum generalization of Hart, Sharir and Pnueli's probabilistic concurrent programs. Some characterizations of the reachable space, uniformly repeatedly reachable space and termination of a concurrent quantum program are derived by the analysis of their mathematical structures. Based on these characterizations, algorithms for computing the reachable space and uniformly repeatedly reachable space and for deciding the termination are given.

Keywords: Quantum computation, concurrent programs, reachability, termination.

1 Introduction

Research on concurrency in quantum computing started about 10 years ago, and it was motivated by two different requirements:

- *Verification of quantum communication protocols*: Quantum communication systems are already commercially available from Id Quantique, MagiQ Technologies, SmartQuantum and NEC. Their advantage over classical communication is that security is provable based on the principles of quantum mechanics. As is well known, it is very difficult to guarantee correctness of even classical communication protocols in the stage of design. Thus, numerous techniques for verifying classical communication protocols have been developed. Human intuition is much better adapted to the classical world than the quantum world. This will make quantum protocol designers to commit many more faults than classical protocol designers. So, it is even more critical to develop formal methods for verification of quantum protocols (see for example [10], [11], [4]). Concurrency is a feature that must be encompassed into the formal models of quantum communication systems.
- *Programming for distributed quantum computing*: A major reason for distributed quantum computing, different from the classical case, comes from the extreme difficulty of the physical implementation of functional quantum computers (see for example [1], [21]). Despite convincing laboratory demonstrations of quantum computing devices, it is beyond the ability of

M. Koutny and I. Ulidowski (Eds.): CONCUR 2012, LNCS 7454, pp. 69–83, 2012.

the current physical technology to scale them. Thus, a natural idea is to use the physical resources of two or more small capacity quantum computers to simulate a large capacity quantum computer. In fact, various experiments in the physical implementation of distributed quantum computing have been frequently reported in recent years. Concurrency naturally arises in the studies of programming for distributed quantum computing.

The majority of work on concurrency in quantum computing is based on process algebras [13], [15], [8], [9], [14], [6], [22], [7], [3]. This paper introduces a new model of concurrent quantum programs in terms of quantum Markov chains. This model is indeed a quantum extension of Hart, Sharir and Pnueli's model of probabilistic concurrent programs [12], [19]. Specifically, a concurrent quantum program consists of a finite set of processes. These processes share a state Hilbert space, and each of them is seen as a quantum Markov chain on the state space. The behaviour of each processes is described by a super-operator. This description of a single process follows Selinger, D'Hont and Panangaden's pioneering works [18], [5] on sequential quantum programs where the denotational semantics of a quantum program is given as a super-operator. The super-operator description of sequential quantum programs was also adopted in one of the authors' work on quantum Floyd-Hoare logic [20]. Similar to the classical and probabilistic cases [12], an execution path of a concurrent quantum program is defined to be an infinite sequence of the labels of their processes, and a certain fairness condition is imposed on an execution path to guarantee that all the processes fairly participate in a computation.

Reachability and termination are two of the central problems in program analysis and verification. The aim of this paper is to develop algorithms that compute the reachable states and decide the termination, respectively, of a concurrent quantum program. To this end, we need to overcome two major difficulties, which are peculiar to the quantum setting and would not arise in the classical case:

- The state Hilbert space of a quantum program is a continuum and thus doomed-to-be infinite even when its dimension is finite. So, a brute-force search is totally ineffective although it may works well to solve a corresponding problem for a classical program. We circumvent the infinity problem of the state space by finding a finite characterization for reachability and termination of a quantum program through a careful analysis of the mathematical structure underlying them.
- The super-operators used to describe the behaviour of the processes are operators on the space of linear operators on the state space, and they are very hard to directly manipulate. In particular, algorithms for computing super-operators are lacking. We adopt a kind of matrix representation for super-operators that allows us to conduct reachability and termination analysis of quantum programs by efficient matrix algorithms.

The paper is organized as follows. For convenience of the reader we briefly recall some basic notions from quantum theory and fix the notations in Sec. 2; but we refer to [17] for more details. A Markov chain model of concurrent quantum programs is defined in Sec. 3, where we also give a running example of quantum walks. In Sec. 4, we present a characterization for reachable space and one for uniformly repeatedly reachable space of a quantum program, and develop two algorithms to compute them. A characterization of termination of a quantum program with fair execution paths and an algorithm for deciding it are given in Sec. 5. It should be pointed out that termination decision in Sec. 5 is based on reachability analysis in Sec. 4. A brief conclusion is drawn in Sec. 6.

2 Preliminaries and Notations

2.1 Hilbert Spaces

The state space of a quantum system is a Hilbert space. In this paper, we only consider a finite dimensional Hilbert space $\mathcal{H}$, which is a complex vector space equipped with an inner product $\langle\cdot|\cdot\rangle$. A pure state of a quantum system is represented by a unit vector, i.e., a vector $|\psi\rangle$ with $\langle\psi|\psi\rangle = 1$. Two vectors $|\varphi\rangle, |\psi\rangle$ in $\mathcal{H}$ are orthogonal, written $|\varphi\rangle \perp |\psi\rangle$, if their inner product is 0. A basis of $\mathcal{H}$ is orthonormal if its elements are mutually orthogonal, unit vectors. The trace of a linear operator A on $\mathcal{H}$ is defined to be $tr(A) = \sum_i \langle i|A|i\rangle$, where $\{|i\rangle\}$ is an orthonormal basis of $\mathcal{H}$. For a subset V of $\mathcal{H}$, the subspace span$V$ spanned by V consists of all linear combinations of vectors in V. For any subspace X of $\mathcal{H}$, its orthocomplement is the subspace $X^\perp = \{|\varphi\rangle \in \mathcal{H} : |\varphi\rangle \perp |\psi\rangle$ for all $|\psi\rangle \in X\}$. The join of a family $\{X_i\}$ of subspaces is $\bigvee_i X_i = \text{span}(\bigcup_i X_i)$. In particular, we write $X \vee Y$ for the join of two subspaces X and Y. A linear operator P is called the projection onto a subspace X if $P|\psi\rangle = |\psi\rangle$ for all $|\psi\rangle \in X$ and $P|\psi\rangle = 0$ for all $|\psi\rangle \in X^\perp$. We write P_X for the projection onto X.

A mixed state of a quantum system is represented by a density operator. A linear operator ρ on $\mathcal{H}$ is called a density operator (resp. partial density operator) if ρ is positive-semidefinite in the sense that $\langle\phi|\rho|\phi\rangle \geq 0$ for all $|\phi\rangle$, and $tr(\rho) = 1$ (resp. $tr(\rho) \leq 1$). For any statistical ensemble $\{(p_i, |\psi_i\rangle)\}$ of pure quantum states with $p_i > 0$ for all i and $\sum_i p_i = 1$, $\rho = \sum_i p_i|\psi_i\rangle\langle\psi_i|$ is a density operator. Conversely, each density operator can be generated by an ensemble of pure states in this way. In particular, we write ψ for the density operator $|\psi\rangle\langle\psi|$ generated by a single pure states $|\psi\rangle$. The support of a partial density operator ρ, written supp(ρ), is the space spanned by its eigenvectors with nonzero eigenvalues.

Lemma 1. *For any $p > 0$ and partial density operators ρ, σ, we have: (1)* $\text{supp}(p\rho) = \text{supp}(\rho)$*; (2)* $\text{supp}(\rho) \subseteq \text{supp}(\rho + \sigma)$*; (3)* $\text{supp}(\rho + \sigma) = \text{supp}(\rho) \vee \text{supp}(\sigma)$.

2.2 Super-Operators

A super-operator is a mathematical formalism used to describe a broad class of transformations that a quantum system can undergo. A super-operator on

$\mathcal{H}$ is a linear operator $\mathcal{E}$ from the space of linear operators on $\mathcal{H}$ into itself, satisfying (1) $tr[\mathcal{E}(\rho)] \leq tr(\rho)$ for any ρ; (2) Complete positivity(CP): for any extra Hilbert space $\mathcal{H}_k$, $(\mathcal{I}_k \otimes \mathcal{E})(A)$ is positive provided A is a positive operator on $\mathcal{H}_k \otimes \mathcal{H}$, where $\mathcal{I}_k$ is the identity operation on $\mathcal{H}_k$. Furthermore, if $tr[\mathcal{E}(\rho)] = tr(\rho)$ for any ρ, then $\mathcal{E}$ is said to be trace-preserving. Each super-operator $\mathcal{E}$ enjoys the Kraus representation: there exists a set of operators $\{E_i\}$ satisfying (1) $\mathcal{E}(\rho) = \sum_i E_i \rho E_i^\dagger$ for all density operators ρ; (2) $\sum_i E_i^\dagger E_i \leq I$, with equality for trace-preserving $\mathcal{E}$, where I is the identity operator. In this case, we write $\mathcal{E} = \sum_i E_i \cdot E_i^\dagger$. The image of subspace X of $\mathcal{H}$ under $\mathcal{E}$ is $\mathcal{E}(X) = \bigvee_{|\psi\rangle \in X} \mathrm{supp}(\mathcal{E}(\psi))$, and the pre-image of X under $\mathcal{E}$ is $\mathcal{E}^{-1}(X) = \{|\psi\rangle \in \mathcal{H} : \mathrm{supp}(\mathcal{E}(\psi)) \subseteq X\}$.

Lemma 2. *(1)* $\mathrm{supp}(\rho) \subseteq \mathrm{supp}(\sigma) \Rightarrow \mathrm{supp}(\mathcal{E}(\rho)) \subseteq \mathrm{supp}(\mathcal{E}(\sigma))$, *and* $\mathrm{supp}(\rho) = \mathrm{supp}(\sigma) \Rightarrow \mathrm{supp}(\mathcal{E}(\rho)) = \mathrm{supp}(\mathcal{E}(\sigma))$.

(2) $\mathrm{supp}(\mathcal{E}(\rho)) \subseteq \mathrm{supp}((\mathcal{E} + \mathcal{F})(\rho))$. *(3)* $\mathcal{E}(X) = \mathrm{supp}(\mathcal{E}(P_X))$.

(4) $X \subseteq Y \Rightarrow \mathcal{E}(X) \subseteq \mathcal{E}(Y)$. *(5)* $\mathcal{E}(X) \subseteq (\mathcal{E} + \mathcal{F})(X)$.

(6) If $\mathcal{E} = \sum_i E_i \cdot E_i^\dagger$, *then* $\mathcal{E}^{-1}(X) = [\mathrm{supp}(\mathcal{E}^*(P_{X^\perp}))]^\perp$, *where* $\mathcal{E}^* = \sum_i E_i^\dagger \cdot E_i$ *is the (Schrödinger-Heisenberg) dual of* $\mathcal{E}$.

2.3 Matrix Representation of Super-Operator

The matrix representation of a super-operator is usually easier to manipulate than the super-operator itself. If $\mathcal{E} = \sum_i E_i \cdot E_i^\dagger$ and $\dim \mathcal{H} = d$, then the matrix representation of $\mathcal{E}$ is the $d^2 \times d^2$ matrix $M = \sum_i E_i \otimes E_i^*$, where A^* stands for the conjugate of matrix A, i.e., $A^* = (a_{ij}^*)$ with a_{ij}^* being the conjugate of complex number a_{ij}, whenever $A = (a_{ij})$. According to [24], we have the following

Lemma 3. *(1) The modulus of any eigenvalue of* M *is less or equal to 1.*

(2) We write $|\Phi\rangle = \sum_j |jj\rangle$ *for the (unnormalized) maximally entangled state in* $\mathcal{H} \otimes \mathcal{H}$, *where* $\{|j\rangle\}$ *is an orthonormal basis of* $\mathcal{H}$. *Then for any* $d \times d$ *matrix* A, *we have* $(\mathcal{E}(A) \otimes I)|\Phi\rangle = M(A \otimes I)|\Phi\rangle$.

2.4 Quantum Measurements

A quantum measurement is described by a collection $\{M_m\}$ of operators, where the indexes m refer to the measurement outcomes. It is required that the measurement operators satisfy the completeness equation $\sum_m M_m^\dagger M_m = I_{\mathcal{H}}$. If the system is in state ρ, then the probability that measurement result m occurs is given by $p(m) = tr(M_m^\dagger M_m \rho)$, and the state of the system after the measurement is $\frac{M_m \rho M_m^\dagger}{p(m)}$.

3 A Model of Concurrent Quantum Programs

Our model is a quantum extension of Hart, Sharir and Pnueli's probabilistic concurrent programs [12]. A concurrent quantum program consists of a finite set

$K = \{1, 2, \cdots, m\}$ of quantum processes, and these processes have a common state space, which is assumed to be a d-dimensional Hilbert space $\mathcal{H}$. With each $k \in K$ we associate a trace-preserving super-operator $\mathcal{E}_k$, describing a single atomic action or evolution of process k. Also, we assume a termination condition for the program. At the end of each execution step, we check whether this condition is satisfied or not. The termination condition is modeled by a yes-no measurement $\{M_0, M_1\}$: if the measurement outcome is 0, then the program terminates, and we can imagine the program state falls into a terminal (absorbing) space and it remains there forever; otherwise, the program will enter the next step and continues to perform a quantum operation chosen from K.

Definition 1. *A concurrent quantum program defined on a d-dimensional Hilbert space $\mathcal{H}$ is a pair $\mathcal{P} = (\{\mathcal{E}_k : k \in K\}, \{M_0, M_1\})$, where:*

1. *$\mathcal{E}_k$ is a super-operator on $\mathcal{H}$ for each $k \in K$;*
2. *$\{M_0, M_1\}$ is a measurement on $\mathcal{H}$ as the termination test.*

Any finite string $s_1s_2 \cdots s_m$ or infinite string $s_1s_2 \cdots s_i \cdots$ of elements of K is called an execution path of the program. Thus, the sets of finite and infinite execution paths of program $\mathcal{P}$ are

$$S = K^\omega = \{s_1s_2 \cdots s_i \cdots : s_i \in K \text{ for every } i \geq 1\},$$
$$S_{fin} = K^* = \{s_1s_2 \cdots s_n : n \geq 0 \text{ and } s_i \in K \text{ for all } 1 \leq i \leq n\},$$

respectively. A subset of S is usually called a schedule.

For simplicity of presentation, we introduce the notation $\mathcal{F}_k$ for any $k \in K$ which stands for the super-operator defined by $\mathcal{F}_k(\rho) = \mathcal{E}_k(M_1\rho M_1^\dagger)$ for all density operators ρ. Assume the initial state is ρ_0. The execution of the program under path $s = s_1s_2 \cdots s_k \cdots \in S$ can be described as follows. At the first step, we perform the termination measurement $\{M_0, M_1\}$ on the initial state ρ_0. The probability that the program terminates; that is, the measurement outcome is 0, is $\mathrm{tr}[M_0\rho_0M_0^\dagger]$. On the other hand, the probability that the program does not terminate; that is, the measurement outcome is 1, is $p_1^s = \mathrm{tr}[M_1\rho_0M_1^\dagger]$, and the program state after the outcome 1 is obtained is $\rho_1^s = M_1\rho_0M_1^\dagger/p_1^s$. We adopt Selinger's normalization convention [18] to encode probability and density operator into a partial density operator $p_1^s\rho_1^s = M_1\rho_0M_1^\dagger$. Then this (partial) state is transformed by the quantum operation $\mathcal{E}_{s_1}$ to $\mathcal{E}_{s_1}(M_1\rho_0M_1^\dagger) = \mathcal{F}_{s_1}(\rho_0)$. The program continues its computation step by step according to the path s. In general, the $(n+1)$th step is executed upon the partial density operator $p_n^s\rho_n^s = \mathcal{F}_{s_n} \circ \cdots \circ \mathcal{F}_{s_2} \circ \mathcal{F}_{s_1}(\rho_0)$, where p_n^s is the probability that the program does not terminate at the nth step, and ρ_n^s is the program state after the termination measurement is performed and outcome 1 is reported at the nth step. For simplicity, let $\mathcal{F}_f$ denote the super-operator $\mathcal{F}_{s_n} \circ \cdots \circ \mathcal{F}_{s_2} \circ \mathcal{F}_{s_1}$ for string $f = s_1s_2 \cdots s_n$. Thus, $p_n^s\rho_n^s = \mathcal{F}_{s[n]}(\rho_0)$, where $s[n]$ is used to denote the head $s_1s_2 \cdots s_n$ for any $s = s_1s_2 \cdots s_n \cdots \in S$. The probability that the program terminates in the $(n+1)$th step is then $\mathrm{tr}(M_0(\mathcal{F}_{s[n]}(\rho_0))M_0^\dagger)$, and the probability that the program does not terminate in the $(n+1)$th step is $p_{n+1}^s = \mathrm{tr}(M_1(\mathcal{F}_{s[n]}(\rho_0))M_1^\dagger)$.

3.1 Fairness

To guarantee that all the processes in a concurrent program can fairly participate in a computation, a certain fairness condition on its execution paths is needed.

Definition 2. *An infinite execution path* $s = s_1 s_2 ... s_i ... \in S$ *is fair if each process appears infinitely often in* s*; that is, for each* $k \in K$*, there are infinitely many* $i \geq 1$ *such that* $s_i = k$.

We write $F = \{s : s \in S \text{ is fair}\}$ for the schedule of all fair execution paths.

Definition 3. *A finite execution path* $\sigma = s_1 s_2 \cdots s_n \in S_{fin}$ *is called a fair piece if each process appears during* σ*; that is, for each* $k \in K$*, there exists* $i \leq n$ *such that* $s_i = k$.

F_{fin} is used to denote the set of all fair pieces: $F_{fin} = \{\sigma : \sigma \in S_{fin} \text{ is a fair piece}\}$. It is obvious that $F = F_{fin}^{\omega}$; in other words, every fair infinite execution path $s \in F$ can be divided into an infinite sequence of fair pieces: $s = f_1 f_2 \cdots f_k \cdots$, where $f_i \in F_{fin}$ for each $i > 0$. The fairness defined above can be generalized by introducing the notion of fairness index, which measures the occurrence frequency of every process in an infinite execution path.

Definition 4. *For any infinite execution path* $s \in F$*, its fairness index* $f(s)$ *is the minimum, over all processes, of the lower limit of the occurrence frequency of the processes in* s*; that is,*

$$f(s) = \min_{k \in K} \lim_{t \to \infty} \inf_{n > t} \frac{s(n,k)}{n},$$

where $s(n,k)$ *is the number of occurrences of* k *in* $s[n]$.

For any $\delta \geq 0$, we write F_δ for the set of infinite execution paths whose fairness index is greater than δ: $F_\delta = \{s : s \in S \text{ and } f(s) > \delta\}$. Intuitively, within an infinite execution path in F_δ, each process will be woken up with frequency greater than δ. It is clear that $F_0 \subsetneq F$.

3.2 Running Example

We consider two quantum walks on a circle $C_3 = (V, E)$ with vertices $V = \{0, 1, 2\}$ and edges $E = \{(0,1), (1,2), (2,0)\}$. The first quantum walk $\mathcal{W}_1 = (\{W_1\}, \{M_0, M_1\})$ is given as follows:

- The state space is the 3−dimensional Hilbert space with computational basis $\{|i\rangle | i \in V\}$;
- The initial state is $|0\rangle$; this means that the walk starts at the vertex 0;
- A single step of the walk is defined by the unitary operator:

$$W_1 = \frac{1}{\sqrt{3}} \begin{pmatrix} 1 & 1 & 1 \\ 1 & w & w^2 \\ 1 & w^2 & w \end{pmatrix},$$

  where $w = e^{2\pi i/3}$. Intuitively, the probabilities of walking to the left and to the right are both 1/3, and there is also a probability 1/3 of not walking.

– The termination measurement $\{M_0, M_1\}$ is defined by

$$M_0 = |2\rangle\langle 2|, \ M_1 = I_3 - |2\rangle\langle 2|,$$

where I_3 is the 3×3 unit matrix.

The second walk $\mathcal{W}_2 = (\{W_2\}, \{M_0, M_1\})$ is similar to the first one, but its single step is described by unitary operator

$$W_2 = \frac{1}{\sqrt{3}} \begin{pmatrix} 1 & 1 & 1 \\ 1 & w^2 & w \\ 1 & w & w^2 \end{pmatrix}.$$

Then we can put these two quantum walks together to form a concurrent program $\mathcal{P} = (\{W_1, W_2\}, \{M_0, M_1\})$. For example, the execution of this concurrent program according to unfair path $1^\omega \notin F$ is equivalent to a sequential program $(\{W_1\}, \{P_0, P_1\})$; and the execution of $\mathcal{P}$ according to fair path $(12)^\omega \in F$ is as follows: we perform the termination measurement $\{M_0, M_1\}$ on the initial state ρ_0, then the nonterminating part of the program state is transformed by the super-operator $\mathcal{U}_1 = W_1 \cdot W_1^\dagger$, followed by the termination measurement, and then the application of the super-operator $\mathcal{U}_2 = W_2 \cdot W_2^\dagger$, and this procedure is repeated infinitely many times.

4 Reachability

Reachability is at the centre of program analysis. A state is reachable if some finite execution starting in the initial state ends in it. What concerns us in the quantum case is the subspace of $\mathcal{H}$ spanned by reachable states.

Definition 5. *The reachable space of program* $\mathcal{P} = (\{\mathcal{E}_k : k \in K\}, \{M_0, M_1\})$ *starting in the initial state* ρ_0 *is*

$$\mathcal{H}_R = \bigvee_{s \in S, j \geq 0} \text{supp } \mathcal{F}_{s[j]}(\rho_0) = \bigvee_{f \in S_{fin}} \text{supp } \mathcal{F}_f(\rho_0).$$

We have the following closed form characterization of the reachable space.

Theorem 1. $\mathcal{H}_R = \text{supp}(\sum_{i=0}^{d-1} \mathcal{F}^i(\rho_0))$, *where* $d = \dim \mathcal{H}$ *is the dimension of* $\mathcal{H}$, *and* $\mathcal{F} = \sum_{k \in K} \mathcal{F}_k$.

Proof: We write X for the right-hand side. From Lemma 1, we see that $X = \bigvee\{\text{supp}\mathcal{F}_f(\rho_0) : f \in S_{fin}, |f| < d\}$, where $|f|$ denotes the length of string f. According to the definition of reachable space, we know that $X \subseteq \mathcal{H}_R$. To prove the inverse part $X \supseteq \mathcal{H}_R$, for each $n \geq 0$, we define subspace Y_n as follows: $Y_n := \text{supp}(\sum_{i=0}^{n} \mathcal{F}^i(\rho_0))$. Due to Lemma 1, we know that $Y_0 \subseteq Y_1 \subseteq \cdots \subseteq Y_n \subseteq \cdots$. Suppose r is the smallest integer satisfying $Y_r = Y_{r+1}$. We observe that $Y_{n+1} = \text{supp}(\rho + \mathcal{F}(P_{Y_n}))$ for all $n \geq 0$. Then it follows that $Y_n = Y_r$ for all $n \geq r$. On the other hand, we have $Y_0 \subsetneq Y_1 \subsetneq \cdots \subsetneq Y_r$.

So, $0 < d_0 < d_1 < \cdots < d_r \leq d$, where d_0 is the rank of ρ_0, and d_i is the dimension of subspace Y_i for $1 \leq i \leq r$. Therefore, we have $r \leq d-1$ and $Y_{d-1} = Y_r \supseteq Y_n$ for all n. Finally, for any $f \in S_{fin}$, it follows from Lemma 2 that $\mathrm{supp}(\mathcal{F}_f(\rho_0)) \subseteq \mathrm{supp}(\mathcal{F}^{|f|}(\rho_0)) \subseteq Y_{|f|} \subseteq Y_{d-1} = X$. Thus, $\mathcal{H}_R \subseteq X$. ■

Now we are able to present an algorithm computing reachable subspace using matrix representation of super-operators. We define $\mathcal{G} = \sum_{k\in K} \mathcal{F}_k/|K|$.

Algorithm 1. Computing reachable space

```
input  : An input state ρ0, and the matrix representation G of 𝒢
output : An orthonormal basis B of ℋR.
|x⟩ ← (I − G/2)^{-1}(ρ0 ⊗ I)|Φ⟩;
(* |Φ⟩ = Σ_j |j_A j_B⟩ is the unnormalized maximally entangled state in ℋ⊗ℋ *)
for j = 1 : d do
    |y_j⟩ ← ⟨j_B|x⟩;
end
set of states B ← ∅;
integer l ← 0;
for j = 1 : d do
    |z⟩ ← |y_j⟩ − Σ_{k=1}^{l} ⟨b_k|y_j⟩|b_k⟩;
    if |z⟩ ≠ 0 then
        l ← l + 1;
        |b_l⟩ ← |z⟩/√⟨z|z⟩;
        B ← B ∪ {|b_l⟩};
    end
end
return
```

Theorem 2. *Algorithm 1 computes the reachable space in time $\mathcal{O}(d^{4.7454})$, where $d = \dim \mathcal{H}$.*

Proof: It follows from Lemma 3(1) that $I - G/2$ is invertible, and $\sum_{i=0}^{\infty}(G/2)^i = (I - G/2)^{-1}$. We write $\rho = \sum_{i=0}^{\infty} \mathcal{G}^i(\rho_0)/2^i$, and have

$$(\rho \otimes I)|\Phi\rangle = \sum_{i=0}^{\infty}(G/2)^i(\rho_0 \otimes I)|\Phi\rangle,$$

and the existence of ρ immediately follows from Lemma 3. We further see that $|x\rangle = (\rho \otimes I)|\Phi\rangle = \sum_j \rho|j_A\rangle|j_B\rangle$ and $|y_i\rangle = \rho|j_A\rangle$. Note that B is obtained from $\{|y_j\rangle\}$ by the Gram-Schmidt procedure. So, $\mathrm{supp}(\rho) = \mathrm{span}\{\rho|j\rangle\} = \mathrm{span}B$. It is clear that $\mathcal{H}_R = \mathrm{supp}(\sum_{i=0}^{d-1} \mathcal{F}^i(\rho_0)) \subseteq \mathrm{supp}(\rho)$. Therefore, $\mathcal{H}_R = \mathrm{supp}(\rho) = \mathrm{span}B$, and the algorithm is correct.

The complexity comes from three the following parts: (1) it costs $\mathcal{O}(d^{2*2.3727})$ to compute $(I - G/2)^{-1}$ by using Coppersmith-Winograd algorithm [2]; (2) it requires $\mathcal{O}(d^4)$ to obtain $|x\rangle$ from $(I - G/2)^{-1}$; (3) the Gram-Schmidt orthonormalization is in time $\mathcal{O}(d^3)$. So, the time complexity is $\mathcal{O}(d^{4.7454})$ in total. ■

An advantage of Algorithm 1 is that we can store $(I - G/2)^{-1}$. Then for any input state ρ_0, we only need $\mathcal{O}(d^4)$ to compute the space reachable from ρ_0.

Definition 6. *The uniformly repeatedly reachable space of program $\mathcal{P} = (\{\mathcal{E}_k : k \in K\}, \{M_0, M_1\})$ starting in the initial state ρ_0 is*

$$\mathcal{H}_{URR} = \bigcap_{n\geq 0} \bigvee_{s\in S, j\geq n} \text{supp } \mathcal{F}_{s[j]}(\rho_0) = \bigcap_{n\geq 0} \bigvee \{\text{supp } \mathcal{F}_f(\rho_0) : f \in S_{fin}, |f| \geq n\}.$$

The uniformly repeatedly reachable space enjoys the following closed form,

Theorem 3. $\mathcal{H}_{URR} = \text{supp}(\sum_{i=d}^{2d-1} \mathcal{F}^i(\rho_0))$, *where $d = \dim \mathcal{H}$, and $\mathcal{F} = \sum_{k\in K} \mathcal{F}_k$.*

Proof: For each $n \geq 0$, we define subspace Z_n as follows: $Z_n := \bigvee_{j\geq n} \text{supp } \mathcal{F}^j(\rho_0)$. It is obvious that $Z_0 \supseteq Z_1 \supseteq \cdots \supseteq Z_n \supseteq \cdots$. Suppose r is the smallest integer satisfying $Z_r = Z_{r+1}$. By noting that $Z_{n+1} = \text{supp}(\mathcal{F}(P_{Z_n}))$, we can show that $Z_n = Z_r$ for all $n \geq r$. On the other hand, we have $Z_0 \supsetneq Z_1 \supsetneq \cdots \supsetneq Z_r$. So, $d_0 > d_1 > \cdots > d_r \geq 0$, and d_i is the dimension of subspace Z_i for $0 \leq i \leq r$. Therefore, we have $r \leq d_0 \leq d$ and $Z_d = Z_r$. Therefore, $\mathcal{H}_{URR} = \bigcap_{n\geq 0} Z_n = Z_d$. It is obvious that Z_d is the reachable space starting in state $\mathcal{F}^d(\rho_0)$. Using Theorem 1 we obtain $Z_d = \text{supp}(\sum_{i=0}^{d-1} \mathcal{F}^i(\mathcal{F}^d(\rho_0))) = \text{supp}(\sum_{i=d}^{2d-1} \mathcal{F}(\rho_0))$. ■

We can give an algorithm computing the uniformly repeatedly reachable space by combining the above theorem and matrix representation of super-operators.

Algorithm 2. Compute uniformly repeatedly reachable space

---

input : An input state ρ_0, and the matrix representation G of $\mathcal{G}$
output : An orthonormal basis B_{URR} of $\mathcal{H}_{URR}$.
$|x\rangle \leftarrow G^d(I - G/2)^{-1}(\rho_0 \otimes I)|\Phi\rangle$;
(* $|\Phi\rangle = \sum_j |j_A j_B\rangle$ is the unnormalized maximally entangled state in $\mathcal{H} \otimes \mathcal{H}$ *)
for $j = 1 : d$ **do**
    $|y_j\rangle \leftarrow \langle j_B|x\rangle$;
end
set of states $B_{URR} \leftarrow \emptyset$;
integer $l \leftarrow 0$;
for $j = 1 : d$ **do**
    $|z\rangle \leftarrow |y_i\rangle - \sum_{k=1}^{l} \langle b_k|y_j\rangle |b_k\rangle$;
    if $|z\rangle \neq 0$ **then**
        $l \leftarrow l + 1$;
        $|b_l\rangle \leftarrow |z\rangle / \sqrt{\langle z|z\rangle}$;
        $B_{URR} \leftarrow B_{URR} \cup \{|b_l\rangle\}$;
    end
end
return

Theorem 4. *Algorithm 2 computes the uniformly repeatedly reachable space in time $\mathcal{O}(d^{4.7454} \log d)$, where $d = \dim \mathcal{H}$.*

Proof: This theorem is a corollary of Theorem 2. Here, $\log d$ in the complexity comes from computing M^d using the method of exponentiation by squaring.

5 Termination

Another important problem concerning the behaviour of a program is its termination.

Definition 7. *Let the program $\mathcal{P} = (\{\mathcal{E}_k : k \in K\}, \{M_0, M_1\})$. Then $\mathcal{P}$ with input ρ_0 terminates for execution path $s \in S$ if $p_n^s \rho_n^s = \mathcal{F}_{s[n]} = 0$ for some positive integer n.*

Definition 8. *1. If a program $\mathcal{P}$ with input ρ_0 terminates for all $s \in A$, then we say that it terminates in schedule A.*
2. If there is a positive integer n such that $p_n^s \rho_n^s = 0$ for all $s \in A$, then it is said that the program $\mathcal{P}$ with input ρ_0 uniformly terminates in schedule A.

We first prove the equivalence between termination and uniform termination. Of course, this equivalence comes from finiteness of the dimension of the state space.

Theorem 5. *The program $\mathcal{P} = (\{\mathcal{E}_k : k \in K\}, \{M_0, M_1\})$ with initial state ρ_0 terminates in the biggest schedule $S = K^\omega$ if and only if it uniformly terminates in schedule S.*

Proof. The "if" part is obvious. We prove the "only if" part in two steps:

(1) We consider the case of $|K| = 1$, where $\{\mathcal{E}_k : k \in K\}$ is a singleton $\{\mathcal{E}\}$. Now the program is indeed a sequential program, and it is a quantum loop [23]. We write $\mathcal{F}(\rho) = \mathcal{E}(M_1 \rho M_1^\dagger)$ for all ρ. What we need to prove is that if $\mathcal{P}$ terminates, i.e., $\mathcal{F}^n(\rho_0) = 0$ for some n, then it terminates within d steps, i.e., $\mathcal{F}^d(\rho_0) = 0$. If ρ_0 is a pure state $|\psi\rangle$, then we define the termination sets as follows: $X_n := \{|\psi\rangle : \mathcal{F}^n(\psi) = 0\}$ for each integer $n > 0$.

(1.1) If $|\varphi\rangle, |\chi\rangle \in X_n$, then $\mathcal{F}^n(\varphi + \chi) = 0$, which leads to $\alpha|\varphi\rangle + \beta|\chi\rangle \in X_n$ for any $\alpha, \beta \in \mathbb{C}$. Thus X_n is a subspace of $\mathcal{H}$.

(1.2) Since $\mathcal{F}^n(\psi) = 0 \Rightarrow \mathcal{F}^{n+1}(\psi) = 0$, it holds that that $X_n \subseteq X_{n+1}$ for any $n > 0$. So, we have the inclusion relation $X_1 \subseteq X_2 \subseteq \cdots \subseteq X_n \subseteq \cdots$.

Now suppose t is the smallest integer satisfying $X_t = X_{t+1}$. Invoking Lemma 2, we obtain that $\mathrm{supp}(\mathcal{F}^{*t}(I)) = X_t^\perp = X_{t+1}^\perp = \mathrm{supp}(\mathcal{F}^{*t+1}(I))$, where $\mathcal{F}^*(\cdot)$ denotes the (Schrödinger-Heisenberg) dual of $\mathcal{F}(\cdot)$. We have $\mathrm{supp}(\mathcal{F}^{*n}(I)) = \mathrm{supp}(\mathcal{F}^{*t}(I))$, which leads to $X_n = X_t$ for all $n \geq t$. Now, it holds that $X_1 \subsetneq X_2 \subsetneq \cdots \subsetneq X_t = X_{t+1} = X_{t+2} = \cdots$. This implies $d_1 < d_2 \cdots < d_t$, where d_i is the dimension of subspace X_i. Thus, $t \leq d$. If $\mathcal{F}^n(\psi) = 0$, then $|\psi\rangle \in X_n \subseteq X_d$, and $\mathcal{F}^d(\psi) = 0$.

In general, if ρ_0 is a mixed input state $\rho_0 = \sum p_i |\psi_i\rangle\langle\psi_i|$ with all $p_i > 0$, and $\mathcal{F}^n(\rho_0) = 0$, then $\mathcal{F}^n(\psi_i) = 0$ for all i. Therefore, $\mathcal{F}^d(\psi_i) = 0$ for all i, and it follows immediately that $\mathcal{F}^d(\rho_0) = 0$.

(2) For the general case of $|K| \geq 2$, we assume that $\mathcal{P}$ starting in ρ_0 terminates in S, i.e., for any $s \in S$, there exists an integer n_s such that $\mathcal{F}_{s[n_s]}(\rho_0) = 0$. Our purpose is to show that there exists an integer n such that $\mathcal{F}_{s[n]}(\rho_0) = 0$ for all $s \in S$. Indeed, we can choose $n = d$. We do this by refutation. Assume that $\mathcal{F}_{s[d]}(\rho_0) \neq 0$ for some $s \in S$. We are going to construct an execution path

$s \in S$ such that $\mathcal{F}_{s[n]}(\rho_0) \neq 0$ for any $n \geq 0$. Let $\mathcal{F} = \sum_{k \in K} \mathcal{F}_k$. Then the assumption means that there exist $f \in K^d$ such that $\mathcal{F}_f(\rho_0) \neq 0$, and it follows that $\mathcal{F}^d(\rho_0) \neq 0$. Now we consider the loop program $(\{\mathcal{F}\}, \{M_0, M_1\})$ with initial state ρ_0. Applying (1) to it, we obtain $\mathcal{F}^{2d}(\rho_0) \neq 0$. Then there exist $g_1, h_1 \in K^d$ such that $\mathcal{F}_{h_1}(\mathcal{F}_{g_1}(\rho_0)) = \mathcal{F}_{g_1 h_1}(\rho_0) \neq 0$, and $\mathcal{F}^d(\mathcal{F}_{g_1}(\rho_0)) \neq 0$. Applying (1) again leads to $\mathcal{F}^{2d}(\mathcal{F}_{g_1}(\rho_0)) \neq 0$, which means that there exist $h_2, g_2 \in K^{2d}$ such that $\mathcal{F}_{h_2}(\mathcal{F}_{g_1 g_2}(\rho_0)) = \mathcal{F}_{g_2 h_2}(\mathcal{F}_{g_1}(\rho_0)) \neq 0$. Thus, we have $\mathcal{F}^d(\mathcal{F}_{g_2 g_1}(\rho_0)) \neq 0$. Repeating this procedure, we can find an infinite sequence $g_1, g_2, ... \in K^d$. Put $s = g_1 g_2 ... \in S$. Then it holds that $\mathcal{T}_{s[kd]}(\rho_0) \neq 0$ for any integer k. Thus, we have $\mathcal{T}_{s[n]}(\rho) \neq 0$ for all n. ■

Now we are ready to consider termination under fairness. Of course, any permutation of K is a fair piece. We write P_K for the set of permutations of K. For $\sigma = s_1 s_2 \cdots s_m \in P_K$, a finite execution path of the form $s_1 \sigma_1 s_2 \sigma_2 \cdots \sigma_{m-1} s_m$ is called an expansion of σ. Obviously, for any $\sigma \in P_K$, all of its expansions are in F_{fin}. We will use a special class of fair pieces generated by permutations:

$$\Pi = \{s_1 \sigma_1 s_2 \sigma_2 \cdots \sigma_{m-1} s_m : s_1 s_2 \cdots s_m \in P_K \text{ and } |\sigma_i| < d \text{ for every } 1 \leq i < m\},$$

where d is the dimension of the Hilbert space $\mathcal{H}$ of program states. It is easy to see that $\Pi \subsetneq F_{fin}$.

Theorem 6. *A program $\mathcal{P} = (\{\mathcal{E}_k : k \in K\}, \{M_0, M_1\})$ with initial state ρ_0 terminates in the fair schedule F if and only if it terminates in the schedule Π^ω.*

Proof. The "only if" part is clear because $\Pi^\omega \subseteq F$. To prove the "if" part, assume $\mathcal{P}$ terminates in the schedule Π^ω. We proceed in four steps:

(1) Since Π is a finite set, we can construct a new program $\mathcal{P}' = (\{\mathcal{F}_f : f \in \Pi\}, \{0, I\})$. (We should point out that $\mathcal{F}_f$ is usually not trace-preserving, and thus $\mathcal{P}'$ is indeed not a program in the sense of Definition 1. However, this does not matter for the following arguments.) It is easy to see that the termination of $\mathcal{P}$ with ρ_0 in schedule Π^ω implies the termination of $\mathcal{P}'$ with ρ_0 in Π^ω. Note that Π^ω is the biggest schedule in $\mathcal{P}'$, although it is not the biggest schedule in $\mathcal{P}$. So, we can apply Theorem 5 to $\mathcal{P}'$ and assert that $(\sum_{f \in \Pi} \mathcal{F}_f)^d(\rho_0) = 0$. That is equivalent to

$$\text{supp}[(\sum_{f \in \Pi} \mathcal{F}_f)^d(\rho_0)] = \{0\} \text{ (0 − dimensional subspace).} \tag{1}$$

(2) For each $\sigma \in P_K$, we set $A_\sigma = \{\sigma' \in \Pi : \sigma' \text{ is an expansion of } \sigma\}$. Then $\bigcup_{\sigma \in P_K} A_\sigma = \Pi$. Moreover, we write $\mathcal{G}_\sigma = \sum_{f \in A_\sigma} \mathcal{F}_f$ for every $\sigma \in P_K$. It is worth noting that $\sum_{\sigma \in P_K} \mathcal{G}_\sigma = \sum_{f \in \Pi} \mathcal{F}_f$ is not true in general because it is possible that $A_{\sigma_1} \cap A_{\sigma_2} \neq \emptyset$ for different σ_1 and σ_2. But by Lemma 1.1 and 3 we have

$$\text{supp}[(\sum_{\sigma \in P_K} \mathcal{G}_\sigma)(\rho_0)] = \text{supp}[(\sum_{f \in \Pi} \mathcal{F}_f)(\rho_0)],$$

and furthermore, it follows from Eq. (1) that

$$\mathrm{supp}[(\sum_{\sigma\in P_K}\mathcal{G}_\sigma)^d(\rho_0)]=\mathrm{supp}[(\sum_{f\in\Pi}\mathcal{F}_f)^d(\rho_0)]=\{0\}. \tag{2}$$

(3) For each fair piece $\sigma'\in F_{fin}$, and for any ρ, we can write $\sigma'=s_1f_1s_2\cdots s_{m-1}f_{m-1}s_m$ for some $\sigma_0=s_1s_2\cdots s_m\in P_K$, and $f_1,...,f_{m-1}\in S_{fin}$. Furthermore, we write $\mathcal{G}=\sum_{i=0}^{d-1}(\sum_{k=1}^m\mathcal{F}_k)^i$. First, a routine calculation leads to $\mathcal{G}_{\sigma_0}=\mathcal{F}_{s_m}\circ\mathcal{G}\circ\mathcal{F}_{s_{m-1}}\cdots\mathcal{F}_{s_2}\circ\mathcal{G}\circ\mathcal{F}_{s_1}$. Second, it follows from Theorem 1 that for each $1\le i\le m-1$, and for any ρ, $\mathrm{supp}(\mathcal{F}_{f_i}(\rho))\subseteq\mathrm{supp}(\mathcal{G}(\rho))$. Repeatedly applying this inclusion together with Lemma 2.1 we obtain

$$\begin{aligned}\mathrm{supp}(\mathcal{F}_{\sigma'}(\rho))&=\mathrm{supp}[(\mathcal{F}_{s_m}\circ\mathcal{F}_{f_{m-1}}\circ\mathcal{F}_{s_{m-1}}\circ\cdots\circ\mathcal{F}_{s_2}\circ\mathcal{F}_{f_1}\circ\mathcal{F}_{s_1})(\rho)]\\&\subseteq\mathrm{supp}[(\mathcal{F}_{s_m}\circ\mathcal{G}\circ\mathcal{F}_{s_{m-1}}\circ\cdots\circ\mathcal{F}_{s_2}\circ\mathcal{G}\circ\mathcal{F}_{s_1})(\rho)]\\&=\mathrm{supp}(\mathcal{G}_{\sigma_0}(\rho))\subseteq\mathrm{supp}(\sum_{\sigma\in\Pi}\mathcal{F}_\sigma)(\rho).\end{aligned} \tag{3}$$

(4) Now we are able to complete the proof by showing that for any fair execution path $s\in F$, s has an initial segment t such that $\mathcal{F}_t(\rho_0)=0$. In fact, s can be written as an infinite sequence of fair piece, i.e., $s=\sigma_1'\sigma_2'\cdots$, where each σ_i' is a fair piece. We take t to be the initial segment of s containing the first d fair pieces, i.e., $t=\sigma_1\sigma_2\cdots\sigma_d$. Repeatedly applying Eq. (3) and Lemma 2.1 we obtain

$$\begin{aligned}\mathrm{supp}\mathcal{F}_t(\rho_0)&=\mathrm{supp}[(\mathcal{F}_{\sigma_d'}\circ\cdots\circ\mathcal{F}_{\sigma_2'}\circ\mathcal{F}_{\sigma_1'})(\rho_0)]\\&\subseteq\mathrm{supp}[(\sum_{p\in\Pi}\mathcal{F}_p)^d(\rho)]=\{0\}.\end{aligned}$$

Thus, $\mathcal{F}_t(\rho)=0$. ■

The above theorem can be slightly strengthened by employing the notion of fairness index in Definition 4. First, we have:

Lemma 4. $\Pi^\omega\subsetneq F_{\frac{1}{md}}$.

Proof. For any $s=\sigma_1\sigma_2\cdots\in\Pi^\omega$ with $\sigma_i\in\Pi$, we know that $\sigma_i(|\sigma_i|,k)\ge1$ for any $k\in K$ and $|\sigma_i|<md$, where $\sigma_i(|\sigma_i|,k)$ is the number of occurrences of k in σ_i. Then the occurrence frequency $f(s)>\frac{1}{md}$, which means that $\Pi^\omega\subseteq F_{\frac{1}{md}}$. On the other hand, we choose an arbitrary $s\in F_{\frac{1}{md}}$. Then $1^{md}s\in F_{\frac{1}{md}}$ but $1^{md}s\notin\Pi^\omega$. ■

Actually, what we proved in Theorem 6 is that for any two schedules A,B between Π^ω and F, i.e., $\Pi^\omega\subset A,B\subset F$, a program terminates in schedule A if and only if it terminates in schedule B . Combining Theorem 6 and Lemma 4 yields:

Corollary 1. *For any* $0 \leq \delta, \epsilon \leq \frac{1}{md}$*, a program terminates in schedule* F_δ *if and only if it terminates in schedule* F_ϵ*.* ■

Now an algorithm checking termination of a concurrent quantum program can be developed based on Theorem 5.

Algorithm 3. Decide termination of a concurrent quantum program

---

input : An input state ρ_0, and the matrix representation of each $\mathcal{F}_i$ *i.e*, N_i
output : b.(If the program terminates under F, $b = 0$; Otherwise, $b = 1$.)

$N \leftarrow 0$;
for $k = 1 : m$ **do**
  $N \leftarrow N_i + N$;
end
$G \leftarrow I$;
for $k = 1 : d - 1$ **do**
  $G \leftarrow I + NG$;
end
(*Compute the matrix representation of $\mathcal{G}$*)
$M \leftarrow 0$;
Generate P_K;
for $p = p_1p_2 \cdots p_m \in P_K$ **do**
  $L \leftarrow N_{p_1}$;
  for $l = 2 : m$ **do**
    $L \leftarrow N_{p_l}GL$;
  end
  (*Compute the matrix representation of $\mathcal{F}_p$*)
  $M \leftarrow M + L$;
end
(*Compute the matrix representation of $\sum_{p\in P_K} \mathcal{F}_p$*)
$|x\rangle \leftarrow M^d(\rho_0 \otimes I)|\Phi\rangle$;
if $|x\rangle \neq 0$ **then**
  $b \leftarrow 1$;
end
if $|x\rangle = 0$ **then**
  $b \leftarrow 0$;
end
return b

Theorem 7. *Algorithm 3 decides termination of a concurrent quantum program in time* $\mathcal{O}((m^m + d)d^{4.7454})$*, where* m *is the number of the processes, and* $d = \dim \mathcal{H}$*.*

Proof: In the algorithm, we use the for loop to compute the matrix representation G of $\mathcal{G} = \sum_{i=0}^{d-1}(\sum_{k=1}^{m} \mathcal{F}_k)^i$. Then the matrix representation of $\mathcal{F}_\sigma = \mathcal{F}_{s_1} \circ \mathcal{G} \circ \mathcal{F}_{s_2} \cdots \mathcal{G} \circ \mathcal{F}_{s_m}(\cdot)$ is obtained for any $\sigma = s_1s_2 \cdots s_m \in P_K$. All $\mathcal{F}_\sigma$s are added up to M. Then M becomes the matrix representation of $\sum_{\sigma\in P_K} \mathcal{F}_\sigma$. Consequently, we can apply Theorem 6 to assert that this algorithm outputs 0 if the program terminates in the fair schedule F; otherwise, 1.

To analyse its complexity, the algorithm can be divided into three steps: (1) Computing G costs $\mathcal{O}(m+d\,d^{2*2.3727}) = \mathcal{O}(m+d^{5.7454})$; (2) Computing M costs $m!*2m*\mathcal{O}(d^{2*2.3727}) = \mathcal{O}(m^m\,d^{4.7454})$; (3) Computing $|x\rangle$ costs $\mathcal{O}(d^{4.7454}\log d)$. So the total cost is $\mathcal{O}((m^m + d)d^{4.7454})$. ■

6 Conclusion

In this paper, we studied two of the central problems, namely, reachability and termination for concurrent quantum programs. A concurrent quantum program is modeled by a family of quantum Markov chains sharing a state Hilbert space and a termination measurement, with each chain standing for a participating process. This model extends Hart, Sharir and Pnueli's model of probabilistic concurrent programs [12] to the quantum setting. We show that the reachable space and the uniformly repeatedly reachable space of a concurrent quantum program can be computed and its termination can be decided in time $\mathcal{O}(d^{4.7454})$, $\mathcal{O}(d^{4.7454}\log d)$, $\mathcal{O}((m^m + d)d^{4.7454})$, respectively, where m is the number of participating processes, and d is the dimension of state space.

For further studies, an obvious problem is: how to improve the above algorithm complexities? In this paper, reachability and termination of quantum programs were defined in a way where probabilities are abstracted out; that is, only reachability and termination with certainty are considered. A more delicate, probability analysis of the reachability and termination is also an interesting open problem. The algorithms for computing the reachable space and checking termination of a *quantum* program presented in this paper are all algorithms for *classical* computers. So, another interesting problem is to find efficient *quantum* algorithms for reachability and termination analysis of a quantum program.

Acknowledgment. We are grateful to Dr Yangjia Li, Runyao Duan and Yuan Feng for useful discussions. This work was partly supported by the Australian Research Council (Grant No. DP110103473).

References

1. Cirac, J.I., Ekert, A.K., Huelga, S.F., Macchiavello, C.: Distributed quantum computation over noisy channels. Physical Review A 59, 4249–4254 (1999)
2. Don, C., Shmuel, W.: Matrix multiplication via arithmetic progressions. Journal of Symbolic Computation 9, 251–280 (1990)
3. Davidson, T.A.S.: Formal Verification Techniques using Quantum Process Calculus, Ph.D. thesis. University of Warwick (2011)
4. Davidson, T.A.S., Gay, S., Nagarajan, R., Puthoor, I.V.: Analysis of a quantum error correcting code using quantum process calculus. In: Proceedingds of QPL 2011, the 8th Workhop on Quantum Physics and Logic, pp. 107–120 (2011)
5. D'Hondt, E., Panangaden, P.: Quantum weakest preconditions. Mathematical Structures in Computer Science 16, 429–451 (2006)
6. Feng, Y., Duan, R.Y., Ji, Z.F., Ying, M.S.: Probabilistic bisimulations for quantum processes. Information and Computation 205, 1608–1639 (2007)

7. Feng, Y., Duan, R.Y., Ying, M.S.: Bisimulation for quantum processes. In: Proceedings of the 38th ACM SIGPLAN-SIGACT Symposium on Principles of Programming Languages (POPL), pp. 523–534 (2011)
8. Gay, S.J., Nagarajan, R.: Communicating Quantum Processes. In: Proceedings of the 32nd ACM Symposium on Principles of Programming Languages (POPL), pp. 145–157 (2005)
9. Gay, S.J., Nagarajan, R.: Types and typechecking for communicating quantum processes. Mathematical Structures in Computer Science 16, 375–406 (2006)
10. Gay, S.J., Nagarajan, R., Papanikolaou, N.: QMC: A Model Checker for Quantum Systems. In: Gupta, A., Malik, S. (eds.) CAV 2008. LNCS, vol. 5123, pp. 543–547. Springer, Heidelberg (2008)
11. Gay, S.J., Papanikolaou, N., Nagarajan, R.: Specification and verification of quantum protocols. In: Gay, S.J., Mackie, I. (eds.) Semantic Techniques in Quantum Computation, pp. 414–472. Cambridge University Press (2010)
12. Hart, S., Sharir, M., Pnueli, A.: Termination of probabilistic concurrent programs. ACM Transactions on Programming Languages and Systems 5, 356–380 (1983)
13. Jorrand, P., Lalire, M.: Toward a quantum process algebra. In: Proceedings of the First ACM Conference on Computing Frontiers, pp. 111–119 (2004)
14. Lalire, M.: Relations among quantum processes: bisimilarity and congruence. Mathematical Structures in Computer Science 16, 407–428 (2006)
15. Lalire, M., Jorrand, P.: A process algebraic approach to concurrent and distributed quantum computation: operational semantics. In: Proceedings of the 2nd International Workshop on Quantum Programming Languages (2004)
16. Li, Y.Y., Yu, N.K., Ying, M.S.: Termination of nondeterministic quantum programs. Short presentation of LICS (2012), (For full paper, see *arXiv*: 1201.0891)
17. Nielsen, M.A., Chuang, I.L.: Quantum Computation and Quantum Information. Cambridge University Press, Cambridge (2000)
18. Selinger, P.: Towards a quantum programming language. Mathematical Structure in Computer Science 14, 527–586 (2004)
19. Sharir, M., Pnueli, A., Hart, S.: Verification of probabilistic programs. SIAM Journal on Computing 13, 292–314 (1984)
20. Ying, M.S.: Floyd-Hoare logic for quantum programs. ACM Transactions on Programming Languages and Systems 33, art. no: 19 (2011)
21. Ying, M.S., Feng, Y.: An algebraic language for distributed quantum computing. IEEE Transactions on Computers 58, 728–743 (2009)
22. Ying, M.S., Feng, Y., Duan, R.Y., Ji, Z.F.: An algebra of quantum processes. ACM Transactions on Computational Logic 10, art. no. 19 (2009)
23. Ying, M.S., Feng, Y.: Quantum loop programs. Acta Informatica 47, 221–250 (2010)
24. Ying, M.S., Yu, N.K., Feng, Y., Duan, R.Y.: Verification of Quantum Programs, arXiv:1106.4063

Making Weighted Containment Feasible: A Heuristic Based on Simulation and Abstraction

Guy Avni and Orna Kupferman

School of Computer Science and Engineering, Hebrew University, Israel

Abstract. Weighted automata map input words to real numbers and are useful in reasoning about quantitative systems and specifications. The containment problem for weighted automata asks, given two weighted automata $\mathcal{A}$ and $\mathcal{B}$, whether for all words w, the value that $\mathcal{A}$ assigns to w is less than or equal to the value $\mathcal{B}$ assigns to w. The problem is of great practical interest, yet is known to be undecidable. Efforts to approximate weighted containment by weighted variants of the simulation pre-order still have to cope with large state spaces. One of the leading approaches for coping with large state spaces is abstraction. We introduce an abstraction-refinement paradigm for weighted automata and show that it nicely combines with weighted simulation, giving rise to a feasible approach for the containment problem. The weighted-simulation pre-order we define is based on a quantitative two-player game, and the technical challenge in the setting origins from the fact the values that the automata assign to words are unbounded. The abstraction-refinement paradigm is based on under- and over-approximation of the automata, where approximation, and hence also the refinement steps, refer not only to the languages of the automata but also to the values they assign to words.

1 Introduction

Traditional automata accept or reject their input, and are therefore Boolean. A weighted finite automaton (WFA, for short) has real-valued weights on its transitions and it maps each word to a real value. Applications of weighted automata include formal verification, where they are used for the verification of quantitative properties [10,11,17,25,32], as well as text, speech, and image processing, where the weights of the automaton are used in order to account for the variability of the data and to rank alternative hypotheses [15,30].

Technically, each transition in a WFA is associated with a weight, the value of a run is the sum of the weights of the transitions traversed along the run, and the value of a word is the value of the maximal run on it.[1] The rich structure of weighted automata makes them intriguing mathematical objects. Fundamental problems that have been solved decades ago for Boolean automata are still open or known to be undecidable in the weighted setting [29]. For example, while in the Boolean setting, nondeterminism does not add to the expressive power of the automata, not all weighted automata can be

[1] The above semantics, which we are going to follow in the paper, is a special case of the general setting, were each weighted automaton is defined with respect to an algebraic semiring.

M. Koutny and I. Ulidowski (Eds.): CONCUR 2012, LNCS 7454, pp. 84–99, 2012.

determinized, and the problem of deciding whether a given nondeterministic weighted automaton can be determinized is still open, in the sense we do not even know whether it is decidable.

A problem of great interest in the context of automata is the *containment* problem. In the Boolean setting, the containment problem asks, given two automata $\mathcal{A}$ and $\mathcal{B}$, whether all the words in Σ^* that are accepted by $\mathcal{A}$ are also accepted by $\mathcal{B}$. In the weighted setting, the "goal" of words is not just to get accepted, but also to do so with a maximal value. Accordingly, the containment problem for WFAs asks, given two WFAs $\mathcal{A}$ and $\mathcal{B}$, whether every word accepted by $\mathcal{A}$ is also accepted by $\mathcal{B}$, and its value in $\mathcal{A}$ is less than or equal to its value in $\mathcal{B}$. We then say that $\mathcal{B}$ contains $\mathcal{A}$, denoted $\mathcal{A} \subseteq \mathcal{B}$. In the Boolean setting, the containment problem is PSPACE-complete [31]. In the weighted setting, the problem is in general undecidable [1,24]. The problem is indeed of great interest: In the automata-theoretic approach to reasoning about systems and their specifications, containment amounts to correctness of systems with respect to their specifications. The same motivation applies for weighted systems, with the specifications being quantitative [10].

Even in the Boolean setting, where the containment problem is decidable, its PSPACE complexity is an obstacle in practice and researchers have suggested two orthogonal methods for coping with it. One is to replace containment by a pre-order that is easier to check, with the leading such pre-order being the *simulation* preorder [28]. Simulation can be checked in polynomial time and symbolically [20,28], and several heuristics for checking containment by variants of simulation have been studied and used in practice [23,26]. A second method, useful also in other paradigms for reasoning about the huge, and possibly infinite, state space of systems is *abstraction* [3,8]. Essentially, in abstraction we hide some of the information about the system. This enables us to reason about systems that are much smaller, yet it gives rise to a 3-valued solution: yes, no, and unknown [5]. In the latter case, the common practice is to refine the abstraction, aiming to add the minimal information that would lead to a definite solution. In particular, in the context of model checking, the method of counterexample guided abstraction-refinement (CEGAR) has proven to be very effective [13].

In this paper we study a combination of the above two methods in the setting of weighted automata. Abstraction frameworks in the 3-valued Boolean semantics are typically based on *modal transition systems* (MTS) [27]. Such systems have two types of transitions: *may* transitions, which over-approximate the transitions of the concrete system, and *must* transitions, which under-approximate them. The over and under approximation refer to the ability of the automaton to take transitions, and hence to its language. In our weighted setting, we combine this with the weights of the transitions: may transitions over-approximate the actual weight and must transitions under-approximate it. This is achieved by defining the weight of may and must transitions according to the maximal and minimal weight, respectively, of the transitions that induce them.

The simulation preorder in the Boolean setting has a game-theoretic characterization. We extend this approach to the weighted setting and define weighted simulation between two WFAs $\mathcal{A}$ and $\mathcal{B}$ by means of a game played between an antagonist, who iteratively generates a word w and an accepting run r of $\mathcal{A}$ on it, and a protagonist, who replies with a run r' of $\mathcal{B}$ on w. The goal of the antagonist is to generate w and r so that either r' is not accepting, or its value is smaller than the value of r. The goal of the protagonist is to continue the game forever without the antagonist reaching his goal. We say that $\mathcal{A}$ is simulated by $\mathcal{B}$, denoted $\mathcal{A} \leq \mathcal{B}$ iff the protagonist has a winning strategy. The above definition is similar to the definition of quantitative simulation in [12,14], and has the flavor of the *energy games* in [4]. In these works, however, the winning condition in the game refers only to the weight along the traversed edges. This corresponds to the case the WFAs in question are such that all states are accepting. Even richer than our setting are *energy parity games* [9]. Both energy games and parity energy games can be decided in NP $\cap$ co-NP. Our main challenge then is to develop an algorithm that would maintain the simplicity of the algorithm in [4] in the richer setting, which is simpler than the one of parity games. We do this by performing a preprocessing on the arena of the game, one after which we can perform only local changes in the algorithm of [4]. This is not easy, as like in parity energy games a winning strategy in the simulation game need not be memoryless. Our main contribution, however, is not the study of simulation games and their solution – the main ideas here are similar to these in [4,9], but the ability to combine simulation with abstraction and refinement, which we see as our main contribution.

Having defined over- and under-approximations of WFAs and the weighted simulation relation, we suggest the following heuristic for checking whether $\mathcal{A} \subseteq \mathcal{B}$. For a WFA $\mathcal{U}$ and an abstraction function α, let $\mathcal{U}^{\alpha}_{\downarrow}$ and $\mathcal{U}^{\alpha}_{\uparrow}$ be the weighted under and over approximations of $\mathcal{U}$ according to α. Let α and β be approximation functions for $\mathcal{A}$ and $\mathcal{B}$, respectively. It is not hard to see that if $\mathcal{A}^{\alpha}_{\uparrow} \subseteq \mathcal{B}^{\beta}_{\downarrow}$, then $\mathcal{A} \subseteq \mathcal{B}$, and that if $\mathcal{A}^{\alpha}_{\downarrow} \not\subseteq \mathcal{B}^{\beta}_{\uparrow}$, then $\mathcal{A} \not\subseteq \mathcal{B}$. We show that the above is valid not just of containment but also for our weighted-simulation relation. This gives rise to the following heuristics. We start by checking $\mathcal{A}^{\alpha}_{\uparrow} \leq \mathcal{B}^{\beta}_{\downarrow}$ and $\mathcal{A}^{\alpha}_{\downarrow} \not\leq \mathcal{B}^{\beta}_{\uparrow}$, for some (typically coarse) initial abstraction functions α and β. As we prove in the paper, if we are lucky and one of them holds, we are done. Otherwise, the winning strategies of the antagonist in the first case and the protagonist in the second case suggest a way to refine α and β, and we repeat the process with the refined abstractions. While refinement in the Boolean case only splits abstract states in order to close the gap between may and must transitions, here we also have refinement steps that tighten the weights along transitions. Note that while repeated refinement can only get us to a solution to the $\mathcal{A} \leq \mathcal{B}$ problem, they also make it more likely that one of our checks returns an answer that would imply a definite solution to the undecidable $\mathcal{A} \subseteq \mathcal{B}$ problem.

Note that our abstraction-refinement procedure combines two games. The first, which corresponds to $\mathcal{A}^{\alpha}_{\uparrow} \leq \mathcal{B}^{\beta}_{\downarrow}$, approximates the simulation question $\mathcal{A} \leq \mathcal{B}$ from below. The second, which corresponds to $\mathcal{A}^{\alpha}_{\downarrow} \leq \mathcal{B}^{\beta}_{\uparrow}$, approximates it from above. Such dual approximations have proven useful also in the Boolean setting [6,16,18,21,22], where games combine may and must transitions, and also in settings in which games that are determined are approximated by means other than abstraction. For example, when LTL realizability is done by checking the realizability of approximations of both the specification and its negation [7].

Due to the lack of space, some proofs are only sketched. The full proofs can be found in the full version in the authors' homepages.

2 Weighted Automata and Their Abstraction

A nondeterministic finite weighted automaton on finite words (WFA, for short) is a tuple $\mathcal{A} = \langle \Sigma, Q, \Delta, Q_0, \tau, F \rangle$, where Σ is an alphabet, Q is a set of states, $\Delta \subseteq Q \times \Sigma \times Q$ is a transition relation, $Q_0 \subseteq Q$ is a set of initial states, $\tau : \Delta \to \mathbb{R}$ is a function that maps each transition to a real value in $\mathbb{R}$, and $F \subseteq Q$ is a set of accepting states. We assume that there are no *dead-end* states in $\mathcal{A}$. That is, for every $q \in Q$ there is a letter $\sigma \in \Sigma$ and state $q' \in Q$ such that $\Delta(q, \sigma, q')$.

A run of $\mathcal{A}$ on a word $u = u_1, \ldots, u_n \in \Sigma^*$ is a sequence of states $r = r_0, r_1, \ldots, r_n$ such that $r_0 \in Q_0$ and for every $0 \leq i < n$ we have $\Delta(r_i, u_{i+1}, r_{i+1})$. The run r is accepting iff $r_n \in F$. The value of the run, denoted $val(r, u)$, is the sum of transitions it traverses. That is, $val(r, u) = \sum_{0 \leq i < n} \tau(\langle r_i, u_{i+1}, r_{i+1} \rangle)$. Since $\mathcal{A}$ is nondeterministic, there can be more than one run on a single word. We define the value that $\mathcal{A}$ assigns to $u \in \Sigma^*$, denoted $val(\mathcal{A}, u)$, as the value of the maximal-valued accepting run of $\mathcal{A}$ on u. That is, $val(\mathcal{A}, u) = max\{val(r, u) : r$ is an accepting run of $\mathcal{A}$ on $u\}$. As in NFAs, the language of $\mathcal{A}$, denoted $L(\mathcal{A})$, is the set of words in Σ^* that $\mathcal{A}$ accepts.

We say that $\mathcal{A}$ is *deterministic* if $|Q_0| = 1$ and for every $q \in Q$ and $\sigma \in \Sigma$, there is at most one state $q' \in Q$ such that $\Delta(q, \sigma, q')$.

An *abstraction function* for a WFA $\mathcal{A}$ is a function $\alpha : Q \to A$, for a set A, which we assume to be smaller than Q. We refer to the members of Q as the *concrete states* and to these of A as the *abstract states*. The function α induces a partition of Q, and we sometimes refer to abstract states as sets of concrete states. In particular, for a concrete state $c \in Q$ and an abstract state $a \in A$, we use the notation $c \in a$ to indicate that $\alpha(c) = a$.

Consider a WFA $\mathcal{A}$ and an abstraction function α. For parameters $\beta \in \{may, must\}$ and $\gamma \in \{max, min\}$, the abstraction of $\mathcal{A}$ according to α, β, and γ is the WFA $\mathcal{A}^{\gamma}_{\beta}[\alpha] = \langle \Sigma, A, \Delta_\beta, A_0, \tau_\gamma, F_\beta \rangle$, where $A_0 = \{\alpha(q_0) : q_0 \in Q_0\}$, and Δ_β, τ_γ, and F_β are defined as follows:

- Consider $a, a' \in A$ and $\sigma \in \Sigma$. We define $\Delta_{must} \subseteq A \times \Sigma \times A$ so that $\Delta_{must}(a, \sigma, a')$ iff for every $c \in a$ there is $c' \in a'$ such that $\Delta(c, \sigma, c')$. We define $\Delta_{may} \subseteq A \times \Sigma \times A$ so that $\Delta_{may}(a, \sigma, a')$ iff there exists $c \in a$ and $c' \in a'$ such that $\Delta(c, \sigma, c')$.
- We define the minimum-value function, denoted τ_{min}, of an abstract transition to be the minimum over the values of concrete transitions that induce it. Formally, for $\langle a, \sigma, a' \rangle \in \Delta_\beta$, we define $\tau_{min}(\langle a, \sigma, a' \rangle) = min\{\tau(\langle c, \sigma, c' \rangle) : c \in a, c' \in a'$, and $\Delta(c, \sigma, c')\}$. Similarly, we define the maximal-value function as τ_{max}, with $\tau_{max}((\langle a, \sigma, a' \rangle) = max\{\tau(\langle c, \sigma, c' \rangle) : c \in a, c' \in a'$, and $\Delta(c, \sigma, c')\}$.
- We define $F_{may} = \{a \in A : a \cap F \neq \emptyset\}$ and $F_{must} = \{a \in A : a \subseteq F\}$.

Note that without weights, our definition coincides with the standard over- and under-approximations studied in the Boolean case. In the weighted setting, the abstraction approximates, in addition to the transitions, the value that the concrete WFA assigns to words. The two interesting combinations are then the under-approximating WFA $\mathcal{A}^{\alpha}_{\downarrow} = \mathcal{A}^{min}_{must}[\alpha]$ and the over-approximating WFA $\mathcal{A}^{\alpha}_{\uparrow} = \mathcal{A}^{max}_{may}[\alpha]$. When α is not important or clear form the context, we omit it.

We refer to runs of $\mathcal{A}_\downarrow$ as *must-runs*, runs of $\mathcal{A}_\uparrow$ as *may-runs*, and runs of $\mathcal{A}$ as *concrete-runs*. Note that for every must-run $r = r_0, \ldots, r_n$ of $\mathcal{A}_\downarrow$ on some word $u \in \Sigma^*$, there is a matching run $r' = r'_0, \ldots, r'_n$ of $\mathcal{A}$ on u such that, for every $0 \leq i \leq n$, we have $r'_i \in r_i$. Similarly, for every run $r = r_0, \ldots, r_n$ of $\mathcal{A}$ on some word u, the sequence $r' = \alpha(r_0), \ldots, \alpha(r_n)$ is a run of $\mathcal{A}_\uparrow$ on u.

In the Boolean setting, *language containment* refers to words accepted by the automaton. That is, for two NFAs $\mathcal{A}$ and $\mathcal{B}$, we say that $\mathcal{A} \subseteq \mathcal{B}$ iff $L(\mathcal{A}) \subseteq L(\mathcal{B})$. In the weighted setting, language containment is more involved, as we also have a requirement on the values the automata assign to words. For two WFAs, we say that $\mathcal{A} \subseteq \mathcal{B}$ iff $L(\mathcal{A}) \subseteq L(\mathcal{B})$ and for every $w \in L(\mathcal{A})$ we have $val(\mathcal{A}, w) \leq val(\mathcal{B}, w)$.

The *containment problem* gets as input two automata $\mathcal{A}$ and $\mathcal{B}$, and decides whether $\mathcal{A} \subseteq \mathcal{B}$. The problem is known to be PSPACE-complete in the Boolean setting [33] and undecidable in the weighted setting [1,24].

Since, in practice, WFAs are typically very large, we would like to reason on their abstractions. As Theorem 1 below shows, $\mathcal{A}_\downarrow$ and $\mathcal{A}_\uparrow$ under- and over-approximates $\mathcal{A}$, making such a reasoning possible.

Theorem 1. *Consider a WFA $\mathcal{A}$ and an abstraction function α. Then, $\mathcal{A}^\alpha_\downarrow \subseteq \mathcal{A} \subseteq \mathcal{A}^\alpha_\uparrow$.*

Proof: We start by proving that $\mathcal{A}_\downarrow \subseteq \mathcal{A}$. Consider a word $u = u_1, \ldots, u_n \in L(\mathcal{A}_\downarrow)$. We prove that $u \in L(\mathcal{A})$ and $val(\mathcal{A}_\downarrow, u) \leq val(\mathcal{A}, u)$. Let $r = a_0, \ldots, a_n \in A^*$ be an accepting run of $\mathcal{A}_\downarrow$ on u. Since $a_0 \in A_0$, there is a concrete state $c_0 \in (a_0 \cap Q_0)$. Since r is a must-run, there is a concrete run $r' = c_0, \ldots, c_n$ of $\mathcal{A}$ on u such that, for $1 \leq i \leq n$, we have $c_i \in a_i$. Since r is accepting, $r_n \subseteq F$, implying that $c_n \in F$. Thus, r' is accepting and $u \in L(\mathcal{A})$.

It is left to prove that $val(\mathcal{A}_\downarrow, u) \leq val(\mathcal{A}, u)$. We show that for every accepting run r of $\mathcal{A}_\downarrow$ on u and every concrete run r' that corresponds to it, $val(r, u) \leq val(r', u)$. Indeed, by the definition of τ_{min}, we have $val(r, u) = \sum_{0 \leq i \leq n} \tau_{min}(r_i, u_{i+1}, r_{i+1}) \leq \sum_{0 \leq i \leq n} \tau(r_i, u_{i+1}, r_{i+1}) = val(r', u)$, so we are done.

The proof of the second claim is similar and is presented in the full version. □

3 Weighted Simulation

As discussed in Section 1, the pre-order of simulation [28] is used in the Boolean setting as a heuristic for checking containment. In this section we define weighted simulation and show that it enjoys the appealing properties of simulation in the Boolean setting. In Section 4, we show that weighted simulation can be checked by reasoning about abstractions of the WFAs in question.

3.1 Defining the Weighted Simulation Relation

Given two WFAs $\mathcal{A}$ and $\mathcal{B}$, deciding whether $\mathcal{A} \subseteq \mathcal{B}$ can be thought of as a two-player game of one round: Player 1, the Player whose goal it is to show that there is no containment, chooses a word w and a run r_1 of $\mathcal{A}$ on w. Player 2 then replies by choosing a run r_2 of $\mathcal{B}$ on w. Player 1 wins if r_1 is accepting and r_2 is not or if $val(r_1, w) > val(r_2, w)$. While this game clearly captures containment, it does not lead to interesting insights or algoritmic ideas about checking containment. A useful way to view simulation is as a "step-wise" version of the above game in which in each round the players proceed according to a single transition of the WFAs.

We continue to describe the simulation game formally. A game between Player 1 and Player 2 is a pair $\langle G, \Gamma \rangle$, for an arena G and an objective Γ for Player 1. Consider two WFAs $\mathcal{A}$ and $\mathcal{B}$, where for $\gamma \in \{\mathcal{A}, \mathcal{B}\}$, let $\gamma = \langle \Sigma, Q_\gamma, \Delta_\gamma, q_0^\gamma, F_\gamma, \tau_\gamma \rangle$. For simplicity, we assume that the WFAs are full, in the sense that each state and letter have at least one successor.

The arena of the game that corresponds to $\mathcal{A} \leq \mathcal{B}$ is $G = \langle V, E, v_0, \tau \rangle$. The set V of vertices is partitioned into two disjoint sets: $V_1 = Q_\mathcal{A} \times Q_\mathcal{B}$ are vertices from which Player 1 proceeds, and $V_2 = Q_\mathcal{A} \times \Sigma \times Q_\mathcal{B}$ are vertices from which Player 2 proceeds. The players alternate moves, thus $E \subseteq (V_1 \times V_2) \cup (V_2 \times V_1)$. Each play starts in the initial vertex $v_0 = \langle q_0^\mathcal{A}, q_0^\mathcal{B} \rangle \in V_1$, and $\tau : E \to \mathbb{R}$ is the weight function. We define $E = E_1 \cup E_2$ and τ as follows:

- $E_1 = \{\langle \langle p, q \rangle, \langle p', \sigma, q \rangle \rangle : \langle p, \sigma, p' \rangle \in \Delta_\mathcal{A} \text{ and } q \in Q_\mathcal{B}\}$.
- $E_2 = \{\langle \langle p, \sigma, q \rangle, \langle p, q' \rangle \rangle : \langle q, \sigma, q' \rangle \in \Delta_\mathcal{B} \text{ and } p \in Q_\mathcal{A}\}$.
- For $e_1 = \langle \langle p, q \rangle, \langle p', \sigma, q \rangle \rangle \in E_1$, we define $\tau(e_1) = \tau_\mathcal{A}(\langle p, \sigma, p' \rangle)$.
- For $e_2 = \langle \langle p, \sigma, q \rangle, \langle p, q' \rangle \rangle \in E_2$, we define $\tau(e_2) = -\tau_\mathcal{B}(\langle q, \sigma, q' \rangle)$.

Thus, edges in E_1 leave vertices in V_1 and correspond to Player 1 choosing a letter and a transition in $\mathcal{A}$. Edges in E_2 leave vertices in V_2 and correspond to Player 2 choosing a transition in $\mathcal{B}$.

A play of the game is a (possibly infinite) sequence of vertices $\pi = \pi_0, \pi_1, \ldots$, where $\pi_0 = v_0$, and for every $i \geq 0$ we have $E(v_i, v_{i+1})$. Every finite play has a value, denoted $val(\pi)$, which is the sum of the edges that are traversed along it: i.e., $val(\pi) = \sum_{0 \leq i < |\pi|} \tau(\langle \pi_i, \pi_{i+1} \rangle)$. We use $\pi[i : j]$, for $i < j$, to refer to the sub-play $\pi_i, \ldots, \pi_j$.

A strategy for player $i \in \{1, 2\}$ is a function $\rho_i : V^* \cdot V_i \to V$. Let $\mathcal{S}_i$ be the set of all strategies for player i. Two strategies $\rho_1 \in \mathcal{S}_1$ and $\rho_2 \in \mathcal{S}_2$, induce a single play obtained when both players follow their strategies. Formally, the outcome of ρ_1 and ρ_2, denoted $out(\rho_1, \rho_2)$, is the infinite play $\pi = \pi_1, \pi_2, \ldots$, where for every $i \geq 0$, we have $\pi_{2i+1} = \rho_1(\pi[0 : 2i])$ and $\pi_{2i+2} = \rho_2(\pi[0 : 2i+1])$. We say that a strategy ρ_i is *memoryless* if it depends only on the current vertex. Formally, $\rho_i(u_1 \cdot v) = \rho_i(u_2 \cdot v)$ for all $u_1, u_2 \in V^*$ and $v \in V_i$.

It is left to define the objective of the game. A finite play π is winning for Player 1 if the last vertex of π is in $F_\mathcal{A} \times (Q_\mathcal{B} \setminus F_\mathcal{B})$ or the last vertex of π is in $F_\mathcal{A} \times F_\mathcal{B}$ and $val(\pi) > 0$. The *objective* $\Gamma \subseteq V^\omega$ of Player 1, namely the set of plays that are winning for Player 1 is defined so that an infinite play π is in Γ iff it has a finite prefix that is winning according to the definition above. Note that for an infinite play π, if $\pi \notin \Gamma$, then it is winning for Player 2. Thus, the objective of *Player* 2 is $\overline{\Gamma} = V^\omega \setminus \Gamma$. Also note that once the play has a prefix that is winning for Player 1, there is no actual need for the play to continue. A *winning strategy* for Player 1 is a strategy $\rho_1 \in \mathcal{S}_1$ such that for every strategy $\rho_2 \in \mathcal{S}_2$, the play $out(\rho_1, \rho_2)$ is in Γ. A winning strategy for Player 2 is defined symmetrically. We define the simulation relation so that $\mathcal{A} \leq \mathcal{B}$ iff Player 2 has a winning strategy in G.

Theorem 2. *Simulation is strictly stronger than containment: (1) for all WFAs $\mathcal{A}$ and $\mathcal{B}$, if $\mathcal{A} \leq \mathcal{B}$, then $\mathcal{A} \subseteq \mathcal{B}$. (2) There are WFAs $\mathcal{A}$ and $\mathcal{B}$ such that $\mathcal{A} \subseteq \mathcal{B}$ and $\mathcal{A} \not\leq \mathcal{B}$.*

Proof: We start with the first claim. Recall that $\mathcal{A} \subseteq \mathcal{B}$ iff $L(\mathcal{A}) \subseteq L(\mathcal{B})$ and for every $u \in L(\mathcal{A})$ we have $val(\mathcal{A}, u) \leq val(\mathcal{B}, u)$. We prove that if $\mathcal{A} \not\subseteq \mathcal{B}$ then Player 1 has a winning strategy. Thus, there is no winning strategy for Player 2 and $\mathcal{A} \not\leq \mathcal{B}$.

Assume that $\mathcal{A} \not\subseteq \mathcal{B}$. That is, there exists a word $u \in \Sigma^*$ such that $u \in L(\mathcal{A}) \setminus L(\mathcal{B})$, or $u \in L(\mathcal{A})$ and $val(\mathcal{A}, u) > val(\mathcal{B}, u)$. Consider the strategy $\rho_1 \in \mathcal{S}_1$ in which Player 1 selects the word u and chooses the run r_1 that maximizes the value of u in $\mathcal{A}$. In the full version, we show that for every strategy $\rho_2 \in \mathcal{S}_2$ of Player 2, the play $out(\rho_1, \rho_2)$ is winning for Player 1. Thus, ρ_1 is a winning strategy of Player 1 and we are done.

The proof of the send claim is described in the full version. While the claim easily follows form the analogous claim in the Boolean setting, the example there is such that $\mathcal{A}$ is simulated by $\mathcal{B}$ in the Boolean sense, and the weights of the WFAs are these that wreck the simulation. □

As in the Boolean setting, simulation and containment do coincide in case the simulating automaton is deterministic. Indeed, then, there is only one Player 2 strategy, so the "step-wise nature" of simulation does not play a role.

Theorem 3. *If $\mathcal{B}$ is a DWFA, then $\mathcal{A} \subseteq \mathcal{B}$ iff $\mathcal{A} \leq \mathcal{B}$.*

Another property of simulation that stays valid in the weighted setting is its transitivity.

Theorem 4. *For WFAs $\mathcal{A}$, $\mathcal{B}$, and $\mathcal{C}$, if $\mathcal{A} \leq \mathcal{B}$ and $\mathcal{B} \leq \mathcal{C}$, then $\mathcal{A} \leq \mathcal{C}$.*

Unlike the Boolean case, here Player 1 need not have a memoryless strategy, as we demonstrate below. The WFAs we use in the example are used also in [9] in order to show that Player 2 has no memoryless winning strategy in energy parity games.

Example 1. We show a family of WFAs $\mathcal{A}_1, \mathcal{A}_2, \ldots$ and a WFA $\mathcal{B}$ such that for all $n \geq 1$, Player 1 wins the simulation game corresponding to $\mathcal{A}_n$ and $\mathcal{B}$, but he has no memoryless winning strategy. Moreover, a winning strategy for Player 1 needs memory of size $\Omega(m \cdot W)$, where m is the size of $\mathcal{A}_n \times \mathcal{B}_n$ and W is the maximal weight.

Consider the WFAs $\mathcal{A}_n$ and $\mathcal{B}$ in Figure 1. Since $L(\mathcal{B}) = a^*$, then clearly $L(\mathcal{A}_n) \subseteq L(\mathcal{B})$. However, $\mathcal{A}_n \not\subseteq \mathcal{B}$, since for $w = a^n \cdot a^{2Wn+1} a^n$, we have $cost(\mathcal{A}_n, w) = 1 > 0 = cost(\mathcal{B}, w)$.

We claim that in the simulation game (on bottom) that corresponds to the two WFAs, there is a winning Player 1 strategy (i.e., $\mathcal{A}_n \not\leq \mathcal{B}$) and that every such winning strategy for Player 1 requires $\Omega(m \cdot W)$ memory. Indeed, a winning Player 1 strategy must proceed to the state (q_n, s_0) and loop there for at least $2Wn+1$ rounds before returning to the initial state. Thus, a winning strategy must "count" to $2Wn + 1$.

Before we turn to study a solution to the simulation game, observe that the set of winning plays for Player 1 is open since it is defined by prefixes. By the Gale-Stewart theorem [19], every game that satisfies this property is determined, hence we have the following.

Theorem 5. *The simulation game is determined. That is, Player 1 or Player 2 has a winning strategy.*

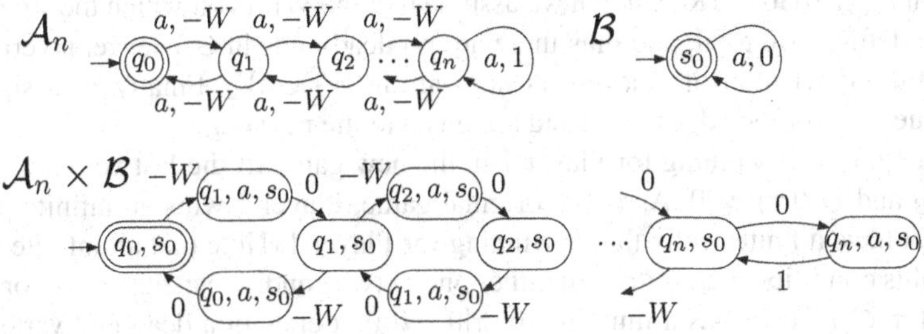

Fig. 1. WFAs $\mathcal{A}_n$ and $\mathcal{B}$ such that $\mathcal{A}_n \not\leq \mathcal{B}$ yet Player 1 does not have a memoryless strategy in the corresponding simulation game

3.2 Solving the Simulation Game

The simulation game stands between the energy games of [4], where the NFAs have no acceptance conditions, and the energy parity games of [9], where the winning condition is richer than the one of WFAs. Both these games are determined and can be decided in NP $\cap$ co-NP. It is thus not surprising that we are going to show that the same holds for our simulation game. Our main challenge is to develop an algorithm that would maintain the simplicity of the algorithm in [4] in the richer setting of WFAs. The setting is indeed richer, and in particular, as in energy parity games, Player 1 need not have a memoryless winning strategy. We do this by performing a preprocessing on the arena of the game, one after which we can perform only local changes in the algorithm of [4]. Our main contribution, however, is not the study of simulation games and their solution – the main ideas here are similar to these in [4,9]. Rather, it is the combination of these ideas in an abstraction-refinement paradigm, to be described in Section 4.

Reducing $\langle G, \Gamma \rangle$ to a Simpler game $\langle G', \Gamma' \rangle$. Consider an arena $G = \langle V, E, v_0, \tau \rangle$.

- Let $W_1 \subseteq V$ be the set of vertices from which Player 1 wins the reachability game with objective $F_\mathcal{A} \times (Q_\mathcal{B} \setminus F_\mathcal{B})$. That is, $v \in W_1$ iff Player 1 can force the game that starts in v to a vertex in $F_\mathcal{A} \times (Q_\mathcal{B} \setminus F_\mathcal{B})$.
- Let $W_2 \subseteq V$ be the vertices from which Player 2 wins the safety game with objective $((Q_\mathcal{A} \setminus F_\mathcal{A}) \times Q_\mathcal{B}) \cup V_2$. That is, $v \in W_2$ iff Player 1 can force the game that starts in v to stay in vertices in $((Q_\mathcal{A} \setminus F_\mathcal{A}) \times Q_\mathcal{B}) \cup V_2$.

It is not hard to see that $W_1 \cap W_2 = \emptyset$. We can therefore distinguish between three cases: If $v_0 \in W_1$, then Player 1 wins the game. If $v_0 \in W_2$, Player 2 wins the game. Otherwise, we define a new game, which excludes states from $W_1 \cup W_2$.

We define the new game $\langle G', \Gamma' \rangle$ on the arena $G' = \langle V', E', v_0, \tau' \rangle$. The set V' of vertices are $\{v_{sink}\} \cup (V \setminus (W_1 \cup W_2))$. The set V_1' of vertices of Player 1 is $V_1 \cap V'$, and the set V_2' of vertices of Player 2 is $V_2 \cap V'$. We say that a vertex $v \in V'$ is a *dead-end* iff $adj(v) \subseteq (W_1 \cup W_2)$, where $adj(v)$ is defined with respect to E. That is, $adj(v) = \{v' \in V : E(v, v')\}$. The set E' of edges restricts the set E to vertices in V' and includes, in addition, an edge from every dead-end vertex in V' to v_{sink} and an edge from v_{sink} to itself. Recall that we assume that the WFAs on which the simulation game are defined are total, and thus there are no dead-ends in G. Hence, a vertex is a dead-end in G' when all its successors in G are in $W_1 \cup W_2$. Finally, τ' assigns the same value as τ for the edges in E, and assigns 0 to the new edges.

A finite play π is winning for Player 1 in the new game iff the last vertex in π is in $F_{\mathcal{A}} \times F_{\mathcal{B}}$ and $val(\pi) > 0$. As in the original game, Player 2 wins an infinite play iff it does not have a finite prefix that is winning for Player 1. Note that an infinite play π satisfies this condition, i.e., $\pi \in \overline{\Gamma'}$, if either one of two conditions: either π is contained in V and $\pi \in \overline{\Gamma}$, or π has a finite prefix $\pi[0:i]$ that ends in a dead-end vertex, i.e., for every $k > i$ we have $\pi_k = v_{sink}$, and for every $j \leq i$, we have that $\pi[0:j]$ is not winning for Player 1.

As we prove in the full version, the characteristics of the vertices in W_1 and W_2, as well as the dead-end states enable us to construct, given a winning strategy for Player 1 in G', a winning strategy for him in G, and similarly for Player 2. Hence, we have the following.

Lemma 1. *Player 1 wins $\langle G, \Gamma \rangle$ iff he wins $\langle G', \Gamma' \rangle$.*

It is thus left to show how to solve the game $\langle G', \Gamma' \rangle$.

Solving the Game $\langle G', \Gamma' \rangle$. We say that a strategy of Player 1 is an *almost memoryless* strategy if, intuitively, in every play, when visiting a vertex, Player 1 plays in the same manner except for, possibly, the last visit to the vertex. Formally, consider a Player 1 strategy ρ_1. Consider a vertex $v \in V_1$. We say that ρ_1 is almost memoryless for v iff there are two vertices $v_1, v_2 \in V_2$ such that for every Player 2 strategy ρ_2, if $out(\rho_1, \rho_2)[0:n] = v$, then either $out(\rho_1, \rho_2)[n+1] = v_1$, or $out(\rho_1, \rho_2)[n+1] = v_2$ and for every index $n' > n+1$ we have $out(\rho_1, \rho_2)[n'] \neq v$. We say that ρ_1 is almost memoryless iff it is almost memoryless for every vertex in V_1.

Lemma 2. *If Player 1 has a winning strategy in $\langle G', \Gamma' \rangle$, then he also has an almost memoryless winning strategy.*

Proof: Assume ρ_1 is a Player 1 winning strategy. Our goal is to construct an almost memoryless winning strategy ρ'_1 from ρ_1. Intuitively, we divide the Player 1 strategy into two "phases": in the first phase, which we refer to as the "accumulation phase", Player 1's goal is to force the game into accumulating a high value. In the second phase, which we refer to as the "reachability phase", his goal is to force the game to a winning position, which is a vertex in $F_{\mathcal{A}} \times F_{\mathcal{B}}$. Since all the vertices in V' are not in W_2, Player 1 can force the game to a winning position from every vertex in V'. Also, since reaching a winning position is done in a memoryless manner, it does not involve a play with cycles, and thus, we bound the maximal value that Player 1 needs to accumulate in the first phase. The technical details can be found in the full version. □

For Player 2, our situation is even better as, intuitively, cycles in the game are either good for Player 2, in which case a strategy for him would always proceed to these cycles, or bad for Player 2, in which case a strategy for him would never enter them. Formally, as proven in the full version, we have the following.

Lemma 3. *If Player 2 has a winning strategy in $\langle G', \Gamma' \rangle$, then he also has a winning memoryless strategy.*

Before turning to prove the complexity results, we remind the reader of the Bellman-Ford algorithm. The algorithm gets as input a weighted directed graph $\langle \mathcal{V}, \mathcal{E}, \theta \rangle$, where $\mathcal{V}$ is a set of vertices, $\mathcal{E} \subseteq \mathcal{V} \times \mathcal{V}$ is a set of edges, and $\theta : \mathcal{E} \to \mathbb{R}$ is a weight function. The algorithm also gets a distinguished source vertex $s \in \mathcal{V}$. It outputs a function $C : \mathcal{V} \to \mathbb{R}$, where for every $v \in \mathcal{V}$, the value $C(v)$ is the value of the shortest path between s and v. If there is a negative cycle connected to s, the algorithm reports that such a cycle exists but it cannot return a correct answer since no shortest path exists.

We continue to prove the complexity that follows.

Theorem 6. *Solving simulation games is in NP $\cap$ co-NP.*

Proof: We first show membership in co-NP. We show that we can check in PTIME, given a memoryless Player 2 strategy, whether it is a winning strategy for Player 2. Given a memoryless Player 2 strategy, we trim every edge that starts from vertices in V_2' and does not agree with the strategy. We run the longest path version of the Bellman-Ford algorithm on the trimmed arena. Given a directed graph and a source vertex, the algorithm returns a function $C : V \to \mathbb{R}$ that assigns to every vertex the longest path from the source vertex, and reports if there is a positive valued cycle in the graph.

In the full version, we prove that the strategy is winning iff there is no positive cycle in the trimmed arena, and if every vertex $v \in F_{\mathcal{A}} \times F_{\mathcal{B}}$ has $C(v) \leq 0$.

We proceed to show membership in NP. For that, we show that we can check in PTIME, given a memoryless Player 1 strategy ρ_1, whether it can serve as the strategy to be used in the "accumulation phase" of the game in a way that induces an almost memoryless winning strategy for Player 1. Intuitively, we check if Player 2 can play against ρ_1 in a way that closes a cycle that is winning for Player 2, or if Player 2 can reach the vertex v_{sink} in a play that is not losing. If he cannot, we show that ρ_1 either forces the game into a vertex in $F_{\mathcal{A}} \times F_{\mathcal{B}}$ after a positive-valued play, or ρ_1 forces the game to close a positive valued cycle.

The algorithm, described in the full version, is similar to the algorithm in [4] with a small adjustment, which in turn is an adjustment of the Bellman-Ford algorithm: we restrict the vertices considered by the algorithm to ones in $F_{\mathcal{A}} \times F_{\mathcal{B}}$, and we take into an account the ability to reach v_{sink}. □

4 An Abstraction-Refinement-Based Algorithm for Deciding Simulation

In this section we solve the weighted-simulation problem $\mathcal{A} \leq \mathcal{B}$ by reasoning about abstractions of $\mathcal{A}$ and $\mathcal{B}$. Recall that for every WFA $\mathcal{A}$, we have that $\mathcal{A}_{\downarrow} \subseteq \mathcal{A} \subseteq \mathcal{A}_{\uparrow}$. We first argue that this order is maintained for the simulation relation. We then use this fact in order to check simulation (and hence, also containment) with respect to abstractions.

Theorem 7. *For every WFA $\mathcal{A}$ and abstraction function α, we have $\mathcal{A}^{\alpha}_{\downarrow} \leq \mathcal{A} \leq \mathcal{A}^{\alpha}_{\uparrow}$.*

Proof: We construct the required winning strategies for Player 2. We start with the claim $\mathcal{A}_{\downarrow} \leq \mathcal{A}$ and show that Player 2 has a winning strategy in the game that corresponds to $\mathcal{A}_{\downarrow}$ and $\mathcal{A}$. Intuitively, whenever Player 1 selects a letter and a must-transition to proceed with in $\mathcal{A}_{\downarrow}$, the winning Player 2 strategy selects a matching concrete transition in $\mathcal{A}$ and proceeds with it. Thus, the winning Player 2 strategy maintains the invariant that when the game reaches a vertex $\langle a, c \rangle$, then $c \in a$. Recall that $\mathcal{A}_{\downarrow}$ under-approximates $\mathcal{A}$ in three ways: the transition relation, the weight function, and the definition of the accepting states. Consequently, as we formally prove in the full version by induction on the length of the prefix, all the prefixes of the play are not winning for Player 1. The proof of the second claim is similar. □

We note that beyond the use of Theorem 7 in practice, it provides an additional witness to the appropriateness of our definition of weighted simulation.

Recall that our algorithm solves the weighted-simulation problem $\mathcal{A} \leq \mathcal{B}$ by reasoning about abstractions of $\mathcal{A}$ and $\mathcal{B}$. We first show that indeed we can conclude about the existence of simulation or its nonexistence by reasoning about the abstractions:

Theorem 8. *Consider two WFAs $\mathcal{A}$ and $\mathcal{B}$ and abstraction functions α and β.*

- *If $\mathcal{A}^{\alpha}_{\uparrow} \leq \mathcal{B}^{\beta}_{\downarrow}$, then $\mathcal{A} \leq \mathcal{B}$.*
- *If $\mathcal{A}^{\alpha}_{\downarrow} \not\leq \mathcal{B}^{\beta}_{\uparrow}$, then $\mathcal{A} \not\leq \mathcal{B}$.*

Our algorithm proceeds as follows. We start by checking whether $\mathcal{A}^{\alpha}_{\uparrow} \leq \mathcal{B}^{\beta}_{\downarrow}$ and $\mathcal{A}^{\alpha}_{\downarrow} \not\leq \mathcal{B}^{\beta}_{\uparrow}$, for some (typically coarse) initial abstraction functions α and β. By Theorem /refrefinement-thm, if we are lucky and one of them holds, we are done. Otherwise, the winning strategies of the Player 2 in the first case and Player 1 in the second case suggest a way to refine α and β, and we repeat the process with the refined abstractions. While refinement in the Boolean case only splits abstract states in order to close the gap between may and must transitions, here we also have refinement steps that tighten the weights along transitions. Below is a formal description of the algorithm.

Input: Two WFAs $\mathcal{A}$ and B, with abstraction functions α and β
Output: *yes* if $\mathcal{A} \leq \mathcal{B}$ and *no* otherwise

```
while true do
    if Player 2 wins the game that corresponds to A^α_↑ and B^β_↓ then return yes
    else let ρ1 be a winning Player 1 strategy in the game
    if Player 1 wins the game that corresponds to A^α_↓ and B^β_↑ then return no
    else let ρ2 be a winning Player 2 strategy in the game
        α', β' = refine(A, B, α, β, ρ1, ρ2)
        set: α = α' and β = β'
end while
```

By Theorem 8, if the algorithm returns *yes*, then $\mathcal{A}$ simulates $\mathcal{B}$, and if the algorithm returns *no*, then $\mathcal{A}$ does not simulate $\mathcal{B}$. If $\mathcal{A}^{\alpha}_{\uparrow} \not\leq \mathcal{B}^{\beta}_{\downarrow}$ and $\mathcal{A}^{\alpha}_{\downarrow} \leq \mathcal{B}^{\beta}_{\uparrow}$, then the answer is indefinite and we refine the abstractions. This is done by the procedure *refine*, described below.

Recall that we refine α and β in case both $\mathcal{A}^{\alpha}_{\uparrow} \not\leq \mathcal{B}^{\beta}_{\downarrow}$ and $\mathcal{A}^{\alpha}_{\downarrow} \leq \mathcal{B}^{\beta}_{\uparrow}$. When this happens, the algorithm for checking simulation generates a winning strategy ρ_1 of Player 1 in the game corresponding to $\mathcal{A}^{\alpha}_{\uparrow} \not\leq \mathcal{B}^{\beta}_{\downarrow}$ and a winning strategy ρ_2 of Player 2 in the game corresponding to $\mathcal{A}^{\alpha}_{\downarrow} \leq \mathcal{B}^{\beta}_{\uparrow}$. The procedure *refine* gets as input the WFAs $\mathcal{A}$ and $\mathcal{B}$, the abstraction functions α and β, and the winning strategies ρ_1 and ρ_2. It returns two new abstraction functions α' and β'.

In order to see the idea behind *refine*, assume that Player 1 wins in the concrete game. Then, ρ_2 is winning in a *spurious* manner in the game that corresponds to $\mathcal{A}^{\alpha}_{\downarrow} \leq \mathcal{B}^{\beta}_{\uparrow}$. Our goal in the refinement process is to remove at least one of the reasons ρ_2 is winning. Also, if Player 1 wins in the concrete game, then refinement in the game corresponding to $\mathcal{A}^{\alpha}_{\uparrow} \leq \mathcal{B}^{\beta}_{\downarrow}$ should reveal the fact that ρ_1 is winning. The situation is dual if Player 2 wins the concrete game. Since during the refinement process we cannot know which of the players wins the concrete game, we perform refinements to the two games simultaneously until we reach a definite answer. Since we assume that the WFAs are finite, we are guaranteed to eventually terminate. Thus, our procedure is complete (it attempts, however, to solve only the simulation, rather than containment, problem).

Observe that the arenas on which the strategies are defined have the same vertices but different edges. Edges that appear in one game but not the other correspond to may transitions that are not must transitions. Our refinement procedure is based on the algorithm for solving the simulation game as described in Section 3.2. Recall that the algorithm first performs a pre-processing stage in which it removes two sets of vertices: vertices from which Player 1 wins (namely the set W_1), and vertices from which Player 2 wins (namely the set W_2). The first set of vertices are the winning vertices in the un-weighted reachability game with objective $F_{\mathcal{A}} \times (Q_{\mathcal{B}} \setminus F_{\mathcal{B}})$. The second set of vertices are the winning vertices in the un-weighted safety game with objective $((Q_{\mathcal{A}} \setminus F_{\mathcal{A}}) \times Q_{\mathcal{B}}) \cup V_2$.

Since the two winning sets depend on the edges of the game, the sets we remove are not the same in the two games. We refer to the vertices after their removal as $V'_{\mathcal{A}_{\uparrow},\mathcal{B}_{\downarrow}}$ and $V'_{\mathcal{A}_{\downarrow},\mathcal{B}_{\uparrow}}$, and we refine them until the initial vertex is in both sets.

We describe the refinement according to the strategy ρ_1. Refinement according to ρ_2 is dual.

Recall that, by Theorem 2, if Player 1 wins, then he has an almost-memoryless winning strategy. Thus, we assume ρ_1 is almost memoryless. Also recall that ρ_1 is winning in the game played on the vertices $V'_{\mathcal{A}_{\uparrow},\mathcal{B}_{\downarrow}}$, and since ρ_2 is winning in the game played on the vertices $V'_{\mathcal{A}_{\downarrow},\mathcal{B}_{\uparrow}}$, the strategy ρ_1 is not winning in this game.

We proceed as in the algorithm for solving simulation games: we "guess" the strategy ρ_1 and check if (actually, how) Player 2 can win against this strategy. Since ρ_1 is not winning in the game played on the vertices $V'_{\mathcal{A}_{\uparrow},\mathcal{B}_{\downarrow}}$, we find at least one path π that is winning for Player 2. As seen in the algorithm, π is either a path that reaches v_{sink} or is a lasso contained in the vertices $V'_{\mathcal{A}_{\uparrow},\mathcal{B}_{\downarrow}} \setminus \{v_{sink}\}$. More formally, π is of the form $\pi_1 \cdot \pi_2^{\omega}$. The path π_1 is a simple path that uses vertices from $V'_{\mathcal{A}_{\uparrow},\mathcal{B}_{\downarrow}} \setminus \{v_{sink}\}$ and it (and every prefix of it) is not losing for Player 2. The path π_2 is either the cycle that is the single vertex v_{sink} or it is a cycle contained in $V'_{\mathcal{A}_{\uparrow},\mathcal{B}_{\downarrow}} \setminus \{v_{sink}\}$. In the second case, $val(\pi_2) \leq 0$, and for every $0 \leq i \leq |\pi_2|$, if $\pi_2[i] \in F_{\mathcal{A}} \times F_{\mathcal{B}}$, then $val(\pi_1) + val(\pi_2[0:i]) \leq 0$.

Since π is not a path in $V'_{\mathcal{A}_\downarrow,\mathcal{B}_\uparrow}$, at least one of the following three cases hold:

- π uses a vertex in $V'_{\mathcal{A}_\uparrow,\mathcal{B}_\downarrow} \setminus V'_{\mathcal{A}_\downarrow,\mathcal{B}_\uparrow}$,
- π traverses an edge that corresponds to a may but not must transition, or
- the sum of the edges traversed in π is larger in the one game than in the other.

In the first case, we refine the vertices $V'_{\mathcal{A}_\uparrow,\mathcal{B}_\downarrow}$ and $V'_{\mathcal{A}_\downarrow,\mathcal{B}_\uparrow}$, as described above. In the second case, the refinement is similar to the one done in the Boolean setting, where we close the gap between may and must transitions. Finally, in the third case, we split states in order to tighten the weights on the transitions. Recall that these weights are defined by taking the minimum or maximum of the corresponding set of transitions. Therefore, splitting of states indeed tightens the weights.

Example 2. Consider the two simulation games $\mathcal{G}_1$ and $\mathcal{G}_2$ in Figure 2. The game $\mathcal{G}_1$ corresponds to $\mathcal{A}_\uparrow$ and $\mathcal{B}_\downarrow$, and $\mathcal{G}_2$ corresponds to $\mathcal{A}_\downarrow$ and $\mathcal{B}_\uparrow$, for some two WFAs $\mathcal{A}$ and $\mathcal{B}$ with abstraction functions. In the figure, we use circle and boxes in order to denote, respectively, the nodes in which Player 1 and Player 2 proceed. In $\mathcal{G}_1$, we define $F_{\mathcal{A}} \times (Q_{\mathcal{B}} \setminus F_{\mathcal{B}}) = \{s_4\}$, $F_{\mathcal{A}} \times F_{\mathcal{B}} = \{s_5, s_6\}$, and $(Q_{\mathcal{A}} \setminus F_{\mathcal{A}}) \times Q_{\mathcal{B}} = \{s_4\}$, and the definition is similar in $\mathcal{G}_2$. Due to lack of space, we omit the letters from the arenas.

We show that Player 1 wins $\mathcal{G}_1$ in three different ways and Player 2 wins $\mathcal{G}_2$. In the first strategy, in $\mathcal{G}_1$, Player 1 proceeds from s_0 to s_1. Player 2 is then forced to continue to s_4, which is losing for Player 2 since it is a vertex in $F_{\mathcal{A}} \times (Q_{\mathcal{B}} \setminus F_{\mathcal{B}})$. In the second winning strategy, Player 1 proceeds from s_0 to s_2. The game continues by alternating between s_2 and s_6. Since the cycle has a positive value and $s_6 \in F_{\mathcal{A}} \times F_{\mathcal{B}}$, Player 1 wins the prefix $s_0 s_2 s_6 s_2 s_6 s_2 s_6$. Finally, in the third strategy, Player 1 proceeds from s_0 to s_3. Player 2 is then forced to proceed to s_6. Since $s_6 \in F_{\mathcal{A}} \times F_{\mathcal{B}}$ and $val(s_0 s_2 s_6) > 0$, Player 1 wins the prefix. Clearly, in $\mathcal{G}_2$, the Player 2 strategy that proceeds from s_1 to s_5 is winning.

We proceed to describe the refinement of the abstractions using these strategies. First, note that in $\mathcal{G}_1$, by playing the first strategy described above, Player 1 can force the game to a vertex in $F_{\mathcal{A}} \times (Q_{\mathcal{B}} \setminus F_{\mathcal{B}})$ from the initial vertex. Thus, $s_0 \notin V'_{\mathcal{A}_\uparrow,\mathcal{B}_\downarrow}$. We start by refining the set of Player 1 winning vertices in the reachability game with objective $F_{\mathcal{A}} \times (Q_{\mathcal{B}} \setminus F_{\mathcal{B}})$. In this process we refine the vertex s_1.

Next, we apply the third Player 1 winning strategy on G_2 and see how Player 2 can win against it. Player 2 wins because Player 1 uses the edge $\langle s_0, s_3 \rangle$, which is not in $\mathcal{G}_2$. We refine s_0, and after the refinement the strategy is no longer valid for Player 1 in $\mathcal{G}_1$. After these two refinements, Player 1 can still win in $\mathcal{G}_1$ using the second strategy, and we apply it in $\mathcal{G}_2$. The outcome of the game against a winning Player 2 strategy is $s_0(s_2 s_6)^\omega$. In this path, we find the failure vertex s_2 and refine it in order to tighten the values of the edges.

The two resulting games after these three refinements are $\mathcal{G}'_1$ and $\mathcal{G}'_2$ (see the right side of Figure 2). Player 1 wins in $\mathcal{G}'_2$ by proceding from s_0 to s_2, and thus we are done.

Note that since not all the values on the edges are the same in $\mathcal{G}'_1$ and $\mathcal{G}'_2$, the refinement is not exauhsted. That is, the arenas are not $Q_{\mathcal{A}} \times Q_{\mathcal{B}}$. Thus, the abstraction-refinement algorithm successfully decides simulation on a smaller state space than the

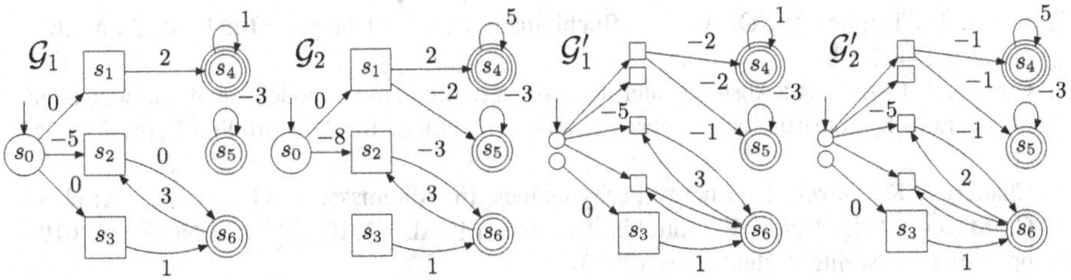

Fig. 2. An example of applying the refinement algorithm on two simulation games

concrete one. Since, however, we found that $\mathcal{A} \not\leq \mathcal{B}$, then by Theorem 2, it might still be the case that $\mathcal{A} \subseteq \mathcal{B}$.

5 Directions for Future Research

We introduced the notions of abstraction and simulation for weighted automata and argue that they form a useful heuristic for checking containment – a problem of practical interest that is known to be undecidable. In the Boolean setting, researchers have suggested ways for closing the gap between containment and simulation [23,26]. Some, like these that extend the definition of simulation with a look ahead, are easy to extend to the weighted setting. Other ways require special treatment of the accumulated weights and are subject to future research. Finally, the rich weighted setting allows one to measure the differences between systems. For example, we can talk about one WFA t-approximating another WFA, in the sense that the value of a word in the second is at most t times its value in the first [2]. Our weighted simulation corresponds to the special case $t = 1$ and we plan to study approximated weighted simulation.

References

1. Almagor, S., Boker, U., Kupferman, O.: What's Decidable about Weighted Automata? In: Bultan, T., Hsiung, P.-A. (eds.) ATVA 2011. LNCS, vol. 6996, pp. 482–491. Springer, Heidelberg (2011)
2. Aminof, B., Kupferman, O., Lampert, R.: Formal Analysis of Online Algorithms. In: Bultan, T., Hsiung, P.-A. (eds.) ATVA 2011. LNCS, vol. 6996, pp. 213–227. Springer, Heidelberg (2011)
3. Ball, T., Bounimova, E., Cook, B., Levin, V., Lichtenberg, J., McGarvey, C., Ondrusek, B., Rajamani, S.K., Ustuner, A.: Thorough static analysis of device drivers. In: EuroSys (2006)
4. Bouyer, P., Fahrenberg, U., Larsen, K.G., Markey, N., Srba, J.: Infinite Runs in Weighted Timed Automata with Energy Constraints. In: Cassez, F., Jard, C. (eds.) FORMATS 2008. LNCS, vol. 5215, pp. 33–47. Springer, Heidelberg (2008)
5. Bruns, G., Godefroid, P.: Model Checking Partial State Spaces with 3-Valued Temporal Logics. In: Halbwachs, N., Peled, D.A. (eds.) CAV 1999. LNCS, vol. 1633, pp. 274–287. Springer, Heidelberg (1999)
6. Ball, T., Kupferman, O.: An abstraction-refinement framework for multi-agent systems. In: Proc. 21st LICS (2006)

7. Boker, U., Kupferman, O.: Co-ing Büchi made tight and helpful. In: Proc. 24th LICS, pp. 245–254 (2009)
8. Cousot, P., Cousot, R.: Abstract interpretation: a unified lattice model for the static analysis of programs by construction or approximation of fixpoints. In: Proc. 4th POPL, pp. 238–252 (1977)
9. Chatterjee, K., Doyen, L.: Energy Parity Games. In: Abramsky, S., Gavoille, C., Kirchner, C., Meyer auf der Heide, F., Spirakis, P.G. (eds.) ICALP 2010, Part II. LNCS, vol. 6199, pp. 599–610. Springer, Heidelberg (2010)
10. Chatterjee, K., Doyen, L., Henzinger, T.A.: Quantative languages. In: Proc. 17th CSL, pp. 385–400 (2008)
11. Chatterjee, K., Doyen, L., Henzinger, T.A.: Probabilistic Weighted Automata. In: Bravetti, M., Zavattaro, G. (eds.) CONCUR 2009. LNCS, vol. 5710, pp. 244–258. Springer, Heidelberg (2009)
12. Chatterjee, K., Doyen, L., Henzinger, T.A.: Expressiveness and closure properties for quantitative languages. LMCS 6(3) (2010)
13. Clarke, E.M., Grumberg, O., Jha, S., Lu, Y., Veith, H.: Counterexample-guided abstraction refinement for symbolic model checking. Journal of the ACM 50(5), 752–794 (2003)
14. Černý, P., Henzinger, T.A., Radhakrishna, A.: Simulation Distances. In: Gastin, P., Laroussinie, F. (eds.) CONCUR 2010. LNCS, vol. 6269, pp. 253–268. Springer, Heidelberg (2010)
15. Culik, K., Kari, J.: Digital images and formal languages. In: Handbook of Formal Languages, vol. 3: Beyond Words, pp. 599–616 (1997)
16. de Alfaro, L., Roy, P.: Solving Games Via Three-Valued Abstraction Refinement. In: Caires, L., Vasconcelos, V.T. (eds.) CONCUR 2007. LNCS, vol. 4703, pp. 74–89. Springer, Heidelberg (2007)
17. Droste, M., Gastin, P.: Weighted Automata and Weighted Logics. In: Caires, L., Italiano, G.F., Monteiro, L., Palamidessi, C., Yung, M. (eds.) ICALP 2005. LNCS, vol. 3580, pp. 513–525. Springer, Heidelberg (2005)
18. Grumberg, O., Lange, M., Leucker, M., Shoham, S.: When not losing is better than winning: Abstraction and refinement for the full μ-calculus. Inf. Comput. 205(8), 1130–1148 (2007)
19. Gale, D., Stewart, F.M.: Infinite games of perfect information. Ann. Math. Studies 28, 245–266 (1953)
20. Henzinger, M.R., Henzinger, T.A., Kopke, P.W.: Computing simulations on finite and infinite graphs. In: Proc. 36th FOCS, pp. 453–462 (1995)
21. Henzinger, T.A., Jhala, R., Majumdar, R.: Counterexample-Guided Control. In: Baeten, J.C.M., Lenstra, J.K., Parrow, J., Woeginger, G.J. (eds.) ICALP 2003. LNCS, vol. 2719, pp. 886–902. Springer, Heidelberg (2003)
22. Henzinger, T.A., Majumdar, R., Mang, F.Y.C., Raskin, J.-F.: Abstract Interpretation of Game Properties. In: SAS 2000. LNCS, vol. 1824, pp. 220–240. Springer, Heidelberg (2000)
23. Kesten, Y., Piterman, N., Pnueli, A.: Bridging the Gap between Fair Simulation and Trace Inclusion. In: Hunt Jr., W.A., Somenzi, F. (eds.) CAV 2003. LNCS, vol. 2725, pp. 381–393. Springer, Heidelberg (2003)
24. Krob, D.: The equality problem for rational series with multiplicities in the tropical semiring is undecidable. International Journal of Algebra and Computation 4(3), 405–425 (1994)
25. Kuperberg, D.: Linear temporal logic for regular cost functions. In: Proc. 28th STACS, pp. 627–636 (2011)
26. Lynch, N.A., Tuttle, M.R.: Hierarchical correctness proofs for distributed algorithms. In: Proc. 6th PODC, pp. 137–151 (1987)
27. Larsen, K.G., Thomsen, G.B.: A modal process logic. In: Proc. 3rd LICS (1988)
28. Milner, R.: An algebraic definition of simulation between programs. In: Proc. 2nd IJCAI, pp. 481–489 (1971)

29. Mohri, M.: Finite-state transducers in language and speech processing. Computational Linguistics 23(2), 269–311 (1997)
30. Mohri, M., Pereira, F.C.N., Riley, M.: Weighted finite-state transducers in speech recognition. Computer Speech and Language 16(1), 69–88 (2002)
31. Meyer, A.R., Stockmeyer, L.J.: The equivalence problem for regular expressions with squaring requires exponential time. In: Proc. 13th SWAT, pp. 125–129 (1972)
32. Schützenberger, M.P.: On the definition of a family of automata. Information and Control 4(2-3), 245–270 (1961)
33. Sistla, A.P., Vardi, M.Y., Wolper, P.: The complementation problem for Büchi automata with applications to temporal logic. Theoretical Computer Science 49, 217–237 (1987)

Avoiding Shared Clocks in Networks of Timed Automata

Sandie Balaguer and Thomas Chatain*

INRIA & LSV (CNRS & ENS Cachan), Cachan, France
{balaguer,chatain}@lsv.ens-cachan.fr

Abstract. Networks of timed automata (NTA) are widely used to model distributed real-time systems. Quite often in the literature, the automata are allowed to share clocks. This is a problem when one considers implementing such model in a distributed architecture, since reading clocks a priori requires communications which are not explicitly described in the model. We focus on the following question: given a NTA $A_1 \parallel A_2$ where A_2 reads some clocks reset by A_1, does there exist a NTA $A'_1 \parallel A'_2$ without shared clocks with the same behavior as the initial NTA? For this, we allow the automata to exchange information during synchronizations only. We discuss a formalization of the problem and give a criterion using the notion of contextual timed transition system, which represents the behavior of A_2 when in parallel with A_1. Finally, we effectively build $A'_1 \parallel A'_2$ when it exists.

Keywords: networks of timed automata, shared clocks, implementation on distributed architecture, contextual timed transition system, behavioral equivalence for distributed systems.

1 Introduction

Timed automata [3] are one of the most famous formal models for real-time systems. They have been deeply studied and very mature tools are available, like UPPAAL [22], EPSILON [16] and KRONOS [13].

Networks of Timed Automata (NTA) are a natural generalization to model real-time distributed systems. In this formalism each automaton has a set of clocks that constrain its real-time behavior. But quite often in the literature, the automata are allowed to share clocks, which provides a special way of making the behavior of one automaton depend on what the others do. Actually shared clocks are relatively well accepted and can be a convenient feature for modeling systems. Moreover, since NTA are almost always given a sequential semantics, shared clocks can be handled very easily even by tools: once the NTA is transformed into a single timed automaton by the classical product construction, the notion of distribution is lost and the notion of shared clock itself becomes meaningless. Nevertheless, implementing a model with shared clocks in a distributed architecture is not straightforward since reading clocks a priori requires communications which are not explicitly described in the model.

* This work is partially supported by the French ANR project ImpRo.

M. Koutny and I. Ulidowski (Eds.): CONCUR 2012, LNCS 7454, pp. 100–114, 2012.

Our purpose is to identify NTA where sharing clocks could be avoided, i.e. NTA which syntactically use shared clocks, but whose semantics could be achieved by another NTA without shared clocks. We are not aware of any previous study about this aspect. To simplify, we look at NTA made of two automata A_1 and A_2 where only A_2 reads clocks reset by A_1. The first step is to formalize what aspect of the semantics we want to preserve in this setting. Then the idea is essentially to detect cases where A_2 can avoid reading a clock because its value does not depend on the actions that are local to A_1 and thus unobservable to A_2. To generalize this idea we have to compute the knowledge of A_2 about the state of A_1. We show that this knowledge is maximized if we allow A_1 to communicate its state to A_2 each time they synchronize on a common action.

In order to formalize our problem we need an appropriate notion of behavioral equivalence between two NTA. We explain why classical comparisons based on the sequential semantics, like timed bisimulation, are not sufficient here. We need a notion that takes the distributed nature of the system into account. That is, a component cannot observe the moves and the state of the other and must choose its local actions according to its partial knowledge of the state of the system. We formalize this idea by the notion of contextual timed transition systems (contextual TTS).

Then we express the problem of avoiding shared clocks in terms of contextual TTS and we give a characterization of the NTA for which shared clocks can be avoided. Finally we effectively construct a NTA without shared clocks with the same behavior as the initial one, when this is possible. A possible interest is to allow a designer to use shared clocks as a high-level feature in a model of a protocol, and rely on our transformation to make it implementable.

Related work. The semantics of time in distributed systems has already been debated. The idea of localizing clocks has already been proposed and some authors [1,6,19] have even suggested to use local-time semantics with independently evolving clocks. Here we stay in the classical setting of perfect clocks evolving at the same speed. This is a key assumption that provides an implicit synchronization and lets us know some clock values without reading them.

Many formalisms exist for real-time distributed systems, among which NTA [3] and time Petri nets [24]. So far, their expressiveness was compared [7,12,15,26] essentially in terms of sequential semantics that forget concurrency. In [5], we defined a concurrency-preserving translation from time Petri nets to networks of timed automata.

While partial-order semantics and unfoldings are well known for untimed systems, they have been very little studied for distributed real-time systems [11,14]. Partial order reductions for (N)TA were proposed in [6,23,25]. Behavioral equivalence relations for distributed systems, like history-preserving bisimulations were defined for untimed systems only [8,20].

Finally, our notion of contextual TTS deals with knowledge of agents in distributed systems. This is the aim of epistemic logics [21], which have been extended to real-time in [18,27]. Our notion of contextual TTS also resembles the technique of partitioning states used in timed games with partial observability [9,17].

Organization of the paper. The paper is organized as follows. Section 2 recalls basic notions about TTS and NTA. Section 3 presents the problem of avoiding shared clocks on examples and rises the problem of comparing NTA component by component. For this, the notion of contextual TTS is developed in Section 4. The problem of avoiding shared clocks is formalized and characterized in terms of contextual TTS. Then Section 5 presents our construction.

The proofs are given in a research report [4].

2 Preliminaries

2.1 Timed Transition Systems

The behavior of timed systems is often described as timed transition systems.

Definition 1. *A timed transition system (TTS) is a tuple* $(S, s_0, \Sigma, \rightarrow)$ *where* S *is a set of states,* $s_0 \in Q$ *is the initial state,* Σ *is a finite set of actions disjoint from* $\mathbb{R}_{\geq 0}$*, and* $\rightarrow \subseteq S \times (\Sigma \cup \mathbb{R}_{\geq 0}) \times S$ *is a set of edges.*

For any $a \in \Sigma \cup \mathbb{R}_{\geq 0}$, we write $s \xrightarrow{a} s'$ if $(s, a, s') \in \rightarrow$, and $s \xrightarrow{a}$ if for some s', $(s, a, s') \in \rightarrow$. A *path* of a TTS is a possibly infinite sequence of transitions $\rho = s \xrightarrow{d_0} s'_0 \xrightarrow{a_0} \cdots s_n \xrightarrow{d_n} s'_n \xrightarrow{a_n} \cdots$, where, for all i, $d_i \in \mathbb{R}_{\geq 0}$ and $a_i \in \Sigma$. A path is *initial* if it starts in s_0. A path $\rho = s \xrightarrow{d_0} s'_0 \xrightarrow{a_0} \cdots s_n \xrightarrow{d_n} s'_n \xrightarrow{a_n} s'_n \cdots$ generates a *timed word* $w = (a_0, t_0)(a_1, t_1) \ldots (a_n, t_n) \ldots$ where, for all i, $t_i = \sum_{k=0}^{i} d_k$. The duration of w is $\delta(w) = \sup_i t_i$ and the untimed word of w is $\lambda(w) = a_0 a_1 \ldots a_n \ldots$, and we denote the set of timed words over Σ and of duration d as $\mathrm{TW}(\Sigma, d) = \{w \mid \delta(w) = d \wedge \lambda(w) \in \Sigma^*\}$. Lastly, we write $s \xrightarrow{w} s'$ if there is a path from s to s' that generates the timed word w.

In the following definitions, we use two TTS $T_1 = (S_1, s_1^0, \Sigma_1, \rightarrow_1)$ and $T_2 = (S_2, s_2^0, \Sigma_2, \rightarrow_2)$, and $\Sigma_i^{\not\varepsilon}$ denotes $\Sigma_i \setminus \{\varepsilon\}$, where ε is the silent action.

Product of TTS. The product of T_1 and T_2, denoted by $T_1 \otimes T_2$, is the TTS $(S_1 \times S_2, (s_1^0, s_2^0), \Sigma_1 \cup \Sigma_2, \rightarrow)$, where $\rightarrow$ is defined as:

- $(s_1, s_2) \xrightarrow{a} (s'_1, s_2)$ iff $s_1 \xrightarrow{a}_1 s'_1$, for any $a \in \Sigma_1 \setminus \Sigma_2^{\not\varepsilon}$,
- $(s_1, s_2) \xrightarrow{a} (s_1, s'_2)$ iff $s_2 \xrightarrow{a}_2 s'_2$, for any $a \in \Sigma_2 \setminus \Sigma_1^{\not\varepsilon}$,
- $(s_1, s_2) \xrightarrow{a} (s'_1, s'_2)$ iff $s_1 \xrightarrow{a}_1 s'_1$ and $s_2 \xrightarrow{a}_2 s'_2$, for any $a \in (\Sigma_1^{\not\varepsilon} \cap \Sigma_2^{\not\varepsilon}) \cup \mathbb{R}_{\geq 0}$.

Timed Bisimulations. Let $\approx$ be a binary relation over $S_1 \times S_2$. We write $s_1 \approx s_2$ for $(s_1, s_2) \in \approx$. $\approx$ is a *strong timed bisimulation* relation between T_1 and T_2 if $s_1^0 \approx s_2^0$ and $s_1 \approx s_2$ implies that, for any $a \in \Sigma \cup \mathbb{R}_{\geq 0}$, if $s_1 \xrightarrow{a}_1 s'_1$, then, for some s'_2, $s_2 \xrightarrow{a}_2 s'_2$ and $s'_1 \approx s'_2$; and conversely, if $s_2 \xrightarrow{a}_2 s'_2$, then, for some s'_1, $s_1 \xrightarrow{a}_1 s'_1$ and $s'_1 \approx s'_2$.

Let $\Rightarrow_i$ (for $i \in \{1, 2\}$) be the transition relation defined as:

- $s \overset{\varepsilon}{\Rightarrow}_i s'$ if $s(\xrightarrow{\varepsilon}_i)^* s'$,
- $\forall a \in \Sigma$, $s \overset{a}{\Rightarrow}_i s'$ if $s(\xrightarrow{\varepsilon}_i)^* \xrightarrow{a}_i (\xrightarrow{\varepsilon}_i)^* s'$,
- $\forall d \in \mathbb{R}_{\geq 0}$, $s \overset{d}{\Rightarrow}_i s'$ if $s(\xrightarrow{\varepsilon}_i)^* \overset{d_0}{\Rightarrow}_i (\xrightarrow{\varepsilon}_i)^* \cdots \overset{d_n}{\Rightarrow}_i (\xrightarrow{\varepsilon}_i)^* s'$, where $\sum_{k=0}^{n} d_k = d$.

Then, $\approx$ is a *weak timed bisimulation* relation between T_1 and T_2 if $s_1^0 \approx s_2^0$ and $s_1 \approx s_2$ implies that, for any $a \in \Sigma \cup \mathbb{R}_{\geq 0}$, if $s_1 \xrightarrow{a}_1 s_1'$, then, for some s_2', $s_2 \overset{a}{\Rightarrow}_2 s_2'$ and $s_1' \approx s_2'$; and conversely. We write $T_1 \approx T_2$ (resp. $T_1 \sim T_2$) when there is a strong (resp. weak) timed bisimulation between T_1 and T_2.

2.2 Networks of Timed Automata

The set $\mathcal{B}(X)$ of clock constraints over the set of clocks X is defined by the grammar $g ::= x \bowtie k \mid g \wedge g$, where $x \in X$, $k \in \mathbb{N}$ and $\bowtie \in \{<, \leq, =, \geq, >\}$. Invariants are clock constraints of the form $i ::= x \leq k \mid x < k \mid i \wedge i$.

Definition 2. *A network of timed automata (NTA) [3] is a parallel composition $A_1 \parallel \cdots \parallel A_n$ of timed automata (TA), with $A_i = (L_i, \ell_i^0, X_i, \Sigma_i, E_i, Inv_i)$ where L_i is a finite set of* locations, *$\ell_i^0 \in L_i$ is the* initial *location, X_i is a finite set of* clocks, *Σ_i is a finite set of* actions, *$E_i \subseteq L_i \times \mathcal{B}(X_i) \times \Sigma_i \times 2^{X_i} \times L_i$ is a set of* edges, *and $Inv_i : L_i \to \mathcal{B}(X_i)$ assigns* invariants *to locations.*

If $(\ell, g, a, r, \ell') \in E_i$, we also write $\ell \xrightarrow{g,a,r} \ell'$. For such an edge, g is the *guard*, a the *action* and r the set of clocks to *reset*. $C_i \subseteq X_i$ is the set of clocks reset by A_i and for $i \neq j$, $C_i \cap C_j$ may not be empty.

Semantics. To simplify, we give the semantics of a network of two TA $A_1 \parallel A_2$. We denote by $((\ell_1, \ell_2), v)$ a *state* of the NTA, where ℓ_1 and ℓ_2 are the current locations, and $v : X \to \mathbb{R}_{\geq 0}$, with $X = X_1 \cup X_2$, is a *clock valuation* that maps each clock to its current value. A state is legal only if its valuation v satisfies the invariants of the current locations, denoted by $v \models Inv_1(\ell_1) \wedge Inv_2(\ell_2)$. For each set of clocks $r \subseteq X$, the valuation $v[r]$ is defined by $v[r](x) = 0$ if $x \in r$ and $v[r](x) = v(x)$ otherwise. For each $d \in \mathbb{R}_{\geq 0}$, the valuation $v + d$ is defined by $(v + d)(x) = v(x) + d$ for each $x \in X$. Then, the *TTS generated by* $A_1 \parallel A_2$ is $\text{TTS}(A_1 \parallel A_2) = (S, s_0, \Sigma_1 \cup \Sigma_2, \to)$, where S is the set of legal states, $s_0 = ((\ell_1^0, \ell_2^0), v_0)$, where v_0 maps each clock to 0, and $\to$ is defined by

- Local action: $((\ell_1, \ell_2), v) \xrightarrow{a} ((\ell_1', \ell_2), v')$ iff $a \in \Sigma_1 \setminus \Sigma_2^{\not\varepsilon}$, $\ell_1 \xrightarrow{g,a,r} \ell_1'$, $v \models g$, $v' = v[r]$ and $v' \models Inv_1(\ell_1')$, and similarly for a local action in $\Sigma_2 \setminus \Sigma_1^{\not\varepsilon}$,
- Synchronization: $((\ell_1, \ell_2), v) \xrightarrow{a} ((\ell_1', \ell_2'), v')$ iff $a \neq \varepsilon$, $\ell_1 \xrightarrow{g_1,a,r_1} \ell_1'$, $\ell_2 \xrightarrow{g_2,a,r_2} \ell_2'$, $v \models g_1 \wedge g_2$, $v' = v[r_1 \cup r_2]$ and $v' \models Inv_1(\ell_1') \wedge Inv_2(\ell_2')$,
- Time delay: $\forall d \in \mathbb{R}_{\geq 0}$, $((\ell_1, \ell_2), v) \xrightarrow{d} ((\ell_1, \ell_2), v + d)$ iff $\forall d' \in [0, d], v + d' \models Inv_1(\ell_1) \wedge Inv_2(\ell_2)$.

A *run* of a NTA is an initial path in its TTS. The semantics of a TA A alone can also be given as a TTS denoted by TTS(A) with only local actions and delay. A TA is *non-Zeno* iff for every infinite timed word w generated by a run, time diverges (i.e. $\delta(w) = \infty$). This is a common assumption for TA. In the sequel, we always assume that the TA we deal with are non-Zeno.

Remark 1. Let $A_1 \parallel A_2$ be such that $X_1 \cap X_2 = \emptyset$. Then $\text{TTS}(A_1) \otimes \text{TTS}(A_2)$ is isomorphic to $\text{TTS}(A_1 \parallel A_2)$. This is not true in general when $X_1 \cap X_2 \neq \emptyset$. For example, in Fig. 2, performing $(b, 0.5)(e, 1)$ is possible in $\text{TTS}(A_1) \otimes \text{TTS}(A_2)$ but not in $\text{TTS}(A_1 \parallel A_2)$, since b resets x which is tested by e.

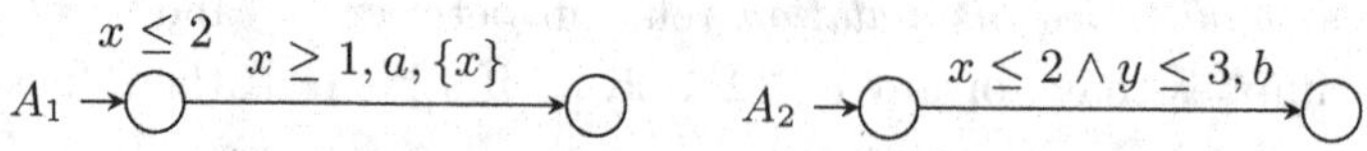

Fig. 1. A_2 could avoid reading clock x which belongs to A_1

3 Need for Shared Clocks

3.1 Problem Setting

We are interested in detecting the cases where it is possible to avoid sharing clocks, so that the model can be implemented using no other synchronization than those explicitly described by common actions.

To start with, let us focus on a network of two TA, $A_1 \parallel A_2$, such that A_1 does not read the clocks reset by A_2, and A_2 may read the clocks reset by A_1. We want to know whether A_2 really needs to read these clocks, or if another NTA $A'_1 \parallel A'_2$ could achieve the same behavior as $A_1 \parallel A_2$ without using shared clocks.

First remark that our problem makes sense only if we insist on the distributed nature of the system, made of two separate components. On the other hand, if the composition operator is simply used as a convenient syntax for describing a system that is actually implemented on a single sequential component, then a product automaton perfectly describes the system and all clocks become local.

So, let us consider the example of Fig. 1, made of two TA, supposed to describe two separate components. Remark that A_2 reads clock x which is reset by A_1. But a simple analysis shows that this reading could be avoided: because of the condition on its clock y, A_2 can only take transition b before time 3; but x cannot reach value 2 before time 3, since it is reset between time 1 and 2. Thus, forgetting the condition on x in A_2 would not change the behavior of the system.

3.2 Transmitting Information during Synchronizations

Consider now the example of Fig. 2. Here also A_2 reads clock x which is reset by A_1, and here also this reading could be avoided. The idea is that A_1 could transmit the value of x when synchronizing, and A_2 could copy this value locally to a new clock x'. Afterwards, any reading of x in A_2 could be replaced by the reading of x'. Therefore A_2 can be replaced by A'_2 pictured in Fig. 2, while preserving the behavior of the NTA, but also the behavior of A_2 w.r.t. A_1.

We claim that we cannot avoid reading x without this copy of clock. Indeed, after the synchronization, the maximal delay depends on the exact value of x, and even if we find a mechanism to allow A'_2 to move to different locations according to the value of x at synchronization time, infinitely many locations would be required (e.g., if s occurs at time 2, x may have any value in $(1, 2]$).

Coding Transmission of Information. In order to model the transmission of information during synchronizations, we allow A'_1 and A'_2 to use a larger synchronization alphabet than A_1 and A_2. This allows A'_1 to transmit discrete information like its current location, to A'_2.

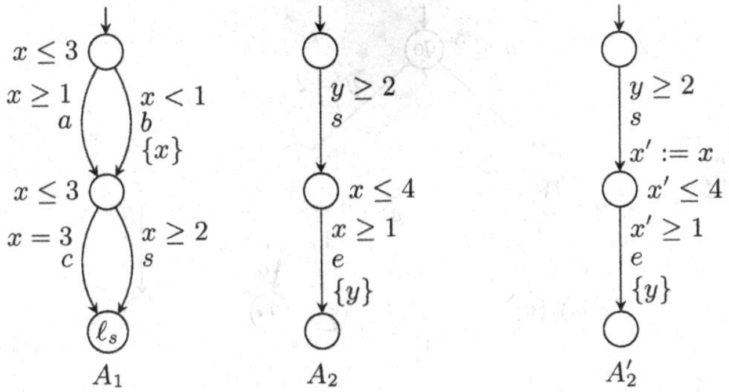

Fig. 2. A_2 reads x which belongs to A_1 and A_2' does not

But we saw that A_1' also needs to transmit the exact value of its clocks. For this we allow an automaton to copy its neighbor's clocks into local clocks during synchronizations. This is denoted as updates of the form $x' := x$ in A_2' (see Fig. 2). This is a special case of updatable timed automata as defined in [10]. Moreover, as shown in [10], the class we consider, with diagonal-free constraints and updates with equality (they allow other operators) is not more expressive than classical TA for the sequential semantics (any updatable TA of the class is bisimilar to a classical TA), and the emptiness problem is PSPACE-complete.

Semantics. TTS($A_1 \parallel A_2$) can be defined as previously, with the difference that the synchronizations are now defined by: $((\ell_1,\ell_2),v) \xrightarrow{a} ((\ell_1',\ell_2'),v')$ iff $\ell_1 \xrightarrow{g_1,a,r_1}_1 \ell_1'$, $\ell_2 \xrightarrow{g_2,a,r_2,u}_2 \ell_2'$ where u is a partial function from X_2 to X_1, $v \models g_1 \wedge g_2$, $v' = (v[r_1 \cup r_2])[u]$, and $v' \models Inv(\ell_1') \wedge Inv(\ell_2')$. The valuation $v[u]$ is defined by $v[u](x) = v(u(x))$ if $u(x)$ is defined, and $v[u](x) = v(x)$ otherwise.

Here, we choose to apply the reset $r_1 \cup r_2$ before the update u, because we are interested in sharing the state reached in A_1 after the synchronization, and r_1 may reset some clocks in $C_1 \subseteq X_1$.

3.3 Towards a Formalization of the Problem

We want to know whether A_2 really needs to read the clocks reset by A_1, or if another NTA $A_1' \parallel A_2'$ could achieve the same behavior as $A_1 \parallel A_2$ without using shared clocks. It remains to formalize what we mean by "having the same behavior" in this context.

First, we impose that the locality of actions is preserved, i.e. A_1' uses the same set of local actions as A_1, and similarly for A_2' and A_2. For the synchronizations, we have explained earlier why we allow A_1' and A_2' to use a larger synchronization alphabet than A_1 and A_2. The correspondence between the two alphabets will be done by a mapping ψ (this point will be refined later).

Now we have to impose that the behavior is preserved. The first idea that comes in mind is to impose bisimulation between $\psi(\text{TTS}(A_1' \parallel A_2'))$ (i.e.

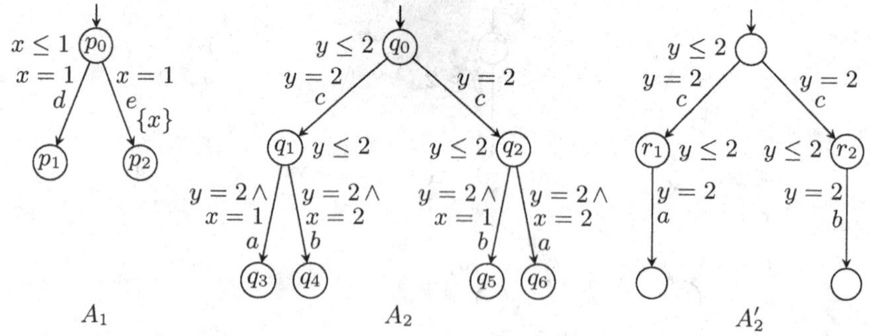

Fig. 3. A_2 needs to read the clocks of A_1 and $\text{TTS}(A_1 \parallel A_2) \sim \text{TTS}(A_1 \parallel A'_2)$

$\text{TTS}(A'_1 \parallel A'_2)$ with synchronization actions relabeled by ψ) and $\text{TTS}(A_1 \parallel A_2)$. But this is not sufficient, as illustrated by the example of Fig. 3 (where ψ is the identity). Intuitively A_2 needs to read x when in q_1 (and similarly in q_2) at time 2, because this reading determines whether it will perform a or b, and the value of x cannot be inferred from its local state given by q_1 and the value of y. Anyway $\text{TTS}(A_1 \parallel A'_2)$ is bisimilar to $\text{TTS}(A_1 \parallel A_2)$, and A'_2 does not read x. For the bisimulation relation $\mathcal{R}$, it suffices to impose $(p_1, q_1)\ \mathcal{R}\ (p_1, r_1)$ and $(p_2, q_1)\ \mathcal{R}\ (p_2, r_2)$.

What we see here is that, if we focus on the point of view of A_2 and A'_2, these two automata do not behave the same. As a matter of fact, when A_2 fires one edge labeled by c, it has not read x yet, and there is still a possibility to fire a or b, whereas when A'_2 fires one edge labeled by c, there is no more choice afterwards. Therefore we need a relation between A'_2 and A_2, and in the general case, a relation between A'_1 and A_1 also.

4 Contextual Timed Transition Systems

As we are interested in representing a partial view of one of the components, we need to introduce another notion, that we call *contextual timed transition system*. This resembles the powerset construction used in game theory to capture the knowledge of an agent about another agent.

Notations. $\mathbb{S} = \Sigma_1^{\not\varepsilon} \cap \Sigma_2^{\not\varepsilon}$ denotes the set of common actions. Q_1 denotes the set of states of $\text{TTS}(A_1)$. When $s = ((\ell_1, \ell_2), v)$ is a state of $\text{TTS}(A_1 \parallel A_2)$, we also write $s = (s_1, s_2)$, where $s_1 = (\ell_1, v_{|X_1})$ is in Q_1, and $s_2 = (\ell_2, v_{|X_2 \setminus X_1})$, where $v_{|X}$ is v restricted to X.

Definition 3 (UR(s))**.** *Let* $\text{TTS}(A_1) = (Q_1, s_0, \Sigma_1, \rightarrow_1)$ *and* $s \in Q_1$. *The set of states of* A_1 *reachable from* s *by local actions in 0 delay (and therefore not observable by* A_2*) is denoted by* $\text{UR}(s) = \{s' \in Q_1 \mid \exists w \in \text{TW}(\Sigma_1 \setminus \Sigma_2^{\not\varepsilon}, 0) : s \xrightarrow{w}_1 s'\}$.

Contextual States. The states of this contextual TTS are called *contextual states.* They can be regarded as possibly infinite sets of states of $\text{TTS}(A_1 \parallel A_2)$ for which A_2 is in the same location and has the same valuation over $X_2 \setminus X_1$. A_2 may not be able to distinguish between some states (s_1, s_2) and (s_1', s_2). In $\text{TTS}_{A_1}(A_2)$, these states are grouped into the same contextual state. However, when $X_2 \cap X_1 \neq \emptyset$, it may happen that A_2 is able to perform a local action or delay from (s_1, s_2) and not from (s_1', s_2), even if these states are grouped in a same contextual state.

Definition 4 (Contextual TTS). *Let* $\text{TTS}(A_1 \parallel A_2) = (Q, q_0, \Sigma_1 \cup \Sigma_2, \Rightarrow)$. *Then, the* TTS *of* A_2 *in the context of* A_1*, denoted by* $\text{TTS}_{A_1}(A_2)$*, is the TTS* $(S, s_0, (\Sigma_2 \setminus \mathbb{S}) \cup (\mathbb{S} \times Q_1), \rightarrow)$*, where*

- $S = \{(S_1, s_2) \mid \forall s_1 \in S_1, (s_1, s_2) \in Q\}$,
- $s_0 = (S_1^0, s_2^0)$, *s.t.* $(s_1^0, s_2^0) = q_0$ *and* $S_1^0 = \text{UR}(s_1^0)$,
- $\rightarrow$ *is defined by*
  - *Local action: for any* $a \in \Sigma_2 \setminus \mathbb{S}$, $(S_1, s_2) \xrightarrow{a} (S_1', s_2')$ *iff* $\exists s_1 \in S_1 : (s_1, s_2) \overset{a}{\Rightarrow} (s_1, s_2')$, *and* $S_1' = \{s_1 \in S_1 \mid (s_1, s_2) \overset{a}{\Rightarrow} (s_1, s_2')\}$
  - *Synchronization: for any* $(a, s_1') \in \mathbb{S} \times Q_1$, $(S_1, s_2) \xrightarrow{a, s_1'} (\text{UR}(s_1'), s_2')$ *iff* $\exists s_1 \in S_1 : (s_1, s_2) \overset{a}{\Rightarrow} (s_1', s_2')$
  - *Local delay: for any* $d \in \mathbb{R}_{\geq 0}$, $(S_1, s_2) \xrightarrow{d} (S_1', s_2')$ *iff* $\exists s_1 \in S_1$, $w \in \text{TW}(\Sigma_1 \setminus \Sigma_2^{\not s}, d) : (s_1, s_2) \overset{w}{\Rightarrow} (s_1', s_2')$, *and* $S_1' = \{s_1' \mid \exists s_1 \in S_1$, $w \in \text{TW}(\Sigma_1 \setminus \Sigma_2^{\not s}, d) : (s_1, s_2) \overset{w}{\Rightarrow} (s_1', s_2')\}$

For example, consider A_1 and A_2 of Fig. 3. The initial state is $(\{(p_0, 0)\}, (q_0, 0))$. From this contextual state, it is possible to delay 2 time units and reach the contextual state $(\{(p_1, 2), (p_2, 1)\}, (q_0, 2))$. Indeed, during this delay, A_1 has to perform either e and reset x, or d. Now, from this contextual state, we can take an edge labeled by c, and reach $(\{(p_1, 2), (p_2, 1)\}, (q_1, 2))$. Lastly, from this new state, a can be fired, because it is enabled by $((p_2, 1), (q_1, 2))$ in the TTS of the NTA, and the reached contextual state is $(\{(p_2, 1)\}, (q_3, 2))$.

We say that there is no restriction in $\text{TTS}_{A_1}(A_2)$ if whenever a local step is possible from a reachable contextual state, then it is possible from all the states (s_1, s_2) that are grouped into this contextual state. In the example above, there is a restriction in $\text{TTS}_{A_1}(A_2)$ because we have seen that a is enabled only by $((p_2, 1), (q_1, 2))$, and not by all states merged in $(\{(p_1, 2), (p_2, 1)\}, (q_1, 2))$. Formally, we use the predicate $noRestriction_{A_1}(A_2)$ defined as follows.

Definition 5 ($noRestriction_{A_1}(A_2)$)**.** *The predicate* $noRestriction_{A_1}(A_2)$ *holds iff for any reachable state* (S_1, s_2) *of* $\text{TTS}_{A_1}(A_2)$*, both*

- $\forall a \in \Sigma_2 \setminus \mathbb{S}, (S_1, s_2) \xrightarrow{a} (S_1', s_2') \iff \forall s_1 \in S_1, (s_1, s_2) \overset{a}{\Rightarrow} (s_1, s_2')$, *and*
- $\forall d \in \mathbb{R}_{\geq 0}, (S_1, s_2) \xrightarrow{d} \iff \forall s_1 \in S_1, \exists w \in \text{TW}(\Sigma_1 \setminus \Sigma_2^{\not s}, d) : (s_1, s_2) \overset{w}{\Rightarrow}$

Remark 2. If A_2 does not read X_1, then $noRestriction_{A_1}(A_2)$.

Fig. 4. $\mathrm{TTS}_{Q_1}(A_1) \otimes \mathrm{TTS}_{A_1}(A_2) \approx \mathrm{TTS}_{Q_1}(A_1 \parallel A_2)$, although there is a restriction in $\mathrm{TTS}_{A_1}(A_2)$

Sharing of Information on the Synchronizations. Later we assume that during a synchronization, A_1 is allowed to transmit all its state to A_2, that is why, in $\mathrm{TTS}_{A_1}(A_2)$, we distinguish the states reached after a synchronization according to the state reached in A_1. We also label the synchronization edges by a pair $(a, s_1) \in \mathbb{S} \times Q_1$ where a is the action and s_1 the state reached in A_1.

For the sequel, let $\mathrm{TTS}_{Q_1}(A_1)$ (resp. $\mathrm{TTS}_{Q_1}(A_1 \parallel A_2)$) denote $\mathrm{TTS}(A_1)$ (resp. $\mathrm{TTS}(A_1 \parallel A_2)$) where the synchronization edges are labeled by (a, s_1), where $a \in \mathbb{S}$ is the action, and s_1 is the state reached in A_1.

We can now state a nice property of unrestricted contextual TTS that is similar to the distributivity of TTS over the composition when considering TA with disjoint sets of clocks (see Remark 1). We say that a TA is *deterministic* if it has no ε-transition and for any location ℓ and action a, there is at most one edge labeled by a from ℓ.

Lemma 1. *If there is no restriction in* $\mathrm{TTS}_{A_1}(A_2)$*, then* $\mathrm{TTS}_{Q_1}(A_1) \otimes \mathrm{TTS}_{A_1}(A_2) \approx \mathrm{TTS}_{Q_1}(A_1 \parallel A_2)$*. Moreover, when* A_2 *is deterministic, this condition becomes necessary.*

The example of Fig. 4 shows that the reciprocal does not hold when A_2 is not deterministic.

4.1 Need for Shared Clocks Revisited

We have argued in Section 3.3 that the existence of a NTA $A'_1 \parallel A'_2$ without shared clocks and such that $\psi(\mathrm{TTS}_{Q'_1}(A'_1 \parallel A'_2)) \sim \mathrm{TTS}_{Q_1}(A_1 \parallel A_2)$ is not sufficient to capture the idea that A_2 does not need to read the clocks of A_1. We are now equipped to define the relations we want to impose on the separate components, namely $\psi(\mathrm{TTS}_{Q'_1}(A'_1)) \sim \mathrm{TTS}_{Q_1}(A_1)$ and $\psi(\mathrm{TTS}_{A'_1}(A'_2)) \sim \mathrm{TTS}_{A_1}(A_2)$. And since we have seen the importance of using labeling the synchronization actions in contextual TTS by labels in $\mathbb{S} \times Q_1$ rather than in $\mathbb{S}$, the correspondence between the synchronization labels of $A'_1 \parallel A'_2$ with those of $A_1 \parallel A_2$ is now done by a mapping $\psi : \mathbb{S}' \times Q'_1 \to \mathbb{S} \times Q_1$.

This settles the problem of the example of Fig. 3 where $\mathrm{TTS}_{A_1}(A'_2) \not\sim \mathrm{TTS}_{A_1}(A_2)$ (here $A'_1 = A_1$), but as shown in Fig. 5, a problem remains. In this example, we can see that A_2 needs to read clock x of A_1 to know whether it has to perform a or b at time 2, and yet $\mathrm{TTS}_{A_1}(A_2) \sim \mathrm{TTS}_{A_1}(A'_2)$ (here again $A'_1 = A_1$). The intuition to understand this is that the contextual TTS merge too many states for the two systems to remain differentiable. However we remark that

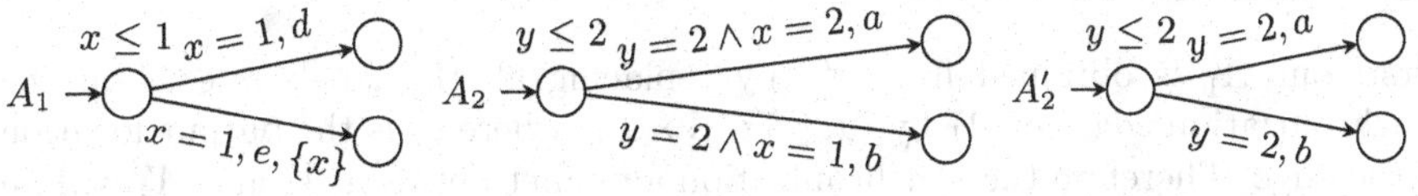

Fig. 5. A_2 needs to read the clocks of A_1 and $\mathrm{TTS}_{A_1}(A_2) \sim \mathrm{TTS}_{A_1}(A_2')$

here, the first condition that we have required in Section 3, namely the global bisimulation between $\psi(\mathrm{TTS}(A_1' \parallel A_2'))$ and $\mathrm{TTS}(A_1 \parallel A_2)$, does not hold.

Now we show that the conjunction of global and local bisimulations actually gives the good definition.

Definition 6 (Need for shared clocks). *Given $A_1 \parallel A_2$ such that A_1 does not read the clocks of A_2, A_2* does not need to read the clocks of A_1 *iff there exists a NTA $A_1' \parallel A_2'$ without shared clocks (but with clock copies during synchronizations), using the same sets of local actions and a synchronization alphabet $\mathbb{S}'$ related to the original one by a mapping $\psi : \mathbb{S}' \times Q_1' \to \mathbb{S} \times Q_1$, and such that*

1. $\psi(\mathrm{TTS}_{Q_1'}(A_1' \parallel A_2')) \sim \mathrm{TTS}_{Q_1}(A_1 \parallel A_2)$ *and*
2. $\psi(\mathrm{TTS}_{Q_1'}(A_1')) \sim \mathrm{TTS}_{Q_1}(A_1)$ *and*
3. $\psi(\mathrm{TTS}_{A_1'}(A_2')) \sim \mathrm{TTS}_{A_1}(A_2)$.

Notice that this does not mean that the clock constraints that read X_1 can simply be removed from A_2 (see Fig. 2).

Lemma 2. *When noRestriction$_{A_1}(A_2)$ holds, any NTA $A_1' \parallel A_2'$ without shared clocks and that satisfies items 2 and 3 of Definition 6 also satisfies item 1.*

We are now ready to give a criterion to decide the need for shared clocks.

Theorem 1. *When noRestriction$_{A_1}(A_2)$ holds, A_2 does not need to read the clocks of A_1. When A_2 is deterministic, this condition becomes necessary.*

We remark from the proof that when there is a restriction in $\mathrm{TTS}_{A_1}(A_2)$, even infinite A_1' and A_2' would not help. Next section will be devoted to the constructive proof of the direct part of this theorem. The indirect part follows from Lemma 1. The counterexample in Fig. 4 also works here to argue that the conditions of Lemma 2 and Theorem 1 are not necessary when A_2 is not deterministic. Indeed A_2' with only one unguarded edge labeled by a and $A_1' = A_1$ satisfy the three items of Definition 6 but there is a restriction in $\mathrm{TTS}_{A_1}(A_2)$.

5 Constructing a NTA without Shared Clocks

This section is dedicated to proving Theorem 1 by constructing suitable A_1' and A_2'. To simplify, we assume that in A_2, the guards on the synchronizations do not read X_1.

5.1 Construction

First, our A'_1 is obtained from A_1 by replacing all the labels $a \in \mathbb{S}$ on the synchronization edges of A_1 by $(a, \ell_1) \in \mathbb{S} \times L_1$, where ℓ_1 is the output location of the edge. Therefore the synchronization alphabet between A'_1 and A'_2 will be $\mathbb{S}' = \mathbb{S} \times L_1$, which allows A'_1 to transmit its location after each synchronization.

Then, the idea is to build A'_2 as a product $A_{1,2} \otimes A_{2,mod}$ ($\otimes$ denotes the product of TA as it is usually defined [3]), where $A_{2,mod}$ plays the role of A_2 and $A_{1,2}$ acts as a local copy of A'_1, from which $A_{2,mod}$ reads clocks instead of reading those of A'_1. For this, as long as the automata do not synchronize, $A_{1,2}$ will evolve, simulating a run of A'_1 that is compatible with what A'_2 knows about A'_1. And, as soon as A'_1 synchronizes with A'_2, A'_2 updates $A_{1,2}$ to the actual state of A'_1. If the clocks of $A_{1,2}$ always give the same truth value to the guards and invariants of $A_{2,mod}$ than the actual value of the clocks of A'_1, then our construction behaves like $A_1 \parallel A_2$. To check that this is the case, we equip A'_2 with an error location, $\frownie$, and edges that lead to it if there is a contradiction between the values of the clocks of A'_1 and the values of the clocks of $A_{1,2}$. The guards of these edges are the only cases where A'_2 reads clocks of A'_1. Therefore, if $\frownie$ is not reachable, they can be removed so that A'_2 does not read the clocks of A'_1. More precisely, a contradiction happens when $A_{2,mod}$ is in a given location and the guard of an outgoing edge is true according to $A_{1,2}$ and false according to A'_1, or vice versa, or when the invariant of the current location is false according to A'_1 (whereas it is true according to $A_{1,2}$, since $A_{2,mod}$ reads the clocks of $A_{1,2}$).

Namely, $\mathcal{S}_{mod} = A'_1 \parallel (A_{1,2} \otimes A_{2,mod})$ where $A_{1,2}$ and $A_{2,mod}$ are defined as follows. $A_{1,2} = (L_1, \ell_1^0, X'_1, \mathbb{S}' \cup \{\varepsilon\}, E'_1, Inv'_1)$, where

- each clock $x' \in X'_1$ is associated with a clock $c(x') = x \in X_1$ (c is a bijection from X'_1 to X_1). γ' denotes the clock constraint where any clock x of X_1 is substituted by x' of X'_1.
- $\forall \ell \in L_1, Inv'_1(\ell) = Inv_1(\ell)'$
- $E'_1 = \{\ell_1 \xrightarrow{g', \varepsilon_a, r'} \ell_2 \mid \exists a \in \Sigma_1 \setminus \Sigma_2^{\not\varepsilon} : \ell_1 \xrightarrow{g, a, c(r')} \ell_2 \in E_1\}$
  $\cup \{\ell \xrightarrow{\top, (a, \ell_2), c} \ell_2 \mid \ell \in L_1 \wedge a \in \mathbb{S} \wedge \exists \ell_1 \xrightarrow{g, a, r} \ell_2 \in E_1\}$
  where $\top$ means true, and c denotes the assignment of any clock $x' \in X'_1$ with the value of its associated clock $c(x') = x \in X_1$ (written $x' := x$ in Fig. 6).

$A_{2,mod} = (L_2 \cup \{\frownie\}, \ell_2^0, X_2 \cup X'_1, (\Sigma_2 \setminus \Sigma_1) \cup \mathbb{S}', E'_2, Inv'_2)$, where

- $\forall \ell \in L_2, Inv'_2(\ell) = Inv_2(\ell)'$ and $Inv'_2(\frownie) = \top$,
- $E'_2 = \{\ell_1 \xrightarrow{g', a, r} \ell_2 \mid \ell_1 \xrightarrow{g, a, r} \ell_2 \in E_2 \wedge a \notin \mathbb{S}\}$
  $\cup \{\ell_1 \xrightarrow{g, (a, \ell), r} \ell_2 \mid \ell_1 \xrightarrow{g, a, r} \ell_2 \in E_2 \wedge a \in \mathbb{S} \wedge \ell \in L_1\}$
  $\cup \{\ell \xrightarrow{\neg Inv_2(\ell), \varepsilon, \emptyset} \frownie \mid \ell \in L_2\}$
  $\cup \{\ell \xrightarrow{g' \wedge \neg g, \varepsilon, \emptyset} \frownie \mid \ell \xrightarrow{g, a, r} \ell' \in E_2 \wedge a \notin \mathbb{S}\}$
  $\cup \{\ell \xrightarrow{\neg g' \wedge g, \varepsilon, \emptyset} \frownie \mid \ell \xrightarrow{g, a, r} \ell' \in E_2 \wedge a \notin \mathbb{S}\}$.

For the example of Fig. 2, $A_{1,2}$ and $A_{2,mod}$ are pictured in Fig. 6.

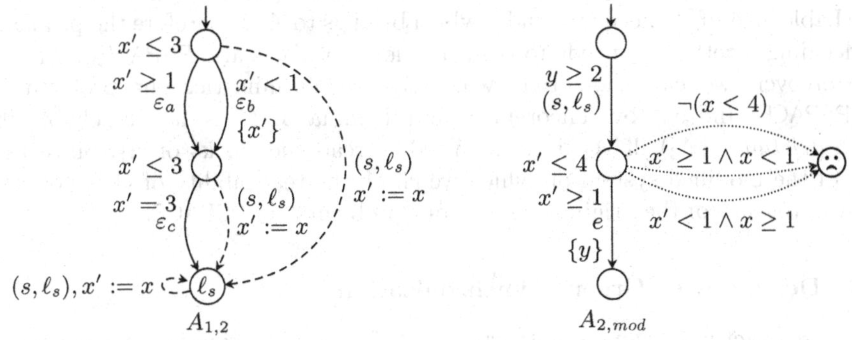

Fig. 6. $A_{1,2}$ and $A_{2,mod}$ for the example of Fig. 2

Lemma 3. ☹ *is reachable in* $\mathcal{S}_{mod}$ *iff there is a restriction in* $\text{TTS}_{A_1}(A_2)$.

We first give a case for which Theorem 1 can be proved easily. We say that A_1 has no urgent synchronization if for any location, when the invariant expires, a local action is enabled. Under this assumption, we show that $A_2' = A_{1,2} \otimes A'_{2,mod}$, where $A'_{2,mod}$ is $A_{2,mod}$ without location ☹ (that is unreachable by Lemma 3) and its ingoing edges, is suitable. Indeed, A_2' does not read X_1 and $\psi(\text{TTS}_{A_1'}(A_2')) \sim \text{TTS}_{A_1}(A_2)$, where for any $((a, \ell_1), s_1) \in \mathbb{S}' \times Q_1'$, $\psi(((a, \ell_1), s_1)) = (a, s_1)$. Item 2 of Definition 6 is immediate, and item 1 holds by Lemma 2.

When A_1 has urgent synchronizations, this construction allows one to check the absence of restriction in $\text{TTS}_{A_1}(A_2)$, but it does not give directly a suitable A_2'. We will give the idea of the construction of A_2' for the general case later.

In the example of Fig. 2, ☹ is not reachable in $\mathcal{S}_{mod}$ (see Fig. 6), therefore A_2 does not need to read X_1. For an example where ☹ is reachable, consider the same example with an additional edge $\xrightarrow{\top, f, \{x\}}$ from the end location of A_1 to a new location. Location ☹ can now be reached in $\mathcal{S}_{mod}$, for example consider a run where s is performed at time 2 leading to a state where $v(x) = 2$ and $v(x') = 2$, and then A_1 immediately performs f and resets x, leading to a state where the valuation v' is such that $v'(x) = 0$ and $v'(x') = 2$, and satisfies guard $x' \geq 1 \wedge x < 1$ in $\mathcal{S}_{mod}$. Therefore, with this additional edge in A_1, A_2 needs to read X_1. Indeed, without this edge, A_2 knows that A_1 cannot modify x after the synchronization, but with this edge, A_2 does not know whether A_1 has performed f and reset x, while this may change the truth value of its guard $x \geq 1$.

5.2 Complexity

The reachability problem for timed automata is known to be PSPACE-complete [2]. We will reduce this problem to our problem of deciding whether A_2 needs to read the clocks of A_1. Consider a TA A over alphabet Σ, with some location ℓ. Build the TA A_2 as A augmented with two new locations ℓ' and ℓ'' and two edges, $\ell \xrightarrow{\top, \varepsilon, \emptyset} \ell'$ and $\ell' \xrightarrow{x=1, a, \emptyset} \ell''$, where x is a fresh clock, and a is some action in Σ. Let A_1 be the one of Fig. 4 with an action $b \notin \Sigma$. Then, ℓ is reachable in A iff A_2 needs to read x which belongs to A_1. Therefore the problem of deciding whether A_2 needs to read the clocks of A_1 is also PSPACE-hard.

Moreover, we can show that when A_2 is deterministic, our problem is in PSPACE. Indeed, by Theorem 1 and Lemma 3, ☹ is not reachable iff $noRestriction_{A_1}(A_2)$ iff A_2 does not need to read the clocks of A_1. Since the size of the modified system on which we check the reachability of ☹ is polynomial in the size of the original system, our problem is in PSPACE.

5.3 Dealing with Urgent Synchronizations

If we use exactly the same construction as before and allow urgent synchronizations, the following problem may occur. Remind that $A_{1,2}$ simulates a possible run of A_1' while A_1' plays its actual run. There is no reason why the two runs should coincide. Thus it may happen that the run simulated by $A_{1,2}$ reaches a state where the invariant expires and only a synchronization is possible. Then A_2' is expecting a synchronization with A_1', but it is possible that the actual A_1' has not reached a state that enables this synchronization. Intuitively, A_2' should then realize that the simulated run cannot be the actual one and try another run compatible with the absence of synchronization.

But it is simpler to avoid this situation, by forcing $A_{1,2}$ to simulate one of the runs of A_1' (from the state reached after the last synchronization) that has maximal duration[1] before it synchronizes again with $A_{2,mod}$ (or never synchronizes again if possible). This choice of a run of A_1' is as valid as the others, and subtle situation described above.

For example, consider automaton A_1 in Fig. 2 without the edge labeled by c and with guard $x \leq 1$ instead of $x < 1$. We can see that $A_{1,2}$ has to fire b at time 1 and is able to wait 3 time units before synchronizing, although it is still able to synchronize at any time (we add the same dashed edges as in Fig. 6). This can be generalized for any A_1. The idea is essentially to force $A_{1,2}$ to follow the appropriate finite or ultimately periodic path in the region automaton [3] of A_1.

6 Conclusion

We have shown that in a distributed framework, when locality of actions and synchronizations matter, NTA with shared clocks cannot be easily transformed into NTA without shared clocks. The fact that the transformation is possible can be characterized using the notion of contextual TTS which represents the knowledge of one TA about the other. Checking the resulting criterion is PSPACE-complete.

One conclusion is that, contrary to what happens when one considers the sequential semantics, NTA with shared clocks are strictly more expressive if we take distribution into account. This somehow justifies why shared clocks were introduced: they are actually more than syntactic sugar.

[1] There may not be any maximum if some time constraints are strict inequalities, but the idea can be adapted even to this case.

Another interesting point is the use of transmitting information during synchronizations. It is noticeable that infinitely precise information is required in general. This advocates the interest of updatable (N)TA used in an appropriate way, and more generally gives a flavor of a class of NTA closer to implementation.

Perspectives. Our first perspective is to generalize our result to the symmetrical case where A_1 also reads clocks from A_2. Then of course we can tackle general NTA with more than two automata.

Another line of research is to focus on transmission of information. The goal would be to minimize the information transmitted during synchronizations, and see for example where are the limits of finite information. Even when infinitely precise information is required to achieve the exact semantics of the NTA, it would be interesting to study how this semantics can be approximated using finitely precise information.

Finally, when shared clocks are necessary, one can discuss how to minimize them, or how to implement the model on a distributed architecture and how to handle shared clocks with as few communications as possible.

References

1. Akshay, S., Bollig, B., Gastin, P., Mukund, M., Narayan Kumar, K.: Distributed Timed Automata with Independently Evolving Clocks. In: van Breugel, F., Chechik, M. (eds.) CONCUR 2008. LNCS, vol. 5201, pp. 82–97. Springer, Heidelberg (2008)
2. Alur, R., Dill, D.: Automata for Modeling Real-Time Systems. In: Paterson, M. (ed.) ICALP 1990. LNCS, vol. 443, pp. 322–335. Springer, Heidelberg (1990)
3. Alur, R., Dill, D.: A theory of timed automata. Theor. Comput. Sci. 126(2), 183–235 (1994)
4. Balaguer, S., Chatain, T.: Avoiding shared clocks in networks of timed automata. Rapport de recherche 7990, INRIA (2012)
5. Balaguer, S., Chatain, T., Haar, S.: A concurrency-preserving translation from time Petri nets to networks of timed automata. FMSD (2012)
6. Bengtsson, J.E., Jonsson, B., Lilius, J., Yi, W.: Partial Order Reductions for Timed Systems. In: Sangiorgi, D., de Simone, R. (eds.) CONCUR 1998. LNCS, vol. 1466, pp. 485–500. Springer, Heidelberg (1998)
7. Bérard, B., Cassez, F., Haddad, S., Lime, D., Roux, O.H.: Comparison of the Expressiveness of Timed Automata and Time Petri Nets. In: Pettersson, P., Yi, W. (eds.) FORMATS 2005. LNCS, vol. 3829, pp. 211–225. Springer, Heidelberg (2005)
8. Best, E., Devillers, R.R., Kiehn, A., Pomello, L.: Concurrent bisimulations in Petri nets. Acta Inf. 28(3), 231–264 (1991)
9. Bouyer, P., D'Souza, D., Madhusudan, P., Petit, A.: Timed Control with Partial Observability. In: Hunt Jr., W.A., Somenzi, F. (eds.) CAV 2003. LNCS, vol. 2725, pp. 180–192. Springer, Heidelberg (2003)
10. Bouyer, P., Dufourd, C., Fleury, E., Petit, A.: Updatable timed automata. Theor. Comput. Sci. 321(2-3), 291–345 (2004)
11. Bouyer, P., Haddad, S., Reynier, P.-A.: Timed Unfoldings for Networks of Timed Automata. In: Graf, S., Zhang, W. (eds.) ATVA 2006. LNCS, vol. 4218, pp. 292–306. Springer, Heidelberg (2006)

12. Boyer, M., Roux, O.H.: On the compared expressiveness of arc, place and transition time Petri nets. Fundam. Inform. 88(3), 225–249 (2008)
13. Bozga, M., Daws, C., Maler, O., Olivero, A., Tripakis, S., Yovine, S.: Kronos: A Model-Checking Tool for Real-Time Systems. In: Hu, A.J., Vardi, M.Y. (eds.) CAV 1998. LNCS, vol. 1427, pp. 546–550. Springer, Heidelberg (1998)
14. Cassez, F., Chatain, T., Jard, C.: Symbolic Unfoldings for Networks of Timed Automata. In: Graf, S., Zhang, W. (eds.) ATVA 2006. LNCS, vol. 4218, pp. 307–321. Springer, Heidelberg (2006)
15. Cassez, F., Roux, O.H.: Structural translation from time Petri nets to timed automata. Jour. of Systems and Software (2006)
16. Cerans, K., Godskesen, J.C., Larsen, K.G.: Timed Modal Specification - Theory and Tools. In: Courcoubetis, C. (ed.) CAV 1993. LNCS, vol. 697, pp. 253–267. Springer, Heidelberg (1993)
17. David, A., Larsen, K.G., Li, S., Nielsen, B.: Timed testing under partial observability. In: ICST, pp. 61–70. IEEE Computer Society (2009)
18. Dima, C.: Positive and negative results on the decidability of the model-checking problem for an epistemic extension of timed CTL. In: TIME, pp. 29–36. IEEE Computer Society (2009)
19. Dima, C., Lanotte, R.: Distributed Time-Asynchronous Automata. In: Jones, C.B., Liu, Z., Woodcock, J. (eds.) ICTAC 2007. LNCS, vol. 4711, pp. 185–200. Springer, Heidelberg (2007)
20. van Glabbeek, R.J., Goltz, U.: Refinement of actions and equivalence notions for concurrent systems. Acta Inf. 37(4/5), 229–327 (2001)
21. Halpern, J.Y., Fagin, R., Moses, Y., Vardi, M.Y.: Reasoning About Knowledge. MIT Press (1995)
22. Larsen, K.G., Pettersson, P., Yi, W.: Uppaal in a nutshell. Jour. on Software Tools for Technology Transfer 1(1-2), 134–152 (1997)
23. Lugiez, D., Niebert, P., Zennou, S.: A partial order semantics approach to the clock explosion problem of timed automata. Theor. Comput. Sci. 345(1), 27–59 (2005)
24. Merlin, P.M., Farber, D.J.: Recoverability of communication protocols – implications of a theorical study. IEEE Transactions on Communications 24 (1976)
25. Minea, M.: Partial Order Reduction for Model Checking of Timed Automata. In: Baeten, J.C.M., Mauw, S. (eds.) CONCUR 1999. LNCS, vol. 1664, pp. 431–446. Springer, Heidelberg (1999)
26. Srba, J.: Comparing the Expressiveness of Timed Automata and Timed Extensions of Petri Nets. In: Cassez, F., Jard, C. (eds.) FORMATS 2008. LNCS, vol. 5215, pp. 15–32. Springer, Heidelberg (2008)
27. Woźna, B., Lomuscio, A.: A Logic for Knowledge, Correctness, and Real Time. In: Leite, J., Torroni, P. (eds.) CLIMA 2004. LNCS (LNAI), vol. 3487, pp. 1–15. Springer, Heidelberg (2005)

Strategy Synthesis for Multi-Dimensional Quantitative Objectives

Krishnendu Chatterjee[1,*], Mickael Randour[2,**], and Jean-François Raskin[3,***]

[1] IST Austria (Institute of Science and Technology Austria)
[2] Institut d'Informatique, Université de Mons (UMONS), Belgium
[3] Départment d'Informatique, Université Libre de Bruxelles (U.L.B.), Belgium

Abstract. Multi-dimensional mean-payoff and energy games provide the mathematical foundation for the quantitative study of reactive systems, and play a central role in the emerging quantitative theory of verification and synthesis. In this work, we study the strategy synthesis problem for games with such multi-dimensional objectives along with a parity condition, a canonical way to express ω-regular conditions. While in general, the winning strategies in such games may require infinite memory, for synthesis the most relevant problem is the construction of a finite-memory winning strategy (if one exists). Our main contributions are as follows. First, we show a tight exponential bound (matching upper and lower bounds) on the memory required for finite-memory winning strategies in both multi-dimensional mean-payoff and energy games along with parity objectives. This significantly improves the triple exponential upper bound for multi energy games (without parity) that could be derived from results in literature for games on VASS (vector addition systems with states). Second, we present an optimal symbolic and incremental algorithm to compute a finite-memory winning strategy (if one exists) in such games. Finally, we give a complete characterization of when finite memory of strategies can be traded off for randomness. In particular, we show that for one-dimension mean-payoff parity games, randomized memoryless strategies are as powerful as their pure finite-memory counterparts.

1 Introduction

Two-player games on graphs provide the mathematical foundation to study many important problems in computer science. Game-theoretic formulations have especially proved useful for synthesis [18,33,31], verification [2], refinement [29], and compatibility checking [19] of reactive systems, as well as in analysis of emptiness of automata [35].

Games played on graphs are repeated games that proceed for an infinite number of rounds. The *state* space of the graph is partitioned into player 1 states and player 2 states (player 2 is adversary to player 1). The game starts at an initial state, and if the

* Author supported by Austrian Science Fund (FWF) Grant No P 23499-N23, FWF NFN Grant No S11407 (RiSE), ERC Start Grant (279307: Graph Games), Microsoft faculty fellowship.

** Author supported by F.R.S.-FNRS. fellowship.

*** Author supported by ERC Starting Grant (279499: inVEST).

M. Koutny and I. Ulidowski (Eds.): CONCUR 2012, LNCS 7454, pp. 115–131, 2012.

current state is a player 1 (resp. player 2) state, then player 1 (resp. player 2) chooses an outgoing *edge*. This choice is made according to a *strategy* of the player: given the sequence of visited states, a *pure* (resp. *randomized*) strategy chooses an outgoing edge (resp. probability distribution over outgoing edges). This process of choosing edges is repeated forever, and gives rise to an outcome of the game, called a *play*, that consists of the infinite sequence of states that are visited.

Traditionally, games on graphs have been studied with Boolean objectives such as reachability, liveness, ω-regular conditions formalized as the canonical parity objectives, strong fairness objectives, etc [28,24,25,38,35,27]. While games with *quantitative* objectives have been studied in the game theory literature [23,39,30], their application in synthesis and other problems in verification is quite recent. The two classical quantitative objectives that are most relevant in verification and synthesis are the *mean-payoff* and *energy* objectives. In games on graphs with quantitative objectives, the game graph is equipped with a weight function that assigns integer-valued weights to every edge. For mean-payoff objectives, the goal of player 1 is to ensure that the long-run average of the weights is above a threshold. For energy objectives, the goal of player 1 is to ensure that the sum of the weights stays above 0 at all times. In applications of verification and synthesis, the quantitative objectives that typically arise are (i) multi-dimensional quantitative objectives (i.e., conjunction of several quantitative objectives), e.g., to express properties like the average response time between a grant and a request is below a given threshold ν_1, and the average number of unnecessary grants is below threshold ν_2; and (ii) conjunction of quantitative objectives with a Boolean objective, such as a mean-payoff parity objective that can express properties like the average response time is below a threshold along with satisfying a liveness property. In summary, the quantitative objectives can express properties related to resource requirements, performance, and robustness; multiple objectives can express the different, potentially dependent or conflicting objectives; and the Boolean objective specifies functional properties such as liveness or fairness. The game theoretic framework of multi-dimensional quantitative games and games with conjunction of quantitative and Boolean objectives has recently been shown to have many applications in verification and synthesis, such as synthesizing systems with quality guarantee [4], synthesizing robust systems [5], performance aware synthesis of concurrent data structure [10], analyzing permissivity in games and synthesis [8], simulation between quantitative automata [14], generalizing Boolean simulation to quantitative simulation distance [11], etc. Moreover, multi-dimensional energy games are equivalent to a decidable class of games on VASS (vector addition systems with states) that are the model to verify games over multi-counter systems and Petri nets [9].

In literature, there are many recent works on the theoretical analysis of multi-dimensional quantitative games, such as, mean-payoff parity games [16,8], energy-parity games [13], multi-dimensional energy games [15], and multi-dimensional mean-payoff games [15,37]. Most of these works focus on establishing the computational complexity of the problem of deciding if player 1 *has* a *winning* strategy. From the perspective of synthesis and other related problems in verification, the most important problem is to obtain a witness *finite-memory* winning strategy (if one exists). The winning strategy in the game corresponds to the desired controller for (or implementation of) the system in synthesis, and for implementability a finite-memory strategy is essential. In this work we consider the problem of finite-memory strategy synthesis in multi-dimensional quantitative games in conjunction with parity objectives, and the problem of existence of memory-efficient randomized strategies for such games. These are the core and foundational problems in the emerging theory of quantitative verification and synthesis.

Our Contributions. In this work, we study for the first time multi-dimensional energy and mean-payoff objectives in conjunction with parity objectives. Conjunction of parity objectives with multi-dimensional quantitative objectives has not been considered before. Since we consider the synthesis of finite-memory strategies, it follows from the results of [15] that both the problems (multi-dimensional energy with parity and multi-dimensional mean-payoff with parity) are equivalent. Our main results for finite-memory strategy synthesis for multi-dimensional energy parity games are as follows. (i) **Optimal memory bounds**. We first show that memory of exponential size is sufficient in multi-dimensional energy parity games. Our result is a significant improvement over the result that can be obtained naively from the results known in literature that yields a triple exponential bound, even in the case of multi-dimensional energy games without parity. Second, we show a matching lower bound by presenting a family of game graphs where exponential memory is necessary in multi-dimensional energy games (without parity), even when all the transition weights belong to $\{-1, 0, +1\}$. Thus we establish *optimal memory bounds* for the finite-memory strategy synthesis problem. (ii) **Symbolic and incremental algorithm.** We present a *symbolic* algorithm (in the sense of [21], i.e., using a compact antichain representation of sets by their minimal elements) to compute a finite-memory winning strategy, if one exists, for multi-dimensional energy parity games. Our algorithm is parameterized by the range of energy levels to consider during its execution. So, we can use it in an *incremental approach*: first, we search for finite-memory winning strategies with a small range, and increment the range only when necessary. We also establish a bound on the maximal range to consider which ensures completeness of the incremental approach. In the worst case the algorithm requires exponential time. Since exponential size memory is required (and also the decision problem is coNP-complete [15]), the worst case exponential bound can be considered as *optimal*. Moreover, as our algorithm is symbolic and incremental, in most relevant problems in practice, it is expected to be efficient. We also consider when the (pure) finite-memory strategies can be traded off for conceptually much simpler randomized strategies. (iii) **Randomized strategies.** We show that for energy objectives randomization is not helpful (as energy objectives are similar in spirit with safety objectives), even with only one player, neither it is for two-player multi-dimensional mean-payoff objectives. However, randomized memoryless strategies suffice for one-player multi-dimensional mean-payoff parity games. For the important special case of mean-payoff parity objectives (conjunction of a single mean-payoff and parity objectives), we show that in games, finite-memory strategies can be traded off for randomized memoryless strategies. An extended version of this work, including proofs, can be found in [17].

Related Works. Games with a single mean-payoff objective have been studied in [23,39], and games with a single energy objective in [12]; their equivalence was established in [7]. One-dimensional mean-payoff parity games problem has been studied in [16]: an exponential algorithm was given to decide if there exists a winning strategy (which in general was shown to require infinite memory); and an improved algorithm was presented in [8]. One-dimensional energy parity games problem has been studied in [13]: it was shown that deciding the existence of a winning strategy is in NP $\cap$ coNP, and an exponential algorithm was given. It was also shown in [13] that, for one-dimensional energy parity objectives, finite-memory strategies with exponential memory are sufficient, and the decision problem for mean-payoff parity objective can be reduced to energy parity objective. Games on VASS with several different winning objectives have been studied in [9], and from the results of [9] it follows that in multi-dimensional energy games, winning strategies with finite memory are sufficient (and a triple exponential bound on memory can be derived from the results). The complexity of multi-dimensional energy and mean-payoff games was studied in [15,37]. It was shown in [15] that in general, winning strategies in multi-dimensional mean-payoff games require infinite memory, whereas for multi-dimensional energy games, finite-memory strategies are sufficient. Moreover, for finite-memory strategies, the multi-dimensional mean-payoff and energy games coincide, and optimal computational complexity for deciding the existence of a winning strategy was established as coNP-complete [15,37]. Multi-dimensional mean-payoff games with infinite-memory strategies were studied in [37], and optimal computational complexity results were established. Various decision problems over multi-dimensional energy games were studied in [26].

2 Preliminaries

We consider two-player game structures and denote the two *players* by $\mathcal{P}_1$ and $\mathcal{P}_2$.

Multi-Weighted Two-Player Game Structures. A *multi-weighted two-player game structure* is a tuple $G = (S_1, S_2, s_{init}, E, k, w)$ where (i) S_1 and S_2 resp. denote the finite sets of *states* belonging to $\mathcal{P}_1$ and $\mathcal{P}_2$, with $S_1 \cap S_2 = \emptyset$; (ii) $s_{init} \in S = S_1 \cup S_2$ is the initial state; (iii) $E \subseteq S \times S$ is the set of *edges* s.t. for all $s \in S$, there exists $s' \in S$ s.t. $(s, s') \in E$; (iv) $k \in \mathbb{N}$ is the *dimension* of the weight vectors; and (v) $w\colon E \to \mathbb{Z}^k$ is the multi-weight labeling function. The game structure G is *one-player* if $S_2 = \emptyset$. A *play* in G is an infinite sequence of states $\pi = s_0 s_1 s_2 \ldots$ s.t. $s_0 = s_{init}$ and for all $i \geq 0$, we have $(s_i, s_{i+1}) \in E$. The *prefix* up to the n-th state of play $\pi = s_0 s_1 \ldots s_n \ldots$ is the finite sequence $\pi(n) = s_0 s_1 \ldots s_n$. Let $\mathsf{First}(\pi(n))$ and $\mathsf{Last}(\pi(n))$ resp. denote s_0 and s_n, the first and last states of $\pi(n)$. A prefix $\pi(n)$ belongs to $\mathcal{P}_i$, $i \in \{1, 2\}$, if $\mathsf{Last}(\pi(n)) \in S_i$. The set of plays of G is denoted by $\mathsf{Plays}(G)$ and the corresponding set of prefixes is denoted by $\mathsf{Prefs}(G)$. The set of prefixes that belong to $\mathcal{P}_i$ is denoted by $\mathsf{Prefs}_i(G)$. The *energy level vector* of a sequence of states $\rho = s_0 s_1 \ldots s_n$ s.t. for all $i \geq 0$, we have $(s_i, s_{i+1}) \in E$, is $\mathsf{EL}(\rho) = \sum_{i=0}^{i=n-1} w(s_i, s_{i+1})$ and the *mean-payoff vector* of a play $\pi = s_0 s_1 \ldots$ is $\mathsf{MP}(\pi) = \liminf_{n \to \infty} \frac{1}{n} \mathsf{EL}(\pi(n))$.

Parity. A game structure G is extended with a priority function $p\colon S \to \mathbb{N}$ to $G_p = (S_1, S_2, s_{init}, E, k, w, p)$. Given a play $\pi = s_0 s_1 s_2 \ldots$, let $\mathsf{Inf}(\pi) = \{s \in S \mid \forall m \geq 0, \exists n > m \text{ s.t. } s_n = s\}$ denote the set of states that appear infinitely often along π. The *parity* of a play π is defined as $\mathsf{Par}(\pi) = \min\{p(s) \mid s \in \mathsf{Inf}(\pi)\}$. In the following definitions, we denote any game by G_p with no loss of generality.

Strategies. Given a finite set A, a *probability distribution* on A is a function $p\colon A \mapsto [0,1]$ s.t. $\sum_{a \in A} p(a) = 1$. We denote the set of probability distributions on A by $\mathcal{D}(A)$. A *pure strategy* for $\mathcal{P}_i$, $i \in \{1,2\}$, in G_p is a function $\lambda_i\colon \mathsf{Prefs}_i(G_p) \to S$ s.t. for all $\rho \in \mathsf{Prefs}_i(G_p)$, we have $(\mathsf{Last}(\rho), \lambda_i(\rho)) \in E$. A *(behavioral) randomized strategy* is a function $\lambda_i\colon \mathsf{Prefs}_i(G_p) \to \mathcal{D}(S)$ s.t. for all $\rho \in \mathsf{Prefs}_i(G_p)$, we have $\{(\mathsf{Last}(\rho), s) \mid s \in S, \lambda_i(\rho)(s) > 0\} \subseteq E$. A pure strategy λ_i for $\mathcal{P}_i$ has *finite-memory* if it can be encoded by a deterministic Moore machine $(M, m_0, \alpha_u, \alpha_n)$ where M is a finite set of states (the memory of the strategy), $m_0 \in M$ is the initial memory state, $\alpha_u\colon M \times S \to M$ is an update function, and $\alpha_n\colon M \times S_i \to S$ is the next-action function. If the game is in $s \in S_i$ and $m \in M$ is the current memory value, then the strategy chooses $s' = \alpha_n(m, s)$ as the next state of the game. When the game leaves a state $s \in S$, the memory is updated to $\alpha_u(m, s)$. Formally, $\langle M, m_0, \alpha_u, \alpha_n\rangle$ defines the strategy λ_i s.t. $\lambda_i(\rho \cdot s) = \alpha_n(\hat{\alpha}_u(m_0, \rho), s)$ for all $\rho \in S^*$ and $s \in S_i$, where $\hat{\alpha}_u$ extends α_u to sequences of states as expected. A pure strategy is *memoryless* if $|M| = 1$, i.e., it does not depend on history but only on the current state of the game. Similar definitions hold for finite-memory randomized strategies, s.t. the next-action function α_n is randomized, while the update function α_u remains deterministic. We resp. denote by $\Lambda_i, \Lambda_i^{PF}, \Lambda_i^{PM}, \Lambda_i^{RM}$ the sets of general (i.e., possibly randomized and infinite-memory), pure finite-memory, pure memoryless and randomized memoryless strategies for player $\mathcal{P}_i$.

Given a prefix $\rho \in \mathsf{Prefs}_i(G_p)$ belonging to player $\mathcal{P}_i$, and a strategy $\lambda_i \in \Lambda_i$ of this player, we define the *support* of the probability distribution defined by λ_i as $\mathsf{Supp}_{\lambda_i}(\rho) = \{s \in S \mid \lambda_i(\rho)(s) > 0\}$, with $\lambda_i(\rho)(s) = 1$ if λ_i is pure and $\lambda_i(\rho) = s$. A play π is said to be *consistent* with a strategy λ_i of $\mathcal{P}_i$ if for all $n \geq 0$ s.t. $\mathsf{Last}(\pi(n)) \in S_i$, we have $\mathsf{Last}(\pi(n+1)) \in \mathsf{Supp}_{\lambda_i}(\pi(n))$. Given two strategies, λ_1 for $\mathcal{P}_1$ and λ_2 for $\mathcal{P}_2$, we define $\mathsf{Outcome}_{G_p}(\lambda_1, \lambda_2) = \{\pi \in \mathsf{Plays}(G_p) \mid \pi \text{ is consistent with } \lambda_1 \text{ and } \lambda_2\}$, the set of possible *outcomes* of the game. Note that if both strategies λ_1 and λ_2 are pure, we obtain a unique play $\pi = s_0 s_1 s_2 \ldots$ s.t. for all $j \geq 0$, $i \in \{1,2\}$, if $s_j \in S_i$, then we have $s_{j+1} = \lambda_i(s_j)$.

Given the initial state s_{init} and strategies for both players $\lambda_1 \in \Lambda_1$, $\lambda_2 \in \Lambda_2$, we obtain a Markov chain. Thus, every *event* $\mathcal{A} \subseteq \mathsf{Plays}(G_p)$, a measurable set of plays, has a uniquely defined probability [36]. We denote by $\mathbb{P}_{s_{init}}^{\lambda_1,\lambda_2}(\mathcal{A})$ the probability that a play belongs to $\mathcal{A}$ when the game starts in s_{init} and is played consistently with λ_1 and λ_2. We use the same notions for prefixes by naturally extending them to their infinite counterparts.

Objectives. An *objective* for $\mathcal{P}_1$ in G_p is a set of plays $\phi \subseteq \mathsf{Plays}(G_p)$. We consider several kinds of objectives:

- *Multi Energy objectives.* Given an initial energy vector $v_0 \in \mathbb{N}^k$, the objective $\mathsf{PosEnergy}_{G_p}(v_0) = \{\pi \in \mathsf{Plays}(G_p) \mid \forall n \geq 0 : v_0 + \mathsf{EL}(\pi(n)) \in \mathbb{N}^k\}$ requires that the energy level in all dimensions stays positive at all times.
- *Multi Mean-payoff objectives.* Given a threshold vector $v \in \mathbb{Q}^k$, the objective $\mathsf{MeanPayoff}_{G_p}(v) = \{\pi \in \mathsf{Plays}(G_p) \mid \mathsf{MP}(\pi) \geq v\}$ requires that for all dimension j, the mean-payoff on this dimension is at least $v(j)$.
- *Parity objectives.* Objective $\mathsf{Parity}_{G_p} = \{\pi \in \mathsf{Plays}(G_p) \mid \mathsf{Par}(\pi) \bmod 2 = 0\}$ requires that the minimum priority visited infinitely often be even. When the set of

priorities is restricted to $\{0,1\}$, we have a *Büchi objective*. Note that every multi-weighted game structure G without parity can trivially be extended to G_p with $p\colon S \to \{0\}$.

- *Combined objectives.* Parity can naturally be combined with multi mean-payoff and multi energy objectives, resp. yielding $\mathsf{MeanPayoff}_{G_p}(v) \cap \mathsf{Parity}_{G_p}$ and $\mathsf{PosEnergy}_{G_p}(v_0) \cap \mathsf{Parity}_{G_p}$.

Sure and Almost-Sure Semantics. A strategy λ_1 for $\mathcal{P}_1$ is *surely winning* for an objective ϕ in G_p if for all plays $\pi \in \mathsf{Plays}(G_p)$ that are consistent with λ_1, we have $\pi \in \phi$. When at least one of the players plays a randomized strategy, the notion of sure winning in general is too restrictive and inadequate, as the set of consistent plays that do not belong to ϕ may have zero probability measure. Therefore, we use the concept of *almost-surely winning*. Given a measurable objective $\phi \subseteq \mathsf{Plays}(G_p)$, a strategy λ_1 for $\mathcal{P}_1$ is *almost-surely winning* if for all $\lambda_2 \in \Lambda_2$, we have $\mathbb{P}^{\lambda_1,\lambda_2}_{s_{init}}(\phi) = 1$.

Strategy Synthesis Problem. For multi energy parity games, the problem is to synthesize a finite initial credit $v_0 \in \mathbb{N}^k$ and a pure *finite-memory* strategy $\lambda_1^{pf} \in \Lambda_1^{PF}$ that is surely winning for $\mathcal{P}_1$ in G_p for the objective $\mathsf{PosEnergy}_{G_p}(v_0) \cap \mathsf{Parity}_{G_p}$, *if one exists*. So, the initial credit is not fixed, but is part of the strategy to synthesize. For multi mean-payoff games, given a threshold $v \in \mathbb{Q}^k$, the problem is to synthesize a pure *finite-memory* strategy $\lambda_1^{pf} \in \Lambda_1^{PF}$ that is surely winning for $\mathcal{P}_1$ in G_p for the objective $\mathsf{MeanPayoff}_{G_p}(v) \cap \mathsf{Parity}_{G_p}$, *if one exists*. Note that multi energy and multi mean-payoff games are equivalent for finite-memory strategies, while in general, infinite memory may be necessary for the latter [15].

Trading Finite Memory for Randomness. We study when finite memory can be traded for randomization. The question is: given a strategy $\lambda_1^{pf} \in \Lambda_1^{PF}$ which ensures surely winning of some objective ϕ, does there exist a strategy $\lambda_1^{rm} \in \Lambda_1^{RM}$ which ensures almost-surely winning for the same objective ϕ?

3 Optimal Memory Bounds

In this section, we establish optimal memory bounds for pure finite-memory winning strategies on multi-dimensional energy parity games (MEPGs). Also, as a corollary, we obtain results for pure finite-memory winning strategies on multi-dimensional mean-payoff parity games (MMPPGs). We show that single exponential memory is both sufficient and necessary for winning strategies. Additionally, we show how the parity condition in a MEPG can be removed by adding additional energy dimensions.

Multi Energy Parity Games. A sample game is depicted on Fig. 1. The key point in the upper bound proof on memory is to understand that for $\mathcal{P}_1$ to win a multi energy parity game, he must be able to force cycles whose energy level is positive in all dimensions and whose minimal parity is even. As stated in the next lemma, finite-memory strategies are sufficient for multi energy parity games for both players.

Lemma 1 (Extension of [15, Lemma 2 and 3]). *If $\mathcal{P}_1$ wins a multi energy parity game, then he has a pure finite-memory winning strategy. If $\mathcal{P}_2$ wins a multi energy parity game, then he has a pure memoryless winning strategy.*

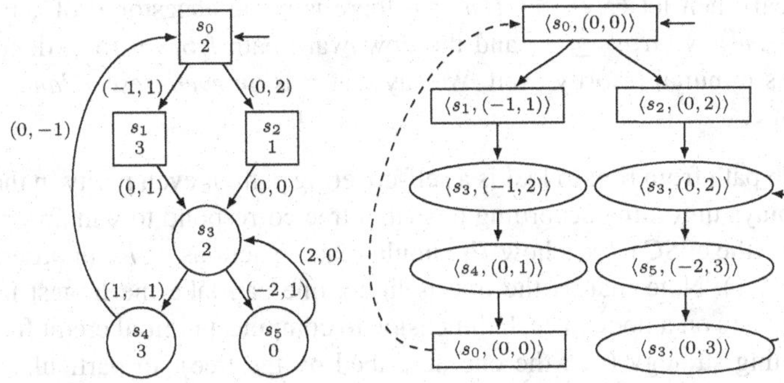

Fig. 1. Two-dimensional energy parity game and epSCT representing an arbitrary finite-memory winning strategy. Circle states belong to $\mathcal{P}_1$, square states to $\mathcal{P}_2$.

By Lemma 1, we know that w.l.o.g. both players can be restricted to play pure finite memory strategies. The property on the cycles can then be formalized as follows.

Lemma 2. *Let $G_p = (S_1, S_2, s_{init}, E, k, w, p)$ be a multi energy parity game. Let $\lambda_1^{pf} \in \Lambda_1^{PF}$ be a winning strategy of $\mathcal{P}_1$ for initial credit $v_0 \in \mathbb{N}^k$. Then, for all $\lambda_2^{pm} \in \Lambda_2^{PM}$, the outcome is a regular play $\pi = \rho \cdot (\eta_\infty)^\omega$, with $\rho \in \mathsf{Prefs}(G), \eta_\infty \in S^+$, s.t. $\mathsf{EL}(\eta_\infty) \geq 0$ and $\mathsf{Par}(\pi) = \min\{p(s) \mid s \in \eta_\infty\}$ is even.*

With the notion of regular play of Lemma 2, we generalize the notion of *self-covering path* to include the parity condition. We show here that, if such a path exists, then the lengths of its cycle and the prefix needed to reach it can be bounded. Bounds on the strategy follow. In [32], Rackoff showed how to bound the length of self-covering paths in *Vector Addition Systems* (VAS). This work was extended to Vector Addition Systems with States (VASS) by Rosier and Yen [34]. Recently, Brázdil *et al.* introduced reachability games on VASS and the notion of *self-covering trees* [9]. Their Zero-safety problem with ω initial marking is equivalent to multi energy games with weights in $\{-1,0,1\}$, and without the parity condition. They showed that if winning strategies exist for $\mathcal{P}_1$, then some of them can be represented as *self-covering trees* of bounded depth. Trees have to be considered instead of paths, as in a game setting all the possible choices of the adversary ($\mathcal{P}_2$) must be considered. Here, we extend the notion of self-covering trees to *even-parity self-covering trees*, in order to handle parity objectives.

Even-Parity Self-covering Tree. An *even-parity self-covering tree* (epSCT) for $s \in S$ is a finite tree $T = (Q, R)$, where Q is the set of nodes, $\Theta\colon Q \mapsto S \times \mathbb{Z}^k$ is a labeling function and $R \subset Q \times Q$ is the set of edges, s.t.

- The root of T is labeled $\langle s, (0, \ldots, 0)\rangle$.
- If $\varsigma \in Q$ is not a leaf, then let $\Theta(\varsigma) = \langle t, u\rangle$, $t \in S$, $u \in \mathbb{Z}^k$, s.t.
  - if $t \in S_1$, then ς has a unique child ϑ s.t. $\Theta(\vartheta) = \langle t', u'\rangle$, $(t, t') \in E$ and $u' = u + w(t, t')$;
  - if $t \in S_2$, then there is a bijection between children of ς and edges of the game leaving t, s.t. for each successor $t' \in S$ of t in the game, there is one child ϑ of ς s.t. $\Theta(\vartheta) = \langle t', u'\rangle$, $u' = u + w(t, t')$.

– If ς is a leaf, then let $\Theta(\varsigma) = \langle t, u \rangle$ s.t. there is some ancestor ϑ of ς in T s.t. $\Theta(\vartheta) = \langle t, u' \rangle$, with $u' \leq u$, and the downward path from ϑ to ς, denoted by $\vartheta \rightsquigarrow \varsigma$, has minimal priority even. We say that ϑ is an *even-descendance energy ancestor* of ς.

Intuitively, each path from root to leaf is a self-covering path of even parity in the game graph so that plays unfolding according to such a tree correspond to winning plays of Lemma 2. Thus, the epSCT fixes how $\mathcal{P}_1$ should react to actions of $\mathcal{P}_2$ in order to win the MEPG (Fig. 1). Note that as the tree is finite, one can take the largest negative number that appears on a node in each dimension to compute an initial credit for which there is a winning strategy (i.e., the one described by the tree). In particular, let W denote the maximal absolute weight appearing on an edge in G_p. Then, for an epSCT T of depth l, it is straightforward to see that the maximal initial credit required is at most $l \cdot W$ as the maximal decrease at each level of the tree is bounded by W. We suppose $W > 0$ as otherwise, any strategy of $\mathcal{P}_1$ is winning for the energy objective, for any initial credit vector $v_0 \in \mathbb{N}^k$.

Let us explicitely state how $\mathcal{P}_1$ can deploy a strategy $\lambda_1^T \in \Lambda_1^{PF}$ based on an epSCT $T = (Q, R)$. We refer to such a strategy as an *epSCT strategy*. It consists in following a path in the tree T, moving a pebble from node to node and playing in the game depending on edges taken by this pebble. Each time a node ς s.t. $\Theta(\varsigma) = \langle t, u \rangle$ is encountered, we do the following.

– If ς is a leaf, the pebble directly goes up to its oldest even-descendance energy ancestor ϑ. By oldest we mean the first encountered when going down in the tree from the root. Note that this choice is arbitrary, in a effort to ease following proof formulations, as any one would suit.
– Otherwise, if ς is not a leaf,
  • if $t \in S_2$ and $\mathcal{P}_2$ plays state $t' \in S$, the pebble is moved along the edge going to the only child ϑ of ς s.t. $\Theta(\vartheta) = \langle t', u' \rangle$, $u' = u + w(t, t')$;
  • if $t \in S_1$, the pebble moves to ϑ, $\Theta(\vartheta) = \langle t', u' \rangle$, the only child of ς, and $\mathcal{P}_1$ strategy is to choose the state t' in the game.

If such an epSCT T of depth l exists for a game G_p, then $\mathcal{P}_1$ can play the strategy $\lambda_1^T \in \Lambda_1^{PF}$ to win the game with initial credit bounded by $l \cdot W$.

Bounding the Depth of epSCTs. Consider a multi energy game *without* parity. Then, the priority condition on downward paths from ancestor to leaf is not needed and self-covering trees (i.e., epSCTs without the condition on priorities) suffice to describe winning strategies. One can bound the size of SCTs using results on the size of solutions for linear diophantine equations (i.e., with integer variables) [6]. In particular, recent work on reachability games over VASS with weights $\{-1, 0, 1\}$, Lemma 7 of [9], states that if $\mathcal{P}_1$ has a winning strategy on a VASS, then he can exhibit one that can be described as a SCT whose *depth* is at most $l = 2^{(d-1)\cdot|S|} \cdot (|S| + 1)^{c \cdot k^2}$, where c is a constant independent of the considered VASS and d its branching degree (i.e., the highest number of outgoing edges on any state). Naive use of this bound for multi energy games with arbitrary integer weights would induce a *triple* exponential bound for memory. Indeed, recall that W denotes the maximal absolute weight that appears in a game

$G_p = (S_1, S_2, s_{init}, E, k, w, p)$. A straightforward translation of a game with arbitrary weights into an equivalent game that uses only weights in $\{-1, 0, 1\}$ induces a blow-up by W in the size of the state space, and thus an exponential blow-up by W in the depth of the tree, which becomes doubly exponential as we have

$$l = 2^{(d-1)\cdot W \cdot |S|} \cdot (W \cdot |S| + 1)^{c \cdot k^2} = 2^{(d-1)\cdot 2^V \cdot |S|} \cdot (W \cdot |S| + 1)^{c \cdot k^2},$$

where V denotes the number of bits used by the encoding of W. Moreover, the width of the tree increases as d^l, i.e., it increases exponentially with the depth. So straight application of previous results provides an overall tree of triple exponential size. In this paper we improve this bound and prove a single exponential upper bound, even for multi energy *parity* games. We proceed in two steps, first studying the depth of the epSCT, and then showing how to compress the tree into a *directed acyclic graph* (DAG) of *single* exponential size.

Lemma 3. *Let $G_p = (S_1, S_2, s_{init}, E, k, w, p)$ be a multi energy parity game s.t. W is the maximal absolute weight appearing on an edge and d the branching degree of G_p. Suppose there exists a finite-memory winning strategy for $\mathcal{P}_1$. Then there is an even-parity self-covering tree for s_{init} of depth at most $l = 2^{(d-1)\cdot|S|} \cdot (W \cdot |S| + 1)^{c \cdot k^2}$, where c is a constant independent of G_p.*

Lemma 3 eliminates the exponential blow-up in depth induced by a naive coding of arbitrary weights into $\{-1, 0, 1\}$ weights, and implies an overall doubly exponential upper bound. Our proof is a generalization of [9, Lemma 7], using a more refined analysis to handle both *parity* and *arbitrary integer weights*. The idea is the following. First, consider the one-player case. The epSCT is reduced to a path. By Lemma 2, it is composed of a finite prefix, followed by an infinitely repeated sequence of positive energy level and even minimal priority. The point is to bound the length of such a sequence by eliminating cycles that are not needed for energy or parity. Second, to extend the result to two-player games, we use an induction on the number of choices available for $\mathcal{P}_2$ in a given state. Intuitively, we show that if $\mathcal{P}_1$ can win with an epSCT T_A when $\mathcal{P}_2$ plays edges from a set A in a state s, and if he can also win with an epSCT T_B when $\mathcal{P}_2$ plays edges from a set B, then he can win when $\mathcal{P}_2$ chooses edges from both A and B, with an epSCT whose depth is bounded by the sum of depths of T_A and T_B.

From Multi Energy Parity Games to Multi Energy Games. Let G_p be a MEPG and assume that $\mathcal{P}_1$ has a winning strategy in that game. By Lemma 3, there exists an epSCT whose depth is bounded by l. As a direct consequence of that bounded depth, we have that $\mathcal{P}_1$, by playing the strategy prescribed by the epSCT, enforces a stronger objective than the parity objective. Namely, this strategy ensures to "never visit more than l states of odd priorities before seeing a smaller even priority" (which is a safety objective). Then, the parity condition can be transformed into additional energy dimensions.

While our transformation shares ideas with the classical transformation of parity objectives into safety objectives, first proposed in [3] (see also [22, Lemma 6.4]), it is technically different because energy levels cannot be reset (as it would be required by those classical constructions). The reduction is as follows. For each odd priority, we add one dimension. The energy level in this dimension is decreased by 1 each time this odd priority is visited, and it is increased by l each time a smaller even priority is visited. If $\mathcal{P}_1$ is able to maintain the energy level positive for all dimensions (for a given initial energy level), then he is clearly winning the original parity objective; on the other hand, an epSCT strategy that wins the original objective also wins the new game.

Lemma 4. *Let $G_p = (S_1, S_2, s_{init}, E, k, w, p)$ be a multi energy parity game with priorities in $\{0, 1, \ldots, 2 \cdot m\}$, s.t. W is the maximal absolute weight appearing on an edge. Then we can construct a multi energy game G with the same set of states, $(k+m)$ dimensions and a maximal absolute weight bounded by l, as defined by Lemma 3, s.t. $\mathcal{P}_1$ has a winning strategy in G iff he has one in G_p.*

Bounding the Width. Thanks to Lemma 4, we continue with multi energy games without parity. In order to bound the overall size of memory for winning strategies, we consider the width of self-covering trees. The following lemma states that SCTs, whose width is at most doubly exponential by application of Lemma 3, can be compressed into *directed acyclic graphs* (DAGs) of single exponential width. Thus we eliminate the second exponential blow-up and give an overall single exponential bound for memory of winning strategies.

Lemma 5. *Let $G = (S_1, S_2, s_{init}, E, k, w)$ be a multi energy game s.t. W is the maximal absolute weight appearing on an edge and d the branching degree of G. Suppose there exists a finite-memory winning strategy for $\mathcal{P}_1$. Then, there exists $\lambda_1^D \in \Lambda_1^{PF}$ a winning strategy for $\mathcal{P}_1$ described by a DAG D of depth at most $l = 2^{(d-1)\cdot|S|} \cdot (W \cdot |S| + 1)^{c \cdot k^2}$ and width at most $L = |S| \cdot (2 \cdot l \cdot W + 1)^k$, where c is a constant independent of G. Thus the overall memory needed to win this game is bounded by the single exponential $l \cdot L$.*

The sketch of this proof is the following. By Lemma 3, we know that there exists a tree T, and thus a DAG, that satisfies the bound on depth. We construct a finite sequence of DAGs, whose first element is T, so that (1) each DAG describes a winning strategy for the same initial credit, (2) each DAG has the same depth, and (3) the last DAG of the sequence has its width bounded by $|S| \cdot (2 \cdot l \cdot W + 1)^k$. This sequence $D_0 = T, D_1, D_2, \ldots, D_n$ is built by merging nodes on the same level of the initial tree depending on their labels, level by level. The key idea of this procedure is that what actually matters for $\mathcal{P}_1$ is only the current energy level, which is encoded in node labels in the self-covering tree T. Therefore, we merge nodes with identical states and energy levels: since $\mathcal{P}_1$ can essentially play the same strategy in both nodes, we only keep one of their subtrees.

Lower Bound. In the next lemma, we show that the upper bound is tight in the sense that there exist families of games which require exponential memory (in the number of dimensions), even for the simpler case of multi energy objectives without parity and weights in $\{-1, 0, 1\}$ (Fig. 2).

Lemma 6. *There exists a family of multi energy games $(G(K))_{K \geq 1}$, $=$ $(S_1, S_2, s_{init}, E, k = 2 \cdot K, w\colon E \to \{-1, 0, 1\})$ s.t. for any initial credit, $\mathcal{P}_1$ needs exponential memory to win.*

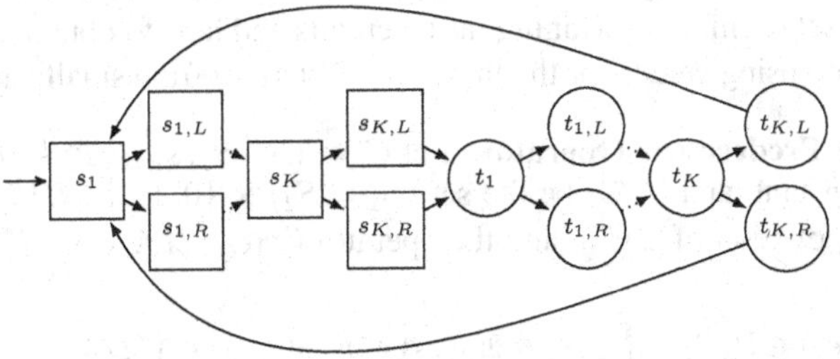

Fig. 2. Family of games requiring exponential memory: $\forall 1 \leq i \leq K$, $\forall 1 \leq j \leq k$, $w((s_i, s_{i,L}))(j) = 1$ if $j = 2 \cdot i - 1$, $= -1$ if $j = 2 \cdot i$, and $= 0$ otherwise; $w((s_i, s_{i,L})) = -w((s_i, s_{i,R})) = w((t_i, t_{i,L})) = -w((t_i, t_{i,R}))$; $w((\circ, s_i)) = w((\circ, t_i)) = (0, \ldots, 0)$.

The idea is the following: in the example of Fig. 2, if $\mathcal{P}_1$ does not remember the exact choices of $\mathcal{P}_2$ (which requires an exponential size Moore machine), there will exist some sequence of choices of $\mathcal{P}_2$ s.t. $\mathcal{P}_1$ cannot counteract a decrease in energy. Thus, by playing this sequence long enough, $\mathcal{P}_2$ can force $\mathcal{P}_1$ to lose, whatever his initial credit is.

We summarize our results in Theorem 1.

Theorem 1 (Optimal memory bounds). *The following assertions hold: (1) In multi energy parity games, if there exists a winning strategy, then there exists a finite-memory winning strategy. (2) In multi energy parity and multi mean-payoff games, if there exists a finite-memory winning strategy, then there exists a winning strategy with at most exponential memory. (3) There exists a family of multi energy games (without parity) with weights in* $\{-1, 0, 1\}$ *where all winning strategies require at least exponential memory.*

4 Symbolic Synthesis Algorithm

We now present a *symbolic, incremental* and *optimal* algorithm to synthesize a finite-memory winning strategy in a MEG.[1] This algorithm outputs a (set of) winning initial credit(s) and a derived finite-memory winning strategy (if one exists) which is exponential in the worst-case. Its running time is at most exponential. So our symbolic algorithm can be considered (worst-case) optimal in the light of the results of previous section.

This algorithm computes the greatest fixed point of a monotone operator that defines the sets of winning initial (vectors of) credits for each state of the game. As those sets are upward-closed, they are symbolically represented by their minimal elements. To ensure convergence, the algorithm considers only credits that are below some *threshold*, noted $\mathbb{C}$. This is without giving up completeness because, as we show below, for a game $G = (S_1, S_2, s_{init}, E, k, w)$, it is sufficient to take the value $2 \cdot l \cdot W$ for $\mathbb{C}$, where l is the bound on the depth on epSCT obtained in Lemma 3 and W is the largest absolute

[1] Note that the symbolic algorithm can be applied to MEPGs and MMPPGs after removal of the parity condition by applying the construction of Lemma 4.

value of weights used in the game. We also show how to extract a finite state Moore machine from this set of minimal winning initial credits and how to obtain an *incremental* algorithm by increasing values for the threshold $\mathbb{C}$ starting from small values.

A Controllable Predecessor Operator. Let $G = (S_1, S_2, s_{init}, E, k, w)$ be a MEG, $\mathbb{C} \in \mathbb{N}$ be a constant, and $U(\mathbb{C})$ be the set $(S_1 \cup S_2) \times \{0, 1, \ldots, \mathbb{C}\}^k$. Let $\mathcal{U}(\mathbb{C}) = 2^{U(\mathbb{C})}$, i.e., the powerset of $U(\mathbb{C})$, and the operator $\mathsf{Cpre}_{\mathbb{C}} : \mathcal{U}(\mathbb{C}) \to \mathcal{U}(\mathbb{C})$ be defined as follows:

$$\mathcal{E}(V) = \{(s_1, e_1) \in U(\mathbb{C}) \mid s_1 \in S_1 \land \exists (s_1, s) \in E, \exists (s, e_2) \in V : e_2 \leq e_1 + w(s_1, s)\},$$
$$\mathcal{A}(V) = \{(s_2, e_2) \in U(\mathbb{C}) \mid s_2 \in S_2 \land \forall (s_2, s) \in E, \exists (s, e_1) \in V : e_1 \leq e_2 + w(s_2, s)\},$$

$$\mathsf{Cpre}_{\mathbb{C}}(V) = \mathcal{E}(V) \cup \mathcal{A}(V). \quad (1)$$

Intuitively, $\mathsf{Cpre}_{\mathbb{C}}(V)$ returns the set of energy levels from which $\mathcal{P}_1$ can force an energy level in V in one step. The operator $\mathsf{Cpre}_{\mathbb{C}}$ is $\subseteq$-monotone over the complete lattice $\mathcal{U}(\mathbb{C})$, and so there exists a *greatest fixed point* for $\mathsf{Cpre}_{\mathbb{C}}$ in the lattice $\mathcal{U}(\mathbb{C})$, denoted by $\mathsf{Cpre}^*_{\mathbb{C}}$. As usual, the greatest fixed point of the operator $\mathsf{Cpre}_{\mathbb{C}}$ can be computed by successive approximations as the last element of the following finite $\subseteq$-descending chain. We define the algorithm CpreFP that computes this greatest fixed point:

$$U_0 = U(\mathbb{C}),\ U_1 = \mathsf{Cpre}_{\mathbb{C}}(U_0),\ \ldots,\ U_n = \mathsf{Cpre}_{\mathbb{C}}(U_{n-1}) = U_{n-1}. \quad (2)$$

The set U_i contains all the energy levels that are sufficient to maintain the energy positive in all dimensions for i steps. Note that the length of this chain can be bounded by $|U(\mathbb{C})|$ and the time needed to compute each element of the chain can be bounded by a polynomial in $|U(\mathbb{C})|$. As a consequence, we obtain the following lemma.

Lemma 7. *Let $G = (S_1, S_2, s_{init}, E, k, w)$ be a multi energy game and $\mathbb{C} \in \mathbb{N}$ be a constant. Then $\mathsf{Cpre}^*_{\mathbb{C}}$ can be computed in time bounded by a polynomial in $|U(\mathbb{C})|$, i.e., an exponential in the size of G.*

Symbolic Representation. To define a symbolic representation of the sets manipulated by the $\mathsf{Cpre}_{\mathbb{C}}$ operator, we exploit the following partial order: let $(s, e), (s', e') \in U(\mathbb{C})$, we define

$$(s, e) \preceq (s', e') \text{ iff } s = s' \text{ and } e \leq e'. \quad (3)$$

A set $V \in \mathcal{U}(\mathbb{C})$ is *closed* if for all $(s, e), (s', e') \in U(\mathbb{C})$, if $(s, e) \in V$ and $(s, e) \preceq (s', e')$, then $(s', e') \in V$. By definition of $\mathsf{Cpre}_{\mathbb{C}}$, we get the following property.

Lemma 8. *All sets U_i in eq.* (2) *are closed for $\preceq$.*

Therefore, all sets U_i in the descending chain of eq. (2) can be symbolically represented by their minimal elements $\mathsf{Min}_{\preceq}(U_i)$ which is an antichain of elements for $\preceq$.

Even if the largest antichain can be exponential in G, this representation is, in practice, often much more efficient, even for small values of the parameters. For example, with $\mathbb{C} = 4$ and $k = 4$, we have that the cardinality of a set can be as large as $|U_i| \leq 625$ whereas the size of the largest antichain is bounded by $|\mathsf{Min}_{\preceq}(U_i)| \leq 35$. Antichains have proved to be very effective: see for example [1,20,21]. Therefore, our algorithm is expected to have good performance in practice.

Correctness and Completeness. The following two lemmas relate the greatest fixed point $\mathsf{Cpre}^*_{\mathbb{C}}$ and the existence of winning strategies for $\mathcal{P}_1$ in G.

Lemma 9 (Correctness). *Let $G = (S_1, S_2, s_{init}, E, k, w)$ be a multi energy game, let $\mathbb{C} \in \mathbb{N}$ be a constant. If there exists $(c_1, \ldots, c_k) \in \mathbb{N}^k$ s.t. $(s_{init}, (c_1, \ldots, c_k)) \in \mathsf{Cpre}^*_{\mathbb{C}}$, then $\mathcal{P}_1$ has a winning strategy in G for initial credit $(c_1, \ldots, c_k)$ and the memory needed by $\mathcal{P}_1$ can be bounded by $|\mathsf{Min}_{\preceq}(\mathsf{Cpre}^*_{\mathbb{C}})|$ (the size of the antichain of minimal elements in the fixed point).*

Given the set of winning initial credits output by algorithm CpreFP, it is straightforward to derive a corresponding winning strategy of at most exponential size. Indeed, for winning initial credit $\bar{c} \in \mathbb{N}^k$, we build a Moore machine which (i) states are the minimal elements of the fixed point (antichain at most exponential in G), (ii) initial state is any element (t, u) among them s.t. $t = s_{init}$ and $u \leq \bar{c}$, (iii) next-action function prescribes an action that ensures remaining in the fixed point, and (iv) update function maintains an accurate energy level in the memory.

Lemma 10 (Completeness). *Let $G = (S_1, S_2, s_{init}, E, k, w)$ be a multi energy game in which all absolute values of weights are bounded by W. If $\mathcal{P}_1$ has a winning strategy in G and $T = (Q, R)$ is a self-covering tree for G of depth l, then $(s_{init}, (\mathbb{C}, \ldots, \mathbb{C})) \in \mathsf{Cpre}^*_{\mathbb{C}}$ for $\mathbb{C} = 2 \cdot l \cdot W$.*

Remark 1. This algorithm is complete in the sense that if a winning strategy exists for $\mathcal{P}_1$, it outputs at least a winning initial credit (and the derived strategy) for $\mathbb{C} = 2 \cdot l \cdot W$. However, this is different from the *fixed initial credit problem*, which consists in deciding if a particular given credit vector is winning and is known to be EXPSPACE-hard [9,26]. In general, there may exist winning credits incomparable to those captured by algorithm CpreFP.

Incrementality. While the threshold $2 \cdot l \cdot W$ is sufficient, it may be the case that $\mathcal{P}_1$ can win the game even if its energy level is bounded above by some smaller value. So, in practice, we can use Lemma 9, to justify an incremental algorithm that first starts with small values for the parameter $\mathbb{C}$ and stops as soon as a winning strategy is found or when the value of $\mathbb{C}$ reaches the threshold $2 \cdot l \cdot W$ and no winning strategy has been found.

Application of the Symbolic Algorithm to MEPGs and MMPGs. Using the reduction of Lemma 4 that allows us to remove the parity condition, and the equivalence between multi energy games and multi mean-payoff games for finite-memory strategies (given by [15, Theorem 3]), along with Lemma 7 (complexity), Lemma 9 (correctness) and Lemma 10 (completeness), we obtain the following result.

Theorem 2 (Symbolic and incremental synthesis algorithm). *Let G_p be a multi energy (resp. multi mean-payoff) parity game. Algorithm* CpreFP *is a symbolic and incremental algorithm that synthesizes a winning strategy in G_p of at most exponential size memory, if a winning (resp. finite-memory winning) strategy exists. In the worst-case, the algorithm* CpreFP *takes exponential time.*

5 Trading Finite Memory for Randomness

In this section, we answer the fundamental question regarding the trade-off of memory for randomness in strategies: we study on which kind of games $\mathcal{P}_1$ can replace a pure finite-memory winning strategy by an equally powerful, yet conceptually simpler, randomized memoryless one and discuss how memory is encoded into probability distributions. We summarize our results in Theorem 3 and give a sketch of how they are obtained in the following.

Energy Games. Randomization is not helpful for energy objectives, even in one-player games. The proof argument is obtained from the intuition that energy objectives are similar in spirit to safety objectives. Indeed, consider a game fitted with an energy objective, and an almost-sure winning strategy λ_1. If there exists a single consistent path that violates the energy objective, then there exists a finite prefix witness to violate the energy objective. As the finite prefix has positive probability, and the strategy λ_1 is almost-sure winning, it follows that no such path exists. In other words, λ_1 is a sure winning strategy. Since randomization does not help for sure winning strategy, it follows that randomization is not helpful for one-player and two-player energy, multi energy, energy parity and multi energy parity games.

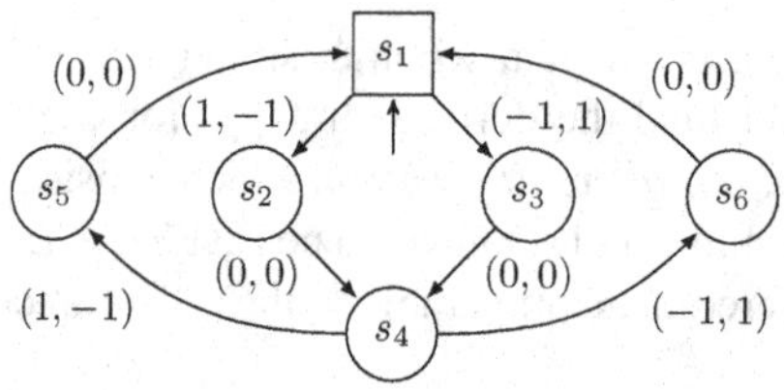

Fig. 3. Memory is needed to enforce perfect long-term balance

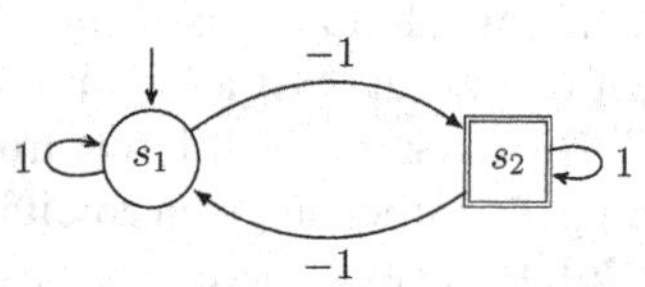

Fig. 4. Mixing strategies that are resp. *good for Büchi* and *good for energy.*

Multi Mean-Payoff (parity) Games. Randomized memoryless strategies can replace pure finite-memory ones in the one-player multi mean-payoff parity case, but not in the two-player one, even without parity. The fundamental difference between energy and mean-payoff is that energy requires a property to be satisfied *at all times* (in that sense, it is similar to safety), while mean-payoff is a *limit* property. As a consequence, what matters here is the long-run frequencies of weights, not their order of appearance, as opposed to the energy case.

For the one-player case, we extract the frequencies of visit for edges of the graph from the regular outcome that arises from the finite-memory strategy of $\mathcal{P}_1$. We build a randomized strategy with probability distributions on edges that yield the exact same frequencies in the long-run. Therefore, if the original pure finite-memory of $\mathcal{P}_1$ is surely winning, the randomized one is almost-surely winning. For the two-player case, this approach cannot be used as frequencies are not well defined, since the strategy of $\mathcal{P}_2$ is unknown. Consider a game which needs perfect balance between frequencies of appearance of two sets of edges in a play to be winning (Fig. 3). To almost-surely achieve mean-payoff vector $(0,0)$, $\mathcal{P}_1$ must ensure that the long-term balance between edges (s_4, s_5) and (s_4, s_6) is the same as the one between edges (s_1, s_3) and (s_1, s_2). This is achievable with memory as it suffices to react immediately to compensate the choice of $\mathcal{P}_2$. However, given a randomized memoryless strategy of $\mathcal{P}_1$, $\mathcal{P}_2$ always has a strategy to enforce that the long-term frequency is unbalanced, and thus the game cannot be won almost-surely by $\mathcal{P}_1$ with such a strategy.

Single Mean-Payoff Parity Games. Randomized memoryless strategies can replace pure finite-memory ones for single mean-payoff parity games. We prove it in two steps. First, we show that it is the case for the simpler case of *MP Büchi games*. Suppose $\mathcal{P}_1$ has a pure finite-memory winning strategy for such a game. We use the existence of particular pure memoryless strategies on winning states: the classical attractor for Büchi states, and a strategy that ensures that cycles of the outcome have positive energy (whose existence follows from [13]). We build an almost-surely randomized memoryless winning strategy for $\mathcal{P}_1$ by mixing those strategies in the probability distributions, with sufficient probability over the strategy that is good for energy. We illustrate this construction on the simple game G_p depicted on Fig. 4. Let $\lambda_1^{pf} \in \Lambda_1^{PF}$ be a strategy of $\mathcal{P}_1$ s.t. $\mathcal{P}_1$ plays (s_1, s_1) for 8 times, then plays (s_1, s_2) once, and so on. This strategy ensures surely winning for the objective $\phi = \mathsf{MeanPayoff}_{G_p}(3/5)$. Obviously, $\mathcal{P}_1$ has a pure memoryless strategy that ensures winning for the Büchi objective: playing (s_1, s_2). On the other hand, he also has a pure memoryless strategy that ensures cycles of positive energy: playing (s_1, s_1). Let $\lambda_1^{rm} \in \Lambda_1^{RM}$ be the strategy defined as follows: play (s_1, s_2) with probability γ and (s_1, s_1) with the remaining probability. This strategy is almost-surely winning for ϕ for sufficiently small values of γ (e.g., $\gamma = 1/9$).

Second, we extend this result to *MP parity games* using an induction on the number of priorities and the size of games. We consider *subgames* that reduce to the MP Büchi and MP coBüchi (where pure memoryless strategies are known to suffice [16]) cases.

Summary. We sum up results for these different classes of games in Theorem 3.

Theorem 3 (Trading finite memory for randomness). *The following assertions hold: (1) Randomized strategies are exactly as powerful as pure strategies for energy objectives. Randomized memoryless strategies are not as powerful as pure finite-memory strategies for almost-sure winning in one-player and two-player energy, multi energy, energy parity and multi energy parity games. (2) Randomized memoryless strategies are not as powerful as pure finite-memory strategies for almost-sure winning in two-player multi mean-payoff games. (3) In one-player multi mean-payoff parity games, and two-player single mean-payoff parity games, if there exists a pure finite-memory sure winning strategy, then there exists a randomized memoryless almost-sure winning strategy.*

6 Conclusion

In this work, we considered the finite-memory strategy synthesis problem for games with multiple quantitative (energy and mean-payoff) objectives along with a parity objective. We established tight (matching upper and lower) exponential bounds on the memory requirements for such strategies (Theorem 1), significantly improving the previous triple exponential bound for multi energy games (without parity) that could be derived from results in literature for games on VASS. We presented an optimal symbolic and incremental strategy synthesis algorithm (Theorem 2). Finally, we also presented a precise characterization of the trade-off of memory for randomness in strategies (Theorem 3).

References

1. Abdulla, P.A., Chen, Y.-F., Holík, L., Mayr, R., Vojnar, T.: When Simulation Meets Antichains. In: Esparza, J., Majumdar, R. (eds.) TACAS 2010. LNCS, vol. 6015, pp. 158–174. Springer, Heidelberg (2010)
2. Alur, R., Henzinger, T.A., Kupferman, O.: Alternating-time temporal logic. J. ACM 49(5), 672–713 (2002)
3. Bernet, J., Janin, D., Walukiewicz, I.: Permissive strategies: from parity games to safety games. ITA 36(3), 261–275 (2002)
4. Bloem, R., Chatterjee, K., Henzinger, T.A., Jobstmann, B.: Better Quality in Synthesis through Quantitative Objectives. In: Bouajjani, A., Maler, O. (eds.) CAV 2009. LNCS, vol. 5643, pp. 140–156. Springer, Heidelberg (2009)
5. Bloem, R., Greimel, K., Henzinger, T.A., Jobstmann, B.: Synthesizing robust systems. In: Proc. of FMCAD, pp. 85–92. IEEE (2009)
6. Borosh, I., Treybig, B.: Bounds on positive integral solutions of linear diophantine equations. Proc. of the American Mathematical Society 55(2), 299–304 (1976)
7. Bouyer, P., Fahrenberg, U., Larsen, K.G., Markey, N.: Timed automata with observers under energy constraints. In: Proc. of HSCC, pp. 61–70. ACM (2010)
8. Bouyer, P., Markey, N., Olschewski, J., Ummels, M.: Measuring Permissiveness in Parity Games: Mean-Payoff Parity Games Revisited. In: Bultan, T., Hsiung, P.-A. (eds.) ATVA 2011. LNCS, vol. 6996, pp. 135–149. Springer, Heidelberg (2011)
9. Brázdil, T., Jančar, P., Kučera, A.: Reachability Games on Extended Vector Addition Systems with States. In: Abramsky, S., Gavoille, C., Kirchner, C., Meyer auf der Heide, F., Spirakis, P.G. (eds.) ICALP 2010, Part II. LNCS, vol. 6199, pp. 478–489. Springer, Heidelberg (2010)
10. Černý, P., Chatterjee, K., Henzinger, T.A., Radhakrishna, A., Singh, R.: Quantitative Synthesis for Concurrent Programs. In: Gopalakrishnan, G., Qadeer, S. (eds.) CAV 2011. LNCS, vol. 6806, pp. 243–259. Springer, Heidelberg (2011)
11. Cerný, P., Henzinger, T.A., Radhakrishna, A.: Simulation distances. Theor. Comput. Sci. 413(1), 21–35 (2012)
12. Chakrabarti, A., de Alfaro, L., Henzinger, T.A., Stoelinga, M.: Resource Interfaces. In: Alur, R., Lee, I. (eds.) EMSOFT 2003. LNCS, vol. 2855, pp. 117–133. Springer, Heidelberg (2003)
13. Chatterjee, K., Doyen, L.: Energy Parity Games. In: Abramsky, S., Gavoille, C., Kirchner, C., Meyer auf der Heide, F., Spirakis, P.G. (eds.) ICALP 2010, Part II. LNCS, vol. 6199, pp. 599–610. Springer, Heidelberg (2010)
14. Chatterjee, K., Doyen, L., Henzinger, T.A.: Quantitative languages. ACM Trans. Comput. Log. 11(4) (2010)
15. Chatterjee, K., Doyen, L., Henzinger, T.A., Raskin, J.-F.: Generalized mean-payoff and energy games. In: Proc. of FSTTCS. LIPIcs, vol. 8, pp. 505–516. Schloss Dagstuhl - LZI (2010)
16. Chatterjee, K., Henzinger, T.A., Jurdzinski, M.: Mean-payoff parity games. In: Proc. of LICS, pp. 178–187. IEEE Computer Society (2005)
17. Chatterjee, K., Randour, M., Raskin, J.-F.: Strategy synthesis for multi-dimensional quantitative objectives. CoRR, abs/1201.5073 (2012), http://arxiv.org/abs/1201.5073

18. Church, A.: Logic, arithmetic, and automata. In: Proceedings of the International Congress of Mathematicians, pp. 23–35. Institut Mittag-Leffler (1962)
19. de Alfaro, L., Henzinger, T.A.: Interface Theories for Component-Based Design. In: Henzinger, T.A., Kirsch, C.M. (eds.) EMSOFT 2001. LNCS, vol. 2211, pp. 148–165. Springer, Heidelberg (2001)
20. De Wulf, M., Doyen, L., Henzinger, T.A., Raskin, J.-F.: Antichains: A New Algorithm for Checking Universality of Finite Automata. In: Ball, T., Jones, R.B. (eds.) CAV 2006. LNCS, vol. 4144, pp. 17–30. Springer, Heidelberg (2006)
21. Doyen, L., Raskin, J.-F.: Antichain Algorithms for Finite Automata. In: Esparza, J., Majumdar, R. (eds.) TACAS 2010. LNCS, vol. 6015, pp. 2–22. Springer, Heidelberg (2010)
22. Doyen, L., Raskin, J.-F.: Games with imperfect information: Theory and algorithms. In: Lectures in Game Theory for Computer Scientists, pp. 185–212 (2011)
23. Ehrenfeucht, A., Mycielski, J.: Positional strategies for mean payoff games. Int. Journal of Game Theory 8(2), 109–113 (1979)
24. Emerson, E.A., Jutla, C.: The complexity of tree automata and logics of programs. In: Proc. of FOCS, pp. 328–337. IEEE (1988)
25. Emerson, E.A., Jutla, C.: Tree automata, mu-calculus and determinacy. In: Proc. of FOCS, pp. 368–377. IEEE (1991)
26. Fahrenberg, U., Juhl, L., Larsen, K.G., Srba, J.: Energy Games in Multiweighted Automata. In: Cerone, A., Pihlajasaari, P. (eds.) ICTAC 2011. LNCS, vol. 6916, pp. 95–115. Springer, Heidelberg (2011)
27. Grädel, E., Thomas, W., Wilke, T. (eds.): Automata, Logics, and Infinite Games. LNCS, vol. 2500. Springer, Heidelberg (2002)
28. Gurevich, Y., Harrington, L.: Trees, automata, and games. In: Proc. of STOC, pp. 60–65. ACM (1982)
29. Henzinger, T.A., Kupferman, O., Rajamani, S.: Fair simulation. Information and Computation 173(1), 64–81 (2002)
30. Martin, D.A.: The determinacy of Blackwell games. The Journal of Symbolic Logic 63(4), 1565–1581 (1998)
31. Pnueli, A., Rosner, R.: On the synthesis of a reactive module. In: Proc. of POPL, pp. 179–190 (1989)
32. Rackoff, C.: The covering and boundedness problems for vector addition systems. Theor. Comput. Sci. 6, 223–231 (1978)
33. Ramadge, P.J., Wonham, W.M.: Supervisory control of a class of discrete-event processes. SIAM Journal of Control and Optimization 25(1), 206–230 (1987)
34. Rosier, L.E., Yen, H.-C.: A multiparameter analysis of the boundedness problem for vector addition systems. J. Comput. Syst. Sci. 32(1), 105–135 (1986)
35. Thomas, W.: Languages, automata, and logic. In: Handbook of Formal Languages, vol.3: Beyond Words, ch. 7, pp. 389–455. Springer (1997)
36. Vardi, M.Y.: Automatic verification of probabilistic concurrent finite-state programs. In: Proc. of FOCS, pp. 327–338. IEEE Computer Society (1985)
37. Velner, Y., Rabinovich, A.: Church Synthesis Problem for Noisy Input. In: Hofmann, M. (ed.) FOSSACS 2011. LNCS, vol. 6604, pp. 275–289. Springer, Heidelberg (2011)
38. Zielonka, W.: Infinite games on finitely coloured graphs with applications to automata on infinite trees. Theoretical Computer Science 200(1-2), 135–183 (1998)
39. Zwick, U., Paterson, M.: The complexity of mean payoff games on graphs. Theoretical Computer Science 158, 343–359 (1996)

Quantitative Languages Defined by Functional Automata*

Emmanuel Filiot[1], Raffaella Gentilini[2], and Jean-François Raskin[1]

[1] Université Libre de Bruxelles
[2] Università degli Studi di Perugia

Abstract. A weighted automaton is functional if any two accepting runs on the same finite word have the same value. In this paper, we investigate functional weighted automata for four different measures: the sum, the mean, the discounted sum of weights along edges and the ratio between rewards and costs. On the positive side, we show that functionality is decidable for the four measures. Furthermore, the existential and universal threshold problems, the language inclusion problem and the equivalence problem are all decidable when the weighted automata are functional. On the negative side, we also study the quantitative extension of the realizability problem and show that it is undecidable for sum, mean and ratio. We finally show how to decide whether the language associated with a given functional automaton can be defined with a deterministic one, for sum, mean and discounted sum. The results on functionality and determinizability are expressed for the more general class of functional weighted automata over groups. This allows one to formulate within the same framework new results related to discounted sum automata and known results on sum and mean automata. Ratio automata do not fit within this general scheme and specific techniques are required to decide functionality.

1 Introduction

Recently, there have been several efforts made to lift the foundations of computer aided verification and synthesis from the basic *Boolean* case to the richer *quantitative* case, e.g. [10,8,2]. This paper belongs to this line of research and contributes to the study of quantitative languages over finite words.

Our paper proposes a systematic study of the algorithmic properties of several classes of *functional* weighted automata (defining quantitative languages). A functional weighted automaton is a *nondeterministic* weighted automaton such that any two accepting runs ρ_1, ρ_2 on a word w associate with this word a unique value $\mathsf{V}(\rho_1) = \mathsf{V}(\rho_2)$. As we show in this paper, several important verification problems are decidable for nondeterministic functional weighted automata while they are undecidable (or not known to be decidable) for the full class of nondeterministic weighted automata. As functional weighted automata are a natural generalization of *unambiguous* weighted automata, and as unambiguity captures most of the nondeterminism that is useful in practice, our

* This work was partially supported by ERC Starting Grant (279499: inVEST). We are very grateful to some anonymous reviewer for suggesting us the encoding of discounted-sum automata as a automata over a left semiring.

M. Koutny and I. Ulidowski (Eds.): CONCUR 2012, LNCS 7454, pp. 132–146, 2012.

results are both theoretically and practically important. Also, the notion of functionality leads to useful insight into the relation between deterministic and nondeterministic weighted automata and into algorithmic idea for testing equivalence for example.

In this paper, we study automata in which an integer weight, or a pair of integer weights, is associated with each of their transitions. From those weights, an (accepting) run ρ on a word w associates a sequence of weights with the word, and this sequence is mapped to a rational value by a *measure function*. We consider four different measure functions[1]: (i) Sum computes the sum of the weights along the sequence, (ii) Avg returns the mean value of the weights, (iii) Dsum computes the discounted sum of the weights for a given discount factor $\lambda \in \mathbb{Q} \cap]0,1[$, and (iv) Ratio is applied to a sequence of pairs of weights, and it returns the ratio between the sum of weights appearing as the first component (rewards) and the sum of the weights appearing as the second component (costs). All those measures are motivated by applications in computer aided verification and synthesis, see for example [12,7]. The value associated with a word w is obtained by combining all the values of the accepting runs on w with a particular operation (usually max or min). The value of w is denoted by $L_A(w)$.

Contributions. Classical results on weighted automata consider operations over semirings: the value of a run is obtained as the multiplication of the values along its transitions, and the values of all runs on the same input word are combined with addition [13]. Since we focus on functional automata, all the accepting runs have the same value, and so we do not need addition. Whenever it is possible, we phrase our results in the general framework of functional weighted automata over a group. In particular, Sum, Avg, and Dsum can be seen as operations over a group. For Ratio however, we always need specific techniques.

We first show that functionality is decidable in PTime for weighted automata over a group (operations on group elements are assumed to be computable in polynomial time). This implies that functionality is PTime for Dsum automata and generalizes know results for Sum and Avg automata. By using a pumping argument, we show that functionality is in CoNP for Ratio-automata.

Then we solve the following decision problems, along the line of [10]. First, we consider *threshold* problems. The *existential* (*universal*, respectively) *threshold* problem asks, given a weighted automaton A and a threshold $\nu \in \mathbb{Q}$, if there exists a word (if for all words, respectively) w accepted by A: $L_A(w) \geq \nu$. Those problems can be seen as generalizations of the emptiness and universality problems for finite state automata. Second, we consider the *quantitative language inclusion problem* that asks, given two weighted automata A and B, if all words accepted by A are also accepted by B, and for all accepted words w of A, we have $L_A(w) \leq L_B(w)$. We show that all those problems are decidable for the four classes of measure functions that we consider in this paper when the automaton is functional. For Ratio, we show decidability of the problem using a recent algorithm to solve quadratic diophantine equations [15], this is a new deep result in mathematics and the complexity of the algorithm is not yet known. We also

[1] We do not consider the measure functions Min and Max that map a sequence to the minimal and the maximal value that appear in the sequence as the nondeterministic automata that use those measure functions can be made deterministic and all the decision problems for them have known and simple solutions.

show that the equivalence problem can be decided in polynomial space for Ratio via an easy reduction to functionality. Note that those decidability results are in sharp contrast with the corresponding results for the full class of nondeterministic weighted automata: for that class, only the existential threshold problem is known to be decidable, the language inclusion problem is undecidable for Sum, Avg, and Ratio while the problem is open for Dsum.

Finally, we consider a (finite word) quantitative variant of the *realizability* problem introduced by Church, which is related to the synthesis of reactive systems [23,25] and can be formalized as a game in which two players (the system and the environment) alternate in choosing letters in their respective alphabet of signals. The system can decide to stop the game. By doing so, they form a word which is obtained by concatenating the successive choices of the players. The realizability problem asks, given a weighted automaton A and an alphabet $\Sigma = \Sigma_1 \times \Sigma_2$, if there exists a strategy for choosing the letters in Σ_1 in the word forming game such that no matter how the adversary chooses his letters in Σ_2, the word w that is obtained belongs to the language of A and $A(w) \geq 0$. We show that this problem is undecidable for Sum, Avg, and Ratio even when considering unambiguous automata (the case Dsum is left open). However, we show that the realizability problem is decidable for the deterministic versions of the automata studied in this paper. This motivates the *determinizability* problem.

The determinizability problem asks, given a functional weighted automaton A, if the quantitative language defined by A is also definable by a *deterministic* automaton. This problem has been solved for Sum, Avg in [17]. It is known that Dsum-automata are not determinizable in general [10]. We give here a decidable *necessary* and *sufficient* condition for the determinizability of functional weighted automata over a group, and we show how to construct a deterministic automaton from the functional one when this is possible. As a corollary, we obtain a decidable characterization of determinizable functional Sum-, Avg- and Dsum-automata. While it was known for Sum and Avg, it is new for Dsum.

Related Works. Motivated by open problems in computer-aided verification, our work follows the same line as [10]. However [10] is concerned with weighted automata on infinite words, either non-deterministic, for which some important problems are undecidable (e.g. inclusion of Avg-automata), or deterministic ones, which are strictly less expressive than functional automata. The Ratio measure is not considered either. Their domains of quantitative languages are assumed to be total (as all states are accepting and their transition relation is total) while we can define partial quantitative languages thanks to an acceptance condition.

Except for realizability, our results for Sum-automata (and to some extent Avg-automata) are not new. Functionality is known to be in PTime [17], and emptiness, inclusion, equivalence (for functional Sum-automata) are already known to be decidable [20,21]. Moreover, it is known that determinizability of functional Sum-automata is decidable in PTime [17], as well as for the strictly more expressive class of polynomially ambiguous Sum-automata [16], for which the termination of Mohri's determinization algorithm [13] is decidable. Weighted automata over semirings have been extensively studied [13], and more generally rational series [5]. Mohri's determinization algorithm has been generalized in [17] to arbitrary semirings, in which a general condition for its termination, called the twins property, is given. However, this sufficient condition only applies to commutative semirings, and therefore cannot directly be used for Dsum automata. However, our determinization algorithm for functional weighted automata over a group is similar to Mohri's algorithm and is, in that sense, not new. We rephrase the twinning property on groups that are not necessarily commutative and prove that it is a sufficient and necessary condition for a functional weighted automata over a group to be determinizable.

The techniques we use for deciding functionality and determinization are also inspired by techniques from word transducers [24,6,4,11,26]. In particular, our procedure to decide functionality of weighted automata also allows us to decide functionality of a word transducer, seen as a weighted automaton over the free group. It generalizes to arbitrary groups the procedure of [4] which was used to show that functionality of word transducers is in PTime. As in [4], it relies on a notion of delay between two runs. This notion of delay is also used for the determinization of weighted automata over a group.

In [9], Boker et. al. show that Dsum-automata on infinite words with a trivial accepting condition (all states are accepting), but not necessarily functional, are determinizable for any discount factor of the form $1/n$ for some $n \in \mathbb{N}_{\geq 2}$, while we consider arbitrary discounted factors. Their proof is based on a notion of *recoverable gap*, similar to that of delays. Finally in [14], the relation between discounted weighted automata over a semiring and weighted logics is studied.

To the best of our knowledge, our results on Dsum and Ratio-automata, as well as on the realizability problem, are new. Our main and most technical results are functionality and inclusion of Ratio-automata, undecidability of the realizability of unambiguous Sum-automata, and solvability of the deterministic versions of the realizability problem. The latter reduce to games on graphs that are to the best of our knowledge new, namely finite Sum, Avg, Dsum, Ratio-games on weighted graphs with a combination of a reachability objective and a quantitative objective.

2 Quantitative Languages and Functionality

Let Σ be a finite alphabet. We denote by Σ^+ the set of non-empty finite words over Σ. A *quantitative language* L over Σ is a mapping $L : \Sigma^+ \to \mathbb{Q} \cup \{\perp\}$[2]. For all $w \in \Sigma^+$, $L(w)$ is called the *value* of w. $L(w) = \perp$ means that the value of w is undefined. We set $\perp < v$ for all $v \in \mathbb{Q}$.

Let $n \geq 0$. Given a finite sequence $v = v_0 \dots v_n$ of integers (resp. a finite sequence $v' = (r_0, c_0) \dots (r_n, c_n)$ of pairs of natural numbers, $c_i > 0$ for all i) and $\lambda \in \mathbb{Q}$ such that $0 < \lambda < 1$, we define the following functions:

$$\mathsf{Sum}(v) = \sum_{i=0}^{n} v_i \quad \mathsf{Avg}(v) = \frac{\mathsf{Sum}(v)}{n+1} \quad \mathsf{Dsum}(v) = \sum_{i=0}^{n} \lambda^i v_i \quad \mathsf{Ratio}(v') = \frac{\sum_{i=0}^{n} r_i}{\sum_{i=0}^{n} c_i}$$

Weighted Automata. Let $V \in \{\mathsf{Sum}, \mathsf{Avg}, \mathsf{Dsum}, \mathsf{Ratio}\}$. A *weighted V-automaton* over Σ is a tuple $A = (Q, q_I, F, \delta, \gamma)$ where Q is a finite set of states, F is a set of final states,

[2] As in [10], we do not consider the empty word as our weighted automata do not have initial and final weight functions. This eases our presentation but all our results carry over to the more general setting with initial and final weight function [13].

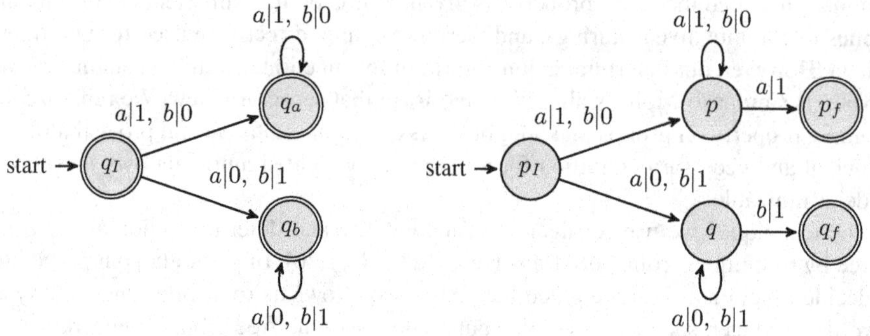

Fig. 1. Examples of Sum-automata

$\delta \subseteq Q \times \Sigma \times Q$ is the transition relation, and $\gamma : \delta \to \mathbb{Z}$ (resp. $\gamma : \delta \to \mathbb{N} \times (\mathbb{N} - 0)$ if V = Ratio) is a *weight function*. The size of A is defined by $|A| = |Q| + |\delta| + \sum_{t \in \delta} log_2(\gamma(t))$. Note that (Q, q_I, F, δ) is a classical finite state automaton. We say that A is *deterministic* (resp. unambiguous) if (Q, q_I, F, δ) is. In the sequel, we use the term V-automata to denote either Sum, Dsum, Avg or Ratio-automata.

A run ρ of A over a word $w = \sigma_0 \ldots \sigma_n \in \Sigma^+$ is a sequence $\rho = q_0\sigma_0 q_1 \sigma_1 \ldots \sigma_n q_{n+1}$ such that $q_0 = q_I$ and for all $i \in \{0, \ldots, n\}$, $(q_i, \sigma_i, q_{i+1}) \in \delta$. It is *accepting* if $q_{n+1} \in F$. We write $\rho : q_0 \xrightarrow{w} q_{n+1}$ to denote that ρ is a run on w starting at q_0 and ending in q_{n+1}. The domain of A, denoted by dom(A), is defined as the set of words $w \in \Sigma^+$ on which there exists some accepting run of A.

The function V is naturally extended to runs as follows:

$$V(\rho) = \begin{cases} V(\gamma(q_0, \sigma_0, q_1) \ldots \gamma(q_n, \sigma_n, q_{n+1})) & \text{if } \rho \text{ is accepting} \\ \bot & \text{otherwise} \end{cases}$$

The relation $R_A^V = \{(w, V(\rho)) \mid w \in \Sigma^+, \rho \text{ is an accepting run of } A \text{ on } w\}$ is called the *relation induced by* A. It is *functional* if for all words $w \in \Sigma^+$, we have $|\{v \mid (w, v) \in R_A^V,\ v \neq \bot\}| \leq 1$. In that case we say that A is functional. The *quantitative language* $L_A : \Sigma^+ \to \mathbb{Q} \cup \{\bot\}$ defined by A is defined by $L_A : w \mapsto \max\{v \mid (w, v) \in R_A^V\}$ where $\max \emptyset = \bot$.

Example 1. Fig. 1 illustrates two Sum-automata over the alphabet $\{a, b\}$. The first automaton (on the left) defines the quantitative language $w \in \Sigma^+ \mapsto \max(\#_a(w), \#_b(w))$, where $\#_\alpha(w)$ denotes the number of occurrences of the letter α in w. Its induced relation is $\{(w, \#_a(w)) \mid w \in \Sigma^+\} \cup \{(w, \#_b(w)) \mid w \in \Sigma^+\}$. The second automaton (on the right) defines the quantitative language that maps any word of length at least 2 to the number of occurrences of its last letter.

We say that a state q is *co-accessible* (resp. *accessible*) by some word $w \in \Sigma^*$ if there exists some run $\rho : q \xrightarrow{w} q_f$ for some $q_f \in F$ (resp. some run $\rho : q_I \xrightarrow{w} q$). If such a word exists, we say that q is co-accessible (resp. accessible). A pair of states (q, q') is co-accessible if there exists a word w such that q and q' are co-accessible by w.

Functional Weighted Automata. The Sum-automaton on the left of Fig. 1 is not functional (e.g. the word *abb* maps to the values 1 and 2), while the one of the right is functional (and even unambiguous). Concerning the expressiveness of functional automata, we can show that deterministic automata are strictly less expressive than functional automata which are again strictly less expressive than non-deterministic automata. Let $V \in \{\mathsf{Sum}, \mathsf{Avg}, \mathsf{Ratio}\}$. The automata of Fig. 1 can be seen as V-automata (with a constant cost 1 if $V = \mathsf{Ratio}$). The right V-automaton cannot be expressed by any deterministic V-automaton because the value of a word depends on its last letter. The left V-automaton cannot be expressed by any functional V-automaton. It is easy to verify that the above results hold also for Dsum-automata. Therefore, for the four measures that we consider, i.e. for $V \in \{\mathsf{Sum}, \mathsf{Avg}, \mathsf{Ratio}, \mathsf{Dsum}\}$, deterministic V-automata are strictly less expressive than functional V-automata which are again strictly less expressive than non-deterministic V-automata.

Functional V-automata are equally expressive as unambiguous V-automata (i.e. at most one accepting run per input word). However we inherit the succinctness property of non-deterministic finite state automata wrt unambiguous finite state automata, as a direct consequence functional V-automata are exponentially more succinct than unambiguous V-automata. Moreover, considering unambiguous V-automata does not simplify the proofs of our results neither lower the computational complexity of the verification and determinizability problems. Finally, testing functionality often relies on a notion of delay that gives strong insights that are useful for determinization procedures, and allows us to test equivalence of functional (and even unambiguous) Ratio-automata with a better complexity than using our results on inclusion.

3 Functionality Problem

In this section, we consider the problem of deciding whether a weighted automaton is functional. In particular, Subsection 3.1 provides a general functionality test applying to a broad class of weighted automata, where the edges are labelled by elements of a weight-set W, having the algebraic structure of a group $(W, \cdot, 1)$. A group is a structure $(S, \cdot, 1)$, where S is a set, $\cdot : S \times S \to S$ is an associative operation, $1 \in S$ is a two sided identity element for $\cdot$ over S, and each element $s \in S$ admits an inverse $s^{-1} \in S$, such that $s^{-1} \cdot s = s \cdot s^{-1} = 1$ (the inverse is unique). Given a run $\rho = q_0\sigma_0 q_1\sigma_1 \dots \sigma_n q_{n+1}$ of a weighted automaton $A = (Q, q_I, F, \delta, \gamma)$ over the weight-set group $(W, \cdot, 1)$, the value $V(\rho)$ is defined as $\perp$ if ρ is not accepting and as the product $\gamma(q_0, \sigma_0, q_1) \cdot \gamma(q_1, \sigma_1, q_2) \cdot \dots \cdot \gamma(q_n, \sigma_n, q_{n+1})$ otherwise. We often write $\rho : p \xrightarrow{w|v} q$ to denote a run from a state p to a state q on $w \in \Sigma^*$ such that the product of the weights along its transitions is v. We assume that the operations over group elements are computable in polynomial time in the size of their representation.

As shown in Remark 1 below, V-automata can be coded as weighted automata over groups, for each measure $V \in \{\mathsf{Sum}, \mathsf{Avg}, \mathsf{Dsum}\}$. Therefore, the functionality test for weighted automata over groups developed in Subsection 3.1 applies to V-automata, $V \in \{\mathsf{Sum}, \mathsf{Avg}, \mathsf{Dsum}\}$, and allows to extend known results on decidability of the functionality problem for Sum-automata [17] to Avg- and Dsum-automata.

Algorithm 1. Functionality test for weighted automata over a group.

Data: A weighted automaton $A = (Q, q_I, F, \delta, \gamma)$ over a group.
Result: Boolean certifying whether A is functional.

$\mathsf{CoAcc} \leftarrow$ all co-accessible pairs of states;
$\mathsf{visited} \leftarrow \emptyset$; $\mathsf{delay}(q_I, q_I) \leftarrow 1$; $\mathsf{PUSH}(S, ((q_I, q_I), (1, 1)))$;
while $S \neq \emptyset$ **do**
  $((p, q), (\alpha, \beta)) \leftarrow \mathsf{POP}(S)$;
  if $(p, q) \in F^2 \wedge \alpha \cdot \beta^{-1} \neq 1$ **then returns** No;
  if $(p, q) \in \mathsf{visited}$ **then**
    if $\mathsf{delay}(p, q) \neq \alpha \cdot \beta^{-1}$ **then returns** No
  else
    $\mathsf{visited} \leftarrow \mathsf{visited} \cup \{(p, q)\}$; $\mathsf{delay}(p, q) \leftarrow \alpha \cdot \beta^{-1}$;
    foreach $(p', q') \in \mathsf{CoAcc}$ *s.t.* $\exists a \in \Sigma \cdot (p, a, p') \in \delta \wedge (q, a, q') \in \delta$ **do**
      $\mathsf{PUSH}(S, ((p', q'), (\alpha \cdot \gamma(p, a, p'), \beta \cdot \gamma(q, a, q'))))$;
return Yes

Remark 1. We show that V-automata, $V \in \{\mathsf{Sum}, \mathsf{Avg}, \mathsf{Dsum}\}$, can be seen as weighted automata over groups. Sum-automata are associated with the group $(\mathbb{Z}, +, 0)$.

For Avg-automata, consider the group $(\mathbb{Z}^2, \cdot, (0, 0))$, where $\cdot$ is the pairwise sum. An Avg-automaton A can be seen as a weighted automaton on $(\mathbb{Z}^2, \cdot, (0, 0))$, by replacing each weight v in A with the pair $(v, 1)$. Then, each run $\rho = (q_0, w_0, q_1) \dots (q_n, w_n, q_{n+1})$ gets valued $V(\rho) = (\sum_{i=0}^{n} \gamma(q_i, w_i, q_{i+1}), n + 1)$ coding $\mathsf{Avg}(\rho) = \frac{\sum_{i=0}^{n} \gamma(q_i, w_i, q_{i+1})}{n+1}$.

For Dsum-automata, consider the group $(W, \cdot, 1)$, where $W = \mathbb{Q}^2$, $\cdot$ is defined by $(a, x) \cdot (b, y) = (\frac{1}{y}a + b, xy)$, $(0, 1)$ is the identity element, and given $(a, x) \in W$, the inverse $(a, x)^{-1}$ is given by $(a, x)^{-1} = (-xa, x^{-1})$. Given $\lambda \in \mathbb{Q} \cap]0, 1[$, a Dsum-automaton A on Σ can be seen as a weighted automaton on $(W, \cdot, 1)$, by replacing each weight a in A with the pair (a, λ), $a \in \mathbb{Z}$. Let $w = w_0 \dots w_n \in \Sigma$, and consider a run $\rho : q_0 \xrightarrow{w} q_{n+1}$ on w in A. Then, ρ is valued by the pair $(a, x) = (\frac{1}{\lambda^n}\gamma(q_0, w_0, q_1) + \dots + \gamma(q_n, w_n, q_{n+1}), \lambda^{n+1})$. Hence, (a, x) codes the value $\frac{ax}{\lambda} = \mathsf{Dsum}(\rho)$.

We also prove that functionality is decidable for Ratio-automata. However it is open if they can be encoded in terms of weighted automata over a group (see Section 3.2).

3.1 Functionality of Weighted Automata over a Group

We start to introduce the notion of *delay* between two runs in a given weighted automaton over a group weight-set $(W, \cdot, 1)$, which turns out to be the main ingredient of the functionality algorithm in Figure 1.

Definition 1 (Delay). *Let $A = (Q, q_I, F, \delta, \gamma)$ be a weighted automaton over a weight-set group $(W, \cdot, 1)$ and let $p, q \in Q$. A value $d \in W$ is a* delay *for (p, q) if A admits two runs $\rho : q_I \xrightarrow{w} p$, $\rho' : q_I \xrightarrow{w} q$ on $w \in \Sigma^*$ s.t.* $\mathsf{delay}(\rho, \rho') =_{def} (V(\rho))^{-1} \cdot V(\rho') = d$.

The following lemma shows that at most one delay can be associated with co-accessible pairs of states in a functional weighted automaton over a weight-set group $(W, \cdot, 1)$. This is related to the uniqueness of inverse elements.

Lemma 1 (One Delay). *Let $A = (Q, q_I, F, \delta, \gamma)$ be a functional weighted automaton over a weight-set group $(W, \cdot, 1)$. For all pairs of states (p, q): If (p, q) is co-accessible, then (p, q) admits at most one delay.*

We are now ready to define an algorithm (Algorithm 1) that checks the functionality of a weighted automaton over a weight-set group $(W\cdot, 1)$. In a first step, such a procedure computes all co-accessible pairs of states. Then, it explores the set of accessible pairs of states in a forward manner and computes the delays associated with those pairs. If two different delays are associated with the same pair, or if a pair of final states with a delay different from 1 (the neutral element of the group) is reached, the test stops and returns that the automaton is not functional (by Lemma 1 and by definition of functionality). Otherwise, it goes on until all co-accessible (and accessible) pairs have been visited and concludes that the automaton is functional.

If the algorithm returns NO, it is either because a pair of accepting states with non-1 delay has been reached, which gives a counter-example to functionality, or because a pair of states with different delays has been found, so A is not functional by Lemma 1.

To establish the converse, we need the following lemma, which says that when A is not functional, it admits two accepting runs witnessing non-functionality (i.e. on the same word w and with different values) satisfying that any pair of states that repeats twice has two different delays.

Lemma 2. *Let $A{=}(Q, q_I, F, \delta, \gamma)$ be a weighted automaton over a weight-set group $(W, \cdot, 1)$. If A is not functional, there exists a word $w{=}\sigma_0 \dots \sigma_n$ and two accepting runs $\rho{=}q_0\sigma_0 \dots q_{n+1}, \rho'{=}q'_0\sigma_0 \dots q'_{n+1}$ on it such that $V(\rho) \neq V(\rho')$ and for all positions $i < j$ in w, if $(p_i, q_i){=}(p_j, q_j)$ then $\mathsf{delay}(\rho_i, \rho'_i){\neq}\mathsf{delay}(\rho_j, \rho'_j)$, where ρ_i and ρ'_i (resp. ρ_j and ρ'_j) denote the prefixes of the runs ρ and ρ' until position i (resp. position j).*

If there are two runs witnessing non-functionality without repetitions of pairs of states, the algorithm can find a pair of final states with a non-1 delay. Otherwise the algorithm will return NO at line 6, if not before. Therefore we get:

Theorem 1. *Let $A = (Q, q_I, F, \delta, \gamma)$ be a weighted automaton over a weight-set group. Algorithm 1 returns* YES *on A iff A is functional and terminates within $O(|A|^2)$ steps.*

Remark 2. Functionality of Sum-automata have been shown decidable in [17]. Our functionality algorithm on weighted automata over groups specialized for Sum-automata corresponds to the functionality algorithm for Sum-automata defined in [17]. Algorithm 1 can also be applied to word transducers for which functionality have been shown decidable in PTIME with similar techniques in [4].

Corollary 1. *Functionality is decidable in* PTime *for V-automata, $V \in \{\mathsf{Avg}, \mathsf{Dsum}\}$.*

Remark 3. Our functionality test can be applied to a more general framework, where functionality is defined modulo an equivalence relation $\sim_W$ (instead of equality) over the values of the weighted automata (on groups). In particular, $\sim_W$ needs to fullfill the following properties to be able to show uniqueness of the delay (modulo $\sim_W$) and termination of the functionality test: (1) it is a *congruence*, i.e. $\forall a, b, c, d \in W$ if $a \sim_W b$ and $c \sim_W d$, then $a \cdot c \sim_W b \cdot d$; (2) for all $a, b, c \in W$ if $a \not\sim_W b$ then $a \cdot c \not\sim_W b \cdot c$.

3.2 Functionality of Ratio-automata

Unlike Sum, Avg and Dsum-automata, it is unclear whether Ratio-automata can be encoded in term of weighted automata over a group. Intuitively, to provide such an encoding we would assign to each edge a pair of natural numbers, where the first component is the reward and the second component is the cost. Thus, each run ρ is assigned the value (n, m), where n (resp. m) is the sum of the rewards (resp. costs) along the run, and two runs ρ, ρ' with values $(n, m), (n', m')$ need to be considered equivalent iff $nm' = n'm$. Unfortunately, the induced equivalence relation (where (n, m) is equivalent to (n', m') iff $nm' = n'm$) is not a congruence. Therefore, the results developed in the previous subsection do not apply to this class of weighted automata (at least to this encoding) as the quotient of the set of pairs by this equivalence relation is not a group (cfr. Remark 3). In fact, it is still open whether there exists a good notion of delay for Ratio-automata that would allow us to design an efficient algorithm to test functionality. However deciding functionality can be done by using a short witness property:

Lemma 3 (Pumping). *Let A be a* Ratio*-automaton with n states. A is not functional iff there exist $w \in \Sigma^+$ s.t. $|w|<4n^2$ and two accepting runs ρ, ρ' on w s.t.* $\mathsf{Ratio}(\rho) \neq \mathsf{Ratio}(\rho')$.

Proof. We prove the existence of a short witness for non-functionality. The other direction is obvious. Let w be a word such that $|w| \geq 4n^2$ and there exists two accepting runs ρ_1, ρ_2 on w such that $\mathsf{Ratio}(\rho) \neq \mathsf{Ratio}(\rho')$. Since $|w| \geq 4n^2$, there exist states $p, q \in Q, p_f, q_f \in F$ and words w_0, w_1, w_2, w_3, w_4 such that $w = w_0w_1w_2w_3w_4$ and ρ, ρ' can be decomposed as follows:

$$\rho : q_I \xrightarrow{w_0|(r_0,c_0)} p \xrightarrow{w_1|(r_1,c_1)} p \xrightarrow{w_2|(r_2,c_2)} p \xrightarrow{w_3|(r_3,c_3)} p \xrightarrow{w_4|(r_4,c_4)} p_f$$
$$\rho' : q_I \xrightarrow{w_0|(r_0',c_0')} q \xrightarrow{w_1|(r_1',c_1')} q \xrightarrow{w_2|(r_2',c_2')} q \xrightarrow{w_3|(r_3',c_3')} q \xrightarrow{w_4|(r_4',c_4')} q_f$$

where r_i, c_i denotes the sum of the rewards and the costs respectively on the subruns of ρ on w_i, and similarly for r_i', c_i'.

By hypothesis we know that $(\sum_{i=0}^4 r_i) \cdot (\sum_{i=0}^4 c_i') \neq (\sum_{i=0}^4 c_i) \cdot (\sum_{i=0}^4 r_i')$. For all subsets $X \subseteq \{1, 2, 3\}$, we denote by w_X the word $w_0 w_{i_1} \dots w_{i_k} w_4$ if $X = \{i_1 < \dots < i_k\}$. For instance, $w_{\{1,2,3\}} = w$, $w_{\{1\}} = w_0w_1w_4$ and $w_{\{\}} = w_0w_4$. Similarly, we denote by ρ_X, ρ_X' the corresponding runs on w_X. We will show that there exists $X \subsetneq \{1, 2, 3\}$ such that $\mathsf{Ratio}(\rho_X) \neq \mathsf{Ratio}(\rho_X')$. Suppose that for all $X \subsetneq \{1, 2, 3\}$, we have $\mathsf{Ratio}(\rho_X) = \mathsf{Ratio}(\rho_X')$. We now show that it implies that $\mathsf{Ratio}(\rho) = \mathsf{Ratio}(\rho')$, which contradicts the hypothesis. For all $X \subseteq \{1, 2, 3\}$, we let:

$$L_X = \Big(\sum_{i \in X \cup \{0,4\}} r_i\Big) \cdot \Big(\sum_{i \in X \cup \{0,4\}} c_i'\Big) \qquad R_X = \Big(\sum_{i \in X \cup \{0,4\}} c_i\Big) \cdot \Big(\sum_{i \in X \cup \{0,4\}} r_i'\Big)$$

By hypothesis, $L_{\{1,2,3\}} \neq R_{\{1,2,3\}}$ and for all $X \subsetneq \{1, 2, 3\}, L_X = R_X$. The following equalities can be easily verified:

$$L_{\{\}} + L_{\{1,2\}} + L_{\{1,3\}} + L_{\{2,3\}} - L_{\{1\}} - L_{\{2\}} - L_{\{3\}} = L_{\{1,2,3\}}$$
$$R_{\{\}} + R_{\{1,2\}} + R_{\{1,3\}} + R_{\{2,3\}} - R_{\{1\}} - R_{\{2\}} - R_{\{3\}} = R_{\{1,2,3\}}$$

Then, since by hypothesis we have $L_X = R_X$ for all $X \subsetneq \{1,2,3\}$, we get $L_{\{1,2,3\}} = R_{\{1,2,3\}}$, which is a contradiction. Thus there exists $X \subsetneq \{1,2,3\}$ such that $L_X \neq R_X$. In other words, there exists $X \subsetneq \{1,2,3\}$ such that $\mathsf{Ratio}(\rho_X) \neq \mathsf{Ratio}(\rho'_X)$. This shows that when a witness of non-functionality has length at least $4n^2$, we can find a strictly smaller witness of functionality. □

As a consequence, we can design an NP procedure that will check non-functionality by guessing runs of length at most $4n^2$, where n is the number of states:

Theorem 2. *Functionality is decidable in* CoNP *for* Ratio-*automata.*

4 Verification Problems

In this section, we investigate several decision problems for functional V-automata as defined in [10], $V \in \{\mathsf{Sum}, \mathsf{Avg}, \mathsf{Dsum}, \mathsf{Ratio}\}$. Given two V-automata A, B over Σ (and with the same discount factor when $V = \mathsf{Dsum}$) and a threshold $\nu \in \mathbb{Q}$, we define the following decision problems, where $\triangleright \in \{>, \geq\}$:

$\triangleright\nu$-Emptiness	$L_A^{\triangleright\nu} \neq \varnothing$	holds if there exists $w \in \Sigma^+$ such that $L_A(w) \triangleright \nu$
$\triangleright\nu$-Universality	$L_A \triangleright \nu$	holds if for all $w \in \mathrm{dom}(A)$, $L_A(w) \triangleright \nu$.
Inclusion	$L_A \leq L_B$	holds if for all $w \in \Sigma^+$, $L_A(w) \leq L_B(w)$
Equivalence	$L_A = L_B$	holds if for all $w \in \Sigma^+$, $L_A(w) = L_B(w)$

Theorem 3. *Let $\nu \in \mathbb{Q}$. The $>\nu$-emptiness (resp. $\geq\nu$-emptiness) problem is in* PTime *for* Sum-, Avg-, Ratio-, *and* Dsum-*automata (resp.* Sum-, Avg-, *and* Ratio-*automata).*

Proof. For Sum-automata, let A be a Sum-automaton. Wlog we assume that all states of A are both accessible from an initial state and co-accessible from a final state (such property can be ensured via a PTime transformation). First, $L_A^{\triangleright\nu} \neq \varnothing$ if A contains a strictly positive cycle, otherwise one inverts the weights and computes a shortest path from an initial to a final state. If the sum β of such a path satisfies $-\nu \triangleright \beta$ then the language is non-empty. Both steps are handled by the classical Bellman-Ford algorithm.

For Avg-automata, let A be an Avg-automaton. We can assume $\nu = 0$ since the $\triangleright\nu$-emptiness problem for Avg-automata reduces to the $\triangleright 0$-emptiness problem for Sum-automata, by simply reweighting the input automaton. $L_A^{\triangleright 0} \neq \emptyset$ iff A admits a path to a final state whose sum of the weights is $\triangleright 0$, that can be easily checked in PTime.

For Dsum, we reduce the problem to deciding whether there exists an infinite path with strictly positive discounted sum in a weighted graph, which is known to be decidable in PTime [3]. The graph is obtained by removing non co-accessible states from the automaton and by adding 0 cost loops on final states. If the language is non-empty, there exists a strictly positive path in the graph to a final state that can be extended into an infinite strictly positive path due to added loops. Conversely, suppose that there exists a strictly positive infinite path in the graph. From any state in this path, we can reach a final state in a bounded number of steps (at most n if the automaton has n states). By playing a sufficiently long prefix of this infinite path we ensure that the discounted sum remains stricly positive if one deviates, in order to reach a final state.

Finally, let A be a Ratio-automaton, let $\nu = m/n$. We consider the Sum automaton A', where each edge of A having reward r and cost c is replaced by an edge of weight $rn - cm$. It can be easily proved that $L_A^{\rhd\nu} \neq \emptyset$ iff $L_{A'}^{\rhd\nu} \neq \emptyset$. □

It is open how to decide $\geq \nu$ for Dsum-automata. Dually:

Theorem 4. *Let $\nu \in \mathbb{Q}$. The $\geq\nu$-universality (resp. $>\nu$-universality) problem is* PTime *for* Sum-, Avg-, Ratio-, *and* Dsum-*automata (resp.* Sum-, Avg-, *and* Ratio-*automata).*

It is known that inclusion is undecidable for non-deterministic Sum-automata [19,1], and therefore also for Avg and Ratio-automata. To the best of our knowledge, it is open whether it is decidable for Dsum-automata. This situation is strikingly different for functional automata as the inclusion problem is decidable for all the measures:

Theorem 5. *Let $V \in \{\mathsf{Sum}, \mathsf{Avg}, \mathsf{Dsum}, \mathsf{Ratio}\}$ and let A, B be two V-automata with B functional. The inclusion problem $L_A \leq L_B$ is decidable. If $V \in \{\mathsf{Sum}, \mathsf{Avg}, \mathsf{Dsum}\}$ then it is* PSpace-c *and if additionally B is deterministic, it is in* PTime.

Proof. Let $V \in \{\mathsf{Sum}, \mathsf{Avg}, \mathsf{Dsum}\}$. In a first step, we test the inclusion of the domains $\mathrm{dom}(A) \subseteq \mathrm{dom}(B)$ (it is well-known from theory of finite automata to be in PSpace-c and in PTime if B is deterministic). Then we construct the product $A \times B$ as follows: $(p, q) \xrightarrow{a|n_A - n_B} (p', q') \in \delta_{A\times B}$ iff $p \xrightarrow{a|n_A} p' \in \delta_A$ and $q \xrightarrow{a|n_B} q' \in \delta_B$. Then $L_A \not\leq L_B$ iff $L_{A\times B}^{>0} \neq \varnothing$, which is decidable by Theorem 3.

Let $V =$ Ratio. As for the other measures we first check inclusion of the domains. We then define the product $A\times B$ of A and B as follows: $(p, q) \xrightarrow{a|(r_1,c_1,r_2,c_2)} (p', q') \in \delta_{A\times B}$ iff $p \xrightarrow{a|(r_1,c_1)} p' \in \delta_A$ and $q \xrightarrow{a|(r_2,c_2)} q' \in \delta_B$. For all $t \in \delta_{A\times B}$, we let $r_A(t)$ be the reward of the transition t projected on A. The values $c_A(t), r_B(t)$ and $c_B(t)$ are defined similarly. We let $F(A \times B)$ be the Parikh image of the transitions of $A \times B$, i.e. the set of total functions $\alpha : \delta_{A\times B} \to \mathbb{N}$ such that there exists $w \in \Sigma^+$ and an accepting run ρ of $A \times B$ on w that passes by t exactly $\alpha(t)$ times, for all $t \in \delta_{A\times B}$. It is well-known by Parikh's theorem that $F(A \times B)$ can be effectively represented by a set of linear constraints. We now define the set of vectors Γ that are the Parikh images of accepting runs of $A\times B$ which, when projected on A, has a strictly bigger ratio value than the one obtained by the projection on B.

$$\Gamma = \{\alpha : \delta_{A\times B} \to \mathbb{N} \mid \alpha \in F(A\times B), \frac{\sum_{t\in\delta_{A\times B}} \alpha(t).r_A(t)}{\sum_{t\in\delta_{A\times B}} \alpha(t).c_B(t)} > \frac{\sum_{t\in\delta_{A\times B}} \alpha(t).r_B(t)}{\sum_{t\in\delta_{A\times B}} \alpha(t).c_A(t)}\}$$

It is easy to check that $\Gamma \neq \varnothing$ iff $L_A \not\leq L_B$. The set Γ can be defined as the solutions over natural numbers of a system of equations in linear and quadratic forms (i.e. in which products of two variables are permitted). There is one variable x_t for each $t \in \delta_{A\times B}$ that gives the number of times t is fired in an accepting run of $A \times B$. It is decidable whether such a system has a solution [27,15]. □

There is no known complexity bound for solving quadratic equations, so the proof above does not give us a complexity bound for the inclusion problem of functional Ratio-automata. However, thanks to the functionality test, which is in PSpace for Ratio-automata, we can test equivalence of two functional Ratio-automata A_1 and A_2 in

PSpace: first check in PSpace that $\text{dom}(A_1) = \text{dom}(A_2)$ and check that the union of A_1 and A_2 is functional. This algorithm can also be used for the other measures:

Theorem 6. *Let* $V \in \{\mathsf{Sum}, \mathsf{Avg}, \mathsf{Dsum}, \mathsf{Ratio}\}$. *Equivalence of functional* V*-automata is* PSpace-c.

5 Realizability Problem

In this section, we consider the problem of *quantitative language realizability*. The realizability problem is better understood as a game between two players: the 'Player input' (the environment, also called Player I) and the 'Player output' (the controller, also called Player O). Player I (resp. Player O) controls the letters of a finite alphabet Σ_I (resp. Σ_O). We assume that $\Sigma_O \cap \Sigma_I = \varnothing$ and that Σ_O contains a special symbol $\#$ whose role is to stop the game. We let $\Sigma = \Sigma_O \cup \Sigma_I$.

Formally, the realizability game is a turn-based game played on an arena defined by a weighted automaton $A{=}(Q{=}Q_O \uplus Q_I, q_0, F, \delta{=}\delta_I \cup \delta_O, \gamma)$, whose set of states is partitioned into two sets Q_O and Q_I, $\delta_O{\subseteq}Q_O{\times}\Sigma_O{\times}Q_I$, $\delta_I{\subseteq}Q_I{\times}\Sigma_I{\times}Q_O$, and such that $\text{dom}(A){\subseteq}(\Sigma\backslash\{\#\})^*\#$. Player O starts by giving an initial letter $o_0 \in \Sigma_O$, Player I responds providing a letter $i_0 \in \Sigma_I$, then Player O gives o_1 and Player I responds i_1, and so on. Player O has also the power to stop the game at any turn with the distinguishing symbol $\#$. In this case, the game results in a finite word $(o_0 i_0)(o_1 i_1)\dots(o_j i_j)\# \in \Sigma^*$, otherwise the outcome of the game is an infinite word $(o_0 i_0)(o_1 i_1)\dots \in \Sigma^\omega$.

The players play according to strategies. A strategy for Player O (resp. Player I) is a mapping $\lambda_O : (\Sigma_O \Sigma_I)^* \to \Sigma_O$ (resp. $\lambda_I : \Sigma_O(\Sigma_I \Sigma_O)^* \to \Sigma_I$). The outcome of the strategies λ_O, λ_I is the word $w = o_0 i_0 o_1 i_1 \dots$ denoted by $\mathsf{outcome}(\lambda_O, \lambda_I)$ such that for all $0 \leq j \leq |w|$ (where $|w| = +\infty$ if w is infinite), $o_j = \lambda_O(o_0 i_0 \dots i_{j-1})$ and $i_j = \lambda(o_0 i_0 \dots o_j)$, and such that if $\# = o_j$ for some j, then $w = o_0 i_0 \dots o_j$. We denote by Λ_O (resp. Λ_I) the set of strategies for Player O (resp. Player I).

A strategy $\lambda_O \in \Lambda_O$ is winning for Player O if for all $\lambda_I \in \Lambda_I$, $\mathsf{outcome}(\lambda_O, \lambda_I)$ is finite and $L_A(\mathsf{outcome}(\lambda_O, \lambda_I)) > 0$. The *quantitative language realizability problem* for the weighted automaton A asks whether Player O has a winning strategy and in that case, we say that A is *realizable*. Our first result on realizability is negative: we show that it is undecidable for weighted functional Sum-, Avg-automata, and Ratio-automata. In particular, we show that the halting problem for deterministic 2-counter Minsky machines [22] can be reduced to the quantitative language realizability problem for (functional) Sum-automata (resp. Avg-automata).

Theorem 7. *Let* $V \in \{\mathsf{Sum}, \mathsf{Avg}, \mathsf{Ratio}\}$. *The realizability problem for functional* V*-automata is undecidable.*

The proof of Theorem 7 relies on the use of a nondeterminism. When the automata are deterministic, we recover decidability by considering suitable variants of classical games played on graphs, and prove that they are solvable in $\mathsf{NP} \cap \mathsf{coNP}$.

Theorem 8. *Let* $V \in \{\mathsf{Sum}, \mathsf{Avg}, \mathsf{Dsum}, \mathsf{Ratio}\}$. *The realizability problem for deterministic* V*-automata is in* $\mathsf{NP} \cap \mathsf{coNP}$.

6 Determinizability Problem

A weighted automaton $A = (Q, q_I, F, \delta, \gamma)$ is *determinizable* if it is effectively equivalent to a deterministic automaton[3]. Weighted automata are not determinizable in general. For example, consider the right automaton on Fig. 1. Seen as a Sum, Avg or Dsum-automaton (for any λ), it cannot be determinized, because there are infinitely many delays associated with the pair of states (p, q). Those delays can for instance be obtained by the family of words of the form a^n. To ease notations, for all weighted automaton A over an alphabet Σ, we assume that there exists a special ending symbol $\# \in \Sigma$ such that any word $w \in \mathrm{dom}(A)$ is of the form $w'\#$ with $w' \in (\Sigma - \#)^*$.

Determinizability is already known to be decidable in PTime for functional Sum-automata [17][4]. Determinizable functional Sum-automata are characterized by the so called *twinning property*, that has been introduced for finite word transducers [11]. It has been used as a sufficient condition for the termination of Mohri's determinization algorithm [13] for (non-functional) weighted automata over the tropical semiring, and as a sufficient condition for the termination of a determinization algorithm for more general commutative semirings [17] (the commutativity hypothesis is necessary). However in this paper, we consider group weight-set that are not necessarily abelian.

As for functionality, we express our results for groups, and get as a corollary the decidability of determinizability for Sum, Avg and Dsum-automata. In particular, we give a general determinization procedure for a functional weighted automaton over a group, and introduce a twinning property that is a sufficient condition of its termination. The procedure is similar to the one of [13] but adapted to groups.

Determinization Procedure. First, we define a determinization procedure that constructs a deterministic automaton $A_d = (Q_d, f_d, F_d, \delta_d, \gamma_d)$ (which may have infinitely many states) from a functional automaton $A = (Q, q_I, F, \delta, \gamma)$ over a weight-set group $(W, \cdot, 1)$. Wlog we assume that all states of A are co-accessible (otherwise we can remove non co-accessible states in linear time) and that δ is totally ordered by some order $\preceq_\delta$. The procedure extends the subset construction to partial functions that associate a delay with a state. At any step, a particular transition of A is chosen and the delays are computed relatively to this transition. We use $\preceq_\delta$ to choose this particular transition, so different orders $\preceq_\delta$ may give different deterministic automata.

We let $\mathcal{D}$ the set of delays $\mathsf{delay}(\rho, \rho')$ for any two runs ρ, ρ' on the same word. We first define $Q' = \mathcal{D}^Q$, the set of partial functions from states Q to delays.We let $f'_I : q_I \mapsto 1$ and F' is defined as $\{f \in Q' \mid \mathrm{dom}(f) \cap F \neq \varnothing\}$. Then, given partial functions $f, f' \in Q'$ and a symbol $a \in \Sigma$, we let t_0 be the smallest transition (for $\preceq_\delta$) from a state $q \in dom(f)$ to a state $q' \in dom(f')$ on a, and we let $\gamma'(f, a, f') = f(q) \cdot \gamma(t_0)$ and $(f, a, f') \in \delta'$ iff for all $q' \in \mathrm{dom}(f')$ there exists $q \in \mathrm{dom}(f)$ such that $(q, a, q') \in \delta$

$$f'(q') = \gamma'(f, a, f')^{-1} \cdot f(p) \cdot \gamma(q, a, q')$$

Let $Q_d \subseteq Q'$ be the accessible states of $A' := (Q', f'_I, F', \delta', \gamma')$. We define $A_d = (Q_d, f_d, \delta_d, \gamma_d)$ as the restriction of A' to the accessible states.

The automaton A_d may be infinite, however it is equivalent to A.

[3] With the existence of an ending symbol, the notion of determinizability corresponds to the notion of subsequentializability [11].

[4] See [18,16] for determinizability results on more general classes of Sum-automata.

Lemma 4. *For all $w \in \Sigma^+$, $L_A(w) = L_{A_d}(w)$.*

Proof. First note that since all states of A are co-accessible and A is functional, if two runs ρ and ρ' over the same input word reach the same state, they have the same value. Next, it is not difficult to show by induction on the length of the input words that if a run of A_d over some word u reaches a state f, then for all states $q \in dom(f)$, $f(q) = \mathsf{delay}(\rho, \rho')$ for any run ρ of A on u that reaches q and any run ρ' on u that reaches some state p such that $f(p) = 1$ (such a state p necessarily exists by construction of A'). Moreover, the value of the run of A_d on u equals the value of any run on u that reaches some state p such that $f(p) = 1$. Finally, since we assume that the words accepted by A all terminate by a unique occurrence of a special symbol # and all states of A are co-accessible, when reading #, A_d necessarily go to a state f such that $f(p) = 1$ for all states $p \in dom(f)$, otherwise A would not be functional. □

We define a twinning property that is sufficient for A_d to be finite:

Definition 2. *Two states p, q of A are twinned if both p and q are co-accessible and for all words $w_1, w_2 \in \Sigma^*$, for all runs $\rho_1 : q_I \xrightarrow{w_1} p$, $\rho_2 : p \xrightarrow{w_2} p$, $\rho_1' : q_I \xrightarrow{w_1} q$, $\rho_2' : q \xrightarrow{w_2} q$, we have $\mathsf{delay}(\rho_1, \rho_1') = \mathsf{delay}(\rho_1\rho_2, \rho_1'\rho_2')$. The automaton A satisfies the twinning property if all pairs of states are twinned.*

Lemma 5. *If A satisfies the twinning property, then there are at most $|\Sigma|^{|Q|^2}$ delays $\mathsf{delay}(\rho, \rho')$ for any two runs ρ, ρ' on the same input, and thus A_d is finite.*

Lemma 6. *It is decidable in* CoNP *whether A satisfies the twinning property.*

Under some condition (called the *infinitary condition*), the twinning property is also a necessary condition. The infinitary condition expresses that iterating two runs on a parallel loop induce infinitely many delays: if we take the premisses of the twinning property, then we require that if $\mathsf{delay}(\rho_1, \rho_1') \neq \mathsf{delay}(\rho_1\rho_2, \rho_1'\rho_2')$ then for all $1 \leq i < j$, we have $\mathsf{delay}(\rho_1(\rho_2)^i, \rho_1'(\rho_2')^i) \neq \mathsf{delay}(\rho_1(\rho_2)^j, \rho_1'(\rho_2')^j)$.

Lemma 7. *If the twinning property does not hold and A satisfies the infinitary condition, then A is not determinizable.*

It is not difficult to show that Sum-, Avg- and Dsum-automata satisfy the infinitary condition, therefore:

Theorem 9. *A functional* Dsum- *(resp.* Sum-, Avg-*) automaton is determinizable iff it satisfies the twinning property. Therefore determinizability is decidable in* CoNP *for functional* Dsum- *(resp.* Sum-, Avg-*) automata.*

References

1. Almagor, S., Boker, U., Kupferman, O.: What's Decidable about Weighted Automata? In: Bultan, T., Hsiung, P.-A. (eds.) ATVA 2011. LNCS, vol. 6996, pp. 482–491. Springer, Heidelberg (2011)
2. Aminof, B., Kupferman, O., Lampert, R.: Rigorous approximated determinization of weighted automata. In: LICS, pp. 345–354 (2011)

3. Andersson, D.: An improved algorithm for discounted payoff games. In: ESSLLI Student Session, pp. 91–98 (2006)
4. Beal, M.-P., Carton, O., Prieur, C., Sakarovitch, J.: Squaring transducers: An efficient procedure for deciding functionality and sequentiality. TCS 292 (2003)
5. Berstel, J., Reutenauer, C.: Rational Series and Their Languages. EATCS Monographs on TCS, vol. 12. Springer (1988)
6. Blattner, M., Head, T.: Single-valued a-transducers. JCSS 15(3), 310–327 (1977)
7. Bloem, R., Greimel, K., Henzinger, T.A., Jobstmann, B.: Synthesizing robust systems. In: FMCAD, pp. 85–92. IEEE (2009)
8. Boker, U., Chatterjee, K., Henzinger, T.A., Kupferman, O.: Temporal specifications with accumulative values. In: LICS, pp. 43–52 (2011)
9. Boker, U., Henzinger, T.A.: Determinizing discounted-sum automata. In: CSL, pp. 82–96 (2011)
10. Chatterjee, K., Doyen, L., Henzinger, T.A.: Quantitative languages. ACM Trans. Comput. Log 11(4) (2010)
11. Choffrut, C.: Une caractérisation des fonctions séquentielles et des fonctions sous-séquentielles en tant que relations rationnelles. TCS 5(3), 325–337 (1977)
12. de Alfaro, L., Faella, M., Henzinger, T.A., Majumdar, R., Stoelinga, M.: Model checking discounted temporal properties. TCS 345(1), 139–170 (2005)
13. Droste, M., Kuich, W., Vogler, H.: Handbook of Weighted Automata. Springer (2009)
14. Droste, M., Rahonis, G.: Weighted automata and weighted logics with discounting. Theor. Comput. Sci. 410(37), 3481–3494 (2009) ISSN: 0304-3975
15. Grunewald, F., Segal, D.: On the integer solutions of quadratic equations. Journal für die reine und angewandte Mathematik 569, 13–45 (2004)
16. Kirsten, D.: A burnside approach to the termination of mohri's algorithm for polynomially ambiguous min-plus-automata. ITA 42(3), 553–581 (2008)
17. Kirsten, D., Mäurer, I.: On the determinization of weighted automata. Journal of Automata, Languages and Combinatorics 10(2/3), 287–312 (2005)
18. Klimann, I., Lombardy, S., Mairesse, J., Prieur, C.: Deciding unambiguity and sequentiality from a finitely ambiguous max-plus automaton. TCS 327(3), 349–373 (2004)
19. Krob, D.: The equality problem for rational series with multiplicities in the tropical semiring is undecidable. Journal of Algebra and Computation 4(3), 405–425 (1994)
20. Krob, D., Litp, P.: Some consequences of a fatou property of the tropical semiring. J. Pure Appl. Algebra 93, 231–249 (1994)
21. Lombardy, S., Mairesse, J.: Series which are both max-plus and min-plus rational are unambiguous. ITA 40(1), 1–14 (2006)
22. Minsky, M.L.: Computation: Finite and Infinite Machines. Prentice-Hall (1967)
23. Pnueli, A., Rosner, R.: On the synthesis of a reactive module. In: ACM Symposium on Principles of Programming Languages (POPL). ACM (1989)
24. Schützenberger, M.P.: Sur Les Relations Rationnelles. In: Brakhage, H. (ed.) GI-Fachtagung 1975. LNCS, vol. 33, pp. 209–213. Springer, Heidelberg (1975)
25. Thomas, W.: Church's Problem and a Tour through Automata Theory. In: Avron, A., Dershowitz, N., Rabinovich, A. (eds.) Trakhtenbrot/Festschrift. LNCS, vol. 4800, pp. 635–655. Springer, Heidelberg (2008)
26. Weber, A., Klemm, R.: Economy of description for single-valued transducers. Inf. Comput. 118(2), 327–340 (1995)
27. Karianto, W., Krieg, A., Thomas, W.: On Intersection Problems for Polynomially Generated Sets. In: Bugliesi, M., Preneel, B., Sassone, V., Wegener, I. (eds.) ICALP 2006. LNCS, vol. 4052, pp. 516–527. Springer, Heidelberg (2006)

A Comparison of Succinctly Represented Finite-State Systems*

Romain Brenguier[1], Stefan Göller[2], and Ocan Sankur[1]

[1] LSV, CNRS & ENS Cachan, France
[2] Institut für Informatik, Universität Bremen, Germany

Abstract. We study the succinctness of different classes of succinctly presented finite transition systems with respect to bisimulation equivalence. Our results show that synchronized product of finite automata, hierarchical graphs, and timed automata are pairwise incomparable in this sense. We moreover study the computational complexity of deciding simulation preorder and bisimulation equivalence on these classes.

1 Introduction

In formal verification *model checking* is one of the most successful approaches; it asks to test automatically whether a given system meets a given specification. Unfortunately, model checking tools have to deal with a combinatorial blow up of the state space, commonly known as the *state explosion problem*, that can be seen as one of the biggest challenges in real-world problems. Different sources of explosion arise, for instance the number of *program variables* or *clocks*, the number of *concurrent components*, or the number of different *subroutines*, just to mention few of them. Numerous techniques to tame the state explosion problem have been introduced such as abstraction methods, partial order reduction or counterexample guided abstraction refinement.

Flip side of the coin, when modeling everyday systems that are potentially exponentially big (also called the *flattened system* or just *flat system*), it is desirable to have succinct representations for them. Three fundamental models include (i) *products of flat systems*, (ii) *timed automata* (more precisely the transitions systems evolving from the time-abstract semantics of timed automata), and (iii) *hierarchical systems*, each of them successfully being used to tame the state explosion problem in their dimension (these dimensions are pairwise orthogonal): (i) Products of flat systems allow to succinctly account for the number of concurrently running components, (ii) Timed automata [2] allow to succinctly model the behavior of programs involving program variables or clocks, and finally (iii) hierarchical systems (also known as hierarchical state machines [3] or hierarchical structures [15]) allow to succinctly represent systems that are decomposed from numerous sub-systems. See also [17] for a recent work, where *web services* are modeled as the asynchronous product of flat systems.

An important algorithmic question in this context is whether two given (succinctly presented) systems behave equivalently, or whether one system can be

* This work has been partly supported by project ImpRo (ANR-10-BLAN-0317).

M. Koutny and I. Ulidowski (Eds.): CONCUR 2012, LNCS 7454, pp. 147–161, 2012.

simulated by another one. For instance, if it turns out that a complex system (implementation) is behaviorally equivalent to a simple system (implementation), the system designer can well replace the complex one by the simple one.

Numerous notions of behavioral equivalences have been proposed by van Glabbeek [20,21]. Among them, *bisimulation equivalence* is undoubtedly the central one of them in formal verification. For instance beautiful characterizations of the bisimulation-invariant fragments of established logics such as first-order logic and monadic second-order have been proven in terms of modal logic [19] and the modal μ-calculus [8], respectively; we refer to [16] for a further such characterization in terms of CTL^*.

Our contributions and related work. In the first part of this paper we study the succinctness with respect to bisimulation equivalence of three established models of succinctly representing finite systems, namely *products of flat systems, timed automata*, and *hierarchical systems*. The main contribution of this paper is to pinpoint to the sources of succinctness when comparing any two of the (orthogonally defined) three models of systems, mainly focusing on the different proof ideas for establishing exponential succinctness. We show that each of the three models *can* be exponentially more succinct than any of the other two. Such a rigorous comparison of fundamental models for succinctly representing finite systems has not yet been carried out in the context of formal verification to the best of the authors' knowledge.

In the second part of this paper we study the computational complexity of simulation preorder and bisimulation equivalence checking for products of flat systems, timed systems and hierarchical systems. We provide a general reduction that shows EXPTIME-hardness (and thus completeness) of checking simulation preorder on hierarchical systems and on timed automata. The former is a new result; the latter was already proven in [13] but we believe our proof is more direct. Moreover, our reduction is quite generic, and can be easily applied to a wide range of succinctly presented models.

We also study the problem of deciding simulation preorder and bisimulation equivalence between one of the three above-mentioned succinct systems and a flat system. We show that checking the simulation preorder of a hierarchical system by a flat system is PSPACE-complete. The problem is known to be EXPTIME-complete for (synchronization-free) non-flat systems and timed automata [5].

Via a standard reduction to model checking EF logic we describe a PSPACE algorithm to check bisimilarity of any of the discussed succinctly presented finite systems and a flat system. Essentially since reachability of all of these systems is in PSPACE, it follows that the problem is PSPACE-complete; the upper bound was left open in [5], where it was shown to be PSPACE-hard.

Finally, we study language inclusion between the three above-mentioned succinct models. We show that checking untimed language equivalence (and in fact language universality) is EXPSPACE-hard (and thus EXPSPACE-complete) for hierarchical systems and timed automata. We would like to mention that this problem has been wrongly cited in the literature as being in PSPACE for timed automata [1,18]. Our results are summarized in Table 1.

Table 1. Complexity results

	Hierarchical	Timed	Prod. of Flat
Simulation	EXPTIME-c	EXPTIME-c [13]	EXPTIME-c [7]
Bisimulation	PSPACE-hard	EXPTIME-c [13]	EXPTIME-c [9]
Bis. with Flat	PSPACE-c	PSPACE-c	PSPACE-c [5]
Sim. by Flat	PSPACE-c	EXPTIME-c [5]	EXPTIME-c [7,5]
Language Inc.	EXPSPACE-c	EXPSPACE-c	EXPSPACE-c [13]

2 Definitions

A *transition system* (also *flat system* or just *system*) over a finite alphabet Σ is a tuple $\mathcal{T} = (S, (\xrightarrow{\sigma})_{\sigma\in\Sigma})$, where S is an arbitrary set of *states* and each relation $\xrightarrow{\sigma}\subseteq S \times S$, is the set of σ-labeled *transitions*. Its size is $|\mathcal{T}| = |S| + \sum_\sigma |\xrightarrow{\sigma}|$. We say that an *action* $\sigma \in \Sigma$ is *enabled* at state $s \in S$ if there is a transition $s \xrightarrow{\sigma} s'$ for some $s' \in S$. $\mathcal{T}$ is *deterministic* if each $\xrightarrow{\sigma}$ is a partial function. An *initialized transition system* is $(S, s_0, (\xrightarrow{\sigma})_{\sigma\in\Sigma})$, where $s_0 \in S$ is the *initial state*. A *simulation* is a relation $R \subseteq S \times S$, with the following property: for any states $s, t \in S$ with sRt, for any $\sigma \in \Sigma$ and $s' \in S$ such that $s \xrightarrow{\sigma} s'$, there exists $t' \in S$ with $t \xrightarrow{\sigma} t'$ and $s'Rt'$. A simulation is a *bisimulation* whenever it is symmetric. For two states $s, t \in S$, we write $s \sqsubseteq t$ (resp. $s \sim t$) if there exists a simulation (resp. bisimulation) $R \subseteq S \times S$ such that sRt. An initialized transition system $\mathcal{T} = (S, s_0, (\xrightarrow{\sigma})_{\sigma\in\Sigma})$ is simulated by an initialized transition system $\mathcal{T}' = (S', s_0', (\xrightarrow{\sigma}')_{\sigma\in\Sigma})$, if there is a simulation R in the disjoint union of $\mathcal{T}$ and $\mathcal{T}'$ such that $s_0 R s_0'$. We extend notations $\sqsubseteq$ and $\sim$ to initialized transition systems. We also define $\sim_k$, *bisimilarity up-to k steps*: we have $s \sim_k t$ for two states $s, t \in S$ if, and only if the unfolding of $\mathcal{T}$ from s up-to k steps is bisimilar to the unfolding at t up-to k steps. A path of $\mathcal{T}$ is a sequence of states that are connected by transitions. The length of a path of a transition system is the number of transitions it contains. For a path π, π_i denotes the i-th state it visits, and we denote by $\pi_{i...j}$ the subpath of π from π_i to π_j. For any initialized transition system $\mathcal{T}$, we define $L(\mathcal{T})$ as the *language* accepted by $\mathcal{T}$, that is the set of words made of the transition labels in all paths of $\mathcal{T}$ starting at s_0.

A *product of flat systems* is a tuple $\mathcal{S} = (\mathcal{T}_1, \ldots, \mathcal{T}_k)$, where $\mathcal{T}_i = (S_i, (\xrightarrow{\sigma}_i)_{\sigma\in\Sigma})$ is a flat system for each $1 \leq i \leq k$. $\mathcal{S}$ defines a transition system $\mathcal{T}(\mathcal{S}) = (\prod_i S_i, (\xrightarrow{\sigma})_{\sigma\in\Sigma})$, where $(s_i)_i \xrightarrow{\sigma} (t_i)_i$ if, and only if, for all $1 \leq i \leq k$, either $s_i \xrightarrow{\sigma} t_i$ in $\mathcal{T}_i$, or $t_i = s_i$ and σ is not enabled at s_i. An example is given in Fig. 1.

Hierarchical systems are a modeling formalism used to succinctly describe finite systems, by allowing the reuse of subsystems. A hierarchical system is defined by a simple grammar that generates a single transition system, in which each nonterminal defines a system by explicitly introducing states and transitions, and using other nonterminals. The reuse relation is required to be acyclic, so as to ensure that the generated transition system is finite. These were introduced in [14] in the context of VLSI design.

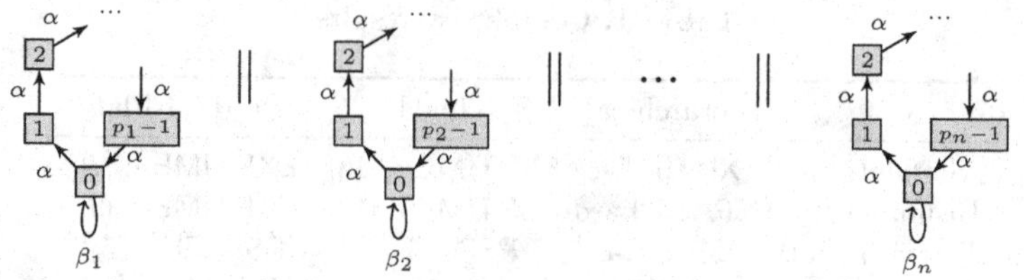

Fig. 1. The system A_n, where $p_1, \ldots, p_n$ are the first n prime numbers, is defined as the product of components F_i made of a α-cycle of length p_i, along where each state corresponds to a value modulo p_i. The self-loop β_i is only available at state 0, which is also the initial state. Then, when the system reads a word α^m, one can read the values $m \mod p_i$ for all $1 \le i \le n$, looking at the states of all components.

An *n-pointed system* is a transition system with n selected states, numbered from 1 to n. It is denoted by a pair $(\mathcal{T}, \tau)$, where $\mathcal{T} = (S, (\xrightarrow{\sigma})_{\sigma \in \Sigma})$ is a transition system and $\tau : \{1, \ldots, n\} \to S$ an injection.

Definition 1. *A hierarchical system [15] is a tuple $H = (N, I, P)$ where*

1. *N is a finite set of* nonterminals. *Each $B \in N$ has a* rank *denoted by $\mathsf{rank}(B) \in \mathbb{N}$. I is the initial nonterminal with $\mathsf{rank}(I) = 0$.*
2. *P is the set of* productions, *that contains for each $B \in N$ a unique production $B \to (\mathcal{A}, \tau, E)$ where $(\mathcal{A}, \tau)$ is a $\mathsf{rank}(B)$-pointed system with the set of states A, and E is the set of* references *with $E \subseteq \{(B', \sigma) \mid B' \in N, \sigma : \{1, \ldots, \mathsf{rank}(B')\} \to A$ is injective$\}$.*
3. *Define relation $\mathcal{E}_H \subseteq N \times N$ as follows: $(B, C) \in \mathcal{E}_H$ if, and only if for the unique production $B \to (\mathcal{A}, \tau, E)$, E contains some reference of the form (C, σ). We require that $\mathcal{E}_H$ is acyclic.*

Its size is defined as $|H| = \sum_{(B \to (\mathcal{A}, \tau, E)) \in P} |\mathcal{A}| + |E|$. For any production $B \to (\mathcal{A}, \tau, E)$, the states $\tau(i)$ are called *contact states.* Each production produces an n-pointed system, that is, a finite system with n contact states. In fact, a hierarchical system $H = (N, I, P)$ describes a single finite system, obtained by taking, for each production $B \to (\mathcal{A}, \tau, E)$, the disjoint union of the (explicitly given) system $\mathcal{A}$ and those systems defined by nonterminals B' for all references $(B', \sigma) \in E$, and merging the i-th contact state of B' with $\sigma(i)$. Thus, the function σ is used to merge the contact states of the references with the states at the current level. Figure 2 gives an example of a hierarchical system.

Formally, each nonterminal B, produces a $\mathsf{rank}(B)$-pointed system denoted $\mathsf{eval}_H(B)$ (also written as $\mathsf{eval}(B)$ in the rest) as follows. If the production $B \to (\mathcal{A}, \tau, E)$ satisfies $E = \varnothing$, then $\mathsf{eval}(B)$ is the $\mathsf{rank}(B)$-pointed system $(\mathcal{A}, \tau)$. Otherwise, let $E = \{(B_1, \sigma_1), \ldots, (B_k, \sigma_k)\}$ and consider systems $\mathsf{eval}(B_i) = (\mathcal{A}_i, \tau_i)$ for each i. Let $\mathcal{U}$ denote the disjoint union of all $\mathcal{A}_i$ and $\mathcal{A}$. We let $\mathsf{eval}(B) = (\mathcal{U}/_{\equiv}, \pi_{\equiv} \circ \tau)$, where $\equiv$ is the equivalence relation generated by $\{(\sigma_i(j), \tau_i(j)), 1 \le i \le k, 1 \le j \le \mathsf{rank}(B_i)\}$, and $\pi_{\equiv}$ is the projection to the equivalence classes. Thus, $\equiv$ merges contact state j of system $\mathcal{A}_i$ with the state $\sigma_i(j)$, for each

$1 \leq i \leq k$. Note that $\mathsf{eval}(B)$ is well-defined since $\mathcal{E}_H$ is acyclic. We define the generated transition system $\mathcal{T}(H)$ of H as $\mathsf{eval}(I)$.

We denote by $\mathsf{unfolding}(H)$ the tree defined as follows. States are labeled by nonterminals, and the root is the initial nonterminal S. The children of each state labeled by nonterminal B are given as follows. If $B \to (\mathcal{A}, \tau, E)$ is the production of nonterminal B, and if $(B_1, \sigma_1), \ldots, (B_k, \sigma_k)$ are the references in E, then B has a child for each $1 \leq i \leq k$, labeled by B_i. Observe that for each state v of $\mathsf{eval}(H)$, there is a unique state in $\mathsf{unfolding}(H)$ labeled by a nonterminal $B \to (\mathcal{A}, \tau, E)$, such that v is an internal state in $\mathcal{A}$, *i.e.* $v \in \mathcal{A} \setminus \mathsf{range}(\tau)$. We denote this state by $\mathsf{unfolding}(H, v)$

For any nonterminal B in H, an *inner path in* B is a path of $\mathsf{eval}(B)$ that does not contain any contact states of $\mathsf{eval}(B)$, except possibly for the first and the last states. An inner path of B is *traversing* if its first and last states are contact states of $\mathsf{eval}(B)$.

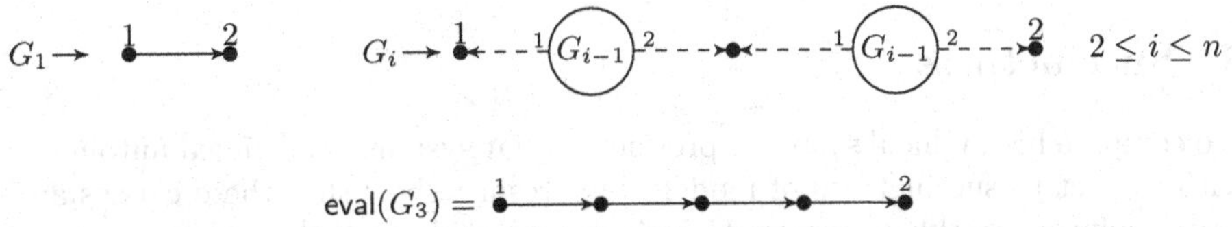

Fig. 2. The figure shows a hierarchical system with nonterminals G_i for $1 \leq i \leq n$. G_1 produces an explicit system with no references, with two contact states (shown by 1 and 2). G_i creates three states, where the leftmost and the rightmost are two contact states, and uses two references to G_{i-1}. The dashed arrows show how to merge the contact states of each copy G_{i-1} with the states of G_i. For instance, the contact state 1 of the leftmost copy of G_{i-1} is merged with contact state 1 of G_i. Then, for $n = 3$, $\mathsf{eval}(G_3)$ is the system depicted on the bottom.

Timed automata are finite automata equipped with a finite set of real-valued clocks. Clocks grow at a constant rate, and are used to enable/disable the transitions of the underlying finite automaton. They can be reset during transitions.

To formally define timed automata, we need the following notations. Given a finite set of clocks $\mathcal{X}$, we call *valuations* the elements of $\mathbb{R}_{\geq 0}^{\mathcal{X}}$. For a subset $R \subseteq \mathcal{X}$ and a valuation v, $v[R \leftarrow 0]$ is the valuation defined by $v[R \leftarrow 0](x) = v(x)$ for $x \in \mathcal{X} \setminus R$ and $v[R \leftarrow 0](x) = 0$ for $x \in R$. Given $d \in \mathbb{R}_{\geq 0}$ and a valuation v, the valuation $v + d$ is defined by $(v + d)(x) = v(x) + d$ for all $x \in \mathcal{X}$. We extend these operations to sets of valuations in the obvious way. We write $\mathbf{0}$ for the valuation that assigns 0 to every clock. An atomic clock constraint is a formula of the form $k \preceq x \preceq' l$ or $k \preceq x - y \preceq' l$ where $x, y \in \mathcal{X}$, $k, l \in \mathbb{Z} \cup \{-\infty, \infty\}$ and $\preceq, \preceq' \in \{<, \leq\}$. *Guards* are conjunctions of atomic clock constraints. The set $\Phi_{\mathcal{X}}$ denotes the guards over clocks $\mathcal{X}$. A valuation v satisfies a guard g, denoted $v \models g$, if all constraints are satisfied when each $x \in \mathcal{X}$ is replaced with $v(x)$.

Definition 2 ([2]). *A timed automaton $\mathcal{A}$ is a tuple $(\mathcal{L}, \Sigma, \mathcal{X}, \ell_0, E)$, consisting of finite sets $\mathcal{L}$ of locations, a finite alphabet Σ, $\mathcal{X}$ of clocks, $E \subseteq \mathcal{L} \times \Phi_{\mathcal{X}} \times \Sigma \times 2^{\mathcal{X}} \times \mathcal{L}$ of edges, and where $\ell_0 \in \mathcal{L}$ is the initial location.*

We are interested in the *time-abstract* semantics of timed automata in the following sense. A timed automaton $\mathcal{A} = (\mathcal{L}, \Sigma, \mathcal{X}, \ell_0, E)$, defines a transition system on the state space $\mathcal{L} \times \mathbb{R}_{\geq 0}^{\mathcal{X}}$, with the initial state $(\ell_0, \mathbf{0})$. There is a transition $(\ell, v) \xrightarrow{\sigma} (\ell', v')$ if, and only if there is $d \geq 0$ and an edge $(\ell, g, \sigma, R, \ell')$ such that $v + d \models g$ and $(v + d)[R \leftarrow 0] = v'$. Although timed automata define infinite transition systems, it is well-known that any timed automaton $\mathcal{A}$ is bisimilar to a computable flat system $\mathcal{T}(\mathcal{A})$, whose size can be exponentially larger than that of $\mathcal{A}$ [2]. See Figure 3 for a timed automaton bisimilar to a large flat system.

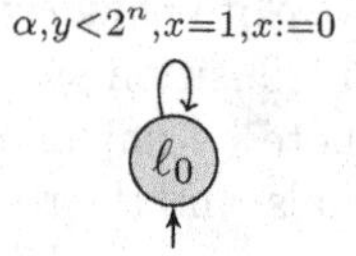

Fig. 3. A timed automaton with one location and two clocks x, y, modelling a "counter" ranging from 0 to 2^n that can only be incremented. At any state (ℓ_0, v) with $v(x) = 0$, $v(y)$ encodes the value of the counter. Taking the self-loop increments the counter. Any run stops after at most 2^n increments.

3 Succinctness

We compare hierarchical systems, products of flat systems, and timed automata with respect to succinctness of models. Our results show that these classes are pairwise incomparable in terms of succinctness: inside each class, there are infinite families of models which are exponentially more succinct than any bisimilar family of models in another class.

3.1 Hierarchical Systems *vs.* Products of Flat Systems

We show that hierarchical systems can be exponentially more succinct than products of flat systems: it is easy to define long finite chains with the former, as in Fig. 2, although this is not possible with the latter.

Theorem 1. *Hierarchical systems can be exponentially more succinct than products of flat systems.*

The other direction, in the next theorem, is more difficult.

Theorem 2. *Products of flat systems can be exponentially more succinct than hierarchical systems.*

This theorem also establishes a non-trivial property of hierarchical systems, giving insight into the differences with the other classes. It shows that any hierarchical graph of size n defining an exponentially large graph contains necessarily two states that are bisimilar up-to $\Omega(n)$ steps. The proof is based on the observation that this is not the case for products of flat systems.

We consider the system A_n described in Fig. 1. We first give simple properties of A_n, based on the Chinese Remainder Theorem:

Theorem 3 (Chinese Remainder Theorem). *Let $p_1, \ldots, p_n$ denote pairwise coprime numbers. For any integers $a_1, \ldots, a_n$, there exists a unique $m \in [0, p_1 p_2 \ldots p_n - 1]$ such that $m \equiv a_i \mod p_i$ for all $1 \leq i \leq n$.*

Let $p_1, \ldots, p_n$ denote the first n prime numbers, and consider A_n given as the product of components $F_1, \ldots, F_n$. Observe that A_n has $p_1 p_2 \cdots p_n$ states. By the Chinese Remainder Theorem, all bisimulation classes of A_n are singletons. In fact, consider a state s reached from the initial state by reading α^m. While executing the word α^{p_n} from s, measuring the minimal distance to some state that enables β_i, we can deduce m modulo p_i for each $1 \leq i \leq n$, and this uniquely determines m modulo $p_1 \cdots p_n$. This is formalized in the following lemma. In the rest of the section, we refer to states of A_n by natural numbers from 0 to $p_1 p_2 \cdots p_n - 1$.

Lemma 1. *For any pair of states $0 \leq c < c' < p_1 p_2 \cdots p_n$ of A_n, $c \not\sim_{p_n} c'$. Moreover, $c \sim_{p_n} c'$ if, and only if $c \sim c'$.*

Let us first explain the idea of the proof of Theorem 2. Any (sufficiently large) hierarchical graph of size polynomial in n that is bisimilar to A_n contains two occurrences of a nonterminal since A_n contains an exponential number of states. Similarly, some contact states of a same nonterminal appear several times. We will show moreover that for any hierarchical graph, there is a bisimilar one whose size is polynomially bounded, with the property that for some nonterminal B, the same contact state of two different copies of $\mathsf{eval}(B)$ belong to inner paths of $\mathsf{eval}(B)$ that are bisimilar up-to p_n steps. Thus, both occurrences of the contact state must be bisimilar to the same state of A_n by Lemma 1. However, we also show that these are reachable from the initial states in less than $p_1 p_2 \cdots p_n$ steps, which leads to a contradiction. We now give a formal proof following these ideas.

The size of A_n can be seen to be polynomially bounded in n from below and above since $p_n \sim n \log(n)$ for large n by the Prime Number Theorem. Assume there are hierarchical systems H_n such that $\mathcal{T}(H_n) \sim \mathcal{T}(A_n)$ for all $n \geq 0$, such that $|H_n| \leq f(n)$ for some polynomial f. We first show, in the following lemma, that each H_n can be assumed to satisfy the following Property ($\star$): for all nonterminals B, all traversing paths of $\mathsf{eval}(B)$ have length either 0 or at least $p_n + 2$.

Lemma 2. *For any family $(H_n)_{n \geq 0}$ of pointed hierarchical systems, there exist pointed hierarchical systems $(H'_n)_{n \geq 0}$ such that $|H'_n| \leq p(|H_n|)$ for some polynomial p, $\mathcal{T}(H_n) \sim \mathcal{T}(H'_n)$ and H'_n satisfies Property ($\star$), for all $n \geq 0$.*

The idea of the transformation is the following. We consider each production $B \to (\mathcal{A}, \tau, E)$, in the reverse topological order w.r.t. $\mathcal{E}_{H_n}$. Then, for all productions $C \to (\mathcal{A}', \tau', E')$ with $(C, B) \in \mathcal{E}_{H_n}$, we add to $\mathcal{A}'$ a copy of each traversing path ρ of $\mathcal{A}$ of size less than $p_n + 2$, and remove all edges labeled by α leaving the first state of ρ. The construction is illustrated in Fig. 4.

Proof of Theorem 2. We assume that Property ($\star$) holds, by Lemma 2. Consider any $n \geq 0$, such that $12 f(n)^4 < p_1 p_2 \cdots p_n$, and let us write $H_n = (N, I, P)$. Consider a path π obtained in H_n by reading $\alpha^{p_1 \cdots p_n}$ from the initial state. For all nonterminals $B \in N$, with the unique production $B \to (\mathcal{A}, \tau, E)$, and $i \in \{1, \ldots, \mathsf{range}(\tau)\}$, let us mark by (B, i) in π all states that are equivalent, under relation $\equiv$, to the state $\tau(i)$ of $\mathcal{A}$. A single state in $\mathsf{eval}(H_n)$ can be marked by several pairs (B, i) since the equivalence $\equiv$ merges states. For example, if we were to apply this marking to the graph of Fig. 2, then the leftmost state would be marked by $(G_1, 1), (G_2, 1), \ldots, (G_n, 1)$, since at each production G_i, this state is merged with contact state 1 of the leftmost occurrence of nonterminal G_{i-1}. Note that at least one state among any consecutive $|H_n|$ states must be marked by some (B, i) in π. Otherwise π would not visit any contact states, and therefore would stay inside the same explicit graph, which has size less than $|H_n|$, and some state would appear twice since $p_1 p_2 \cdots p_n > f(n) \geq |H_n|$. Then, a same state of $\mathcal{T}(H_n)$ would be bisimilar to two distinct states of $\mathcal{T}(A_n)$, which contradicts Lemma 1. Since the number of pairs (B, i) is bounded by $|H_n|$ at least $m = \frac{|\pi|}{|H_n|^2}$ states of π are marked by some pair (B, i). Observe that $m = |\pi|/|H_n|^2 = \Omega(2^n/f(n)^2)$. Now, at least half the states marked by (B, i) mark the beginning of traversing paths of $\mathsf{eval}(B)$.

Among these states, assume that there are π_j and $\pi_{j'}$ for $0 \leq j < j' < p_1 \cdots p_n$, such that the traversing paths starting at these states have positive length (therefore, at least $p_n + 2$, thus contain at least p_n inner states). By assumption, these states are bisimilar to the states of A_n corresponding to the numbers j and j' respectively. Consider the inner paths $\pi_{j \ldots j+p_n}$ and $\pi_{j' \ldots j'+p_n}$ of $\mathsf{eval}(B)$. These paths belong to different instances of the production of B, so the visited states are pairwise disjoint. However, states π_j and $\pi_{j'}$, seen as states of $\mathsf{eval}(B)$ are bisimilar, since they correspond to the same contact state of $\mathsf{eval}(B)$. Since all α-labelled transitions from π_j lead to bisimilar states in $\mathsf{eval}(B)$, all internal paths starting at π_j are bisimilar. In particular, π_j and $\pi_{j'}$ are bisimilar up-to p_n steps, since they stay inside $\mathsf{eval}(B)$. So, each β_i is enabled in π_{j+k} iff it is enabled at $\pi_{j'+k}$, for all $1 \leq k \leq p_n$. But then π_j and $\pi_{j'}$ must be bisimilar to the same state of A_n by Lemma 1, and this is a contradiction.

Assume now that there is no more than one state π_j marked by (B, i) with a positive-length traversing path; so there are at least $m/2 - 1$ states corresponding to beginnings of traversing paths of length 0 (consisting of single states). Let $(\alpha_j)_{1 \leq j}$ denote the indices such that π_{α_j} is marked by (B, i) and is a traversing path of length 0. We argue that some state marked by a pair (B', i') with $(B, i) \neq (B', i')$, that is the beginning or the end of a traversing path of positive length must occur in $\pi_{\alpha_1 \ldots \alpha_1 + |H_n|}$. Consider the nonterminal C labeling the state $\mathsf{unfolding}(H_n, \pi_{\alpha_1})$. By definition, π_{α_1} is an inner state of C, so π_{α_1} is part of an inner path of $\mathsf{eval}(C)$. Since the structure defined in the production of C has size less than $|H_n|$, $\pi_{\alpha_1 \ldots \alpha_1 + |H_n|}$ must visit a state labeled by (B', i') that is the beginning or the end of an inner path of positive length: this is either a contact state of $\mathsf{eval}(C)$ (the end of the inner path containing π_{α_1}), or the beginning of an inner path inside $\mathsf{eval}(B')$, where $(C, B') \in \mathcal{E}_{H_n}$. In fact, if this subpath does not visit contact states of C and if it only contains inner paths of length 0 for other nonterminals B', then it stays inside the explicit graph defined in the production of C. This is again a contradiction with the bisimilarity with A_n since a state then must appear twice. This shows that every chunk of $|H_n|$ starting at some π_{α_i} contains a state marked by some other (B', i'), which is the beginning or the end of some traversing path of positive length of $\mathsf{eval}(B')$. Then, at least

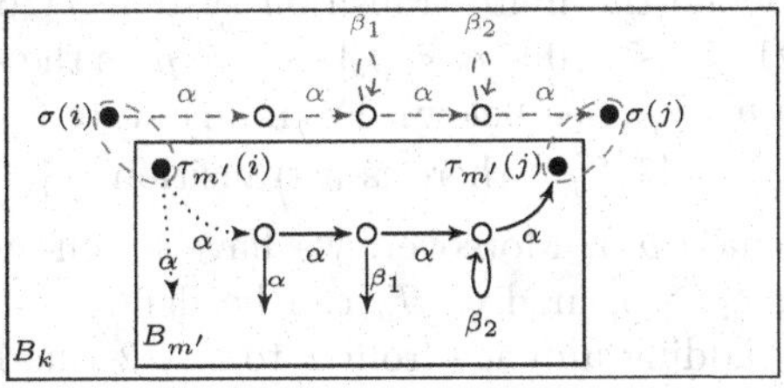

Fig. 4. The construction of Theorem 2 that removes a small traversing path created in a production $B_{m'} \to (\mathcal{A}_{m'}, \tau_{m'}, E_{m'})$. Here, $B_{m'}$ has an internal path of length 4 between $\tau_{m'}(i)$ and $\tau_{m'}(j)$, where internal states are represented by unfilled states. The contact states $\tau_{m'}(i)$ and $\tau_{m'}(j)$ are to be merged with the states $\sigma(i)$ and $\sigma(j)$ created in the production of B_k. The construction removes all edges of $\mathcal{A}_{m'}$ leaving $\tau_{m'}(i)$ (shown by dotted arrows). Then, the red dashed path ρ' is added instead from $\sigma(i)$ and $\sigma(j)$ in $\mathcal{A}_k$.

$\frac{m/2-1}{2|H_n|^2}$ states are marked by the same (B', i'), and are the beginning of traversing paths of positive length, and we can apply the previous case.

3.2 Timed Automata *vs.* Product of Flat Systems

Theorem 4. *Timed automata can be exponentially more succinct than products of flat systems.*

Proof. The proof immediately follows from Theorem 1 and the fact that the timed automaton of Fig. 3 is time-abstract bisimilar to the system G_n. □

We now show that products of flat systems can be more succinct than timed automata. This result requires new techniques since the nature of state-space explosion of timed automata is different; it is due to the complex relation between its clock values, rather than to its structure. To show this result, we use the well-known notion of *zones*, which are convex sets of the state space with integer corners. We only need the fact that zones are closed under basic operations such as time predecessors and intersection. We refer to [4] for definitions and properties of zones.

The main idea behind the proof is the following: a state in the transition system defined by a timed automaton can have an exponential number of a priori pairwise non-bisimilar successors but we show that the pairwise non-bisimilarity of an exponential number of successors of a state cannot be detected by looking only one step further in the transition system. This important property is established using geometric properties of regions, and it is inherent to transition systems defined by timed automata. We show, on the other hand, that such a system can be defined by a small product of automata (system A'_n defined below), which yields the following theorem.

Theorem 5. *Products of flat systems can be exponentially more succinct than timed automata.*

For any $n \geq 1$, we define the finite transition system $\mathcal{T}_n$ on the set of states $S_n = \{(c_1, \ldots, c_n) \mid \forall 1 \leq i \leq n, 0 \leq c_i < p_i\}$, where p_i is the $i+2$-th prime number (so that we have $p_i \geq 5$, see below). From any state $(c_1, \ldots, c_n) \in S_n$ and any vector $(b_1, \ldots, b_n) \in \{1,2\}^n$, there is a transition $(c_1, \ldots, c_n) \xrightarrow{\alpha} (c_1 + b_1 \mod p_1, \ldots, c_n + b_n \mod p_n)$. Moreover, we have a self-loop $(c_1, \ldots, c_n) \xrightarrow{\beta_i} (c_1, \ldots, c_n)$ whenever $c_i \equiv 0 \mod p_i$. $\mathcal{T}_n$ can be defined by adapting the system A_n of Fig. 1, by adding an edge from x to $x+2$ (modulo p_i) inside each component F_i. Let us call A'_n this product of flat systems. It is clear that A'_n has size $O(n^2 \log(n))$ since $p_n \sim n \log n$.

The following lemma shows that states of $\mathcal{T}_n$ cannot simulate each other.

Lemma 3. *For all states $\mathbf{c}, \mathbf{c}'$ of $\mathcal{T}_n$, there is no simulation R such that $\mathbf{c} \mathrel{R} \mathbf{c}'$.*

Proof (of Thm. 5). We consider any timed automaton T_n bisimilar to $\mathcal{T}_n$ (thus, to A'_n). By definition, all states of $\mathcal{T}_n$ have 2^n transitions, all leading to pairwise non-bisimilar states. We show that such a branching is not possible in T_n unless T_n has exponential size.

We consider the state $\mathbf{c} = (p_1 - 1, \ldots, p_n - 1)$ of $\mathcal{T}_n$, which is reachable. Let (ℓ, v) be any state of T_n that is bisimilar to $\mathbf{c}$. In $\mathcal{T}_n$, $\mathbf{c}$ has 2^n α-successors. Moreover, for each $1 \leq i \leq n$, β_i is enabled in exactly half of these successor states. In fact, for any subset $P \subseteq \{\beta_1, \ldots, \beta_n\}$, there is a successor where the set of enabled transition labels is exactly $P \cup \{\alpha\}$. Let $E(\ell)$ denote the number of edges from ℓ. For each successor $\mathbf{c}'$ of $\mathbf{c}$, pick a transition from (ℓ, v) in T_n, leading to a state bisimilar to $\mathbf{c}'$. Then, at least $2^n/E(\ell)$ of these transitions are along some edge $e = (\ell, \phi, \alpha, R, \ell')$. This means that there exist $d_1, \ldots, d_m \geq 0$ with $m = \lfloor 2^n/E(\ell) \rfloor$ such that states $(\ell, v + d_i)$ satisfy the guard ϕ; and the states $(\ell', v'_i) = (\ell', (v + d_i)[R \leftarrow 0])$ are each bisimilar to a successor of $\mathbf{c}$. States (ℓ, v'_i) are therefore pairwise non-simulating, by Lemma 3. Let us note here that R cannot be empty, since otherwise $(\ell', v + d_i)$ can simulate $(\ell', v + d_j)$ whenever $d_i \leq d_j$, which contradicts Lemma 3. We are going to show that there must be $\Omega(2^n)$ edges leaving ℓ'.

Valuations $v + d_i$ belong to a line of direction $\mathbf{1}$, that contains v. So the projections $v'_i = (v + d_i)[R \leftarrow 0]$ also belong to a line $\mathcal{D}$. Consider the set $g_1, \ldots, g_m$ of guards of the edges leaving ℓ'. Such a transition can be taken from v'_i if, and only if $v'_i + d \in g_j$ for some delay $d \geq 0$. This condition is equivalent to $v'_i \in \bigwedge_{x \in R}(x = 0) \wedge \mathsf{Pre}(g_i)$, where Pre gives the set of *time-predecessors* of g_i, *i.e.* $\mathsf{Pre}(g_i) = \{v \mid \exists d \geq 0, v + d \models g_i\}$. It is well-known that the right hand side of the above expression can be expressed by a guard [4]. Therefore, for simplicity, but without loss of generality, let us replace g_i by the right hand side of the above. Thus, we have now a line $\mathcal{D}$ that contains all valuations v'_i, and convex sets defined by the guards. The intersection of each guard with $\mathcal{D}$ is a segment. From now on, we are only interested in valuations and segments that lie in $\mathcal{D}$. Each segment along $\mathcal{D}$ thus can be seen as an interval.

Now, we will show that only a small number of bisimulation classes can be distinguished inside $\mathcal{D}$, looking only at the immediate enablement of m guards. For a set of real intervals $\mathcal{I} = \{I_1, \ldots, I_n\}$, we denote by $\chi_{\mathcal{I}}$ the equivalence relation among real numbers given by $(x, y) \in \chi_{\mathcal{I}}$ if, and only if $x \in I \Leftrightarrow y \in I$, for all $I \in \mathcal{I}$. When $\mathcal{I}$ is finite, this relation is finite too. For instance, if $\mathcal{I} = \{[a, b]\}$, then $\chi_{\mathcal{I}}$ has index 2. We denote by $|\chi_{\mathcal{I}}|$ the index of $\chi_{\mathcal{I}}$.

Lemma 4. *Let $\mathcal{I}$ be a finite set of real intervals, and let J be a real interval. Then $|\chi_{\mathcal{I}\cup\{J\}}| \leq |\chi_{\mathcal{I}}| + 2$.*

Now, using m guards, one can only define $2m$ subsets of $\mathcal{D}$ which are pairwise distinguished with respect to the satisfaction of all guards g_i. By the previous lemma, there are at most $2m$ equivalence classes defined by $\chi_{\{g_1,\dots,g_{E(\ell')}\}}$. On the other hand, any pair of states v'_i and v'_j can be distinguished by the satisfaction of some guard g_k, since this is the case for the 2^n successors of $\mathbf{c} = (p_1-1, \dots, p_n-1)$ inside $\mathcal{T}_n$. It follows that $2m \geq 2^n/E(\ell)$. Therefore, $|T_n| \geq m = \Omega(2^n)$. □

3.3 Timed Automata *vs.* Hierarchical Systems

Theorem 6. *Timed automata can be exponentially more succinct than hierarchical systems, and vice versa.*

The proof of the first direction is similar to that of Theorem 2: we give a timed automaton that describes a system similar to A_n. The other direction uses the techniques of Theorem 5.

4 Complexity of Preorder Checking

4.1 Hardness of Simulation

The main result of this section is that deciding simulation between two hierarchical systems is EXPTIME-complete. Our proof is based on a simple reduction from countdown games [10]. Our reduction is quite generic, and it can be applied to any class with a set of simple properties (discussed at the end of the section). As an example, we apply the reduction to timed automata. Note the EXPTIME-hardness of checking simulation for timed automata was already proved in [13] by a reduction based on Turing machines; we obtain here a simpler proof.

Theorem 7. *Checking simulation between two hierarchical systems (resp. two timed automata) is* EXPTIME*-complete.*

Our reduction is based on *countdown games* [10], defined as follows. A countdown game $\mathcal{C}$ is played on a weighted graph (S, T), whose edges are labeled with positive integer weights encoded in binary. A *move* of the game from configuration $(s, c) \in S \times \mathbb{N}$ is determined jointly by both players, as follows. First, Eve chooses a number $d \leq c$ such that $(s, d, s') \in T$ for some state s'. Then Adam chooses a state $s' \in S$ such that $(s, d, s') \in T$. The resulting configuration is $(s', c-d)$. The game stops when Eve has no available moves: configuration (s, c) is *winning* for Eve if $c = 0$. Given a countdown game, one can build an equivalent turn-based graph game of exponential size with a reachability objective. We note that given a countdown game and an initial configuration, the existence of a winning strategy for Eve is EXPTIME -complete [10].

We first reduce the problem of determining the winner in countdown games to the simulation problem on finite automata, that may have exponential size. We then show how these automata can be described in polynomial size by hierarchical systems and timed automata. This proves the EXPTIME-hardness (thus, completeness) of the simulation problem on these classes.

Consider a countdown game $\mathcal{C} = (S, T)$ with initial state $q \in S$ and initial value c. Let Σ denote the set of constants used in $\mathcal{C}$. We define two finite automata on the alphabet $\Gamma = \Sigma \cup \{e, \alpha, \beta\}$. The first one, called $\text{Counter}_{\mathcal{C}}(c)$, is a directed path of length c with some additional states, defined in Fig. 5. The bottom left state is the initial state. Intuitively, this is used to count down from c when simulating the countdown game.

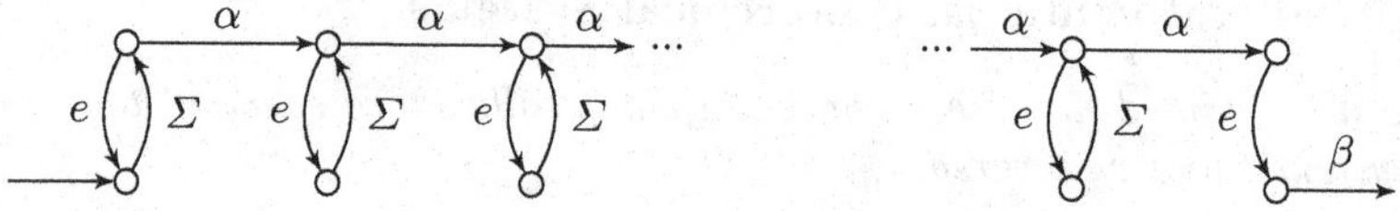

Fig. 5. System $\text{Counter}_{\mathcal{C}}(c)$

The second automaton is called $\text{Control}_{\mathcal{C}}$, and has the same structure as the game $\mathcal{C} = (S, T)$, except that each transition labeled by $k \in \Sigma$ is replaced by a module $\text{Chain}_{\mathcal{C}}(k)$, which is roughly a directed path of length $k+1$ labeled by α^k. In addition, in every state, an edge leads to a sink state by any symbol of $\Gamma \setminus \{\alpha\}$ from all but the last state, and by any symbol in $\Gamma \setminus \{e\}$ from the last state. Sink states have self-loops on all symbols. The module is given in Fig. 6.

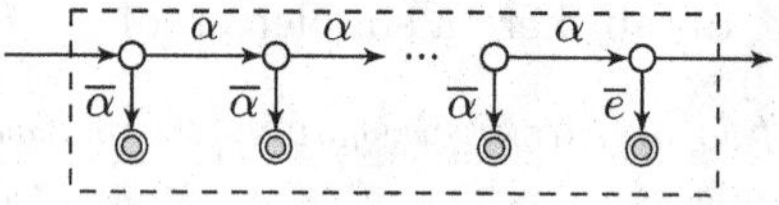

Fig. 6. Module $\text{Chain}_{\mathcal{C}}(k)$. Here, $\overline{x}$ denotes the complement of the set $\{x\}$. All gray states at the bottom in the figure are sink states with (omitted) self-loops on all symbols.

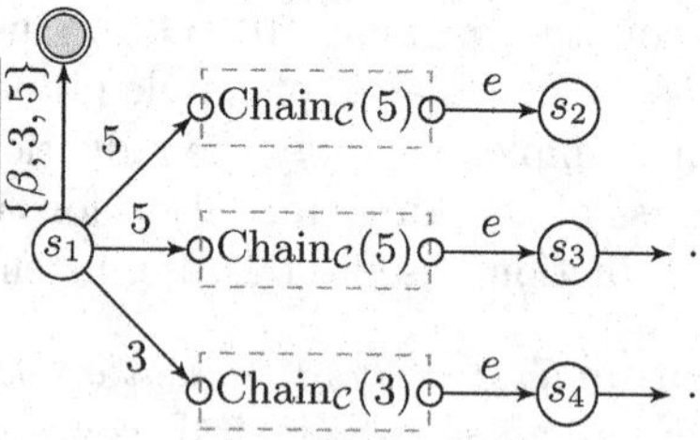

Fig. 7. A part of $\text{Control}_{\mathcal{C}}$ for a countdown game $\mathcal{C}$ with states s_1, s_2, s_3, s_4 and edges $(s_1, 5, s_2), (s_1, 5, s_3), (s_1, 3, s_4)$

Now, automaton $\text{Control}_{\mathcal{C}}$ is defined by replacing each transition labeled by k in the game $\mathcal{C}$, with an instance of module $\text{Chain}_{\mathcal{C}}(k)$, as shown in Fig. 7. Moreover, from each state s_i, there is an edge going to a sink state, labeled by all labels in $\Gamma \setminus (\Sigma(s_i) \cup \{\beta\})$, where $\Sigma(s_i)$ denotes the set of labels of the edges leaving s_i in game $\mathcal{C}$. This ensures that a path in $\text{Control}_\mathcal{C}$ encodes a correct simulation of the game. The initial state of $\text{Control}_\mathcal{C}$ is the initial state of $\mathcal{C}$.

Proposition 1. *For any countdown game $\mathcal{C} = (S, T)$ with initial state s_1 and initial value c, $\text{Counter}_\mathcal{C}(c) \sqsubseteq \text{Control}_\mathcal{C}$ if, and only if Eve does not have a winning strategy in $\mathcal{C}$ from configuration (s_1, c).*

We now explain how this reduction can be applied to hierarchical systems and timed automata, in polynomial time. For hierarchical systems, in order to succinctly represent $\text{Counter}_\mathcal{C}(c)$ and modules $\text{Chain}_\mathcal{C}(k)$, we use the trick of Fig. 2. For instance, in order to define $\text{Chain}_\mathcal{C}(k)$, one can generate all systems $G_1, G_2, \ldots, G_{\lceil \log(k) \rceil}$ and combine these according to the binary representation of k. For timed automata, a pair of clocks can be simply used to count up-to k, as in Fig. 3. Thus, modules $\text{Counter}_\mathcal{C}(c)$ and $\text{Chain}_\mathcal{C}(k)$ can be defined in polynomial space in these classes, which yields a polynomial-time reduction.

4.2 Simulation and Bisimulation with a Flat System

We show that checking whether a hierarchical graph is simulated by a finite automaton is PSPACE-complete. The PSPACE-membership follows from the fact that simulation by a finite automaton can reduced to μ-calculus model-checking (see e.g. [12]), which is in turn in PSPACE [6]. The corresponding lower bound can in fact be deduced from results from [11] and [12] by using lengthy definitions, however, we decided to give a direct reduction from quantified Boolean satisfiability problem.

Theorem 8. *Checking whether a flat system simulates a hierarchical system is* PSPACE*-complete.*

Second, we show that the problems of checking bisimilarity between a timed automaton and a flat system, and between a hierarchical system and a flat system are PSPACE-complete. In fact, one can reduce bisimilarity with a flat system to model checking CTL's fragment EF (where formulas are represented as DAGs) in polynomial time [12]. This yields a polynomial space algorithm for this problem since EF model-checking is easily seen to be in PSPACE for products of flat systems, timed automata and hierarchical systems since reachability for all these systems is in PSPACE.

Theorem 9. *Checking bisimilarity between a timed automaton (resp. hierarchical system, product of flat systems) and a flat system is* PSPACE*-complete.*

The PSPACE-hardness for product of finite automata was already proved in [5]. For timed automata, it follows from PSPACE-hardness of control state reachability that checking *any* relation between time-abstract language equivalence and time-abstract bisimulation between a timed automaton and a finite automaton is PSPACE-hard. For hierarchical systems, we observe that the reduction of [12] that shows the PSPACE-hardness of checking bisimulation between a pushdown automaton and a finite automaton can be adapted to hierarchical systems.

4.3 Language Inclusion and Universality

Given any timed automaton $\mathcal{A}$, one can effectively construct an exponential-size finite automaton, called the *region automaton* that is time-abstract bisimilar to $\mathcal{A}$ [2]. Then, using region automata, one can decide the inclusion between the untimed languages of two timed automata in exponential space. The exact complexity of these problems had not been characterized, and the problem was wrongly cited in the literature as being PSPACE in [1,18]. In this section, we prove that untimed language universality and inclusion are actually EXPSPACE-complete. The result holds already for two clocks. For one clock, the problem is PSPACE-complete. Language inclusion can also be decided in exponential space for hierarchical systems, since the system generated has at most exponential size. We adapt the proof to hierarchical systems, and obtain the same complexity results.

Theorem 10. *Checking untimed language universality is* EXPSPACE-*complete for timed automata with two clocks, and* PSPACE-*complete with one clock. Language universality is* EXPSPACE-*complete for hierarchical systems.*

To prove this, we consider the acceptance problem on exponential-space Turing machines, and show how to compute timed automata (resp. hierarchical systems) that accept all words but those encoding correct accepting executions.

5 Conclusion

In this paper, we compared products of automata, timed automata and hierarchical systems, which are used to succinctly describe finite-state systems. We showed that each of them contains models that are exponentially more succinct than the others, formalizing the intuition that the nature of the state space explosion is different in each formalism. Several variants of these systems were not considered in this paper. For instance, silent transitions improve succinctness in general: the main argument in the proof of Theorem 5 does not hold for timed automata with silent transitions. One could also study different synchronization semantics for products of automata. We also studied the computational complexity of several preorder and equivalence relations. The complexity of bisimilarity between hierarchical systems remains open.

References

1. Aceto, L., Ingólfsdóttir, A., Larsen, K.G., Srba, J.: Reactive Systems: Modelling, Specification and Verification. Cambridge University Press, NY (2007)
2. Alur, R., Dill, D.L.: A theory of timed automata. Theoretical Computer Science 126, 183–235 (1994)
3. Alur, R., Yannakakis, M.: Model checking of hierarchical state machines. ACM Trans. Program. Lang. Syst. 23(3), 273–303 (2001)

4. Bengtsson, J.E., Yi, W.: Timed Automata: Semantics, Algorithms and Tools. In: Desel, J., Reisig, W., Rozenberg, G. (eds.) ACPN 2003. LNCS, vol. 3098, pp. 87–124. Springer, Heidelberg (2004)
5. Bozzelli, L., Legay, A., Pinchinat, S.: Hardness of Preorder Checking for Basic Formalisms. In: Clarke, E.M., Voronkov, A. (eds.) LPAR-16 2010. LNCS, vol. 6355, pp. 119–135. Springer, Heidelberg (2010)
6. Göller, S., Lohrey, M.: Fixpoint logics over hierarchical structures. Theory Comput. Syst. 48(1), 93–131 (2011)
7. Harel, D., Kupferman, O., Vardi, M.Y.: On the complexity of verifying concurrent transition systems. Inf. Comput. 173, 143–161 (2002)
8. Janin, D., Walukiewicz, I.: On the Expressive Completeness of the Propositional mu-Calculus with Respect to Monadic Second Order Logic. In: Montanari, U., Sassone, V. (eds.) CONCUR 1996. LNCS, vol. 1119, pp. 263–277. Springer, Heidelberg (1996)
9. Jategaonkar, L., Meyer, A.R.: Deciding true concurrency equivalences on safe, finite nets. Theoretical Computer Science 154(1), 107–143 (1996)
10. Jurdziński, M., Laroussinie, F., Sproston, J.: Model Checking Probabilistic Timed Automata with One or Two Clocks. In: Grumberg, O., Huth, M. (eds.) TACAS 2007. LNCS, vol. 4424, pp. 170–184. Springer, Heidelberg (2007)
11. Kučera, A., Mayr, R.: Why Is Simulation Harder than Bisimulation? In: Brim, L., Jančar, P., Křetínský, M., Kučera, A. (eds.) CONCUR 2002. LNCS, vol. 2421, pp. 594–610. Springer, Heidelberg (2002)
12. Kučera, A., Mayr, R.: On the complexity of checking semantic equivalences between pushdown processes and finite-state processes. Information and Computation 208(7), 772–796 (2010)
13. Laroussinie, F., Schnoebelen, P.: The State Explosion Problem from Trace to Bisimulation Equivalence. In: Tiuryn, J. (ed.) FOSSACS 2000. LNCS, vol. 1784, pp. 192–207. Springer, Heidelberg (2000)
14. Lengauer, T., Wanke, E.: Efficient solution of connectivity problems on hierarchically defined graphs. SIAM J. Comput. 17(6), 1063–1080 (1988)
15. Lohrey, M.: Model-checking hierarchical structures. J. Comput. Syst. Sci. 78(2), 461–490 (2012)
16. Moller, F., Rabinovich, A.M.: Counting on CTL^*: on the expressive power of monadic path logic. Inf. Comput. 184(1), 147–159 (2003)
17. Muscholl, A., Walukiewicz, I.: A lower bound on web services composition. Logical Methods in Computer Science 4(2) (2008)
18. Srba, J.: Comparing the Expressiveness of Timed Automata and Timed Extensions of Petri Nets. In: Cassez, F., Jard, C. (eds.) FORMATS 2008. LNCS, vol. 5215, pp. 15–32. Springer, Heidelberg (2008)
19. van Benthem, J.: Modal Correspondence Theory. PhD thesis, University of Amsterdam (1976)
20. van Glabbeek, R.J.: The Linear Time-Branching Time Spectrum (Extended Abstract). In: Baeten, J.C.M., Klop, J.W. (eds.) CONCUR 1990. LNCS, vol. 458, pp. 278–297. Springer, Heidelberg (1990)
21. van Glabbeek, R.J.: The Linear Time - Branching Time Spectrum II. In: Best, E. (ed.) CONCUR 1993. LNCS, vol. 715, pp. 66–81. Springer, Heidelberg (1993)

All Linear-Time Congruences for Familiar Operators Part 2: Infinite LTSs

Antti Valmari

Tampere University of Technology,
Department of Software Systems,
Tampere, Finland
Antti.Valmari@tut.fi

Abstract. In a previous publication, we enumerated all stuttering-insensitive linear-time (in a well-defined sense) congruences with respect to action prefix, hiding, relational renaming, and parallel composition for finite labelled transition systems. There are 20 of them. They are built from the alphabet, traces, two kinds of divergence traces, and five kinds of failures. Now we remove the finiteness assumption. To re-establish the congruence property, four kinds of infinite traces are needed. Some congruences split to two and some to three, yielding altogether 40 congruences. Like its predecessor, because of lack of space, also this publication concentrates on proving the absence of more congruences.

Keywords: process algebra, semantics, compositionality, verification.

1 Introduction

Process algebra researchers have introduced numerous equivalence notions for comparing the behaviours of systems or subsystems. It is desirable that an equivalence is a congruence, that is, if a subsystem is replaced by an equivalent subsystem, then the system as a whole remains equivalent. Whether or not an equivalence is a congruence depends on the set of operators used in building systems from subsystems.

We say that "$\cong_1$" is *weaker* than "$\cong_2$" or that "$\cong_2$" *implies* "$\cong_1$", if and only if $P \cong_2 Q$ implies $P \cong_1 Q$ for every P and Q, but not vice versa. We say that "$\cong$" *preserves* a property, if and only if $P \cong Q$ implies that either none or both of P and Q have the property. If, for instance, "$\cong$" preserves deadlocks, P is complicated, Q is simple, and we can reason that $P \cong Q$, then we can analyse the deadlocks of P by analysing Q. On the other hand, if "$\cong$" also preserves some other information (say, livelocks) about which P and Q disagree, then $P \not\cong Q$, and we cannot reason that $P \cong Q$. Therefore, we would ideally like to use the weakest possible deadlock-preserving congruence in this analysis task.

Finding the weakest congruence that preserves a given property has been tedious. A handful of such results has been published (e.g., [1,3,5,6,8,11], please see [9] for comments on some of them), but if none of them directly matches, then the user is more or less left with empty hands. Two more powerful results

M. Koutny and I. Ulidowski (Eds.): CONCUR 2012, LNCS 7454, pp. 162–176, 2012.

were discussed in Chapters 11 and 12 of [7]. With the CSP set of operators and a certain notion of finite linear-time observations, there are only three congruences. Therefore, if the given property meets that notion, to find the weakest congruence that preserves it, it suffices to test the three congruences. If also infinite behaviour is observable, another set of only three congruences is obtained.

Behaviours of (sub)systems are often represented as *labelled transition systems*, abbreviated *LTS*. In [9], we proved — but only for finite LTSs — that another region contains precisely twenty congruences. Four of them are the same as in [7] and two are trivial. The remaining fourteen are obtained because [9] covers a different set of properties and uses a smaller set of operators than [7]. The operators in [9] are parallel composition, hiding, relational renaming, and action prefix. Only execution of visible actions, deadlock, and livelock were considered as directly observable. That is what was meant by *abstract linear-time*. It is slightly more general than the stuttering-insensitive linear temporal logic of [4]. Then the congruence requirement brought refusal sets into consideration in the end, but not in the middle, of a trace. The additional two congruences in [7] assume the ability to also observe refusal sets in the middle of a trace.

In this publication we extend the results of [9] by removing the finiteness assumption. Because of lack of space, we concentrate on proving that there are no other congruences than those that we discuss, and skip the proofs that they indeed are congruences.

Section 2 presents the background definitions and introduces the strongest abstract linear-time congruence (in our sense). Congruences that are weaker than it are found in Sections 3 to 5. Finally Fig. 6 summarizes the publication.

2 Basic Definitions

We reserve the symbol τ to denote so-called invisible actions. A *labelled transition system* or *LTS* is the tuple $(S, \Sigma, \Delta, \hat{s})$, where $\tau \notin \Sigma$, $\Delta \subseteq S \times (\Sigma \cup \{\tau\}) \times S$, and $\hat{s} \in S$. We call S the set of *states*, Σ the *alphabet*, Δ the set of *transitions*, and $\hat{s}$ the *initial state*. Unless otherwise stated, L_1 denotes the LTS $(S_1, \Sigma_1, \Delta_1, \hat{s}_1)$, and similarly with L, L', L_2, and so on. When we show an LTS as a drawing, *unless otherwise stated, its alphabet is precisely the labels in the drawing excluding* τ.

LTSs L_1 and L_2 are *bisimilar*, denoted with $L_1 \equiv L_2$, if and only if there is a relation "$\sim$" $\subseteq S_1 \times S_2$ such that (1) $\Sigma_1 = \Sigma_2$, (2) $\hat{s}_1 \sim \hat{s}_2$, and (3) for every $s_1 \in S_1$, $s_2 \in S_2$, $s_1' \in S_1$, $s_2' \in S_2$, and $a \in \Sigma \cup \{\tau\}$ such that $s_1 \sim s_2$, (3a) if $(s_1, a, s_1') \in \Delta_1$, then there is an s' such that $s_1' \sim s'$ and $(s_2, a, s') \in \Delta_2$, and (3b) if $(s_2, a, s_2') \in \Delta_2$, then there is an s' such that $s' \sim s_2'$ and $(s_1, a, s') \in \Delta_1$. It is well known that bisimilarity is a very strong equivalence. For the purposes of this publication, it can and will be used like identity. This implies that only the states and transitions that are reachable from the initial state matter, because any LTS is bisimilar to its reachable part.

If Φ is any set of pairs, we define $\mathcal{D}(\Phi) := \{a \mid \exists b : (a,b) \in \Phi\}$, $\mathcal{R}(\Phi) := \{b \mid \exists a : (a,b) \in \Phi\}$, and $\Phi(a,b) :\Leftrightarrow (a,b) \in \Phi \vee a = b \notin \mathcal{D}(\Phi)$. The operators that we use for building systems are defined as follows:

Action prefix. Let $a \neq \tau$. The LTS $L' = a.L$ is defined as $S' = S \cup \{\hat{s}'\}$, where $\hat{s}' \notin S$, $\Sigma' = \Sigma \cup \{a\}$, and $\Delta' = \Delta \cup \{(\hat{s}', a, \hat{s})\}$. That is, $a.L$ executes a and then behaves like L.

Hiding. Let A be a set. The LTS $L' = L \setminus A$ is defined as $S' = S$, $\Sigma' = \Sigma \setminus A$, $\Delta' = \{(s, a, s') \mid \exists b : (s, b, s') \in \Delta \wedge (a = b \notin A \vee a = \tau \wedge b \in A)\}$, and $\hat{s}' = \hat{s}$. That is, $L \setminus A$ behaves otherwise like L, but all labels in A are replaced by τ.

Relational renaming. Let Φ be a set of pairs such that $\tau \notin \mathcal{D}(\Phi) \cup \mathcal{R}(\Phi)$. The LTS $L' = L\Phi$ is defined as $S' = S$, $\hat{s}' = \hat{s}$, $\Sigma' = \{b \mid \exists a \in \Sigma : \Phi(a, b)\}$, and $\Delta' = \{(s, b, s') \mid \exists a : (s, a, s') \in \Delta \wedge \Phi(a, b)\}$. That is, $L\Phi$ behaves otherwise like L, but the labels of transitions are changed. A label may be replaced by more than one label, resulting in more than one copy of the original transition. If Φ does not specify any new label for a transition, it keeps its original label. This is in particular the case with τ-transitions.

Parallel composition. The LTS $L = L_1 \,||\, L_2$ is defined as $S = S_1 \times S_2$, $\Sigma = \Sigma_1 \cup \Sigma_2$, $\hat{s} = (\hat{s}_1, \hat{s}_2)$, and $((s_1, s_2), a, (s_1', s_2')) \in \Delta$ if and only if (1) $a \notin \Sigma_2$, $(s_1, a, s_1') \in \Delta_1$, and $s_2' = s_2$, (2) $a \notin \Sigma_1$, $s_1' = s_1$, and $(s_2, a, s_2') \in \Delta_2$, or (3) $a \in \Sigma_1 \cap \Sigma_2$, $(s_1, a, s_1') \in \Delta_1$, and $(s_2, a, s_2') \in \Delta_2$. That is, if a belongs to the alphabets of both L_1 and L_2, it is executed simultaneously by both. If $a = \tau$ or a belongs to the alphabet of precisely one of L_1 and L_2, then it is executed by one of L_1 and L_2 while the other stays in the state where it is. Clearly $L_2 \,||\, L_1 \equiv L_1 \,||\, L_2$ and $L_1 \,||\, (L_2 \,||\, L_3) \equiv (L_1 \,||\, L_2) \,||\, L_3$, so we may write $L_1 \,||\, \cdots \,||\, L_n$ without confusion.

The CSP language [2,7] has these operators (and many more), and every major process-algebraic language has at least something similar. Therefore, requiring the congruence property with respect to these operators is justified. One has to keep in mind, however, that if the language does not have all these operators, then it may have more abstract linear-time congruences than the ones in this publication. Indeed, we will see after Theorem 1 that the difference between functional and relational renaming matters. It is thus a good idea to declare:

> *In the theorems of this publication, "$\cong$" is a congruence means that it is an equivalence and for all LTSs L and L', if $L \cong L'$, then $a.L \cong a.L'$, $L \setminus A \cong L' \setminus A$, $L\Phi \cong L'\Phi$, $L \,||\, L'' \cong L' \,||\, L''$, and $L'' \,||\, L \cong L'' \,||\, L'$.*

It follows by structural induction that if $f(L_1, \ldots, L_n)$ is any expression only made of these four operators and $L_i \cong L_i'$ for $1 \leq i \leq n$, then $f(L_1, \ldots, L_n) \cong f(L_1', \ldots, L_n')$.

For discussing abstract equivalences, it is handy to have notation for talking about paths between states such that only the non-τ labels along the path are shown. Let Σ^* and Σ^ω denote the sets of all finite and infinite sequences of elements of Σ. By $s = \!\varepsilon\!\Rightarrow s'$ we mean that there are $s_0, \ldots, s_n$ such that $s = s_0$, $s_n = s'$, and $(s_{i-1}, \tau, s_i) \in \Delta$ for $1 \leq i \leq n$. By $s = \!a_1 a_2 \cdots a_n\!\Rightarrow s'$, where $a_1 a_2 \cdots a_n \in \Sigma^*$, we mean that there are $s_0, s_0', \ldots, s_n, s_n'$ such that $s_0 = s$, $s_n' = s'$, $s_i = \!\varepsilon\!\Rightarrow s_i'$ for $0 \leq i \leq n$, and $(s_{i-1}', a_i, s_i) \in \Delta$ for $1 \leq i \leq n$. If we do not want to mention s', we write $s = \!a_1 a_2 \cdots a_n\!\Rightarrow$, and $s = \!a_1 a_2 \cdots\!\Rightarrow$ denotes the similar notion for infinite sequences $a_1 a_2 \cdots$. An infinite path can also consist of an uninterrupted infinite sequence of invisible transitions. This is denoted with $s \, {-\tau^\omega\!\!\rightarrow}$.

Let $s \in S$. We say that s is *a deadlock* or *deadlocked* if and only if $\forall a : \forall s' : (s, a, s') \notin \Delta$. We say that s is *stable* if and only if $\forall s' : (s, \tau, s') \notin \Delta$.

The linear-time semantics of L (in our sense) consists of its complete — i.e., deadlocking or infinite — executions. The abstract linear-time semantics consists of their abstractions, i.e., *deadlocking traces*, *infinite traces*, and *divergence traces*. It is well known that to obtain a congruence and preserve deadlocks, the semantics must also preserve *stable failures* (see, e.g., [8]). We also define *traces*.

- $Tr(L) := \{\sigma \in \Sigma^* \mid \hat{s} \,{=\sigma\!\!\Rightarrow}\}$
- $Inf(L) := \{\xi \in \Sigma^\omega \mid \hat{s} \,{=\xi\!\!\Rightarrow}\}$
- $Div(L) := \{\sigma \in \Sigma^* \mid \exists s : \hat{s} \,{=\sigma\!\!\Rightarrow}\, s \wedge s \,{-\tau^\omega\!\!\rightarrow}\}$
- $Sf(L) := \{(\sigma, A) \in \Sigma^* \times 2^\Sigma \mid \exists s : \hat{s} \,{=\sigma\!\!\Rightarrow}\, s \wedge \forall a \in A \cup \{\tau\} : \forall s' : (s, a, s') \notin \Delta\}$

We do not introduce notation for deadlocking traces, because σ is a deadlocking trace if and only if $(\sigma, \Sigma) \in Sf(L)$.

For uniformity, from now on we denote the alphabet of L with $\Sigma(L)$. We say that *the equivalence induced by* Σ, *Sf*, *Div*, *and Inf* is the one defined by $\Sigma(L) = \Sigma(L') \wedge Sf(L) = Sf(L') \wedge Div(L) = Div(L') \wedge Inf(L) = Inf(L')$. It is a congruence [10]. It has traditionally been called *chaos-free failures divergences equivalence* or *CFFD-equivalence*. We will denote it with "$\doteq$".

CFFD-equivalence preserves full information on traces even without explicitly mentioning them, because of the following easily proven fact:

$$Tr(L) \;=\; Div(L) \cup \{\sigma \mid (\sigma, \emptyset) \in Sf(L)\} \tag{1}$$

We will also need the following.

$$Inf(L) \;\subseteq\; \{a_1 a_2 \cdots \in \Sigma^\omega \mid \forall i : a_1 a_2 \cdots a_i \in Tr(L)\} \tag{2}$$

In [9], the so-called *finite CFFD-equivalence* was used whose definition is otherwise the same but lacks $Inf(L) = Inf(L')$. In the case of finite LTSs, it coincides with CFFD-equivalence, because of the following (see, e.g., [10]):

$$Inf(L) \;=\; \{a_1 a_2 \cdots \in \Sigma^\omega \mid \forall i : a_1 a_2 \cdots a_i \in Tr(L)\}\ \text{, if } L \text{ is finite.}$$

Our goal is to find all congruences that are implied by "$\doteq$". For any stuttering-insensitive linear-time property in the sense of [4] (and a bit more), its optimal congruence is among them. To break our task into smaller parts, let us consider all possibilities when $\Sigma = \emptyset$. Then $Sf(L)$ is either $\emptyset$ or $\{(\varepsilon, \emptyset)\}$ and $Div(L)$ is either $\emptyset$ or $\{\varepsilon\}$. By (1) they cannot both be empty, because ε is a trace of every LTS. This leaves three possibilities. They can be drawn as follows.

We will study each of the cases  $\cong$ 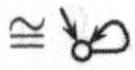,  $\cong$  $\not\cong$ , and  $\not\cong$  $\not\cong$  (not assuming  $\not\cong$ 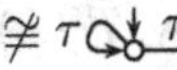) in turn.

3 When Deadlock ≅ Livelock

We define *the dullest congruence* by $L \cong L'$ holds for every L and L'. It is obviously the weakest of all congruences. The next theorem implies that it is the only congruence that does not imply $\Sigma(L) = \Sigma(L')$, that is, preserve Σ. Its proof in [9] does not rely on the finiteness assumption. (However, it does rely on how the definitions of $L \setminus A$ and $L\Phi$ treat actions who are not in $\Sigma(L)$.)

Theorem 1. *If "≅" is implied by "≡", is a congruence, and does not preserve Σ, then "≅" is the dullest congruence.*

With only functional renaming, the following would be a congruence: $L \cong L'$ if and only if $(\Sigma(L) \setminus \Sigma(L')) \cup (\Sigma(L') \setminus \Sigma(L))$ is finite.

It is easy to check from the definitions that the equivalence induced by Σ is a congruence. The next lemma will be needed soon.

Lemma 1. *Any congruence that preserves Inf also preserves Σ and Tr.*

Proof. Let "≅" be a congruence that preserves *Inf*. Then $\searrow\!\circ\!\circlearrowleft a \not\cong \searrow\!\circ\!\xrightarrow{a}\!\circ$, so "≅" preserves Σ by Theorem 1. Let $L \cong L'$, $\Sigma = \Sigma(L) = \Sigma(L')$, and $b \notin \Sigma \cup \{\tau\}$. If $\sigma = a_1 a_2 \cdots a_n \in Tr(L)$, then let T_σ^b be $\searrow\!\circ\!\xrightarrow{a_1}\!\circ\!\xrightarrow{a_2} \ldots \xrightarrow{a_n}\!\circ\!\circlearrowleft b$ with the alphabet $\Sigma \cup \{b\}$. We have $\sigma b^\omega \in Inf(L \,||\, T_\sigma^b) = Inf(L' \,||\, T_\sigma^b)$, yielding $\sigma \in Tr(L')$. So $Tr(L) \subseteq Tr(L')$. By symmetry, $Tr(L') \subseteq Tr(L)$. □

Many of the subsequent proofs use the following lemma. In it, $X_1, \ldots, X_k$ are functions from LTSs to sets, like *Tr* and *Sf*. A similar lemma without *Inf* was presented and proven in [9]. The lemma is so central that we show its proof, although it is essentially the same as in [9].

Lemma 2. *Assume that "≅" is an equivalence, is implied by "≐", and preserves Σ and $X_1, \ldots, X_k$. Assume that there is a function f such that for every LTS L we have $L \cong f(L)$, and $Sf(f(L))$, $Div(f(L))$, and $Inf(f(L))$ can be represented as functions of $\Sigma(L)$ and $X_1(L), \ldots, X_k(L)$. Then "≅" is the equivalence induced by Σ and $X_1, \ldots, X_k$.*

Proof. Obviously "≅" implies the equivalence induced by Σ and $X_1, \ldots, X_k$.

To prove the implication in the opposite direction, let $\Sigma(L) = \Sigma(L')$ and $X_i(L) = X_i(L')$ for $1 \leq i \leq k$. We need to prove that $L \cong L'$. We have $\Sigma(f(L)) = \Sigma(L) = \Sigma(L') = \Sigma(f(L'))$, because $L \cong f(L)$ and "≅" preserves Σ. When $X \in \{Sf, Div, Inf\}$, let λ_X be the function that represents $X(f(L))$ as was promised. Then $X(f(L)) = \lambda_X(\Sigma(L), X_1(L), \ldots, X_k(L)) = \lambda_X(\Sigma(L'), X_1(L'), \ldots, X_k(L')) = X(f(L'))$. We get $f(L) \doteq f(L')$. So $L \cong f(L) \doteq f(L') \cong L'$ and $L \cong L'$. □

The following theorem and its proof are adapted from [9] by adding *Inf* and not assuming that *Tr* is preserved. The proof illustrates, in a simple context, the use of Lemma 2. Although the f in the proof preserves the congruence, it throws away all information on *Sf* and *Div*. This is possible because of the assumption $\searrow\!\circ \cong \searrow\!\circ\!\circlearrowleft \tau$. Although $Div(f(L))$ is neither $\emptyset$ nor $\Sigma(L)^*$, it contains no genuine information, because it is fully determined by $Tr(L)$.

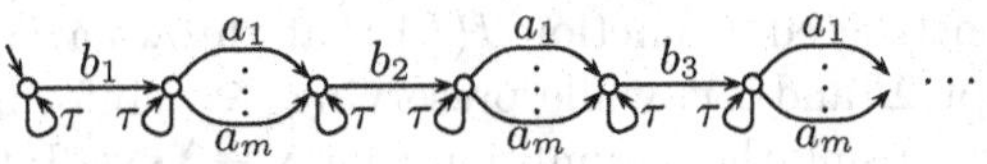

Fig. 1. An LTS for detecting the infinite trace $b_1b_2\cdots$. $\{a_1,\ldots,a_m\}$ may be infinite

Theorem 2. *If "$\cong$" is a congruence, "$\doteq$" implies "$\cong$", "$\cong$" preserves Inf, and* $\searrow\!\circ \cong \searrow\!\circ\!\circlearrowleft\tau$*, then "$\cong$" is the equivalence induced by Σ, Tr, and Inf.*

Proof. By Lemma 1, "$\cong$" preserves Σ and *Tr*. Let $f(L) = L \,||\, \searrow\!\circ\!\circlearrowleft\tau$. We have $L \equiv L \,||\, \searrow\!\circ \cong L \,||\, \searrow\!\circ\!\circlearrowleft\tau = f(L)$. Clearly $\mathit{Sf}(f(L)) = \emptyset$, $\mathit{Div}(f(L)) = \mathit{Tr}(L)$, and $\mathit{Inf}(f(L)) = \mathit{Inf}(L)$. Lemma 2 gives the claim if we choose $k = 2$, $X_1 = \mathit{Tr}$, and $X_2 = \mathit{Inf}$. □

In forthcoming proofs, we will play trickery with renaming and hiding so that precisely those actions synchronize whom we want to synchronize. To facilitate that, we introduce the following notation for temporarily attaching an integer i to symbols other than τ.

- If $a \neq \tau \notin A$ and $a_j \neq \tau$ for $1 \leq j$, then $a^{[i]} := (a, i)$, $A^{[i]} := \{a^{[i]} \mid a \in A\}$, $(a_1a_2\cdots a_n)^{[i]} := a_1^{[i]}a_2^{[i]}\cdots a_n^{[i]}$, and $(a_1a_2\cdots)^{[i]} := a_1^{[i]}a_2^{[i]}\cdots$.
- $\lceil L \rceil^{[i]} := L\Phi$, where $\Phi = \{(a, a^{[i]}) \mid a \in \Sigma\}$.
- $\lfloor L \rfloor_{[i]} := L\Phi$, where $\Phi = \{(a^{[i]}, a) \mid a^{[i]} \in \Sigma\}$.

Let $\mathsf{Run}(A)$ denote the LTS whose alphabet is A, who has one state, and whose transitions are $\{(\hat{s}, a, \hat{s}) \mid a \in A\}$. We are ready to present the first significantly new result of this publication.

Theorem 3. *If "$\cong$" is a congruence, "$\doteq$" implies "$\cong$", "$\cong$" preserves Tr but not Inf, and* $\searrow\!\circ \cong \searrow\!\circ\!\circlearrowleft\tau$*, then "$\cong$" is the equivalence induced by Σ and Tr.*

Proof. There are M_1, M_2, and ξ such that $M_1 \cong M_2$ and $\xi \in \mathit{Inf}(M_1) \setminus \mathit{Inf}(M_2)$. Because "$\cong$" preserves *Tr*, Theorem 1 implies that it also preserves Σ, so we may let $\Sigma_M = \Sigma(M_1) = \Sigma(M_2)$. Let $b_1b_2\cdots = \xi^{[1]}$. Let A be any set such that $\tau \notin A$. Let $\{a_1, a_2, \ldots [, a_m]\} = A^{[2]}$, where "$[, a_m]$" emphasizes that A may be finite or infinite. When $i \in \{1, 2\}$, let

$$M_i^A \;=\; \lfloor (T_\xi \,||\, \lceil M_i \rceil^{[1]}) \setminus \Sigma_M^{[1]} \rfloor_{[2]} \;,$$

where $\Sigma(T_\xi) = \Sigma_M^{[1]} \cup A^{[2]}$ and otherwise T_ξ is like in Fig. 1. Because $X^{[i]}$ and $Y^{[j]}$ are disjoint whenever $i \neq j$, we have $\Sigma(M_1^A) = \Sigma(M_2^A) = A$. Thanks to the τ-loops in Fig. 1, $\mathit{Sf}(M_1^A) = \mathit{Sf}(M_2^A) = \emptyset$. By (2), M_1 can execute any finite prefix of ξ. This yields $\mathit{Tr}(M_1^A) = \mathit{Div}(M_1^A) = A^*$. By the congruence property $M_1^A \cong M_2^A$. Because "$\cong$" preserves *Tr*, also $\mathit{Tr}(M_2^A) = \mathit{Div}(M_2^A) = A^*$. Since M_1 can but M_2 cannot execute ξ completely, we get $\mathit{Inf}(M_1^A) = A^\omega$ and $\mathit{Inf}(M_2^A) = \emptyset$.

Let L be any LTS and $A = \Sigma(L)$. We can reason $\mathsf{Run}(A) \equiv \mathsf{Run}(A) \,||\, \searrow\!\circ \cong \mathsf{Run}(A) \,||\, \searrow\!\circ\!\circlearrowleft\tau \doteq M_1^A \cong M_2^A$, and $L \equiv L \,||\, \mathsf{Run}(A) \cong L \,||\, M_2^A$. Lemma 2 gives the claim if we choose $k = 1$, $X_1 = \mathit{Tr}$, and $f(L) = L \,||\, M_2^A$, because then $L \cong f(L)$, $\mathit{Sf}(f(L)) = \emptyset$, $\mathit{Div}(f(L)) = \mathit{Tr}(L)$, and $\mathit{Inf}(f(L)) = \emptyset$. □

The above proof constructed a function $f(L)$ that throws away all information (modulo "$\doteq$") except Σ and Tr, while preserving "$\cong$". Information on Sf and Div was thrown away using the assumption that $\searrow\!\circ \cong \searrow\!\circ\!\circlearrowright\tau$. Information on Inf was thrown away by starting with an arbitrary difference on Inf, and amplifying it to a function $f'(L,M) = L|||\lfloor(T_\xi||\lceil M\rceil^{[1]})\backslash\Sigma_M^{[1]}\rfloor_{[2]}$ so that $f'(L,M_1)$ preserves $Inf(L)$ while $f'(L,M_2)$ wipes it out. The permission to also throw away all information on Sf and Div simplified the design. We have $L \cong f'(L,M_1) \cong f'(L,M_2) = f(L)$, where the first "$\cong$" takes care of Sf and Div, and the second of Inf. In the construction of f, despite the use of notation defined in this section, ultimately only operators from Section 2 were used.

The following theorem was proven in [9] with the same method. The proof did not discuss Inf, but its f has $Inf(f(L)) = \emptyset$ by (2), because it has $Tr(f(L)) = \{\varepsilon\}$. So Lemma 2 of this publication applies.

Theorem 4. *If "$\cong$" is a congruence, "$\doteq$" implies "$\cong$", "$\cong$" preserves Σ but not Tr, and $\searrow\!\circ \cong \searrow\!\circ\!\circlearrowright\tau$, then "$\cong$" is the equivalence induced by Σ.*

In conclusion, altogether precisely four abstract linear-time congruences satisfy $\searrow\!\circ \cong \searrow\!\circ\!\circlearrowright\tau$: those induced by the first zero, one, two, or three of Σ, Tr, and Inf. That also the last two are congruences is widely known and proven, e.g., in [10].

4 When Deadlock $\cong$ Bothlock $\ncong$ Livelock

The following results are from [9], with easy modifications to cover Inf:

Theorem 5. *If "$\cong$" is a congruence, "$\doteq$" implies "$\cong$", and $\tau\circlearrowright\!\overset{\downarrow}{\circ}\xrightarrow{\tau}\circ \ncong \searrow\!\circ\!\circlearrowright\tau$, then "$\cong$" preserves Sf.*

If "$\cong$" is a congruence, "$\doteq$" implies "$\cong$", "$\cong$" preserves Sf but not Tr, and $\searrow\!\circ \cong \tau\circlearrowright\!\overset{\downarrow}{\circ}\xrightarrow{\tau}\circ$, then "$\cong$" is the equivalence induced by Σ and Sf.

If "$\cong$" is a congruence, "$\doteq$" implies "$\cong$", "$\cong$" preserves Sf and Inf, and $\searrow\!\circ \cong \tau\circlearrowright\!\overset{\downarrow}{\circ}\xrightarrow{\tau}\circ$, then "$\cong$" is the equivalence induced by Σ, Tr, Sf, and Inf.

These leave a gap between (Σ, Tr, Sf) and (Σ, Tr, Sf, Inf). To fill it, we need a more complicated construction than in the proof of Theorem 3, because this time Sf has to be preserved. We will use the "internal choice" operator of CSP. It is equivalent to the CCS expression $\tau.P + \tau.Q$, and it can be built from our operators as follows:

$$L_1 \sqcap L_2 \;:=\; ((L_C \,||\, c_1.\lceil L_1\rceil^{[1]} \,||\, c_2.\lceil L_2\rceil^{[2]}) \setminus \{c_1, c_2\})\Phi\,,$$

where $\Phi = \{(a^{[i]}, a) \mid 1 \le i \le 2 \land a \in \Sigma_i\}$, $c_1 = 1^{[0]}$, $c_2 = 2^{[0]}$, and L_C has $S_C = \{\hat{s}_C, s_C\}$, $\Sigma_C = \{c_1, c_2\}$, $\Delta_C = \{(\hat{s}_C, c_1, s_C), (\hat{s}_C, c_2, s_C)\}$, and $\hat{s}_C \ne s_C$. (Here c_1 and c_2 could be any distinct new symbols.)

The CFFD-semantics of this operator is simple:

$$\begin{array}{rclrcl}
\Sigma(L \sqcap L') & = & \Sigma(L) \cup \Sigma(L') & \quad Div(L \sqcap L') & = & Div(L) \cup Div(L') \\
Sf(L \sqcap L') & = & Sf(L) \cup Sf(L') & \quad Inf(L \sqcap L') & = & Inf(L) \cup Inf(L')
\end{array}$$

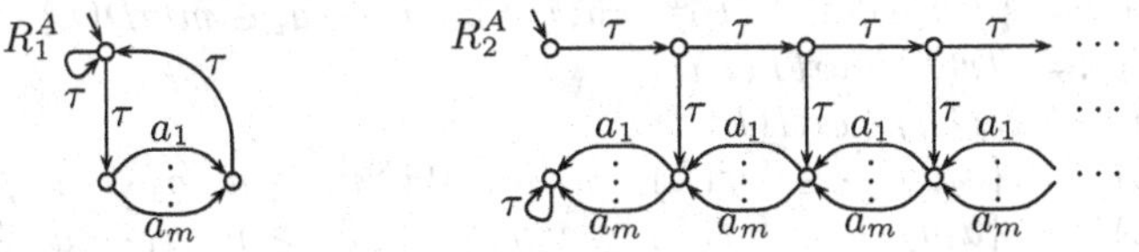

Fig. 2. R_1^A has $\Sigma(R_1^A) = A = \{a_1, \ldots [, a_m]\}$, $Sf(R_1^A) = A^* \times \{\emptyset\}$, $Div(R_1^A) = A^*$, and $Inf(R_1^A) = A^\omega$. R_2^A has the same except $Inf(R_2^A) = \emptyset$.

Theorem 6. *If "$\cong$" is a congruence, "$\doteq$" implies "$\cong$", "$\cong$" preserves Tr and Sf but not Inf, and* $\searrow\!\circ \cong \tau\circlearrowleft\!\searrow\!\circ\!\xrightarrow{\tau}\!\circ$, *then "$\cong$" is the equivalence induced by Σ, Tr, and Sf.*

Proof. Let $M_1 \cong M_2$, $\xi \in Inf(M_1) \setminus Inf(M_2)$, $b_1 b_2 \cdots = \xi^{[1]}$, and A be any set such that $\tau \notin A$. By Theorem 1, "$\cong$" preserves Σ. Let $\Sigma_M = \Sigma(M_1) = \Sigma(M_2)$. When $i \in \{1, 2\}$, let

$$M_i^A = \lfloor (T_\xi \,||\, \lceil M_i \rceil^{[1]}) \setminus \Sigma_M^{[1]} \rfloor_{[2]} ,$$

where $\Sigma(T_\xi) = \Sigma_M^{[1]} \cup A^{[2]}$ and otherwise T_ξ is like in Fig. 1.

Because T_ξ does not have stable states, we have $Sf(M_1^A) = Sf(M_2^A) = \emptyset$. Because $\lceil M_2 \rceil^{[1]}$ lacks the infinite trace $b_1 b_2 \cdots$, M_2^A has no infinite traces. Let R_1^A and R_2^A be the LTSs in Fig. 2. We have $Div(R_2^A) = A^*$. These imply $M_2^A \sqcap R_2^A \doteq R_2^A$. On the other hand, M_1^A has A^ω as its infinite traces, $Inf(R_1^A) = A^\omega$, $Sf(R_1^A) = Sf(R_2^A)$, and also $Div(R_1^A) = A^*$, so $M_1^A \sqcap R_2^A \doteq R_1^A$. As a consequence, $R_1^A \doteq M_1^A \sqcap R_2^A \cong M_2^A \sqcap R_2^A \doteq R_2^A$.

By choosing $A = \Sigma(L)$ and $f(L) = L \,||\, R_2^A$ we get $L \equiv L \,||\, \searrow\!\circ \cong L \,||\, \tau\circlearrowleft\!\searrow\!\circ\!\xrightarrow{\tau}\!\circ \doteq L \,||\, R_1^A \cong L \,||\, R_2^A$, so $L \cong f(L)$. We have $Sf(f(L)) = Sf(L)$, $Div(f(L)) = Tr(f(L)) = Tr(L)$, and $Inf(f(L)) = \emptyset$. Lemma 2 gives the claim. □

To summarize, precisely three absract linear-time congruences satisfy $\searrow\!\circ \cong \tau\circlearrowleft\!\searrow\!\circ\!\xrightarrow{\tau}\!\circ \not\cong \searrow\!\circ\!\circlearrowright\tau$: those induced by (Σ, Sf), (Σ, Tr, Sf), and (Σ, Tr, Sf, Inf).

5 When Deadlock $\not\cong$ The Other Two

In this section we need new semantic sets. *Minimal divergence traces minD* are divergence traces whose proper prefixes are not divergence traces. Finite extensions of minimal divergence traces *extT* are an alternative representation for the same information (assuming that Σ is available). Also infinite extensions *extI* can be derived from *minD*. *Always-nondivergent traces anT* are traces who and whose proper prefixes are not divergence traces, and similarly with *always-nondivergent infinite traces anI*. *Eventually-always-nondivergent infinite traces eanI* may have a finite number of divergence traces as prefixes. *Always-eventually-nondivergent infinite traces aenI* have an infinite number of prefixes that are not divergence traces.

- $minD(L) := \{a_1 \cdots a_n \in Div(L) \mid \forall i; 0 \leq i < n : a_1 \cdots a_i \notin Div(L)\}$
- $extT(L) := \{a_1 \cdots a_n \in \Sigma(L)^* \mid \exists i; 0 \leq i \leq n : a_1 \cdots a_i \in minD(L)\}$

- $extI(L) := \{a_1a_2\cdots \in \Sigma(L)^\omega \mid \exists i; i \geq 0 : a_1\cdots a_i \in minD(L)\}$
- $anT(L) := Tr(L) \setminus extT(L)$
- $anI(L) := Inf(L) \setminus extI(L)$
- $eanI(L) := \{a_1a_2\cdots \in Inf(L) \mid \exists n; n \geq 0 : \forall i; i \geq n : a_1\cdots a_i \notin Div(L)\}$
- $aenI(L) := \{a_1a_2\cdots \in Inf(L) \mid \forall n; n \geq 0 : \exists i; i \geq n : a_1\cdots a_i \notin Div(L)\}$

Lemma 3. *Any congruence that preserves minD also preserves anT and anI. Any congruence that preserves Div also preserves Tr and eanI.*

Proof. The anT- and Tr-claims have been proven in [9].

Let $L \cong L'$ and $a_1a_2\cdots \in anI(L)$. Then $\Sigma(L) = \Sigma(L')$ by Theorem 1, and none of $a_1\cdots a_i$ is in $minD(L)$. Furthermore, $\varepsilon \in minD((L \,||\, T) \setminus \Sigma(L))$, where $T = \rightarrow\circ\xrightarrow{a_1}\circ\xrightarrow{a_2}\cdots$ with $\Sigma(T) = \Sigma(L)$. So $\varepsilon \in minD((L' \,||\, T) \setminus \Sigma(L'))$. Since $minD(L' \,||\, T) = minD(L \,||\, T) = \emptyset$, we have $a_1a_2\cdots \in anI(L')$.

Let $\Sigma_L = \Sigma(L)$, $\xi \in eanI(L)$, and $L \cong L'$. If no prefix of ξ is in $Div(L)$, then let $i = 1$, and otherwise let i be 2 plus the length of the longest prefix of ξ that is in $Div(L)$. Let $a_i \notin \Sigma_L \cup \{\tau\}$ and, when $1 \leq j \neq i$, let a_j be such that $\xi = a_1\cdots a_{i-1}a_{i+1}\cdots$. Let T be the LTS whose alphabet is $\Sigma_L \cup \{a_i\}$ and whose graph is $\rightarrow\circ\xrightarrow{a_1}\circ\xrightarrow{a_2}\cdots$. We have $a_i \in Div((L||T)\setminus\Sigma_L) = Div((L'||T)\setminus\Sigma_L)$. When $j \geq 0$, none of $a_1\cdots a_{i-1}a_{i+1}\cdots a_{i+j}$ is in $Div(L')$, because $Div(L') = Div(L)$. As a consequence, $\xi \in Inf(L')$ and $\xi \in eanI(L')$. □

In [9], the following four additional kinds of failures were defined.

- $nF(L) := \{(\sigma, A) \in Sf(L) \mid \sigma \notin Div(L)\}$
- $snF(L) := \{(\sigma, A) \in nF(L) \mid \forall a \in A : \sigma a \notin Div(L)\}$
- $anF(L) := \{(\sigma, A) \in Sf(L) \mid \sigma \notin extT(L)\}$
- $sanF(L) := \{(\sigma, A) \in anF(L) \mid \forall a \in A : \sigma a \notin minD(L)\}$

In [9] it was proven that for finite LTSs, only the following 15 congruences (without Y_1, Y_2, and Y_3) exist in addition to those found in Sections 3 and 4:

- $(\Sigma, X, minD, Y_1)$ where X is anT, $sanF$, anF, or Sf.
- $(\Sigma, Tr, X, minD, Y_2)$ where X is none, $sanF$, anF, or Sf.
- (Σ, X, Div, Y_3) where X is
  Tr, $(Tr \;\&\; sanF)$, $(Tr \;\&\; anF)$, snF, $(anF \;\&\; snF)$, nF, or Sf.

Without the finiteness assumption, some Y_i are needed by Lemma 3. Similar adaptations of the results in [9] as in Section 3 tell that Y_1 is anI, but let Y_2 and Y_3 be anything between what Lemma 3 says and Inf. Other than that, they do not leave room for additional congruences. Using functions f of Lemma 2 of the form $g(f_2(L))$, where the f_2 are given below and the g are from [9], it is possible to prove that Y_2 is anI or Inf, and Y_3 is $eanI$, $aenI$, or Inf. Because of lack of space, we only show the proofs when g is the identity function (that is, $X = Sf$).

We need a construction that preserves anI but not Inf. Our construction will block infinite traces after a minimal divergence trace, while not affecting them before a minimal divergence trace. Blocking does not have the desired effect unless *all* executions of the same minimal divergence trace switch it on. Forcing the execution of the switch at every divergent state does not suffice, because the same trace may have two executions, one leading to a divergent and the other to a nondivergent state. Even if we knew that this is the case with some nondivergent state, we could not blindly implement the switch there, because it may also be reachable via another, always-nondivergent trace.

To cope with this problem, we use the function Una that was defined in [9] to solve another problem of a similar nature. We first define the *determinization* of L as the LTS $\mathsf{Det}(L) := (S_\mathsf{D}, \Sigma, \Delta_\mathsf{D}, \hat{s}_\mathsf{D})$, where $S_\sigma = \{s \mid \hat{s} =\sigma\Rightarrow s\}$, $S_\mathsf{D} = \{S_\sigma \mid \sigma \in Tr(L)\}$, $\Delta_\mathsf{D} = \{(S_\sigma, a, S_{\sigma a}) \mid a \neq \tau \wedge \sigma a \in Tr(L)\}$, and $\hat{s}_\mathsf{D} = S_\varepsilon$. We define $\mathsf{Una}(L) := L \,||\, \mathsf{Det}(L)$. One may check that $\mathsf{Det}(L)$ and $\mathsf{Una}(L)$ are LTSs, and $\mathsf{Una}(L) \equiv L$. We say that a state of $\mathsf{Una}(L)$ is *potentially divergent* if it can be reached via a divergence trace, and *certainly nondivergent* otherwise. The following lemma is from [9].

Lemma 4. *If state s_U of $\mathsf{Una}(L)$ is potentially divergent, then all traces that lead to it belong to $Div(L)$. If state s_U of $\mathsf{Una}(L)$ is certainly nondivergent, then no trace that leads to it belongs to $Div(L)$.*

Then we define a function PD that makes the following property hold while preserving CFFD-equivalence: for every state s, either no or all traces that lead to s has a divergence trace as a prefix. This is obtained by adding a component to $\mathsf{Una}(L)$ that remembers if the execution has gone through a divergence trace. Formally, by $\mathsf{PD}(L)$ we mean the LTS $(S_\mathsf{P}, \Sigma, \Delta_\mathsf{P}, \hat{s}_\mathsf{P})$ that is obtained as follows. Let $[\sigma] = \mathsf{pre}$ if $\sigma \in anT(L)$ and $[\sigma] = \mathsf{post}$ otherwise. Let $\sigma^\tau = \sigma$ and $\sigma^a = \sigma a$ if $a \in \Sigma$. First L is replaced by $\mathsf{Una}(L) = (S_\mathsf{U}, \Sigma, \Delta_\mathsf{U}, \hat{s}_\mathsf{U})$. Then let

- $S_\mathsf{P} \;=\; \{(s_\mathsf{U}, [\sigma]) \mid \hat{s}_\mathsf{U} =\sigma\Rightarrow s_\mathsf{U}\}$,
- $\Delta_\mathsf{P} \;=\; \{((s_\mathsf{U}, [\sigma]), a, (s'_\mathsf{U}, [\sigma^a])) \mid \hat{s}_\mathsf{U} =\sigma\Rightarrow s_\mathsf{U} \wedge (s_\mathsf{U}, a, s'_\mathsf{U}) \in \Delta_\mathsf{U}\}$, and
- $\hat{s}_\mathsf{P} \;=\; (\hat{s}_\mathsf{U}, [\varepsilon])$.

We say that (s_U, x) is *pre-divergent* if $x = \mathsf{pre}$ and *post-divergent* otherwise.

Lemma 5. *We have $\mathsf{PD}(L) \equiv L$. If state s_P of $\mathsf{PD}(L)$ is pre-divergent, then all traces that lead to it belong to $anT(L)$. If state s_P of $\mathsf{PD}(L)$ is post-divergent, then no trace that leads to it belongs to $anT(L)$.*

Proof. The subscripts $_\mathsf{U}$ or $_\mathsf{P}$ of states reveal which LTS is in question. We have $\mathsf{PD}(L) \equiv \mathsf{Una}(L) \equiv L$, because the relation $(s_\mathsf{U}, [\sigma]) \sim s'_\mathsf{U} \Leftrightarrow s_\mathsf{U} = s'_\mathsf{U}$ is a bisimulation between S_P and S_U. If $[\sigma^a] = \mathsf{pre}$, then $\sigma^a \in anT(L)$, implying $\sigma \in anT(L)$ and $[\sigma] = \mathsf{pre}$. Thus $\mathsf{PD}(L)$ has no transitions from post-divergent to pre-divergent states. Let $\hat{s}_\mathsf{P} =\rho\Rightarrow (s_\mathsf{U}, x)$ and $\rho \in Div(L)$. Because $(s_\mathsf{U}, x) \in S_\mathsf{P}$, there is a σ such that $\hat{s}_\mathsf{U} =\sigma\Rightarrow s_\mathsf{U}$ and $x = [\sigma]$. Because $\rho \in Div(L)$, s_U is potentially divergent. So all traces that lead to it are divergence traces. That includes σ, thus $x = \mathsf{post}$. As a consequence, each trace that has a divergence trace as a prefix only leads to post-divergent states.

If an execution of $\mathsf{PD}(L)$ leads to a post-divergent state, then $\hat{s}_\mathsf{P}$ is post-divergent or the execution contains a transition of the form $((s_\mathsf{U}, \mathsf{pre}), a, (s'_\mathsf{U}, \mathsf{post}))$. In the first case, $[\varepsilon] = \mathsf{post}$, so $\varepsilon \in Div(L)$. In the second case, by the definition

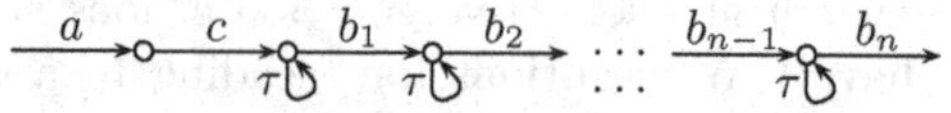

Fig. 3. An LTS fragment for detecting the divergence trace $b_1 b_2 \cdots b_n$

of Δ_{P}, there is a σ such that $\hat{s}_{\mathsf{U}} {=}\sigma{\Rightarrow}\, s_{\mathsf{U}}$, $\sigma \in anT(L)$, and $\sigma a \notin anT(L)$. This implies $\sigma a \in Div(L)$. So s'_{U} is potentially divergent and all traces that lead to it are divergence traces. As a consequence, each post-divergent state has a divergence trace in each of its histories. □

Armed with PD, we can attack the case where *Tr*, *Sf*, and *minD* are preserved, but *Div* and *Inf* are not. This time there is no unique next congruence, but two. Therefore, the proof consists of two parts, where the first throws away information on divergence traces that are not minimal, and the second on infinite traces that are not always-nondivergent. To be compatible with the functions in [9], we must have $Sf(f_2(L)) = Sf(L)$, complicating the construction.

Theorem 7. *If "≅" is a congruence, "≐" implies "≅", and "≅" preserves Tr, Sf, and minD but neither Div nor Inf, then "≅" is the equivalence induced by Σ, Tr, Sf, minD, and anI.*

Proof. Let $M_1 \cong M_2$, $\sigma \in Div(M_1) \setminus Div(M_2)$, $b_1 \cdots b_n = \sigma^{[1]}$, $c = 1^{[0]}$, and $d = 2^{[0]}$. Let $\Sigma_M = \Sigma(M_1) = \Sigma(M_2)$. For any LTS L, let $\Sigma_L = \Sigma(L)$ and let $g(L)$ be the LTS that is obtained as follows. First L is replaced by $\mathsf{PD}(\lceil L \rceil^{[2]})$. Then each transition (s, a, s') where s is pre-divergent and s' is post-divergent is replaced by a copy of the LTS fragment shown in Fig. 3. If $\hat{s}_{\mathsf{P}}$ is pre-divergent, then it is the new initial state. Otherwise a copy of Fig. 3 is added such that its a-transition is left out, the start state of the c-transition is the new initial state, and the LTS fragment leads to $\hat{s}_{\mathsf{P}}$. The alphabet of $g(L)$ is $\{c\} \cup \Sigma_M^{[1]} \cup \Sigma_L^{[2]}$. When completing a minimal divergence trace of $\lceil L \rceil^{[2]}$, $g(L)$ executes $c\sigma^{[1]}$ before continuing, but otherwise it behaves like $\lceil L \rceil^{[2]}$.

Let $N'_0 = \searrow\!\circ$. We will introduce N'_1, N'_2, and Σ_N later. When $i \in \{1, 2\}$ and $j \in \{0, 1, 2\}$, let $M'_i = c.\lceil M_i \sqcap M_2 \rceil^{[1]}$ and

$$f_{i,j}(L) \;=\; \lfloor\, (g(L) \,||\, M'_i \;\, ||\, N'_j\,) \setminus (\{c, d\} \cup \Sigma_M^{[1]} \cup \Sigma_N^{[3]}) \,\rfloor_{[2]} \;.$$

We show now that $L \doteq f_{2,0}(L)$. Clearly N'_0 has no effect to the behaviour. Before completing any minimal divergence trace, $f_{2,0}(L)$ behaves like L. When $g(L)$ executes c, one of the two copies of M_2 in M'_2 is switched on. Then $g(L)$ tries to execute $\sigma^{[1]}$. If it fails because M_2 blocks it, then $f_{2,0}(L)$ diverges due to the τ-loops in Fig. 3. That is still equivalent to L, because the trace that has been executed is a minimal divergence trace. For the same reason it is okay if M_2 diverges before completing σ. The execution of σ may also succeed, because $\sigma \in Div(M_1) \subseteq Tr(M_1) = Tr(M_2)$. In that case, $g(L)$ continues like L. Because $\sigma \notin Div(M_2)$, M_2 is left in a nondivergent state, having no effect on the further behaviour.

Because M'_1 has a copy of both M_1 and M_2, $f_{1,0}(L)$ behaves otherwise like $f_{2,0}(L)$, but it has additional behaviour caused by M_1 starting in M'_1, executing σ

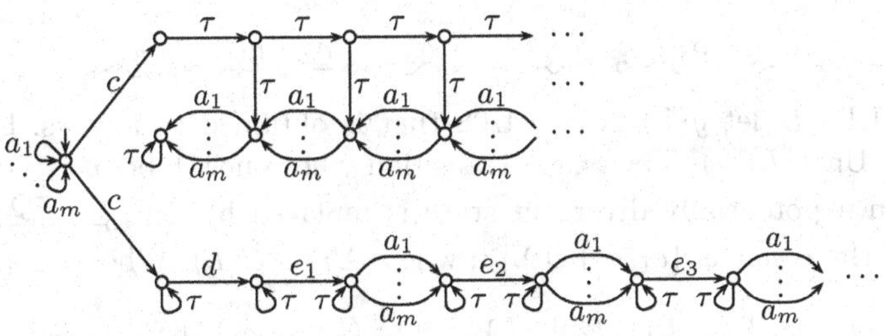

Fig. 4. A switchable LTS for detecting the infinite trace $e_1e_2\cdots$

completely, and diverging. In that case, every subsequent state of $f_{1,0}(L)$ is divergent. Thus $L \doteq f_{2,0}(L) \cong f_{1,0}(L)$, $Tr(f_{1,0}(L)) = Tr(L)$, $Sf(f_{1,0}(L)) = Sf(L)$, $minD(f_{1,0}(L)) = minD(L)$, $Div(f_{1,0}(L)) = extT(L) \cap Tr(L)$, $anI(f_{1,0}(L)) = anI(L)$, and $Inf(f_{1,0}(L)) = Inf(L)$.

Because Inf is not preserved, there are N_1, N_2, and ξ such that $N_1 \cong N_2$ and $\xi \in Inf(N_1) \setminus Inf(N_2)$. Let $e_1e_2\cdots = \xi^{[3]}$, $\Sigma_N = \Sigma(N_1) = \Sigma(N_2)$, and $\{a_1, a_2, \ldots [, a_m]\} = \Sigma_L^{[2]}$. When $j \in \{1,2\}$, let $N_j' = T_\xi \parallel d.\lceil N_j \rceil^{[3]}$, where T_ξ is the LTS in Fig. 4 with the alphabet $\{c,d\} \cup \Sigma_L^{[2]} \cup \Sigma_N^{[3]}$. (We have $\Sigma(N_0') \neq \Sigma(N_1')$, but that will not matter.)

If $j \in \{1,2\}$, c makes T_ξ enter one of its two branches. Its initial state and upper branch can parallel any finite execution of $g(L)$. Because T_ξ never refuses any other subset of $\Sigma_L^{[2]}$ than $\emptyset$, and because of the stable states initially and in its upper branch, $Sf(f_{1,j}(L)) = Sf(f_{1,0}(L))$. Furthermore, $Div(f_{1,j}(L)) = Div(f_{1,0}(L))$, because T_ξ cannot diverge before executing c, and all traces that involve the execution of c are in $Div(f_{1,0}(L))$. In its lower branch T_ξ switches N_j on by executing d. Thanks to the initial state of T_ξ and because N_2 cannot execute ξ, we have $Inf(f_{1,2}(L)) = anI(f_{1,0}(L))$. Because N_1 can execute ξ, we have $Inf(f_{1,1}(L)) = Inf(f_{1,0}(L))$. We get $f_{1,0}(L) \doteq f_{1,1}(L) \cong f_{1,2}(L)$.

For compatibility with the naming conventions outside this proof, let $f_2(L) = f_{1,2}(L)$. So $L \cong f_2(L)$, $Sf(f_2(L)) = Sf(L)$, $Div(f_2(L)) = extT(L) \cap Tr(L)$, and $Inf(f_2(L)) = anI(L)$. By Lemma 3, "$\cong$" preserves anI. Therefore, f_2 qualifies as the f of Lemma 2. □

The case where Div is preserved but Inf is not splits to two.

Theorem 8. *If "$\cong$" is a congruence, "$\doteq$" implies "$\cong$", and "$\cong$" preserves Sf and Div but not aenI, then "$\cong$" is the equivalence induced by Σ, Sf, Div, and eanI.*

Proof. Let $M_1 \cong M_2$ and $\xi \in aenI(M_1) \setminus aenI(M_2)$. Let $\Sigma_M = \Sigma(M_1) = \Sigma(M_2)$, $c = 0^{[0]}$, $c_1 = 1^{[0]}$, and $c_2 = 2^{[0]}$. Because Div is preserved, M_1 and M_2 agree on which prefixes of ξ are divergence traces. Infinitely many of them are not, by the definition of $aenI$. So non-empty σ_1, σ_2, σ_3, ... exist such that $\sigma_1\sigma_2\sigma_3\cdots = \xi^{[1]}$ and σ_1, $\sigma_1\sigma_2$, $\sigma_1\sigma_2\sigma_3$, ... are not divergence traces. Let T_ξ be the LTS whose alphabet is $\{c, c_1, c_2\} \cup \Sigma_M^{[1]}$ and whose graph is

For any LTS L, let $g(L)$ be the LTS that is obtained as follows. First L is replaced by $\mathsf{Una}(\lceil L \rceil^{[2]})$. Then each transition whose new label a is visible and who ends in a potentially divergent state is replaced by $\xrightarrow{a}\circ\xrightarrow{c_1}\overset{\tau}{\circlearrowleft}\xrightarrow{c_2}$. The alphabet of the result is $\{c_1, c_2\} \cup \Sigma_L^{[2]}$, where $\Sigma_L = \Sigma(L)$. When $i \in \{1,2\}$, let

$$f_i(L) \;=\; \lfloor\, (g(L) \,||\, T_\xi \,||\, c.\lceil M_i \rceil^{[1]}\,) \setminus (\{c, c_1, c_2\} \cup \Sigma_M^{[1]})\, \rfloor_{[2]}\ .$$

Each time when $g(L)$ is about to enter a potentially divergent state, it executes c_1. This makes T_ξ move one step and then let $c.\lceil M_i \rceil^{[1]}$ try to execute up to a nondivergent state. If it succeeds, T_ξ lets $g(L)$ continue by executing c_2. In the opposite case, $g(L)$ is trapped in the τ-loop between c_1 and c_2.

The LTS M_1 has every prefix of ξ as its trace. By Lemma 3, "$\cong$" preserves *Tr*. So both $\lceil M_1 \rceil^{[1]}$ and $\lceil M_2 \rceil^{[1]}$ may succeed in executing $\sigma_1\sigma_2\cdots\sigma_i$ for any i. This implies $\mathit{Tr}(f_1(L)) = \mathit{Tr}(f_2(L)) = \mathit{Tr}(L)$. Clearly $g(L)$ mimics the divergence traces of L. When M_1 or M_2 diverges, $g(L)$ is in a τ-loop and the trace that has been executed is a divergence trace. Thus $\mathit{Div}(f_1(L)) = \mathit{Div}(f_2(L)) = \mathit{Div}(L)$.

When $g(L)$ is in a stable state (other than the start states of c_1), then $c.\lceil M_1 \rceil^{[1]}$ and $c.\lceil M_2 \rceil^{[1]}$ do not diverge, so $\mathit{Sf}(f_1(L)) = \mathit{Sf}(f_2(L)) = \mathit{Sf}(L)$. Because M_2 does but M_1 does not necessarily prevent $g(L)$ from infinitely many times continuing after a divergence trace, we have $\mathit{Inf}(f_1(L)) = \mathit{Inf}(L)$ but $\mathit{Inf}(f_2(L)) = \mathit{eanI}(L)$. So $L \doteq f_1(L) \cong f_2(L)$. By Lemma 3, "$\cong$" preserves *eanI*. Lemma 2 yields the claim. □

Theorem 9. *If "$\cong$" is a congruence, "$\doteq$" implies "$\cong$", and "$\cong$" preserves Sf, Div, and aenI but not Inf, then "$\cong$" is the equivalence induced by Σ, Sf, Div, and aenI.*

Proof. We proceed similarly to earlier proofs. Because *Div* is preserved, M_1 and M_2 agree on which prefixes of a $\xi \in \mathit{Inf}(M_1) \setminus \mathit{Inf}(M_2)$ are divergence traces. From some point on all of them are, because *aenI* is preserved.

We abbreviate potentially divergent as *pd* and certainly nondivergent as *cn*. To get $g(L)$, each transition of $\mathsf{Una}(L)$ whose label a is visible is replaced by

- $\xrightarrow{a^{[2]}}\circ\xrightarrow{c_1}$, if it starts in a cn and ends in a pd state;
- $\xrightarrow{a^{[2]}}\circ\xrightarrow{c_2}$, if it starts and ends in a pd state;
- $\xrightarrow{a^{[3]}}$, if it starts in a pd and ends in a cn state;
- $\xrightarrow{a^{[2]}}$, if it starts and ends in a cn state.

If the initial state of $\mathsf{Una}(L)$ is pd, then a c_1-transition is added to its front. The alphabet of $g(L)$ is $\{c_1, c_2\} \cup \Sigma_L^{[2]} \cup \Sigma_L^{[3]}$.

Let $b_1 b_2 \cdots = \xi^{[1]}$. Let T_ξ be the LTS whose alphabet is $\{c, c_1, c_2\} \cup \Sigma_M^{[1]} \cup \Sigma_L^{[3]}$ and whose graph is in Fig. 5. When $i \in \{1,2\}$, let

$$f_i(L) \;=\; ((g(L) \,||\, T_\xi \,||\, c.\lceil M_i \rceil^{[1]}) \setminus (\{c, c_1, c_2\} \cup \Sigma_M^{[1]}))\varPhi\ ,$$

where $\varPhi$ renames each $a^{[2]}$ and each $a^{[3]}$ to a.

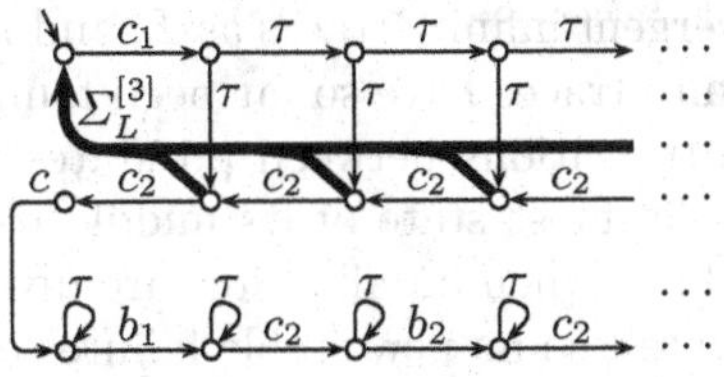

Fig. 5. An LTS for detecting an infinite trace with only finitely many nondivergent prefixes. The thick arrows with $\Sigma_L^{[3]}$ denote that there is a transition from each start state of the thick arrows to their common end state for each $a \in \Sigma_L^{[3]}$.

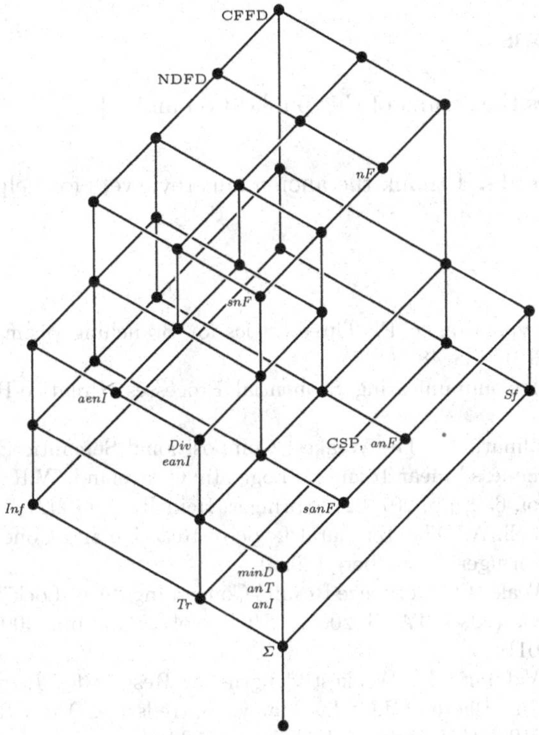

Fig. 6. All abstract linear-time congruences with respect to $a.L$, $L \setminus A$, $L\Phi$, and $L \,||\, L'$. Names in *italics* indicate the new preserved set(s). Other names are the names of the congruences. There is a path from "$\cong_1$" down to "$\cong_2$" if and only if "$\cong_1$" implies "$\cong_2$".

While $g(L)$ traverses among cn states, $f_1(L)$ and $f_2(L)$ behave like L. When $g(L)$ enters a pd state, T_ξ prepares for an arbitrary finite number of transitions between pd states. As long as T_ξ is in its middle row excluding its leftmost state, $g(L)$ can execute transitions at will. These states of T_ξ are stable and offer all actions in $\Sigma(g(L)) \cap \Sigma(T_\xi)$ except c_1 that also $g(L)$ refuses, so *Sf* is preserved. If $g(L)$ enters a cn state, then T_ξ goes back to its initial state. As a consequence, $f_1(L)$ and $f_2(L)$ have at least the same stable failures, divergence traces, and always-eventually-nondivergent infinite traces as L, and no extra stable failures, divergence traces, or infinite traces have so far been found.

If $g(L)$ executes more transitions between pd states than T_ξ has been prepared for, T_ξ reaches the leftmost state of its middle row. Then it executes c, switching M_1 or M_2 on. From then on all states are divergent and $g(L)$ is prevented from leaving pd states, so no new stable failures or divergence traces are introduced. $f_2(L)$ does not introduce new infinite traces either, while $f_1(L)$ may execute all the remaining infinite traces of L. So $Sf(f_1(L)) = Sf(f_2(L)) = Sf(L)$, $Div(f_1(L)) = Div(f_2(L)) = Div(L)$, $Inf(f_1(L)) = Inf(L)$, and $Inf(f_2(L)) = aenI(L)$. Clearly $L \doteq f_1(L) \cong f_2(L)$, thus Lemma 2 yields the claim. □

6 Conclusions

Fig. 6 summarizes the results of this publication and [9].

Acknowledgements. I thank the anonymous reviewers for helpful comments.

References

1. De Nicola, R., Vaandrager, F.: Three Logics for Branching Bisimulation. Journal of the ACM 42(2), 458–487 (1995)
2. Hoare, C.A.R.: Communicating Sequential Processes. Prentice-Hall, Englewood Cliffs (1985)
3. Kaivola, R., Valmari, A.: The Weakest Compositional Semantic Equivalence Preserving Nexttime-less Linear Temporal Logic. In: Cleaveland, W.R. (ed.) CONCUR 1992. LNCS, vol. 630, pp. 207–221. Springer, Heidelberg (1992)
4. Manna, Z., Pnueli, A.: The Temporal Logic of Reactive and Concurrent Systems: Specification. Springer, Heidelberg (1992)
5. Puhakka, A.: Weakest Congruence Results Concerning "Any-Lock". In: Kobayashi, N., Pierce, B.C. (eds.) TACS 2001. LNCS, vol. 2215, pp. 400–419. Springer, Heidelberg (2001)
6. Puhakka, A., Valmari, A.: Weakest-Congruence Results for Livelock-Preserving Equivalences. In: Baeten, J.C.M., Mauw, S. (eds.) CONCUR 1999. LNCS, vol. 1664, pp. 510–524. Springer, Heidelberg (1999)
7. Roscoe, A.W.: Understanding Concurrent Systems. Springer, Heidelberg (2010)
8. Valmari, A.: The Weakest Deadlock-Preserving Congruence. Information Processing Letters 53(6), 341–346 (1995)
9. Valmari, A.: All Linear-Time Congruences for Finite LTSs and Familiar Operators. In: Brandt, J., Heljanko, K. (eds.) 12th Int. Conf. on Application of Concurrency to System Design, pp. 12–21. IEEE, USA (2012)
10. Valmari, A., Tienari, M.: Compositional Failure-Based Semantic Models for Basic LOTOS. Formal Aspects of Computing 7(4), 440–468 (1995)
11. van Glabbeek, R.J.: The Coarsest Precongruences Respecting Safety and Liveness Properties. In: Calude, C.S., Sassone, V. (eds.) TCS 2010. IFIP AICT, vol. 323, pp. 32–52. Springer, Heidelberg (2010)

Quantified CTL: Expressiveness and Model Checking (Extended Abstract)

Arnaud Da Costa[1], François Laroussinie[2], and Nicolas Markey[1]

[1] LSV – CNRS & ENS Cachan
[2] LIAFA – Univ. Paris Diderot & CNRS

Abstract. While it was defined long ago, the extension of CTL with quantification over atomic propositions has never been studied extensively. Considering two different semantics (depending whether propositional quantification refers to the Kripke structure or to its unwinding tree), we study its expressiveness (showing in particular that QCTL coincides with Monadic Second-Order Logic for both semantics) and characterize the complexity of its model-checking problem, depending on the number of nested propositional quantifiers (showing that the structure semantics populates the polynomial hierarchy while the tree semantics populates the exponential hierarchy). We also show how these results apply to model checking ATL-like temporal logics for games.

1 Introduction

Temporal logics. Temporal logics extend propositional logics with modalities for specifying constraints on the order of events in time. Since [25,5,26], they have received much attention from the computer-aided-verification community, since they fit particularly well for expressing and automatically verifying (*e.g.* via *model checking*) properties of reactive systems. Two important families of temporal logics have been considered: linear-time temporal logics (*e.g.* LTL [25]) can be used to express properties of one single execution of the system under study, while branching-time temporal logics (*e.g.* CTL [5,26] and CTL* [10]) consider the execution tree. Since the 90s, many extensions of these logics have been introduced, of which alternating-time temporal logics (such as ATL, ATL* [1]) extend CTL towards the study of open systems (involving several agents).

In this landscape of temporal logics, both CTL and ATL enjoy the nice property of having polynomial-time model-checking algorithms. In return for this, both logics have quite limited expressiveness. Several extensions have been defined in order to increase this limited expressive power.

Our Contributions. We are interested in the present paper in the extension of CTL (and CTL*) with *propositional quantification* [28,11]. In that setting, propositional quantification can take different meaning, depending whether the extra propositions label the Kripke structure under study (*structure semantics*) or its

M. Koutny and I. Ulidowski (Eds.): CONCUR 2012, LNCS 7454, pp. 177–192, 2012.

execution tree (*tree semantics*). While these extensions of CTL with propositional quantification have been in the air for thirty years, they have not been extensively studied yet: some complexity results have been published for existential quantification [15], for the two-alternation fragment [16] and for the full extension [12]; but expressiveness issues, as well as a complete study of model checking for the whole hierarchy, have been mostly overlooked. We answer these questions in the present paper: in terms of expressiveness, we prove that QCTL and QCTL* are equally expressive, and coincide with Monadic Second-Order Logic. Regarding model checking, we consider both prenex-normal-form formulas (EQCTL) and general formulas (QCTL), and our results are summarized in the table below (where k in $\mathsf{EQ}^k\mathsf{CTL}$ and $\mathsf{Q}^k\mathsf{CTL}$ refers to some measure of quantification height of formulas, see Section 2.4). Finally, we also characterize the model- and formula-complexities of our problems, when one of the inputs to the model-checking problem is fixed. By lack of spaces, most proofs are omitted. They can be found in [8].

	structure semantics	tree semantics
$\mathsf{EQ}^k\mathsf{CTL}$	$\Sigma^{\mathsf{P}}_{\mathsf{k}}$-c.	k-EXPTIME-c.
$\mathsf{Q}^k\mathsf{CTL}$	$\Delta^{\mathsf{P}}_{\mathsf{k+1}}[O(\log n)]$-c.	
$\mathsf{EQ}^k\mathsf{CTL}^*$, $\mathsf{Q}^k\mathsf{CTL}^*$	PSPACE-c.	k+1-EXPTIME-c.
EQCTL, QCTL, EQCTL*, QCTL*		non-elementary

Applications to alternating-time temporal logics. ATL also has several flaws in terms of expressiveness: namely, it can only focus on (some) zero-sum properties, *i.e.*, on purely antagonist games, in which two coalitions fight with opposite objectives. In many situations, games are not purely antagonist, but involve several independent systems, each having its own objective. Recently, several extensions of ATL have been defined to express properties of such non-zero-sum games. Among those, our logic ATL_{sc} [7] extends ATL with *strategy contexts*, which provides a way of expressing interactions between strategies. Other similar approaches include Strategy Logics [4,19] or (B)SIL [32].

Interestingly, the model-checking problem for these extensions of ATL_{sc} (and also for Strategy Logics) can be seen as a QCTL model-checking problem[1]: strategy quantification in ATL is naturally encoded using propositional quantification of QCTL; since this labelling is *persistent*, it can encode interactions between strategies. We give the full encoding in Section 5. Notice that while the *tree semantics* of QCTL encodes plain strategies, the *structure semantics* also finds a meaning in that translation, as it may correspond to *memoryless strategies*.

Related Works. Propositional quantification was also defined and studied on LTL [28,29,14], where the model-checking problem for the k-alternation fragment

[1] Notice that the link between games and propositional quantification already emerges in QDμ [24], which extends the *decision μ-calculus* with some flavour of propositional quantification. Also, the main motivation of [16] for studying the two-alternation fragment of QCTL is a hardness result for the control and synthesis of open systems.

was settled complete for k-EXPSPACE. In the branching-time setting, the results are more sparse: CTL and CTL* with only existential quantification was studied in [15], where model checking is shown NP- and PSPACE-complete resp. (for the structure semantics) and EXPTIME- and 2-EXPTIME-complete resp. (for the tree semantics). The two-alternation fragment was then studied in [16] (only for the tree semantics): model checking is 2-EXPTIME- and 3-EXPTIME-complete, respectively for CTL or CTL*. Finally, satisfiability of the full extension (with arbitrary quantification) was studied in [12].

Several other semantics have also been defined in the literature: the amorphous semantics is somewhat intermediary between structure- and tree semantics, and considers bisimilar structures before labelling with extra atomic propositions [12]. Alternative semantics are proposed and studied in [27,23].

Besides the above-mentioned applications of QCTL to open systems, let us mention that QCTL has also been used in the setting of three-valued model checking, where *partial* Kripke structures are considered (*i.e.*, Kripke structures where the truth value of some atomic propositions may be unknown) [3].

2 Preliminaries

2.1 Kripke Structures and Trees

We fix once and for all a set AP of atomic propositions.

Definition 1. *A* Kripke structure $\mathcal{S}$ *is a* 3*-tuple* $\langle Q, R, \ell\rangle$ *where* Q *is a countable set of states,* $R \subseteq Q^2$ *is a total*[2] *relation and* $\ell\colon Q \to 2^{\mathsf{AP}}$ *is a labelling function.*

An execution (or path) in $\mathcal{S}$ is an infinite sequence $\rho = (q_i)_{i\in\mathbb{N}}$ s.t. $(q_i, q_{i+1}) \in R$ for all i. We use $\mathsf{Exec}(q)$ to denote the set of executions issued from q and $\mathsf{Exec}^{\mathsf{f}}(q)$ for the set of all finite prefixes of executions of $\mathsf{Exec}(q)$. Given $\rho \in \mathsf{Exec}(q)$ and $i \in \mathbb{N}$, we write ρ^i for the path $(q_{i+k})_{k\in\mathbb{N}}$ of $\mathsf{Exec}(q_i)$ (the i-th suffix of ρ), ρ_i for the finite prefix $(q_k)_{k\leq i}$ (the i-th prefix), and $\rho(i)$ for the i-th state q_i.

Definition 2. *Let* Σ *and* S *be two finite sets. A* Σ-labelled S-tree *is a pair* $\mathcal{T} = \langle T, l\rangle$*, where* $T \subseteq S^*$ *is a non-empty set of finite words on* S *s.t. for any non-empty word* $n = m \cdot s$ *in* T *with* $m \in S^*$ *and* $s \in S$*, the word* m *is also in* T*; and* $l\colon T \to \Sigma$ *is a labelling function.*

The unwinding of a finite-state Kripke structure $\mathcal{S} = \langle Q, R, \ell\rangle$ from a state $q \in Q$ is the (finitely-branching) 2^{AP}-labelled Q-tree $\mathcal{T}_{\mathcal{S}}(q) = \langle \mathsf{Exec}^{\mathsf{f}}(q), \ell_{\mathcal{T}}\rangle$ with $\ell_{\mathcal{T}}(q_0 \cdots q_i) = \ell(q_i)$. Note that $\mathcal{T}_{\mathcal{S}}(q) = \langle \mathsf{Exec}^{\mathsf{f}}(q), \ell_{\mathcal{T}}\rangle$ can be seen as an (infinite-state) Kripke structure where the set of states is $\mathsf{Exec}^{\mathsf{f}}(q)$, labelled according to $\ell_{\mathcal{T}}$, and with transitions $(m, m \cdot s)$ for all $m \in \mathsf{Exec}^{\mathsf{f}}(q)$ and $s \in Q$ s.t. $m \cdot s \in \mathsf{Exec}^{\mathsf{f}}(q)$.

Definition 3. *For* $P \subseteq \mathsf{AP}$*, two (possibly infinite-state) Kripke structures* $\mathcal{S} = \langle Q, R, \ell\rangle$ *and* $\mathcal{S}' = \langle Q', R', \ell'\rangle$ *are* P-equivalent *(denoted by* $\mathcal{S} \equiv_P \mathcal{S}'$*) whenever* $Q = Q'$*,* $R = R'$*, and* $\ell(q) \cap P = \ell'(q) \cap P$ *for any* $q \in Q$*.*

[2] *I.e.*, for all $q \in Q$, there exists $q' \in Q$ s.t. $(q, q') \in R$.

In other terms, $\mathcal{S} \equiv_P \mathcal{S}'$ if $\mathcal{S}'$ can be obtained from $\mathcal{S}$ by modifying the labelling function of $\mathcal{S}$ for propositions in P.

2.2 CTL and Quantified Extensions

Definition 4. *The syntax of* QCTL* *is defined by the following grammar:*

$$\varphi_{\mathsf{state}}, \psi_{\mathsf{state}} ::= p \mid \neg\varphi_{\mathsf{state}} \mid \varphi_{\mathsf{state}} \vee \psi_{\mathsf{state}} \mid \mathbf{E}\varphi_{\mathsf{path}} \mid \mathbf{A}\varphi_{\mathsf{path}} \mid \exists p.\ \varphi_{\mathsf{state}}$$
$$\varphi_{\mathsf{path}}, \psi_{\mathsf{path}} ::= \varphi_{\mathsf{state}} \mid \neg\varphi_{\mathsf{path}} \mid \varphi_{\mathsf{path}} \vee \psi_{\mathsf{path}} \mid \mathbf{X}\,\varphi_{\mathsf{path}} \mid \varphi_{\mathsf{path}}\,\mathbf{U}\,\psi_{\mathsf{path}}$$

where p ranges over AP. *Formulas defined as φ_{state} are called* state-formulas, *while φ_{path} defines* path-formulas. *Only state formulas are* QCTL* *formulas.*

We use standard abbreviations as: $\top = p \vee \neg p$, $\bot = \neg\top$, $\mathbf{F}\varphi = \top\,\mathbf{U}\,\varphi$, $\mathbf{G}\varphi = \neg\mathbf{F}\neg\varphi$, and $\forall p \cdot \varphi = \neg\exists p \cdot \neg\varphi$. The logic QCTL is a fragment of QCTL* where temporal modalities are under the immediate scope of path quantifiers:

Definition 5. *The syntax of* QCTL *is defined by the following grammar:*

$$\varphi_{\mathsf{state}}, \psi_{\mathsf{state}} ::= p \mid \neg\varphi_{\mathsf{state}} \mid \varphi_{\mathsf{state}} \vee \psi_{\mathsf{state}} \mid \exists p.\ \varphi_{\mathsf{state}} \mid$$
$$\mathbf{E}\varphi_{\mathsf{state}}\,\mathbf{U}\,\psi_{\mathsf{state}} \mid \mathbf{A}\varphi_{\mathsf{state}}\,\mathbf{U}\,\psi_{\mathsf{state}} \mid \mathbf{EX}\,\varphi_{\mathsf{state}} \mid \mathbf{AX}\,\varphi_{\mathsf{state}}.$$

Standard definition of CTL* and CTL are obtained by removing the use of quantification over atomic proposition ($\exists p.\varphi$) in the formulas. In the following, $\exists$ and $\forall$ are called *(proposition) quantifiers*, while $\mathbf{E}$ and $\mathbf{A}$ are *path quantifiers.*

Given QCTL* (state) formulas φ and $(\psi_i)_i$ and atomic propositions $(p_i)_i$ appearing free in φ (*i.e.*, not appearing as quantified propositions), we write $\varphi[(p_i \to \psi_i)_i]$ (or $\varphi[(\psi_i)_i]$ when $(p_i)_i$ are understood from the context) for the formula obtained from φ by replacing each occurrence of p_i with ψ_i. Given two sublogics L_1 and L_2 of QCTL*, we write $L_1[L_2] = \{\varphi[(\psi_i)_i] \mid \varphi \in L_1,\ (\psi_i)_i \in L_2\}$.

2.3 Structure- and Tree Semantics

Formulas of the form $\exists p.\varphi$ can be interpreted in different manners (see [15,12,27]). Here we consider two semantics: the *structure semantics* and the *tree semantics.*

Structure Semantics. Given a QCTL* state formula φ, a (possibly infinite-state) Kripke structure $\mathcal{S} = \langle Q, R, \ell\rangle$ and a state $q \in Q$, we write $\mathcal{S}, q \models_s \varphi$ to denote that φ holds at q under the structure semantics. This is defined as for CTL*, with the following addition:

$$\mathcal{S}, q \models_s \exists p.\varphi_{\mathsf{state}} \quad \text{iff} \quad \exists \mathcal{S}' \equiv_{\mathsf{AP}\setminus\{p\}} \mathcal{S} \text{ s.t. } \mathcal{S}', q \models_s \varphi_{\mathsf{state}}$$

Intuitively, $\exists p.\varphi$ holds true at state q of structure $\mathcal{S}$ if it is possible to modify the p-labelling of $\mathcal{S}$ in such a way that φ holds at q.

Example 6. As an example, consider the formula $\mathsf{selfloop} = \forall z.(z \Rightarrow \mathbf{EX}\, z)$. If a state q in $\mathcal{S}$ satisfies this formula, then the particular labelling in which only q is labelled with z implies that q has to carry a self-loop. Conversely, any state that carries a self-loop satisfies this formula (for the structure semantics).

Let φ be a QCTL* formula, and consider now the formula

$$\mathsf{uniq}(\varphi) = \mathbf{EF}\,(\varphi) \wedge \forall z.\Big(\mathbf{EF}\,(\varphi \wedge z) \Rightarrow \mathbf{AG}\,(\varphi \Rightarrow z)\Big).$$

In order to satisfy such a formula, at least one φ-state must be reachable. Assume now that two different such states q and q' are reachable: then for the particular labelling where only q is labelled with z, the second part of the formula fails to hold. Hence $\mathsf{uniq}(\varphi)$ holds in a state (under the structure semantics) if, and only if, exactly one reachable state satisfies φ.

Tree Semantics. The tree-semantics is obtained from the structure semantics by seeing the execution tree as an infinite-state Kripke structure. We write $\mathcal{S}, q \models_t \varphi$ to denote that formula φ holds at q under the tree semantics. Formally, seeing $\mathcal{T}_{\mathcal{S}}(q)$ as an infinite-state Kripke structure, we define:

$$\mathcal{S}, q \models_t \varphi \quad \text{iff} \quad \mathcal{T}_{\mathcal{S}}(q), q \models_s \varphi$$

Clearly enough, $\mathsf{selfloop}$ is always false under the tree semantics, while $\mathsf{uniq}(\varphi)$ holds if, and only if, φ holds at only one node of the execution tree.

Example 7. Formula $\mathsf{acyclic} = \mathbf{AG}\,\big(\exists z.\ (z \wedge \mathsf{uniq}(z) \wedge \mathbf{AX}\ \mathbf{AG}\,\neg z)\big)$ expresses that all infinite paths (starting from the current state) are acyclic, which for *finite* Kripke structures is always false under the structure semantics and always true under the tree semantics.

Equivalences between QCTL* Formulas. We consider two kinds of equivalences depending on the semantics we use. Two state formulas φ and ψ are said s-equivalent (resp. t-equivalent), written $\varphi \equiv_s \psi$ (resp. written $\varphi \equiv_t \psi$) if for any finite-state Kripke structure $\mathcal{S}$ and any state q of $\mathcal{S}$, it holds $\mathcal{S}, q \models_s \varphi$ iff $\mathcal{S}, q \models_s \psi$ (resp. $\mathcal{S}, q \models_t \varphi$ iff $\mathcal{S}, q \models_t \psi$). We write $\varphi \equiv_{s,t} \psi$ when the equivalence holds for both $\equiv_s$ and $\equiv_t$.

Note that both equivalences $\equiv_s$ and $\equiv_t$ are *substitutive*, *i.e.*, a subformula ψ can be replaced with any equivalent formula ψ' without changing the truth value of the global formula. Formally, if $\psi \equiv_s \psi'$ (resp. $\psi \equiv_t \psi'$), we have $\Phi[\psi] \equiv_s \Phi[\psi']$ (resp. $\Phi[\psi] \equiv_t \Phi[\psi']$) for any QCTL* formula Φ.

2.4 Fragments of QCTL*.

In the sequel, besides QCTL and QCTL*, we study several interesting fragments. The first one is the fragment of QCTL in *prenex normal form*, *i.e.*, in which propositional quantification must be external to the CTL formula. We write EQCTL and EQCTL* for the corresponding logics[3]

[3] Notice that the logics named EQCTL and EQCTL* defined in [15] are restrictions of our prenex-normal-form logics where only existential quantification is allowed. They correspond to our fragments $\mathsf{EQ}^1\mathsf{CTL}$ and $\mathsf{EQ}^1\mathsf{CTL}^*$.

We also study the fragments of these logics with limited quantification. For prenex-normal-form formulas, the fragments are defined as follows:

- for any $\varphi \in \mathsf{CTL}$ and any $p \in \mathsf{AP}$, $\exists p.\varphi$ is an $\mathsf{EQ}^1\mathsf{CTL}$ formula, and $\forall p.\varphi$ is in $\mathsf{AQ}^1\mathsf{CTL}$;
- for any $\varphi \in \mathsf{EQ}^k\mathsf{CTL}$ and any $p \in \mathsf{AP}$, $\exists p.\varphi$ is in $\mathsf{EQ}^k\mathsf{CTL}$ and $\forall p.\varphi$ is in $\mathsf{AQ}^{k+1}\mathsf{CTL}$. Symmetrically, if $\varphi \in \mathsf{AQ}^k\mathsf{CTL}$, then $\exists p.\varphi$ is in $\mathsf{EQ}^{k+1}\mathsf{CTL}$ while $\forall p.\varphi$ remains in $\mathsf{AQ}^k\mathsf{CTL}$.

Using similar ideas, we define fragments of QCTL and QCTL*. Again, the definition is inductive: $\mathsf{Q}^1\mathsf{CTL}$ is the logic $\mathsf{CTL}[\mathsf{EQ}^1\mathsf{CTL}]$, and $\mathsf{Q}^{k+1}\mathsf{CTL} = \mathsf{Q}^1\mathsf{CTL}[\mathsf{Q}^k\mathsf{CTL}]$.

The corresponding extensions of CTL*, which we respectively denote with $\mathsf{EQ}^k\mathsf{CTL}^*$, $\mathsf{AQ}^k\mathsf{CTL}^*$ and $\mathsf{Q}^k\mathsf{CTL}^*$, are defined in a similar way.

Remark 8. Notice that $\mathsf{EQ}^k\mathsf{CTL}$ and $\mathsf{AQ}^k\mathsf{CTL}$ are (syntactically) included in $\mathsf{Q}^k\mathsf{CTL}$, and $\mathsf{EQ}^k\mathsf{CTL}^*$ and $\mathsf{AQ}^k\mathsf{CTL}^*$ are fragments of $\mathsf{Q}^k\mathsf{CTL}^*$.

3 Expressiveness

In this section we present several results about the expressiveness of our logics for both semantics. We show that QCTL, QCTL* and Monadic Second-Order Logic are equally expressive. First we show that any QCTL formula is equivalent to a formula in prenex normal form (which extends to QCTL* thanks to Proposition 12).

3.1 Prenex Normal Form

By translating path quantification into propositional quantification, we can extract propositional quantification out of purely temporal formulas: for instance, $\mathbf{EX}\,(\mathcal{Q}.\varphi)$ where $\mathcal{Q}$ is some propositional quantification is equivalent to $\exists z.\mathcal{Q}.\big(\mathsf{uniq}(z) \wedge \mathbf{EX}\,(z \wedge \varphi)\big)$. This generalizes to full QCTL for both semantics:

Proposition 9. *In both semantics,* EQCTL *and* QCTL *are equally expressive.*

3.2 QCTL and Monadic Second-Order Logic

We briefly review Monadic Second-Order Logic (MSO) over trees and over finite Kripke structures (*i.e.*, labeled finite graphs). In both case, we use constant monadic predicates P_a for $a \in \mathsf{AP}$ and a relation Edge either for the immediate successor relation in an S-tree $\langle T, l\rangle$ or for the relation R in a finite KS $\langle Q, R, \ell\rangle$.

MSO is built with first-order (or individual) variables for nodes or vertices (denoted with lowercase letters $x, y, ...$), monadic second-order variables for sets of nodes (denoted with uppercase letters $X, Y, ...$). Atomic formulas are of the form $x = y$, $\mathsf{Edge}(x, y)$, $x \in X$, $\mathsf{P}_a(x)$. Formulas are constructed from atomic formulas using the Boolean connectives and the first- and second-order quantifier $\exists$. We write $\varphi(x_1, ..., x_n, X_1, ..., X_k)$ to state that $x_1, ..., x_n$ and $X_1, ..., X_k$ may appear free (*i.e.* not within the scope of a quantifier) in φ. A closed formula contains no free variable. We use the standard semantics for MSO, writing $\mathcal{M}, s_1, ..., s_n, S_1, ..., S_k \models \varphi(x_1, ..., x_n, X_1, ..., X_k)$ when φ holds on $\mathcal{M}$ when s_i (resp. S_j) is assigned to the variable x_i (resp. X_j) for $i = 1, ..., n$ (resp. $j = 1, ..., k$).

In the following, we compare the expressiveness of our logics with MSO over the finite Kripke structures (the structure semantics) and the execution trees corresponding to a finite Kripke structure (tree semantics). First note that MSO formulas may express properties directly over trees or graphs, while our logics are interpreted over *states* of these structures. Therefore we use MSO formulas with one free variable x, which represents the state where the formula is evaluated. Moreover, we restrict the evaluation of MSO formulas to the *reachable* part of the model from the given state. This last requirement makes an important difference for the structure semantics, since MSO can express that a graph is connected.

Formally, for the tree semantics, we say that $\varphi(x) \in$ MSO is t-equivalent to some QCTL* formula ψ (written $\varphi(x) \equiv_t \psi$) when for any finite Kripke structure $\mathcal{S}$ and any state $q \in \mathcal{T}_\mathcal{S}$, it holds $\mathcal{T}_\mathcal{S}(q), q \models \varphi(x)$ iff $\mathcal{T}_\mathcal{S}(q), q \models \psi$. Similarly, for the structure semantics: $\varphi(x)$ is s-equivalent to ψ (written $\varphi(x) \equiv_s \psi$) iff for any finite Kripke structure $\mathcal{S}$ and any state $q \in \mathcal{S}$, it holds $\mathcal{S}_q, q \models \varphi(x)$ iff $\mathcal{S}_q, q \models \psi$, where $\mathcal{S}_q$ is the reachable part of $\mathcal{S}$ from q. For these definitions, we have:

Proposition 10. *Under both semantics,* MSO *and* QCTL *are equally expressive.*

Sketch of proof. One inclusion is straightforward: CTL is easily translated into MSO, and propositional quantification (for both semantics) can be encoded using second-order quantification. Conversely, every MSO formula $\Phi(x)$ can be translated into an equivalent QCTL formula $\widehat{\Phi}$. QCTL propositional quantifications are used to encode both first-order and second-order quantification in Φ (but in the first-order case, we require that only one state is labeled by the dedicated proposition). Then an MSO subformula of the form $x_i \in X_j$ is rewritten in QCTL as $\mathbf{EF}\,(\mathsf{p}_{x_i} \wedge \mathsf{p}_{X_j})$ where p_{x_i} (resp. p_{X_j}) is the proposition associated with x_i (resp. X_j). A formula of the form $\mathsf{Edge}(x_i, x_j)$ is rewritten as $\mathbf{EF}\,(\mathsf{p}_{x_i} \wedge \mathbf{EX}\,\mathsf{p}_{x_j})$, and $x_i = x_j$ is replaced by $\mathbf{EF}\,(\mathsf{p}_{x_i} \wedge \mathsf{p}_{x_j})$. Other cases use the same ideas. □

Remark 11. One can also notice that it is easy to express fixpoint operators with QCTL in both semantics, thus μ-calculus can be translated into QCTL. This provides another proof of the previous result for the tree semantics, since the μ-calculus extended with counting capabilities has the same expressiveness as MSO on trees [20].

3.3 QCTL and QCTL*

Finally, we show that QCTL* and QCTL are equally expressive for both semantics. The main idea of the proof is an inductive replacement of quantified subformulas with extra atomic propositions.

Proposition 12. *In the tree and structure semantics, every* QCTL* *formula is equivalent to some* QCTL *formula.*

Proof. This was shown in [12] for the tree semantic. We give another translation, which is correct for both semantics. Consider a QCTL* formula Φ, and write k for the number of subformulas of Φ that are not in QCTL. If $k = 0$, Φ already belongs to QCTL. Otherwise let ψ be one of the inner-most Φ-subformulas in QCTL* \ QCTL. Let $(\alpha_i)_{1\leq i\leq m}$ be the largest ψ-subformulas belonging to QCTL. These are state formulas, so that ψ is equivalent (for both semantics) to:

$$\exists p_1 \ldots \exists p_m . \Big(\psi[(\alpha_i \leftarrow p_i)_{i=1,\ldots,m}] \wedge \bigwedge_{i=1,\ldots,m} \mathbf{AG}\,(p_i \Leftrightarrow \alpha_i)\Big)$$

Let Ω be $\psi[(\alpha_i \leftarrow p_i)_{i=1,\ldots,m}]$. Then Ω is a CTL* formula: every subformula of the form $\exists p.\xi$ in ψ appears in some QCTL formula α_i, since ψ is one of the smallest QCTL*\QCTL subformula. As every CTL* formula is equivalent to some μ-calculus formula, Ω is equivalent to some QCTL formula $\widetilde{\Omega}$ (see Remark 11). Hence

$$\psi \equiv_{s,t} \exists p_1 \ldots \exists p_m . \Big(\widetilde{\Omega} \wedge \bigwedge_{i=1,\ldots,m} \mathbf{AG}\,(p_i \Leftrightarrow \alpha_i)\Big)$$

Now, consider the formula obtained from Φ by replacing ψ with the right-hand-side formula above. This formula is equivalent to Φ and has at most $k-1$ subformulas in QCTL* \ QCTL, so that the induction hypothesis applies. □

From Propositions 9, 10 and 12, we get:

Corollary 13. *In both semantics,* EQCTL, QCTL *and* QCTL* *and* MSO *are equally expressive.*

Remark 14. In [12], French considers a variant of QCTL* (which we call FQCTL*), with propositional quantification within path formulas: $\exists p.\ \varphi_{\mathsf{path}}$ is a valid path formula, meaning that φ_{path} holds along ρ after modifying the labelling with p:

$$\mathcal{S}, \rho \models_s \exists p.\varphi_{\mathsf{path}} \quad \text{iff} \quad \exists \mathcal{S}' \equiv_{\mathsf{AP}\setminus\{p\}} \mathcal{S} \text{ s.t. } \mathcal{S}', \rho \models_s \varphi_{\mathsf{path}}.$$

For the tree semantics, QCTL is as expressive as FQCTL* [12]. For the structure semantics, we show that FQCTL* is strictly more expressive than MSO. Formula

$$\mathbf{EG}\,\big(\exists z.\forall z'.[\mathsf{uniq}(z) \wedge \mathsf{uniq}(z') \wedge z \wedge \neg z'] \Rightarrow \mathbf{X}\,(\neg z\, \mathbf{U}\, z')\big).$$

expresses the existence of an (infinite) path along which, between any two occurrences of the same state, all the other reachable states will be visited. This precisely characterizes the existence of a Hamilton cycle. This is known not to be expressible in MSO [9, Cor. 6.3.5], it can be expressed in Guarded Second Order Logic GSO (also called MS_2 in [6]), in which quantification over sets of *edges* is allowed (in addition to quantification over sets of states). Still, FQCTL* is strictly more expressive than GSO, as it is easy to modify the above formula to express the existence of *Euler* cycles:

$$\mathbf{EG}\Big(\exists x.\exists y.\forall x'.\forall y'.\Big[\mathsf{tr}(x,y)\wedge \mathsf{tr}(x',y')\wedge \mathsf{next\_tr}(x,y)\wedge\neg\,\mathsf{next\_tr}(x',y')\Big]$$
$$\Rightarrow \mathbf{X}\,(\neg\,\mathsf{next\_tr}(x,y)\,\mathbf{U}\,\mathsf{next\_tr}(x',y'))\Big)$$

where $\mathsf{tr}(x,y) = \mathsf{uniq}(x)\wedge\mathsf{uniq}(y)\wedge\mathbf{EF}\,(x\wedge\mathbf{X}\,y)$ states that x and y mark the source and target of a reachable transition, and $\mathsf{next\_tr}(x,y) = x\wedge\mathbf{X}\,y$ states that the next transition along the current path jumps from x to y.

Proposition 15. *Under the structure semantics,* FQCTL* *is more expressive than* QCTL* *and* MSO.

Still, FQCTL* model checking (see next section) is decidable: for the tree semantics, it suffices to translate FQCTL* to QCTL [12]. The problem in the structure semantics can then be encoded in the tree semantics: we first assume that each state of the input Kripke structure $\mathcal{S}$ is labelled with its name (so that any two different states can be distinguished). Then any quantification $\exists p.\varphi$ in the structure semantics is considered in the tree semantics, with the additional requirement that any two copies of the same state receive the same p-labelling.

4 QCTL Model Checking

We now consider the model-checking problem for QCTL* and its fragments under both semantics: given a finite Kripke structure $\mathcal{S}$, a state q and a formula[4] φ, is φ satisfied in state q in $\mathcal{S}$ under the structure (resp. tree) semantics? Some results already exist, *e.g.* for $\mathsf{EQ}^1\mathsf{CTL}$ and $\mathsf{EQ}^1\mathsf{CTL}^*$ under both semantics [15]. Hardness results for $\mathsf{EQ}^2\mathsf{CTL}$ and $\mathsf{EQ}^2\mathsf{CTL}^*$ under the tree semantics can be found in [16]. Here we extend these results to all the fragments of QCTL* we have defined. We also characterize the model- and formula-complexities [31] of model-checking for these fragments.

4.1 Model Checking for the Structure Semantics

Formulas in Prenex Normal Form. Prenex-normal-form formulas are (technically) easy to handle: a formula in $\mathsf{EQ}^k\mathsf{CTL}$ can be model-checked by nondeterminisitically guessing a labelling and applying a model-checking procedure for $\mathsf{AQ}^{k-1}\mathsf{CTL}$. We easily derive the following results.

Theorem 16. *Under the structure semantics, model checking* $\mathsf{EQ}^k\mathsf{CTL}$ *is* $\Sigma^{\mathsf{P}}_{\mathsf{k}}$*-complete, model checking* $\mathsf{AQ}^k\mathsf{CTL}$ *is* $\Pi^{\mathsf{P}}_{\mathsf{k}}$*-complete, and model checking* $\mathsf{EQ}^k\mathsf{CTL}^*$, $\mathsf{AQ}^k\mathsf{CTL}^*$, EQCTL *and* EQCTL* *is* PSPACE*-complete.*

[4] For standard notions of size for $\mathcal{S}$ and φ, unless specified otherwise (see Theorem 18).

General Case. If we drop the prenex-normal-form restriction, we get

Theorem 17. *For the structure semantics, model checking is* $\Delta^{\mathsf{P}}_{\mathsf{k}+1}[O(\log n)]$*-complete for* $\mathsf{Q}^k\mathsf{CTL}$*, and* PSPACE*-complete for* $\mathsf{Q}^k\mathsf{CTL}^*$*,* QCTL *and* QCTL^**.*

Sketch of proof. The algorithm in $\Delta^{\mathsf{P}}_{\mathsf{k}+1}[O(\log n)]$ is obtained by first noticing that a formula $\varphi \in \mathsf{Q}^{k+1}\mathsf{CTL}$ can be written as $\Phi[(q_i \to \exists P_i.\ \psi_i)_i]$ with Φ being a CTL formula involving fresh atomic propositions q_i, and $\exists P_i.\ \psi_i$ (with $\exists P_i$ denoting a sequence of existential quantifications) are subformulas of φ with $\psi_i \in \mathsf{Q}^k\mathsf{CTL}$. The algorithm then consists in asking independant oracles for the sets of states satisfying $\exists P_i.\ \psi_i$, and applying a CTL model-checking algorithm. Hardness is proved by encoding PARITY ($\Sigma^{\mathsf{P}}_{\mathsf{k}}$), which aims at deciding whether the number of positive instances of $\Sigma^{\mathsf{P}}_{\mathsf{k}}$ in a given set of instances is even [13]. □

Formula- and Program-Complexity. Most of the proofs above can be adapted to use a fixed formula or a fixed model. One notable exception is QCTL: when model checking a fixed formula of QCTL (hence with fixed alternation depth), there is no hope of being able to encode arbitrary alternation: the program complexity of QCTL model checking thus lies in the small gap between PH and PSPACE (unless the polynomial-time hierarchy collapses).

Theorem 18. *Under the structure semantics, the formula-complexity (i.e., when the model is fixed) of model checking is* $\Sigma^{\mathsf{P}}_{\mathsf{k}}$*-complete for* $\mathsf{EQ}^k\mathsf{CTL}$*,* $\Pi^{\mathsf{P}}_{\mathsf{k}}$*-complete for* $\mathsf{AQ}^k\mathsf{CTL}$*; it is* $\Delta^{\mathsf{P}}_{\mathsf{k}+1}[O(\log n)]$*-complete for* $\mathsf{Q}^k\mathsf{CTL}$ *when considering the* DAG-size *of the formula. It is* PSPACE*-complete for* $\mathsf{EQ}^k\mathsf{CTL}^*$*,* $\mathsf{AQ}^k\mathsf{CTL}^*$*,* $\mathsf{Q}^k\mathsf{CTL}^*$*,* EQCTL*,* QCTL*,* EQCTL^**, and* QCTL^**.*

The program-complexity (i.e., when the formula is fixed) of model checking is $\Sigma^{\mathsf{P}}_{\mathsf{k}}$*-complete for* $\mathsf{EQ}^k\mathsf{CTL}$ *and* $\mathsf{EQ}^k\mathsf{CTL}^*$*,* $\Pi^{\mathsf{P}}_{\mathsf{k}}$*-complete for* $\mathsf{AQ}^k\mathsf{CTL}$ *and* $\mathsf{AQ}^k\mathsf{CTL}^*$*, and* $\Delta^{\mathsf{P}}_{\mathsf{k}+1}[O(\log n)]$*-complete for* $\mathsf{Q}^k\mathsf{CTL}$ *and* $\mathsf{Q}^k\mathsf{CTL}^*$ *(for positive k). It is* PH*-hard but not in* PH *(unless the polynomial-time hierarchy collapses), and in* PSPACE *but not* PSPACE*-hard for* EQCTL*,* QCTL*,* EQCTL^* *and* QCTL^**.*

4.2 Model Checking for the Tree Semantics

Theorem 19. *Model checking* $\mathsf{EQ}^k\mathsf{CTL}$*,* $\mathsf{AQ}^k\mathsf{CTL}$ *and* $\mathsf{Q}^k\mathsf{CTL}$ *under the tree semantics is* k-EXPTIME*-complete (for positive k).*

Sketch of proof. Since $\mathsf{EQ}^k\mathsf{CTL}$ and $\mathsf{AQ}^k\mathsf{CTL}$ are dual and contained in $\mathsf{Q}^k\mathsf{CTL}$, it suffices to prove hardness for $\mathsf{EQ}^k\mathsf{CTL}$ and membership for $\mathsf{Q}^k\mathsf{CTL}$. We briefly sketch the proof here.

▶ *Hardness in* k-EXPTIME. The reduction uses the ideas of [16,29]: we encode an alternating Turing machine $\mathcal{M}$ whose tape has size k-exponential. An execution of $\mathcal{M}$ on an input word y of length n is then a tree. Our reduction consists in building a Kripke structure K and an $\mathsf{EQ}^k\mathsf{CTL}$ formula φ such that φ holds true in K (for the tree semantics) iff $\mathcal{M}$ accepts y. The encoding is depicted on Fig. 1.

The main tool in this proof is a set of (polynomial-size) formulas of $\mathsf{EQ}^k\mathsf{CTL}$ that are able to relate two states that are at distance k-exponential. This is used in our reduction to ensure that the content of one cell of the Turing machine is preserved from one configuration to the next one, unless the tape head is around.

Our set of formulas will ensure the following (see Fig. 2): given a tree labeled with propositions s and t (among others), both s and t appear exactly once along each branch, and the distance between them is $F(k,n)$, defined as

$$F(0,n) = n \qquad\qquad F(k+1,n) = F(k,n) \cdot 2^{F(k,n)}.$$

The formulas for $k=0$ are easy to write. Given a formula for level k, we build the formula for level $k+1$ as follows: we add a new proposition r, which is required to hold at s and t, and at distance $F(k,n)$ from each other inbetween. We then use existential quantification over another proposition in order to implement a counter enforcing that there are exactly $2^{F(k,n)}$ occurrences of r between s and t.

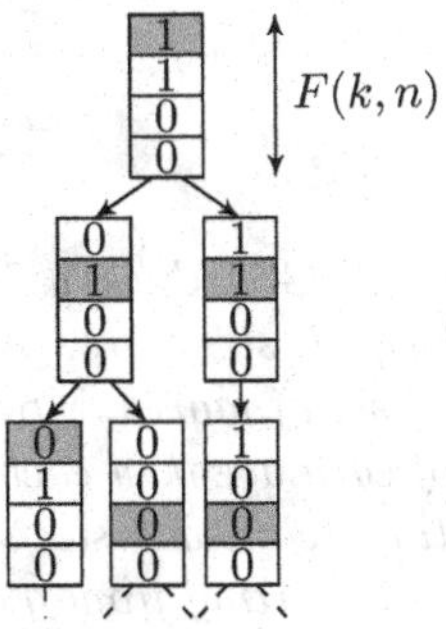

Fig. 1. A run of $\mathcal{M}$

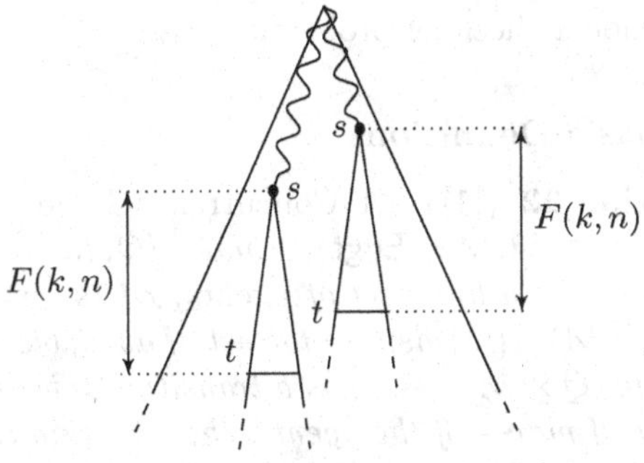

Fig. 2. Chunks of height $F(k,n)$

▶ *Membership in* k-EXPTIME. Our algorithm for $\mathsf{Q}^k\mathsf{CTL}$ model checking uses alternating parity tree automata[21,30]. The construction is inductive: we begin with building automata for the innermost CTL formulas [18], and then use projection to encode existential quantification. This requires turning the alternating automata into non-deterministic ones, which comes with an exponential blowup [22]. We apply this procedure recursively, until the last propositional quantifier. We end up with a non-deterministic parity tree automaton with size k-exponential and index $(k-1)$-exponential; emptiness is then solved in time k-exponential [17]. We apply a CTL model-checking algorithm to handle the possible outermost CTL operators. This whole algorithm runs in k-EXPTIME. □

Theorem 20. *Model checking* $\mathsf{EQ}^k\mathsf{CTL}^*$, $\mathsf{AQ}^k\mathsf{CTL}^*$ *and* $\mathsf{Q}^k\mathsf{CTL}^*$ *under the tree semantics are* (k+1)-EXPTIME*-complete (for positive k).*

Proof. The proof techniques are the same as in the previous proof. Membership requires that we build an automaton for a CTL^* formula, which entails an additional exponential blowup. Hardness is proven by using CTL^* to have $\mathsf{yardstick}_0^n(s,t)$ enforce that the distance between s and t is 2^n. □

Formula- and Program-Complexity. The reductions above can be made to work with a fixed model. When fixing the formula, the problem becomes much easier (in terms of theoretical complexity):

Theorem 21. *Under the tree semantics, the formula-complexity of model-checking is* k-EXPTIME*-complete for* $\mathsf{EQ}^k\mathsf{CTL}$, $\mathsf{Q}^k\mathsf{CTL}$, $\mathsf{EQ}^k\mathsf{CTL}^*$ *and* $\mathsf{Q}^k\mathsf{CTL}^*$ *with* $k \geq 1$. *It is non-elementary for* EQCTL, QCTL, EQCTL^* *and* QCTL^*.

The program-complexity of model-checking is PTIME*-complete for all those fragments of* QCTL^*.

5 Using QCTL for Specifying Multi-Agent Systems

Extending CTL with propositional quantification has already found several applications for reasoning about complex systems. In this section, we show how a model-checking problem involving a multi-agent system (typically a concurrent game) and a property written in ATL_{sc} (see below) is logspace-reducible to a QCTL model-checking problem.

5.1 Basic Definitions

Definition 22 ([1]). *A* Concurrent Game Structure *(CGS)* $\mathcal{C}$ *is a 7-tuple* $\langle Q, R, \ell, \mathsf{Agt}, \mathcal{M}, \mathsf{Mov}, \mathsf{Edge}\rangle$ *where:* $\langle Q, R, \ell\rangle$ *is a Kripke structure,* $\mathsf{Agt} = \{A_1, ..., A_p\}$ *is a finite set of* agents, $\mathcal{M}$ *is a non-empty set of moves,* $\mathsf{Mov}\colon Q \times \mathsf{Agt} \to \mathcal{P}(\mathcal{M}) \smallsetminus \{\varnothing\}$ *defines the set of available moves of each agent in each state, and* $\mathsf{Edge}\colon Q \times \mathcal{M}^{\mathsf{Agt}} \to R$ *is a transition table associating, with each state* q *and each set of moves of the agents, the resulting transition departing from* q.

The size of a CGS $\mathcal{C}$ is $|Q|+|\mathsf{Edge}|$. For a state $q \in Q$, we write $\mathsf{Next}(q)$ for the set of all transitions corresponding to possible moves from q, and $\mathsf{Next}(q, A_j, m_j)$, with $m_j \in \mathsf{Mov}(q, A_j)$, for the restriction of $\mathsf{Next}(q)$ to possible transitions from q when player A_j plays move m_j. We extend Mov and Next to coalitions (*i.e.*, sets of agents) in the natural way. A path in $\mathcal{C}$ is a path in its underlying Kripke structure. For a finite prefix π of a path, we write $\mathsf{last}(\pi) = \pi_i$ for its last state.

A *strategy* for some player $A_i \in \mathsf{Agt}$ is a function f_i that maps any history to a possible move for A_i, *i.e.*, satisfying $f_i(\pi) \in \mathsf{Mov}(\mathsf{last}(\pi), A_i)$. A strategy for a coalition A is a mapping assigning a strategy to each agent in A. The set of strategies for A is denoted $\mathsf{Strat}(A)$. The *domain* $\mathsf{dom}(F_A)$ of $F_A \in \mathsf{Strat}(A)$ is A. Given a coalition B, the strategy $(F_A)_{|B}$ (resp. $(F_A)_{\smallsetminus B}$) denotes the restriction of F_A to the coalition $A \cap B$ (resp. $A \smallsetminus B$). Given two strategies $F \in \mathsf{Strat}(A)$ and $F' \in \mathsf{Strat}(B)$, we define $F \circ F' \in \mathsf{Strat}(A \bigcup B)$ as $(F \circ F')_{|A_j}(\rho) = F_{|A_j}(\rho)$ (resp. $F'_{|A_j}(\rho)$) if $A_j \in A$ (resp. $A_j \in B \smallsetminus A$).

Let ρ be a history. A strategy $F_A = (f_j)_{A_j \in A}$ for some coalition A induces a set of paths from ρ, called the *outcomes* of F_A after ρ, and denoted $\mathsf{Out}(\rho, F_A)$: an infinite path $\pi = \rho \cdot q_1 q_2 \ldots$ is in $\mathsf{Out}(\rho, F_A)$ iff, writing $q_0 = \mathsf{last}(\rho)$, for all $i \geq 0$ there is a set of moves $(m_k^i)_{A_k \in \mathsf{Agt}}$ such that $m_k^i \in \mathsf{Mov}(q_i, A_k)$ for all $A_k \in \mathsf{Agt}$, $m_k^i = f_{A_k}(\pi_{|\rho|+i})$ if $A_k \in A$, and $q_{i+1} \in \mathsf{Next}(q_i, \mathsf{Agt}, (m_k^i)_{A_k \in \mathsf{Agt}})$.

We now introduce the extension of ATL with strategy contexts [2,7]:

Definition 23. *The syntax of* ATL_{sc} *is defined by the following grammar (where* p *ranges over* AP *and* A *over* 2^{Agt}*):*

$$\varphi_{\text{state}}, \psi_{\text{state}} ::= p \mid \neg\,\varphi_{\text{state}} \mid \varphi_{\text{state}} \vee \psi_{\text{state}} \mid \cdot\rangle A \langle\cdot\, \varphi_{\text{state}} \mid \langle\cdot A\cdot\rangle\, \varphi_{\text{path}}$$
$$\varphi_{\text{path}}, \psi_{\text{path}} ::= \mathbf{X}\, \varphi_{\text{state}} \mid \varphi_{\text{state}}\, \mathbf{U}\, \psi_{\text{state}} \mid \varphi_{\text{state}}\, \mathbf{W}\, \psi_{\text{state}}.$$

That a formula φ in ATL_{sc} is satisfied by a state q of a CGS $\mathcal{C}$ under a strategy context $F \in \mathsf{Strat}(B)$ (for some coalition B), denoted $\mathcal{C}, q \models_F \varphi$, is defined as follows (omitting Boolean operators and path modalities):

$$\mathcal{C}, q \models_F \cdot\rangle A \langle\cdot\, \varphi_{\text{state}} \text{ iff } \mathcal{C}, q \models_{F_{\smallsetminus A}} \varphi_{\text{state}}$$
$$\mathcal{C}, q \models_F \langle\cdot A\cdot\rangle\, \varphi_{\text{path}} \text{ iff } \exists F_A \in \mathsf{Strat}(A). \forall \rho' \in \mathsf{Out}(q, F_A \circ F).\ \mathcal{C}, \rho' \models_{F_A \circ F} \varphi_{\text{path}}$$

In the following we will use $\langle\cdot A\cdot\rangle\, \varphi_{\text{state}}$ as a shorthand for $\langle\cdot A\cdot\rangle \perp \mathbf{U}\, \varphi_{\text{state}}$.

5.2 From ATL_{sc} to QCTL^* and QCTL Model Checking

Let $\mathcal{C} = \langle Q, R, \ell, \mathsf{Agt}, \mathcal{M}, \mathsf{Mov}, \mathsf{Edge}\rangle$ be a CGS, and $\mathcal{M}$ be $\{m_1, \ldots, m_k\}$. We consider the following sets of fresh atomic propositions: $\mathsf{P}_Q = \{\mathsf{p}_q \mid q \in Q\}$, $\mathsf{P}^j_{\mathcal{M}} = \{\mathsf{m}^j_1, \ldots, \mathsf{m}^j_k\}$ for every $A_j \in \mathsf{Agt}$, and $\mathsf{P}_{\mathcal{M}} = \bigcup_{A_j \in \mathsf{Agt}} \mathsf{P}^j_{\mathcal{M}}$.

Let $\mathcal{S}_{\mathcal{C}}$ be the Kripke structure $\langle Q, R, \ell_+\rangle$ where for any state q, we have: $\ell_+(q) = \ell(q) \cup \{\mathsf{p}_q\}$. $\mathcal{S}_{\mathcal{C}}$ is the Kripke structure underlying $\mathcal{C}$, in which every state q is labelled with its own atomic proposition p_q. In the following, every labelling function we consider coincides with ℓ_+ on $\mathsf{AP}\backslash\mathsf{P}_{\mathcal{M}}$.

A strategy for an agent A_j can be seen as a function labelling the execution tree of $\mathcal{S}_{\mathcal{C}}$ with $\mathsf{P}^j_{\mathcal{M}}$. More precisely, a strategy for A_j is a labelling function $f_j \colon \mathsf{Exec}^{\mathsf{f}}(\ell) \to \mathsf{P}^j_{\mathcal{M}}$. A memoryless strategy for A_j corresponds to a labelling function $f_j \colon Q \to \mathsf{P}^j_{\mathcal{M}}$, *i.e.*, a labelling of the Kripke structure $\mathcal{S}_{\mathcal{C}}$.

Let $F \in \mathsf{Strat}(C)$ be a strategy context and $\Phi \in \mathsf{ATL}_{sc}$. We reduce the question whether $\mathcal{C}, q \models_F \Phi$ to a model-checking instance for QCTL^* over $\mathcal{S}_{\mathcal{C}}$. For this, we define a QCTL^* formula $\widehat{\Phi}^C$ inductively; for non-temporal formulas,

$$\widehat{\cdot\rangle A \langle\cdot\, \varphi}^C = \widehat{\varphi}^{C \smallsetminus A} \qquad \widehat{\varphi \wedge \psi}^C = \widehat{\varphi}^C \wedge \widehat{\psi}^C \qquad \widehat{\neg \psi}^C = \neg\, \widehat{\varphi}^C \qquad \widehat{P}^C = P$$

For a formula of the form $\langle\cdot A\cdot\rangle\, \mathbf{X}\, \varphi$ with $A = \{A_{j_1}, \ldots, A_{j_l}\}$, we let:

$$\widehat{\langle\cdot A\cdot\rangle\, \mathbf{X}\, \varphi}^C = \exists \mathsf{m}^{j_1}_1 \ldots \mathsf{m}^{j_1}_k \ldots \mathsf{m}^{j_l}_1 \ldots \mathsf{m}^{j_l}_k.\ \bigwedge_{A_j \in A} \mathbf{AG}\,(\Phi_{\mathsf{strat}}(A_j)) \wedge \mathbf{A}\Big(\Phi^{[A \cup C]}_{\mathsf{out}} \Rightarrow \mathbf{X}\, \widehat{\varphi}^{C \cup A}\Big)$$

where:
$$\Phi_{\mathsf{strat}}(A_j) = \bigvee_{q \in Q} \Big(\mathsf{p}_q \wedge \bigvee_{m_i \in \mathsf{Mov}(q, A_j)} (\mathsf{m}^j_i \wedge \bigwedge_{l \neq i} \neg\, \mathsf{m}^j_l)\Big)$$
$$\Phi^{[A]}_{\mathsf{out}} = \mathbf{G} \bigwedge_{\substack{q \in Q \\ m \in \mathsf{Mov}(q, A)}} \Big((\mathsf{p}_q \wedge P_m) \Rightarrow \mathbf{X}\big(\bigvee_{q' \in \mathsf{Next}(q, A, m)} \mathsf{p}_{q'}\big)\Big)$$

where m is a move $(m^j)_{A_j \in A} \in \mathsf{Mov}(q, A)$ for A and P_m is the propositional formula $\bigwedge_{A_j \in A} m^j$ characterizing m. Formula $\Phi_{\mathsf{strat}}(A_j)$ ensures that, the labelling of propositions m_i^js describes a feasible strategy for A_j. Formula $\Phi_{\mathsf{out}}^{[A]}$ characterizes the outcomes of the strategy for A that is described by the atomic propositions in the model. Note that $\Phi_{\mathsf{out}}^{[A]}$ is based on the transition table Edge of $\mathcal{C}$. Then:

Theorem 24. *Let q be a state in $\mathcal{C}$. Let Φ be an ATL_{sc} formula and F be a strategy context for some coalition C. Let $\mathcal{T}'$ be the execution tree $\mathcal{T}_{\mathcal{S}_\mathcal{C}}(q)$ with a labelling function ℓ' s.t. for every $\pi \in \mathsf{Exec}^{\mathsf{f}}(q)$ of length i and any $A_j \in C$, $\ell'(\pi) \cap \mathsf{P}_\mathcal{M}^j = \mathsf{m}_i^j$ iff $F(\pi)_{|A_j} = m_i$. Then $\mathcal{C}, q \models_F \Phi$ iff $\mathcal{T}', q \models \widehat{\Phi}^C$.*

We get a non-elementary model-checking algorithm for ATL_{sc}, similar to [7].

Remark 25. The translation above assumes the tree semantics. However, it also makes sense in the structure semantics, where quantification then corresponds to the selection of a *memoryless* strategy. A variant of Theorem 24 can be stated for the structure semantics for QCTL and memoryless strategies for ATL_{sc}.

Remark 26. Our reduction above is into QCTL* but we can use Proposition 12 to get an equivalent QCTL formula. This may increase the quantifier height of the formula. For the tree semantics, a direct translation into QCTL exists: instead of using $\Phi_{\mathsf{out}}^{[A]}$, we can use an extra atomic proposition p_{out} for labelling outcomes. This yields a QCTL formula with the same quantifier height.

Using a converse translation, from QCTL to ATL_{sc}, we can prove:

Theorem 27. *Model-checking the fragment of* ATL_{sc} *with at most k non-trivial nested strategy quantifiers is* k-EXPTIME-*complete.*

Strategy logic (SL) [4,19] is another temporal logic for non-zero-sum games, which has explicit first-order quantification over strategies. Our results above can be adapted to SL, correcting a wrong claim in [19, Theorem 4.2]:

Theorem 28. *The model-checking problems for* QCTL, ATL_{sc} *and* SL *are inter-reducible (in logarithmic space). They all are non-elementary.*

6 Conclusions and Future Works

We have proposed a complete picture of CTL extended with propositional quantifiers w.r.t. expressiveness and model-checking. On the expressiveness side, we proved how adding quantification on top of CTL fills in the gap between temporal logics and monadic second-order logic. As for model checking, we exhaustively characterized the complexity of QCTL and its variants, completing the earlier results from [15,12]. Finally, we provided an application (which was our original motivation) of QCTL for reasonning about multi-agent systems. Satisfiability of fragments of QCTL* is part of our future work.

References

[1] Alur, R., Henzinger, T.A., Kupferman, O.: Alternating-time temporal logic. J. ACM 49(5), 672–713 (2002)

[2] Brihaye, T., Da Costa, A., Laroussinie, F., Markey, N.: ATL with Strategy Contexts and Bounded Memory. In: Artemov, S., Nerode, A. (eds.) LFCS 2009. LNCS, vol. 5407, pp. 92–106. Springer, Heidelberg (2008)

[3] Bruns, G., Godefroid, P.: Model Checking Partial State Spaces with 3-Valued Temporal Logics. In: Halbwachs, N., Peled, D.A. (eds.) CAV 1999. LNCS, vol. 1633, pp. 274–287. Springer, Heidelberg (1999)

[4] Chatterjee, K., Henzinger, T.A., Piterman, N.: Strategy Logic. In: Caires, L., Vasconcelos, V.T. (eds.) CONCUR 2007. LNCS, vol. 4703, pp. 59–73. Springer, Heidelberg (2007)

[5] Clarke, E.M., Emerson, E.A.: Design and Synthesis of Synchronization Skeletons using Branching-Time Temporal Logic. In: Kozen, D. (ed.) Logic of Programs 1981. LNCS, vol. 131, pp. 52–71. Springer, Heidelberg (1982)

[6] Courcelle, B., Engelfriet, J.: Graph Structure and Monadic Second-Order Logic, a Language Theoretic Approach. Cambridge University Press (2011)

[7] Da Costa, A., Laroussinie, F., Markey, N.: ATL with strategy contexts: Expressiveness and model checking. In: FSTTCS 2010. LIPIcs, vol. 8, pp. 120–132. LZI (2010)

[8] Da Costa, A., Laroussinie, F., Markey, N.: Quantified CTL: expressiveness and model checking. Research Report LSV-12-02, Laboratoire Spécification et Vérification, ENS Cachan, France (2012)

[9] Ebbinghaus, H.-D., Flum, J.: Finite Model Theory. Springer (1995)

[10] Emerson, E.A., Halpern, J.Y.: "Sometimes" and "not never" revisited: On branching versus linear time temporal logic. J. ACM 33(1), 151–178 (1986)

[11] Emerson, E.A., Sistla, A.P.: Deciding full branching time logic. Inf.& Cont. 61(3), 175–201 (1984)

[12] French, T.: Decidability of Quantifed Propositional Branching Time Logics. In: Stumptner, M., Corbett, D.R., Brooks, M. (eds.) AI 2001. LNCS (LNAI), vol. 2256, pp. 165–176. Springer, Heidelberg (2001)

[13] Gottlob, G.: NP trees and Carnap's modal logic. J. ACM 42(2), 421–457 (1995)

[14] Kesten, Y., Pnueli, A.: A complete proof systems for QPTL. In: LICS 1995, pp. 2–12. IEEE Comp. Soc. Press (1995)

[15] Kupferman, O.: Augmenting Branching Temporal Logics with Existential Quantification over Atomic Propositions. In: Wolper, P. (ed.) CAV 1995. LNCS, vol. 939, pp. 325–338. Springer, Heidelberg (1995)

[16] Kupferman, O., Madhusudan, P., Thiagarajan, P.S., Vardi, M.Y.: Open Systems in Reactive Environments: Control and Synthesis. In: Palamidessi, C. (ed.) CONCUR 2000. LNCS, vol. 1877, pp. 92–107. Springer, Heidelberg (2000)

[17] Kupferman, O., Vardi, M.Y.: Weak alternating automata and tree automata emptiness. In: STOC 1998, pp. 224–233. ACM Press (1998)

[18] Kupferman, O., Vardi, M.Y., Wolper, P.: An automata-theoretic approach to branching-time model-checking. J. ACM 47(2), 312–360 (2000)

[19] Mogavero, F., Murano, A., Vardi, M.Y.: Reasoning about strategies. In: FSTTCS 2010. LIPIcs, vol. 8, pp. 133–144. LZI (2010)

[20] Moller, F., Rabinovich, A.: Counting on CTL*: on the expressive power of monadic path logic. Inf.& Comp. 184(1), 147–159 (2003)

[21] Muller, D.E., Schupp, P.E.: Alternating automata on infinite trees. TCS 54(2-3), 267–276 (1987)

[22] Muller, D.E., Schupp, P.E.: Simulating alternating tree automata by nondeterministic automata: New results and new proofs of the theorems of Rabin, McNaughton and Safra. TCS 141(1-2), 69–107 (1995)

[23] Patthak, A.C., Bhattacharya, I., Dasgupta, A., Dasgupta, P., Chakrabarti, P.P.: Quantified computation tree logic. IPL 82(3), 123–129 (2002)

[24] Pinchinat, S.: A Generic Constructive Solution for Concurrent Games with Expressive Constraints on Strategies. In: Namjoshi, K.S., Yoneda, T., Higashino, T., Okamura, Y. (eds.) ATVA 2007. LNCS, vol. 4762, pp. 253–267. Springer, Heidelberg (2007)

[25] Pnueli, A.: The temporal logic of programs. In: FOCS 1977, pp. 46–57. IEEE Comp. Soc. Press (1977)

[26] Queille, J.-P., Sifakis, J.: Specification and Verification of Concurrent Systems in CESAR. In: Dezani-Ciancaglini, M., Montanari, U. (eds.) Programming 1982. LNCS, vol. 137, pp. 337–351. Springer, Heidelberg (1982)

[27] Riedweg, S., Pinchinat, S.: Quantified Mu-Calculus for Control Synthesis. In: Rovan, B., Vojtáš, P. (eds.) MFCS 2003. LNCS, vol. 2747, pp. 642–651. Springer, Heidelberg (2003)

[28] Sistla, A.P.: Theoretical Issues in the Design and Verification of Distributed Systems. PhD thesis, Harvard University, Cambridge, Massachussets, USA (1983)

[29] Sistla, A.P., Vardi, M.Y., Wolper, P.: The complementation problem for Büchi automata with applications to temporal logics. TCS 49, 217–237 (1987)

[30] Thomas, W.: Languages, automata and logics. In: Handbook of Formal Languages, pp. 389–455. Springer (1997)

[31] Vardi, M.Y.: The complexity of relational query languages. In: STOC 1982, pp. 137–146. ACM Press (1982)

[32] Wang, F., Huang, C.-H., Yu, F.: A Temporal Logic for the Interaction of Strategies. In: Katoen, J.-P., König, B. (eds.) CONCUR 2011. LNCS, vol. 6901, pp. 466–481. Springer, Heidelberg (2011)

What Makes ATL* Decidable? A Decidable Fragment of Strategy Logic

Fabio Mogavero[1,*], Aniello Murano[1,**], Giuseppe Perelli[1], and Moshe Y. Vardi[2,***]

[1] Università degli Studi di Napoli "Federico II", Napoli, Italy
[2] Rice University, Houston, TX-USA
{mogavero,murano}@na.infn.it,
perelli.gi@gmail.com, vardi@cs.rice.edu

Abstract. *Strategy Logic* (SL, for short) has been recently introduced by Mogavero, Murano, and Vardi as a formalism for reasoning explicitly about strategies, as first-order objects, in multi-agent concurrent games. This logic turns out to be very powerful, strictly subsuming all major previously studied modal logics for strategic reasoning, including ATL, ATL*, and the like. The price that one has to pay for the expressiveness of SL is the lack of important model-theoretic properties and an increased complexity of decision problems. In particular, SL does not have the bounded-tree model property and the related satisfiability problem is *highly undecidable* while for ATL* it is 2EXPTIME-COMPLETE. An obvious question that arises is then what makes ATL* decidable. Understanding this should enable us to identify decidable fragments of SL. We focus, in this work, on the limitation of ATL* to allow only one temporal goal for each strategic assertion and study the fragment of SL with the same restriction. Specifically, we introduce and study the syntactic fragment *One-Goal Strategy Logic* (SL[1G], for short), which consists of formulas in prenex normal form having a single temporal goal at a time for every strategy quantification of agents. We show that SL[1G] is strictly more expressive than ATL*. Our main result is that SL[1G] has the bounded tree-model property and its satisfiability problem is 2EXPTIME-COMPLETE, as it is for ATL*.

1 Introduction

In open-system verification [4,14], an important area of research is the study of modal logics for strategic reasoning in the setting of multi-agent games [2,11,22]. An important contribution in this field has been the development of *Alternating-Time Temporal Logic* (ATL*, for short), introduced by Alur, Henzinger, and Kupferman [2]. ATL* allows reasoning about strategic behavior of agents with temporal goals. Formally, it is obtained as a generalization of the branching-time temporal logic CTL* [6], where the path quantifiers *there exists* "E" and *for all* "A" are replaced with strategic modalities of the form "⟨⟨A⟩⟩" and "[[A]]", for a set A of *agents*. Such strategic modalities are used to express cooperation and competition among agents in order to achieve certain temporal

* Part of this research was done while visiting the Rice University.

** Work supported in part by University of Naples Federico II under the F.A.R.O. project.

*** Work supported in part by NSF grants CNS 1049862 and CCF-1139011, by BSF grant 9800096, and by gift from Intel.

M. Koutny and I. Ulidowski (Eds.): CONCUR 2012, LNCS 7454, pp. 193–208, 2012.

goals. In particular, these modalities express selective quantifications over those paths that are the results of infinite games between a coalition and its complement. ATL* formulas are interpreted over *concurrent game structures* (CGS, for short) [2], which model interacting processes. Given a CGS $\mathcal{G}$ and a set A of agents, the ATL* formula $\langle\langle A \rangle\rangle \psi$ holds at a state s of $\mathcal{G}$ if there is a set of strategies for the agents in A such that, no matter which strategy is executed by the agents not in A, the resulting outcome of the interaction in $\mathcal{G}$ satisfies ψ at s. Several decision problems have been investigated about ATL*; both its model-checking and satisfiability problems are decidable in 2EXPTIME [26].

Despite its powerful expressiveness, ATL* suffers from the strong limitation that strategies are treated only implicitly through modalities that refer to games between competing coalitions. To overcome this problem, Chatterjee, Henzinger, and Piterman introduced *Strategy Logic* (CHP-SL, for short) [3], a logic that treats strategies in *two-player turn-based games* as *first-order objects*. The explicit treatment of strategies in this logic allows the expression of many properties not expressible in ATL*. Although the model-checking problem of CHP-SL is known to be decidable, with a non-elementary upper bound, it is not known if the satisfiability problem is decidable [3]. While the basic idea exploited in [3] of explicitly quantify over strategies is powerful and useful [8], CHP-SL still suffers from various limitations. In particular, it is limited to two-player turn-based games. Furthermore, CHP-SL does not allow different players to share the same strategy, suggesting that strategies have yet to become truly first-class objects in this logic. For example, it is impossible to describe the classic strategy-stealing argument of combinatorial games such as Hex and the like [1].

These considerations led us to introduce a new *Strategy Logic*, denoted SL, as a more general framework than CHP-SL, for explicit reasoning about strategies in multi-agent concurrent games [18]. Syntactically, SL extends the linear-time temporal-logic LTL [24] by means of *strategy quantifiers*, the existential $\langle\langle x \rangle\rangle$ and the universal $[[x]]$, as well as *agent binding* (a, x), where a is an agent and x a variable. Intuitively, these elements can be read as *"there exists a strategy x"*, *"for all strategies x"*, and *"bind agent a to the strategy associated with x"*, respectively. For example, in a CGS $\mathcal{G}$ with agents α, β, and γ, consider the property "α and β have a common strategy to avoid a failure". This property can be expressed by the SL formula $\langle\langle \mathsf{x} \rangle\rangle [[\mathsf{y}]] (\alpha, \mathsf{x})(\beta, \mathsf{x})(\gamma, \mathsf{y})(\mathsf{G} \neg \mathit{fail})$. The variable x is used to select a strategy for the agents α and β, while y is used to select another one for agent γ such that their composition, after the binding, results in a play where *fail* is never met. Additional material can be found in [16].

The price that one has to pay for the expressiveness of SL w.r.t. ATL* is the lack of important model-theoretic properties and an increased complexity of decision problems. In particular, in [18], it was shown that SL does not have the bounded-tree model property and the related satisfiability problem is *highly undecidable*, precisely, Σ_1^1-HARD. Hence, a natural question that arises is what makes ATL* decidable. Understanding the reasons for the decidability of ATL* should enable us to identify decidable fragments of SL.

In this work, we focus on the limitation of ATL* to allow only one temporal goal for each strategic assertion and study the fragment of SL with the same restriction. Specifically, we introduce the syntactic fragment *One-Goal Strategy Logic* (SL[1G], for short), which consists of formulas in a special prenex normal form having a single temporal goal at a time, for every strategy quantification of agents. This means that every temporal formula ψ is prefixed with a quantification-binding prefix that quantifies over a tuple of strategies and bind all agents to strategies. It is worth noting that SL[1G] still retains the ability to alternate strategy quantifiers as it is for SL, which is not allowed in ATL*. Roughly speaking, SL[1G] is ATL* augmented with this no-limitation on quantifier alternation and with the possibility to force agents to share strategies. This makes SL[1G] strictly more expressive and much more flexible than ATL*, as is shown in [16]. With SL[1G] one can express, for example, visibility constraints on strategies among agents, i.e., only some agents from a coalition have knowledge of the strategies taken by those in the opponent coalition, via the quantifier alternation. Also, by means of strategy sharing, one can describe the fact that, in the Hex game, the strategy-stealing argument does not let the player who adopts it to win. Observe that these properties cannot be expressed neither in ATL* nor in CHP-SL.

In this paper, we show that the satisfiability problem for SL[1G] is also 2EXPTIME-COMPLETE. Thus, in spite of its expressiveness, SL[1G] has the same computational complexities as ATL*. From this result, we conclude that the one-goal restriction is the key aspect to the elementary complexity of ATL*, while the arbitrary quantifier alternation does not let the complexity of the satisfiability problem to rise to non-elementary, as it usually happens in other logics, such as MSOL [25]. In [16], we also introduce SL[NG] and SL[BG] as two additional fragments of SL that strictly include SL[1G]. In SL[NG] we allow writing nesting and boolean combinations of temporal goals, while in SL[BG] we forbid the nesting, but still allow the boolean combinations. Both fragments do not satisfy important model-theoretic properties and have an highly undecidable satisfiability problem. Hence, at the present time, SL[1G] is the most general fragment of SL that subsumes ATL* while keeping its positive model-theoretic and computational properties.

To achieve our main result, we use a fundamental property of the semantics of SL[1G] called *elementariness*, which allows us to simplify reasoning about strategies by reducing it to a set of reasonings about actions. This intrinsic characteristic of SL[1G] means that, to choose an existential strategy, we do not need to know the entire structure of universally-quantified strategies, as it is the case for SL, but only their values on the histories of interest. Technically, to formally describe this property, we make use of the machinery of *dependence maps*, which is introduced to define a Skolemization procedure for SL, inspired by the one in first-order logic. Using elementariness, we show that SL[1G] satisfies the *bounded tree-model property*. This allows us to efficiently make use of a *tree automata-theoretic approach* [27,29] to solve the satisfiability problem. Given a formula φ, we build an *alternating co-Büchi tree automaton* [13,21], whose size is only exponential in the size of φ, accepting all bounded-branching tree models of the formula. Then, together with the complexity of automata-nonemptiness checking, we get that the satisfiability procedure for SL[1G] is 2EXPTIME. For completeness, we report that in [16] we already prove that the model-checking problem for SL[1G] remains 2EXPTIME-COMPLETE, while it is non-elementarily decidable for SL.

Related works. Several works have focused on extensions of ATL* to incorporate more powerful strategic constructs. Among them, we recall the *Alternating-Time* μCALCULUS (AμCALCULUS, for short) [2], *Game Logic* (GL, for short) [2], *Quantified Decision Modality* μCALCULUS (QDμ, for short) [23], *Coordination Logic* (CL, for short) [7], and some other extensions considered in [5], [19], and [30]. AμCALCULUS and QDμ are intrinsically different from SL[1G] (as well as from CHP-SL and ATL*) as they are obtained by extending the propositional μ-calculus [12] with strategic modalities. CL is similar to QDμ, but with LTL temporal operators instead of explicit fixpoint constructors. GL and CHP-SL are orthogonal to SL[1G]. Indeed, they both use more than a temporal goal, GL has quantifier alternation fixed to one, and CHP-SL only works for two agents.

Due to lack of space, proofs are reported in [17]. Also, see [16] for more on SL[1G].

2 Preliminaries

A *concurrent game structure* (CGS, for short) [2] is a tuple $\mathcal{G} \triangleq \langle \text{AP}, \text{Ag}, \text{Ac}, \text{St}, \lambda, \tau, s_0 \rangle$, where AP and Ag are finite non-empty sets of *atomic propositions* and *agents*, Ac and St are enumerable non-empty sets of *actions* and *states*, $s_0 \in \text{St}$ is a designated *initial state*, and $\lambda : \text{St} \to 2^{\text{AP}}$ is a *labeling function* that maps each state to the set of atomic propositions true in that state. Let $\text{Dc} \triangleq \text{Ac}^{\text{Ag}}$ be the set of *decisions*, i.e., functions from Ag to Ac representing the choices of an action for each agent. Then, $\tau : \text{St} \times \text{Dc} \to \text{St}$ is a *transition function* mapping a pair of a state and a decision to a state. If the set of actions is finite, i.e., $b = |\text{Ac}| < \omega$, we say that $\mathcal{G}$ is b-bounded, or simply bounded. If both the sets of actions and states are finite, we say that $\mathcal{G}$ is finite.

A *track* (resp., *path*) in a CGS $\mathcal{G}$ is a finite (resp., an infinite) sequence of states $\rho \in \text{St}^*$ (resp., $\pi \in \text{St}^\omega$) such that, for all $i \in [0, |\rho| - 1[$ (resp., $i \in \mathbb{N}$), there exists a decision $\mathsf{d} \in \text{Dc}$ such that $(\rho)_{i+1} = \tau((\rho)_i, \mathsf{d})$ (resp., $(\pi)_{i+1} = \tau((\pi)_i, \mathsf{d})$). A track ρ is *non-trivial* if $|\rho| > 0$, i.e., $\rho \neq \varepsilon$. $\text{Trk} \subseteq \text{St}^+$ (resp., $\text{Pth} \subseteq \text{St}^\omega$) denotes the set of all non-trivial tracks (resp., paths). Moreover, $\text{Trk}(s) \triangleq \{\rho \in \text{Trk} : \mathsf{fst}(\rho) = s\}$ (resp., $\text{Pth}(s) \triangleq \{\pi \in \text{Pth} : \mathsf{fst}(\pi) = s\}$) indicates the subsets of tracks (resp., paths) starting at a state $s \in \text{St}$.

A *strategy* is a partial function $\mathsf{f} : \text{Trk} \rightharpoonup \text{Ac}$ that maps each non-trivial track in its domain to an action. For a state $s \in \text{St}$, a strategy f is said s-*total* if it is defined on all tracks starting in s, i.e., $\mathsf{dom}(\mathsf{f}) = \text{Trk}(s)$. $\text{Str} \triangleq \text{Trk} \rightharpoonup \text{Ac}$ (resp., $\text{Str}(s) \triangleq \text{Trk}(s) \to \text{Ac}$) denotes the set of all (resp., s-total) strategies.

For all tracks $\rho \in \text{Trk}$, by $(\mathsf{f})_\rho \in \text{Str}$ we denote the *translation* of f along ρ, i.e., the strategy with $\mathsf{dom}((\mathsf{f})_\rho) \triangleq \{\mathsf{lst}(\rho) \cdot \rho' : \rho \cdot \rho' \in \mathsf{dom}(\mathsf{f})\}$[1] such that $(\mathsf{f})_\rho(\mathsf{lst}(\rho) \cdot \rho') \triangleq \mathsf{f}(\rho \cdot \rho')$, for all $\rho \cdot \rho' \in \mathsf{dom}(\mathsf{f})$.

Let Var be a fixed set of *variables*. An *assignment* is a partial function $\chi : \text{Var} \cup \text{Ag} \rightharpoonup \text{Str}$ mapping variables and agents in its domain to a strategy. An assignment χ is *complete* if it is defined on all agents, i.e., $\text{Ag} \subseteq \mathsf{dom}(\chi)$. For a state $s \in \text{St}$, it is said that χ is s-*total* if all strategies $\chi(l)$ are s-total, for $l \in \mathsf{dom}(\chi)$. $\text{Asg} \triangleq \text{Var} \cup \text{Ag} \rightharpoonup \text{Str}$ (resp., $\text{Asg}(s) \triangleq \text{Var} \cup \text{Ag} \rightharpoonup \text{Str}(s)$) denotes the set of all (resp., s-total) assignments. Moreover, $\text{Asg}(\mathrm{X}) \triangleq \mathrm{X} \to \text{Str}$ (resp., $\text{Asg}(\mathrm{X}, s) \triangleq \mathrm{X} \to \text{Str}(s)$) indicates the subset of X-*defined* (resp., s-total) assignments, i.e., (resp., s-total) assignments defined on the set $\mathrm{X} \subseteq \text{Var} \cup \text{Ag}$. For all tracks $\rho \in \text{Trk}$, by $(\chi)_\rho \in \text{Asg}(\mathsf{lst}(\rho))$ we denote the *translation* of χ along ρ, i.e., the $\mathsf{lst}(\rho)$-total assignment with $\mathsf{dom}((\chi)_\rho) \triangleq \mathsf{dom}(\chi)$, such that $(\chi)_\rho(l) \triangleq (\chi(l))_\rho$, for all $l \in \mathsf{dom}(\chi)$. For all elements $l \in \text{Var} \cup \text{Ag}$, by

[1] By $\mathsf{lst}(\rho) \triangleq (\rho)_{|\rho|-1}$ we denote the last state of ρ.

$\chi[l \mapsto \mathsf{f}] \in \mathrm{Asg}$ we denote the new assignment defined on $\mathsf{dom}(\chi[l \mapsto \mathsf{f}]) \triangleq \mathsf{dom}(\chi) \cup \{l\}$ that returns f on l and χ otherwise, i.e., $\chi[l \mapsto \mathsf{f}](l) \triangleq \mathsf{f}$ and $\chi[l \mapsto \mathsf{f}](l') \triangleq \chi(l')$, for all $l' \in \mathsf{dom}(\chi) \setminus \{l\}$.

A path $\pi \in \mathrm{Pth}(s)$ starting at a state $s \in \mathrm{St}$ is a *play* w.r.t. a complete s-total assignment $\chi \in \mathrm{Asg}(s)$ ((χ, s)-*play*, for short) if, for all $i \in \mathbb{N}$, it holds that $(\pi)_{i+1} = \tau((\pi)_i, \mathsf{d})$, where $\mathsf{d}(a) \triangleq \chi(a)((\pi)_{\leq i})$, for each $a \in \mathrm{Ag}$. The partial function $\mathsf{play} : \mathrm{Asg} \times \mathrm{St} \rightharpoonup \mathrm{Pth}$, with $\mathsf{dom}(\mathsf{play}) \triangleq \{(\chi, s) : \mathrm{Ag} \subseteq \mathsf{dom}(\chi) \wedge \chi \in \mathrm{Asg}(s) \wedge s \in \mathrm{St}\}$, returns the (χ, s)-play $\mathsf{play}(\chi, s) \in \mathrm{Pth}(s)$, for all (χ, s) in its domain.

For a state $s \in \mathrm{St}$ and a complete s-total assignment $\chi \in \mathrm{Asg}(s)$, the *i-th global translation* of (χ, s), with $i \in \mathbb{N}$, is the pair of a complete assignment and a state $(\chi, s)^i \triangleq ((\chi)_{(\pi)_{\leq i}}, (\pi)_i)$, where $\pi = \mathsf{play}(\chi, s)$.

From now on, we use CGS names with subscript to extract the components from their tuple-structures. For example, $s_{0\mathcal{G}} = \mathsf{s}_0$ is the starting state of the CGS $\mathcal{G}$.

3 One-Goal Strategy Logic

In this section, we introduce syntax and semantics of One-Goal Strategy Logic (SL[1G], for short), as a syntactic fragment of SL, which we also report here for technical reasons. For more about SL[1G], see [16].

SL Syntax. SL syntactically extends LTL by means of two *strategy quantifiers*, existential $\langle\langle x \rangle\rangle$ and universal $[[x]]$, and *agent binding* (a, x), where a is an agent and x is a variable. Intuitively, these elements can be read, respectively, as *"there exists a strategy x"*, *"for all strategies x"*, and *"bind agent a to the strategy associated with the variable x"*. The formal syntax of SL follows.

Definition 1 (SL Syntax). SL formulas *are built inductively from the sets of atomic propositions* AP, *variables* Var, *and agents* Ag, *by using the following grammar, where* $p \in \mathrm{AP}$, $x \in \mathrm{Var}$, *and* $a \in \mathrm{Ag}$*:*

$$\varphi ::= p \mid \neg\varphi \mid \varphi \wedge \varphi \mid \varphi \vee \varphi \mid \mathsf{X}\,\varphi \mid \varphi\,\mathsf{U}\,\varphi \mid \varphi\,\mathsf{R}\,\varphi \mid \langle\langle x \rangle\rangle\varphi \mid [[x]]\varphi \mid (a, x)\varphi.$$

By $\mathsf{sub}(\varphi)$ we denote the set of all *subformulas* of the SL formula φ. By $\mathsf{free}(\varphi)$ we denote the set of *free agents/variables* of φ defined as the subset of $\mathrm{Ag} \cup \mathrm{Var}$ containing *(i)* all agents a for which there is no binding (a, x) before the occurrence of a temporal operator and *(ii)* all variables x for which there is a binding (a, x) but no quantification $\langle\langle x \rangle\rangle$ or $[[x]]$. A formula φ without free agents (resp., variables), i.e., with $\mathsf{free}(\varphi) \cap \mathrm{Ag} = \emptyset$ (resp., $\mathsf{free}(\varphi) \cap \mathrm{Var} = \emptyset$), is named *agent-closed* (resp., *variable-closed*). If φ is both agent- and variable-closed, it is named *sentence*. By $\mathsf{snt}(\varphi)$ we denote the set of all sentences that are subformulas of φ.

SL Semantics. As for ATL*, we define the semantics of SL w.r.t. concurrent game structures. For a CGS $\mathcal{G}$, a state s, and an s-total assignment χ with $\mathsf{free}(\varphi) \subseteq \mathsf{dom}(\chi)$, we write $\mathcal{G}, \chi, s \models \varphi$ to indicate that the formula φ holds at s under the assignment χ. The semantics of SL formulas involving p, $\neg$, $\wedge$, and $\vee$ is defined as usual in LTL and we omit it here (see [16], for the full definition). The semantics of the remaining part, which involves quantifications, bindings, and temporal operators follows.

Definition 2 (SL Semantics). *Given a* CGS $\mathcal{G}$, *for all* SL *formulas* φ, *states* $s \in \mathrm{St}$, *and s-total assignments* $\chi \in \mathrm{Asg}(s)$ *with* $\mathsf{free}(\varphi) \subseteq \mathsf{dom}(\chi)$, *the relation* $\mathcal{G}, \chi, s \models \varphi$ *is inductively defined as follows.*

1. $\mathcal{G}, \chi, s \models \langle\langle x \rangle\rangle \varphi$ *iff there is an s-total strategy* $\mathsf{f} \in \mathrm{Str}(s)$ *such that* $\mathcal{G}, \chi[x \mapsto \mathsf{f}], s \models \varphi$;
2. $\mathcal{G}, \chi, s \models [[x]] \varphi$ *iff for all s-total strategies* $\mathsf{f} \in \mathrm{Str}(s)$ *it holds that* $\mathcal{G}, \chi[x \mapsto \mathsf{f}], s \models \varphi$.

Moreover, if $\mathsf{free}(\varphi) \cup \{x\} \subseteq \mathsf{dom}(\chi) \cup \{a\}$ *for an agent* $a \in \mathrm{Ag}$, *it holds that:*

3. $\mathcal{G}, \chi, s \models (a, x)\varphi$ *iff* $\mathcal{G}, \chi[a \mapsto \chi(x)], s \models \varphi$.

Finally, if χ *is also complete, it holds that:*

4. $\mathcal{G}, \chi, s \models \mathsf{X}\, \varphi$ *if* $\mathcal{G}, (\chi, s)^1 \models \varphi$;
5. $\mathcal{G}, \chi, s \models \varphi_1 \mathsf{U}\, \varphi_2$ *if there is an index* $i \in \mathbb{N}$ *with* $k \leq i$ *such that* $\mathcal{G}, (\chi, s)^i \models \varphi_2$ *and, for all indexes* $j \in \mathbb{N}$ *with* $k \leq j < i$, *it holds that* $\mathcal{G}, (\chi, s)^j \models \varphi_1$;
6. $\mathcal{G}, \chi, s \models \varphi_1 \mathsf{R}\, \varphi_2$ *if, for all indexes* $i \in \mathbb{N}$ *with* $k \leq i$, *it holds that* $\mathcal{G}, (\chi, s)^i \models \varphi_2$ *or there is an index* $j \in \mathbb{N}$ *with* $k \leq j < i$ *such that* $\mathcal{G}, (\chi, s)^j \models \varphi_1$.

Intuitively, at Items 1 and 2, respectively, we evaluate the existential $\langle\langle x \rangle\rangle$ and universal $[[x]]$ quantifiers over strategies, by associating them to the variable x. Moreover, at Item 3, by means of an agent binding (a, x), we commit the agent a to a strategy associated with the variable x. It is evident that the LTL semantics is simply embedded into the SL one.

A CGS $\mathcal{G}$ is a *model* of an SL sentence φ, denoted by $\mathcal{G} \models \varphi$, iff $\mathcal{G}, \emptyset, s_0 \models \varphi$, where $\emptyset$ is the empty assignment. Moreover, φ is *satisfiable* iff there is a model for it. Given two CGSs $\mathcal{G}_1, \mathcal{G}_2$ and a sentence φ, we say that φ is *invariant* under $\mathcal{G}_1$ and $\mathcal{G}_2$ iff it holds that: $\mathcal{G}_1 \models \varphi$ iff $\mathcal{G}_2 \models \varphi$. Finally, given two SL formulas φ_1 and φ_2 with $\mathsf{free}(\varphi_1) = \mathsf{free}(\varphi_2)$, we say that φ_1 *implies* φ_2, in symbols $\varphi_1 \Rightarrow \varphi_2$, if, for all CGSs $\mathcal{G}$, states $s \in \mathrm{St}$, and $\mathsf{free}(\varphi_1)$-defined s-total assignments $\chi \in \mathrm{Asg}(\mathsf{free}(\varphi_1), s)$, it holds that if $\mathcal{G}, \chi, s \models \varphi_1$ then $\mathcal{G}, \chi, s \models \varphi_2$. Accordingly, we say that φ_1 is *equivalent* to φ_2, in symbols $\varphi_1 \equiv \varphi_2$, if $\varphi_1 \Rightarrow \varphi_2$ and $\varphi_2 \Rightarrow \varphi_1$.

As an example, consider the SL sentence $\varphi = \langle\langle \mathsf{x} \rangle\rangle [[\mathsf{y}]] \langle\langle \mathsf{z} \rangle\rangle ((\alpha, \mathsf{x})(\beta, \mathsf{y})(\mathsf{X}\, \mathsf{p}) \wedge (\alpha, \mathsf{y})(\beta, \mathsf{z})(\mathsf{X}\, \mathsf{q}))$. Note that both agents α and β use the strategy associated with y to achieve simultaneously the LTL goals $\mathsf{X}\, \mathsf{p}$ and $\mathsf{X}\, \mathsf{q}$, respectively. A model for φ is the CGS $\mathcal{G} \triangleq \langle \{\mathsf{p}, \mathsf{q}\}, \{\alpha, \beta\}, \{0, 1\}, \{\mathsf{s}_0, \mathsf{s}_1, \mathsf{s}_2, \mathsf{s}_3\}, \lambda, \tau, \mathsf{s}_0 \rangle$, where $\lambda(\mathsf{s}_0) \triangleq \emptyset$, $\lambda(\mathsf{s}_1) \triangleq \{\mathsf{p}\}$, $\lambda(\mathsf{s}_2) \triangleq \{\mathsf{p}, \mathsf{q}\}$, $\lambda(\mathsf{s}_3) \triangleq \{\mathsf{q}\}$, $\tau(\mathsf{s}_0, (0, 0)) \triangleq \mathsf{s}_1$, $\tau(\mathsf{s}_0, (0, 1)) \triangleq \mathsf{s}_2$, $\tau(\mathsf{s}_0, (1, 0)) \triangleq \mathsf{s}_3$, and all the remaining transitions go to s_0. See the representation of $\mathcal{G}$ depicted in Figure 1, in which vertexes are states of the game and labels on edges represent decisions of agents or sets of them, where the symbol $*$ is used in place of every possible action. Clearly, $\mathcal{G} \models \varphi$ by letting, on s_0, the variables x to chose action 0 (the formula $(\alpha, \mathsf{x})(\beta, \mathsf{y})(\mathsf{X}\, \mathsf{p})$ is satisfied for any choice of y, since we can move from s_0 to either s_1 or s_2, both labeled with p) and z to choose action 1 when y has action 0 and, vice versa, 0 when y has 1 (in both cases, the formula $(\alpha, \mathsf{y})(\beta, \mathsf{z})(\mathsf{X}\, \mathsf{q})$ is satisfied, since one can move from s_0 to either s_2 or s_3, both labeled with q).

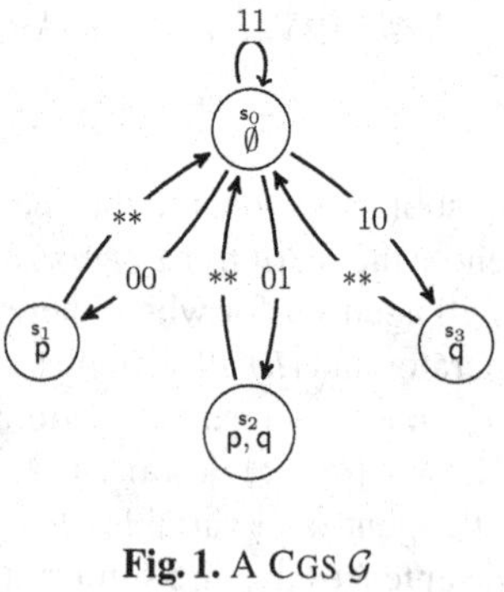

Fig. 1. A CGS $\mathcal{G}$

SL[1G] Syntax. To formalize the syntactic fragment SL[1G] of SL, we need first to define the concepts of *quantification* and *binding prefixes*.

Definition 3 (Prefixes). *A* quantification prefix *over a set* $V \subseteq \mathrm{Var}$ *of variables is a finite word* $\wp \in \{\langle\langle x\rangle\rangle, [[x]] : x \in V\}^{|V|}$ *of length* $|V|$ *such that each variable* $x \in V$ *occurs just once in* $\wp$. *A* binding prefix *over a set* $V \subseteq \mathrm{Var}$ *of variables is a finite word* $\flat \in \{(a, x) : a \in \mathrm{Ag} \wedge x \in V\}^{|\mathrm{Ag}|}$ *of length* $|\mathrm{Ag}|$ *such that each agent* $a \in \mathrm{Ag}$ *occurs just once in* $\flat$. *Finally,* $\mathrm{Qnt}(V) \subseteq \{\langle\langle x\rangle\rangle, [[x]] : x \in V\}^{|V|}$ *and* $\mathrm{Bnd}(V) \subseteq \{(a, x) : a \in \mathrm{Ag} \wedge x \in V\}^{|\mathrm{Ag}|}$ *denote, respectively, the sets of all quantification and binding prefixes over variables in* V.

We can now define the syntactic fragment we want to analyze. The idea is to force each group of agent bindings, represented by a binding prefix, to be coupled with a quantification prefix.

Definition 4 (SL[1G] Syntax). SL[1G] *formulas are built inductively from the sets of atomic propositions* AP, *quantification prefixes* Qnt(V), *for* $V \subseteq \mathrm{Var}$, *and binding prefixes* Bnd(Var), *by using the following grammar, with* $p \in \mathrm{AP}$, $\wp \in \cup_{V \subseteq \mathrm{Var}} \mathrm{Qnt}(V)$, *and* $\flat \in \mathrm{Bnd}(\mathrm{Var})$*:*

$$\varphi ::= p \mid \neg\varphi \mid \varphi \wedge \varphi \mid \varphi \vee \varphi \mid \mathsf{X}\,\varphi \mid \varphi\,\mathsf{U}\,\varphi \mid \varphi\,\mathsf{R}\,\varphi \mid \wp\flat\varphi,$$

with $\wp \in \mathrm{Qnt}(\mathsf{free}(\flat\varphi))$, *in the formation rule* $\wp\flat\varphi$.

In the following, for a *goal* we mean an SL agent-closed formula of the kind $\flat\psi$, where ψ is variable-closed and $\flat \in \mathrm{Bnd}(\mathsf{free}(\psi))$. Note that, since $\flat\varphi$ is a goal, it is agent-closed, so, $\mathsf{free}(\flat\varphi) \subseteq \mathrm{Var}$. Moreover, an SL[1G] sentence φ is *principal* if it is of the form $\varphi = \wp\flat\psi$, where $\flat\psi$ is a goal and $\wp \in \mathrm{Qnt}(\mathsf{free}(\flat\psi))$. By $\mathsf{psnt}(\varphi) \subseteq \mathsf{snt}(\varphi)$ we denote the set of *principal subsentences* of the SL[1G] formula φ.

As an example, let $\varphi_1 = \wp\flat_1\psi_1$ and $\varphi_2 = \wp(\flat_1\psi_1 \wedge \flat_2\psi_2)$, where $\wp = [[\mathsf{x}]]\langle\langle \mathsf{y}\rangle\rangle[[\mathsf{z}]]$, $\flat_1 = (\alpha, \mathsf{x})(\beta, \mathsf{y})(\gamma, \mathsf{z})$, $\flat_2 = (\alpha, \mathsf{y})(\beta, \mathsf{z})(\gamma, \mathsf{y})$, $\psi_1 = \mathsf{X}\,\mathsf{p}$, and $\psi_2 = \mathsf{X}\,\mathsf{q}$. Then, it is evident that $\varphi_1 \in$ SL[1G] but $\varphi_2 \notin$ SL[1G], since the quantification prefix $\wp$ of the latter does not have in its scope a unique goal.

It is fundamental to observe that the formula φ_1 of the above example cannot be expressed in ATL*, as proved in [16] and reported in the following theorem, since its 2-quantifier alternation cannot be encompassed in the 1-alternation ATL* modalities. On the contrary, each ATL* formula of the type $\langle\langle \mathrm{A}\rangle\rangle\psi$, where $\mathrm{A} = \{\alpha_1, \ldots, \alpha_n\} \subseteq \mathrm{Ag} = \{\alpha_1, \ldots, \alpha_n, \beta_1, \ldots, \beta_m\}$ can be expressed in SL[1G] as follows: $\langle\langle \mathsf{x}_1\rangle\rangle \cdots \langle\langle x_n\rangle\rangle[[\mathsf{y}_1]] \cdots [[\mathsf{y}_m]](\alpha_1, \mathsf{x}_1) \cdots (\alpha_n, \mathsf{x}_n)(\beta_1, \mathsf{y}_1) \cdots (\beta_m, \mathsf{y}_m)\psi$.

Theorem 1. SL[1G] *is strictly more expressive than* ATL*.

We now give two examples in which we show the importance of the ability to write specifications with alternation of quantifiers greater than 1 along with strategy sharing.

Example 1 (Escape from Alcatraz[2]). Consider the situation in which an Alcatraz prisoner tries to escape from jail by helicopter with the help of an accomplice. Due to his panoramic point of view, assume that the accomplice has the full visibility on the behaviors of guards, while the prisoner does not have the same ability. Therefore, the latter

[2] We thank Luigi Sauro for having pointed out this example.

has to put in practice an escape strategy that, independently of guards moves, can be supported by his accomplice to escape. We can formalize such an intricate situation by means of an SL[1G] sentence with alternation 2, where the prisoner has to choose a uniform strategy w.r.t. those chosen by the guards, as follows. First, let $\mathcal{G}_A$ be a CGS modeling the possible situations in which the agents "p" prisoner, "g" guards, and "a" accomplice can reside, together with all related possible moves. Then, verify the existence of an escape strategy by checking $\mathcal{G}_A \models \langle\langle \mathsf{x} \rangle\rangle [[\mathsf{y}]] \langle\langle \mathsf{z} \rangle\rangle (\mathsf{p}, \mathsf{x})(\mathsf{g}, \mathsf{y})(\mathsf{a}, \mathsf{z})(\mathsf{F}\ \mathsf{free}_{\mathsf{P}})$.

Example 2 (Stealing-Strategy in Hex). Hex is a two-player game, red vs blue, in which each player in turn places a stone of his color on a single empty hexagonal cell of the rhomboidal playing board having opposite sides equally colored, either red or blue. The goal of each player is to be the first to form a path connecting the opposing sides of the board marked by his color. It is easy to prove that the stealing-strategy argument does not lead to a winning strategy in Hex, i.e., if the player that moves second copies the moves of the opponent, he surely loses the play. It is possible to formalize this fact in SL[1G] as follows. First model Hex with a CGS $\mathcal{G}_H$ whose states represent a possible possible configurations reached during a play between "r" red and "b" blue. Then, verify the negation of the stealing-strategy argument by checking $\mathcal{G}_H \models \langle\langle \mathsf{x} \rangle\rangle (\mathsf{r}, \mathsf{x})(\mathsf{b}, \mathsf{x})(\mathsf{F}\ \mathsf{cnc}_{\mathsf{r}})$. Intuitively, this sentence says that agent r has a strategy that, once it is copied (bound) by b it allows the former to win, i.e., to be the first to connect the related red edges ($\mathsf{F}\ \mathsf{cnc}_{\mathsf{r}}$).

4 Strategy Quantifications

We now define the concept of *dependence map*. The key idea is that every quantification prefix of an SL formula can be represented by a suitable choice of a dependence map over strategies. Such a result is at the base of the definition of the *elementariness* property and allows us to prove that SL[1G] is elementarily satisfiable, i.e., we can simplify a reasoning about strategies by reducing it to a set of local reasonings about actions [16].

Dependence Map. First, we introduce some notation regarding quantification prefixes. Let $\wp \in \mathrm{Qnt}(\mathrm{V})$ be a quantification prefix over a set $\mathrm{V}(\wp) \triangleq \mathrm{V} \subseteq \mathrm{Var}$ of variables. By $\langle\langle \wp \rangle\rangle \triangleq \{x \in \mathrm{V} : \exists i \in [0, |\wp|[\,.\, (\wp)_i = \langle\langle x \rangle\rangle\}$ and $[[\wp]] \triangleq \mathrm{V} \setminus \langle\langle \wp \rangle\rangle$ we denote, respectively, the sets of *existential* and *universal variables* quantified in $\wp$. For two variables $x, y \in \mathrm{V}$, we say that x *precedes* y in $\wp$, in symbols $x <_\wp y$, if x occurs before y in $\wp$. Moreover, by $\mathrm{Dep}(\wp) \triangleq \{(x, y) \in \mathrm{V} \times \mathrm{V} : x \in [[\wp]], y \in \langle\langle \wp \rangle\rangle \wedge x <_\wp y\}$ we denote the set of *dependence pairs*, i.e., a dependence relation, on which we derive the parameterized version $\mathrm{Dep}(\wp, y) \triangleq \{x \in \mathrm{V} : (x, y) \in \mathrm{Dep}(\wp)\}$ containing all variables from which y depends. Also, we use $\overline{\wp} \in \mathrm{Qnt}(\mathrm{V})$ to indicate the quantification derived from $\wp$ by *dualizing* each quantifier contained in it, i.e., for all $i \in [0, |\wp|[$, it holds that $(\overline{\wp})_i = \langle\langle x \rangle\rangle$ iff $(\wp)_i = [[x]]$, with $x \in \mathrm{V}$. Clearly, $\langle\langle \overline{\wp} \rangle\rangle = [[\wp]]$ and $[[\overline{\wp}]] = \langle\langle \wp \rangle\rangle$. Finally, we define the notion of *valuation* of variables over a generic set D as a partial function $\mathsf{v} : \mathrm{Var} \rightharpoonup \mathrm{D}$ mapping every variable in its domain to an element in D. By $\mathrm{Val}_{\mathrm{D}}(\mathrm{V}) \triangleq \mathrm{V} \to \mathrm{D}$ we denote the set of all valuation functions over D defined on $\mathrm{V} \subseteq \mathrm{Var}$.

We now give the semantics for quantification prefixes via the following definition of *dependence map*.

Definition 5 (Dependence Maps). *Let $\wp \in \mathrm{Qnt}(\mathrm{V})$ be a quantification prefix over a set of variables $\mathrm{V} \subseteq \mathrm{Var}$, and D a set. Then, a* dependence map *for $\wp$ over D is a function $\theta : \mathrm{Val_D}([\![\wp]\!]) \to \mathrm{Val_D}(\mathrm{V})$ satisfying the following properties:* (i) $\theta(\mathsf{v})_{\restriction [\![\wp]\!]} = \mathsf{v}$, *for all* $\mathsf{v} \in \mathrm{Val_D}([\![\wp]\!])$*;* (ii) $\theta(\mathsf{v}_1)(x) = \theta(\mathsf{v}_2)(x)$, *for all* $\mathsf{v}_1, \mathsf{v}_2 \in \mathrm{Val_D}([\![\wp]\!])$ *and* $x \in \langle\!\langle \wp \rangle\!\rangle$ *such that* $\mathsf{v}_{1\restriction \mathrm{Dep}(\wp,x)} = \mathsf{v}_{2\restriction \mathrm{Dep}(\wp,x)}$. $\mathrm{DM_D}(\wp)$ *denotes the set of all dependence maps of $\wp$ on D.*

Intuitively, Item (i) asserts that θ takes the same values of its argument w.r.t. the universal variables in $\wp$ and Item (ii) ensures that the value of θ w.r.t. an existential variable x in $\wp$ does not depend on variables not in $\mathrm{Dep}(\wp, x)$. To get better insight into this definition, a dependence map θ for $\wp$ can be considered as a set of *Skolem functions* that, given a value for each universal variable, return a possible value for all the existential variables in a way that is consistent w.r.t. the order of quantifications in $\wp$.

We now state a fundamental theorem that describes how to eliminate strategy quantifications of an SL formula via a choice of a dependence map over strategies. This procedure, easily proved to be correct by induction on the structure of the formula in [16], can be seen as the equivalent of the *Skolemization* in first order logic [10].

Theorem 2 (SL Strategy Quantification). *Let $\mathcal{G}$ be a CGS and $\varphi = \wp\psi$ an SL sentence, where ψ is agent-closed and $\wp \in \mathrm{Qnt}(\mathsf{free}(\psi))$. Then, $\mathcal{G} \models \varphi$ iff there exists a dependence map $\theta \in \mathrm{DM}_{\mathrm{Str}(s_0)}(\wp)$ such that $\mathcal{G}, \theta(\chi), s_0 \models \psi$, for all $\chi \in \mathrm{Asg}([\![\wp]\!], s_0)$.*

The above theorem substantially characterizes SL semantics by means of the concept of dependence map. In particular, it shows that if a formula is satisfiable then it is always possible to find a suitable dependence map returning the existential strategies in response to the universal ones. Such a characterization enables the definition of an alternative semantics of SL, based on the choice of a subset of dependence maps that meet a certain given property. We do this with the aim of identifying semantic fragments of SL having better model properties and easier decision problems. With more details, given a CGS $\mathcal{G}$, one of its states s, and a property P, we say that a sentence $\wp\psi$ is P-satisfiable in $\mathcal{G}$, in symbols $\mathcal{G} \models_{\mathsf{P}} \wp\psi$, if there exists a dependence map θ meeting P such that, for all assignment $\chi \in \mathrm{Asg}([\![\wp]\!], s)$, it holds that $\mathcal{G}, \theta(\chi), s \models \psi$. An alternative semantics identified by a property P is even more interesting if there exists a syntactic fragment corresponding to it, i.e., each satisfiable sentence of such a fragment is P-satisfiable and vice versa. In the following, we put in practice this idea in order to show that SL[1G] has the same complexity of ATL*w.r.t. the satisfiability problem.

Elementary Quantifications. According to the above description, we now introduce a suitable property of dependence maps, called elementariness, together with the related alternative semantics. Then, in Theorem 3, we state that SL[1G] has the elementariness property, i.e., each SL[1G] sentence is satisfiable iff it is elementarily satisfiable. Intuitively, a dependence map $\theta \in \mathrm{DM}_{\mathrm{T}\to\mathrm{D}}(\wp)$ over functions from a set T to a set D is elementary if it can be split into a set of dependence maps over D, one for each element of T, represented by a function $\widetilde{\theta} : \mathrm{T} \to \mathrm{DM_D}(\wp)$. This idea allows us to greatly simplify the reasoning about strategy quantifications, since we can reduce them to a set of quantifications over actions, one for each track in their domains.

Note that sets D and T, as well as U and V used in the following, are generic and in our framework they may refer to actions and strategies (D), tracks (T), and variables

(U and V). In particular, observe that functions from T to D represent strategies. We prefer to use abstract name, as the properties we describe hold generally.

To formally develop the above idea, we have first to introduce the generic concept of *adjoint function*. From now on, we denote by $\widehat{\mathsf{g}} : \mathrm{Y} \rightarrow (\mathrm{X} \rightarrow \mathrm{Z})$ the operation of *flipping* of a generic function $\mathsf{g} : \mathrm{X} \rightarrow (\mathrm{Y} \rightarrow \mathrm{Z})$, i.e., the transformation of g by swapping the order of its arguments. Such a flipping is well-grounded due to the following chain of isomorphisms: $\mathrm{X} \rightarrow (\mathrm{Y} \rightarrow \mathrm{Z}) \cong (\mathrm{X} \times \mathrm{Y}) \rightarrow \mathrm{Z} \cong (\mathrm{Y} \times \mathrm{X}) \rightarrow \mathrm{Z} \cong \mathrm{Y} \rightarrow (\mathrm{X} \rightarrow \mathrm{Z})$.

Definition 6 (Adjoint Functions). *Let* D, T, U, *and* V *be four sets, and* $\mathsf{m} : (\mathrm{T} \rightarrow \mathrm{D})^{\mathrm{U}} \rightarrow (\mathrm{T} \rightarrow \mathrm{D})^{\mathrm{V}}$ *and* $\widetilde{\mathsf{m}} : \mathrm{T} \rightarrow (\mathrm{D}^{\mathrm{U}} \rightarrow \mathrm{D}^{\mathrm{V}})$ *two functions. Then,* $\widetilde{\mathsf{m}}$ *is the* adjoint *of* m *if* $\widetilde{\mathsf{m}}(t)(\widehat{\mathsf{g}}(t))(x) = \mathsf{m}(\mathsf{g})(x)(t)$, *for all* $\mathsf{g} \in (\mathrm{T} \rightarrow \mathrm{D})^{\mathrm{U}}$, $x \in \mathrm{V}$, *and* $t \in \mathrm{T}$.

Intuitively, a function m transforming a map of kind $(\mathrm{T} \rightarrow \mathrm{D})^{\mathrm{U}}$ into a new map of kind $(\mathrm{T} \rightarrow \mathrm{D})^{\mathrm{V}}$ has an adjoint $\widetilde{\mathsf{m}}$ if such a transformation can be done pointwisely w.r.t. the set T, i.e., we can put out as a common domain the set T and then transform a map of kind D^{U} in a map of kind D^{V}. Observe that, if a function has an adjoint, this is unique. Similarly, from an adjoint function it is possible to determine the original function unambiguously. Thus, it is established a one-to-one correspondence between functions admitting an adjoint and the adjoint itself.

The formal meaning of the elementariness of a dependence map over generic functions follows.

Definition 7 (Elementary Dependence Maps). *Let* $\wp \in \mathrm{Qnt}(\mathrm{V})$ *be a quantification prefix over a set* $\mathrm{V} \subseteq \mathrm{Var}$ *of variables,* D *and* T *two sets, and* $\theta \in \mathrm{DM}_{\mathrm{T} \rightarrow \mathrm{D}}(\wp)$ *a dependence map for* $\wp$ *over* $\mathrm{T} \rightarrow \mathrm{D}$*. Then,* θ *is* elementary *if it admits an adjoint function.* $\mathrm{EDM}_{\mathrm{T} \rightarrow \mathrm{D}}(\wp)$ *denotes the set of all elementary dependence maps for* $\wp$ *over* $\mathrm{T} \rightarrow \mathrm{D}$.

As mentioned above, we now introduce an important variant of SL[1G] semantics based on the property of elementariness of dependence maps over strategies. We refer to the related satisfiability concept as *elementary satisfiability*, in symbols $\models_{\mathrm{E}}$.

The new semantics of SL[1G] formulas involving atomic propositions, Boolean connectives, temporal operators, and agent bindings is defined as for the classic one, where the modeling relation $\models$ is substituted with $\models_{\mathrm{E}}$, and we omit to report it here. In the following definition, we only describe the part concerning the quantification prefixes. Observe that by $\zeta_{\flat} : \mathrm{Ag} \rightarrow \mathrm{Var}$, for $\flat \in \mathrm{Bnd}(\mathrm{Var})$, we denote the function associating to each agent the variable of its binding in $\flat$.

Definition 8 (SL[1G] Elementary Semantics). *Let* $\mathcal{G}$ *be a* CGS, $s \in \mathrm{St}$ *one of its states, and* $\wp\flat\psi$ *an* SL[1G] *principal sentence. Then* $\mathcal{G}, \varnothing, s \models_{\mathrm{E}} \wp\flat\psi$ *iff there is an elementary dependence map* $\theta \in \mathrm{EDM}_{\mathrm{Str}(s)}(\wp)$ *for* $\wp$ *over* $\mathrm{Str}(s)$ *such that* $\mathcal{G}, \theta(\chi) \circ \zeta_{\flat}, s \models_{\mathrm{E}} \psi$, *for all* $\chi \in \mathrm{Asg}([\![\wp]\!], s)$.

It is immediate to see a strong similarity between the statement of Theorem 2 of SL strategy quantification and the previous definition. The only crucial difference resides in the choice of the kind of dependence map. Moreover, observe that, differently from the classic semantics, the quantifications in a prefix are not treated individually but as an atomic block. This is due to the necessity of having a strict correlation between the point-wise structure of the quantified strategies.

Finally, we state the following fundamental theorem which is a key step in the proof of the bounded model property and decidability of the satisfiability for SL[1G], whose correctness has been proved in [16]. The idea behind the proof of the elementariness property resides in the strong similarity between the statement of Theorem 2 of SL strategy quantification and the definition of the winning condition in a classic turn-based two-player game. Indeed, on one hand, we say that a sentence is satisfiable iff "there exists a dependence map such that, for all all assignments, it holds that ...". On the other hand, we say that the first player wins a game iff "there exists a strategy for him such that, for all strategies of the other player, it holds that ...". The gap between these two formulations is solved in SL[1G] by using the concept of elementary quantification. So, we build a two-player turn-based game in which the two players are viewed one as a dependence map and the other as a valuation over universal quantified variables, both over actions, such that the formula is satisfied iff the first player wins the game. This construction is a deep technical evolution of the proof method used for the dualization of alternating automata on infinite objects [20]. Precisely, it uses Martin's Determinacy Theorem [15] on the auxiliary turn-based game to prove that, if there is no dependence map of a given prefix that satisfies the given property, there is a dependence map of the dual prefix satisfying its negation.

Theorem 3 (SL[1G] Elementariness). *Let $\mathcal{G}$ be a* CGS *and φ an* SL[1G] *sentence. Then,* $\mathcal{G} \models \varphi$ *iff* $\mathcal{G} \models_{\mathrm{E}} \varphi$.

In order to understand what elementariness means from a syntactic point of view, note that in SL[1G] it holds that $\wp\flat \mathsf{X}\, \psi \equiv \wp\flat \mathsf{X}\, \wp\flat\psi$, i.e., we can requantify the strategies to satisfy the inner subformula ψ. This equivalence is a generalization of what is well know to hold for CTL*: $\mathsf{EX}\, \psi \equiv \mathsf{EX}\, \mathsf{E}\psi$. Moreover, note that, as reported in [16], elementariness does not hold for more expressive fragments of SL, such as SL[BG].

5 Model Properties

We now investigate basic model properties of SL[1G] that turn out to be important on their own and useful to prove the decidability of the satisfiability problem.

First, recall that the satisfiability problem for branching-time logics can be solved via tree automata, once a kind of bounded tree-model property holds. Indeed, by using it, one can build an automaton accepting all models of formulas, or their encoding. So, we first introduce the concepts of *concurrent game tree*, *decision tree*, and *decision-unwinding* and then show that SL[1G] is *invariant under decision-unwinding*, which directly implies that it satisfies an *unbounded tree-model property*. Finally, by using a sharp technique that is precisely described in [17], we further prove that the above property is actually a *bounded tree-model property*.

Tree-Model Property. We now introduce two particular kinds of CGS whose structure is a directed tree. As already explained, we do this since the decidability procedure we give in the last section of the paper is based on alternating tree automata.

Definition 9 (Concurrent Game Trees). *A* concurrent game tree *(*CGT*, for short) is a* CGS $\mathcal{T} \triangleq \langle \mathrm{AP}, \mathrm{Ag}, \mathrm{Ac}, \mathrm{St}, \lambda, \tau, \varepsilon \rangle$, *where* (i) $\mathrm{St} \subseteq \Delta^*$ *is a Δ-tree for a given set Δ of* *directions and* (ii) *if* $t \cdot e \in \mathrm{St}$ *then there is a decision* $\mathsf{d} \in \mathrm{Dc}$ *such that* $\tau(t, \mathsf{d}) = t \cdot e$, *for all* $t \in \mathrm{St}$ *and* $e \in \Delta$. *Furthermore,* $\mathcal{T}$ *is a* decision tree *(*DT*, for short) if* (i) $\mathrm{St} = \mathrm{Dc}^*$ *and* (ii) *if* $t \cdot \mathsf{d} \in \mathrm{St}$ *then* $\tau(t, \mathsf{d}) = t \cdot \mathsf{d}$, *for all* $t \in \mathrm{St}$ *and* $\mathsf{d} \in \mathrm{Dc}$.

Intuitively, CGTs are CGSs with a tree-shaped transition relation and DTs have, in addition, states uniquely determining the history of computation leading to them.

At this point, we can define a generalization for CGSs of the classic concept of *unwinding* of labeled transition systems, namely decision-unwinding. Note that, in general and differently from ATL*, SL is not invariant under decision-unwinding, as we show later. On the contrary, SL[1G] satisfies such an invariance property. This fact allows us to show that this logic has the unbounded tree-model property.

Definition 10 (Decision-Unwinding). *Let* $\mathcal{G}$ *be a* CGS. *Then, the* decision-unwinding *of* $\mathcal{G}$ *is the* DT $\mathcal{G}_{DU} \triangleq \langle \mathrm{AP}, \mathrm{Ag}, \mathrm{Ac}_{\mathcal{G}}, \mathrm{Dc}_{\mathcal{G}}^*, \lambda, \tau, \varepsilon \rangle$ *for which there is a surjective function* $\mathsf{unw} : \mathrm{Dc}_{\mathcal{G}}^* \to \mathrm{St}_{\mathcal{G}}$ *such that* (i) $\mathsf{unw}(\varepsilon) = s_{0\mathcal{G}}$, (ii) $\mathsf{unw}(\tau(t, \mathsf{d})) = \tau_{\mathcal{G}}(\mathsf{unw}(t), \mathsf{d})$, *and* (iii) $\lambda(t) = \lambda_{\mathcal{G}}(\mathsf{unw}(t))$, *for all* $t \in \mathrm{Dc}_{\mathcal{G}}^*$ *and* $\mathsf{d} \in \mathrm{Dc}_{\mathcal{G}}$.

Note that each CGS $\mathcal{G}$ has a unique associated decision-unwinding $\mathcal{G}_{DU}$.

We say that a sentence φ has the *decision-tree model property* if, for each CGS $\mathcal{G}$, it holds that $\mathcal{G} \models \varphi$ iff $\mathcal{G}_{DU} \models \varphi$. By using a standard proof by induction on the structure of SL[1G] formulas, we can show that this logic is invariant under decision-unwinding, i.e., each SL[1G] sentence has decision-tree model property, and, consequently, that it satisfies the unbounded tree-model property. For the case of the combined quantification and binding prefixes $\wp\flat\psi$, we can use a technique that allows to build, given an elementary dependence map θ satisfying the formula on a CGS $\mathcal{G}$, an elementary dependence map θ' satisfying the same formula over the DT $\mathcal{G}_{DU}$, and vice versa. This construction is based on a step-by-step transformation of the adjoint of a dependence maps into another, which is done for each track of the original model. This means that we do not actually transform the strategy quantifications but the equivalent infinite set of action quantifications.

Theorem 4 (SL[1G] Positive Model Properties). *For* SL[1G] *it holds that:* (i) *it is invariant under decision-unwinding and* (ii) *it has the decision-tree model property.*

Although this result is a generalization of that proved to hold for ATL*, it actually represents an important demarcation line between SL[1G] and SL. Indeed, as we show in the following theorem, SL does not satisfy neither the tree-model property nor, consequently, the invariance under decision-unwinding.

Theorem 5 (SL Negative Model Properties). *For* SL *it holds that:* (i) *it does not have the decision-tree model property and* (ii) *it is not invariant under decision-unwinding.*

Bounded Tree-Model Property. We now have all tools we need to prove the bounded tree-model property for SL[1G], which we recall SL does not satisfy [18]. Actually, we prove here a stronger property, which we name *bounded disjoint satisfiability*.

To this aim, we first introduce the new concept, called *disjoint satisfiability*, regarding the satisfiability of different instances of the same subsentence of the original specification, which intuitively states that these instances can be checked on disjoint subtrees of the tree model. With more detail, this property asserts that, if two instances use part of the same subtree, they are forced to use the same dependence map as well. This intrinsic characteristic of SL[1G] is fundamental to build a unique automaton that checks the truth of all subsentences, by simply merging their respective automata, without using a projection operation that eliminates their proper alphabets, which otherwise can be in conflict. In this way, we can avoid an exponential blow-up.

In the following theorem, we finally describe the crucial step behind our automata-theoretic decidability procedure for SL[1G]. At an high-level, the proof proceeds as follows. We start from the satisfiability of the specification φ over a DT $\mathcal{T}$, whose existence is ensured by Item *(ii)* of Theorem 4 of SL[1G] positive model properties. Then, by means of Theorem 3 on the SL[1G] elementariness, we construct the adjoint functions of the dependence maps used to verify the satisfiability of the sentences on $\mathcal{T}$. Finally, by using a fundamental and very technical property of dependence maps, called *overlapping* [17], we transform the dependence maps over actions, contained in the ranges of the adjoint functions, in a bounded version, which preserves the satisfiability of the sentences on a bounded pruning $\mathcal{T}'$ of $\mathcal{T}$.

Theorem 6 (SL[1G] Bounded Tree-Model Property). *Let φ be an* SL[1G] *satisfiable sentence. Then, there exists a bounded* CGT $\mathcal{T}$ *such that* $\mathcal{T} \models \varphi$. *Moreover, for all* $\phi \in \mathsf{psnt}(\varphi)$, *it holds that* $\mathcal{T}$ *satisfies* ϕ *disjointly over the set* $\{s \in \mathrm{St} : \mathcal{T}, \emptyset, s \models \phi\}$.

6 Satisfiability Procedure

We finally solve the satisfiability problem for SL[1G] and show that it is 2EXPTIME-COMPLETE, as for ATL*. The algorithmic procedures is based on an automata-theoretic approach, which reduces the decision problem for the logic to the emptiness problem of a suitable universal Co-Büchi tree automaton (UCT, for short) [9]. From an high-level point of view, the automaton construction seems similar to what was proposed in literature for CTL* [13] and ATL* [26]. However, our technique is completely new, since it is based on the novel notions of elementariness and disjoint satisfiability.

Principal Sentences. To proceed with the satisfiability procedure, we have to introduce a concept of encoding for an assignment and the labeling of a DT.

Definition 11 (Assignment-Labeling Encoding). *Let $\mathcal{T}$ be a* DT, $t \in \mathrm{St}_{\mathcal{T}}$ *one of its states, and* $\chi \in \mathrm{Asg}_{\mathcal{T}}(\mathrm{V}, t)$ *an assignment defined on the set* $\mathrm{V} \subseteq \mathrm{Var}$. *A* $(\mathrm{Val}_{\mathrm{Ac}_{\mathcal{T}}}(\mathrm{V}) \times 2^{\mathrm{AP}})$*-labeled* $\mathrm{Dc}_{\mathcal{T}}$*-tree* $\mathcal{T}' \triangleq \langle \mathrm{St}_{\mathcal{T}}, \mathsf{u} \rangle$ *is an* assignment-labeling encoding *for* χ *on* $\mathcal{T}$ *if* $\mathsf{u}(\mathsf{lst}((\rho)_{\geq 1})) = (\widehat{\chi}(\rho), \lambda_{\mathcal{T}}(\mathsf{lst}(\rho)))$, *for all* $\rho \in \mathrm{Trk}_{\mathcal{T}}(t)$.

Observe that there is a unique assignment-labeling encoding for each assignment over a given DT.

Now, we prove the existence of a UCT $\mathcal{U}^{\mathrm{Ac}}_{\flat\psi}$ for each SL[1G] goal $\flat\psi$ having no principal subsentences. $\mathcal{U}^{\mathrm{Ac}}_{\flat\psi}$ recognizes all the assignment-labeling encodings $\mathcal{T}'$ of an a priori given assignment χ over a generic DT $\mathcal{T}$, once the goal is satisfied on $\mathcal{T}$ under χ. Intuitively, we start with a UCW, recognizing all infinite words on the alphabet 2^{AP} that satisfy the LTL formula ψ, obtained by a simple variation of the Vardi-Wolper construction [28]. Then, we run it on the encoding tree $\mathcal{T}'$ by following the directions imposed by the assignment in its labeling.

Lemma 1 **(SL[1G] Goal Automaton).** *Let $\flat\psi$ an SL[1G] goal without principal subsentences and Ac a finite set of actions. Then, there exists an UCT $\mathcal{U}^{\mathrm{Ac}}_{\flat\psi} \triangleq \langle \mathrm{Val}_{\mathrm{Ac}}(\mathsf{free}(\flat\psi)) \times 2^{\mathrm{AP}}, \mathrm{Dc}, \mathrm{Q}_{\flat\psi}, \delta_{\flat\psi}, q_{0\flat\psi}, \aleph_{\flat\psi}\rangle$ such that, for all DTs $\mathcal{T}$ with $\mathrm{Ac}_{\mathcal{T}} = \mathrm{Ac}$, states $t \in \mathrm{St}_{\mathcal{T}}$, and assignments $\chi \in \mathrm{Asg}_{\mathcal{T}}(\mathsf{free}(\flat\psi), t)$, it holds that $\mathcal{T}, \chi, t \models \flat\psi$ iff $\mathcal{T}' \in \mathrm{L}(\mathcal{U}^{\mathrm{Ac}}_{\flat\psi})$, where $\mathcal{T}'$ is the assignment-labeling encoding for χ on $\mathcal{T}$.*

We now introduce a new concept of encoding regarding the elementary dependence maps over strategies.

Definition 12 **(Elementary Dependence-Labeling Encoding).** *Let $\mathcal{T}$ be a DT, $t \in \mathrm{St}_{\mathcal{T}}$ one of its states, and $\theta \in \mathrm{EDM}_{\mathrm{Str}_{\mathcal{T}}(t)}(\wp)$ an elementary dependence map over strategies for a quantification prefix $\wp \in \mathrm{Qnt}(\mathrm{V})$ over the set $\mathrm{V} \subseteq \mathrm{Var}$. A $(\mathrm{DM}_{\mathrm{Ac}_{\mathcal{T}}}(\wp) \times 2^{\mathrm{AP}})$-labeled Δ-tree $\mathcal{T}' \triangleq \langle \mathrm{St}_{\mathcal{T}}, \mathsf{u}\rangle$ is an* elementary dependence-labeling encoding *for θ on $\mathcal{T}$ if $\mathsf{u}(\mathsf{lst}((\rho)_{\geq 1})) = (\widetilde{\theta}(\rho), \lambda_{\mathcal{T}}(\mathsf{lst}(\rho)))$, for all $\rho \in \mathrm{Trk}_{\mathcal{T}}(t)$.*

Observe that also in this case there exists a unique elementary dependence-model encoding for each elementary dependence map over strategies.

Finally, in the next lemma, we show how to handle locally the strategy quantifications on each state of the model, by simply using a quantification over actions modeled by the choice of an action dependence map. Intuitively, we guess in the labeling what is the right part of the dependence map over strategies for each node of the tree and then verify that, for all assignments of universal variables, the corresponding complete assignment satisfies the inner formula.

Lemma 2 **(SL[1G] Sentence Automaton).** *Let $\wp\flat\psi$ be an SL[1G] principal sentence without principal subsentences and Ac a finite set of actions. Then, there exists an UCT $\mathcal{U}^{\mathrm{Ac}}_{\wp\flat\psi} \triangleq \langle \mathrm{DM}_{\mathrm{Ac}}(\wp) \times 2^{\mathrm{AP}}, \mathrm{Dc}, \mathrm{Q}_{\wp\flat\psi}, \delta_{\wp\flat\psi}, q_{0\wp\flat\psi}, \aleph_{\wp\flat\psi}\rangle$ such that, for all DTs $\mathcal{T}$ with $\mathrm{Ac}_{\mathcal{T}} = \mathrm{Ac}$, states $t \in \mathrm{St}_{\mathcal{T}}$, and elementary dependence maps over strategies $\theta \in \mathrm{EDM}_{\mathrm{Str}_{\mathcal{T}}(t)}(\wp)$, it holds that $\mathcal{T}, \theta(\chi), t \models_{\mathrm{E}} \flat\psi$, for all $\chi \in \mathrm{Asg}_{\mathcal{T}}([\![\wp]\!], t)$, iff $\mathcal{T}' \in \mathrm{L}(\mathcal{U}^{\mathrm{Ac}}_{\wp\flat\psi})$, where $\mathcal{T}'$ is the elementary dependence-labeling encoding for θ on $\mathcal{T}$.*

Full Sentences. By summing up all previous results, we are now able to solve the satisfiability problem for the full SL[1G] fragment.

To construct the automaton for a given SL[1G] sentence φ, we first consider all UCT $\mathcal{U}^{\mathrm{Ac}}_{\phi}$, for an assigned bounded set Ac, previously described for the principal sentences $\phi \in \mathsf{psnt}(\varphi)$, in which the inner subsentences are considered as atomic propositions. Then, thanks to the disjoint satisfiability property, we can merge them into a unique UCT $\mathcal{U}_{\varphi}$ that supplies the dependence map labeling of internal components $\mathcal{U}^{\mathrm{Ac}}_{\phi}$, by using the two functions head and body contained into its labeling. Moreover, observe that the final automaton runs on a b-bounded decision tree, where b is obtained from Theorem 6 on the bounded-tree model property.

Theorem 7 **(SL[1G] Automaton).** *Let φ be an SL[1G] sentence. Then, there exists an UCT $\mathcal{U}_{\varphi}$ such that φ is satisfiable iff $\mathrm{L}(\mathcal{U}_{\varphi}) \neq \emptyset$.*

Finally, by a simple calculation of the size of $\mathcal{U}_{\varphi}$ and the complexity of the related emptiness problem, we state in the next theorem the precise computational complexity of the satisfiability problem for SL[1G].

Theorem 8 (SL[1G] Satisfiability). *The satisfiability problem for* SL[1G] *is* 2EXPTIME-COMPLETE.

References

1. Albert, M.H., Nowakowski, R.J., Wolfe, D.: Lessons in Play: An Introduction to Combinatorial Game Theory. AK Peters (2007)
2. Alur, R., Henzinger, T.A., Kupferman, O.: Alternating-Time Temporal Logic. JACM 49(5), 672–713 (2002)
3. Chatterjee, K., Henzinger, T.A., Piterman, N.: Strategy Logic. IC 208(6), 677–693 (2010)
4. Clarke, E.M., Grumberg, O., Peled, D.A.: Model Checking. MIT Press (2002)
5. Da Costa, A., Laroussinie, F., Markey, N.: ATL with Strategy Contexts: Expressiveness and Model Checking. In: FSTTCS 2010. LIPIcs, vol. 8, pp. 120–132 (2010)
6. Emerson, E.A., Halpern, J.Y.: "Sometimes" and "Not Never" Revisited: On Branching Versus Linear Time. JACM 33(1), 151–178 (1986)
7. Finkbeiner, B., Schewe, S.: Coordination Logic. In: Dawar, A., Veith, H. (eds.) CSL 2010. LNCS, vol. 6247, pp. 305–319. Springer, Heidelberg (2010)
8. Fisman, D., Kupferman, O., Lustig, Y.: Rational Synthesis. In: Esparza, J., Majumdar, R. (eds.) TACAS 2010. LNCS, vol. 6015, pp. 190–204. Springer, Heidelberg (2010)
9. Grädel, E., Thomas, W., Wilke, T. (eds.): Automata, Logics, and Infinite Games. LNCS, vol. 2500. Springer, Heidelberg (2002)
10. Hodges, W.: Model theory. Encyclopedia of Mathematics and its Applications. Cambridge University Press (1993)
11. Jamroga, W., van der Hoek, W.: Agents that Know How to Play. FI 63(2-3), 185–219 (2004)
12. Kozen, D.: Results on the Propositional mu-Calculus. TCS 27(3), 333–354 (1983)
13. Kupferman, O., Vardi, M.Y., Wolper, P.: An Automata Theoretic Approach to Branching-Time Model Checking. JACM 47(2), 312–360 (2000)
14. Kupferman, O., Vardi, M.Y., Wolper, P.: Module Checking. IC 164(2), 322–344 (2001)
15. Martin, A.D.: Borel Determinacy. AM 102(2), 363–371 (1975)
16. Mogavero, F., Murano, A., Perelli, G., Vardi, M.Y.: Reasoning About Strategies: On the Model-Checking Problem. Technical Report 1112.6275, arXiv (December 2011)
17. Mogavero, F., Murano, A., Perelli, G., Vardi, M.Y.: A Decidable Fragment of Strategy Logic. Technical Report 1202.1309, arXiv (February 2012)
18. Mogavero, F., Murano, A., Vardi, M.Y.: Reasoning About Strategies. In: FSTTCS 2010. LIPIcs, vol. 8, pp. 133–144 (2010)
19. Mogavero, F., Murano, A., Vardi, M.Y.: Relentful Strategic Reasoning in Alternating-Time Temporal Logic. In: Clarke, E.M., Voronkov, A. (eds.) LPAR-16 2010. LNCS, vol. 6355, pp. 371–386. Springer, Heidelberg (2010)
20. Muller, D.E., Schupp, P.E.: Alternating Automata on Infinite Trees. TCS 54(2-3), 267–276 (1987)
21. Muller, D.E., Schupp, P.E.: Simulating Alternating Tree Automata by Nondeterministic Automata: New Results and New Proofs of Theorems of Rabin, McNaughton, and Safra. TCS 141(1-2), 69–107 (1995)
22. Pauly, M.: A Modal Logic for Coalitional Power in Games. JLC 12(1), 149–166 (2002)
23. Pinchinat, S.: A Generic Constructive Solution for Concurrent Games with Expressive Constraints on Strategies. In: Namjoshi, K.S., Yoneda, T., Higashino, T., Okamura, Y. (eds.) ATVA 2007. LNCS, vol. 4762, pp. 253–267. Springer, Heidelberg (2007)
24. Pnueli, A.: The Temporal Logic of Programs. In: FOCS 1977, pp. 46–57 (1977)
25. Rabin, M.O.: Decidability of Second-Order Theories and Automata on Infinite Trees. TAMS 141, 1–35 (1969)

26. Schewe, S.: ATL* Satisfiability Is 2EXPTIME-Complete. In: Aceto, L., Damgård, I., Goldberg, L.A., Halldórsson, M.M., Ingólfsdóttir, A., Walukiewicz, I. (eds.) ICALP 2008, Part II. LNCS, vol. 5126, pp. 373–385. Springer, Heidelberg (2008)
27. Vardi, M.Y.: Why is Modal Logic So Robustly Decidable? In: DCFM 1996, pp. 149–184. American Mathematical Society (1996)
28. Vardi, M.Y., Wolper, P.: An Automata-Theoretic Approach to Automatic Program Verification. In: LICS 1986, pp. 332–344. IEEE Computer Society (1986)
29. Vardi, M.Y., Wolper, P.: Automata-Theoretic Techniques for Modal Logics of Programs. JCSS 32(2), 183–221 (1986)
30. Wang, F., Huang, C.-H., Yu, F.: A Temporal Logic for the Interaction of Strategies. In: Katoen, J.-P., König, B. (eds.) CONCUR 2011 – Concurrency Theory. LNCS, vol. 6901, pp. 466–481. Springer, Heidelberg (2011)

Specifying Stateful Asynchronous Properties for Distributed Programs

Tzu-Chun Chen and Kohei Honda

Queen Mary College, University of London

Abstract. Having *stateful* specifications to track the states of processes, such as the balance of a customer for online shopping or the booking number of a transaction, is needed to verify real-life interacting systems. For safety assurance of distributed IT infrastructures, specifications need to capture states in the presence of asynchronous interactions. We demonstrate that not all specifications are suitable for asynchronous observations because they implicitly rely on an order-preservation assumption. To establish a theory of asynchronous specifications, we use the interplay between synchronous and asynchronous semantics, through which we characterise the class of specifications suitable for verifications through asynchronous interactions. The resulting theory offers a general semantic setting as well as concrete methods to analyse and determine semantic well-formedness (healthiness) of specifications with respect to asynchronous observations, for both static and dynamic verifications. In particular, our theory offers a key criterion for suitability of specifications for distributed dynamic verifications.

1 Introduction

The purpose of this paper is to introduce a theory of specification for communicating processes under the condition that the observation is done asynchronously, motivated by a semantic problem in specifications for distributed systems.

The semantic problem arose in a concrete engineering setting, through our collaboration with the design and development of a large IT infrastructure for ocean sciences [17], which is a typical large-scale distributed system. In that infrastructure, applications are predominantly built as asynchronous interactions among distributed components. Since some of these components may be contributed by the third party so that they may be buggy or untrusted, we cannot completely rely on static verification. To detect undesirable behaviours during runtime is thus needed. We start from consider having system-level observers observe the endpoint behaviours, and wish to provide a basis for *dynamically* safe-behaviours enforcement. However, putting system-level observer at every endpoint is expensive and they might be polluted by the malicious endpoint. To concur this problem, an ideal setting comes to have *remotely* located observer (e.g., "outline monitor" [9]), who would be asynchronously inspecting behaviours of a component against a specification. For this endeavour, we need to formulate an expressive *specification language* usable for asynchronously monitoring components. We then came across a basic issue in the *semantics* of a specification language in the presence of asynchronous communication. The issue makes naturally written specifications *semantically nonsensical*, thus posing a fundamental challenge to our endeavour to provide a consistent specification-verification framework.

M. Koutny and I. Ulidowski (Eds.): CONCUR 2012, LNCS 7454, pp. 209–224, 2012.

The combination of asynchrony and *state* is omnipresent in specifications for distributed systems capturing real-life scenarios, where e.g. the (expected) states of participants in the applications, such as the credit of a client for online shopping, or the purchase number for a transaction, play a critical role. When an observer (e.g. a trusted monitor) is located at an observee, the order of the observee's actions the observer sees is exactly the same as the one happening at the observee. However, when she sits remotely outside the observee, the order of actions that she observes may not necessarily be the same as the one happening at the observee. We call the former kind of observation *synchronous*, and the latter *asynchronous*. Although the synchronous observation can capture more precisely the "actual" behaviour of the observee, in distributed systems, asynchronous observations are the norm and often a necessity.

Contributions. In the remainder, §2 illustrates the background, including the semantic issue in asynchronous specifications, through concrete examples. Starting from these motivating examples, the paper presents the following contributions:

1. Introduction of an intuitive, semantically well-founded protocol-centred specification method suitable for asynchronous stateful behaviour (called SP for stateful protocols), enriching [4] with set-based stateful operations (§2, §3).
2. Identification (first to our knowledge) of a semantic issue when specifying asynchronous interaction behaviour combined with updatable states (§2).
3. Formal analysis of the issue through asynchronous trace semantics, reaching several criteria for asynchronous verifiability of specifications (healthiness conditions [11]) including a decidable one admitting a rich set of specifications (§4).

Finally in §5, we examine the practical implications of the theory, discuss related work and conclude with further topics. For the space sake, the proofs of the technical results as well as further examples are left to the full version [5].

2 Motivating Examples

2.1 Using State(s) in Protocol Specifications

Before formally introducing the syntax and semantics of specifications, we discuss key ideas through simple examples. Our specification language is based on multiparty session types [3, 13] annotated by logical formulae, extending [4] with local state(s).

We first motivate the use of state in specifications, considering the scenario below:

(step 1). Buyer sends a *product name* (denoted by *PName*) to Seller, then Seller replies with its *price*, and Buyer decides to purchase (then go to step 2) or not (then terminate). We assume shipping is done independently.

(step 2). Seller sends the Buyer an *invoice* for the purchased product.

In [4, 8, 13], this scenario can only be realised as a single protocol between Buyer and Seller; while, by using state(s), it can be realised using *two* protocols, one for each step. Separating protocols has a merit in flexibility: when Buyer and Seller finish step 1, both can terminate, and an invoice may be issued any time later. Below we present a *stateful* specification that realising using two separate protocols.

Example 1 (SP for a cross-session Purchase-and-Invoice scenario)

$$G_{\mathsf{pcs}} = B \to S : \mathit{Request}(\mathit{PName} : \mathsf{string}).$$
$$S \to B : \mathit{Confirm}(\mathit{PNameConf} : \mathsf{string}, \mathit{Price} : \mathsf{int})\langle \mathit{PNameConf} = \mathit{PName} \wedge \mathit{Price} \geq 0\ ;\ \varepsilon\rangle\langle \mathsf{truth}; \varepsilon\rangle.$$
$$B \to S : \{\mathit{OK}(\mathit{UserID} : \mathsf{int})\langle \mathit{UserID} \neq 0; \varepsilon\rangle\langle \mathsf{truth}; \varepsilon\rangle.$$
$$S \to B : (\mathit{PNo} : \mathsf{int})\langle \mathit{PNo} \notin \mathsf{dom}(\mathbf{PLog}); \mathbf{PLog} := \mathbf{PLog} \cup \{\mathit{PNo} \mapsto (\mathit{UserID}, \mathit{PName}, \mathit{Price})\}\rangle\langle \mathsf{truth}; \varepsilon\rangle$$
$$\mathsf{end}$$
$$\mathit{KO}().\mathsf{end}\}$$
$$G_{\mathsf{ivc}} = S \to B : (\mathit{PNo} : \mathsf{string}, \mathit{Invoice} : \mathsf{int})\langle \mathit{PNo} \in \mathsf{dom}(\mathbf{PLog}) \wedge \mathit{Invoice} = \mathbf{PLog}(\mathit{PNo})\ ;\ \varepsilon\rangle\langle \mathsf{truth}; \varepsilon\rangle.\mathsf{end}$$

Above G_{pcs} and G_{ivc} denote *stateful protocols*, or SPs from now on for short, respectively corresponding to steps 1 and 2. Each specifies the flow of interactions which the participants, S (for seller) and B (for buyer), should realise at each session. $\langle ...; ...\rangle\langle ...; ...\rangle$ are the obligations for sender (the former) and receiver (the latter), where the block before ";" is the predicate and the one after is the state(s) updating rule. $\langle \mathsf{truth}; \varepsilon\rangle$ means no obligation. The syntax is formally introduced in §3. In this example, the state of S, represented by the field **PLog** (the Purchase Log, which we consider to be a key-value store, mapping distinct keys to values), links the two protocols. Both specifications can be read intuitively. First, in G_{pcs},

1. B first sends a request (*Request* is an operator name), with the message value *PName* of type string, which is a product name.
2. S confirms by sending the same product name and its price, where the latter should be a non-negative integer as annotated.
3. If B says *OK* and sends its identity, then (in practice, after authentication etc.) S sends back a *fresh* purchase number *PNo*, i.e. it should not be in the domain of **PLog**. As a result, this new key and the corresponding information is added to **PLog**. On the other hand, if B says *KO*, the conversation terminates.

Note our specifications use local state to record an abstraction of preceding interactions across sessions, used for constraining future behaviours. Our ultimate aim is to specify visible behaviours: thus the stipulated state does not have to come from an actual state of a process: we may call it a "ghost state" following JML [1].

2.2 Synchrony and Asynchrony in Specification

The next example illustrates the central topic of this paper, asynchrony in specifications, showing how a specification can be "too synchronous" for asynchronous observations. We focus on a part of the previous example. The purchase number allocator S will, upon a request from a buyer B at each session, issue a purchase number incrementing the previously issued one: so S issues e.g. 1, 2, 3, ... in a sequence of sessions. Figure 2 (a) shows the corresponding protocol G_{sync} which the participants, S and B, should realise at each session. $\mathbf{c}$ is a local state of S, denoting the next purchase number.

Example 2 (SPs for purchase number allocator: synchronous v.s. asynchronous)

(a) synchronous spec

$$G_{\mathsf{sync}} = B \to S : \mathsf{req}(\varepsilon).$$
$$S \to B : \mathsf{ans}(x : \mathsf{int})$$
$$\langle x = \mathbf{c};\ \mathbf{c} := \mathbf{c} + 1\rangle\langle \mathsf{truth}; \varepsilon\rangle.$$
$$\mathsf{end}$$

(b) asynchronous spec

$$G_{\mathsf{async}} = B \to S : \mathsf{req}(\varepsilon).$$
$$S \to B : \mathsf{ans}(x : \mathsf{int})$$
$$\langle x \notin \mathbf{c};\ \mathbf{c} := \mathbf{c} \cup \{x\}\rangle\langle \mathsf{truth}; \varepsilon\rangle.$$
$$\mathsf{end}$$

In the first line of G_{sync}, B requests S a purchase number by sending req(ε), where ε means there is no message value in this request. In the second line, an integer x is sent from S to B, for which $\langle x = \mathbf{c}; \mathbf{c} := \mathbf{c}+1\rangle$ specifies the *obligation* for S, while no obligation i.e. $\langle \mathsf{truth}; \varepsilon\rangle$ for B. The first part "$x = \mathbf{c}$" says that x should be equal to $\mathbf{c}$. The second part "$\mathbf{c} := \mathbf{c}+1$" says that, after sending, S will increase $\mathbf{c}$ by 1, which constrains further behaviours of S in later sessions.

G_{sync} is an example of a SP which makes sense synchronously but *not* asynchronously. It seems an intuitively sensible specification: however, for a remote observer, even if S *actually* sends the series of purchase numbers $1,2,3,4,\ldots$ in this order, they may arrive at the observer as e.g. $2,4,1,3,\ldots$, under the practical assumption that the order of messages belonging to *distinct* sessions may not be preserved. In particular, this remote observer will consider S as being *ill-behaved with respect to* G_{sync}: the correctness for S (which is synchronous) and the correctness for its observer (which is asynchronous) are incongruent.

As a remedy, we present G_{async} in Example 2(b), which is intended for asynchronous observation. We now use the *set* of purchase numbers: $\mathbf{c}$, whose type is a set of integers, corresponds to **PLog** in Example 2.1. The new specification just says, in brief, that "S always sends a fresh number". If the behaviour of S satisfies this condition at S, then even though messages from S may arrive out-of-order, the remote observer can verify that they are correct w.r.t. G_{async}, so that the actions of S and their asynchronous observation by a remote observer coincide. We shall later verify this statement formally.

2.3 Capturing Causality Using Sets

While G_{async} gives a reasonable specification, it is not a strongest possible specification if our target is a server that issues purchase numbers incrementally based on the previous numbers. For example, if the same buyer sequentially repeats a series of request-reply sessions, that buyer (and an observer sitting in-between) will surely observe $1,2,3,4$ in this order, but this point is not captured by G_{async}.

Example 3 (A refinement of G_{async})

$$\begin{aligned} G_{\mathsf{ass}} = {} & B \to S : \mathsf{req}(\varepsilon)\langle \mathsf{truth}\ ;\ \varepsilon\rangle\langle \mathsf{truth}\ ;\ \mathbf{t} := \mathbf{t}+1, \mathbf{c} := \mathbf{c} \uplus \{\mathbf{t}\}\rangle. \\ & S \to B : \mathsf{ans}(x : \mathsf{int})\langle x \in \mathbf{c};\ \mathbf{c} := \mathbf{c} \setminus \{x\}\rangle\langle \mathsf{truth}\ ;\ \varepsilon\rangle. \\ & \mathsf{end} \end{aligned}$$

G_{ass} in Example 3 is a refinement of G_{async} in Example 2: while still being suitable for asynchronous observations, it can capture a stronger causal constraint. It uses two states: $\mathbf{t}$, a counter, and $\mathbf{c}$, a collection of valid numbers to be issued. $\mathbf{t}$ and $\mathbf{c}$ are incremented when receiving a request, while the sent value is taken off from $\mathbf{c}$. The basic idea is that, if S receives n requests, then (assuming the server issues the purchase numbers starting from 1) as a whole the numbers which can be issued are among $\{1,2,..,n\}$. And if S issues a number from this set, the remaining numbers are what it can issue.

To understand G_{ass} as a specification, consider two sessions following the protocol, s_1 and s_2. Assume the initial states are $\mathbf{t} \mapsto 0$ and $\mathbf{c} \mapsto \{\}$. Then G_{ass} says the traces in Figure 1 are valid ones (we list the traces together with step-by-step state change: (I,II,III) are categories each stipulating how states will change).

cases	1st	2nd	3rd	4th
(I) actions:	$s_1[B,S]?\text{req}(\varepsilon)$	$s_2[B,S]?\text{req}(\varepsilon)$	$s_1[S,B]!\text{ans}(1)$	$s_2[S,B]!\text{ans}(2)$
	$s_2[B,S]?\text{req}(\varepsilon)$	$s_1[B,S]?\text{req}(\varepsilon)$	$s_1[S,B]!\text{ans}(1)$	$s_2[S,B]!\text{ans}(2)$
	$s_1[B,S]?\text{req}(\varepsilon)$	$s_2[B,S]?\text{req}(\varepsilon)$	$s_2[S,B]!\text{ans}(1)$	$s_1[S,B]!\text{ans}(2)$
	$s_2[B,S]?\text{req}(\varepsilon)$	$s_1[B,S]?\text{req}(\varepsilon)$	$s_2[S,B]!\text{ans}(1)$	$s_1[S,B]!\text{ans}(2)$
(I) states:	$\mathbf{t}\mapsto 1, \mathbf{c}\mapsto \{1\}$	$\mathbf{t}\mapsto 2, \mathbf{c}\mapsto \{1,2\}$	$\mathbf{t}\mapsto 2, \mathbf{c}\mapsto \{2\}$	$\mathbf{t}\mapsto 2, \mathbf{c}\mapsto \{\}$
(II) actions:	$s_1[B,S]?\text{req}(\varepsilon)$	$s_2[B,S]?\text{req}(\varepsilon)$	$s_1[S,B]!\text{ans}(2)$	$s_2[S,B]!\text{ans}(1)$
	$s_2[B,S]?\text{req}(\varepsilon)$	$s_1[B,S]?\text{req}(\varepsilon)$	$s_1[S,B]!\text{ans}(2)$	$s_2[S,B]!\text{ans}(1)$
	$s_1[B,S]?\text{req}(\varepsilon)$	$s_2[B,S]?\text{req}(\varepsilon)$	$s_2[S,B]!\text{ans}(2)$	$s_1[S,B]!\text{ans}(1)$
	$s_2[B,S]?\text{req}(\varepsilon)$	$s_1[B,S]?\text{req}(\varepsilon)$	$s_2[S,B]!\text{ans}(2)$	$s_1[S,B]!\text{ans}(1)$
(II) states:	$\mathbf{t}\mapsto 1, \mathbf{c}\mapsto \{1\}$	$\mathbf{t}\mapsto 2, \mathbf{c}\mapsto \{1,2\}$	$\mathbf{t}\mapsto 2, \mathbf{c}\mapsto \{1\}$	$\mathbf{t}\mapsto 2, \mathbf{c}\mapsto \{\}$
(III) actions:	$s_1[B,S]?\text{req}(\varepsilon)$	$s_1[S,B]!\text{ans}(1)$	$s_2[B,S]?\text{req}(\varepsilon)$	$s_2[S,B]!\text{ans}(2)$
	$s_2[B,S]?\text{req}(\varepsilon)$	$s_2[S,B]!\text{ans}(1)$	$s_1[B,S]?\text{req}(\varepsilon)$	$s_1[S,B]!\text{ans}(2)$
(III) states:	$\mathbf{t}\mapsto 1, \mathbf{c}\mapsto \{1\}$	$\mathbf{t}\mapsto 1, \mathbf{c}\mapsto \{\}$	$\mathbf{t}\mapsto 2, \mathbf{c}\mapsto \{2\}$	$\mathbf{t}\mapsto 2, \mathbf{c}\mapsto \{\}$

Fig. 1. The valid traces from G_{ass}

Above, $s_1[B,S]?\text{req}(\varepsilon)$ denotes an input ? from B to S at session s_1 carrying a req-message without value; $s_1[S,B]!\text{ans}(1)$ is an output ! from S to B at s_1 carrying a ans-message with value 1. (I) and (II) are the traces where a remote observer observes that two consecutive inputs have arrived first. Note that, even if S may have indeed outputted immediately after the first input, we can have these traces, due to asynchrony. Even then, unlike G_{async}, the observer is sure that the returned values should be no more than 2, i.e. it is either 1 or 2. In (III), the observer observes the second request only after the answer to the first request: the request-answer order in each session is preserved because without the request, its answer cannot occur. Unlike G_{async}, the observer can expect, based on G_{ass}, that the first answer is surely 1; and the second is surely 2. This example shows how we can represent causality while (intuitively) keeping the asynchronous nature of specifications.

3 Asynchronous Specifications

3.1 Syntax of Protocols and Specifications

Grammar of global and local stateful protocols. Figure 2 summarises the grammar of global SPs ($G, \ldots$), which specify the interaction structure of a session from a global viewpoint; and local SPs ($T, \ldots$) which specify protocols for endpoints, to be projected from G. Their syntax extends [4] with local states and operations on them: by adding simple state update, we obtain a rich class of stateful specifications.

$$S ::= \mathsf{nat} \mid \mathsf{bool} \mid \mathsf{string} \mid \ldots \qquad A ::= \mathsf{truth} \mid \mathsf{false} \mid e_1 = e_2 \mid e_1 > e_2$$
$$\mid S_1 \times S_2 \mid \mathsf{set}(S) \mid \mathsf{map}(S_1, S_2) \qquad \mid e_1 \in e_2 \mid A_1 \wedge A_2 \mid \neg A$$
$$e ::= x \mid v \mid \mathbf{f} \mid op(e_1, \ldots, e_n) \qquad E ::= \varepsilon \mid E, \mathbf{f} := e$$

$$G ::= \mathsf{p} \to \mathsf{q} : \{l_i(x_i : S_i)\langle A_i; E_i\rangle\langle A'_i; E'_i\rangle.G_i\}_{i \in I} \;\text{G-cm} \quad T ::= \mathsf{p}!\{l_i(x_i : S_i)\langle A_i; E_i\rangle.T_i\}_{i \in I} \;\text{L-sel}$$
$$\mid G_1 \mid G_2,\ role(G_1) \cap role(G_2) = \emptyset \;\text{G-par} \quad \mid \mathsf{p}?\{l_i(x_i : S_i)\langle A_i; E_i\rangle.T_i\}_{i \in I} \;\text{L-bra}$$
$$\mid \mathsf{end} \;\text{G-end} \quad \mid \mathsf{end} \;\text{L-end}$$

Fig. 2. The grammar of stateful protocols

A SP uses a state consisting of zero or more *fields*. A field gets read in a *predicate* A and gets read and written in an *update* E. We call $\langle A; E\rangle$ *obligation*. We use updates instead of post-conditions for usability in runtime verification. $(S, \ldots)$ are sorts (types of expressions), and $(e, \ldots)$ are expressions, where $op(e_1, \ldots, e_n)$ is the operation op on parameters $e_1, \ldots, e_n$. We use product $S_1 \times S_2$, set $\mathsf{set}(S)$ and (finite) function $\mathsf{map}(S_1, S_2)$. Sets and functions play important roles in asynchronous specifications. In expressions, x is a variable, v is a value, $\mathbf{f}$ is a (mutable) field. In E, $\mathbf{f} := e$ is assigned by e. The grammar of G and T is simplified for distilled presentation. In particular we omit recursion, which however can be added preserving all results, see §5.

In G, $\mathsf{p} \to \mathsf{q}$ describes the communication from sender p to receiver q, while $\mathsf{p}!$ and $\mathsf{p}?$ are endpoint actions for output (to p) and input (from p). In $l_i(x_i : S_i)$, l_i is the label for a branch: when l_i is chosen, the interaction variable is x_i, and S_i is its type. In G-cm, the first obligation $\langle A; E\rangle$ is for the sender, indicating a sender should guarantee that its message satisfies A and as a result E is done; the second obligation $\langle A'; E'\rangle$ is for the receiver, indicating it can expect a message to satisfy A' and as a result E' is done. In G-par, its side condition (where $role(G)$ denotes the set of roles in G) demands no role is shared by G_1 and G_2, Rule L-sel is for sender's behaviours, while rule L-bra is for receiver's behaviours. Parallel composition specifies two interactions in parallel, while end denotes the end of interactions.

As a notational convention, if an obligation is trivial (i.e. the predicate is truth and the update is ε) then it is omitted. Further, if either the predicate or the update is trivial in an obligation, then it is omitted.

Well-formedness and projection. Assume $\mathsf{p} \to \mathsf{q} : \{l_i(x_i : S_i)\langle A_i; E_i\rangle\langle A'_i; E'_i\rangle.G_i\}_{i \in I}$ is inside a context, with possibly preceding interactions. The following well-formedness conditions, based on [4], stipulate consistency of global protocols:

(1) (a) $\forall i \in I, \mathit{field}(A'_i) = \emptyset$ (where $\mathit{field}(A)$ denotes the sets of field names occurring in A); and (b) $\forall i \in I, A_i$ implies A'_i.
(2) (history sensitivity) A_i and E_i only refer to interaction variables which p, a sender, has sent or received before, as well as x_i. Similarly for A'_i and E'_i for a receiver.
(3) (temporal satisfiability) at each step, and for any state, there is always a branch i and a value x_i that satisfy A_i (hence A'_i, i.e. at each step).

(1-a) says that a predicate of a receiver is stateless (generally, if a receiving-side predicate relies on its own local state, then a sender may not be able to find a "proper" value to send). (1-b) says that, in every interaction, the predicate at sender always imply the predicate at the receiver: together with (1-a), this means that if a sender sends a message that satisfies the sender's predicate, then automatically the receiver's predicate is satisfied (the latter however is useful for the receiver to know what it can expect). (2) and (3) are from [4]. All examples treated in this paper are easily well-formed. *Henceforth we assume all global SPs we treat are well-formed.*

A global protocol is useful to capture the overall interaction scenario, while a local protocol specifies what the endpoint is expected to do. They are linked by *endpoint projection*. Leaving its formal definition to [5], we illustrate the idea by an example.

Example 4 (endpoint projection). The local SPs projected from G_{ass} are:

$$G_{\text{ass}} \upharpoonright B = T_B = S!\mathsf{req}(\varepsilon).S?\mathsf{ans}(x:\mathsf{int}).\mathsf{end}$$
$$G_{\text{ass}} \upharpoonright S = T_S = B?\mathsf{req}(\varepsilon)\langle\mathsf{truth};\mathbf{t}:=\mathbf{t}+1\ \ \mathbf{c}:=\mathbf{c}\uplus\{\mathbf{t}\}\rangle.B!\mathsf{ans}(x:\mathsf{int})\langle x\in\mathbf{c}\,;\ \mathbf{c}:=\mathbf{c}\setminus\{x\}\rangle.\mathsf{end}$$

Specifications. A *specification* is a triple $\Theta ::= \langle\Gamma;\Delta;D\rangle$ which gives a behavioural specification of a local process (endpoint) as its interface. Γ, Δ and D, separated by ";" in Θ, are given by:

$$\Gamma ::= \emptyset \mid \Gamma, a:\mathtt{I}(G[\mathrm{p}]) \mid \Gamma, a:\mathtt{O}(G[\mathrm{p}]) \mid \Gamma, \mathbf{f}:S \qquad \Delta ::= \emptyset \mid \Delta, s[\mathrm{p}]:T \qquad D ::= \emptyset \mid D, \mathbf{f}\mapsto v$$

Above, $\mathtt{I}$ (resp. $\mathtt{O}$) is a mode denoting input (resp. output) capability. Γ, *shared environment*, describes the permitted behaviour at each shared channel; and the type of each field. When a process has $a:\mathtt{I}(G[\mathrm{p}])$, it can *accept* invitations via a shared channel a to play the role p following what (the p-projection of) G specifies; while $a:\mathtt{O}(G[\mathrm{p}])$ is its dual. In Δ, *session environment*, $s[\mathrm{p}] : T$ describes the session behaviour (T) in a session s as p. D is a set of (ghost) states of a local process (endpoint): the states in $D \in \Theta$ belong to an endpoint participant in a session. Each D is a map from fields to values. In formulae, a field $\mathbf{f}$ itself represents its current value.

Example 5. Based on G_{ass} in Example 3 and its local SPs in Example 4, we give a local specification Θ_{ass} for server, playing role S, and Θ_{B_1} and Θ_{B_2} for two buyers B_1 and B_2, each playing role B in G_{ass}, assuming there are two ongoing sessions s_1 and s_2.

$$T_S = B?\mathsf{req}(\varepsilon)\langle\mathsf{truth};\mathbf{t}:=\mathbf{t}+1\ \ \mathbf{c}:=\mathbf{c}\uplus\{\mathbf{t}\}\rangle.B!\mathsf{ans}(x:\mathsf{int})\langle x\in\mathbf{c}\,;\ \mathbf{c}:=\mathbf{c}\setminus\{x\}\rangle.\mathsf{end}$$
$$\Theta_{\text{ass}} = \langle\Gamma'_{Ser}, \mathtt{ser}:\mathtt{I}(G_{\text{ass}}[S])\,;\ \Delta'_{Ser}, s_1[S]:T_S, s_2[S]:T_S\,;\ D'_{Ser}, \mathbf{t}\mapsto 0, \mathbf{c}\mapsto\{\}\rangle$$

$$T_B = S!\mathsf{req}(\varepsilon).S?\mathsf{ans}(x:\mathsf{int}).\mathsf{end}, \quad \Theta_{B_1} = \langle\Gamma'_{B_1}, \mathtt{b}_1:\mathtt{O}(G_{\text{ass}}[B]);\ \Delta'_{B_1},\ s_1[B]:T_B;\ D_{B_1}\rangle$$
$$\Theta_{B_2} = \langle\Gamma'_{B_2}, \mathtt{b}_2:\mathtt{O}(G_{\text{ass}}[B]);\ \Delta'_{B_2}, s_2[B]:T_B;\ D_{B_2}\rangle$$

The data storage in Θ_{ass} is $D'_{Ser}, \mathbf{t}, \mathbf{c}$. In this protocol, no state in D'_{Ser} is used. Similarly, no state in D_{B_1} or D_{B_2} is used. Although we do not illustrate the whole procedures of session establishment (by using rules [REQ-INI], [REQ] and [ACC] defined in Figure 3), it shows that buyers B_1 and B_2 are the invitors requesting S to join session s_1 and s_2.

3.2 Semantics of Specifications

We present the semantics of specifications as a labelled transition system (LTS). The transition is of the form $\Theta \xrightarrow{\ell} \Theta'$, which intuitively means Θ as a specification *allows* a process to do an action ℓ, and the resulting process should conform to Θ'. For actions labels, we use $\overline{a}(s[\mathtt{p}] : G)$ for sending an invitation when s is fresh to the sender, and use $\overline{a}\langle s[\mathtt{p}] : G\rangle$ for sending an invitation when s is not fresh. $a(s[\mathtt{p}] : G)$ for accepting an invitation when s is fresh to the receiver (which is the only case we consider), and $s[\mathtt{p},\mathtt{q}]!l(v)$ and $s[\mathtt{p},\mathtt{q}]?l(v)$ for sending and receiving in a session. We do not use τ since it is irrelevant in the present work (because, in brief, τ is always possible and has no effects on specifications). The LTS is defined in Figure 3 below: the induced transition is deterministic: if $\Theta \xrightarrow{\ell} \Theta'$ and $\Theta \xrightarrow{\ell} \Theta''$, then $\Theta' = \Theta''$.

$$[\textsc{Req-ini}]\quad \frac{a:\mathtt{O}(G[\mathtt{p}_j]) \in \Gamma,\ s \notin \mathsf{dom}(\Delta),\ \mathit{role}(G) = \{\mathtt{p}_i\}_{i\in I}}{\langle \Gamma;\Delta,\{s[\mathtt{p}_i] : G\upharpoonright \mathtt{p}_i\}_{i\in I}; D\rangle \xrightarrow{\overline{a}(s[\mathtt{p}_j]:G)} \langle \Gamma;\Delta,\{s[\mathtt{p}_i] : G\upharpoonright \mathtt{p}_i\}_{i\in I\setminus\{j\}}; D\rangle}$$

$$[\textsc{Req}]\quad \frac{a:\mathtt{O}(G[\mathtt{p}_j]) \in \Gamma,\ \mathit{role}(G) = \{\mathtt{p}_i\}_{i\in I}}{\langle \Gamma;\Delta,s[\mathtt{p}_j] : G\upharpoonright \mathtt{p}_j; D\rangle \xrightarrow{\overline{a}\langle s[\mathtt{p}_j]:G\rangle} \langle \Gamma;\Delta;D\rangle}$$

$$[\textsc{Acc}]\quad \frac{s \notin \mathsf{dom}(\Delta),\ T = G\upharpoonright \mathtt{q},\ \mathit{field}(T) \in D}{\langle \Gamma, a:\mathtt{I}(G[\mathtt{q}]);\Delta;D\rangle \xrightarrow{a(s[\mathtt{q}]:G)} \langle \Gamma, a:\mathtt{I}(G[\mathtt{q}]);\Delta,s[\mathtt{q}]:T;D\rangle}$$

$$[\textsc{Sel}]\quad \frac{T = \mathtt{q}!\{l_i(x_i:S_i)\langle A_i;E_i\rangle.T_i'\}_{i\in I},\ \Gamma\vdash v:S_j,\ \Gamma \models A_j\{v/x_j\},\ s\notin \mathsf{dom}(\Delta)}{\langle \Gamma;\Delta,s[\mathtt{p}]:T;D\rangle \xrightarrow{s[\mathtt{p},\mathtt{q}]!l_j(v)} \langle \Gamma;\Delta,s[\mathtt{p}]:T_j'\{v/x_j\}; D\,\mathtt{after}\,E\{v/x_j\}\rangle}$$

$$[\textsc{Bra}]\quad \frac{T = \mathtt{p}?\{l_i(x_i:S_i)\langle A_i;E_i\rangle.T_i'\}_{i\in I},\ \Gamma\vdash v:S_j,\ \Gamma \models A_j\{v/x_j\},\ s\notin \mathsf{dom}(\Delta)}{\langle \Gamma;\Delta,s[\mathtt{q}]:T;D\rangle \xrightarrow{s[\mathtt{p},\mathtt{q}]?l_j(v)} \langle \Gamma;\Delta,s[\mathtt{q}]:T_j'\{v/x_j\}; D\,\mathtt{after}\,E\{v/x_j\}\rangle}$$

$$[\textsc{Par}]\quad \frac{\Theta_1 \xrightarrow{\ell} \Theta_2,\quad \mathsf{bn}(\ell)\cap\mathsf{n}(\Theta_3) = \emptyset}{\Theta_1,\Theta_3 \xrightarrow{\ell} \Theta_2,\Theta_3}$$

Fig. 3. Labelled transition system for specifications

The first two rules are for invitations. [REQ-INI] is used when s is fresh, i.e. when the first request happens to the sender to ask someone for playing role $\mathtt{p}_j$ in a fresh s. The round parenthesis in $\overline{a}(s[\mathtt{p}_j] : G)$ indicates s in this label is a binding occurrence and we record all capabilities except the passed one in the linear typing environment; otherwise we use [REQ]. [REQ] says that, when s is *not* fresh in the session environment, and if Θ has an output channel a with G, (1) the target behaviour is permitted to send a request $\overline{a}\langle s[\mathtt{p}_j] : G\rangle$ to ask someone to play role $\mathtt{p}_j$ in session s; and (2) after requesting, we take off the capability at $\mathtt{p}_j$. Rule [ACC] says that, if s is a new session, and all states declared in $G\upharpoonright \mathtt{q}$, $\mathit{field}(G\upharpoonright \mathtt{q})$, are in D, when Θ has an input channel a with G for accepting to play role q, it accepts this request and plays session role $s[\mathtt{q}]$ specified by $G\upharpoonright \mathtt{q}$.

Rule [SEL] is for sending a message in a session. The premise says that, first, the type T should be a selection type; the passed value v has type S_j from the j-th branch of T under Γ (note that, when v is a name, Γ needs to have the knowledge of its type, but it is not needed if v is a non-channel value, like 3 or "*hello*" whose type is automatically known without Γ); and A_j after substitution holds under Γ. The condition $s \notin \mathsf{dom}(\Delta)$ says that, when an agent communicates in a session, it is playing only a single role (this restriction can be taken off but simplifies the technical development). In the conclusion, T_j' substitutes v for x_j and prepares for the next action, and the state is updated by $D\,\mathtt{after}\,E_j\{v/x_j\}$. To illustrate the updating of D by E_j, assume E_j is defined as $\mathbf{f} := \mathbf{f} \uplus \{x_j\}$, and currently $\mathbf{f} \mapsto \{10\}$. After substituting 5 for x_j, D is updated to $\mathbf{f} \mapsto \{10, 5\}$. Rule [BRA] is a symmetric rule of [SEL]. Finally [PAR], where $\mathsf{bn}(\cdot)$ is the set of bound names and $\mathsf{n}(\cdot)$ is the set of names, says if Θ_1 and Θ_3 are composable, after action happens and Θ_1 becomes as Θ_2, they are still composable.

3.3 Processes and Satisfaction

Definition 6 (trace). A *trace* $(\mathtt{s}, \mathtt{s}', \ldots)$ is a sequence of actions where we assume a request/accept action introducing the session channel, say s, binds the later occurrences of s. Based on this binding, we only consider traces which satisfy the standard binding conventions, i.e. two binding occurrences never coincide and if free s occurs then it cannot do so before a binding occurrence (by an accept or request).

Below $\mathsf{sbj}(\ell)$ denotes the *subject* of ℓ, given as, for a request/accept, the initial shared channel (e.g. $\mathsf{sbj}(\overline{a}\langle s[\mathtt{p}_j] : G\rangle) = a$); and, for a session action, the session channel with the interacting role (e.g. $\mathsf{sbj}(s[\mathtt{p},\mathtt{q}]!l_j(v)) = s[\mathtt{q}]$, $\mathsf{sbj}(s[\mathtt{p},\mathtt{q}]?l_j(v)) = s[\mathtt{p}]$).

Definition 7 (legal unit permutation). Let $\ell_1 \cdot \ell_2$ be a trace. Then a permutation from $\ell_1 \cdot \ell_2$ to $\ell_2 \cdot \ell_1$ is *legal* if one of the following conditions holds:

1. ℓ_1 and ℓ_2 are both inputs and either both are session actions and $\mathsf{sbj}(\ell_1) \neq \mathsf{sbj}(\ell_2)$ to the same receiver, or one of them is an accept action and ℓ_1 does not bind ℓ_2.
2. ℓ_1 and ℓ_2 are both outputs and either both are session actions and $\mathsf{sbj}(\ell_1) \neq \mathsf{sbj}(\ell_2)$ to the same sender, or one of them is a request action and ℓ_1 does not bind ℓ_2.
3. ℓ_1 is an output and ℓ_2 is an input and ℓ_1 does not bind ℓ_2.

Such a permutation is called a *legal unit permutation*. We write $\mathtt{s} \curvearrowright \mathtt{s}'$ when $\mathtt{s}'$ is the result of applying zero or more legal unit permutations. In this case $\mathtt{s}'$ is *a permutation variant of* $\mathtt{s}$ and this permutation is called a *legal permutation*.

Example 8 (legal permutation). In Figure 1, all traces in (I) and (II) are permutation variants to each other. The traces in (III) can legally permute to any trace in (I) and (II), but not the converse.

The following simple definition of processes is enough for our purpose: we can readily use the π-calculus with session primitives and its weak (τ-abstracted) LTS to induce this abstract notion of processes.

Definition 9 (process). A *process* $(P, Q, ..)$ is a prefix-closed set of traces.

The following defines the notion of synchronous and asynchronous observables as the sets of traces observed by a synchronous observer (i.e. as it is) and by an asynchronous observer (i.e. up to legal permutations).

Definition 10 (synchronous and asynchronous observable). (1) $\mathsf{Obs}_s(P) \stackrel{\text{def}}{=} P$. (2) $\mathsf{Obs}_a(P)$ is the set of all legal permutation variants of the traces in P.

Definition 11 **($|\Theta|$: valid traces of Θ).** We define $|\Theta|$, the set of *valid traces* of Θ, as finite sequences from the LTS of Θ defined in Figure 3.

Intuitively, a valid trace is a trace that Θ approves. The following says that a process P synchronously (resp. asynchronously) satisfies Θ if, w.r.t. synchronous (resp. asynchronous) observables, P always does valid outputs as far as it receives valid inputs.

Definition 12 **(satisfaction up to observables).** A process $\mathsf{Obs}_s(P)$ *synchronously satisfies* Θ, denoted $P \models_{\mathtt{sync}} \Theta$, when the following two conditions hold:

1. (output safety) $\mathsf{Obs}_s(P) \subset |\Theta|$.

2.a (input consistency) Whenever $\mathtt{s} \in \mathsf{Obs}_s(P)$ and $\mathtt{s} \cdot \ell \in |\Theta|$ where ℓ is an input, $\mathtt{s} \cdot \ell' \in \mathsf{Obs}_s(P)$ and ℓ' is an input with the same subject as ℓ, then $\mathtt{s} \cdot \ell \in \mathsf{Obs}_s(P)$.

A process P *asynchronously satisfies* Θ, denoted $P \models_{\mathtt{async}} \Theta$, if, after replacing each $\mathsf{Obs}_s(P)$ with $\mathsf{Obs}_a(P)$, it satisfies condition 1. above, as well as:

2.b (input consistency) Whenever $\mathtt{s} \in \mathsf{Obs}_a(P)$ and $\mathtt{s} \cdot \ell \in |\Theta|$ where ℓ is an input, then $\mathtt{s} \cdot \ell \in \mathsf{Obs}_a(P)$.

Note that a synchronous process (2.a) can accept a valid input only when it is ready to receive it; while an asynchronous process (2.b) can, and should, accept any valid input.

Example 13 **(valid/invalid traces of G_{ass}).** We consider Θ_{ass} from Example 5 which uses the local SP from G_{ass} in Example 3 for the server side. Then, for example, the trace $s_2[B,S]?\mathrm{req}(\varepsilon) \cdot s_2[S,B]!\mathrm{ans}(1) \cdot s_1[B,S]?\mathrm{req}(\varepsilon) \cdot s_1[S,B]!\mathrm{ans}(2)$ is valid for Θ_{ass}, but $s_2[B,S]?\mathrm{req}(\varepsilon) \cdot s_2[S,B]!\mathrm{ans}(2) \cdot s_1[B,S]?\mathrm{req}(\varepsilon) \cdot s_1[B,S]!\mathrm{ans}(1)$ is not its trace (violation is at the second step), i.e. it is not permitted by Θ_{ass}.

4 Theory of Asynchronous Specifications

4.1 Asynchronously Verifiable Specifications

We say Θ is *asynchronous* if it is suitable for a remote observer to verify a process behaviour. In this case, we do not want the conformance of a trace to change depending on an accidental reordering due to asynchrony: i.e. we want its validity to be robust w.r.t. legal permutations.

Definition 14 **(asynchronously verifiable specification).** We say Θ is *asynchronously verifiable* or simply *asynchronous* when $\mathtt{s} \in |\Theta|$ and $\mathtt{s} \curvearrowright \mathtt{s}'$ imply $\mathtt{s}' \in |\Theta|$.

To check violation of asynchrony of a specification, we only have to find a single acceptable trace whose permutation is not acceptable.

Example 15. Let T_{sync} be the local SP at server, projected from G_{sync}. Then $\Theta_{\mathsf{sync}} = \langle \Gamma'_{Ser}, \mathtt{ser} : \mathtt{I}(G_{\mathsf{sync}}[S])\ ;\ \Delta'_{Ser}, s[S] : T_{\mathsf{sync}}\ ;\ D'_{Ser}, \mathbf{c} \rangle$, where I contains the sessions using G_{sync}, is *not* asynchronous by the traces given in §2.

On the other hand, checking asynchrony by Definition 14 means we should verify the property for all traces, which are usually infinitely many. Later we shall find methods by which we can validate the asynchrony of, for example, Θ_{ass} and all the corresponding specifications that use $G_{\mathsf{pcs}}/G_{\mathsf{ivc}}$ and G_{async}.

The following characterisation says that, if a specification Θ is asynchronous, the anomaly we discussed in §2.2, for G_{sync} in Figure 2(a), can never take place: if a synchronous observer recognises that P conforms to Θ, i.e. if P conforms to Θ synchronously, then an asynchronous observer will also do the same.

Proposition 16. *Θ is asynchronous iff, for each P, $P \models_{\mathtt{sync}} \Theta$ implies $P \models_{\mathtt{async}} \Theta$.*

The next result says that asynchronous verifiability is consistent with the asynchronous trace equivalence. Below let $P \approx_{\mathtt{async}} Q$ mean $\mathsf{Obs}_a(P) = \mathsf{Obs}_a(Q)$. In [14], we have shown how $\approx_{\mathtt{async}}$ (but not its synchronous counterpart) can be used for non-trivial optimising transformation.

Proposition 17. *If $P \approx_{\mathtt{async}} Q$ and $P \models_{\mathtt{async}} \Theta$ then $Q \models_{\mathtt{async}} \Theta$.*

4.2 Asynchrony in Specifications through Commutativity

A basic issue in Definition 14 and its characterisation in Proposition 16 is that they do not directly mention the (intensional) structure of specifications. Thus it does not offer engineers insights as to how one may design her/his specifications. Extending the usage of the term in [11], we may call a criterion for specifications which a designer can use for ensuring robustness w.r.t. asynchrony, *healthiness condition*. The following definition is a first step towards such a criterion.

Definition 18 (confluence). Θ is *confluent* if, whenever $\Theta \xrightarrow{\mathtt{s}} \Theta'$, if $\Theta' \xrightarrow{\ell_1 \cdot \ell_2} \Theta''$ and $\ell_2 \cdot \ell_1 \curvearrowright \ell_1 \cdot \ell_2$, then $\Theta' \xrightarrow{\ell_2 \cdot \ell_1} \Theta''$ again.

I.e. the specification accepts the same sequence of values regardless of legal permutations and the resulting states are the same. Immediately confluence means asynchrony.

Lemma 19. *Θ is asynchronous iff $\mathtt{s} \cdot \ell_1 \cdot \ell_2 \in |\Theta|$ and $\ell_1 \cdot \ell_2 \curvearrowright \ell_2 \cdot \ell_1$ imply $\mathtt{s} \cdot \ell_2 \cdot \ell_1 \in |\Theta|$ for each $\mathtt{s}$, ℓ_1 and ℓ_2.*

Proposition 20. *If Θ is confluent then it is asynchronous.*

Note that the other way round is not true. Given Θ is asynchronous, for any $\mathtt{s}, \ell_1$, and ℓ_2, $\mathtt{s} \cdot \ell_1 \cdot \ell_2 \in |\Theta|$ implies $\mathtt{s} \cdot \ell_2 \cdot \ell_1 \in |\Theta|$. However, it is possible that $\Theta \xrightarrow{\mathtt{s}} \Theta' \xrightarrow{\ell_1 \cdot \ell_2} \Theta''$ while $\Theta \xrightarrow{\mathtt{s}} \Theta' \xrightarrow{\ell_2 \cdot \ell_1} \Theta'''$, where $\Theta'' \neq \Theta'''$.

We can easily find a specification which is not confluent (for example, if a specification just does the same counting as G_{sync}). To check confluence, we still need to consider all possible transition derivatives of Θ. However we can observe that, in such a derivative, *the obligations used to check confluence are already present in Θ*. This suggests we only have to look at the obligations occurring in Θ and check their commutativity w.r.t. their legal unit permutations. This method demands designers to look at only Θ, so that it clearly helps her/his design process. The method treats a predicate and an update in an obligation as functions (operations) on state, as follows. Let $\dagger \in \{?, !\}$.

Definition 21 (predicate/update functions). Let $\xi \stackrel{\text{def}}{=} \mathtt{r} \dagger l(x:S)\langle A;E\rangle$ with the associated state D whose domain is $\mathbf{f}_1,...,\mathbf{f}_n$. W.l.o.g. we regard E to be a simultaneous substitution of the form $\mathbf{f}_1 := e_1,...,\mathbf{f}_n := e_n$. Then we define:

$$\mathtt{pred}(\xi) \stackrel{\text{def}}{=} \lambda x,\mathbf{f}_1,...,\mathbf{f}_n.(A) \qquad \mathtt{upd}(\xi) \stackrel{\text{def}}{=} \lambda x,\mathbf{f}_1,...,\mathbf{f}_n.\langle e_1,..,e_n\rangle$$

We call $\mathtt{pred}(\xi)$ (resp. $\mathtt{upd}(\xi)$) the *predicate function* (resp. *update function*) of ξ.

Example 22. Below we project G_{sync} and G_{ass} (all from §2) to the server. For simplicity we assume its local state only consists of those fields specified in global SP.

$$G_{\mathsf{sync}} \upharpoonright S = B?\mathrm{req}(\varepsilon)\langle \mathsf{truth};\varepsilon\rangle \,.\, B!\mathrm{ans}(x:\ \mathsf{int})\langle x=\mathbf{c}\ ;\ \mathbf{c}:=\mathbf{c}+1\rangle$$

$$G_{\mathsf{ass}} \upharpoonright S = B?\mathrm{req}(\varepsilon)\langle \mathsf{truth};\mathtt{t}:=\mathtt{t}+1\ \ \mathbf{c}:=\mathbf{c}\uplus\{\mathtt{t}\}\rangle \,.\, B!\mathrm{ans}(x:\ \mathsf{int})\langle x\in\mathbf{c}\ ;\ \mathbf{c}:=\mathbf{c}\setminus\{x\}\rangle$$

Then the following table gives the functions induced by obligations in these local types.

	input	output
$G_{\mathsf{sync}} \upharpoonright S$	$\xi_0 \stackrel{\text{def}}{=} B?\mathrm{req}(\varepsilon)\langle \mathsf{truth};\varepsilon\rangle$	$\xi_1 \stackrel{\text{def}}{=} B!\mathrm{ans}(x:\mathsf{int})\langle x=\mathbf{c};\mathbf{c}:=\mathbf{c}+1\rangle$
	$\mathtt{pred}(\xi_0) \stackrel{\text{def}}{=} \lambda\varepsilon,\mathbf{c}.(\mathsf{truth})$ $\mathtt{upd}(\xi_0) \stackrel{\text{def}}{=} \lambda\varepsilon,\mathbf{c}.\langle\varepsilon\rangle$	$\mathtt{pred}(\xi_1) \stackrel{\text{def}}{=} \lambda x,\mathbf{c}.(x=\mathbf{c})$ $\mathtt{upd}(\xi_1) \stackrel{\text{def}}{=} \lambda x,\mathbf{c}.\langle\mathbf{c}+1\rangle$
$G_{\mathsf{ass}} \upharpoonright S$	$\xi_2 \stackrel{\text{def}}{=} B?\mathrm{req}(\varepsilon)\langle \mathsf{truth};\mathtt{t}:=\mathtt{t}+1\ \ \mathbf{c}:=\mathbf{c}\uplus\{\mathtt{t}\}\rangle$	$\xi_3 \stackrel{\text{def}}{=} B!\mathrm{ans}(x:\ \mathsf{int})\langle x\in\mathbf{c}\ ;\ \mathbf{c}:=\mathbf{c}\setminus\{x\}\rangle$
	$\mathtt{pred}(\xi_2) \stackrel{\text{def}}{=} \lambda\varepsilon,\mathbf{c}.(\mathsf{truth})$ $\mathtt{upd}(\xi_2) \stackrel{\text{def}}{=} \lambda\varepsilon,\mathbf{c}.\langle\mathtt{t}+1\ \ \mathbf{c}\cup\{\mathtt{t}\}\rangle$	$\mathtt{pred}(\xi_3) \stackrel{\text{def}}{=} \lambda x,\mathbf{c}.(x\in\mathbf{c})$ $\mathtt{upd}(\xi_3) \stackrel{\text{def}}{=} \lambda x,\mathbf{c}.\langle\mathbf{c}\setminus\{x\}\rangle$

Once we can treat obligations as operations on state(s), we can define their commutativity. Since the commutativity we need is asymmetric (corresponding to asymmetric permutations induced by asynchrony, cf. Definition 7), we define semi-commutativity, which plays a key role in validating specifications later. A precursor of the following construction in a different setting is found in [7] (see §5 for discussions).

Definition 23 (semi-commutativity). Assume w.l.o.g., ξ_i and ξ_j use $\mathbf{f}$ as the field. Then we say ξ_i *commutes over* ξ_j if, for any message values v_i and v_j (for ξ_i and ξ_j), and the value of initial state w (for $\mathbf{f}$), the following conditions hold. If $\mathtt{pred}(\xi_i)(v_i,w)$ and $\mathtt{pred}(\xi_j)(v_j,\mathtt{upd}(\xi_i)(v_i,w))$ are both true, then

1. $\mathtt{pred}(\xi_j)(v_j,w)$ and $\mathtt{pred}(\xi_i)(v_i,\mathtt{upd}(\xi_j)(v_j,w))$ are both true.
2. $\mathtt{upd}(\xi_j)(v_j,\mathtt{upd}(\xi_i)(v_i,w)) = \mathtt{upd}(\xi_i)(v_i,\mathtt{upd}(\xi_j)(v_j,w))$.

If ξ_i commutes over ξ_j and vice versa, then we say *ξ_i and ξ_j are commutative.*

Example 24. We show ξ_1 in Example 22 does not commute over itself (i.e. ξ_1, ξ_1 is not commutative). Let $\mathbf{f}=\mathbf{c}$. We know $\mathtt{pred}(\xi_1)(1,1)$, $\mathtt{pred}(\xi_1)(2,\mathtt{upd}(\xi_1)(1,1))$ and $\mathtt{pred}(\xi_1)(2,2)$ are all truth, however $\mathtt{pred}(\xi_1)(2,1) = \mathsf{false}$. Similarly, ξ_0 does not commute over ξ_1 (however ξ_0, ξ_0 are commutative).

Using this notion, the healthiness condition for asynchronous specification can be concisely stated as follows. Below we say an obligation is *usable in* Θ if it occurs in a local SP in Θ or in the projection of a global SP in Θ to its potentially local role, where by "potentially local" we mean that the role has a potential to be played locally (e.g. for the global SP carried by an input shared channel type, only the specified role is potentially local).

Definition 25 (commutativity). Given Θ, let $\xi_1,..,\xi_n$ be all the obligations usable in Θ. Then we say Θ is *commutative* if the following conditions hold.

1. For (possibly identical) ξ_1' and ξ_2' from $\{\xi_1,..,\xi_n\}$, if both are inputs or both are outputs, then ξ_1' and ξ_2' are commutative.
2. For distinct ξ_1' and ξ_2' from $\{\xi_1,..,\xi_n\}$, if ξ_1' is an output and ξ_2' is an input then ξ_1' commutes over ξ_2'.

I.e. Θ is action confluent when all obligations used in the specifications for the target process commute over each other up to legal permutations. We can easily show:

Proposition 26. *If Θ is commutative then it is confluent (hence asynchronous).*

Note that the other way round is not true: Θ is confluent does not imply that it is commutative. Since, based on Definition 18, Θ is confluent, then whenever $\Theta \xrightarrow{\mathsf{s}} \Theta'$, $\Theta' \xrightarrow{\ell_1 \cdot \ell_2} \Theta''$ and $\ell_1 \cdot \ell_2 \curvearrowright \ell_2 \cdot \ell_1$ imply $\Theta' \xrightarrow{\ell_2 \cdot \ell_1} \Theta''$. Θ' is commutative, but Θ' cannot imply that Θ is commutative.

This method can be strengthened by adding an invariant (including correlation among states) in state and checking that invariant continues to hold at each step. We can now show all our example specifications except the one induced by G_{sync} is asynchronous. Below we let Θ_{async}'s shared environment contains $a : I(G_{\mathsf{async}}[S])$, and let Θ_{async}'s data storage contains $\mathbf{c} \mapsto \{\}$. By inspecting the (semi-)commutativity of induced predicates and operations, we easily obtain:

Proposition 27. *Θ_{async} and Θ_{ass} at server are both commutative, hence asynchronous.*

We can similarly check a specification induced by G_{pcs} and G_{ivc} are commutative.

The valuation of commutativity is essentially satisfiability of a formula whose free variables are universally quantified. Thus if the logic (for predicates) we use for our specification language is decidable, commutativity is decidable. In particular, by [20]:

Proposition 28. *With the SP language given in §3 restricting operations on integers to be the addition and the subtraction, then the commutativity is decidable.*

We discuss practical implications of these results in the next section.

5 Related Work and Further Topics

Practical implications of the Theory The characterisation results in §4 offer not only a decision procedure for a rich subset of specifications, but also a basic insight on the design methodology for asynchronous specifications. In particular it sheds light on the use of operations on sets in our examples in §2. Because checking commutativity solely relies on the obligations occurring in protocols, adding the recursion to the syntax:

$$G \ ::= \ \dots \ | \ \mu X.G \ | \ X \qquad T \ ::= \ \dots \ | \ \mu X.T \ | \ X$$

does not change the nature of commutativity checking nor the resulting guarantee.

If Θ is asynchronous and a process behaves properly w.r.t. Θ synchronously, an asynchronous observer will also judge the induced (permuted) trace to be proper w.r.t. Θ. It is however easy to see that the converse is *not* true: consider a server that violates Θ_{ass} by responding 2 to the first request, 1 to the second, but these are delayed by asynchrony, leading to a valid trace when they arrive at the remote observer (for a concrete analysis, see the Appendix in our full version [5]). A key consistency property is that any further legal permutation of this valid trace is again valid. For example, if a system monitor for the server is sitting between Client and Server, and if this monitor observes a valid trace of Server against the specification she has, Client will observe no worse behaviour. This monotonicity gives a basis for an application of the presented framework such as runtime monitoring.

Related works and further topics The semantic differences between synchronous and asynchronous communications have been studied for several decades: early works include [2,6,10,12]. The permutations associated with asynchronous communication used in Definition 7 are noted in these works (and implicit in such work as [15]). Their more explicit presentation in the categorical setting is found in [19]. There is also a study in component validation based on asynchronous histories such as [18]. In spite of these precursors and close technical connection, the existing works (except [16] which however focuses on synchronous specifications and proof rules for their verifications) may not have pointed out the concrete semantic issues which stateful behavioural specifications and asynchronous observables can induce, and how this issue can be resolved through the interplay between synchronous and asynchronous semantics.

As observed in §4.2, a close analogue of commutativity of operations used for our characterisation result (Definition 23) appears in [7], where the authors study a method for checking commutativity (called *diamond connectivity*) of operations with pre-conditions in object-oriented programs, with a view to preventing the simultaneous issuance of these operations when they are not commutative. They translate the original model of methods in OCL to Alloy, which is analysed through simulation by Alloy Analyser. They do not (aim to) determine a class of specifications suitable for asynchronously communicating processes. In contrast, our aim is to stipulate a general class of specifications for communicating processes suitable for asynchronous observations, and identify its subclass amenable for automatic verification. Following this principle, we use a semi-commutativity to capture asymmetry in asynchronous communications: as seen in the Proposition 27 (the proofs are in our full version [5]), we crucially use this semi-commutativity when verifying G_{ass} is asynchronous.

Among further topics, we are currently exploring and analysing concrete forms of asynchronously verifiable specifications with different structures, informed by use cases from [17] as well as our theory, with a view to their usage in monitoring. One of the challenges is to find a solid (asynchronous) specification framework for inherently conflicting operations, such as two consecutive and overwriting updates on the same datum.

Acknowledgements. We thank the reviewers for their valuable comments and our colleagues in Mobility Reading Group for discussions. This work is supported by Ocean Observatories Initiative [17] and EPSRC grants EP/F002114/1 and EP/G015481/1.

References

1. The Java Modeling Language (JML) homepage, `http://www.jmlspecs.org/`
2. Amadio, R., Castellani, I., Sangiorgi, D.: On Bisimulations for the Asynchronous π-Calculus. In: Montanari, U., Sassone, V. (eds.) CONCUR 1996. LNCS, vol. 1119, pp. 147–162. Springer, Heidelberg (1996)
3. Bettini, L., Coppo, M., D'Antoni, L., De Luca, M., Dezani-Ciancaglini, M., Yoshida, N.: Global Progress in Dynamically Interleaved Multiparty Sessions. In: van Breugel, F., Chechik, M. (eds.) CONCUR 2008. LNCS, vol. 5201, pp. 418–433. Springer, Heidelberg (2008)
4. Bocchi, L., Honda, K., Tuosto, E., Yoshida, N.: A Theory of Design-by-Contract for Distributed Multiparty Interactions. In: Gastin, P., Laroussinie, F. (eds.) CONCUR 2010. LNCS, vol. 6269, pp. 162–176. Springer, Heidelberg (2010)
5. Chen, T.-C., Honda, K.: Full Version of this paper, to appear as an EECS technical report, Queen Mary. University of London
6. de Boer, F.S., Kok, J.N., Palamidessi, C., Rutten, J.J.M.M.: The Failure of Failures in a Paradigm for Asynchronous Communication. In: Groote, J.F., Baeten, J.C.M. (eds.) CONCUR 1991. LNCS, vol. 527, pp. 111–126. Springer, Heidelberg (1991)
7. Dennis, G., Seater, R., Rayside, D., Jackson, D.: Automating commutativity analysis at the design level. In: ISSTA 2004, pp. 165–174. ACM, New York (2004)
8. Chen, T.-C., Bocchi, L., Deniélou, P.-M., Honda, K., Yoshida, N.: Asynchronous Distributed Monitoring for Multiparty Session Enforcement. In: Bruni, R., Sassone, V. (eds.) TGC 2011. LNCS, vol. 7173, pp. 25–45. Springer, Heidelberg (2012)
9. Falcone, Y.: You Should Better Enforce Than Verify. In: Barringer, H., Falcone, Y., Finkbeiner, B., Havelund, K., Lee, I., Pace, G., Roşu, G., Sokolsky, O., Tillmann, N. (eds.) RV 2010. LNCS, vol. 6418, pp. 89–105. Springer, Heidelberg (2010)
10. He, J., Josephs, M., Hoare, T.: A theory of synchrony and asynchrony. In: Programming Concepts and Methods. IFIP, pp. 459–478 (1990)
11. Hoare, C., Jifeng, H.: Unifying theories of programming. Prentice Hall series in computer science. Prentice Hall (1998)
12. Honda, K., Tokoro, M.: An Object Calculus for Asynchronous Communication. In: America, P. (ed.) ECOOP 1991. LNCS, vol. 512, pp. 133–147. Springer, Heidelberg (1991)
13. Honda, K., Yoshida, N., Carbone, M.: Multiparty Asynchronous Session Types. In: POPL 2008, pp. 273–284. ACM (2008)
14. Hu, R., Kouzapas, D., Pernet, O., Yoshida, N., Honda, K.: Type-Safe Eventful Sessions in Java. In: D'Hondt, T. (ed.) ECOOP 2010. LNCS, vol. 6183, pp. 329–353. Springer, Heidelberg (2010)
15. Lamport, L.: Time, clocks, and the ordering of events in a distributed system. Communications of the ACM 21(7), 558–564 (1978)

16. A multiparty multi-session logic, http://www.cs.le.ac.uk/people/lb148/StatefulAssertions/main-long.pdf
17. Ocean Observatories Initiative (OOI), http://www.oceanleadership.org/programs-and-partnerships/ocean-observing/ooi/
18. Owe, O., Steffen, M., Torjusen, A.B.: Model Testing Asynchronously Communicating Objects using Modulo AC Rewriting. ENCS 264(3), 69–84 (2010)
19. Selinger, P.: First-Order Axioms for Asynchrony. In: Mazurkiewicz, A., Winkowski, J. (eds.) CONCUR 1997. LNCS, vol. 1243, pp. 376–390. Springer, Heidelberg (1997)
20. Zarba, C.G.: Combining Sets with Integers. In: Armando, A. (ed.) FroCoS 2002. LNCS (LNAI), vol. 2309, pp. 103–116. Springer, Heidelberg (2002)

Synthesising Choreographies from Local Session Types*

Julien Lange and Emilio Tuosto

Department of Computer Science, University of Leicester, UK

Abstract. Designing and analysing multiparty distributed interactions can be achieved either by means of a global view (e.g. in choreography-based approaches) or by composing available computational entities (e.g. in service orchestration).

This paper proposes a typing systems which allows, under some conditions, to synthesise a choreography (i.e. a multiparty global type) from a set of local session types which describe end-point behaviours (i.e. local types).

1 Introduction

Communication-centred applications are paramount in the design and implementation of modern distributed systems such as those in service-oriented or cloud computing. Session types [8] and their multiparty variants [7,9] offer an effective formal framework for designing, analysing, and implementing this class of applications. Those theories feature rather appealing methodologies that consists of (*i*) designing a global view of the interactions – aka *global type* –, (*ii*) effective analysis of such a global view, (*iii*) automatic projection of the global view to local end-points – aka *local types* –, and (*iv*) type checking end-point code against local types. Such theories guarantee that, when the global view enjoys suitable properties (phase (*ii*)), the end-points typable with local types enjoy e.g., liveness properties like progress.

A drawback of such approaches is that they cannot be applied when the local types describing the communication patterns of end-points are not obtained by an a priori designed global view. For instance, in service-oriented computing, one typically has independently developed end-points that have to be combined to form larger services. Hence, deciding if the combined service respects its specification becomes non trivial. To illustrate this, we introduce a simple example used throughout the paper.

Consider a system $S_{\text{BS}} = \mathtt{b}_1[P_1] \mid \mathtt{s}_1[S_1] \mid \mathtt{b}_2[P_2] \mid \mathtt{s}_2[S_2]$ consisting of two buyers ($\mathtt{b}_1$ and $\mathtt{b}_2$) and two servers ($\mathtt{s}_1$ and $\mathtt{s}_2$) running in parallel, so that

$$P_1 = t_1!\mathtt{order}.p_1?\mathtt{price}.r?\mathtt{price}.(c_1!.t_1!\mathtt{addr} \oplus c_2!.no_1!) \quad \text{is the behaviour of } \mathtt{b}_1$$

$$P_2 = t_2!\mathtt{order}.p_2?\mathtt{price}.r!\mathtt{price}.(c_2?.t_2!\mathtt{addr} + c_1?.no_2!) \quad \text{is the behaviour of } \mathtt{b}_2$$

$$S_i = t_i?\mathtt{order}.p_i!\mathtt{price}.(t_i?\mathtt{addr} + no_i?), \quad i \in \{1,2\} \quad \text{is the behaviour of } \mathtt{s}_i$$

with $a!\mathtt{e}$ (resp. $a?\mathtt{e}$) representing the action of sending (resp. receiving) a message of type $\mathtt{e}$ on a channel a (we omit $\mathtt{e}$ when the message is immaterial), $\oplus$ representing an internal choice, and $+$ a choice made by the environment. Intuitively, the overall behaviour of S_{BS} should be that either $\mathtt{b}_1$ or $\mathtt{b}_2$ purchase from their corresponding seller.

* Work partially supported by the Leverhulme Trust Programme Award "Tracing Networks".

M. Koutny and I. Ulidowski (Eds.): CONCUR 2012, LNCS 7454, pp. 225–239, 2012.

A natural question arises: is this intended behaviour actually realised by S_{BS}? Arguably, it is not immediate to answer such a question, even more so if a system involves a large number of participants, with possibly complex behaviours.

We propose to construct a global view of distributed end-points like S_{BS} by a straightforward extension of the multiparty session types introduced in [9]. Such types formalise a global view of the behaviour which, for S_{BS}, resembles the informal diagram below, where the choreography of the overall protocol becomes much clearer.

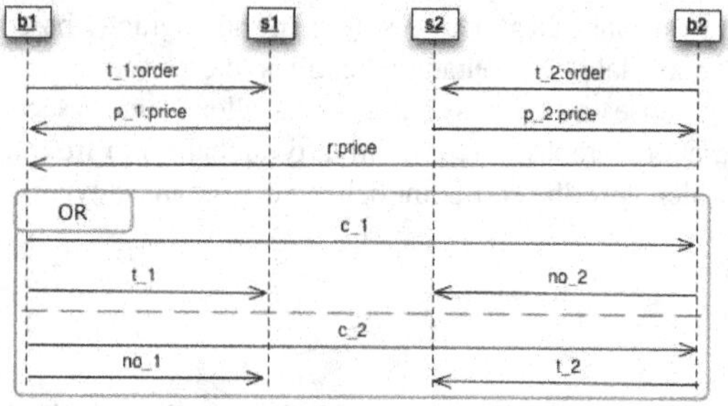

An advantage of our approach is that we can reuse the results of the theory of multiparty session types to prove properties of end-points e.g. safety and progress. In fact, we show that when the choreography can be constructed, its projections correspond to the initial end-points. Therefore, the well-formedness of the synthesised global choreography guarantees progress and safety properties of end-points.

We assume that session types are extracted from programs (relying on e.g. [6,8,9]), and that they are readily available before addressing the construction of a global type.

Contributions. We introduce a theory to assign a global type to a set of local types. If it exists, such global type is unique (Theorem 2) and well-formed (Theorem 3); also, its projections are equivalent to the original local types (Theorem 7). We show a subject reduction result (Theorem 4) as well as progress and safety properties (Theorems 5 and 6) guaranteed by our theory. Finally, we show that for every well-formed global type, an equivalent global type can be assigned to its projections (Theorem 8).

Synopsis. In § 2, we give the syntax and semantics of the local types from which it is possible to construct a global type. In § 3, we present an extension of the global types in [9]. In § 4, we introduce a typing systems for local types and we give our main results. Finally, in § 5 we conclude, and discuss related and future work. Due to space restriction, we omitted the proofs, which are available in [11].

2 Local Types

We use CCS-like processes (with guarded external and internal choices) to infer a global type from *local types* that correspond to the participants in the inferred choreography. Hereafter, $\mathbb{P}$ is a denumerable set of *participant names* (ranged over by $\mathtt{s}, \mathtt{r}, \mathtt{n}, \ldots$) and $\mathbb{C}$ is a denumerable set of *channel names* (ranged over by $a, b, \ldots$).

Syntax. The syntax of local types below is parametrised wrt basic data types such as bool, int, ... (ranged over by $\mathtt{e}$):

$$S,T ::= S \mid S' \quad \mid \quad \mathtt{n}[P] \quad \mid \quad a:\rho \quad \mid \quad \mathbf{0}$$

$$P,Q ::= \bigoplus_{i\in I} a_i!\mathtt{e_i}.P_i \quad \mid \quad \sum_{i\in I} a_i?\mathtt{e_i}.P_i \quad \mid \quad \mu\mathbf{x}.P \quad \mid \quad \mathbf{x}$$

A system S consists of the parallel composition of *processes* and *queues*. A *process* $\mathtt{n}[P]$ is a behaviour P identified by $\mathtt{n} \in \mathbb{P}$; we assume that the participant names are all different. A behaviour is either an external choice, an internal choice, or a recursive process. An internal choice $\bigoplus_{i\in I} a_i!\mathtt{e_i}.P_i$ is guarded by output prefixes $a_i!\mathtt{e_i}$ representing the sending of a value of sort $\mathtt{e}_i$ on channel a_i. An external choice $\sum_{i\in I} a_i?\mathtt{e_i}.P_i$ is guarded by input prefixes $a_i?\mathtt{e_i}$ representing the reception of a value of type $\mathtt{e}_i$ on channel a_i. (we overload $\mathbf{0}$ to denote either an internal or external choice where $I = \emptyset$). We adopt asynchronous (order-preserving) communications and assume that the channels in the guards of choices are pairwise distinct. In $\mu\mathbf{x}.P$, $\mu\mathbf{x}$ is a binder for the free occurrences of $\mathbf{x}$ in P. Moreover, all such free occurrences are prefix guarded in P. We consider closed behaviours only that is, behaviours with no free occurrences of recursion variables, and, for simplicity, we assume that bound variables are pairwise distinct.

A *program* is a system with no queues, while a *runtime system* is a system S having exactly one queue $a:\rho$ per channel name $a \in \mathbb{C}$ in S. In the following, $S,T,\ldots$ denote either a program or runtime system.

Semantics. The semantics of local types is a labelled transition system (LTS) with labels

$$\lambda ::= \alpha \mid a\cdot\mathtt{e} \mid \mathtt{e}\cdot a \mid \mathtt{n}[\alpha] \mid \mathtt{n}:\alpha \qquad \text{where} \qquad \alpha ::= a!\mathtt{e} \mid a?\mathtt{e}$$

Label α indicates either sending or reception by a process. Labels $a\cdot\mathtt{e}$ and $\mathtt{e}\cdot a$ respectively indicate push and pop operations on queues. Label $\mathtt{n}[\alpha]$ indicates a communication action done by participant $\mathtt{n}$ while $\mathtt{n} : a!\mathtt{e}$ and $\mathtt{n} : a?\mathtt{e}$ indicate a synchronisation between $\mathtt{n}$ and a queue.

Assume the usual laws for commutative monoids for $\mid$ and $\mathbf{0}$ on systems and $\mu\mathbf{x}.P \equiv P[\mu\mathbf{x}.P/\mathbf{x}]$. The LTS $\xrightarrow{\lambda}$ is the smallest relation closed under the following rules:

$$\text{[INT]}\ \bigoplus_{i\in I} a_i!\mathtt{e_i}.P_i \xrightarrow{a_j!\mathtt{e_j}} P_j \quad j\in I \qquad\qquad \text{[EXT]}\ \sum_{i\in I} a_i?\mathtt{e_i}.P_i \xrightarrow{a_j?\mathtt{e_j}} P_j \quad j\in I$$

$$\text{[PUSH]}\ a:\rho \xrightarrow{a\cdot\mathtt{e}} a:\rho\cdot\mathtt{e} \qquad\qquad \text{[POP]}\ a:\mathtt{e}\cdot\rho \xrightarrow{\mathtt{e}\cdot a} a:\rho$$

$$\text{[IN]}\ \frac{S \xrightarrow{\mathtt{n}[a?\mathtt{e}]} S' \quad T \xrightarrow{\mathtt{e}\cdot a} T'}{S \mid T \xrightarrow{\mathtt{n}:a?\mathtt{e}} S' \mid T'} \qquad \text{[OUT]}\ \frac{S \xrightarrow{\mathtt{n}[a!\mathtt{e}]} S' \quad T \xrightarrow{a\cdot\mathtt{e}} T'}{S \mid T \xrightarrow{\mathtt{n}:a!\mathtt{e}} S' \mid T'} \qquad \text{[BOX]}\ \frac{P \xrightarrow{\alpha} P'}{\mathtt{n}[P] \xrightarrow{\mathtt{n}[\alpha]} \mathtt{n}[P']}$$

$$\text{[EQ-P]}\ \frac{P \equiv Q \xrightarrow{\alpha} Q' \equiv P'}{P \xrightarrow{\alpha} P'} \qquad\qquad \text{[EQ-S]}\ \frac{S \equiv T \xrightarrow{\lambda} T' \equiv S'}{S \xrightarrow{\lambda} S'}$$

Rules [INT] and [EXT] are trivial. By [PUSH] (resp. [POP]), a queue receives a (resp. sends the first) datum (resp. if any). Processes can synchronise with queues according to rules [IN] and [OUT]. The remaining rules are standard. Let $S \longrightarrow$ iff there are S' and λ s.t. $S \xrightarrow{\lambda} S'$ and $\xRightarrow{\lambda_1\ldots\lambda_n}$ (resp. $\Longrightarrow$) be the reflexive transitive closure of $\xrightarrow{\lambda}$ (resp. $\longrightarrow$).

3 Global Types

Global types specify an ordering of the interactions in choreographies. The syntax for global types in [9] is extended with a generalised sequencing $\mathcal{G}\,;\mathcal{G}'$ so that (*i*) our theory can type more systems and (*ii*) subject reduction can be established (cf. Example 3).

Global types have the following syntax:

$$\mathcal{G} ::= \mathtt{s}\to\mathtt{r}\!:\!a\langle\mathtt{e}\rangle\,.\,\mathcal{G} \;\mid\; \mathcal{G}\,;\mathcal{G}' \;\mid\; \mathcal{G}+\mathcal{G}' \;\mid\; \mathcal{G} \mid \mathcal{G}' \;\mid\; \mu\chi.\mathcal{G} \;\mid\; \chi \;\mid\; \mathbf{0}$$

The prefix $\mathtt{s}\to\mathtt{r}\!:\!a\langle\mathtt{e}\rangle$ represents an interaction where $\mathtt{s}\in\mathbb{P}$ sends a value of sort $\mathtt{e}$ to $\mathtt{r}\in\mathbb{P}$ on $a\in\mathbb{C}$ (we let ι range over interactions $\mathtt{s}\to\mathtt{r}\!:\!a\langle\mathtt{e}\rangle$ and assume that $\mathtt{s}\neq\mathtt{r}$). In generalised sequencing $\mathcal{G}\,;\mathcal{G}'$, the interactions in $\mathcal{G}'$ are enabled only after the ones in $\mathcal{G}$. The production $\mathcal{G}+\mathcal{G}'$ indicates a (exclusive) choice of interactions. Concurrent interactions are written $\mathcal{G} \mid \mathcal{G}'$. In a recursive global type $\mu\chi.\mathcal{G}$, χ is bound and guarded in $\mathcal{G}$. We assume that global types are closed and often omit trailing occurrences of $\mathbf{0}$.

Example 1. The first two interactions between $\mathtt{b_i}$ and $\mathtt{s_i}$ in the example of § 1 are

$$\mathcal{G}_i = \mathtt{b_i}\to\mathtt{s_i}\!:\!t_i\langle\mathtt{order}\rangle\,.\,\mathtt{s_i}\to\mathtt{b_i}\!:\!p_i\langle\mathtt{price}\rangle \quad i\in\{1,2\} \tag{3.1}$$

The type $\mathcal{G}_i$ says that a participant $\mathtt{b_i}$ sends a message of type $\mathtt{order}$ to participant $\mathtt{s_i}$ on channel t_i, then $\mathtt{s_i}$ replies with a message of type $\mathtt{price}$ on channel p_i. ◇

The smallest equivalence relation satisfying the laws for commutative monoids for $\mid$, $+$, and $\mathbf{0}$ and the axioms below is the structural congruence for global types:

$$\mathcal{G};\mathbf{0}\equiv\mathcal{G} \qquad \mathbf{0};\mathcal{G}\equiv\mathcal{G} \qquad (\mathcal{G};\mathcal{G}');\mathcal{G}''\equiv\mathcal{G};(\mathcal{G}';\mathcal{G}'')$$
$$\iota.(\mathcal{G};\mathcal{G}')\equiv(\iota.\,\mathcal{G});\mathcal{G}' \qquad \mu\chi.\mathcal{G}\equiv\mathcal{G}[\mu\chi.\mathcal{G}/\chi]$$

The syntax of global types may specify behaviours that are not implementable. The rest of this section borrows from [5] and [9] and adapts the requirements a global type must fulfil to ensure that the ordering relation it prescribes is indeed feasible.

3.1 Channel Usage and Linearity

It is paramount that no race occurs on the channels of a global type (i.e. a datum sent on a channel is received by its intended recipient). As in [9], we require that a global type is *linear*, that is actions on channels shared by different participants are temporally ordered. For this, we use generic environments (ranged over by C) which keep track of channel usage. Such environments are trees defined as follows:

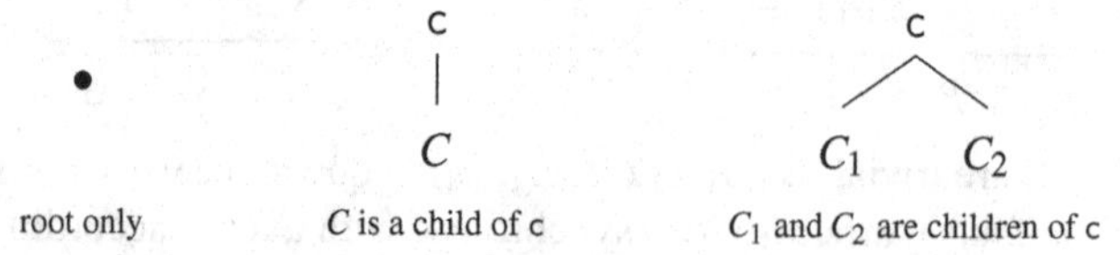

Each node c has a label $\underline{\mathrm{c}}$ of the form $\circ$, $\mathtt{s}\to\mathtt{r}\!:\!a$, or $\mu\chi$ respectively representing the root of choice or concurrent branches, an interaction between $\mathtt{s}$ and $\mathtt{r}$ on a, and a recursive behaviour. Immaterial components of a label are left unspecified by using a wild-card $\_$, e.g. $\_ \rightarrow \_ : a$ matches any label representing an interaction on a. Write $\mathtt{c} \in C$ when $\mathtt{c}$ is a node in C, and $\mathtt{c}_1 \prec \mathtt{c}_2$ iff $\mathtt{c}_1, \mathtt{c}_2 \in C$ and $\mathtt{c}_2$ is a node in the sub-tree rooted at $\mathtt{c}_1$.

We adapt the definitions in [9] to our framework.

Definition 1 (Dependency relations [9]). *Fix C, we define the following relations:*

$$\begin{array}{l}
\mathtt{c}_1 \prec_{\mathtt{II}} \mathtt{c}_2 \textit{ if } \mathtt{c}_1 \prec \mathtt{c}_2 \textit{ and } \underline{\mathtt{c}_i} = \mathtt{s}_i \rightarrow \mathtt{r} : a_i \quad i \in \{1,2\} \\
\mathtt{c}_1 \prec_{\mathtt{IO}} \mathtt{c}_2 \textit{ if } \mathtt{c}_1 \prec \mathtt{c}_2 \textit{ and } \underline{\mathtt{c}_1} = \mathtt{s}_1 \rightarrow \mathtt{r} : a_1 \textit{ and } \underline{\mathtt{c}_2} = \mathtt{r} \rightarrow \mathtt{s}_2 : a_2 \\
\mathtt{c}_1 \prec_{\mathtt{OO}} \mathtt{c}_2 \textit{ if } \mathtt{c}_1 \prec \mathtt{c}_2 \textit{ and } \underline{\mathtt{c}_i} = \mathtt{s} \rightarrow \mathtt{r}_i : a \quad i \in \{1,2\}
\end{array}$$

An input dependency *from $\mathtt{c}_1$ to $\mathtt{c}_2$ is a chain of the form $\mathtt{c}_1 \prec_{\phi_1} \cdots \prec_{\phi_k} \mathtt{c}_2$ ($k \geq 0$) such that $\phi_i \in \{\mathtt{II}, \mathtt{IO}\}$ for $1 \leq i \leq k-1$ and $\phi_k = \mathtt{II}$. An* output dependency *from $\mathtt{c}_1$ to $\mathtt{c}_2$ is a chain $\mathtt{c}_1 \prec_{\phi_1} \cdots \prec_{\phi_k} \mathtt{c}_2$ ($k \geq 1$) such that $\phi_i \in \{\mathtt{OO}, \mathtt{IO}\}$.*

Definition 2 (Linearity [9]). *C is linear if and only if whenever $\mathtt{c}_1 \prec \mathtt{c}_2$ with $\underline{\mathtt{c}_1} = \_ \rightarrow \_ : a$ and $\underline{\mathtt{c}_2} = \_ \rightarrow \_ : a$ then there is both input and output dependencies from $\mathtt{c}_1$ to $\mathtt{c}_2$.*

We also define a function $\_ \star \_$ to append trees as follows

$$\begin{array}{c} \mathtt{c} \\ | \\ C_0 \end{array} \star C' = \begin{array}{c} \mathtt{c} \\ | \\ C_0 \star C' \end{array}, \qquad \bullet \star C = C, \qquad \begin{array}{c} \mathtt{c} \\ \diagup \quad \diagdown \\ C_1 \qquad C_2 \end{array} \star C' = \begin{array}{c} \mathtt{c} \\ \diagup \quad \diagdown \\ C_1 \star C' \quad C_2 \star C' \end{array}$$

and a partial function to append a tree C' to a tree C while preserving linearity: $C \prec C' = C \star C'$ if $C \star C'$ is linear, otherwise $C \prec C' = \bot$. Also, let $\mathcal{T}(\mathcal{G})$ be the total function (cf. [11]) which returns a tree C corresponding to the use of channels in $\mathcal{G}$.

3.2 Well-Formed Global Types

We define the conditions for a global type to be well-formed. We write $\mathcal{P}(\mathcal{G})$ (resp. $C(\mathcal{G})$) for the set of participant (resp. channel) names in $\mathcal{G}$, and $\mathtt{fv}(\mathcal{G})$ for the set of free variables in $\mathcal{G}$, similarly for a system S. We give a few accessory functions. Let

$$\mathtt{R}(\mathcal{G}) \stackrel{\text{def}}{=} \{\mathtt{s} \rightarrow \mathtt{r} : a \mid \mathcal{G} \equiv (\mathtt{s} \rightarrow \mathtt{r} : a\langle \mathtt{e} \rangle . \mathcal{G}_1 + \mathcal{G}_2 \mid \mathcal{G}_3) ; \mathcal{G}_4\}$$

$$\mathtt{F_P}(\mathcal{G}) \stackrel{\text{def}}{=} \begin{cases} \mathtt{F_P}(\mathcal{G}_1) \cup \mathtt{F_P}(\mathcal{G}_2), & \mathcal{G} = \mathcal{G}_1 \mid \mathcal{G}_2 \\ \{\mathcal{P}(\mathcal{G})\}, & \text{otherwise} \end{cases}$$

$$\mathtt{F_O}(\mathcal{P}, \mathcal{G}) \stackrel{\text{def}}{=} \begin{cases} \mathtt{F_O}(\{\mathtt{s}, \mathtt{r}\} \cup \mathcal{P}, \mathcal{G}_1), & \mathcal{G} = \mathtt{s} \rightarrow \mathtt{r} : a\langle \mathtt{e} \rangle . \mathcal{G}_1 \\ \mathtt{F_O}(\emptyset, \mathcal{G}_1) \cup \mathtt{F_O}(\emptyset, \mathcal{G}_2), & \mathcal{G} = \mathcal{G}_1 \mid \mathcal{G}_2 \\ \mathtt{F_O}(\mathcal{P}, \mathcal{G}_1), & \mathcal{G} = \mathcal{G}_1 + \mathcal{G}_2 \text{ and } \mathtt{F_O}(\mathcal{P}, \mathcal{G}_1) = \mathtt{F_O}(\mathcal{P}, \mathcal{G}_2) \\ \mathtt{F_O}(\mathcal{P}, \mathcal{G}_1), & \mathcal{G} = \mu\chi . \mathcal{G}_1 \\ \mathtt{F_O}(\emptyset, \mathcal{G}_2), & \mathcal{G} = \mathcal{G}_1 ; \mathcal{G}_2 \\ \{\mathcal{P}\}, & \mathcal{G} = \mathbf{0} \text{ or } \mathcal{G} = \chi \\ \bot, & \text{otherwise} \end{cases}$$

$\mathtt{R}(\mathcal{G})$ is the *ready set* of $\mathcal{G}$, and $\mathtt{F_P}(\mathcal{G})$ is the family of sets of its participants running in different concurrent branches. That is, $N \in \mathtt{F_P}(\mathcal{G})$ iff all $\mathtt{n} \in N$ are in a same top-level thread of $\mathcal{G}$. $\mathtt{F_O}(\mathcal{G}, \mathcal{P})$ is the family of sets of participants of $\mathcal{G}$, so that for all $N, M \in \mathtt{F_O}(\mathcal{P}, \mathcal{G})$, the participants in N and those in M are in different concurrent branches in the last part of $\mathcal{G}$; define $\mathtt{F_O}(\mathcal{G}) \stackrel{\text{def}}{=} \mathtt{F_O}(\emptyset, \mathcal{G})$. Note that $\mathtt{F_O}(\_,\_)$ is a partial function.

Example 2. Let $\mathcal{G}_{i,j} = \mathtt{b_1} \to \mathtt{b_2} : c_i\langle\rangle.(\mathtt{b_i} \to \mathtt{s_i} : t_i\langle\mathtt{addr}\rangle \mid \mathtt{b_j} \to \mathtt{s_j} : no_j\langle\rangle)$ describe each of the branches of the *or* box in the example of § 1, where $i \neq j \in \{1,2\}$, then

$$\mathtt{R}(\mathcal{G}_{1,2}) = \{\mathtt{b_1} \to \mathtt{b_2} : c_1\},\ \mathtt{F_P}(\mathcal{G}_{1,2}) = \{\mathtt{b_1}, \mathtt{s_1}, \mathtt{b_2}, \mathtt{s_2}\},\ \mathtt{F_O}(\mathcal{G}_{1,2}) = \{\{\mathtt{b_1}, \mathtt{s_1}\}, \{\mathtt{b_2}, \mathtt{s_2}\}\}$$

The global type below corresponds to the whole protocol of § 1

$$\mathcal{G} = (\mathcal{G}_1 \mid \mathcal{G}_2); \mathtt{b_2} \to \mathtt{b_1} : r\langle\mathtt{price}\rangle.(\mathcal{G}_{1,2} + \mathcal{G}_{2,1})$$

hence $\mathtt{R}(\mathcal{G}) = \{\mathtt{b_i} \to \mathtt{s_i} : t_i\}_{i=1,2}$, $\mathtt{F_P}(\mathcal{G}) = \mathtt{F_P}(\mathcal{G}_{1,2})$, and $\mathtt{F_O}(\mathcal{G}) = \mathtt{F_O}(\mathcal{G}_{1,2})$. $\diamond$

Well-Formedness. The well-formedness of a global type $\mathcal{G}$ depends on how it uses channels; a judgement of the form $C \vdash \mathcal{G}$ states that $\mathcal{G}$ is well-formed according to the channel environment C (cf. § 3.1); $\mathcal{G}$ is *well-formed* if $\bullet \vdash \mathcal{G}$ can be derived from the rules given in Fig. 1. We assume that each premise of the rules in Fig. 1 does not hold if any of the functions used are not defined (e.g., in [WF-;], if $\mathtt{F_O}(\mathcal{G}) = \perp$ then $C \vdash \mathcal{G}; \mathcal{G}'$ is not derivable). Hereafter, we assume that a node $\mathtt{c}$ is fresh (i.e. $\mathtt{c} \notin C$). The environment C permits to tackle one of the main requirements for a global type to be well-formed: there should not be any race on channels. In the following, we discuss the rules of Fig. 1, which are grouped according to three other requirements: sequentiality, single threadness, and knowledge of choice.

Sequentiality [5]. Rules [WF-.], [WF-;] and [WF-;-0] ensure that sequentiality is preserved. In [WF-.], the ordering dependency between a prefix and its continuation allows us to implement each participant so that at least one action of the first prefix always happens before an action of the second prefix. More concretely, this rules out, e.g.

$$\mathtt{s_1} \to \mathtt{r_1} : a\langle\mathtt{e}\rangle.\mathtt{s_2} \to \mathtt{r_2} : b\langle\mathtt{e}'\rangle \quad ✘$$

where, evidently, it is not possible to guarantee that $\mathtt{s_2}$ sends after $\mathtt{r_1}$ receives on a. Since we are working in an asynchronous setting, we do not want to force both send and receive actions of the first prefix to happen before both actions of the second one. Rule [WF-;] requires the following for generalised sequencing. (*i*) For each pair of "first" participants in $\mathcal{G}'$, there exist two concurrent branches of $\mathcal{G}$ such that these two participants appear in different branches. This is to avoid global types of the form, e.g.

$$(\mathtt{s_1} \to \mathtt{r_1} : a\langle\mathtt{e}\rangle \mid \mathtt{s_2} \to \mathtt{r_2} : b\langle\mathtt{e}\rangle); \mathtt{s_1} \to \mathtt{r_1} : c\langle\mathtt{e}\rangle \quad ✘$$

since there is no possible sequencing between the prefix on b and the one on c. (*ii*) For all top-level concurrent branches in $\mathcal{G}$, there is a participant in that branch which is also in one of the branches of $\mathcal{G}'$. This requirement discards global types of the form, e.g.

$$(\mathtt{s_1} \to \mathtt{r_1} : a\langle\mathtt{e}\rangle \mid \mathtt{s_2} \to \mathtt{r_2} : b\langle\mathtt{e}\rangle \mid \mathtt{s_3} \to \mathtt{r_3} : c\langle\mathtt{e}\rangle); \mathtt{s_1} \to \mathtt{r_2} : d\langle\mathtt{e}\rangle \quad ✘$$

$$[\text{WF-.}]\ \frac{\forall\, \mathtt{s}' \to \mathtt{r}' : \_ \in \mathtt{R}(\mathcal{G}) : \{\mathtt{s}',\mathtt{r}'\} \cap \{\mathtt{s},\mathtt{r}\} \neq \emptyset \qquad C \prec \mathtt{c} \vdash \mathcal{G} \qquad \underline{\mathtt{c}} = \mathtt{s} \to \mathtt{r} : a}{C \vdash \mathtt{s} \to \mathtt{r} : a\langle \mathtt{e} \rangle \,.\, \mathcal{G}}$$

$$[\text{WF-;}]\ \frac{\begin{array}{c}\forall\, \mathtt{s} \to \mathtt{r} : \_ \in \mathtt{R}(\mathcal{G}').\exists N_1 \neq N_2 \in \mathtt{F_0}(\mathcal{G}).\mathtt{s} \in N_1 \wedge \mathtt{r} \in N_2 \\ \forall N \in \mathtt{F_P}(\mathcal{G}).\exists N' \in \mathtt{F_P}(\mathcal{G}').N \cap N' \neq \emptyset \qquad C \vdash \mathcal{G} \qquad C \prec \mathcal{T}(\mathcal{G}) \vdash \mathcal{G}'\end{array}}{C \vdash \mathcal{G} ; \mathcal{G}'}$$

$$[\text{WF-}\mid]\ \frac{\mathcal{P}(\mathcal{G}) \cap \mathcal{P}(\mathcal{G}') = \emptyset \qquad C(\mathcal{G}) \cap C(\mathcal{G}') = \emptyset \qquad C \vdash \mathcal{G} \qquad C \vdash \mathcal{G}'}{C \vdash \mathcal{G} \mid \mathcal{G}'}$$

$$[\text{WF-}\mu\chi]\ \frac{\chi \in \mathtt{fv}(\mathcal{G}) \Rightarrow \#\mathtt{F_0}(\mathcal{G}) = 1 \qquad C \star \mathtt{c} \vdash \mathcal{G} \qquad \underline{\mathtt{c}} = \mu\chi}{C \vdash \mu\chi.\mathcal{G}}$$

$$[\text{WF-;-}\mathbf{0}]\ \frac{C \vdash \mathcal{G}}{C \vdash \mathcal{G} ; \mathbf{0}} \qquad [\text{WF-}\chi]\ \frac{C \prec C(\mu\chi)}{C \vdash \chi} \qquad [\text{WF-}\mathbf{0}]\ \frac{}{C \vdash \mathbf{0}}$$

$$[\text{WF-+}]\ \frac{\forall\, \mathtt{s} \to \mathtt{r} : a \in \mathtt{R}(\mathcal{G}).\forall\, \mathtt{s}' \to \mathtt{r}' : b \in \mathtt{R}(\mathcal{G}').\, \mathtt{s} = \mathtt{s}' \wedge a \neq b \qquad C \vdash \mathcal{G} \qquad C \vdash \mathcal{G}'}{C \vdash \mathcal{G} + \mathcal{G}'}$$

Fig. 1. Rules for Well-formedness

since it is not possible to enforce an order between $\mathtt{s}_3$ and $\mathtt{r}_3$ and the others. *(iii)* $\mathcal{G}$ and $\mathcal{G}'$ are also well-formed. Observe that *(i)* implies that for $\mathcal{G} ; \mathcal{G}'$ to be well-formed, $\mathcal{G}$ is of the form $\mathcal{G}_1 \mid \mathcal{G}_2$, with $\mathcal{G}_1 \neq \mathbf{0}$ and $\mathcal{G}_2 \neq \mathbf{0}$. Both [WF-.] and [WF-;] are only applicable when linearity is preserved. Finally, rule [WF-;-0] is a special case of $\mathcal{G} ; \mathcal{G}'$.

Single threadness [9]. A participant should not appear in different concurrent branches of a global type, so that each participant is single threaded. This is also reflected in the calculus of § 2, where parallel composition is only allowed at the system level. Therefore, in [WF-|], the participant (resp. channel) names in concurrent branches must be disjoints. Rule [WF-$\mu\chi$] adds a new node in C to keep track of recursive usage of the channels, and requires that $\mathcal{G}$ is single threaded, i.e. concurrent branches cannot appear under recursion. If that was the case, a participant would appear in different concurrent branches of the unfolding of a recursive global type. Rule [WF-χ] unfolds C at $\mu\chi$ to ensure that the one-time unfolding of C preserves linearity (see [9] for details). For this we define $C(\mu\chi)$ to be the subtree of C rooted at the *deepest* node of C labelled by $\mu\chi$ (note that this node is unique since bound variables are distinct).

Knowledge of choice [5, 9]. Whenever a global type specifies a choice of two sets of interactions, the decision should be made by exactly one participant. For instance,

$$\mathtt{s}_1 \to \mathtt{r}_1 : a_1\langle \mathtt{e} \rangle \,.\, \mathcal{G}_1 \quad + \quad \mathtt{s}_2 \to \mathtt{r}_2 : a_2\langle \mathtt{e}' \rangle \,.\, \mathcal{G}_2 \quad ✘$$

specifies a choice made by $\mathtt{s}_1$ in the first branch and by $\mathtt{s}_2$ in the second one; this kind of choreographies cannot be implemented (without using hidden interactions). Also, we want to avoid global types where a participant $\mathtt{n}$ behaves differently in choice branches without being aware of the choice made by others. For instance, in

$$\mathtt{s} \to \mathtt{r} : a\langle \mathtt{e} \rangle \,.\, \mathtt{n} \to \mathtt{r} : c\langle \mathtt{e} \rangle \,.\, \mathcal{G}_1 \quad + \quad \mathtt{s} \to \mathtt{r} : b\langle \mathtt{e} \rangle \,.\, \mathtt{n} \to \mathtt{r} : d\langle \mathtt{e} \rangle \,.\, \mathcal{G}_2 \qquad ✘$$

where n ignores the choice of s and behaves differently in each branch. On the other hand, we want global types of the following form to be accepted.

$$\begin{array}{c}\mathtt{s}\to\mathtt{r}:a\langle\mathtt{e}\rangle.\mathtt{n}\to\mathtt{s}:b\langle\mathtt{e}\rangle.\mathtt{s}\to\mathtt{n}:c\langle\mathtt{e}\rangle.\mathtt{n}\to\mathtt{r}:d\langle\mathtt{e}\rangle\\ + \\ \mathtt{s}\to\mathtt{r}:a'\langle\mathtt{e}\rangle.\mathtt{n}\to\mathtt{s}:b\langle\mathtt{e}\rangle.\mathtt{s}\to\mathtt{n}:c'\langle\mathtt{e}\rangle.\mathtt{n}\to\mathtt{r}:d'\langle\mathtt{e}\rangle\end{array} \quad \checkmark$$

Indeed, in this case n behaves differently in each branch, but only *after* "being informed" by s about the chosen branch.

Together with the projection map defined below, rule [WF-+] guarantees that "knowledge of choice" is respected. In particular, the rule requires that the participant who makes the decision is the same in every branch of a choice, while the channels guarding the choice must be distinct.

Definition 3 ($\_\!\restriction\!\_$). *The* projection of a global type $\mathcal{G}$ wrt. $\mathtt{n} \in \mathcal{P}(\mathcal{G})$ *is defined as*

$$\mathcal{G}\restriction_{\mathtt{n}} \stackrel{def}{=} \begin{cases} a?\mathtt{e}.\mathcal{G}'\restriction_{\mathtt{n}}, & \text{if } \mathcal{G} = \mathtt{s}\to\mathtt{n}:a\langle\mathtt{e}\rangle.\mathcal{G}' \\ a!\mathtt{e}.\mathcal{G}'\restriction_{\mathtt{n}}, & \text{if } \mathcal{G} = \mathtt{n}\to\mathtt{r}:a\langle\mathtt{e}\rangle.\mathcal{G}' \\ \mathcal{G}'\restriction_{\mathtt{n}}, & \text{if } \mathcal{G} = \mathtt{s}\to\mathtt{r}:a\langle\mathtt{e}\rangle.\mathcal{G}' \text{ and } \mathtt{s}\neq\mathtt{n}\neq\mathtt{r} \\ \mathcal{G}_1\restriction_{\mathtt{n}} \uplus \mathcal{G}_2\restriction_{\mathtt{n}}, & \text{if } \mathcal{G} = \mathcal{G}_1 + \mathcal{G}_2 \\ \mathcal{G}_i\restriction_{\mathtt{n}}, & \text{if } \mathcal{G} = \mathcal{G}_1 \mid \mathcal{G}_2 \text{ and } \mathtt{n} \notin \mathcal{P}(\mathcal{G}_j), i \neq j \in \{1,2\} \\ \mathcal{G}_1\restriction_{\mathtt{n}} [\mathcal{G}_2\restriction_{\mathtt{n}}/\mathbf{0}], & \text{if } \mathcal{G} = \mathcal{G}_1 ; \mathcal{G}_2 \\ \mu\chi.\mathcal{G}'\restriction_{\mathtt{n}}, & \text{if } \mathcal{G} = \mu\chi.\mathcal{G}' \\ \mathcal{G}, & \text{if } \mathcal{G} = \chi \text{ or } \mathcal{G} = \mathbf{0} \\ \bot, & \text{otherwise} \end{cases}$$

We say that a global type is projectable *if* $\mathcal{G}\restriction_{\mathtt{n}}$ *is defined for all* $\mathtt{n} \in \mathcal{P}(\mathcal{G})$.

The projection map is similar to the one given in [9], but for the generalised sequencing case and the use of $\_\uplus\_$ to project choice branches. Observe that if $\mathcal{G} = \mathcal{G}_1 ; \mathcal{G}_2$, we replace $\mathbf{0}$ by the projection of $\mathcal{G}_2$ in the projection of $\mathcal{G}_1$. Function $\_\uplus\_$ basically merges (if possible) the behaviour of a participant in different choice branches; $\_\uplus\_$ is defined only when the behaviour is the same in all branches, or if it differs after having received enough information about the branch which was chosen. The definition of $\_\uplus\_$ is given in [11]. A global type may be projected even if is not well-formed, but in that case none of the properties given below are guaranteed to hold.

4 Synthesising Global Types

We now introduce a typing systems to synthesise a global type $\mathcal{G}$ from a system S so that S satisfies safety and progress properties (e.g. no race on channels and no participant gets stuck). Also, the set of typable systems corresponds exactly to the set of systems obtained by projecting well-formed global types. To synthesise $\mathcal{G}$ from a system S, a careful analysis of what actions can occur at each possible state of S is necessary.

If $S \equiv \mathtt{n}[P] \mid S'$ then $S(\mathtt{n})$ denotes P (if $S \not\equiv \mathtt{n}[P] \mid S'$ then $S(\mathtt{n}) = \perp$). We define the *ready set* of a system as follows:

$$\mathtt{R}(S) = \begin{cases} \{a_i | i \in I\} \cup \mathtt{R}(S') & \text{if } S \equiv \mathtt{r}[\sum_{i \in I} a_i?\mathtt{e}_i.P_i] \mid S' \\ \{\overline{a_i} | i \in I\} \cup \mathtt{R}(S') & \text{if } S \equiv \mathtt{s}[\bigoplus_{i \in I} a_i!\mathtt{e}_i.P_i] \mid S' \\ \{\overline{a}\} \cup \mathtt{R}(S') & \text{if } S \equiv a : \mathtt{e} \cdot \rho \mid S' \\ \emptyset & \text{if } S \equiv \mathbf{0} \end{cases}$$

We overload $\mathtt{R}(\_)$ on behaviours as expected, and define $\overline{\mathtt{R}}(S) \stackrel{\text{def}}{=} \{a \in \mathbb{C} \,|\, a \in \mathtt{R}(S) \text{ or } \overline{a} \in \mathtt{R}(S)\}$, and $S\updownarrow \iff \exists a \in \mathbb{C} : a \in \mathtt{R}(S) \wedge \overline{a} \in \mathtt{R}(S)$; we write $S\not\updownarrow$ if $S\updownarrow$ does not hold.

4.1 Validation Rules

A judgement of the form $A\,;\Gamma; C \vdash S \blacktriangleright \mathcal{G}$ says that the system S forms a choreography defined by a global type $\mathcal{G}$, under the environments A, Γ, and C. The environment A is a superset of the channel names used in S, and corresponds to the channels that S is entitled to use. The environment Γ maps participant names and local recursion variables to global recursion variables ($\circ$ is the empty context Γ). The channel environment C records the use of channels. Hereafter, we use $\cdot$ for the disjoint union of environments.

Programs. A global type $\mathcal{G}$ can be synthesised from the *program* S if the judgement

$$C(S)\,;\circ\,;\bullet \vdash S \blacktriangleright \mathcal{G}$$

(stating that S is entitled to use all its channels in empty environments) is derivable from the rules in Fig. 2 (driven by the ready set of S and the structure of its processes).

Rule [.] validates prefixes provided that the system is entitled to linearly use the channel a, that the continuation is typable, and that no other interactions are possible in S. For instance, [.] does not apply to

$$\mathtt{s}_1[a!\mathtt{e}.P_1] \mid \mathtt{r}_1[a?\mathtt{e}.Q_1] \mid \mathtt{s}_2[b!\mathtt{e}.P_2] \mid \mathtt{r}_2[b?\mathtt{e}.Q_2] \quad ✘$$

because there is no ordering relation between the actions on a and b; in this case either [|] or [;] should be used. Rule [|] validates concurrent branches when they can be validated using a partition A_1 and A_2 of the channels (recall that $\mathcal{P}(S) \cap \mathcal{P}(S') = \emptyset$). Rule [;] splits the system into two sequential parts and it relies on the function $\mathtt{split}(\_)$ defined in § 4.2; for now it suffices to notice that linearity is checked for in the second part of the split by adding the channel environment corresponding to $\mathcal{G}_1$ to C (recall that $C \prec C'$ is undefined if $C \star C'$ is not linear).

Rule [$\oplus$] introduces the global type choice operator, it requires that both branches are typable and that no other interactions are possible in S. Rule [+] allows to discharge a branch of an external choice; together with the premises of [|], rule [+] discards systems such as the one on the left below (due to a race on b) but permits those like the one on the right (as only the channels guarding the choice must be in A).

$\mathtt{r}_1[a?\mathtt{e}+b?\mathtt{e}] \mid \mathtt{s}_2[b!\mathtt{e}] \mid \mathtt{r}_2[b?\mathtt{e}]$ ✘ $\qquad$ $\mathtt{s}_1[a!\mathtt{e}] \mid \mathtt{r}_1[a?\mathtt{e}+c?\mathtt{e}.b?\mathtt{e}] \mid \mathtt{s}_2[b!\mathtt{e}] \mid \mathtt{r}_2[b?\mathtt{e}]$ ✔

$$[.]\ \frac{\{a\}\cup A;\Gamma;C\prec \mathtt{c}\vdash \mathtt{s}[P]\mid \mathtt{r}[Q]\mid S\blacktriangleright \mathcal{G} \qquad \underline{\mathtt{c}}=\mathtt{s}\to\mathtt{r}:a \qquad S\updownarrow\!\!\!\!/}{\{a\}\cup A;\Gamma;C\vdash \mathtt{s}[a!\mathtt{e}.P]\mid \mathtt{r}[a?\mathtt{e}.Q]\mid S\blacktriangleright \mathtt{s}\to\mathtt{r}:a\langle\mathtt{e}\rangle.\mathcal{G}}$$

$$[\mid]\ \frac{A_1;\circ;C\vdash S\blacktriangleright \mathcal{G} \qquad A_2;\circ;C\vdash S'\blacktriangleright \mathcal{G}' \qquad A_1\cap A_2=\emptyset}{A_1\cup A_2;\Gamma;C\vdash S\mid S'\blacktriangleright \mathcal{G}\mid \mathcal{G}'}$$

$$[;]\ \frac{A;\circ;C\vdash S_1\blacktriangleright \mathcal{G}_1 \qquad \mathtt{split}(S)=(S_1,S_2) \qquad A;\circ;C\prec\mathcal{T}(\mathcal{G}_1)\vdash S_2\blacktriangleright \mathcal{G}_2}{A;\Gamma;C\vdash S\blacktriangleright \mathcal{G}_1;\mathcal{G}_2}$$

$$[\oplus]\ \frac{A;\Gamma;C\vdash \mathtt{s}[P]\mid S\blacktriangleright \mathcal{G} \qquad A;\Gamma;C\vdash \mathtt{s}[Q]\mid S\blacktriangleright \mathcal{G}' \qquad S\updownarrow\!\!\!\!/}{A;\Gamma;C\vdash \mathtt{s}[P\oplus Q]\mid S\blacktriangleright \mathcal{G}+\mathcal{G}'}$$

$$[+]\ \frac{\overline{\mathtt{R}}(Q)\subseteq A \qquad A;\Gamma;C\vdash \mathtt{r}[P]\mid S\blacktriangleright \mathcal{G} \qquad S\updownarrow\!\!\!\!/}{A;\Gamma;C\vdash \mathtt{r}[P+Q]\mid S\blacktriangleright \mathcal{G}}$$

$$[\mu]\ \frac{\begin{array}{c}\exists 1\le i,j\le k.(\mathtt{n_i}[P_i]\mid \mathtt{n_j}[P_j])\updownarrow\\ A;\Gamma\cdot(\mathtt{n}_1,\mathtt{x}_1):\chi,\ldots,(\mathtt{n}_k,\mathtt{x}_k):\chi;C\star\mu\chi\vdash \mathtt{n}_1[P_1]\mid\ldots\mid \mathtt{n_k}[P_k]\blacktriangleright \mathcal{G}\end{array}}{A;\Gamma;C\vdash \mathtt{n}_1[\mu\mathtt{x}_1.P_1]\mid\ldots\mid \mathtt{n_k}[\mu\mathtt{x}_k.P_k]\blacktriangleright \mu\chi.\mathcal{G}}$$

$$[\mathtt{x}]\ \frac{\forall 1\le i\le k.\Gamma(\mathtt{n_i},\mathtt{x}_i)=\chi \quad C\prec C(\mu\chi)}{A;\Gamma;C\vdash \mathtt{n}_1[\mathtt{x}_1]\mid\ldots\mid \mathtt{n_k}[\mathtt{x}_k]\blacktriangleright\chi}$$

$$[eq]\ \frac{S\equiv S' \qquad A;\Gamma;C\vdash S'\blacktriangleright \mathcal{G}}{A;\Gamma;C\vdash S\blacktriangleright \mathcal{G}} \qquad [\mathbf{0}]\ \frac{\forall \mathtt{n}\in\mathcal{P}(S).S(\mathtt{n})=\mathbf{0} \quad C(S)=\emptyset}{A;\Gamma;C\vdash S\blacktriangleright\mathbf{0}}$$

Fig. 2. Validation Rules for Programs

Rules $[\mu]$ and $[\mathtt{x}]$ handle recursive systems. The former rule "guesses" the participants involved in a recursive behaviour. If two of them interact, $[\mu]$ validates the recursion provided that the system can be typed when such participants are associated to the global recursion variable χ (assuming that χ is not in Γ). Rule $[\mathtt{x}]$ checks that all the participants in the recursion have reached a local recursion variable corresponding to the global recursion, and that the unfolding of C on $\mu\chi$ preserves linearity.

Rule $[\mathbf{0}]$ only applies when all the participants in S end, while $[eq]$ validates a system up to structural congruence.

Theorem 1 (Decidability). *Typability is decidable.*

The proofs follows from the fact that the typing is done wrt to the (finite) partitions of channels in a system, and that the number of required behaviour unfoldings is finite.

Theorem 2 (Unique typing). *If $A;\Gamma;C\vdash S\blacktriangleright \mathcal{G}$ and $A;\Gamma;C\vdash S\blacktriangleright \mathcal{G}'$ then $\mathcal{G}\equiv\mathcal{G}'$.*

Theorem 3 (Well-formedness). *If $A;\Gamma;C\vdash S\blacktriangleright \mathcal{G}$ then $\bullet\vdash\mathcal{G}$ and $\mathcal{G}$ is projectable.*

The proofs for these two theorems are by induction on the structure of the derivation.

Runtime systems. To prove subject reduction we have to deal with queues. Hereafter, $*\notin\mathbb{P}$ is a distinguished name to denote an anonymous participant, and $*\to\mathtt{r}:a\langle\mathtt{e}\rangle.\mathcal{G}$ denotes the presence of message of sort $\mathtt{e}$ on channel a for participant $\mathtt{r}$.

Example 3. Let $S = \mathtt{s}[a!\mathsf{e}.b!\mathsf{e}] \mid \mathtt{r}[b?\mathsf{e}.c?\mathsf{e}] \mid \mathtt{n}[a?\mathsf{e}.c!\mathsf{e}] \mid a : [] \mid b : [] \mid c : []$. Consider the judgement

$$A; \Gamma; C \vdash S \blacktriangleright \mathtt{s} \to \mathtt{n}{:}a\langle \mathsf{e} \rangle . \mathtt{s} \to \mathtt{r}{:}b\langle \mathsf{e} \rangle . \mathtt{n} \to \mathtt{r}{:}c\langle \mathsf{e} \rangle$$

If S evolves to $S' = \mathtt{s}[b!\mathsf{e}] \mid \mathtt{r}[b?\mathsf{e}.c?\mathsf{e}] \mid \mathtt{n}[a?\mathsf{e}.c!\mathsf{e}] \mid a : \mathsf{e} \mid b : [] \mid c : []$, the identity of the sender of e on a (i.e. $\mathtt{s}$) is lost. However, the judgement

$$A; \Gamma; C \vdash S' \blacktriangleright (* \to \mathtt{n}{:}a\langle \mathsf{e} \rangle \mid \mathtt{s} \to \mathtt{r}{:}b\langle \mathsf{e} \rangle) ; \mathtt{n} \to \mathtt{r}{:}c\langle \mathsf{e} \rangle$$

types S' using $*$. Observe that general sequencing (;) is now used to type S'. ◇

Runtime systems can be handled by slightly extending Def. 1 so that we have[1]

$$\mathsf{c}_1 \prec_{00} \mathsf{c}_2 \text{ if } \mathsf{c}_1 \prec \mathsf{c}_2 \text{ and } \underline{\mathsf{c}_1} = * \to \mathtt{r}{:}a \text{ and } \underline{\mathsf{c}_2} = \mathtt{s} \to \mathtt{r}{:}a$$

and by adding two rules to the validation rules for handling queues:

$$[\rho]\ \frac{\{a\} \cup A; \circ; C \prec \mathsf{c} \vdash a : \rho \mid \mathtt{r}[P] \mid S \blacktriangleright \mathcal{G} \qquad \underline{\mathsf{c}} = * \to \mathtt{r}{:}a \qquad S \updownarrow\!\!\!/}{\{a\} \cup A; \Gamma; C \vdash a : \mathsf{e} \cdot \rho \mid \mathtt{r}[a?\mathsf{e}.P] \mid S \blacktriangleright * \to \mathtt{r}{:}a\langle \mathsf{e} \rangle . \mathcal{G}} \qquad [[]]\ \frac{A; \Gamma; C \vdash S \blacktriangleright \mathcal{G}}{A; \Gamma; C \vdash a : [] \mid S \blacktriangleright \mathcal{G}}$$

Rule $[\rho]$ is similar to rule $[.]$, except that a non-empty queue replaces the sender, and Γ is emptied. Rule $[[]]$ simply allows to remove empty queues from the system.

Theorem 4. *If* $A; \circ; C \vdash S \blacktriangleright \mathcal{G}$, $S \xrightarrow{\lambda} S'$, *and* $C(\lambda) \notin C$ *then* $A; \circ; C \vdash S' \blacktriangleright \mathcal{G}'$

The proof is by case analysis on the different types of transitions a system can make. The recursive case follows from the fact that reduction preserves closeness of behaviours.

4.2 Splitting Systems

The purpose of systems' splitting is to group participants according to their interactions. For this we use judgements of the form

$$\Psi; \Theta \vdash S \mathrel{\hat{=}} \Omega \tag{4.1}$$

which reads as "S splits as Ω under Ψ and Θ". The environment Ψ is a set of (pairwise disjoint) *ensembles* that is disjoint sets $N \subseteq \mathcal{P}(S)$ containing participants that interact with each other for a while; and then some of them may interact with participants in other ensembles in Ψ. The environment Θ is a set of (pairwise disjoint) *duos*, that is two-element sets of participants $\{\mathtt{s}, \mathtt{r} \in \mathcal{P}(S) : \mathtt{r} \neq \mathtt{s}\}$ representing the first participants able to interact once the first part of the split is finished. Under suitable conditions, one could identify when $\mathtt{n} \in N$ has to interact with a participant of another ensemble. In other words, one can divide $S(\mathtt{n})$ as $P_1 \cdot \varepsilon \cdot P_2$: the interactions in P_1 happen with participants in the ensemble of $\mathtt{n}$, while P_2 starts interacting with a participant in another ensemble. Finally, the environment Ω assigns behaviours augmented with a separator ε to participant names, and lists of sorts to queues a.

Given a judgement as (4.1), we say that $N, M \in \Psi$ are Θ-*linked* ($N \overset{\Theta}{\frown} M$ in symbols) iff $\exists D \in \Theta : N \cap D \cap M \neq \emptyset$; also, we say that $\mathtt{n}, \mathtt{m} \in \mathcal{P}(S)$ are Ω-*linked* ($\mathtt{n} \overset{\Omega}{\frown} \mathtt{m}$ in symbols) iff $C(\Omega(\mathtt{n})) \cap C(\Omega(\mathtt{m})) \neq \emptyset$. We define $S[N] \overset{\text{def}}{=} \prod_{\mathtt{n} \in N} \mathtt{n}[S(\mathtt{n})] \mid \prod_{a \in C(S)} a : S(a)$.

[1] This extension makes sense since the order of messages is preserved in the calculus.

$$[\varepsilon]\ \frac{\mathtt{n} \in N, \mathtt{m} \in M \qquad (\mathtt{n}[P] \mid \mathtt{m}[Q]) \updownarrow \qquad \Psi \cdot N \backslash \{\mathtt{n}\} \cdot M \backslash \{\mathtt{m}\}; \Theta \vdash S \mathrel{\supset\!\subset} \Omega}{\Psi \cdot N \cdot M; \Theta \cdot \{\mathtt{n},\mathtt{m}\} \vdash \mathtt{n}[P] \mid \mathtt{m}[Q] \mid S \mathrel{\supset\!\subset} \Omega \cdot \mathtt{n} : \varepsilon \cdot \mathtt{m} : \varepsilon}$$

$$[sync]\ \frac{\mathtt{s},\mathtt{r} \in N \qquad \Psi \cdot N; \Theta \vdash \mathtt{s}[P] \mid \mathtt{r}[Q] \mid S \mathrel{\supset\!\subset} \Omega \cdot \mathtt{s} : \pi \cdot \mathtt{r} : \varphi}{\Psi \cdot N; \Theta \vdash \mathtt{s}[a!\mathsf{e}.P] \mid \mathtt{r}[a?\mathsf{e}.Q] \mid S \mathrel{\supset\!\subset} \Omega \cdot \mathtt{s} : a!\mathsf{e}.\pi \cdot \mathtt{r} : a?\mathsf{e}.\varphi}$$

$$[+]\ \frac{\mathtt{m},\mathtt{n} \in N \qquad (\mathtt{m}[P] \mid \mathtt{n}[Q]) \updownarrow \qquad \Psi \cdot N; \Theta \vdash \mathtt{m}[P] \mid \mathtt{n}[Q] \mid S \mathrel{\supset\!\subset} \Omega \cdot \mathtt{m} : \pi}{\Psi \cdot N; \Theta \vdash \mathtt{m}[P+P'] \mid \mathtt{n}[Q] \mid S \mathrel{\supset\!\subset} \Omega \cdot \mathtt{m} : \pi}$$

$$[\oplus]\ \frac{\begin{array}{c}\mathtt{n},\mathtt{m} \in N \qquad (\mathtt{n}[P \oplus P'] \mid \mathtt{m}[Q]) \updownarrow \qquad \Omega \asymp \Omega' \\ \Psi \cdot N; \Theta \vdash \mathtt{n}[P] \mid \mathtt{m}[Q] \mid S \mathrel{\supset\!\subset} \Omega \cdot \mathtt{n} : \pi \qquad \Psi \cdot N; \Theta \vdash \mathtt{n}[P'] \mid \mathtt{m}[Q] \mid S \mathrel{\supset\!\subset} \Omega' \cdot \mathtt{n} : \varphi\end{array}}{\Psi \cdot N; \Theta \vdash \mathtt{n}[P \oplus P'] \mid \mathtt{m}[Q] \mid S \mathrel{\supset\!\subset} \Omega \sqcup \Omega' \cdot \mathtt{n} : \pi \oplus \varphi}$$

$$[ax]\ \frac{}{\{\emptyset\}; \emptyset \vdash \mathbf{0} \mathrel{\supset\!\subset} \emptyset} \qquad [0]\ \frac{\Psi \backslash \mathtt{n}; \Theta \vdash S \mathrel{\supset\!\subset} \Omega}{\Psi; \Theta \vdash \mathtt{n}[\mathbf{0}] \mid S \mathrel{\supset\!\subset} \Omega \cdot \mathtt{n} : \mathbf{0}}$$

$$[rem]\ \frac{(\mathtt{n}[P] \mid S) \not\updownarrow \qquad P \not\equiv \mathbf{0} \qquad \Psi \backslash \mathtt{n}; \Theta \vdash S \mathrel{\supset\!\subset} \Omega}{\Psi; \Theta \vdash \mathtt{n}[P] \mid S \mathrel{\supset\!\subset} \Omega \cdot \mathtt{n} : \varepsilon}$$

$$[q]\ \frac{\mathtt{r} \in N \qquad \Psi \cdot N; \Theta \vdash \mathtt{r}[P] \mid S \mathrel{\supset\!\subset} \Omega \cdot \mathtt{r} : \pi \cdot \mathtt{a} : \rho}{\Psi \cdot N; \Theta \vdash \mathtt{r}[a?\mathsf{e}.P] \mid a : \mathsf{e} \cdot \rho \mid S \mathrel{\supset\!\subset} \Omega \cdot \mathtt{r} : a?\mathsf{e}.\pi \cdot \mathtt{a} : \mathsf{e} \cdot \rho}$$

Fig. 3. Splitting Systems

Definition 4. *The judgement* $\Psi; \Theta \vdash S \mathrel{\supset\!\subset} \Omega$ *is* coherent *if it can be derived from the rules in Fig. 3,* $\Theta \neq \emptyset$*, and for all* $N \in \Psi$*,* $S[N] \updownarrow$ *and the following conditions hold*

$$\exists! \mathtt{n} \in N : \left((\exists! \mathtt{m} \in N \setminus \{\mathtt{n}\} : S[N \setminus \{\mathtt{n}\}] \not\updownarrow \wedge S[N \setminus \{\mathtt{m}\}] \not\updownarrow) \text{ or } (S[N \setminus \{\mathtt{n}\}] \not\updownarrow) \right) \tag{4.2}$$

$$\circledast \text{ is total on } N \text{ and } \leftrightarrow_\Theta \text{ is total on } \Psi \tag{4.3}$$

where $\leftrightarrow_\Theta \overset{def}{=} \overset{\Theta}{\frown}{}^*$ *is the reflexive and transitive closure of* $\overset{\Theta}{\frown}$ *and* $\circledast \overset{def}{=} \overset{\Omega}{\frown}{}^+$ *is the transitive closure of* $\overset{\Omega}{\frown}$.

Essentially, Def. 4 ensures that rule [;] is the only rule of Fig. 2 applicable when the system can be split. Condition (4.2) ensures that, in each ensemble N, there is a unique pair of synchronising participants or there is a unique participant that can synchronise with a queue a. Condition (4.3) is the local counterpart of the well-formedness rule for global types of the form $\mathcal{G}; \mathcal{G}'$. The totality of $\circledast$ on N guarantees that the participants in an ensemble share channels. The totality of $\leftrightarrow_\Theta$ on Ψ guarantees that each ensemble in Ψ has one "representative" which is one of the first participants to interact in the second part of the split. Together with condition $\Theta \neq \emptyset$, the condition on $\leftrightarrow_\Theta$ ensures that there are (at least) two ensembles of participants in Ψ. Note that (4.3) also ensures that all the set of participants in Ψ are interdependent (i.e. one cannot divide them into independent systems, in which case rule [|] should be used).

A judgement (4.1) is to be derived with the rules of Fig.3 (we omit rules for commutativity and associativity of systems). The derivation is driven by the structure of up to two processes in S, and whether they are in the same ensemble and/or form a duo.

Rule $[\varepsilon]$ marks two processes $\mathtt{m}$ and $\mathtt{n}$ as "to be split" when $\mathtt{m}$ and $\mathtt{n}$ form a duo in Θ and are in different ensembles of Ψ. The continuation of the system is to be split as well, with $\mathtt{m}$ and $\mathtt{n}$ removed from the system and from the environments. Rule $[sync]$ records in Ω the interactions of participants in a same ensemble of Ψ. Rule $[+]$ discharges the branch of an external choice for participants in a same ensemble while $[\oplus]$ deals with internal choice. The premise $\Omega \asymp \Omega'$ holds only when Ω and Ω' have the same domain and differ only up to external choice, i.e. for each $\mathtt{n}$ either its split is the same in both branches, or its split is an external choice (guarded by different channels); $\Omega \sqcup \Omega'$ merges Ω and Ω' accordingly (cf. [11]). The additional premise $\mathtt{s}[P \oplus P'] \mid \mathtt{r}[Q] \updownarrow$ is required so that the split is done *before* a branching if a participant cannot interact with one of its peer in N after the branching. Rule $[ax]$ terminates a derivation (all environments emptied) while $[\mathbf{0}]$ completes the split of a process (abusing notation, $\Psi \setminus \mathtt{n}$ denotes the removal of $\mathtt{n}$ from any $N \in \Psi$). Rule $[rem]$ marks a process to be split when it cannot interact with anyone in S. The premise $P \not\equiv \mathbf{0}$ allows to differentiate a process which terminates after the split, from others which terminate before. In the latter case, rule $[\mathbf{0}]$ is to be used. Rule $[q]$ records in Ω interactions with non-empty queues.

We now define a (partial) function $\mathtt{split}$ which splits a system into two parts.

Definition 5 ($\mathtt{split}(\_)$). *Let $\Psi;\Theta \vdash S \,\hat{\approx}\, \Omega$ be a coherent judgement. Define* $\mathtt{split}(S) = (S_1, S_2)$ *where*

- $\forall \mathtt{n} \in \mathcal{P}(S).\, S_1(\mathtt{n}) = S(\mathtt{n}) - \Omega(\mathtt{n})$ *and* $S_2(\mathtt{n}) = S(\mathtt{n}) \,\%\, \Omega(\mathtt{n})$
- $\forall a \in C(S).\, S_1(a) = \Omega(a)$ *and* $S_2(a) = S(a) \setminus \Omega(a)$

if $S(\mathtt{n}) \,\%\, \Omega(\mathtt{n}) \neq \bot$ *for all* $\mathtt{n} \in \mathcal{P}(S)$, *and* $\mathtt{split}(S) = \bot$ *otherwise.*

The auxiliary functions $\_ - \_$ and $\_ \% \_$ used in Def. 5 are defined in [11]; we give here their intuitive description. Let $\mathtt{n} \in \mathcal{P}(S)$, and $\Psi;\Theta \vdash S \,\hat{\approx}\, \Omega$ be a coherent judgement. Function $S(\mathtt{n}) - \Omega(\mathtt{n})$ returns the "first part" of the split of $\mathtt{n}$, that is the longest common prefix of $S(\mathtt{n})$ and $\Omega(\mathtt{n})$, while $S(\mathtt{n}) \,\%\, \Omega(\mathtt{n})$ is partial and returns the remaining part of the behaviour of $S(\mathtt{n})$ after $\Omega(\mathtt{n})$.

Example 4. Taking S_{BS} as in § 1, we have $\mathtt{split}(S_{\text{BS}}) = (S_1, S_2)$ so that

$$S_1(\mathtt{b}_1) = t_1!\mathtt{order}.p_1?\mathtt{price} \qquad S_2(\mathtt{b}_1) = r?\mathtt{price}.(c_1!.t_1!\mathtt{addr} \oplus c_2!.no_1!)$$
$$S_1(\mathtt{s}_i) = t_i?\mathtt{order}.p_i!\mathtt{price} \qquad S_2(\mathtt{s}_i) = t_i?\mathtt{addr} + no_i?$$

Note that $\{\{\mathtt{b}_1, \mathtt{s}_1\}, \{\mathtt{b}_2, \mathtt{s}_2\}\}; \{\{\mathtt{b}_1, \mathtt{b}_2\}\} \vdash S_{\text{BS}} \,\hat{\approx}\, \Omega$ is coherent. ◇

4.3 Properties of Synthesised Global Type

Progress and safety. If a system is typable, then it will either terminate or be able to make further transitions (e.g. if there are recursive processes).

Theorem 5. *If $A;\circ;C \vdash S \blacktriangleright G$ then $S \longrightarrow S'$, or $\forall \mathtt{n} \in \mathcal{P}(S).\, S(\mathtt{n}) = \mathbf{0}$ and all queues in S are empty.*

Let us add the rule [ERROR] below to the semantics given in § 2.

$$[\text{ERROR}]\ \frac{S \xrightarrow{a?\mathsf{e}'} S' \qquad T \xrightarrow{\mathsf{e}\cdot a} T'}{S \mid T \longrightarrow \mathtt{error}} \qquad \mathsf{e} \neq \mathsf{e}'$$

Theorem 6. *If* $A ; \circ ; C \vdash S \blacktriangleright \mathcal{G}$*, then* S *is race free and* $S \Longrightarrow\longrightarrow \mathtt{error}$ *is not possible.*

The proofs of Theorems 5 and 6 are by contradiction, using Theorem 4.

Behavioural equivalences. We show that there is a correspondence between the original system and the projections of its global type. First, let us introduce two relations.

Definition 6 ($\lesssim$ **and** $\approx$)**.** $P \lesssim Q$ *if and only if* $Q \xrightarrow{\alpha} Q'$ *implies* $P \xrightarrow{\alpha} P'$ *for some* $P' \lesssim Q'$*. Also,* $S \approx T$ *iff whenever* $S \xrightarrow{\lambda} S'$ *then* $T \xrightarrow{\lambda} T'$ *and* $S' \approx T'$*; and whenever* $T \xrightarrow{\lambda} T'$ *then* $S \xrightarrow{\lambda} S'$ *and* $S' \approx T'$ *where* $\lambda \in \{\mathtt{n} : a!\mathtt{e}, \mathtt{n} : a?\mathtt{e}\}$*.*

The behaviour of a participant in S is a simulation of the projection of a synthesised global type from S onto this participant. Intuitively, the other direction is lost due to rule [+], indeed external choice branches which are never chosen are not "recorded" in the synthesised global type.

Lemma 1. *If* $A ; \circ ; C \vdash S \blacktriangleright \mathcal{G}$ *then* $\forall \mathtt{n} \in \mathcal{P}(S) \,.\, \mathcal{G}\lfloor_{\mathtt{n}} \lesssim S(\mathtt{n})$.

The proof is by case analysis on the transitions of S, using Theorem 4.

Since the branches that are not recorded in a synthesised global type are only those which are never chosen, we have the following result.

Theorem 7. *If* $A ; \circ ; C \vdash S \blacktriangleright \mathcal{G}$ *then* $\prod_{\mathtt{n} \in \mathcal{P}(S)} \mathtt{n}[\mathcal{G}\lfloor_{\mathtt{n}}] \approx S$*.*

The proof is by case analysis on the transitions of S, using Theorem 4 and Lemma 1.

Our completeness result shows that every well-formed and projectable global type is inhabited by the system consisting of the parallel composition of all its projections.

Theorem 8. *If* $\bullet \vdash \mathcal{G}$ *and* $\mathcal{G}$ *is projectable, then there is* $\mathcal{G}' \equiv \mathcal{G}$ *such that* $A ; \Gamma ; C \vdash \prod_{\mathtt{n} \in \mathcal{P}(\mathcal{G})} \mathtt{n}[\mathcal{G}\lfloor_{\mathtt{n}}] \blacktriangleright \mathcal{G}'$*.*

The proof is by induction on the structure of (well-formed) $\mathcal{G}$.

5 Concluding Remarks

We presented a typing systems to synthesise a choreography (i.e. a global type) from a set of end-point types (i.e. local types). Such a global type is unique, well-formed, and its projections are equivalent to the original local types. We have shown safety and progress properties for the local session types which also enjoy a subject reduction theorem.

In [12] *local and global graphs* are used to construct choreographies. A global graph is a disjoint union of local graphs, which resemble local types. We contend that global types are more suitable than global graphs to represent choreographies; in fact, differently from the approach in [12], our work allows us to reuse most of the theories and techniques based on multiparty global types.

Our work lies on the boundary between theories based on *global types* (e.g. [1,5,7,9]) and the ones based on the *conversation types* [3]. Our work relies on global types, but uses it the other way around. We start from local types and construct a global type. We have discussed the key elements of the global types in § 3. Conversation types [3] abandon global views of distributed interactions in favour of a more flexible type structure allowing participants to dynamically join and leave sessions. The approach in [6] fills the gap between the theories based on session types and those based on behavioural contracts [4]. We are also inspired from [13], where session types are viewed as CCS-like "projections" of process behaviours. The *connectedness* conditions for a choreography given in [2] is similar to our notion of *well-formed* global type.

We aim to extend our framework to session delegation and to expand our theory to indicate designers the reasons why a choreography cannot be synthesised so to improve specifications. We will study a more precise comparison between our work and the different theories cited above, in particular with [2] and [3]. Finally, we are considering implementing an algorithm from the rules of Fig. 2 and Fig. 3, and integrate it in an existing tool [10] implementing the framework from [1].

Acknowledgements. We thank the anonymous reviewers for their valuable comments.

References

1. Bocchi, L., Honda, K., Tuosto, E., Yoshida, N.: A Theory of Design-by-Contract for Distributed Multiparty Interactions. In: Gastin, P., Laroussinie, F. (eds.) CONCUR 2010. LNCS, vol. 6269, pp. 162–176. Springer, Heidelberg (2010)
2. Bravetti, M., Lanese, I., Zavattaro, G.: Contract-Driven Implementation of Choreographies. In: Kaklamanis, C., Nielson, F. (eds.) TGC 2008. LNCS, vol. 5474, pp. 1–18. Springer, Heidelberg (2009)
3. Caires, L., Vieira, H.T.: Conversation Types. In: Castagna, G. (ed.) ESOP 2009. LNCS, vol. 5502, pp. 285–300. Springer, Heidelberg (2009)
4. Carpineti, S., Castagna, G., Laneve, C., Padovani, L.: A Formal Account of Contracts for Web Services. In: Bravetti, M., Núñez, M., Zavattaro, G. (eds.) WS-FM 2006. LNCS, vol. 4184, pp. 148–162. Springer, Heidelberg (2006)
5. Castagna, G., Dezani-Ciancaglini, M., Padovani, L.: On Global Types and Multi-party Sessions. In: Bruni, R., Dingel, J. (eds.) FMOODS/FORTE 2011. LNCS, vol. 6722, pp. 1–28. Springer, Heidelberg (2011)
6. Castagna, G., Padovani, L.: Contracts for Mobile Processes. In: Bravetti, M., Zavattaro, G. (eds.) CONCUR 2009. LNCS, vol. 5710, pp. 211–228. Springer, Heidelberg (2009)
7. Deniélou, P.-M., Yoshida, N.: Dynamic multirole session types. In: POPL (2011)
8. Honda, K., Vasconcelos, V.T., Kubo, M.: Language Primitives and Type Discipline for Structured Communication-Based Programming. In: Hankin, C. (ed.) ESOP 1998. LNCS, vol. 1381, pp. 122–138. Springer, Heidelberg (1998)
9. Honda, K., Yoshida, N., Carbone, M.: Multiparty asynchronous session types. In: POPL (2008)
10. Lange, J., Tuosto, E.: A modular toolkit for distributed interactions. In: PLACES (2010)
11. Lange, J., Tuosto, E.: Synthesising choreographies from local session types (extended version). CoRR, abs/1204.2566 (2012)
12. Mostrous, D., Yoshida, N., Honda, K.: Global Principal Typing in Partially Commutative Asynchronous Sessions. In: Castagna, G. (ed.) ESOP 2009. LNCS, vol. 5502, pp. 316–332. Springer, Heidelberg (2009)
13. Padovani, L.: On projecting processes into session types. MSCS 22, 237–289 (2012)

A Theory of History Dependent Abstractions for Learning Interface Automata*

Fides Aarts, Faranak Heidarian**, and Frits Vaandrager

Institute for Computing and Information Sciences, Radboud University Nijmegen
P.O. Box 9010, 6500 GL Nijmegen, The Netherlands

Abstract. History dependent abstraction operators are the key for scaling existing methods for active learning of automata to realistic applications. Recently, Aarts, Jonsson & Uijen have proposed a framework for history dependent abstraction operators. Using this framework they succeeded to automatically infer models of several realistic software components with large state spaces, including fragments of the TCP and SIP protocols. Despite this success, the approach of Aarts et al. suffers from limitations that seriously hinder its applicability in practice. In this article, we get rid of some of these limitations and present four important generalizations/improvements of the theory of history dependent abstraction operators. Our abstraction framework supports: (a) interface automata instead of the more restricted Mealy machines, (b) the concept of a learning purpose, which allows one to restrict the learning process to relevant behaviors only, (c) a richer class of abstractions, which includes abstractions that overapproximate the behavior of the system-under-test, and (d) a conceptually superior approach for testing correctness of the hypotheses that are generated by the learner.

1 Introduction

Within process algebra [10], the most prominent abstraction operator is the τ_I operator from ACP, which renames actions from a set I into the internal action τ. In order to establish that an implementation *Imp* satisfies a specification *Spec*, one typically proves $\tau_I(\mathit{Imp}) \approx \mathit{Spec}$, where $\approx$ is some behavioral equivalence or preorder that treats τ as invisible. In state based models of concurrency, such as TLA+ [22], the corresponding abstraction operator is existential quantification, which hides certain state variables. Both τ_I and $\exists$ abstract in a way that does not depend on the history of the computation. In practice, however, we frequently describe and reason about reactive systems in terms of history dependent abstractions. For instance, most of us have dealt with the following protocol: "If you forgot your password, enter your email and user name in the form below. You will then receive a new, temporary password. Use this temporary password

* Supported by STW project 11763 ITALIA. For a full version with all the proofs we refer to `http://www.mbsd.cs.ru.nl/publications/papers/fvaan/AHV12/`

** Supported by NWO/EW project 612.064.610 ARTS.

M. Koutny and I. Ulidowski (Eds.): CONCUR 2012, LNCS 7454, pp. 240–255, 2012.

to login and immediately select a new password." Here, essentially, the huge name spaces for user names and passwords are abstracted into small sets with abstract values such as "temporary password" and "new password". The choice which concrete password is mapped to which abstract value depends on the history, and may change whenever the user selects a new password.

History dependent abstractions turn out to be the key for scaling methods for active learning of automata to realistic applications. During the last two decades, important developments have taken place in the area of automata learning, see e.g. [6, 9, 17, 18, 23, 27, 30, 31]. Tools that are able to learn automata models automatically, by systematically "pushing buttons" and recording outputs, have numerous applications in different domains. For instance, they support understanding and analyzing legacy software, regression testing of software components [20], protocol conformance testing based on reference implementations, reverse engineering of proprietary/classified protocols, fuzz testing of protocol implementations [12], and inference of botnet protocols [11]. State-of-the-art methods for learning automata such as LearnLib [18, 27, 30], the winner of the 2010 Zulu competition on regular inference, are currently able to only learn automata with at most in the order of 10,000 states. Hence, powerful abstraction techniques are needed to apply these methods to practical systems. Dawn Song et al. [11], for instance, succeeded to infer models of realistic botnet command and control protocols by placing an emulator between botnet servers and the learning software, which concretizes the alphabet symbols into valid network messages (for instance, by adding sequence numbers) and sends them to botnet servers. When responses are received, the emulator does the opposite — it abstracts the response messages into the output alphabet and passes them on to the learning software. The idea of an intermediate component that takes care of abstraction and concretization is very natural and is used, implicitly or explicitly, in many case studies on automata learning and model-based testing.

History dependent abstractions can be described formally using the state operator known from process algebra [8], but this operator has been mostly used to model state bearing processes, rather than as an abstraction device. Implicitly, history dependent abstractions play an important role in the work of Pistore et al. [16, 29]: whereas the standard automata-like models for name-passing process calculi are infinite-state and infinite-branching, they provide models using the notion of a history dependent automaton which, for a wide class of processes (e.g. finitary π-calculus agents), are finite-state and may be explored using model checking techniques. Aarts, Jonsson and Uijen [2] formalized the concept of history dependent abstractions within the context of automata learning. Inspired by ideas from predicate abstraction [24] and abstract interpretation [13], they defined the notion of a *mapper* $\mathcal{A}$, which is placed in between the teacher or system-under-test (SUT), described by a Mealy machine $\mathcal{M}$, and the learner. The mapper transforms the concrete actions of $\mathcal{M}$ (in a history dependent manner) into a small set of abstract actions. Each mapper $\mathcal{A}$ induces an abstraction operator $\alpha_{\mathcal{A}}$ that transforms a Mealy machine over the concrete signature into a Mealy machine over the abstract signature. A teacher for $\mathcal{M}$ and a mapper

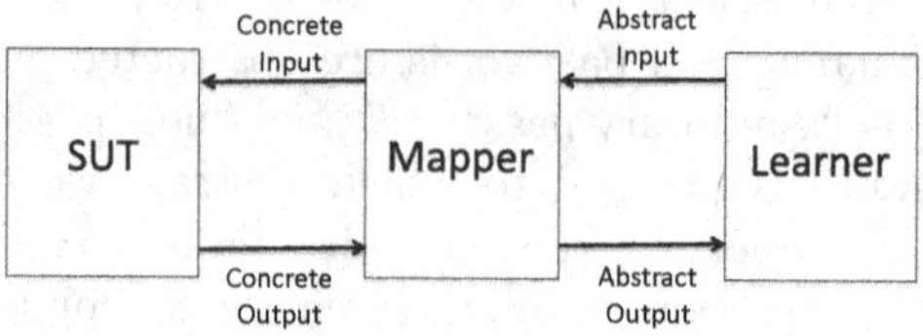

Fig. 1. Active learning with an abstraction mapping

for $\mathcal{A}$ together behave like a teacher for $\alpha_{\mathcal{A}}(\mathcal{M})$. Hence, by interacting with the mapper component, the learner may learn an abstract Mealy machine $\mathcal{H}$ that is equivalent ($\approx$) to $\alpha_{\mathcal{A}}(\mathcal{M})$. Mapper $\mathcal{A}$ also induces a concretization operator $\gamma_{\mathcal{A}}$. The main technical result of [2] is that, under some strong assumptions, $\alpha_{\mathcal{A}}(\mathcal{M}) \approx \mathcal{H}$ implies $\mathcal{M} \approx \gamma_{\mathcal{A}}(\mathcal{H})$. Aarts et al. [2] demonstrated the feasibility of their approach by learning models of fragments of realistic protocols such as SIP and TCP [2], and the new biometric passport [3]. The learned SIP model, for instance, is an extended finite state machine with 29 states, 3741 transitions, and 17 state variables with various types (booleans, enumerated types, (long) integers, character strings,..). This corresponds to a state machine with an astronomical number of states and transitions, thus far fully out of reach of automata learning techniques.

Despite its success, we observed that the theory of [2] has several limitations that seriously hinder its applicability in practice. In this article, we overcome some of these limitations by presenting four important improvements to the theory of history dependent abstraction operators.

From Mealy machines to interface automata. The approach of [2] is based on Mealy machines, in which each input induces exactly one output. In practice, however, inputs and outputs often do not alternate: a single input may sometimes be followed by a series of outputs, sometimes by no output at all, etc. For this reason, our approach is based on interface automata [15], which have separate input and output transitions, rather than the more restricted Mealy machines.

In a (deterministic) Mealy machine, each sequence of input actions uniquely determines a corresponding sequence of output actions. This means that the login protocol that we described above cannot be modeled in terms of a Mealy machine, since a single input (a request for a temporary password) may lead to many possible outputs (one for each possible password). Our theory applies to interface automata that are determinate in the sense of Milner [28]. In a determinate interface automaton multiple output actions may be enabled in a single state, which makes it straightforward to model the login protocol. In order to learn the resulting model, it is crucial to define an abstraction that merges all outputs that are enabled in a given state to a single abstract output.

Learning purposes. In practice, it is often neither feasible nor necessary to learn a model for the complete behavior of the SUT. Typically, it is better to concentrate the learning efforts on certain parts of the state space. This can be achieved using the concept of a *learning purpose* [4] (known as *test purpose* within model-based testing theory [21, 32, 36]), which allows one to restrict the learning process to relevant interaction patterns only. In our theory, we integrate the concept of a mapper component of [2] with the concept of a learning purpose of [4]. This integration constitutes one of the main technical contributions of this article.

Forgetful abstractions. The main result of [2] only applies to abstractions that are output predicting. This means that no information gets lost and the inferred model is behaviorally equivalent to the model of the teacher: $\mathcal{M} \approx \gamma_{\mathcal{A}}(\mathcal{H})$. In order to deal with the complexity of real systems, we need to support also forgetful abstractions that *overapproximate* the behavior of the teacher. For this reason, we replace the notion of equivalence $\approx$ by the **ioco** relation, which is one of the main notions of conformance in model-based black-box testing [33, 34] and closely related to the alternating simulations of [5].

Handling equivalence queries. Active learning algorithms in the style of Angluin [6] alternate two phases. In the first phase an hypothesis is constructed and in the second phase, called an *equivalence query* by Angluin [6], the correctness of this hypothesis is checked. In general, no guarantees can be given that the answer to an equivalence query is correct. Tools such as LearnLib, "approximate" equivalence queries via long test sequences, which are computed using some established algorithms for model-based testing of Mealy machines. In the approach of [2], one needs to answer equivalence queries of the form $\alpha_{\mathcal{A}}(\mathcal{M}) \approx \mathcal{H}$. In order to do this, a long test sequence for $\mathcal{H}$ that is computed by the learner is concretized by the mapper. The resulting output of the SUT is abstracted again by the mapper and sent back to the learner. Only if the resulting output agrees with the output of $\mathcal{H}$ the hypothesis is accepted. This means that the outcome of an equivalence query depends on the choices of the mapper. If, for instance, the mapper always picks the same concrete action for a given abstract action and a given history, then it may occur that the test sequence does not reveal any problem, even though $\alpha_{\mathcal{A}}(\mathcal{M}) \not\approx \mathcal{H}$. Hence the task of generating a good test sequence is divided between the learner and the mapper, with an unclear division of responsibilities. This makes it extremely difficult to establish good coverage measures for equivalence queries. A more sensible approach, which we elaborate in this article, is to test whether the concretization $\gamma_{\mathcal{A}}(\mathcal{H})$ is equivalent to $\mathcal{M}$, using state-of-the-art model based testing algorithms and tools for systems with data, and to translate the outcomes of that experiment back to the abstract setting.

We believe that the theoretical advances that we describe in this article will be vital for bringing automata learning tools and techniques to a level where they can be used routinely in industrial practice.

2 Preliminaries

2.1 Interface Automata

We model reactive systems by a simplified notion of *interface automata* [15], essentially labeled transition systems with input and output actions.

Definition 1 (IA). *An* interface automaton (IA) *is a tuple* $\mathcal{I} = \langle I, O, Q, q^0, \rightarrow \rangle$ *where I and O are disjoint sets of input and output actions, respectively, Q is a set of states, $q^0 \in Q$ is the initial state, and* $\rightarrow \subseteq Q \times (I \cup O) \times Q$ *is the transition relation.*

We write $q \xrightarrow{a} q'$ if $(q, a, q') \in \rightarrow$. An action a is *enabled* in state q, denoted $q \xrightarrow{a}$, if $q \xrightarrow{a} q'$ for some state q'. We extend the transition relation to sequences by defining, for $\sigma \in (I \cup O)^*$, $\xrightarrow{\sigma}_*$ to be the least relation that satisfies, for $q, q', q'' \in Q$ and $a \in I \cup O$, $q \xrightarrow{\epsilon}_* q$, and if $q \xrightarrow{\sigma}_* q'$ and $q' \xrightarrow{a} q''$ then $q \xrightarrow{\sigma a}_* q''$. Here we use ϵ to denote the empty sequence. We say that state q is *reachable* if $q^0 \xrightarrow{\sigma}_* q$, for some σ. We write $q \xrightarrow{\sigma}_*$ if $q \xrightarrow{\sigma}_* q'$, for some q'. We say that $\sigma \in (I \cup O)^*$ is a *trace* of $\mathcal{I}$ if $q^0 \xrightarrow{\sigma}_*$, and write $Traces(\mathcal{I})$ for the set of traces of $\mathcal{I}$.

A *bisimulation* on $\mathcal{I}$ is a symmetric relation $R \subseteq Q \times Q$ s.t. $(q^0, q^0) \in R$ and

$$(q_1, q_2) \in R \wedge q_1 \xrightarrow{a} q_1' \Rightarrow \exists q_2' : q_2 \xrightarrow{a} q_2' \wedge (q_1', q_2') \in R.$$

We say that two states $q, q' \in Q$ are *bisimilar*, denoted $q \sim q'$, if there exists a bisimulation on $\mathcal{I}$ that contains (q, q'). Recall that relation $\sim$ is the largest bisimulation and that $\sim$ is an equivalence relation [28].

Interface automaton $\mathcal{I}$ is said to be:

- *deterministic* if for each state $q \in Q$ and for each action $a \in I \cup O$, whenever $q \xrightarrow{a} q'$ and $q \xrightarrow{a} q''$ then $q' = q''$.
- *determinate* [28] if for each reachable state $q \in Q$ and for each action $a \in I \cup O$, whenever $q \xrightarrow{a} q'$ and $q \xrightarrow{a} q''$ then $q' \sim q''$.
- *output-determined* if for each reachable state $q \in Q$ and for all output actions $o, o' \in O$, whenever $q \xrightarrow{o}$ and $q \xrightarrow{o'}$ then $o = o'$.
- *behavior-deterministic* if $\mathcal{I}$ is both determinate and output-determined.
- *active* if each reachable state enables an output action.
- *output-enabled* if each state enables each output action.
- *input-enabled* if each state enables each input action.

An *I/O automaton (IOA)* is an input-enabled IA. Our notion of an I/O automaton is a simplified version of the notion of IOA of Lynch & Tuttle [25] in which the set of internal actions is empty, the set of initial states has only one member, and the task partition has only one equivalence class.

2.2 The ioco Relation

A state q of $\mathcal{I}$ is *quiescent* if it enables no output actions. Let δ be a special action symbol. In this article, we only consider IAs $\mathcal{I}$ in which δ is not an input action. The *δ-extension* of $\mathcal{I}$, denoted $\mathcal{I}^\delta$, is the IA obtained by adding δ to the set of output actions, and δ-loops to all the quiescent states of $\mathcal{I}$. Write $O^\delta = O \cup \{\delta\}$. Write $out_{\mathcal{I}}(q)$, or just $out(q)$ if $\mathcal{I}$ is clear from the context, for $\{a \in O \mid q \xrightarrow{a}\}$, the set of output actions enabled in state q. For $S \subseteq Q$ a set of states, write

$out_{\mathcal{I}}(S)$ for $\bigcup\{out_{\mathcal{I}}(q) \mid q \in S\}$. Write $\mathcal{I}$ **after** σ for the set $\{q \in Q \mid q^0 \xrightarrow{\sigma}_* q\}$ of states of $\mathcal{I}$ that can be reached via trace σ. Let $\mathcal{I}_1 = \langle I_1, O_1, Q_1, q_1^0, \rightarrow_1\rangle$, $\mathcal{I}_2 = \langle I_2, O_2, Q_2, q_2^0, \rightarrow_2\rangle$ be IAs with $I_1 = I_2$ and $O_1^\delta = O_2^\delta$. Then $\mathcal{I}_1$ and $\mathcal{I}_2$ are *input-output conforming*, denoted $\mathcal{I}_1$ **ioco** $\mathcal{I}_2$, if

$$\forall \sigma \in \mathit{Traces}(\mathcal{I}_2^\delta) : out(\mathcal{I}_1^\delta \textbf{ after } \sigma) \subseteq out(\mathcal{I}_2^\delta \textbf{ after } \sigma).$$

Informally, an implementation $\mathcal{I}_1$ is **ioco**-conforming to specification $\mathcal{I}_2$ if any experiment derived from $\mathcal{I}_2$ and executed on $\mathcal{I}_1$ leads to an output from $\mathcal{I}_1$ that is allowed by $\mathcal{I}_2$. The **ioco** relation is one of the main notions of conformance in model-based black-box testing [33, 34].

2.3 XY-Simulations

In the technical development of this paper, a major role is played by the notion of an XY-simulation. Below we recall the definition of XY-simulation, as introduced in [4].

Let $\mathcal{I}_1 = \langle I, O, Q_1, q_1^0, \rightarrow_1\rangle$ and $\mathcal{I}_2 = \langle I, O, Q_2, q_2^0, \rightarrow_2\rangle$ be IAs with the same sets of input and output actions. Write $A = I \cup O$ and let $X, Y \subseteq A$. An *XY-simulation* from $\mathcal{I}_1$ to $\mathcal{I}_2$ is a binary relation $R \subseteq Q_1 \times Q_2$ that satisfies, for all $(q, r) \in R$ and $a \in A$,

- if $q \xrightarrow{a} q'$ and $a \in X$ then there exists a $r' \in Q_2$ s.t. $r \xrightarrow{a} r'$ and $(q', r') \in R$, and
- if $r \xrightarrow{a} r'$ and $a \in Y$ then there exists a $q' \in Q_1$ s.t. $q \xrightarrow{a} q'$ and $(q', r') \in R$.

We write $\mathcal{I}_1 \sim_{XY} \mathcal{I}_2$ if there exists an XY-simulation from $\mathcal{I}_1$ to $\mathcal{I}_2$ that contains (q_1^0, q_2^0). Since the union of XY-simulations is an XY-simulation, $\mathcal{I}_1 \sim_{XY} \mathcal{I}_2$ implies that there exists a unique maximal XY-simulation from $\mathcal{I}_1$ to $\mathcal{I}_2$. The notion of XY-simulation offers a natural generalization of several fundamental concepts from concurrency theory: AA-simulations are just *bisimulations* [28], $A\emptyset$-simulations are *(forward) simulations* [26], OI-simulations are *alternating simulations* [5], and, for $B \subseteq A$, AB-simulations are *partial bisimulations* [7]. We write $\mathcal{I}_1 \sim \mathcal{I}_2$ instead of $\mathcal{I}_1 \sim_{AA} \mathcal{I}_2$.

2.4 Relating Alternating Simulations and ioco

The results below link alternating simulation and the **ioco** relation. Variations of these results occur in [4, 35].

Definition 2 ($\lesssim$ **and** $\lessapprox$)**.** *Let $\mathcal{I}_1$ and $\mathcal{I}_2$ be IAs with inputs I and outputs O, and let $A = I \cup O$ and $A^\delta = A \cup \{\delta\}$. Then $\mathcal{I}_1 \lesssim \mathcal{I}_2 \Leftrightarrow \mathcal{I}_1^\delta \sim_{O^\delta I} \mathcal{I}_2^\delta$ and $\mathcal{I}_1 \lessapprox \mathcal{I}_2 \Leftrightarrow \mathcal{I}_1^\delta \sim_{A^\delta I} \mathcal{I}_2^\delta$.*

In general, $\mathcal{I}_1 \lesssim \mathcal{I}_2$ implies $\mathcal{I}_1 \sim_{OI} \mathcal{I}_2$, but the converse implication does not hold. Similarly, $\mathcal{I}_1 \lessapprox \mathcal{I}_2$ implies $\mathcal{I}_1 \sim_{AI} \mathcal{I}_2$, but not vice versa.

Lemma 1. *Let $\mathcal{I}_1$ and $\mathcal{I}_2$ be determinate IAs. Then $\mathcal{I}_1 \lesssim \mathcal{I}_2$ implies $\mathcal{I}_1$* **ioco** *$\mathcal{I}_2$.*

Lemma 2. *Let $\mathcal{I}_1$ be an IOA and let $\mathcal{I}_2$ be a determinate IA. Then $\mathcal{I}_1$* **ioco** *$\mathcal{I}_2$ implies $\mathcal{I}_1 \lesssim \mathcal{I}_2$.*

3 Basic Framework for Inference of Automata

We present (a slight generalization of) the framework of [4] for learning interface automata. We assume there is a *teacher*, who knows a determinate IA $\mathcal{T} = \langle I, O, Q, q^0, \rightarrow \rangle$, called the *system under test (SUT)*. There is also a *learner*, who has the task to learn about the behavior of $\mathcal{T}$ through experiments. The type of experiments which the learner may do is restricted by a *learning purpose* [4,21,32,36], which is a determinate IA $\mathcal{P} = \langle I, O^\delta, P, p^0, \rightarrow_\mathcal{P} \rangle$, satisfying $\mathcal{T} \lesssim \mathcal{P}$.

In practice, there are various ways to ensure that $\mathcal{T} \lesssim \mathcal{P}$. If $\mathcal{T}$ is an IOA then $\mathcal{T} \lesssim \mathcal{P}$ is equivalent to $\mathcal{T}$ **ioco** $\mathcal{P}$ by Lemmas 1 and 2, and so we may use model-based black-box testing to obtain evidence for $\mathcal{T} \lesssim \mathcal{P}$. Alternatively, if $\mathcal{T}$ is an IOA and $\mathcal{P}$ is output-enabled then $\mathcal{T} \lesssim \mathcal{P}$ trivially holds.

After doing a number of experiments, the learner may formulate a *hypothesis*, which is a determinate IA $\mathcal{H}$ with outputs O^δ satisfying $\mathcal{H} \lessapprox \mathcal{P}$. Informally, the requirement $\mathcal{H} \lessapprox \mathcal{P}$ expresses that $\mathcal{H}$ only displays behaviors that are allowed by $\mathcal{P}$, but that any input action that must be explored according to $\mathcal{P}$ is indeed present in $\mathcal{H}$. Hypothesis $\mathcal{H}$ is *correct* if $\mathcal{T}$ **ioco** $\mathcal{H}$. In practice, we will use black-box testing to obtain evidence for the correctness of the hypothesis. In general, there will be many $\mathcal{H}$'s satisfying $\mathcal{T}$ **ioco** $\mathcal{H} \lessapprox \mathcal{P}$ (for instance, we may take $\mathcal{H} = \mathcal{P}$), and additional conditions will be imposed on $\mathcal{H}$, such as behavior-determinacy. In fact, in the full version of this article we establish that if $\mathcal{T}$ is behavior-determininistic there always exists a behavior-deterministic IA $\mathcal{H}$ such that $\mathcal{T}$ **ioco** $\mathcal{H} \lessapprox \mathcal{P}$. If, in addition, $\mathcal{T}$ is an IOA then this $\mathcal{H}$ is unique up to bisimulation equivalence.

Example 1 (Learning purpose). A trivial learning purpose $\mathcal{P}_{triv}$ is displayed in Figure 2 (left). Here notation $i : I$ means that we have an instance of the transition for each input $i \in I$. Notation $o : O$ is defined similarly. Since $\mathcal{P}_{triv}$ is output-enabled, $\mathcal{T} \lesssim \mathcal{P}_{triv}$ holds for each IOA $\mathcal{T}$. If $\mathcal{H}$ is a hypothesis, then $\mathcal{H} \lessapprox \mathcal{P}_{triv}$ just means that $\mathcal{H}$ is input enabled.

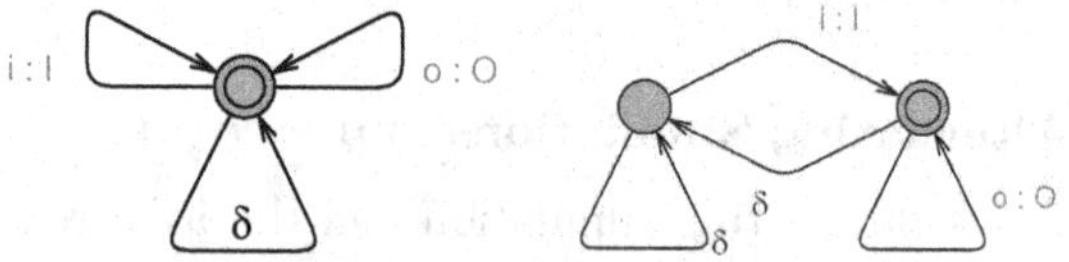

Fig. 2. A trivial learning purpose (left) and a learning purpose with a nontrivial δ-transition (right)

The learning purpose $\mathcal{P}_{wait}$ displayed in Figure 2 (right) contains a nontrivial δ-transition. It expresses that after each input the learner has to wait until the SUT enters a quiescent state before offering the next input. It is straightforward to check that $\mathcal{T} \lesssim \mathcal{P}_{wait}$ holds if $\mathcal{T}$ is an IOA.

We now present the protocol that learner and teacher must follow. At any time, the teacher records the current state of $\mathcal{T}$, initially q^0, and the learner records the current state of $\mathcal{P}$, initially p^0. Suppose the teacher is in state q and the learner is in state p. In order to learn about the behavior of $\mathcal{T}$, the learner may engage in four types of interactions with the teacher:

1. *Input.* If a transition $p \xrightarrow{i}_{\mathcal{P}} p'$ is enabled in $\mathcal{P}$, then the learner may present input i to the teacher. If i is enabled in q then the teacher jumps to a state q' with $q \xrightarrow{i} q'$ and returns reply $\top$ to the learner. Otherwise, the teacher returns reply $\bot$. If the learner receives reply $\top$ it jumps to p', otherwise it stays in p.
2. *Output.* The learner may send an *output query* Δ to the teacher. Now there are two possibilities. If state q is quiescent, the teacher remains in q and returns answer δ. Otherwise, the teacher selects an output transition $q \xrightarrow{o} q'$, jumps to q', and returns o. The learner jumps to a state p' that can be reached by the answer o or δ.
3. *Reset.* The learner may send a **reset** to the teacher. In this case, both learner and teacher return to their respective initial states.
4. *Hypothesis.* The learner may present a *hypothesis* to the teacher: a determinate IA $\mathcal{H}$ with outputs O^δ such that $\mathcal{H} \lesssim \mathcal{P}$. If $\mathcal{T}$ **ioco** $\mathcal{H}$ then the teacher returns answer **yes**. Otherwise, by definition, $\mathcal{H}^\delta$ has a trace σ such that an output o that is enabled by $\mathcal{T}^\delta$ **after** σ, is not enabled by $\mathcal{H}^\delta$ **after** σ. In this case, the teacher returns answer **no** together with counterexample σo, and learner and teacher return to their respective initial states.

The next lemma, which is easy to prove, implies that the teacher never returns $\bot$ to the learner: whenever the learner performs an input transition $p \xrightarrow{i}_{\mathcal{P}} p'$, the teacher can perform a matching transition $q \xrightarrow{i} q'$. Moreover, whenever the teacher performs an output transition $q \xrightarrow{o} q'$, the learner can perform a matching transition $p \xrightarrow{o}_{\mathcal{P}} p'$.

Lemma 3. *Let R be the maximal alternating simulation from $\mathcal{T}^\delta$ to $\mathcal{P}^\delta$. Then, for any configuration of states q and p of teacher and learner, respectively, that can be reached after a finite number of steps (1)-(4) of the learning protocol, we have $(q, p) \in R$.*

We are interested in effective procedures which, for any finite (and some infinite) $\mathcal{T}$ and $\mathcal{P}$ satisfying the above conditions, allows a learner to come up with a correct, behavior-deterministic hypothesis $\mathcal{H}$ after a finite number of interactions with the teacher. In [4], it is shown that any algorithm for learning Mealy machines can be transformed into an algorithm for learning finite, behavior-deterministic IOAs. Efficient algorithms for learning Mealy machines have been implemented in the tool Learnlib [30].

4 Mappers

In order to learn a "large" IA $\mathcal{T}$, with inputs I and outputs O, we place a *mapper* in between the teacher and the learner, which translates concrete actions in I

and O to abstract actions in (typically smaller) sets X and Y, and vice versa. The task of the learner is then reduced to inferring a "small" IA with alphabet X and Y. Our notion of mapper is essentially the same as the one of [2].

Definition 3 (Mapper). *A* mapper *for a set of inputs I and a set of outputs O is a tuple $\mathcal{A} = \langle \mathcal{I}, X, Y, \Upsilon \rangle$, where*

- *$\mathcal{I} = \langle I, O^\delta, R, r^0, \rightarrow \rangle$ is a deterministic IA that is input- and output-enabled and has trivial δ-transitions: $r \xrightarrow{\delta} r' \Leftrightarrow r = r'$.*
- *X and Y are disjoint sets of abstract input and output actions with $\delta \in Y$.*
- *$\Upsilon : R \times A^\delta \rightarrow Z$, where $A = I \cup O$ and $Z = X \cup Y$, maps concrete actions to abstract ones. We write $\Upsilon_r(a)$ for $\Upsilon(r, a)$ and require that Υ_r respects inputs, outputs and quiescence: $(\Upsilon_r(a) \in X \Leftrightarrow a \in I) \wedge (\Upsilon_r(a) = \delta \Leftrightarrow a = \delta)$.*

Mapper $\mathcal{A}$ is output-predicting *if $\forall o, o' \in O : \Upsilon_r(o) = \Upsilon_r(o') \Rightarrow o = o'$, that is, Υ_r is injective on outputs, for each $r \in R$. Mapper $\mathcal{A}$ is* surjective *if $\forall z \in Z\ \exists a \in A^\delta : \Upsilon_r(a) = z$, that is, Υ_r is surjective, for each $r \in R$. Mapper $\mathcal{A}$ is* state-free *if R is a singleton set.*

Example 2. Consider a system with input actions $LOGIN(p_1)$, $SET(p_2)$ and $LOGOUT$. Assume that the system only triggers certain outputs when a user is properly logged in. Then we may not abstract from the password parameters p_1 and p_2 entirely, since this will lead to nondeterminism. We may preserve behavior-determinism by considering just two abstract values for p_1: ok and nok. Since passwords can be changed using the input $SET(p_2)$ when a user is logged in, the mapper may not be state-free: it has to record the current password and whether or not the user is logged (T and F, respectively). The input transitions are defined by:

$$(p, b) \xrightarrow{LOGIN(p)} (p, \mathsf{T}), \quad p \neq p_1 \Rightarrow (p, b) \xrightarrow{LOGIN(p_1)} (p, b),$$
$$(p, \mathsf{T}) \xrightarrow{SET(p_2)} (p_2, \mathsf{T}), \quad (p, \mathsf{F}) \xrightarrow{SET(p_2)} (p, \mathsf{F}), \qquad (p, b) \xrightarrow{LOGOUT} (p, \mathsf{F})$$

For input actions, abstraction Υ is defined by

$$\Upsilon_{(p,b)}(LOGIN(p_1)) = \begin{cases} LOGIN(\mathsf{ok}) & \text{if } p_1 = p \\ LOGIN(\mathsf{nok}) & \text{otherwise} \end{cases}$$
$$\Upsilon_{(p,b)}(SET(p_2)) = SET$$

For input $LOGOUT$ and for output actions, $\Upsilon_{(p,b)}$ is the identity. This mapper is surjective, since no matter how the password has been set, a user may always choose either a correct or an incorrect login.

Example 3. Consider a system with three inputs $IN1(n_1)$, $IN2(n_2)$, and $IN3(n_3)$, in which an $IN3(n_3)$ input triggers an output OK if and only if the value of n_3 equals either the latest value of n_1 or the latest value of n_2. In this case, we may not abstract away entirely from the values of the parameters, since that leads to nondeterminism. We may preserve behavior-determinism by a mapper that records the last values of n_1 and n_2. Thus, if D is the set of parameter values, we define the set of mapper states by $R = (D \cup \{\bot\}) \times (D \cup \{\bot\})$, choose $r^0 = (\bot, \bot)$ as initial state, and define the input transitions by

$$(v_1, v_2) \xrightarrow{IN1(n_1)} (n_1, v_2), \quad (v_1, v_2) \xrightarrow{IN2(n_2)} (v_1, n_2), \quad (v_1, v_2) \xrightarrow{IN3(n_3)} (v_1, v_2)$$

Abstraction Υ abstracts from the specific value of a parameter, and only records whether it is fresh, or equals the last value of *IN1* or *IN2*. For $i = 1, 2, 3$:

$$\Upsilon_{(v_1,v_2)}(INi(n_i)) = \begin{cases} INi(\mathsf{old}_1) & \text{if } n_i = v_1 \\ INi(\mathsf{old}_2) & \text{if } n_i = v_2 \wedge n_i \neq v_1 \\ INi(\mathsf{fresh}) & \text{otherwise} \end{cases}$$

This abstraction is not surjective: for instance, in the initial state $IN1(\mathsf{old}_1)$ is not possible as an abstract value, and in any state of the form (v, v), $IN1(\mathsf{old}_2)$ is not possible.

Each mapper $\mathcal{A}$ induces an abstraction operator on interface automata, which abstracts an IA with actions in I and O into an IA with actions in X and Y. This abstraction operator is essentially just a variation of the state operator well-known from process algebras [8].

Definition 4 (Abstraction). *Let $\mathcal{T} = \langle I, O, Q, q^0, \rightarrow \rangle$ be an IA and let $\mathcal{A} = \langle \mathcal{I}, X, Y, \Upsilon \rangle$ be a mapper with $\mathcal{I} = \langle I, O^\delta, R, r^0, \rightarrow \rangle$. Then $\alpha_{\mathcal{A}}(\mathcal{T})$, the* abstraction *of $\mathcal{T}$, is the IA $\langle X, Y, Q \times R, (q^0, r^0), \rightarrow_{\mathsf{abst}} \rangle$, where transition relation $\rightarrow_{\mathsf{abst}}$ is given by the rule:*

$$\frac{q \xrightarrow{a} q' \quad r \xrightarrow{a} r' \quad \Upsilon_r(a) = z}{(q, r) \xrightarrow{z}_{\mathsf{abst}} (q', r')}$$

Observe that if $\mathcal{T}$ is determinate then $\alpha_{\mathcal{A}}(\mathcal{T})$ does not have to be determinate. Also, if $\mathcal{T}$ is an IOA then $\alpha_{\mathcal{A}}(\mathcal{T})$ does not have to be an IOA (if $\mathcal{A}$ is not surjective, as in Example 3, then an abstract input will not be enabled if there is no corresponding concrete input). If $\mathcal{T}$ is output-determined then $\alpha_{\mathcal{A}}(\mathcal{T})$ is output-determined, but the converse implication does not hold. The following lemma gives a positive result: abstraction is monotone with respect to the alternating simulation preorder.

Lemma 4. *If $\mathcal{T}_1 \lesssim \mathcal{T}_2$ then $\alpha_{\mathcal{A}}(\mathcal{T}_1) \lesssim \alpha_{\mathcal{A}}(\mathcal{T}_2)$.*

The concretization operator is the dual of the abstraction operator. It transforms each IA with abstract actions in X and Y into an IA with concrete actions in I and O.

Definition 5 (Concretization). *Let $\mathcal{H} = \langle X, Y, S, s^0, \rightarrow \rangle$ be an IA and let $\mathcal{A} = \langle \mathcal{I}, X, Y, \Upsilon \rangle$ be a mapper with $\mathcal{I} = \langle I, O^\delta, R, r^0, \rightarrow \rangle$. Then $\gamma_{\mathcal{A}}(\mathcal{H})$, the* concretization *of $\mathcal{H}$, is the IA $\langle I, O^\delta, R \times S, (r^0, s^0), \rightarrow_{\mathsf{conc}} \rangle$, where transition relation $\rightarrow_{\mathsf{conc}}$ is given by the rule:*

$$\frac{r \xrightarrow{a} r' \quad s \xrightarrow{z} s' \quad \Upsilon_r(a) = z}{(r, s) \xrightarrow{a}_{\mathsf{conc}} (r', s')}$$

Whereas the abstraction operator does not preserve determinacy in general, the concretization of a determinate IA is always determinate. Also, the concretization of an output-determined IA is output-determined, provided the mapper is output-predicting.

Lemma 5. *If $\mathcal{H}$ is determinate then $\gamma_{\mathcal{A}}(\mathcal{H})$ is determinate.*

Lemma 6. *If $\mathcal{A}$ is output-predicting and $\mathcal{H}$ is output-determined then $\gamma_{\mathcal{A}}(\mathcal{H})$ is output-determined.*

In an abstraction of the form $\gamma_{\mathcal{A}}(\mathcal{H})$ it may occur that a reachable state (r, s) is quiescent, even though the contained state s of $\mathcal{H}$ enables some abstract output y: this happens if there exists no concrete concrete output o such that $\Upsilon_r(o) = y$. This situation is ruled out by following definition.

Definition 6. $\gamma_{\mathcal{A}}(\mathcal{H})$ *is* quiescence preserving *if, for each reachable state (r, s), (r, s) quiescent implies s quiescent.*

Concretization is monotone with respect to the $\lessapprox$ preorder, provided the concretization of the first argument is quiescence preserving.

Lemma 7. *Suppose $\gamma_{\mathcal{A}}(\mathcal{H}_1)$ is quiescence preserving. Then $\mathcal{H}_1 \lessapprox \mathcal{H}_2$ implies $\gamma_{\mathcal{A}}(\mathcal{H}_1) \lessapprox \gamma_{\mathcal{A}}(\mathcal{H}_2)$.*

The lemma below is a key result of this article. It says that if $\mathcal{T}$ is **ioco**-conforming to the concretization of an hypothesis $\mathcal{H}$, and this concretization is quiescence preserving, then the abstraction of $\mathcal{T}$ is **ioco**-conforming to $\mathcal{H}$ itself.

Lemma 8. *If $\gamma_{\mathcal{A}}(\mathcal{H})$ is quiescence preserving then $\mathcal{T}$ **ioco** $\gamma_{\mathcal{A}}(\mathcal{H}) \Rightarrow \alpha_{\mathcal{A}}(\mathcal{T})$ **ioco** $\mathcal{H}$.*

By using a mapper $\mathcal{A}$, we may reduce the task of learning an IA $\mathcal{H}$ such that $\mathcal{T}$ **ioco** $\mathcal{H} \lessapprox \mathcal{P}$ to the simpler task of learning an IA $\mathcal{H}'$ such that $\alpha_{\mathcal{A}}(\mathcal{T})$ **ioco** $\mathcal{H}' \lessapprox \alpha_{\mathcal{A}}(\mathcal{P})$. However, in order to establish the correctness of this reduction, we need two technical lemmas that require some additional assumptions on $\mathcal{P}$ and $\mathcal{A}$. It is straightforward to check that these assumptions are met by the mappers of Examples 2 and 3, and the learning purposes of Example 1.

Definition 7. *Let $\mathcal{A} = \langle \mathcal{I}, X, Y, \Upsilon \rangle$ be a mapper for I and O. We define $\equiv_{\mathcal{A}}$ to be the equivalence relation on $I \cup O^{\delta}$ which declares two concrete actions equivalent if, for some states of the mapper, they are mapped to the same abstract action: $a \equiv_{\mathcal{A}} b \Leftrightarrow \exists r, r' : \Upsilon_r(a) = \Upsilon_{r'}(b)$. Let $\mathcal{T} = \langle I, O, Q, q^0, \rightarrow \rangle$ be an IA. We call $\mathcal{P}$ and $\mathcal{A}$* compatible *if, for all concrete actions a, b with $a \equiv_{\mathcal{A}} b$ and for all $p, p_1, p_2 \in P$, $(p \xrightarrow{a} \Leftrightarrow p \xrightarrow{b}) \wedge (p \xrightarrow{a} p_1 \wedge p \xrightarrow{b} p_2 \Rightarrow p_1 \sim p_2)$.*

Lemma 9. *Suppose $\alpha_{\mathcal{A}}(\mathcal{P})$ is determinate and $\mathcal{P}$ and $\mathcal{A}$ are compatible. Then $\gamma_{\mathcal{A}}(\alpha_{\mathcal{A}}(\mathcal{P})) \lessapprox \mathcal{P}$.*

Lemma 10. *Suppose $\mathcal{A}$ and $\mathcal{P}$ are compatible, $\alpha_{\mathcal{A}}(\mathcal{P})$ is determinate and $\mathcal{H} \lessapprox \alpha_{\mathcal{A}}(\mathcal{P})$. Then $\gamma_{\mathcal{A}}(\mathcal{H})$ is quiescence preserving.*

5 Inference Using Abstraction

Suppose we have a teacher equipped with a determinate IA $\mathcal{T}$, and a learner equipped with a determinate learning purpose $\mathcal{P}$ such that $\mathcal{T} \lesssim \mathcal{P}$. The learner has the task to infer some $\mathcal{H}$ satisfying $\mathcal{T}$ **ioco** $\mathcal{H} \lessapprox \mathcal{P}$. After the preparations from the previous section, we are now ready to show how, in certain cases, the learner may simplify her task by defining a mapper $\mathcal{A}$ such that $\alpha_\mathcal{A}(\mathcal{T})$ and $\alpha_\mathcal{A}(\mathcal{P})$ are determinate, $\mathcal{P}$ and $\mathcal{A}$ are compatible, and $\mathcal{T}$ *respects* $\mathcal{A}$ in the sense that, for $i, i' \in I$ and $q \in Q$, $i \equiv_\mathcal{A} i' \Rightarrow (q \xrightarrow{i} \Leftrightarrow q \xrightarrow{i'})$. Note that if $\mathcal{T}$ is an IOA it trivially respects $\mathcal{A}$. In these cases, we may reduce the task of the learner to learning an IA $\mathcal{H}'$ satisfying $\alpha_\mathcal{A}(\mathcal{T})$ **ioco** $\mathcal{H}' \lessapprox \alpha_\mathcal{A}(\mathcal{P})$. Note that $\alpha_\mathcal{A}(\mathcal{P})$ is a proper learning purpose for $\alpha_\mathcal{A}(\mathcal{T})$ since it is determinate and, by monotonicity of abstraction (Lemma 4), $\alpha_\mathcal{A}(\mathcal{T}) \lesssim \alpha_\mathcal{A}(\mathcal{P})$.

We construct a teacher for $\alpha_\mathcal{A}(\mathcal{T})$ by placing a mapper component in between the teacher for $\mathcal{T}$ and the learner for $\mathcal{P}$, which translates concrete and abstract actions to each other in accordance with $\mathcal{A}$. Let $\mathcal{T} = \langle I, O, Q, q^0, \rightarrow \rangle$, $\mathcal{P} = \langle I, O^\delta, P, p^0, \rightarrow_\mathcal{P} \rangle$, $\mathcal{A} = \langle \mathcal{I}, X, Y, \Upsilon \rangle$, and $\mathcal{I} = \langle I, O^\delta, R, r^0, \rightarrow \rangle$. The mapper component maintains a state variable of type R, which initially is set to r^0. The behavior of the mapper component is defined as follows:

1. *Input.* If the mapper is in state r and receives an abstract input $x \in X$ from the learner, it picks a concrete input $i \in I$ such that $\Upsilon_r(i) = x$, forwards i to the teacher, and waits for a reply $\top$ or $\bot$ from the teacher. This reply is then forwarded to the learner. In case of a $\top$ reply, the mapper updates its state to the unique r' with $r \xrightarrow{i} r'$. If there is no $i \in I$ such that $\Upsilon_r(i) = x$ then the mapper returns a $\bot$ reply to the learner right away.
2. *Output.* If the mapper receives an output query Δ from the learner, it forwards Δ to the teacher. It then waits until it receives an output $o \in O^\delta$ from the teacher, and forwards $\Upsilon_r(o)$ to the learner.
3. *Reset.* If the mapper receives a **reset** from the learner, it resets its state to r^0 and forwards **reset** to the teacher.
4. *Hypothesis.* If the mapper receives a hypothesis $\mathcal{H}$ from the learner then, by Lemma 10, $\gamma_\mathcal{A}(\mathcal{H})$ is quiescence preserving, Since $\mathcal{H} \lessapprox \alpha_\mathcal{A}(\mathcal{P})$, monotonicity of concretization (Lemma 7) implies $\gamma_\mathcal{A}(\mathcal{H}) \lessapprox \gamma_\mathcal{A}(\alpha_\mathcal{A}(\mathcal{P}))$. Hence, by Lemma 9, $\gamma_\mathcal{A}(\mathcal{H}) \lessapprox \mathcal{P}$. This means that the mapper may forward $\gamma_\mathcal{A}(\mathcal{H})$ as a hypothesis to the teacher. If the mapper receives response **yes** from the teacher, it forwards **yes** to the learner. If the mapper receives response **no** with counterexample σo, where $\sigma = a_1 \cdots a_n$, then it constructs a run $(r_0, s_0) \xrightarrow{a_1} (r_1, s_1) \xrightarrow{a_2} \cdots \xrightarrow{a_n} (r_n, s_n)$ of $(\gamma_\mathcal{A}(\mathcal{H}))^\delta$ with $(r_0, s_0) = (r^0, s^0)$. It then forwards **no** to the learner, together with counterexample $z_1 \cdots z_n y$, where, for $1 \leq j \leq n$, $z_j = \Upsilon_{r_{j-1}}(a_j)$ and $y = \Upsilon_{r_n}(o)$. Finally, the mapper returns to its initial state.

The next lemma implies that, whenever the learner presents an abstract input x to the mapper, there exists a concrete input i such that $\Upsilon_r(i) = x$, and the teacher will accept input i from the mapper. So no $\bot$ replies will be sent. Moreover, whenever the teacher sends a concrete output o to the mapper, the learner accepts the corresponding abstract output $\Upsilon_r(o)$ from the mapper.

Lemma 11. *Let S be the maximal alternating simulation from $\mathcal{T}^\delta$ to $\mathcal{P}^\delta$. Then, for any configuration of states q, r_1 and (p, r_2) of teacher, mapper and learner, respectively, that can be reached after a finite number of steps (1)-(5) of the learning protocol, we have $(q, p) \in S$ and $(p, r_1) \sim (p, r_2)$ (here $\sim$ denotes bisimulation equivalence in $\alpha_\mathcal{A}(\mathcal{P})$).*

We claim that, from the perspective of a learner with learning purpose $\alpha_\mathcal{A}(\mathcal{P})$, a teacher for $\mathcal{T}$ and a mapper for $\mathcal{A}$ together behave exactly like a teacher for $\alpha_\mathcal{A}(\mathcal{T})$. Since we have not formalized the notion of behavior for a teacher and a mapper, the mathematical content of this claim may not be immediately obvious. Clearly, it is routine to describe the behavior of teachers and mappers formally in some concurrency formalism, such as Milner's CCS [28] or another process algebra [10]. For instance, we may define, for each IA $\mathcal{T}$, a CCS process $\mathsf{Teacher}(\mathcal{T})$ that describes the behavior of a teacher for $\mathcal{T}$, and for each mapper $\mathcal{A}$ a CCS process $\mathsf{Mapper}(\mathcal{A})$ that models the behavior of a mapper for $\mathcal{A}$. These two CCS processes may then synchronize via actions taken from A^δ, actions Δ, δ, $\top$, $\bot$ and **reset**, and actions $\mathsf{hypothesis}(\mathcal{H})$, where $\mathcal{H}$ is an interface automaton. If we compose $\mathsf{Teacher}(\mathcal{T})$ and $\mathsf{Mapper}(\mathcal{A})$ using the CCS composition operator $|$, and apply the CCS restriction operator $\setminus$ to internalize all communications between teacher and mapper, the resulting process is observation equivalent (weakly bisimilar) to process $\mathsf{Teacher}(\alpha_\mathcal{A}(\mathcal{T}))$: $(\mathsf{Teacher}(\mathcal{T}) \mid \mathsf{Mapper}(\mathcal{A})) \setminus L \approx \mathsf{Teacher}(\alpha_\mathcal{A}(\mathcal{T}))$, where $L = A^\delta \cup \{\Delta, \delta, \top, \bot, \mathbf{reset}, \mathsf{hypothesis}\}$. It is in this precise, formal sense that one should read the following theorem.

Theorem 1. *Let $\mathcal{T}$, $\mathcal{A}$ and $\mathcal{P}$ be as above. A teacher for $\mathcal{T}$ and a mapper for $\mathcal{A}$ together behave like a teacher for $\alpha_\mathcal{A}(\mathcal{T})$.*

Since a teacher for $\mathcal{T}$ and a mapper for $\mathcal{A}$ together behave like a teacher for $\alpha_\mathcal{A}(\mathcal{T})$, it follows that we have reduced the task of learning an $\mathcal{H}$ such that $\mathcal{T}$ **ioco** $\mathcal{H} \lessapprox \mathcal{P}$ to the simpler task of learning an $\mathcal{H}$ such that $\alpha_\mathcal{A}(\mathcal{T})$ **ioco** $\mathcal{H} \lessapprox \alpha_\mathcal{A}(\mathcal{P})$: whenever the learner receives the answer **yes** from the mapper, indicating that $\alpha_\mathcal{A}(\mathcal{T})$ **ioco** $\mathcal{H}$ we know, by definition of the behavior of the mapper component, that $\gamma_\mathcal{A}(\mathcal{H})$ is quiescent preserving and $\mathcal{T}$ **ioco** $\gamma_\mathcal{A}(\mathcal{H})$. Moreover, by Lemmas 7 and 9, $\gamma_\mathcal{A}(\mathcal{H}) \lessapprox \mathcal{P}$.

Recall that for output-predicting abstractions, if $\mathcal{H}$ is behavior-deterministic then $\gamma_\mathcal{A}(\mathcal{H})$ is behavior-deterministic. This implies that, for such abstractions, provided $\mathcal{T}$ is an IOA, whenever the mapper returns **yes** to the learner, $\gamma_\mathcal{A}(\mathcal{H})$ is the unique IA (up to bisimulation) that satisfies $\mathcal{T}$ **ioco** $\gamma_\mathcal{A}(\mathcal{H}) \lessapprox \mathcal{P}$.

6 Conclusions and Future Work

We have provided several generalizations of the framework of [2], leading to a general theory of history dependent abstractions for learning interface automata. Our work establishes some interesting links between previous work on concurrency theory, model-based testing, and automata learning.

The theory of abstractions presented in this paper is not complete yet and deserves further study. The link between our theory and the theory of abstract interpretation [13, 14] needs to be investigated further. Also the notion of XY-simulation, which offers a natural generalization of several fundamental concepts from concurrency theory (bisimulations, simulations, alternating simulations and partial bisimulations), deserves further study.

A major challenge will be the development of algorithms for the automatic construction of mappers: the availability of such algorithms will boost the applicability of automata learning technology. In [19], a method is presented that is able to automatically construct certain state-free mappers. In [1], we present our prototype tool Tomte, which is able to automatically construct mappers for a restricted class of scalarset automata, in which one can test for equality of data parameters, but no operations on data are allowed. Both [1,19] use the technique of counterexample-guided abstraction refinement: initially, the algorithms starts with a very course abstraction $\mathcal{A}$, which is subsequently refined if it turns out that $\alpha_{\mathcal{A}}(\mathcal{T})$ is not behavior-deterministic.

Finally, an obvious challenge is to generalize the theory of this paper to SUTs that are not determinate.

References

1. Aarts, F., Heidarian, F., Kuppens, H., Olsen, P., Vaandrager, F.: Automata Learning through Counterexample-Guided Abstraction Refinement. In: Proc. FM 2012. LNCS. Springer (to appear, 2012)
2. Aarts, F., Jonsson, B., Uijen, J.: Generating Models of Infinite-State Communication Protocols Using Regular Inference with Abstraction. In: Petrenko, A., Simão, A., Maldonado, J.C. (eds.) ICTSS 2010. LNCS, vol. 6435, pp. 188–204. Springer, Heidelberg (2010)
3. Aarts, F., Schmaltz, J., Vaandrager, F.: Inference and Abstraction of the Biometric Passport. In: Margaria, T., Steffen, B. (eds.) ISoLA 2010. LNCS, vol. 6415, pp. 673–686. Springer, Heidelberg (2010)
4. Aarts, F., Vaandrager, F.: Learning I/O Automata. In: Gastin, P., Laroussinie, F. (eds.) CONCUR 2010. LNCS, vol. 6269, pp. 71–85. Springer, Heidelberg (2010)
5. Alur, R., Henzinger, T.A., Kupferman, O., Vardi, M.Y.: Alternating Refinement Relations. In: Sangiorgi, D., de Simone, R. (eds.) CONCUR 1998. LNCS, vol. 1466, pp. 163–178. Springer, Heidelberg (1998)
6. Angluin, D.: Learning regular sets from queries and counterexamples. Inf. Comput. 75(2), 87–106 (1987)
7. Baeten, J.C.M., van Beek, D.A., Luttik, B., Markovski, J., Rooda, J.E.: A process-theoretic approach to supervisory control theory. In: ACC 2011, pp. 4496–4501(2011)
8. Baeten, J.C.M., Bergstra, J.A.: Global renaming operators in concrete process algebra. Information and Computation 78(3), 205–245 (1988)
9. Berg, T., Grinchtein, O., Jonsson, B., Leucker, M., Raffelt, H., Steffen, B.: On the Correspondence Between Conformance Testing and Regular Inference. In: Cerioli, M. (ed.) FASE 2005. LNCS, vol. 3442, pp. 175–189. Springer, Heidelberg (2005)
10. Bergstra, J.A., Ponse, A., Smolka, S.A. (eds.): Handbook of Process Algebra. North-Holland (2001)

11. Cho, C.Y., Babic, D., Shin, E.C.R., Song, D.: Inference and analysis of formal models of botnet command and control protocols. In: ACM Conference on Computer and Communications Security, pp. 426–439. ACM (2010)
12. Comparetti, P., Wondracek, G., Krügel, C., Kirda, E.: Prospex: Protocol specification extraction. In: IEEE Symposium on Security and Privacy, pp. 110–125. IEEE (2009)
13. Cousot, P., Cousot, R.: Abstract interpretation: a unified lattice model for static analysis of programs by construction or approximation of fixpoints. In: Proc. POPL, pp. 238–252 (1977)
14. Dams, D., Gerth, R., Grumberg, O.: Abstract interpretation of reactive systems. ACM TOPLS 19(2), 253–291 (1997)
15. de Alfaro, L., Henzinger, T.A.: Interface automata. SIGSOFT Softw. Eng. Notes 26, 109–120 (2001)
16. Ferrari, G., Gnesi, S., Montanari, U., Pistore, M.: A model-checking verification environment for mobile processes. ACM TOSEM 12(4), 440–473 (2003)
17. de la Higuera, C.: Grammatical Inference: Learning Automata and Grammars. Cambridge University Press (April 2010)
18. Howar, F., Steffen, B., Merten, M.: From ZULU to RERS. In: Margaria, T., Steffen, B. (eds.) ISoLA 2010. LNCS, vol. 6415, pp. 687–704. Springer, Heidelberg (2010)
19. Howar, F., Steffen, B., Merten, M.: Automata Learning with Automated Alphabet Abstraction Refinement. In: Jhala, R., Schmidt, D. (eds.) VMCAI 2011. LNCS, vol. 6538, pp. 263–277. Springer, Heidelberg (2011)
20. Hungar, H., Niese, O., Steffen, B.: Domain-Specific Optimization in Automata Learning. In: Hunt Jr., W.A., Somenzi, F. (eds.) CAV 2003. LNCS, vol. 2725, pp. 315–327. Springer, Heidelberg (2003)
21. Jard, C., Jéron, T.: TGV: theory, principles and algorithms. STTT 7(4), 297–315 (2005)
22. Lamport, L.: Specifying Systems: The TLA+ Language and Tools for Hardware and Software Engineers. Addison-Wesley Longman Publishing Co., Inc. (2002)
23. Leucker, M.: Learning Meets Verification. In: de Boer, F.S., Bonsangue, M.M., Graf, S., de Roever, W.-P. (eds.) FMCO 2006. LNCS, vol. 4709, pp. 127–151. Springer, Heidelberg (2007)
24. Loiseaux, C., Graf, S., Sifakis, J., Boujjani, A., Bensalem, S.: Property preserving abstractions for the verification of concurrent systems. FMSD 6(1), 11–44 (1995)
25. Lynch, N., Tuttle, M.: An introduction to input/output automata. CWI Quarterly 2(3), 219–246 (1989)
26. Lynch, N., Vaandrager, F.: Forward and backward simulations, I: Untimed systems. Inf. Comput. 121(2), 214–233 (1995)
27. Merten, M., Steffen, B., Howar, F., Margaria, T.: Next Generation LearnLib. In: Abdulla, P.A., Leino, K.R.M. (eds.) TACAS 2011. LNCS, vol. 6605, pp. 220–223. Springer, Heidelberg (2011)
28. Milner, R.: Communication and Concurrency. Prentice-Hall (1989)
29. Montanari, U., Pistore, M.: Checking Bisimilarity for Finitary Pi-Calculus. In: Lee, I., Smolka, S.A. (eds.) CONCUR 1995. LNCS, vol. 962, pp. 42–56. Springer, Heidelberg (1995)
30. Raffelt, H., Steffen, B., Berg, T., Margaria, T.: LearnLib: a framework for extrapolating behavioral models. STTT 11(5), 393–407 (2009)
31. Rivest, R., Schapire, R.: Inference of finite automata using homing sequences. In: Proc. STOC, pp. 411–420. ACM (1989)

32. Rusu, V., du Bousquet, L., Jéron, T.: An Approach to Symbolic Test Generation. In: Grieskamp, W., Santen, T., Stoddart, B. (eds.) IFM 2000. LNCS, vol. 1945, pp. 338–357. Springer, Heidelberg (2000)
33. Tretmans, J.: Test generation with inputs, outputs, and repetitive quiescence. Software–Concepts and Tools 17, 103–120 (1996)
34. Tretmans, J.: Model Based Testing with Labelled Transition Systems. In: Hierons, R.M., Bowen, J.P., Harman, M. (eds.) FORTEST 2008. LNCS, vol. 4949, pp. 1–38. Springer, Heidelberg (2008)
35. Veanes, M., Bjørner, N.: Input-Output Model Programs. In: Leucker, M., Morgan, C. (eds.) ICTAC 2009. LNCS, vol. 5684, pp. 322–335. Springer, Heidelberg (2009)
36. de Vries, R.G., Tretmans, J.: Towards Formal Test Purposes. In: FATES 2001, BRICS Notes NS-01-4, pp. 61–76. Univ. Aarhus (2001)

Linearizability with Ownership Transfer

Alexey Gotsman and Hongseok Yang

[1] IMDEA Software Institute
[2] University of Oxford

Abstract. Linearizability is a commonly accepted notion of correctness for libraries of concurrent algorithms. Unfortunately, it assumes a complete isolation between a library and its client, with interactions limited to passing values of a given data type. This is inappropriate for common programming languages, where libraries and their clients can communicate via the heap, transferring the ownership of data structures, and can even run in a shared address space without any memory protection. In this paper, we present the first definition of linearizability that lifts this limitation and establish an Abstraction Theorem: while proving a property of a client of a concurrent library, we can soundly replace the library by its abstract implementation related to the original one by our generalisation of linearizability. We also prove that linearizability with ownership transfer can be derived from the classical one if the library does not access some of data structures transferred to it by the client.

1 Introduction

The architecture of concurrent software usually exhibits some forms of modularity. For example, concurrent algorithms are encapsulated in libraries and complex algorithms are often constructed using libraries of simpler ones. This lets developers benefit from ready-made libraries of concurrency patterns and high-performance concurrent data structures, such as `java.util.concurrent` for Java and Threading Building Blocks for C++. To simplify reasoning about concurrent software, we need to exploit the available modularity. In particular, in reasoning about a client of a concurrent library, we would like to abstract from the details of a particular library implementation. This requires an appropriate notion of library correctness.

Correctness of concurrent libraries is commonly formalised by *linearizability* [12], which fixes a certain correspondence between the library and its specification. The latter is usually just another library, but implemented atomically using an abstract data type. A good notion of linearizability should validate an *Abstraction Theorem* [9]: it is sound to replace a library with its specification in reasoning about its client.

The classical linearizability assumes a complete isolation between a library and its client, with interactions limited to passing values of a given data type as parameters or return values of library methods. This notion is not appropriate for low-level heap-manipulating languages, such as C/C++. There the library and the client run in a shared address space; thus, to prove the whole program correct, we need to verify that one of them does not corrupt the data structures used by the other. Type systems [5] and program logics [13] usually establish this using the concept of *ownership* of data structures by a program component. When verifying realistic programs, this ownership of data structures cannot be assigned statically; rather, it should be *transferred*

M. Koutny and I. Ulidowski (Eds.): CONCUR 2012, LNCS 7454, pp. 256–271, 2012.

between the client and the library at calls to and returns from the latter. The times when ownership is transferred are not determined operationally, but set by the proof method: as O'Hearn famously put it, "ownership is in the eye of the asserter" [13]. However, ownership transfer reflects actual interactions between program components via the heap, e.g., alternating accesses to a shared area of memory. Such interactions also exist in high-level languages providing basic memory protection, such as Java.

For an example of ownership transfer between concurrent libraries and their clients consider a memory allocator accessible concurrently to multiple threads. We can think of the allocator as owning the blocks of memory on its free-list; in particular, it can store free-list pointers in them. Having allocated a block, a thread gets its exclusive ownership, which allows accessing it without interference from the other threads. When the thread frees the block, its ownership is returned to the allocator.

As another example, consider any container with concurrent access, such as a concurrent set from `java.util.concurrent` or Threading Building Blocks. A typical use of such a container is to store pointers to a certain type of data structures. However, when verifying a client of the container, we usually think of the latter as holding the ownership of the data structures whose addresses it stores [13]. Thus, when a thread inserts a pointer to a data structure into a container, its ownership is transferred from the thread to the container. When another thread removes a pointer from the container, it acquires the ownership of the data structure the pointer identifies. If the first thread tries to access a data structure after a pointer to it has been inserted into the container, this may result in a race condition. Unlike a memory allocator, the container code usually does not access the contents of the data structures its elements identify, but merely ferries their ownership between different threads. For this reason, correctness proofs for such containers [1,6,17] have so far established their classical linearizability, without taking ownership transfer into account.

We would like to use the notion of linearizability and, in particular, an Abstraction Theorem to reason about above libraries and their clients in isolation, taking into account only the memory that they own. When clients use the libraries to implement the ownership transfer paradigm, the correctness of the latter cannot be defined only in terms of passing pointers between the library and the client; we must also show that they perform ownership transfer correctly. So far, there has been no notion of linearizability that would allow this. In the case of concurrent containers, we cannot use classical linearizability established for them to validate an Abstraction Theorem that would be applicable to clients performing ownership transfer. This paper fills in these gaps.

Contributions. In this paper, we generalise linearizability to a setting where a library and its client execute in a shared address space, and boundaries between their data structures can change via ownership transfers (Section 3). Linearizability is usually defined in terms of *histories*, which are sequences of calls to and returns from a library in a given program execution, recording parameters and return values passed. To handle ownership transfer, histories also have to include descriptions of memory areas transferred. However, in this case, some histories cannot be generated by any pair of a client and a library. For example, a client that transfers an area of memory upon a call to a library not communicating with anyone else cannot then transfer the same area again before getting it back from the library upon a method return.

We propose a notion of *balancedness* that characterises those histories that treat ownership transfer correctly. We then define a *linearizability relation* between balanced histories, matching histories of an implementation and a specification of a library (Section 3). We show that the proposed linearizability relation on histories is correct in the sense that it validates a Rearrangement Lemma (Lemma 13, Section 4): if a history H' linearizes another history H, and it can be produced by some execution of a library, then so can the history H. The need to consider ownership transfer makes the proof of the lemma highly non-trivial. This is because changing the history from H' to H requires moving calls and returns to different points in the computation. In the setting without ownership transfer, these actions are thread-local and can be moved easily; however, once they involve ownership transfer, they become global and the justification of their moves becomes subtle, in particular, relying on the fact that the histories involved are balanced (see the discussion in Section 4).

To lift the linearizability relation on histories to libraries and establish the Abstraction Theorem, we define a novel compositional semantics for a language with libraries that defines the denotation of a library or a client considered separately in an environment that communicates with the component correctly via ownership transfers (Section 6). To define such a semantics for a library, we generalise the folklore notion of its *most general client* to allow ownership transfers, which gives us a way to generate all possible library histories and lift the notion of linearizabiliy to libraries. We prove that our compositional semantics is sound and adequate with respect to the standard non-compositional semantics (Lemmas 16 and 17). This, together with the Rearrangement Lemma, allows us to establish the Abstraction Theorem (Theorem 19, Section 7).

To avoid having to prove the new notion of linearizability from scratch for libraries that do not access some of the data structures transferred to them, such as concurrent containers, we propose a *frame rule for linearizability* (Theorem 22, Section 8). It ensures the linearizability of such libraries with respect to a specification with ownership transfer given their linearizability with respect to a specification without one.

The Abstraction Theorem is not just a theoretical result: it enables compositional reasoning about complex concurrent algorithms that are challenging for existing verification methods (Section 7). We have also developed a logic, based on separation logic [14], for establishing our linearizability. Due to space constraints, the details of the logic are outside the scope of this paper. For the same reason, proofs of most theorems are given in [10, Appendix B].

2 Footprints of States

Our results hold for a class of models of program states called *separation algebras* [4], which allow expressing the dynamic memory partitioning between libraries and clients.

Definition 1. *A **separation algebra** is a set Σ, together with a partial commutative, associative and cancellative operation $*$ on Σ and a unit element $\epsilon \in \Sigma$. Here unity, commutativity and associativity hold for the equality that means both sides are defined and equal, or both are undefined. The property of cancellativity says that for each $\theta \in \Sigma$, the function $\theta * \cdot : \Sigma \rightharpoonup \Sigma$ is injective.*

We think of elements of a separation algebra Σ as *portions* of program states and the $*$ operation as combining such portions. The partial states allow us to describe parts of the program state belonging to a library or the client. When the $*$-combination of two states is defined, we call them ***compatible***. We sometimes use a pointwise lifting $* : 2^\Sigma \times 2^\Sigma \to 2^\Sigma$ of $*$ to sets of states.

Elements of separation algebras are often defined using partial functions. We use the following notation: $g(x)\downarrow$ means that the function g is defined on x, $\mathsf{dom}(g)$ denotes the set of arguments on which g is defined, and $g[x : y]$ denotes the function that has the same value as g everywhere, except for x, where it has the value y. We also write $\_$ for an expression whose value is irrelevant and implicitly existentially quantified.

Below is an example separation algebra RAM:

$$\mathsf{Loc} = \{1, 2, \ldots\}; \qquad \mathsf{Val} = \mathbb{Z}; \qquad \mathsf{RAM} = \mathsf{Loc} \rightharpoonup_{\mathit{fin}} \mathsf{Val}.$$

A (partial) state in this model consists of a finite partial function from allocated memory locations to the values they store. The $*$ operation on RAM is defined as the disjoint function union $\uplus$, with the everywhere-undefined function $[\,]$ as its unit. Thus, the $*$ operation combines disjoint pieces of memory.

We define a partial operation $\setminus : \Sigma \times \Sigma \rightharpoonup \Sigma$, called ***state subtraction***, as follows: $\theta_2 \setminus \theta_1$ is a state in Σ such that $\theta_2 = (\theta_2 \setminus \theta_1) * \theta_1$; if such a state does not exist, $\theta_2 \setminus \theta_1$ is undefined. When reasoning about ownership transfer between a library and a client, we use the $*$ operation to express a state change for the component that is receiving the ownership of memory, and the $\setminus$ operation, for the one that is giving it up.

Our definition of linearizability uses a novel formalisation of a *footprint* of a state, which, informally, describes the amount of memory or permissions the state includes.

Definition 2. *A* ***footprint*** *of a state θ in a separation algebra Σ is the set of states $\delta(\theta) = \{\theta' \mid \forall \theta''. (\theta' * \theta'')\downarrow \Leftrightarrow (\theta * \theta'')\downarrow\}$.*

The function δ computes the equivalence class of states with the same footprint as θ. In the case of RAM, we have $\delta(\theta) = \{\theta' \mid \mathsf{dom}(\theta) = \mathsf{dom}(\theta')\}$ for every $\theta \in \mathsf{RAM}$. Thus, states with the same footprint contain the same memory cells.

Let $\mathcal{F}(\Sigma) = \{\delta(\theta) \mid \theta \in \Sigma\}$ be the set of footprints in a separation algebra Σ. We now lift the $*$ and $\setminus$ operations on Σ to $\mathcal{F}(\Sigma)$. First, we define the operation $\circ : \mathcal{F}(\Sigma) \times \mathcal{F}(\Sigma) \rightharpoonup \mathcal{F}(\Sigma)$ for adding footprints. Consider $l_1, l_2 \in \mathcal{F}(\Sigma)$ and $\theta_1, \theta_2 \in \Sigma$ such that $l_1 = \delta(\theta_1)$ and $l_2 = \delta(\theta_2)$. If $\theta_1 * \theta_2$ is defined, we let $l_1 \circ l_2 = \delta(\theta_1 * \theta_2)$; otherwise $l_1 \circ l_2$ is undefined. Choosing θ_1 and θ_2 differently does not lead to a different result [10, Appendix B]. For RAM, $\circ$ is just a pointwise lifting of $*$. To define a subtraction operation on footprints, we use the following condition.

Definition 3. *The $*$ operation of a separation algebra Σ is* ***cancellative on footprints*** *when for all $\theta_1, \theta_2, \theta_1', \theta_2' \in \Sigma$, if $\theta_1 * \theta_2$ and $\theta_1' * \theta_2'$ are defined, then*

$$(\delta(\theta_1 * \theta_2) = \delta(\theta_1' * \theta_2') \wedge \delta(\theta_1) = \delta(\theta_1')) \Rightarrow \delta(\theta_2) = \delta(\theta_2').$$

For example, the $*$ operation on RAM satisfies this condition.

When $*$ of Σ is cancellative on footprints, we can define an operation $\setminus : \mathcal{F}(\Sigma) \times \mathcal{F}(\Sigma) \rightharpoonup \mathcal{F}(\Sigma)$ of ***footprint subtraction*** as follows. Consider $l_1, l_2 \in \mathcal{F}(\Sigma)$. If for some $\theta_1, \theta_2, \theta \in \Sigma$, we have $l_1 = \delta(\theta_1)$, $l_2 = \delta(\theta_2)$ and $\theta_2 = \theta_1 * \theta$, then we let

$l_2 \setminus l_1 = \delta(\theta)$. When such $\theta_1, \theta_2, \theta$ do not exist, $l_2 \setminus l_1$ is undefined. Again, we can show that this definition is well-formed [10, Appendix B]. We say that a footprint l_1 is ***smaller*** than l_2, written $l_1 \preceq l_2$, when $l_2 \setminus l_1$ is defined. In the rest of the paper, we fix a separation algebra Σ with the $*$ operation cancellative on footprints.

3 Linearizability with Ownership Transfer

In the following, we consider descriptions of computations of a library providing several methods to a multithreaded client. We fix the set ThreadID of thread identifiers and the set Method of method names. A good definition of linearizability has to allow replacing a concrete library implementation with its abstract version while keeping client behaviours reproducible. For this, it should require that the two libraries have similar client-observable behaviours. Such behaviours are recorded using *histories*, which we now define in our setting.

Definition 4. *An **interface action** ψ is an expression of the form $(t, \mathsf{call}\ m(\theta))$ or $(t, \mathsf{ret}\ m(\theta))$, where $t \in \mathsf{ThreadID}$, $m \in \mathsf{Method}$ and $\theta \in \Sigma$.*

An interface action records a call to or a return from a library method m by thread t. The component θ in $(t, \mathsf{call}\ m(\theta))$ specifies the part of the state transferred upon the call from the client to the library; θ in $(t, \mathsf{ret}\ m(\theta))$ is transferred in the other direction. For example, in the algebra RAM (Section 2), the annotation $\theta = [42 : 0]$ implies the transfer of the cell at the address 42 storing 0.

Definition 5. *A **history** H is a finite sequence of interface actions such that for every thread t, its projection $H|_t$ to actions by t is a sequence of alternating call and return actions over matching methods that starts from a call action.*

In the following, we use the standard notation for sequences: ε is the empty sequence, $\alpha(i)$ is the i-th element of a sequence α, and $|\alpha|$ is the length of α.

Not all histories make intuitive sense with respect to the ownership transfer reading of interface actions. For example, let $\Sigma = \mathsf{RAM}$ and consider the history

$$(1, \mathsf{call}\ m_1([10:0]))\ (2, \mathsf{call}\ m_2([10:0]))(2, \mathsf{ret}\ m_2([\,]))\ (1, \mathsf{ret}\ m_1([\,])).$$

The history is meant to describe *all* the interactions between the library and the client. According to the history, the cell at the address 10 was first owned by the client, and then transferred to the library by thread 1. However, before this state was transferred back to the client, it was again transferred from the client to the library, this time by thread 2. This is not consistent with the intuition of ownership transfer, as executing the second action requires the cell to be owned both by the library and by the client, which is impossible in RAM.

As we show in this paper, histories that do not respect the notion of ownership, such as the one above, cannot be generated by any program, and should not be taken into account when defining linearizability. We use the notion of footprints of states from Section 2 to characterise formally the set of histories that respect ownership.

A finite history H induces a partial function $[\![H]\!]^\sharp : \mathcal{F}(\Sigma) \rightharpoonup \mathcal{F}(\Sigma)$, which tracks how a computation with the history H changes the footprint of the library state:

$$[\![\varepsilon]\!]^\sharp l = l; \qquad [\![H\psi]\!]^\sharp l = [\![H]\!]^\sharp l \circ \delta(\theta), \text{ if } \psi = (\_, \mathsf{call}\,\_(\theta)) \wedge ([\![H]\!]^\sharp l \circ \delta(\theta))\downarrow;$$
$$[\![H\psi]\!]^\sharp l = [\![H]\!]^\sharp l \setminus \delta(\theta), \text{ if } \psi = (\_, \mathsf{ret}\,\_(\theta)) \wedge ([\![H]\!]^\sharp l \setminus \delta(\theta))\downarrow;$$
$$[\![H\psi]\!]^\sharp l = \text{undefined}, \quad \text{otherwise.}$$

Definition 6. *A history H is **balanced** from $l \in \mathcal{F}(\Sigma)$ if $[\![H]\!]^\sharp(l)$ is defined.*

Let $\mathsf{BHistory} = \{(l, H) \mid H$ is balanced from $l\}$ be the set of balanced histories and their initial footprints.

Definition 7. ***Linearizability** is a binary relation $\sqsubseteq$ on $\mathsf{BHistory}$ defined as follows: $(l, H) \sqsubseteq (l', H')$ holds iff (i) $l' \preceq l$; (ii) $H|_t = H'|_t$ for all $t \in \mathsf{ThreadID}$; and (iii) there exists a bijection $\pi \colon \{1, \dots, |H|\} \to \{1, \dots, |H'|\}$ such that for all i and j,*

$$H(i) = H'(\pi(i)) \wedge ((i < j \wedge H(i) = (\_, \mathsf{ret}\,\_) \wedge H(j) = (\_, \mathsf{call}\,\_)) \Rightarrow \pi(i) < \pi(j)).$$

A history H' linearizes a history H when it is a permutation of the latter preserving the order of actions within threads and non-overlapping method invocations. We additionally require that the initial footprint of H' be smaller than that of H, which is a standard requirement in data refinement [8]. It does not pose problems in practice, as the abstract library generating H' usually represents some of the data structures of the concrete library as abstract data types, which do not use the heap.

Definition 7 treats parts of memory whose ownership is passed between the library and the client in the same way as parameters and return values in the classical definition [12]: they are required to be the same in the two histories. In fact, the setting of the classical definition can be modelled in ours if we pass parameters and return values via the heap. The novelty of our definition lies in restricting the histories considered to balanced ones. This restriction is required for our notion of linearizability to be correct in the sense of the Rearrangement Lemma established in the next section.

4 Rearrangement Lemma

Intuitively, the Rearrangement Lemma says that, if $H \sqsubseteq H'$, then every execution trace of a library producing H' can be transformed into another trace of the same library that differs from the original one only in interface actions and produces H, instead of H'. This property is the key component for establishing the correctness of linearizability *on libraries*, formulated by the Abstraction Theorem in Section 7.

Primitive Commands. We first define a set of primitive commands that clients and libraries can execute to change the memory atomically. Consider the set $2^\Sigma \cup \{\top\}$ of subsets of Σ with a special element $\top$ used to denote an error state, resulting, e.g., from dereferencing an invalid pointer. We assume a collection of primitive commands PComm and an interpretation of every $c \in \mathsf{PComm}$ as a transformer $f_c^t : \Sigma \to (2^\Sigma \cup \{\top\})$, which maps pre-states to states obtained when thread $t \in \mathsf{ThreadID}$ executes c from a pre-state. The fact that our transformers are parameterised by t allows atomic accesses to areas of memory indexed by thread identifiers. This idealisation simplifies the setting in that it lets us do without special thread-local or method-local storage for passing method parameters and return values. For our results to hold, we need to place some standard restrictions on the transformers f_c^t (see [10, Appendix A]).

Traces. We record information about a program execution, including internal actions by components, using *traces*.

Definition 8. *An* ***action*** φ *is either an interface action or an expression of the form* (t, c)*, where* $t \in \mathsf{ThreadID}$ *and* $c \in \mathsf{PComm}$*. We denote the set of all actions by* Act.

Definition 9. *A* ***trace*** τ *is a finite sequence of actions such that its projection* $\mathsf{history}(\tau)$ *to interface actions is a history. A trace* η *is a* ***client trace****, if*

$$\forall i, j, t, c.\, i < j \wedge \eta(i) = (t, \mathsf{call}\ \_) \wedge \eta(j) = (t, c) \Rightarrow \exists k.\, i < k < j \wedge \eta(k) = (t, \mathsf{ret}\ \_).$$

A trace ξ *is a* ***library trace****, if*

$$\forall i, t, c.\, \xi(i) = (t, c) \Rightarrow \exists j.\, j < i \wedge \xi(j) = (t, \mathsf{call}\ \_) \wedge \neg\exists k.\, i < k < j \wedge \xi(k) = (t, \mathsf{ret}\ \_).$$

In other words, a thread in a client trace cannot execute actions inside a library method, and in a library trace, outside it. We denote the set of all traces by Trace. In the following, η denotes client traces, ξ, library traces, and τ, arbitrary ones.

In this section, we are concerned with library traces only. For a library trace ξ, we define a function $[\![\xi]\!]_{\mathsf{lib}} : 2^{\Sigma} \to (2^{\Sigma} \cup \{\top\})$ that ***evaluates*** ξ, computing the state of the memory after executing the sequence of actions given by the trace. We first define the evaluation of a single action φ by $[\![\varphi]\!]_{\mathsf{lib}} : \Sigma \to (2^{\Sigma} \cup \{\top\})$:

$$[\![(t, c)]\!]_{\mathsf{lib}}\theta = f_c^t(\theta); \qquad [\![(t, \mathsf{call}\ m(\theta_0))]\!]_{\mathsf{lib}}\theta = \text{if } (\theta * \theta_0)\!\downarrow \text{then } \{\theta * \theta_0\} \text{ else } \emptyset;$$
$$[\![(t, \mathsf{ret}\ m(\theta_0))]\!]_{\mathsf{lib}}\theta = \text{if } (\theta \setminus \theta_0)\!\downarrow \text{then } \{\theta \setminus \theta_0\} \text{ else } \top.$$

The evaluation of call and return actions follows their ownership transfer reading explained in Section 3: upon a call to a library, the latter gets the ownership of the specified piece of state; upon a return, the library gives it up. In the former case, only transfers of states compatible with the current library state are allowed. In the latter case, the computation faults when the required piece of state is not available, which ensures that the library respects the contract with its client.

Let us lift $[\![\varphi]\!]_{\mathsf{lib}}$ to 2^{Σ} pointwise: for $p \in 2^{\Sigma}$ we let $[\![\varphi]\!]_{\mathsf{lib}}p = \bigcup\{[\![\varphi]\!]_{\mathsf{lib}}\theta \mid \theta \in p\}$, if $\forall \theta \in p.\, [\![\varphi]\!]_{\mathsf{lib}}\theta \neq \top$; otherwise, $[\![\varphi]\!]_{\mathsf{lib}}p = \top$. We then define the evaluation $[\![\xi]\!]_{\mathsf{lib}} : 2^{\Sigma} \to (2^{\Sigma} \cup \{\top\})$ of a library trace ξ as follows:

$$[\![\varepsilon]\!]_{\mathsf{lib}}p = p; \quad [\![\xi\varphi]\!]_{\mathsf{lib}}p = \text{if } ([\![\xi]\!]_{\mathsf{lib}}p \neq \top) \text{ then } [\![\varphi]\!]_{\mathsf{lib}}([\![\xi]\!]_{\mathsf{lib}}p) \text{ else } \top.$$

In the following, we write $[\![\xi]\!]_{\mathsf{lib}}\theta$ for $[\![\xi]\!]_{\mathsf{lib}}(\{\theta\})$. Using trace evaluation, we can define when a particular trace can be safely executed.

Definition 10. *A library trace* ξ *is* ***executable*** *from* θ *when* $[\![\xi]\!]_{\mathsf{lib}}\theta \notin \{\emptyset, \top\}$.

Proposition 11. *If* ξ *is a library trace executable from* θ*, then* $\mathsf{history}(\xi)$ *is balanced from* $\delta(\theta)$.

Definition 12. *Library traces* ξ *and* ξ' *are* ***equivalent****, written* $\xi \sim \xi'$*, if* $\xi|_t = \xi'|_t$ *for all* $t \in \mathsf{ThreadID}$*, and the projections of* ξ *and* ξ' *to non-interface actions are identical.*

Lemma 13 (Rearrangement). *Assume* $(\delta(\theta), H) \sqsubseteq (\delta(\theta'), H')$*. If a trace* ξ' *is executable from* θ' *and* $\mathsf{history}(\xi') = H'$*, then there exists a trace* ξ *executable from* θ' *such that* $\mathsf{history}(\xi) = H$ *and* $\xi \sim \xi'$.

The proof transforms ξ' into ξ by repeatedly swapping adjacent actions according to a certain strategy to make the history of the trace equal to H. The most subtle place in the proof is swapping $(t_1, \mathsf{ret}\ m_1(\theta_1))$ and $(t_2, \mathsf{call}\ m_2(\theta_2))$, where $t_1 \neq t_2$. The justification of this transformation relies on the fact that the target history H is balanced. Consider the case when $\theta_1 = \theta_2 = \theta$. Then the two actions correspond to the library first transferring θ to the client and then getting it back. It is impossible for the client to transfer θ to the library earlier, unless it already owned θ before the return in the original trace (this may happen when θ describes only partial permissions for a piece of memory, and thus, its instances can be owned by the client and the library at the same time). Fortunately, using the fact that H is balanced, we can prove that the latter is indeed the case, and hence, the actions commute.

So far we have used the notion of linearizability on histories, without taking into account library implementations that generate them. In the rest of the paper, we lift this notion to libraries, written in a particular programming language, and prove an Abstraction Theorem, which guarantees that a library can be replaced by another library linearizing it when we reason about its client program.

5 Programming Language

We consider a simple concurrent programming language:

$$C ::= c \mid m \mid C;C \mid C+C \mid C^* \quad L ::= \{m{=}C;\ \ldots;\ m{=}C\} \quad S ::= \mathsf{let}\ L\ \mathsf{in}\ C \parallel \ldots \parallel C$$

A program consists of a ***library*** L implementing methods $m \in \mathsf{Method}$ and its ***client*** $C_1 \parallel \ldots \parallel C_n$, given by a parallel composition of threads. The commands include primitive commands $c \in \mathsf{PComm}$, method calls $m \in \mathsf{Method}$, sequential composition $C; C'$, nondeterministic choice $C + C'$ and iteration C^*. We use $+$ and * instead of conditionals and while loops for theoretical simplicity: the latter can be defined in the language as syntactic sugar. Methods do not take arguments and do not return values: these can be passed via special locations on the heap associated with the identifier of the thread calling the method. We assume that every method called in the program is defined by the library, and that there are no nested method calls.

An ***open program*** is one without a library (denoted $\mathcal{C}$) or a client (denoted $\mathcal{L}$):

$$\mathcal{C} ::= \mathsf{let}\ [-]\ \mathsf{in}\ C \parallel \ldots \parallel C \qquad \mathcal{L} ::= \mathsf{let}\ L\ \mathsf{in}\ [-] \qquad \mathcal{P} ::= \mathcal{S} \mid \mathcal{C} \mid \mathcal{L}$$

In $\mathcal{C}$, we allow the client to call methods that are not defined in the program (but belong to the missing library). We call $\mathcal{S}$ a ***complete program***. Open programs represent a library or a client considered in isolation. The novelty of the kind of open programs we consider here is that we allow them to communicate with their environment via ownership transfers. We now define a way to specify a contract this communication follows.

A ***predicate*** is a set of states from Σ, and a ***parameterised predicate*** is a mapping from thread identifiers to predicates. We use the same symbols p, q, r for ordinary and parameterised predicates. When p is a parameterised predicate, we write p_t for the predicate obtained by applying p to a thread t. Both kinds of predicates can be described syntactically, e.g., using separation logic assertions ([14] and [10, Appendix C]).

We describe possible ownership transfers between components with the aid of ***method specifications*** Γ, which are sets of Hoare triples $\{p\}\, m\, \{q\}$, at most one for each method. Here p and q are parameterised predicates such that p_t describes pieces of state transferred when thread t calls the method m, and q_t, those transferred at its return. Note that the pre- and postconditions in method specifications only identify the areas of memory transferred; in other words, they describe the "type" of the returned data structure, but not its "value". As usual for concurrent algorithms, a complete specification of a library is given by its abstract implementation (Section 7).

For example, as we discussed in Section 1, clients of a memory allocator transfer the ownership of memory cells at calls to and returns from it. In particular, the specifications of the allocator methods look approximately as follows:

$$\{\mathsf{emp}\}\mathtt{alloc}\{(\mathtt{r}=0 \wedge \mathsf{emp}) \vee (\mathtt{r} \neq 0 \wedge \mathsf{Block}(\mathtt{r}))\} \quad \{\mathsf{Block}(\mathtt{blk})\}\mathtt{free}(\mathtt{blk})\{\mathsf{emp}\}$$

Here `r` denotes the return value of `alloc`; `blk`, the actual parameter of `free`; emp, the empty heap ϵ; and $\mathsf{Block}(\mathtt{r})$, a block of memory at address `r` managed by the allocator.

To define the semantics of ownership transfers unambiguously, we require pre- and postconditions to be *precise*.

Definition 14. *A predicate $r \in 2^{\Sigma}$ is* ***precise*** *[13] if for every state θ there exists at most one substate θ_1 satisfying r, i.e., such that $\theta_1 \in r$ and $\theta = \theta_1 * \theta_2$ for some θ_2.*

Note that, since the $*$ operation is cancellative, when such a substate θ_1 exists, the corresponding substate θ_2 is unique and is denoted by $\theta \setminus r$. Informally, a precise predicate carves out a unique piece of the heap. A parameterised predicate r is precise if so is r_t for every t.

A ***specified open program*** is of the form $\Gamma \vdash \mathcal{C}$ or $\mathcal{L} : \Gamma$. In the former, the specification Γ describes all the methods without implementations that $\mathcal{C}$ may call. In the latter, Γ provides specifications for the methods in the open program that can be called by its external environment. In both cases, Γ specifies the type of another open program that can fill in the hole in $\mathcal{C}$ or $\mathcal{L}$. When we are not sure which form a program has, we write $\Gamma \vdash \mathcal{P} : \Gamma'$, where Γ is empty if $\mathcal{P}$ does not have a client, Γ' is empty if it does not have a library, and both of them are empty if the program is complete.

For open programs $\Gamma \vdash \mathcal{C} = \mathsf{let}\ [-]\ \mathsf{in}\ C_1 \parallel \ldots \parallel C_n$ and $\mathcal{L} : \Gamma = \mathsf{let}\ L\ \mathsf{in}\ [-]$, we denote by $\mathcal{C}(\mathcal{L})$ the complete program $\mathsf{let}\ L\ \mathsf{in}\ C_1 \parallel \ldots \parallel C_n$.

6 Client-Local and Library-Local Semantics

We now give the semantics to complete and open programs. In the latter case, we define component-local semantics that include all behaviours of an open program under any environment satisfying the specification associated with it. In Section 7, we use these to lift linearizability to libraries and formulate the Abstraction Theorem.

We define program semantics in two stages. First, given a program, we generate the set of all its traces possible. This is done solely based on the structure of its statements, without taking into account restrictions arising from the semantics of primitive commands or ownership transfers. The next step filters out traces that are not consistent with these restrictions using a trace evaluation process similar to that in Section 4.

$$(\!|c|\!)_t^\Gamma S = \{(t,c)\}; \quad (\!|C_1 + C_2|\!)_t^\Gamma S = (\!|C_1|\!)_t^\Gamma S \cup (\!|C_2|\!)_t^\Gamma S; \quad (\!|C^*|\!)_t^\Gamma S = (((\!|C|\!)_t^\Gamma)S)^*;$$
$$(\!|m|\!)_t^\Gamma S = \{(t, \mathsf{call}\ m(\theta_p))\,\tau\,(t, \mathsf{ret}\ m(\theta_q)) \mid \tau \in S(m,t) \wedge \theta_p \in p_t^m \wedge \theta_q \in q_t^m\};$$
$$(\!|C_1; C_2|\!)_t^\Gamma S = \{\tau_1\tau_2 \mid \tau_1 \in (\!|C_1|\!)_t^\Gamma S \wedge \tau_2 \in (\!|C_2|\!)_t^\Gamma S\};$$
$$(\!|C_1 \parallel \ldots \parallel C_n|\!)^\Gamma S = \bigcup\{\tau_1 \parallel \ldots \parallel \tau_n \mid \forall t = 1..n.\, \tau_t \in (\!|C_t|\!)_t^\Gamma S\};$$
$$(\!|\mathsf{let}\ \{m = C_m \mid m \in M\}\ \mathsf{in}\ C_1 \parallel \ldots \parallel C_n|\!) = \mathsf{prefix}((\!|C_1 \parallel \ldots \parallel C_n|\!)^{\Gamma_\epsilon}(\lambda m, t.\, (\!|C_m|\!)_{\bar{t}}(\_)));$$
$$(\!|\Gamma \vdash \mathsf{let}\ [-]\ \mathsf{in}\ C_1 \parallel \ldots \parallel C_n|\!) = \mathsf{prefix}((\!|C_1 \parallel \ldots \parallel C_n|\!)^\Gamma(\lambda m, t.\, \{\varepsilon\}));$$
$$(\!|\mathsf{let}\ \{m = C_m \mid m \in M\}\ \mathsf{in}\ [-] : \Gamma|\!) =$$
$$\mathsf{prefix}\left(\bigcup_{k\geq 1} (\!|C_{\mathsf{mgc}} \parallel \ldots (k \text{ times}) \ldots \parallel C_{\mathsf{mgc}}|\!)^\Gamma(\lambda m, t.\, (\!|C_m|\!)_{\bar{t}}(\_))\right).$$

Fig. 1. Trace sets of commands and programs. Here $\Gamma_\epsilon = \{\{\{\epsilon\}\}\, m\, \{\{\epsilon\}\} \mid m \in M\}$, $\Gamma = \{\{p^m\}\, m\, \{q^m\} \mid m \in M\}$, $M = \{m_1, \ldots, m_j\}$, $C_{\mathsf{mgc}} = (m_1 + \ldots + m_j)^*$, and $\mathsf{prefix}(T)$ is the prefix closure of T. Also, $\tau \in \tau_1 \parallel \ldots \parallel \tau_n$ if and only if every action in τ is done by a thread $t \in \{1, \ldots, n\}$ and for all such t, we have $\tau|_t = \tau_t$.

Trace Sets. Consider a program $\Gamma \vdash \mathcal{P} : \Gamma'$ and let $M \subseteq \mathsf{Method}$ be the set of methods implemented by its library or called by its client. We define the trace set $(\!|\Gamma \vdash \mathcal{P} : \Gamma'|\!) \in 2^{\mathsf{Trace}}$ of $\mathcal{P}$ in Figure 1. We first define the trace set $(\!|C|\!)_t^\Gamma S$ of a command C, parameterised by the identifier t of the thread executing it, a method specification Γ, and a mapping $S \in M \times \mathsf{ThreadID} \to 2^{\mathsf{Trace}}$ giving the trace set of the body of every method that C can call when executed by a given thread. The trace set of a client $(\!|C_1 \parallel \ldots \parallel C_n|\!)^\Gamma S$ is obtained by interleaving traces of its threads.

The trace set $(\!|\mathcal{C}(\mathcal{L})|\!)$ of a complete program is that of its client computed with respect to a mapping $\lambda m, t.\, (\!|C_m|\!)_{\bar{t}}(\_)$ associating every method m with the trace set of its body C_m. Since we prohibit nested method calls, $(\!|C_m|\!)$ does not depend on the Γ and S parameters. Since the program is complete, we use a method specification Γ_ϵ with empty pre- and postconditions for computing $(\!|C_1 \parallel \ldots \parallel C_n|\!)$. We prefix-close the resulting trace set to take into account incomplete executions. A program $\Gamma \vdash \mathcal{C}$ generates client traces $(\!|\Gamma \vdash \mathcal{C}|\!)$, which do not include internal library actions. This is enforced by associating an empty trace with every library method. Finally, a program $\mathcal{L} : \Gamma'$ generates all possible library traces $(\!|\mathcal{L} : \Gamma'|\!)$. This is achieved by running the library under its *most general client*, where every thread executes an infinite loop, repeatedly invoking arbitrary library methods.

Evaluation. The set of traces generated using $(\!|\cdot|\!)$ may include those not consistent with the semantics of primitive commands or expected ownership transfers. We therefore define the meaning of a program $[\![\Gamma \vdash \mathcal{P} : \Gamma']\!] \in \Sigma \rightharpoonup (2^{\mathsf{Trace}} \cup \{\top\})$ by evaluating every trace in $(\!|\Gamma \vdash \mathcal{P} : \Gamma'|\!)$ to determine whether it is executable.

First, consider a library $\mathcal{L} : \Gamma'$. In this case we use the evaluation function $[\![\cdot]\!]_{\mathsf{lib}}$ defined in Section 4. We let $[\![\mathcal{L} : \Gamma']\!]\theta = \top$, if

$$\exists \xi, t.\, (\exists c.\, [\![\xi]\!]_{\mathsf{lib}}\theta \neq \top \wedge \xi\,(t,c) \in (\!|\mathcal{L} : \Gamma'|\!) \wedge f_c^t(\theta) = \top) \vee$$
$$(\exists m, \theta_q.\, [\![\xi]\!]_{\mathsf{lib}}\theta \neq \top \wedge \xi\,(t, \mathsf{ret}\ m(\theta_q)) \in (\!|\mathcal{L} : \Gamma'|\!)$$
$$\wedge\, \forall \theta_q'.\, \xi\,(t, \mathsf{ret}\ m(\theta_q')) \in (\!|\mathcal{L} : \Gamma'|\!) \Rightarrow [\![\xi\,(t, \mathsf{ret}\ m(\theta_q'))]\!]_{\mathsf{lib}}\theta = \top).$$

Thus, the library has no semantics if a primitive command in one of its executions faults, or the required piece of state is not available for transferring to the client at a method return. Otherwise, $[\![\mathcal{L} : \Gamma']\!]\theta = \{\xi \mid \xi \in (\!|\mathcal{L} : \Gamma'|\!) \wedge [\![\xi]\!]_{\mathsf{lib}}\theta \notin \{\emptyset, \top\}\}$. This gives a ***library-local*** semantics to $\mathcal{L}$, in the sense that it takes into account only the part of the program state owned by the library and considers its behaviour under any client respecting Γ'. This generalises the standard notion of the most general client to situations where the library performs ownership transfers. Lemma 16 below confirms that the client defined by $(\!|\mathcal{L} : \Gamma'|\!)$ and $[\![\cdot]\!]_{\mathsf{lib}}$ is indeed most general, as it reproduces library behaviours under any possible clients.

To give a semantics to $\Gamma \vdash \mathcal{C}$, we define an evaluation function $[\![\eta]\!]_{\mathsf{client}} : 2^{\Sigma} \to (2^{\Sigma} \cup \{\top\})$ for client traces η. To this end, we define the evaluation of a single action φ by $[\![\varphi]\!]_{\mathsf{client}} : \Sigma \to (2^{\Sigma} \cup \{\top\})$ and then lift it to client traces as in Section 4:

$$[\![(t,c)]\!]_{\mathsf{client}}\theta = f_c^t(\theta); \qquad [\![(t, \mathsf{call}\ m(\theta_0))]\!]_{\mathsf{client}}\theta = \text{if } (\theta \setminus \theta_0)\!\downarrow \text{then } \{\theta \setminus \theta_0\} \text{ else } \top;$$
$$[\![(t, \mathsf{ret}\ m(\theta_0))]\!]_{\mathsf{client}}\theta = \text{if } (\theta * \theta_0)\!\downarrow \text{then } \{\theta * \theta_0\} \text{ else } \emptyset.$$

When a thread t calls a method m in Γ, it transfers the ownership of the specified piece of state to the library being called. The evaluation faults if the state to be transferred is not available, which ensures that the client respects the specifications of the library. When the method returns, the client receives the ownership of the specified piece of state, which has to be compatible with the state of the client. We let $[\![\Gamma \vdash \mathcal{C}]\!]\theta = \top$, if

$$\begin{aligned}\exists \eta, t.\ (\exists c.\ [\![\eta]\!]_{\mathsf{client}}\theta \neq \top \wedge \eta\,(t,c) \in (\!|\Gamma \vdash \mathcal{C}|\!) \wedge f_c^t(\theta) = \top) \vee \\ (\exists m, \theta_p.\ [\![\eta]\!]_{\mathsf{client}}\theta \neq \top \wedge \eta\,(t, \mathsf{call}\ m(\theta_p)) \in (\!|\Gamma \vdash \mathcal{C}|\!) \\ \wedge \forall \theta'_p.\ \eta\,(t, \mathsf{call}\ m(\theta'_p)) \in (\!|\Gamma \vdash \mathcal{C}|\!) \Rightarrow [\![\eta\,(t, \mathsf{ret}\ m(\theta'_p))]\!]_{\mathsf{client}}\theta = \top).\end{aligned}$$

Otherwise, $[\![\Gamma \vdash \mathcal{C}]\!]\theta = \{\eta \mid \eta \in (\!|\Gamma \vdash \mathcal{C}|\!) \wedge [\![\eta]\!]_{\mathsf{client}}\theta \notin \{\emptyset, \top\}\}$. This gives a ***client-local*** semantics to $\mathcal{C}$, in the sense that it takes into account only the part of the state owned by the client and considers its behaviour when using any library respecting Γ.

Finally, for a complete program $\mathcal{C}(\mathcal{L})$, we let $[\![\mathcal{C}(\mathcal{L})]\!]\theta = \top$, if $\exists \tau.\ \tau \in (\!|\mathcal{C}(\mathcal{L})|\!) \wedge [\![\tau]\!]_{\mathsf{lib}}\theta = \top$; otherwise, $[\![\mathcal{C}(\mathcal{L})]\!]\theta = \{\tau \mid \tau \in (\!|\mathcal{C}(\mathcal{L})|\!) \wedge [\![\tau]\!]_{\mathsf{lib}}\theta \neq \emptyset\}$ (note that using $[\![\cdot]\!]_{\mathsf{client}}$ here would yield the same result). For a set of initial states $I \subseteq \Sigma$, let

$$[\![(\Gamma \vdash \mathcal{P} : \Gamma'), I]\!] = \{(\theta, \tau) \mid \theta \in I \wedge \tau \in [\![\Gamma \vdash \mathcal{P} : \Gamma']\!]\theta\}.$$

Definition 15. *A program $\Gamma \vdash \mathcal{P} : \Gamma'$ is **safe** at θ, if $[\![\Gamma \vdash \mathcal{P} : \Gamma']\!]\theta \neq \top$; $\mathcal{P}$ is safe for $I \subseteq \Sigma$, if it is safe at θ for all $\theta \in I$.*

Commands fault when accessing memory cells that are not present in the state they are run from. Thus, the safety of a program guarantees that it does not touch the part of the heap belonging to its environment. Besides, calls to methods in Γ and returns from methods in Γ' fault when the piece of state they have to transfer is not available. Thus, the safety of the program also ensures that it respects the contract with its environment given by Γ or Γ'.

While decomposing the verification of a closed program into the verification of its components, we rely on the above properties to ensure that we can indeed reason about the components in isolation, without worrying about the interference from their environment. In particular, our definition of linearizability on libraries considers only safe libraries (Section 7).

Soundness and Adequacy. The client-local and library-local semantics are sound and adequate with respect to the global semantics of the complete program. These properties are used in the proof of the Abstraction Theorem.

Let ground be a function on traces that replaces the state annotations θ of all interface actions with ϵ. For a trace τ, we define its projection $\mathsf{client}(\tau)$ to actions executed by the client code: we include $\varphi = (t, \_)$ with $\tau = \tau' \varphi \tau''$ into the projection, if (i) φ is an interface action; or (ii) φ is outside an invocation of a method, i.e., it is not the case that $\tau|_t = \tau_1\, (t, \mathsf{call}\ \_)\, \tau_2 \varphi \tau_3$, where τ_2 does not contain a $(t, \mathsf{ret}\ \_)$ action. We also use a similar projection $\mathsf{lib}(\tau)$ to library actions.

The following lemma shows that a trace of $\mathcal{C}(\mathcal{L})$ generates two traces in the client-local and library-local semantics with the same history. The lemma thus carries over properties of the local semantics, such as safety, to the global one, and in this sense is the statement of the soundness of the former with respect to the latter.

Lemma 16 (Soundness). *Assume $\Gamma \vdash \mathcal{C}$ and $\mathcal{L} : \Gamma$ safe for I_1 and I_2, respectively. Then so is $\mathcal{C}(\mathcal{L})$ for $I_1 * I_2$ and*

$$\forall (\theta, \tau) \in [\![\mathcal{C}(\mathcal{L}), I_1 * I_2]\!].\, \exists (\theta_1, \eta) \in [\![\mathcal{C}, I_1]\!].\, \exists (\theta_2, \xi) \in [\![\mathcal{L}, I_2]\!].\, \theta = \theta_1 * \theta_2 \wedge \\ \mathsf{history}(\eta) = \mathsf{history}(\xi) \wedge \mathsf{client}(\tau) = \mathsf{ground}(\eta) \wedge \mathsf{lib}(\tau) = \mathsf{ground}(\xi).$$

The following lemma states that any pair of client-local and library-local traces agreeing on the history can be combined into a trace of $\mathcal{C}(\mathcal{L})$. It thus carries over properties of the global semantics to the local ones, stating the adequacy of the latter.

Lemma 17 (Adequacy). *If $\mathcal{L} : \Gamma$ and $\Gamma \vdash \mathcal{C}$ are safe for I_1 and I_2, respectively, then*

$$\forall (\theta_1, \eta) \in [\![\mathcal{C}, I_1]\!].\, \forall (\theta_2, \xi) \in [\![\mathcal{L}, I_2]\!].\, ((\theta_1 * \theta_2){\downarrow} \wedge \mathsf{history}(\eta) = \mathsf{history}(\xi)) \Rightarrow \\ \exists \tau.\, (\theta_1 * \theta_2, \tau) \in [\![\mathcal{C}(\mathcal{L}), I_1 * I_2]\!] \wedge \mathsf{client}(\tau) = \mathsf{ground}(\eta) \wedge \mathsf{lib}(\tau) = \mathsf{ground}(\xi).$$

7 Abstraction Theorem

We are now in a position to lift the notion of linearizability on histories to libraries and prove the central technical result of this paper—the Abstraction Theorem. We define linearizability between specified libraries $\mathcal{L} : \Gamma$, together with their sets of initial states I. First, using the library-local semantics, we define the set of histories of a library $\mathcal{L}$ with the set of initial states I: $\mathsf{history}(\mathcal{L}, I) = \{(\delta(\theta_0), \mathsf{history}(\tau)) \mid (\theta_0, \tau) \in [\![\mathcal{L}, I]\!]\}$.

Definition 18. *Consider $\mathcal{L}_1 : \Gamma$ and $\mathcal{L}_2 : \Gamma$ safe for I_1 and I_2, respectively. We say that $(\mathcal{L}_2, I_2)$ **linearizes** $(\mathcal{L}_1, I_1)$, written $(\mathcal{L}_1, I_1) \sqsubseteq (\mathcal{L}_2, I_2)$, if*

$$\forall (l_1, H_1) \in \mathsf{history}(\mathcal{L}_1, I_1).\, \exists (l_2, H_2) \in \mathsf{history}(\mathcal{L}_2, I_2).\, (l_1, H_1) \sqsubseteq (l_2, H_2).$$

Thus, $(\mathcal{L}_2, I_2)$ linearizes $(\mathcal{L}_1, I_1)$ if every behaviour of the latter may be reproduced in a linearized form by the former without requiring more memory.

Theorem 19 (Abstraction). *If $\mathcal{L}_1 : \Gamma$, $\mathcal{L}_2 : \Gamma$, $\Gamma \vdash \mathcal{C}$ are safe for I_1, I_2, I, respectively, and $(\mathcal{L}_1, I_1) \sqsubseteq (\mathcal{L}_2, I_2)$, then $\mathcal{C}(\mathcal{L}_1)$ and $\mathcal{C}(\mathcal{L}_2)$ are safe for $I * I_1$ and $I * I_2$, respectively, and*

$$\forall (\theta_1, \tau_1) \in [\![\mathcal{C}(\mathcal{L}_1), I * I_1]\!].\, \exists (\theta_2, \tau_2) \in [\![\mathcal{C}(\mathcal{L}_2), I * I_2]\!].\, \mathsf{client}(\tau_1) = \mathsf{client}(\tau_2).$$

Thus, when reasoning about a client $\mathcal{C}(\mathcal{L}_1)$ of a library $\mathcal{L}_1$, we can soundly replace $\mathcal{L}_1$ with a library $\mathcal{L}_2$ linearizing it: if a linear-time safety property over client actions holds of $\mathcal{C}(\mathcal{L}_2)$, it will also hold of $\mathcal{C}(\mathcal{L}_1)$. In practice, we are usually interested in ***atomicity abstraction***, a special case of this transformation when methods in $\mathcal{L}_2$ are atomic. The theorem is restricted to safety properties as, for simplicity, in this paper we consider only finite histories and traces. Our results can be generalised to the infinite case as in [9]. The requirement that $\mathcal{C}$ be safe in the theorem restricts its applicability to *healthy* clients that do not access library internals.

To prove Theorem 19, we first lift Lemma 13 to traces in the library-local semantics.

Corollary 20. *If* $(\delta(\theta), H) \sqsubseteq (\delta(\theta'), H')$ *and* $\mathcal{L}$ *is safe at* θ', *then*

$$\forall \xi' \in [\![\mathcal{L}]\!]\theta'.\,\mathsf{history}(\xi') = H' \Rightarrow \exists \xi \in [\![\mathcal{L}]\!]\theta'.\,\mathsf{history}(\xi) = H.$$

Thus, if $(\mathcal{L}_1, I_1) \sqsubseteq (\mathcal{L}_2, I_2)$, then the set of histories of $\mathcal{L}_1$ is a subset of those of $\mathcal{L}_2$: linearizability is a sound criterion for proving that one library simulates another.

Proof of Theorem 19. The safety of $\mathcal{C}(\mathcal{L}_1)$ and $\mathcal{C}(\mathcal{L}_2)$ follows from Lemma 16. Take $(\theta, \tau_1) \in [\![\mathcal{C}(\mathcal{L}_1), I * I_1]\!]$. We transform the trace τ_1 of $\mathcal{C}(\mathcal{L}_1)$ into a trace τ_2 of $\mathcal{C}(\mathcal{L}_2)$ with the same client projection using the local semantics of $\mathcal{L}_1$, $\mathcal{L}_2$ and $\mathcal{C}$. Namely, we first apply Lemma 16 to generate a pair of a library-local initial state and a trace $(\theta_l^1, \xi_1) \in [\![\mathcal{L}_1, I_1]\!]$ and a client-local pair $(\theta_c, \eta) \in [\![\mathcal{C}, I]\!]$, such that $\theta = \theta_c * \theta_l^1$, $\mathsf{client}(\tau_1) = \mathsf{ground}(\eta)$ and $\mathsf{history}(\eta) = \mathsf{history}(\xi_1)$. Since $(\mathcal{L}_1, I_1) \sqsubseteq (\mathcal{L}_2, I_2)$, for some $(\theta_l^2, \xi_2) \in [\![\mathcal{L}_2, I_2]\!]$, we have $\delta(\theta_l^2) \preceq \delta(\theta_l^1)$ and $(\delta(\theta_l^1), \mathsf{history}(\xi_1)) \sqsubseteq (\delta(\theta_l^2), \mathsf{history}(\xi_2))$. By Corollary 20, ξ_2 can be transformed into a trace ξ_2' such that $(\theta_l^2, \xi_2') \in [\![\mathcal{L}_2, I_2]\!]$ and $\mathsf{history}(\xi_2') = \mathsf{history}(\xi_1) = \mathsf{history}(\eta)$. Since $\delta(\theta_l^2) \preceq \delta(\theta_l^1)$ and $(\theta_c * \theta_l^1)\!\downarrow$, we have $(\theta_c * \theta_l^2)\!\downarrow$. We then use Lemma 17 to compose the library-local trace ξ_2' with the client-local one η into a trace τ_2 such that $(\theta_c * \theta_l^2, \tau_2) \in [\![\mathcal{C}(\mathcal{L}_2), I * I_2]\!]$ and $\mathsf{client}(\tau_2) = \mathsf{ground}(\eta) = \mathsf{client}(\tau_1)$. □

Establishing Linearizability with Ownership Transfer and Its Applications. We have developed a logic for proving linearizability in the sense of Definition 18, which generalises an existing proof system [16] based on separation logic [14] to the setting with ownership transfer. The logic uses the usual method of proving linearizability based on linearization points [1, 12, 16] and treats ownership transfers between a library and its environment in the same way as transfers between procedures and their callers in separation logic. Due to space constraints, the details of the logic are beyond the scope of this paper and are described in [10, Appendix D]. We mention the logic here to emphasise that our notion of linearizability can indeed be established effectively.

The Abstraction Theorem is not just a theoretical result: it enables compositional reasoning about complex concurrent algorithms that are challenging for existing verification methods. For example, the theorem can be used to justify Vafeiadis's compositional proof [16, Section 5.3] of the multiple-word compare-and-swap (MCAS) algorithm implemented using an auxiliary operation called RDCSS [11] (the proof used an abstraction of the kind enabled by Theorem 19 without justifying its correctness). If the MCAS algorithm were verified together with RDCSS, its proof would be extremely compicated. Fortunately, we can consider MCAS as a client of RDCSS, with the two components performing ownership transfers between them. The Abstraction Theorem then makes the proof tractable by allowing us to verify the linearizability of MCAS assuming an atomic specification of the inner RDCSS algorithm.

8 Frame Rule for Linearizability

Libraries such as concurrent containers are used by clients to transfer the ownership of data structures, but do not actually access their contents. We show that for such libraries, the classical linearizability implies linearizability with ownership transfer.

Definition 21. *A method specification* $\Gamma' = \{\{r^m\}\, m\, \{s^m\} \mid m \in M\}$ ***extends*** *a specification* $\Gamma = \{\{p^m\}\, m\, \{q^m\} \mid m \in M\}$, *if* $\forall t.\, r^m_t \subseteq p^m_t * \Sigma \wedge s^m_t \subseteq q^m_t * \Sigma$.

For example, Γ might say that a method m receives a pointer x as a parameter: $\{\exists x.\, \mathtt{param}[t] \mapsto x\}\, m\, \{\mathtt{param}[t] \mapsto \_\}$, where t is the identifier of the thread calling m. Then Γ' may mandate that the cell the pointer identifies be transferred to the method: $\{\exists x.\, \mathtt{param}[t] \mapsto x * x \mapsto \_\}\, m\, \{\mathtt{param}[t] \mapsto \_\}$. For a history H, let $\lfloor\!\lfloor H \rfloor\!\rfloor_\Gamma$ be the result of replacing every action φ in H by the action $\lfloor\!\lfloor \varphi \rfloor\!\rfloor_\Gamma$ defined as follows:

$$\lfloor\!\lfloor (t, \mathsf{call}\ m(\theta)) \rfloor\!\rfloor_\Gamma = (t, \mathsf{call}\ m(\theta \setminus p^m_t)); \quad \lfloor\!\lfloor (t, \mathsf{ret}\ m(\theta)) \rfloor\!\rfloor_\Gamma = (t, \mathsf{ret}\ m(\theta \setminus q^m_t)).$$

$\lfloor\!\lfloor H \rfloor\!\rfloor_\Gamma$ is undefined if so is the result of any of the $\setminus$ operations above. The operation selects the extra pieces of state not required by Γ.

Theorem 22 (Frame rule). *Assume (i) for all* $i \in \{1, 2\}$, $\mathcal{L}_i : \Gamma$ *and* $\mathcal{L}_i : \Gamma'$ *are safe for* I_i *and* $I_i * I$, *respectively; (ii)* $(\mathcal{L}_1 : \Gamma, I_1) \sqsubseteq (\mathcal{L}_2 : \Gamma, I_2)$; *(iii)* Γ' *extends* Γ; *and (iv) for every* $(\theta_0, \theta'_0) \in I_1 \times I$ *and* $\xi \in [\![\mathcal{L}_1 : \Gamma']\!](\theta_0 * \theta'_0)$, *the trace* $\lfloor\!\lfloor \mathsf{history}(\xi) \rfloor\!\rfloor_\Gamma$ *is executable from* θ'_0. *Then* $(\mathcal{L}_1 : \Gamma', I_1 * I) \sqsubseteq (\mathcal{L}_2 : \Gamma', I_2 * I)$.

The proof of the theorem relies on Corollary 20. The linearizability relation established in the theorem enables the use of the Abstraction Theorem for clients performing ownership transfer. The safety requirement on $\mathcal{L}_1$ and $\mathcal{L}_2$ with respect to Γ' is needed because Γ' not only transfers extra memory to the library in its preconditions, but also takes it back in its postconditions. The requirement (iv) ensures that the extra memory required by postconditions in Γ' comes from the extra memory provided in its preconditions and the extension of the initial state, not from the memory transferred according to Γ.

9 Related Work

In our previous work, we proved Abstraction Theorems for definitions of linearizability supporting reasoning about liveness properties [9] and weak memory models [3]. These definitions assumed that the library and its client operate in disjoint address spaces and, hence, are guaranteed not to interfere with each other and cannot communicate via the heap. Lifting this restriction is the goal of the present paper. Although we borrow the basic proof structure of Theorem 19 from [3], including the split into Lemmas 13, 16 and 17, the formulations and proofs of the Abstraction Theorem and the lemmas here have to deal with technical challenges posed by ownership transfer that did not arise in previous work. First, their formulations rely on the novel forms of client-local and library-local semantics, and in particular, the notion of the most general client (Section 6), that allow a component to communicate with its environment via ownership transfers. Proving Lemmas 16 and 17 then involves a delicate tracking of a splitting between the parts of the state owned by the library and the client, and how ownership transfers affect it. Second, the key result needed to establish the Abstraction Theorem is the Rearrangement Lemma (Lemma 13). What makes the proof of this lemma difficult in our case is the need to deal with subtle interactions between concurrency and ownership transfer that have not been considered in previous work. Namely, changing the history of a sequential library specification for one of its concurrent implementation in the lemma requires commuting ownership transfer actions; justifying the correctness of these transformations is non-trivial and relies on the notion of history balancedness that we propose.

Recently, there has been a lot of work on verifying linearizability of common algorithms; representative papers include [1, 6, 16]. All of them proved classical linearizability, where libraries and their clients exchange values of a given data type and do not perform ownership transfers. This includes even libraries such as concurrent containers discussed in Section 1, that are actually used by client threads to transfer the ownership of data structures. The frame rule for linearizability we propose (Theorem 22) justifies that classical linearizability established for concurrent containers entails linearizability with ownership transfer. This makes our Abstraction Theorem applicable, enabling compositional reasoning about their clients.

Turon and Wand [15] have proposed a logic for establishing refinements between concurrent modules, likely equivalent to linearizability. Their logic considers libraries and clients residing in a shared address space, but not ownership transfer. It assumes that the client does not access the internal library state; however, their paper does not provide a way of checking this condition. As a consequence, Turon and Wand do not propose an Abstraction Theorem strong enough to support separate reasoning about a library and its client in realistic situations of the kind we consider.

Elmas et al. [6, 7] have developed a system for verifying concurrent programs based on repeated applications of atomicity abstraction. They do not use linearizability to perform the abstraction. Instead, they check the commutativity of an action to be incorporated into an atomic block with *all* actions of other threads. In particular, to abstract a library implementation in a program by its atomic specification, their method would have to check the commutativity of every internal action of the library with all actions executed by the client code of other threads. Thus, the method of Elmas et al. does not allow decomposing the verification of a program into verifying libraries and their clients separately. In contrast, our Abstraction Theorem ensures the atomicity of a library under *any* healthy client.

Ways of establishing relationships between different sequential implementations of the same library have been studied in *data refinement*, including cases of interactions via ownership transfer [2, 8]. Our results can be viewed as generalising data refinement to the concurrent setting.

Acknowledgements. We would like to thank Anindya Banerjee, Josh Berdine, Xinyu Feng, Hongjin Liang, David Naumann, Peter O'Hearn, Matthew Parkinson, Noam Rinetzky and Julles Villard for helpful comments. Yang was supported by EPSRC.

References

1. Amit, D., Rinetzky, N., Reps, T., Sagiv, M., Yahav, E.: Comparison Under Abstraction for Verifying Linearizability. In: Damm, W., Hermanns, H. (eds.) CAV 2007. LNCS, vol. 4590, pp. 477–490. Springer, Heidelberg (2007)
2. Banerjee, A., Naumann, D.A.: Ownership confinement ensures representation independence in object-oriented programs. JACM 52(6) (2005)
3. Burckhardt, S., Gotsman, A., Musuvathi, M., Yang, H.: Concurrent Library Correctness on the TSO Memory Model. In: Seidl, H. (ed.) Programming Languages and Systems. LNCS, vol. 7211, pp. 87–107. Springer, Heidelberg (2012)
4. Calcagno, C., O'Hearn, P., Yang, H.: Local action and abstract separation logic. In: LICS (2007)
5. Clarke, D.G., Noble, J., Potter, J.M.: Simple Ownership Types for Object Containment. In: Lee, S.H. (ed.) ECOOP 2001. LNCS, vol. 2072, pp. 53–76. Springer, Heidelberg (2001)
6. Elmas, T., Qadeer, S., Sezgin, A., Subasi, O., Tasiran, S.: Simplifying Linearizability Proofs with Reduction and Abstraction. In: Esparza, J., Majumdar, R. (eds.) TACAS 2010. LNCS, vol. 6015, pp. 296–311. Springer, Heidelberg (2010)
7. Elmas, T., Qadeer, S., Tasiran, S.: A calculus of atomic actions. In: POPL (2009)
8. Filipović, I., O'Hearn, P., Torp-Smith, N., Yang, H.: Blaiming the client: On data refinement in the presence of pointers. FAC 22(5) (2010)
9. Gotsman, A., Yang, H.: Liveness-Preserving Atomicity Abstraction. In: Aceto, L., Henzinger, M., Sgall, J. (eds.) ICALP 2011, Part II. LNCS, vol. 6756, pp. 453–465. Springer, Heidelberg (2011)
10. Gotsman, A., Yang, H.: Linearizability with ownership transfer (extended version) (2012), `www.software.imdea.org/~gotsman`
11. Harris, T., Fraser, K., Pratt, I.: A Practical Multi-Word Compare-and-Swap Operation. In: Malkhi, D. (ed.) DISC 2002. LNCS, vol. 2508, pp. 265–279. Springer, Heidelberg (2002)
12. Herlihy, M., Wing, J.M.: Linearizability: a correctness condition for concurrent objects. TOPLAS 12(3) (1990)
13. O'Hearn, P.: Resources, concurrency and local reasoning. TCS 375(1-3) (2007)
14. Reynolds, J.C.: Separation logic: A logic for shared mutable data structures. In: LICS (2002)
15. Turon, A., Wand, M.: A separation logic for refining concurrent objects. In: POPL (2011)
16. Vafeiadis, V.: Modular fine-grained concurrency verification. PhD Thesis. University of Cambridge (2008)
17. Vafeiadis, V.: Automatically Proving Linearizability. In: Touili, T., Cook, B., Jackson, P. (eds.) CAV 2010. LNCS, vol. 6174, pp. 450–464. Springer, Heidelberg (2010)

Nested Protocols in Session Types

Romain Demangeon and Kohei Honda

Queen Mary, University of London

Abstract. We propose an improvement to session-types, introducing nested protocols, the possibility to call a subprotocol from a parent protocol. This feature adds expressiveness and modularity to the existing session-type theory, allowing arguments to be passed and enabling higher-order protocols definition. Our theory is introduced through a new type system for protocols handling subprotocol calls, and its implementation in a session-calculus. We propose validation and satisfaction relations between specification and implementation. Sound behaviour is enforced thanks to the usage of kinds and well-formedness, allowing us to ensure progress and subject reduction. In addition, we describe an extension of our framework allowing subprotocols to send back results.

1 Introduction

Decentralised computation is becoming more and more popular thanks to the fast growth of web services and other distributed computing technologies. In such a distributed framework, agents (users, servers, applications) are interacting through message-passing communications, without central control. The programmatic coordination of a large number of independent entities interacting with each other inside a network is a challenging task: without global control, the only place where coordination can come from is local endpoints. How can we specify and ensure correctly coordinated behaviour without having any global control? Session types [11] provide a powerful expressive framework to help solving this issue, focusing on the notion of *session* seen as a unit of conversation among participants called *roles*. The expected scenario of the session is described in a global protocol given as a *global type*, projected into end-point specifications called *local types*, describing the behaviour of each role. Those are enforced locally, either through a static analysis of programs (static validation [8,3,13]) or at run-time (monitoring [2]). If each agent in the network conforms to its local type, it is guaranteed that their overall interactions conform to the global specification. In the past few years, the theory of session types has been extended in several directions. On the one hand, new features added to the language of the global types allow one to specify more accurately the interactions inside a protocol, for instance by including logical assertions [3], or information flow [4]. This "internal expressiveness" ensure the satisfaction of auxiliary properties: security ("the messages between Alice and Bob cannot be read by Carol"), or governance ("Alice can send a buying request to Bob only if she has enough money on her bank account"). On the other hand, extensions of the session mechanisms allow greater control over, for example, how participants join or leave a session

M. Koutny and I. Ulidowski (Eds.): CONCUR 2012, LNCS 7454, pp. 272–286, 2012.

(through dynamic multiparty session [9] or through a reputation system [10]) or how sessions can be parametrised, increasing "external expressiveness".

Real-world specifications for decentralised networks are large, complex and often highly modular: for example, such specifications are found in many use cases from the development of a large-scale distributed infrastructure for ocean sciences, Ocean Observatories Initiative [15], with whom we are collaborating. Among the use cases in the project, several protocols, used in different contexts, share the same shape. Moreover, some protocols call other protocols. In order to be able to specify, verify, simplify and organise such complex protocol frameworks effectively, solid improvements to the theory of session-types are needed.

In this paper, we present a novel approach to session-types that addresses the structuring principle itself of protocols, increasing both internal and external expressiveness. We introduce *nesting* of protocols, that is, the possibility to define a subprotocol independently of its parent protocol, which calls the subprotocol explicitly. Through a call, arguments can be passed, such as values, roles and other protocols, allowing higher-order description. At the programming level, subprotocols are realised as *subsessions*: one agent creates a new private session, inviting roles of the parent session (*internal invitations*) as well as other agents from the network (*external invitations*). Uninvited participants of the parent session do not have access to the subsession, allowing one to model private interactions inside public sessions. This contrasts with the current use of subprotocols in the protocol description language Scribble [16], where they only correspond to the in-lining mechanism. As an example, we noticed that in several use cases described in [15], a negotiation procedure *Nego* between two agents is invoked inside a main protocol, and other participants do not take part in that negotiation. The *Nego* procedure has its own description, subject to independent modifications and can be invoked in different contexts for different purposes. The theory we propose introduces such modularity in the framework of session types, yielding a solid, formal verification method for distributed programs.

One strong motivation for introducing subprotocols and subsession is that they are a powerful structuring tool: cross-cutting features such as login, negotiations or security controls can be abstracted from the targeted protocols in a compositional way, becoming subprotocols. If we update a login protocol to enforce stronger security checks, specifications of applications using it do not need be updated. Moreover, nesting allows one to call multiple copies of the same protocol with different arguments, improving flexibility and readability. This allows us to clean up and reorganise a large protocol database in [15], by unifying many protocols with the same shape into one parametrised protocol. Another direct benefit from nesting is allowing a better separation of the different branches by inviting participants only when necessary, reducing complexity and resource usage. For instance, in protocol $\mathcal{P}$ involving Alice, Bob and Carol, if Carol interacts only if a certain condition is met, we can have Carol act in a separate subprotocol, inviting Carol only if her presence is required. In our framework, internal invitations to a subsession are sent *inside the parent-session*, targeting a specific participant through a linear channel. This extends the existing session-calculi where invitations are always done externally, through shared channels.

We propose in Section 2 a syntax for nested protocols, with dedicated constructors for protocol definitions and protocol calls. In order to ensure sound composition, we introduce the notion of *kinds*, "types for types", and define a notion of well-formedness. In Section 3, we describe a session-calculus (based on the π-calculus [14]) handling subsessions. We describe in Section 4 a static validation and a run-time satisfaction, each linking specifications and processes in the session-calculus. We sketch the main properties of typed processes. Finally we propose an extension to our theory in Section 5, allowing a subsession to have a goal: a *result* that is returned to its parent session.

2 Nested Protocols

Global types. Throughout the paper, we use G for global types, T for local types, l for communication labels, s, k for session names, a, b for shared channels, ℓ for transition labels, $\mathtt{r}, \mathtt{r}'$ for role identifiers and $\mathcal{P}$ for protocol identifiers. We use v to describe *values*, which can be base type variables (integers, strings, ...), labels or protocol identifiers. x, y are variables, possibly abstracting any value. For any identifier e, we use $\widetilde{e}$ to abstract the sequence $e_1, \ldots, e_n$ of unspecified length n. We use $\mathcal{R}^+$ (resp. $\mathcal{R}^*$) for the reflexive (resp. reflexive-transitive) closure of the relation $\mathcal{R}$. We assume a Barendregt convention for bound variables.

Global types describe protocols from the network point of view: they consist of sequences of interactions between *roles*. We choose the already existing syntax of multi-party session types (e.g., in [3,1]) as a basis. The syntax for our global types is given by the following grammar:

$$
\begin{array}{rcll}
G & ::= & \mathtt{let}\ \mathcal{P} = \lambda\widetilde{\mathtt{r}}^1, \widetilde{y} \mapsto \mathtt{new}\ \widetilde{\mathtt{r}}^2.G\ \mathtt{in}\ G' & \text{(declaration)} \\
 & | & \mathtt{r}\ \mathtt{calls}\ \mathcal{P}\langle\widetilde{\mathtt{r}}, \widetilde{y}\rangle.G & \text{(call)} \\
 & | & \mathtt{r}_1 \to \mathtt{r}_2 : \Sigma_{i\in I}\{l_i(x_i).G_i\} & \text{(com)} \\
 & | & G_1 \oplus^{\mathtt{r}} G_2 \mid G_1 \parallel G_2 \mid \mu\mathtt{t}.G \mid \mathtt{t} & \text{(choice,par,rec,rec-var)}
\end{array}
$$

Communications between two roles are specified with $\mathtt{r}_1 \to \mathtt{r}_2 : \Sigma_{i\in I}\{l_i(x_i : S_i).G_i\}$, stating that $\mathtt{r}_1$ has a *directed choice* between several labels $\widetilde{l}$ proposed by $\mathtt{r}_2$. Each branch expects a value x_i and executes the continuation G_i. When I is a singleton, we write $\mathtt{r}_1 \to \mathtt{r}_2 : l(x : S)$. Primitive $\oplus^{\mathtt{r}}$ is *located choice*: the choice for one participant $\mathtt{r}$ between two distinct protocol branches. Parallel composition is denoted by $\parallel$ and recursion by the two operators $\mu\mathtt{t}$ and $\mathtt{t}$. We assume a congruence over global types, handling implicit unfolding of recursion.

The new primitives addressing protocol stratification are `let` and `calls`. We describe the declaration of an auxiliary protocol, to be called by a main protocol, by the notation $\mathtt{let}\ \mathcal{P} = \lambda\widetilde{\mathtt{r}}^1, \widetilde{y} \mapsto \mathtt{new}\ \widetilde{\mathtt{r}}^2.G_1\ \mathtt{in}\ G_2$. In this notation, the protocol G_1 is identified by $\mathcal{P}$ in the main protocol G_2. The participants of G_1 are explicitly separated into two groups, $\widetilde{\mathtt{r}}^1$ are internally invited from the parent session and thus given as arguments to $\mathcal{P}$ together with values $\widetilde{y}$; whereas $\widetilde{\mathtt{r}}^2$ are externally invited from the network at the beginning of G_1. The counterpart of this constructor is the *protocol call* $\texttt{r calls } \mathcal{P}(\widetilde{\texttt{r}}, \widetilde{v})$ stating that participant $\texttt{r}$ executes an auxiliary protocol $\mathcal{P}$ with role arguments $\widetilde{\texttt{r}}$, value arguments $\widetilde{v}$. Note that $\widetilde{v}$ can contain protocol identifiers, thus allowing higher-order programming.

Kinds. As protocols can be abstracted, called and used as arguments, we introduce a simple and concise discipline for protocols, which ensures that they are used in an adequate way, *well-formedness*. In order to formalise this notion, we type all objects appearing in specifications with *kinds* (types for types) $K, S ::= \texttt{Role} \mid \texttt{Val} \mid \diamond \mid (K_1 \times \cdots \times K_n) \to K$. We use $\texttt{Val}$ to denote the value-kinds, which are first-order types for values (like $\texttt{Nat}$ for integers) or data types (such as $\texttt{Req}$ in Section 2), $\diamond$ to denote protocol type and $\to$ to denote parametrisation. The presence of higher-order calls allows us to treat protocols whose kinds have shapes like $\texttt{Role} \times (\texttt{Role} \to \diamond) \to \diamond$, describing a protocol parametrised by a role and another protocol, the latter parametrised by a role. In the following, we will sometimes adopt an *à la Church* notation for protocol constructors, as in $\texttt{let } P = \lambda \text{buyer} : \texttt{Role}, \textit{price} : \texttt{Nat} \mapsto \texttt{new } \widetilde{r}.G \texttt{ in } G'$, in order to specify the kinds of the arguments passed to a protocol.

We define well-formedness to rule out unsound protocols. For instance, a protocol where $\mathcal{P}$ has kind $\texttt{Role} \to \diamond$ but is used with kind $\texttt{Nat} \to \diamond$ is not *well-kinded*. A protocol containing $(\texttt{r}_1 \to \texttt{r}_2 : \text{ok}) \oplus^{\texttt{r}_0} (\texttt{r}_2 \to \texttt{r}_1 : \text{ko})$ is not *projectable* as $\texttt{r}_1$ has no mean to know which branch $\texttt{r}_0$ chooses, and thus is not able to know if it must perform an input or an output. In order to define projectability, which ensures that a global type can be coherently projected into local types, we define the *restriction* of a protocol to a role, noted $(G)|_{\texttt{r}}$ as the global type obtained by removing every constructor of G where $\texttt{r}$ does not appear. A protocol is projectable if for every choice (directed or located), the difference between the branches are only visible to the roles involved in that choice.

Definition 1 (Well-Formedness).
A global-type G is well-kinded *if there exists τ from all identifiers of G to types satisfying, for all subprotocols of G:*

1. $\texttt{let } \mathcal{P} = (\lambda \widetilde{y} \mapsto \texttt{new } \widetilde{r} \cdot) \texttt{ in } \cdot$ *is s.t.* $\tau(\mathcal{P}) = \tau(\widetilde{y}) \to \diamond$, *and* $\forall i, \tau(r_i) = \texttt{Role}$.
2. $\texttt{r calls } \mathcal{P}\langle \widetilde{y} \rangle.G$ *is s.t.* $\tau(\texttt{r}) = \texttt{Role}$, $\tau(\mathcal{P}) = \tau(\widetilde{y}) \to \diamond$.
3. *for all identifiers* $\texttt{r}$ *in* $\texttt{r} \to \texttt{r}' : l(x : S).G$ *and* $G_1 \oplus^{\texttt{r}} G_2$, $\tau(\texttt{r}) = \texttt{Role}$.

A global type G is projectable *if:*

1. *for each subterm of G of the form $G_1 \oplus^{\texttt{r}_0} G_2$, for any free $\texttt{r} \neq \texttt{r}_0$, $(G_1)|_{\texttt{r}} = (G_2)|_{\texttt{r}}$.*
2. *for each subterm of G of the form $\texttt{r} \to \texttt{r}' : \Sigma_{i \in I}\{l_i(x_i : S_i).G_i\}$, for any role free role $\texttt{r} \notin \{\texttt{r}, \texttt{r}'\}$ and for all $\{i, j\} \subseteq I$, $(G_i)|_{\texttt{r}} = (G_j)|_{\texttt{r}}$.*

A protocol G is well-formed *when it is well-kinded and projectable, and satisfies the standard linearity condition [1].*

There exists in [9,12] *mergeability conditions* that allows the authors to be less restrictive in the definition of projectability. Our framework could accommodate this refinement. We do not present it here, for the sake of clarity.

Motivating Examples. In this section, we motivate our contribution with three examples extracted from concrete specifications and illustrate higher-order programming with a fourth one.

Resource usage. The following example is inspired by the use cases (UC R2.34, UC R2.32) from the OOI project [15]. A negotiation procedure *Nego* is first defined independently, to be used in several different protocols. This negotiation procedure involves two participants trying to agree on a contract: first participant specifies a request, second participant offers a corresponding contract, then both participants enter a loop when the first one can either accept the contract, which ends the protocol or make a counter-offer.

$$
\begin{array}{l}
\texttt{let}\ \mathit{Nego} = \lambda \mathtt{r}_1, \mathtt{r}_2 \mapsto \\
\qquad \mathtt{r}_1 \to \mathtt{r}_2 : \mathrm{ask}(\mathit{terms}). \\
\qquad \mu\mathtt{t}. \\
\qquad \mathtt{r}_2 \to \mathtt{r}_1 : \mathrm{proposition}(\mathit{contract}_2). \\
\qquad \mathtt{r}_1 \to \mathtt{r}_2 : \{\mathrm{accept}.\mathbf{end} \\
\qquad\qquad\qquad \mathrm{counter}(\mathit{contract}_1).\mathtt{t}\} \\
\texttt{in} \\
\mathrm{client} \to \mathrm{agent} : \mathrm{request}(\mathit{coord}).\ \mathrm{agent} \to \mathrm{instr} : \mathrm{connect} \\
\mathrm{instr} \to \mathrm{agent} : \mathrm{available}.\ \mathrm{agent} \to \mathrm{client} : \mathrm{ack}. \\
\mathrm{agent}\ \texttt{calls}\ \mathit{Nego}(\mathrm{agent}, \mathrm{client}). \\
\mu\mathtt{t}. \\
\quad \mathrm{client} \to \mathrm{instr} : \{\mathrm{abort}(\mathit{coord}).\mathbf{end} \\
\qquad\qquad\qquad \mathrm{command}(\mathit{code}). \\
\qquad\qquad\qquad\quad \mathrm{instr} \to \mathrm{client} : \mathrm{result}(\mathit{data}).\mathtt{t}\}
\end{array}
$$

The main protocol *UseRes* consists of several interactions between three participants (client, agent, instr), processed in the following order: first client sends a request to agent for an instrument he wants to use, agent tries to connect to instr which acknowledges when available. Then, agent negotiates a contract with client (by calling protocol *Nego*). After a successful negotiation, client and instr interact inside a loop, the client sending commands and receiving data. The negotiation phase is considered external: should the auxiliary protocol be modified, for instance to enforce another negotiation policy, the main protocol would remain the same.

Client-Middleware-Server. The protocol CMS, presented of the left side of Figure 1 describing a typical service interaction. This protocol initially involves two participants, client starts the interactions by sending a request to the middleware middle. If the latter is able to treat the request directly, it answers to client, if not, it contacts server, calling subprotocol *Contact* with itself as role argument. In the subprotocol, middle performs an external invitation of server, forwards the request and waits for an answer. After the subprotocol is completed, the answer is forwarded to the client. Nesting, in this example, allows us to invite server to participate only when necessary: if middle can treat the request, server is not even invited. Using subprotocols in such a way allows us to cut a great deal of unnecessary traffic caused by external invitations, saving bandwidth.

```
let Contact = λagent, req ↦
        new server.
        agent → server : request(req).
        server → agent : answer(ans).
        end
in
client → middle : request(req0).
        (middle → client : answer(ans0).end)
⊕middle
        (middle calls Contact(middle, req0).
        middle → client : answer(ans0).end)
```

```
let Treat =
λr1, r2 ↦
        new worker.
        r1 → worker : raw(data).
        worker → r2 : processed(data).
        end
in
parallel_n(
        source calls Treat(source, target)
        ).
end
```

Fig. 1. Protocols CMS and ANF

Dynamic distribution. We then describe on the right side of Figure 1 a third example, inspired by a concrete protocol from the Array Network Facility, used for processing seismic data. Here, the operator $\mathtt{parallel}_n(G)$ is used as a shortcut for n parallel copies of the protocol G. In this protocol, data comes in a raw state from a participant source and should reach participant target processed. In the body of each of the n parallel executions, source calls the subprotocol $Treat$ inviting a new participant worker and using it to process data. This protocol is run in networks where many computing units can accept temporarily the worker role. In this example, stratification is used to present in a clean way the execution of thousands of copies of the same protocol. As each copy is implemented by a different session, the different calls to the subprotocol are actually independent from each other.

Marketplace. Finally, we propose a protocol for a virtual marketplace in which participants have the possibility to engage in trade actions with other participants. General protocols *Buy* and *Sell* are defined to handle these buying and selling. The encounter between two agents follows the same procedure (handshake, authentication, possibility to cancel the transaction) whatever the reason of their meeting is. This common procedure is abstracted in $Meet$ and a protocol identifier *Action* is given as an argument to $Meet$ calls, meant to be substituted by *Buy* or *Sell* (or any similar protocol). Thus, $Meet$ is an higher-order protocol, parametrised with protocol *Action*.

```
let Buy = λ agent : Role, seller : Role, item : Tradable ↦ ...
in let Sell = λ agent : Role, buyer : Role, item : Tradable ↦ ...
in let Meet = λ agent : Role, partner : Role,
                item : Tradable, Action : (Role → Role → Tradable → ◇) ↦ ...
agent calls Action⟨partner, item⟩ ...
in ...
alice calls Meet⟨bob, kettle, Buy⟩. carol calls Meet⟨bob, teacup, Sell⟩ ...
```

The protocols presented in this section are well-formed: notice that protocol CMS is projectable, in each branch of the choice $\oplus^{\text{middle}}$, the restriction on client is "middle → client : answer.end". Kinds for subprotocols presented in the examples are as follows: *Nego* : $\texttt{Role} \times \texttt{Role} \to \diamond$, *Contact* : $\texttt{Role} \times \texttt{Req} \to \diamond$, *Treat* : $\texttt{Role} \times \texttt{Role} \to \diamond$, *Buy*, *Sell* : $\texttt{Role} \times \texttt{Role} \times \texttt{Tradable} \to \diamond$, *Meet* : $\texttt{Role} \times \texttt{Role} \times \texttt{Tradable} \times (\texttt{Role} \times \texttt{Role} \times \texttt{Tradable} \to \diamond) \to \diamond$

Local types and Projection. Local types describe a global conversation from the partial point-of-view of a participant and are used to validate and monitor distributed programs. Their syntax is given by:

$$\begin{array}{rcl} T & ::= & \texttt{get}[\texttt{r}]?_{i\in I}\{l_i(x_i : S_i).T_i\} \ \mid\ \texttt{send}[\texttt{r}]!_{i\in I}\{l_i(x_i : S_i).T_i\} \\ & \mid & T \parallel T \ \mid\ T \oplus T \ \mid\ \mu \texttt{t}.T \ \mid\ \texttt{t} \ \mid\ \texttt{end} \\ & \mid & \texttt{call}\ \mathcal{P} : G\ \texttt{with}\ (\widetilde{v}\ \texttt{as}\ \widetilde{y} : \widetilde{S})\&(\widetilde{\texttt{r}}^2).T \\ & \mid & \texttt{ent}\ \mathcal{P}[\texttt{r}]\langle\widetilde{v}\rangle\ \texttt{from}\ \texttt{r}.T \ \mid\ \texttt{req}\ \mathcal{P}[\texttt{r}]\langle\widetilde{v}\rangle\ \texttt{to}\ \texttt{r}.T \end{array}$$

Creating a subsession for protocol $\mathcal{P}$ having global type G is specified by $\texttt{call}\ \mathcal{P} : G\, \texttt{with}\, (\widetilde{v}\, \texttt{as}\, \widetilde{y} : \widetilde{S})\&(\widetilde{\texttt{r}}^2)$, with $\widetilde{v}$ as value arguments and involving external invitations for roles $\widetilde{\texttt{r}}^2$. Internal invitations are handled using two specific constructors, as they are meant to be performed on the parent session channel: `ent` specifies the act of accepting such an invitation, `req` specifies the dual action. Syntax contains endpoint primitives for communications, specified by `get` for the receiver side and `send` for the sender side, as well as constructors for parallel, choice and recursion. We handle equivalence of types through recursions and parallel compositions implicitly. In the following, we omit trailing occurrences of `end`.

Projection from global to local types is defined w.r.t. a protocol environment, associating protocols identifiers to their contents. Environment is updated by `let in` constructors. We present below the projection rule for `call` and `let`. For the former the result of the projection depends on the participant we project on, $\texttt{r}_{\text{proj}}$. If it is the subprotocol initiator $\texttt{r}^A$ it is responsible for creating the subsession (`call`) and sending the internal invitations (`req`). If it participates in the subprotocol, it has to accept an internal invitation (`ent`). Projection on other constructors is standard.

$$(\texttt{let}\ \mathcal{P} = \lambda\widetilde{\texttt{r}}^1.\widetilde{y} \mapsto \texttt{new}\ \widetilde{\texttt{r}}^2.G_{\mathcal{P}}\ \texttt{in}\ G') \Downarrow^{\textbf{Env}}_{\texttt{r}^p} = G' \Downarrow^{\textbf{Env},\mathcal{P}\mapsto(\widetilde{\texttt{r}}^1,\widetilde{y};\widetilde{\texttt{r}}^2;G_{\mathcal{P}})}_{\texttt{r}^p}$$

$$(\texttt{r}^A\ \texttt{calls}\ \mathcal{P}(\widetilde{\texttt{r}}^0,\widetilde{v}).G) \Downarrow^{\textbf{Env},\mathcal{P}\mapsto(\widetilde{\texttt{r}}^1,\widetilde{y};\widetilde{\texttt{r}}^2;G_{\mathcal{P}})}_{\texttt{r}^p} =$$
$$\begin{cases} \text{if } \texttt{r}^p = \texttt{r}^A,\ \texttt{r}^A \notin \widetilde{\texttt{r}}^0 \\ \quad \texttt{call}\ \mathcal{P} : G_{\mathcal{P}}\ \texttt{with}\ (\widetilde{v}\ \texttt{as}\ \widetilde{y})\&(\widetilde{\texttt{r}}^2).[(G) \Downarrow^{\textbf{Env},\mathcal{P}\mapsto(\widetilde{\texttt{r}}^1,\widetilde{y};\widetilde{\texttt{r}}^2;G_{\mathcal{P}})}_{\texttt{r}^p} \\ \quad \parallel \texttt{req}\ \mathcal{P}[\texttt{r}^1_0]\langle\widetilde{v}\rangle\ \texttt{to}\ \texttt{r}^0_0 \parallel \cdots \parallel \texttt{req}\ \mathcal{P}[\texttt{r}^1_n]\langle\widetilde{v}\rangle\ \texttt{to}\ \texttt{r}^0_n] \\ \text{if } \texttt{r}^p = \texttt{r}^A \text{ and } \texttt{r}^A = \texttt{r}^0_i \\ \quad \texttt{call}\ \mathcal{P} : G_{\mathcal{P}}\ \texttt{with}\ (\widetilde{v}\ \texttt{as}\ \widetilde{y})\&(\widetilde{\texttt{r}}^2).[(G) \Downarrow^{\textbf{Env},\mathcal{P}\mapsto(\widetilde{\texttt{r}}^1,\widetilde{y};\widetilde{\texttt{r}}^2,G_{\mathcal{P}})}_{\texttt{r}^p} \\ \quad \parallel \texttt{ent}\ \mathcal{P}[\texttt{r}^1_i]\langle\widetilde{v}\rangle\ \texttt{from}\ \texttt{r}^A \parallel \texttt{req}\ \mathcal{P}[\texttt{r}^1_0]\langle\widetilde{v}\rangle\ \texttt{to}\ \texttt{r}^0_0 \parallel \cdots \parallel \texttt{req}\ \mathcal{P}[\texttt{r}^1_n]\langle\widetilde{v}\rangle\ \texttt{to}\ \texttt{r}^0_n] \\ \text{if } \texttt{r}^p \neq \texttt{r}^A \text{ and } \texttt{r}^p = \texttt{r}^0_i \\ \quad \texttt{ent}\ \mathcal{P}[\texttt{r}^1_i]\langle\widetilde{v}\rangle\ \texttt{from}\ \texttt{r}^A.(G) \Downarrow^{\textbf{Env},\mathcal{P}\mapsto(\widetilde{\texttt{r}}^1,\widetilde{y};\widetilde{\texttt{r}}^2;G_{\mathcal{P}})}_{\texttt{r}^p} \\ \text{Otherwise} \\ \quad (G) \Downarrow^{\textbf{Env},\mathcal{P}\mapsto(\widetilde{\texttt{r}}^1,\widetilde{y};\widetilde{\texttt{r}}^2;G_{\mathcal{P}})}_{\texttt{r}^p} \end{cases}$$

If the initiator $\mathtt{r}^{\mathcal{A}}$ of the subsession also takes part in it, the projection on $\mathtt{r}^{\mathcal{A}}$ specifies that it invites itself. It is easy to add to our language a dedicated constructor handling session-invitation directly, without inducing communication at the network level. For the sake of clarity, we do not include such a constructor in this paper.

We present below the projection of CMS on its two roles. G_{CMS} is the global type of the whole protocol and G_C the global type of $Contact$.

$$\begin{array}{ll} G_{CMS} \Downarrow^{\emptyset}_{\text{client}} & = \mathtt{send}[\text{middle}]!\{\text{request}(req_{\mathrm{O}})\}.\mathtt{get}[\text{middle}]?\{\text{answer}(ans_{\mathrm{O}})\} \\ G_{CMS} \Downarrow^{\emptyset}_{\text{middlew}} & = \mathtt{get}[\text{client}]?\{\text{request}(req_{\mathrm{O}})\}. \\ & \quad \mathtt{send}[\text{client}]!\{\text{answer}(ans_{\mathrm{O}})\} \\ & \quad \oplus \\ & \quad (\mathtt{call}\ Contact : G_C\ \mathtt{with}\ (req_{\mathrm{O}}\ \mathtt{as}\ req : \mathtt{Req})\&(\text{server}). \\ & \quad\quad (\mathtt{req}\ Contact[\text{agent}]\langle req\rangle\ \mathtt{to}\ \text{middle} \parallel \\ & \quad\quad \mathtt{ent}\ Contact[\text{agent}]\langle req\rangle\ \mathtt{from}\ \text{middle} \parallel \\ & \quad\quad \mathtt{send}[\text{client}]!\{\text{answer}(ans_{\mathrm{O}})\})) \end{array}$$

3 Session-Calculus

Our session-calculus, based on the π-calculus [14], contains usual primitives from existing session-calculi [3], as well as dedicated primitives for session creation and internal (on-session) invitations. Names are divided into shared channels a, b, u (standard π-names) and session channels s, k. The former are used to send and receive external invitations, the latter to handle all session interactions.

$$\begin{array}{rcl} P & ::= & \mathbf{0} \mid P|P \mid a(x).P \mid \overline{a}\langle s\rangle.P \mid P+P \\ & \mid & k?[\mathtt{r},\mathtt{r}]_{i\in I}\{l_i(x_i).P_i\} \mid k![\mathtt{r},\mathtt{r}]l\langle v\rangle.P \mid (\nu u)\ P \\ & \mid & \mathtt{new}\ s\ \mathtt{on}\ s\ \mathtt{with}\ (\widetilde{v})\&(\widetilde{a}\ \mathtt{as}\ \widetilde{\mathtt{r}}).P \\ & \mid & s\downarrow[\mathtt{r},\mathtt{r}:\mathtt{r}](x).P \mid s\uparrow[\mathtt{r},\mathtt{r}:\mathtt{r}]\langle s\rangle.P \mid \mu X(x).P\langle v\rangle \mid X\langle v\rangle \end{array}$$

We denote by $k?[\mathtt{r}_1,\mathtt{r}_2]_{i\in I}\{l_i(x_i).P_i\}$ a branching input on session k from $\mathtt{r}_1$ to $\mathtt{r}_2$, with continuations $(P_i)_{i\in I}$. The dual primitive is $k![\mathtt{r}_1,\mathtt{r}_2]l\langle v\rangle.P$. Creation of a subsession is done with $\mathtt{new}\ s\ \mathtt{on}\ k\ \mathtt{with}\ (\widetilde{v})\&(\widetilde{a}\ \mathtt{as}\ \widetilde{\mathtt{r}}^2)$ with s being the subsession, k the parent session, $\widetilde{v}$ the arguments and $\widetilde{a}$ the channels on which the external invitations are sent. Operator $s\downarrow[\mathtt{r}^1,\mathtt{r}^2:\mathtt{r}^3](x).P$ is the action of waiting on s for an internal invitation sent by $\mathtt{r}^1$ to $\mathtt{r}^2$ in order to play role $\mathtt{r}^3$ in a subsession x. Finally, $s\uparrow[\mathtt{r}^1,\mathtt{r}^2:\mathtt{r}^3]\langle s\rangle.P$ is its dual action. Inputs and outputs on shared channels, choice, parallel composition and inactive process $\mathbf{0}$ are inherited from the π-calculus. We omit trailing occurrences of $\mathbf{0}$. Structural congruence $\equiv$ for processes is defined in the usual way.

Semantics is given by reduction rules below, defined w.r.t. a notion of evaluation context $\mathbf{E} ::= [\,] \mid P \mid \mathbf{E} \mid (\nu a)\ \mathbf{E}$. The crucial rule of our system is (**subs**) where a session creation operator `new` is destructed in order to create external invitations on shared channels. (**join**) handles internal session invitation, other rules are standard:

$$(\textbf{comS})\quad \frac{}{\mathbf{E}[s![\mathtt{r}_1,\mathtt{r}_2]l_j\langle\tilde{v}\rangle.P \mid s?[\mathtt{r}_1,\mathtt{r}_2]_{i\in I}\{l_i(\tilde{x}_i).P_i\}] \to \mathbf{E}[P \mid P_j\{\tilde{v}/\tilde{x}_j\}]}$$

$$(\textbf{comC})\quad \frac{}{\mathbf{E}[\overline{a}\langle\tilde{v}\rangle.P \mid a(\tilde{y}).Q] \to \mathbf{E}[P \mid Q\{\tilde{v}/\tilde{y}\}]}$$

$$(\textbf{subs})\quad \frac{\tilde{\mathtt{r}}^2 = (\mathtt{r}^2_1,\ldots,\mathtt{r}^2_n) \qquad \tilde{a} = (a_1,\ldots,a_n)}{\mathbf{E}[\mathtt{new}\ s\ \mathtt{on}\ k\ \mathtt{with}\ (\tilde{v})\&(\tilde{a}\ \mathtt{as}\ \tilde{\mathtt{r}}^2).P] \to \mathbf{E}[P \mid \overline{a_1}\langle s[\mathtt{r}^2_1]\rangle \mid \ldots \mid \overline{a_n}\langle s[\mathtt{r}^2_n]\rangle]}$$

$$(\textbf{join})\quad \frac{}{\mathbf{E}[s\uparrow[\mathtt{r},\mathtt{r}':\mathtt{r}'']\langle k\rangle.P \mid s\downarrow[\mathtt{r},\mathtt{r}':\mathtt{r}''](x).Q] \to \mathbf{E}[P \mid Q\{k/x\}]}$$

$$(\textbf{choice})\quad \frac{P_i \to P'_i}{\mathbf{E}[(P_1+P_2)] \to \mathbf{E}[P'_i]}$$

As an example consider the following processes:

$$\begin{aligned}
P_{\mathsf{alice}} &= a(x).x![\mathsf{client},\mathsf{middle}]\mathsf{request}(\text{“kettle”}).x?[\mathsf{middle},\mathsf{client}]\mathsf{answer}(ans_{\mathsf{O}})\\
P_{\mathsf{bob}} &= \overline{a}\langle s\rangle.s?[\mathsf{client},\mathsf{middle}]\mathsf{request}(req_{\mathsf{O}}).\\
&\qquad (s![\mathsf{middle},\mathsf{client}]\mathsf{answer}(ans_{\mathsf{O}})\\
&\quad + (\mathtt{new}\ k\ \mathtt{on}\ s\ \mathtt{with}\ (req_{\mathsf{O}})\&(c\ \mathtt{as}\ \mathsf{server}).\\
&\qquad s\uparrow[\mathsf{middle},\mathsf{middle}:\mathsf{agent}]\langle k\rangle \mid s\downarrow[\mathsf{middle},\mathsf{middle}:\mathsf{agent}](z).\\
&\qquad z![\mathsf{agent},\mathsf{server}]\mathsf{request}\langle req_{\mathsf{O}}\rangle.z?[\mathsf{server},\mathsf{agent}]\mathsf{answer}(ans_r).\\
&\qquad s![\mathsf{middle},\mathsf{client}]\mathsf{answer}\langle ans_r\rangle)\\
P_{\mathsf{carol}} &= c(y).y?[\mathsf{agent},\mathsf{server}]\mathsf{request}(req).y![\mathsf{server},\mathsf{agent}]\mathsf{answer}(ans)
\end{aligned}$$

P_{alice}, P_{bob} and P_{carol} are processes ready to play, respectively roles client, middle and server in the CMS protocol. P_{alice} (resp. P_{carol}) is a simple process, ready to accept an external invitation to the parent session on a (resp. to the child session on c) and to behave as expected. P_{bob} is more complex: it sends an invitation on a, and after receiving a request it chooses, as specified in Figure 1, between answering directly on the session channel or contacting the server through a subsession. In this case, the new session channel k is created and one internal invitation to play role agent in k is sent and accepted by P_{bob} itself, then it proceeds as expected. We describe a reduction sequence for the composition of these three processes:

$$\begin{aligned}
P_{\mathsf{alice}} \mid P_{\mathsf{carol}} \mid P_{\mathsf{bob}} \to\to\quad & s?[\mathsf{middle},\mathsf{client}]\mathsf{answer}(ans_{\mathsf{O}}) \mid P_{\mathsf{carol}}\\
& \mid (\ldots) + (\mathtt{new}\ k\ \mathtt{on}\ s\ \mathtt{with}\ (req_{\mathsf{O}})\&(c\ \mathtt{as}\ \mathsf{server})\ldots)\\
\to\quad & s?[\mathsf{middle},\mathsf{client}]\mathsf{answer}(ans_{\mathsf{O}}) \mid P_{\mathsf{carol}} \mid \overline{c}\langle k\rangle\\
& \mid s\uparrow[\mathsf{middle},\mathsf{middle}:\mathsf{agent}]\langle k\rangle \mid s\downarrow[\mathsf{middle},\mathsf{middle}:\mathsf{agent}](z)\ldots\\
\to\quad & s?[\mathsf{middle},\mathsf{client}]\mathsf{answer}(ans_{\mathsf{O}}) \mid P_{\mathsf{carol}}\\
& \mid \overline{c}\langle k\rangle \mid k![\mathsf{middle},\mathsf{server}]\mathsf{request}(req_{\mathsf{O}})\ldots\\
\to\quad & s?[\mathsf{middle},\mathsf{client}]\mathsf{answer}(ans_{\mathsf{O}})\\
& \mid k![\mathsf{agent},\mathsf{server}]\mathsf{request}(req_{\mathsf{O}})\ldots\\
& \mid k?[\mathsf{agent},\mathsf{server}]\mathsf{request}(req)\ldots \quad \to\to\to \quad \mathbf{0}
\end{aligned}$$

After two communications on a and s, the reduct of P_{bob} reaches the located choice. We suppose it chooses the second branch. Thus, an output on c containing session name k is created. Then the internal self-invitation for k is performed, and, finally, the external invitation of P_{carol} on c. Three reductions can still be played, two on k and one on s.

Validation. We describe a static way to ensuring that processes conforms to formal specifications. The *global environment* Γ relates shared channels to the type of the invitation they carry, protocol names to their code and session channels to the global type they implement. $a : T[\mathtt{r}]$ means that a is used to send and receive invitations to play role $\mathtt{r}$ with local type T, $\mathcal{P} : (\widetilde{\mathtt{r}}^1, \widetilde{y}; \widetilde{\mathtt{r}}^2; G_{\mathcal{P}})$ describes the participants, arguments and code of protocol $\mathcal{P}$, finally, $s : G$ means that protocol G can be implemented on s. The *session environment* Δ relates pairs of session channels and roles $s[\mathtt{r}]$ to local types. $s[\mathtt{r}] : T$ means that in session s, participant $\mathtt{r}$ still has to perform the actions of T. $s[\mathtt{r}]^\bullet : T$ (resp. $s[\mathtt{r}]^\circ : T$) stands for the *capability* to invite externally (resp. internally) someone to play role $\mathtt{r}$ in s. In the following, we consider only environments which are mappings, and we will write $\Delta(s[\mathtt{r}])$. Additionally, we write $\Delta(s) = 0$ when s does not appear in Δ and $s[\mathtt{r}]^-$ to denote either $s[\mathtt{r}]^\circ$, $s[\mathtt{r}]^\bullet$ or $s[\mathtt{r}]$. We allow "garbage collection" for session environment: $(\Delta, s[\mathtt{r}] : \mathbf{end}) = \Delta$.

$$\begin{array}{rcl} \Gamma & ::= & \emptyset \mid \Gamma, a : T[\mathtt{r}] \mid \Gamma, \mathcal{P} : (\widetilde{\mathtt{r}}^1, \widetilde{y}; \widetilde{\mathtt{r}}^2; G_{\mathcal{P}}) \mid \Gamma, s : G \\ \Delta & ::= & \emptyset \mid \Delta, s[\mathtt{r}] : T \mid \Delta, s[\mathtt{r}]^\bullet : T \mid \Delta, s[\mathtt{r}]^\circ : T \end{array}$$

A typing judgement $\Gamma \vdash P \triangleright \Delta$ means that under the global environment Γ, the process P is validated by the session environment Δ. We use $\vdash v : S$ to notify that value v has kind S. The validation rules are as follows:

$$\textbf{(I, O)}\ \frac{\Gamma \vdash P \triangleright \Delta, x[\mathtt{r}] : T \qquad \Gamma(a) = T[\mathtt{r}]}{\Gamma \vdash a(x).P \triangleright \Delta} \qquad \frac{\Gamma \vdash P \triangleright \Delta \qquad \Gamma(a) = T[\mathtt{r}]}{\Gamma \vdash \overline{a}\langle s\rangle.P \triangleright \Delta, s[\mathtt{r}]^\bullet : T}$$

$$\textbf{(C)}\ \frac{(\Gamma \vdash P_i \triangleright \Delta, s[\mathtt{r}'] : T_i \qquad \vdash y_i : S_i)_{i\in I}}{\Gamma \vdash s?[\mathtt{r}, \mathtt{r}']_{i\in I}\{l_i(y_i).P_i\} \triangleright \Delta, s[\mathtt{r}'] : \mathtt{get}[\mathtt{r}]?_{i\in I}\{l_i(x_i : S_i).T_i\}}$$

$$\textbf{(S)}\ \frac{\Gamma \vdash P \triangleright \Delta, s[\mathtt{r}] : T_j \qquad \vdash v : S_j}{\Gamma \vdash s![\mathtt{r}, \mathtt{r}']l_j\langle v\rangle.P \triangleright \Delta, s[\mathtt{r}] : \mathtt{send}[\mathtt{r}']!_{i\in I}\{l_i(x_i : S_i).T_i\}}$$

$$\textbf{(P)}\ \frac{\Gamma \vdash P \triangleright \Delta, s[\mathtt{r}] : T \qquad \Gamma(\mathcal{P}) = (\widetilde{\mathtt{r}}^1, \widetilde{y}; \widetilde{\mathtt{r}}^2; G) \qquad G\{\widetilde{v}/\widetilde{y}\} \Downarrow_{\mathtt{r}''} = T''}{\Gamma \vdash s \uparrow [\mathtt{r}, \mathtt{r}' : \mathtt{r}'']\langle k\rangle.P \triangleright \Delta, s[\mathtt{r}] : \mathtt{req}\ \mathcal{P}[\mathtt{r}'']\langle\widetilde{v}\rangle\ \mathtt{to}\ \mathtt{r}'.T, k[\mathtt{r}'']^\circ : T''}$$

$$\textbf{(J)}\ \frac{\Gamma \vdash P \triangleright \Delta, s[\mathtt{r}'].T, x[\mathtt{r}''] : T'' \qquad \Gamma(\mathcal{P}) = (\widetilde{\mathtt{r}}^1, \widetilde{y}; \widetilde{\mathtt{r}}^2; G) \qquad G\{\widetilde{v}/\widetilde{y}\} \Downarrow_{\mathtt{r}''} = T''}{\Gamma \vdash s \downarrow [\mathtt{r}, \mathtt{r}' : \mathtt{r}''](x).P \triangleright \Delta, s[\mathtt{r}'] : \mathtt{ent}\ \mathcal{P}[\mathtt{r}'']\langle\widetilde{v}\rangle\ \mathtt{from}\ \mathtt{r}.T}$$

$$\textbf{(New)}\ \frac{\begin{array}{c} \Gamma \vdash P \triangleright \Delta, s[\mathtt{r}] : T, k[\mathtt{r}^1_1]^\circ : T'_1, \ldots, k^\circ[\mathtt{r}^1_n] : T'_n, k^\bullet[\mathtt{r}^2_1] : T'_{n+1}, \ldots, k^\bullet[\mathtt{r}^2_m] : T'_{n+m} \\ \Gamma(\mathcal{P}) = (\widetilde{\mathtt{r}}^1, \widetilde{y}; \widetilde{\mathtt{r}}^2; G) \qquad \forall i, \Gamma(a_i) = T'_{i+n}[\mathtt{r}_{i+n}] \\ \forall i, G\{\widetilde{v}/\widetilde{y}\} \Downarrow_{\mathtt{r}^1_i} = T'_i \qquad \forall j, G\{\widetilde{v}/\widetilde{y}\} \Downarrow_{\mathtt{r}^2_j} = T'_{j+n} \qquad \vdash \widetilde{v} : S \qquad \Gamma(k) : \mathcal{P}\{\widetilde{v}/\widetilde{y}\} \end{array}}{\Gamma \vdash \mathtt{new}\ k\ \mathtt{on}\ s\ \mathtt{with}\ (\widetilde{v})\&(\widetilde{a}\ \mathtt{as}\ \widetilde{\mathtt{r}}^2).P \triangleright \Delta, s[\mathtt{r}] : \mathtt{call}\ \mathcal{P} : G\ \mathtt{with}\ (\widetilde{v}\ \mathtt{as}\ \widetilde{y} : \widetilde{S})\&(\widetilde{\mathtt{r}}^2).T}$$

$$\textbf{(N, P)}\ \frac{}{\Gamma \vdash \mathbf{0} \triangleright \emptyset} \qquad \frac{\Gamma \vdash P_1 \triangleright \Delta_1 \qquad \Gamma \vdash P_2 \triangleright \Delta_2}{\Gamma \vdash P_1 \mid P_2 \triangleright \Delta_1 \otimes \Delta_2}$$

$$\textbf{(S1)}\ \frac{\Gamma \vdash P_1 \triangleright \Delta, s[\mathtt{r}] : T_1 \qquad \Gamma \vdash P_2 \triangleright \Delta, s[\mathtt{r}] : T_2}{\Gamma \vdash P_1 + P_2 \triangleright \Delta, s[\mathtt{r}] : T_1 \oplus T_2}$$

$$\textbf{(S2, R)}\ \frac{\Gamma \vdash P \triangleright \Delta, s[\mathtt{r}] : T_i \qquad i \in \{1, 2\}}{\Gamma \vdash P \triangleright \Delta, s[\mathtt{r}] : T_1 \oplus T_2} \qquad \frac{\Gamma, a : T[\mathtt{r}] \vdash P \triangleright \Delta}{\Gamma \vdash (\nu a)\ P \triangleright \Delta}$$

Rule (**New**) is the crux of this type system, as it ensures subsessions are called in a sound way. To type the process $\mathtt{new}\ k\ \mathtt{on}\ s\ \mathtt{with}\ (\widetilde{v})\&(\widetilde{a}\ \mathtt{as}\ \widetilde{\mathtt{r}}^2).P$, the session channel k should be associated with a protocol $G\{\widetilde{v}/\widetilde{y}\}$ matching the one present in the local type of $\mathtt{r}$ in the parent session s: $\mathtt{call}\ \mathcal{P} : G\ \mathtt{with}\ (\widetilde{v}\ \mathtt{as}\ \widetilde{y} : \widetilde{S})\&(\widetilde{\mathtt{r}}^2).T$ and global environment Γ should map $\mathcal{P}$ to $(\widetilde{\mathtt{r}}^1, \widetilde{y}; \widetilde{\mathtt{r}}^2; G)$. The endpoint projections $(T_p)_{1\leq p\leq n+m}$ of $\mathcal{P}$ are divided into two sets, the ones that correspond to roles $(\mathtt{r}^1_i)_{1\leq i\leq n}$ internally invited, and the ones that correspond to roles $(\mathtt{r}^2_j)_{1\leq j\leq m}$ externally invited through $\widetilde{a}$. Capabilities $(k[\mathtt{r}_i]^\circ : T_i)_i, (k[\mathtt{r}_j]^\bullet : T_j)_j$ for both types of invitations are given to the continuation process P. Rule (**P**) types a process whose role $\mathtt{r}$ on session s consists in sending a internal invitation to play role $\mathtt{r}''$ in session k. The process is required to hold the capability for $k[\mathtt{r}'']$, we ensure it corresponds to the type of the invitation. Its counterpart (**J**) ensures that role $\mathtt{r}$ of session s after receiving an invitation for $k[\mathtt{r}'']$, gets the corresponding local type T'' in its Δ. Rules (**I**) and (**O**) handle external invitations. As in the internal case, we ensure that the sending process has the corresponding capability. Rules (**C**) and (**S**) address branching communications on session channels. In both rules we ensure that the values communicated x_i, v have the same value-type as the identifiers y_i in the type. Summations are handled by two rules (**S1**) and (**S2**). If the local type specifies a choice between two branches, the process can either implement this choice with the $+$ constructor, or implement only one branch of the choice. This illustrates the fact that the decision can be made at implementation time (for instance a middleware implementing CMS which always contacts the server) or at run-time (a middleware which can proceed both ways according to the request). Rule (**Pa**) requires a small explanation, as it allows one to split local types into two branches. We define the $\otimes$ operator with $\Delta_1 \otimes \emptyset = \Delta_1$, $\Delta_1 \otimes (\Delta_2, s[\mathtt{r}]^- : T) = (\Delta_1, s[\mathtt{r}]^- : T) \otimes \Delta_2$ if $\Delta_1(s[\mathtt{r}]) = 0$ and $(\Delta_1, s[\mathtt{r}]^- : T_1) \otimes (\Delta_2, s[\mathtt{r}]^- : T_2) = (\Delta_1, s[\mathtt{r}]^- : T_1 \parallel T_2) \otimes \Delta_2$. Thus, when splitting the session environment in a parallel constructor, we allow the splitting of a single local type composed of two parallel subtypes. Finally, rule (**N**) specifies that the session environment should be empty to type $\mathbf{0}$. This ensures that the processes eventually complete the local types of their specification.

Following the typing rules, one can type the processes introduced in Section 3 as follows: $\Gamma \vdash P_{\text{alice}} \triangleright \emptyset$, $\Gamma \vdash P_{\text{bob}} \triangleright s[\text{middle}] : T_{\text{middle}}, s[\text{client}]^\bullet : T_{\text{client}}$, $\Gamma \vdash P_{\text{carol}} \triangleright \emptyset$ with $\Gamma = a : T_{\text{client}}, c : T_{\text{server}}, \mathit{Contact} : (\text{agent}, \text{req}; \text{server}; G_{\mathit{Contact}}), s : \mathit{CMS}, k : \mathit{Contact}$, $G_{\mathit{Contact}} \Downarrow^{\emptyset}_{\text{server}} = T_{\text{server}}$, and $T_{\text{client}} = G_{CMS} \Downarrow^{\emptyset}_{\text{client}}$, $T_{\text{middle}} = G_{CMS} \Downarrow^{\emptyset}_{\text{middle}}$ as defined in Section 2.

Session environments for P_{alice} and P_{carol} are empty: processes are not bound to do anything as long as they did not receive an invitation. Session environment for P_{bob} contains both the local type for the role middle played by the process and the capability to send an external invitation for client in the same session. The capability to send an external invitation to server is not created yet.

4 Properties

In this section we justify our theory with two main propositions, subject reduction and progress. First, we define a satisfaction relation relating dynamically processes and specifications. We introduce Labelled Transition Systems for both the processes and the specification. Labels are defined by $\ell ::= \quad \tau \mid \overline{a}\langle v\rangle \mid a\langle v\rangle \mid s?[\mathtt{r},\mathtt{r}']l\langle k\rangle \mid s![\mathtt{r},\mathtt{r}']l\langle k\rangle \mid s\downarrow[\mathtt{r},\mathtt{r}':\mathtt{r}'']\langle k\rangle \mid s\uparrow[\mathtt{r},\mathtt{r}':\mathtt{r}'']\langle k\rangle$ The subject of a label $\mathbf{sbj}(\ell)$ is defined intuitively for all labels, knowing that $\mathbf{sbj}(\tau)=0$. Labels $\overline{a}\langle v\rangle, a\langle v\rangle, s![\mathtt{r},\mathtt{r}']l\langle k\rangle$, $s\uparrow[\mathtt{r},\mathtt{r}':\mathtt{r}'']\langle k\rangle$ and τ (resp. $s?[\mathtt{r},\mathtt{r}']l\langle k\rangle$ and $s\downarrow[\mathtt{r},\mathtt{r}':\mathtt{r}'']\langle k\rangle$) are denoted as *output labels* (resp. *input labels*). In the satisfaction relation defined below, output labels are the ones played by the process, to which the specification must answer (thus τ and $a\langle v\rangle$ are considered outputs), and the input labels are the ones the specification plays, to which the process must answer. Transitions for processes $P \xrightarrow{\ell} P'$ follow the reduction semantics. The most relevant transitions for specifications, defined w.r.t. a global environment Γ, are presented in Figure 2.

Definition 2 (Satisfaction). *We say that $\mathcal{R}_\Gamma$ is a satisfaction relation between process P and specification Δ, if:*

whenever $\Delta \xrightarrow[\Gamma]{\ell} \Delta'$ with an input label ℓ, then $P \xrightarrow{\ell} P'$ and $P'\mathcal{R}_\Gamma\Delta'$,

whenever $P \xrightarrow{\ell} P'$ with an output label ℓ, then $\Delta \xrightarrow[\Gamma]{\ell} \Delta'$ and $P'\mathcal{R}_\Gamma\Delta'$.

The largest relation $\mathcal{R}_\Gamma$ is called satisfaction w.r.t. Γ *denoted* $\mathbf{sat}(P,\Delta)_\Gamma$. *In this case, we say that P satisfies Δ w.r.t. Γ (we omit this last part when Γ is clear from context)*

We justify the soundness of our framework by relating the static validation to the dynamic satisfaction, through *correspondence*. If a process is validated by a specification Δ, it is able to behave as described in Δ. From this property, we derive subject reduction, which ensures that validation is preserved by reduction. A session environment is *coherent* if it is composed of projections of well-formed global types. A coherent session environment is *simple* if it consists of a single

$$\textbf{(Ssub)}\frac{\Gamma(\mathcal{P})=(\widetilde{\mathtt{r}}^1,\widetilde{y}:\widetilde{S};\widetilde{\mathtt{r}}^2;G_{\mathcal{P}}) \qquad \forall i, G_{\mathcal{P}}\{\widetilde{v}/\widetilde{y}\}\Downarrow_{\mathtt{r}^1_i}=T'_i \qquad \forall j, G_{\mathcal{P}}\{\widetilde{v}/\widetilde{y}\}\Downarrow_{\mathtt{r}^2_j}=T''_j \qquad \Gamma(k)=G\{\widetilde{v}/\widetilde{y}\}}{s[\mathtt{r}]:\mathtt{call}\ \mathcal{P}:G\ \mathtt{with}\ (\widetilde{v}\ \mathtt{as}\ \widetilde{y}:\widetilde{S})\&(\widetilde{\mathtt{r}}^2).T \xrightarrow[\Gamma]{\tau} s[\mathtt{r}]:T,(k[\mathtt{r}^1_i]:T'_i)_i,(k[\mathtt{r}^2_j]:T''_j)_j}$$

$$\textbf{(Sout)}\frac{\Gamma(a)=T[\mathtt{r}]}{k[\mathtt{r}]^\bullet:T\xrightarrow[\Gamma]{\overline{a}\langle k\rangle}\emptyset} \qquad \textbf{(Sin)}\frac{\Gamma(a)=T[\mathtt{r}]}{\emptyset\xrightarrow[\Gamma]{a\langle k\rangle}k[\mathtt{r}]:T} \qquad \textbf{(ScomC)}\frac{}{k[\mathtt{r}'']^\bullet:T''\xrightarrow[\Gamma]{\tau}k[\mathtt{r}'']:T''}$$

$$\textbf{(Sjoin)}\frac{\Gamma(\mathcal{P})=(\widetilde{\mathtt{r}}^1,\widetilde{y}:\widetilde{S};\widetilde{\mathtt{r}}^2;G_{\mathcal{P}}) \qquad G_{\mathcal{P}}\{\widetilde{v}/\widetilde{y}\}\Downarrow_{\mathtt{r}''}=T''}{s[\mathtt{r}']:\mathtt{ent}\ \mathcal{P}[\mathtt{r}'']\langle\widetilde{v}\rangle\ \mathtt{from}\ \mathtt{r}.T\xrightarrow[\Gamma]{s\downarrow[\mathtt{r},\mathtt{r}':\mathtt{r}'']\langle k\rangle}s[\mathtt{r}']:T,k:[\mathtt{r}'']:T''}$$

$$\textbf{(Sparti)}\frac{\Gamma(\mathcal{P})=(\widetilde{\mathtt{r}}^1,\widetilde{y}:\widetilde{S};\widetilde{\mathtt{r}}^2;G_{\mathcal{P}}) \qquad G_{\mathcal{P}}\{\widetilde{v}/\widetilde{y}\}\Downarrow_{\mathtt{r}''}=T''}{s[\mathtt{r}]:\mathtt{req}\ \mathcal{P}[\mathtt{r}'']\langle\widetilde{v}\rangle\ \mathtt{to}\ \mathtt{r}'.T,k[\mathtt{r}'']^\circ:T''\xrightarrow[\Gamma]{s\uparrow[\mathtt{r},\mathtt{r}':\mathtt{r}'']\langle k\rangle}s[\mathtt{r}]:T}$$

$$\textbf{(Sinvit)}\frac{\Gamma(\mathcal{P})=(\widetilde{\mathtt{r}}^1,\widetilde{y}:\widetilde{S};\widetilde{\mathtt{r}}^2;G_{\mathcal{P}}) \qquad G_{\mathcal{P}}\{\widetilde{v}/\widetilde{y}\}\Downarrow_{\mathtt{r}''}=T''}{\begin{array}{c}s[\mathtt{r}]:\mathtt{ent}\ \mathcal{P}[\mathtt{r}'']\langle\widetilde{v}\rangle\ \mathtt{from}\ \mathtt{r}.T,s[\mathtt{r}']:\mathtt{req}\ \mathcal{P}[\mathtt{r}'']\langle\widetilde{v}\rangle\ \mathtt{to}\ \mathtt{r}.T',k[\mathtt{r}'']^\circ:T''\\ \xrightarrow[\Gamma]{\tau}s[\mathtt{r}]:T,s[\mathtt{r}']:T',k[\mathtt{r}'']:T''\end{array}}$$

Fig. 2. Transitions for specifications (excerpt)

session. A process is *unblocked* if it does not contain hidden channels and if its session channel is never under a prefix whose subject is a shared channel, except when the latter binds the former. If an unblocked process is validated by a simple coherent session environment, interactions at session channels can proceed. If, further, the original global type is non-recursive, the process can eventually complete all interactions at its session-environment.

Proposition 3 (Soundness of the type system)

(Correspondence) If $\Gamma \vdash P \triangleright \Delta$ *then* $\mathbf{sat}(P, \Delta)_{\Gamma}$.

(Subject Reduction) If $\Gamma \vdash P \triangleright \Delta$ *and* $P \to P'$ *then there exists* Δ' *s.t.* $\Gamma \vdash P' \triangleright \Delta'$.

(Progress) If P *is unblocked and* $\Gamma \vdash P \triangleright \Delta$ *such that* Δ *is simple, then there exists* P' *s.t.* $P \to^{+} P'$, $\Gamma \vdash P' \triangleright \Delta'$ *and* Δ' *is coherent.*

(Coherence) If P *is unblocked and* $\Gamma \vdash P \triangleright \Delta$ *such that* Δ *is simple, and moreover* Δ *does not contain recursions, then there exists* P' *s.t.* $P \to^{*} P'$ *and* $\Gamma \vdash P' \triangleright \emptyset$.

5 Returning a Result

We introduce the notion of *result* of a session as an object (which can be a value or even a protocol), sent back to the initiator of the session. *Protocols with results* allow us to describe complex governance properties, such as ensuring that a privately negotiated price corresponds to the one proposed publicly in the parent protocol. Suppose we want to ensure that, in CMS, the answer ans given in the subprotocol *Contact* by server is the same as ans_0 sent by middle to client. Information can be transmitted from a parent session to a subsession, but the converse is not possible. Continuation-Passing-Style is a possible solution: we convert the end of the CMS protocol into a continuation K, send it as argument when calling *Contact* and call K inside *Contact* with ans. However, this may not lead to a clean descriptive framework. Thus we choose to use a dedicated mechanism. The syntax of global types with results adds $\mathtt{r}\ \mathtt{returns}(res : S)$ and $(res : S) \leftarrow \mathtt{r}\ \mathtt{calls}\ \mathcal{P}\langle \widetilde{\mathtt{r}}, \widetilde{v}\rangle$ (replacing $\mathtt{end}$ and $\mathtt{r}\ \mathtt{calls}\ \mathcal{P}\langle \widetilde{v}\rangle$). The former constructor ends the session by specifying that the protocol returns the value identified in the session by res and that $\mathtt{r}$ is responsible for doing it, the latter specifies that we call a subprotocol which eventually produces a result res. Kinds ensure that the returned result has the type expected by the initiator.

We present corresponding modifications to CMS. Inside the *Contact* protocol, we ask agent to send the result ans back to the parent protocol. In the latter, the result ans_0 is expected when calling *Contact*, thus we ensure that the answer sent by the server in the subprotocol is the same as the one sent to client in the parent one. Local types use similar constructors and implementation of result is done through cross-session communications.

$$\begin{array}{l} \mathtt{let}\ \mathit{Contact} = (\text{agent}, \mathit{req} : \mathtt{Req})\{ \\ \ldots \text{agent}\ \mathtt{returns}(\mathit{ans} : \mathtt{Req}) \\ \mathtt{in} \\ \ldots \mathit{ans}_0 : \mathtt{Req} \leftarrow \text{middle}\ \mathtt{calls}\ \mathit{Contact}\langle \text{middle}, \mathit{req}_0\rangle \ldots \end{array}$$

In the framework presented above, subsessions are executed in parallel with the parent session. The result mechanism allows one to include synchronisation between the two sessions:

$$\ldots \text{ Alice } \texttt{waits for } \mathit{contract} \texttt{ calling } \text{Nego(Alice, Carol)}.$$
$$\text{Alice} \rightarrow \text{Bob} : \texttt{Data}(\mathit{contract}) \ldots$$

Here participant Alice starts a negotiation subsession with Carol. When the negotiation is over, she sends the result of the subsession to Bob, participant of the parent session not invited in the subsession. This has two advantages, first Bob can know the result of a subsession without going through the internal invitation procedure, and it prevents both Alice and Bob to perform actions in the parent session as long as the subsession is not over.

6 Conclusion and Future Works

To our knowledge, there does not exist other works addressing the notion of nested session types, or protocol calls inside session types. The closest contribution is [9], which introduces parametrisation of protocols through *dynamic session types*. Parametrisation allows one single two-party protocol to be applied to each pair of agents in a large network. Our framework contains more than simple parametrisation, it presents nesting and introduces kinds and higher-order programming. Another related work is [7]: the authors describe a global language for *choreographies*, implementing global types, protocols interleaved in the same choreography can be merged together into a single global type, removing costly invitations. The authors actually proceed in a direction different from ours, by trying to unify every protocol into a single superprotocol. Their approach focuses on implementation, while ours focus on types. We believe session type theory benefits independently from both methods. Our contribution makes use of the same formal framework as [3,13,2]. Each of these contributions adds expressiveness, in different directions (logical assertions, ghost states, monitoring), to a large common theory for validation of distributed programs with session types. The whole theory (including this work) is put in practise by the development of the Scribble language [16] and the collaboration with the OOI project [15].

We are currently investigating how the result mechanism can be improved (in the context of [16]). Currently, the result is sent to the initiator. Broadcasting the result to every member of the subsession might also be a desirable feature. Moreover, our results are restricted to value-types, but some use cases of [15] specify that a negotiation subprotocol produces a contract that is used in the parent protocol to control interactions. Although it leads to technical challenges, we believe our framework can eventually accommodate such behaviours by using dependent types, introducing abstract logical predicate decided at run-time inside global types. Exceptions handling in a distributed asynchronous framework, remains a challenging task, even if some progress have been made in [6] and [5]. Yet exceptions are absolutely necessary when specifying real-world protocols. We believe that nested protocols give a simple way to handle exceptions, by making explicit blocks of computation.

Acknowledgements. We thank the CONCUR reviewers for their comments, our colleagues in Mobility Reading Group for discussions, and the OOI project and Matthew Arrott for their feedback. This work is supported by Ocean Observatories Initiative [15] and EPSRC grants EP/F002114/1 and EP/G015481/1.

References

1. Bettini, L., Coppo, M., D'Antoni, L., De Luca, M., Dezani-Ciancaglini, M., Yoshida, N.: Global Progress in Dynamically Interleaved Multiparty Sessions. In: van Breugel, F., Chechik, M. (eds.) CONCUR 2008. LNCS, vol. 5201, pp. 418–433. Springer, Heidelberg (2008)
2. Bocchi, L., Denéilou, P.-M., Demangeon, R., Honda, K., Hu, R., Neykova, R., Yoshida, N.: Dynamic and static safety validation in distributed programs through multiparty sessions (submitted, 2012)
3. Bocchi, L., Honda, K., Tuosto, E., Yoshida, N.: A Theory of Design-by-Contract for Distributed Multiparty Interactions. In: Gastin, P., Laroussinie, F. (eds.) CONCUR 2010. LNCS, vol. 6269, pp. 162–176. Springer, Heidelberg (2010)
4. Capecchi, S., Castellani, I., Dezani-Ciancaglini, M.: Information flow safety in multiparty sessions. In: EXPRESS. EPTCS, vol. 64, pp. 16–30 (2011)
5. Capecchi, S., Giachino, E., Yoshida, N.: Global escape in multiparty sessions. In: Lodaya, K., Mahajan, M. (eds.) FSTTCS. LIPIcs, vol. 8, pp. 338–351. Schloss Dagstuhl - Leibniz-Zentrum fuer Informatik (2010)
6. Carbone, M., Honda, K., Yoshida, N.: Structured Interactional Exceptions in Session Types. In: van Breugel, F., Chechik, M. (eds.) CONCUR 2008. LNCS, vol. 5201, pp. 402–417. Springer, Heidelberg (2008)
7. Carbone, M., Montesi, F.: Merging multiparty protocols in multiparty choreographies (unpublished, presented at PLACES, 2012)
8. Coppo, M., Dezani-Ciancaglini, M.: Structured Communications with Concurrent Constraints. In: Kaklamanis, C., Nielson, F. (eds.) TGC 2008. LNCS, vol. 5474, pp. 104–125. Springer, Heidelberg (2009)
9. Deniélou, P.-M., Yoshida, N.: Dynamic multirole session types. In: POPL, pp. 435–446 (2011)
10. Bono, V., Capecchi, S., Castellani, I., Dezani-Ciancaglini, M.: A Reputation System for Multirole Sessions. In: Bruni, R., Sassone, V. (eds.) TGC 2011. LNCS, vol. 7173, pp. 1–24. Springer, Heidelberg (2012)
11. Honda, K., Vasconcelos, V.T., Kubo, M.: Language Primitives and Type Discipline for Structured Communication-Based Programming. In: Hankin, C. (ed.) ESOP 1998. LNCS, vol. 1381, pp. 122–138. Springer, Heidelberg (1998)
12. Lanese, I., Guidi, C., Montesi, F., Zavattaro, G.: Bridging the gap between interaction- and process-oriented choreographies. In: Cerone, A., Gruner, S. (eds.) SEFM, pp. 323–332. IEEE Computer Society (2008)
13. Bocchi, L., Demangeon, R., Yoshida, N.: A multiparty multi-session logic (submitted, 2012)
14. Milner, R.: A Calculus of Communicating Systems. LNCS, vol. 92. Springer, Heidelberg (1980)
15. Ocean Observatories Initiative (OOI), `http://www.oceanleadership.org/programs-and-partnerships/ocean-observing/ooi/`
16. Scribble Project homepage, `www.scribble.org`

Intensional and Extensional Characterisation of Global Progress in the π-Calculus

Luca Fossati[1,2], Kohei Honda[1], and Nobuko Yoshida[2]

[1] Queen Mary University of London
[2] Imperial College London

Abstract. We introduce an observational theory of global progress properties such as non-blockingness and wait-freedom based on a linear π-calculus. The theory uniformly captures such properties both extensionally and intensionally, by using fair transition relations and partial failures, which represent stalling activities. A fairness-enriched bisimilarity preserves these properties and is a congruence. The framework is applied to the semantic characterisation and separation results for concurrent data structures including different queue implementations.

1 Introduction

Imperative concurrent data structures such as lock-based and lock-free queues play a fundamental role in practice, and have been extensively studied from the algorithmic viewpoint [13,24]. But our understanding still lacks a rigorous semantic foundation that supports diverse engineering concerns, from observational specification and verification of properties to correctness arguments for optimisation.

For example, we may wish to replace a queue implementation [9,20,21] with a better one sharing the same interface. Can we exactly identify the similarities and differences in their observable effects? Can such identifications be extended to concurrent data structures based on message passing? To answer these questions, we need a uniform theory based on externally observable behaviour, which is applicable to a large class of concurrent data structures and which can accurately identify and classify their global progress properties such as non-blockingness (lock-freedom) and wait-freedom.

Previous studies presented *intensional* definitions of global progress that mainly pertain to internal structures of programs. For example, the standard algorithmic understanding of non-blockingness (lock-freedom) [12, 24] says that, in a non-blocking data structure, "some process can always complete its pending operation in a finite number of its own steps, regardless of the execution speed of other processes" (the quote is from [24]). Wait-freedom is obtained by replacing "some process" with "all processes". This description critically relies on the internal functioning of a program (e.g. "its own steps"). Existing formal accounts [5, 10], based on program logics, are along the same line (cf. §5). But for some engineering concerns such as comparing the observable behaviour of two components for substitutivity, an extensional understanding is essential.

This paper introduces a behavioural theory of imperative concurrent data structures based on a linear π-calculus [15, 16, 28], where global progress properties are characterised both intensionally and extensionally. The intensional characterisations offer a

M. Koutny and I. Ulidowski (Eds.): CONCUR 2012, LNCS 7454, pp. 287–301, 2012.

faithful formalisation of the existing notions of global progress, while their extensional counterparts capture a wider class of properties solely based on external observables, independently of internal implementations. The theory uses fair transitions and partial failures to capture global progress, and linear interactions to encode atomic operations such as semaphores and compare-and-swap (`cas`). Exploiting the fine-grainedness and expressiveness of the π-calculus, our theory is independent from synchronisation primitives and programming language constructs and it is uniformly applicable to a large class of behaviours, extending global progress properties to (say) higher-order functions, objects and message-passing programs.

Summary of Contributions. In §**2** we introduce a linear π-calculus with the key atomic agents and its properties used in the paper. Our main technical contributions include:

- A behavioural theory of the linear π-calculus based on an asynchronous fair typed LTS with partial failures, rigorously characterising intensional and extensional global progress, the latter preserved by a fairness-enriched bisimilarity (§**3**).
- A classification of global progress properties from the literature and beyond, showing inclusions and separations among them (cf. Theorems 3.11 and 3.14).
- An application to the semantic analysis of lock-based and non-lock-based queues in the π-calculus (Theorem 4.2) (§**4**), which leads to concise proofs of semantic linearisability (Theorem 4.3) and separation (Theorem 4.6).

To our knowledge, the present work offers the first comprehensive observational theory of global progress applicable to a wide range of concurrent data structures, as well as being the first to verify non-blockingness of a non-trivial concurrent data structure [21] as a behavioural property in the π-calculus. § **5** presents comparisons with related works. [6] lists auxiliary definitions, further reasoning examples and proofs.

2 The π-Calculus with Linear Types

2.1 Processes, Reduction and Types

Processes. Following [15,25,28], we use the asynchronous π-calculus augmented with branching. We use *channel names* $(a, b, c, g, h, r, u, \ldots)$; *value variables* $(x, y, \ldots)$; *process variables* $(X, Y, \ldots)$; *constants* $(\mathsf{k}, \mathsf{k}', \ldots)$, including booleans and numerals; *values* $(v, v', \ldots)$ which are the union of channel names and constants; and *expressions* $(e, e', \ldots)$, inductively generated from values, value variables and first-order operations on them (e.g. $-e$, $e_1{+}e_2$, $e_1{\wedge}e_2$, $\neg e$ and $e_1{=}e_2$. We write $\vec{x}$ $(\vec{e})$ for a vector of variables (resp. expressions). *Processes* $(P, Q, \ldots)$ are given by the following grammar.

$$\begin{aligned} P \ ::= \ & u\{l_i(\vec{x}_i).P_i\}_{i\in I} \ \mid \ \overline{u}\,l\langle\vec{e}\rangle \ \mid \ \texttt{if}\ e\ \texttt{then}\ P\ \texttt{else}\ Q \\ \mid \ & P|Q \ \mid \ (\boldsymbol{\nu}\,u)P \ \mid \ (\mu X(\vec{x}).P)\langle\vec{e}\rangle \ \mid \ X\langle\vec{x}\rangle \ \mid \ \mathbf{0} \end{aligned}$$

A *branching* $u\{l_i(\vec{x}_i).P_i\}_{i\in I}$ offers a non-empty set of branches, each with a *branch label* l_i, formal parameters $\vec{x}_i$ and continuation P_i. Dually, a *selection* $\overline{u}\,l\langle\vec{e}\rangle$ chooses l and passes $\vec{e}$ after evaluation. In both, u occurs as *subject*; $\vec{x}_i$ and $\vec{e}$ as *objects*. Branchings/selections are encodable but play a key role in typing [15]. We also use the conditional `if` e `then` P `else` Q; parallel composition $P|Q$; hiding $(\boldsymbol{\nu}\,u)P$ where u is bound in P; recursion $(\mu X(\vec{x}).P)\langle\vec{e}\rangle$, where $X, \vec{x}$ are bound in P and P is an input prefix. $X\langle\vec{e}\rangle$ instantiates X with actual parameters $\vec{e}$.

Branchings and selections are often called *inputs* and *outputs*, respectively. W.l.o.g. we use a unique fixed branch label for all single-branch inputs and omit it, as in $u(\vec{x}).P$ for input and $\overline{u}\langle\vec{e}\rangle$ for output. We write $\overline{u}(\vec{a})P$ for $(\boldsymbol{\nu}\,\vec{a})(\overline{u}\langle\vec{a}\rangle|P)$; $\overline{a}$ and $a.P$ for $\overline{a}\langle\rangle$ and $a().P$, resp.; and the replication $!u\{l_i(\vec{x}_i).P_i\}_i$ for $(\mu X().u\{l_i(\vec{x}_i).(P_i|X\langle\rangle)\})\langle\rangle$.

Reduction. The *structural congruence* $\equiv$ is defined by the standard rules including the unfolding of recursion: $(\mu X(\vec{x}).P)\langle\vec{e}\rangle \equiv P\{(\mu X(\vec{x}).P)/X\}\{\vec{e}/\vec{x}\}$. The *reduction relation* $\longrightarrow$ over processes modulo $\equiv$, is generated from:

$$u\{l_i(\vec{x}_i).P_i\}_{i\in I} \mid \overline{u}\,l_j\langle\vec{e}\rangle \;\longrightarrow\; P_j\{\vec{v}/\vec{x}_j\} \quad (j\in I,\ \vec{e}\downarrow\vec{v})$$

$$\texttt{if}\ e\ \texttt{then}\ P\ \texttt{else}\ Q \longrightarrow P \quad (e\downarrow\texttt{tt}) \qquad \texttt{if}\ e\ \texttt{then}\ P\ \texttt{else}\ Q \longrightarrow Q \quad (e\downarrow\texttt{ff})$$

where $\vec{e}\downarrow\vec{v}$ says that the pointwise evaluation of $\vec{e}$ is $\vec{v}$. The first rule says that an input interacts with an output at u, the former's j-th branch P_j is chosen, and $\vec{x}_j$ are instantiated with the evaluation of $\vec{e}$. We close the relation under $|$ and $\boldsymbol{\nu}$.

Types and Environments. Given base types θ, types $(\tau, \tau', \ldots)$ are as follows:

$$\tau \ ::=\ \&^{\mathsf{L}}_{i\in I} l_i(\vec{\tau}_i) \mid \oplus^{\mathsf{L}}_{i\in I} l_i(\vec{\tau}_i) \mid \&^{\mathsf{NL}}_{i\in I} l_i(\vec{\tau}_i) \mid \oplus^{\mathsf{NL}}_{i\in I} l_i(\vec{\tau}_i) \mid \bot \mid \theta \qquad \theta\ ::=\ \mathsf{bool} \mid \mathsf{int}$$

The types of both input ($\&$) and output ($\oplus$) channels have either a linear (L) or a non-linear (NL) modality. Each element in the vector $\vec{\tau}_i$ should not be $\bot$. Type $\bot$ indicates that both an input and an output are present at a linear channel. We define $\overline{\tau}$, the *dual* of τ, by exchanging all occurrences of $\&$ in τ with $\oplus$ and vice versa. We write $\uparrow^{\mathsf{L}}(\vec{\tau})$ for a singleton index set $\oplus^{\mathsf{L}}_{1\in\{1\}} l_1(\vec{\tau})$. Similarly for $\downarrow^{\mathsf{L}}(\vec{\tau})$, $\uparrow^{\mathsf{NL}}(\vec{\tau})$ and $\downarrow^{\mathsf{NL}}(\vec{\tau})$.

An *environment* $(\Gamma, \Delta, \ldots)$ is a finite map of *type assignments* of the form $u : \tau$ (channel/variable to type) or $X : \vec{\tau}$ (process variable to a vector of its argument types). A typing judgement is written $\Gamma \vdash P$ which reads: "*P has typing Γ*". The typing rules follow [15] and are left to [6]. They ensure: for a linear input (output) channel, exactly one input (resp. output) occurs; for a non-linear input, at most one input and zero or arbitrarily many outputs occur; similarly for a non-linear output except an input never occurs there. The typing also prohibits the use of name matching from expressions.

The subsequent development does not depend on details of typing rules as far as the basic properties of typed processes are preserved, which we shall discuss later in §2.2

Linearity Annotations. We add linear annotations to typable processes. A linearly typed input/output name u corresponds to a *linear input/output*, $u^{\mathsf{L}}\{l_i(\vec{x}_i).P_i\}_{i\in I}$ and $\overline{u}^{\mathsf{L}}l\langle\vec{e}\rangle$ respectively. If P and/or Q contain free linear channel names/variables, we write $\texttt{if}^{\mathsf{L}} v\ \texttt{then}\ P\ \texttt{else}\ Q$ (*linear conditional*). A *linear reduction*, denoted $\longrightarrow_{\mathsf{L}}$, is induced by interaction at a linear channel or by reducing a linear conditional.

Example 2.1 (atomicity through linearity). We encode atomic operations such as atomic read, write and `cas`, as reduction sequences starting with an initial non-linear interaction for invocation, and ending with a series of linear interactions, the last being the final response. An example follows (for readability, we use recursive equations, which are easily encodable through recursions).

$$\mathsf{Ref}\langle u,v\rangle \stackrel{\text{def}}{=} u\,\{\, \mathit{read}(z) : \overline{z}^{\mathsf{L}}\langle v\rangle \mid \mathsf{Ref}\langle u,v\rangle,\ \mathit{write}(y,z) : \overline{z}^{\mathsf{L}} \mid \mathsf{Ref}\langle u,y\rangle \}$$

$$\mathsf{Ref}^{\mathsf{cas}}\langle u,v\rangle \stackrel{\text{def}}{=} u \left\{ \begin{array}{l} \mathit{read}(z) : \overline{z}^{\mathsf{L}}\langle v\rangle \mid \mathsf{Ref}^{\mathsf{cas}}\langle u,v\rangle,\ \mathit{write}(y,z) : \overline{z}^{\mathsf{L}} \mid \mathsf{Ref}^{\mathsf{cas}}\langle u,y\rangle, \\ \mathit{cas}(x,y,z) : \mathtt{if}^{\mathsf{L}}\, x = v\ \mathtt{then}\ \overline{z}^{\mathsf{L}}\langle \mathtt{tt}\rangle \mid \mathsf{Ref}^{\mathsf{cas}}\langle u,y\rangle \\ \qquad\qquad\qquad \mathtt{else}\ \overline{z}^{\mathsf{L}}\langle \mathtt{ff}\rangle \mid \mathsf{Ref}^{\mathsf{cas}}\langle u,v\rangle \end{array} \right\}$$

Above, $\mathsf{Ref}\langle u,v\rangle$ represents an atomic reference, to which $\mathsf{Ref}^{\mathsf{cas}}\langle u,v\rangle$ adds the standard cas operation. The following example performs a cas atomic operation:

$$\begin{array}{l} \mathsf{Ref}^{\mathsf{cas}}\langle a,0\rangle | (\boldsymbol{\nu}\, c)(\overline{a}\mathit{cas}\langle 0,1,c\rangle | c^{\mathsf{L}}(x).P) \\ \longrightarrow (\boldsymbol{\nu}\, c)((\mathtt{if}\ 0=0\ \mathtt{then}\ \overline{c}\langle \mathtt{tt}\rangle \mid \mathsf{Ref}^{\mathsf{cas}}\langle a,1\rangle\ \mathtt{else}\ \overline{c}\langle \mathtt{ff}\rangle \mid \mathsf{Ref}^{\mathsf{cas}}\langle a,0\rangle) \mid c^{\mathsf{L}}(x).P) \\ \longrightarrow_{\mathsf{L}} (\boldsymbol{\nu}\, c)(\overline{c}^{\mathsf{L}}\langle \mathtt{tt}\rangle \mid \mathsf{Ref}^{\mathsf{cas}}\langle a,1\rangle \mid c^{\mathsf{L}}(x).P) \longrightarrow_{\mathsf{L}} \mathsf{Ref}^{\mathsf{cas}}\langle a,1\rangle \mid P\{\mathtt{tt}/x\} \end{array}$$

it is atomic since linear reductions necessarily take place (i.e. no other reduction may suppress them or interfere with their outcome). We shall formalise this shortly.

Example 2.2 (mutex agents). The following are two different mutex implementations. Let $\mathtt{if}\ \mathtt{cas}(u,v,w)\ \mathtt{then}\ P\ \mathtt{else}\ Q \stackrel{\text{def}}{=} (\boldsymbol{\nu}\, c)(\overline{u}\ \mathit{cas}\langle v,w,c\rangle | c(x).\mathtt{if}\ x\ \mathtt{then}\ P\ \mathtt{else}\ Q)$ and $\mathtt{CAS}(u,v,w) \stackrel{\text{def}}{=} \mathtt{if}\ \mathtt{cas}(u,v,w)\ \mathtt{then}\ \mathbf{0}\ \mathtt{else}\ \mathbf{0}$. Then:

$$\begin{array}{l} \mathsf{Mtx}\langle u\rangle \stackrel{\text{def}}{=} u(x).\overline{x}(h)h.\mathsf{Mtx}\langle u\rangle \\ \mathsf{Mtx}^{\mathsf{spin}}\langle u\rangle \stackrel{\text{def}}{=} (\boldsymbol{\nu}\, c)(\mathsf{Ref}^{\mathsf{cas}}\langle c,0\rangle \mid !u(x).\mu X.(\mathtt{if}\ \mathtt{cas}(c,0,1)\ \mathtt{then}\ \overline{x}(h)h.\mathtt{CAS}(c,1,0)\ \mathtt{else}\ X)) \end{array}$$

When $\mathsf{Mtx}\langle u\rangle$ gets locked, u becomes unavailable until it gets unlocked [17]; while $\mathsf{Mtx}^{\mathsf{spin}}\langle u\rangle$ is always available and uses cas to make clients spin until they are served.

2.2 Labelled Transition and Bisimilarity

Untyped Labelled Transitions. The LTS uses the *actions* ($\ell, \ell', \ldots$) given as:

$$\ell \quad ::= \quad \tau \mid (\boldsymbol{\nu}\, \vec{c})a\, l\langle \vec{v}\rangle \mid (\boldsymbol{\nu}\, \vec{c})\overline{a}\, l\langle \vec{v}\rangle$$

Above the channels in $\vec{c}$ are pairwise distinct and disjoint from a, and occur in $\vec{v}$. For single-branch value passing, we write $(\boldsymbol{\nu}\, \vec{c})a\langle \vec{v}\rangle$ and $(\boldsymbol{\nu}\, \vec{c})\overline{a}\langle \vec{v}\rangle$. If $\vec{c}$ is empty, we omit $(\boldsymbol{\nu}\, \vec{c})$, writing e.g. $\overline{a}\, l\langle \vec{v}\rangle$. We now define the *untyped* LTS over closed processes, i.e. processes without free process/value variables. First let $P \xrightarrow{\tau} Q$ iff $P \longrightarrow Q$. Then:

$$\text{(Bra)}\quad P \xrightarrow{(\boldsymbol{\nu}\, \vec{c})a\, l\langle \vec{v}\rangle} P|\overline{a}\, l\langle \vec{v}\rangle \qquad\qquad \text{(Sel)}\quad (\boldsymbol{\nu}\, \vec{c})(P|\overline{a}\, l\langle \vec{v}\rangle) \xrightarrow{(\boldsymbol{\nu}\, \vec{c})\overline{a}\, l\langle \vec{v}\rangle} P$$

In (Bra), we assume no name in $\vec{c}$ occurs in P. In (Sel), the names in $\vec{c}$ occur in $\vec{v}$. We close the relation under $\equiv$ by $P \xrightarrow{\ell} Q$ when $P \equiv P_0$, $P_0 \xrightarrow{\ell} Q_0$ and $Q_0 \equiv Q$.

Typed Transitions. The typed LTS requires environment transitions [28], denoted $\Gamma \xrightarrow{\ell} \Gamma'$ (which reads: "Γ *allows* the action ℓ and becomes Γ' *after* that action") generated from the rules below. For readability we assume carried types consist only of: a base type and a non-base type, for input transitions; a base type and three non-base types, for output transitions (where the message carries a constant, a free linear name, a free non-linear name, and a bound name). The rules can be easily generalised (i.e. an output message may carry zero or more base type expressions, free linear names, and so on).

$$\Gamma, a\!:\!\&^{\mathsf{NL}}\{l_i(\theta_i\tau_i)\}_{i\in I} \xrightarrow{(\nu\, c)al_j\langle wc\rangle} \Gamma, c\!:\!\tau_j, a\!:\!\&^{\mathsf{NL}}\{l_i(\theta_i\tau_i)\}_{i\in I}$$

$$\begin{matrix}\Gamma,\, b'\!:\!\tau_j',\, b''\!:\!\tau_j'', \\ a\!:\!\oplus^{\mathsf{NL}}_{i\in I} l_i(\theta_i\,\tau_i'\,\tau_i''\,\tau_i''')\end{matrix} \xrightarrow{(\nu\, c)\overline{a}\,l_j\langle wb'b''c\rangle} \begin{matrix}\Gamma,\, b''\!:\!\tau_j'',\, c\!:\!\tau_j''', \\ a\!:\!\oplus^{\mathsf{NL}}_{i\in I} l_i(\theta_i\,\tau_i'\,\tau_i''\,\tau_i''')\end{matrix} \qquad (j\in I)$$

$$\Gamma, a\!:\!\&^{\mathsf{L}}\{l_i(\theta_i\tau_i)\}_{i\in I} \xrightarrow{(\nu\, c)al_j\langle wc\rangle} \Gamma, c\!:\!\tau_j, a\!:\!\bot$$

$$\Gamma,\, b'\!:\!\tau_j', b''\!:\!\tau_j'', a\!:\!\oplus^{\mathsf{L}}_{i\in I} l_i(\theta_i\,\tau_i'\,\tau_i''\,\tau_i''') \xrightarrow{(\nu\, c)\overline{a}\,l_j\langle wb'b''c\rangle} \Gamma, b''\!:\!\tau_j'', c\!:\!\tau_j''' \qquad (j\in I)$$

where, for all $i \in I$, τ_i' is a linear type, while τ_i'' is a non-linear type. In the first rule, the type of a allows an input via a and, by its non-linearity, it does not change afterwards. Similarly in the second rule; further a linear b' disappears; a non-linear b'' does not; and a bound c becomes free. The last two rules are the linear variants of the former two, only differing in the resulting type of a. We also set $\Gamma \xrightarrow{\tau} \Gamma$ for each Γ. We then set:

$$\Gamma \vdash P \xrightarrow{\ell} \Delta \vdash Q \quad \overset{\text{def}}{\Leftrightarrow} \quad \Gamma \vdash P,\ P \xrightarrow{\ell} Q \text{ and } \Gamma \xrightarrow{\ell} \Delta.$$

Proposition 2.3. *Our typed LTS is consistent:* $(\Gamma \vdash P \wedge \Gamma \xrightarrow{\ell} \Delta \wedge P \xrightarrow{\ell} Q) \Rightarrow \Delta \vdash Q$.

The following example highlights how the typing controls transitions.

Example 2.4 (typed LTS). Let $\tau \stackrel{\text{def}}{=} \uparrow^{\mathsf{L}}(\mathsf{int})$, $\tau' \stackrel{\text{def}}{=} \downarrow^{\mathsf{NL}}(\tau)$ and $\Gamma \stackrel{\text{def}}{=} a:\tau', c:\tau$. Let $P \stackrel{\text{def}}{=} !a(x).\overline{x}\langle 2\rangle \mid \overline{a}\langle c\rangle$. Then: $\Gamma \vdash P \xrightarrow{(\nu\, g)a\langle g\rangle} \Gamma, g:\tau \vdash P|\overline{a}\langle g\rangle$. But $\Gamma \vdash P \not\xrightarrow{\overline{a}\langle c\rangle}$ since $\Gamma \not\xrightarrow{\overline{a}\langle c\rangle}$. This message is to be consumed by the unique input $!a(x).\overline{x}\langle 2\rangle$.

Henceforth we always assume that processes and transitions are typed, even when we leave environments implicit as in $P \xrightarrow{\ell} Q$. We use the standard notation $P \overset{\hat{\ell}}{\Longrightarrow} Q$ standing for $P \xrightarrow{\tau}{}^{*} Q$ when $\ell = \tau$ and $P \xrightarrow{\tau}{}^{*}\xrightarrow{\ell}\xrightarrow{\tau}{}^{*} Q$ otherwise. $P \xrightarrow{s} P'$ stands for $P \xrightarrow{\ell_1} \ldots \xrightarrow{\ell_n} P'$, where $s = \ell_1 \ldots \ell_n$; we say that P' is a *transition derivative of* P.

Proposition 2.5. *The key properties of linear actions/reductions follow.*

(1 - partial confluence [16]) *Let* $P \xrightarrow{\ell} Q_1$ *and* $P \longrightarrow_{\mathsf{L}} Q_2$, *where* $Q_1 \not\equiv Q_2$. *Then there is* R *s.t.* $Q_1 \longrightarrow_{\mathsf{L}} R$ *and* $Q_2 \xrightarrow{\ell} R$.

(2 - linear normal form) *For any* P, *we have* $P \longrightarrow_{\mathsf{L}}^{*} Q \not\longrightarrow_{\mathsf{L}}$ *for a unique* Q.

(3 - asynchrony) *Let* ℓ *be an input whose subject is not bound in* s, *then* $P \xrightarrow{s}\xrightarrow{\ell} Q$ *implies* $P \xrightarrow{\ell}\xrightarrow{s} Q$. *While if* ℓ *is a free output,* $P \xrightarrow{\ell}\xrightarrow{s} Q$ *implies* $P \xrightarrow{s}\xrightarrow{\ell} Q$.

Bisimilarity. Based on the typed LTS, we introduce the standard typed weak bisimilarity [28]. Henceforth we assume a relation $\mathcal{R}$ over typed processes is *typed*, relating $\Gamma \vdash P$ and $\Delta \vdash Q$ only if $\Gamma = \Delta$, in which case we write $\Gamma \vdash P\mathcal{R}Q$.

Definition 2.6 (bisimilarity). A symmetric relation $\mathcal{R}$ over closed terms is a *(weak) bisimulation* if $P\mathcal{R}Q$ and $P \xrightarrow{\ell} P'$ imply $Q \overset{\hat{\ell}}{\Longrightarrow} Q'$ such that $P'\mathcal{R}Q'$. The largest bisimulation, denoted $\approx$, is extended to open terms in the standard way.

Proposition 2.7. *(1)* $\approx$ *is a typed congruence. (2)* $\longrightarrow_{\mathsf{L}} \subset \approx$.

By Prop. 2.5 (1) and Prop. 2.7 (2), linear reductions are semantically neutral. Further by Prop. 2.5 (2) any transition can be completed by consuming all linear reductions. This is why a reduction sequence like the one in Ex. 2.1, consisting of one non-linear reduction followed by some linear ones, may be semantically considered as a single action.

3 An Observational Theory of Global Progress

The framework given in this section allows unboundedly many concurrent operations, hence also an execution in which new requests keep on coming and no operation makes progress (i.e. no request is answered). To avoid such anomalies, we shall use:

- *Fairness* : ensuring that every active operation eventually makes progress.

But this prevents the standard representation of *stalling* activities. Consider a concurrent thread inside a critical section protected by a lock. By fairness it will eventually exit, then we cannot model the effect of the thread stalling inside and blocking other threads. To avoid this issue, we combine fairness with:

- *Failures* : allowing an active output process to arbitrarily reduce to the inaction **0**.

With fairness and failures, we accurately represent and differentiate a wide range of global progress properties over a general class of concurrent behaviours.

3.1 Fair and Failing Sequences

Fairness. First we define enabledness: a conditional is *enabled* if it can reduce; an input/output message is *enabled* if it can reduce by synchronisation.

Henceforth $\Phi, \Psi, \ldots$ range over possibly infinite typed transition sequences, also written $\Phi : P_1 \xrightarrow{\ell_1} P_2 \xrightarrow{\ell_2} \cdots$, omitting environments. A transition sequence Φ is *maximal* if it is either infinite or ends with a process in which no occurrence of conditional, output or linear input is *enabled*. We assume we can identify an occurrence across transitions through residuals (a rigorous treatment is in [4]). Now we define fairness.

Definition 3.1 (fairness). A transition sequence Φ is *fair* if Φ is maximal and no single occurrence of conditional, output or linear input is infinitely often enabled in Φ.

Def. 3.1 uses strong fairness [8]. This does not lose generality because strongly fair transition sequences in the π-calculus correspond to weakly fair runs in concurrent programs. We encode an execution step which is continuously enabled in a program, as an output which is infinitely often enabled by a recursively re-appearing dual input.

Example 3.2 (fairness). In $(!a.\overline{a})|\overline{a} \mid (!b.\overline{b})|\overline{b}$, if we always reduce the a redex, we have a non-fair transition sequence, because the same occurrence of $\overline{b}$ is enabled infinitely often. By alternating the reductions on a and b we have a fair sequence, as each output occurrence is enabled twice, before the reduction on the other side and before its own.

Failing reduction and blocking. We capture stalling by adding the following *failing transitions* (or *failures*), where we assume neither u nor the conditional are linear.

$$\overline{u}\, l_j\langle\vec{e}\rangle \longrightarrow \mathbf{0} \qquad\qquad \texttt{if } v \texttt{ then } P \texttt{ else } Q \longrightarrow \mathbf{0}$$

Since linear transitions are non-failing, so are *atomic operations* (cf. Example 2.1).

Definition 3.3 (failing sequence). A transition sequence is *failing* if it contains a failing transition. It is *finitely failing* if the number of failing transitions is finite.

The purpose is to observationally capture how a failure in a component blocks others. Given a transition sequence Φ and assuming no request came prior to Φ, $\texttt{ended}(\Phi, Q_i)$ is the set of output subjects occurring in Φ *before* Q_i (by abusing notation, we denote an *occurrence* of Q_i in Φ by Q_i). Intuitively, it denotes the set of "threads which have answered". Let $\texttt{allowed}(\Gamma)$ be the set of subjects of transition labels allowed by Γ (i.e. the subject of ℓ in $\Gamma \xrightarrow{\ell} \Gamma'$). A channel g is *pending at a process occurrence* $\Gamma_i \vdash P_i$ *in* Φ, if it is allowed by Γ_i but the corresponding answer has not been sent yet. Then:

$$\texttt{pending}(\Phi,\, \Gamma_i \vdash P_i) \stackrel{\text{def}}{=} \texttt{allowed}(\Gamma_i) \setminus \texttt{ended}(\Phi, P_i) \tag{3.1}$$

denotes the set of pending channels at $\Gamma_i \vdash P_i$ in Φ.

Definition 3.4 (blocked output). Let Φ be a possibly failing transition sequence. c is *blocked at* $\Gamma \vdash P$ *in* Φ if $c \in \texttt{pending}(\Phi, \Gamma \vdash P)$ and no output at c appears in any transition sequence from $\Gamma \vdash P$, not restricted to the remaining of Φ. $\texttt{blocked}(\Phi, \Gamma \vdash P)$ (or $\texttt{blocked}(\Gamma \vdash P)$, or $\texttt{blocked}(P)$, if Φ and Γ are implicit) denotes the set of blocked names at P. We set $\texttt{blocked}(\Phi) = \cup_{i \geq 0}\texttt{blocked}(P_i)$.

Example 3.5 (blocked output). To see how failing reductions induce blocked outputs, consider $\mathsf{Lck}\langle u\rangle \stackrel{\text{def}}{=} (\boldsymbol{\nu}\, m)(!u(z).\overline{m}(c)c(h).(\overline{z}|\overline{h}) \mid \mathsf{Mtx}\langle m\rangle)$ which represents a server offering one operation, to take a lock and release it immediately. Then consider $\Gamma \vdash \mathsf{Lck}\langle u\rangle \mid \overline{u}\langle z'\rangle \mid \overline{u}\langle z''\rangle$ where $\Gamma \vdash \overline{z'}$ and $\Gamma \vdash \overline{z''}$. This reduces to the following process, where a failure at $\overline{h'}$ would block z'', since m would become permanently unavailable:

$$(\boldsymbol{\nu}\, m)(!u(z).\overline{m}(c)c(h).(\overline{z}|\overline{h}) \mid \overline{z'} | (\boldsymbol{\nu}\, h')(\overline{h'} \mid h'.\mathsf{Mtx}\langle m\rangle)) \mid \overline{u}\langle z''\rangle$$

3.2 Intensional Global Progress Properties

We start from *resilience*, laying the basis for uniformly defining diverse global progress properties. Varying resilience gives intensional/extensional variants of such properties: the former faithfully formalise the standard understanding; the latter generalise it. We first give the intensional version. Below, $|S|$ indicates the cardinality of a set S.

Definition 3.6 (strict resilience). A closed P is *strictly resilient* if for each finitely failing and fair Φ from P, $|\texttt{blocked}(\Phi)|$ is not greater than the number of failures in Φ.

By requiring less blocked outputs than failures, strict resilience ensures each failure may block only locally. It is intensional, as it assumes the number of failures is known.

Strict resilience can be weakened by requiring the number of blocked outputs to be less than, say, n times the number of failures. This gives a whole range of resilience properties, with the extensional one (defined shortly) representing a limiting point, while the others are intensional in nature. Here is an example of strict resilience.

Example 3.7 (strict resilience). 1. Consider $\Gamma \vdash \mathsf{Lck}\langle u\rangle \,|\, \overline{u}\langle z'\rangle \,|\, \overline{u}\langle z''\rangle \,|\, \overline{u}\langle z'''\rangle$, obtained by adding another request in parallel to Ex. 3.5. By the same reductions as in Ex. 3.5, both z'' and z''' become blocked. Hence this process is not strictly resilient.
2. In contrast, $\mathsf{Ref}\langle u, v\rangle$ (an atomic reference) is strictly resilient: since u is continuously available, it is impossible that an operation gets blocked by another's failure.

We show informally (details in [6]) that strict resilience coincides with *obstruction-freedom (OF)* [12], assuming each operation is performed by one sequential thread. *OF* ensures the completion of an operation that is performed in isolation. Since *OF* allows any operation that has not failed to complete, it implies strict resilience. Now assume strict resilience. Executing op_i in isolation is equivalent to making all other operations fail first, so that only op_i progresses, and by strict resilience it completes, obtaining *OF*.

Using strict resilience, we formalise non-blockingness and wait-freedom in our calculus. $\mathsf{FT}(P)$ denotes the set of finitely-failing and fair transition sequences from P.

Definition 3.8 (intensional NB/WF). A strictly resilient P is:

1. *intensionally non-blocking* (INB) if for any $\Phi \in \mathsf{FT}(P)$ s.t. $\Delta \vdash Q$ is in Φ and $\mathtt{allowed}(\Delta) \setminus \mathtt{blocked}(\Phi) \neq \emptyset$, some output occurs in Φ after Q.
2. *intensionally wait-free* (IWF) if for any $\Phi \in \mathsf{FT}(P)$ s.t. $\Delta \vdash Q$ is in Φ and $c \in \mathtt{allowed}(\Delta) \setminus \mathtt{blocked}(\Phi)$, an output at c occurs in Φ after Q.

INB asks that, in *every* execution, *some* non-blocked outputs eventually occur; IWF replaces "some" with "all". Without resilience, the set $\mathtt{allowed}(\Delta) \setminus \mathtt{blocked}(\Phi)$ could be empty for all Φ and Δ, i.e. when a failure in one component blocks all other components. Then both properties would be trivially satisfied and any lock-based implementation would become non-blocking, defying the general understanding. $\mathsf{Ref}^{\mathsf{cas}}\langle u, v\rangle$ is a simple example of both INB and IWF, more complex examples are in § 4. We write **INB** and **IWF**, for the sets of INB and IWF processes, resp.

3.3 Extensional Global Progress and Classification Results

First we relax strict resilience to get "extensional" properties which are strictly more inclusive than their intensional counterparts, offering an observational basis for reasoning about global progress. Then we classify these extensional properties.

Definition 3.9 (extensional resilience/NB/WF). P is *(extensionally) resilient* iff, for any finitely failing and fair Φ from P, $|\mathtt{blocked}(\Phi)|$ is finite. P is *non-blocking, NB* (resp. *wait-free, WF*) if it satisfies (1) (resp. (2)) of Def. 3.8, replacing strict resilience with resilience. Henceforth **NB** and **WF** denote, resp., the sets of NB and WF processes.

Example 3.10. Let $\mathsf{eR}_K\langle u\rangle \stackrel{\text{def}}{=} (\boldsymbol{\nu}\, u_0)(\mathsf{Mtx}\langle u_0\rangle | \mathsf{eR}_K\langle u{,}0{,}u_0\rangle)$, where:

$$\mathsf{eR}_K\langle u, n, u_i\rangle \stackrel{\text{def}}{=} !u(x).\mathtt{if}^{\mathsf{L}}\, n = K \;\mathtt{then}\; (\boldsymbol{\nu}\, u_{i+1})(\mathsf{C}(u_{i+1}, x) | \mathsf{Mtx}\langle u_{i+1}\rangle | \mathsf{eR}_K\langle u, 0, u_{i+1}\rangle)$$
$$\mathtt{else}\; (\mathsf{C}(u_i, x) | \mathsf{eR}_K\langle u, n+1, u_i\rangle)$$

representing a server which, after invocation on u, spawns unboundedly many dedicated servers ($u_0, u_1, \ldots$), each realising a mutex and treating up to K (reasonably defined) clients $\mathsf{C}(u_i, x)$. A failure inside the critical section of a dedicated server only blocks up to K outputs, while u is always available: $\mathsf{eR}_K\langle u\rangle$ is resilient but not strictly so.

Extensional resilience abstracts away from counting failures. This makes sense, just as it makes sense to abstract away from τ-actions in weak process equivalences.

Theorem 3.11 (relating prop. (1)). IWF $\subsetneq$ INB, INB $\subsetneq$ NB *and* IWF $\subsetneq$ WF.

The inclusions are by definition. $\mathsf{CQemp}(r)$ in § 4 shows the first strictness. Ex. 3.10 shows the last one, since all non-blocked threads enter their critical section by strong fairness. By a slight modification (external "spinning" cas) we show the second.

Next we define the variants of NB and WF obtained by disabling failures.

Definition 3.12 (WNB, WWF, RBL). P is *weakly non-blocking* (WNB) (*weakly wait-free*, WWF) if it satisfies (1) (resp. (2)) of Def. 3.8 restricted to non-failing transitions. It is *reliable* (RBL) if it is strictly resilient w.r.t. non-failing transitions (i.e. no blocked outputs). **RBL / WNB / WWF** denote the sets of RBL/WNB/WWF processes, resp.

Example 3.13. 1. $\mathsf{Lck}\langle u\rangle$ (Ex. 3.5) is WWF, as every request is served, by fairness.
2. Let $\mathsf{Lck}^{\mathsf{spin}}\langle u\rangle$ be the same agent but replacing $\mathsf{Mtx}\langle m\rangle$ with $\mathsf{Mtx}^{\mathsf{spin}}\langle m\rangle$. $\mathsf{Lck}^{\mathsf{spin}}\langle u\rangle$ is WNB but not WWF, since in an infinite execution a thread may spin forever.

Theorem 3.14. *1. $P \approx Q$ implies ($P \in$ **RBL** $\iff Q \in$ **RBL**).*
2. We have **NB** $\cup$ **WWF** $\subsetneq$ **WNB** $\subsetneq$ **RBL** *and* **WF** $\subsetneq$ **NB** $\cap$ **WWF**.

(1) is because reliability is an existential requirement. (2) underpins the inclusions among behavioural properties. **NB** $\subsetneq$ **WNB** also says that, if an execution of a NB process shows no output, a failure has occurred. The diagram below contains the examples seen so far plus $\mathsf{LQemp}(r)$ and $\mathsf{CQemp}(r)$ from § 4. While not in this picture, **NB** $\subsetneq$ **INB** and **IWF** $\subsetneq$ **WF** (cf. Theorem 3.11). Also, resilience contains **NB** and is contained in **RBL** (both by definition), but is incomparable with **WNB** and **WWF**.

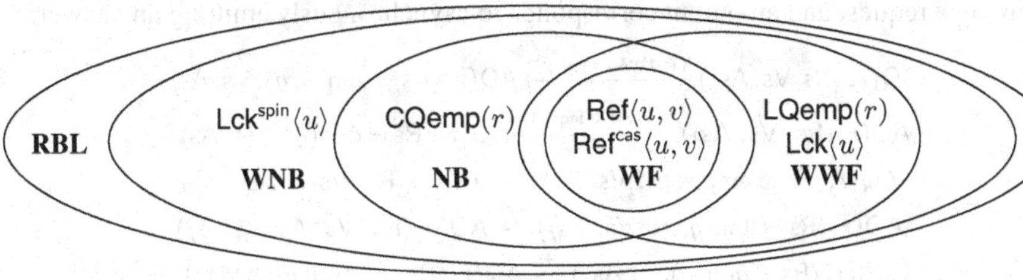

3.4 Fair Preorder and Preservation

We defined observable generalisations of global progress properties. Now we identify a behavioural pre-order/equivalence which preserves them, and offers a basis to reason about them. Define $\widehat{\Phi}$ by abstracting away all τ-actions from Φ. Then let:

$$\mathsf{WFT}(\Gamma \vdash P) \stackrel{\text{def}}{=} \{\langle \widehat{\Phi}, \mathtt{blocked}(\Phi)\rangle \mid \Phi \in \mathsf{FT}(\Gamma \vdash P)\}$$

where: $\widehat{\Phi}$ tells us what visible sequences are possible in the presence of stalled threads; and $\mathtt{blocked}(\Phi)$ is used to identify such stalled threads. And now the fair pre-order:

Definition 3.15. A *fair preorder* $\mathcal{R}$ is a weak bisimulation s.t. for any $\Gamma \vdash P\mathcal{R}Q$, $\mathsf{WFT}(\Gamma \vdash P) \supseteq \mathsf{WFT}(\Gamma \vdash Q)$. A *fair bisimulation* is a symm. fair preorder, $\precsim_{\mathsf{fair}}$ is the max. fair preorder, $\approx_{\mathsf{fair}}$ is the max. fair bisimulation and $\precnsim_{\mathsf{fair}} = (\precsim_{\mathsf{fair}} \setminus \approx_{\mathsf{fair}})$.

$\precapprox_{\mathsf{fair}}$ is preserved by all operators except a parallel composition involving a free non-linear input (which may be unavailable). Since such channel can be replaced by a replicated channel up to $\approx_{\mathsf{fair}}$, $\precapprox_{\mathsf{fair}}$ is practically a pre-congruence. Since $\mathsf{WFT}(\Gamma \vdash P)$ includes blocked outputs information, $\precapprox_{\mathsf{fair}}$ preserves WF and NB.

Theorem 3.16. *Let $P \precapprox_{\mathsf{fair}} Q$. Then if $P \in$ **NB** so is Q, and if $P \in$ **WF** so is Q.*

Example 3.17 (reasoning with $\precapprox_{\mathsf{fair}}$). We separate bisimilar processes by showing fair witnesses which distinguish them. $\mathsf{Lck}^{\mathsf{spin}}\langle u\rangle \approx \mathsf{Lck}\langle u\rangle$ but $\mathsf{Lck}^{\mathsf{spin}}\langle u\rangle \not\precapprox_{\mathsf{fair}} \mathsf{Lck}\langle u\rangle$. For the latter, we have a fair sequence from $\mathsf{Lck}^{\mathsf{spin}}\langle u\rangle$ where a thread does infinitely many (useless but fair) cycles and never answers, which is impossible in $\mathsf{Lck}\langle u\rangle$.

4 Application: Semantic Separation of Queues

Specification. We now apply the observational theory of §3 to the semantic analysis of two imperative queues. We start from an abstract specification of a queue, which is given as an intuitive state-based abstraction. A *queue state* $(\mathtt{st}, \mathtt{st}', \ldots)$ is a triple $\langle \mathsf{Rs}, \mathsf{Vs}, \mathsf{As}\rangle$, where (1) Rs is a set of *requests*, each of the form $\mathtt{enq}(v, g)$ or $\mathtt{deq}(g)$ s.t. v and g are respectively its *value* and *continuation name* (2) Vs is a *value sequence* $v_1 \cdots v_n$, s.t. v_1 is the head and v_n is the tail; (3) As is a set of *answers* of the form $\overline{g}\langle\vec{v}\rangle$, in which g is the *continuation name* and $\vec{v}$ a single *value* or ε. An *abstract queue* $(p, q, \ldots)$ is a pair $\mathsf{AQ}(r, \mathtt{st})$ of a queue state $\mathtt{st}$ and a channel r, its *subject* (e.g. $\mathsf{AQ}(r, \langle\{\mathtt{enq}(6, g_1), \mathtt{deq}(g_2)\}, 2\cdot 3\cdot 1, \{\overline{g_3}\langle 5\rangle\}\rangle)$ is an abstract queue with subject r, two requests, three values and one answer). A special case is the empty queue:

$$\mathsf{AQemp}(r) \stackrel{\text{def}}{=} \mathsf{AQ}(r, \langle\emptyset,\ \varepsilon,\ \emptyset\rangle)$$

We define a LTS over abstract queues, where an input corresponds to asynchronously receiving a request and an output corresponds to asynchronously emitting an answer:

$$\mathsf{AQ}(r, \langle\mathsf{Rs}, \mathsf{Vs}, \mathsf{As}\rangle) \xrightarrow{(\boldsymbol{\nu}\, g) r \& \mathtt{enq}\langle v, g\rangle} \mathsf{AQ}(r, \langle\mathsf{Rs} \uplus \mathtt{enq}(v, g), \mathsf{Vs}, \mathsf{As}\rangle)$$
$$\mathsf{AQ}(r, \langle\mathsf{Rs},\ \mathsf{Vs},\ \mathsf{As}\rangle) \xrightarrow{(\boldsymbol{\nu}\, g) r \& \mathtt{deq}\langle g\rangle} \mathsf{AQ}(r, \langle\mathsf{Rs} \uplus \mathtt{deq}(g),\ \mathsf{Vs},\ \mathsf{As}\rangle)$$
$$\mathsf{AQ}(r, \langle\mathsf{Rs} \uplus \mathtt{enq}(v, g),\ \mathsf{Vs},\ \mathsf{As}\rangle) \xrightarrow{\tau} \mathsf{AQ}(r, \langle\mathsf{Rs},\ \mathsf{Vs}\cdot v,\ \mathsf{As} \uplus \overline{g}\rangle)$$
$$\mathsf{AQ}(r, \langle\mathsf{Rs} \uplus \mathtt{deq}(g),\ v\cdot\mathsf{Vs},\ \mathsf{As}\rangle) \xrightarrow{\tau} \mathsf{AQ}(r, \langle\mathsf{Rs},\ \mathsf{Vs},\ \mathsf{As} \uplus \overline{g}\langle v\rangle\rangle)$$
$$\mathsf{AQ}(r, \langle\mathsf{Rs} \uplus \mathtt{deq}(g),\ \varepsilon,\ \mathsf{As}\rangle) \xrightarrow{\tau} \mathsf{AQ}(r, \langle\mathsf{Rs},\ \varepsilon,\ \mathsf{As} \uplus \overline{g}\langle\mathtt{null}\rangle\rangle)$$
$$\mathsf{AQ}(r, \langle\mathsf{Rs},\ \mathsf{Vs},\ \mathsf{As} \uplus \overline{g}\langle v\rangle\rangle) \xrightarrow{\overline{g}\langle v\rangle} \mathsf{AQ}(r, \langle\mathsf{Rs},\ \mathsf{Vs},\ \mathsf{As}\rangle)$$

where $\mathsf{Rs} \uplus \mathtt{deq}(g)$ denotes the union of Rs and $\{\mathtt{deq}(g)\}$ if $\mathtt{deq}(g) \notin \mathsf{Rs}$. Above and henceforward, we use `null` as a special value which can be given any type but which differs from any channel name. This can be translated away through branching/selection in the standard way (cf. [6]). A τ-action is also denoted $\mathsf{AQ}(r, \mathtt{st}) \xrightarrow{\mathrm{com}(g)} \mathsf{AQ}(r, \mathtt{st}')$ and called *commit action* or *commit*. It represents a state change.

Equipping abstract queues with our linear typing is straightforward. Then we get a typed LTS over abstract queues. For instance, the example above is typed under:

$$r : \&^{\mathsf{NL}}\{\mathtt{enq}(\mathtt{int} \uparrow^{\mathsf{NL}} ()),\ \mathtt{deq}(\uparrow^{\mathsf{NL}} (\mathtt{int}))\},\ g_1 : \uparrow^{\mathsf{NL}} (),\ g_2 : \uparrow^{\mathsf{NL}} (\mathtt{int}),\ g_3 : \uparrow^{\mathsf{NL}} (\mathtt{int})$$

Lock-Based Queue. Define a lock-based queue from empty configuration $\mathsf{LQemp}(r)$:

$$\mathsf{LQemp}(r) \stackrel{\text{def}}{=} (\nu h,t,s,l)(\mathsf{Mtx}\langle l\rangle \mid \mathsf{LQ}(r,h,t,l) \mid \mathsf{LPtr}(h,s) \mid \mathsf{LPtr}(t,s) \mid \mathsf{LENode}(s,0))$$

$$\mathsf{LQ}(r,h,t,l) \stackrel{\text{def}}{=} !\,r\&\{enq(v,u): \bar{l}(g)g(y).P^{lck}_{\mathsf{enq}}(v,t,y,u),\ deq(u): \bar{l}(g)g(y).P^{lck}_{\mathsf{deq}}(h,t,y,u)\}$$

where $\mathsf{LPtr}(h,s)$, $\mathsf{LPtr}(t,s)$ and $\mathsf{LENode}(s,0)$ are (non-CAS) references from § 2. The queue is represented as a linked list. Pointers h and t store the names of the head and tail nodes, resp.: when they coincide, the list is empty, with a single dummy node (as above). The key steps are the *non-linear* interactions with $\mathsf{Mtx}\langle l\rangle$. $P^{lck}_{\mathsf{enq}}(v,t,y)$ and $P^{lck}_{\mathsf{deq}}(h,t,y)$ are the obvious list manipulation followed by lock release, and are omitted.

CAS-Based Queue. The cas-based queue (cf. [21]) is also encoded as a linked list:

$$\mathsf{CQemp}(r) \stackrel{\text{def}}{=} (\nu h,t,nd_0,nxt_0)\begin{pmatrix}\mathsf{CQ}(r,h,t) \mid \mathsf{Ptr}(h,nd_0,0) \mid \mathsf{Ptr}(t,nd_0,0) \mid \\ \mathsf{Node}(nd_0,0,nxt_0) \mid \mathsf{Ptr}(nxt_0,\mathsf{null},0)\end{pmatrix}$$

$$\mathsf{CQ}(r,h,t) \stackrel{\text{def}}{=} !\,r\&\{\mathsf{enq}(v,g) : \mathsf{Enqueue}_{\mathsf{cas}}\langle v,t,g\rangle,\ \mathsf{deq}(g) : \mathsf{Dequeue}_{\mathsf{cas}}\langle h,t,g\rangle\}$$

$\mathsf{Node}(nd,v,ptr) \stackrel{\text{def}}{=} \mathsf{Ref}\langle nd,\langle v,ptr\rangle\rangle$ and $\mathsf{Ptr}(ptr,nxt,ctr) \stackrel{\text{def}}{=} \mathsf{Ref}^{\mathsf{cas}}\langle ptr,\langle nxt,ctr\rangle\rangle$ represent *nodes* and *pointers*, resp. A node stores a value and the name of a pointer, which stores the name of the next node, or null, and a *counter* incremented at each successful cas. To scan, from h, we reach the initial (dummy) node, read its pointer name, then the first value node, and so on. Enqueue and dequeue are as follows:

```
Enqueue_cas⟨x, tail, u⟩ = (ν node) ((ν nlPtr)
  (Ptr(nlPtr, null, 0) | Node(node, x, nlPtr)) |
  (μX_tag(u').
   tail ⊲ read(last, ctrT).
   last ⊲ read(tPtr, ∗).
   tPtr ⊲ read(next, ctr).
   if^L (next = null) then
    if^L cas(tPtr,⟨next,ctr⟩,⟨node,ctr + 1⟩)
    then CAS(t,⟨last, ctrT⟩,⟨node, ctrT + 1⟩);
     u'‾
     else X_tag⟨u'⟩
   else CAS(t, ⟨last, ctrT⟩, ⟨next, ctrT + 1⟩);
X_tag⟨u'⟩) ⟨u⟩)
```

```
Dequeue_cas⟨head, tail, u⟩ = (μX_tag(u').
 head ⊲ read(hn, h_ctr).
 tail ⊲ read(tn, t_ctr).
 hn ⊲ read(∗, hp).
 hp ⊲ read(next, ∗).
 if^L (hn = tn) then
  if^L (next = null) then
   u'‾⟨null⟩
  else
   CAS(tail,⟨tn,t_ctr⟩,⟨next,t_ctr + 1⟩);X_tag⟨u'⟩
 else
  next ⊲ read(x, ∗).
  if^L (cas(head, ⟨hn, ctr⟩, ⟨next, ctr + 1⟩)) then
   u'‾⟨x⟩
  else X_tag⟨u'⟩)⟨u⟩
```

The notations `if` $\mathtt{cas}(u,v,w)$ `then` P `else` Q and $\mathtt{CAS}(u,v,w); P$ are from § 2; $x \triangleleft read(\vec{y}).P$ is short for $(\nu c)(\overline{x}\, read\langle c\rangle | c^{\mathsf{L}}(\vec{y}).P)$, where $*$ is for irrelevant values. $\mathsf{Enqueue}_{\mathsf{cas}}\langle x,\mathtt{t},u\rangle$ uses cas to *append* a node and to *swing* the tail pointer t. $\mathsf{Dequeue}_{\mathsf{cas}}\langle h,t,g\rangle$ uses it to swing head and tail forward. Both slightly simplify the original algorithms [21]. $\mathsf{CQemp}(r)$, $\mathsf{LQemp}(r)$ and $\mathsf{AQ}(r,\langle\emptyset,\ \varepsilon,\ \emptyset\rangle)$ are all typed under $r : \&^{\mathsf{NL}}\{\mathsf{enq}(\alpha\uparrow^{\mathsf{NL}}()),\mathsf{deq}(\uparrow^{\mathsf{NL}}(\alpha))\}$, for some type α.

Functional Correctness. We outline the proof of functional correctness of $\mathsf{CQemp}(r)$, given as its bisimilarity to the empty abstract queue $\mathsf{AQemp}(r)$ (details in [6]). We use *molecular actions* $P \stackrel{\ell}{\mapsto} Q$, which consist of a transition $P \stackrel{\ell}{\rightarrow}$ followed by all available linear actions (thus representing atomic operations, cf. Ex. 2.1). The one-step transition $\stackrel{\ell}{\mapsto}$ is justified by Prop. 2.5(1,2) and does not change $\approx$ nor global progress properties. We call cas-*queue process* any molecular action derivative of $\mathsf{CQemp}(r)$.

Among molecular actions, a *commit action* marks an irreversible state change: in an enqueue operation, it is a successful cas action on the last pointer in the linked list, adding a new node; in a dequeue operation on a non-empty queue, it is the cas on the head pointer; while if the queue is empty, it is the last *read* action before checking that the successor of the first (dummy) node is $null$. All other actions are *non-commit*.

In the proof, a cas-queue process is reduced to a unique *normal form*, of the shape:

$$(\nu h, t, nd_0..nd_n, nxt_0..nxt_n)(\mathsf{CQ}(r,h,t) \mid LL \mid \textstyle\prod_{1\le i\le m} P_i)$$

$$\text{where } LL \stackrel{\text{def}}{=} \begin{pmatrix} \mathsf{Ptr}(h, nd_H, ctr_H)|\mathsf{Ptr}(t, nd_T, ctr_T)| \\ \Pi_{0\le i\le n}(\mathsf{Node}(nd_i, v_i, nxt_i)|\mathsf{Ptr}(nxt_i, nd_{i+1}, ctr_i)) \end{pmatrix}, \quad \begin{matrix} nd_{n+1} = \mathsf{null} \\ \wedge \\ 0 \le H \le T = n \end{matrix}$$

LL is called the *linked-list sub-process* and each P_i is a *thread sub-process* in a *local normal form* (LNF): i.e. either P_i is ready to commit in the next step or it is an answer, say $\overline{g}\langle\vec{v}\rangle$, to an enqueue/dequeue request. The idea is that we can reach a normal form just using non-commit actions, written $\stackrel{\mathsf{nc}}{\longmapsto}$ below.

Proposition 4.1. *If P is a* cas*-queue process, $P \stackrel{\mathsf{nc}}{\longmapsto}^* P'$ and P' is in NF.*

The above normalisability result is obtained as a corollary of a stronger *linearisability* result, transforming an execution into a chain of enqueue/dequeue operations. This is achieved through *local permutations* among molecular actions from different threads. The permutation cases reflect the classification of molecular actions.

Given a relation $\mathcal{R}_{\mathsf{cas}}$ between cas-queue processes and abstract queues s.t.: (1) $\mathsf{CQemp}(r)\,\mathcal{R}_{\mathsf{cas}}\mathsf{AQemp}(r)$; (2) If $P\,\mathcal{R}_{\mathsf{cas}}Q$, $P \stackrel{\ell}{\longmapsto} P'$, $Q \stackrel{\ell}{\to} Q'$ and ℓ is an input/output/commit label, then $P'\,\mathcal{R}_{\mathsf{cas}}Q'$; (3) If $P\,\mathcal{R}_{\mathsf{cas}}Q$ and $P \stackrel{\mathsf{nc}}{\longmapsto} P'$ then $P'\,\mathcal{R}_{\mathsf{cas}}Q$. By Prop. 4.1, we can normalise each cas-queue process. Then we show that a normal form has the same action capability as the related abstract queue, thus establishing the bisimilarity of $\mathcal{R}_{\mathsf{cas}}$. By a similar but simpler argument for $\mathsf{LQemp}(r)$, we obtain:

Theorem 4.2 (functional correctness). $\mathsf{CQemp}(r) \approx \mathsf{LQemp}(r) \approx \mathsf{AQemp}(r)$.

Global Progress and Separation. By linearising executions of $\mathsf{CQemp}(r)$, we easily see that a failure blocks exactly one output, i.e. $\mathsf{CQemp}(r)$ is strictly resilient. As for non-blockingness, consider a process $\Delta \vdash P$ in the non-failing post-fix of a finitely failing fair transition sequence Φ from $\mathsf{CQemp}(r)$, s.t. $c \in \mathtt{allowed}(\Delta) \setminus \mathtt{blocked}(\Phi)$. Since c is not blocked, its sub-process either reduces to normal form and outputs or engages in an infinite loop without committing (fairness). But in the latter case (infinitely many) other threads would commit and output: $\mathsf{CQemp}(r)$ is NB but *not* WF.

$\mathsf{LQemp}(r)$ is not resilient because a failure in the critical section blocks all threads. Then it is neither WF nor NB. But in the absence of failures, every thread in a transition sequence from $\mathsf{LQemp}(r)$ can enter the critical section by fairness. To summarise:

Theorem 4.3 (glob. prog.). $\mathsf{CQemp}(r) \in$ (**NB** $\setminus$ **WF**) *and* $\mathsf{LQemp}(r) \in$ (**WWF** $\setminus$ **NB**).

We show that $\mathsf{CQemp}(r)$ and $\mathsf{LQemp}(r)$ are strictly ordered by $\precsim_{\mathsf{fair}}$. A key lemma is:

Lemma 4.4 $\mathsf{WFT}(P) \subseteq \mathsf{WFT}(Q)$ *iff it is so w.r.t. molecular action sequences.*

The above allows us to use molecular action sequences to show the following:

Lemma 4.5 $\mathsf{WFT}(\mathsf{CQemp}(r)) \subsetneq \mathsf{WFT}(\mathsf{LQemp}(r))$.

For inclusion, given two processes in the bisimulation from the proof of Theorem 4.2, we map a fair finitely failing molecular trace of the cas-queue process to one of the lock-queue process, where a failure is mapped to a failure *before* lock acquisition.

For strictness suppose, in a molecular transition sequence from $\mathsf{LQemp}(r)$, a thread fails in the critical section and then infinitely many other requests come, generating threads which may only progress up to some point and then are blocked. Such a sequence is finitely failing, maximal (because no thread can progress further) and trivially fair. Since $\mathsf{CQemp}(r)$ is resilient, it admits no fair and finitely failing sequence with the same external behaviour. The bisimilarity comes from Theorem 4.2. Then:

Theorem 4.6 $\mathsf{LQemp}(r) \precnapprox_{\mathsf{fair}} \mathsf{CQemp}(r)$.

5 Related Work and Further Topics

Logical Formalisation of Global Progress. To our knowledge, [5] offered the first formal characterisation of intensional non-blockingness and wait-freedom, using linear temporal logic. That work uses fairness and stalling actions as ours, but over simple *while* programs, rather than the π-calculus. Later, [10] captured stalling actions by an unfair scheduler, which leads to a simple setup, but forces the execution of an atomic operation in a single step, unlike what happens in practice. Both of these works aim to give formal accounts of *intensional* global progress, referring to program counters ([5]) and state transformations (atomic formulae in [10]). In contrast, we emphasise observationality through an LTS-based characterisation, thus capturing both extensional and intensional properties in a uniform way. Further, through the π-calculus, our theory can cover a wide range of behaviours beyond first-order concurrent data structures. The simple linear π-calculus used in this paper can already represent higher-order functions, objects, higher-order pointers, and client-server interactions.

Another limitation of previous formalisations is that they only allow boundedly many threads, whereas our extensional setting allows new operations to be requested at any time, spawning unboundedly many concurrent threads. As we showed in [6], such different approaches induce two semantically distinct classes: there exists a π-calculus process which is non-blocking if the execution model allows only a bounded number of threads, but not so in general.

Fairness and Progress in Process Algebras. We adapted *fairness* from [4] to our asynchronous, typed framework, where types play a key role (defining "enabled transitions"). The use of fairness in defining progress properties was first suggested in [27]. In [7], a well-known distributed consensus algorithm is studied through a transition relation on configurations with state changes in the algorithm, where fairness is combined with failures to capture a global termination. Indeed, our π-calculus approach could be applied to uniformly encompass such properties as those found in [7], to compare them to and distinguish them from those we have already defined.

Several recent works [1, 17, 28] study progress properties enforced by typing in the π-calculus, where they statically ensure liveness by compositional typing rules. Among them, [17] defines two notions of progress using fairness, which essentially correspond to our reliability and weak wait-freedom. While linear typing is also a key element in our theory, [1,17,28] ensure liveness by inductively building up local causal chains, thus enforcing local progress at *every* interaction in the chain. Michael-Scott queue satisfies a more subtle notion of progress, where *some* output eventually occurs. Further, [1, 17] study progress through an invisible action at a specified redex, while we use visible transitions to capture progress as an observational property. This allows us to reason about its preservation by different kinds of behavioural equivalences.

Linearisability. The proofs of functional correctness in § 4 use a version of linearisability [14], relying on local permutability of actions. Linearisability has already been applied to Michael-Scott's queue ([2] and others). [11] shows the composition of linearisable libraries preserves non-blockingness. They abstractly define linearisation relying on separate tools for its concrete realisation. Their definition is based on *begin-end* (less fine-grained) rather than *commit*. [2] uses commits, but coarser than ours: instead of local permutations, it suspends execution of the simulating process B until the simulated one A commits. Then A is suspended and B completes. [23] exploits modularity in the search for atomicity violations, and reduces the state-explosion by requesting non-commuting operations before and after the one being tested.

The above works share with ours: a semantic understanding of non-blockingness, modularity, and reasoning with critical permutations; but the formal framework is quite different. Apart from the intensional/extensional characterisation of global progress, the π-calculus allows a uniform behavioural analysis at a very fine granularity level, enabling a rigorous operational reasoning on linearisability through local permutations of transitions. It would be interesting to see if we can apply our bisimilarity technique to justify the automated proofs in [2].

Further discussions on related works are found in the long version [6].

Further Results and Topics. The current formal framework and proof techniques for concrete data structures outlined in §4, are readily applicable to a wide range of concurrent behaviours. We chose Michael-Scott's `cas`-based queue because it is arguably one of the most subtle non-blocking data structures widely used in practice and not requiring atomic operations more powerful than `cas`. As a further result, in [6] we have reasoned about stacks including Treiber's stack [26], obtaining the corresponding results with isomorphic (but much simpler) arguments.

As another line of study, the intensional formalisations and reasoning techniques on them can be exploited further, enriched by existing studies, to obtain a comprehensive technical framework for verifying both intensional and extensional properties of concurrent data structures.

References

1. Acciai, L., Boreale, M.: Responsiveness in process calculi. TCS 409(1), 59–93 (2008)
2. Amit, D., Rinetzky, N., Reps, T., Sagiv, M., Yahav, E.: Comparison Under Abstraction for Verifying Linearizability. In: Damm, W., Hermanns, H. (eds.) CAV 2007. LNCS, vol. 4590, pp. 477–490. Springer, Heidelberg (2007)

3. Berger, M., Honda, K., Yoshida, N.: Sequentiality and the π-Calculus. In: Abramsky, S. (ed.) TLCA 2001. LNCS, vol. 2044, pp. 29–45. Springer, Heidelberg (2001)
4. Cacciagrano, D., Corradini, F., Palamidessi, C.: Explicit fairness in testing semantics. LMCS 5(2:15), 27 pages (2007)
5. Dongol, B.: Formalising Progress Properties of Non-blocking Programs. In: Liu, Z., Kleinberg, R.D. (eds.) ICFEM 2006. LNCS, vol. 4260, pp. 284–303. Springer, Heidelberg (2006)
6. Fossati, L., Honda, K., Yoshida, N.: The extended version of the present paper (June 2012), `http://www.eecs.qmul.ac.uk/~luca/CONCURextended.pdf`
7. Fuzzati, R., Merro, M., Nestmann, U.: Distributed Consensus, revisited. Acta Inf. 44(6), 377–425 (2007)
8. Francez, N.: Fairness. Springer (1986)
9. Goetz, B.: Java Concurrency in Practice. Addison-Wesley (2008)
10. Gotsman, A., Cook, B., Parkinson, M., Vafeiadis, V.: Proving that non-blocking algorithms don't block. In: POPL 2009, pp. 16–28. ACM (2009)
11. Gotsman, A., Yang, H.: Liveness-Preserving Atomicity Abstraction. In: Aceto, L., Henzinger, M., Sgall, J. (eds.) ICALP 2011, Part II. LNCS, vol. 6756, pp. 453–465. Springer, Heidelberg (2011)
12. Herlihy, M., Luchangco, V., Moir, M.: Obstruction-free synchronization: double-ended queues as an example. In: ICDCS 2003, pp. 522–529. IEEE Computer Society (2003)
13. Herlihy, M., Sharit, B.: The Art of Multiprocessor Programming. Morgan Kaufmann (2009)
14. Herlihy, M.P., Wing, J.M.: Linearizability: a correctness condition for concurrent objects. TOPLAS 12(3), 463–492 (1990)
15. Honda, K., Yoshida, N.: A uniform type structure for secure information flow. In: POPL 2002, pp. 81–92. ACM (2002)
16. Kobayashi, N., Pierce, B.C., Turner, D.N.: Linearity and the Pi-calculus. TOPLAS 21(5), 914–947 (1999)
17. Kobayashi, N., Sangiorgi, D.: A Hybrid Type System for Lock-Freedom of Mobile Processes. TOPLAS 32(5:16), 49 pages (2010)
18. Lamport, L.: Time, clocks, and the ordering of events in a distributed system. Communications of the ACM 21(7), 558–564 (1978)
19. Lauer, H.C., Needham, R.M.: On the duality of operating system structures. SIGOPS Operating Systems Review 13(2), 3–19 (1979)
20. Lea, D., et al.: Java Concurrency Package (2003), `http://gee.cs.oswego.edu/dl`
21. Michael, M.M., Scott, M.L.: Simple, fast, and practical non-blocking and blocking concurrent queue algorithms. In: PODC 1996, pp. 267–275. ACM (1996)
22. Sangiorgi, D.: The name discipline of uniform receptiveness. TCS 221(1-2), 457–493 (1999)
23. Schacham, O., Bronson, N., Aiken, A., Sagiv, M., Vechev, M., Yahav, E.: Testing atomicity of composed concurrent operations. In: OOPSLA 2011, pp. 51–64. ACM (2011)
24. Taubenfeld, G.: Synchronization Algorithms and Concurrent Programming. Pearson–Prentice Hall (2006)
25. Tokoro, M., Vasconcelos, V.: A Typing System for a Calculus of Objects. In: Nishio, S., Yonezawa, A. (eds.) ISOTAS 1993. LNCS, vol. 742, pp. 460–474. Springer, Heidelberg (1993)
26. Treiber, R.K.: Systems programming: Coping with parallelism. Technical Report RJ 5118, IBM Almaden Research Center (1986)
27. Walker, D.: Automated analysis of mutual exclusion algorithms using CCS. Formal Aspects of Computing 1(3), 273–292 (1989)
28. Yoshida, N., Berger, M., Honda, K.: Strong Normalisation in the π-Calculus. Information and Computation 191(2), 145–202 (2004)

Duality and i/o-Types in the π-Calculus

Daniel Hirschkoff[1], Jean-Marie Madiot[1], and Davide Sangiorgi[2]

[1] ENS Lyon, Université de Lyon, CNRS, INRIA, France
[2] INRIA/Università di Bologna, Italy

Abstract. We study duality between input and output in the π-calculus. In dualisable versions of π, including πI and fusions, duality breaks with the addition of ordinary input/output types. We introduce $\overline{\pi}$, intuitively the minimal symmetrical conservative extension of π with input/output types. We prove some duality properties for $\overline{\pi}$ and we study embeddings between $\overline{\pi}$ and π in both directions. As an example of application of the dualities, we exploit the dualities of $\overline{\pi}$ and its theory to relate two encodings of call-by-name λ-calculus, by Milner and by van Bakel and Vigliotti, syntactically quite different from each other.

1 Introduction

It is common in mathematics to look for dualities; dualities may reveal underlying structure and lead to simpler theories. In turn, dualities can be used to relate different mathematical entities. In this work, our goal is to study dualities in the typed π-calculus, and to exploit them to understand the possible relationships between encodings of functions as π-calculus processes.

Reasoning about processes usually involves proving behavioural equivalences. In the case of the π-calculus, there is a well-established theory of equivalences and proof techniques. In some cases, it is necessary to work in a *typed* setting. Types allow one to express constraints about the observations available to the context when comparing two processes. One of the simplest and widely used such discipline is given by input/output-types [SW01] — i/o-types in the sequel.

In the π-calculus (simply called π below), the natural form of duality comes from the symmetry between input and output. There are several variants of π where processes can be 'symmetrised' by replacing inputs with outputs and vice versa. The π-calculus with internal mobility, πI [San96], is a subcalculus of π where only bound outputs are allowed (a bound output, that we shall note $\overline{a}(x).P$, is the emission of a private name x on some channel a). In πI, duality can be expressed at an operational level, by exchanging (bound) inputs and bound outputs: the dual of $a(x).\overline{x}(y).0$ is $\overline{a}(x).x(y).0$.

Other well-known variants of π with dualities are the calculi in the fusion family [PV98, Fu97, GW00]. In fusions, a construct for *free input* acts as the dual of the free output construct of π, and the calculus has only one binder, restriction. Interaction on a given channel has the effect of *fusing* (that is, identifying) names.

The discipline of simple types can be adapted both to πI and to fusions, while preserving dualities. The situation is less clear for i/o-types, which can be very

M. Koutny and I. Ulidowski (Eds.): CONCUR 2012, LNCS 7454, pp. 302–316, 2012.

useful to establish equivalences between processes. Let us give some intuitions about why it is so. In i/o-types, types are assigned to channels and express *capabilities*: a name of type oT can be used only to emit values of type T, and similarly for the input capability (iT). This is expressed by the following typing rules for i/o-types in π:

$$\frac{\Gamma \vdash a : iT \qquad \Gamma, x : T \vdash P}{\Gamma \vdash a(x).P} \qquad \frac{\Gamma \vdash a : oT \qquad \Gamma \vdash b : T \qquad \Gamma \vdash P}{\Gamma \vdash \overline{a}b.P}$$

The rule for input can be read as follows: process $a(x).P$ is well-typed provided (i) the typing environment, Γ, ensures that the input capability on a can be derived, and (ii) the continuation of the input can be typed in an environment where x is used according to T. The typing rule for output checks that (i) the output capability on a is derivable, (ii) the emitted value, b, has the right type, and (iii) the continuation P can be typed. As an example, $a : i(iT) \vdash a(x).\overline{x}t.0$ cannot be derived, because only the input capability is received on a, which prevents $\overline{x}t.0$ from being typable.

I/o-types come with a notion of subtyping, that makes it possible to relate type $\sharp T$ (which stands for both input and output capabilities) with input and output capabilities (in particular, we have $\sharp T \leq iT$ and $\sharp T \leq oT$). We stress an asymmetry between the constraints attached to the transmitted name in the two rules above. Indeed, while in a reception we somehow enforce a "contract" on the usage of the received name, in the rule for output this is not the case: we can use subtyping in order to derive type, say, iU for b when typechecking the output, while b's type can be $\sharp U$ when typechecking the continuation P.

The starting point of this work is the conflict between the asymmetry inherent to i/o-types and the symmetries we want to obtain via duality. For example i/o-types can be adapted to πI, but duality cannot be applied to the resulting typings. In fusion calculi, the conflict with the asymmetry of i/o-types is even more dramatic. Indeed, subtyping in i/o-types is closely related to substitution, since replacing a name with another makes sense only if the latter has a more general type. Fusions are intuitively substitutions operating in both directions, which leaves no room for subtyping. In work in preparation [HMS12], we investigate this relationship between subtyping and substitution, and compare several variants of existing calculi, including the one presented in this paper.

In this paper, in order to work in a setting that provides a form of duality and where i/o-types can be used, we introduce a calculus named $\overline{\pi}$ (Section 2). $\overline{\pi}$ is an extension of π with constructs for free input and bound output (note that bound output is not seen as a derived construct in $\overline{\pi}$). In $\overline{\pi}$, we rely on substitutions as the main mechanism at work along interactions. To achieve this, we forbid interactions involving a free input and a free output: the type system rules out processes that use both kinds of prefixes on the same channel.

Calculus $\overline{\pi}$ contains π, and any π process that can be typed using i/o-types can be typed in exactly the same way in $\overline{\pi}$. Moreover $\overline{\pi}$ contains a 'dualised' version of π: one can choose to use some channels in free input and bound output. For such channels, the typing rules intuitively enforce a 'contract' on the usage of the transmitted name *on the side of the emitter* (dually to the typing rules presented above). We show how $\overline{\pi}$ can be related to π, by translating $\overline{\pi}$ into a variant of the π-calculus with i/o-types in a fully abstract way. This result shows that π and $\overline{\pi}$ are rather close in terms of expressiveness.

We also define a notion of typed barbed congruence in $\overline{\pi}$, which allows us to validate at a behavioural level the properties we have mentioned above: two processes are equivalent if and only if their duals are. To our knowledge, no existing calculus with i/o-types enjoys this form of duality for behaviours.

As an application of $\overline{\pi}$, its dualities, and its behavioural theory, we use $\overline{\pi}$ to relate two encodings of call-by-name λ-calculus. The first one is the ordinary encoding by Milner [Mil92], the second one is by van Bakel and Vigliotti [vBV09]. The two encodings are syntactically quite different. Milner's is *input-based*, in that an abstraction interacts with its environment via an input. In contrast, van Bakel and Vigliotti's is *output-based*. Moreover, only the latter makes use of *link processes*, that is, forwarders that under certain conditions act as substitutions.

Van Bakel and Vigliotti actually encode *strong* call-by-name — reductions may also take place inside a λ-abstraction. We therefore compare van Bakel and Vigliotti's encoding with the strong variant of Milner's encoding, obtained by replacing an input with a delayed input, following [Mer00] (in a delayed input $a(x){:}P$, the continuation P may perform transitions not involving the binder x even when the head input at a has not been consumed).

We exploit $\overline{\pi}$ (in fact the extension of $\overline{\pi}$ with delayed input) to prove that the two encodings are the dual of one another. This is achieved by first embedding the π-terms of the λ-encodings into $\overline{\pi}$, and then applying behavioural laws of $\overline{\pi}$. The correctness of these transformations is justified using i/o-types (essentially to express the conditions under which a link can be erased in favour of a substitution). Some of the transformations needed for the λ-encodings, however, are proved in this paper only for barbed bisimilarity; see the concluding section for a discussion.

Paper outline. Section 2 introduces $\overline{\pi}$, and presents its main properties. To analyse dualities in encodings of λ into π, in Section 3, we extend $\overline{\pi}$, notably with delayed prefixes. As the addition of these constructs is standard, they are omitted from the original syntax so to simplify the presentation. Section 4 gives concluding remarks.

2 $\overline{\pi}$, a Symmetric π-Calculus

In this section, we present $\overline{\pi}$, a π-calculus with i/o-types that enjoys duality properties. We define the syntax and operational semantics for $\overline{\pi}$ processes in Section 2.1, introduce types and barbed congruence in Section 2.2, establish duality in Section 2.3, and present results relating π and $\overline{\pi}$ in Section 2.4.

2.1 Syntax and Operational Semantics

We consider an infinite set of names, ranged over using $a, b, \ldots, x, y, \ldots$. The syntax of $\overline{\pi}$ is as follows:

$$P ::= 0 \mid P|P \mid !P \mid \alpha.P \mid (\nu a)P \qquad \alpha ::= \rho b \mid \rho(x) \qquad \rho ::= a \mid \overline{a}$$

$\overline{\pi}$ differs from the usual π-calculus by the presence of the free input ab and bound output $\overline{a}(x)$ prefixes. Note that in $\overline{\pi}$, the latter is *not* a notation for $(\nu x)\overline{a}x.P$, but a primitive construct. These prefixes are the symmetric counterpart of $\overline{a}b$ and $a(x)$ respectively. Given a process P, $\text{fn}(P)$ stands for the set of free names of P — restriction, bound input and bound output are binding constructs. Given ρ of the form a or $\overline{a}$, $\text{n}(\rho)$ is defined by $\text{n}(\overline{a}) = \text{n}(a) = a$.

Structural congruence is standard, and defined as in π (in particular, there are no axioms involving prefixes). The reduction laws allow communication involving two prefixes *only if at least one of them is bound*:

$$\begin{array}{rlrl} \overline{a}b.P \mid a(x).Q \to P \mid Q[b/x] & & P \to Q & \text{if } P \equiv\to\equiv Q \\ ab.P \mid \overline{a}(x).Q \to P \mid Q[b/x] & & (\nu a)P \to (\nu a)Q & \text{if } P \to Q \\ \overline{a}(x).P \mid a(x).Q \to (\nu x)(P \mid Q) & & P \mid R \to Q \mid R & \text{if } P \to Q \end{array}$$

Note that $\overline{a}b \mid ac$ is a process of $\overline{\pi}$ that has no reduction; this process is ruled out by the type system presented below.

2.2 Types and Behavioural Equivalence

Types are a refinement of standard i/o-types: in addition to capabilities (ranged over using c), we annotate types with *sorts* (s), that specify whether a name can be used in free input (sort $\mathbf{e}$) or in free output ($\mathbf{r}$) — note that a name cannot be used to build both kinds of free prefixes.

$$T ::= c^s T \mid \mathbf{1} \qquad c ::= i \mid o \mid \sharp \qquad s ::= \mathbf{e} \mid \mathbf{r}$$

If name a has type $c^{\mathbf{r}}T$, we shall refer to a as an $\mathbf{r}$-*name*, and similarly for $\mathbf{e}$.

The subtyping relation is the smallest reflexive and transitive relation $\leq$ satisfying the rules of Figure 1. As in the π-calculus $i^{\mathbf{r}}$ is covariant and $o^{\mathbf{r}}$ is contravariant. Dually, $i^{\mathbf{e}}$ is contravariant and $o^{\mathbf{e}}$ is covariant. Note that sorts ($\mathbf{e}$, $\mathbf{r}$) are not affected by subtyping.

The type system is defined as a refinement of input/output types, and is given by the rules of Figure 2. There is a dedicated typing rule for every kind of prefix (free, ρb, or bound, $\rho(x)$), according to the sort of the involved name. We write $\Gamma(a)$ for the type associated to a in Γ. $T^{\leftrightarrow}$ stands for T where we switch the top-level capability: $(c^s T)^{\leftrightarrow} = \overline{c}^s T$ where $\overline{o} = i, \overline{i} = o, \overline{\sharp} = \sharp$.

The typing rules for $\mathbf{r}$-names impose a constraint on the receiving side: all inputs on an $\mathbf{r}$-channel should be bound. Note that $\overline{a}(x).P$ and $(\boldsymbol{\nu} x)\overline{a}x.P$ are *not* equivalent from the point of view of typing: typing a bound output on an $\mathbf{r}$-channel (a) imposes that the transmitted name (x) is used according to the "dual constraint" w.r.t. what a's type specifies: this is enforced using $T^{\leftrightarrow}$ (while names received on a are used according to T). Symmetrical considerations can be made for $\mathbf{e}$-names, that impose constraints on the emitting side.

We write $\Gamma \vdash P, Q$ when both $\Gamma \vdash P$ and $\Gamma \vdash Q$ can be derived.

$$\frac{}{\sharp^s T \leq i^s T} \qquad \frac{}{\sharp^s T \leq o^s T}$$

$$\frac{T_1 \leq T_2}{i^{\mathbf{r}} T_1 \leq i^{\mathbf{r}} T_2} \qquad \frac{T_1 \leq T_2}{o^{\mathbf{r}} T_2 \leq o^{\mathbf{r}} T_1} \qquad \frac{T_1 \leq T_2}{i^{\mathbf{e}} T_2 \leq i^{\mathbf{e}} T_1} \qquad \frac{T_1 \leq T_2}{o^{\mathbf{e}} T_1 \leq o^{\mathbf{e}} T_2}$$

Fig. 1. Subtyping

$$\frac{\Gamma \vdash a : i^{\mathbf{r}} T \qquad \Gamma, x : T \vdash P}{\Gamma \vdash a(x).P} \qquad \frac{\Gamma \vdash a : i^{\mathbf{e}} T \qquad \Gamma, x : T^{\leftrightarrow} \vdash P}{\Gamma \vdash a(x).P}$$

$$\frac{\Gamma \vdash a : o^{\mathbf{e}} T \qquad \Gamma, x : T \vdash P}{\Gamma \vdash \overline{a}(x).P} \qquad \frac{\Gamma \vdash a : o^{\mathbf{r}} T \qquad \Gamma, x : T^{\leftrightarrow} \vdash P}{\Gamma \vdash \overline{a}(x).P}$$

$$\frac{\Gamma \vdash a : i^{\mathbf{e}} T \qquad \Gamma \vdash b : T \qquad \Gamma \vdash P}{\Gamma \vdash ab.P} \qquad \frac{\Gamma \vdash a : o^{\mathbf{r}} T \qquad \Gamma \vdash b : T \qquad \Gamma \vdash P}{\Gamma \vdash \overline{a}b.P}$$

$$\frac{\Gamma, a : T \vdash P}{\Gamma \vdash (\nu a)P} \qquad \frac{\Gamma \vdash P \qquad \Gamma \vdash Q}{\Gamma \vdash P \mid Q} \qquad \frac{\Gamma \vdash P}{\Gamma \vdash !P} \qquad \frac{}{\Gamma \vdash 0} \qquad \frac{\Gamma(a) \leq T}{\Gamma \vdash a : T}$$

Fig. 2. $\overline{\pi}$: Typing rules

Remark 1 ("Double contract"). We could adopt a more liberal typing for bound outputs on $\mathbf{r}$ names, and use the rule

$$\frac{\Gamma \vdash a : o^{\mathbf{r}} T \qquad \Gamma, x : T' \vdash P \qquad T' \leq T}{\Gamma \vdash \overline{a}(x).P}$$

(and its counterpart for inputs on $\mathbf{e}$-names). This would have the effect of typing $\overline{a}(x).P$ like $(\boldsymbol{\nu} x)\overline{a}x.P$. We instead chose to enforce what we call a *"double contract"*: the same way a receiving process uses the bound name according to the type specified in the channel that is used for reception, the continuation of a bound output uses the emitted name according to $T^{\leftrightarrow}$, the *symmetrised version* of T. This corresponds to a useful programming idiom in π, where it is common to create a name, transmit one capability on this name and use locally the other, dual capability. This idiom is used e.g. in [Vas09] and in [SW01, Sect. 5.7.3]. This choice moreover makes the proofs in Section 3.2 easier.

Observe that when a typable process reduces according to

$$\overline{a}(x).P \mid a(x).Q \to (\nu x)(P \mid Q) \ ,$$

if a has type, say, $\sharp^{\mathbf{r}}(o^s T)$, then in the right hand side process, name x is given type $\sharp^s T$, and the $\sharp$ capability is "split" into $i^s T$ (used by P) and $o^s T$ (used by Q) — it would be the other way around if a's sort were $\mathbf{e}$.

Lemma 1 (Properties of typing)

1. *(Weakening) If $\Gamma \vdash P$ then $\Gamma, a : T \vdash P$.*
2. *(Strengthening) If $\Gamma, a : T \vdash P$ and $a \notin fn(P)$ then $\Gamma \vdash P$.*
3. *(Narrowing) If $\Delta \leq \Gamma$ and $\Gamma \vdash P$ then $\Delta \vdash P$.*
4. *(Substitution) If $\Gamma, x : T \vdash P$ and $\Gamma \vdash b : T$ then $\Gamma \vdash P[b/x]$.*

Proposition 1 (Subject reduction). *If $\Gamma \vdash P$ and $P \to Q$ then $\Gamma \vdash Q$.*

Proof. By transition induction. Lemma 1 (4) is used when a bound prefix communicates with a free prefix; Lemma 1 (3) is used for the interaction between two bound prefixes, since T and $T^{\leftrightarrow}$ have a common subtype. □

Definition 1 (Contexts). *Contexts are processes with one occurrence of the hole, written $[-]$. They are defined by the following grammar:*

$$C ::= [-] \mid C|P \mid P|C \mid !C \mid \alpha.C \mid (\nu a)C\ .$$

Definition 2. *Let Γ, Δ be typing environments. We say that Γ* extends *Δ if the support of Δ is included in the support of Γ, and if $\Delta \vdash x : T$ entails $\Gamma \vdash x : T$ for all x. A context C is a (Γ/Δ)-context, written $\Gamma/\Delta \vdash C$, if C can be typed in the environment Γ, the hole being well-typed in any context that extends Δ.*

As a consequence of the previous definition and of Lemma 1, it is easy to show that if $\Delta \vdash P$ and $\Gamma/\Delta \vdash C$, then $\Gamma \vdash C[P]$.

We now move to the definition of behavioural equivalence.

Definition 3 (Barbs). *Given $\rho \in \{a, \overline{a}\}$, where a is a name, we say that P exhibits barb ρ, written $P\downarrow_\rho$, if $P \equiv (\nu c_1 \dots c_n)(\alpha.Q \mid R)$ where $\alpha \in \{\rho(x), \rho b\}$ with $a \notin \{c_1, \dots, c_n\}$. We extend the definition to* weak barbs*: $P \Downarrow_\rho$ stands for $P \Rightarrow\downarrow_\rho$ where $\Rightarrow$ is the reflexive transitive closure of $\to$.*

Definition 4 (Typed barbed congruence). Barbed bisimilarity *is the largest symmetric relation $\dot{\approx}$ such that whenever $P \dot{\approx} Q$, $P\downarrow_\rho$ implies $Q \Downarrow_\rho$ and $P \to P'$ implies $Q \Rightarrow \dot{\approx} P'$. When $\Delta \vdash P, Q$, we say that P and Q are* barbed congruent *at Δ, written $\Delta \rhd P \cong^c Q$, if for all (Γ/Δ)-context C, $C[P] \dot{\approx} C[Q]$.*

2.3 Duality

Definition 5 (Dual of a process). *The dual of a process P, written $\overline{P}$, is the process obtained by transforming prefixes as follows: $\overline{\overline{a}b} = ab$, $\overline{ab} = \overline{a}b$, $\overline{\overline{a}(x)} = a(x)$, $\overline{a(x)} = \overline{a}(x)$, and applying dualisation homeomorphically to the other constructs.*

Lemma 2 (Duality for reduction). *If $P \to Q$ then $\overline{P} \to \overline{Q}$.*

Dualising a type means swapping i/o capabilities and $\mathbf{e}/\mathbf{r}$ sorts.

Definition 6 (Dual of a type). *The dual of T, written $\overline{T}$, is defined by setting $\overline{c^s T} = \overline{c}^{\overline{s}}\,\overline{T}$, with $\overline{\mathbf{r}} = \mathbf{e}, \overline{\mathbf{e}} = \mathbf{r}, \overline{i} = o$, and $\overline{o} = i$. We extend the definition to typing environments, and write $\overline{\Gamma}$ for the dual of Γ.*

Lemma 3 (Duality for typing)

1. *If* $T_1 \leq T_2$ *then* $\overline{T_1} \leq \overline{T_2}$.
2. *If* $\Gamma \vdash P$ *then* $\overline{\Gamma} \vdash \overline{P}$.
3. *If* $\Gamma/\Delta \vdash C$ *then* $\overline{\Gamma}/\overline{\Delta} \vdash \overline{C}$.

Proof. (1): the covariant type operators ($i^{\mathtt{r}}$ and $o^{\mathtt{e}}$) are dual of each other, and so are the contravariant operators ($o^{\mathtt{r}}$ and $i^{\mathtt{e}}$). (2) follows from the shape of the typing rules, e.g., the dual of the rule for $i^{\mathtt{r}}$ is an instance of the rule for $\overline{i^{\mathtt{r}}} = o^{\mathtt{e}}$. (3) holds because if Φ extends Δ then $\overline{\Phi}$ extends $\overline{\Delta}$ (item (1)). □

Most importantly, duality holds for typed barbed congruence. The result is easy in the untyped case, since duality preserves reduction and dualises barbs. On the other hand, we are not aware of the existence of another system having this property in presence of i/o-types.

Theorem 1 (Duality for $\cong^c$). *If* $\Delta \rhd P \cong^c Q$ *then* $\overline{\Delta} \rhd \overline{P} \cong^c \overline{Q}$.

Proof. By Lemma 3, we only have to prove that if $P \dot{\approx} Q$ then $\overline{P} \dot{\approx} \overline{Q}$, i.e., duality preserves reduction and swaps barbs. □

2.4 Embeddings between π and $\overline{\pi}$

From $\overline{\pi}$ *to* π^{io}. As explained in Section 1, the π-calculus with i/o-types (that we note π^{io}) is an asymmetric calculus. In some sense, $\overline{\pi}$ can be seen as a 'dualisation' of π^{io}. This can be formulated rigorously by projecting $\overline{\pi}$ into π^{io}. To define this projection, which we call a *partial dualisation*, we work in an extended version of π^{io}, where capabilities are duplicated: in addition to the $i, o, \sharp$ capabilities, we also have capabilities $\underline{i}, \underline{o}$ and $\underline{\sharp}$, that intuitively correspond to the image of the "e-part" of $\overline{\pi}$ through the encoding. The additional capabilities act exactly like the corresponding usual capabilities, in particular w.r.t. subtyping and duality. We write π^{io}_2 for the resulting calculus. We discuss below (Remark 3) to what extent the addition of these capabilities is necessary. We also rely on π^{io}_2 to prove that $\overline{\pi}$ is a conservative extension of the π-calculus in Theorem 2 — π^{io}_2 is actually close, operationally, to both calculi.

Definition 7 (Partial dualisation). *We define a translation from typed processes in* $\overline{\pi}$ *to* π^{io}_2. *The translation acts on typing derivations: given a derivation* δ *of* $\Gamma \vdash P$ *(written* $\delta :: \Gamma_\delta \vdash P$*), we define a* π^{io}_2 *process noted* $[P]^\delta$ *as follows:*

$$\begin{array}{rll} [\rho b.P]^\delta &= \overline{\rho} b.[P]^{\delta'} & \text{if } \Gamma_\delta(\mathrm{n}(\rho)) = c^{\mathtt{e}}T \\ [\rho b.P]^\delta &= \rho b.[P]^{\delta'} & \text{if } \Gamma_\delta(\mathrm{n}(\rho)) = c^{\mathtt{r}}T \\ [\rho(x).P]^\delta &= \overline{\rho}(x).[P]^{\delta'} & \text{if } \Gamma_\delta(\mathrm{n}(\rho)) = c^{\mathtt{e}}T \\ [\rho(x).P]^\delta &= \rho(x).[P]^{\delta'} & \text{if } \Gamma_\delta(\mathrm{n}(\rho)) = c^{\mathtt{r}}T \end{array}$$

$$[(\nu a)P]^\delta = [P]^{\delta'} \qquad [0]^\delta = 0 \qquad [!P]^\delta = ![P]^{\delta'} \qquad [P \mid Q]^\delta = [P]^{\delta'_1} \mid [Q]^{\delta'_2}$$

In the above definition, δ' *is the subderivation of* δ*, in case there is only one, and* δ'_1 *and* δ'_2 *are the obvious subderivations in the case of parallel composition.*

We extend the definition to types: T^* stands for T where all occurrences of $\mathrm{c}^{\mathbf{r}}$ (resp. $\mathrm{c}^{\mathbf{e}}$) are replaced with c (resp. $\overline{\mathrm{c}}$, the dual of c). We define accordingly Γ^*.

Remark 2. The same translation could be defined for a simply typed version of $\overline{\pi}$. Indeed, $[\cdot]^{-}$ does not depend on capabilities ($i/o/\sharp$), but only on sorts ($\mathbf{r}/\mathbf{e}$).

Lemma 4. *If $\delta :: \Gamma \vdash P$ (in $\overline{\pi}$), then $\Gamma^* \vdash [P]^\delta$ (in π_2^{io}).*

Proof. In moving from Γ to Γ^*, we replace $i^{\mathbf{e}}$ (resp. $o^{\mathbf{e}}$, $i^{\mathbf{r}}$, $o^{\mathbf{r}}$) with $\underline{o}$ (resp. $\underline{i}$, i, o). This transformation preserves the subtyping relation. Moreover, the rules to type prefixes $i^{\mathbf{r}}, o^{\mathbf{r}}, i^{\mathbf{e}}, o^{\mathbf{e}}$ in $\overline{\pi}$ correspond to the rules for $i, o, \underline{o}, \underline{i}$ in π_2^{io}. □

Lemma 5. *Whenever $\delta_1 :: \Gamma \vdash P$ and $\delta_2 :: \Gamma \vdash P$, we have $\Gamma^* \rhd [P]^{\delta_1} \simeq^c [P]^{\delta_2}$.*

Proof. The relation $\mathcal{R} \triangleq \{([P]^{\delta_1}, [P]^{\delta_2}) \mid \delta_1, \delta_2 :: \Gamma \vdash P\}$ is a strong bisimulation in π and is substitution-closed; hence $\mathcal{R}$ is included in $\simeq^c$, since $[P]^{\delta_i}$ is typable in Γ^* (by Lemma 4). □

Lemma 6. *If $\delta_P :: \Gamma \vdash P$ and $\delta_Q :: \Gamma \vdash Q$ then we have the following:*

1. *(P and Q have the same barbs) iff ($[P]^{\delta_P}$ and $[Q]^{\delta_Q}$ have the same barbs)*
2. *if $P \to P'$ then $[P]^{\delta_P} \to [P']^\delta$ for some $\delta :: \Gamma \vdash P'$.*
3. *if $[P]^{\delta_P} \to P_1$ then $P_1 = [P']^\delta$ with $P \to P'$ for some $\delta :: \Gamma \vdash P'$.*
4. *$P \stackrel{\cdot}{\approx} Q$ iff $[P]^{\delta_P} \stackrel{\cdot}{\approx} [Q]^{\delta_Q}$.*

Proof. (4) is a consequence of (1), (2), (3). For (1) remark that if $\Gamma(a) = \mathrm{c}^{\mathbf{r}}T$ then P and $[P]^{\delta_P}$ have the same barbs on a; if $\Gamma(a) = \mathrm{c}^{\mathbf{e}}T$, they have dual barbs on a, but in this case so do Q and $[Q]^{\delta_Q}$. For (2) and (3), we remark that $[\cdot]^\delta$ is compositional and preserves the fact that two prefixes can interact — even when moving to a different δ. □

Proposition 2 (Full abstraction). *If $\delta_P :: \Gamma \vdash P$ and $\delta_Q :: \Gamma \vdash Q$ then*

$$\Gamma \rhd P \cong^c Q \ (\text{in } \overline{\pi}) \quad \text{iff} \quad \Gamma^* \rhd [P]^{\delta_P} \cong^c [Q]^{\delta_Q} \ (\text{in } \pi_2^{\mathrm{io}}) \ .$$

Proof. Soundness: given a derivation $\gamma :: \Delta/\Gamma \vdash C$, we build $[C]^\gamma$ which is a (Δ^*/Γ^*)-context. Then $[C]^\gamma[[P]^{\delta_P}] = [C[P]]^{\beta_P}$ for some β_P and we can rely on barbed congruence in π_2^{io} to establish $[C[P]]^{\beta_P} \stackrel{\cdot}{\approx} [C[Q]]^{\beta_Q}$. By Lemma 6, we deduce $C[P] \stackrel{\cdot}{\approx} C[Q]$.
Completeness: we define the reverse translation $\{\cdot\}^{-}$ of $[\cdot]^{-}$ and reason as above to prove its soundness. Thanks to the fact that $\delta_P :: \Gamma \vdash P$ implies $\{[P]^{\delta_P}\}^{\delta_P^*} = P$ where $\delta_P^* :: \Gamma^* \vdash [P]^\delta$ is the derivation obtained by Lemma 4, the soundness of $\{\cdot\}^{-}$ implies the completeness of $[\cdot]^{-}$, and vice versa. □

Remark 3 (π_2^{io} vs π^{io}). We can make two remarks about the above result.

First, it would seem natural to project directly onto π^{io}, by mapping capabilities $i^{\mathbf{r}}$ and $o^{\mathbf{e}}$ into i, and $o^{\mathbf{r}}$ and $i^{\mathbf{e}}$ into o. However, the result of Proposition 2 would not hold in this case. The intuitive reason is that in doing so, we would allow two names having different sorts in $\overline{\pi}$ to be equated in the image of the encoding, thus giving rise to additional observations (since we cannot equate names having different sorts in $\overline{\pi}$). Technically, this question is reminiscent of the problem of closure of bisimilarity under substitutions in the π-calculus.

Second, the key ingredient in the definition of partial dualisation is to preserve the distinction between names having originally different sorts in the $\overline{\pi}$ process. It is possible to define an encoding of π_2^{io} into *a dyadic version* of π^{io} (without the extra capabilities), in order to do so.

Lemma 7. *Suppose $\Delta \vdash P, Q$ holds in π^{io}.*
Then $\Delta \rhd P \cong^c Q$ (in π^{io}) iff $\Delta \rhd P \cong^c Q$ (in π_2^{io}).

Proof. The right-to-left implication is immediate because any π^{io}-context is a π_2^{io}-context. To show the converse, we observe that a (Γ/Δ)-context in π_2^{io} is a (Γ'/Δ)-context in π^{io}, where Γ' is Γ where every $\underline{c}$ capability is replaced with c.

From π^{io} to $\overline{\pi}$. $\overline{\pi}$ contains π^{io}, the π-calculus with i/o-types: the rules for **r**-channels are exactly those of π^{io}, and typability of **e**-free processes coincides with typability in π^{io}. More precisely we can say that $\overline{\pi}$ is a conservative extension of π^{io}. In π^{io} we rely on typed barbed congruence as defined in [SW01], which is essentially the same as $\cong^c$ in $\overline{\pi}$. Before presenting the result, the following remark introduces some notation.

Remark 4. Suppose $\delta :: \Gamma \vdash P$, in π^{io}. Then $\delta^{\mathbf{r}} :: \Gamma^{\mathbf{r}} \vdash P$ in $\overline{\pi}$, where $\Gamma^{\mathbf{r}}$ stands for Γ in which all types are decorated with **r** and $\delta^{\mathbf{r}}$ stands for δ where all usages of the typing rule for restriction introduce an **r**-type. Moreover $[P]^{\delta^{\mathbf{r}}} = P$.

Theorem 2 (Conservative extension). *Suppose $\Gamma \vdash P, Q$ holds in π^{io}.*
Then $\Gamma \rhd P \cong^c Q$ (in π^{io}) iff $\Gamma^{\mathbf{r}} \rhd P \cong^c Q$ (in $\overline{\pi}$).

Proof. We use π_2^{io} as an intermediate calculus. By Remark 4, let δ_P, δ_Q be derivations of $\Gamma^{\mathbf{r}} \vdash P$ and $\Gamma^{\mathbf{r}} \vdash Q$ such that $P = [P]^{\delta_P}$ and $Q = [Q]^{\delta_Q}$. By Proposition 2, the right hand side is equivalent to $(\Gamma^{\mathbf{r}})^* \rhd [P]^{\delta_P} \cong^c [Q]^{\delta_Q}$ (in π_2^{io}). By hypothesis, and since $(\Gamma^{\mathbf{r}})^* = \Gamma$, the latter is equivalent to $\Gamma \rhd P \cong^c Q$ (in π_2^{io}). Lemma 7 allows us to finish the proof. □

The result above shows that π can be embedded rather naturally into $\overline{\pi}$. This is in contrast with fusion calculi, where the equivalence on π-calculus terms induced by the embedding into fusions does not coincide with a barbed congruence or equivalence in the π-calculus.

Remark 5 ($\overline{\pi}$ and existing symmetric calculi). $\overline{\pi}$ contains the π-calculus, and hence contains (the typed version of) πI, the π-calculus with internal mobility (see [SW01]). On the other hand, because free inputs and free outputs are not allowed to interact in $\overline{\pi}$, $\overline{\pi}$ fails to represent the fusion calculus. As mentioned above, we have not succeeded in defining a 'symmetrical version' of i/o-types that would be suitable for fusions.

3 Application: Relating Encodings of the λ-Calculus

In this section, we use $\overline{\pi}$ to reason about encodings of the (call-by-name) λ-calculus into the π-calculus. To do so, we need to extend $\overline{\pi}$ (Section 3.1). We then justify the validity of a transformation that makes use of link processes in Section 3.2. Finally, we show how duality, together with the latter transformation, allows us to relate Milner's encoding with the one of van Bakel and Vigliotti.

3.1 Extending $\overline{\pi}$

Based on $\overline{\pi}$, we develop an extension, called $\overline{\pi}^{\mathbf{a}}$, with forms of asynchronous communication and polyadicity. The extension to polyadic communication is standard. Asynchronous communication is added via the inclusion of *delayed* prefixes: $a(x){:}P$ (resp. $\overline{a}(x){:}P$) stands for a *(bound) delayed input (resp. output)* prefix. The intuition behind delayed prefixes is that they allow the continuation of the prefix to interact, as long as the performed action is not causally dependent on the prefix itself — this is made more precise below. Intuitively asynchrony is useful when reasoning about encodings of the λ-calculus because in a β-reduction $(\lambda x.M)N \to M[N/x]$ the "output" part N has no continuation. It is also useful to have asynchrony in input because the considered λ-strategy allows reduction under a λ-abstraction. Moreover asynchrony allows us to derive some transformation laws involving link processes (Section 3.2). Note that synchronous prefixes are still necessary, to encode the argument of an application.

Delayed prefixes are typed like bound input and output prefixes in Section 2. Types are refined with two new sorts that enforce asynchrony: **d** to force inputs to be bound and delayed, **a** to force outputs to be bound and delayed — we call such outputs *asynchronous*. For instance, if we have $a : \sharp^{\mathbf{r}}_{\mathbf{d}}T$ for some T, then all inputs at a are bound and delayed. We also include recursive types.

$$T ::= c_t\langle {}^{s_1}T_1, \ldots, {}^{s_n}T_n\rangle \mid \mathbf{1} \mid \mu X.T \mid X \qquad s ::= \mathbf{e} \mid \mathbf{r} \qquad t ::= \mathbf{d} \mid \mathbf{a}$$

In the polyadic case, **e**/**r** sorts are given to each element of the transmitted tuple. We present here only the typing rule for delayed input, in polyadic form, to illustrate how we extend the type system of Section 2.

$$\frac{\Gamma \vdash a : i_t\langle {}^{s_1}T_1, \ldots {}^{s_n}T_n\rangle \quad \Gamma, x_1 : T_1^{s_1}, \ldots, x_n : T_n^{s_n} \vdash P}{\Gamma \vdash a(x_1, \ldots, x_n){:}P}$$

(with $T^{\mathbf{r}} = T$ and $T^{\mathbf{e}} = T^{\leftrightarrow}$). The sort **d** (resp. **a**) is forbidden in the rules to type non-delayed input (resp. output) prefixes.

The definition of operational semantics is extended as follows to handle delayed prefixes (below, $\overline{\rho}(y)P$ stands for either $\overline{\rho}(y).P$ or $\overline{\rho}(y){:}P$):

$$\begin{array}{ll} P \mid \rho(x){:}Q \equiv \rho(x){:}(P \mid Q) & \text{if } x \notin \mathrm{fn}(P) \\ \rho_1(y){:}\rho_2(x){:}P \equiv \rho_2(x){:}\rho_1(y){:}P & \text{if } \mathrm{n}(\rho_1) \neq x, x \neq y, y \neq \mathrm{n}(\rho_2) \\ (\nu y)\rho(x){:}P \equiv \rho(x){:}(\nu y)P & \text{if } x \neq y, y \neq \mathrm{n}(\rho) \end{array}$$

$$\rho(x){:}(\overline{\rho}(y)P \mid Q) \to (\nu y)(P \mid Q)[y/x] \qquad \rho(x){:}P \to \rho(x){:}Q \quad \text{if } P \to Q$$
$$\rho(x){:}(\overline{\rho}b.P \mid Q) \to (P \mid Q)[b/x]$$

Barbs are defined as in Section 2, with an additional clause saying that if ρ is a barb of P and $\mathrm{n}(\rho) \neq x$, then ρ is a barb of $\rho'(x){:}P$.

The results of Section 2 hold for this extended calculus, with similar proofs:

Proposition 3 (Duality, extended calculus)

1. *Duality of typing:* $\Gamma \vdash P \Rightarrow \overline{\Gamma} \vdash \overline{P}$.
2. *Duality of barbed congruence:* $\Gamma \rhd P \cong^{c} Q \Rightarrow \overline{\Gamma} \rhd \overline{P} \cong^{c} \overline{Q}$.

The counterpart of Theorem 2 also holds in $\overline{\pi}^{\mathbf{a}}$, which stands for the extended calculus of this section, where types also specify how names have to be used in delayed prefixes. It can be stated w.r.t. $\pi^{\mathrm{io},\mathbf{a}}$, which is defined as π^{io} with additional typing information to specify which names have to be used asynchronously.

Theorem 3 (Conservative extension, extended calculus). *Suppose we have $\Gamma \vdash P, Q$ in $\pi^{\mathrm{io},\mathbf{a}}$. Then $\Gamma \rhd P \cong^{c} Q$ (in $\pi^{\mathrm{io},\mathbf{a}}$) iff $\Gamma^{\mathbf{r}} \rhd P \cong^{c} Q$ (in $\overline{\pi}^{\mathbf{a}}$) .*

The extensions $\overline{\pi}^{\mathbf{a}}$ and $\pi^{\mathrm{io},\mathbf{a}}$ are asynchronous versions of $\overline{\pi}$ and π^{io} in the sense that interaction is no longer a synchronous handshaking between two processes: for at least one of the processes, the occurrence of the interaction is not observable because the consumed action is not blocking for a continuation.

3.2 Reasoning about Links, a transformation from $o^{\mathbf{e}}_{\mathbf{a}}$ to $i^{\mathbf{r}}_{\mathbf{a}}$

The main result of this section is a technical lemma about the validity of a transformation which is used for the analysis of λ-calculus encodings in Section 3.3. A reader not interested in this result may safely skip this section.

Differently from partial dualisation (Definition 7), the transformation, written $\langle\!\langle\cdot\rangle\!\rangle^{\mathbf{er}}$, modifies prefixes, beyond simple dualisation, by introducing link processes. It also acts on types, by mapping **e**-names onto **r**-names.

Definition 8. *We set $\langle\!\langle ab.P\rangle\!\rangle^{\mathbf{er}} = a(x).(x \multimap b \mid \langle\!\langle P\rangle\!\rangle^{\mathbf{er}})$, where $x \multimap b = !x(z).\overline{b}z$ is called a* link process*. We also define $\langle\!\langle \rho(x).P\rangle\!\rangle^{\mathbf{er}} = \rho(x).\langle\!\langle P\rangle\!\rangle^{\mathbf{er}}$ and similarly for delayed prefixes. $\langle\!\langle\cdot\rangle\!\rangle^{\mathbf{er}}$ leaves free outputs unchanged and acts homeomorphically on the other constructors.*

The transformation $\langle\!\langle\cdot\rangle\!\rangle^{\mathbf{er}}$ removes all free inputs and inserts free outputs (in the link process). We therefore expect it to return plain π processes. Moreover, the process computed in the translation of free input behaves as expected provided only the *input capability* is transmitted (the link process *at the receiver's side* exerts the input capability on x). Accordingly, we define $T_{o\mathbf{e}} = \mu X.o^{\mathbf{e}}_{\mathbf{a}}X = o^{\mathbf{e}}_{\mathbf{a}}o^{\mathbf{e}}_{\mathbf{a}}o^{\mathbf{e}}_{\mathbf{a}}\cdots$, and $T_{i\mathbf{r}} = \mu X.i^{\mathbf{r}}_{\mathbf{a}}X = i^{\mathbf{r}}_{\mathbf{a}}i^{\mathbf{r}}_{\mathbf{a}}i^{\mathbf{r}}_{\mathbf{a}}\cdots$. We let $\Gamma_{i\mathbf{r}}$ (resp. $\Gamma_{o\mathbf{e}}$) range over environments mapping all names to some $c^{\mathbf{r}}_{\mathbf{a}}T_{i\mathbf{r}}$ (resp. $c^{\mathbf{e}}_{\mathbf{a}}T_{o\mathbf{e}}$), for $c \in \{i, o, \sharp\}$.

Lemma 8 (Typing for $\langle\!\langle\cdot\rangle\!\rangle^{\mathbf{er}}$). *If $\Gamma_{o\mathbf{e}} \vdash P$ then $\Gamma_{i\mathbf{r}} \vdash \langle\!\langle P\rangle\!\rangle^{\mathbf{er}}$ for some $\Gamma_{i\mathbf{r}}$.*

Proof. We prove by induction on P that if $\Gamma \vdash P$ then $\overline{\Gamma} \vdash \langle\!\langle P\rangle\!\rangle^{\mathbf{er}}$. In the case for ν we always introduce the type $\sharp^{\mathbf{r}}_{\mathbf{a}}T_{i\mathbf{r}}$. For bound prefixes we replace $c^{\mathbf{e}}_{\mathbf{a}}T_{o\mathbf{e}}$ with $\overline{c}^{\mathbf{r}}_{\mathbf{a}}T_{i\mathbf{r}}$, and for free inputs we type links with $T_{i\mathbf{r}}$ types. □

As this result shows, $\langle\!\langle\cdot\rangle\!\rangle^{\mathbf{er}}$ yields processes that only transmit the input capability. This is reminiscent of the localised π-calculus [SW01] where only the output capability is passed.

It can be noted that Lemma 8 holds because we enforce a "double contract" in the typing rules (cf. Remark 1), which allows us to typecheck bound prefixes as **e**-names (before the transformation) and as **r**-names (after).

The relationship between P and $\langle\!\langle P\rangle\!\rangle^{\mathbf{er}}$ is given in terms of barbed expansion precongruence, which is a preorder in between strong and weak barbed congruence.

Definition 9 (Barbed expansion precongruence). Barbed expansion *is the largest relation* $\dot{\lesssim}$ *such that whenever* $P \dot{\lesssim} Q$,

- *if* $P \to P'$ *then* $Q \to\Rightarrow Q'$ *with* $P' \dot{\lesssim} Q'$;
- *if* $Q \to Q'$ *then* $P \to P'$ *or* $P = P'$ *with* $P' \dot{\lesssim} Q'$;
- $P \downarrow \rho$ *implies* $Q \Downarrow \rho$, *and* $Q \downarrow \rho$ *implies* $P \downarrow \rho$.

We call (resp. typed) barbed expansion precongruence ($\lesssim^c$) *the induced (resp. typed) precongruence.*

Lemma 9 (Properties of links)

1. $a : i^{\mathbf{r}}_{\mathbf{a}}T_{\mathbf{ir}}, b : o^{\mathbf{r}}_{\mathbf{a}}T_{\mathbf{ir}} \rhd a \twoheadrightarrow b \lesssim^c (\nu x)(a \twoheadrightarrow x \mid x \twoheadrightarrow b)$.
2. *If* $\Gamma_{\mathbf{oe}}, a : T_{\mathbf{oe}} \vdash P$ *then* $\Gamma_{\mathbf{ir}} \rhd \langle\!\langle P\rangle\!\rangle^{\mathbf{er}}[b/a] \lesssim^c (\nu a)(a \twoheadrightarrow b \mid \langle\!\langle P\rangle\!\rangle^{\mathbf{er}})$.

Proof. 1. The law is valid for the ordinary π-calculus (and is substitution-closed); Lemma 3 transfers the result to $\overline{\pi}$.

2. By typing, a free output involving a in $\langle\!\langle P\rangle\!\rangle^{\mathbf{er}}$ is necessarily in a link; in this case, we can use (1). The other kind of interaction is with some $\overline{a}(x){:}Q$ in $\langle\!\langle P\rangle\!\rangle^{\mathbf{er}}$, and $\overline{b}(x){:}Q[b/a]$ behaves like $(\nu a)(a \twoheadrightarrow b \mid \overline{a}(x){:}Q[b/a])$. □

We use Lemma 9 to deduce operational correspondence.

Lemma 10 (Operational correspondence). *Suppose that* $\Gamma_{\mathbf{oe}} \vdash P$.

1. $P \downarrow \rho$ *iff* $\langle\!\langle P\rangle\!\rangle^{\mathbf{er}} \downarrow \rho$.
2. *If* $P \to P'$ *then* $\langle\!\langle P\rangle\!\rangle^{\mathbf{er}} \to\gtrsim^c \langle\!\langle P'\rangle\!\rangle^{\mathbf{er}}$.
3. *If* $\langle\!\langle P\rangle\!\rangle^{\mathbf{er}} \to P_1$ *then* $P \to P'$ *and* $P_1 \gtrsim^c \langle\!\langle P'\rangle\!\rangle^{\mathbf{er}}$ *for some* P'.

A version of these results in the weak case can also be proved, for barbed expansion. Notably, P and $\langle\!\langle P\rangle\!\rangle^{\mathbf{er}}$ exhibit the same weak barbs.

Lemma 11. *If* $\Gamma_{\mathbf{oe}} \vdash P, Q$ *then* $P \approx Q$ *iff* $\langle\!\langle P\rangle\!\rangle^{\mathbf{er}} \approx \langle\!\langle Q\rangle\!\rangle^{\mathbf{er}}$.

Proof. We show that $\dot{\gtrsim}\{(\langle\!\langle P\rangle\!\rangle^{\mathbf{er}}, \langle\!\langle Q\rangle\!\rangle^{\mathbf{er}}) \mid P \dot{\approx} Q\}\dot{\lesssim}$ and $\{(P, Q) \mid \langle\!\langle P\rangle\!\rangle^{\mathbf{er}} \dot{\approx} \langle\!\langle Q\rangle\!\rangle^{\mathbf{er}}\}$ are weak barbed bisimulations. We then use the adaptation of Lemma 10 to the weak case, for barbed expansion. □

Lemma 12. *If $\Gamma_{oe} \vdash P, Q$ and $\Gamma_{ir} \rhd \langle\!\langle P\rangle\!\rangle^{er} \cong^c \langle\!\langle Q\rangle\!\rangle^{er}$ then $\Gamma_{oe} \rhd P \cong^c Q$.*

Proof. We define a type system with marks on types, such that only T_{ir}-types are marked. The marking propagates onto the names of the typed processes. We modify the encoding $\langle\!\langle\cdot\rangle\!\rangle^{er}$ to only operate on marked prefixes. For every (Δ/Γ_{oe})-context C, its encoding $\langle\!\langle C\rangle\!\rangle^{er}$ is a (Δ'/Γ_{ir})-context. Thanks to the compositionality of $\langle\!\langle\cdot\rangle\!\rangle^{er}$, the hypothesis of the lemma implies the equivalence $\langle\!\langle C[P]\rangle\!\rangle^{er} \approx \langle\!\langle C[Q]\rangle\!\rangle^{er}$. We then adapt the proof of Lemma 11 to this marked encoding. □

3.3 An Analysis of van Bakel and Vigliotti's Encoding

As announced in Section 1, we start from an adaptation of Milner's call-by-name (cbn) encoding of [Mil92] to *strong* cbn, which also allows reductions to occur under λ. We obtain this by using a delayed prefix in the clause for λ-abstraction. The encoding, noted $[\![\cdot]\!]^{\mathcal{M}}$, is defined as follows:

$$[\![x]\!]^{\mathcal{M}}_p = \overline{x}p \qquad\qquad [\![\lambda x.M]\!]^{\mathcal{M}}_p = p(x,q){:}[\![M]\!]^{\mathcal{M}}_q$$
$$[\![MN]\!]^{\mathcal{M}}_p = (\nu q)\big([\![M]\!]^{\mathcal{M}}_q \mid (\nu x)(\overline{q}\langle x,p\rangle \mid !x(r).[\![N]\!]^{\mathcal{M}}_r)\big)$$

The other encoding we analyse, taken from [vBV09], is written $[\![\cdot]\!]^{\mathcal{B}}$:

$$[\![x]\!]^{\mathcal{B}}_p = x(p'){:}p' \twoheadrightarrow p \qquad\qquad [\![\lambda x.M]\!]^{\mathcal{B}}_p = \overline{p}(x,q){:}[\![M]\!]^{\mathcal{B}}_q$$
$$[\![MN]\!]^{\mathcal{B}}_p = (\nu q)\big([\![M]\!]^{\mathcal{B}}_q \mid q(x,p').(p' \twoheadrightarrow p \mid !\overline{x}(r).[\![N]\!]^{\mathcal{B}}_r)\big)$$

Note that $[\![\cdot]\!]^{\mathcal{B}}$ is written in [vBV09] using asynchronous free output and restriction instead of delayed bound output. We can adopt this more concise notation since $(\nu x)(\overline{a}x \mid P)$ and $\overline{a}(x){:}P$ are strongly bisimilar processes, and similarly for $x(p'){:}p' \twoheadrightarrow p$ and $x(p').p' \twoheadrightarrow p$. (Another difference is that the replication in the encoding of the application is guarded, as in [vBV10], to force a tighter operational correspondence between reductions in λ and in the encodings.)

As remarked above, $[\![\cdot]\!]^{\mathcal{B}}$ and $[\![\cdot]\!]^{\mathcal{M}}$ differ considerably because they engage in quite different dialogues with their environments: in $[\![\cdot]\!]^{\mathcal{M}}$ a function receives its argument via an input, in $[\![\cdot]\!]^{\mathcal{B}}$ it interacts via an output. Differences are also visible in the encodings of variables and application (e.g. the use of links).

To compare the encodings $[\![\cdot]\!]^{\mathcal{M}}$ and $[\![\cdot]\!]^{\mathcal{B}}$, we introduce an intermediate encoding, noted $[\![\cdot]\!]^{\mathcal{I}}$, which is defined as the dual of $[\![\cdot]\!]^{\mathcal{M}}$ (in $\overline{\pi}$):

$$[\![x]\!]^{\mathcal{I}}_p = xp \qquad\qquad [\![\lambda x.M]\!]^{\mathcal{I}}_p = \overline{p}(x,q){:}[\![M]\!]^{\mathcal{I}}_q$$
$$[\![MN]\!]^{\mathcal{I}}_p = (\nu q)\big([\![M]\!]^{\mathcal{I}}_q \mid (\nu x)(q\langle x,p\rangle \mid !\overline{x}(r).[\![N]\!]^{\mathcal{I}}_r)\big)$$

Note that while $[\![\cdot]\!]^{\mathcal{M}}$ and $[\![\cdot]\!]^{\mathcal{B}}$ can be expressed in π, $[\![\cdot]\!]^{\mathcal{I}}$ uses free input, and does thus not define π-calculus processes.

The three encodings given above are based on a similar usage of names. Two kinds of names are used: we refer to names that represent continuations (p, p', q, r in the encodings) as *handles*, and to names that stand for λ-calculus parameters (x, y, z) as *λ-variables*. Here is how these encodings can be typed in $\overline{\pi}$:

Lemma 13 (Typing the encodings). *$[\![\cdot]\!]^{\mathcal{M}}$, $[\![\cdot]\!]^{\mathcal{B}}$ and $[\![\cdot]\!]^{\mathcal{I}}$ yield processes which are typable with the respective typing environments $\Gamma_{\mathcal{M}}, \Gamma_{\mathcal{B}}, \Gamma_{\mathcal{I}}$, where:*

- *$\Gamma_{\mathcal{M}}$ types λ-variables with $o^{\mathrm{r}}_{\mathbf{a}}H$ and handles with $H = \mu X.i^{\mathrm{r}}_{\mathbf{d}}\langle o^{\mathrm{r}}_{\mathbf{a}}X, X\rangle$;*
- *$\Gamma_{\mathcal{B}}$ uses respectively $i^{\mathrm{r}}_{\mathbf{d}}G$ and $o^{\mathrm{r}}_{\mathbf{a}}\langle o^{\mathrm{r}}_{\mathbf{d}}G, G\rangle$ where $G = \mu Y.i^{\mathrm{r}}_{\mathbf{a}}\langle o^{\mathrm{r}}_{\mathbf{d}}Y, Y\rangle$;*
- *$\Gamma_{\mathcal{I}}$ is the dual of $\Gamma_{\mathcal{M}}$ (that is, it uses $i^{\mathrm{e}}_{\mathbf{d}}\overline{H}$ and $\overline{H} = \mu Z.o^{\mathrm{e}}_{\mathbf{a}}\langle i^{\mathrm{e}}_{\mathbf{d}}Z, Z\rangle$).*

Encoding $[\![\cdot]\!]^{\mathcal{I}}$ can be obtained from $[\![\cdot]\!]^{\mathcal{M}}$ by duality. The only difference between $[\![\cdot]\!]^{\mathcal{I}}$ and $[\![\cdot]\!]^{\mathcal{B}}$ is the presence of two links. We rely on a link transformation similar to the one of Section 3.2 to move from $[\![\cdot]\!]^{\mathcal{I}}$ to $[\![\cdot]\!]^{\mathcal{B}}$. Thus, by composing the results on duality and on the transformation, we are able to go from $[\![\cdot]\!]^{\mathcal{M}}$ to $[\![\cdot]\!]^{\mathcal{B}}$.

Proposition 4. *Given two λ-terms M and N, we have $[\![M]\!]^{\mathcal{M}}_p \dot{\approx} [\![N]\!]^{\mathcal{M}}_p$ if and only if $[\![M]\!]^{\mathcal{B}}_p \dot{\approx} [\![N]\!]^{\mathcal{B}}_p$ (both equivalences are in $\pi^{\mathrm{io,a}}$).*

Proof. By duality, $[\![M]\!]^{\mathcal{M}}_p \dot{\approx} [\![N]\!]^{\mathcal{M}}_p$ iff $[\![M]\!]^{\mathcal{I}}_p \dot{\approx} [\![N]\!]^{\mathcal{I}}_p$. To establish that this is equivalent to $[\![M]\!]^{\mathcal{B}}_p \dot{\approx} [\![N]\!]^{\mathcal{B}}_p$, we rely on an adaptation of Lemma 11. For this, we define a transformation that exploits the ideas presented in Section 3.2. In particular, handles (p, p', q, r) are treated like in Definition 8. The handling of λ-variables (x, y, z) is somehow orthogonal, and raises no major difficulty, because such names are always transmitted as bound (fresh) names. □

Remark 6 (Call by name). To forbid reductions under λ-abstractions, we could adopt Milner's original encoding, and use an input prefix instead of delayed input in the translation of abstractions. Accordingly, adapting Van Bakel and Vigliotti's encoding to this strategy would mean introducing a free input prefix — which is rather natural in $\overline{\pi}$, but is not in the π-calculus.

4 Concluding Remarks

We have presented several properties of $\overline{\pi}$, and established relationships with the π-calculus with i/o-types (π^{io}).

The calculus $\overline{\pi}$ enjoys properties of dualities while being "large", in the sense that it incorporates many of the forms of prefix found in dialects of the π-calculus (free input, bound input, and, in the extension in Section 3.1, also delayed input, plus the analogue for outputs), and a non-trivial type system based on i/o-types. This syntactic abundance makes $\overline{\pi}$ a possibly interesting model in which to study various forms of dualities. This is exemplified in our study of encodings of the λ-calculus, where we have applied $\overline{\pi}$ and its theory to explain a recent encoding of cbn λ-calculus by van Bakel and Vigliotti: it can be related, via dualities, to Milner's encoding.

It would be interesting to strengthen the full abstraction in Lemma 11 from barbed bisimilarity to barbed congruence. This would allow us to replace barbed bisimilarity with typed barbed congruence in Proposition 4 as well (using the type environments of Lemma 13). While we believe the result to be true, the proof appears difficult because the link transformation modifies both processes and types, so that the types needed for barbed congruence in the two encodings are different. Therefore also the sets of contexts to be taken into account are different. The problem could be tackled by combining the theory on delayed input and the link bisimilarity in [MS04], and adapting it to a typed setting.

We plan to further investigate the behavioural theory of $\overline{\pi}$, and study in particular other transformations along the lines of Section 3.2, where link processes are used to implement substitutions. It would be interesting to provide general results on process transformations in terms of links, when the direction and the form of the links vary depending on the types of the names involved. Currently we only know how to handle them when the calculus is asynchronous and localised [MS04].

As already mentioned, another interesting issue is how to accommodate i/o-types into πI and fusion calculi while maintaining the dualities of the untyped calculi.

Acknowledgments. This work was supported by the french ANR projects Recre, 2009-BLAN-0169-02 Panda, and 2010-BLAN-0305-01 PiCoq.

References

[Fu97] Fu, Y.: The χ-calculus. In: Proc. of APDC 1997, pp. 74–81. IEEE Computer Society Press (1997)

[GW00] Gardner, P., Wischik, L.: Explicit Fusions. In: Nielsen, M., Rovan, B. (eds.) MFCS 2000. LNCS, vol. 1893, pp. 373–382. Springer, Heidelberg (2000)

[HMS12] Hirschkoff, D., Madiot, J.M., Sangiorgi, D.: On subtyping in symmetric versions of the π-calculus (in preparation, 2012)

[Mer00] Merro, M.: Locality in the pi-calculus and applications to distributed objects. PhD thesis, École des Mines, France (2000)

[Mil92] Milner, R.: Functions as processes. Mathematical Structures in Computer Science 2(2), 119–141 (1992)

[MS04] Merro, M., Sangiorgi, D.: On asynchrony in name-passing calculi. Mathematical Structures in Computer Science 14(5), 715–767 (2004)

[PV98] Parrow, J., Victor, B.: The fusion calculus: expressiveness and symmetry in mobile processes. In: Proc. of LICS, pp. 176–185. IEEE (1998)

[San96] Sangiorgi, D.: π-calculus, internal mobility, and agent-passing calculi. Selected papers from TAPSOFT 1995, pp. 235–274. Elsevier (1996)

[SW01] Sangiorgi, D., Walker, D.: The Pi-Calculus: a theory of mobile processes. Cambridge University Press (2001)

[Vas09] Vasconcelos, V.T.: Fundamentals of Session Types. In: Bernardo, M., Padovani, L., Zavattaro, G. (eds.) SFM 2009. LNCS, vol. 5569, pp. 158–186. Springer, Heidelberg (2009)

[vBV09] van Bakel, S., Vigliotti, M.G.: A Logical Interpretation of the λ-Calculus into the π-Calculus, Preserving Spine Reduction and Types. In: Bravetti, M., Zavattaro, G. (eds.) CONCUR 2009. LNCS, vol. 5710, pp. 84–98. Springer, Heidelberg (2009)

[vBV10] van Bakel, S., Vigliotti, M.G.: Implicative logic based encoding of the λ-calculus into the π-calculus (2010), `http://www.doc.ic.ac.uk/~svb/`

Spatial and Epistemic Modalities in Constraint-Based Process Calculi

Sophia Knight[2], Catuscia Palamidessi[2], Prakash Panangaden[3], and Frank D. Valencia[1]

[1] CNRS and LIX École Polytechnique de Paris
[2] INRIA and LIX École Polytechnique de Paris
[3] School of Computer Science, McGill University

Abstract. We introduce spatial and epistemic process calculi for reasoning about spatial information and knowledge distributed among the agents of a system. We introduce domain-theoretical structures to represent spatial and epistemic information. We provide operational and denotational techniques for reasoning about the potentially infinite behaviour of spatial and epistemic processes. We also give compact representations of infinite objects that can be used by processes to simulate announcements of common knowledge and global information.

Introduction

Distributed systems have changed substantially in the recent past with the advent of phenomena like social networks and cloud computing. In the previous incarnation of distributed computing [16] the emphasis was on consistency, fault tolerance, resource management and related topics; these were all characterized by *interaction between processes*. Research proceeded along two lines: the algorithmic side which dominated the Principles Of Distributed Computing conferences and the more process algebraic approach epitomized by CONCUR where the emphasis was on developing compositional reasoning principles. What marks the new era of distributed systems is an emphasis on managing access to information to a much greater degree than before.

Epistemic concepts were crucial in distributed computing as was realized in the mid 1980s with Halpern and Moses' groundbreaking paper on common knowledge [13]. This led to a flurry of activity in the next few years [11] with many distributed protocols being understood from an epistemic point of view. The impact of epistemic ideas in the concurrency theory community was slower in coming. In an invited talk by one of us [20] at a joint PODC-CONCUR conference in 2008, this point was emphasized and a plea was made for epistemic ideas to be exploited more by concurrency theorists.

The goal of the present paper is simple: to put epistemic concepts in the hands of programmers rather than just appearing in post-hoc theoretical analyses. One could imagine the incorporation of these ideas in a variety of process algebraic settings – and indeed we expect that such formalisms will appear in due course – but what is particularly appealing about the *concurrent constraint programming (ccp)* paradigm [24,25] is that it was designed to give programmers explicit access to the concept of *partial information* and, as such, had close ties with logic [21,18]. This makes it ideal for the incorporation of epistemic concepts by expanding the logical connections to include

M. Koutny and I. Ulidowski (Eds.): CONCUR 2012, LNCS 7454, pp. 317–332, 2012.

modal logic [15]. In particular, agents posting and querying information in the presence of *spatial hierarchies for sharing information and knowledge*, e.g. friend circles and shared albums in social networks or shared folders in cloud storage, provide natural examples of managing information access. These domains raise important problems such as the design of models to predict and prevent privacy breaches, which are commonplace nowadays.

Contributions. In ccp [24,25] processes interact with each other by querying and posting information to a single centralized shared-store. The information and its associated partial order are specified as a *constraint system*, which can be seen as a *Scott information system* without consistency structure [1]. The centralized notion of store, however, makes ccp unsuitable for systems where information and processes can be shared or spatially distributed among certain groups of agents. In this paper we enhance and generalize the theory of ccp for systems with spatial distribution of information.

In Section 1 we generalize the underlying theory of constraint systems by adding *space functions* to their structure. These functions can be seen as topological and closure operators and they provide for the specification of spatial and epistemic information. In Section 2 we extend ccp with a *spatial/epistemic* operator. The spatial operator can specify a process, or a local store of information, that resides within the *space* of a given agent (e.g., an application in some user's account, or some private data shared with a specific group). This operator can also be interpreted as an *epistemic* construction to specify that the information computed by a process will be known to a given agent. It is crucial that one make the distinction between agent and process. The processes are programs, they are mindless and do not "know" anything; the agents are other primitive entities in our model that can be viewed as spatial locations (a passive view) or as active entities that control a locus of information and interact with the global system by launching processes.

It also worth noticing that the ccp concept of local variables cannot faithfully model what we are calling local spaces, since in our spatial framework we can have inconsistent local stores without propagating their inconsistencies towards the global store.

In Section 3 we give a natural notion of observable behaviour for spatial/epistemic processes. Recursive processes are part of our framework, accordingly the notion of observable may involve limits of the spatial information in fair, possibly infinite, computations. These limits may result in infinite or, more precisely, *non-compact* objects involving unbounded nestings of spaces, or epistemic specifications such as *common knowledge*. We then provide a finitary characterization of these observables avoiding complex concepts such as fairness and limits. We also provide a compositional denotational characterization of the observable behaviour. Finally, in Section 4 we address the technical issue of giving *finite approximations* of non-compact information. (An extended version of this work is at http://www.lix.polytechnique.fr/~fvalenci/papers/eccp-extended.pdf.)

1 Space and Knowledge in Constraint Systems

In this section we introduce two new notions of constraint system for reasoning about distributed information and knowledge in ccp. We presuppose basic knowledge of domain theory and modal logic [1,22].

Flat Constraint Systems. The ccp model is parametric in a *constraint system (cs)* specifying the structure and interdependencies of the information that processes can ask of and add to a *central shared store*. This information is represented as assertions traditionally referred to as *constraints*. Following [8,21] we regard a cs as a complete algebraic lattice in which the ordering $\sqsubseteq$ is the reverse of an entailment relation: $c \sqsubseteq d$ means d *entails* c, i.e., d contains "more information" than c. The top element *false* represents inconsistency, the bottom element *true* is the empty constraint, and the *least upper bound* (lub) $\sqcup$ is the join of information. $\bigsqcup S$ is the lub of the elements in S.

Definition 1 (cs). *A* constraint system (cs) $\mathbf{C} = (Con, Con_0, \sqsubseteq, \sqcup, true, false)$ *is a complete algebraic lattice where* Con*, the set of constraints, is a partially ordered set wrt* $\sqsubseteq$*,* Con_0 *is the subset of* compact *elements of* Con*,* $\sqcup$ *is the lub operation defined on all subsets, and true, false are the least and greatest elements of* Con*, respectively.*

Remark 1. Recall that $\mathbf{C}$ is a *complete lattice* iff each subset of Con has a least upper bound in Con. Also $c \in Con$ is *compact (finite)* iff for any directed subset D of Con, $c \sqsubseteq \bigsqcup D$ implies $c \sqsubseteq d$ for some $d \in D$. $\mathbf{C}$ is *algebraic* iff for each $c \in Con$, the set of compact elements below it forms a directed set and the lub of this directed set is c.

Example 1. We briefly explain the *Herbrand* cs from [24,25]. This cs captures *syntactic* equality between terms $t, t', \ldots$ built from a first-order alphabet $\mathcal{L}$ with countably many variables $x, y, \ldots$, function symbols, and equality $=$. The constraints are sets of equalities over the terms of $\mathcal{L}$ (e.g., $\{x = t, y = t\}$ is a constraint). The relation $c \sqsubseteq d$ holds if the equalities in c follow from those in d (e.g., $\{x = y\} \sqsubseteq \{x = t, y = t\}$). The constraint *false* is the set of all term equalities in $\mathcal{L}$ and *true* is (the equivalence class of) the empty set. The compact elements are the (equivalence clases of) finite sets of equalities. The lub is (the equivalence class of) set union. (See [24,25] for full details).

Spatial Constraint Systems. A crucial issue in distributed and multi-agent scenarios is that agents may have their own space for their local information or for performing their computations. We shall address this issue by introducing a notion of space for agents. In our approach each agent i has a *space* $\mathfrak{s}_i$. We can then think of $\mathfrak{s}_i(c)$ as an assertion stating that c holds *within a space attributed to agent* i. Thus, given a store $s = \mathfrak{s}_i(c) \sqcup \mathfrak{s}_j(d) \sqcup e$ we may think of c and d as holding within the spaces that agents i and j have in s, respectively. Similarly, $\mathfrak{s}_i(\mathfrak{s}_j(c))$ can be viewed as a hierarchical spatial specification stating that c holds within the space the agent i attributes to agent j.

An n-agent *spatial constraint system (n-scs)* is a cs parametric in n structure-preserving constraint mappings $\mathfrak{s}_1, \ldots, \mathfrak{s}_n$ capturing the above intuitions.

Definition 2 (scs). *An n-agent* spatial constraint system (n-scs) $\mathbf{C}$ *is a cs equipped with n lub and bottom preserving maps* $\mathfrak{s}_1, \ldots, \mathfrak{s}_n$ *over its set of constraints Con. More precisely, each* $\mathfrak{s}_i : Con \to Con$ *must satisfy the following properties:* (S.1) $\mathfrak{s}_i(true) = true$*, and* (S.2) $\mathfrak{s}_i(c \sqcup d) = \mathfrak{s}_i(c) \sqcup \mathfrak{s}_i(d)$.

Henceforth, given an n-scs $\mathbf{C}$*, we refer to each* $\mathfrak{s}_i$ *as the* space *(function) of agent* i *in* $\mathbf{C}$*. We use* $(Con, Con_0, \sqsubseteq, \sqcup, true, false, \mathfrak{s}_1, \ldots, \mathfrak{s}_n)$ *to denote the corresponding*

n-scs with space functions $\mathfrak{s}_1, \ldots, \mathfrak{s}_n$. We shall simply write "scs" when n is unimportant. Intuitively, S.1 states that having an empty local store amounts to nothing and S.2 allows us to join pieces of information of agent i. From S.2 one can draw the immediate inference that space functions are monotone: Property S.3 below says that if c can be derived from d then any agent should be able to derive c from d within its own space.

Corollary 1. *Let $\mathbf{C}$ be an n-scs with space functions $\mathfrak{s}_1, \ldots, \mathfrak{s}_n$. Then for each $\mathfrak{s}_i$ the following property holds:* (S.3) *If $c \sqsubseteq d$ then $\mathfrak{s}_i(c) \sqsubseteq \mathfrak{s}_i(d)$.*

Inconsistency Confinement. In an scs nothing prevents us from having $\mathfrak{s}_i(\mathit{false}) \neq \mathit{false}$. Intuitively, inconsistencies generated by an agent may be confined within its own space. It is also possible to have $\mathfrak{s}_i(c) \sqcup \mathfrak{s}_j(d) \neq \mathit{false}$ even when $c \sqcup d = \mathit{false}$; i.e. we may have agents whose information is inconsistent with that of other agents. This reflects the distributive nature of the agents as they may have different information about the same incident. The following notions capture the above-mentioned situations.

Definition 3. *An n-scs $\mathbf{C} = (Con, Con_0, \sqsubseteq, \sqcup, \mathit{true}, \mathit{false}, \mathfrak{s}_1, \ldots, \mathfrak{s}_n)$ is said to be (i, j)* space-consistent *wrt (c, d) iff $\mathfrak{s}_i(c) \sqcup \mathfrak{s}_j(d) \neq \mathit{false}$. Also, $\mathbf{C}$ is said to be (i, j)* space-consistent *iff it is (i, j) space-consistent wrt to each $(c, d) \in Con \times Con$. Furthermore, $\mathbf{C}$ is space-consistent iff it is (i, j) space-consistent for all $i, j \in \{1, \ldots, n\}$.*

We will see an important class of logical structures characterized as space-consistent scs's in Applications (Section 1). From the next proposition we conclude that to check (i, j) space-consistency it is sufficient to verify whether $\mathfrak{s}_i(\mathit{false}) \sqcup \mathfrak{s}_j(\mathit{false}) \neq \mathit{false}$.

Proposition 1. *Let $\mathbf{C}$ be an n-scs with space functions $\mathfrak{s}_1, \ldots, \mathfrak{s}_n$. Then (1) $\mathbf{C}$ is (i, j) space-consistent if $\mathfrak{s}_i(\mathit{false}) \sqcup \mathfrak{s}_j(\mathit{false}) \neq \mathit{false}$ and (2) if $\mathbf{C}$ is (i, j) space-consistent then $\mathfrak{s}_i(\mathit{false}) \neq \mathit{false}$.*

Distinctness preservation. Analogous to inconsistency confinement, we could have $\mathfrak{s}_i(c) = \mathfrak{s}_i(d)$ for $c \neq d$. Depending on the intended model this could be interpreted as saying that agent i cannot distinguish c from d. For some applications, however, one may require the space functions to preserve distinctness

Definition 4. *An n-scs $\mathbf{C}$* preserves distinctness *iff all its space functions are injective.*

Shared and Global Information. We conclude by introducing a lub construction that captures the intuition that a given constraint holds in a shared space and globally.

Definition 5. *Let $\mathbf{C}$ be an n-scs with space functions $\mathfrak{s}_1, \ldots, \mathfrak{s}_n$.* Group-spaces *$\mathfrak{s}_G(\cdot)$ and* global information *$\mathfrak{g}_G(\cdot)$ of $G \subseteq \{1, \ldots, n\}$ are defined thus: $\mathfrak{s}_G(c) = \bigsqcup_{i \in G} \mathfrak{s}_i(c)$ and $\mathfrak{g}_G(c) = \bigsqcup_{j=0}^{\infty} \mathfrak{s}_G^j(c)$, where $\mathfrak{s}_G^0(c) = c$ and $\mathfrak{s}_G^{k+1}(c) = \mathfrak{s}_G(\mathfrak{s}_G^k(c))$.*

The constraint $\mathfrak{g}_G(c)$ is easily seen to entail c and $\mathfrak{s}_{i_1}(\mathfrak{s}_{i_2}(\ldots(\mathfrak{s}_{i_m}(c))\ldots))$ for any $\{i_1, \ldots, i_m\} \subseteq G$. Thus it realizes the intuition that c holds *globally* wrt G: c holds in each nested space involving only the agents in G.

Epistemic Constraint Systems. We now wish to use $\mathfrak{s}_i(c)$ to represent not only some information c that agent i has but rather a *fact* that he knows. In this case, (i, j)-space consistency wrt any pair of inconsistent information (Definition 3) would not be considered admissible. For in epistemic reasoning if an agent knows facts, those facts must be true, hence asserting that an agent i knows *false* or inconsistent information would be a fallacy. Thus, $\mathfrak{s}_i(\mathit{false}) = \mathit{false}$ and $\mathfrak{s}_i(c) \sqcup \mathfrak{s}_j(d) = \mathit{false}$ if $c \sqcup d = \mathit{false}$.

The domain theoretical nature of constraint systems allows for a rather simple and elegant characterization of knowledge by requiring our space functions to be *Kuratowski closure operators* [17]: i.e., lub and bottom preserving closure operators.

Definition 6 (n**-ecs).** *An n-agent* epistemic constraint system (n-ecs) $\mathbf{C}$ *is an n-scs whose space functions $\mathfrak{s}_1, \ldots, \mathfrak{s}_n$ are also* closure operators. *Thus, in addition to* S.1, S.2 *in Def. 2, each $\mathfrak{s}_i$ also satisfies:* (E.1) $c \sqsubseteq \mathfrak{s}_i(c)$ *and* (E.2) $\mathfrak{s}_i(\mathfrak{s}_i(c)) = \mathfrak{s}_i(c)$.

Intuitively, in an n-ecs, $\mathfrak{s}_i(c)$ states that the agent i has knowlege of c in its store $\mathfrak{s}_i$. The axiom E.1 says that if agent i knows c then c must hold, hence $\mathfrak{s}_i(c)$ has at least as much information as c. The epistemic principle that an agent i is aware of its own knowledge (the agent knows what he knows) is realized by E.2. Also the epistemic assumption that agents are idealized reasoners follows from S.3 in Corollary 1; for if c is a consequence of d ($c \sqsubseteq d$) then if d is known to agent i, so is c, $\mathfrak{s}_i(c) \sqsubseteq \mathfrak{s}_i(d)$.

Common Knowledge. Epistemic constructions such as "the agent i knows that agent j knows c" can be expressed as $\mathfrak{s}_i(\mathfrak{s}_j(c))$. The *group knowledge* of a fact c in a group of agents G happens when all the agents in G know c. This can be represented as $\mathfrak{s}_G(c)$ in Definition 5. Similarly, *common knowlege* of a fact c in a group G happens when all the agents in G know c, they all know that they know c, and so on ad infinitum. This can be captured by the lub construction $\mathfrak{g}_G(c)$ in Definition 5.

Remark 2. Consider an n-ecs $\mathbf{C}$ whose compact elements Con_0 are closed under the space functions: i.e., if $c \in Con_0$ the $\mathfrak{s}_i(c) \in Con_0$. Clearly Con_0 is closed under group knowledge $\mathfrak{s}_G(c)$ since G is finite. It is not necessarily closed under common knowledge $\mathfrak{g}_G(c)$ because, in general, $\bigsqcup_{j=1}^{\infty} \mathfrak{s}_G^j(c)$ cannot be finitely approximated. Nevertheless, in Applications (Section 1) we shall identify families of scs's where Con_0 is closed under common knowledge, and in Section 4 we address the issue of using suitable over-approximations of common knowledge.

The following proposition states two distinctive properties of ecs's: They are not space-consistent, as argued above, and those whose space function is not the identity do not preserve distinctness. We use *id* for the identity space function.

Proposition 2. *Let* $\mathbf{C}$ *be an n-ecs with space functions $\mathfrak{s}_1, \ldots, \mathfrak{s}_n$. For each $i, j \in \{1, \ldots, n\}$: (1)* $\mathbf{C}$ *is not (i, j)-space consistent, and (2) if $\mathfrak{s}_i \neq id$ then $\mathfrak{s}_i$ is not injective.*

Applications. We shall now illustrate important families of scs's. The families reveal meaningful connections between our scs's and models of knowledge and belief [11].

Aumann Constraint Systems. Aumann structures [11] are an alternative *event-based* approach to modelling knowledge. An Aumann structure is a tuple $\mathcal{A} = (S, \mathcal{P}_1, ..., \mathcal{P}_n)$ where S is a set of states and each $\mathcal{P}_i$ is a partition on S for agent i. We call these partitions *information sets.* If two states t and u are in the same information set for agent i, it means that in state t agent i considers state u possible, and vice versa. An *event* in an Aumann structure is any subset of S. Event e holds at state t if $t \in e$. The conjunction of two events is their intersection and knowledge operators are defined as $\mathsf{K}_i(e) = \{t \in S \mid \mathcal{P}_i(t) \subseteq e\}$ where $\mathcal{P}_i(t)$ denotes the set where t appears in $\mathcal{P}_i$.

We define the Aumann n-ecs $\mathbf{C}(\mathcal{A})$ as follows: The constraints are the events, i.e., $Con = \{e \mid e \text{ is an event in } \mathcal{A}\}$, $e_1 \sqsubseteq e_2$ iff $e_2 \subseteq e_1$, $\sqcup$ is the set intersection of two events, $true$ is the event containing every state in S, and *false* is the event containing no states. The space function for each agent i is given by $\mathfrak{s}_i(e) = \mathsf{K}_i(e)$. □

Theorem 1. *For any Aumann structure* $\mathcal{A} = (S, \mathcal{P}_1, ..., \mathcal{P}_n)$*,* $\mathbf{C}(\mathcal{A})$ *is an n-ecs.*

Aumann constraint systems are ecs's, thus they are not space-consistent (Proposition 2). We shall now identify a meaningful scs that is space-consistent.

Kripke Constraint Systems. A Kripke structure can be seen as a labeled transition system (LTS) where the labels represent agents and the transitions represent accessibility relations for the agents: if $s \xrightarrow{i} t$ then in state s, agent i considers t possible. An epistemic Kripke structure is an LTS where the transition relations are equivalences. In the following scs, the constraints are sets of *pointed Kripke structures*, i.e., sets of pairs (M, s) where M is a Kripke structure and s is a state of M.

Consider a set of Kripke structures $\mathfrak{M}$ over agents $\{1, ..., n\}$. Let $\Delta_{\mathfrak{M}}$ be the set $\{(M, t) \mid M \in \mathfrak{M} \text{ and } t \in St(M)\}$ where $St(M)$ denotes the set of states of M. Define an n-scs $\mathbf{C}(\Delta_{\mathfrak{M}})$ as follows: Let $Con = \mathcal{P}(\Delta_{\mathfrak{M}})$ and $c_1 \sqsubseteq c_2$ iff $c_2 \subseteq c_1$. This generates a complete algebraic lattice, where $c_1 \sqcup c_2$ is the set intersection of c_1 and c_2. The compact elements of the lattice are the cofinite sets, that is, if $\Delta_{\mathfrak{M}} \backslash c$ is a finite set, then c is a compact element in the lattice. Finally, define $\mathfrak{s}_i(c) = \{(M, t) \mid \forall t' \in St(M) \left[t \xrightarrow{i}_M t' \Longrightarrow (M, t') \in c\right]\}$– this definition is reminiscent of the semantics of the box modality in modal logic [22]. □

The following theorem gives us a taxonomy of scs's for the above construction.

Theorem 2. *For any non-empty set of Kripke structures* $\mathfrak{M}$ *over agents* $\{1, ..., n\}$*, (1)* $\mathbf{C}(\Delta_{\mathfrak{M}})$ *is an n-scs, (2) if* $\mathfrak{M}$ *is the set of all pointed Kripke structures,* $\mathbf{C}(\Delta_{\mathfrak{M}})$ *is a space-consistent n-scs, and (3) if* $\mathfrak{M}$ *is the set of all pointed Kripke structures whose accessibility relations are equivalences then* $\mathbf{C}(\Delta_{\mathfrak{M}})$ *is an n-ecs.*

Remark 3. Consider the modal formulae given by $\phi := p \mid \phi \wedge \phi \mid \Box_i \phi$, where p is a basic proposition, and the corresponding usual notion of satisfaction over Kripke models for propositions, conjunction and the box modality (see [22]). We abuse the notation and use a formula ϕ to denote the set of all pointed Kripke structures that satisfy ϕ. With the help of the above theorem, one can establish a correspondence between the n-scs satisfying the premise in (2) and the modal system K_n [11] in the sense that ϕ is above ϕ' in the lattice iff we can derive in K_n that ϕ implies ϕ' (written $\vdash_{K_N} \phi \Rightarrow \phi'$). Similarly, for the n-scs satisfying (3) and the epistemic system $S4_n$ [11].

We conclude by giving sufficient conditions for compactness of the constraints in $\mathbf{C}(\Delta_{\mathfrak{M}})$. The compact elements of $\mathbf{C}(\Delta_{\mathfrak{M}})$ are the cofinite subsets of $\Delta_{\mathfrak{M}}$. If $\Delta_{\mathfrak{M}}$ is a finite set (this occurs if $\mathfrak{M}$ is a finite set of finite state Kripke structures), then every subset of $\Delta_{\mathfrak{M}}$ is cofinite, and therefore each element of the lattice is compact, even $\mathfrak{g}_G(c)$ (Remark 2). Thus, if $\Delta_{\mathfrak{M}}$ is finite then each constraint in $\mathbf{C}(\Delta_{\mathfrak{M}})$ is compact.

2 Space and Knowledge in Processes

We now introduce two ccp variants: *spatial ccp (sccp)* and *epistemic ccp (eccp)*. The former is a conservative extension of ccp to model agents with spaces, possibly nested, in which they can store information and run processes. Its underlying cs is an scs. The latter extends the former with additional rules to model agents that interact by asking and computing knowledge within the spatial information distribution. Its underlying scs is an ecs. For semantic reasons, we require our scs be continuous and space-compact.

Definition 7. *An n-scs $\mathbf{C} = (Con, Con_0, \sqsubseteq, \sqcup, true, false, \mathfrak{s}_1, \ldots, \mathfrak{s}_n)$ is said to be* continuous *iff for every directed set $S \subseteq Con$ and every $\mathfrak{s}_i$, $\mathfrak{s}_i(\bigsqcup S) = \bigsqcup_{e \in S} \mathfrak{s}_i(e)$. Furthermore $\mathbf{C}$ is said to be* space-compact *iff for every $\mathfrak{s}_i$, $\mathfrak{s}_i(c) \in Con_0$ if $c \in Con_0$.*

Our examples (Applications, Section 1) can be shown to be continuous. Aumann ecs's are space-compact under the additional condition that every set in each partition is finite. A Kripke scs is space-compact if the inverse of the accessibility relation is finitely-branching. In the special case of Kripke ecs's this is the same as requiring each agent's accessibility relation to be finitely-branching since these relations are reflexive.

Syntax. The following syntax of processes will be common to both calculi. [1]

Definition 8. *Let $\mathbf{C} = (Con, Con_0, \sqsubseteq, \sqcup, true, false, \mathfrak{s}_1, \ldots, \mathfrak{s}_n)$ be a continuous and space compact n-scs. Let $A = \{1, ..., n\}$ be the set of agents. Assume a countable set of variables $Vars = \{X, Y, \ldots\}$. The terms are given by the following syntax:*

$$P, Q \ldots ::= \mathbf{0} \mid \mathbf{tell}(c) \mid \mathbf{ask}(c) \rightarrow P \mid P \parallel Q \mid [P]_i \mid X \mid \mu X.P$$

where $c \in Con_0$, $i \in A$, and $X \in Vars$. A term T is said to be closed iff every variable X in T occurs in the scope of an expression $\mu X.P$. We shall refer to closed terms as processes *and use Proc to denote the corresponding set.*

Before giving semantics to our processes, we give some intuitions about their behaviour. The *basic processes* are tell, ask, and parallel composition and they are defined as in standard ccp [25]. Intuitively, $\mathbf{tell}(c)$ in a store d adds c to d to make c available to other processes with access to this store. This addition, represented as $d \sqcup c$, is performed whether or not $d \sqcup c = false$. The process $\mathbf{ask}(c) \rightarrow P$ in a store e may execute P if c is entailed by e, i.e., $c \sqsubseteq e$. The process $P \parallel Q$ stands for the *parallel execution* of P and Q. The following example will be referred to throughout the paper.

Example 2. Let us take $P = \mathbf{tell}(c)$ and $Q = \mathbf{ask}(c) \rightarrow \mathbf{tell}(d)$. From the above intuitions, it follows that in $P \parallel Q$ both c and d will be added to the store.

[1] For the sake of space and clarity, we dispense with the local/hiding operator.

Spatial Processes. Our spatial ccp variant can be thought of as a *shared-spaces* model of computation. Each agent $i \in A$ may have computational spaces of the form $[\cdot]_i$ where processes as well as other agents' spaces may reside. It also has a space function $\mathfrak{s}_i$ representing the information stored in its spaces. Recall that $\mathfrak{s}_i(c)$ states that c holds in the space of agent i. Similarly, $\mathfrak{s}_i(\mathfrak{s}_j(c))$ means that c holds in the store that agent j has within the space of agent i. Unlike any other ccp calculus, it is possible to have agents with inconsistent information since $c \sqcup d = \mathit{false}$ does not necessarily imply $\mathfrak{s}_i(c) \sqcup \mathfrak{s}_j(d) = \mathit{false}$ (see space-consistent ecs in Definition 3).

The spatial construction $[P]_i$ represents a process P running within the space of agent i. Any information c that P produces is available to processes that lie within the same space. We shall use $[P]_G$, where $G \subseteq A$, as an abbreviation of $\|_{i \in G} [P]_i$.

Example 3. Consider $[P]_i \parallel [Q]_i$ with P and Q as in Ex. 2. From the above intuitions it follows that both c and d will be added to store of agent i, i.e., we will have $\mathfrak{s}_i(c) \sqcup \mathfrak{s}_i(d)$. Similarly, $[P \parallel Q]_i$ will produce $c \sqcup d$ in the store of agent i, i.e., $\mathfrak{s}_i(c \sqcup d)$ which from the scs axioms is equivalent to $\mathfrak{s}_i(c) \sqcup \mathfrak{s}_i(d)$. In fact, we will equate the behaviour of $[P]_i \parallel [Q]_i$ with that of $[P \parallel Q]_i$. In $[P]_j \parallel [Q]_i$ for $i \neq j$, d will not necessarily be added to the space of i because c is not made available for agent i. Also in $P \parallel [Q]_i$, d is not added to the the space of i. In this case, however, we may view the c told by P as being available at an outermost space that *does not belong to any agent.* This does not mean that c holds everywhere, i.e., *globally* (Def. 5). Finally, consider $[P]_{\{i,j\}} \parallel [[Q]_i]_j$. Here d will not necessarily be added to the space agent i has within the space of agent j because in an scs although $\mathfrak{s}_i(c)$ and $\mathfrak{s}_j(c)$ hold, $\mathfrak{s}_j(\mathfrak{s}_i(c))$ may not hold.

Epistemic Processes. For our epistemic ccp variant, we shall further require that the underlying scs be epistemic, i.e., an ecs. This gives the operator $[P]_i$ additional behaviour. From an epistemic point of view, the information c produced by P not only becomes available to agent i, as in the spatial case, but also it becomes a *fact.* This does not necessarily mean, of course, that c will be available everywhere, as there are facts that some agents may not know. It does mean, however, that unlike the spatial case, we cannot allow agents' spaces to include inconsistent information, as facts *cannot be contradictory*–in an ecs, $c \sqcup d = \mathit{false}$ implies $\mathfrak{s}_i(c) \sqcup \mathfrak{s}_j(d) = \mathit{false}$.

Operationally, $[P]_i$ causes any information c produced by P to become available not only in the space of agent i but also in any space in which $[P]_i$ is included. This is because epistemically $\mathfrak{s}_i(c) = c \sqcup \mathfrak{s}_i(c)$ so if $\mathfrak{s}_j(\mathfrak{s}_i(c))$ holds, then $\mathfrak{s}_j(c \sqcup \mathfrak{s}_i(c))$ also holds, and similarly $c \sqcup \mathfrak{s}_j(c \sqcup \mathfrak{s}_i(c))$. This can be viewed as saying that c propagates outward in space.

Example 4. Consider $[Q \parallel [P]_i]_j$ with P and Q as in Example 2. Notice that from executing P we obtain $\mathfrak{s}_j(\mathfrak{s}_i(c))$. In the spatial case, Q will not necessarily tell d because in an scs, $\mathfrak{s}_j(\mathfrak{s}_i(c))$ may not entail $\mathfrak{s}_j(c)$. On the other hand, in the epistemic case, Q will tell d since in any ecs, $\mathfrak{s}_j(\mathfrak{s}_i(c)) = \mathfrak{s}_j(c \sqcup \mathfrak{s}_i(c))$ which entails $\mathfrak{s}_j(c)$.

Infinite Processes. Unbounded behaviour is specified using recursive definitions of the form $\mu X.P$ whose behaviour is that of $P[\mu X.P/X]$, i.e., P with every free occurrence of X replaced with $\mu X.P$. We assume that recursion is *ask guarded*: i.e., for every

Table 1. Rules for sccp and eccp (see Convention 1). The projection c^i is given in Definition 9. The symmetric right rule for PL, PR, is omitted. Rule E only applies to eccp.

$$\mathbf{T}\ \langle \mathbf{tell}(c), d\rangle \longrightarrow \langle \mathbf{0}, d \sqcup c\rangle \qquad \mathbf{A}\ \frac{c \sqsubseteq d}{\langle \mathbf{ask}\ (c)\ \rightarrow\ P, d\rangle \longrightarrow \langle P, d\rangle} \qquad \mathbf{PL}\ \frac{\langle P, d\rangle \longrightarrow \langle P', d'\rangle}{\langle P \parallel Q, d\rangle \longrightarrow \langle P' \parallel Q, d'\rangle}$$

$$\mathbf{R}\ \frac{\langle P[\mu X.P/X], d\rangle \longrightarrow \gamma}{\langle \mu X.P, d\rangle \longrightarrow \gamma} \qquad \mathbf{S}\ \frac{\langle P, c^i\rangle \longrightarrow \langle P', c'\rangle}{\langle [P]_i, c\rangle \longrightarrow \langle [P']_i, c \sqcup \mathfrak{s}_i(c')\rangle} \qquad \mathbf{E}\ \frac{\langle P, c\rangle \longrightarrow \langle P', c'\rangle}{\langle [P]_i, c\rangle \longrightarrow \langle [P]_i \parallel P', c'\rangle}$$

$\mu X.P$, each occurrence of X in P occurs under the scope of an ask process. For simplicity we assume an implicit "**ask**$(true) \rightarrow$" in unguarded occurrences of X.

Recursive definitions allow us to define complex spatial and epistemic situations. Given $G \subseteq A$ and a basic process P we define $global(G, P) \stackrel{\text{def}}{=} P \parallel \mu X. [P \parallel X]_G$. Intuitively, in $global(G, P)$ any information c produced by P will be available at any space or any nesting of spaces involving only the agents in G. Consider the process $global(G, P) \parallel \left[[\ldots [Q]_{k_m} \cdots]_{k_2}\right]_{k_1}$ where $G = \{k_1, ..., k_m\} \subseteq A$, with P and Q as in Example 2. The process $global(G, P)$ eventually makes c available in the (nested) space $\left[[\ldots [\cdot]_{k_m} \cdots]_{k_2}\right]_{k_1}$ and thus Q will tell d in that space.

Spatial and Epistemic Reduction Semantics. We now define a structural operational semantics (sos) for sccp and eccp. We begin with the sos for the spatial case. The sos for the epistemic case extends the spatial one with an additional rule and the assumption that the underlying scs is an ecs. Henceforth we shall use the following convention:

Convention 1. *The relations in following sections assume an underlying continuous and space-compact n-scs* $\mathbf{C} = (Con, Con_0, \sqsubseteq, \sqcup, true, false, \mathfrak{s}_1, \ldots, \mathfrak{s}_n)$. *We sometimes index them with "s" if they are interpreted for sccp, and with "e" if they are interpreted for eccp. We often omit the indexes when they are irrelevant or obvious.*

A configuration is a pair $\langle P, c\rangle \in Proc \times Con$ where c represents the current *spatial distribution* of information in P. We use $Conf$ with typical elements $\gamma, \gamma', \ldots$ to denote the set of configurations. The sos for sccp is given by means of the transition relation between configurations $\longrightarrow_{\mathtt{s}} \subseteq Conf \times Conf$ obtained by replacing $\longrightarrow$ with $\longrightarrow_{\mathtt{s}}$ in the rules A, T, PL (and its symmetric version), R, and S in Table 1.

The rules A, T, PL, and R for the basic processes and recursion are standard in ccp and they are easily seen to realize the above intuitions (see [25]). The rule S for the new spatial operator is more involved and we explain it next. First we introduce the following central notion defining the projection of a spatial constraint c for agent i.

Definition 9 (Views). *The agent i's* view *of c, c^i, is given by* $c^i = \bigsqcup\{d \mid \mathfrak{s}_i(d) \sqsubseteq c\}$.

Intuitively, c^i represents all the information the agent i may see or have in c. For example if $c = \mathfrak{s}_i(d) \sqcup \mathfrak{s}_j(e)$ then agent i sees d, so $d \sqsubseteq c^i$. Observe that if $\mathfrak{s}_i(d) = \mathfrak{s}_i(d')$ then $(\mathfrak{s}_i(d))^i$ entails both d and d'. This is intended because $\mathfrak{s}_i(d) = \mathfrak{s}_i(d')$ means that agent i cannot distinguish d from d'. The constraint c^i enjoys the following property which will be useful later on.

Lemma 1. *For any constraint* c, $c \sqcup \mathfrak{s}_i(c^i) = c$.

Let us now describe the rule S for the spatial operator. First, in order for $[P]_i$ with store c to make a reduction, the information agent i sees or has in c must allow P to make the reduction. Hence we run P with store c^i. Second, the information d that P's reduction would add to c^i is what $[P]_i$ adds to the space of agent i as stated in Proposition 3 below.

Proposition 3. *If* $\langle P, c^i\rangle \rightarrow \langle P', c^i \sqcup d\rangle$ *then* $\langle [P]_i, c\rangle \rightarrow \langle [P']_i, c \sqcup \mathfrak{s}_i(d)\rangle$.

Next we show an instructive reduction involving the use of the S rule.

Example 5. Take $R = [P]_i \parallel [Q]_i$ with P and Q as in Example 2. One can verify that $\langle R, \mathit{true}\rangle \longrightarrow \langle [\mathbf{0}]_i \parallel [Q]_i, \mathfrak{s}_i(c)\rangle \longrightarrow \langle [\mathbf{0}]_i \parallel [\mathbf{0}]_i, \mathfrak{s}_i(c) \sqcup \mathfrak{s}_i(d)\rangle$. Recall that $\mathfrak{s}_i(c) \sqcup \mathfrak{s}_i(d) = \mathfrak{s}_i(c \sqcup d)$. A more interesting example is $T = [\mathbf{tell}(c')]_i \parallel [Q]_i$ under the assumption that $\mathfrak{s}_i(c) = \mathfrak{s}_i(c')$. We have $\langle T, \mathit{true}\rangle \longrightarrow \langle [\mathbf{0}]_i \parallel [Q]_i, \mathfrak{s}_i(c')\rangle \longrightarrow \langle [\mathbf{0}]_i \parallel [\mathbf{0}]_i, \mathfrak{s}_i(c') \sqcup \mathfrak{s}_i(d)\rangle$. d is told by Q within the space of i because $\mathfrak{s}_i(c) = \mathfrak{s}_i(c')$, so c and c' are regarded as equivalent by i.

Epistemic Semantics. The eccp sos assumes that the underlying scs is an ecs. As explained earlier given $[P]_i$, the information c produced by P not only becomes available to agent i but also becomes a *fact* within the hierarchy of spaces in which $[P]_i$ is included. This means that c is available not only in the space of agent i but also in any space in which $[P]_i$ is included. We can view this as saying that c propagates *outwards* through the spaces $[P]_i$ is in and this is partly realized by the equation $\mathfrak{s}_i(c) = c \sqcup \mathfrak{s}_i(c)$ which follows from E.1 in ecs (Definition 6). Mirroring this constraint equation and epistemic reasoning, the behaviour of $[P]_i$ and $P \parallel [P]_i$ must also be equated (since P can only produce factual information). This makes $[P]_i$ reminiscent of the replication/bang operator in the π-calculus [19]. For eccp we include Rule E in Table 1. As illustrated in Example 6, Rule E is necessary for the behaviour of $[P]_i$ and $P \parallel [P]_i$ to be the same, corresponding to the epistemic principles we wish to mimic.

The sos of eccp is given by the transition relation between configurations $\longrightarrow_{\mathsf{e}} \subseteq \mathit{Conf} \times \mathit{Conf}$ obtained by replacing $\longrightarrow$ with $\longrightarrow_{\mathsf{e}}$ in the rules in Table 1 and assuming the underlying scs to be an ecs.

Example 6. Let $R = [P \parallel [Q]_i]_j$ and $T = [P \parallel [Q]_i \parallel Q]_j$ with P and Q as in Example 2. We wish to equate R and T to mimic epistemic principles. Even assuming an ecs, with only the rules of sccp (i.e., without Rule E), T can produce $\mathfrak{s}_j(d)$, d in the store of agent j, but R is not necessarily able to do this: One can verify that there are T', e' s.t. $\langle T, \mathit{true}\rangle \longrightarrow_{\mathsf{s}}^{*} \langle T', e'\rangle$ and $\mathfrak{s}_j(d) \sqsubseteq e'$, while, in general, for all R', e'' s.t., $\langle R, \mathit{true}\rangle \longrightarrow_{\mathsf{s}}^{*} \langle R', e''\rangle$ we have $\mathfrak{s}_j(d) \not\sqsubseteq e''$. With the rules of eccp, however, one can verify for each e' s.t. $\langle T, \mathit{true}\rangle \longrightarrow_{\mathsf{e}}^{*} \langle T', e'\rangle$ there exists e'', $\langle R, \mathit{true}\rangle \longrightarrow_{\mathsf{e}}^{*} \langle R', e''\rangle$ such that $e' \sqsubseteq e''$ (and vice-versa with the roles of R and T interchanged).

3 Observable Behaviour of Space and Knowledge

A standard notion of observable behaviour in ccp involves infinite fair computations and information constructed as the limit of finite approximations. For our calculi, however, these limits may result in infinite (or non-compact) objects involving arbitrary nesting of spaces, or epistemic specifications such as common knowledge. In this section we provide techniques useful for analyzing the observable behaviour of such processes using simpler finitary concepts and compositional reasoning.[2]

The notion of *fairness* is central to the definition of observational equivalence for ccp. We introduce this notion following [12]. Any derivation of a transition involves an application of Rule A or Rule T. We say that P is *active* in a transition $t = \gamma \longrightarrow \gamma'$ if there exists a derivation of t where rule A or T is used to produce a transition of the form $\langle P, d\rangle \longrightarrow \gamma''$. Moreover, we say that P is *enabled* in γ if there exists γ' such that P is active in $\gamma \longrightarrow \gamma'$. A computation $\gamma_0 \longrightarrow \gamma_1 \longrightarrow \gamma_2 \longrightarrow \dots$ is said to be *fair* if for each process enabled in some γ_i there exists $j \geq i$ such that the process is active in γ_j.

Observing Limits. A standard notion of observables for ccp is the *results* computed by a process for a given initial store. The result of a computation is defined as the least upper bound of all the stores occurring in the computation, which, thanks to the monotonic properties of our calculi, form an increasing chain. More formally, given a finite or infinite computation ξ of the form $\langle Q_0, d_0\rangle \longrightarrow \langle Q_1, d_1\rangle \longrightarrow \langle Q_2, d_2\rangle \longrightarrow \dots$ the result of ξ, denoted by $\mathit{Result}(\xi)$, is the constraint $\bigsqcup_i d_i$. In our calculi all fair computations from a configuration have the same result: Let γ be a configuration and let ξ_1 and ξ_2 be two computations of γ. We can show that if ξ_1 and ξ_2 are fair, then $\mathit{Result}(\xi_1) = \mathit{Result}(\xi_2)$. We can then set $\mathit{Result}(\gamma) \stackrel{\text{def}}{=} \mathit{Result}(\xi)$ for any fair computation ξ of γ.

Definition 10. (Observational equivalence) *Let $\mathcal{O} : \mathit{Proc} \rightarrow \mathit{Con}_0 \rightarrow \mathit{Con}$ be given by $\mathcal{O}(P)(d) = \mathit{Result}(\langle P, d\rangle)$. We say that P and Q are observationally equivalent, written $P \sim_o Q$, iff $\mathcal{O}(P) = \mathcal{O}(Q)$.*

Example 7. The observation we make of the recursive process $\mathit{global}(G, \mathbf{tell}(c))$ on input true is the limit $\mathfrak{g}_G(c)$ (Definition 5). I.e., $\mathcal{O}(\mathit{global}(G, \mathbf{tell}(c)))(\mathit{true}) = \mathfrak{g}_G(c)$.

The relation $\sim_o$ can be shown to be a congruence, i.e., it is preserved under arbitrary contexts. Recall that a context C is a term with a hole $\bullet$, so that replacing it with a process P yields a process term $C(P)$. E.g., if $C = [\bullet]_i$ then $C(\mathbf{tell}(d)) = [\mathbf{tell}(d)]_i$.

Theorem 3. *$P \sim_o Q$ iff for every context C, $C(P) \sim_o C(Q)$.*

Observing Barbs. In the next section we shall show that the above notion of observation has pleasant and useful closure properties like those of basic ccp. Some readers, however, may feel uneasy with observable behaviour involving notions such as *infinite fair* computations and limits, i.e., possibly *infinite* (or non-compact) elements. Nevertheless, we can give a finitary characterization of behavioral equivalence for our calculi, involving only finite computations and compact elements.

[2] See Convention 1.

A barb is an element of Con_0, i.e., a compact element. We say that $\gamma = \langle P, d\rangle$ *satisfies* the barb c, written $\gamma \downarrow_c$, iff $c \sqsubseteq d$; γ *weakly satisfies* the barb c, written $\gamma \Downarrow_c$, iff there is γ' s.t. $\gamma \longrightarrow^* \gamma'$ and $\gamma' \downarrow_c$. E.g., $\langle \mathbf{tell}(c) \parallel \mathbf{ask}\, c \rightarrow [\mathbf{tell}(d)]_i, \mathit{true}\rangle \Downarrow_{\mathfrak{s}_i(d)}$.

Definition 11. *P and Q are* barb equivalent, *written $P \sim_b Q$, iff $\forall d \in Con_0$, $\langle P, d\rangle$ and $\langle Q, d\rangle$ weakly satisfy the same barbs.*

We now establish the correspondence between our process equivalences. First we recall some facts from domain theory central to our proof of the correspondence. Two (possibly infinite) chains $d_0 \sqsubseteq d_1 \sqsubseteq \cdots \sqsubseteq d_n \sqsubseteq \ldots$ and $e_0 \sqsubseteq e_1 \sqsubseteq \cdots \sqsubseteq e_n \sqsubseteq \ldots$ are said to be *cofinal* if for all d_i there exists an e_j such that $d_i \sqsubseteq e_j$ and vice versa.

Lemma 2. *Let $d_0 \sqsubseteq d_1 \sqsubseteq \cdots \sqsubseteq d_n \sqsubseteq \ldots$ and $e_0 \sqsubseteq e_1 \sqsubseteq \cdots \sqsubseteq e_n \sqsubseteq \ldots$ be two chains. (1) If they are cofinal, then they have the same limit, i.e., $\bigsqcup d_i = \bigsqcup e_i$. (2) If all elements of both chains are* compact *and $\bigsqcup d_i = \bigsqcup e_i$, then the two chains are cofinal.*

The proof of the correspondence shows that the stores of any pair of *fair* computations of equivalent processes form pairs of cofinal chains. It also uses a relation between weak barbs and fair computations: Let $\langle P_0, d_0\rangle \longrightarrow \langle P_1, d_1\rangle \longrightarrow \ldots \longrightarrow \langle P_n, d_n\rangle \longrightarrow \ldots$ be a fair computation. We can show that if $\langle P_0, d_0\rangle \Downarrow_c$ then there exists a store d_i s.t., $c \sqsubseteq d_i$. With these observations we can show that two processes are not observationally equivalent on a given input iff there is a compact element that tells them apart.

Theorem 4. $\sim_o \; = \sim_b$.

Denotational Semantics. Here we define a denotational characterization of observable behaviour that allows us to reason compositionally about our spatial/epistemic processes. First we can show that the behaviour of a process P, $\mathcal{O}(P)$, is a closure operator on $\sqsubseteq$. The importance of $\mathcal{O}(P)$ being a closure operator on $\sqsubseteq$ is that it is fully determined by its fixed points $\mathit{fix}(\mathcal{O}(P)) = \{d \mid \mathcal{O}(P)(d) = d\}$. More precisely, $\mathcal{O}(P)(c) = \bigsqcup\{d \in Con \mid c \sqsubseteq d \text{ and } d \in \mathit{fix}(\mathcal{O}(P))\}$. Therefore,

Corollary 2. $\mathcal{O}(P) = \mathcal{O}(Q)$ *iff* $\mathit{fix}(\mathcal{O}(P)) = \mathit{fix}(\mathcal{O}(Q))$.

We now give a compositional denotational semantics $[\![P]\!]$ that captures exactly the set of fixed points of $\mathcal{O}(P)$. More precisely, let I be an assignment function from Var, the set of process variables, to $\mathcal{P}(Con)$. Given a term T, $[\![T]\!]_I$ is meant to capture the fixed points of T under the assignment I. Notice that if T is a process P, i.e., a closed term, the assignment is irrelevant so we simply write $[\![P]\!]$. The denotation for processes in sccp is given by the equations DX, D0, DT, DA, DP and DS in Table 2. The denotation for the processes in eccp is given by the same rules except that the rule DS is replaced with the rule DE in Table 2.

The denotations of the basic operators are the same as in standard ccp [25] and are given by equations D0, DT, DA and DP. E.g., DA says that the set of fixed points of $\mathbf{ask}\, c \rightarrow P$ are those d that do not entail c or that if they do entail c then they are fixed points of P. The denotation of a term X under I is $I(X)$ (see DX). The equation DR for $\mu X.P$ follows from the Knaster-Tarski theorem in the complete lattice $(\mathcal{P}(Con), \subseteq)$.

Table 2. Denotational Equations for sccp and eccp. $I : Var \to \mathcal{P}(Con)$.

DX $[\![X]\!]_I = I(X)$ **DP** $[\![P \parallel Q]\!]_I = [\![P]\!]_I \cap [\![Q]\!]_I$ **D0** $[\![0]\!]_I = \{d \mid d \in Con\}$
DT $[\![\mathbf{tell}(c)]\!]_I = \{d \mid c \sqsubseteq d\}$ **DA** $[\![\mathbf{ask}(c) \to P]\!]_I = \{d \mid c \sqsubseteq d \text{ and } d \in [\![P]\!]_I\} \cup \{d \mid c \not\sqsubseteq d\}$
DR $[\![\mu X.P]\!]_I = \bigcap\{S \subseteq \mathcal{P}(Con) \mid [\![P]\!]_{I[X:=S]} \subseteq S\}$
DS $[\![[P]_i]\!]_I = \{d \mid d^i \in [\![P]\!]_I\}$ (for sccp) **DE** $[\![[P]_i]\!]_I = \{d \mid d^i \in [\![P]\!]_I\} \cap [\![P]\!]_I$ (for eccp)

The denotation of $[P]_i$ in the spatial case is given by equation DS. It says that d is a fixed point for $[P]_i$ if $d^i \in [\![P]\!]$. Recall that d^i is i's view of d, so if $d^i \in [\![P]\!]$, then i's view of d is a fixed point for P. In the operational semantics, the S rule is the only applicable rule for this case. We can use Lemma 1, which says that $d = d \sqcup \mathfrak{s}_i(d^i)$, to prove that if d^i is a fixed point for P then d is a fixed point for $[P]_i$.

The denotation of $[P]_i$ in the epistemic case is given by DE instead of DS. It says that d is a fixed point for $[P]_i$ if $d^i \in [\![P]\!]$, as in the spatial case, and d is fixed point of P. The additional requirement follows from the operational semantics rule E which it amounts to run $[P]_i$ in parallel with (an evolution of) P.

From the above observations we can show that in fact $[\![P]\!] = \mathit{fix}(\mathcal{O}(P))$. Hence, from Corollary 2 we obtain a compositional characterization of observational equivalence, and thus from Theorem 4 also for barb equivalence.

Theorem 5. *$P \sim_o Q$ iff $[\![P]\!] = [\![Q]\!]$.*

4 Compact Approximation of Space and Knowledge

An important semantic property of global information/common knowledge $\mathfrak{g}_G(c)$ (Definition 5) in the underlying scs is that it preserves the *continuity* of the space functions. I.e., one can verify that $\mathfrak{g}_G(\bigsqcup D) = \bigsqcup_{d \in D} \mathfrak{g}_G(d)$ for any directed set $D \subseteq Con$.

In contrast $\mathfrak{g}_G(c)$ does not preserve the *compactness* of the space functions (Remark 2). This means that, although, the limit of infinite computation may produce $\mathfrak{g}_G(c)$, we cannot have a process that refers directly to $\mathfrak{g}_G(c)$ since processes can only ask and tell compact elements. The reason for this syntactic restriction is illustrated below:

Example 8. Suppose we had a process $P = \mathbf{ask}\ \mathfrak{g}_G(c) \to \mathbf{tell}(d)$ asking whether group G has common knowledge of c and if so posting d. Note that $\mathcal{O}(P)(\mathit{true}) = \mathit{true}$ and $\mathcal{O}(P)(\mathfrak{g}_G(c)) = \mathfrak{g}_G(c) \sqcup d$. Now for $Q = \mathit{global}(G, \mathbf{tell}(c))$ we have $\mathcal{O}(Q)(\mathit{true}) = \mathfrak{g}_G(c)$. But one can verify that $\mathcal{O}(P \parallel Q)(\mathit{true}) = \mathfrak{g}_G(c)$, and thus $\mathcal{O}(P \parallel Q)(\mathcal{O}(P \parallel Q)(\mathit{true})) = \mathcal{O}(P \parallel Q)(\mathfrak{g}_G(c)) = \mathfrak{g}_G(c) \sqcup d$. This would mean that the observation function is not idempotent, contradicting the fact that $\mathcal{O}(P)$ is a closure operator, a crucial property for full abstraction of our denotational semantics.

Nevertheless, asking and telling information of the form $\mathfrak{g}_G(c)$ could be useful in certain protocols to state in one computational step, rather than computing as a limit, common knowledge or global information about certain states of affairs c (e.g., mutual agreement). To address this issue we extend the underlying scs with *compact elements* of the form $\mathfrak{a}_G(c)$ which can be thought of as (over-)approximations of $\mathfrak{g}_G(c)$. The approximation $\mathfrak{a}_G(c)$ can then be used in our processes to simulate the use of $\mathfrak{g}_G(c)$. We refer to $\mathfrak{a}_G(c)$ as a *announcement* of c for the group G to convey the meaning that $\mathfrak{g}_G(c)$ is attained in one step as in a public announcement. We can only define the announcements over a finite subset of compact elements S, since an infinite set would conflict with the continuity $\mathfrak{a}_G(\cdot)$. We only consider announcements for the entire set of agents A (for arbitrary groups the construction follows easily). The above-mentioned extension of an scs $\mathbf{C}^1$ into an scs $\mathbf{C}^2(S)$ with announcement over S is given below:

Definition 12. *Let* $\mathbf{C}^1 = (Con^1, Con_0^1, \sqsubseteq_1, \mathfrak{s}_1^1, \ldots, \mathfrak{s}_n^1)$ *be an scs over agents* $A = \{1, \ldots, n\}$. *For* $S \subseteq_{fin} Con_0^1$, *define lattice* $\mathbf{C}^2(S) = (Con^2, Con_0^2, \sqsubseteq_2, \mathfrak{s}_1^2, \ldots, \mathfrak{s}_n^2)$ *as follows. The set* Con^2 *is given by two rules: (1)* $Con^1 \subseteq Con^2$, *and (2) for any finite nonempty indexing set* I, *if* $c_i \in S$ *for all* $i \in I$ *then* $\mathfrak{a}_A(\bigsqcup_{i \in I} c) \in Con^2$. *The ordering* $\sqsubseteq_2$ *is given by the following rules: (1)* $\sqsubseteq_1 \subseteq \sqsubseteq_2$, *(2)* $d \sqsubseteq_2 \mathfrak{a}_A(\bigsqcup_{i \in I} c_i)$ *if* $d \in Con^1$ *and* $d \sqsubseteq_1 \mathfrak{g}_A(\bigsqcup_{i \in I} c_i)$, *and (3)* $\mathfrak{a}_A(\bigsqcup_{i \in I} c_i) \sqsubseteq_2 \mathfrak{a}_A(\bigsqcup_{j \in J} c_j)$ *if* $\mathfrak{g}_A(\bigsqcup_{i \in I} c_i) \sqsubseteq_1 \mathfrak{g}_A(\bigsqcup_{j \in J} c_j)$. *Furthermore, for all* $i \in A$, *for any* $\mathfrak{a}_A(d) \in Con^2$, $\mathfrak{s}_i^2(\mathfrak{a}_A(d)) = \mathfrak{a}_A(d)$ *and for each* $e \in Con^1$, $\mathfrak{s}_i^2(e) = \mathfrak{s}_i^1(e)$.

The next theorem states the correctness of the above construction. Intuitively, the lattice $\mathbf{C}^2(S)$ above must be an scs and the announcement of a certain fact in $c \in S$ must behave similarly to common knowledge or global information of the same fact.

Theorem 6. *Let* $\mathbf{C}^1 = (Con^1, Con_0^1, \sqsubseteq_1, \ldots)$ *be a continuous space-compact n-scs (n-ecs) and let* $S \subseteq_{fin} Con_0^1$. *Let* $\mathbf{C}^2(S) = (Con^2, Con_0^2, \sqsubseteq_2, \ldots)$ *as in Def. 12, then (1)* $\mathbf{C}^2(S)$ *is a continuous, space-compact n-scs (n-ecs), (2)* $\forall \mathfrak{a}_A(c) \in Con^2$, $\mathfrak{a}_A(c) \in Con_0^2$, *and (3)* $\forall d \in Con^1$, $\forall \mathfrak{a}_A(c) \in Con^2$, $d \sqsubseteq_2 \mathfrak{a}_A(c)$ *iff* $d \sqsubseteq_1 \mathfrak{g}_A(c)$.

Related Work. There is a huge volume of work on epistemic logic and its applications to distributed systems; [11] gives a good summary of the subject. This work is all aimed at analyzing distributed protocols using epistemic logic as a reasoning tool. While it has been very influential in setting the stage for the present work it is not closely connected to the present proposal to put epistemic concepts into the programming formalism.

Epistemic logic for process calculi has been discussed in [7,9,14]. In all of these works, however, the epistemic logic is defined outside of the process calculus, with the processes as models for the logic, whereas our processes have epistemic (or spatial) logic terms within the constraint system, as well as knowledge or space constructions on the processes.

The issue of extending ccp to provide for distributed information has been previously addressed in [23]. In [23] processes can send constraints using communication channels much like in the π-calculus. This induces a distribution of information among the processes in the system. This extension, however, is not conservative wrt to ccp and hence does not share the goal of the present paper.

Another closely related work is the Ambient calculus [6], an important calculus for spatial mobility. Ambient allows the specification of processes that can move in and out within their spatial hierarchy. It does not, however, address posting and querying epistemic information within a spatial distribution of processes. Adding Ambient-like mobility to our calculi is a natural research direction.

One very interesting approach related to ours in spirit – but not in conception or details – is the spatial logic of Caires and Cardelli [4,5]. In this work they also take spatial location as the fundamental concept and develop modalities that reflect locativity. Rather than using modal logic, they use the name quantifier which has been actively studied in the theory of freshness of names in programming languages. Their language is better adapted to the calculi for mobility where names play a fundamental role. In effect, the concept of freshness of a name is exploited to control the flow of information. It would be interesting to see how a name quantified scs would look and to study the relationship with the Caires-Cardelli framework.

Finally, the process calculi in [2,3,10] provide for the use of assertions within π-like processes. They are not concerned with spatial distribution of information and knowledge. These frameworks are very generic and offer several reasoning techniques. Therefore, it would be interesting to see how the ideas here developed can be adapted to them.

Acknowledgments. We thank Raluca Diaconu for her insights and discussions on some preliminary ideas of this work. This work has been partially supported by the project ANR-09-BLAN-0169-01 PANDA and European project MEALS.

References

1. Abramsky, S., Jung, A.: Domain theory. In: Maibaum, T.S.E., Abramsky, S., Gabbay, D.M. (eds.) Handbook of Logic in Computer Science, vol. III. Oxford University Press (1994)
2. Bengtson, J., Johansson, M., Parrow, J., Victor, B.: Psi-calculi: Mobile processes, nominal data, and logic. In: LICS (2009)
3. Buscemi, M.G., Montanari, U.: CC-Pi: A Constraint-Based Language for Specifying Service Level Agreements. In: De Nicola, R. (ed.) ESOP 2007. LNCS, vol. 4421, pp. 18–32. Springer, Heidelberg (2007)
4. Caires, L., Cardelli, L.: A spatial logic for concurrency - i. Inf. and Comp (2003)
5. Caires, L., Cardelli, L.: A spatial logic for concurrency - ii. Theor. Comp. Sci. (2004)
6. Cardelli, L., Gordon, A.D.: Mobile ambients. Theor. Comput. Sci. 240(1), 177–213 (2000)
7. Chadha, R., Delaune, S., Kremer, S.: Epistemic Logic for the Applied Pi Calculus. In: Lee, D., Lopes, A., Poetzsch-Heffter, A. (eds.) FMOODS/FORTE 2009. LNCS, vol. 5522, pp. 182–197. Springer, Heidelberg (2009)
8. de Boer, F.S., Pierro, A.D., Palamidessi, C.: Nondeterminism and infinite computations in constraint programming. Theor. Comput. Sci. 151(1), 37–78 (1995)
9. Dechesne, F., Mousavi, M.R., Orzan, S.: Operational and Epistemic Approaches to Protocol Analysis: Bridging the Gap. In: Dershowitz, N., Voronkov, A. (eds.) LPAR 2007. LNCS (LNAI), vol. 4790, pp. 226–241. Springer, Heidelberg (2007)
10. Fages, F., Ruet, P., Soliman, S.: Linear concurrent constraint programming: Operational and phase semantics. Inf. Comput. 165(1), 14–41 (2001)
11. Fagin, R., Halpern, J.Y., Moses, Y., Vardi, M.Y.: Reasoning About Knowledge. MIT Press (1995)
12. Falaschi, M., Gabbrielli, M., Marriott, K., Palamidessi, C.: Confluence in concurrent constraint programming. Theor. Comput. Sci. 183(2), 281–315 (1997)
13. Halpern, J.Y., Moses, Y.: Knowledge and common knowledge in a distributed environment. In: Proc. of Principles of Distributed Computing, pp. 50–61 (1984)
14. Hughes, D., Shmatikov, V.: Information hiding, anonymity and privacy: a modular approach. Journal of Computer Security 12(1), 3–36 (2004)

15. Kripke, S.: Semantical analysis of modal logic. Zeitschrift fur Mathematische Logik und Grundlagen der Mathematik (1963)
16. Lynch, N.: Distributed Algorithms. Morgan Kaufmann Publishers (1996)
17. McKinsey, J.C.C., Tarski, A.: The algebra of topology. The Annals of Mathematics, second series (1944)
18. Mendler, N.P., Panangaden, P., Scott, P.J., Seely, R.A.G.: A logical view of concurrent constraint programming. Nordic Journal of Computing 2, 182–221 (1995)
19. Milner, R., Parrow, J., Walker, D.: A calculus of mobile processes i and ii. Information and Computation 100, 1–77 (1992)
20. Panangaden, P.: Knowledge and Information in Probabilistic Systems. In: van Breugel, F., Chechik, M. (eds.) CONCUR 2008. LNCS, vol. 5201, p. 4. Springer, Heidelberg (2008)
21. Panangaden, P., Saraswat, V., Scott, P., Seely, R.: A Hyperdoctrinal View of Concurrent Constraint Programming. In: de Bakker, J.W., de Roever, W.-P., Rozenberg, G. (eds.) REX 1992. LNCS, vol. 666, pp. 457–476. Springer, Heidelberg (1993)
22. Popkorn, S.: First Steps in Modal Logic. Cambridge University Press (1994)
23. Réty, J.-H.: Distributed concurrent constraint programming. Fundam. Inform. (1998)
24. Saraswat, V.A.: Concurrent Constraint Programming Languages. PhD thesis, CMU (1989)
25. Saraswat, V.A., Rinard, M., Panangaden, P.: Semantic foundations of concurrent constraint programming. In: POPL 1991 (1991)

Fluid Model Checking

Luca Bortolussi[1] and Jane Hillston[2]

[1] Department of Mathematics and Geosciences
University of Trieste, Italy
CNR/ISTI, Pisa, Italy
luca@dmi.units.it

[2] Laboratory for the Foundations of Computer Science,
School of Informatics, University of Edinburgh, UK
jane.hillston@ed.ac.uk

Abstract. In this paper we investigate a potential use of fluid approximation techniques in the context of stochastic model checking of CSL formulae. We focus on properties describing the behaviour of a single agent in a (large) population of agents, exploiting a limit result known also as fast simulation. In particular, we will approximate the behaviour of a single agent with a time-inhomogeneous CTMC which depends on the environment and on the other agents only through the solution of the fluid differential equation. We will prove the asymptotic correctness of our approach in terms of satisfiability of CSL formulae and of reachability probabilities. We will also present a procedure to model check time-inhomogeneous CTMC against CSL formulae.

Keywords: Stochastic model checking, fluid approximation, mean field approximation, reachability probability.

1 Introduction

In recent years, there has been growing interest in fluid approximation techniques in the formal methods community [3, 7, 16, 20]. These techniques, also known as mean field approximation, are useful for analysing quantitative models of population processes based on continuous time Markov Chains (CTMC), when populations are large. They work by approximating the discrete state space of the CTMC by a continuous one, and by approximating the stochastic dynamics of the process with a deterministic one, expressed by means of a set of ordinary differential equations (ODE). The asymptotic correctness of this approach is guaranteed by limit theorems [11, 22], showing the convergence of the CTMC to the fluid ODE for systems of increasing population numbers.

Another possibility to analyse such quantitative systems is to use techniques like quantitative model checking. As far as stochastic model checking is considered, there are some consolidated approaches based mainly on checking Continuous Stochastic Logic (CSL) formulae [2], which have led to widespread software tools [24]. All these methods, however, suffer (in a more or less relevant way) from the curse of state space explosion, which severely hampers their practical

M. Koutny and I. Ulidowski (Eds.): CONCUR 2012, LNCS 7454, pp. 333–347, 2012.

applicability. In order to mitigate these combinatorial barriers, many techniques have been developed, often based on some notion of abstraction or approximation of the original process [18, 19].

In this paper, we will precisely target this problem, trying to see to what extent fluid approximation techniques can be used to scale up the model checking of CTMC. We will not tackle this problem in general, but rather we will focus on a restricted subset of system properties: the behaviour of single agents within a large population. In fact, even if large systems behave almost deterministically, the evolution of a single agent in a large population is always stochastic. Single agent properties are interesting in many application domains. For instance, in performance models of computer networks, like client-server interaction, one is often interested in the behaviour and in quality-of-service metrics of a single client (or a single server), such as the waiting time of the client or the probability of a time-out. Single agent properties also hold interest in other contexts, like ecology, socio-technical systems, emergency egress.

The use of fluid approximation in this context is based on the *fast simulation* theorem [11, 13], which characterizes the limit behaviour of a single agent as depending on the rest of the system only through the solution of the fluid equation. Our idea is simply to abstract the system and study the evolution of a single agent (or of a subset of agents) by means of this limit characterization. This has the effect of drastically reducing the dimension of the state space by several orders of magnitude. Furthermore, the limit CTMC is independent of the population size. The unavoidable error introduced by mean field approximation will be small for systems with large populations, which are precisely those in which current tools suffer severely from state space explosion, and that can benefit most from a fluid approximation. However, fluid approximation is often acceptably good also for small populations. Related work in this direction is [13], in which the authors study policies to balance the load between servers, and [14, 15], in which an approach similar to fast simulation is considered to study first passage times in PEPA models, using a probe-based specification.

In the rest of the paper, we will focus on how to analyse single agent properties expressed by means of the branching-time temporal logic CSL. In order to do this, we have to cope with the fact that the limit of the model of a single agent is a time-inhomogeneous CTMC (ICTMC). This introduces some additional complexity in the approach, as reachability and model checking of ICTMC are far more difficult than the homogeneous-time case. To the best of the authors' knowledge, in fact, there is no known algorithm to solve CSL model checking in general. Related work on ICTMC focussed on uniformization [1], on the Hennessy-Milner Logics [17], under the assumption of piecewise constant rates, and on time-unbounded LTL properties [9]. We will discuss a general method in Sections 3 and 4, based on the solution of variants of the Kolmogorov equations, which is expected to work for small state spaces and controlled dynamics of the fluid approximation. The main problem with ICTMC model checking is that the truth of a formula can depend on the time at which the formula is evaluated. This creates problems especially when nesting until formulae. Hence, we need to impose some regularity on the dependency of rates on time to control the complexity of time-dependent truth. We will see that the requirement, that the rate functions are piecewise analytic, is intimately connected not only with the decidability of the model checking for ICTMC, but also with the lifting of convergence results from CTMC and their reachability probability to truth values of CSL formulae (Theorems 3 and 5).

The paper is organized as follows: in Section 2, we introduce preliminary notions, while in Section 3 we consider the reachability problem. In Section 4, instead, we focus on the CSL model checking problem for ICTMC, exploiting the routines for reachability developed earlier. We also consider the convergence of truth values for formulae about single agent properties. Finally, in Section 5, we discuss open issues and future work. Proof of lemmas and theorems can be found in [6].

2 Preliminaries

We first introduce a notation to describe population CTMC models, following [4, 5]. Let $Y_i^{(N)}(t) \in S$, $S = \{1, \ldots, n\}$, be the state of agent i in a pool of N agents, at time t. We assume that its $n \times n$ infinitesimal generator matrix is $Q^{(N)}(\mathbf{x})$, depending on the fraction of agents $\mathbf{x} \in [0,1]^n$ in each state of S. This last quantity is computed from $Y_i^{(N)}$ as $\hat{X}_i^{(N)}(t) = \frac{1}{N}\sum_{j=1}^{N} \mathbf{1}\{Y_j^{(N)}(t) = i\}$, where $\mathbf{1}\{\ldots\}$ is the indicator function. It can be shown that $\hat{\mathbf{X}}^{(N)}(t)$ is a CTMC [4] on the state space $\mathcal{D}^{(N)} = \{0, \frac{1}{N}, \frac{2}{N}, \ldots, 1\}^n$, and it is usually called the *occupancy measure*. We will denote such a model by $\hat{\mathcal{X}}^{(N)} = (S, N, Q^{(N)}, \mathbf{x}_0^{(N)})$, where $\mathbf{x}_0^{(N)} \in \mathcal{D}^{(N)}$ is the initial state.

Example 1. *We now introduce a running example: we will consider a model of a simple client-server system, in which a pool of clients submits queries to a group of servers, waiting for a reply. For simplicity, we assume a fixed server capacity and ignore their dynamics, so that we only need to describe clients. The client model is shown in Fig. 1(a): a client submits a request to a server and waits for it to reply. It can time-out if too much time passes, after which it takes a period to recover. Hence, a client has four states* $S = \{1(request), 2(wait), 3(recover), 4(think)\}$. *To aid readability we will denote the states as* $S = \{rq = 1, w = 2, rc = 3, t = 4\}$, *and the global system by the 4 variables* X_{rq}, X_w, X_{rc}, *and* X_t. *Let* k_i *denote the rate at which a single client completes action* i. *The generator matrix* $Q^{(N)} = Q$ *of the single client is*

$$Q(\mathbf{X}) = \begin{pmatrix} q_{rq,rq}(\mathbf{X}) & k_r q \min\{1, m/X_{rq}\} & 0 & 0 \\ 0 & q_{w,w}(\mathbf{X}) & \min\{k_w, k_{rp} m/X_{rq}\} & k_{to} \\ k_t & 0 & q_{t,t}(\mathbf{X}) & 0 \\ k_{rc} & 0 & 0 & q_{rc,rc}(\mathbf{X}) \end{pmatrix} \begin{matrix} rq \\ w \\ t \\ rc \end{matrix}$$

In the previous rate functions, m *represents the server to client ratio, so that we have* $M = mN$ *servers in total. The use of min guarantees that at most* M *clients can be served at a given time. The assumption of a constant number of available servers is obviously a simplification. However, more realistic models require a modelling language allowing explicit synchronization. All results of this paper still hold in such a larger setting [6].*

Given a model $\hat{\mathcal{X}}^{(N)}$, its drift (i.e., the average infinitesimal variation given that the process is in state $\mathbf{x}$) is $F^{(N)}(\mathbf{x}) = \mathbf{x}^T Q^{(N)}(\mathbf{x})$ (with $\mathbf{x}$ column vector of length n). Assume that $Q^{(N)}(\mathbf{x})$ converges uniformly to $Q(x)$, a Lipschitz continuous generator matrix, when $N \to \infty$, and that $\mathbf{x}_0^{(N)} \to x_0$. Let $\mathbf{x}(t)$ be the solution of the ODE $\frac{d\mathbf{x}}{dt} = F(\mathbf{x}) = \mathbf{x}^T Q(\mathbf{x})$. Then

Theorem 1 (Deterministic approximation [10,22]). *Let $\hat{\mathbf{X}}^{(N)}(t)$ and $\mathbf{x}(t)$ be defined as before. Then, for any finite time horizon $T < \infty$, it holds that $\sup_{0 \le t \le T} ||\hat{\mathbf{X}}^{(N)}(t) - \mathbf{x}(t)|| \to 0$ almost surely, as $N \to \infty$.*

We now turn our attention back to a single or few individuals in the population, whose dynamics remains stochastic also in the limit. However, Theor. 1 implies that this dynamics, in the limit, becomes essentially dependent on the other agents only through the solution of the fluid equation. This result is often known in the literature [11] as *fast simulation* [13]. To formalize this, fix an integer $k > 0$ and let $Z_k^{(N)} = (Y_1^{(N)}, \ldots, Y_k^{(N)})$ be the process tracking the state of k selected agents among the population, with state space $\mathcal{S} = S^k$. Notice that k is fixed and independent of N. We stress that $Z_k^{(N)}$ is not a CTMC. In fact, it is the projection of the Markov process $(Y_1^{(N)}(t), \ldots, Y_N^{(N)}(t))$ on the first k coordinates, and the projection of a Markov process is generally not Markov. However, the process $(Z_k^{(N)}(t), \hat{\mathbf{X}}^{(N)}(t))$ is Markov. Consider now $z_k(t)$, a *time-inhomogeneous* CTMC on $\mathcal{S}$ defined by $\mathbb{P}\{z_k(t + dt) = (z_1, \ldots, j, \ldots, z_k) \mid z_k(t) = (z_1, \ldots, i, \ldots, z_k)\} = q_{i,j}(\mathbf{x}(t))dt$, where $Q(\mathbf{x}) = (q_{ij}(\mathbf{x}))$ is the limit of $Q^{(N)}(\mathbf{x})$. We have the following

Theorem 2 (Fast simulation theorem [11]). *For any $T < \infty$, $\mathbb{P}\{Z_k^{(N)}(t) \neq z_k(t), \text{for some } t \le T\} \to 0$, as $N \to \infty$.*

This theorem states that, in the limit of an infinite population, each fixed set of k agents will behave independently, sensing only the mean state of the global system, described by the fluid limit $\mathbf{x}(t)$.

Continuous Stochastic Logic. We recall the definition of CSL formulae and their satisfiability, for a generic stochastic process $Z(t)$, with state space $\mathcal{S}$. Let the labelling function $L : \mathcal{S} \to 2^{\mathcal{P}}$ associate with each state $s \in \mathcal{S}$ the subset of atomic propositions $L(s) \subset \mathcal{P} = \{a_1, \ldots, a_k \ldots\}$ true in that state. A path of $Z(t)$ is a sequence $\sigma = s_0 \xrightarrow{t_0} s_1 \xrightarrow{t_1} \ldots$, such that the probability of going from s_i to s_{i+1} at time $T_i = \sum_{j=0}^{i} t_i$, is greater than zero. Denote with $\sigma@t$ the state of σ at time t. We assume that all subsets of paths considered are measurable; this will hold for all sets considered here. A time-bounded CSL formula φ is defined by the following syntax:

$$\varphi = a \mid \varphi_1 \wedge \varphi_2 \mid \neg\varphi \mid \mathcal{P}_{\bowtie p}(\varphi_1 U^{[T_1,T_2]} \varphi_2).$$

The satisfiability relation of φ with respect to a labelled stochastic process $Z(t)$ is given by the following rules (we report only non-trivial ones):

- $s, t_0 \models \mathcal{P}_{\bowtie p}(\varphi_1 U^{[T_1,T_2]} \varphi_2)$ if and only if $\mathbb{P}\{\sigma \mid \sigma, t_0 \models \varphi_1 U^{[T_1,T_2]} \varphi_2\} \bowtie p$.
- $\sigma, t_0 \models \varphi_1 U^{[T_1,T_2]} \varphi_2$ if and only if $\exists \bar{t} \in [t_0 + T_1, t_0 + T_2]$ s.t. $\sigma@\bar{t}, \bar{t} \models \varphi_2$ and $\forall t_0 \leq t < \bar{t}$, $\sigma@t, t \models \varphi_1$.

Notice that we are considering a fragment of CSL without the next temporal operator, and allowing only time-bounded properties. This last restriction is connected with the nature of convergence theorems 1 and 2, which hold only on finite time horizons (see also Remark 1). Model checking a *time-homogeneous CTMC* $Z(t)$ against an until CSL formula can be reduced to the computation of two reachability problems, which themselves can be solved by transient analysis [2].

3 Reachability

In this section, we will focus on reachability properties of a single agent (or a fixed set of agents), in a population of increasing size. Essentially, we want to compute the probability of the set of traces reaching some goal state $G \subseteq \mathcal{S}$ within T units of time, starting at time t_0 from state s and avoiding unsafe states in $U \subseteq \mathcal{S}$. This probability will be denoted by $P_{reach}(Z, t_0, T, G, U)[s]$, where $Z(t)$ is a stochastic process (either $Z_k^{(N)}(t)$ or $z_k(t)$). The key point is that the reachability probability of the limit CTMC $z_k(t)$ obtained by Theorem 2 approximates the reachability probability of a single agent in a large population of size N, i.e. the reachability probability for $Z_k^{(N)}(t)$.

In the rest of the section, we will focus specifically on the time-varying reachability for an ICTMC $Z(t)$, assuming that goal and unsafe sets depend on time t (i.e. a state may belong to G or U depending on time t). The interest in time-varying sets is intimately connected with CSL model checking. In fact, the reachability probability and *a-fortiori* the truth value of a CSL formula in a state s for a ICTMC $Z(t)$, depends on the initial time at which we start evaluating the formula.

Let $Z(t)$ be an ICTMC on $\mathcal{S}$, with rate matrix $Q(t)$ and initial state $Z(0) = Z_0 \in \mathcal{S}$. Let $\Pi(t_1, t_2)$ be the probability matrix of $Z(t)$, in which entry $\pi_{s_1,s_2}(t_1, t_2)$ gives the probability of being in state s_2 at time t_2, given that we were in state s_1 at time t_1 [26]. The *Kolmogorov forward and backward equations* describe the time evolution of $\Pi(t_1, t_2)$ as a function of t_2 and t_1, respectively. More precisely, the forward equation is $\frac{\partial \Pi(t_1,t_2)}{\partial t_2} = \Pi(t_1, t_2)Q(t_2)$, while the backward equation is $\frac{\partial \Pi(t_1,t_2)}{\partial t_1} = -Q(t_1)\Pi(t_1, t_2)$.

We will solve the reachability problem in a standard way, by reducing it to the computation of transient probabilities in a modified ICTMC [2], in which goal and unsafe sets are made absorbing. The main difficulty with time varying sets is that, at each time T_i in which the goal or the unsafe set changes, also the modified Markov chain that we need to consider to compute the reachability probability changes structure. This can have the effect of introducing a discontinuity in the probability matrix. In particular, if at time T_i a state s becomes a goal state, then the probability $\pi_{s_1,s}(t, T_i)$ suddenly needs to be added to the reachability probability of s_1: A change in the goal set at time T_i introduces a discontinuity in the reachability probability at time T_i. Similarly, if a state s was safe and then becomes unsafe at time T_i, we have to discard the probability of trajectories being in it at time T_i, as those trajectories become suddenly unsafe.

In the following, let $G(t)$ and $U(t)$ be the goal and unsafe sets, and assume that the set of time points in which G or U change value (in at least one state) is finite and equal to $T_1 \leq T_2 \ldots \leq T_k$. Let $T_0 = t$ and $T_{k+1} = t + T$.

In order to compute the reachability probability, we can exploit the semi-group property of the Markov process: $\Pi(T_0, T_{k+1}) = \prod_{i=0}^{k} \Pi(T_i, T_{i+1})$. We proceed in the following way:

1. We double the state space, letting $\tilde{\mathcal{S}} = \mathcal{S} \cup \bar{\mathcal{S}}$, where a state $\bar{s} \in \bar{\mathcal{S}}$ represents state s when it is a goal state. Hence, in the probability matrix $\tilde{\Pi}$, $\tilde{\pi}_{s_1,\bar{s}_2}$ is the probability of having reached s_2 avoiding unsafe states, while s_2 was a goal state.
2. Consider a discontinuity time T_i and let $t_1 \in [T_{i-1}, T_i)$ and $t_2 \in (T_i, T_{i+1}]$. Define $W(t) = \mathcal{S} \setminus (G(t) \cup U(t))$. Then, for $s_1 \in W(t_1)$ and $s_2 \in W(t_2)$, the probability of being in s_2 at time t_2, given that we were in s_1 at time t_1 and avoiding both unsafe and goal sets, can be written as $\tilde{\pi}_{s_1,s_2}(t_1, t_2) = \sum_{s \in W(t_1) \cap W(t_2)} \tilde{\pi}_{s_1,s}(t_1, T_i)\tilde{\pi}_{s,s_2}(T_i, t_2)$.
3. Consider again a discontinuity time T_i and let $t_1 \in [T_{i-1}, T_i)$ and $t_2 \in (T_i, T_{i+1}]$. Suppose $s_2 \in W(t_1)$ and $s_2 \in G(t_2)$. Then, the probability of reaching the goal state s_2 at time t_2, given that at time t_1 we were in s_1, can be written as $\tilde{\pi}_{s_1,s_2}(t_1, T_i) + \sum_{s \in W(t_1) \cap W(t_2)} \tilde{\pi}_{s_1,s}(t_1, T_i)\tilde{\pi}_{s,\bar{s}_2}(T_i, t_2)$. The first term is needed because all safe trajectories that are in state s_2 at time T_i suddenly become trajectories satisfying the reachability problem, hence we have to add them to the reachability probability.

All the previous remarks can be formally incorporated into the semi-group expansion of $\tilde{\Pi}(t, t+T)$ by multiplying on the right each term $\tilde{\Pi}(T_i, T_{i+1})$ by a suitable 0/1 matrix, depending only on the structural changes at time T_{i+1}. Let $|\mathcal{S}| = n$ and let $\zeta_W(T_i)$ be the $n \times n$ matrix equal to 1 only on the diagonal elements corresponding to states s_j belonging to both $W(T_i^-)$ and $W(T_i^+)$ (i.e. states that are safe and not goals both before and after T_i), and equal to 0 elsewhere. Furthermore, let $\zeta_G(T_i)$ be the $n \times n$ matrix equal to 1 in the diagonal elements corresponding to states s_j belonging to $W(T_i^-) \cap G(T_i^+)$, and zero elsewhere. Finally, let $\zeta(T_i)$ be the $2n \times 2n$ matrix $\zeta(T_i) = \begin{pmatrix} \zeta_W(T_i) & \zeta_G(T_i) \\ 0 & I \end{pmatrix}$.

Consider now the ICTMC $\tilde{Z}$ on $\tilde{\mathcal{S}}$, with rate matrix $\tilde{Q}(t)$, defined by making absorbing (and hence setting their exit rate to zero) all unsafe and goal states, and all states in $\bar{\mathcal{S}}$. Furthermore, transitions leading from a safe state s to a goal state s' are readdressed to the copy $\bar{s}'$ of s'. Non-null rates are derived from $Q(t)$. Now let $\tilde{\Pi}(t_1, t_2)$ be the probability matrix associated with the ICTMC $\tilde{Q}(t)$. Given the interval $I = [t, t+T]$, we indicate with $T_1, \ldots, T_{k_I}$ the ordered sequence of discontinuity points of goal and unsafe sets internal to I. Let

$$\Upsilon(t, t+T) = \tilde{\Pi}(t, T_1)\zeta(T_1)\tilde{\Pi}(T_1, T_2)\zeta(T_2)\cdots\zeta(T_{k_I})\tilde{\Pi}(T_{k_I}, t+T).$$

Then, it holds that $P_s(t) = P_{reach}(Z, t, T, G, U)[s] = \sum_{\bar{s}_1 \in \bar{S}} \Upsilon_{s,\bar{s}_1}(t, t+T) + \mathbf{1}\{s \in G(t)\}$, where the first term takes into account the probability of reaching a goal state starting from a non-goal state, while the second term is needed to properly account for states $s \in G(t)$, for which $P_s(t)$ has to be equal to 1 (a formal proof can be given by induction on the number of discontinuity points). $\Upsilon(t, t+T)$ can be obtained by computing each $\tilde{\Pi}(T_i, T_{i+1})$, by solving the associated forward Kolmogorov equation and then multiplying those matrices and the appropriate ζ ones, according to the definition of Υ.

If we want to compute $P(t)$ as a function of t, we can derive a differential equation for computing $\Upsilon(t, t+T)$ as a function of t. Defining $\Gamma(T_1, T_k) = \zeta(T_1)\tilde{\Pi}(T_1, T_2)\zeta(T_2)\cdots\tilde{\Pi}(T_{k-1}, T_k)\zeta(T_k)$, writing $\Upsilon(t, t+T) = \tilde{\Pi}(t, T_1)\Gamma(T_1, T_k)$ $\tilde{\Pi}(T_k, t+T)$, differentiating with respect to t and applying the forward or backward equation for $\tilde{\Pi}$, we derive that $\frac{d\Upsilon(t,t+T)}{dt} = -\tilde{Q}(t)\Upsilon(t, t+T) + \Upsilon(t, t+T)\tilde{Q}(t+T)$. This equation holds until either t or $t+T$ becomes equal to a discontinuity point. When this happens, the integration has to be stopped and restarted, recomputing Υ accordingly. This procedure can be easily turned into a proper algorithm.

Limit Behaviour. We consider now the limit behaviour of the time-varying reachability probability for $Z_k^{(N)}$, proving that it converges (almost everywhere) to that of z_k. We state this result in a more general form, assuming that also the goal and unsafe sets depend on N, and converge (in a sense specified below) to some limit sets G and U. This is needed to reason about CSL model checking.

However, both the previous algorithm to compute reachability for time-varying sets and the convergence proof rely on some regularity assumptions of the functions involved. In particular, we want a guarantee that the number of discontinuities in goal and unsafe sets, hence the number of zeros of $P(t) - p$, where $P(t)$ is the reachability probability, is finite in any compact time interval $[0, T]$. This is unfortunately not true in general, as even a smooth function can be equal to zero on infinitely many points. To avoid these issues, we will require that the rate functions of z_k and of $Z_k^{(N)}$ are *piecewise real analytic functions.*

A function $f : I \to \mathbb{R}$, I an open subset of $\mathbb{R}$, is said to be analytic [21] in I if and only if for each point t_0 of I there is an open neighbourhood of I in which f coincides with its Taylor series expansion around t_0. Hence, f is locally a power series. For a piecewise analytic function, we intend a function from $I \to \mathbb{R}$, I interval, such that there exists $I_1, \ldots, I_k$ disjoint open intervals, with $I = \bigcup_j \bar{I}_j$, such that f is analytic in each I_j. A similar definition holds for functions from $\mathbb{R}^n$ to $\mathbb{R}$, considering their multi-dimensional Taylor expansion. Most of the functions encountered in practice are piecewise analytic (PWA). In fact, PWA functions include polynomials, the exponential, logarithm, sine, cosine. Furthermore, they are closed by addition, product, composition, division (for non-zero analytic functions), differentiation and integration. Furthermore, the number of zeros of a PWA function f, different from the constant function zero, in any bounded interval I, is finite. This holds also for all derivatives of f. Furthermore, the solution of an ODE defined by an analytic vector field is analytic. Hence, if the rate functions of z_k and $Z_k^{(N)}$ are PWA, then all the probability functions computed solving the differential equations introduced above are PWA.

Additionally, we also need some regularity on the time-dependency of goal and unsafe sets (at least for the limit model) and on the way goal and unsafe sets at level N converge to these limit sets.

Definition 1. *A time-dependent subset $V(t)$ of $\mathcal{S}$, $t \in I$, is* robust *if and only if for each $s \in \mathcal{S}$, the indicator function $V_s : I \to \{0,1\}$ of s has only a finite number of discontinuities and it is either right or left continuous in those discontinuity points. Let $Disc(V)$ be the set of all discontinuities of V.*

A sequence of time-varying sets $V^{(N)}(t)$, $t \in I$, converges robustly *to a time-varying set $V(t)$, $t \in I$, if and only if, for each open neighbourhood U of $Disc(V)$, there is an $N_0 \in \mathbb{N}$ such that, $\forall N \geq N_0$, $V^{(N)}(t) = V(t)$, for each $t \in I \setminus U$*

The following lemma contains the convergence result for the reachability problem with respect to robust (limit) goal and unsafe sets. Its proof, which can be found in [6], relies on the notion of robustness introduced above and on properties of PWA functions.

Lemma 1. *Let $\mathcal{X}^{(N)}$ be a sequence of CTMC models and let $Z_k^{(N)}$ and z_k be defined from $\mathcal{X}^{(N)}$, as in Section 2, with piecewise analytic rates in a compact interval $[0, T']$, for T' sufficiently large.*

Let $G(t)$, $U(t)$, $t \in [t_0, t_1 + T]$ be robust *time-varying sets, and let $G^{(N)}(t)$, $U^{(N)}(t)$ be sequences of time-varying sets converging robustly to G and U, respectively. Furthermore, let $P(t) = P_{reach}(z_k, t, T, G, U)$ and $P^{(N)}(t) = P_{reach}(Z_k^{(N)}, t, T, G^{(N)}, U^{(N)})$, $t \in [t_0, t_1]$.*

Finally, fix $p \in [0,1]$, $\bowtie \in \{\leq, <, >, \geq\}$, and let $V_p(t) = \mathbf{1}\{P(t) \bowtie p\}$, $V_p^{(N)}(t) = \mathbf{1}\{P^{(N)}(t) \bowtie p\}$, with $\mathbf{1}\{\cdot\}$ the indicator function. Then

1. *For all but finitely many $t \in [t_0, t_1]$, $P^{(N)}(t) \to P(t)$ in probability, with uniform speed (i.e. independently of t).*
2. *For almost every $p \in [0,1]$, V_p is robust and the sequence $V_p^{(N)}$ converges robustly to V_p.*

The values of p that we need to discard in point 2 above are essentially those for which the zeros of $P_s(t) - p$ are tangential to p, for some s (i.e., for which $P_s'(t) = 0$). These generate removable discontinuities in the time dependent truth (for which the left and right limits coincide) and convergence may fail for them (suppose we are solving $P_s(t) > p$, and in such a zero, $V_s(t) = 0$ but $V_s(t^-) = V_s(t^+) = 1$, if $P_s^{(N)}(t) > P_s(t)$ for all N, then $V_s^{(N)}(t) = 1$ for all N, even when $P_s^{(N)}(t) \to P_s(t)$).

Example 2. *Let's go back to our running example, and consider the reachability property $[F^{[0,T]} timeout]$, i.e. $[true\ U^{[0,T]} timeout]$, the probability of doing a timeout within T units of time. In Fig. 1(b), we show the reachability probability of $z_1(t)$, for a single client, starting at $t_0 = 0$ as a function of T (for state rq). In Fig. 1(c), instead, we show the dependency of such a reachability probability on the*

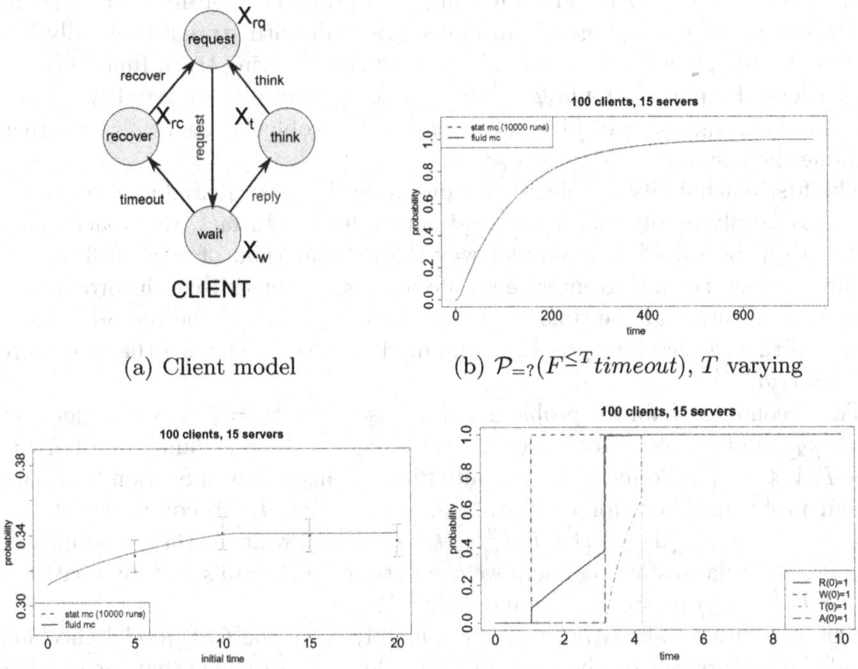

(a) Client model
(b) $\mathcal{P}_{=?}(F^{\leq T} timeout)$, T varying
(c) $\mathcal{P}_{=?}(F^{\leq 50} timeout)$, t_0 varying
(d) $[\mathcal{P}_{=?}(F^{\leq T}(\mathcal{P}_{>0.325}(F^{\leq 50} timeout))$

Fig. 1. Figure 1(a): client model of Section 2. Figure 1(b): reachability probability of $\mathcal{P}_{=?}[F^{\leq T} timeout]$, as a function of T. Parameters are: $N = 100$, $m = 0.15$, $k_r =$, $k_{rp} = 0.5$, $k_t = 1$, $k_{to} = 0.01$, $k_w = k_{rc} = 100$. The stochastic trajectory is generated using statistical sampling from 10000 runs. It took about 285 seconds to be generated. The fluid trajectory took instead 0.2 seconds. Figure 1(c): reachability probability of $\mathcal{P}_{=?}[F^{\leq 50} timeout]$, as a function of the initial time t_0. Each point of the statistical model has been generated in about 16-20 seconds. The whole fluid trajectory took 0.12 seconds. Figure 1(d): probability of $\mathcal{P}_{=?}[F^{\leq T}(\mathcal{P}_{>0.325}[F^{\leq 50} timeout]]$ as a function of T. Notice discontinuities in the probability, caused by states changing status from non-goal to goal.

initial time t_0, for $T = 50$. Furthermore, we compare the results with those estimated for $Z_1^{(N)}(t)$, with $N = 100$, using a statistical model checking-based approach. The results for the fluid approximation are quite accurate, and the speed-up achieved is of about 3 orders of magnitude (for the probability shown in Fig. 1(b)).

4 CSL Model Checking

We turn now to consider the model checking of CSL formulae and the relationship between the truth of formulae for $Z_k^{(N)}$ and z_k. As mentioned above, the truth value of until formulae in each state for a ICTMC depends on the time at which we evaluate them. When we consider *nested* until formulae, we are therefore forced to solve reachability problems for time-varying sets, using the method of Section 3. We will focus on computing path probability of until formulae, as boolean combination and atomic formulae are dealt with straightforwardly (for conjunction/disjunction, take the min/max of time-varying truth functions).

Consider the path formula $\varphi_1 U^{[T,T']} \varphi_2$. To compute its probability for initial time $t_0 \in [t_0, t_1]$,[1] we solve two reachability problems separately and then combine the results.

The first reachability problem is for unsafe set $U = [\![\neg\varphi_1]\!]$ and goal set $G(t+T) = [\![\varphi_1]\!]$ (only at the final time) and empty before. In fact, this reachability problem can be solved in a simpler way than the method of Section 3: it just requires trajectories not to enter an unsafe state, and then collects the probability to be in a safe state at the time $t+T$, for $t \in [t_0, t_1]$.[2] Let Υ^1 be the probability matrix of this reachability problem computed with (a variant of) the procedure of the section 3.

The second reachability problem is for unsafe set $U = [\![\neg\varphi_1]\!]$ and goal set $G = [\![\varphi_2]\!]$, and is solved for initial time $t \in [t_0 + T, t_1 + T]$, and time horizon $T' - T$. Let Υ^2 be the function computed by the algorithm in Section 3 for this second problem. Then, for each state s, safe at time t, we compute $P_s(t) = \sum_{s_1 \in \neg U(t+T)} \sum_{s_2 \in S} \Upsilon^1_{s,s_1}(t, t+T)\Upsilon^2_{s_1,\bar{s}_2}(t+T, t+T')$, which is the probability of the until formula in state s. Then, we can determine if state s at time t satisfies $\mathcal{P}_{\bowtie p}(\varphi_1 U^{[T,T']} \varphi_2)$ by solving the inequality $P_s(t) \bowtie p$.

This provides an algorithm to approximately solve the CSL model checking for ICTMC recursively on the structure of the formula, provided that the number of discontinuities of sets satisfying a formula is finite and that we are able to find all the zeros of the computed probability functions, to construct the appropriate time-dependent satisfiability sets (or approximations thereof).

In order to study in more detail the previous algorithm, in particular for what concerns its correctness and its termination, we assume to carry out computations using interval arithmetic procedures, in such a way that the approximation error can be made arbitrarily small [25].

The approach presented above relies, in addition to the solution of ODEs, also on two other key numerical operations: given a computable real number p, determine if p is zero and and given an analytic function f, find all the zeros of such a function (or better an interval approximation of these zeros of arbitrary accuracy). However, it is not known if these two operations can be carried out effectively for any input that we can generate.[3] To avoid these problems, we will restrict the admissible constants

---

[1] The appropriate values of t_0 and t_1 are to be deduced from φ_1, φ_2 and the superformula of the until, in a standard way.

[2] In particular, we can get rid of the copy $\bar{S}$ of the state space, and define a simplified Υ function using ζ_W matrices instead of ζ ones.

[3] The decidability of the zero test, at least for a subset of transcendental numbers generated using the exponential, is equivalent to the decidability of first order formulae on the real field extended with the exponential, which in turn is equivalent to the Schaunel conjecture [27]. Identifying zeros of a PWA function, instead, is troublesome when the zeros are not simple, i.e. when the function and derivatives up to order $j \geq 1$ are all zero [29].

in the path quantification of until CSL formulae, in order to guarantee that we will always find decidable instances of both problems above. Following [12], we thus introduce a notion of *robust CSL formula* and prove decidability for this subset of formulae. This will make CSL model checking for ICTMC quasi-decidable [12], which should be enough in practice, as the set of CSL formulae which is not robust is a closed set of measure zero (see Theor. 4).

In order to introduce the concept of robust CSL formula, consider a CSL formula φ and let $p_1, \ldots, p_k$ be the constants appearing in the $\mathcal{P}_{\bowtie p}$ operators of until sub-formulae of φ. We will treat $\varphi = \varphi(p_1, \ldots, p_k)$ as a function of those $p_1, \ldots, p_k$. Furthermore, we will call the until sub-formulae of φ *top until sub-formulae* if they are not sub-formulae of other until formulae. The other until formulae will be called *dependent*. Finally, given two robust time-varying sets V_1 and V_2, we say that V_1 and V_2 are *boolean compatible* if they do not have discontinuities for the same state s happening at the same time instant t.

Definition 2. *A CSL formula $\varphi = \varphi(\mathbf{p})$, $\mathbf{p} \in [0,1]^k$ is robust if and only if*

1. *there is an open neighbourhood W of $\mathbf{p}$ in $[0,1]^k$ such that for each $\mathbf{p_1} \in W$,*
$$s, 0 \models \varphi(\mathbf{p}) \Leftrightarrow s, 0 \models \varphi(\mathbf{p_1}).$$
2. *The time-varying sets of states in which any dependent until sub-formula of φ holds are* robust *and* boolean compatible *among them.*

Condition 1 in the previous definition guarantees that $P(0) \neq p$ for top until formulae, so that the zero test is decidable, while condition 2 guarantees that all zeros of function $P(t) - p$ that we encounter are simple. These facts, combined with properties of PWA functions and with the arbitrary precision of interval arithmetic routines, are the key ingredients to prove the following

Theorem 3. *The CSL model checking for ICTMC, for piecewise analytic interval computable rate functions, is correct and decidable for a robust CSL formula $\varphi(p_1, \ldots, p_k)$.*

We turn now to characterise the set of robust formulae from a topological and measure-theoretic point on view. Again, exploiting the conditions of robustness of CSL formulae and the properties of PWA functions, we have the following

Theorem 4. *Given a CSL formula $\varphi(\mathbf{p})$, with $\mathbf{p} \in [0,1]^k$, then the set $\{\mathbf{p} \mid \varphi(\mathbf{p})$ is robust$\}$ is (relatively) open in $[0,1]^k$ and has Lebesgue measure 1.*

The fact that the robust set of thresholds for a formula is open and has measure one implies that it is very unlikely that we will find an instance of the CSL model checking problem that behaves badly (if we choose threshold randomly from a grid of rationals, we can make this probability smaller than any $\varepsilon > 0$, for a grid sufficiently large [6]). In addition, decidability (and the truth value of a formula) is resistant to small perturbations of the thresholds, explaining the use of the term robust. In particular, Theor. 3 and 4 make the CSL model checking for ICTMC quasi-decidable, according to the definition of [12].

A complexity analysis of the algorithm presented here is sketched in [6].

Convergence for CSL Formulae. We now focus attention on the convergence of CSL model checking when looking at single agent properties, restricting to robust CSL formulae. The following theorem is proved by structural induction, applying Lemma 1 in order to deal with the case of until formulae.

Theorem 5. *Let $\mathcal{X}^{(N)}$ be a sequence of CTMC models and let $Z_k^{(N)}$ and z_k be defined from $\mathcal{X}^{(N)}$, as in Section 2.*
Assume that $Z_k^{(N)}$, z_k have piecewise analytic infinitesimal generator matrices. Let $\varphi(p_1, \ldots, p_k)$ be a robust CSL formula. Then, there exists an N_0 such that, for $N \geq N_0$ and each $s \in \mathcal{S}$

$$s, 0 \models_{Z_k^{(N)}} \varphi \Leftrightarrow s, 0 \models_{z_k} \varphi.$$

Corollary 1. *Given a CSL formula $\varphi(\mathbf{p})$, with $\mathbf{p} \in [0,1]^k$, then the subset of $[0,1]^k$ in which convergence holds has Lebesgue measure 1 and is open in $[0,1]^k$.*

The previous theorem shows that the results that we obtain abstracting a single agent in a population of size N by means of the fluid approximation is consistent. However, the theorem excludes the sets of constants $\mathbf{p}$ for which the formula is not robust. This shows that convergence and decidability are intimately connected. Notice that this limitation for convergence is unavoidable and is present also in the case of sequences of processes converging to a time-homogeneous CTMC. In this case, in fact, the reachability probability of an until formula is constant with respect to the initial time, and if it equals the constant p appearing in its path quantifier (in the limit model) convergence of truth values can fail (by the same argument sketched at the end of Section 3).

However, the constants p appearing in a formula that can make convergence fail depend only on the limit CTMC z_k, hence we can detect potentially dangerous situations while solving the CSL model checking for the limit process.

Remark 1. The version of CSL considered in this paper lacks the (time bounded) next operator $\mathbf{X}^I \varphi_1$. However, it can be easily dealt with by computing the integrals giving associated path probability, taking into account discontinuities of $[\![\varphi_1]\!]$, and proving decidability and convergence with arguments similar to those used here. Dealing with steady state operators, instead is more difficult, as limit theorems 1 and 2 hold only for finite time horizons. However, for "well-behaved" fluid ODEs, convergence can be extended to the time-limit [4]. Finally, dealing with time unbounded operators for ICTMC requires additional regularity properties of rate functions, in order to control the behaviour on non-compact time domains (e.g., convergence to steady state or periodic behaviour).

Remark 2. The CSL model checking problems for the processes $Z_k^{(N)}(t)$ and $(Z_k^{(N)}(t), \hat{\mathbf{X}}^{(N)}(t))$ are different, in the sense that the same formula can have different truth values in those two models. This is because the state spaces of the two processes are different: $Z_k^{(N)}(t)$ is defined on $\mathcal{S}$, while $(Z_k^{(N)}(t), \hat{\mathbf{X}}^{(N)}(t))$ on $\mathcal{S} \times \mathcal{D}^{(N)}$. Furthermore, while the latter process is a time-homogeneous

CTMC, the former is not a Markov process and the reachability probability, even for time-constant sets, depends on the initial time. We can see this as follows: compute the reachability probability $P_{U,G}(s,x,T)$ for each state $(s,\mathbf{x})$ of $(Z_k^{(N)}, \hat{\mathbf{X}}^{(N)})$ with time horizon T. Fix a state $s \in \mathcal{S}$ of $Z_k^{(N)}$, and consider the probability $P_{s,\mathbf{x}}(t|s)$ of being in $(s,\mathbf{x})$ conditional of being in state s. Then $P_{reach}(Z_k^{(N)}, t, T, G, U)[s] = \sum_{\mathbf{x}\in\hat{\mathcal{D}}} P_{s,\mathbf{x}}(t|s) P_{U,G}(s,x,T)$, which depends on time via $P_{s,\mathbf{x}}(t|s)$. Hence, CSL satisfiability for $Z_k^{(N)}$ depends on the time at which we evaluate the formula. Therefore, we need to consider time-varying sets also in this case, and this can introduce discontinuities on the path probability of until formulae, while no discontinuities can be observed in $(Z_k^{(N)}, \hat{\mathbf{X}}^{(N)})$. However, in [6], it is shown that this discrepancy is absorbed in the limit: for N large enough, CSL formulas evaluated in $Z_k^{(N)}(t)$ and $(Z_k^{(N)}(t), \hat{\mathbf{X}}^{(N)}(t))$ will be equi-satisfiable.

Example 3. *Going back to Ex. 1, consider the path formula* $(F^{[0,50]} timeout)$ *for the limit model of a single client. Its path probability depends on the initial time, and so does the truth value of the CSL formula* $\mathcal{P}_{>0.325}(F^{[0,50]} timeout)$. *In Fig. 1(d), the probability of the path formula*

$$F^{[0,T]}(\mathcal{P}_{>0.325}(F^{[0,50]} timeout)),$$

is shown as a function of the time horizon T. *In the figure, it is evident how this probability has discontinuities at those time instants in which the truth value function of its until sub-formula change.*

5 Conclusions

In this paper we exploited a corollary of fluid limit theorems to approximate properties of the behaviour of single agents in large population models. In particular, we focussed on reachability and stochastic model checking of CSL formulae. The method proposed requires us to model check a time-inhomogeneous CTMC of size equal to the number of internal states of the agent (which is usually very small). The approach can provide in some cases a good approximation also for moderately small populations, as the examples here and in [6] show, giving a huge improvement in terms of computational efficiency.

We then focussed on the reachability problem for ICTMC, in the case of time varying sets. We provided an algorithm for this problem, and we also proved convergence of the reachability probabilities computed for the single agent in a finite population of size N to those of the limit fluid CTMC. Finally, we focussed on model checking CSL formulae for ICTMC proposing an algorithm working for a subset of CSL with only the time bounded until operator. We also showed a decidability and a convergence result for robust formulae, proving that the set of non-robust formulae is closed and has measure zero.

There are many issues that we wish to tackle in the future. First, we would like to better understand the quality of convergence both theoretically and experimentally. In this direction, we need to investigate in more detail the effect of nesting of temporal operators on the quality of the approximation. From a theoretical point of view, this can be done by lifting the error bounds on fast simulation [11] to bounds on the probability for a path formula (also with nested temporal operators) and on truth profiles.

Furthermore, we want to investigate the connections between single agent properties and system level properties. We believe this approach can become a powerful tool to investigate the relationship between microscopic and macroscopic characterisations of systems, and to understand their emergent behaviour. In addition, we would like to provide a working implementation of the model checking algorithm for ICTMC, studying its computational cost in practice (and how easy is in practice to find a non computable instance). Furthermore, we aim at extending the CSL model checking for ICTMC to include time bounded next operator, time unbounded and steady state operators, and rewards. Another line of investigation is to consider different temporal logics, such as MTL [8, 9].

References

1. Andreychenko, A., Crouzen, P., Wolf, V.: On-the-fly Uniformization of Time-Inhomogeneous Infinite Markov Population Models. In: Proceedings of QAPL 2011. ENTCS, vol. 57, pp. 1–15 (2011)
2. Baier, C., Haverkort, B., Hermanns, H., Katoen, J.P.: Model Checking Continuous-Time Markov Chains by Transient Analysis. In: Emerson, E.A., Sistla, A.P. (eds.) CAV 2000. LNCS, vol. 1855, pp. 358–372. Springer, Heidelberg (2000)
3. Bakhshi, R., Cloth, L., Fokkink, W., Haverkort, B.R.: Mean-field analysis for the evaluation of gossip protocols. In: Proceedings of QEST 2009, pp. 247–256. IEEE Computer Society (2009)
4. Benaïm, M., Le Boudec, J.: A class of mean field interaction models for computer and communication systems. Performance Evaluation (2008)
5. Bobbio, A., Gribaudo, M., Telek, M.: Analysis of large scale interacting systems by mean field method. In: Proceedings of QEST 2008, pp. 215–224. IEEE Computer Society (2008)
6. Bortolussi, L., Hillston, J.: Fluid model checking. *CoRR 1203.0920* (2012), `http://arxiv.org/abs/1203.0920`
7. Bortolussi, L., Policriti, A.: Dynamical systems and stochastic programming — from ordinary differential equations and back. Trans. Comp. Sys. Bio. XI (2009)
8. Chen, T., Diciolla, M., Kwiatkowska, M., Mereacre, A.: Time-Bounded Verification of CTMCs against Real-Time Specifications. In: Fahrenberg, U., Tripakis, S. (eds.) FORMATS 2011. LNCS, vol. 6919, pp. 26–42. Springer, Heidelberg (2011)
9. Chen, T., Han, T., Katoen, J.-P., Mereacre, A.: LTL Model Checking of Time-Inhomogeneous Markov Chains. In: Liu, Z., Ravn, A.P. (eds.) ATVA 2009. LNCS, vol. 5799, pp. 104–119. Springer, Heidelberg (2009)
10. Darling, R.W.R.: Fluid limits of pure jump Markov processes: A practical guide (2002), `http://arxiv.org/abs/math.PR/0210109`
11. Darling, R.W.R., Norris, J.R.: Differential equation approximations for Markov chains. Probability Surveys 5 (2008)
12. Franek, P., Ratschan, S., Zgliczynski, P.: Satisfiability of Systems of Equations of Real Analytic Functions Is Quasi-decidable. In: Murlak, F., Sankowski, P. (eds.) MFCS 2011. LNCS, vol. 6907, pp. 315–326. Springer, Heidelberg (2011)

13. Gast, N., Gaujal, B.: A mean field model of work stealing in large-scale systems. In: Proceedings of ACM SIGMETRICS 2010, pp. 13–24 (2010)
14. Hayden, R.A., Bradley, J.T., Clark, A.: Performance Specification and Evaluation with Unified Stochastic Probes and Fluid Analysis. IEEE Trans. Soft. Eng.
15. Hayden, R.A., Stefanek, A., Bradley, J.T.: Fluid computation of passage-time distributions in large Markov models. Theor. Comput. Sci. 413(1), 106–141 (2012)
16. Hillston, J.: Fluid flow approximation of PEPA models. In: Proceedings of QEST 2005, pp. 33–42. IEEE Computer Society (2005)
17. Katoen, J.-P., Mereacre, A.: Model Checking HML on Piecewise-Constant Inhomogeneous Markov Chains. In: Cassez, F., Jard, C. (eds.) FORMATS 2008. LNCS, vol. 5215, pp. 203–217. Springer, Heidelberg (2008)
18. Kattenbelt, M., Kwiatkowska, M.Z., Norman, G., Parker, D.: Game-based probabilistic predicate abstraction in PRISM. Electr. Notes Theor. Comput. Sci. 220(3), 5–21 (2008)
19. Kattenbelt, M., Kwiatkowska, M., Norman, G., Parker, D.: Abstraction Refinement for Probabilistic Software. In: Jones, N.D., Müller-Olm, M. (eds.) VMCAI 2009. LNCS, vol. 5403, pp. 182–197. Springer, Heidelberg (2009)
20. Kolesnichenko, A., Remke, A., de Boer, P.-T., Haverkort, B.R.: Comparison of the Mean-Field Approach and Simulation in a Peer-to-Peer Botnet Case Study. In: Thomas, N. (ed.) EPEW 2011. LNCS, vol. 6977, pp. 133–147. Springer, Heidelberg (2011)
21. Krantz, S., Harold, P.R.: A Primer of Real Analytic Functions, 2nd edn. Birkhäuser (2002)
22. Kurtz, T.G.: Solutions of ordinary differential equations as limits of pure jump Markov processes. Journal of Applied Probability 7, 49–58 (1970)
23. Kwiatkowska, M., Norman, G., Parker, D.: Probabilistic symbolic model checking with PRISM: A hybrid approach. Int. Journal on Software Tools for Technology Transfer 6(2), 128–142 (2004)
24. Kwiatkowska, M., Norman, G., Parker, D.: Probabilistic symbolic model checking with PRISM: A hybrid approach. Int. Journal on Software Tools for Technology Transfer 6(2), 128–142 (2004)
25. Neumaier, A.: Interval Methods for Systems of Equations. University Press, Cambridge (1990)
26. Norris, J.R.: Markov Chains. Cambridge University Press (1997)
27. Richardson, D.: Zero tests for constants in simple scientific computation. Mathematics in Computer Science 1(1), 21–37 (2007)
28. Rudin, W.: Principles of Mathematical Analysis. McGraw-Hill (1976)
29. Taylor, P.: A lambda calculus for real analysis. Journal of Logic and Analysis 2(5), 1–115 (2010)

Playing Stochastic Games Precisely

Taolue Chen[1], Vojtěch Forejt[1], Marta Kwiatkowska[1], Aistis Simaitis[1], Ashutosh Trivedi[2], and Michael Ummels[3]

[1] Department of Computer Science, University of Oxford, Oxford, UK
[2] University of Pennsylvania, Philadelphia, USA
[3] Technische Universität Dresden, Germany

Abstract. We study stochastic two-player games where the goal of one player is to achieve *precisely* a given expected value of the objective function, while the goal of the opponent is the opposite. Potential applications for such games include controller synthesis problems where the optimisation objective is to maximise or minimise a given payoff function while respecting a strict upper or lower bound, respectively. We consider a number of objective functions including reachability, ω-regular, discounted reward, and total reward. We show that precise value games are not determined, and compare the memory requirements for winning strategies. For stopping games we establish necessary and sufficient conditions for the existence of a winning strategy of the controller for a large class of functions, as well as provide the constructions of compact strategies for the studied objectives.

1 Introduction

Two-player zero-sum stochastic games [13] naturally model controller synthesis problems [12] for systems exhibiting both the controllable and the uncontrollable nondeterminism coupled with stochastic behaviour. In such games two players—Min (the *controller*) and Max (the *environment*)—move a token along the edges of a graph, called a *stochastic game arena*, whose vertices are partitioned into those controlled by either of the players and the *stochastic* vertices. Player chooses an outgoing edge when the token is in a state controlled by her, while in a stochastic state the outgoing edge is chosen according to a state-dependent probability distribution. Starting from an initial state, choices made by players and at the stochastic vertices characterise a run in the game. Edge-selection choices of players are often specified by means of a *strategy*, which is a partial function from the set of finite runs to probability distributions over enabled edges. Fixing an initial state and strategies for both players determines a *probability space* on the runs of the stochastic game. In classical stochastic games players Min and Max are viewed as *optimisers* as their goals are to minimise and maximise, respectively, the expectation of a given real-valued function of the run called the *payoff function*. Payoff functions are often specified by annotating the vertices with rewards, and include total reward, discounted reward, average reward [8], and more recently ω-regular objectives [3].

M. Koutny and I. Ulidowski (Eds.): CONCUR 2012, LNCS 7454, pp. 348–363, 2012.

In this paper we take a different stand from the well-established notion of viewing players as optimisers which, even though useful in many applications, is inadequate for the problems requiring precision. Among others, such precision requirements may stem from: a) controller design under strict regulatory or safety conditions, or b) optimal controller design minimising or maximising some payoff function while requiring that a given lower or upper bound is respected. For instance, consider the task of designing a gambling machine to maximise profit to the "house" while ensuring the minimum expected *payback* to the customers established by a law or a regulatory body [14,2]. Given that such a task can be cast as a controller synthesis problem using stochastic games, the objective of the controller is to ensure that the machine achieves the expected payback *exactly* equal to the limit set by the regulatory body—higher paybacks will result in a substantial decrease in profits, while lower paybacks will make the design illegal. There are examples from other domains, e.g., ensuring precise 'coin flipping' in a *security protocol* (e.g., Crowds), keeping the expected voltage constant in *energy grid*, etc.

In order to assist in designing the above-mentioned controllers, we consider the problem of achieving a *precise* payoff value in a stochastic game. More specifically, we study games played over a stochastic game arena between two players, Preciser and Spoiler, where the goal (the winning objective) of the Preciser is to ensure that the expected payoff is *precisely* a given payoff value, while the objective of the Spoiler is the contrary, i.e., to ensure that the expected value is anything but the given value. We say that the Preciser wins from a given state if he has a winning strategy, i.e., if he has a strategy such that, for all strategies of Spoiler, the expected payoff for the given objective function is *precisely* a given value x. Similarly, the Spoiler wins from a given state if she has a strategy such that, for all strategies of Preciser, the payoff for the given objective function is not equal to x. The winning region of a player is the set of vertices from which that player wins. Observe that the winning regions of Preciser and Spoiler are disjoint. We say that a game is *determined* if winning regions of the players form a partition of the states set of the arena. Our first result (Section 3.1) is that stochastic games with precise winning objectives are *not* determined even for reachability problems. Given the non-determinacy of the stochastic precise value games, we study the following two dual problems. For a fixed stochastic game arena $\mathcal{G}$, an objective function f, and a target value x,

- the *synthesis problem* is to decide whether there exists a strategy π of Preciser such that, for all strategies σ of Spoiler, the expected value of the payoff is equal to x, and to construct such a strategy if it exists;
- the *counter-strategy problem* is to decide whether, for a given strategy σ of Spoiler, there exists a counter-strategy π of Preciser such that the expected value of the payoff is equal to x[1].

Consider the case when Spoiler does not control any states, i.e., when the stochastic game arena is a *Markov decision process* [11]. In this case, both the synthesis

[1] We do not consider the construction of π here. Note that the problem of constructing a counter-strategy is not well defined, because the strategy σ can be an arbitrary (even non-recursive) function.

and the counter-strategy problems overlap and they can be solved using optimisation problems for the corresponding objective function. Assuming that, for some objective function, Preciser achieves the value h while maximising, and value l while minimising, then any value $x \in [l, h]$ is precisely achievable by picking minimising and maximising strategies with probability θ and $(1 - \theta)$ respectively, where $\theta = \frac{h-x}{h-l}$ if $l \neq h$ and $\theta = 1$ if $l = h$. Notice that such a strategy will require just one bit of memory for all the objectives for which there exist memoryless strategies for the corresponding optimisation problems in a Markov decision process, including a large class of objective functions [11], such as expected reachability reward, discounted reward, and total reward objectives.

It seems natural to conjecture that a similar approach can be used for the game setting, i.e., Preciser can achieve any value between his minimising and maximising strategies by picking one of the strategies with an appropriate probability. Unfortunately, the same intuition does *not* carry over to stochastic games because, once Preciser fixes his strategy, Spoiler can choose any of her sub-optimal (i.e., not optimising) counter-strategies to ensure a payoff different from the target value. Intuitively, the strategy of Preciser may need to be responsive to Spoiler actions and, therefore, it should require memory.

Strategies are expressed as *strategy automata* [6,1] that consist of—i) a set of *memory elements*, ii) a *memory update function* that specifies how memory is updated as the transitions occur in the game arena, and iii) a *next move function* that specifies a distribution over the successors of game state, depending on the memory element. Memory update functions in strategy automata can be either deterministic or stochastic [1]. We show that the choice of how the memory is updated drastically influences the size of memory required. In Section 3.2 we show that deterministic update winning strategies require at least exponential memory size in precise value games. Although we are not aware of the exact memory requirement for deterministic memory update strategies, we show in Section 4 that, if *stochastic update* strategies are used, then memory need is linear in the size of the arena for the reachability, ω-regular properties and discounted and total reward objectives. We study precise value problems for these objectives and show necessary and sufficient conditions for the existence of winning strategies for controller synthesis problem in stopping games (Section 4) and counter-strategy problem in general (Section 5).

Contributions. The contributions of the paper can be summarised as follows.

- We show that stochastic games with precise value objectives are not determined even for reachability objectives, and we compare the memory requirements for different types of strategies.
- We solve the *controller synthesis* problem for precise value in stopping games for a large class of functions and provide a construction for compact winning strategies. We illustrate that for non-stopping games the problem is significantly harder to tackle.
- We solve the *counter strategy* as well as discounted reward controller synthesis problem for general games.

The proofs that have been omitted from this paper can be found in [5].

Related Work. We are not aware of any other work studying precise value problem for any objective function. There is a wealth of results [8,10,3] studying two-player stochastic games with various objective functions where players optimise their objectives. The precise value problem studied here is a special case of *multi-objective optimisation*, where a player strives to fulfill several (in our case two) objectives at once, each with a certain minimum probability. Multi-objective optimisation has been studied for Markov decision processes with discounted rewards [4], long-run average rewards [1], as well as reachability and ω-regular objectives [7]; however, none of these works consider multi-player optimisation.

2 Preliminaries

We begin with some background on stochastic two-player games.

Stochastic Game Arena. Before we present the definition, we introduce the concept of discrete probability distributions. A *discrete probability distribution* over a (countable) set S is a function $\mu : S \to [0,1]$ such that $\sum_{s \in S} \mu(s) = 1$. We write $\mathcal{D}(S)$ for the set of all discrete distributions over S. Let $\mathsf{supp}(\mu) = \{s \in S \mid \mu(s){>}0\}$ be the *support set* of $\mu \in \mathcal{D}(S)$. We say a distribution $\mu \in \mathcal{D}(S)$ is a *Dirac distribution* if $\mu(s) = 1$ for some $s \in S$. Sometimes we abuse the notation to identify a Dirac distribution μ with its unique element in $\mathsf{supp}(\mu)$.

We represent a discrete probability distribution $\mu \in \mathcal{D}(S)$ on a set $S = \{s_1, \ldots, s_n\}$ as a map $[s_1 \mapsto \mu(s_1), \ldots, s_n \mapsto \mu(s_n)] \in \mathcal{D}(S)$ and we omit the states outside $\mathsf{supp}(\mu)$ to improve presentation.

Definition 1 (Stochastic Game Arena). *A* stochastic game arena *is a tuple* $\mathcal{G} = \langle S, (S_\Box, S_\Diamond, S_\bigcirc), \Delta \rangle$ *where:*

- *S is a countable set of states partitioned into sets of states $S_\Box$, $S_\Diamond$, and $S_\bigcirc$;*
- *$\Delta : S \times S \to [0,1]$ is a probabilistic transition function such that $\Delta(\langle s,t \rangle) \in \{0,1\}$ if $s \in S_\Box \cup S_\Diamond$ and $\sum_{t \in S} \Delta(\langle s,t \rangle) = 1$ if $s \in S_\bigcirc$.*

A stochastic game arena is *finite* if S is a finite set. In this paper we omit the keyword "finite" as we mostly work with finite stochastic game arenas and explicitly use "countable" for the arenas for emphasise when they are not finite.

The sets $S_\Box$ and $S_\Diamond$ represent the sets of states controlled by players Preciser and Spoiler, respectively, while the set $S_\bigcirc$ is the set of stochastic states. A game arena is a *Markov decision process* if the set of states controlled by one of the players in an empty set, while it is a *Markov chain* if the sets of states controlled by both players are empty. For a state $s \in S$, the set of successor states is denoted by $\Delta(s) \stackrel{\text{def}}{=} \{t \in S \mid \Delta(\langle s,t \rangle){>}0\}$. We assume that $\Delta(s) \neq \emptyset$ for all $s \in S$.

Paths. An infinite *path* λ of a stochastic game arena $\mathcal{G}$ is an infinite sequence $s_0 s_1 \ldots$ of states such that $s_{i+1} \in \Delta(s_i)$ for all $i \geq 0$. A finite path is a finite such sequence. For a finite or infinite path λ we write $\mathsf{len}(\lambda)$ for the number of states in the path. For $i < \mathsf{len}(\lambda)$ we write λ_i to refer to the i-th state s_i of

λ. Similarly, for $k \leq \mathsf{len}(\lambda)$ we denote the prefix of length k of the path λ by $\mathrm{Pref}(\lambda, k) \stackrel{\text{def}}{=} s_0 s_1 \ldots s_{k-1}$. For a finite path $\lambda = s_0 s_1 \ldots s_n$ we write $\mathsf{last}(\lambda)$ for the last state of the path, here $\mathsf{last}(\lambda) = s_n$. For a stochastic game arena $\mathcal{G}$ we write $\Omega_{\mathcal{G}}{}^{+}$ for the set of all finite paths, $\Omega_{\mathcal{G}}$ for the set of all infinite paths, $\Omega_{\mathcal{G},s}$ for the set of infinite paths starting in state s. If the starting state is given as a distribution $\alpha : S \to [0,1]$ then we write $\Omega_{\mathcal{G},\alpha}$ for the set of infinite paths starting from some state in $\mathsf{supp}(\alpha)$.

Strategy. Classically, a *strategy* of Preciser is a partial function $\pi\colon \Omega_{\mathcal{G}}{}^{+} \to \mathcal{D}(S)$, which is defined for $\lambda \in \Omega_{\mathcal{G}}{}^{+}$ only if $\mathsf{last}(\lambda) \in S_{\Box}$, such that $s \in \mathsf{supp}(\pi(\lambda))$ only if $\Delta(\langle \mathsf{last}(\lambda), s\rangle) = 1$. Such a strategy π is *memoryless* if $\mathsf{last}(\lambda) = \mathsf{last}(\lambda')$ implies $\pi(\lambda) = \pi(\lambda')$ for all $\lambda, \lambda' \in \Omega_{\mathcal{G}}{}^{+}$. If π is a memoryless strategy for Preciser then we identify it with a mapping $\pi\colon S_{\Box} \to \mathcal{D}(S)$. Similar concepts for a strategy σ of the Spoiler are defined analogously. In this paper we use an alternative formulation of strategy [1] that generalises the concept of strategy automata [6].

Definition 2. *A* strategy *of Preciser in a game arena* $\mathcal{G} = \langle S, (S_{\Box}, S_{\Diamond}, S_{\circ}), \Delta\rangle$ *is a tuple* $\pi = \langle \mathcal{M}, \pi_u, \pi_n, \alpha\rangle$, *where:*

- $\mathcal{M}$ *is a countable set of* memory elements.
- $\pi_u\colon \mathcal{M} \times S \to \mathcal{D}(\mathcal{M})$ *is a* memory update function,
- $\pi_n\colon S_{\Box} \times \mathcal{M} \to \mathcal{D}(S)$ *is a* next move function *such that* $\pi_n(s,m)[s'] = 0$ *for all* $s' \in S \setminus \Delta(s)$,
- $\alpha\colon S \to \mathcal{D}(\mathcal{M})$ *defines an* initial distribution *on the memory elements for a given initial state of* $\mathcal{G}$.

A strategy σ for Spoiler is defined in an analogous manner. We denote the set of all strategies for Preciser and Spoiler by Π and Σ, respectively.

A strategy is *memoryless* if $|\mathcal{M}| = 1$. We say that a strategy requires finite memory if $|\mathcal{M}| < \infty$ and infinite memory if $|\mathcal{M}| = \infty$. We also classify the strategies based on the use of randomisation. A strategy $\pi = \langle \mathcal{M}, \pi_u, \pi_n, \alpha\rangle$ is *pure* if π_u, π_n, and α map to Dirac distributions; *deterministic update* if π_u and α map to Dirac distributions, while π_n maps to an arbitrary distributions; and *stochastic update* where π_u, π_n, and α can map to arbitrary distributions. Stochastic update strategies are convenient because, for example, they allow to randomly choose between several other strategies in α, thus making the implementation of exact value problem for MDPs (as discussed in the introduction) straightforward. Note that from an implementation point of view, the controller using a *stochastic update* or a *deterministic update* strategy where π_n uses randomisation has to be equipped with a random number generator to provide a correct realisation of the strategy.

Markov Chain Induced by Strategy Pairs. Given a stochastic game arena $\mathcal{G}$ and an initial state distribution α, a strategy $\pi = \langle \mathcal{M}_1, \pi_u, \pi_n, \alpha_1\rangle$ of Preciser and a strategy $\sigma = \langle \mathcal{M}_2, \sigma_u, \sigma_n, \alpha_2\rangle$ of Spoiler induce a countable Markov chain $\mathcal{G}(\alpha, \pi, \sigma) = \langle S', (\emptyset, \emptyset, S'), \Delta'\rangle$ with starting state distribution $\alpha(\pi, \sigma)$ where

- $S' = S \times \mathcal{M}_1 \times \mathcal{M}_2$,
- $\Delta' \colon S' \times S' \to [0,1]$ is such that for all $(s, m_1, m_2), (s', m_1', m_2') \in S'$ we have
$$\Delta'(\langle (s, m_1, m_2), (s', m_1', m_2') \rangle) = \begin{cases} \pi_n(s, m_1)[s'] \cdot \pi_u(m_1, s')[m_1'] \cdot \sigma_u(m_2, s')[m_2'] & \text{if } s \in S_\Box, \\ \sigma_n(s, m_2)[s'] \cdot \pi_u(m_1, s')[m_1'] \cdot \sigma_u(m_2, s')[m_2'] & \text{if } s \in S_\Diamond, \\ \Delta(\langle s, s' \rangle) \cdot \pi_u(m_1, s')[m_1'] \cdot \sigma_u(m_2, s')[m_2'] & \text{if } s \in S_\circ. \end{cases}$$
- $\alpha(\pi, \sigma) : S' \to [0,1]$ is defined such that for all $(s, m_1, m_2) \in S'$ we have that $\alpha(\pi, \sigma)[s, m_1, m_2] = \alpha[s] \cdot \alpha_1(s)[m_1] \cdot \alpha_2(s)[m_2]$.

To analyze a stochastic game $\mathcal{G}$ under a strategy pair $(\pi, \sigma) \in \Pi \times \Sigma$ and a starting state distribution α we define the probability measure over the set of paths $\Omega^{\pi,\sigma}_{\mathcal{G},\alpha}$ of $\mathcal{G}(\alpha, \pi, \sigma)$ with starting state distribution $\alpha(\pi, \sigma)$ in the following manner. The basic open sets of $\Omega^{\pi,\sigma}_{\mathcal{G},\alpha}$ are the *cylinder sets* $\mathrm{Cyl}(P) \stackrel{\text{def}}{=} P \cdot S'^\omega$ for every finite path $P = s_0' s_1' \ldots s_k'$ of $\mathcal{G}(s, \pi, \sigma)$, and the probability assigned to $\mathrm{Cyl}(P)$ equals $\alpha(\pi, \sigma)[s_1'] \cdot \prod_{i=0}^{k} \Delta'(\langle s_i', s_{i+1}' \rangle)$. This definition induces a probability measure on the algebra of cylinder sets which, by Carathéodory's extension theorem, can be extended to a unique probability measure on the σ-algebra $\mathfrak{B}'$ generated by these sets. We denote the resulting probability measure by $\mathrm{Pr}^{\pi,\sigma}_{\mathcal{G},\alpha}$. Often, we are only interested in the states visited on a path through $\mathcal{G}(s, \pi, \sigma)$ and not the memory contents. Let $\mathfrak{B}$ be the σ-algebra generated by the cylinder subsets of S^ω. We obtain a probability measure P on $\mathfrak{B}$ by setting $P(A) = \mathrm{Pr}^{\pi,\sigma}_{\mathcal{G},\alpha}(\rho^{-1}(A))$, where ρ is the natural projection from S'^ω to S^ω. We abuse notation slightly and denote this probability measure also by $\mathrm{Pr}^{\pi,\sigma}_{\mathcal{G},\alpha}$. Our intended measurable space will always be clear form the context.

The xpected value of a measurable function $f \colon S'^\omega \to \mathbb{R} \cup \{\infty\}$ or $f \colon S^\omega \to \mathbb{R} \cup \{\infty\}$ under a strategy pair $(\pi, \sigma) \in \Pi \times \Sigma$ and a starting state distribution α is defined as $\mathbb{E}^{\pi,\sigma}_{\mathcal{G},\alpha}[f] \stackrel{\text{def}}{=} \int f \, d\mathrm{Pr}^{\pi,\sigma}_{\mathcal{G},\alpha}$. The *conditional expectation* of a measurable function f *given* an event $A \in \mathfrak{B}$ ($A \in \mathfrak{B}'$) such that $\mathrm{Pr}^{\pi,\sigma}_{\mathcal{G},\alpha}(A) > 0$ is defined analogously, i.e. $\mathbb{E}^{\pi,\sigma}_{\mathcal{G},\alpha}[f \mid A] = \int f \, d\mathrm{Pr}^{\pi,\sigma}_{\mathcal{G},\alpha}(\cdot \mid A)$, where $\mathrm{Pr}^{\pi,\sigma}_{\mathcal{G},\alpha}(\cdot \mid A)$ denotes the usual conditional probability measure (conditioned on A).

3 Stochastic Games with Precise Objectives

We start this section by providing generic definitions of the two types of problems that we consider – *controller synthesis* and *counter strategy*. Then we show that the games are not determined even for reachability objectives and discuss the memory requirements for deterministic update strategies.

In a stochastic game with precise objective on arena $\mathcal{G}$, with starting state s, *objective function* $f \colon \Omega_{\mathcal{G},s} \to \mathbb{R}$, and target value $x \in \mathbb{Q}$, we say that a strategy π of player Preciser is *winning* if $\mathbb{E}^{\pi,\sigma}_{\mathcal{G},s}[f] = x$ for all $\sigma \in \Sigma$. Analogously, a strategy σ of player Spoiler is winning if $\mathbb{E}^{\pi,\sigma}_{\mathcal{G},s}[f] \neq x$ for all $\pi \in \Pi$. It is straightforward to see that for every starting state at most one player has a winning strategy. In Section 3.1 we show via an example that there are games where no

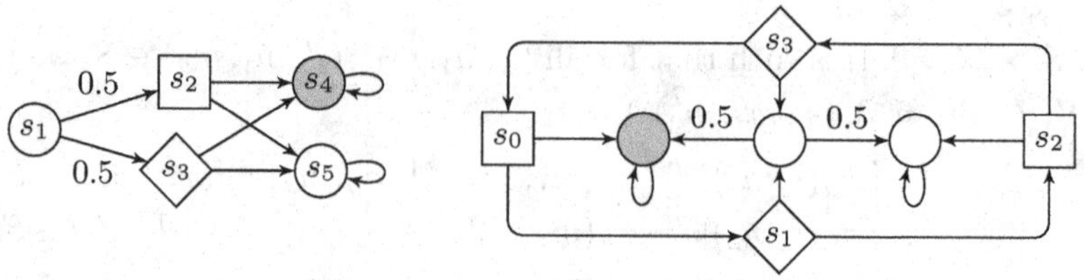

Fig. 1. Two stochastic game arenas where we depict stochastic vertices as circles and vertices of players Preciser and Spoiler as boxes and diamonds, respectively

player has a winning strategy from some given state, i.e. stochastic games with precise objective are in general not determined. Hence, we study the following two problems with applications in controller synthesis of systems.

Definition 3 (Controller synthesis problem). *Given a game $\mathcal{G}$, a state s, an* objective function $f\colon \Omega_{\mathcal{G},s} \to \mathbb{R}$, *and a target value $x \in \mathbb{Q}$, the* controller synthesis problem *is to decide whether player Preciser has a winning strategy.*

Definition 4 (Counter-strategy problem). *Given a game $\mathcal{G}$, a state s, an objective function $f\colon \Omega_{\mathcal{G},s} \to \mathbb{R}$, and a target value $x \in \mathbb{Q}$, the* counter-strategy problem *asks whether Spoiler has no winning strategy, i.e., whether for every strategy σ of Spoiler there exists a strategy π of Preciser such that $\mathbb{E}^{\pi,\sigma}_{\mathcal{G},s}[f] = x$.*

In this paper we study the study controller synthesis and counter-strategy problems for the following objective functions:

- *Reachability* (with respect to a target set $T \subseteq S$) defined as $f^T_{\text{reach}}(\lambda) \stackrel{\text{def}}{=} 1$ if $\exists i \in \mathbb{N} : \lambda_i \in T$, and $f^T_{\text{reach}}(\lambda) \stackrel{\text{def}}{=} 0$ otherwise.
- *ω-regular* (with respect to an ω-regular property given as a deterministic parity automaton $\mathcal{A}$ [9]; we write $\mathcal{L}(\mathcal{A})$ for the language accepted by $\mathcal{A}$) defined as $f^{\mathcal{A}}_{\text{omega}}(\lambda) \stackrel{\text{def}}{=} 1$ if $\lambda \in \mathcal{L}(\mathcal{A})$, and $f^{\mathcal{A}}_{\text{omega}}(\lambda) \stackrel{\text{def}}{=} 0$ otherwise.
- *Total reward* (with respect to a *reward structure* $r\colon S \to \mathbb{R}^{\geq 0}$) defined as $f^r_{\text{total}}(\lambda) \stackrel{\text{def}}{=} \sum_{i=0}^{\infty} r(\lambda_i)$.
- *Discounted reward* (with respect to a discount factor $\delta \in [0,1)$ and a reward structure $r\colon S \to \mathbb{R}^{\geq 0}$) defined as $f^{\delta,r}_{\text{disct}}(\lambda) \stackrel{\text{def}}{=} \sum_{i=0}^{\infty} r(\lambda_i) \cdot \delta^i$.

3.1 Determinacy

In this section, we show that our games are, in general, *not determined*, i.e., a positive answer to the counter-strategy problem does not imply a positive answer to the controller synthesis problem. To see this, consider the game arena $\mathcal{G}$ given in Figure 1 (left) w.r.t the reachability function f^T_{reach} with target set $T = \{s_4\}$.

Proposition 1. *Preciser has no winning strategy on $\mathcal{G}$ from state s_1 for objective function f^T_{reach} and target value $x = 0.5$.*

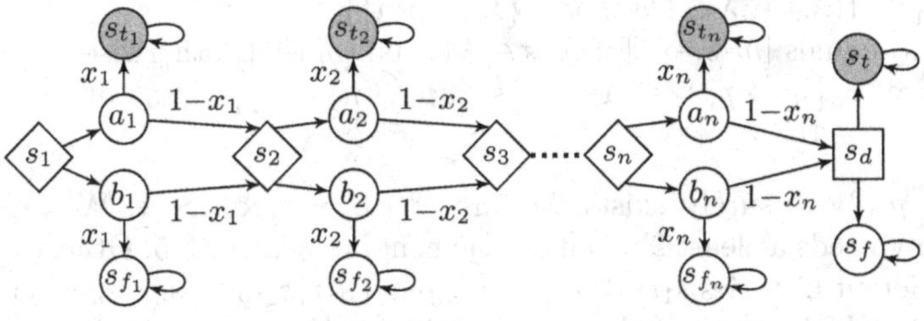

Fig. 2. Exponential deterministic update memory for Preciser

Proof. Assume that $\pi = \langle \mathcal{M}, \pi_u, \pi_n, \alpha \rangle$ is a solution the controller synthesis problem. We define two memoryless Spoiler strategies $\sigma = \langle \mathcal{M}_2, \sigma_u, \sigma_n, \alpha_2 \rangle$ and $\sigma' = \langle \mathcal{M}_2, \sigma_u, \sigma'_n, \alpha_2 \rangle$, where $\mathcal{M}_2 = \{\mathit{init}\}$, $\sigma_u(\mathit{init}, s_1) = \alpha_2(s_1) = \mathit{init}$, $\sigma_n(s_3, \mathit{init}) = s_4$, and $\sigma'_n(s_3, \mathit{init}) = s_5$. From the strategy construction and the fact that 0.5 of the probability mass is under control of Spoiler in s_3, we get that

$$\mathbb{E}^{\pi,\sigma}_{\mathcal{G},s_1}[f^T_{\text{reach}}] - \mathbb{E}^{\pi,\sigma'}_{\mathcal{G},s_1}[f^T_{\text{reach}}] = 0.5 \Longrightarrow \mathbb{E}^{\pi,\sigma}_{\mathcal{G},s_1}[f^T_{\text{reach}}] \neq 0.5 \text{ or } \mathbb{E}^{\pi,\sigma'}_{\mathcal{G},s_1}[f^T_{\text{reach}}] \neq 0.5,$$

and thus π cannot be a solution to the controller synthesis problem. □

Proposition 2. *Spoiler has no winning strategy on $\mathcal{G}$ from state s_1 for objective function f^T_{reach} and target value $x = 0.5$.*

Proof. Let $\sigma = \langle \mathcal{M}, \sigma_u, \sigma_n, \alpha \rangle$ be any strategy for Spoiler. Then any strategy $\pi = \langle \mathcal{M}, \pi_u, \pi_n, \alpha \rangle$ for Preciser with $\pi_u(m, s_2) = \sigma_u(m, s_3)$ and $\pi_n(s_2, m)[s_4] = \sigma_n(s_3, m)[s_5]$ for all $m \in \mathcal{M}$ satisfies $\mathbb{E}^{\pi,\sigma}_{\mathcal{G},s_1}[f^T_{\text{reach}}] = 0.5$. □

3.2 Memory Requirements

In this section we show that if *deterministic update* strategies are used, then the required size of the memory may be exponential in the size of the game. On the other hand, we later prove that *stochastic update* strategies require memory linear in the size of the game arena.

Proposition 3. *In the* controller synthesis *problem, Preciser may need memory exponential in the size of the game while using* deterministic update *strategy.*

Proof. Consider the game $\mathcal{G}$ in Figure 2 with the target set T shaded in gray, and constants x_i set to $2^{-(i+1)}$. Observe that under any strategy of Spoiler, the probability of runs that end in state s_{t_i} or s_{f_i} is exactly $\sum_{i=1}^{n} x_i \cdot \beta(i-1)$, where $\beta(k) = \prod_{j=1}^{k}(1 - x_j)$.

We now construct a deterministic update strategy $\pi = \langle \mathcal{M}, \pi_u, \pi_n, \alpha \rangle$, which ensures that the probability to reach T is exactly 0.5. Intuitively, the strategy remembers the exact history, and upon arriving to s_d it looks at which states a_i for $1 \leq i \leq n$ were visited on a prefix of a history (and hence how much of the probability mass was directed to s_{t_i}), and sets the probability of going to s_f so that it "compensates" for these paths to target states to get the overall probability to reach target equal to 0.5. Formally,

- $\mathcal{M} = \{\text{Pref}(\lambda, k) \colon \lambda \in \Omega_{\mathcal{G},s_1}, k \in \{1, \ldots, 2n\}\}$
- $\pi_u(m, s)$ equals $[m{\cdot}s \mapsto 1]$ if $m{\cdot}s \in \mathcal{M}$, and $[m \mapsto 1]$ otherwise.
- $\pi_n(s_d, m) = [s_t \mapsto p, s_f \mapsto 1 - p]$, s. t. $p \cdot \beta(n) + \sum_{a_i \in m} x_i \cdot \beta(i-1) = 0.5$
- $\alpha(s) = [s \mapsto 1]$

Note that p above surely exists, because $\beta(n) \geq \beta(\infty) > \frac{1}{2}$. We argue that any strategy needs at least 2^n memory elements to achieve 0.5. Otherwise, there are two different histories $s_1 t_1 s_2 t_2 \ldots s_n t_n s_d$ and $s_1 t'_1 s_2 t'_2 \ldots s_n t'_n s_d$ where $t_i, t'_i \in \{a_i, b_i\}$ after which π assigns the same distribution $[s_t \mapsto y, s_f \mapsto 1-y]$. Let k be the smallest number such that $t_k \neq t'_k$, and w.l.o.g. suppose $t_k = a_k$. Let $\sigma \in \Sigma$ be a deterministic strategy that chooses to go to t_i in s_i, and let $\sigma' \in \Sigma$ be a deterministic strategy that chooses to go to t'_i in s_i. Then the probability to reach a target state under π and σ is at least $\sum_{i<k, t_i=a_i} x_i{\cdot}\beta(i-1) + x_k{\cdot}\beta(k-1) + y{\cdot}\beta(n)$, and under π and σ' — at most $\sum_{i<k, t_i=a_i} x_i{\cdot}\beta(i-1) + \sum_{k<i\leq n} x_i{\cdot}\beta(i-1) + y{\cdot}\beta(n)$. Because $x_k{\cdot}\beta(k-1) > (\sum_{k<i\leq n} x_i){\cdot}\beta(k-1) > \sum_{k<i\leq n} x_i{\cdot}\beta(i-1)$, we obtain a contradiction.

Note that by replacing the states a_i and b_i with gadgets of $i+1$ stochastic states the example can be altered so that the only probabilities assigned by the probabilistic transition function are 0, 1 and $\frac{1}{2}$.

4 Controller Synthesis Problem

In this section we present our results on controller synthesis problem. We say that a state is *terminal* if no other state is reachable from it under any strategy pair. We call a stochastic game *stopping* if a terminal state is reached with probability 1 under any pair of strategies. We define conditions under which the controller synthesis problem has a solution for a general class of functions, the so-called linearly bounded functions—under stopping games assumption. We say that an objective function is *linearly bounded* if there are x_1 and x_2 such that for any ω that contains k nonterminal states we have $|f(\omega)| \leq x_1 \cdot k + x_2$. We observe that objective functions define in previous section are linearly-bounded and present compact winning strategies for those objective.

4.1 Conditions for the Existence of Winning Strategies

We define $\mathit{Exact}_{\mathcal{G}}(s, f) \stackrel{\text{def}}{=} \{x \in \mathbb{R} \mid \exists \pi \in \Pi \,.\, \forall \sigma \in \Sigma : \mathbb{E}^{\pi,\sigma}_{\mathcal{G},s}[f] = x\}$ to be the set of values for which Preciser has a winning strategy on $\mathcal{G}$ from s with objective function f. Given a function $f : \Omega_{\mathcal{G}} \to \mathbb{R}$, a finite path $u{\cdot}s \in {\Omega_{\mathcal{G}}}^+$ and an infinite path $v \in \Omega_{\mathcal{G}}$, we define a curried function $f_{u\cdot s}(s{\cdot}v) = f(u{\cdot}s{\cdot}v)$, where $s \in S$. Given a finite path as the history of the game, the following lemma presents conditions under which player Preciser cannot win the game for any value.

Lemma 1. *Given a game $\mathcal{G}$, a finite path $w{\cdot}s \in {\Omega_{\mathcal{G}}}^+$, where $s \in S$ and a function f, if $\inf_{\pi\in\Pi} \sup_{\sigma\in\Sigma} \mathbb{E}^{\pi,\sigma}_{\mathcal{G},s}[f_{w\cdot s}] > \sup_{\pi\in\Pi} \inf_{\sigma\in\Sigma} \mathbb{E}^{\pi,\sigma}_{\mathcal{G},s}[f_{w\cdot s}]$, then Preciser cannot achieve any exact value after that path, i.e., $\mathit{Exact}_{\mathcal{G}}(s, f_{w\cdot s}) = \emptyset$.*

Proof. For every Preciser strategy $\pi \in \Pi$, we have that

$$\inf_{\sigma\in\Sigma} \mathbb{E}^{\pi,\sigma}_{\mathcal{G},s}[f_{w\cdot s}] \leq \sup_{\pi\in\Pi}\inf_{\sigma\in\Sigma} \mathbb{E}^{\pi,\sigma}_{\mathcal{G},s}[f_{w\cdot s}] < \inf_{\pi\in\Pi}\sup_{\sigma\in\Sigma} \mathbb{E}^{\pi,\sigma}_{\mathcal{G},s}[f_{w\cdot s}] \leq \sup_{\sigma\in\Sigma} \mathbb{E}^{\pi,\sigma}_{\mathcal{G},s}[f_{w\cdot s}].$$

Hence, for any of the strategy π of Preciser, Spoiler can ensure one of the two *distinct* values $\inf_{\sigma\in\Sigma} \mathbb{E}^{\pi,\sigma}_{\mathcal{G},s}[f_{w\cdot s}]$ or $\sup_{\sigma\in\Sigma} \mathbb{E}^{\pi,\sigma}_{\mathcal{G},s}[f_{w\cdot s}]$, and therefore Preciser cannot guarantee any exact value after history $w\cdot s$, so $Exact_{\mathcal{G}}(s, f_{w\cdot s}) = \emptyset$. □

Let $\Omega^{\mathrm{no}}_{\mathcal{G},f} \subseteq \Omega_{\mathcal{G}}{}^{+}$ be a set paths in $\mathcal{G}$ such that a path w is in $\Omega^{\mathrm{no}}_{\mathcal{G},f}$ if and only if w satisfies the condition in Lemma 1, i.e., after w Preciser cannot guarantee any exact value for a function f. The above proposition characterises the states from which Preciser cannot achieve any exact value.

Proposition 4. *In a game $\mathcal{G}$, and a state $s \in S$, if for any strategy of Preciser, Spoiler has a strategy to make sure that at least one path from $\Omega^{no}_{\mathcal{G},f}$ has positive probability, then $Exact_{\mathcal{G}}(s, f) = \emptyset$, i.e.,*

$$\forall \pi \in \Pi\,.\,\exists \sigma \in \Sigma : \mathrm{Pr}^{\pi,\sigma}_{\mathcal{G},s}\Big(\bigcup_{w\in\Omega^{no}_{\mathcal{G},f}} \mathrm{Cyl}(w)\Big) > 0 \Rightarrow Exact_{\mathcal{G}}(s, f) = \emptyset.$$

In the next theorem we complement the proposition by describing the states with nonempty sets $Exact_{\mathcal{G}}(s, f)$, for the class of linearly-bounded objective functions.

Theorem 1. *Given a stopping game $\mathcal{G}$, a linearly bounded objective function f satisfying $\Omega^{no}_{\mathcal{G},f} = \emptyset$, a state $s \in S$, and a value $x \in \mathbb{R}$,*

$$x \in Exact_{\mathcal{G}}(s, f) \iff \inf_{\pi\in\Pi}\sup_{\sigma\in\Sigma} \mathbb{E}^{\pi,\sigma}_{\mathcal{G},s}[f] \leq x \leq \sup_{\pi\in\Pi}\inf_{\sigma\in\Sigma} \mathbb{E}^{\pi,\sigma}_{\mathcal{G},s}[f].$$

Proof (Sketch). The "⇒" direction of the theorem is straightforward. To show "⇐" direction, we construct a strategy to achieve any given probability x.

Let π^- and π^+ be minimising and maximising pure deterministic update strategies [2]. Let $w\cdot s \in \Omega_{\mathcal{G}}{}^{+}$. We define minimum and maximum expected values achievable by Preciser after a finite path $w\cdot s$ as:

$$\mathrm{val}^-(w\cdot s) = \inf_{\pi\in\Pi}\sup_{\sigma\in\Sigma} \mathbb{E}^{\pi,\sigma}_{\mathcal{G},s}[f_{w\cdot s}] \quad\text{and}\quad \mathrm{val}^+(w\cdot s) = \sup_{\pi\in\Pi}\inf_{\sigma\in\Sigma} \mathbb{E}^{\pi,\sigma}_{\mathcal{G},s}[f_{w\cdot s}].$$

We will now construct a stochastic update strategy for Preciser, which is winning from all $s \in S$. Given any $l \leq y \leq h$, we define $c(y, l, h)$ as $\frac{h-y}{h-l}$ if $l \neq h$ and 1 otherwise. For a finite path $w \in \Omega_{\mathcal{G}}{}^{+}$ such that $\mathrm{val}^-(w) \leq y \leq \mathrm{val}^+(w)$, we define $\beta(y, w) = c(y, \mathrm{val}^-(w), \mathrm{val}^+(w))$. The strategy $\pi = \langle \mathcal{M}, \pi_u, \pi_n, \alpha\rangle$ is defined by

[2] Note that thanks to our restrictions on f and $\mathcal{G}$ these always exist.

- $\mathcal{M} = \{\langle w, \mathrm{val}^-(w)\rangle, \langle w, \mathrm{val}^+(w)\rangle \mid w \in \Omega_{\mathcal{G}}{}^+\}$,

- $$\pi_u(\langle w{\cdot}s, y\rangle, t) = \begin{cases} \langle w{\cdot}s{\cdot}t, y\rangle, & \text{if } s \in S_\Box, \\ [\langle w{\cdot}s{\cdot}t, \mathrm{val}^-(w{\cdot}s{\cdot}t)\rangle \mapsto \beta(y, w{\cdot}s{\cdot}t), & \\ \ \langle w{\cdot}s{\cdot}t, \mathrm{val}^+(w{\cdot}s{\cdot}t)\rangle \mapsto 1 - \beta(y, w{\cdot}s{\cdot}t)], & \text{if } s \in S_\Diamond, \\ \langle w{\cdot}s{\cdot}t, \mathrm{val}^-(w{\cdot}s{\cdot}t)\rangle, & \text{if } s \in S_\bigcirc \text{ and } y = \mathrm{val}^-(w{\cdot}s), \\ \langle w{\cdot}s{\cdot}t, \mathrm{val}^+(w{\cdot}s{\cdot}t)\rangle, & \text{if } s \in S_\bigcirc \text{ and } y = \mathrm{val}^+(w{\cdot}s), \end{cases}$$

- $$\pi_n(s, \langle w, y\rangle) = \begin{cases} \pi^-(w) & \text{if } y = \mathrm{val}^-(w), \\ \pi^+(w) & \text{otherwise} \end{cases}$$

- $\alpha(s) = [\langle s, \mathrm{val}^-(s)\rangle \mapsto \beta(x, s), \langle s, \mathrm{val}^+(s)\rangle \mapsto 1 - \beta(x, s)]$,

for all $w \in \Omega_{\mathcal{G}}{}^+$, $s, t \in S$, and $\langle w, y\rangle, \langle w{\cdot}s, y\rangle \in \mathcal{M}$. The correctness of the strategy follows from the proof in [5]. □

4.2 Compact Strategies for Objective Functions

In this section, using the results from Theorem 1, we construct stochastic update strategies for the functions defining reachability, total expected reward, discounted reward and ω-regular objectives, all of which are linearly bounded. For all games, and objective functions in this section we assume that $\Omega^{\mathrm{no}}_{\mathcal{G},f} = \emptyset$.

Proposition 5. *Reachability, ω-regular, total reward and discounted reward objectives are linearly-bounded.*

From Theorem 1 and Proposition 5 it follows that for in a game $\mathcal{G}$, a state s and value x, if f is reachability, ω-regular, total reward or discounted reward objectives satisfying the assumptions of Theorem 1, then player Preciser has a winning strategy if and only if $\inf_{\pi \in \Pi} \sup_{\sigma \in \Sigma} \mathbb{E}^{\pi,\sigma}_{\mathcal{G},s}[f] \leq x \leq \sup_{\pi \in \Pi} \inf_{\sigma \in \Sigma} \mathbb{E}^{\pi,\sigma}_{\mathcal{G},s}[f]$. The construction from Theorem 1 only provides strategy having countable memory. In this section we show that these objectives allow for a compact strategy.

Proposition 6 (Reachability). *If there exists a winning strategy for Preciser in stopping game $\mathcal{G}$ for reachability function f^T_{reach}, then there exists a stochastic update winning strategy $\pi = \langle \mathcal{M}, \pi_u, \pi_n, \alpha\rangle$ such that $|\mathcal{M}| \leq 2{\cdot}|S|$.*

Proof (Sketch). Let $f = f^T_{\mathrm{reach}}$ and π^- and π^+ be the pure memoryless deterministic update strategies achieving, for every $w \cdot s \in \Omega_{\mathcal{G}}{}^+$, the minimum and maximum expected value for f. By Theorem 1 there exists a stochastic update strategy $\pi^\star$, which achieves the precise reachability probability. However, the construction only provides a strategy having countable memory. We will construct a stochastic update strategy which is equivalent to $\pi^\star$, but has memory size at most $2{\cdot}|S|$. The strategy $\pi = \langle \mathcal{M}, \pi_u, \pi_n, \alpha\rangle$ is defined as follows:

- $\mathcal{M} = \{\langle s, \text{val}^-(s)\rangle, \langle s, \text{val}^+(s)\rangle \mid s \in S\}$,
- $\pi_u(\langle s, y\rangle, t) = \begin{cases} \langle t, y\rangle & \text{if } s \in S_\Box, \\ [\langle t, \text{val}^-(t)\rangle \mapsto \beta(y,t), \\ \ \langle t, \text{val}^+(t)\rangle \mapsto 1-\beta(y,t)] & \text{if } s \in S_\Diamond, \\ \langle t, \text{val}^-(t)\rangle & \text{if } s \in S_\circ \text{ and } y = \text{val}^-(s), \\ \langle t, \text{val}^+(t)\rangle & \text{if } s \in S_\circ \text{ and } y = \text{val}^+(s), \end{cases}$
- $\pi_n(s, \langle s, y\rangle) = \begin{cases} \pi^-(s) & \text{if } y = \text{val}^-(s), \\ \pi^+(s) & \text{otherwise} \end{cases}$
- $\alpha(s) = [\langle s, \text{val}^-(s)\rangle \mapsto \beta(x,s), \langle s, \text{val}^+(s)\rangle \mapsto 1-\beta(x,s)]$,

for all $s, t \in S$, and $\langle s, y\rangle \in \mathcal{M}$.

Let us look at the functions of the strategy individually. The initial distribution functions of $\pi^\star$ and π are the same. For the next move functions, since π^- and π^+ are memoryless, we have that for any path $w{\cdot}s \in \Omega_{\mathcal{G}}{}^+$, $\pi^-(w{\cdot}s) = \pi^-(s)$ and $\pi^+(w{\cdot}s) = \pi^+(s)$. It follows that $\pi_n(s, \langle w{\cdot}s, y\rangle) = \pi_n(s, \langle s, y\rangle)$. For the memory update function π_u, it is equivalent to the memory update function of $\pi^\star$ (i.e., produces the same distributions for all paths) if the target states are treated as terminal, i.e., for reachability function it does not matter what actions are played after the target has been reached. □

The proofs for the following two propositions are similar (see [5] for details).

Proposition 7 (ω-regular). *If there exists a winning strategy for Preciser in stopping game $\mathcal{G}$ for ω-regular objective function $f^{\mathcal{A}}_{\text{omega}}$ and objective given as a deterministic parity automaton $\mathcal{A}$, then there exists a stochastic update winning strategy $\pi = \langle \mathcal{M}, \pi_u, \pi_n, \alpha\rangle$ such that $|\mathcal{M}| \le 2{\cdot}|S|{\cdot}|\mathcal{A}|$.*

Proposition 8 (Total reward). *If there exists a winning strategy for Preciser in a stopping game $\mathcal{G}$ for total reward function f^r_{total}, then there exists a stochastic update winning strategy $\pi = \langle \mathcal{M}, \pi_u, \pi_n, \alpha\rangle$ such that $|\mathcal{M}| \le 2{\cdot}|S|$.*

Since discounted objective implicitly mimics stopping mechanism, using Proposition 8 and Theorem 1 we show that for the discounted objectives we can construct compact strategies for arbitrary finite games without the stopping assumption.

Theorem 2. *Given a game arena $\mathcal{G}$, a discounted reward function $f = f^{\delta,r}_{\text{disct}}$, satisfying $\Omega^{no}_{\mathcal{G},f} = \emptyset$, a state $s \in S$, and a value $x \in \mathbb{R}$.*

$$x \in \mathit{Exact}_{\mathcal{G}}(s, f) \iff \inf_{\pi\in\Pi}\sup_{\sigma\in\Sigma} \mathbb{E}^{\pi,\sigma}_{\mathcal{G},s}[f] \le x \le \sup_{\pi\in\Pi}\inf_{\sigma\in\Sigma} \mathbb{E}^{\pi,\sigma}_{\mathcal{G},s}[f].$$

Proof. The proof employs a standard construction [11] that reduces the expected discounted reward problem to expected total reward problem. Let $\mathcal{G} = \langle S, (S_\Box, S_\Diamond, S_\circ), \Delta\rangle$, and let $f^{\delta,r}_{\text{disct}}$ be given by a reward structure r and a discount factor $0 < \delta < 1$, we define a stopping game $\mathcal{G}' = \langle S \cup S', (S_\Box, S_\Diamond, S_\circ \cup S'), \Delta'\rangle$ and a *total reward* objective function f^r_{total} as follows. The set S' contains states

$\bar{s}$ for all $s \in S$ and a distinguished state $\star$. The set Δ' is defined as follows: for all s, t we define $\Delta'(s, \bar{t}) = \Delta(s, t)$, $\Delta(\bar{t}, t) = 1 - \delta$ and $\Delta(\bar{t}, \star) = \delta$. We make the state $\star$ terminal by putting $\Delta'(\star, \star) = 1$. The reward structure r' for f^r_{total} in $\mathcal{G}'$ is defined by $r'(s) = r(s)$ for all $s \in S$ and $r(s') = 0$ otherwise. There is a straightforward bijection between the strategies of $\mathcal{G}$ and $\mathcal{G}'$ that for any π and σ returns π' and σ' such that $\mathbb{E}^{\pi,\sigma}_{\mathcal{G},s}[f^{\delta,r}_{\text{disct}}] = \mathbb{E}^{\pi',\sigma'}_{\mathcal{G}',s}[f^r_{\text{total}}]$. The theorem is then obtained by using Theorem 1 and Proposition 8. □

4.3 Complexity

We discuss the complexity of the controller synthesis problem for the objectives considered in Section 4.2 where compact strategies do exist. As we discussed in previous section, controller synthesis essentially boils down to computing the extreme values of the corresponding game. Assume that we have an oracle to decide the following: (1) given any state of the game s, whether $\sup_{\pi\in\Pi}\inf_{\sigma\in\Sigma}\mathbb{E}^{\pi,\sigma}_{\mathcal{G},s}[f] \geq \inf_{\pi\in\Pi}\sup_{\sigma\in\Sigma}\mathbb{E}^{\pi,\sigma}_{\mathcal{G},s}[f]$ and (2) given any state of the game s, whether $\inf_{\pi\in\Pi}\sup_{\sigma\in\Sigma}\mathbb{E}^{\pi,\sigma}_{\mathcal{G},s}[f] \leq x \leq \sup_{\pi\in\Pi}\inf_{\sigma\in\Sigma}\mathbb{E}^{\pi,\sigma}_{\mathcal{G},s}[f]$. By Proposition 4 and Theorem 1, together with Proposition 6 – 8 the controller synthesis problem is decidable in polynomial time if we have oracles for (1) and (2).

For the considered objectives, (1) and (2) are decidable in NP ∩ co-NP since games with these objectives admit pure memoryless strategies for both players (in the product of the game with the deterministic parity automaton at least in the case of ω-regular objectives; cf. [3]). It is easy to see that $\mathrm{P}^{\mathrm{NP}\cap\mathrm{co\text{-}NP}} = \mathrm{NP}\cap\mathrm{co\text{-}NP}$. Hence, we can conclude that the controller-synthesis problem is in NP ∩ co-NP for the objectives studied in Section 4.2.

4.4 Non-stopping Games

It is natural to ask whether the result of Theorem 1 can be transferred to non-stopping games. The following proposition provides a negative answer.

Proposition 9. *There is a game $\mathcal{G}$ and a reachability objective f, a state $s \in S$ and a number* $\inf_{\pi\in\Pi}\sup_{\sigma\in\Sigma}\mathbb{E}^{\pi,\sigma}_{\mathcal{G},s}[f] \leq x \leq \sup_{\pi\in\Pi}\inf_{\sigma\in\Sigma}\mathbb{E}^{\pi,\sigma}_{\mathcal{G},s}[f]$ *such that* $\Omega^{no}_{\mathcal{G},f} = \emptyset$ *and* $x \notin \mathit{Exact}_{\mathcal{G}}(s, f)$.

To prove Proposition 9, consider the game $\mathcal{G}$ from Figure 1 (right), where the target state is marked with gray colour. For each state $s \in \{s_0, s_1, s_3\}$ we have $\inf_{\pi\in\Pi}\sup_{\sigma\in\Sigma}\mathbb{E}^{\pi,\sigma}_{\mathcal{G},s}[f] = 0.5$, and for state s_2 we have $\inf_{\pi\in\Pi}\sup_{\sigma\in\Sigma}\mathbb{E}^{\pi,\sigma}_{\mathcal{G},s_2}[f] = 0.0$. On the other hand, for each state $s \in \{s_1, s_2, s_3\}$ we have that $\sup_{\pi\in\Pi}\inf_{\sigma\in\Sigma}\mathbb{E}^{\pi,\sigma}_{\mathcal{G},s}[f] = 0.5$, while for state s_0 we have $\sup_{\pi\in\Pi}\inf_{\sigma\in\Sigma}\mathbb{E}^{\pi,\sigma}_{\mathcal{G},s_0}[f] = 1$. However, for example in state s_0 we get $\mathit{Exact}(s, f) = \{1\}$. For any value $0.5 \leq x < 1$, any strategy π that should achieve x must in s_0 pick the transition to the terminal state with probability $2 \cdot x - 1$, because otherwise Spoiler could propose a counter strategy σ which deterministically goes up from s_1, and thus $\mathbb{E}^{\pi,\sigma}_{\mathcal{G},s}[f] \neq x$. Let us suppose that π has this property, then it must further ensure that from s_1

the target state is reached with probability 0.5, which means that it can *never* randomise in s_0 or s_1, except for the very first step: if it randomised, Spoiler could propose a winning counter-strategy that would go to central vertex immediately after the first randomisation took place. But this means that the strategy π must always keep going from s_2 to s_3 and from s_0 to s_1 deterministically, to which Spoiler can respond by a strategy σ that always goes from s_1 to s_2 and from s_3 to s_0 deterministically, hence avoiding to enter the target state at all.

An interesting point to make is that even though Preciser has not any strategy that would ensure reaching the target from s_0 in $\mathcal{G}$ with probability x for a given $0.5 \leq x < 1$, he has got an "ε-optimal" strategy for any $\varepsilon > 0$, i.e. for any x there is a strategy π of Preciser such that for all σ of Spoiler we get $x - \varepsilon \leq \mathbb{E}^{\pi,\sigma}_{\mathcal{G},s_0}[f] \leq x + \varepsilon$. For example, if $x = 0.5$, the strategy π can be defined so that in s_0 it picks the transition to s_1 with probability $1 - \varepsilon$, and the other available transition with probability ε, while in s_2 it takes the transition to s_3 with probability $1 - \frac{\varepsilon}{1-\varepsilon}$, and the other available transition with probability $\frac{\varepsilon}{1-\varepsilon}$.

Again, one might ask whether ε-optimal strategies always exist. Unfortunately, this is also not the case, as can be seen when the transition from s_0 to the target state is redirected to the non-target terminal state.

5 Counter-Strategy Problem

In this section we discuss the *counter-strategy* problem, which, given a game $\mathcal{G}$, a state s, and an objective function f, asks whether for any strategy of Spoiler there exists a counter-strategy for Preciser such that the expected value of f is exactly x. Let us characterise the set of all values for which counter-strategy exists by defining $\mathit{CExact}_{\mathcal{G}}(s, f) = \{x \in \mathbb{R} \mid \forall \sigma \in \Sigma \,.\, \exists \pi \in \Pi : \mathbb{E}^{\pi,\sigma}_{\mathcal{G},s}[f] = x\}$.

Lemma 2. *Given a game $\mathcal{G}$, a finite path $w \cdot s \in \Omega_{\mathcal{G}}{}^{+}$, where $s \in S$ and a function f, if $\sup_{\sigma\in\Sigma} \inf_{\pi\in\Pi} \mathbb{E}^{\pi,\sigma}_{\mathcal{G},s}[f_{w\cdot s}] > \inf_{\sigma\in\Sigma} \sup_{\pi\in\Pi} \mathbb{E}^{\pi,\sigma}_{\mathcal{G},s}[f_{w\cdot s}]$, then Preciser cannot achieve any exact value after that path, i.e., $\mathit{CExact}_{\mathcal{G}}(s, f_{w\cdot s}) = \emptyset$.*

Proof. Let $x^* = \sup_{\sigma\in\Sigma} \inf_{\pi\in\Pi} \mathbb{E}^{\pi,\sigma}_{\mathcal{G},s}[f_{w\cdot s}]$ and $x_* = \inf_{\sigma\in\Sigma} \sup_{\pi\in\Pi} \mathbb{E}^{\pi,\sigma}_{\mathcal{G},s}[f_{w\cdot s}]$ such that $x^* > x_*$; and let $\sigma^*, \sigma_* \in \Sigma$ be the corresponding strategies of Spoiler. Notice that for any arbitrary strategy π of Preciser we have that

$$\mathbb{E}^{\pi,\sigma_*}_{\mathcal{G},w_0}[f_{w\cdot s}] \leq x_* < x^* \leq \mathbb{E}^{\pi,\sigma^*}_{\mathcal{G},w_0}[f_{w\cdot s}].$$

Hence, if $x \leq x_*$ then there is no strategy of Preciser that yields expectation at most x against σ^*, while if $x > x_*$ then there is no strategy of Preciser that yields expectation at least x against σ_*. Hence, $\mathit{CExact}_{\mathcal{G}}(s, f_{w\cdot s}) = \emptyset$. □

Let $\Omega^{\mathrm{no}_c}_{\mathcal{G},f} \subseteq \Omega_{\mathcal{G}}{}^{+}$ be a set paths in $\mathcal{G}$ such that a path w is in $\Omega^{\mathrm{no}_c}_{\mathcal{G},f}$ if and only if w satisfies the condition in Lemma 2, i.e., after w Preciser cannot propose a counter strategy to achieve any exact value, for a function f.

Proposition 10. *In an game $\mathcal{G}$, and a state $s \in S$, if there exists a strategy of Spoiler, such that for all strategies of Preciser at least one path from $\Omega^{no_c}_{\mathcal{G},f}$ has a positive probability, then $CExact_{\mathcal{G}}(s,f) = \emptyset$, i.e.,*

$$\exists \sigma \in \Sigma \,.\, \forall \pi \in \Pi : \mathrm{Pr}^{\pi,\sigma}_{\mathcal{G},s}\Big(\bigcup_{w \in \Omega^{no_c}_{\mathcal{G},f}} \mathrm{Cyl}(w)\Big) > 0 \Rightarrow CExact_{\mathcal{G}}(s,f) = \emptyset.$$

Using the results above we are now ready to characterise the states from which Preciser has, for any Spoiler strategy, a winning counter strategy to achieve exactly the specified value x. The following theorem is proved in [5].

Theorem 3. *In a game $\mathcal{G}$ with $\Omega^{no_c}_{\mathcal{G},f} = \emptyset$, and a state $s \in S$, $x \in CExact_{\mathcal{G}}(s,f)$ if and only if $\sup_{\sigma \in \Sigma} \inf_{\pi \in \Pi} \mathbb{E}^{\pi,\sigma}_{\mathcal{G},s}[f] \le x \le \inf_{\sigma \in \Sigma} \sup_{\pi \in \Pi} \mathbb{E}^{\pi,\sigma}_{\mathcal{G},s}[f]$.*

6 Conclusion and Future Work

In this paper we studied a novel kind of objectives for two-player stochastic games, in which the role of one player is to achieve exactly a given expected value, while the role of the other player is to get any other value. We settled the controller synthesis problem for stopping games with linearly bounded objective functions and for arbitrary finite games with discounted reward objective. We solved the counter strategy problem for arbitrary finite games and arbitrary payoff functions. There are two main directions for future work: 1. relaxing the restrictions on the game arenas, i.e., studying the controller-synthesis problem for non-stopping games; 2. modifying the problem so that the role of preciser is to reach a value from certain interval, rather than one specific number.

Acknowledgments. The authors are part supported by ERC Advanced Grant VERIWARE and EPSRC grant EP/F001096/1. Vojtěch Forejt is supported by a Royal Society Newton Fellowship. Ashutosh Trivedi is supported by NSF awards CNS 0931239, CNS 1035715, CCF 0915777. Michael Ummels is supported by the DFG project SYANCO.

References

1. Brázdil, T., Brožek, V., Chatterjee, K., Forejt, V., Kučera, A.: Two views on multiple mean-payoff objectives in Markov decision processes. In: LICS, pp. 33–42 (2011)
2. Cabot, A.N., Hannum, R.C.: Gaming regulation and mathematics: A marriage of necessity. John Marshall Law Review 35(3), 333–358 (2002)
3. Chatterjee, K., Henzinger, T.A.: A survey of stochastic ω-regular games. J. Comput. Syst. Sci. 78(2), 394–413 (2012)
4. Chatterjee, K., Majumdar, R., Henzinger, T.A.: Markov Decision Processes with Multiple Objectives. In: Durand, B., Thomas, W. (eds.) STACS 2006. LNCS, vol. 3884, pp. 325–336. Springer, Heidelberg (2006)

5. Chen, T., Forejt, V., Kwiatkowska, M., Simaitis, A., Trivedi, A., Ummels, M.: Playing stochastic games precisely. Technical Report No. CS-RR-12-03, Department of Computer Science, University of Oxford (June 2012)
6. Dziembowski, S., Jurdzinski, M., Walukiewicz, I.: How much memory is needed to win infinite games? In: LICS, pp. 99–110. IEEE Computer Society (1997)
7. Etessami, K., Kwiatkowska, M.Z., Vardi, M.Y., Yannakakis, M.: Multi-objective model checking of Markov decision processes. LMCS 4(4) (2008)
8. Filar, J., Vrieze, K.: Competitive Markov Decision Processes. Springer (1997)
9. Grädel, E., Thomas, W., Wilke, T. (eds.): Automata, Logics, and Infinite Games. LNCS, vol. 2500. Springer, Heidelberg (2002)
10. Neyman, A., Sorin, S. (eds.): Stochastic Games and Applications. NATO Science Series C, vol. 570. Kluwer Academic Publishers (2004)
11. Puterman, M.L.: Markov Decision Processes: Discrete Stochastic Dynamic Programming. Wiley (1994)
12. Ramadge, P., Wonham, W.: The control of discrete event systems. Proc. IEEE 77(1) (1989)
13. Shapley, L.S.: Stochastic games. Proc. Nat. Acad. Sci. U.S.A. 39 (1953)
14. State of New Jersey, 214th legislature, as amended by the General Assembly on 01/10/2011 (November 2010), `http://www.njleg.state.nj.us/2010/Bills/S0500/12_R4.PDF`

Efficient Modelling and Generation of Markov Automata*

Mark Timmer[1], Joost-Pieter Katoen[1,2], Jaco van de Pol[1], and Mariëlle I.A. Stoelinga[1]

[1] Formal Methods and Tools, Faculty of EEMCS
University of Twente, The Netherlands
{timmer,vdpol,m.i.a.stoelinga}@cs.utwente.nl
[2] Software Modeling and Verification Group
RWTH Aachen University, Germany
katoen@cs.rwth-aachen.de

Abstract. This paper introduces a framework for the efficient modelling and generation of Markov automata. It consists of (1) the data-rich process-algebraic language MAPA, allowing concise modelling of systems with nondeterminism, probability and Markovian timing; (2) a restricted form of the language, the MLPPE, enabling easy state space generation and parallel composition; and (3) several syntactic reduction techniques on the MLPPE format, for generating equivalent but smaller models.

Technically, the framework relies on an encoding of MAPA into the existing prCRL language for probabilistic automata. First, we identify a class of transformations on prCRL that can be lifted to the Markovian realm using our encoding. Then, we employ this result to reuse prCRL's linearisation procedure to transform any MAPA specification to an equivalent MLPPE, and to lift three prCRL reduction techniques to MAPA. Additionally, we define two novel reduction techniques for MLPPEs. All our techniques treat data as well as Markovian and interactive behaviour in a fully symbolic manner, working on specifications instead of models and thus reducing state spaces prior to their construction. The framework has been implemented in our tool SCOOP, and a case study on polling systems and mutual exclusion protocols shows its practical applicability.

1 Introduction

In the past decade, much research has been devoted to improving the efficiency of probabilistic model checking: verifying properties on systems that are governed by, in general, both probabilistic and nondeterministic choices. This way, many models in areas like distributed systems, networking, security and systems biology have been successfully used for dependability and performance analysis.

Recently, a new type of model that captures much richer behaviour was introduced: Markov automata (MAs) [5,4,3]. In addition to nondeterministic and

* This research has been partially funded by NWO under grants 612.063.817 (SYRUP) and Dn 63-257 (ROCKS).

M. Koutny and I. Ulidowski (Eds.): CONCUR 2012, LNCS 7454, pp. 364–379, 2012.

probabilistic choices, MAs also contain Markovian transitions, i.e., transitions subject to an exponentially distributed delay. Hence, MAs can be seen as a unification of probabilistic automata (PAs) [16,18] (containing nondeterministic and probabilistic transitions) and interactive Markov chains (IMCs) [8] (containing nondeterministic and Markovian transitions). They provide a natural semantics for a wide variety of specification languages for concurrent systems, including Generalized Stochastic Petri Nets [12], the domain-specific language AADL [2] and (dynamic) fault trees [1]; i.e., MAs are very general and, except for hard real-time deadlines, can describe most behaviour that is modelled today.

Example 1. Figure 1 shows the state space of a polling system with two arrival stations and probabilistically erroneous behaviour (inspired by [17]). Although probability can sometimes be encoded in rates (e.g., having $(0,0,0) \xrightarrow{0.1\lambda_1} (1,0,1)$ and $(0,0,0) \xrightarrow{0.9\lambda_1} (0,0,1)$ instead of the current λ_1-transition from $(0,0,0)$ and the τ-transition from $(1,0,0)$), the transitions leaving $(1,1,0)$ cannot be encoded like that, due to the nondeterminism between them. Thus, this system could not be represented by an IMC (and neither a PA, due to the Markovian rates). □

Although several formalisms to specify PAs and IMCs exist [10,6], no data-rich specification language for MAs has been introduced so far. Since realistic systems often consist of a very large number of states, such a method to model systems on a higher level, instead of explicitly providing the state space, is vital. Additionally, the omnipresent state space explosion also applies to MAs. Therefore, high-level specifications are an essential starting point for syntactic optimisations that aim to reduce the size of the state spaces to be constructed.

Our approach. We introduce a new process-algebraic specification language for MAs, called MAPA (Markov Automata Process Algebra). It is based on the prCRL language for PAs [10], which was in turn based on μCRL [7]. MAPA supports the use of data for efficient modelling in the presence of nondeterministic and probabilistic choices, as well as Markovian delays. We define a normal form

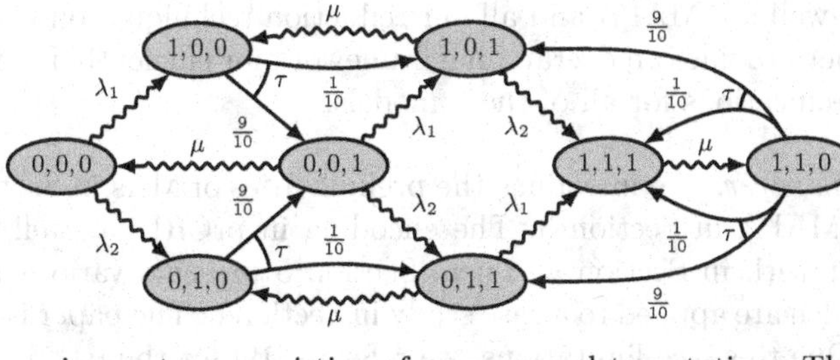

Fig. 1. A queueing system, consisting of a server and two stations. The two stations have incoming requests with rates λ_1, λ_2, which are stored until fetched by the server. If both stations contain a job, the server chooses nondeterministically. Jobs are processed with rate μ, and when polling a station, there is a $\frac{1}{10}$ probability that the job is erroneously kept in the station after being fetched. Each state is represented as a tuple (s_1, s_2, j), with s_i the number of jobs in station i, and j the number of jobs in the server. For simplicity we assume that each component can hold at most one job.

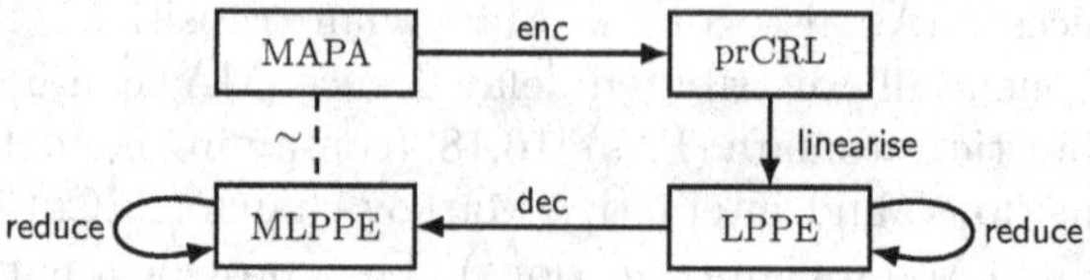

Fig. 2. Linearising MAPA specifications using prCRL linerarisation

for MAPA: the Markovian Linear Probabilistic Process Equation (MLPPE). Like the LPPE for prCRL, it allows for easy state space generation and parallel composition, and simplifies the definition of syntactic reduction techniques. These reduce the MA underlying a MAPA specification prior to its generation.

We present an encoding of MAPA into prCRL, to exploit many useful results from the prCRL context. This is non-trivial, since strong bisimulation (or even isomorphism) of PAs does not guarantee bisimulation of the MAs obtained after decoding. Therefore, we introduce a notion of bisimulation on prCRL terms, based on the preservation of derivations. We show that, for any prCRL transformation f that respects our *derivation-preserving bisimulation*, $\mathsf{dec} \circ f \circ \mathsf{enc}$ preserves strong bisimulation, i.e., $\mathsf{dec}\,(f(\mathsf{enc}\,(M)))$ is strongly bisimilar to M for every MAPA specification M. This implies that many useful prCRL transformations are directly applicable to MAPA specifications. We show that this is the case for the linearisation procedure of [10]; as a result, we can reuse it to transform any MAPA specifications to an equivalent MLPPE. We show that three previously defined reduction techniques also respect derivation-preserving bisimulation. Hence, they can now be applied to Markovian models as well. Moreover, we describe two novel reduction techniques for MLPPEs. We implemented the complete framework in our tool SCOOP [21], and show its applicability using the aforementioned polling system and a probabilistic mutual exclusion protocol.

Figure 2 summarises the procedure of encoding a specification into prCRL, linearising, reducing, decoding, and possibly reducing some more, obtaining an efficient MLPPE that is strongly bisimilar to the original specification. Since MAs generalise many existing formalisms (LTSs, DTMCs, CTMCs, IMCs, PAs), we can just as well use MAPA and all our reduction techniques on such models. Thus, this paper provides an overarching framework for efficiently modelling and optimising specifications for all of these models.

Overview of the paper. We introduce the preliminaries of MAs in Section 2, and the language MAPA in Section 3. The encoding in prCRL, as well as linearisation, is dealt with in Section 4. Then, Section 5 presents various reductions techniques, which are applied to a case study in Section 6. The paper is concluded in Section 7. Due to space limitations, we refer to [19] for the (straightforward) definition of parallel composition and all complete proofs.

2 Preliminaries

Definition 1 (Basics). *Given a set S, an element $s \in S$ and a sequence $\sigma = \langle s_1, s_2, \ldots, s_n \rangle \in S^*$, we use $s + \sigma$ to denote $\langle s, s_1, s_2, \ldots, s_n \rangle$.*

A probability distribution *over a countable set* S *is a function* $\mu\colon S \to [0,1]$ *such that* $\sum_{s\in S}\mu(s) = 1$. *We denote by* $\mathsf{Distr}(S)$ *the sets of all such functions. For* $S' \subseteq S$, *let* $\mu(S') = \sum_{s\in S'}\mu(s)$. *We define the lifting* $\mu_f \in \mathsf{Distr}(T)$ *of* μ *over a function* $f\colon S \to T$ *by* $\mu_f(t) = \mu(f^{-1}(t))$. *Note that, for injective* f, $\mu_f(f(s)) = \mu(s)$ *for every* $s \in S$. *We let* $\mathsf{supp}(\mu) = \{s \in S \mid \mu(s) > 0\}$ *be the* support *of* μ, *and write* $\mathbb{1}_s$ *for the* Dirac distribution *for* s, *determined by* $\mathbb{1}_s(s) = 1$.

Given an equivalence relation $R \subseteq S \times S$, *we write* $[s]_R$ *for the equivalence class induced by* s, *i.e.,* $[s]_R = \{s' \in S \mid (s,s') \in R\}$. *We denote the set of all such equivalence classes by* S/R. *Given two probability distributions* μ, μ' *over* S, *we write* $\mu \equiv_R \mu'$ *to denote that* $\mu([s]_R) = \mu'([s]_R)$ *for every* $s \in S$.

An MA is a transition system in which the set of transitions is partitioned into interactive transitions (which are equivalent to the transitions of a PA) and Markovian transitions (which are equivalent to the transitions of an IMC). The following definition formalises this, and provides notations for MAs. We assume a countable universe *Act* of actions, with $\tau \in Act$ the invisible internal action.

Definition 2 (Markov automata). *A* Markov automaton (MA) *is a tuple* $\mathcal{M} = \langle S, s^0, A, \hookrightarrow, \rightsquigarrow\rangle$, *where*

- S *is a countable set of* states, *of which* $s^0 \in S$ *is the* initial state*;*
- $A \subseteq Act$ *is a countable set of* actions*;*
- $\hookrightarrow\ \subseteq S \times A \times \mathsf{Distr}(S)$ *is the* interactive transition relation*;*
- $\rightsquigarrow\ \subseteq S \times \mathbb{R}_{>0} \times S$ *is the* Markovian transition relation.

If $(s,a,\mu) \in \hookrightarrow$, *we write* $s \xhookrightarrow{a} \mu$ *and say that the action* a *can be* executed *from state* s, *after which the probability to go to* $s' \in S$ *is* $\mu(s')$. *If* $(s,\lambda,s') \in \rightsquigarrow$, *we write* $s \overset{\lambda}{\rightsquigarrow} s'$ *and say that* s *moves to* s' *with rate* λ.

The rate between two states $s, s' \in S$ *is* $rate(s,s') = \sum_{(s,\lambda,s')\in\rightsquigarrow}\lambda$, *and the* outgoing rate of s *is* $rate(s) = \sum_{s'\in S} rate(s,s')$. *We require* $rate(s) < \infty$ *for every state* $s \in S$. *If* $rate(s) > 0$, *the* branching probability distribution *after this delay is denoted by* $\mathbb{P}_s$ *and defined by* $\mathbb{P}_s(s') = \frac{rate(s,s')}{rate(s)}$ *for every* $s' \in S$.

Remark 1. As we focus on data with possibly infinite domains, we need countable state spaces. Although this is problematic for weak bisimulation [5], it does not hinder us since we only depend on strong bisimulation.

We do need a finite exit rate for every state. After all, given a state s with $rate(s) = \infty$, there is no obvious measure for the next state distribution of s. Also, if all states reachable from s would be considered equivalent by a bisimulation relation, the bisimulation quotient would be ill-defined as it would yield a Markovian transition with rate ∞ (which is not allowed). Fortunately, restricting to finite exit rates is no severe limitation; it still allows infinite chains of states connected by finite rates, as often seen in the context of queueing systems. Also, it still allows infinite branching with for instance rates $\frac{1}{2}\lambda$, $\frac{1}{4}\lambda$, $\frac{1}{8}\lambda$, ... □

Following [5], we define a special action $\chi(r)$ to denote a delay with rate r, enabling a uniform treatment of interactive and Markovian transitions via *extended actions*. As usual [8,5], we employ the *maximal progress assumption*: time is only allowed to progress in states without outgoing τ-transitions (since they are assumed to be infinitely fast). This is taken into account by only having extended actions representing Markovian delay from states that do not enable an interactive transition $s \xhookrightarrow{\tau} \mu'$.

Definition 3 (Extended action set). *Let $\mathcal{M} = \langle S, s^0, A, \hookrightarrow, \rightsquigarrow \rangle$ be an MA, then the* extended action set *of $\mathcal{M}$ is given by $A^\chi = A \cup \{\chi(r) \mid r \in \mathbb{R}_{>0}\}$. Given a state $s \in S$ and an action $\alpha \in A^\chi$, we write $s \xrightarrow{\alpha} \mu$ if either*

- *$\alpha \in A$ and $s \xhookrightarrow{\alpha} \mu$, or*
- *$\alpha = \chi(rate(s))$, $rate(s) > 0$, $\mu = \mathbb{P}_s$ and there is no μ' such that $s \xhookrightarrow{\tau} \mu'$.*

Based on extended actions, we introduce strong bisimulation and isomorphism.

Definition 4 (Strong bisimulation). *Let $\mathcal{M} = \langle S, s^0, A, \hookrightarrow, \rightsquigarrow \rangle$ be an MA, then an equivalence relation $R \subseteq S \times S$ is a* strong bisimulation *if for every pair $(s, s') \in R$, action $a \in A^\chi$ and transition $s \xrightarrow{a} \mu$, there is a μ' such that $s' \xrightarrow{a} \mu'$ and $\mu \equiv_R \mu'$.*

Two states $s, t \in S$ are strongly bisimilar (denoted by $s \sim t$) if there exists a bisimulation relation R such that $(s, t) \in R$. Two MAs $\mathcal{M}_1, \mathcal{M}_2$ are strongly bisimilar (denoted $\mathcal{M}_1 \sim \mathcal{M}_2$) if their initial states are strongly bisimilar in their disjoint union.

Definition 5 (Isomorphism). *Let $\mathcal{M} = \langle S, s^0, A, \hookrightarrow, \rightsquigarrow \rangle$ be an MA, then two states $s, s' \in S$ are* isomorphic *(denoted by $s \cong s'$) if there exists a bijection $f \colon S \to S$ such that $f(s) = s'$ and $\forall t \in S, \mu \in \mathsf{Distr}(S), a \in A^\chi \,.\, t \xrightarrow{a} \mu \Leftrightarrow f(t) \xrightarrow{a} \mu_f$. Two MAs $\mathcal{M}_1, \mathcal{M}_2$ are isomorphic (denoted $\mathcal{M}_1 \cong \mathcal{M}_2$) if their initial states are isomorphic in their disjoint union.*

Obviously, isomorphism implies strong probabilistic bisimulation, as the reflexive and symmetric closure of $\{(s, f(s)) \mid s \in S\}$ is a bisimulation relation.

MAs generalise many classes of systems. Most importantly for this paper, they generalise Segala's PAs [16].

Definition 6 (Probabilistic automata). *A* probabilistic automaton *(PA) is an MA $\mathcal{M} = \langle S, s^0, A, \hookrightarrow, \rightsquigarrow \rangle$ without any Markovian transitions, i.e., $\rightsquigarrow = \emptyset$.*

The definitions of strong bisimulation and isomorphism for MAs correspond to those for PAs, if the MA only contains interactive transitions. So, if two PAs are strongly bisimilar or isomorphic, so are their corresponding MA representations. Therefore, we use the same notations for strong bisimulation and isomorphism of PAs as we do for MAs.

Additionally, we can obtain IMCs by restricting to Dirac distributions for the interactive transitions, CTMCs by taking $\hookrightarrow = \emptyset$, DTMCs by taking $\rightsquigarrow = \emptyset$ and having only one transition $(s, a, \mu) \in \hookrightarrow$ for every $s \in S$, and LTSs by taking $\rightsquigarrow = \emptyset$ and using only Dirac distributions for the interactive transitions [4]. Hence, the results in this paper can be applied to all these models.

3 Markov Automata Process Algebra

We introduce Markov Automata Process Algebra (MAPA), a language in which all conditions, nondeterministic and probabilistic choices, and Markovian delays may depend on data parameters. We assume an external mechanism for the evaluation of expressions (e.g., equational logic, or a fixed data language), able to handle at least boolean and real-valued expressions. Also, we assume that any expression that does not contain variables can be evaluated. Note that this restricts the expressiveness of the data language. In the examples we use an intuitive data language, containing basic arithmetic and boolean operators.

We generally refer to data types with upper-case letters $D, E, \ldots$, and to variables with lower-case letters $u, v, \ldots$.

Definition 7 (Process terms). *A* process term *in MAPA is any term that can be generated by the following grammar:*

$$p ::= Y(\boldsymbol{t}) \ \mid\ c \Rightarrow p \ \mid\ p + p \ \mid\ \textstyle\sum_{\boldsymbol{x}:\boldsymbol{D}} p \ \mid\ a(\boldsymbol{t}) \textstyle\sum_{\boldsymbol{x}:\boldsymbol{D}} f : p \ \mid\ (\lambda) \cdot p$$

Here, Y is a process name, $\boldsymbol{t}$ a vector of expressions, c a boolean expression, $\boldsymbol{x}$ a vector of variables ranging over a (possibly infinite) type $\boldsymbol{D}$, $a \in Act$ a (parameterised) atomic action, f a real-valued expression yielding values in $[0, 1]$, and λ an expression yielding positive real numbers (rates). We write $p = p'$ for syntactically identical process terms. Note that, if $|\boldsymbol{x}| > 1$, $\boldsymbol{D}$ is a Cartesian product, as for instance in $\sum_{(m,i):\{m_1,m_2\}\times\{1,2,3\}} \text{send}(m, i) \ldots$.

Given an expression t, a process term p and two vectors $\boldsymbol{x} = (x_1, \ldots, x_n)$, $\boldsymbol{d} = (d_1, \ldots, d_n)$, we use $t[\boldsymbol{x} := \boldsymbol{d}]$ to denote the result of substituting every x_i in t by d_i, and $p[\boldsymbol{x} := \boldsymbol{d}]$ for the result of applying this to every expression in p.

In a process term, $Y(\boldsymbol{t})$ denotes *process instantiation*, where $\boldsymbol{t}$ instantiates Y's process variables as defined below (allowing recursion). The term $c \Rightarrow p$ behaves as p if the *condition* c holds, and cannot do anything otherwise. The $+$ operator denotes *nondeterministic choice*, and $\sum_{\boldsymbol{x}:\boldsymbol{D}} p$ a (possibly infinite) *nondeterministic choice over data type* $\boldsymbol{D}$. The term $a(\boldsymbol{t}) \sum_{\boldsymbol{x}:\boldsymbol{D}} f : p$ performs the action $a(\boldsymbol{t})$ and then does a *probabilistic choice* over $\boldsymbol{D}$. It uses the value $f[\boldsymbol{x} := \boldsymbol{d}]$ as the probability of choosing each $\boldsymbol{d} \in \boldsymbol{D}$. Finally, $(\lambda) \cdot p$ can behave as p after a delay, determined by a negative exponential distribution with rate λ.

Definition 8 (Specifications). *A* MAPA specification *is given by a tuple* $M = (\{X_i(\boldsymbol{x_i} : \boldsymbol{D_i}) = p_i\}, X_j(\boldsymbol{t}))$ *consisting of a set of uniquely-named* processes X_i, *each defined by a* process equation $X_i(\boldsymbol{x_i} : \boldsymbol{D_i}) = p_i$, *and an* initial process $X_j(\boldsymbol{t})$. *In a process equation,* $\boldsymbol{x_i}$ *is a vector of* process variables *with type* $\boldsymbol{D_i}$, *and* p_i *(the* right-hand side*) is a* process term *specifying the behaviour of* X_i.

A variable v *in an expression in a right-hand side* p_i *is* bound *if it is an element of* $\boldsymbol{x_i}$ *or it occurs within a construct* $\sum_{\boldsymbol{x}:\boldsymbol{D}}$ *or* $\textstyle\sum_{\boldsymbol{x}:\boldsymbol{D}}$ *such that* v *is an element of* $\boldsymbol{x}$. *Variables that are not bound are said to be* free.

A prCRL specification [10] is a MAPA specification without rates.

We generally refer to process terms with lower-case letters p, q, r, and to processes with capitals X, Y, Z. Also, we will often write $X(x_1 : D_1, \ldots, x_n : D_n)$ for

$\textbf{constant } \mathit{queueSize} = 10, \mathit{nrOfJobTypes} = 3$

$\textbf{type } \mathit{Stations} = \{1, 2\},\ \mathit{Jobs} = \{1, \ldots, \mathit{nrOfJobTypes}\}$

$$\begin{aligned}
&\mathit{Station}(i : \mathit{Stations}, q : \text{Queue}, \mathit{size} : \{0..\mathit{queueSize}\}) \\
&\quad = \mathit{size} < \mathit{queueSize} \Rightarrow (2i+1) \cdot \textstyle\sum_{j:\mathit{Jobs}} \mathit{arrive}(j) \cdot \mathit{Station}(i, \text{enqueue}(q, j), \mathit{size}+1) \\
&\quad + \mathit{size} > 0 \qquad\quad \Rightarrow \mathit{deliver}(i, \text{head}(q)) \sum_{k \in \{1,9\}} \tfrac{k}{10} : k = 1 \Rightarrow \mathit{Station}(i, q, \mathit{size}) \\
&\qquad\qquad\qquad\qquad\qquad\qquad\qquad\qquad + k = 9 \Rightarrow \mathit{Station}(i, \text{tail}(q), \mathit{size} - 1)
\end{aligned}$$

$$\mathit{Server} = \textstyle\sum_{n:\mathit{Stations}} \sum_{j:\mathit{Jobs}} \mathit{poll}(n, j) \cdot (2 * j) \cdot \mathit{finish}(j) \cdot \mathit{Server}$$

$$\gamma(\mathit{poll}, \mathit{deliver}) = \mathit{copy}$$

$$\mathit{System} = \tau_{\{\mathit{copy},\mathit{arrive},\mathit{finish}\}}(\partial_{\{\mathit{poll},\mathit{deliver}\}}(\mathit{Station}(1, \text{empty}, 0) \,||\, \mathit{Station}(2, \text{empty}, 0) \,||\, \mathit{Server}))$$

Fig. 3. Specification of a polling system

$X((x_1, \ldots, x_n) : (D_1 \times \cdots \times D_n))$. The syntactic sugar introduced for prCRL [10] can be lifted directly to MAPA. Most importantly, we write $a(\boldsymbol{t}) \cdot p$ for the action $a(\boldsymbol{t})$ that goes to p with probability 1.

Parallel composition. Using MAPA processes as basic building blocks, we support the modular construction of large systems via top-level parallelism, encapsulation, hiding, and renaming. This can be defined straightforwardly [19].

Example 2. Figure 3 shows the specification for a slightly more involved variant of the system explained in Example 1. Instead of having just one type of job, as was the case there, we now allow a number of different kinds of jobs (with different service rates). Also, we allow the stations to have larger buffers.

The specification uses three data types: a set *Stations* with identifiers for the two stations, a set *Jobs* with the possible incoming jobs, and a built-in type *Queue*. The arrival rate for station i is set to $2i + 1$, so in terms of the rates in Figure 1 we have $\lambda_1 = 3$ and $\lambda_2 = 5$. Each job j is served with rate $2j$.

The stations receive jobs if their queue is not full, and are able to deliver jobs if their queue is not empty. As explained before, removal of jobs from the queue fails with probability $\frac{1}{10}$. The server continuously polls the stations and works on their jobs. The system is composed of the server and two stations, communicating via the *poll* and *deliver* actions. □

3.1 Static and Operational Semantics

Not all syntactically correct MAPA specifications are meaningful. The following definition formulates additional well-formedness conditions. The first two constraints ensure that a specification does not refer to undefined variables or processes, the third is needed to obtain valid probability distributions, and the fourth ensures that the specification has a unique solution (modulo strong probabilistic bisimulation). Additionally, all exit rates should be finite. This is discussed in Remark 2, after providing the operational semantics and MLPPE format.

To define well-formedness, we require the concept of *unguardedness*. We say that a process term $Y(\boldsymbol{t})$ can go *unguarded* to Y. Moreover, $c \Rightarrow p$ can go unguarded to Y if p can, $p+q$ if either p or q can, and $\sum_{\boldsymbol{x}:\boldsymbol{D}} p$ if p can, whereas $a(\boldsymbol{t})\sum_{\boldsymbol{x}:\boldsymbol{D}} f : p$ and $(\lambda) \cdot p$ cannot go unguarded anywhere.

Definition 9 (Well-formed). *A MAPA specification $M = (\{X_i(\boldsymbol{x_i} : \boldsymbol{D_i}) = p_i\}, X_j(\boldsymbol{t}))$ is* well-formed *if the following four constraints are all satisfied:*

- *There are no free variables.*
- *For every instantiation $Y(\boldsymbol{t}')$ occurring in some p_i, there exists a process equation $(X_k(\boldsymbol{x_k} : \boldsymbol{D_k}) = p_k) \in M$ such that $X_k = Y$ and $\boldsymbol{t}'$ is of type $\boldsymbol{D_k}$. Also, the vector $\boldsymbol{t}$ used in the initial process is of type $\boldsymbol{D_j}$.*
- *For every construct $a(\boldsymbol{t})\sum_{\boldsymbol{x}:\boldsymbol{D}} f : p$ occurring in a right-hand side p_i it holds that $\sum_{\boldsymbol{d}\in\boldsymbol{D}} f[\boldsymbol{x} := \boldsymbol{d}] = 1$ for every possible valuation of the free variables in $f[\boldsymbol{x} := \boldsymbol{d}]$ (the summation now used in the mathematical sense).*
- *For every process Y, there is no sequence of processes $X_1, X_2, \ldots, X_n$ (with $n \geq 2$) such that $Y = X_1 = X_n$ and every p_j can go unguarded to p_{j+1}.*

We assume from now on that every MAPA specification is well-formed.

The operational semantics of well-formed MAPA is given by an MA, based on the SOS rules in Figure 4. These rules provide derivations for process terms, like for classical process algebras, but additionally keep track of the rules used in a derivation. A mapping to MAs is only provided for process terms without free variables; this is consistent with our notion of well-formedness. Note that, without the new MStep rule, the semantics corresponds precisely to prCRL [10].

Definition 10 (Derivations). *An* α-derivation *from p to β is a sequence of SOS rules $\mathcal{D}$ such that $p \xrightarrow{\alpha}_{\mathcal{D}} \beta$. We denote the set of all derivations by Δ, and the set of* Markovian derivations *from p to p' by*

$$\mathsf{MD}(p, p') = \{(\lambda, \mathcal{D}) \in \mathbb{R} \times \Delta \mid p \xrightarrow{\lambda}_{\mathcal{D}} p', \text{MStep} \in \mathcal{D}\}.$$

Note that NSum is instantiated with a data element to distinguish between, for instance, $\sum_{d:\{1,2\}} a(d) \cdot p \xrightarrow{a(d_1)}_{\text{NSum}(d_1)} p$ and $\sum_{d:\{1,2\}} a(d) \cdot p \xrightarrow{a(d_2)}_{\text{NSum}(d_2)} p$.

$$\text{Inst}\ \frac{p[\boldsymbol{x} := \boldsymbol{d}] \xrightarrow{\alpha}_{\mathcal{D}} \beta}{Y(\boldsymbol{d}) \xrightarrow{\alpha}_{\text{Inst}+\mathcal{D}} \beta}\ \text{if } Y(\boldsymbol{x} : \boldsymbol{D}) = p \qquad \text{Implies}\ \frac{p \xrightarrow{\alpha}_{\mathcal{D}} \beta}{c \Rightarrow p \xrightarrow{\alpha}_{\text{Implies}+\mathcal{D}} \beta}\ \text{if } c \text{ holds}$$

$$\text{NChoiceL}\ \frac{p \xrightarrow{\alpha}_{\mathcal{D}} \beta}{p + q \xrightarrow{\alpha}_{\text{NChoiceL}+\mathcal{D}} \beta} \qquad \text{NChoiceR}\ \frac{q \xrightarrow{\alpha}_{\mathcal{D}} \beta}{p + q \xrightarrow{\alpha}_{\text{NChoiceR}+\mathcal{D}} \beta}$$

$$\text{NSum}(\boldsymbol{d})\ \frac{p[\boldsymbol{x} := \boldsymbol{d}] \xrightarrow{\alpha}_{\mathcal{D}} \beta}{\sum_{\boldsymbol{x}:\boldsymbol{D}} p \xrightarrow{\alpha}_{\text{NSum}(\boldsymbol{d})+\mathcal{D}} \beta}\ \text{if } \boldsymbol{d} \in \boldsymbol{D} \qquad \text{MStep}\ \frac{-}{(\lambda) \cdot p \xrightarrow{\lambda}_{\text{MSum}} p}$$

$$\text{PSum}\ \frac{-}{a(\boldsymbol{t}) \sum_{\boldsymbol{x}:\boldsymbol{D}} f : p \xrightarrow{a(\boldsymbol{t})}_{\text{PSum}} \mu}\ \text{where } \mu(p[\boldsymbol{x} := \boldsymbol{d}]) = \sum_{\substack{\boldsymbol{d}' \in \boldsymbol{D} \\ p[\boldsymbol{x}:=\boldsymbol{d}] = p[\boldsymbol{x}:=\boldsymbol{d}']}} f[\boldsymbol{x} := \boldsymbol{d}'],\ \text{for every } \boldsymbol{d} \in \boldsymbol{D}$$

Fig. 4. SOS rules for MAPA

Example 3. Consider $p = (\lambda_1) \cdot q + (\sum_{n:\{1,2,3\}} n < 3 \Rightarrow (\lambda_2) \cdot q)$. We derive

$$\dfrac{\dfrac{\dfrac{\dfrac{-}{(\lambda_2) \cdot q \xrightarrow{\lambda_2}_{\langle \text{MSTEP} \rangle} q}\ \text{MSTEP}}{1 < 3 \Rightarrow (\lambda_2) \cdot q \xrightarrow{\lambda_2}_{\langle \text{IMPLIES}, \text{MSTEP} \rangle} q}\ \text{IMPLIES}}{\sum_{n:\{1,2,3\}} n < 3 \Rightarrow (\lambda_2) \cdot q \xrightarrow{\lambda_2}_{\langle \text{NSUM}(1), \text{IMPLIES}, \text{MSTEP} \rangle} q}\ \text{NSUM}(1)}{(\lambda_1) \cdot q + \sum_{n:\{1,2,3\}} n < 3 \Rightarrow (\lambda_2) \cdot q \xrightarrow{\lambda_2}_{\langle \text{NCHOICER}, \text{NSUM}(1), \text{IMPLIES}, \text{MSTEP} \rangle} q}\ \text{NCHOICER}$$

So, $p \xrightarrow{\lambda_2}_{\mathcal{D}} q$ with $\mathcal{D} = \langle \text{NCHOICER}, \text{NSUM}(1), \text{IMPLIES}, \text{MSTEP} \rangle$. Similarly, we can find one other derivation $\mathcal{D}'$ with rate λ_2 using NSUM(2), and finally $p \xrightarrow{\lambda_1}_{\mathcal{D}''} q$ with $\mathcal{D}'' = \langle \text{NCHOICEL}, \text{MSTEP} \rangle$. Since these are the only derivations from p to q, we find $\mathsf{MD}(p, q) = \{(\lambda_2, \mathcal{D}), (\lambda_2, \mathcal{D}'), (\lambda_1, \mathcal{D}'')\}$. □

Definition 11 (Operational semantics). *The semantics of a MAPA specification $M = (\{X_i(\boldsymbol{x_i} : \boldsymbol{D_i}) = p_i\}, X_j(\boldsymbol{t}))$ is an MA $\mathcal{M} = \langle S, s^0, A, \hookrightarrow, \rightsquigarrow \rangle$, where*

- *S is the set of all MAPA process terms without free variables, and $s^0 = X_j(\boldsymbol{t})$;*
- *$A = \{a(\boldsymbol{t}) \mid a \in Act, \boldsymbol{t}$ is a vector of expressions without free variables$\}$*
- *$\hookrightarrow$ is the smallest relation such that $(p, a, \mu) \in \hookrightarrow$ if $p \xrightarrow{a}_{\mathcal{D}} \mu$ is derivable using the SOS rules in Figure 4 for some $\mathcal{D}$ such that MSTEP $\notin \mathcal{D}$;*
- *$\rightsquigarrow$ is the smallest relation such that $(p, \lambda, p') \in \rightsquigarrow$ if $\mathsf{MD}(p, p') \neq \emptyset$ and $\lambda = \sum_{(\lambda', \mathcal{D}) \in \mathsf{MD}(p,p')} \lambda'$.*

Note that, for $\rightsquigarrow$, we sum the rates of all Markovian derivations from p to p'. For Example 3, this yields $p \overset{\lambda}{\rightsquigarrow} q$ with $\lambda = \lambda_1 + 2\lambda_2$. Just applying the SOS rules as for $\hookrightarrow$ would yield $(\lambda) \cdot p' + (\lambda) \cdot p' \overset{\lambda}{\rightsquigarrow} p'$. However, as the race between the two exponentially distributed transitions doubles the speed of going to p, we want to obtain $(\lambda) \cdot p' + (\lambda) \cdot p' \overset{2\lambda}{\rightsquigarrow} p'$. This issue has been recognised before, leading to state-to-function transition systems [11], multi-transition systems [9], and derivation-labelled transitions [15]. Our approach is based on the latter.

An appealing implication of the derivation-based semantics is that parallel composition can easily be defined for MAPA: we can do without the extra clause for parallel self-loops that was needed in [5]. See [19] for more details.

Given a MAPA specification M and its underlying MA $\mathcal{M}$, two process terms in M are isomorphic if their corresponding states in $\mathcal{M}$ are isomorphic. Two specifications with underlying MAs $\mathcal{M}_1, \mathcal{M}_2$ are isomorphic if $\mathcal{M}_1$ is isomorphic to $\mathcal{M}_2$. Bisimilar process terms and specifications are defined in the same way.

3.2 Markovian Linear Probabilistic Process Equations

To simplify state space generation and enable reduction techniques, we introduce a normal form for MAPA: the MLPPE. It generalises the LPPE format for prCRL [10], which in turn was based on the LPE format for μCRL [7]. In the LPPE format, there is precisely one process, which consists of a nondeterministic choice between a set of *summands*. Each of these summands potentially contains a nondeterministic choice, followed by a condition, an interactive action and a probabilistic choice that determines the next state. The MLPPE additionally allows summands with a rate instead of an action.

Definition 12 (MLPPEs). *An* MLPPE (Markovian linear probabilistic process equation) *is a MAPA specification of the following format:*

$$X(\boldsymbol{g} : \boldsymbol{G}) = \sum_{i \in I} \sum_{\boldsymbol{d_i} : \boldsymbol{D_i}} c_i \Rightarrow a_i(\boldsymbol{b_i}) \sum_{\boldsymbol{e_i} : \boldsymbol{E_i}} f_i : X(\boldsymbol{n_i})$$
$$+ \sum_{j \in J} \sum_{\boldsymbol{d_j} : \boldsymbol{D_j}} c_j \Rightarrow (\lambda_j) \cdot X(\boldsymbol{n_j})$$

The first $|I|$ nondeterministic choices are referred to as interactive summands, *the last $|J|$ as* Markovian summands.

The two outer summations are abbreviations of nondeterministic choices between the summands. The expressions c_i, $\boldsymbol{b_i}$, f_i and $\boldsymbol{n_i}$ may depend on $\boldsymbol{g}$ and $\boldsymbol{d_i}$, and f_i and $\boldsymbol{n_i}$ also on $\boldsymbol{e_i}$. Similarly, c_j, λ_j and $\boldsymbol{n_j}$ may depend on $\boldsymbol{g}$ and $\boldsymbol{d_j}$.

Each state of an MLPPE corresponds to a valuation of its global variables, due to the recursive call immediately after each action or delay. Therefore, every reachable state in the underlying MA can be uniquely identified with one of the vectors $\boldsymbol{g'} \in \boldsymbol{G}$ (with the initial vector identifying the initial state). From the SOS rules, it follows that for all $\boldsymbol{g'} \in \boldsymbol{G}$, there is a transition $\boldsymbol{g'} \xrightarrow{a(\boldsymbol{q})} \mu$ if and only if for at least one summand $i \in I$ there is a local choice $\boldsymbol{d'_i} \in \boldsymbol{D_i}$ such that

$$c_i \wedge a_i(\boldsymbol{b_i}) = a(\boldsymbol{q}) \wedge \forall \boldsymbol{e'_i} \in \boldsymbol{E_i} \,.\, \mu(\boldsymbol{n_i}[\boldsymbol{e_i} := \boldsymbol{e'_i}]) = \sum_{\substack{\boldsymbol{e''_i} \in \boldsymbol{E_i} \\ \boldsymbol{n_i}[\boldsymbol{e_i} := \boldsymbol{e'_i}] = \boldsymbol{n_i}[\boldsymbol{e_i} := \boldsymbol{e''_i}]}} f_i[\boldsymbol{e_i} := \boldsymbol{e''_i}],$$

where, for readability, the substitution $[(\boldsymbol{g}, \boldsymbol{d_i}) := (\boldsymbol{g'}, \boldsymbol{d'_i})]$ is omitted from c_i, $\boldsymbol{b_i}$, $\boldsymbol{n_i}$ and f_i. Additionally, there is a transition $\boldsymbol{g'} \overset{\lambda}{\rightsquigarrow} \boldsymbol{g''}$ if and only if $\lambda > 0$ and

$$\lambda = \sum_{\substack{(j, \boldsymbol{d'_j}) \in J \times \boldsymbol{D_j} \\ c_j[(\boldsymbol{g}, \boldsymbol{d_j}) := (\boldsymbol{g'}, \boldsymbol{d'_j})] \wedge \boldsymbol{n_j}[(\boldsymbol{g}, \boldsymbol{d_j}) := (\boldsymbol{g'}, \boldsymbol{d'_j})] = \boldsymbol{g''}}} \lambda_j[(\boldsymbol{g}, \boldsymbol{d_j}) := (\boldsymbol{g'}, \boldsymbol{d'_j})]$$

Remark 2. For the semantics to be an MA with finite outgoing rates, we need $\sum_{p'} \sum_{(\lambda, \mathcal{D}) \in \mathsf{MD}(p, p')} \lambda < \infty$ for every process term p. One way of enforcing this syntactically is to require all data types in Markovian summands to be finite. □

4 Encoding in prCRL

To apply MLPPE-based reductions while modelling in the full MAPA language, we need an automated way for transforming MAPA specifications to strongly bisimilar MLPPEs. Instead of defining such a *linearisation* procedure for MAPA, we exploit the existing linearisation procedure for prCRL. That is, we show how to encode a MAPA specification into a prCRL specification and how to decode a MAPA specification from a prCRL specification. That way, we can apply the existing linearisation procedure, as depicted earlier in Figure 2. Additionally, the encoding enables us to immediately apply many other useful prCRL transformations to MAPA specifications. In this section we explain the encoding and decoding procedures, and prove the correctness of our method.

$\mathsf{enc}\,(Y(\boldsymbol{t}))$	$= Y(\boldsymbol{t})$	$\mathsf{dec}\,(Y(\boldsymbol{t}))$	$= Y(\boldsymbol{t})$
$\mathsf{enc}\,(c \Rightarrow p)$	$= c \Rightarrow \mathsf{enc}\,(p)$	$\mathsf{dec}\,(c \Rightarrow p)$	$= c \Rightarrow \mathsf{dec}\,(p)$
$\mathsf{enc}\,(p + q)$	$= \mathsf{enc}\,(p) + \mathsf{enc}\,(q)$	$\mathsf{dec}\,(p + q)$	$= \mathsf{dec}\,(p) + \mathsf{dec}\,(q)$
$\mathsf{enc}\,(\sum_{\boldsymbol{x}:\boldsymbol{D}} p)$	$= \sum_{\boldsymbol{x}:\boldsymbol{D}} \mathsf{enc}\,(p)$	$\mathsf{dec}\,(\sum_{\boldsymbol{x}:\boldsymbol{D}} p)$	$= \sum_{\boldsymbol{x}:\boldsymbol{D}} \mathsf{dec}\,(p)$
$\mathsf{enc}\,(a(\boldsymbol{t}) \textstyle\sum_{\boldsymbol{x}:\boldsymbol{D}} f : p)$	$= a(\boldsymbol{t}) \textstyle\sum_{\boldsymbol{x}:\boldsymbol{D}} f : \mathsf{enc}\,(p)$	$\mathsf{dec}\,(a(\boldsymbol{t}) \textstyle\sum_{\boldsymbol{x}:\boldsymbol{D}} f : p)$	$= a(\boldsymbol{t}) \textstyle\sum_{\boldsymbol{x}:\boldsymbol{D}} f : \mathsf{dec}\,(p)$ $(a \neq \mathsf{rate})$

$$\mathsf{enc}\,((\lambda) \cdot p) = \mathsf{rate}(\lambda) \textstyle\sum_{x:\{*\}} 1 : \mathsf{enc}\,(p) \qquad (x \text{ does not occur in } p)$$
$$\mathsf{dec}\,(\mathsf{rate}(\lambda) \textstyle\sum_{x:\{*\}} 1 : p) = (\lambda) \cdot \mathsf{dec}\,(p)$$

Fig. 5. Encoding and decoding rules for process terms

4.1 Encoding and Decoding

The encoding of MAPA terms is straightforward. The $(\lambda) \cdot p$ construct of MAPA is the only one that has to be encoded, since the other constructs all are also present in prCRL. We chose to encode exponential rates by an action $\mathsf{rate}(\lambda)$ (which is assumed not to occur in the original specification). Since actions in prCRL require a probabilistic choice for the next state, we use $\sum_{x:\{*\}} 1 : p$ such that x is not used in p. Here, $\{*\}$ is a singleton set with an arbitrary element. Figure 5 shows the appropriate encoding and decoding functions.

Definition 13 (Encoding). *Given a MAPA specification* $M = (\{X_i(\boldsymbol{x_i} : \boldsymbol{D_i}) = p_i\}, X_j(\boldsymbol{t}))$ *and a prCRL specification* $P = (\{Y_i(\boldsymbol{y_i} : \boldsymbol{E_i}) = q_i\}, Y_j(\boldsymbol{u}))$, *let*

$$\mathsf{enc}\,(M) = (\{X_i(\boldsymbol{x_i} : \boldsymbol{D_i}) = \mathsf{enc}\,(p_i)\}, X_j(\boldsymbol{t}))$$
$$\mathsf{dec}\,(P) = (\{Y_i(\boldsymbol{y_i} : \boldsymbol{E_i}) = \mathsf{dec}\,(q_i)\}, Y_j(\boldsymbol{u}))$$

where the functions enc *and* dec *for process terms are given in Figure 5.*

Remark 3. It may appear that, given the above encoding and decoding rules, bisimilar prCRL specifications always decode to bisimilar MAPA specifications. However, this is not the case. Consider the bisimilar prCRL terms $\mathsf{rate}(\lambda) \cdot X + \mathsf{rate}(\lambda) \cdot X$ and $\mathsf{rate}(\lambda) \cdot X$. The decodings of these two terms, $(\lambda) \cdot X + (\lambda) \cdot X$ and $(\lambda) \cdot X$, are clearly not bisimilar in the context of MAPA.

An obvious solution may seem to encode each rate by a unique action, yielding $\mathsf{rate}_1(\lambda) \cdot X + \mathsf{rate}_2(\lambda) \cdot X$, preventing the above erroneous reduction. However, this does not work in all occasions either. Take for instance a MAPA specification consisting of two processes $X = Y + Y$ and $Y = (\lambda) \cdot X$. Encoding this to $X = Y + Y$ and $Y = \mathsf{rate}_1(\lambda) \cdot X$ enables the reduction to $X = Y$ and $Y = \mathsf{rate}_1(\lambda) \cdot X$, which is incorrect since it halves the rate of X.

Note that an 'encoding scheme' that does yield bisimilar MAPA specifications for bisimilar prCRL specifications exists. We could generate the complete state space of a MAPA specification, determine the total rate from p to p' for every pair of process terms p, p', and encode each of these as a unique action in the prCRL specification. When decoding, potential copies of this action that may arise when looking at bisimilar specifications can then just be ignored. However, this clearly renders useless the whole idea of reducing a linear specification before generation of the entire state space. □

Derivation-preserving bisimulation. The observations above suggest that we need a stronger notion of bisimulation if we want two bisimilar prCRL specifications to decode to bisimilar MAPA specifications: all bisimilar process terms should have an equal number of $\mathsf{rate}(\lambda)$ derivations to every equivalence class (as given by the bisimulation relation). We formalise this by means of a *derivation-preserving bisimulation.* It is defined on prCRL terms instead of states in a PA.

Definition 14 (Derivation preservation[1]). *Let R be a bisimulation relation over prCRL process terms. Then, R is* derivation preserving *if for every pair $(p, q) \in R$, every equivalence equivalence class $[r]_R$ and every rate λ:*

$$|\{\mathcal{D} \in \Delta \mid \exists r' \in [r]_R \,.\, p \xrightarrow{\mathsf{rate}(\lambda)}_{\mathcal{D}} \mathbb{1}_{r'}\}| =$$
$$|\{\mathcal{D} \in \Delta \mid \exists r' \in [r]_R \,.\, q \xrightarrow{\mathsf{rate}(\lambda)}_{\mathcal{D}} \mathbb{1}_{r'}\}|.$$

Two prCRL terms p, q are derivation-preserving bisimilar, *denoted $p \sim_{\mathrm{dp}} q$, if there exists a derivation-preserving bisimulation relation R such that $(p, q) \in R$.*

The next theorem states that derivation-preserving bisimulation is a congruence for every prCRL operator. The proof can be found in [19].

Theorem 1. *Derivation-preserving bisimulation is a congruence for prCRL.*

Our encoding scheme and notion of derivation-preserving bisimulation allow us to reuse prCRL transformations for MAPA specifications. The next theorem confirms that a function $\mathsf{dec} \circ f \circ \mathsf{enc}\colon$ MAPA $\to$ MAPA respects bisimulation if $f\colon$ prCRL $\to$ prCRL respects derivation-preserving bisimulation.

Theorem 2. *Let $f\colon$ prCRL $\to$ prCRL such that $f(P) \sim_{\mathrm{dp}} P$ for every prCRL specification P. Then, $\mathsf{dec}\,(f(\mathsf{enc}\,(M))) \sim M$ for every MAPA specification M without any* rate *action.*

Proof (sketch). It can be shown that (a) $m \xhookrightarrow{a} \mu$ (with $a \neq \mathsf{rate}$) is a transition in an MA if and only if $\mathsf{enc}\,(m) \xrightarrow{a} \mu_{\mathsf{enc}}$, and that (b) every derivation $m \xrightarrow{\lambda}_{\mathcal{D}} m'$ in an MA corresponds one-to-one to a derivation $\mathsf{enc}\,(m) \xrightarrow{\mathsf{rate}(\lambda)}_{\mathcal{D}'} \mathbb{1}_{\mathsf{enc}(m')}$, with $\mathcal{D}'$ obtained from $\mathcal{D}$ by substituting PSUM for MSTEP. Using these two observations, and taking R as the derivation-preserving bisimulation relation for $f(P) \sim_{\mathrm{dp}} P$, it can be shown that $R' = \{(\mathsf{dec}\,(p), \mathsf{dec}\,(q)) \mid (p, q) \in R\}$ is a bisimulation relation, and hence $\mathsf{dec}\,(f(P)) \sim \mathsf{dec}\,(P)$. Taking $P = \mathsf{enc}\,(M)$, and noting that $\mathsf{dec}\,(\mathsf{enc}\,(M)) = M$, the theorem follows. □

We can now state that the linearisation procedure from [10] (here referred to by linearise) can be used to transform a MAPA specification to an MLPPE. Under the observation that a prCRL specification P and its linearisation are derivation-preserving bisimilar (proven in [19]), it is an immediate consequence of Theorem 2. The fact that M' is an MLPPE follows from the proof in [10] that linearise(enc (M)) is an LPPE, and the observation that decoding does not change the structure of a specification.

[1] We could even be a bit more liberal (although technically slightly more involved), only requiring equal sums of the λs of all rate-transitions to each equivalence class.

Theorem 3. *Let M be a MAPA specification without any* rate *action, and let* $M' = \mathsf{dec}(\mathsf{linearise}(\mathsf{enc}(M)))$. *Then,* $M \sim M'$ *and* M' *is an MLPPE.*

5 Reductions

We discuss three symbolic prCRL reduction techniques that, by Theorem 2, can directly be applied to MAPA specifications. Also, we discuss two new techniques that are specific to MAPA. Note that, since MAs generalise LTSs, CTMCs, DTMCs, PAs and IMCs, all techniques also are applicable to these subclasses.

5.1 Novel Reduction Techniques

Maximal progress reduction. No Markovian transitions can be taken from states that also allow a τ-transition. Hence, such Markovian transitions (and their target states) can safely be omitted. This maximal progress reduction can be applied during state space generation, but it is more efficient to already do this on the MLPPE level: we can just omit all Markovian summands that are always enabled together with non-Markovian summands. Note that, to detect such scenarios, some heuristics or theorem proving have to be applied, as in [14].

Summation elimination. Summation elimination [10] aims to remove unnecessary summations, transforming $\sum_{d:\mathbb{N}} d = 5 \Rightarrow \mathit{send}(d) \cdot X$ to $\mathit{send}(5) \cdot X$ (as there is only one possible value for d) and $\sum_{d:\{1,2\}} a \cdot X$ to $a \cdot X$ (as the summation variable is not used). This technique would fail for MAPA, as the second transformation changes the number of a-derivations; for $a = \mathsf{rate}(\lambda)$, this would change behaviour. Therefore, we generalise summation elimination to MLPPEs. Interactive summands are handled as before, but for Markovian summands the second kind of reduction is altered. Instead of reducing $\sum_{d:D} (\lambda) \cdot X$ to $(\lambda) \cdot X$, we now reduce to $(|D| \times \lambda) \cdot X$. That way, the total rate to X remains the same.

5.2 Generalisation of Existing Techniques

Constant elimination [10] detects if a parameter of an LPPE never changes value. Then, the parameter is omitted and every reference to it replaced by its initial value. *Expression simplification* [10] evaluates functions for which all parameters are constants and applies basic laws from logic. These techniques do not change the state space, but improve readability and speed up state space generation. *Dead-variable reduction* [14] additionally reduces the number of states. It takes into account the control flow of an LPPE and tries to detect states in which the value of some data variable is irrelevant. Basically, this is the case if that variable will be overwritten before being used for all possible futures.

It is easy to see that all three techniques are derivation preserving. Hence, by Theorem 2 we can reuse them unchanged for MAPA using $\mathsf{dec}(\mathsf{reduce}(\mathsf{enc}(M)))$.

6 Case Study and Implementation

We extended our tool SCOOP [21], enabling it to handle MAPA. We implemented the encoding scheme, linked it to the original linearisation and derivation-preserving reduction techniques, and implemented the novel reductions. Table 1 shows statistics of the MAs generated from several variations of Figure 3; `queue-i-j` denotes the variant with buffers of size `i` and `j` types of jobs[2]. The primed specifications were modified to have a single rate for all types of jobs. Therefore, dead-variable reduction detects that the queue contents are irrelevant.

We also modelled a probabilistic mutex exclusion protocol, based on [13]. Each process is in the critical section for an amount of time governed by an exponential rate, depending on a nondeterministically chosen job type. We denote by `mutex-i-j` the variant with `i` processes and `j` types of jobs.

Note that the MLPPE optimisations impact the MA generation time significantly, even for cases without state space reduction. Also note that earlier case studies for prCRL or μCRL would still give the same results; e.g., the results in [14] that showed the benefits of dead-variable reduction are still applicable.

Table 1. State space generation using SCOOP on a 2.4 GHz 8 GB Intel Core 2 Duo MacBook (MLPPE in number of parameters / symbols, time in seconds)

	Original				Reduced				
Spec.	States	Trans.	MLPPE	Time	States	Trans.	MLPPE	Time	Red.
queue-3-5	316,058	581,892	15 / 335	87.4	218,714	484,548	8 / 224	20.7	76%
queue-3-6	1,005,699	1,874,138	15 / 335	323.3	670,294	1,538,733	8 / 224	64.7	80%
queue-3-6'	1,005,699	1,874,138	15 / 335	319.5	74	108	5 / 170	0.0	100%
queue-5-2	27,659	47,130	15 / 335	4.3	23,690	43,161	8 / 224	1.9	56%
queue-5-3	1,191,738	2,116,304	15 / 335	235.8	926,746	1,851,312	8 / 224	84.2	64%
queue-5-3'	1,191,738	2,116,304	15 / 335	233.2	170	256	5 / 170	0.0	100%
queue-25-1	3,330	5,256	15 / 335	0.5	3,330	5,256	8 / 224	0.4	20%
queue-100-1	50,805	81,006	15 / 335	8.9	50,805	81,006	8 / 224	6.6	26%
mutex-3-2	17,352	40,200	27 / 3,540	12.3	10,560	25,392	12 / 2,190	4.6	63%
mutex-3-4	129,112	320,136	27 / 3,540	95.8	70,744	169,128	12 / 2,190	30.3	68%
mutex-3-6	425,528	1,137,048	27 / 3,540	330.8	224,000	534,624	12 / 2,190	99.0	70%
mutex-4-1	27,701	80,516	36 / 5,872	33.0	20,025	62,876	16 / 3,632	13.5	59%
mutex-4-2	360,768	1,035,584	36 / 5,872	435.9	218,624	671,328	16 / 3,632	145.5	67%
mutex-4-3	1,711,141	5,015,692	36 / 5,872	2,108.0	958,921	2,923,300	16 / 3,632	644.3	69%
mutex-5-1	294,882	1,051,775	45 / 8,780	549.7	218,717	841,750	20 / 5,430	216.6	61%

7 Conclusions and Future Work

We introduced a new process-algebraic framework with data, called MAPA, for modelling and generating Markov automata. We defined a special restricted format, the MLPPE, that allows easy state space generation and parallel composition. We showed how MAPA specifications can be encoded in prCRL, an existing language for probabilistic automata. Based on the novel concept of derivation-preservation bisimulation, we proved that many useful prCRL transformations

[2] See `fmt.cs.utwente.nl/~timmer/scoop/papers/concur/` for the tool and models.

can directly be used on MAPA specifications. This includes a linearisation procedure to turn MAPA processes into strongly bisimilar MLPPEs, and several existing reduction techniques. Also, we introduced two new reduction techniques. A case study demonstrated the use of the framework and the strength of the reduction techniques. Since MAs generalise LTS, DTMCs, CTMCs, IMCs and PAs, we can use MAPA and all our reduction techniques on all such models.

Future work will focus on developing more reduction techniques for MAPA. Most importantly, we will investigate a generalisation of confluence reduction [20].

Acknowledgements. We thank Erik de Vink for his many helpful comments on an earlier draft of this paper, as well as Pedro d'Argenio for his useful insights.

References

1. Boudali, H., Crouzen, P., Stoelinga, M.I.A.: Dynamic fault tree analysis using Input/Output interactive Markov chains. In: DSN, pp. 708–717 (2007)
2. Bozzano, M., Cimatti, A., Katoen, J.P., Nguyen, V.Y., Noll, T., Roveri, M.: Safety, dependability and performance analysis of extended AADL models. The Computer Journal 54(5), 754–775 (2011)
3. Deng, Y., Hennessy, M.: On the Semantics of Markov Automata. In: Aceto, L., Henzinger, M., Sgall, J. (eds.) ICALP 2011, Part II. LNCS, vol. 6756, pp. 307–318. Springer, Heidelberg (2011)
4. Eisentraut, C., Hermanns, H., Zhang, L.: Concurrency and Composition in a Stochastic World. In: Gastin, P., Laroussinie, F. (eds.) CONCUR 2010. LNCS, vol. 6269, pp. 21–39. Springer, Heidelberg (2010)
5. Eisentraut, C., Hermanns, H., Zhang, L.: On probabilistic automata in continuous time. In: LICS, pp. 342–351 (2010)
6. Garavel, H., Lang, F., Mateescu, R., Serwe, W.: CADP 2010: A Toolbox for the Construction and Analysis of Distributed Processes. In: Abdulla, P.A., Leino, K.R.M. (eds.) TACAS 2011. LNCS, vol. 6605, pp. 372–387. Springer, Heidelberg (2011)
7. Groote, J.F., Ponse, A.: The syntax and semantics of μCRL. In: Algebra of Communicating Processes, Workshops in Computing, pp. 26–62 (1995)
8. Hermanns, H.: Interactive Markov Chains. LNCS, vol. 2428. Springer, Heidelberg (2002)
9. Hillston, J.: Process algebras for quantitative analysis. In: LICS, pp. 239–248 (2005)
10. Katoen, J.P., van de Pol, J., Stoelinga, M., Timmer, M.: A linear process-algebraic format with data for probabilistic automata. TCS 413(1), 36–57 (2012)
11. Latella, D., Massink, M., de Vink, E.P.: Bisimulation of labeled state-to-function transition systems of stochastic process languages. In: ACCAT (to appear, 2012)
12. Marsan, M.A., Conte, G., Balbo, G.: A class of generalized stochastic Petri nets for the performance evaluation of multiprocessor systems. ACM Transactions on Computer Systems 2(2), 93–122 (1984)
13. Pnueli, A., Zuck, L.D.: Verification of multiprocess probabilistic protocols. Distributed Computing 1(1), 53–72 (1986)
14. van de Pol, J., Timmer, M.: State Space Reduction of Linear Processes Using Control Flow Reconstruction. In: Liu, Z., Ravn, A.P. (eds.) ATVA 2009. LNCS, vol. 5799, pp. 54–68. Springer, Heidelberg (2009)

15. Priami, C.: Stochastic pi-calculus. The Computer Journal 38(7), 578–589 (1995)
16. Segala, R.: Modeling and Verification of Randomized Distributed Real-Time Systems. Ph.D. thesis, MIT (1995)
17. Srinivasan, M.M.: Nondeterministic polling systems. Management Science 37(6), 667–681 (1991)
18. Stoelinga, M.I.A.: An introduction to probabilistic automata. Bulletin of the EATCS 78, 176–198 (2002)
19. Timmer, M., Katoen, J.P., van de Pol, J., Stoelinga, M.I.A.: Efficient modelling and generation of Markov automata (extended version). Tech. Rep. TR-CTIT-12-16, CTIT, University of Twente (2012)
20. Timmer, M., Stoelinga, M., van de Pol, J.: Confluence Reduction for Probabilistic Systems. In: Abdulla, P.A., Leino, K.R.M. (eds.) TACAS 2011. LNCS, vol. 6605, pp. 311–325. Springer, Heidelberg (2011)
21. Timmer, M.: SCOOP: A tool for symbolic optimisations of probabilistic processes. In: QEST, pp. 149–150 (2011)

Exact Fluid Lumpability for Markovian Process Algebra

Max Tschaikowski and Mirco Tribastone

Institut für Informatik
Ludwig-Maximilians-Universität Munich, Germany
{tschaikowski,tribastone}@pst.ifi.lmu.de

Abstract. We study behavioural relations for process algebra with a fluid semantics given in terms of a system of ordinary differential equations (ODEs). We introduce *label equivalence*, a relation which is shown to induce an *exactly lumped fluid model*, a potentially smaller ODE system which can be exactly related to the original one. We show that, in general, for two processes that are related in the fluid sense nothing can be said about their relationship from stochastic viewpoint. However, we identify a class of models for which label equivalence implies a correspondence, called *semi-isomorphism*, between their transition systems that are at the basis of the Markovian interpretation.

Keywords: Stochastic process algebra, ordinary differential equations, equivalence relations.

1 Introduction

Aggregation of discrete-state models has been a long-standing research problem to tackle the complexity of large-scale parallel systems. In the case of continuous-time Markov chains (CTMCs) induced by a process algebra (e.g., [10,8,2]) a classical solution has been offered by notions of behavioural equivalence which induce *lumping*, where a (hopefully much smaller) CTMC may be defined which preserves most of the system's original stochastic behaviour (e.g., [4]).

More recently, fluid semantics for process algebra have become popular for a description based on a system of ordinary differential equations (ODEs) which, especially in the case of large *population processes*, is very accurate but typically much more compact than the lumped CTMC. The relationship between the CTMC and the fluid semantics has been studied in the context of PEPA [9], Cardelli's stochastic interacting processes [5], and stochastic Concurrent Constraint Programming [3]. The significant computational savings provided by differential analysis, together with its widespread use in computational systems biology, have also stimulated the development of process algebra directly equipped with an ODE semantics [13].

Unfortunately, ODE models of realistic complex systems may still be too large for feasible analysis. This problem has motivated work on ODE aggregations in diverse contexts such as control theory [1], theoretical ecology [12], and economics [11].

M. Koutny and I. Ulidowski (Eds.): CONCUR 2012, LNCS 7454, pp. 380–394, 2012.

In this paper, for the first time, we study aggregation of ODEs induced by a stochastic process algebra. We carry out this investigation in the context of a fluid framework for PEPA [7], *grouped PEPA* (GPEPA), which we overview in Section 2. In principle, however, with suitable syntactical changes our approach is applicable to other compositional methods equipped with a fluid semantics. At the core of this study is the general notion of *exact fluid lumpability* (Section 3) which, intuitively, is defined as a partition over the ODEs of a model whereby two ODEs belonging to the same partition element have undistinguishable solutions; an aggregated ODE model may be defined which only considers such elements. In Section 4, we define a notion of behavioural equivalence, called *label equivalence*, which induces exactly fluid lumpable partitions. We also study conditions under which it is possible to construct coarser ODE partitions by suitably merging distinct label equivalences. A running example, presented for the illustrative purposes, suggests that this theory is particularly convenient in practice to exploit symmetries in large-scale models with replicated behaviour, as the lumped ODE model becomes independent from the number of replicas. The paper is concluded with a characterisation of the relationship between label equivalence and stochastic notions of behavioural equivalence for PEPA, in Section 4.2, and by concluding remarks in Section 5.

An extended version of this paper with proofs is available as a technical report at the authors' web pages.

2 Preliminaries

We study PEPA (cf. [10]) without the hiding operator. The syntax and semantics are briefly overviewed in Sect. 2.1. The full language does not pose technical difficulties but comes at the cost of extra definitions, sacrificing space. This caveat notwithstanding, for the sake of conciseness we shall refer to our simplified version still as PEPA. In Sect. 2.2, we introduce a new, but simple, behavioural relation between PEPA processes, called *semi-isomorphism*, which will be instrumental for the characterisation of label equivalence.

2.1 PEPA

Definition 1. *The syntax of a PEPA component is given by the grammar*

$$S ::= (\alpha, r).S \mid S + S \mid A \qquad P ::= S \mid P \underset{L}{\bowtie} P \quad \textit{with} \quad A \stackrel{\text{def}}{=} S \quad \textit{(constant)}.$$

The first rule describes *sequential components*. The term $(\alpha, r).S$ (prefix) denotes a process which can perform a transition of type $\alpha \in \mathcal{A}$, with an exponentially distributed delay with mean $1/r$, after which the process behaves as S. The (positive) real r is called the *rate* of action α. (Passive rates are not allowed in our fluid framework.) The $S + S$ (choice) is capable of performing the transitions of its operands. The second rule describes a *model component*, which may simply be a sequential component or a *cooperation* $P \underset{L}{\bowtie} P$: The two operands

$$\frac{}{(\alpha,r).P \xrightarrow{(\alpha,r)} P} \qquad \frac{P \xrightarrow{(\alpha,r)} P'}{A \xrightarrow{(\alpha,r)} P'} \; A \stackrel{\text{def}}{=} P$$

$$\frac{P \xrightarrow{(\alpha,r)} P'}{P+Q \xrightarrow{(\alpha,r)} P'} \qquad \frac{Q \xrightarrow{(\alpha,r)} Q'}{P+Q \xrightarrow{(\alpha,r)} Q'}$$

$$\frac{P_1 \xrightarrow{(\alpha,r_1)} P_1'}{P_1 \underset{L}{\bowtie} P_2 \xrightarrow{(\alpha,r_1)} P_1' \underset{L}{\bowtie} P_2} \; \alpha \notin L \qquad \frac{P_2 \xrightarrow{(\alpha,r_2)} P_2'}{P_1 \underset{L}{\bowtie} P_2 \xrightarrow{(\alpha,r_2)} P_1 \underset{L}{\bowtie} P_2'} \; \alpha \notin L$$

$$\frac{P_1 \xrightarrow{(\alpha,r_1)} P_1' \quad P_2 \xrightarrow{(\alpha,r_2)} P_2'}{P_1 \underset{L}{\bowtie} P_2 \xrightarrow{(\alpha,R)} P_1' \underset{L}{\bowtie} P_2'} \; \alpha \in L, \quad R = \frac{r_1}{r_\alpha(P_1)} \frac{r_2}{r_\alpha(P_2)} \min(r_\alpha(P_1), r_\alpha(P_2))$$

Fig. 1. Structured operational semantics of PEPA

behave independently of each other whenever they do not perform transitions with actions belonging to the *cooperation set* L. Otherwise, a synchronisation occurs and the operands proceed together.

In this paper, we will present simple examples which are slight variations of

$$\underbrace{(A \underset{\emptyset}{\bowtie} \dots \underset{\emptyset}{\bowtie} A)}_{N_A \text{ copies}} \underset{\{\alpha\}}{\bowtie} \underbrace{(B \underset{\emptyset}{\bowtie} \dots \underset{\emptyset}{\bowtie} B)}_{N_B = N_A \text{ copies}} \underset{\{\alpha\}}{\bowtie} \underbrace{(C \underset{\emptyset}{\bowtie} \dots \underset{\emptyset}{\bowtie} C)}_{N_C \text{ copies}} \tag{1}$$

where the sequential components are defined as follows:

$$A \stackrel{\text{def}}{=} (\alpha, r).A' \qquad B \stackrel{\text{def}}{=} (\alpha, r/2).B' + (\alpha, r/2).B' \qquad C \stackrel{\text{def}}{=} (\alpha, u).C'$$
$$A' \stackrel{\text{def}}{=} (\beta, s).A \qquad B' \stackrel{\text{def}}{=} (\beta, s).B \qquad C' \stackrel{\text{def}}{=} (\gamma, w).C$$

Actions of type α are synchronised, whereas β- and γ-actions may be performed independently by each component. The total rate at which some action may be performed is defined through the following.

Definition 2 (Apparent Rate). *The apparent rate of action α in a PEPA component P, denoted by $r_\alpha(P)$, is defined as follows:*

$$r_\alpha((\beta, r).S) := \begin{cases} r & , \beta = \alpha \\ 0 & , \textit{else} \end{cases} \qquad r_\alpha(A) := r_\alpha(S), \; A \stackrel{\text{def}}{=} S$$

$$r_\alpha(P \underset{L}{\bowtie} Q) := \begin{cases} r_\alpha(P) + r_\alpha(Q) & , \alpha \notin L \\ \min(r_\alpha(P), r_\alpha(Q)) & , \textit{else.} \end{cases} \qquad r_\alpha(P+Q) := r_\alpha(P) + r_\alpha(Q)$$

Using the structured operational semantics of PEPA, cf. Figure 1, we write $P \xrightarrow{(\alpha,r)} P'$ whenever there is an α-transition with rate r from process P to process P'. We say that P' is a *derivative* of P. For instance, if $A \stackrel{\text{def}}{=} (\alpha, r).A'$, then $A \xrightarrow{(\alpha,r)} A'$ may be inferred. The following definitions formalise the notion of state space of a PEPA component.

Definition 3 (Derivative Set). *The derivative set of a PEPA component P, denoted by $ds(P)$, is defined as the smallest set such that $P \in ds(P)$; and if $P' \in ds(P)$ and $P' \xrightarrow{(\alpha,r)} P''$ then $P'' \in ds(P)$.*

Definition 4 (Derivation Graph). *Let $\mathcal{A}ct := \mathcal{A} \times \mathbb{R}_{>0}$ denote the set of all activities of PEPA. The derivation graph $dg(P)$ of a PEPA component P has $ds(P)$ as the set of nodes. The multiset of transitions $\mathcal{T} \subseteq ds(P) \times \mathcal{A}ct \times ds(P)$ is such that*

$$P_0 \xrightarrow{(\alpha,r)} P_1 \Leftrightarrow (P_0, (\alpha, r), P_1) \in \mathcal{T},$$

with multiplicity equal to the number of distinct derivations of $P_0 \xrightarrow{(\alpha,r)} P_1$.

2.2 Semi-isomorphism

In PEPA, isomorphism is defined as a map between the derivative sets of two processes which induces a one-to-one correspondence, i.e., a *graph isomorphism*, between their derivation graphs [10, Sect. 6.2]. Here we introduce a slightly weaker notion, called *semi-isomorphism*, which relates two processes with respect to their *merged derivation graphs* (cf. Definition 6), defined as the graphs obtained by replacing multiple equally-labelled transitions between two states with a single transition with the same action type and a rate which is the sum across all such transition rates.

Definition 5 (Semi-Isomorphism). *Two PEPA processes P and Q are semi-isomorphic if there is a bijection $\sigma : ds(P) \to ds(Q)$ which satisfies $\sum_{P_i \xrightarrow{(\alpha,r)} P_j} r = \sum_{\sigma(P_i) \xrightarrow{(\alpha,r)} \sigma(P_j)} r$ for all $P_i, P_j \in ds(P)$ and $\alpha \in \mathcal{A}$. We shall call such a σ a semi-isomorphism.*

Definition 6 (Merged Derivation Graph). *The merged derivation graph $dg_m(P)$ of P arises from $dg(P)$, if, for all $\alpha \in \mathcal{A}$, all α-transitions between any two states whose rate-sum across all transitions is equal to q are replaced by a single transition (α, q).*

Though easy to prove, due to its importance the following is stated as a theorem.

Theorem 1. *Let $\sigma : ds(P) \to ds(Q)$ be a semi-isomorphism between the PEPA processes P and Q. Then it holds that $dg_m(P)$ and $dg_m(Q)$ stand in a one-to-one correspondence.*

For instance, let us consider processes A and B in (1). Then, it can be shown that A is semi-isomorphic to B. However, A and B are not isomorphic because the number of transitions in their derivation graphs is different.

In general, it is easy to see that PEPA isomorphism induces semi-isomorphism and that the CTMCs of semi-isomorphic PEPA processes stand in a one-to-one correspondence.

2.3 Fluid Process Algebra

The derivative set of (1) is known to have $2^{N_A+N_A+N_C}$ states (recall that $N_B := N_A$). The fluid semantics of GPEPA provides an approximation to the expectation values of the population of components exhibiting states A, A', B, B', C and C', using a system of only 2+2+2 coupled ODEs. In the interest of clarity and succinctness, we also provide here a simplified version of GPEPA, called Fluid Process Algebra (FPA), which can be shown to be as expressive as the full GPEPA (without the hiding operator).

Definition 7 (FPA Model). *An FPA model M is given by the grammar*

$$M ::= M \underset{L}{\bowtie} M \mid H\{P\}$$

where $L \subseteq \mathcal{A}$, P is as in Definition 1, and H is a label. We require that each label be unique in an FPA model.

We call $H\{P\}$ a *fluid atom*. The size of the ODE system will be as large as the sum of the sizes of the derivative sets of all fluid atoms in a model. We denote by *Triple* the FPA model to be studied for the differential analysis of (1), i.e.,

$$\mathit{Triple} := \mathbb{A}_1\{A\} \underset{\{\alpha\}}{\bowtie} \mathbb{B}_1\{B\} \underset{\{\alpha\}}{\bowtie} \mathbb{C}_1\{C\} \tag{2}$$

The next definitions will be needed for the setup of the fluid framework.

Definition 8. *Let M be an FPA model. We define then*

- *$\mathcal{G}(M)$ as the set of labels of M, e.g., $\mathcal{G}(\mathit{Triple}) = \{\mathbb{A}_1, \mathbb{B}_1, \mathbb{C}_1\}$.*
- *$\mathcal{B}(M, H)$ as the PEPA derivative set of the fluid atom which is labelled with H, e.g. $\mathcal{B}(\mathit{Triple}, \mathbb{A}_1) = ds(A) = \{A, A'\}$.*
- *$\mathcal{B}(M)$ as $\{(H, P) \mid H \in \mathcal{G}(M) \wedge P \in \mathcal{B}(M, H)\}$.*
- *A population function $V : X \to \mathbb{R}_{\geq 0}$ with $\mathcal{B}(M) \subseteq X$.*
- *An* initial *population function $V(0) : X \to \mathbb{N}_0$.*

Function $V(0)$ deserves more explanation. It essentially encodes the size of the system. For instance, the initial populations present in (1) are recovered by

$$\begin{aligned} &V_{(\mathbb{A}_1,A)}(0) = N_A, \qquad && V_{(\mathbb{B}_1,B)}(0) = N_A, \qquad && V_{(\mathbb{C}_1,C)}(0) = N_C, \\ &V_{(\mathbb{A}_1,A')}(0) = 0, && V_{(\mathbb{B}_1,B')}(0) = 0, && V_{(\mathbb{C}_1,C')}(0) = 0. \end{aligned} \tag{3}$$

Definition 9 (Parameterised Apparent Rate). *Let M be an FPA model, $\alpha \in \mathcal{A}$ and V a population function. The apparent rate of M with respect to V is defined as*

$$r_\alpha(M_0 \underset{L}{\bowtie} M_1, V) := \begin{cases} \min(r_\alpha(M_0, V), r_\alpha(M_1, V)) & , \alpha \in L, \\ r_\alpha(M_0, V) + r_\alpha(M_1, V) & , \alpha \notin L. \end{cases}$$

$$r_\alpha(H\{P\}, V) := \sum_{P_i \in ds(P)} V_{(H,P_i)} r_\alpha(P_i),$$

where $r_\alpha(P_i)$ denotes the apparent rate of a PEPA component P_i according to Definition 2.

For instance, in (2) it holds that $r_\alpha(\mathbb{A}_1\{A\}, V) = rV_{(\mathbb{A}_1,A)}$, which gives the apparent rate at which a population of $V_{(\mathbb{A}_1,A)}$ A-components exhibits action α.

Definition 10 (Parameterised Component Rate). *Let M be an FPA model, $\alpha \in \mathcal{A}$ and V a population function. The component rate of $(H,P) \in \mathcal{B}(M)$ with respect to V is then defined as follows.*

- Synchronised cooperation: *if $H \in \mathcal{G}(M_i)$, $i = 0,1$, and $\alpha \in L$ then*

$$\mathcal{R}_\alpha(M_0 \underset{L}{\bowtie} M_1, V, H, P) := \frac{\mathcal{R}_\alpha(M_i, V, H, P)}{r_\alpha(M_i, V)} \min(r_\alpha(M_0, V), r_\alpha(M_1, V)).$$

- Unsynchronised cooperation: *if $H \in \mathcal{G}(M_i)$, $i = 0,1$, and $\alpha \notin L$ then*

$$\mathcal{R}_\alpha(M_0 \underset{L}{\bowtie} M_1, V, H, P) := \mathcal{R}_\alpha(M_i, V, H, P).$$

- Fluid atom:

$$\mathcal{R}_\alpha(H'\{P'\}, V, H, P) := \begin{cases} V(H,P)r_\alpha(P) & , H = H' \wedge P \in ds(P') \\ 0 & , \textit{otherwise.} \end{cases}$$

These quantities are used to define the ODE system to be analysed.

Notation. The derivative of $V_{(H,P)}$ is denoted by Newton's dot notation $\dot{V}_{(H,P)}$. To enhance readability, time t will be suppressed in the representation of ODEs, i.e. $\dot{V}_{(H,P)}$ denotes $\dot{V}_{(H,P)}(t)$ and $V_{(H,P)}$ denotes $V_{(H,P)}(t)$.

Definition 11. *Let M be an FPA model. The initial value problem for M is*

$$\dot{V}_{(H,P)} = \sum_{\alpha \in \mathcal{A}} \Big(\Big(\sum_{P' \in \mathcal{B}(M,H)} p_\alpha(P',P) \mathcal{R}_\alpha(M, V, H, P') \Big) - \mathcal{R}_\alpha(M, V, H, P) \Big)$$

where $p_\alpha(P,P') := (1/r_\alpha(P)) \sum_{P \xrightarrow{(\alpha,r)} P'} r$, with initial condition given by $V(0)$.

For instance, the initial value problem of (2) and (3) is given by the initial condition (3) and the ODE system

$$\begin{aligned}
\dot{V}_{(\mathbb{A}_1,A)} &= -\min\big(rV_{(\mathbb{A}_1,A)}, rV_{(\mathbb{B}_1,B)}, uV_{(\mathbb{C}_1,C)}\big) + sV_{(\mathbb{A}_1,A')} \\
\dot{V}_{(\mathbb{A}_1,A')} &= -sV_{(\mathbb{A}_1,A')} + \min\big(rV_{(\mathbb{A}_1,A)}, rV_{(\mathbb{B}_1,B)}, uV_{(\mathbb{C}_1,C)}\big) \\
\dot{V}_{(\mathbb{B}_1,B)} &= -\min\big(rV_{(\mathbb{A}_1,A)}, rV_{(\mathbb{B}_1,B)}, uV_{(\mathbb{C}_1,C)}\big) + sV_{(\mathbb{B}_1,B')} \\
\dot{V}_{(\mathbb{B}_1,B')} &= -sV_{(\mathbb{B}_1,B')} + \min\big(rV_{(\mathbb{A}_1,A)}, rV_{(\mathbb{B}_1,B)}, uV_{(\mathbb{C}_1,C)}\big) \\
\dot{V}_{(\mathbb{C}_1,C)} &= -\min\big(rV_{(\mathbb{A}_1,A)}, rV_{(\mathbb{B}_1,B)}, uV_{(\mathbb{C}_1,C)}\big) + wV_{(\mathbb{C}_1,C')} \\
\dot{V}_{(\mathbb{C}_1,C')} &= -wV_{(\mathbb{C}_1,C')} + \min\big(rV_{(\mathbb{A}_1,A)}, rV_{(\mathbb{B}_1,B)}, uV_{(\mathbb{C}_1,C)}\big).
\end{aligned} \tag{4}$$

Remark 1. In general, it can be shown that for any fluid atom $H\{P\}$ it holds that $\sum_{P' \in \mathcal{B}(M,H)} \dot{V}_{(H,P')} = 0$. For instance, in (2) we have that $\dot{V}_{(\mathbb{A}_1,A)} + \dot{V}_{(\mathbb{A}_1,A')} = 0$. Throughout the paper, for the sake of brevity we will write one of the ODEs for a fluid atom in terms of the derivatives of its other states, e.g., $\dot{V}_{(\mathbb{A}_1,A')} = -\dot{V}_{(\mathbb{A}_1,A)}$ instead of its explicit form as in (4).

3 Exact Fluid Lumpability

The goal of this section is to develop a simplification technique to reduce the computational cost of fluid analysis. The idea is to partition the set $\mathcal{G}(M)$ of an FPA model M in such a way that the fluid atoms belonging to the same block have, intuitively, the same ODE trajectories. Notice that a necessary condition is that any two fluid atoms within the same block must have the same initial condition. Such a partitioning allows one to relate the solution of the original ODE system to that of a smaller, collapsed ODE system with the ODEs of only one label for each element of the partition. The name of *exactly fluid lumpable partitions* stems from the parallel with the theory of exact lumpability for Markov chains, where a partition over the state space has to satisfy the requirement that states within the same block must have the same initial probability [4].

3.1 Motivating Example

Let us consider a variation of *Triple* (2) which corresponds to the PEPA model where (1) is replicated D times and further composed with N_U components defined as $U \stackrel{def}{=} (\gamma, z).U'$, $U' \stackrel{def}{=} (\delta, z').U$. The FPA encoding is given then by

$$Sys' := \Big(\big(\mathbb{A}_1\{A\} \underset{\{\alpha\}}{\bowtie} \mathbb{B}_1\{B\} \underset{\{\alpha\}}{\bowtie} \mathbb{C}_1\{C\}\big) \underset{\emptyset}{\bowtie} \ldots$$
$$\ldots \underset{\emptyset}{\bowtie} \big(\mathbb{A}_D\{A\} \underset{\{\alpha\}}{\bowtie} \mathbb{B}_D\{B\} \underset{\{\alpha\}}{\bowtie} \mathbb{C}_D\{C\}\big)\Big) \underset{\{\gamma\}}{\bowtie} \mathbb{U}\{U\} \quad (5)$$

with initial values

$$\begin{array}{lll} V_{(\mathbb{A}_d,A)}(0) = N_A & V_{(\mathbb{B}_d,B)}(0) = N_A & V_{(\mathbb{C}_d,C)}(0) = N_C \\ V_{(\mathbb{A}_d,A')}(0) = 0 & V_{(\mathbb{B}_d,B')}(0) = 0 & V_{(\mathbb{C}_d,C')}(0) = 0 \\ V_{(\mathbb{U},U)}(0) = N_U & V_{(\mathbb{U},U')}(0) = 0 & \end{array} \quad (6)$$

for $1 \leq d \leq D$. Since each $\mathbb{A}_d\{A\} \underset{\{\alpha\}}{\bowtie} \mathbb{B}_d\{B\} \underset{\{\alpha\}}{\bowtie} \mathbb{C}_d\{C\}$, with $1 \leq d \leq D$, contributes $|ds(A)|+|ds(B)|+|ds(C)| = 6$ ODEs, the size of the fluid approximation of Sys' is $6D + |ds(U)| = 6D + 2$, which is given by the following ODE system.

$$\begin{aligned}
\dot{V}_{(\mathbb{A}_d,A)} &= -\min\big(rV_{(\mathbb{A}_d,A)}, rV_{(\mathbb{B}_d,B)}, uV_{(\mathbb{C}_d,C)}\big) + sV_{(\mathbb{A}_d,A')} \\
\dot{V}_{(\mathbb{A}_d,A')} &= -\dot{V}_{(\mathbb{A}_d,A)} \\
\dot{V}_{(\mathbb{B}_d,B)} &= -\min\big(rV_{(\mathbb{A}_d,A)}, rV_{(\mathbb{B}_d,B)}, uV_{(\mathbb{C}_d,C)}\big) + sV_{(\mathbb{B}_d,B')} \\
\dot{V}_{(\mathbb{B}_d,B')} &= -\dot{V}_{(\mathbb{B}_d,B)} \\
\dot{V}_{(\mathbb{C}_d,C)} &= -\min\big(rV_{(\mathbb{A}_d,A)}, rV_{(\mathbb{B}_d,B)}, uV_{(\mathbb{C}_d,C)}\big) + \\
&\quad + \frac{wV_{(\mathbb{C}_d,C')}}{w\sum_{d'=1}^{D} V_{(\mathbb{C}_{d'},C')}} \min\Big(w\sum_{d'=1}^{D} V_{(\mathbb{C}_{d'},C')}, zV_{(\mathbb{U},U)}\Big) \\
\dot{V}_{(\mathbb{C}_d,C')} &= -\dot{V}_{(\mathbb{C}_d,C)} \\
\dot{V}_{(\mathbb{U},U)} &= -\min\Big(w\sum_{d'=1}^{D} V_{(\mathbb{C}_{d'},C')}, zV_{(\mathbb{U},U)}\Big) + z'V_{(\mathbb{U},U')} \\
\dot{V}_{(\mathbb{U},U')} &= -\dot{V}_{(\mathbb{U},U)}
\end{aligned} \quad (7)$$

for all $1 \leq d \leq D$. When D is large, ODE analysis may become problematic from a computational viewpoint.

Assume now that the solution satisfies

$$\begin{array}{ll} V_{(\mathbb{A}_1,A)}(t) = V_{(\mathbb{A}_d,A)}(t) & V_{(\mathbb{A}_1,A')}(t) = V_{(\mathbb{A}_d,A')}(t) \\ V_{(\mathbb{B}_1,B)}(t) = V_{(\mathbb{B}_d,B)}(t) & V_{(\mathbb{B}_1,B')}(t) = V_{(\mathbb{B}_d,B')}(t) \\ V_{(\mathbb{C}_1,C)}(t) = V_{(\mathbb{C}_d,C)}(t) & V_{(\mathbb{C}_1,C')}(t) = V_{(\mathbb{C}_d,C')}(t) \end{array} \tag{8}$$

and

$$V_{(\mathbb{A}_d,A)}(t) = V_{(\mathbb{B}_d,B)}(t) \qquad V_{(\mathbb{A}_d,A')}(t) = V_{(\mathbb{B}_d,B')}(t) \tag{9}$$

for all $1 \leq d \leq D$ and $t \geq 0$. Although these can be written as

$$\begin{array}{ll} V_{(\mathbb{A}_1,A)}(t) = V_{(\mathbb{A}_d,A)}(t) & V_{(\mathbb{A}_1,A')}(t) = V_{(\mathbb{A}_d,A')}(t) \\ V_{(\mathbb{A}_1,A)}(t) = V_{(\mathbb{B}_d,B)}(t) & V_{(\mathbb{A}_1,A')}(t) = V_{(\mathbb{B}_d,B')}(t) \\ V_{(\mathbb{C}_1,C)}(t) = V_{(\mathbb{C}_d,C)}(t) & V_{(\mathbb{C}_1,C')}(t) = V_{(\mathbb{C}_d,C')}(t) \end{array} \tag{10}$$

for all $1 \leq d \leq D$ and $t \geq 0$, we prefer to state them as two separate groups of equations because (8) and (9) will be shown to be inferred from two relations, called *projected label equivalences* (cf. Definition 15), directly arising from two distinct label equivalences on $\mathcal{G}(Sys')$; (10) is instead induced by the transitive closure of the union of such relations, which will yield a coarser partition but does not arise from a label equivalence.

Simplifying (7) for a fixed d, say $d = 1$, and using (10) allows us to rewrite the fractions and summations in the right-hand sides in a way that is independent from labels different than $\mathbb{A}_1$, $\mathbb{C}_1$, and $\mathbb{U}$:

$$\begin{array}{ll} \dot{V}_{(\mathbb{A}_1,A)} = -\min\left(rV_{(\mathbb{A}_1,A)}, uV_{(\mathbb{C}_1,C)}\right) + sV_{(\mathbb{A}_1,A')} & \dot{V}_{(\mathbb{A}_1,A')} = -\dot{V}_{(\mathbb{A}_1,A)} \\ \dot{V}_{(\mathbb{C}_1,C)} = -\min\left(rV_{(\mathbb{A}_1,A)}, uV_{(\mathbb{C}_1,C)}\right) + & \dot{V}_{(\mathbb{C}_1,C')} = -\dot{V}_{(\mathbb{C}_1,C)} \\ \qquad + (1/D)\min\left(wD \cdot V_{(\mathbb{C}_1,C')}, zV_{(\mathbb{U},U)}\right) & \\ \dot{V}_{(\mathbb{U},U)} = -\min\left(wD \cdot V_{(\mathbb{C}_1,C')}, zV_{(\mathbb{U},U)}\right) + z'V_{(\mathbb{U},U')} & \dot{V}_{(\mathbb{U},U')} = -\dot{V}_{(\mathbb{U},U)} \end{array} \tag{11}$$

By using the same initial populations as in (7) and assuming that the above ODE system has a unique solution, through (10) we can exactly relate the solution of (7), which has $(2 + 2 + 2)D + 2$ equations, to that of (11), which has only $(2 + 2) + 2$ equations, thus making the problem independent from D.

3.2 Definitions

Definition 12 (Exact Fluid Lumpability). *Let M be an FPA model and $\overline{H} = \{\overline{H}_1, \ldots, \overline{H}_n\}$ a partition of $\mathcal{G}(M)$. We call $\overline{H}$ exactly fluid lumpable, if, for all $\overline{H}_i \in \overline{H}$, there are $H_i \in \overline{H}_i$ and a family of bijections $\sigma_\bullet$,*

$$\sigma_H : \mathcal{B}(M, H_i) \longrightarrow \mathcal{B}(M, H), \qquad \text{for all} \quad H \in \overline{H}_i \setminus \{H_i\},$$

such that for all initial populations $V(0)$ which satisfy

$$\forall \overline{H}_i \in \overline{H} \forall H \in \overline{H}_i \setminus \{H_i\} \forall P \in \mathcal{B}(M, H_i)\big(V_{(H_i,P)}(0) = V_{(H,\sigma_H(P))}(0)\big),$$

the same holds for all $t \geq 0$ *in the corresponding fluid approximation* V, *i.e.*

$$\forall t \geq 0 \forall \overline{H}_i \in \overline{H} \forall H \in \overline{H}_i \setminus \{H_i\} \forall P \in \mathcal{B}(M, H_i)\big(V_{(H_i,P)}(t) = V_{(H,\sigma_H(P))}(t)\big).$$

We shall say that $\sigma_\bullet$ *establishes the exact fluid lumpability of* $\overline{H}$ *and that* $\overline{H}_i \setminus \{H_i\}$ is related to H_i, $1 \leq i \leq n$.

For instance, assumption (10) holds if

$$\{\overline{H}_1, \overline{H}_2, \overline{H}_3\} = \{\{\mathbb{A}_1, \mathbb{B}_1, \ldots, \mathbb{A}_D, \mathbb{B}_D\}, \{\mathbb{C}_1, \ldots, \mathbb{C}_D\}, \{\mathbb{U}\}\} \tag{12}$$

is an exactly fluid lumpable partition which is established by the family

$$\begin{aligned} \sigma_H(\mathbb{A}_1, T) &:= \begin{cases} (H, T) & , H \in \{\mathbb{A}_2, \ldots, \mathbb{A}_D\} \wedge T \in \{A, A'\} \\ (H, B) & , H \in \{\mathbb{B}_2, \ldots, \mathbb{B}_D\} \wedge T = A \\ (H, B') & , H \in \{\mathbb{B}_2, \ldots, \mathbb{B}_D\} \wedge T = A' \end{cases} \\ \sigma_H(\mathbb{C}_1, T) &:= (H, T), \quad H \in \{\mathbb{C}_2, \ldots, \mathbb{C}_D\} \wedge T \in \{C, C'\} \end{aligned} \tag{13}$$

Remark 2. Note that Definition 12 requires, for all $1 \leq i \leq n$, the existence of an $H_i \in \overline{H}_i$ such that $\overline{H}_i \setminus \{H_i\}$ is related to H_i. However, if one such H_i can be found for each $1 \leq i \leq n$, then a suitable family of bijections exists for all $H_i' \in \overline{H}_i$, where $1 \leq i \leq n$.

Let us fix an FPA model M and assume that $\overline{H} = \{\overline{H}_1, \ldots, \overline{H}_n\}$ is exactly fluid lumpable. We consider the ODE of $V_{(H_i,P_i)}$

$$\dot{V}_{(H_i,P_i)} = \sum_{\alpha \in \mathcal{A}} \Big(\sum_{P' \in \mathcal{B}(M,H_i)} p_\alpha(P', P_i) \mathcal{R}_\alpha(M, V, H_i, P') - \mathcal{R}_\alpha(M, V, H_i, P_i) \Big)$$

and fix some $V_{(H,P)}(t)$, with $H \in \overline{H}_j \setminus \{H_j\}$, $1 \leq j \leq n$, on the right-hand-side of the ODE. Using the assumption on $\overline{H}$ we infer then that $V_{(H,P)}(t) = V_{(H_j, \sigma_H^{-1}(P))}(t)$, i.e., we can express the right-hand-side of the ODE using only the functions $\{V_{(H_j,P_j)} \mid 1 \leq j \leq n, P_j \in \mathcal{B}(M, H_j)\}$.

This observation leads to the following notion.

Definition 13 (Exactly Lumped Fluid Model). *Let* $\overline{H} = \{\overline{H}_1, \ldots \ldots, \overline{H}_n\}$ *be an exactly fluid lumpable partition of* $\mathcal{G}(M)$ *which is established by* $\sigma_\bullet$. *Moreover, let* $D^l_{(H_i,P_i)}$ *denote the equation which arises from*

$$D_{(H_i,P_i)} := \sum_{\alpha \in \mathcal{A}} \Big(\sum_{P' \in \mathcal{B}(M,H_i)} p_\alpha(P', P_i) \mathcal{R}_\alpha(M, V, H_i, P') - \mathcal{R}_\alpha(M, V, H_i, P_i) \Big)$$

by replacing all $V_{(H,P)}$, *where* $H \in \overline{H}_j \setminus \{H_j\}$ *for some* $1 \leq j \leq n$, *with* $V_{(H_j,\sigma_H^{-1}(P))}$. The exactly lumped fluid model *of* M *with respect to* $\sigma_\bullet$ *and* $V(0)$ *is the solution of the lumped ODE system* $\dot{V}_{(H_i,P_i)} = D^l_{(H_i,P_i)}$, $(H_i, P_i) \in \mathcal{B}^l(M)$, *subjected to the initial value* $V(0)_{|\mathcal{B}^l(M)}$, *where* $\mathcal{B}^l(M) := \{(H, P) \in \mathcal{B}(M) \mid \exists 1 \leq i \leq n(H = H_i)\}$.

For instance, if (12) is established by (13) we infer that the exactly lumped fluid model of (5) with respect to (13) and (6) is the solution of (11).

Recall that we assumed that the lumped ODE system has a unique solution. To see this, note that a restriction of a Lipschitz function is again Lipschitz and that the original ODE system is Lipschitz [6].

4 Construction of Exactly Fluid Lumpable Partitions

This section discusses two related equivalences for the construction of exactly fluid lumpable partitions. The first, *label equivalence*, relates tuples of labels. If two tuples, say $(H_1, \ldots, H_n)$ and $(H'_1, \ldots, H'_n)$ are related, then this implies that the fluid atoms tagged with H_i and H'_i, $1 \leq i \leq n$, have the same fluid approximation. The second relation, called *projected label equivalence*, is shown to induce exactly fluid lumpable partitions.

4.1 Label Equivalence and Projected Label Equivalence

Definition 14 (Label Equivalence). *Let M be an FPA model and let $\mathcal{H} = (\boldsymbol{H}^1, \ldots, \boldsymbol{H}^N)$, $\boldsymbol{H}^i = (H^i_1, \ldots, H^i_{K_i})$, be a* tuple partition *on $\mathcal{G}(M)$, i.e. such that for each $H \in \mathcal{G}(M)$ there exist unique $1 \leq i \leq N$ and $1 \leq k \leq K_i$ with $H = H^i_k$. $\boldsymbol{H}^i$ and $\boldsymbol{H}^j$ are said to be* label equivalent, *written $\boldsymbol{H}^i \sim_{\mathcal{H}} \boldsymbol{H}^j$, if*

i) $K_i = K_j$ and there exist bijections $\sigma_k : \mathcal{B}(M, H^i_k) \to \mathcal{B}(M, H^j_k)$, for all $1 \leq k \leq K_i$, such that
- *the α-component rate out of (H^i_k, P) with respect to V is equal to the α-component rate out of $(H^j_k, \sigma_k(P))$ with respect to V^σ,*

$$\mathcal{R}_\alpha(M, V, H^i_k, P) = \mathcal{R}_\alpha(M, V^\sigma, H^j_k, \sigma_k(P))$$

- *the sum of α-component rates into (H^i_k, P) with respect to V is equal to the sum of the α-component rates into $(H^j_k, \sigma_k(P))$ with respect to V^σ,*

$$\sum_{P' \in \mathcal{B}(M, H^i_k)} p_\alpha(P', P) \mathcal{R}_\alpha(M, V, H^i_k, P') = \sum_{P' \in \mathcal{B}(M, H^j_k)} p_\alpha(P', \sigma_k(P)) \mathcal{R}_\alpha(M, V^\sigma, H^j_k, P')$$

- *for all $(H, P) \in \mathcal{B}(M)$ such that $H \notin \boldsymbol{H}^i, \boldsymbol{H}^j$ it holds $\mathcal{R}_\alpha(M, V, H, P) = \mathcal{R}_\alpha(M, V^\sigma, H, P)$ and*

$$\sum_{P' \in \mathcal{B}(M,H)} p_\alpha(P', P) \mathcal{R}_\alpha(M, V, H, P') = \sum_{P' \in \mathcal{B}(M,H)} p_\alpha(P', P) \mathcal{R}_\alpha(M, V^\sigma, H, P')$$

ii) $r_\alpha(M, V) = r_\alpha(M, V^\sigma)$

hold for all *population functions V and*
$$V^\sigma_{(H,P)} := \begin{cases} V_{(H^j_k, \sigma_k(P))} & , H = H^i_k \\ V_{(H^i_k, \sigma_k^{-1}(P))} & , H = H^j_k \\ V_{(H,P)} & , \textit{otherwise.} \end{cases}$$

Informally, two tuples $\boldsymbol{H}^i, \boldsymbol{H}^j$ are label equivalent if the component and apparent rates respect an exchange of fluid atom populations within the tuples. Hence, label equivalence especially applies to symmetries within the model under study. For instance, let us fix the subprocess of (5)

$$Sys := (\mathbb{A}_1\{A\} \underset{\{\alpha\}}{\bowtie} \mathbb{B}_1\{B\} \underset{\{\alpha\}}{\bowtie} \mathbb{C}_1\{C\}) \underset{\emptyset}{\bowtie} \ldots \underset{\emptyset}{\bowtie} (\mathbb{A}_D\{A\} \underset{\{\alpha\}}{\bowtie} \mathbb{B}_D\{B\} \underset{\{\alpha\}}{\bowtie} \mathbb{C}_D\{C\}),$$

the tuple partition $\mathcal{H}_1 := \{(\mathbb{A}_1, \mathbb{B}_1, \mathbb{C}_1), \ldots, (\mathbb{A}_D, \mathbb{B}_D, \mathbb{C}_D)\}$ of $\mathcal{G}(Sys)$ and two arbitrary $1 \leq i, j \leq D$. The bijections

$$\begin{aligned} \sigma_1^{(\mathbb{A}_i,\mathbb{B}_i,\mathbb{C}_i),(\mathbb{A}_j,\mathbb{B}_j,\mathbb{C}_j)} &: \mathcal{B}(Sys, \mathbb{A}_i) \to \mathcal{B}(Sys, \mathbb{A}_j),\ (\mathbb{A}_i, T) \mapsto (\mathbb{A}_j, T), \\ \sigma_2^{(\mathbb{A}_i,\mathbb{B}_i,\mathbb{C}_i),(\mathbb{A}_j,\mathbb{B}_j,\mathbb{C}_j)} &: \mathcal{B}(Sys, \mathbb{B}_i) \to \mathcal{B}(Sys, \mathbb{B}_j),\ (\mathbb{B}_i, T) \mapsto (\mathbb{B}_j, T), \\ \sigma_3^{(\mathbb{A}_i,\mathbb{B}_i,\mathbb{C}_i),(\mathbb{A}_j,\mathbb{B}_j,\mathbb{C}_j)} &: \mathcal{B}(Sys, \mathbb{C}_i) \to \mathcal{B}(Sys, \mathbb{C}_j),\ (\mathbb{C}_i, T) \mapsto (\mathbb{C}_j, T), \end{aligned} \tag{14}$$

establish then $(\mathbb{A}_i, \mathbb{B}_i, \mathbb{C}_i) \sim_{\mathcal{H}_1} (\mathbb{A}_j, \mathbb{B}_j, \mathbb{C}_j)$. The next theorem relates the fluid trajectories of label equivalent tuples.

Theorem 2. *Let M be an FPA model with fluid approximation V, and $\mathcal{H}$ be a tuple partition on $\mathcal{G}(M)$. Then $\boldsymbol{H}^i \sim_{\mathcal{H}} \boldsymbol{H}^j$ implies*

$$\forall (H,P) \in \mathcal{B}(M)\Big(V_{(H,P)}(0) = V^{\sigma}_{(H,P)}(0)\Big) \quad \Rightarrow$$
$$\forall (H,P) \in \mathcal{B}(M) \forall t \geq 0 \Big(V_{(H,P)}(t) = V^{\sigma}_{(H,P)}(t)\Big),$$

where V^{σ} is as in Definition 14.

For instance, $(\mathbb{A}_i, \mathbb{B}_i, \mathbb{C}_i) \sim_{\mathcal{H}_1} (\mathbb{A}_j, \mathbb{B}_j, \mathbb{C}_j)$ and Theorem 2 show that

$$\begin{array}{lll} V_{(\mathbb{A}_i,A)}(0) = V_{(\mathbb{A}_j,A)}(0) & V_{(\mathbb{B}_i,B)}(0) = V_{(\mathbb{B}_j,B)}(0) & V_{(\mathbb{C}_i,C)}(0) = V_{(\mathbb{C}_j,C)}(0) \\ V_{(\mathbb{A}_i,A')}(0) = V_{(\mathbb{A}_j,A')}(0) & V_{(\mathbb{B}_i,B')}(0) = V_{(\mathbb{B}_j,B')}(0) & V_{(\mathbb{C}_i,C')}(0) = V_{(\mathbb{C}_j,C')}(0) \end{array}$$

implies

$$\begin{array}{lll} V_{(\mathbb{A}_i,A)}(t) = V_{(\mathbb{A}_j,A)}(t) & V_{(\mathbb{B}_i,B)}(t) = V_{(\mathbb{B}_j,B)}(t) & V_{(\mathbb{C}_i,C)}(t) = V_{(\mathbb{C}_j,C)}(t) \\ V_{(\mathbb{A}_i,A')}(t) = V_{(\mathbb{A}_j,A')}(t) & V_{(\mathbb{B}_i,B')}(t) = V_{(\mathbb{B}_j,B')}(t) & V_{(\mathbb{C}_i,C')}(t) = V_{(\mathbb{C}_j,C')}(t) \end{array}$$

for all $t \geq 0$, where V denotes the fluid approximation of *Sys* with respect to a given $V(0)$.

This example also illustrates that, in general, one has to consider relations between *tuples* of labels, rather than just labels. For clarification, assume that our tuple partition of $\mathcal{G}(Sys)$ consists only of trivial tuples, i.e. $\mathcal{H}_2 := \{(H) \mid H \in \mathcal{G}(Sys)\}$. Then, for instance,

$$\sigma_1^{(\mathbb{A}_i),(\mathbb{A}_j)} : \mathcal{B}(Sys, \mathbb{A}_i) \to \mathcal{B}(Sys, \mathbb{A}_j), (\mathbb{A}_i, T) \mapsto (\mathbb{A}_j, T),$$

where $1 \leq i < j \leq D$, does not establish $(\mathbb{A}_i) \sim_{\mathcal{H}_2} (\mathbb{A}_j)$. This is because the fluid atoms tagged with $\mathbb{B}_i$ and $\mathbb{B}_j$ or the fluid atoms tagged with $\mathbb{C}_i$ and $\mathbb{C}_j$

may have different initial populations. This problem does not manifest itself if we use the tuple partition $\mathcal{H}_1$, where the populations of larger processes, rather than that of single fluid atoms, are exchanged.

The next theorem states that label equivalence is a congruence with respect to the parallel composition of FPA.

Theorem 3 (Label Equivalence is a Congruence). *Let M be an FPA model and $\mathcal{H}$ be a tuple partition on $\mathcal{G}(M)$. Then the following hold:*

- *$\sim_{\mathcal{H}}$ is an equivalence relation on $\mathcal{H}$.*
- *Fix an action set L, an FPA model M_0 and a tuple partition $\mathcal{H}_0$ on $\mathcal{G}(M_0)$. If $\boldsymbol{H}^i \sim_{\mathcal{H}} \boldsymbol{H}^j$ then $\boldsymbol{H}^i \sim_{\mathcal{H}'} \boldsymbol{H}^j$, where $\mathcal{H}' := \mathcal{H} \cup \mathcal{H}_0$ is a tuple partition on $M \underset{L}{\bowtie} M_0$.*

As usual, this is a useful tool for compositional reasoning. For instance, let us consider Sys' defined in (5) and fix the tuple partition $\mathcal{H}_1' := \mathcal{H}_1 \cup \mathcal{H}_0$ of $\mathcal{G}(Sys')$, where $\mathcal{H}_0 := \{(\mathbb{U})\}$ is obviously the only possible tuple partition of $\mathcal{G}(\mathbb{U}\{U\})$. Theorem 3 implies $(\mathbb{A}_i, \mathbb{B}_i, \mathbb{C}_i) \sim_{\mathcal{H}_1'} (\mathbb{A}_j, \mathbb{B}_j, \mathbb{C}_j)$, which yields

$$\mathcal{H}_1' / \sim_{\mathcal{H}_1'} = \{\{(\mathbb{A}_1, \mathbb{B}_1, \mathbb{C}_1), \ldots, (\mathbb{A}_D, \mathbb{B}_D, \mathbb{C}_D)\}, \{(\mathbb{U})\}\},$$

as $1 \leq i, j \leq D$ were chosen arbitrarily. This and Theorem 2 show then that

$$\{\{\mathbb{A}_1, \ldots, \mathbb{A}_D\}, \{\mathbb{B}_1, \ldots, \mathbb{B}_D\}, \{\mathbb{C}_1, \ldots, \mathbb{C}_D\}, \{\mathbb{U}\}\} \tag{15}$$

is an exactly fluid lumpable partition. This motivates the following.

Definition 15 (Projected Label Equivalence). *Fix an FPA model M and a tuple partition $\mathcal{H}$ of $\mathcal{G}(M)$. The labels $H_1, H_2 \in \mathcal{G}(M)$ are projected label equivalent, $H_1 \approx_{\mathcal{H}} H_2$, if $\boldsymbol{H}^i \sim_{\mathcal{H}} \boldsymbol{H}^j$ and $k_i = k_j$ in the unique assignment $H_1 = H^i_{k_i}$, $H_2 = H^j_{k_j}$.*

Theorem 4. *Fix an FPA model M and a tuple partition $\mathcal{H}$ of $\mathcal{G}(M)$. The relation $\approx_{\mathcal{H}}$ is then an equivalence relation on $\mathcal{G}(M)$ and $\mathcal{G}(M)/\approx_{\mathcal{H}}$ is an exactly fluid lumpable partition.*

Note that $\mathcal{H}_1'$ induces the exactly fluid lumpable partition (15) via $\approx_{\mathcal{H}_1'}$ which shows assumption (8) in our running example. Intuitively, this partition relates all fluid atoms expressed with the same sequential component, A, B, and C, if they are initialised with the same conditions. However, in general, for the same model there might be more tuple partitions which allow for a simplification: The partition $\mathcal{H}_2' := \mathcal{H}_2 \cup \mathcal{H}_0$, the family of bijections

$$\sigma_1^{(\mathbb{A}_i),(\mathbb{B}_i)} : \mathcal{B}(Sys, \mathbb{A}_i) \to \mathcal{B}(Sys, \mathbb{B}_i), (\mathbb{A}_i, T) \mapsto \begin{cases} (\mathbb{B}_i, B) & , T = A \\ (\mathbb{B}_i, B') & , T = A' \end{cases} \tag{16}$$

and Theorem 3 yield $(\mathbb{A}_i) \sim_{\mathcal{H}_2'} (\mathbb{B}_i)$ for all $1 \leq i \leq D$. As these are the only nontrivial relations on $\mathcal{H}_2'$, we get $\mathcal{H}_2' / \sim_{\mathcal{H}_2'} = \{\{(\mathbb{U})\}, \{(\mathbb{A}_1), (\mathbb{B}_1)\}, \{(\mathbb{C}_1)\}, \ldots$ $\ldots, \{(\mathbb{A}_D), (\mathbb{B}_D)\}, \{(\mathbb{C}_D)\}\}$. This shows, in turn, that $\mathcal{H}_2'$ induces the exactly fluid lumpable partition

$$\mathcal{G}(Sys')/\approx_{\mathcal{H}'_2} = \{\{\mathbb{A}_1, \mathbb{B}_1\}, \{\mathbb{C}_1\}, \ldots, \{\mathbb{A}_D, \mathbb{B}_D\}, \{\mathbb{C}_D\}, \{\mathbb{U}\}\}.$$

Such a partition, instead, relates fluid atoms exhibiting distinct sequential components, A and B. This shows the assumption (9) in the example.

However, none of these partitions allows us to consider the *coarser* one (12) which shows (10), that is, (8) and (9) at the same time. We now remark that (12) would be obtained by $\mathcal{G}(Sys')/(\approx_{\mathcal{H}'_1} \cup \approx_{\mathcal{H}'_2})^*$, where * denotes the transitive closure. Crucially, we observe that there exists no tuple partition $\mathcal{H}$ of $\mathcal{G}(Sys')$ such that $\mathcal{G}(Sys')/\approx_{\mathcal{H}} = \mathcal{G}(Sys')/(\approx_{\mathcal{H}'_1} \cup \approx_{\mathcal{H}'_2})^*$, i.e., a combination of several projected label equivalences cannot be expressed as a projected label equivalence in general.

Fortunately, Theorem 5 states that these can be always merged as discussed, if the model satisfies a property of well-posedness in the following sense.

Definition 16 (Well-Posedness). *An FPA model M is well-posed if for all occurrences $M_1 \bowtie_L M_2$ in M it holds $\exists V_1\big(r_\alpha(M_1, V_1) > 0\big) \wedge \exists V_2\big(r_\alpha(M_2, V_2) > 0\big)$ for all $\alpha \in L$.*

Theorem 5. *Fix a well-posed FPA model M and a nonempty set of tuple partitions $S = \{\mathcal{H}_1, \ldots, \mathcal{H}_n\}$ of $\mathcal{G}(M)$. Then the partition $\mathcal{G}(M)/(\approx_{\mathcal{H}_1} \cup \ldots \cup \approx_{\mathcal{H}_n})^*$ is exactly fluid lumpable.*

We wish to stress here that the proof of Theorem 5 is constructive in that it provides a family of semi-isomorphisms which establish the exact fluid lumpability of $\mathcal{G}(M)/(\approx_{\mathcal{H}_1} \cup \ldots \cup \approx_{\mathcal{H}_n})^*$.

We argue that the assumption of well-posedness is not particularly restrictive. Essentially, it is introduced to rule out conditions where a fluid atom is capable of performing an activity of some action type, and it is synchronised with a process which cannot perform that action. Clearly, this is weaker than a deadlock situation, where no progress can be made whatsoever, but it may be a symptom of potential problems in the model description in practice. For instance, let $P \stackrel{\text{def}}{=} (\alpha, r).P' + (\beta, s).P'$, $P' \stackrel{\text{def}}{=} (\gamma, w).P$ and $Q \stackrel{\text{def}}{=} (\beta, s).Q'$, $Q' \stackrel{\text{def}}{=} (\gamma, w).Q$. Then

$$\mathit{Illposed} := H_1\{P\} \underset{\{\alpha,\beta\}}{\bowtie} H_2\{Q\} \tag{17}$$

is not well-posed (alternatively, it is *ill-posed*), because α-activities cannot be performed, therefore the contribution of the parametrised component rates for α will be zero. However, the fluid atom tagged with H_1 is allowed to cycle between its states P and P' through β-activities. Thus, (17) essentially behaves like the well-posed model defined by the sequential components

$$\tilde{P} \stackrel{\text{def}}{=} (\beta, s).\tilde{P}', \quad \tilde{P}' \stackrel{\text{def}}{=} (\gamma, w).\tilde{P}, \quad \tilde{Q} \stackrel{\text{def}}{=} (\beta, s).\tilde{Q}', \quad \tilde{Q}' \stackrel{\text{def}}{=} (\gamma, w).\tilde{Q}$$

and by the model component $\tilde{H}_1\{\tilde{P}\} \underset{\{\beta\}}{\bowtie} \tilde{H}_2\{\tilde{Q}\}$, since it holds that $V_{(H,T)}(t) = V_{(\tilde{H},\tilde{T})}(t)$ for all $(H,T) \in \mathcal{B}(\mathit{Illposed})$ and all $t > 0$, if the same holds for $t = 0$. That is, the ill-posed model (17) is transformed into a well-posed one which has the same ODE solution.

We leave for future work further investigations on well-posedness — e.g., whether Theorem 5 still holds also for ill-posed FPA models, or if any ill-posed model can be systematically transformed into a well-posed one.

4.2 Relationship with Stochastic Behavioural Equivalences

We shall investigate now the relation between the fluid atoms $H^i_k\{P^i_k\}$ and $H^j_k\{P^j_k\}$ in a relation between tuples $(H^i_1, \ldots, H^i_K) \sim_{\mathcal{H}} (H^j_1, \ldots, H^j_K)$.

The first observation is that even syntactical equivalence between fluid atoms is not *sufficient* for $(H^i_k) \sim_{\mathcal{H}} (H^j_k)$ in general. To see this, consider the model $(\mathbb{A}_1\{A\} \underset{\{\alpha\}}{\bowtie} \mathbb{C}\{C\}) \underset{\emptyset}{\bowtie} \mathbb{A}_2\{A\}$, where A and C are as in (1) and the tuple partition $\mathcal{H} = \{(\mathbb{A}_1), (\mathbb{C}), (\mathbb{A}_2)\}$ is used. Then it does not hold that $(\mathbb{A}_1) \sim_{\mathcal{H}} (\mathbb{A}_2)$, as $\mathbb{A}_1\{A\}$ is in a context where it is synchronised with $\mathbb{C}\{C\}$, whereas $\mathbb{A}_2\{A\}$ progresses independently. Using similar ideas, one can easily construct counterexamples for tuples of length greater than one.

We turn now to a *necessary* condition for label equivalence to hold. The theorem below states that label equivalence and projected label equivalence imply the notion of semi-isomorphism in the case of well-posed models.

Theorem 6. *Fix a well-posed FPA model M, a tuple partition $\mathcal{H} = \{\boldsymbol{H}^1, \ldots \ldots, \boldsymbol{H}^N\}$ on $\mathcal{G}(M)$ and assume that $\boldsymbol{H}^i \sim_{\mathcal{H}} \boldsymbol{H}^j$. Then P^i_k is semi-isomorphic to P^j_k for all $1 \leq k \leq K_i$. Specifically, $H^i_k \approx_{\mathcal{H}} H^j_k$ implies that P^i_k is semi-isomorphic to P^j_k for all $1 \leq k \leq K_i$.*

However, if the model is ill-posed, in general label equivalence does not imply any of the stochastic notions of behavioural equivalence for PEPA [10]. To see this, consider (17) and fix the tuple partition $\mathcal{H} = \{(H_1), (H_2)\}$. One can show then that $(H_1) \sim_{\mathcal{H}} (H_2)$, essentially because P is hindered in performing its α action. Because of this, we conclude that label equivalence implies neither isomorphism, nor strong bisimulation, nor strong equivalence, since each such relation distinguishes between the types of action performed by a process, and, clearly, P performs an α-activity whereas Q does not.

5 Conclusion

In Markovian process algebra, notions of equivalence for *discrete-state* aggregation are essentially based on equalities between the transition rates from states of the underlying continuous-time Markov chain. In an analogous way, in this paper we have presented a behavioural equivalence which relates the *continuous states* of the fluid semantics, i.e., the functions that are solutions of the underlying ODE system. The comparison here is between the fluxes that define the vector field governing such a system.

We have taken the path of considering as (fluid) *atoms* the sequential components that make up a model, therefore *label equivalence* was defined as a relation over such atoms. There are also other possibilities that we intend to explore in future work. For instance, a fluid atom in effect does not give rise to a single ODE, but it induces as many ODEs as the size of its derivative set. Therefore, it is natural to ask whether another behavioural relation could be devised over elements of derivative sets instead. In principle, such an approach could give rise to coarser partitions, hence more aggregated systems, than those that are obtainable through label equivalence. However, the simple running example used in this paper suggests that label equivalence may be highly effective when a model exhibits replicated behaviour of composite processes.

Exact fluid lumpability, at the basis of label equivalence, considers a form of invariance between models which holds for all time points for which the ODE solution exists. Of the possible directions for future research, particularly pressing for us is the characterisation of approximate relations for further state-space reduction, and the study of equivalences which hold in specific points, for instance at equilibrium.

Acknowledgement. This work has been partially supported by the EU project ASCENS, 257414, and by the DFG project FEMPA.

References

1. Aoki, M.: Control of large-scale dynamic systems by aggregation. IEEE Trans. Autom. Control 13(3), 246–253 (1968)
2. Bernardo, M., Gorrieri, R.: A tutorial on EMPA: A theory of concurrent processes with nondeterminism, priorities, probabilities and time. Theor. Comput. Sci. 202(1-2), 1–54 (1998)
3. Bortolussi, L., Policriti, A.: Dynamical systems and stochastic programming: To ordinary differential equations and back. T. Comp. Sys. Biology 11, 216–267 (2009)
4. Buchholz, P.: Exact and ordinary lumpability in finite Markov chains. J. Applied Probability 31, 59–74 (1994)
5. Cardelli, L.: On process rate semantics. Theor. Comput. Sci. 391, 190–215 (2008)
6. Hayden, R.: Scalable performance analysis of massively parallel stochastic systems. Ph.D. thesis, Imperial College London (2011)
7. Hayden, R.A., Bradley, J.T.: A fluid analysis framework for a Markovian process algebra. Theor. Comput. Sci. 411(22-24), 2260–2297 (2010)
8. Hermanns, H., Rettelbach, M.: Syntax, semantics, equivalences, and axioms for MTIPP. In: Proceedings of Process Algebra and Probabilistic Methods, Erlangen, pp. 71–87 (1994)
9. Hillston, J.: Fluid flow approximation of PEPA models. In: Proceedings of Quantitative Evaluation of Systems, pp. 33–43. IEEE Computer Society Press (2005)
10. Hillston, J.: A compositional approach to performance modelling. Cambridge University Press, New York (1996)
11. Ijiri, Y.: Fundamental queries in aggregation theory. Journal of the American Statistical Association 66(336), 766–782 (1971)
12. Iwase, Y., Levin, S.A., Andreasen, V.: Aggregation in model ecosystems I: perfect aggregation. Ecological Modelling 37 (1987)
13. Kwiatkowski, M., Stark, I.: The Continuous π-Calculus: A Process Algebra for Biochemical Modelling. In: Heiner, M., Uhrmacher, A.M. (eds.) CMSB 2008. LNCS (LNBI), vol. 5307, pp. 103–122. Springer, Heidelberg (2008)

Compositionality of Probabilistic Hennessy-Milner Logic through Structural Operational Semantics

Daniel Gebler[1] and Wan Fokkink[1,2]
{e.d.gebler,w.j.fokkink}@vu.nl

[1] VU University Amsterdam
[2] Eindhoven University of Technology

Abstract. We present a method to decompose HML formulae for reactive probabilistic processes. This gives rise to a compositional modal proof system for the satisfaction relation of probabilistic process algebras. The satisfaction problem of a probabilistic HML formula for a process term is reduced to the question of whether its subterms satisfy a derived formula obtained via the operational semantics.

1 Introduction

Probabilistic process algebras allow one to specify and reason about both qualitative and quantitative aspects of system behavior [2,5,12,17]. Transition system specifications (TSSs) associate to each process term a labeled transition system (LTS). We consider reactive probabilistic LTSs [22] (essentially Labeled Markov Chains), which are pure probabilistic systems for which the internal nondeterminism (i.e. how does the system react to an action) is fully probabilistic, while the external nondeterminism (i.e. which action label is selected by the environment for the system to perform) is unquantified. Modal logics have been designed to express properties of states in reactive probabilistic LTSs [22].

Larsen and Xinxin [21,23] developed for process languages in the de Simone format [27] a general approach to obtain a compositional proof system for the satisfaction relation of Hennessy-Milner logic (HML) formulae [16]. This technique was extended to TSSs in ready simulation and tyft/tyxt format [11]. We carry over this line of research to reactive probabilistic LTSs. In particular we extend the decomposition method from terms to distributions, as well as to modal operators for probabilistic processes. Thus, we obtain a compositional proof system for a probabilistic version of HML [24]. Moreover, the decomposition developed in this paper provides a basis for investigating connections between behavioral semantics, modal characterizations and structural operational semantics of probabilistic systems. In particular, it opens the door to deriving expressive and elegant congruence formats for probabilistic semantics in a structured way, following the approach of [6].

We develop a number of proof-theoretic facts for probabilistic TSSs. In detail, we provide an extension of proofs for probabilistic TSSs [20] to support the

M. Koutny and I. Ulidowski (Eds.): CONCUR 2012, LNCS 7454, pp. 395–409, 2012.

derivation that a transition does not hold. Furthermore, we construct a collection of derived rules, called ruloids [7], that determine completely the behavior of each open term. Transition rules of probabilistic TSSs can be partitioned such that every partition allows to derive transitions of a total probability of 1 and different partitions are mutually exclusive [20]. We show that this partitioning can be lifted to ruloids. This fact is a corner stone of our compositional proof systems for probabilistic HML. Ruloids and ruloid partitions are used to decompose the diamond modality.

2 Preliminaries

In probabilistic labeled transition systems, transitions carry probabilities. We consider reactive probabilistic systems where each state is required to be semistochastic, i.e. the sum of the probabilities of all outgoing transitions for an action is either 0 (action cannot be performed) or 1 (fully quantified dynamic behavior). $Dist(S)$ is the set of probability measures on a countable set S, i.e. all functions $\mu \in S \to [0,1]$ with $\sum_{s \in S} \mu(s) = 1$. Let $\mu(T) = \sum_{s \in T} \mu(s)$ for $T \subseteq S$; $Supp(\mu) = \{s \in S \mid \mu(s) > 0\}$ denotes the support of μ; δ_s for $s \in S$ is the Dirac distribution with $\delta_s(s) = 1$ and $\delta_s(s') = 0$ for $s' \neq s$. $\{\!|$ and $|\!\}$ denotes multisets.

Definition 1. *A* probabilistic labeled transition system (PLTS) *is a tuple* $\mathcal{M} = (S, Act, I, \to)$, *with* S *a set of states,* Act *a set of actions,* I *a set of indices, and* $\to \subseteq S \times Act \times (0,1] \times I \times S$, *where for each* $s \in S, a \in Act$,

$$\sum \{\!| p \mid \exists i \in I, s' \in S : (s,a,p,i,s') \in \to |\!\} \in \{0,1\}$$

$s \xrightarrow{a,p}_i s'$ denotes $(s,a,p,i,s') \in \to$, and $d(s,a) \in Dist(S)$ the measure with $d(s,a)(s') = \sum \{\!| p \mid \exists i \in I : s \xrightarrow{a,p}_i s' |\!\}$. Let $s \xrightarrow{a} \mu$ denote that the system evolves from state s by action a to distribution $\mu = d(s,a)$.

The first logical characterization of probabilistic bisimilarity for fully probabilistic reactive systems was provided in [22]. This logic is derived from Hennessy-Milner logic (HML) by decorating the diamond operator with a probability. It was generalized to the probabilistic modal logic L^N [24] for nondeterministic probabilistic systems (probabilistic automata). In the following we use this logic.

Definition 2. *[24] The syntax of probabilistic HML is:*

$$\varphi ::= \top \mid \neg\varphi \mid \bigwedge_{j \in J} \varphi_j \mid \langle a \rangle \varphi \mid [\varphi]_p$$

with $p \in [0,1]$, J *a countable index set, and* $a \in Act$. *Let* $\mathbb{O}$ *denote the set of probabilistic HML formulae.*

Definition 3. *[24] Let* $\mathcal{M} = (S, Act, I, \to)$ *be a PLTS. The satisfaction relation of probabilistic HML formulae* $\models \subseteq Dist(S) \times \mathbb{O}$ *is defined as follows:*

- $\mu \models \top$ *for each measure* μ
- $\mu \models \neg\varphi$ *iff* $\mu \not\models \varphi$
- $\mu \models \bigwedge_{j \in J} \varphi_j$ *iff* $\mu \models \varphi_j$ *for each* $j \in J$
- $\mu \models \langle a \rangle \varphi$ *iff for each* $s \in Supp(\mu)$ *there is a* $\nu \in Dist(S)$ *with* $s \xrightarrow{a} \nu$ *and* $\nu \models \varphi$
- $\mu \models [\varphi]_p$ *iff* $\mu(\{s \in S \mid \delta_s \models \varphi\}) \geq p$

We write $s \models \varphi$ for $\delta_s \models \varphi$.

Structural operational semantics (SOS) is defined by a transition system specification (TSS), which induces an LTS whose states are closed terms over an algebraic signature. Transitions are obtained inductively from the transition rules of the TSS. For a signature Σ and an infinite set of variables *Var*, $\mathbb{T}(\Sigma, Var)$ denotes the set of open Σ-terms over variables *Var*, and $T(\Sigma)$ the set of closed Σ-terms. Substitutions $\sigma : Var \to \mathbb{T}(\Sigma, Var)$ are extended to open Σ-terms as usual. Let $var(t)$ denote the set of variables in Σ-term t. Following [1], we develop separately the concepts of literals, rules and proofs, to emphasize the required probabilistic extensions to generate well-formed PLTSs. Labels are either pairs of an action and a probability denoting that the action can be executed with the given probability, or sets of actions denoting that all actions in the set can (or cannot) be executed with an unquantified probability.

Definition 4. *Let* $t, t' \in \mathbb{T}(\Sigma, Var)$. *A probabilistic* Σ*-literal is an expression* $t \xrightarrow{a,\pi}_{\iota} t'$ *(positive probabilistic* Σ*-literal),* $t \xrightarrow{B}$ *(positive unquantified* Σ*-literal) or* $t \stackrel{C}{\not\to}$ *(negative unquantified* Σ*-literal), with* $a \in Act$ *and* $B, C \subseteq Act$. *In an open positive probabilistic* Σ*-literal, not only* t *and* t' *are open terms, but also* π *is a linear function on variables ranging over* $(0, 1]$, *and* ι *is a variable ranging over* $\mathcal{I}$. *A* Σ*-literal is closed if* $t, t' \in T(\Sigma)$, $\pi \in (0, 1]$ *and* $\iota \in \mathcal{I}$.

A positive Σ-literal is either a positive probabilistic Σ-literal or a positive unquantified Σ-literal. An unquantified Σ-literal is either a positive or negative unquantified Σ-literal. Subscript ι allows to distinguish different occurrences of the same probabilistic transition [15]. Subscripts are omitted if they are clear from the context. We say literal for Σ-literal if Σ is clear from the context.

Definition 5. *A probabilistic transition rule is of the form* $r = \dfrac{H}{t \xrightarrow{a,\pi}_{\iota} t'}$ *with* H *a set of open* Σ*-literals, called premises, and* $t \xrightarrow{a,\pi}_{\iota} t'$ *an open positive probabilistic* Σ*-literal, called the conclusion. We call* t *the source and* t' *the target, and write* $premises(r) = H$, $conc(r) = t \xrightarrow{a,\pi}_{\iota} t'$, $action(r) = a$, $index(r) = \iota$, $source(r) = t$ *and* $target(r) = t'$.

Open positive probabilistic and negative unquantified Σ-literals are called active resp. negative premises in [20]; open positive unquantified Σ-literals are called unquantified premises in [20] and move premises in [28].

A probabilistic TSS (PTSS) consists of a signature Σ, set of actions *Act*, and set of probabilistic transition rules *R*.

Definition 6. *[20] A reactive probabilistic transition rule r, for $f \in \Sigma$ and $a \in Act$, is of the form*

$$\frac{\{x_k \xrightarrow{a_k,\pi_k}_{\iota_k} y_k \mid k \in K\} \quad \{x_l \xrightarrow{B_l} \mid l \in L\} \quad \{x_m \not\xrightarrow{C_m} \mid m \in M\}}{f(x_1,\ldots,x_n) \xrightarrow{a,\pi}_{\iota} t}$$

with $t \in \mathbb{T}(\Sigma, \{x_1,\ldots,x_n\} \cup \{y_k \mid k \in K\})$, $K, L, M \subseteq \{1,\ldots,ar(f)\}$, for all $k \in K, l \in L, m \in M$, $a_k \in Act$, $B_l, C_m \subseteq Act$, π_k are variables ranging over $(0,1]$, ι_k are variables ranging over $\mathcal{I}$, $w_r \in (0,1]$, $\pi = w_r * \prod_{k\in K} \pi_k$ and $\iota = (r, [\iota_k]_{k\in K})$. We denote $weight(r) = w_r$, $pppremises(r) = \{x_k \xrightarrow{a_k,\pi_k}_{\iota_k} y_k \mid k \in K\}$, $pupremises(r) = \{x_l \xrightarrow{B_l} \mid l \in L\}$, $nupremises(r) = \{x_m \not\xrightarrow{C_m} \mid m \in M\}$, $var(r) = \{x_1,\ldots,x_n\} \cup \{y_k \mid k \in K\} \cup var(t)$.

We assume that the set of indices $\mathcal{I}$ is totally ordered and closed under building pairs of a rule name and a list of indices, i.e. for every rule r with positive probabilistic literals $\{x_k \xrightarrow{a_k,\pi_k}_{\iota_k} y_k \mid k \in K\}$ with $\iota_k \in \mathcal{I}$, we have $(r, [\iota_k]_{k\in K}) \in \mathcal{I}$. The weight of a rule defines the conditional probability of the conclusion, assuming that all premises hold. We define the operator $unquant(t \xrightarrow{a,\pi} t') = t \xrightarrow{\{a\}}$ that eliminates the quantification and the target term from a positive probabilistic literal and is identity for unquantified literals. It lifts in a natural way to sets of literals. Furthermore, for a set of literals H, the normalized set of literals is defined by merging actions of unquantified literals with equal source, i.e. $norm(H) = \{t \xrightarrow{a,\pi} t' \mid t \xrightarrow{a,\pi} t' \in H\} \cup \{t \xrightarrow{\hat{B}} \mid t \in \mathbb{T}(\Sigma, Var), \hat{B} = \cup_{t \xrightarrow{B} \in H} B, \hat{B} \neq \emptyset\} \cup \{t \not\xrightarrow{\hat{C}} \mid t \in \mathbb{T}(\Sigma, Var), \hat{C} = \cup_{t \not\xrightarrow{C} \in H} C, \hat{C} \neq \emptyset\}$.

A PTSS guarantees congruence of probabilistic bisimilarity [20]. A PTSS is well-formed if its induced PLTS satisfies the semi-stochasticity property. The following specification format ensures well-formedness. It is defined using rule partitions that describe sets of rules for which a given process either allows that from each rule a transition can be derived (premises of all rules are satisfied) or no transition can be derived (none of the premises is satisfied) and the rule weights sum up to a total probability mass of 1. The format is a mild relaxation of [20, Def. 7.2] by not enforcing equality of positive unquantified premises of rules in a partition, but only equality of positive premises irrespective of its quantification. This allows for more compact rules, without semantically redundant positive unquantified premises just to enforce the partitioning.

Definition 7. *[20] In a PTSS (Σ, Act, R), the set $R^{f,a}$ of reactive probabilistic transition rules for $f \in \Sigma$ and $a \in Act$, is partitioned into sets $R_1^{f,a},\ldots,R_n^{f,a}$ such that the following conditions hold:*

1. *For each set $R_u^{f,a}$:*
   (a) *For each pair $r_1, r_2 \in R_u^{f,a}$ we have $norm(unquant(pppremises(r_1)) \cup pupremises(r_1)) = norm(unquant(pppremises(r_2)) \cup pupremises(r_2))$.*
   (b) *For each pair $r_1, r_2 \in R_u^{f,a}$ we have $nupremises(r_1) = nupremises(r_2)$.*
   (c) *The sum of weights of rules in $R_u^{f,a}$ is 1.*

2. *Given two sets $R_u^{f,a} \neq R_v^{f,a}$. For any rules $r_u \in R_u^{f,a}$ and $r_v \in R_v^{f,a}$ there is an index $1 \leq i \leq ar(f)$ such that r_u has a positive premise $x_i \xrightarrow{a_i,\pi_i}_{\iota_i} y_i$ or $x_i \xrightarrow{B_i}$ and r_v has a negative premise $x_i \stackrel{C_i}{\not\longrightarrow}$ with $a_i \in C_i$ or $C_i \cap B_i \neq \emptyset$, respectively, or vica versa.*

1(a) and 1(b) ensure that either none or all rules of a partition can be applied, and 2 that only rules from one single partition can be applied. By 1(c), induced PLTSs satisfy the semi-stochasticity property [20, Thm. 7.8].

Example 1. If t_1 can perform an a-transition to t_1' with probability p_1 and t_2 to t_2' with probability p_2, their probabilistic alternative composition $t_1 +^p t_2$ can perform an a-transitions to t_1' with probability $p_1 * p$ and to t_2' with probability $p_2 * (1-p)$. If only one of the processes can perform an a-transition and this transition goes to t' with probability p', then $t_1 +^p t_2$ can perform an a-transition to t' with probability p'.

$$(r_a^{+1})\ \frac{x_1 \xrightarrow{a,\pi_1}_{\iota} y_1 \quad x_2 \xrightarrow{\{a\}}}{x_1 +^p x_2 \xrightarrow{a,\pi_1 * p}_{(r_a^{+1},\iota)} y_1} \qquad \frac{x_2 \xrightarrow{a,\pi_2}_{\iota} y_2 \quad x_1 \xrightarrow{\{a\}}}{x_1 +^p x_2 \xrightarrow{a,\pi_2 * (1-p)}_{(r_a^{+2},\iota)} y_2}\ (r_a^{+2})$$

$$(r_a^{+3})\ \frac{x_1 \xrightarrow{a,\pi_1}_{\iota} y_1 \quad x_2 \stackrel{\{a\}}{\not\longrightarrow}}{x_1 +^p x_2 \xrightarrow{a,\pi_1}_{(r_a^{+3},\iota)} y_1} \qquad \frac{x_2 \xrightarrow{a,\pi_2}_{\iota} y_2 \quad x_1 \stackrel{\{a\}}{\not\longrightarrow}}{x_1 +^p x_2 \xrightarrow{a,\pi_2}_{(r_a^{+4},\iota)} y_2}\ (r_a^{+4})$$

Rules r_a^{+1} to r_a^{+4} for operator $+$ and action a specify a PTSS with partitions $R_1^{+,a} = \{r_a^{+1}, r_a^{+2}\}$, $R_2^{+,a} = \{r_a^{+3}\}$ and $R_3^{+,a} = \{r_a^{+4}\}$. We note that the original rule format of [20, Def. 7.2] would require additionally the premises $x_1 \xrightarrow{\{a\}}$ in r_a^{+1} and $x_2 \xrightarrow{\{a\}}$ in r_a^{+2}. ■

Derivations are defined as inductive applications of closed transition rules. Negative literals are proved using the negation as failure principle [9] and the supported proof notion [13, Def. 8].

Definition 8. *[20] Let $P = (\Sigma, Act, R)$ be a PTSS and $t, s \in T(\Sigma)$. A closed Σ-literal $t \xrightarrow{a,p}_i s$ is derivable, denoted by $P \vdash t \xrightarrow{a,p}_i s$, if there is a closed substitution instance*

$$\frac{\{t_k \xrightarrow{a_k,p_k}_{i_k} s_k \mid k \in K\} \quad \{t_l \xrightarrow{B_l} \mid l \in L\} \quad \{t_m \stackrel{C_m}{\not\longrightarrow} \mid m \in M\}}{t \xrightarrow{a,p}_i s}$$

of a rule $r \in R$, $p = w_r * \prod_{k \in K} p_k$ and $i = (r, [i_k]_{k \in K})$ such that

- *for all $k \in K$, $P \vdash t_k \xrightarrow{a_k,p_k}_{i_k} s_k$*
- *for all $l \in L$ and for all $b_l \in B_l$, $P \vdash t_l \xrightarrow{b_l,p_l}_{i_l} u_l$ for some p_l, i_l, u_l*

– *for all* $m \in M$ *and for all* $c_m \in C_m$*,* $P \nvdash t_m \xrightarrow{c_m, p_m}_{i_m} u_m$ *for all* p_m, i_m, u_m*.*

$P \nvdash t \xrightarrow{a,p}_i u$ *denotes there is no derivation of this transition.*

$P \vdash t \stackrel{a}{\nrightarrow}$ denotes there are no p, i, s such that $P \vdash t \xrightarrow{a,p}_i s$. By $P \vdash t \xrightarrow{B}$ we denote that for all $b \in B$ there are some p, s such that $P \vdash t \xrightarrow{b,p} s$. By $P \vdash t \stackrel{C}{\nrightarrow}$ we denote that $P \vdash t \stackrel{c}{\nrightarrow}$ for all $c \in C$. We write $P \vdash t \xrightarrow{a,p} s$ if there is a rule r and a list of indices $[i_k]_{k \in K}$ such that $P \vdash t \xrightarrow{a,p}_{(r,[i_k]_{k \in K})} s$.

We say that literals $t \xrightarrow{a,p} s$ and $t \stackrel{a}{\nrightarrow}$ deny each other. A proof system is consistent if it does not admit proofs of literals denying each other. Consistency of Def. 8 can be shown similar to consistency of the well-supported proof notion for nondeterministic TSSs [13]. A TSS is complete if for any $t \in T(\Sigma)$ either $P \vdash t \xrightarrow{a,p} s$ for some $s \in T(\Sigma)$ and $p \in (0, 1]$ or $P \vdash t \stackrel{a}{\nrightarrow}$. PTSSs are GSOS-type TSSs [7], which guarantees the existence of a strict finite stratification [13]. Stratifiability of a PTSS is a sufficient condition for completeness.

3 Decomposition of Modal Formulae

This section shows how to decompose probabilistic HML formulae wrt. distributions over process terms. Section 3.1 constructs ruloids that are derived rules describing completely the set of provable literals of a PTSS. Furthermore, the partitioning of rules to ensure the semi-stochasticity property is lifted to ruloids. Section 3.2 provides the decomposition method for probabilistic HML formulae.

3.1 Ruloids and Ruloid Partitioning

Ruloids are derived transition rules describing completely the behavior of open terms [7]. Intuitively, they are compact proofs where intermediate proof steps are removed. While the source can be any term, the premises are simple and consist of only variables. Their proof-theoretical closure property (Thm. 1) gives them a prominent role in decomposing modalities.

The construction of ruloids is motivated by [7, Def. 7.4.2 and Thm. 7.4.3] and its reformulation in [14, Def. 14]. We prefer the constructive approach of the latter reference, which separates the definition of ruloids from the proof of their properties. Ruloids are constructed inductively by composing rules. The base case is defined by rules being ruloids. A ruloid ρ is constructed by taking an instance of a rule r and acting for each premise α as follows: If α is a positive literal, then a ruloid ρ_α with conclusion α is selected, and all premises of ρ_α are included in the premise of ρ. If α is a negative literal, then for every ruloid with conclusion being negated α, one of its premises is negated and included in the premises of ρ.

Literals(P) denotes the set of literals of PTSS P, and $RHS(r)$ the set of right-hand side variables of positive probabilistic premises of ruloid ρ. Just like rules the conclusion of a ruloid is indexed by a pair consisting of the ruloid name and a list of indices of the positive probabilistic premises. The ruloid name is the concatenation of the rule name and the ruloid names applied to its positive premises.

Definition 9. *Let $P = (\Sigma, Act, R)$ be a PTSS. The set of P-ruloids $\mathcal{R}$ is the smallest set such that:*

– $\dfrac{x \xrightarrow{a,\pi}_\iota y}{x \xrightarrow{a,\pi}_\iota y}$ *is a P-ruloid with weight 1 for $x, y \in Var$, $a \in Act$, π a variable ranging over $(0,1]$ and ι a variable ranging over $\mathcal{I}$.*

–
$$\frac{norm(\bigcup_{k\in K} H_k \ \cup\ \bigcup_{l\in L} H_l \ \cup\ \bigcup_{m\in M} H_m)}{\sigma(f(x_1,\dots,x_n)) \xrightarrow{a,\pi}_\iota \sigma(t)}$$

is a P-ruloid with weight $w = w_r * \prod_{k\in K} w_k$, transition probability $\pi = w * \prod_{k\in K}\prod_{k'\in K_k} \pi_{k,k'}$, rules $rs = r \cdot [\rho_k]_{k\in K} \cdot [\rho_l]_{l\in L}$ and index $\iota = (rs, [\iota_{k,k'}]_{k\in K, k'\in K_k})$ if there is a rule r

$$\frac{\{x_k \xrightarrow{a_k,\pi_k}_{\iota_k} y_k \mid k \in K\} \quad \{x_l \xrightarrow{B_l} \mid l \in L\} \quad \{x_m \not\xrightarrow{\mathcal{C}_m} \mid m \in M\}}{f(x_1,\dots,x_n) \xrightarrow{a, w_r * \prod_{k\in K}\pi_k}_{(r,[\iota_k]_{k\in K})} t}$$

in R, and a substitution σ, such that the following properties hold:

- *For every positive probabilistic literal $x_k \xrightarrow{a_k,\pi_k}_{\iota_k} y_k$, either*
  - $*$ *$\sigma(x_k)$ and $\sigma(y_k)$ are variables and $H_k = \{\sigma(x_k) \xrightarrow{a_k,\pi_k}_{\iota_k} \sigma(y_k)\}$, or*
  - $*$ *there is a P-ruloid $\rho_k = \dfrac{H_k}{\sigma(x_k) \xrightarrow{a_k,\pi_k}_{\iota_k} \sigma(y_k)}$ with weight w_k, the positive probabilistic premises in H_k are indexed by K_k and have probabilistic variables $\pi_{k,k'}$ and index variables $\iota_{k,k'}$ with $k' \in K_k$.*
- *For every positive unquantified literal $x_l \xrightarrow{B_l}$, either*
  - $*$ *$\sigma(x_l)$ is a variable and $H_l = \{\sigma(x_l) \xrightarrow{B_l}\}$, or*
  - $*$ *for all $b \in B_l$ there is a P-ruloid $\rho_b = \dfrac{H_b}{\sigma(x_l) \xrightarrow{b,\pi_b} s}$ for some π_b, s and $H_l = \cup_{b\in B_l} unquant(H_b)$, $\rho_l = [\rho_b]_{b\in B_l}$.*
- *For every negative unquantified literal $x_m \not\xrightarrow{\mathcal{C}_m}$, either*
  - $*$ *$\sigma(x_m)$ is a variable and $H_m = \{\sigma(x_m) \not\xrightarrow{\mathcal{C}_m}\}$, or*
  - $*$ *$H_m = neg_{\mathcal{C}_m}(h_{\mathcal{C}_m}(\mathcal{R}_{\mathcal{C}_m}))$ with*
    - · *Define $\mathcal{R}_{\mathcal{C}_m} = \{premises(\rho) \mid \rho \in \mathcal{R}, conc(\rho) = \sigma(x_m) \xrightarrow{c,\pi_c} s, c \in \mathcal{C}_m\}$ the set of premises of all P-ruloids with conclusion $\sigma(x_m) \xrightarrow{c,\pi_c} s$ for some $c \in \mathcal{C}_m$, π_c, s.*
    - · *Define any mapping $h_{\mathcal{C}_m} : \mathcal{R}_{\mathcal{C}_m} \to Literals(P)$ by $h_{\mathcal{C}_m}(L) = l$ with $l \in L$ for $L \in \mathcal{R}_{\mathcal{C}_m}$.*
    - · *Define any mapping $neg_{\mathcal{C}_m} : Literals(P) \to Literals(P)$ that satisfies $neg_{\mathcal{C}_m}(x \xrightarrow{a,\pi} y) = x \not\xrightarrow{\{a\}}$, $neg_{\mathcal{C}_m}(x \xrightarrow{A}) = x \not\xrightarrow{\{a\}}$ for some $a \in A$ and $neg_{\mathcal{C}_m}(x \not\xrightarrow{A}) = x \xrightarrow{\{a\}}$ for some $a \in A$.*
- *Right-hand side variables $RHS(\rho_k)$ are all pairwise disjoint and each $RHS(\rho_k)$ is disjoint with $\{x_1,\dots,x_n\}$. All probabilistic variables $\pi_{k,k'}$ and index variables $\iota_{k,k'}$ are distinct.*

The ruloid construction for unquantified literals, i.e. the mapping $unquant(H_b)$ for positive unquantified literals and neg_{C_m} for negative unquantified literals, prevents that new probabilistic variables are introduced that would modify the probabilistic weight of the ruloid. Operators denoting parameters of rules like *premises*, *conc*, *source* carry over to ruloids. Furthermore, the rules applied to a ruloid ρ are denoted by $rules(\rho) = r \cdot [\rho_k]_{k \in K} \cdot [\rho_l]_{l \in L}$. The set of P-ruloids for a term $t \in \mathbb{T}(\Sigma, Var)$ and action $a \in Act$ is denoted by $\mathcal{R}^{t,a} = \{\rho \mid \rho \in \mathcal{R}, source(\rho) = t, action(\rho) = a\}$.

Example 2. Let $P = (\Sigma, Act, R)$ be the PTSS from Example 1. Consider the probabilistic summation $(x_1 +^{p_{12}} x_2) +^{p_{23}} x_3$, where only x_3 is able to perform an a-transition. The construction tree of the ruloid is as follows:

$$\dfrac{\dfrac{x_1 \overset{\{a\}}{\not\longrightarrow} \quad x_2 \overset{\{a\}}{\not\longrightarrow}}{x_1 +^{p_{12}} x_2 \overset{\{a\}}{\not\longrightarrow}}\,(1) \qquad x_3 \xrightarrow{a,\pi_3}_{\iota} y_3}{(x_1 +^{p_{12}} x_2) +^{p_{23}} x_3 \xrightarrow{a,\pi_3}_{(\rho_a^{+4},\iota)} y_3}\,(2)$$

At (1) the rules ρ_a^{+1} to ρ_a^{+4} were applied to assure $x_1 +^{p_{12}} x_2 \overset{\{a\}}{\not\longrightarrow}$ by disproving $x_1 +^{p_{12}} x_2 \xrightarrow{\{a\}}$. In fact, the mapping h_{C_m} selects for each rule to disprove one literal from its premise and neg_{C_m} generates the literal which refutes it. The resulting ruloid is:

$$\frac{x_1 \overset{\{a\}}{\not\longrightarrow} \quad x_2 \overset{\{a\}}{\not\longrightarrow} \quad x_3 \xrightarrow{a,\pi_3}_{\iota} y_3}{(x_1 +^{p_{12}} x_2) +^{p_{23}} x_3 \xrightarrow{a,\pi_3}_{(\rho_a^{+4},\iota)} y_3}$$

■

The following theorem states the key property of ruloids (called soundness and specifically witnessing property in [7]). It formalizes a kind of completeness property of the form that every transition that can be proven from P has a corresponding P-ruloid where the provable transition is an instance of the conclusion of the P-ruloid. This shows that ruloids are exhaustive wrt. provable transitions. This will be used to decompose the diamond modality over an action a by providing a complete logical characterization of the preconditions and effects of the possible transitions with label a.

Theorem 1 (Ruloid theorem). *Let $P = (\Sigma, Act, R)$ be a PTSS. Then $P \vdash \sigma(t) \xrightarrow{a,p} u$ for $t \in \mathbb{T}(\Sigma, Var)$, $u \in T(\Sigma)$ and σ a closed substitution, iff there is a P-ruloid $\frac{H}{t \xrightarrow{a,p} v}$ and a closed substitution σ' with $P \vdash \sigma'(\alpha)$ for all $\alpha \in H$, $\sigma'(t) = \sigma(t)$ and $\sigma'(v) = u$.*

Next we construct the partitioning of ruloids. Intuitively, the partitioning of a set of ruloids is defined as lifting of the partitionings of the rules involved in their construction. The partitioning of ruloids with variables or terms with only one function symbol in the source handles explicitly α-equivalence. The partitioning of ruloids with source $t = f(t_1, \ldots, t_n)$ with at least one t_i being no variable handles α-equivalence indirectly by referring to the partitioning of rules involved in the construction. Like rule partitions, the ruloid partitions are well-formed under an adapted notion of derivability. This is required for the decomposition of the modalities.

Definition 10. *Let $P = (\Sigma, Act, R)$ be a PTSS, $t \in \mathbb{T}(\Sigma, Var)$ and $a \in Act$. The partitioning of ruloids $\mathcal{R}^{t,a}$ is defined by:*

- $t = x$: *There is one ruloid partition* $\left\{ \frac{x \xrightarrow{a,\pi}_{\iota} y}{x \xrightarrow{a,\pi}_{\iota} y} \mid y \in Var \right\}$.
- $t = f(x_1, \ldots, x_n)$: *For every rule partition $R^{f,a}_u$ there is a ruloid partition $\mathcal{R}^{f(x_1,\ldots,x_n),a}_u = \{\sigma(r) \mid r \in R^{f,a}_u, \sigma$ a variable subsitution, $\sigma(x_i) = x_i$ for $1 \leq i \leq n\}$.*
- $t = f(t_1, \ldots, t_n)$, *some t_i is no variable: $\rho_1, \rho_2 \in \mathcal{R}^{t,a}_u$ iff $rules(\rho^1) = r^1 \cdot [\rho^1_k]_{k \in K^1} \cdot [\rho^1_l]_{l \in L^1}$, $rules(\rho^2) = r^2 \cdot [\rho^2_k]_{k \in K^2} \cdot [\rho^2_l]_{l \in L^2}$, for some v we have $r^1, r^2 \in R^{f,a}_v$ and for each $i \in K^1 \cup L^1$ we have $\rho^1_i, \rho^2_i \in \mathcal{R}^{t_i,a_i}_{u_i}$ for some u_i.*

The ruloid partitioning of a term is fully defined by the ruloid partitionings of its subterms and the rule partitioning of its outermost function symbol. Note that for case $t = f(t_1, \ldots, t_n)$ the rule partitioning (Def. 7.1a) guarantees that $K^1 \cup L^1 = K^2 \cup L^2$. The ruloid partitions $\mathcal{R}^{f(x_1,\ldots,x_n),a}_u$ are the rule partitions $R^{f,a}_u$ including renaming of variables that are not used in the source.

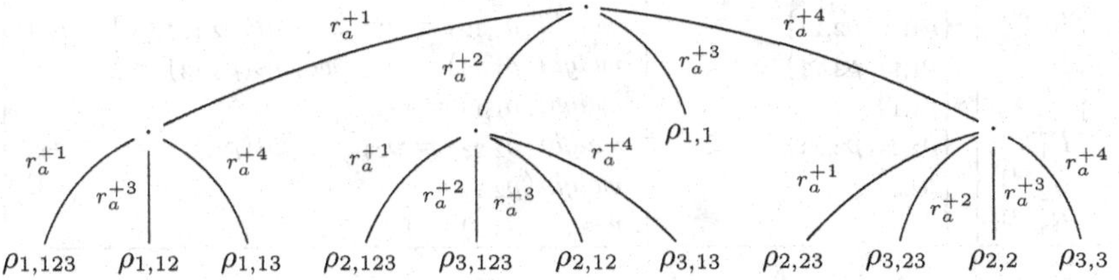

Fig. 1. Ruloid derivations for the 3-fold probabilistic sum

Example 3. $t = x_1 +^{p_{12}} (x_2 +^{p_{23}} x_3)$ generates 12 ruloids (up to α-equivalence and variants generated by negative unquantified premises). The derivation tree in Fig. 1 shows the deduction of ruloids by rule concatenation. Ruloid names denote in the first parameter the target variable and in the second parameter which variables can perform an a-move. E.g., ruloid $\rho_{1,12}$ denotes that the target is y_1 and that x_1, x_2 can move but not x_3. The 4 ruloids with target y_3 are:

$$\frac{x_1 \xrightarrow{\{a\}} \qquad x_2 \xrightarrow{\{a\}} \qquad x_3 \xrightarrow{a,\pi_3}_{\iota} y_3}{x_1 +^{p_{12}} (x_2 +^{p_{23}} x_3) \xrightarrow{a,\pi_3 * (1-p_{12})(1-p_{23})}_{(r_a^{+2} r_a^{+3}, \iota)} y_3} \; (\rho_{3,123})$$

$$\frac{x_1 \not\xrightarrow{\{a\}} \quad x_2 \xrightarrow{\{a\}} \quad x_3 \xrightarrow{a,\pi_3}_{\iota} y_3}{x_1 +^{p_{12}} (x_2 +^{p_{23}} x_3) \xrightarrow{a,\pi_3 * (1-p_{23})}_{(r_a^{+4} r_a^{+2}, \iota)} y_3} \; (\rho_{3,23})$$

$$\frac{x_1 \xrightarrow{\{a\}} \quad x_2 \not\xrightarrow{\{a\}} \quad x_3 \xrightarrow{a,\pi_3}_{\iota} y_3}{x_1 +^{p_{12}} (x_2 +^{p_{23}} x_3) \xrightarrow{a,\pi_3 * (1-p_{12})}_{(r_a^{+2} r_a^{+4}, \iota)} y_3} \; (\rho_{3,13})$$

$$\frac{x_1 \not\xrightarrow{\{a\}} \quad x_2 \not\xrightarrow{\{a\}} \quad x_3 \xrightarrow{a,\pi_3}_{\iota} y_3}{x_1 +^{p_{12}} (x_2 +^{p_{23}} x_3) \xrightarrow{a,\pi_3}_{(r_a^{+4} r_a^{+4}, \iota)} y_3} \; (\rho_{3,3})$$

Ruloids with target y_1 or y_2 are constructed similarly. Table 1 shows all ruloid partitions of the 3-fold probabilistic sum. The weights of every ruloid partition sum up to 1. E.g., ruloid partition $[R_1^{+,a}, R_1^{+,a}]$ with ruloids $\{\rho_{1,123}, \rho_{2,123}, \rho_{3,123}\}$ has weight $p_{12} + (1 - p_{12})p_{23} + (1 - p_{12})(1 - p_{23}) = 1$. There are 12 ruloids for $x_1 +^{p_{12}} (x_2 +^{p_{23}} x_3)$, because 3 of the 4 rules of P have a positive literal on x_2 which can be instantiated by the 4 rules specifying the probabilistic sum. ■

Table 1. Ruloid partitions for the 3-fold probabilistic sum

Partition	Ruloids	Ruloid weights
$[R_1^{+,a}, R_1^{+,a}]$	$\{\rho_{1,123}, \rho_{2,123}, \rho_{3,123}\}$	$weight(\rho_{1,123}) = p_{12}$ $weight(\rho_{2,123}) = (1 - p_{12})p_{23}$ $weight(\rho_{3,123}) = (1 - p_{12})(1 - p_{23})$
$[R_1^{+,a}, R_2^{+,a}]$	$\{\rho_{1,12}, \rho_{2,12}\}$	$weight(\rho_{1,12}) = p_{12}$, $weight(\rho_{2,12}) = 1 - p_{12}$
$[R_1^{+,a}, R_3^{+,a}]$	$\{\rho_{1,13}, \rho_{3,13}\}$	$weight(\rho_{1,13}) = p_{12}$, $weight(\rho_{3,13}) = 1 - p_{12}$
$[R_2^{+,a}]$	$\{\rho_{1,1}\}$	$weight(\rho_{1,1}) = 1$
$[R_3^{+,a}, R_1^{+,a}]$	$\{\rho_{2,23}, \rho_{3,23}\}$	$weight(\rho_{2,23}) = p_{23}$, $weight(\rho_{3,23}) = 1 - p_{23}$
$[R_3^{+,a}, R_2^{+,a}]$	$\{\rho_{2,2}\}$	$weight(\rho_{2,2}) = 1$
$[R_3^{+,a}, R_3^{+,a}]$	$\{\rho_{3,3}\}$	$weight(\rho_{3,3}) = 1$

We define $[\rho]_\alpha = \{\rho' \mid rules(\rho) = rules(\rho')\}$, the ruloid equivalence class containing all ruloids that were constructed by the same rules applied in the same order as ρ. This set contains beside ρ all those ruloids which differ from ρ only by α-equivalence (renaming) or by the selection of premises of rules to refute in the construction of negative unquantified literals. All ruloids in $[\rho]_\alpha$ have equal weight. The weight of $[\rho]_\alpha$ is defined to be $weight(\rho')$ for any $\rho' \in [\rho]_\alpha$. The weight of a set of ruloids R is defined as $\sum_{\varrho \in [R]_\alpha} weight(\varrho)$.

Well-formedness of rule partitions was proved in [20]. The following theorem shows well-formedness of ruloid partitions. A set of transitions is derivable from a ruloid partition $\mathcal{R}_u^{t,a}$ if each transition is derivable from a ruloid $\rho \in \mathcal{R}_u^{t,a}$ and different transitions $t \xrightarrow{a,p_1} t_1$ derived from ρ_1 and $t \xrightarrow{a,p_2} t_2$ derived from ρ_2 are derived from ruloids of different equivalence classes $[\rho_1]_\alpha \neq [\rho_2]_\alpha$.

Theorem 2 (Well-formedness of ruloid partitions). *Let $P = (\Sigma, Act, R)$ be a PTSS, $t \in \mathbb{T}(\Sigma, Var)$ a term and $\sigma : var(t) \to T(\Sigma)$ a closed substitution. If for each $x_i \in var(t)$ and $a_i \in Act$ the probability of transitions of $\sigma(x_i)$ with label a_i, if there are any, sum up to 1, then for each $a \in Act$ the probability of transitions of $\sigma(t)$ derivable from any ruloid partition $\mathcal{R}_u^{t,a}$, if there are any, sum up to 1.*

3.2 Decomposition of HML Formulae

We present a method to reduce the question whether a probability distribution over process terms satisfies a formula φ to the question whether its subterms satisfy one of those formulae obtained by decomposing the formula φ using the SOS rules of the process algebra. A formula φ is decomposed wrt. a distribution μ in multiple mappings $\psi : Var \to \mathbb{O}$ (Def. 11) such that for each closed substitution $\sigma : Var \to T(\Sigma)$ there is one mapping ψ such that for each variable x of a term in the support of μ its instance $\sigma(x)$ satisfies the decomposed formula $\psi(x)$ (Thm. 3).

The decomposition of propositional connectives is from [6,11]. The decomposition of $\neg\varphi$ expresses that none of the decompositions of φ hold. The decomposition of $\langle a\rangle\varphi$ wrt. distribution μ states that for each term t in the support of μ the decomposition of φ wrt. the distribution induced by some ruloid partition $\mathcal{R}_u^{t,a}$ holds. The decomposition of $[\varphi]_p$ characterizes that the decomposition of φ holds for some set of terms with probability mass at least p. Different variants to refute a ruloid (decomposition of negation), different ruloid partitions $\mathcal{R}_u^{t,a}, \mathcal{R}_v^{t,a}$ of a process term t and action a (decomposition of diamond modality) and probabilistic branching (decomposition of probability measure modality) lead to multiple decompositions $\psi \in \mathcal{P}(Var \to \mathbb{O})$.

For $\mu \in Dist(\mathbb{T}(\Sigma, Var))$ we define $var(\mu) = \bigcup_{t\in Supp} var(t)$. A set of ruloids R is target variable disjoint if for $\rho, \rho' \in R$ with $\rho \neq \rho'$ we have $(var(\rho) - var(source(\rho))) \cap (var(\rho') - var(source(\rho'))) = \emptyset$. Variable disjointness of sets of ruloids prevents unintended variable binding in decompositions where multiple ruloids are applied. For R a set of ruloids we call $R' \subseteq R$ minimal representative if $weight(R') = weight(R)$ and for each $\rho, \rho' \in R'$ with $\rho \neq \rho'$ we have $[\rho]_\alpha \neq [\rho']_\alpha$. Minimal representative subsets of a ruloid partition have only one representative for each equivalence class while still preserving the total probability mass of 1. A substitution $\sigma : Var \to \mathbb{T}(\Sigma, Var)$ is lifted to $\mu \in Dist(\mathbb{T}(\Sigma, Var))$ by $\sigma(\mu)(t) = \mu(\sigma^{-1}(t))$. A substitution σ is called μ-well-formed if for $t, t' \in Supp(\mu)$ with $t \neq t'$ we have $\sigma(t) \neq \sigma(t')$. A distribution $\mu \in Dist(\mathbb{T}(\Sigma, Var))$ is called well-formed if there is some μ-well-formed substitution. $\mathbb{DT}(\Sigma, Var) \subseteq Dist(\mathbb{T}(\Sigma, Var))$ denotes all well-formed distributions.

Definition 11. *Let $P = (\Sigma, Act, R)$ be a PTSS. We define $\cdot^{-1} : \mathbb{DT}(\Sigma, Var) \to (\mathbb{O} \to \mathcal{P}(Var \to \mathbb{O}))$ as the smallest function satisfying the following conditions:*

1. $\mu^{-1}(\top) = \{\psi\}$ *with* $\psi(x) = \top$ *for all* $x \in Var$
2. $\psi \in \mu^{-1}(\neg\varphi)$ *iff there is a function* $h : \mu^{-1}(\varphi) \to var(\mu)$ *such that*

$$\psi(x) = \begin{cases} \bigwedge_{\chi \in h^{-1}(x)} \neg\chi(x) & \text{if } x \in var(\mu) \\ \top & \text{if } x \notin var(\mu) \end{cases}$$

3. $\psi \in \mu^{-1}(\bigwedge_{i\in I} \varphi_i)$ *iff there are* $\psi_i \in \mu^{-1}(\varphi_i)$ *for each* $i \in I$ *such that*

$$\psi(x) = \bigwedge_{i \in I} \psi_i(x) \quad \text{for all } x \in Var$$

4. $\psi \in \mu^{-1}(\langle a\rangle\varphi)$ *iff for each* $t \in Supp(\mu)$ *there is some minimal representative and target variable disjoint* $R^t \subseteq \mathcal{R}_u^{t,a}$, *a distribution* $\nu^t \in Dist(\mathbb{T}(\Sigma, Var))$ *defined by* $\nu^t(target(\rho)) = weight(\rho)$ *for* $\rho \in R^t$, *some* $\chi^t \in (\nu^t)^{-1}(\varphi)$ *s.t.*

$$\psi^t(x) = \begin{cases} \bigwedge_{\substack{\rho \in R^t \\ H = premises(\rho)}} \Bigg[\chi^t(x) \wedge \Big(\bigwedge_{(x \xrightarrow{a_k,\pi_k} y) \in H} \langle a_k\rangle \chi^t(y) \Big) \wedge \\ \quad \Big(\bigwedge_{(x \xrightarrow{B_l}) \in H} \bigwedge_{b \in B_l} \langle b\rangle \top \Big) \wedge \Big(\bigwedge_{(x \not\xrightarrow{C_m}) \in H} \bigwedge_{c \in C} \neg\langle c\rangle \top \Big) \Bigg] & \text{if } x \in var(\mu) \\ \top & \text{if } x \notin var(\mu) \end{cases}$$

and $\psi(x) = \bigwedge_{t \in Supp(\mu)} \psi^t(x)$

5. $\psi \in \mu^{-1}([\varphi]_p)$ *iff there is some* $T \subseteq Supp(\mu)$ *with* $\mu(T) \geq p$ *and for each* $t \in T$ *there is a* $\psi^t \in \delta_t^{-1}(\varphi)$ *such that*

$$\psi(x) = \bigwedge_{t \in T} \psi^t(x) \quad \text{for all } x \in Var$$

The decomposition of φ wrt. a term t is defined by $t^{-1}(\varphi) = \delta_t^{-1}(\varphi)$. The decomposition of $\langle a\rangle\varphi$ wrt. a distribution reflects the universal nature of the diamond modality that every term in the support of the distribution has to satisfy $\langle a\rangle\varphi$. The decomposition of $\langle a\rangle\varphi$ wrt. a term t, denoted $\psi^t \in t^{-1}(\langle a\rangle\varphi)$, uses a set of ruloids with total weight 1, i.e. the diamond modality reasons over all probabilistic moves (internal nondeterminism), but employs a minimal set of ruloids (only one single representative per ruloid equivalence class) to prevent double counting of probabilities.

The main theorem shows that using modal decomposition, the satisfaction problem of a probabilistic HML formula for a distribution over process terms can be reduced to the question whether its subterms satisfy the decomposed formulae.

Theorem 3 (Decomposition theorem). *Let* $P = (\Sigma, Act, R)$ *be a PTSS. For any well-formed distribution* $\mu \in \mathbb{DT}(\Sigma, Var)$, *closed* μ*-well-formed substitution* $\sigma : Var \to T(\Sigma)$ *and modal assertion* $\varphi \in \mathbb{O}$:

$$\sigma(\mu) \models \varphi \quad \Leftrightarrow \quad \exists \psi \in \mu^{-1}(\varphi). \forall t \in Supp(\mu). \forall x \in var(t) : \sigma(x) \models \psi(x)$$

4 Example: Decomposition of the Probabilistic Sum

Example 4. Consider the probabilistic sum of Example 1. The decomposition of $(x_1 +^p x_2)^{-1}(\langle a\rangle[\varphi]_q)$ leads for the partitions $R_1^{+,a}$ to $R_3^{+,a}$ to the calculation of $\mu_i^{-1}([\varphi]_q)$ with $\mu_1 = \{y_1 \mapsto p, y_2 \mapsto 1-p\}$ (partition $R_1^{+,a}$), $\mu_2 = \delta_{y_1}$ (partition $R_2^{+,a}$) and $\mu_3 = \delta_{y_2}$ (partition $R_3^{+,a}$). The calculation of $\mu_2^{-1}([\varphi]_q) = \{\psi_2\}$ with $\psi_2(y_1) = \varphi$ and $\psi_2(z) = \top$ for $z \neq y_1$, and $\mu_3^{-1}([\varphi]_q) = \{\psi_3\}$ with $\psi_3(y_2) = \varphi$ and $\psi_3(z) = \top$ for $z \neq y_2$ is trivial. For partition $R_2^{+,a}$ this gives $\psi_2(x_1) = \langle a\rangle\varphi$, $\psi_2(x_2) = \neg\langle a\rangle\top$ and for $R_3^{+,a}$ this gives $\psi_3(x_1) = \neg\langle a\rangle\top$, $\psi_3(x_2) = \langle a\rangle\varphi$. For $\mu_1^{-1}([\varphi]_q)$ there are four cases to distinguish, depending on the arithmetic relation between q, p and $1-p$ (Def. 11.5):

Case	Condition	$T \subseteq Supp(\mu_1)$
1	$q > p,\ q > 1-p$	$\{y_1, y_2\}$
2	$q < p,\ q > 1-p$	$\{y_1\}$
3	$q > p,\ q < 1-p$	$\{y_2\}$
4	$q < p,\ q < 1-p$	$\{y_1\}, \{y_2\}$

We omitted the cases where T contains more terms than necessary to satisfy the required probability mass q. We exemplify the decomposition by instantiating p and q. The decomposition of case 1 (say for $p = 0.3, q = 0.8$) gives $(x_1 +^{0.3} x_2)^{-1}(\langle a\rangle[\varphi]_{0.8}) = \{\psi_1^1\}$ with $\psi_1^1(x_1) = \psi_1^1(x_2) = \langle a\rangle\varphi$. The conditions $q > p$ and $q > 1-p$ assert that if both processes x_1,x_2 can move, none of both alone has enough probability mass to satisfy the probability measure modality. The decomposition reflects the intuition that if both processes x_1,x_2 can perform an a transition then φ has to hold after both transitions. Case 2 (say for $p = 0.8, q = 0.3$) gives $(x_1 +^{0.8} x_2)^{-1}(\langle a\rangle[\varphi]_{0.3}) = \{\psi_1^2\}$ with $\psi_1^2(x_1) = \langle a\rangle\varphi$, $\psi_1^2(x_2) = \langle a\rangle\top$. Case 3 (say for $p = 0.2, q = 0.7$) leads to $(x_1 +^{0.2} x_2)^{-1}(\langle a\rangle[\varphi]_{0.7}) = \{\psi_1^3\}$ with $\psi_1^3(x_1) = \langle a\rangle\top, \psi_1^3(x_2) = \langle a\rangle\varphi$. Cases 2 and 3 express that if one of the processes can perform a transition with enough probability mass to satisfy the probability measure modality then the target of this transition has to satisfy φ, i.e. y_1 satisfies φ if $p > q$ or y_2 satisfies φ if $1-p > q$. Case 4 (say for $p = 0.7, q = 0.2$) results in $(x_1 +^{0.7} x_2)^{-1}(\langle a\rangle[\varphi]_{0.2}) = \{\psi_1^4, \psi_2^4\}$ with $\psi_1^4(x_1) = \langle a\rangle\varphi$, $\psi_1^4(x_2) = \langle a\rangle\top$, $\psi_2^4(x_1) = \langle a\rangle\top, \psi_2^4(x_2) = \langle a\rangle\varphi$. In this case both probabilistic transitions have enough probability mass to satisfy the probability measure modality. Thus, the probabilistic branching lead to two different decompositions ψ_1^4 and ψ_2^4. ■

5 Future Work

The decomposition method presented in this paper can be extended in the following directions. The modal logic employed is L^N [24], which takes into account probabilistic branching. Segala and Lynch provided a variant of probabilistic simulation where state transitions need to be matched only by convex combinations of distributions (combined transition) [26]. The decomposition method could be extended to the corresponding logic L_p^N that provides a modified diamond operator which uses combined transitions instead of state transitions.

Furthermore, the decomposition method could be adapted to generative PLTSs, to probabilistic automata [25] which combine nondeterministic and probabilistic choice using the recently introduced rule format by [10], and to continuous-space Markov processes using Modular Markovian Logic [8].

Following the approach of [6], the decomposition method can be applied to systematically develop congruence formats for different behavioral semantics of probabilistic systems, such as strong and weak variants of bisimulation, simulation, and testing semantics. Behavioral equivalences for stochastic systems are e.g. Markovian bisimulation, Markovian testing, and probabilistic and Markovian trace semantics. Congruence formats have so far only been developed for probabilistic bisimulation for reactive probabilistic systems [4,20], generative probabilistic systems [20] and bisimulation for stochastic systems [18].

Bialgebraic semantics abstracts away from concrete notions of syntax and system behavior [29]. Klin combines bialgebraic semantics with a coalgebraic approach to modal logic to prove compositionality of process equivalences for languages defined by SOS [19]. He developed the SGSOS format to define well-behaved Markovian stochastic transition systems [18]. A closely related approach was taken by Bacci and Miculan for probabilistic processes with continuous probabilities [3]. It is worth investigating how our modal decomposition approach relates to bialgebraic methods.

Acknowledgements. We are grateful to Simone Tini for discussions on structural properties of operational semantics for PLTSs, and to Bas Luttik for constructive feedback on the presentation of the research results.

References

1. Aceto, L., Fokkink, W., Verhoef, C.: Structural operational semantics. In: Handbook of Process Algebra, pp. 197–292. Elsevier (2001)
2. Aldini, A., Bravetti, M., Gorrieri, R.: A process-algebraic approach for the analysis of probabilistic noninterference. J. Comput. Secur. 12, 191–245 (2004)
3. Bacci, G., Miculan, M.: Structural Operational Semantics for Continuous State Probabilistic Processes. In: Pattinson, D., Schröder, L. (eds.) CMCS 2012. LNCS, vol. 7399, pp. 71–89. Springer, Heidelberg (2012)
4. Bartels, F.: GSOS for probabilistic transition systems. In: Proc. CMCS 2002. ENTCS, vol. 65, pp. 29–53. Elsevier (2002)
5. Bergstra, J., Baeten, J., Smolka, S.: Axiomatizing probabilistic processes: ACP with generative probabilities. Inf. Comput. 121, 234–254 (1995)
6. Bloom, B., Fokkink, W., van Glabbeek, R.: Precongruence formats for decorated trace semantics. ACM TOCL 5, 26–78 (2004)
7. Bloom, B., Istrail, S., Meyer, A.R.: Bisimulation can't be traced. J. ACM 42, 232–268 (1995)
8. Cardelli, L., Larsen, K.G., Mardare, R.: Modular Markovian Logic. In: Aceto, L., Henzinger, M., Sgall, J. (eds.) ICALP 2011, Part II. LNCS, vol. 6756, pp. 380–391. Springer, Heidelberg (2011)
9. Clark, K.L.: Negation as failure. In: Logic and Data Bases, pp. 293–322. Plenum Press (1978)

10. D'Argenio, P.R., Lee, M.D.: Probabilistic Transition System Specification: Congruence and Full Abstraction of Bisimulation. In: Birkedal, L. (ed.) FOSSACS 2012. LNCS, vol. 7213, pp. 452–466. Springer, Heidelberg (2012)
11. Fokkink, W., van Glabbeek, R., de Wind, P.: Compositionality of Hennessy-Milner logic by structural operational semantics. Theor. Comput. Sci. 354, 421–440 (2006)
12. Giacalone, A., Jou, C., Smolka, S.: Algebraic reasoning for probabilistic concurrent systems. In: Proc. IFIP ProCoMet 1990, pp. 443–458. North-Holland (1990)
13. van Glabbeek, R.: The meaning of negative premises in transition system specifications II. J. Logic Algebr. Program. 60-61, 229–258 (2004)
14. van Glabbeek, R.: On cool congruence formats for weak bisimulations. Theor. Comput. Sci. 412, 3283–3302 (2011)
15. van Glabbeek, R., Smolka, S., Steffen, B.: Reactive, generative, and stratified models of probabilistic processes. Inf. Comput. 121, 59–80 (1995)
16. Hennessy, M., Milner, R.: Algebraic laws for nondeterminism and concurrency. J. ACM 32, 137–161 (1985)
17. Jonsson, B., Yi, W., Larsen, K.G.: Probabilistic extensions of process algebras. In: Handbook of Process Algebra, pp. 685–710. Elsevier (2001)
18. Klin, B., Sassone, V.: Structural Operational Semantics for Stochastic Process Calculi. In: Amadio, R.M. (ed.) FOSSACS 2008. LNCS, vol. 4962, pp. 428–442. Springer, Heidelberg (2008)
19. Klin, B.: Structural operational semantics and modal logic, revisited. In: Proc. CMCS 2010. ENTCS, vol. 264, pp. 155–175. Elsevier (2010)
20. Lanotte, R., Tini, S.: Probabilistic bisimulation as a congruence. ACM TOCL 10, 1–48 (2009)
21. Larsen, K.G.: Context-Dependent Bisimulation Between Processes. Ph.D. thesis, University of Edinburgh (1986)
22. Larsen, K.G., Skou, A.: Bisimulation through probabilistic testing. Inf. Comput. 94, 1–28 (1991)
23. Larsen, K.G., Xinxin, L.: Compositionality through an operational semantics of contexts. J. Log. Comput. 1, 761–795 (1991)
24. Parma, A., Segala, R.: Logical Characterizations of Bisimulations for Discrete Probabilistic Systems. In: Seidl, H. (ed.) FOSSACS 2007. LNCS, vol. 4423, pp. 287–301. Springer, Heidelberg (2007)
25. Segala, R.: Modeling and Verification of Randomized Distributed Real-Time Systems. Ph.D. thesis, MIT (1995)
26. Segala, R., Lynch, N.: Probabilistic simulations for probabilistic processes. Nordic J. of Computing 2, 250–273 (1995)
27. de Simone, R.: Higher-level synchronising devices in Meije-SCCS. Theor. Comput. Sci. 37, 245–267 (1985)
28. Tini, S.: Non-expansive epsilon-bisimulations for probabilistic processes. Theor. Comput. Sci. 411, 2202–2222 (2010)
29. Turi, D., Plotkin, G.: Towards a mathematical operational semantics. In: Proc. LICS 1997, pp. 280–291. IEEE (1997)

Coalgebraic Trace Semantics for Probabilistic Transition Systems Based on Measure Theory

Henning Kerstan and Barbara König

Universität Duisburg-Essen, Duisburg, Germany
{henning.kerstan,barbara_koenig}@uni-due.de

Abstract. Coalgebras in a Kleisli category yield a generic definition of trace semantics for various types of labelled transition systems. In this paper we apply this generic theory to generative *probabilistic transition systems*, short *PTS*, with *arbitrary (possibly uncountable) state spaces*. We consider the *sub-probability monad* and the *probability monad (Giry monad)* on the category of measurable spaces and measurable functions. Our main contribution is that the existence of a final coalgebra in the Kleisli category of these monads is closely connected to the measure-theoretic extension theorem for sigma-finite pre-measures. In fact, we obtain a practical definition of the trace measure for both *finite* and *infinite traces* of PTS that subsumes a well-known result for discrete probabilistic transition systems.

1 Introduction

Coalgebra [11,16] is a general framework in which several types of transition systems can be studied (deterministic and non-deterministic automata, weighted automata, transition systems with non-deterministic and probabilistic branching, etc.). One of the strong points of coalgebra is that it induces – via the notion of coalgebra homomorphism and final coalgebra – a notion of behavioural equivalence for all these types of systems. The resulting behavioural equivalence is usually some form of bisimilarity. However, [10] has shown that by modifying the category in which the coalgebra lives, one can obtain different notions of behavioural equivalence, such as trace equivalence.

We will shortly describe the basic idea: given a functor F, describing the branching type of the system, a coalgebra in the category **Set** is a function $\alpha\colon X \to FX$, where X is a set. Consider, for instance, the functor $FX = \mathcal{P}_{fin}(\mathcal{A} \times X + \mathbf{1})$, where $\mathcal{P}_{fin}$ is the finite powerset functor and $\mathcal{A}$ is the given alphabet. This setup allows us to specify finitely branching non-deterministic automata where a state $x \in X$ is mapped to a set of tuples of the form (a, y), where $a \in \mathcal{A}, y \in X$, describing transitions. The set contains the symbol $\checkmark$ (for termination) – the only element contained in the one-element set $\mathbf{1}$ – whenever x is a final state.

A coalgebra homomorphism maps sets of states of a coalgebra to sets of states of another coalgebra, preserving the branching structure. Furthermore, the final coalgebra – if it exists – is the final object in the category of coalgebras. Every coalgebra has a unique homomorphism into the final coalgebra and two states are mapped to the same state in the final coalgebra iff they are behaviourally equivalent.

M. Koutny and I. Ulidowski (Eds.): CONCUR 2012, LNCS 7454, pp. 410–424, 2012.

Now, applying this notion to the example above induces bisimilarity, whereas usually the appropriate notion of behavioural equivalence for non-deterministic finite automata is language equivalence. One of the ideas of [10] is to view a coalgebra $X \to \mathcal{P}(\mathcal{A} \times X + \mathbf{1})$ not as an arrow in **Set**, but as an arrow $X \to \mathcal{A} \times X + \mathbf{1}$ in **Rel**, the Kleisli category of the powerset monad. This induces trace equivalence, instead of bisimilarity, with the underlying intuition that non-determinism is a side-effect that is "hidden" within the monad. This side effect is not present in the final coalgebra (which consists of the set $\mathcal{A}^*$ with a suitable coalgebra structure), but in the arrow from a state $x \in X$ to $\mathcal{A}^*$, which is a relation, and relates each state with all words accepted from this state.

In [10] it is also proposed to obtain probabilistic trace semantics for the Kleisli category of the (discrete) subdistribution monad $\mathcal{D}$. Hence coalgebras in this setting are functions of the form $X \to \mathcal{D}(\mathcal{A} \times X + \mathbf{1})$ (modelling probabilistic branching and termination), seen as arrows in the corresponding Kleisli category. From a general result in [10] it again follows that the final coalgebra is carried by $\mathcal{A}^*$, where the mapping into the final coalgebra assigns to each state a probability distribution over its traces. In this way one obtains the finite trace semantics of generative probabilistic systems [17,8].

The contribution in [10] is restricted to discrete probability spaces, where the probability distributions always have at most countable support [18]. This might seem sufficient for practical applications at first glance, but it has two important drawbacks: first, it excludes several interesting systems that involve uncountable state spaces (see for instance the examples in [15]). Second, it excludes the treatment of infinite traces, as detailed in [10], since the set of all infinite traces is uncountable and hence needs measure theory to be treated appropriately. This is an intuitive reason for the choice of the subdistribution monad – instead of the distribution monad – in [10]: for a given state, it might always be the case that a non-zero "probability mass" is associated to the infinite traces leaving this state, which – in the discrete case – can not be specified by a probability distribution over all words.

Hence, we generalize the results concerning probabilistic trace semantics from [10] to the case of uncountable state spaces, by working in the Kleisli category of the (continuous) subprobability monad over **Meas** (the category of measurable spaces). Unlike in [10] we do not derive the final coalgebra via a generic construction (building the initial algebra of the functor), but we define the final coalgebra directly. Furthermore we consider the Kleisli category of the (continuous) probability monad (Giry monad) and treat the case with and without termination. In the former case we obtain a coalgebra over the set $\mathcal{A}^\infty$ (finite and infinite traces over $\mathcal{A}$) and in the letter over the set $\mathcal{A}^\omega$ (infinite traces), which shows the naturality of the approach. For completeness we also consider the case of the subprobability monad without termination, which results in a trivial final coalgebra over the empty set. In all cases we obtain the natural trace measures as instances of the generic coalgebraic theory.

Since, to our knowledge, there is no generic construction of the final coalgebra for these cases, we construct the respective final coalgebras directly and show their correctness by proving that each coalgebra admits a unique homomorphism into the final coalgebra. Here we rely on the measure-theoretic extension theorem for sigma-finite pre-measures.

2 Background Material and Preliminaries

We assume that the reader is familiar with the basic definitions of category theory. However, we will provide a brief introduction to measure theory and integration, coalgebra, coalgebraic trace semantics and Kleisli categories - of course all geared to our needs. For a more detailed analysis of many of the given proofs we refer to [12] which is the primary source for the results presented in this paper. Moreover, there is a long version of this paper ([13]) including all the missing proofs.

2.1 Notation

By **1** we denote a singleton set, its unique element is $\checkmark$. For arbitrary sets X, Y we write $X \times Y$ for the usual cartesian product and the disjoint union $X + Y$ is the set $\{(x,0),(y,1) \mid x \in X, y \in Y\}$. Whenever $X \cap Y = \emptyset$ this coincides with (is isomorphic to) the usual union $X \cup Y$ in an obvious way and we often write $X \uplus Y$. For set inclusion we write $\subset$ for strict inclusion and $\subseteq$ otherwise. The set of extended reals is the set $\overline{\mathbb{R}} := \mathbb{R} \cup \{\pm\infty\}$ and $\overline{\mathbb{R}}_+$ is the set of non-negative extended reals.

2.2 A Brief Introduction to Measure Theory [2,6]

Measure theory generalizes the idea of length, area or volume. Its most basic definition is that of a *σ-algebra (sigma-algebra)*. Given an arbitrary set X we call a set Σ of subsets of X a *σ-algebra* iff it contains the empty set and is closed under absolute complement and countable union. The tuple (X, Σ) is called a *measurable space*. We will sometimes call the set X itself a measurable space, keeping in mind that there is an associated σ-algebra which we will then denote by Σ_X. For any subset $\mathcal{G} \subseteq \mathcal{P}(X)$ we can always uniquely construct the smallest σ-algebra on X containing $\mathcal{G}$ which is denoted by $\sigma_X(\mathcal{G})$. We call $\mathcal{G}$ the *generator* of $\sigma_X(\mathcal{G})$, which in turn is called *the σ-algebra generated by* $\mathcal{G}$. It is known, that σ_X is a monotone and idempotent operator. The elements of a σ-algebra on X are called the *measurable sets* of X.

Similar to the definition of a σ-algebra we call a subset $\mathcal{S} \subseteq \mathcal{P}(X)$ a *semi-ring of sets* iff it contains the empty set, is closed under pairwise intersection and any relative complement of two sets in $\mathcal{S}$ is the disjoint union of finitely many sets in $\mathcal{S}$. It is easy to see that every σ-algebra is a semi-ring of sets but the reverse is false.

A non-negative function $\mu\colon \mathcal{S} \to \overline{\mathbb{R}}_+$ defined on a semi-ring $\mathcal{S}$ is called a *pre-measure* on X if it assigns 0 to the empty set and is σ-additive, i.e. for a sequence $(S_n)_{n\in\mathbb{N}}$ of mutually disjoint sets in $\mathcal{S}$ where $(\biguplus_{n\in\mathbb{N}} S_n) \in \mathcal{S}$ we must have $\mu\left(\biguplus_{n\in\mathbb{N}} S_n\right) = \sum_{n\in\mathbb{N}} \mu\left(S_n\right)$. A pre-measure is called *σ-finite* if there is a sequence $(S_n)_{n\in\mathbb{N}}$ of sets in $\mathcal{S}$ such that their union is X and $\mu\left(S_n\right) < \infty$ for all $n \in \mathbb{N}$. Whenever $\mathcal{S}$ is a σ-algebra we call μ a *measure* and the tuple $(X, \mathcal{S}, \mu)$ a *measure space*. In that case μ is said to be *finite* iff $\mu(X) < \infty$ and for the special cases $\mu(X) = 1$ (or $\mu(X) \leq 1$) μ is called a *probability measure* (or *sub-probability measure* respectively). The most significant theorem from measure theory which we will use in this paper is the extension theorem for σ-finite pre-measures, for which a proof can be found e.g. in [6].

Proposition 1 (Extension Theorem for σ-finite Pre-Measures). *Let X be an arbitrary set, $\mathcal{S} \subseteq \mathcal{P}(X)$ be a semi-ring of sets and $\mu \colon \mathcal{S} \to \overline{\mathbb{R}}_+$ be a σ-finite pre-measure. Then there exists a uniquely determined measure $\hat{\mu} \colon \sigma_X(\mathcal{S}) \to \overline{\mathbb{R}}_+$ such that $\hat{\mu}|_{\mathcal{S}} = \mu$.*

This theorem can on the one hand be used to construct measures and on the other hand it provides an equality test for σ-finite measures.

Corollary 2 (Equality of σ-finite Measures). *Let X be an arbitrary set, $\mathcal{S} \subseteq \mathcal{P}(X)$ be a semi-ring of sets and $\mu, \nu \colon \sigma_X(\mathcal{S}) \to \overline{\mathbb{R}}$ be σ-finite measures. Then μ and ν are equal iff they agree on all elements of the semi-ring.*

2.3 The Category of Measurable Spaces and Functions

Let X and Y be measurable spaces. A function $f \colon X \to Y$ is called *measurable* iff the pre-image of any measurable set of Y is a measurable set of X. The category **Meas** has measurable spaces as objects and measurable functions as arrows. Composition of arrows is function composition and the identity arrow is the identity function.

The product of two measurable spaces (X, Σ_X) and (Y, Σ_Y) is the set $X \times Y$ endowed with the σ-algebra generated by $\Sigma_X * \Sigma_Y$, the set of so-called "rectangles" which is $\{S_X \times S_Y \mid S_X \in \Sigma_X, S_Y \in \Sigma_Y\}$. It is called the *product σ-algebra* of Σ_X and Σ_Y and is denoted by $\Sigma_X \otimes \Sigma_Y$. Whenever Σ_X and Σ_Y have suitable generators, we can also construct a possibly smaller generator for the product σ-algebra than the set of all rectangles.

Proposition 3 (Generators for the Product σ-Algebra, [6]). *Let X, Y be arbitrary sets and $\mathcal{G}_X \subseteq \mathcal{P}(X), \mathcal{G}_Y \subseteq \mathcal{P}(Y)$ such that $X \in \mathcal{G}_X$ and $Y \in \mathcal{G}_Y$. Then the following holds: $\sigma_{X \times Y}(\mathcal{G}_X * \mathcal{G}_Y) = \sigma_X(\mathcal{G}_X) \otimes \sigma_Y(\mathcal{G}_Y)$.*

We remark that we can construct product endofunctors on the category of measurable spaces and functions.

Definition 4 (Product Functors). *Let Z be a measurable space. The endofunctor $Z \times \mathrm{Id}_{\mathbf{Meas}}$ maps a measurable space X to $(Z \times X, \Sigma_Z \otimes \Sigma_X)$ and a measurable function $f \colon X \to Y$ to the measurable function $F(f) \colon Z \times X \to Z \times Y, (z, x) \mapsto (z, f(x))$. The functor $\mathrm{Id}_{\mathbf{Meas}} \times Z$ is constructed analogously.*

The co-product of two measurable spaces (X, Σ_X) and (Y, Σ_Y) is the set $X + Y$ endowed with $\Sigma_X \oplus \Sigma_Y := \{S_X + S_Y \mid S_X \in \Sigma_X, S_Y \in \Sigma_Y\}$ as σ-algebra, the *disjoint union σ-algebra*. Note that in contrast to the product no σ-operator is needed because $\Sigma_X \oplus \Sigma_Y$ itself is already a σ-algebra whereas $\Sigma_X * \Sigma_Y$ is usually no σ-algebra. For generators of the disjoint union σ-algebra there is a comparable result to the one given above for the product σ-algebra.

Proposition 5 (Generators for the Disjoint Union σ-Algebra). *Let X, Y be arbitrary sets and $\mathcal{G}_X \subseteq \mathcal{P}(X), \mathcal{G}_Y \subseteq \mathcal{P}(Y)$ such that $\emptyset \in \mathcal{G}_X$ and $Y \in \mathcal{G}_Y$. Then the following holds: $\sigma_{X+Y}(\mathcal{G}_X \oplus \mathcal{G}_Y) = \sigma_X(\mathcal{G}_X) \oplus \sigma_Y(\mathcal{G}_Y)$.*

A short proof for this can be found in [13]. As before we can construct endofunctors, the co-product functors.

Definition 6 (Co-Product Functors). *Let Z be a measurable space. The endofunctor* $\mathrm{Id}_{\mathbf{Meas}}+Z$ *maps a measurable space X to $(X+Z,\Sigma_X \oplus \Sigma_Z)$ and a measurable function $f\colon X \to Y$ to the measurable function $F(f)\colon X+Z \to Y+Z$ which acts like f on X and like the identity on Z. The functor* $\mathrm{Id}_{\mathbf{Meas}}+Z$ *is constructed analogously.*

For isomorphisms in **Meas** we provide the following characterization, where again the proof can be found in [13].

Proposition 7 (Isomorphisms in Meas). *Two measurable spaces X and Y are isomorphic in* **Meas** *iff there is a bijective function $\varphi\colon X \to Y$ such that*[1] $\varphi(\Sigma_X) = \Sigma_Y$. *If Σ_X is generated by a set $\mathcal{S} \subseteq \mathcal{P}(X)$ then X and Y are isomorphic iff there is a bijective function $\varphi\colon X \to Y$ such that Σ_Y is generated by $\varphi(\mathcal{S})$. In this case $\mathcal{S}$ is a semi-ring of sets (a σ-algebra) iff $\varphi(\mathcal{S})$ is a semi-ring of sets (a σ-algebra).*

2.4 Kleisli Categories and Liftings of Endofunctors

Given a monad (T,η,μ) on a category **C** we can define a new category, the Kleisli category of T, where the objects are the same as in **C** but every arrow in the new category corresponds to an arrow $f\colon X \to TY$ in **C**. Thus, arrows in the Kleisli category incorporate side effects specified by a monad [10,1]. In the following definition we will adopt the notation used by S. Mac Lane [14, Theorem VI.5.1], as it allows us to distinguish between objects and arrows in the base category **C** and their associated objects and arrows in the Kleisli category $\mathcal{K}\ell(T)$.

Definition 8 (Kleisli Category). *Let (T,η,μ) be a monad on a category* **C**. *To each object X of* **C** *we associate a new object X_T and to each arrow $f\colon X \to TY$ of* **C** *we associate a new arrow $f^\flat\colon X_T \to Y_T$. Together these objects and arrows form a new category $\mathcal{K}\ell(T)$, the* Kleisli category of T, *where composition of arrows $f^\flat\colon X_T \to Y_T$ and $g^\flat\colon Y_T \to Z_T$ is defined as: $g^\flat \circ f^\flat := (\mu_Z \circ T(g) \circ f)^\flat$. For every object X_T the identity arrow is $\mathrm{id}_{X_T} = (\eta_X)^\flat$.*

Given an endofunctor F on **C**, we now want to construct an endofunctor $\overline{F}$ on $\mathcal{K}\ell(T)$ that "resembles" F: Since objects in **C** and objects in $\mathcal{K}\ell(T)$ are basically the same, we want $\overline{F}$ to coincide with F on objects i.e. $\overline{F}(X_T) = (FX)_T$. It remains to define how $\overline{F}$ shall act on arrows $f^\flat\colon X_T \to Y_T$ such that it "resembles" F. We note that for the associated arrow $f\colon X \to TY$ we have $F(f)\colon FX \to FTY$. If we had a map $\lambda_Y\colon FTY \to TFY$ to "swap" the endofunctors F and T, we could simply define $\overline{F}(f^\flat) := (\lambda_Y \circ F(f))^\flat$ which is exactly what we are going to do.

Definition 9 (Distributive Law). *Let (T,η,μ) be a monad on a category* **C** *and F be an endofunctor on* **C**. *A natural transformation $\lambda\colon FT \Rightarrow TF$ is called a distributive law iff for all X we have $\lambda_X \circ F(\eta_X) = \eta_{FX}$ and $\mu_{FX} \circ T(\lambda_X) \circ \lambda_{TX} = \lambda_X \circ F(\mu_X)$.*

Whenever we have a distributive law we can define the lifting of a functor.

Definition 10 (Lifting of a Functor). *Let (T,η,μ) be a monad on a category* **C** *and F be an endofunctor on* **C** *with a distributive law $\lambda\colon FT \Rightarrow TF$. The distributive law*

[1] For $\mathcal{S} \subseteq \mathcal{P}(X)$ and a function $f\colon X \to Y$ let $\varphi(\mathcal{S}) = \{\varphi(S_X) \mid S_X \in \mathcal{S}\}$.

induces a lifting *of* F *to an endofunctor* $\overline{F}\colon \mathcal{K}\ell(T) \to \mathcal{K}\ell(T)$ *where for each object* X_T *of* $\mathcal{K}\ell(T)$ *we define* $\overline{F}(X_T) = (FX)_T$ *and for each arrow* $f^\flat\colon X_T \to Y_T$ *we define* $\overline{F}(f^\flat)\colon \overline{F}(X_T) \to \overline{F}(Y_T)$ *via* $\overline{F}(f^\flat) := (\lambda_Y \circ Ff)^\flat$.

2.5 Coalgebraic Trace Semantics

We recall that for an endofunctor F on a category $\mathbf{C}$ an (F-)coalgebra is a pair (X,α) where X is an object and $\alpha\colon X \to FX$ is an arrow of $\mathbf{C}$. An F-coalgebra homomorphism between two F-coalgebras $(X,\alpha),(Y,\beta)$ is an arrow $\varphi\colon X \to Y$ in $\mathbf{C}$ such that $\beta \circ \varphi = F(\varphi) \circ \alpha$. We call an F-coalgebra (Ω,κ) final iff for every F-coalgebra (X,α) there is a unique F-coalgebra-homomorphism $\varphi_X : X \to \Omega$.

By choosing a suitable category and a suitable endofunctor, many (labelled) transition systems can be modelled as F-coalgebras. The final coalgebra - if it exists - can be seen as the "universe of all possible behaviours" and the unique map into it yields a behavioural equivalence: Two states are equivalent iff they are mapped identically into the final coalgebra. Whenever transition systems incorporate side-effects, these can be "hidden" in a monad. In this case the final coalgebra of an endofunctor in the Kleisli category of this monad yields a notion of trace semantics ([9], [18]). In this case, the side-effects from the original system are not part of the final coalgebra, but are contained in the unique map into the final coalgebra.

2.6 The Lebesgue Integral

Before we can define the probability and the sub-probability monad, we give a crash course in integration loosely based on [2,6]. For that purpose let us fix a measurable space X, a measure μ on X and a Borel-measurable[2] function $f\colon X \to \overline{\mathbb{R}}$. We call f *simple* iff it attains only finitely many values, say $f(X) = \{\alpha_1,...,\alpha_N\}$. The integral of such a simple function f is then defined to be the μ-weighted sum of the α_n, formally $\int_X f \,\mathrm{d}\mu = \sum_{n=1}^{N} \alpha_n \mu(S_n)$ where $S_n = f^{-1}(\alpha_n) \in \Sigma_X$. Whenever f is non-negative we can approximate it from below using non-negative simple functions. In this case we define the integral to be $\int_X f \,\mathrm{d}\mu := \sup\{\int_X s \,\mathrm{d}\mu \mid s \text{ non-negative and simple s.t. } 0 \le s \le f\}$. For arbitrary f we decompose it into its positive part $f^+ = \max\{f,0\}$ and negative part $f^- := \max\{-f,0\}$ which are both non-negative and Borel-measurable. We denote that $f = f^+ - f^-$ and consequently we define the integral of f to be the difference $\int_X f \,\mathrm{d}\mu := \int_X f^+ \,\mathrm{d}\mu - \int_X f^- \,\mathrm{d}\mu$ if not both integrals on the right hand side are $+\infty$. In the latter case we say that the integral does not exist. Whenever it exists and is finite we call f a (μ-)integrable function. Instead of $\int_X f \,\mathrm{d}\mu$ we will sometimes write $\int_X f(x) \,\mathrm{d}\mu(x)$ or $\int_{x\in X} f(x) \,\mathrm{d}\mu(x)$ which is useful if we have functions with more than one argument or multiple integrals. Note that this does not imply that singleton sets are measurable.

For every measurable set $S \in \Sigma_X$ its characteristic function $\chi_S\colon X \to \{0,1\}$, which is 1 iff $x \in S$ and 0 otherwise, is integrable and for integrable f the product $\chi_S \cdot f$ is also integrable and we write $\int_S f \,\mathrm{d}\mu$ for $\int_X \chi_S \cdot f \,\mathrm{d}\mu$. Some useful properties of the integral are that it is linear, i.e. for integrable $f,g\colon X \to \overline{\mathbb{R}}$ we have $\int \alpha f + \beta g \,\mathrm{d}\mu = \alpha \int f \,\mathrm{d}\mu + \beta \int g \,\mathrm{d}\mu$ and monotone, i.e. $f \le g$ implies $\int f \,\mathrm{d}\mu \le \int g \,\mathrm{d}\mu$. We will state one result explicitly which we will use in our proofs.

[2] A function $f\colon X \to \overline{\mathbb{R}}$ is Borel-measurable iff $\forall t \in \overline{\mathbb{R}} : f^{-1}([-\infty,t]) \in \Sigma_X$.

Proposition 11 ([2, Theorem 1.6.12]). *Let X, Y be measurable spaces, μ be a measure on X, $f\colon Y \to \overline{\mathbb{R}}$ be a Borel-measurable function and $g\colon X \to Y$ be a measurable function. Then $\mu_g := \mu \circ g^{-1}$ is a measure on Y, the so-called* image-measure *and f is μ_g-integrable iff $f \circ g$ is μ-integrable and in this case we have $\int_S f \,\mathrm{d}\mu_g = \int_{g^{-1}(S)} f \circ g \,\mathrm{d}\mu$ for all $S \in \Sigma_Y$.*

2.7 The Probability and the Sub-probability Monad

We are now going to present the probability monad (Giry monad) and the sub-probability monad as presented e.g. in [7] and [15]. First, we define the endofunctors of these monads.

Definition 12 (Probability and Sub-Probability Functor). *The* probability-functor $\mathbb{P}\colon \mathbf{Meas} \to \mathbf{Meas}$ *maps a measurable space (X, Σ_X) to the measurable space $\left(\mathbb{P}(X), \Sigma_{\mathbb{P}(X)}\right)$ where $\mathbb{P}(X)$ is the set of all probability measures on Σ_X and $\Sigma_{\mathbb{P}(X)}$ is the smallest σ-algebra such that the* evaluation maps*:*

$$\forall S \in \Sigma_X : \quad p_S\colon \mathbb{P}(X) \to [0,1], P \mapsto P(S) \tag{1}$$

are Borel-measurable. For any measurable function $f\colon X \to Y$ between measurable spaces $(X, \Sigma_X), (Y, \Sigma_Y)$ the arrow $\mathbb{P}(f)$ maps a probability measure P to its image measure:

$$\mathbb{P}(f)\colon \mathbb{P}(X) \to \mathbb{P}(Y), P \mapsto P_f := P \circ f^{-1} \tag{2}$$

If we take sub-probabilities instead of probabilities we can construct the sub-probability functor $\mathbb{S}$ analogously.

Having defined the endofunctors, we continue by constructing the unit and multiplication natural tranformations.

Definition 13 (Unit and Multiplication). *Let $T \in \{\mathbb{S}, \mathbb{P}\}$. We obtain two natural transformations $\eta\colon \mathrm{Id}_{\mathbf{Meas}} \Rightarrow T$ and $\mu\colon T^2 \Rightarrow T$ by defining η_X, μ_X for every measurable space (X, Σ_X) as follows:*

$$\eta_X\colon X \to T(X),\ x \mapsto \delta_x^X \tag{3}$$

$$\mu_X\colon T^2(X) \to T(X),\ \mu_X(P)(S) := \int p_S \mathrm{d}P \quad \forall S \in \Sigma_X \tag{4}$$

where $\delta_x^X\colon \Sigma_X \to [0,1]$ is the Dirac measure which is 1 on $S \in \Sigma_X$ iff $x \in S$ and 0 otherwise. The map p_S ist the evaluation map (1) *from above.*

If we combine all the ingredients we obtain the following result which also guarantees the soundness of the previous definitions:

Proposition 14 ([7]). $(\mathbb{S}, \eta, \mu)$ *and* $(\mathbb{P}, \eta, \mu)$ *are monads on* **Meas**.

3 Main Results

There is a big variety of probabilistic transition systems [18,8]. We will deal with four slightly different versions of so-called *generative* PTS. The underlying intuition is that, according to a probability measure, an action from the alphabet $\mathcal{A}$ and a set of possible successor states are chosen. We distinguish between probabilistic branching according to sub-probability and probability measures and furthermore we treat systems without and with termination.

Definition 15 (Probabilistic Transition System (PTS)). *A* probabilistic transition system *is a tuple* $(\mathcal{A}, X, \alpha)$ *where* $\mathcal{A}$ *is a finite alphabet (endowed with* $\mathcal{P}(\mathcal{A})$ *as* σ*-algebra),* X *is the* state space, *an arbitrary measurable space with* σ*-algebra* Σ_X *and* $\alpha \in \{\alpha_0, \alpha_*, \alpha_\omega, \alpha_\infty\}$ *is the* transition function *where:*

$$\alpha_0 : X \to \mathbb{S}(\mathcal{A} \times X),\ \alpha_* : X \to \mathbb{S}(\mathcal{A} \times X + \mathbf{1})$$
$$\alpha_\omega : X \to \mathbb{P}(\mathcal{A} \times X),\ \alpha_\infty : X \to \mathbb{P}(\mathcal{A} \times X + \mathbf{1})$$

Depending on the type of the transition function, we call the PTS a $\diamond$*-PTS with*[3] $\diamond \in \{0, *, \omega, \infty\}$*. For every* $x \in X$ *and every* $a \in \mathcal{A}$ *we define the finite sub-probability measure* $\mathbf{P}_{x,a} : \Sigma_X \to [0,1]$ *where* $\mathbf{P}_{x,a}(S) := \alpha(x)(\{a\} \times S)$ *for every* $S \in \Sigma_X$*. Intuitively,* $\mathbf{P}_{x,a}(S)$ *is the probability of making an a-transition from the state* $x \in X$ *to any state* $y \in S$*. Whenever* X *is a countable set and* $\Sigma_X = \mathcal{P}(X)$ *we call the PTS* discrete.

We will now take a look at a small example ∞-PTS before we continue to build up our theory.

Example 16 (Discrete PTS with Finite and Infinite Traces). Let $\mathcal{A} = \{a, b\}$, $X = \{0, 1, 2\}$, $\Sigma_X = \mathcal{P}(X)$ and $\alpha := \alpha_\infty : X \to \mathbb{P}(\mathcal{A} \times X + \mathbf{1})$ such that we obtain the following system:

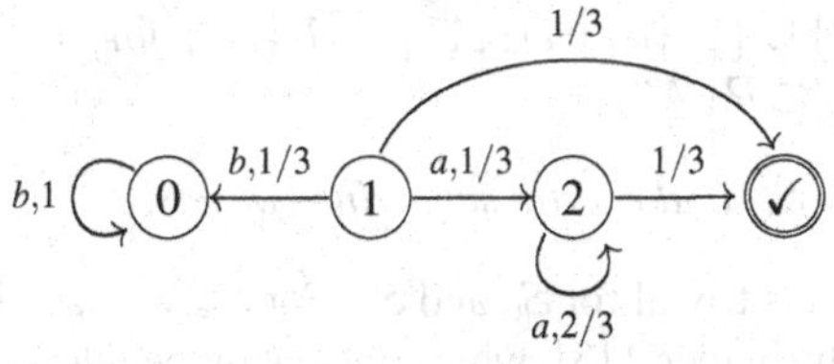

Obviously ✓ is the unique final state which has only incoming transitions bearing probabilities and no labels. This should be interpreted as follows: "From state 1 the system terminates immediately with probability $1/3$".

In order to define a trace measure on these probabilistic transition systems, we need suitable σ-algebras on the sets of words. While the set of all finite words, $\mathcal{A}^*$, is rather simple - we take $\mathcal{P}(\mathcal{A}^*)$ as σ-algebra - the set of all infinite words, $\mathcal{A}^\omega$, and also the set of all finite and infinite words, $\mathcal{A}^\infty$, needs some consideration. For a word $u \in \mathcal{A}^*$ we call the set of all infinite words that have u as a prefix the ω-cone of u, denoted by

[3] The reason for choosing these symbols as type-identifiers will be revealed later in this paper.

$\uparrow_\omega\{u\}$, and similarily we call the set of all finite and infinite words having u as a prefix the ∞-cone ([15, p. 23]) of u and denote it with $\uparrow_\infty\{u\}$.

A cone can be visualized in the following way: We consider the undirected, rooted and labelled tree given by $T = (\mathcal{A}^*, E, l)$ with edges $E := \{\{u, uv\} \mid u \in \mathcal{A}^*, v \in \mathcal{A}\}$, edge-labelling function $l\colon E \to \mathcal{A}, \{u, uv\} \mapsto v$ and $\varepsilon \in \mathcal{A}^*$ as the dedicated root. For $\mathcal{A} = \{a, b, c\}$ the first three levels of the tree can be depicted as follows:

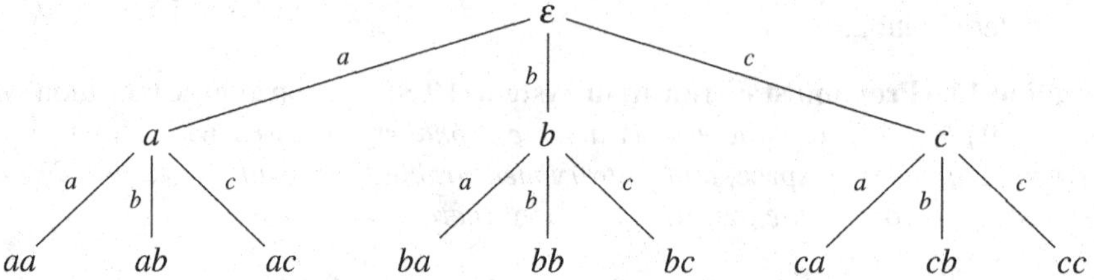

Given a finite word $u \in \mathcal{A}^*$, the ω-cone of u is the set of all infinite paths that begin in ε and contain the vertex u and the ∞-cone of u is the set of all finite and infinite simple paths that begin in ε and contain the vertex u (and thus necessarily have a length which is greater or equal to the length of u). Since the sets of cones are no σ-algebras, we will of course take the σ-algebra generated by them. However, the sets of cones can be augmented in such a way that we obtain semi-rings of sets.

Definition 17 (Cones). *Let $\mathcal{A}$ be a finite alphabet and let $\sqsubseteq \subset \mathcal{A}^* \times \mathcal{A}^\infty$ denote the usual prefix relation on words. For $u \in \mathcal{A}^*$ we define its* ω-cone *to be the set $\uparrow_\omega\{u\} := \{v \in \mathcal{A}^\omega \mid u \sqsubseteq v\}$ and analgously we call $\uparrow_\infty\{u\} := \{v \in \mathcal{A}^\infty \mid u \sqsubseteq v\}$ the* ∞-cone *of u. Furthermore we define $\uparrow_0\{u\} := \emptyset, \uparrow_*\{u\} := \{u\}$.*

With this definition at hand, we can now define the semi-rings we will use to generate σ-algebras on $\mathcal{A}^*, \mathcal{A}^\omega$ and $\mathcal{A}^\infty$.

Definition 18 (Semi-Rings of Sets of Words). *Let $\mathcal{A}$ be a finite alphabet. We define the sets $\mathcal{S}_\diamond := \{\emptyset\} \cup \{\uparrow_\diamond\{u\} \mid u \in \mathcal{A}^\infty\} \subset \mathcal{P}(\mathcal{A}^\diamond)$ for $\diamond \in \{0, *, \omega\}$ and $\mathcal{S}_\infty := \{\uparrow_\infty\{u\} \mid u \in \mathcal{A}^\infty\} \cup \mathcal{S}_* \subset \mathcal{P}(\mathcal{A}^\infty)$.*

Proposition 19. *$\mathcal{S}_0, \mathcal{S}_*, \mathcal{S}_\omega$ and $\mathcal{S}_\infty$ are semi-rings of sets.*

Proving this Proposition is trivial for $\mathcal{S}_0$ and $\mathcal{S}_*$. For $\mathcal{S}_\infty$ we have included a short proof in the long version of this paper, [13], which can easily be adopted to $\mathcal{S}_\omega$.

We remark that many interesting sets will be measurable in the σ-algebra generated by the cones. The singleton-set $\{u\}$ will be measurable for every $u \in \mathcal{A}^\omega$ because $\{u\} = \bigcap_{v \sqsubseteq u} \uparrow_\omega\{v\} = \bigcap_{v \sqsubseteq u} \uparrow_\infty\{v\}$ which are countable intersections, or (for ∞-cones only) the set $\mathcal{A}^* = \bigcup_{u \in \mathcal{A}^*}\{u\}$ and consequently also the set $\mathcal{A}^\omega = \mathcal{A}^\infty \setminus \mathcal{A}^*$ will have to be measurable. The latter will be useful to check to what "extent" a state of a ∞-PTS accepts finite or infinite words/behaviour. One thing about $\mathcal{S}_0$ is worth mentioning: In fact, the above definition yields $\mathcal{S}_0 = \{\emptyset\}$. While this is certainly odd at first sight, it will turn out to be a reasonable specification in our setting.

We will now give a definition of the trace measure which can be understood as the behaviour of a state: it measures the probability of accepting a set of words.

Definition 20 (The Trace Measure). *Let $(\mathcal{A}, X, \alpha)$ be a $\diamond$-PTS. For every state $x \in X$ the trace (sub-)probability measure $\mathbf{tr}_\diamond(x)\colon \sigma_{\mathcal{A}^\diamond}(\mathcal{S}_\diamond) \to [0,1]$ is uniquely defined by the following equations:*

$$\forall a \in \mathcal{A}, \forall u \in \mathcal{A}^*: \quad \mathbf{tr}_\diamond(x)(\uparrow_\diamond \{au\}) := \int_{x' \in X} \mathbf{tr}_\diamond(x')(\uparrow_\diamond \{u\})\, \mathrm{d}\mathbf{P}_{x,a}(x') \tag{5}$$

and $\mathbf{tr}_\diamond(x)(\emptyset) = 0$, $\mathbf{tr}_*(x)(\uparrow_* \{\varepsilon\}) = \alpha(x)(\mathbf{1})$, $\mathbf{tr}_\omega(x)(\uparrow_\omega \{\varepsilon\}) = 1$, $\mathbf{tr}_\infty(x)(\uparrow_\infty \{\varepsilon\}) = 1$ and $\mathbf{tr}_\infty(x)(\{u\}) = \mathbf{tr}_\infty(x)(\uparrow_\infty \{u\}) - \sum_{a \in \mathcal{A}} \mathbf{tr}_\infty(x)(\uparrow_\infty \{au\})$ where applicable.

We need to verify that everything is well-defined. In the next proposition we explicitly state what has to be shown.

Proposition 21. *The equations in Definition 20 yield a σ-finite pre-measure $\mathbf{tr}_\diamond(x)\colon \mathcal{S}_\diamond \to [0,1]$ for $\diamond \in \{0, *, \omega, \infty\}$ and every $x \in X$. Moreover, the unique extension of this pre-measure is a (sub-)probability measure.*

Before we prove this proposition, let us try to get a more intuitive understanding of Definition 20 and especially equation (5). First we check how the above definition reduces when we consider discrete systems.

Remark 22. Let $(\mathcal{A}, X, \alpha)$ be a discrete[4] $*$-PTS, i.e. $\alpha\colon X \to \mathbb{S}(\mathcal{A} \times X + \mathbf{1})$. Then $\mathbf{tr}_*(x)(\varepsilon) := \alpha(x)(\checkmark)$ and (5) is equivalent to:

$$\forall a \in \mathcal{A}, \forall u \in \mathcal{A}^*: \quad \mathbf{tr}_*(x)(au) := \sum_{x' \in X} \mathbf{tr}_*(x')(u) \cdot \mathbf{P}_{x,a}(x')$$

which is equivalent to the discrete trace distribution presented in [9] for the sub-distribution monad $\mathcal{D}$ on **Set**.

Having seen this coincidence with known results, we proceed to calculate the trace measure for our example (Ex. 16) which we can only do in our more general setting because this ∞-PTS is a discrete probabilistic transition system which exhibits both finite and infinite behaviour.

Example 23 (Example 16 cont.). We calculate the trace measures for the ∞-PTS from Example 16. We have $\mathbf{tr}_\infty(0) = \delta_{b^\omega}^{\mathcal{A}^\infty}$ because

$$\begin{aligned}
\mathbf{tr}_\infty(0)(\{b^\omega\}) &= \mathbf{tr}_\infty(0)\left(\cap_{k=0}^\infty \uparrow_\infty \{b^k\}\right) = \mathbf{tr}_\infty(0)\left(\mathcal{A}^\infty \setminus \cup_{k=0}^\infty \left(\mathcal{A}^\infty \setminus \uparrow_\infty \{b^k\}\right)\right) \\
&= \mathbf{tr}_\infty(0)\,(\mathcal{A}^\infty) - \mathbf{tr}(0)\left(\cup_{k=0}^\infty \left(\mathcal{A}^\infty \setminus \uparrow_\infty \{b^k\}\right)\right) \\
&\geq 1 - \sum_{k=0}^\infty \mathbf{tr}_\infty(0)\left(\mathcal{A}^\infty \setminus \uparrow_\infty \{b^k\}\right) \\
&= 1 - \sum_{k=0}^\infty \left(1 - \mathbf{tr}_\infty(0)\left(\uparrow_\infty \{b^k\}\right)\right) = 1 - \sum_{k=0}^\infty (1-1) = 1
\end{aligned}$$

Thus we have $\mathbf{tr}_\infty(0)(\mathcal{A}^*) = \mathbf{tr}_\infty(0)\,(\uplus_{u \in \mathcal{A}^*} \{u\}) = 0$ and $\mathbf{tr}_\infty(0)(\mathcal{A}^\omega) = 1$. By induction we can show that $\mathbf{tr}_\infty(2)(\{a^k\}) = (1/3) \cdot (2/3)^k$ and thus $\mathbf{tr}_\infty(2)(\mathcal{A}^*) = 1$ and $\mathbf{tr}_\infty(2)(\mathcal{A}^\omega) = 0$. Furthermore we calculate $\mathbf{tr}_\infty(1)(\{b^\omega\}) = 1/3$, $\mathbf{tr}_\infty(1)(\uparrow_\infty \{a\}) = 1/3$ and $\mathbf{tr}_\infty(1)(\{\varepsilon\}) = 1/3$ yielding $\mathbf{tr}_\infty(1)(\mathcal{A}^*) = 2/3$ and $\mathbf{tr}_\infty(1)(\mathcal{A}^\omega) = 1/3$.

[4] If Z is a countable set and $\mu\colon \mathcal{P}(Z) \to [0,1]$ is a measure, we write $\mu(z)$ for $\mu(\{z\})$.

Recall, that we still have to prove Proposition 21. In order to simplify this proof, we provide a few technical results about the sets $\mathcal{S}_*, \mathcal{S}_\omega, \mathcal{S}_\infty$ for which proofs are given in [13] or in [12].

Lemma 24 (Countable Unions). *Let $(S_n)_{n\in\mathbb{N}}$ be a sequence of mutually disjoint sets in $\mathcal{S}_\omega$ or in $\mathcal{S}_\infty$ such that $\biguplus_{n\in\mathbb{N}} S_n$ is itself an element of $\mathcal{S}_\omega$ or $\mathcal{S}_\infty$. Then $S_n = \emptyset$ for all but finitely many n.*

Lemma 25 (Sigma-Finiteness 1). *A non-negative map $\mu\colon \mathcal{S}_* \to \overline{\mathbb{R}}_+$ where $\mu(\emptyset) = 0$ is always σ-additive and thus a pre-measure.*

Lemma 26 (Sigma-Finiteness 2). *A non-negative map $\mu\colon \mathcal{S}_\omega \to \overline{\mathbb{R}}_+$ where $\mu(\emptyset) = 0$ is σ-additive and thus a pre-measure iff $\mu(\uparrow_\omega \{u\}) = \sum_{a\in\mathcal{A}} \mu(\uparrow_\omega \{ua\})$ for all $u \in \mathcal{A}^*$.*

Lemma 27 (Sigma-Finiteness 3). *A non-negative map $\mu\colon \mathcal{S}_\infty \to \overline{\mathbb{R}}_+$ where $\mu(\emptyset) = 0$ is σ-additive and thus a pre-measure iff $\mu(\uparrow_\infty \{u\}) = \mu(\{u\}) + \sum_{a\in\mathcal{A}} \mu(\uparrow_\infty \{ua\})$ for all $u \in \mathcal{A}^*$.*

Using these results, we can now prove Proposition 21.

Proof (of Proposition 21). For $\diamond = 0$ nothing has to be shown because $\sigma_\emptyset(\{\emptyset\}) = \{\emptyset\}$ and $\mathbf{tr}_0(x)\colon \{\emptyset\} \to [0,1]$ is already uniquely defined by $\mathbf{tr}_0(x)(\emptyset) = 0$. Lemma 25 and Lemma 27 yield immediately that for $\diamond \in \{*,\infty\}$ the equations define a pre-measure. The only difficult case is $\diamond = \omega$ where we will, of course, apply Lemma 26. Let $u = u_1...u_m \in \mathcal{A}^*$ with $u_k \in \mathcal{A}$ for every k, then multiple application of (5) yields:

$$\mathbf{tr}_\omega(x)(\uparrow_\omega \{u\}) = \int_{x_1\in X} \cdots \int_{x_m\in X} 1 \, \mathbf{dP}_{x_{m-1},u_m}(x_m) \ldots \mathbf{dP}_{x,u_1}(x_1)$$

and for arbitrary $a \in \mathcal{A}$ we obtain analogously:

$$\mathbf{tr}_\omega(x)(\uparrow_\omega \{ua\}) = \int_{x_1\in X} \cdots \int_{x_m\in X} \mathbf{P}_{x_m,a}(X) \, \mathbf{dP}_{x_{m-1},u_m}(x_m) \ldots \mathbf{dP}_{x,u_1}(x_1).$$

All integrals exist and are bounded above by 1 so we can use the linearity and monotonicity of the integral to exchange the finite sum and the integrals to obtain that indeed $\sum_{a\in\mathcal{A}} \mathbf{tr}_\omega(x)(\uparrow_\omega \{ua\}) = \mathbf{tr}_\omega(x)(\uparrow_\omega \{u\})$ is valid using the fact that $\sum_{a\in\mathcal{A}} \mathbf{P}_{x_m,a}(X) = \sum_{a\in\mathcal{A}} \alpha(x)(\{a\}\times X) = \alpha(x)(\mathcal{A}\times X) = 1$. Hence also $\mathbf{tr}_\omega(x)\colon \mathcal{S}_\omega \to \overline{\mathbb{R}}_+$ is σ-additive and thus a pre-measure.

Now let us check that the pre-measures are σ-finite. For $\diamond \in \{\omega,\infty\}$ this is obvious and in these cases the unique extension must be a (sub-)probability measure because by definition we have $\mathbf{tr}_\omega(x)(\mathcal{A}^\omega) = 1$ and $\mathbf{tr}_\infty(x)(\mathcal{A}^\infty) = 1$ respectively. For the remaining case ($\diamond = *$) we remark that $\mathcal{A}^* = \biguplus_{u\in\mathcal{A}^*} \{u\}$ which is countable and disjoint. Using induction on the length of $u \in \mathcal{A}^*$ and monotonicity of the integral we can easily verify that $\mathbf{tr}_*(x)(\{u\})$ is always bounded by 1 and hence also in this case $\mathbf{tr}_*(x)$ is σ-finite. Again by induction we can see that for all $n \in \mathbb{N}_0$ we have $\mathbf{tr}_*(x)\left(\mathcal{A}^{\leq n}\right) \leq 1$. Since $\mathbf{tr}_*(x)$ is a measure (and thus non-negative and σ-additive), the sequence given by $\left(\mathbf{tr}_*(x)\left(\mathcal{A}^{\leq n}\right)\right)_{n\in\mathbb{N}_0}$ is a monotonically increasing sequence of real numbers bounded above by 1 and hence has a limit. Furthermore, $\mathbf{tr}_*(x)$ is continuous from below as a measure and we have $\mathcal{A}^{\leq n} \subseteq \mathcal{A}^{\leq n+1}$ for all $n \in \mathbb{N}_0$ and thus can conclude that

$$\mathbf{tr}_*(x)\,(\mathcal{A}^*) = \mathbf{tr}_*(x)\left(\bigcup_{n=1}^{\infty} \mathcal{A}^{\leq n}\right) = \lim_{n\to\infty} \mathbf{tr}_*(x)\,(\mathcal{A}^{\leq n}) = \sup_{n\in\mathbb{N}_0} \mathbf{tr}_*(x)\,(\mathcal{A}^{\leq n}) \leq 1.$$

For more details take a look at [12, Proofs of Theorems 4.14 and 4.24]. □

Now that we know that our definition of a trace measure is mathematically sound, we remember that we wanted to show that it is "natural", meaning that it arises from the final coalgebra in the Kleisli category of the (sub-)probability monad. We now state our main theorem which presents a close connection between the unique existence of the map into the final coalgebra and the unique extension of a family of σ-finite measures.

Theorem 28 (Main Theorem). *Let $T \in \{\mathbb{S}, \mathbb{P}\}$, F be an endofunctor on* **Meas** *with a distributive law $\lambda\colon FT \Rightarrow TF$ and $(\Omega_T, \kappa^\flat)$ be an $\overline{F}$-coalgebra where $\Sigma_{F\Omega} = \sigma_{F\Omega}(\mathcal{S}_{F\Omega})$ for a semi-ring $\mathcal{S}_{F\Omega}$. Then $(\Omega_T, \kappa^\flat)$ is final iff for every $\overline{F}$-coalgebra $(X_T, \alpha^\flat)$ there is a unique (sub-)probability measure $\mathbf{tr}(x)\colon \Sigma_\Omega \to [0,1]$ for every $x \in X$ such that:*

$$\forall S \in \mathcal{S}_{F\Omega}: \quad \int_\Omega p_S \circ \kappa \,\mathrm{d}\mathbf{tr}(x) = \int_{FX} p_S \circ \lambda_\Omega \circ F(\mathbf{tr})\,\mathrm{d}\alpha(x) \tag{6}$$

Proof. We consider the final coalgebra diagram in $\mathcal{K}\ell(T)$:

$$\begin{array}{ccc} X_T & \xrightarrow{\alpha^\flat} & \overline{F}X_T \\ {\scriptstyle \mathbf{tr}^\flat}\downarrow & & \downarrow{\scriptstyle \overline{F}(\mathbf{tr}^\flat) = (\lambda_\Omega \circ F(\mathbf{tr}))^\flat} \\ \Omega_T & \xrightarrow{\kappa^\flat} & \overline{F}\Omega_T \end{array}$$

By definition $(\Omega_T, \kappa^\flat)$ is final iff for every $\overline{F}$-coalgebra $(X_T, \alpha^\flat)$ there is a unique arrow $\mathbf{tr}^\flat\colon X_T \to \Omega_T$ making the diagram commute. We define:

$$g^\flat := \kappa^\flat \circ \mathbf{tr}^\flat \text{ (down, right)} \quad h^\flat := \overline{F}(\mathbf{tr}^\flat) \circ \alpha^\flat \text{ (right, down)}$$

and note that commutativity of this diagram is equivalent to:

$$\forall x \in X, \forall S \in \mathcal{S}_{F\Omega}: \quad g(x)(S) = h(x)(S) \tag{7}$$

because for every $x \in X$ both $g(x)$ and $h(x)$ are (sub-)probability measures and thus σ-finite measures which allows us to apply Corollary 2. We calculate:

$$\begin{aligned} g(x)(S) &= (\mu_{F\Omega} \circ T(\kappa) \circ \mathbf{tr})(x)(S) = \mu_{F\Omega}\,(T(\kappa)(\mathbf{tr}(x)))\,(S) \\ &= \mu_{F\Omega}\,(\mathbf{tr}(x)_\kappa)\,(S) = \int p_S \,\mathrm{d}\mathbf{tr}(x)_\kappa = \int p_S \circ \kappa \,\mathrm{d}\mathbf{tr}(x) \end{aligned}$$

and if we define $\rho := \lambda_\Omega \circ F(\mathbf{tr})\colon FX \to TF\Omega$ we obtain:

$$\begin{aligned} h(x)(S) &= (\mu_{F\Omega} \circ T(\rho) \circ \alpha)(x)(S) = \mu_{F\Omega}\,(T(\rho)(\alpha(x)))\,(S) = \mu_{F\Omega}\left(\alpha(x)_\rho\right)(S) \\ &= \int p_S \,\mathrm{d}\alpha(x)_\rho = \int p_S \circ \rho \,\mathrm{d}\alpha(x) = \int p_S \circ \lambda_\Omega \circ F(\mathbf{tr})\,\mathrm{d}\alpha(x) \end{aligned}$$

and thus (7) is equivalent to (6). □

We immediately obtain the following corollary.

Corollary 29. *Let in Theorem 28 $\kappa = \eta_{F\Omega} \circ \varphi$, for an isomorphism $\varphi\colon \Omega \to F\Omega$ in* **Meas** *and let $\mathcal{S}_\Omega \subseteq \mathcal{P}(\Omega)$ be a semi-ring such that $\Sigma_\Omega = \sigma_\Omega(\mathcal{S}_\Omega)$. Then equation (6) is equivalent to:*

$$\forall S \in \mathcal{S}_\Omega: \quad \mathbf{tr}(x)(S) = \int p_{\varphi(S)} \circ \lambda_\Omega \circ F(\mathbf{tr})\, \mathrm{d}\alpha(x) \tag{8}$$

Proof. Since φ is an isomorphism in **Meas** we know from Proposition 7 that $\Sigma_{F\Omega} = \sigma_\Omega(\varphi(\mathcal{S}_\Omega))$. For every $S \in \Sigma_\Omega$ and every $u \in \Omega$ we calculate:

$$p_{\varphi(S)} \circ \kappa(u) = p_{\varphi(S)} \circ \eta_{F\Omega} \circ \varphi(u) = \delta^{F\Omega}_{\varphi(u)}(\varphi(S)) = \chi_{\varphi(S)}(\varphi(u)) = \chi_S(u)$$

and hence we have $\int p_{\varphi(S)} \circ \kappa\, \mathrm{d}\mathbf{tr}(x) = \int \chi_S\, \mathrm{d}\mathbf{tr}(x) = \mathbf{tr}(x)(S)$. □

Since we want to apply this corollary to sets of words, we now define the necessary isomorphism φ using the characterization given in Proposition 7.

Proposition 30. *Let $\varphi\colon \mathcal{A}^\infty \to \mathcal{A} \times \mathcal{A}^\infty + \mathbf{1}$, $\varepsilon \mapsto \checkmark$, $au \mapsto (a,u)$. Then φ, $\varphi|_{\mathcal{A}^*}$ and $\varphi|_{\mathcal{A}^\omega}$ are bijective functions[5] and the following holds:*

$$\sigma_{\mathcal{A}\times\mathcal{A}^\omega}(\varphi(\mathcal{S}_\omega)) = \mathcal{P}(\mathcal{A}) \otimes \sigma_{\mathcal{A}^\omega}(\mathcal{S}_\omega) \tag{9}$$

$$\sigma_{\mathcal{A}\times\mathcal{A}^*+\mathbf{1}}(\varphi(\mathcal{S}_*)) = \mathcal{P}(\mathcal{A}) \otimes \sigma_{\mathcal{A}^*}(\mathcal{S}_*) \oplus \mathcal{P}(\mathbf{1}) \tag{10}$$

$$\sigma_{\mathcal{A}\times\mathcal{A}^\infty+\mathbf{1}}(\varphi(\mathcal{S}_\infty)) = \mathcal{P}(\mathcal{A}) \otimes \sigma_{\mathcal{A}^\infty}(\mathcal{S}_\infty) \oplus \mathcal{P}(\mathbf{1}) \tag{11}$$

We recall that – in order to get a lifting of an endofunctor on **Meas** – we also need a distributive law for the functors we are using to define PTS. A proof for the following proposition is given in [12, Prop. and Def. 4.12 and 4.22].

Proposition 31 (Distributive Laws for the (Sub-)Probability Monad). *Let $T \in \{\mathbb{S}, \mathbb{P}\}$. For every measurable space (X, Σ_X) we define*

$$\lambda_X\colon \mathcal{A} \times TX \to T(\mathcal{A} \times X),\ (a,P) \mapsto \delta^{\mathcal{A}}_a \otimes P$$

where $\delta^{\mathcal{A}}_a \otimes P$ denotes the product measure[6] of $\delta^{\mathcal{A}}_a$ and P. Then we obtain a distributive law $\lambda\colon \mathcal{A} \times T \Rightarrow T(\mathcal{A} \times \mathrm{Id}_{\mathbf{Meas}})$. In an analogous manner we obtain another distributive law $\lambda\colon \mathcal{A} \times T + \mathbf{1} \Rightarrow T(\mathcal{A} \times \mathrm{Id}_{\mathbf{Meas}} + \mathbf{1})$ if we define

$$\lambda_X\colon \mathcal{A} \times TX + \mathbf{1} \to T(\mathcal{A} \times X + \mathbf{1}),\ (a,P) \mapsto \delta^{\mathcal{A}}_a \odot P,\ \checkmark \mapsto \delta^{\mathcal{A}\times X+\mathbf{1}}_{\checkmark}$$

for every measurable space (X, Σ_X) where $(\delta^{\mathcal{A}}_a \odot P)(S) := (\delta^{\mathcal{A}}_a \otimes P)(S \cap (\mathcal{A} \times X))$ for every $S \in \mathcal{P}(\mathcal{A}) \otimes \Sigma_X \oplus \mathcal{P}(\mathbf{1})$.

With this result at hand we can finally apply Corollary 29 to the measurable spaces $\emptyset, \mathcal{A}^*, \mathcal{A}^\omega, \mathcal{A}^\infty$, each of which is of course equipped with the σ-algebra generated by the semi-rings $\mathcal{S}_0, \mathcal{S}_*, \mathcal{S}_\omega, \mathcal{S}_\infty$ as defined in Proposition 19, to obtain the final coalgebra and the induced trace semantics for PTS as presented in the following corollary.

[5] For a function $f\colon X \to Y$ and $X' \subset X$ we consider $f|_{X'}$ to be $f|_{X'}\colon X' \to f(X')$.

[6] $\delta^{\mathcal{A}}_a \otimes P$ is the unique extension of the measure defined via $\delta^{\mathcal{A}}_a \otimes P(S_{\mathcal{A}} \times S_X) := \delta^{\mathcal{A}}_a(S_{\mathcal{A}}) \cdot P(S_X)$ for all $S_{\mathcal{A}} \times S_X \in \mathcal{P}(\mathcal{A}) * \Sigma_X$.

Corollary 32 (Final Coalgebra and Trace Semantics for PTS). *A PTS $(\mathcal{A},X,\alpha)$ is an $\overline{F}$-coalgebra $(X_T,\alpha^\flat)$ in $\mathcal{K}\ell(T)$ and vice versa. In the following table we present the (carriers of) final $\overline{F}$-coalgebras $(\Omega_T,\kappa^\flat)$ in $\mathcal{K}\ell(T)$ for all suitable choices of T and F (depending on the type of the PTS).*

Type	*Monad T*	*Endofunctor F*	*Carrier Ω_T*
0	$\mathbb{S}$	$\mathcal{A}\times X$	$(\emptyset,\{\emptyset\})_T$
$*$	$\mathbb{S}$	$\mathcal{A}\times X+\mathbf{1}$	$(\mathcal{A}^*,\sigma_{\mathcal{A}^*}(\mathcal{S}_*))_T$
ω	$\mathbb{P}$	$\mathcal{A}\times X$	$(\mathcal{A}^\omega,\sigma_{\mathcal{A}^\omega}(\mathcal{S}_\omega))_T$
∞	$\mathbb{P}$	$\mathcal{A}\times X+\mathbf{1}$	$(\mathcal{A}^\infty,\sigma_{\mathcal{A}^\infty}(\mathcal{S}_\infty))_T$

In all cases $\kappa=\eta_{F\Omega}\circ\varphi$ where φ is the isomorphism as defined before. The unique map $\mathbf{tr}^\flat$ into the final coalgebra is $\mathbf{tr}_\diamond(x)$ as given in Definition 20 for every $x\in X$.

4 Conclusion, Related and Future Work

We have shown how to obtain coalgebraic trace semantics in a general measure-theoretic setting, thereby allowing uncountable state spaces and infinite trace semantics.

Our work is clearly inspired by [10], generalizing their instantiation to generative probabilistic systems. Probabilistic systems in the general measure-theoretic setting were in detail studied by [21], but note that the author considers bisimilarity and constructs coalgebras in **Meas**, whereas we are working in Kleisli categories based on **Meas**.

In [5] and [15] a very thorough and general overview of properties of labelled Markov processes including the treatment of temporal logics is given. However, the authors do not explicitly cover a coalgebraic notion of trace semantics.

Infinite traces in a general coalgebraic setting have already been studied in [4]. However, this generic theory, once applied to probabilistic systems, is restricted to coalgebras with countable carrier while our setting, which is undoubtedly specific, allows arbitrary carriers for coalgebras of probabilistic systems.

As future work we plan to apply the minimization algorithm introduced in [1] and adapt it to this general setting, by working out the notion of canonical representatives for probabilistic transition system.

Furthermore we plan to define and study a notion of probabilistic trace distance, similar to the distance measure studied in [20,19]. We are also interested in algorithms for calculating this distance, perhaps similar to what has been proposed in [3] for probabilistic bisimilarity.

Acknowledgement. We would like to thank Paolo Baldan, Filippo Bonchi, Mathias Hülsbusch and Alexandra Silva for discussing this topic with us and giving us some valuable hints. Moreover, we are grateful for the detailed feedback from our reviewers.

References

1. Adámek, J., Bonchi, F., Hülsbusch, M., König, B., Milius, S., Silva, A.: A Coalgebraic Perspective on Minimization and Determinization. In: Birkedal, L. (ed.) FOSSACS 2012. LNCS, vol. 7213, pp. 58–73. Springer, Heidelberg (2012)

2. Ash, R.B.: Real Analysis and Probability. Probability and Mathematical Statistics – A Series of Monographs and Textbooks. Academic Press, New York (1972)
3. Chen, D., van Breugel, F., Worrell, J.: On the Complexity of Computing Probabilistic Bisimilarity. In: Birkedal, L. (ed.) FOSSACS 2012. LNCS, vol. 7213, pp. 437–451. Springer, Heidelberg (2012)
4. Cîrstea, C.: Generic infinite traces and path-based coalgebraic temporal logics. Electronic Notes in Theoretical Computer Science 264(2), 83–103 (2010)
5. Doberkat, E.: Stochastic relations: foundations for Markov transition systems. Chapman & Hall/CRC studies in informatics series. Chapman & Hall/CRC (2007)
6. Elstrodt, J.: Maß- und Integrationstheorie, 5th edn. Springer (2007)
7. Giry, M.: A categorical approach to probability theory. In: Categorical Aspects of Topology and Analysis. Lecture Notes in Mathematics, vol. 915, pp. 68–86. Springer (1981)
8. van Glabbeek, R., Smolka, S.A., Steffen, B., Tofts, C.M.N.: Reactive, generative and stratified models of probabilistic processes. Information and Computation 121, 59–80 (1995)
9. Hasuo, I., Jacobs, B., Sokolova, A.: Generic trace theory. In: International Workshop on Coalgebraic Methods in Computer Science. Electronic Notes in Theoretical Computer Science, vol. 164, pp. 47–65. Elsevier (2006)
10. Hasuo, I., Jacobs, B., Sokolova, A.: Generic trace semantics via coinduction. Logical Methods in Computer Science 3(4:11), 1–36 (2007)
11. Jacobs, B., Rutten, J.: A tutorial on (co)algebras and (co)induction. Bulletin of the European Association for Theoretical Computer Science 62, 222–259 (1997)
12. Kerstan, H.: Trace Semantics for Probabilistic Transition Systems - A Coalgebraic Approach. Diploma thesis, Universität Duisburg-Essen (September 2011), `http://jordan.inf.uni-due.de/publications/kerstan/kerstan_diplomathesis.pdf`
13. Kerstan, H., König, B.: Coalgebraic trace semantics for probabilistic transition systems based on measure theory. Tech. rep., Abteilung für Informatik und Angewandte Kognitionswissenschaft, Universität Duisburg-Essen (2012), `http://jordan.inf.uni-due.de/publications/kerstan/coalgpts_concur12_long.pdf`
14. Mac Lane, S.: Categories for the Working Mathematician, 2nd edn. Springer (1998)
15. Panangaden, P.: Labelled Markov Processes. Imperial College Press (2009)
16. Rutten, J.: Universal coalgebra: a theory of systems. Theoretical Computer Science 249, 3–80 (2000)
17. Sokolova, A.: Coalgebraic Analysis of Probabilistic Systems. Ph.D. thesis, Technische Universiteit Eindhoven (2005)
18. Sokolova, A.: Probabilistic systems coalgebraically: A survey. Theoretical Computer Science 412(38), 5095–5110 (2011); cMCS Tenth Anniversary Meeting
19. van Breugel, F., Worrell, J.: Approximating and computing behavioural distances in probabilistic transition systems. Theoretical Computer Science 360, 373–385 (2005)
20. van Breugel, F., Worrell, J.: A behavioural pseudometric for probabilistic transition systems. Theoretical Computer Science 331, 115–142 (2005)
21. Viglizzo, I.D.: Final Sequences and Final Coalgebras for Measurable Spaces. In: Fiadeiro, J.L., Harman, N.A., Roggenbach, M., Rutten, J. (eds.) CALCO 2005. LNCS, vol. 3629, pp. 395–407. Springer, Heidelberg (2005)

Modeling Interval Order Structures with Partially Commutative Monoids*

Ryszard Janicki, Xiang Yin, and Nadezhda Zubkova

Department of Computing and Software, McMaster University,
Hamilton, Canada L8S 4K1
{janicki,yinx5,zubkovna}@mcmaster.ca

Abstract. *Interval order structures* are useful tools to model abstract concurrent histories, i.e. sets of equivalent system runs, when system runs are modeled with *interval orders*. The paper shows how interval order structures can be modeled by *partially commutative monoids*, called *interval traces*.

1 Introduction

Most observational semantics of concurrent systems are defined either in terms of sequences (i.e. total orders) or step-sequences (i.e. stratified orders). When concurrent histories are fully described by *causality relations*, i.e. *partial orders*, Mazurkiewicz traces [2,15,16] allow a representation of the entire partial order by a single sequence (plus *independency* relation), which provides a simple and elegant connection between observational and process semantics of concurrent systems. Other relevant observations can be derived as just stratified or interval extensions of appropriate partial orders.

However when we want to model both causality and "not later than" relationship, we have to use *stratified order structures* [2,15], when *all* observations are step-sequences, or *interval order structures* [13,9], when *all* observations are interval orders.

Comtraces [8] allow a representation of stratified order structures by single step-sequences (with appropriate *simultaneity* and *serializability* relations).

It was argued by Wiener in 1914 [19] (and later more formally in [7]) that any execution that can be observed by a single observer must be an interval order. It implies that the most precise observational semantics is defined in terms of interval orders. However generating interval orders directly is problematic for most models of concurrency. Unfortunately, the only feasible sequence representation of interval order is by using sequences of *beginnings* and *endings* of events involved [3,7].

The goal of this paper is to provide a monoid based model that would allow a single sequence of beginning and endings (enriched with appropriate *simultaneity* and *serializability* relations) to represent the entire *stratified order structures* as well as all equivalent interval order observations. This will be done by introducing the concept of *interval traces*, a mixture of ideas from both Mazurkiewicz traces [2] and comtraces [8], and proving that each interval trace uniquely determines an interval order structure.

For details regarding order structures models of concurrency and more adequate references the reader is referenced to [4,5,12].

* Partially supported by NSERC Grant of Canada, ORF Grant of Ontario, and McMaster Centre for Safety-Critical Software Certification.

M. Koutny and I. Ulidowski (Eds.): CONCUR 2012, LNCS 7454, pp. 425–439, 2012.

2 Partial Orders and Mazurkiewicz Traces

In this section, we recall some well-known mathematical concepts, notations and results that will be used frequently in this paper.

Definition 1. *A relation* $< \subseteq X \times X$ *is a (strict)* partial order *if it is irreflexive and transitive, i.e. for all* $a,c,b \in X$, $a \not< a$ *and* $a < b < c \implies a < c$. *We also define:*

$$a \frown_< b \overset{df}{\iff} \neg(a<b) \wedge \neg(b<a) \wedge a \neq b,$$
$$a <^\frown b \overset{df}{\iff} a < b \vee a \frown_< b.$$

Note that $a \frown_< b$ *means* a *and* b *are* incomparable *(w.r.t.* $<$*) elements of* X. □

Let $<$ be a partial order on a set X. Then:

1. $<$ is *total* if $\frown_< = \emptyset$. In other words, for all $a,b \in X$, $a < b \vee b < a \vee a = b$. For clarity, we will reserve the symbol $\lhd$ to denote total orders;
2. $<$ is *stratified* if $a \frown_< b \frown_< c \implies a \frown_< c \vee a = c$, i.e., the relation $\frown_< \cup\, id_X$, where id_X is the identity on X, is an equivalence relation on X;
3. $<$ is *interval* if for all $a,b,c,d \in X$, $a < c \wedge b < d \implies a < d \vee b < c$, i.e., $<$ has no restriction that is isomorphic to $<_4$ from Figure 1.

It is clear from these definitions that every total order is stratified and every stratified order is interval. The following simple concept will often be used in this paper.

Definition 2. *For a relation* $R \subseteq X \times X$*, any relation* $Q \subseteq X \times X$ *is an* extension *of* R *if* $R \subseteq Q$. □

For convenience, we define $\mathsf{Total}(<) \overset{df}{=} \{\lhd \subseteq X \times X \mid \lhd \text{ is a total order and } < \subseteq \lhd\}$.

In other words, the set $\mathsf{Total}(<)$ consists of all the *total order extensions* of $<$.

By Szpilrajn's Theorem [18], we know that every partial order $<$ is uniquely represented by the the set $\mathsf{Total}(<)$. Szpilrajn's Theorem can be stated as follows:

Theorem 1 (Szpilrajn [18]). *For every partial order* $<$, $< = \bigcap_{\lhd \in \mathsf{Total}(<)} \lhd$. □

For the interval orders, the name and intuition follow from Fishburn's Theorem:

Theorem 2 (Fishburn [3]). *A partial order* $<$ *on* X *is* interval *iff there exists a total order* $\lhd$ *on some* T *and two mappings* $B,E : X \to T$ *such that for all* $x,y \in X$,

1. $B(x) \lhd E(x)$ *2.* $x < y \iff E(x) \lhd B(y)$ □

Usually $B(x)$ is interpreted as the beginning and $E(x)$ as the end of an *interval* x. The intuition of Fishburn's theorem is illustrated in Figure 1 with $<_3$ and $\lhd_3$. For all $x,y \in \{a,b,c,d\}$, we have $B(x) \lhd_3 E(x)$ and $x <_3 y \iff E(x) \lhd_3 B(y)$. For better readability in the future we will skip parentheses in $B(x)$ and $E(x)$, and just write Bx and Ex.

A triple $(X, *, \mathbb{1})$, where X is a set, $*$ is a total binary operation on X, and $\mathbb{1} \in X$, is called a *monoid*, if for all $a,b,c \in X$, $(a*b)*c = a*(b*c)$, $a * \mathbb{1} = \mathbb{1} * a = a$.

An equivalence relation $\sim \subseteq X \times X$ is a *congruence* in the monoid $(X,*,\mathbb{1})$ if for all $a_1,a_2,b_1,b_2 \in X$, $a_1 \sim b_1 \wedge a_2 \sim b_2 \Rightarrow (a_1 * a_2) \sim (b_1 * b_2)$. Traditionally, $[a]_\sim$ (or just $[a]$) will denote the equivalence class containing a.

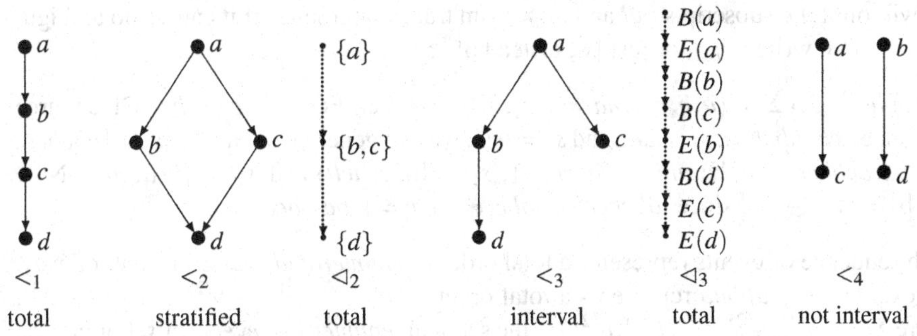

Fig. 1. Various types of partial orders (represented as Hasse diagrams). The partial order $<_1$ is an extension of $<_2$, $<_2$ is an extension of $<_3$, and $<_3$ is and extension of $<_4$. Note that order $<_1$, being total, is uniquely represented by a sequence $abcd$, the stratified order $<_2$ is uniquely represented by a step sequence $\{a\}\{b,c\}\{d\}$, and the interval order $<_3$ is (*not* uniquely) represented by a sequence that represents $\lhd_3$, i.e. $B(a)E(a)B(b)B(c)E(b)B(d)E(c)E(d)$.

The triple $(X/\sim, \circledast, [\mathbb{1}])$, where $[a] \circledast [b] = [a * b]$, is called the *quotient monoid* of $(X, *, 1)$ under the congruence $\sim$. The symbols $*$ and $\circledast$ are often omitted if this does not lead to any discrepancy.

Let $M = (X, *, \mathbb{1})$ be a *monoid* and let $EQ = \{ x_i = y_i \mid x_i, y_i \in X,\ i = 1, \ldots, n \}$ be a finite set of *equations*. Define $\equiv_{EQ}$ (or just $\equiv$) to be the *least congruence* on M satisfying, $x_i = y_i \implies x_i \equiv_{EQ} y_i$, for each equation $x_i = y_i \in EQ$. We call the relation $\equiv_{EQ}$ the *congruence defined by EQ*, or *EQ-congruence*.

The *quotient monoid* $M_{\equiv_{EQ}} = (X/\equiv_{EQ}, \circledast, [\mathbb{1}])$, where $[x] \circledast [y] = [x * y]$, is called an *equational monoid* (see [10,14] for more details).

Monoids of *Mazurkiewicz traces* (or *traces*) (cf. [2,15]) are *equational monoids over sequences*. The theory of traces has been utilized to tackle problems from quite diverse areas including combinatorics, graph theory, algebra, logic and, especially concurrency theory [2,15]. Applications of traces in concurrency theory are originated from the fact that traces are *sequence representation of partial orders*, which gives traces the ability to model "true concurrency" semantics. We will now recall the definition of a *trace monoid*.

Definition 3 ([2,15]). *Let $M = (\Sigma^*, *, \lambda)$ be the* free monoid *generated by Σ, and let the relation $ind \subseteq \Sigma \times \Sigma$ be an irreflexive and symmetric relation (called* independency*), and $EQ = \{ab = ba \mid (a,b) \in ind\}$. Let $\equiv_{ind}$, called* trace congruence*, be the congruence defined by EQ. Then the equational monoid $M_{\equiv_{ind}} = (\Sigma^*/\equiv_{ind}, \circledast, [\lambda])$ is a monoid of* traces. *The pair (Σ, ind) is called a* trace alphabet. □

The following folklore result (see for example [10] for a proof) allows us to define the congruence $\equiv_{ind}$ explicitly.

Proposition 1. *For every monoid of traces the congruence $\equiv_{ind}$ can be defined explicitly as the reflexive and transitive closure of the relation $\approx$, i.e. $\equiv = \approx^*$, where $\approx \subseteq \Sigma^* \times \Sigma^*$, and*

$$x \approx y \iff \exists\, x_1, x_2 \in \Sigma^*.\ \exists\, (u = v) \in EQ.\ x = x_1 * u * x_2 \wedge y = x_1 * v * x_2.$$ □

We will omit the subscripts *ind* and $\equiv_{sim}$ from trace congruence if it causes no ambiguity, and often write $[x]_{ind}$, or just $[x]$, instead of $[x]_{\equiv_{ind}}$.

Example 1. Let $\Sigma = \{a,b,c\}$, $ind = \{(b,c),(c,b)\}$, i.e., $EQ = \{\ bc = cb\ \}$. Given three sequences $s = abcbca$, $s_1 = abc$ and $s_2 = bca$, we can generate the traces $[s] = \{abcbca, abccba, acbbca, acbcba, abbcca, accbba\}$, $[s_1] = \{abc, acb\}$ and $[s_2] = \{bca, cba\}$. Note that $[s] = [s_1] \circledast [s_2]$ since $[abcbca] = [abc] \circledast [bca] = [abc * bca]$. □

Each sequence of events represents a total order of *enumerated events* in a natural way. For example $s = abbaa$ represents a total order: $a^{(1)} \rightarrow b^{(1)} \rightarrow b^{(2)} \rightarrow a^{(2)} \rightarrow a^{(3)}$, where $\widehat{\Sigma}_s = \{a^{(1)}, a^{(2)}, a^{(3)}, b^{(1)}, b^{(2)}\}$ is the set of all *enumerated events* of s. For precise definitions see for example [8], here we will be using the following notation.

Definition 4. *1. For each set of events Σ, let $\widehat{\Sigma} = \{a^{(i)} \mid a \in \Sigma, i = 1,2,...,\infty\}$.*

2. *For each sequence $s \in \Sigma^*$, let $\hat{s} \in \widehat{\Sigma}^*$ denote its enumerated representation. For example if $s = abbaa$ then $\hat{s} = a^{(1)}b^{(1)}b^{(2)}a^{(2)}a^{(3)}$.*
3. *For each sequence $s \in \Sigma^*$, $\widehat{\Sigma}_s$ denotes the set of all* enumerated events *of s.*
4. *For each trace $[s]$, we define $\widehat{\Sigma}_{[s]} = \widehat{\Sigma}_s$.* □

Each trace represents a finite partial order in the following sense. For the trace $[s]$ from Example 1, we have $\widehat{\Sigma}_{[s]} = \{a^{(1)}, b^{(1)}, c^{(1)}, b^{(2)}, c^{(2)}, a^{(2)}\}$.

The partially ordered set $(\widehat{\Sigma}_{[s]}, <_{[s]})$ represented by $[s]$ is depicted as Hasse diagram on the right. In fact, the total orders induced by the elements of $[s]$ comprise *all* the total extensions of $<_{[s]}$ (see [15,16]), which by Theorem 1 implies that $[s]$ *uniquely determines* the partial order $<_{[s]}$ (called *occurrence graph* in [16]).

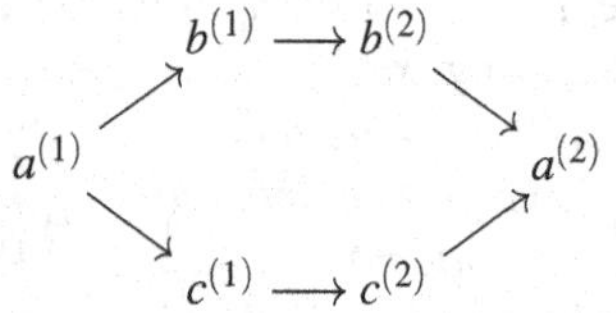

3 Interval Order Structures and Their Partial Order Representations

Interval order structures provide a more general formalism for analysis of concurrent systems than partial orders and stratified order structures, as discussed in [9]. The main goal of this section is to show that each interval trace uniquely determines an interval order structure.

Definition 5 ([6,13]). *An* interval order structure *is a relational structure $S = (X, \prec, \sqsubset)$, such that for all $a,b,c,d \in X$:*

I1: $a \not\sqsubset a$	*I4:* $a \prec b \sqsubset c \vee a \sqsubset b \prec c \Longrightarrow a \sqsubset c$
I2: $a \prec b \Longrightarrow a \sqsubset b$	*I5:* $a \prec b \sqsubset c \prec d \Longrightarrow a \prec d$
I3: $a \prec b \prec c \Longrightarrow a \prec c$	*I6:* $a \sqsubset b \prec c \sqsubset d \Longrightarrow a \sqsubset d \vee a = d$. □

Interval order structures were introduced in [13][1] and rediscovered independently in [6]. Some of their properties have been presented in [9], yet their theory is not as well-developed and much less often applied than for instance simpler stratified order structures (c.f. [4,8,11,14]), not to mention just plain partial orders.

In this model the *causality* relation $\prec$ represents the "earlier than" relationship, and the *weak causality* relation $\sqsubset$ represents the "not later than" relationship but under the assumption that the system runs are interval orders. The relation $\prec$ is always a partial order, while the relation $\sqsubset$ may not. The main interpretational difference between interval order structures and stratified order structures is that for the latter it is assumed that the systems runs are modeled with stratified orders.

From Definition 5 we can get immediately that $\prec$ is a partial order, and if $<$ is an interval order on X, then $(X,<,<^\frown)$ is an interval order structure, i.e. interval orders can be interpreted as simple instances of interval order structures.

Definition 6 **([9])**

1. *An interval order* $<$ *on* X *is an* interval extension *of an interval order structure* $S=(X,\prec,\sqsubset)$ *if* $\prec\subseteq<$ *and* $\sqsubset\subseteq<^\frown$, *i.e. if* $<$ *is an extension of* $\prec$ *and* $<^\frown$ *is an extension of* $\sqsubset$.
2. *The set of all interval extensions of* S *will be denoted by* $\mathsf{Interv}(S)$. □

Theorem 1 states that each partial order is uniquely represented by its set of total extensions, we have the similar relationship between interval order structures and interval orders.

Theorem 3 **([9]).** *For each interval order structure* $S=(X,\prec,\sqsubset)$, *we have*

$$S=\left(X,\bigcap_{<\in\mathsf{Interv}(S)}<,\bigcap_{<\in\mathsf{Interv}(S)}<^\frown\right).$$ □

The above theorem is a generalization of Szpilrajn's Theorem to interval order structures. It is interpreted as the proof of the claim that interval order structures uniquely represent sets of equivalent system runs, provided that the system's operational semantics can be fully described in terms of interval orders (see [4,9] for details).

An example of a simple interval order structure which illustrates the main ideas behind this concept is shown in Figure 2. The orders $<_1$ and $<_2$ are total, $<_3$ and $<_4$ are stratified and $<_5$ is interval but not stratified. The elements of $\mathsf{Interv}(S_P)$ are all equivalent runs (executions) of the program P and the net N_P involving the actions a, b, c and d, so the interval order structure uniquely defines a concurrent behaviour (history) of P (see [4] for details). In the present case $\prec$ equals $<_5$, as there are not so many partial orders over the four elements set, but the interpretations of $<_5$ and $\prec$ are different. The incomparability in $<_5$ is interpreted as *simultaneity* while in $\prec$ as *having no causal relationship*.

It turns out that every interval order structure can be represented by an appropriate partial order of beginnings and ends. We will later use this relationship to construct a monoid model of interval order structures.

[1] In a slightly different but equivalent form, with a different interpretation of the relation $\sqsubset$, and initially without Axiom I6, which was added later. Evolution of the definition from [13] is discussed in [1]. Definition 5 is a little bit modified version of that from [6]. See also [9].

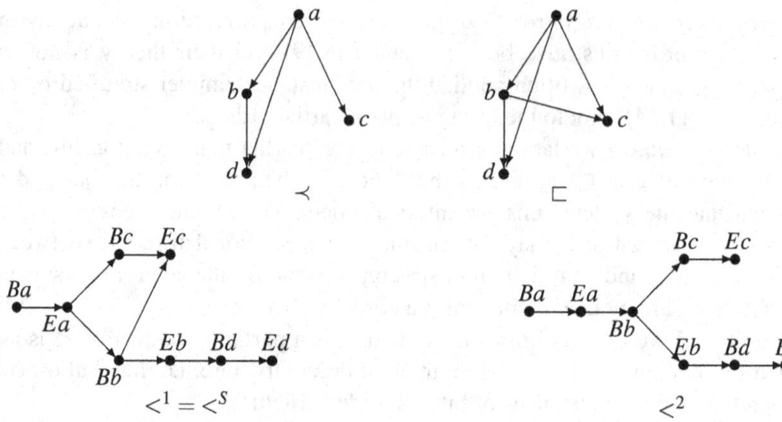

Fig. 2. An example of a simple interval order structure $S_P = (X, \prec, \sqsubset)$, with $X = \{a,b,c,d\}$. Its set of all interval extensions $\mathsf{Interv}(S_P)$ equals to $\{<_1, <_2, <_3, <_4, <_5\}$, where $<_1, <_2, <_3, <_4, <_5$, are partial orders from Figure 3. Partial orders $<^1$ and $<^2$ (in the form of Hasse Diagrams) represent the interval order structure S via Theorem 4. The partial order $<^1$ is $<^S$, the minimal partial order for S that satisfies Theorem 4.

Theorem 4 (Abraham, Ben-David, Magidor [1]). *A triple* $S = (X, \prec, \sqsubset)$ *is an interval order structure if and only if there exists a partial order* $<$ *on some* Y *and two mappings* $B, E : X \to Y$ *such that* $B(X) \cap E(X) = \emptyset$ *and for each* $x, y \in X$*:*
1. $B(x) < E(x)$, *2.* $x \prec y \iff Ex < By$, *3.* $x \sqsubset y \iff Bx < Ey$. □

Theorem 4 can be seen as a generalization of Theorem 2 (Fisburn's Theorem) from interval orders to interval order structures.

The partial order from Theorem 4 is not unique (see Figure 2), but the least partial order that satisfies Theorem 4 clearly does exist. We will denote it by $<^S$. Moreover one can show that the original construction from [1] is such least partial order.

4 Intuition and Motivation of the Model

When a concurrent history (i.e. a set of equivalent systems runs) can fully be represented by a partial order, trace approach allows to represent it by just one sequence. For instance a sequence *abcbca* from Example 1 (together with the relation $ind = \{(b,c),(c,b)\}$) defines uniquely the partial order from the end of Section 2. Any particular and legal system run can then be obtained as an extension of the partial order that represent the concurrent history.

If proper modeling of 'not later than' relationship is an issue, but possible systems runs are restricted to stratified orders, then concurrent histories can be adequately modeled by *stratified order structures* that can be uniquely represented by equational monoids called *comtraces* [8]. In this case a single step-sequence (together with appropriate simultaneity and serializability relations) uniquely defines the entire concurrent history [4,5].

Simple example in Figure 3 (originating form [4]) illustrates the difficulties of modeling 'not later than' relationship when no restrictions on the shape of system runs. Here we have a simple program P and corresponding inhibitor Petri net[2] representation of P. For this example, all possible system runs (observations) that involve all four events a, b, c, and d, are represented by the set of partial orders $Obs(P) = \{<_1, <_2, <_3, <_4, <_5\}$. The orders $<_1$ and $<_2$ are total, $<_3$ and $<_4$ are stratified and $<_5$ is *interval but not stratified*. However, to derive the observation $<_5$ is in general a non-trivial task, since the event c is executed *simultaneously* with the whole sequence bd. Classical semantics for inhibitor nets generate the set $\{<_1, <_2, <_3, <_4\}$ (c.f. [8]) at most, they are unable to generate $<_5$. The same incompleteness of observations is typical for practically any popular model of concurrency.

The concurrent history can in this case be represented by the *interval order structure* $S_P = (\{a,b,c,d\}, \prec, \sqsubset)$ from Figure 2. One can verify by inspection that $\mathsf{Interv}(S_P) = \{<_1, <_2, <_3, <_4, <_5\}$. However, how to derive S_P from either P or N_P is not clear either (as opposed to both stratified order structures [5,11] and partial orders [16,17]).

A natural solution is to use Fishburn's Theorem (Theorem 2) to represent interval orders by total orders of beginnings and ends since total orders, i.e. sequences, are easily generated in virtually all formal models of concurrency.

Our goal is to provide a monoid based model that would allow any sequence of beginnings and ends[3] that represent *any* order from $\mathsf{Interv}(S)$ to represent the entire $S = (X, \prec, \sqsubset)$. For example $BaEaBbEbBcEcBdEd$, that represents $<_1$ of Figure 3 via Theorem 2, or $BaEaBbBcEbBdEcEd$, that represents $<_5$, or any other representation of any order from $\mathsf{Interv}(S_P)$, should also be able to represent the entire interval order structure S_P (from Figure 3).

Our model will use the results and consequences of Theorems 2, 3 and 4.

5 Interval Traces

Interval traces stem from both Mazurkiewicz traces and *comtraces*, an extension of Mazurkiewicz traces introduced in [8]. The comtraces were invented to handle explicitly 'simultaneity' and 'not later than' relationships. The major innovation was to use two relations *sim* and *ser* on a given set of events Σ instead of just one. The relation *sim*, called *simultaneity*, is symmetric and irreflexive, the relation *ser*, called *serializability* is a subset of *sim*. If $(a,b) \in sim$ then a and b can be executed simultaneously, while $(a,b) \in ser$ means a and b can either be executed simultaneously, or a precedes b. When operational semantics is expressed in terms of stratified orders or step sequences, $(a,b) \in sim$ means the step $\{a,b\}$ is allowed, and $(a,b) \in ser$ means the both the step $\{a,b\}$ and the sequence $\{a\}\{b\}$ are allowed (see [5,8] for details). Unfortunately a convenient representation of interval orders by sequences, but without using Ba and Ea

[2] As inhibitor nets are now a part of popular folklore knowledge, no formal definition is given, see for instance [8], but the inhibitor arc here forbids the execution of transition b if there is a token in place s_6.

[3] A method for generating such sequences of beginning and ends needs to be defined for any specific model of concurrency, for inhibitor nets one may use for instance "3-phase-firing" construction first proposed in [20].

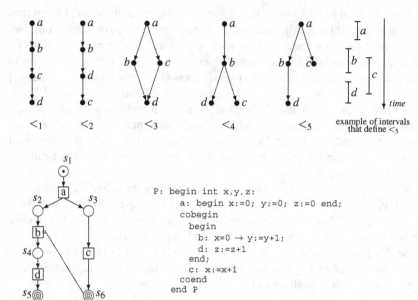

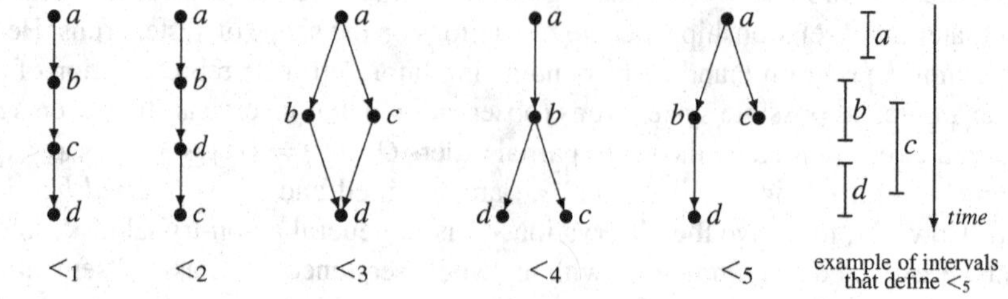

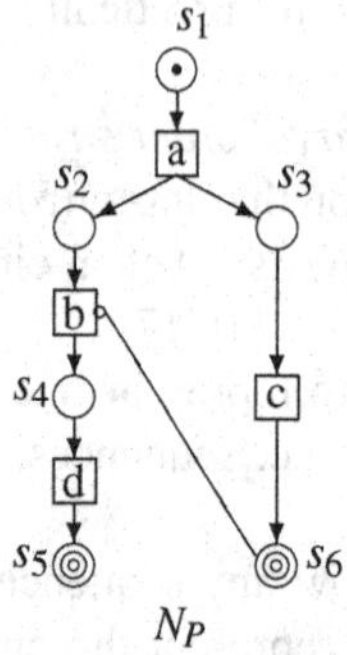


```
P: begin int x,y,z:
     a: begin x:=0; y:=0; z:=0 end;
     cobegin
       begin
         b: x=0 → y:=y+1;
         d: z:=z+1
       end;
       c: x:=x+1
     coend
   end P
```

Fig. 3. An example of a simple concurrent program P and its interval order operational semantics. The program P can also be adequately modeled by the inhibitor Petri Net N_P and partial orders $Obs(P) = \{<_1, <_2, <_3, <_4, <_5\}$ constitute its all possible observations.

concepts and Fishburn Theorem, has not been invented yet (the one proposed in [7] is problematic). When 'beginnings' and 'ends' are used to represent events, $(a,b) \in sim$ means that the occurrence Ba before Eb and Bb before Ea is allowed, while $(a,b) \in ser$ means that the occurrences Ba before Eb and Bb before Ea (i.e. a and b simultaneously), and Ea before Bb (i.e. a precedes b) are both allowed. It turns out that when events are represented by their beginning and endings, the two relations *sim* and *ser* can be represented by just one, independency in the sense of Mazurkiewicz traces.

Let Σ be a finite set of events and let $\mathscr{E} = \{Ba \mid a \in \Sigma\} \cup \{Ea \mid a \in \Sigma\}$, be the set of all beginnings and ends of events in Σ.

Definition 7. *1. A triple (Σ, sim, ser), where $sim, ser \subseteq \Sigma \times \Sigma$ are relations, sim is a symmetric and irreflexive relation, and $ser \subseteq sim$, is called an* external interval trace alphabet.

2. *A pair $(\mathscr{E}, ind_{(sim,ser)})$ is called an* internal interval trace alphabet *derived from (Σ, sim, ser) (or just* interval trace alphabet*), where $ind_{(sim,ser)} \subseteq \mathscr{E} \times \mathscr{E}$ is a symmetric and irreflexive relation defined as follows:*
   (a) $(\{Ba, Ea\} \times \{Ba, Ea\}) \cap ind_{(sim,ser)} = \emptyset$,
   (b) $(Bb, Ea) \in ind_{(sim,ser)} \overset{\text{def}}{\Longleftrightarrow} (a,b) \in ser$,
   (c) $((Ba, Bb) \in ind_{(sim,ser)} \wedge (Ea, Eb) \in ind_{(sim,ser)}) \overset{\text{def}}{\Longleftrightarrow} (a,b) \in sim$. □

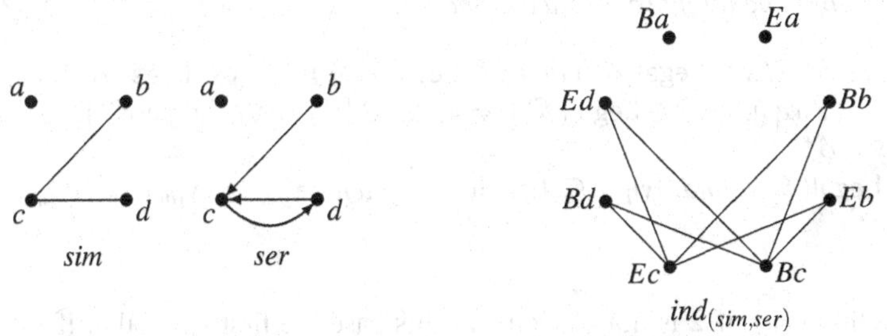

Fig. 4. An example of external and internal trace alphabet where $\Sigma = \{a,b,c,d\}$, $\mathscr{E} = \{Ba,Ea,Bb,Eb,Bc,Ec,Bd,Ed\}$

The relations *sim*, *ser*, $ind_{(sim,ser)}$ are called *simultaneity*, *serializability* and *independency*, respectively. In the rest of this paper we will usually write just *ind* instead of $ind_{(sim,ser)}$.

The first definition simply characterizes the relations *sim* and *ser*. The definition 2(a) just says that the beginning and the end of the same event are always dependent (as the end must follow the beginning). The definition 2(b) says that if $(a,b) \in ser$ then a and b may either overlap or a may precede b. The definition 2(c) is based on the observation that by Fishburn Theorem (Theorem 2) either of the sequences $BaBb$ and $EaEb$ implies that neither b follows a nor a follows b, i.e. the intervals a and b are just overlapping.

Definition 7 is illustrated in Figure 4, where the relations *sim* and *ser* represent the concurrency structure of the program and an inhibitor net from Figure 3.

Note that $(\mathscr{E}, ind)$ is still a trace alphabet, so we can apply the standard theory of Mazurkiewicz traces. The problem is that not all sequences from $\mathscr{E}^*$ can be interpreted as representations of interval orders, for example if $a \in \Sigma$ then $EaBa \in \mathscr{E}^*$, while the end must always follow the beginning.

Let $\mathscr{D} \subseteq \mathscr{E}$ and let $s \in \mathscr{E}^*$. We define the projection of s onto $\mathscr{D}$ standardly as:

$$\pi_{\mathscr{D}}(\varepsilon) = \varepsilon \quad \text{and} \quad \pi_{\mathscr{D}}(s\alpha) = \text{ if } \alpha \in \mathscr{D} \text{ then } \pi_{\mathscr{D}}(s)\alpha \text{ else } \pi_{\mathscr{D}}(s).$$

For example $\pi_{\{Ba,Ea,Bc,Ec\}}(BbBaEbBaEaEc) = BaBaEaEc$.

We can now define the subset $\mathsf{Legal}(\mathscr{E}^*)$ of $\mathscr{E}^*$ that contains all sequences of $\mathscr{E}^*$ that can be interpreted as a proper sequence of beginnings and ends.

Definition 8. *A string $x \in \mathscr{E}^*$ is a legal sequence iff*

$$\forall a,b \in \Sigma,\ (a,b) \notin sim \iff \pi_{\{Ba,Ea,Bb,Eb\}}(x) \in (BaEa \cup BbEb)^*.$$

We use $\mathsf{Legal}(\mathscr{E}^*)$ *to denote the set of all legal sequences of* $\mathscr{E}^*$. □

For example the string $BbBaEbBaEaEc \notin \mathsf{Legal}(\mathscr{E}^*)$ since $BaBaEa \notin (BaEa)^*$.

If $(a,c) \in sim$, the string $x = BbBaEbBcEaEcBcBaEaEc \in \mathsf{Legal}(\mathscr{E}^*)$, since we have $\pi_{\{Ba,Ea\}}(x) = BaEaBaEa \in (BaEa)^*$, $\pi_{\{Bb,Eb\}}(x) = BbEb \in (BbEb)^*$ and $\pi_{\{Bc,Ec\}}(x) = BcEcBcEc \in (BcEc)^*$. However, if $(a,c) \notin sim$, the same string $x = BbBaEbBcEaEcBcBaEaEc \notin \mathsf{Legal}(\mathscr{E}^*)$, since $\pi_{\{Ba,Ea,Bc,Ec\}}(x) = BaBcEaEcBcBaEaEc \notin (BaEa \cup BcEc)^*$.

It is worth noting that the set $\mathsf{Legal}(\mathscr{E}^*)$ can be easily shown to be a regular language. We will now show that legality is preserved by all trace operations.

Lemma 1. *Let $(\mathcal{E}, ind)$ be an interval trace alphabet.*

1. *For each $x,y \in \mathcal{E}^*$, if $x \in \mathsf{Legal}(\mathcal{E}^*)$ and $y \in \mathsf{Legal}(\mathcal{E}^*)$ then $xy \in \mathsf{Legal}(\mathcal{E}^*)$.*
2. *For each $s \in \mathcal{E}^*$, we have: $s \in \mathsf{Legal}(\mathcal{E}^*) \iff \forall x \in [s]_{ind}.\ x \in \mathsf{Legal}(\mathcal{E}^*)$.*
3. *For each $x,y \in \mathcal{E}^*$,*
   if $[x]_{ind} \subseteq \mathsf{Legal}(\mathcal{E}^*)$ and $[y]_{ind} \subseteq \mathsf{Legal}(\mathcal{E}^*)$, then $[x]_{ind} \circledast [y]_{ind} = [xy]_{ind} \subseteq \mathsf{Legal}(\mathcal{E}^*)$.

Proof. (sketch) Only ($\Rightarrow$) of 2 is not obvious. In this case we first show that if $s \approx x$ then $x \in \mathsf{Legal}(\mathcal{E}^*)$ and next use Proposition 1. □

The above three results enable us to provide the following definition:

Definition 9. *A trace $[x]_{ind}$ over the interval trace alphabet $(\mathcal{E}, ind)$ is called an* interval trace *if $[x]_{ind} \subseteq \mathsf{Legal}(\mathcal{E}^*)$.* □

Example 2. We can easily check that if $\Sigma = \{a,b,c,d\}$, $ind_{(sim,ser)}$ is that of Figure 4 and

$$\mathbf{x} = \left\{ \begin{array}{c} BaEaBbEbBcEcBdEd, BaEaBbEbBdEdBcEc, BaEaBbBcEbEcBdEd, \\ BaEaBcBbEbEcEdEd, BaEaBcBbEcEbBdEd, BaEaBbBcEcEbBdEd, \\ BaEaBbEbBcBdEcEd, BaEaBbEbBdBcEcEd, BaEaBbEbBdBcEdEc, \\ BaEaBbEbBcBdEdEc, BaEaBbBcEbBdEcEd, BaEaBbBcEbBdEdEc, \\ BaEaBcBbEbBdEdEc, BaEaBcBbEbBdEcEd \end{array} \right\}.$$

then $\mathbf{x} = [x]_{ind_{(sim,ser)}}$ for any $x \in \mathbf{x}$, for example $[x]_{ind_{(sim,ser)}} = [BaEaBbEbBcEcBdEd]_{ind_{(sim,ser)}}$. Moreover one can show that $\mathbf{x}$ is the set of all sequences of beginnings and ends that are generated by both the program P and the net N_P. □

6 Interval Order Structures and Interval Traces

We will now show the exact relationship between interval traces and interval order structures.

First we recall how one can construct a partial order of beginnings and ends from an interval trace. Assume that a set of events Σ and an interval trace alphabet $(\mathcal{E}, ind)$ are given. Recall that for each sequence $x \in \mathcal{E}^*$, $\widehat{\mathcal{E}}_x$ is the set of all elements of $\hat{x}$, the enumerated version of x (see Definition 4).

Definition 10. *Let $x \in \mathcal{E}^*$ be a sequence, $\hat{x}$ its enumerated version and α, β be elements of $\hat{x}$ (i.e. of the form $Ba^{(i)}$ or $Ea^{(i)}$), such that $\alpha \neq \beta$, and $[x]$ be an interval trace generated by x. Then $\lhd_x \subseteq \widehat{\mathcal{E}}_x \times \widehat{\mathcal{E}}_x$ and $\lessdot_{[x]} \subseteq \widehat{\mathcal{E}}_x \times \widehat{\mathcal{E}}_x$ are the relations defined as follows:*

1. *$\lhd_x$ is a total order such that $\alpha \lhd_x \beta \iff \alpha$ occurs before β in the sequence x;*
2. *$\lessdot_{[x]}$ is a partial order such that $\alpha \lessdot_{[x]} \beta \iff \alpha \lhd_t \beta$ for every $t \in [x]$.* □

Note that the relation $<_{[x]}$ is just the standard partial order (or dependency graph) generated by $[x]$ (treated as standard Mazurkiewicz trace), as illustrated at the end of Section 2 (c.f. [5,16]).

Now, we are ready to define an interval order structure induced by a single sequence $x \in \mathscr{E}^*$.

Definition 11. *For each* $x \in \mathscr{E}^*$, *let* $S^x = (\widehat{\mathscr{E}_x^\Sigma}, \prec_x, \sqsubset_x)$, *where* $\widehat{\mathscr{E}_x^\Sigma} = \{a^{(i)} \mid Ba^{(i)} \in \widehat{\mathscr{E}_x}\} \cup \{a^{(i)} \mid Ea^{(i)} \in \widehat{\mathscr{E}_x}\}$, *and* $\prec_x$ *and* $\sqsubset_x$ *are relations on* $\widehat{\mathscr{E}_x^\Sigma}$ *defined as follows, for all* $a,b \in \Sigma$*:*

1. $a^{(i)} \prec_x b^{(j)} \overset{df}{\iff} Ea^{(i)} <_{[x]} Bb^{(j)}$. *2.* $a^{(i)} \sqsubset_x b^{(j)} \overset{df}{\iff} Ba^{(i)} <_{[x]} Eb^{(j)}$. □

The resemblance of Definition 11 to the points (2) and (3) of Theorem 4 is not a coincidence, the triple $S^x = (\widehat{\mathscr{E}_x^\Sigma}, \prec_x, \sqsubset_x)$, is indeed an interval order structure.

Proposition 2. *If* $x \in \mathsf{Legal}(\mathscr{E}^*)$, *then* $S^x = (\widehat{\mathscr{E}_x^\Sigma}, \prec_x, \sqsubset_x)$ *is an interval order structure.*

Proof. Since $x \in \mathsf{Legal}(\mathscr{E}^*)$, then the property (1) of Theorem 4 is satisfied. Definition 11 implies satisfying (2) and (3) of Theorem 4. Hence, by Theorem 4, S^x is an interval order structure. □

We will call $S^x = (\widehat{\mathscr{E}_x^\Sigma}, \prec_x, \sqsubset_x)$ the *interval order structure* S^x *induced by a legal sequence* x. We will show that S^x plays the same role in our model as a partial order derived from a single sequence plays in standard trace theory [16], or a stratified order structure derived from a single step-sequence place the theory of comtraces [8]. To do this we need to show that $x \equiv y \iff S^x = S^y$, and that the set of interval orders $\mathsf{Interv}(S^x)$ is uniquely defined by the elements of $[x]$.

We need the following two lemmas to prove one of our main results. First lemma is quite technical one, it characterizes the relationships $Ba^{(i)} <_{[x]} Bb^{(j)}$ and $Ea^{(i)} <_{[x]} Eb^{(j)}$.

Lemma 2. *For any interval trace alphabet* $(\mathscr{E}, ind)$, *every* $x \in \mathsf{Legal}(\mathscr{E}^*)$, *and for all* $a^{(i)}, b^{(j)} \in \widehat{\mathscr{E}_x^\Sigma}$, *we have:*

1. $Ba^{(i)} <_{[x]} Bb^{(j)} \iff (Ea^{(i)} <_{[x]} Bb^{(j)}) \vee (\exists c^{(k)} \in \widehat{\mathscr{E}_x^\Sigma}.\ Ba^{(i)} <_{[x]} Ec^{(k)} <_{[x]} Bb^{(j)})$,

2. $Ea^{(i)} <_{[x]} Eb^{(j)} \iff (Ea^{(i)} <_{[x]} Bb^{(j)}) \vee (\exists c^{(k)} \in \widehat{\mathscr{E}_x^\Sigma}.\ Ea^{(i)} <_{[x]} Bc^{(k)} <_{[x]} Eb^{(j)})$.

Proof. 1. ($\Leftarrow$) Obvious.
($\Rightarrow$) Since $x \in \mathsf{Legal}(\mathscr{E}^*)$, we have that if $(Ba, Bb) \notin ind$ then a and b never overlap, so $Ea^{(i)} <_{[x]} Bb^{(j)}$. Suppose that $(Ba, Bb) \in ind$. This means that if there is $x_1 \in [x]$ such that $x_1 = uBaBbw$ and $\hat{x}_1 = \hat{u}Ba^{(i)}Bb^{(j)}\tilde{w}$ ($\tilde{w} \neq \hat{w}$ as in $\tilde{w}$ enumeration does not start from one of the symbols that are also in $uBaBb$), then $x_2 = uBbBaw$ is also in $[x]$, so $Ba^{(i)} \lhd_{x_1} Bb^{(j)}$ and $Bb^{(j)} \lhd_{x_2} Ba^{(i)}$. Hence $\neg(Ba^{(i)} <_{[x]} Bb^{(j)})$. If $Ba^{(i)} <_{[x]} Bb^{(j)}$ then the situation described above does not happen. This means there is $\gamma \in \widehat{\mathscr{E}_x}$ such that $Ba^{(i)} <_{[x]} \gamma <_{[x]} Bb^{(j)}$. If all γ between $Ba^{(i)}$ and $Bb^{(j)}$ are of type $Bc^{(k)}$, by the same reasoning as above we conclude that $\neg(Ba^{(i)} <_{[x]} Bc^{(k)})$ and $\neg(Bc^{(k)} <_{[x]} Bb^{(j)})$. Hence at least one γ between $Ba^{(i)}$ and $Bb^{(j)}$ must be equal to $Ec^{(k)}$. If $c^{(k)} = a^{(i)}$, then we have the case $Ea^{(i)} <_{[x]} Bb^{(j)}$ again.
2. Dually, by exchanging B with E. □

We will now show that the relationship between $\lessdot_{[x]}$ and S^x is a one-to-one correspondence.

Lemma 3. *For all* $x,y \in \mathsf{Legal}(\mathscr{E}^*)$, $\lessdot_{[x]} = \lessdot_{[y]}$ *if and only if* $S^x = S^y$.

Proof. ($\Rightarrow$) From Definition 11, we clearly have $S^x = S^y$.
($\Leftarrow$) (*sketch*) To prove that $\lessdot_{[x]} = \lessdot_{[y]}$ we need to show that $\alpha \lessdot_{[x]} \beta \iff \alpha \lessdot_{[y]} \beta$ where $\alpha,\beta \in \{Ba^{(i)},Ea^{(i)},Bb^{(j)},Eb^{(j)}\}$ and $a^{(i)},b^{(j)} \in \widehat{\mathscr{E}}_x^{\Sigma}$. From Theorem 4(1) we have $Ba^{(i)} \lessdot_{[x]} Ea^{(i)}$, $Bb^{(j)} \lessdot_{[x]} Eb^{(j)}$ and $Ba^{(i)} \lessdot_{[y]} Ea^{(i)}$, $Bb^{(j)} \lessdot_{[y]} Eb^{(j)}$.

We have to consider five cases, in all cases $u \in \{x,y\}$: (1) $a^{(i)} \prec_u b^{(j)}$, (2) $a^{(i)} \sqsubset_u b^{(j)}$ and $b^{(j)} \sqsubset_u a^{(i)}$, (3) $a^{(i)} \sqsubset_u b^{(j)}$ and $\neg(a^{(i)} \prec_u b^{(j)})$, (4) $a^{(i)} \sqsubset_u b^{(j)}$ and $\neg(b^{(j)} \sqsubset_u a^{(i)})$, and (5) $\neg(a^{(i)} \sqsubset_u b^{(j)})$ and $\neg(b^{(j)} \sqsubset_u a^{(i)})$.

The proofs of all five cases are similar. We provide only the proof of case 2 as cases 3,4,5 are at some points reduced to the case 2, and the case 1 is quite simple.
(*Case* 2). We have $a^{(i)} \sqsubset_u b^{(j)}$ and $b^{(j)} \sqsubset_u a^{(i)}$ where $u \in \{x,y\}$. From Def. 11 and Th. 4(1) we conclude: $Ba^{(i)} \lessdot_{[u]} Ea^{(i)}$, $Bb^{(j)} \lessdot_{[u]} Eb^{(j)}$, $Ba^{(i)} \lessdot_{[u]} Eb^{(j)}$, and $Bb^{(j)} \lessdot_{[u]} Ea^{(i)}$, i.e. only the relationships between $Ba^{(i)}$ and $Bb^{(j)}$, and between $Ea^{(i)}$ and $Eb^{(j)}$, are not described yet. Suppose $Ba^{(i)} \lessdot_{[x]} Bb^{(j)}$ and $\neg(Ba^{(i)} \lessdot_{[y]} Bb^{(j)})$, i.e. $(Ba^{(i)} \lessdot_{[x]} Bb^{(j)} \wedge Bb^{(j)} \lessdot_{[y]} Ba^{(i)})$ or $(Ba^{(i)} \lessdot_{[x]} Bb^{(j)} \wedge Bb^{(j)} \frown_{\lessdot_{[y]}} Ba^{(i)})$. By Lemma 2 and Def. 11, $Ba^{(i)} \lessdot_{[x]} Bb^{(j)}$ implies $(a^{(i)} \prec_x b^{(j)}) \vee (\exists c^{(k)} \in \widehat{\mathscr{E}}_x^{\Sigma}.\ a^{(i)} \sqsubset_x c^{(k)} \wedge c^{(k)} \prec_x b^{(j)})$. Since $\prec_x = \prec_y$ and $\sqsubset_x = \sqsubset_y$, it also implies $(a^{(i)} \prec_y b^{(j)})$ or $(\exists c^{(k)} \in \widehat{\mathscr{E}}_x^{\Sigma}.\ a^{(i)} \sqsubset_y c^{(k)} \wedge c^{(k)} \prec_y b^{(j)})$. Since $a^{(i)} \prec_y b^{(j)}$ implies $Ea^{(i)} \lessdot_{[y]} Bb^{(j)}$, it clearly contradicts both $Bb^{(j)} \lessdot_{[y]} Ba^{(i)}$ and $Bb^{(j)} \frown_{\lessdot_{[y]}} Ba^{(i)}$. Consider now the case $\exists c^{(k)} \in \widehat{\mathscr{E}}_x^{\Sigma}.\ a^{(i)} \sqsubset_y c^{(k)} \wedge c^{(k)} \prec_y b^{(j)}$. From Proposition 2 and axioms I1, I4 of Definition 5 it follows that $a^{(i)} \sqsubset_y c^{(k)}$ implies $\neg(c^{(k)} \prec_y a^{(i)})$. But $c^{(k)} \prec_y b^{(j)}$ and $Bb^{(j)} \lessdot_{[y]} Ba^{(i)}$ implies $c^{(k)} \prec_y a^{(i)}$, a contradiction; while $c^{(k)} \prec_y b^{(j)}$ and $Bb^{(j)} \frown_{\lessdot_{[y]}} Ba^{(i)})$ implies $\neg(Ba^{(i)} \lessdot_{[y]} Ec^{(k)})$, i.e. $\neg(a^{(i)} \sqsubset_x c^{(k)})$, a contradiction again. Hence $Ba^{(i)} \lessdot_{[x]} Bb^{(j)} \iff Ba^{(i)} \lessdot_{[y]} Bb^{(j)}$. Similarly we can show that $Ba^{(i)} \frown_{\lessdot_{[x]}} Bb^{(j)} \iff Ba^{(i)} \frown_{\lessdot_{[y]}} Bb^{(j)}$. The proof that $Ea^{(i)} \lessdot_{[x]} Eb^{(j)} \iff Ea^{(i)} \lessdot_{[y]} Eb^{(j)}$ and $Ea^{(i)} \frown_{\lessdot_{[x]}} Eb^{(j)} \iff Ea^{(i)} \frown_{\lessdot_{[y]}} Eb^{(j)}$ is similar.
Hence $\alpha \lessdot_{[x]} \beta \iff \alpha \lessdot_{[y]} \beta$ where $\alpha,\beta \in \{Ba^{(i)},Ea^{(i)},Bb^{(j)},Eb^{(j)}\}$. □

The following result, that belongs to the standard trace theory, characterizes the set of all total extensions of the partial order $\lessdot_{[x]}$.

Theorem 5 (Theorem 6.31 in [5], also follows from [16])
For every $x \in \mathsf{Legal}(\mathscr{E}^*)$, $\mathsf{Total}(\lessdot_{[x]}) = \{\lhd_t \mid t \in [x]\}$. □

We are now able to prove one of our main results, namely that every interval trace uniquely determines an interval order structure.

Theorem 6. *For all* $x,y \in \mathsf{Legal}(\mathscr{E}^*)$, $x \equiv y$ *if and only if* $S^x = S^y$.

Proof. ($\Rightarrow$) If $x \equiv y$ then $[x] = [y]$, so $\lessdot_{[x]} = \lessdot_{[y]}$. Then by Lemma 3, $S^x = S^y$.
($\Leftarrow$) If $S^x = S^y$ then, by Lemma 3, we have $\lessdot_{[x]} = \lessdot_{[y]}$, and now by Theorem 5, $\{\lhd_t \mid t \in [x]\} = \{\lhd_t \mid t \in [y]\}$. From Definition 10 it follows that $t = u \iff \lhd_t = \lhd_u$, so $[x] = [y]$, i.e. $x \equiv y$. □

The above theorem makes possible the following definition.

Definition 12. *For each interval trace* $[x]$*, the interval order structure* $S^{[x]}$ *induced by* $[x]$*, in defined as* $S^{[x]} = S^t$*, where* $t \in [x]$. □

Theorem 6 alone is not enough to claim that interval traces can represent all the properties of interval order structures. We also have to show that for any $x \in \mathsf{Legal}(\mathscr{E}^*)$, $\mathsf{Interv}(S^x)$, the set of all interval order extensions of S^s (see Definition 6) is equal to the set of all interval orders generated via Fishburn's Theorem (Theorem 2) from all $\hat{t}$ (enumerated version of t) such that $t \in [x]$.

Definition 13. *Let* $x \in \mathsf{Legal}(\mathscr{E}^*)$*, and let* $\blacktriangleleft_x$ *be a relation on* $\widehat{\mathscr{E}_x^{\Sigma}}$*, defined by*

$$a^{(i)} \blacktriangleleft_x b^{(j)} \iff Ea^{(i)} \lhd_x Bb^{(j)}.$$

By Theorem 2, the relation $\blacktriangleleft_x$ *is an interval order.* □

Our second main result is the following.

Theorem 7. *For every* $x \in \mathsf{Legal}(\mathscr{E}^*)$*,* $\quad \mathsf{Interv}(S^x) = \{\blacktriangleleft_t \mid t \in [x]\}$.

Proof. ($\Leftarrow$) Let $t \in [x]$ and $a^{(i)}, b^{(j)} \in$. Let us consider the relation $\prec_x$ first. We have $a^{(i)} \prec_x b^{(j)} \overset{\text{Def.11}}{\iff} Ea^{(i)} \lessdot_{[x]} Bb^{(j)} \overset{\text{Def.10(2)}}{\Longrightarrow} Ea^{(i)} \lhd_t Bb^{(j)} \overset{\text{Def.13}}{\iff} a^{(i)} \blacktriangleleft_x b^{(j)}$. Hence, by Definition 2, the relation $\blacktriangleleft_x$ is an extension of $\prec_x$. Let us now consider the relation $\sqsubset_x$. Here we have $a^{(i)} \sqsubset_x b^{(j)} \overset{\text{Def.11}}{\iff} Ba^{(i)} \lessdot_{[x]} Eb^{(j)} \overset{\text{Def.10(2)}}{\Longrightarrow} Ba^{(i)} \lhd_t Eb^{(j)}$. Because $\lhd_t$ is a total order, $Ba^{(i)} \lhd_t Eb^{(j)} \iff \neg(Eb^{(j)} \lhd_t Ba^{(i)})$. But $\neg(Eb^{(j)} \lhd_t Ba^{(i)}) \overset{\text{Def.13}}{\iff} \neg(b^{(j)} \blacktriangleleft_x a^{(i)}) \iff a^{(i)}) \blacktriangleleft_x^{\frown} b^{(j)}$. Hence $a^{(i)} \sqsubset_x b^{(j)} \implies a^{(i)} \blacktriangleleft_x^{\frown} b^{(j)}$, so, by Definition 2, $\blacktriangleleft_x$ an extension of $\sqsubset_x$ as well, which means, now by Definition 6, $\blacktriangleleft_x \in \mathsf{Interv}(S^x)$.

($\Rightarrow$) (*sketch*) Let $< \in \mathsf{Interv}(S^x)$ and let $\lhd_< \subseteq \widehat{\mathscr{E}_x^{\Sigma}} \times \widehat{\mathscr{E}_x^{\Sigma}}$ be a total order representation of $<$ via Fishburn Theorem (Theorem 2), i.e. $a^{(i)} < b^{(j)} \iff Ea^{(i)} \lhd_< Bb^{(j)}$. Furthermore let $t_< \in \mathscr{E}^*$ be the sequence representation of the total order $\lhd_<$, i.e. $\lhd_< = \lhd_{t_<}$, where $\lhd_{t_<}$ is the total order generated by $t_<$ as in Definition 10(1). Note that, by Definition 13, the interval order $<$ equals the interval order $\blacktriangleleft_{t_<}$. To show that $< \in \{\blacktriangleleft_t \mid t \in [x]\}$, we have to prove that $t_< \in [x]$. Since $< \in \mathsf{Interv}(S^x)$ then $<$ is an extension of $\prec_x$ and $\sqsubset_x$, i.e., by Definition 6, $\prec_x \subseteq <$ and $\sqsubset_x \subseteq <^{\frown}$. We will show that $\lhd_<$ is a total extension of $\lessdot_{[x]}$, i.e. $\lhd_< \in \mathsf{Total}(\lessdot_{[x]})$. To prove this we will just show that for all $\alpha, \beta \in \{Ba^{(i)}, Ea^{(i)}, Bb^{(j)}, Eb^{(j)}\}$ we have $\alpha \lessdot_{[x]} \beta \implies \alpha \lhd_< \beta$.

First note that from Theorem 4(1) and Theorem 2(1) we have $Ba^{(i)} \lessdot_{[x]} Ea^{(i)}$, $Bb^{(j)} \lessdot_{[x]} Eb^{(j)}$, and $Ba^{(i)} \lhd_< Ea^{(i)}$, $Bb^{(j)} \lhd_< Eb^{(j)}$. For the remaining four cases we will provide a proof to one case only, as the proofs of other cases are structurally similar.

Consider $Ea^{(i)}$ and $Bb^{(j)}$. By Definitions 11, 6 and Theorem 2(2), we have: $Ea^{(i)} \lessdot_{[x]} Bb^{(j)} \overset{\text{Def.11}}{\iff} a^{(i)} \prec_x b^{(j)} \overset{\text{Def.6}}{\Longrightarrow} a^{(i)} < b^{(j)} \overset{\text{Th.2(2)}}{\iff} Ea^{(i)} \lhd_< Bb^{(j)}$.

For all other three case we proceed in a vary similar fashion. This means that indeed $\lhd_< \in \mathsf{Total}(\lessdot_{[x]})$. By Theorem 5, $\lhd_< \in \{\lhd_t \mid t \in [x]\}$. But $\lhd_< = \lhd_{t_x}$, so $t_x \in [x]$, which end the proof of ($\Rightarrow$). □

Theorems 6 and 7 show that interval traces, i.e. sets of legal sequences of beginnings and ends, correspond to interval order structures in the same way as Mazurkiewicz traces correspond to partial orders (dependency graphs of [16]) and comtraces correspond to stratified order structures.

We will now show that the partial order $\lessdot_{[x]}$ equals $<^{S^x}$, i.e. it is the least partial order that satisfies Theorem 4 for S^x.

Proposition 3. *For every* $x \in \mathsf{Legal}(\mathscr{E}^*)$, $\lessdot_{[x]} = <^{S^x}$.

Proof. (*sketch*) We will show that for each $<$ that satisfies Theorem 4, and every $\alpha,\beta \in \widehat{\mathscr{E}}_x$, we have $\alpha \lessdot_{[x]} \beta \implies \alpha < \beta$. Since α and β are of the form $Ba^{(i)}$ or $Ea^{(i)}$ where $a \in \Sigma$, we have to consider four cases, but again we will provide the full proof for only one case.

Assume that $\alpha = Ba^{(i)}, \beta = Eb^{(j)}$. In this case we have

$$Ba^{(i)} \lessdot_{[x]} Eb^{(j)} \overset{\text{Def.11}}{\iff} a^{(i)} \sqsubset_x b^{(j)} \overset{\text{Th.4}}{\iff} Ba^{(i)} < Eb^{(j)}.$$

The remaining three cases are similar. □

Example 3. Let $\Sigma = \{a,b,c,d\}$. Then we have $\mathscr{E} = \{Ba,Ea,Bb,Eb,Bc,Ec,Bd,Ed\}$. Let $ser \subseteq sim \subset \Sigma \times \Sigma$ be those from Figure 4. From Definition 7 it follows that the relation $ind \subseteq \mathscr{E} \times \mathscr{E}$ is also that of Figure 4.

Let $x = BaEaBbEbBcEcBdEd \in \mathscr{E}^*$. Since $x \in \mathsf{Legal}(\mathscr{E}^*)$ then the interval trace $[x]$ is defined, and $[x] = \mathbf{x}$, where $\mathbf{x}$ is that from Example 2 (it contains fourteen sequences).

The interval order structure $S^{[x]} = S^x = (\widehat{\mathscr{E}}^{\Sigma}_x, \prec, \sqsubset)$, where $\widehat{\mathscr{E}}^{\Sigma}_x = \{a^{(1)},b^{(1)},c^{(1)},d^{(1)}\}$, and the relations $\prec$ and $\sqsubset$ are these from Figure 2, after replacing a with $a^{(1)}$, b with $b^{(1)}$, etc. The set $\widehat{\mathscr{E}}_x = \{Ba^{(1)},Ea^{(1)},Bb^{(1)},Eb^{(1)},Bc^{(1)},Ec^{(1)},Bd^{(1)},Ed^{(1)}\}$ and the relation $\lessdot_{[x]} \subseteq \widehat{\mathscr{E}}_x \times \widehat{\mathscr{E}}_x$ equals $<^1$ also from Figure 2, after replacing Ba with $Ba^{(1)}$, Ea with $Ea^{(1)}$, etc.

The set $\mathsf{Interv}(S^{[x]}) = \{<_1,<_2,<_3,<_4,<_5\}$, where $<_1$, $<_2$, $<_3$, $<_4$ and $<_5$ are interval orders from Figure 3, again after replacing a with $a^{(1)}$, b with $b^{(1)}$, etc.

Moreover $<_1 = \blacktriangleleft_{BaEaBbEbBcEcBdEd}$, $<_2 = \blacktriangleleft_{BaEaBbEbBdEdBcEc}$,
$<_3 = \blacktriangleleft_{BaEaBbBcEbEcBdEd} = \blacktriangleleft_{BaEaBcBbEbEcEdEd} = \blacktriangleleft_{BaEaBcBbEcEbBdEd} = \blacktriangleleft_{BaEaBbBcEcEbBdEd}$,
$<_4 = \blacktriangleleft_{BaEaBbEbBcBdEcEd} = \blacktriangleleft_{BaEaBbEbBdBcEcEd} = \blacktriangleleft_{BaEaBbEbBdBcEdEc} = \blacktriangleleft_{BaEaBbEbBcBdEdEc}$,
$<_4 = \blacktriangleleft_{BaEaBbBcEbBdEcEd} = \blacktriangleleft_{BaEaBbBcEbBdEdEc} = \blacktriangleleft_{BaEaBcBbEbBdEdEc} = \blacktriangleleft_{BaEaBcBbEbBdEcEd}$.

Finally note that the results would be the same if x would be replaced by any $t \in [x]$. □

7 Final Comment

We have introduced the concept of interval traces, a special kind of Mazurkiewicz traces, that can provide an abstract semantics of concurrent systems when the operational semantics involves interval orders.

It was proven that interval traces can model interval order structures in the same manner as classical Mazurkiewicz traces can model partial orders [16] and comtraces can model stratified order structures [8].

The concept and theory of interval traces stems from three sources: classical traces, comtraces and the representation theorem of Abraham, Ben-David and Magidor ([1], Theorem 4 in this paper). Like comtraces, interval traces are generated by two relations *sim* and *ser* on a given set of events, and the interpretation of these relations is the same as for comtraces. However, comtraces are sets of step sequences of event occurrences, interval traces are just sets of ordinary sequences (like classical traces) but beginnings and ends of event occurrences. Like in classical traces, the structure of interval traces is generated by a single independency relation $ind_{(sim,ser)}$ which is derived from the relations *sim* and *ser*. Technically, interval traces are just a special case of classical traces that are defined on the set of beginnings and ends of events. The representation theorem of Abraham, Ben-David and Magidor allows representing interval order structures by appropriate partial orders of beginnings and ends. We have shown that the partial order generated by a given interval trace uniquely defines an interval order structure via the Abraham, Ben-David and Magidor theorem. Moreover this partial order is the least partial order representation of the derived interval order structure.

References

1. Abraham, U., Ben-David, S., Magidor, M.: On global-time and inter-process communication. In: Semantics for Concurrency, Workshops in Computing, pp. 311–323. Springer, Heiderberg (1990)
2. Diekert, V., Rozenberg, G. (eds.): The Book of Traces. World Scientific, Singapore (1995)
3. Fishburn, P.C.: Intransitive indifference with unequal indifference intervals. Journal of Mathematical Psychology 7, 144–149 (1970)
4. Janicki, R.: Relational Structures Model of Concurrency. Acta Inform. 45, 279–320 (2008)
5. Janicki, R., Kleijn, J., Koutny, M.: Quotient Monoids and Concurrent Behaviours. In: Martin-Vide, C. (ed.) Scientific Applications of Language Methods, pp. 311–385. Imperial College Press, London (2010)
6. Janicki, R., Koutny, M.: Invariants and Paradigms of Concurrency Theory. In: Aarts, E.H.L., van Leeuwen, J., Rem, M. (eds.) PARLE 1991. LNCS, vol. 506, pp. 59–74. Springer, Heidelberg (1991)
7. Janicki, R., Koutny, M.: Structure of Concurrency. Theor. Comput. Sci. 112, 5–52 (1993)
8. Janicki, R., Koutny, M.: Semantics of Inhibitor Nets. Inf. Comput. 123(1), 1–16 (1995)
9. Janicki, R., Koutny, M.: Fundamentals of Modelling Concurrency Using Discrete Relational Structures. Acta Inform. 34, 367–388 (1997)
10. Janicki, R., Lê, D.T.M.: Modelling Concurrency with Comtraces and Generalized Comtraces. Inf. Comput. 209, 1355–1389 (2011)
11. Kleijn, H.C.M., Koutny, M.: Process Semantics of General Inhibitor Nets. Inf. Comput. 190, 18–69 (2004)
12. Kleijn, J., Koutny, M.: Formal Languages and Concurrent Behaviour. Studies in Computational Intelligence 113, 125–182 (2008)
13. Lamport, L.: The mutual exclusion problem: Part I - a theory of interprocess communication; Part II - statements and solutions. Journal of ACM 33(2), 313–326 (1986)
14. Lê, D.T.M.: On Three Alternative Characterizations of Combined Traces. Fundam. Informaticae 113, 265–293 (2011)
15. Mazurkiewicz, A.: Concurrent Program Schemes and Their Interpretation. TR DAIMI PB-78, Comp. Science Depart. Aarhus University (1977)
16. Mazurkiewicz, A.: Introduction to Trace Theory. In: [2], pp. 3–42
17. Nielsen, M., Rozenberg, G., Thiagarajan, P.S.: Behavioural Notions for Elementary Net Systems. Distributed Computing 4, 45–57 (1990)
18. Szpilrajn, E.: Sur l'extension de l'ordre partiel. Fundam. Mathematicae 16, 386–389 (1930)
19. Wiener, N.: A contribution to the theory of relative position. Proc. of the Cambridge Philosophical Society 17, 441–449 (1914)
20. Zuberek, W.M.: Timed Petri nets and preliminary performance evaluation. In: Proc. of the 7th Annual Symp. on Computer Architecture, La Baule, France, pp. 89–96 (1980)

A Polynomial Translation of π-Calculus (FCP) to Safe Petri Nets

Roland Meyer[1], Victor Khomenko[2], and Reiner Hüchting[1]

[1] University of Kaiserslautern
{meyer,huechting}@cs.uni-kl.de
[2] Newcastle University
Victor.Khomenko@ncl.ac.uk

Abstract. We develop a polynomial translation from finite control processes (an important fragment of π-calculus) to safe low-level Petri nets. To our knowledge, this is the first such translation. It is natural (there is a close correspondence between the control flow of the original specification and the resulting Petri net), enjoys a bisimulation result, and it is suitable for practical model checking.

Keywords: finite control process, π-calculus, Petri net, model checking.

1 Introduction

Mobile and reconfigurable systems are common nowadays, e.g. ad-hoc networks serve a dynamically changing number of clients, and at hardware level, some Networks-on-Chips can temporarily shut down individual cores to save power. Even the traditional concurrent systems are notoriously hard to design correctly, and designing reconfigurable systems, where the interconnect topology evolves over time, has an additional layer of complexity. Hence formal modelling and verification become an essential part of the design cycle for such systems.

Several formalisms have been proposed for modelling mobile and reconfigurable systems. The main concern in choosing a formalism is the tradeoff between expressiveness and tractability of the associated verification problems. Expressive formalisms like π-calculus [15] are Turing complete and so not decidable in general. Fortunately, the ability to change the linkage *per se* does not lead to undecidability. One can impose restrictions on dimensions like communication [1,11], control [4,19], and interconnection shape [10,11] to recover decidability.

Finite Control Processes (FCP) [4] are a fragment of π-calculus that restricts the control flow to be finite. More precisely, an FCP is a parallel composition of sequential threads. The control of each thread can be represented by a finite automaton, and the number of threads is bounded in advance. The threads communicate synchronously via channels that they create, exchange and destroy at runtime. These capabilities are often sufficient for modelling mobile applications and instances of parameterised systems, and the appeal of FCPs is due to combining this modelling power with decidability of verification [4,14].

M. Koutny and I. Ulidowski (Eds.): CONCUR 2012, LNCS 7454, pp. 440–455, 2012.

In this paper, we contribute to FCP verification, following an established approach: we translate the process into a safe low-level Petri net (PN). This translation bridges the gap between expressiveness and verifiability: While π-calculus is suitable for modelling mobile systems but difficult to verify due to the complicated semantics, PNs are a low-level formalism equipped with efficient analysis algorithms. With the translation, all verification techniques and tools that are available for PNs can be applied to analysing the (translated) process.

There is a large body of literature on π-calculus to PN translations (cf. Section 1.1 for a detailed discussion). Complexity-theoretic considerations, however, suggest that they are all suboptimal for FCPs — either in terms of size [3, 11, 12, 14] or because of a too powerful target formalism [1, 5, 8]. Indeed, the following argument shows that a polynomial translation of FCPs into safe low-level PNs must exist: An FCP can be simulated by a Turing machine with a tape of length linear in the FCP's size, which in turn can be simulated by a safe PN of polynomial (in the tape's length) size [6]. (This argument is in fact constructive, but the resulting PN would be large and ugly.)

This reasoning motivated us to look for a *natural* polynomial translation of FCPs to safe PNs, which is the main contribution of this paper. We stress that our translation is not just a theoretical result, but also quite practical: the transition systems of the FCP and that of its PN representation are bisimilar, which makes the latter suitable for checking temporal properties of the former. Moreover, we propose a number of optimisations that significantly reduce the size of the resulting nets. Finally, we perform several experiments to confirm our claim for practicality.

Technically, our translation relies on three insights: (i) the behaviour of an FCP $\nu a.(S_1 \mid S_2)$ coincides with the behaviour of $(S_1\{n/a\} \mid S_2\{n/a\})$ where the restricted name a has been replaced by a fresh public name n (a set of fresh names that is linear in the size of the FCP will be sufficient); (ii) we have to recycle fresh names, and so implement reference counters for them; and (iii) we hold substitutions explicit and give them a compact representation by decomposing, e.g., $\{a, b/x, y\}$ into $\{a/x\}$ and $\{b/y\}$.

The formal proof of the correctness of our translation and some further details can be found in the technical report [13].

1.1 Related Work

There are two main approaches to verification of FCPs. The first is to directly generate the state space of the model as is done (on the fly) in the Mobility Workbench (MWB) [21]. Scalability of this approach is poor due to the complex π-calculus semantics, restricting the use of heuristics for pruning and imposing the need for expensive operations (like equivalence checks [9]) when a new state is generated. Moreover, symbolic representations are difficult to apply.

The second approach, and the one followed here, is to translate FCPs into an automata-theoretic model that is then analysed. Although for the π-calculus several translations have been proposed, none of them provides a polynomial translation of FCPs into safe PNs. We discuss some of these below.

Montanari and Pistore translate FCPs into *history dependent automata (HDA)*—finite automata where states are labelled by sets of names that represent restrictions [16, 19]. For model checking, these automata are further translated to finite automata [7]. Like in our approach, the idea is to replace restrictions with fresh names. But their translation stores full substitutions, which may yield an exponential blow up of the finite automaton. The translation presented here avoids this blow up by compactly representing substitutions by PN markings. This, however, needs careful substitution manipulation and reference counting.

To deal with restrictions, Amadio and Meyssonnier [1] replace unused names by generic free names, and handle a π-calculus subset that is incomparable with FCPs. This translation instantiates the substitution, i.e. a process like $(\overline{x_1}\langle y_1\rangle.\overline{x_2}\langle y_2\rangle)\{a,b,a,b/x_1,y_1,x_2,y_2\}$ is represented by $\overline{a}\langle b\rangle.\overline{a}\langle b\rangle$. This creates an exponential blow up: since the substitution changes over time, m public names and n variables may yield m^n instantiated terms. Moreover, as the number of processes to be modified by replacement is not bounded, PNs with transfer are used. As the results of this paper show, transfer nets are an unnecessarily powerful target formalism for FCPs — e.g. reachability is undecidable in such nets.

Busi and Gorrieri study non-interleaving and causal semantics for the π-calculus and provide decidability results for model checking [3, 12]. The translations may be exponential for FCPs due to the instantiation of substitutions.

Devillers et al. [5] achieve a bisimilar translation of π-calculus into high-level Petri nets, thus using a Turing complete formalism. In [8], this translation is used for unfolding-based model checking; to avoid undecidability, the processes are restricted to be recursion-free — a class of limited practical applicability.

In the approach developed in [18], a graphical variant of π-calculus is translated into high-level PNs. The technique works on a fragment that is equivalent to FCPs. However, the target formalism is unnecessarily powerful, and the paper provides no experimental evaluation.

Our earlier translation [11] identifies groups of processes that share restricted names. In [14], we modify it to generate safe low-level PNs, and use an unfolding based model checking. The experiments indicate that this technique is more scalable than the ones above, and it has the advantage of generating low-level rather than high-level PNs. However, the PN may still be exponentially large.

2 Basic Notions

Petri Nets. A *Petri net* (PN) is a tuple $N \overset{\text{df}}{=} (P, T, F, M_0)$ such that P and T are disjoint sets of *places* and *transitions*, $F \subseteq (P \times T) \cup (T \times P)$ is a *flow relation*, and M_0 is the *initial marking* of N. A *marking* $M : P \to \mathbb{N} \overset{\text{df}}{=} \{0, 1, 2, \ldots\}$ of N is a multiset of places. We draw PNs in the standard way: places are represented as circles, transitions as boxes, the flow relation by arcs, and a marking by tokens within circles. The *size* of N is $\|N\| \overset{\text{df}}{=} |P| + |T| + |F| + |M_0|$.

We denote by ${}^\bullet z \overset{\text{df}}{=} \{y \mid (y, z) \in F\}$ and $z^\bullet \overset{\text{df}}{=} \{y \mid (z, y) \in F\}$ the *pre-* and *postset* of $z \in P \cup T$. A transition t is *enabled at marking* M, denoted by $M[t\rangle$, if $M(p) \geq 0$ for every $p \in {}^\bullet t$. Such a transition can be *fired*, leading to the marking

M' with $M'(p) \stackrel{\mathrm{df}}{=} M(p) - F(p,t) + F(t,p)$ for every $p \in P$. We denote the firing relation by $M[t\rangle M'$ or by $M \rightarrow M'$ if the identity of the transition is irrelevant. The set of *reachable markings of* N is denoted by $\mathcal{R}(N)$.

A PN N is k-*bounded* if $M(p) \leq k$ for every reachable marking $M \in \mathcal{R}(N)$ and every place $p \in P$, and *safe* if it is 1-bounded. We will focus on safe PNs.

Finite Control Processes. In π-calculus [15, 20], threads communicate via synchronous message exchange. The key idea in the model is that messages and the channels they are sent on have the same type: they are just *names* from some set $\Phi \stackrel{\mathrm{df}}{=} \{a, b, x, y, i, f, r, \ldots\}$. This means a name that has been received as message in one communication may serve as channel in a later interaction. To communicate, processes consume *prefixes* π of the form $\pi ::= \overline{a}\langle b\rangle \mid a(x) \mid \tau$. The *output prefix* $\overline{a}\langle b\rangle$ sends name b along channel a. The *input prefix* $a(i)$ receives a name that replaces i on channel a. Prefix τ stands for a *silent action*.

Threads, also called *sequential processes*, are constructed as follows. A *choice process* $\sum_{i\in I} \pi_i.S_i$ over a finite and non-empty set of indices I executes a prefix π_i and then behaves like S_i. The special case with $I = \emptyset$ is denoted by $\mathbf{0}$ — such a process has no behaviour. A *restriction* $\nu r.S$ generates a name r that is different from all other names in the system. We denote a (perhaps empty) sequence of restrictions $\nu r_1 \ldots \nu r_k$ by $\nu\tilde{r}$ with $\tilde{r} = r_1 \ldots r_k$. To implement parameterised recursion, we use *calls to process identifiers* $K\lfloor\tilde{a}\rfloor$. We defer the explanation of this construct for a moment. To sum up, threads take the form

$$S ::= K\lfloor\tilde{a}\rfloor \mid \textstyle\sum_{i\in I} \pi_i.S_i \mid \nu r.S.$$

We use $\mathcal{S}$ to refer to the set of all threads. A *finite control process (FCP)* F is a parallel composition of a fixed number of threads $S_{Init,i}$:

$$F ::= \nu\tilde{a}.(S_{Init,1} \mid \ldots \mid S_{Init,n}).$$

Our presentation of parameterized recursion using calls $K\lfloor\tilde{a}\rfloor$ follows [20]. Process identifiers K are taken from some set $\Psi \stackrel{\mathrm{df}}{=} \{H, K, L, \ldots\}$ and have a defining equation $K(\tilde{f}) := S$. Thread S can be understood as the implementation of identifier K. The process has a list of *formal parameters* $\tilde{f} = f_1, \ldots, f_k$ that are replaced by *factual parameters* $\tilde{a} = a_1, \ldots, a_k$ when $K\lfloor\tilde{a}\rfloor$ is executed. Note that both lists $\tilde{a}$ and $\tilde{f}$ have the same length. When we talk about an *FCP specification* F, we mean process F with all its defining equations.

To implement the replacement of $\tilde{f}$ by $\tilde{a}$ in calls to process identifiers, we use *substitutions.* A substitution is a function $\sigma : \Phi \rightarrow \Phi$ that maps names to names. If we make domain and codomain explicit, $\sigma : A \rightarrow B$ with $A, B \subseteq \Phi$, we require $\sigma(a) \in B$ for all $a \in A$ and $\sigma(x) = x$ for all $x \in \Phi \setminus A$. We use $\{\tilde{a}/\tilde{f}\}$ to denote the substitution $\sigma : \tilde{f} \rightarrow \tilde{a}$ with $\sigma(f_i) \stackrel{\mathrm{df}}{=} a_i$ for $i \in \{1, \ldots, k\}$. The *application of substitution* σ *to* S is denoted by $S\sigma$ and defined in the standard way [20].

Input prefix $a(i)$ and restriction νr *bind* the names i and r, respectively. The *set of bound names* in a process $P = S$ or $P = F$ is *bn* (P). A name which is not bound is *free*, and the *set of free names* in P is *fn* (P). We permit α-conversion of bound names. Therefore, w.l.o.g., we make the following assumptions common in π-calculus theory and collectively referred to as no clash **(NC)** henceforth.

For every FCP specification F, we require that: (i) a name is bound at most once, bound and free names are disjoint, a name f is used at most once in a formal parameter list, bound names and formal parameters are disjoint, formal parameters and free names in F are disjoint; (ii) in $K(\tilde{f}) := S$ we have $fn\,(S) = \tilde{f}$; and (iii) if $\sigma = \{\tilde{a}/\tilde{x}\}$ is applied to S then $bn\,(S) \cap (\tilde{a} \cup \tilde{x}) = \emptyset$.

Assuming **(NC)**, the names in an FCP specification F can be partitioned into the following sets: set $\mathcal{P} = fn\,(F)$ of public names that are free in F, set $\mathcal{R}$ of names bound by restriction operators, set $\mathcal{I}$ of names bound by input prefixes, and set $\mathcal{F}$ of names used as formal parameters in defining equations.

We are interested in the relation between the size of an FCP specification and the size of its Petri net representation. The *size* of an FCP specification is defined as the size of its initial term plus the sizes of the defining equations:

$$\|\mathbf{0}\| \stackrel{\text{df}}{=} 1 \quad \|\textstyle\sum_{i\in I} \pi_i.S_i\| \stackrel{\text{df}}{=} 3|I|-1+\sum_{i\in I}\|S_i\| \quad \|\nu r.P\| \stackrel{\text{df}}{=} 1+\|P\| \quad \|K\lfloor\tilde{a}\rfloor\| \stackrel{\text{df}}{=} 1+|\tilde{a}|$$
$$\|S_{Init,1} \mid \ldots \mid S_{Init,n}\| \stackrel{\text{df}}{=} n-1+\textstyle\sum_{1\le i\le n}\|S_{Init,i}\| \quad \|K(\tilde{f}) := S\| \stackrel{\text{df}}{=} 1+|\tilde{f}|+\|S\|.$$

To define the behaviour of a process, we rely on *structural congruence* $\equiv$. It is the smallest congruence on processes where α-conversion of bound names is allowed, $+$ and $\mid$ are commutative and associative with $\mathbf{0}$ as the neutral element, and the following laws for restriction hold:

$$\nu x.\mathbf{0} \equiv \mathbf{0} \qquad \nu x.\nu y.P \equiv \nu y.\nu x.P \qquad \nu x.(P \mid Q) \equiv P \mid (\nu x.Q), \text{ if } x \notin fn\,(P).$$

The behaviour of π-calculus processes is determined by the *reaction relation* $\rightarrow$ [15, 20]. It has the following two axioms for communications and identifier calls, and an axiom for silent steps (omitted):

$$(x(y).S + M) \mid (\overline{x}\langle z\rangle.S' + N) \rightarrow S\{z/y\} \mid S' \qquad K\lfloor\tilde{a}\rfloor \rightarrow S\{\tilde{a}/\tilde{f}\}, \text{ if } K(\tilde{f}) := S.$$

The remaining rules define $\rightarrow$ to be closed under parallel composition, restriction, and structural congruence. By $\mathcal{R}(F)$ we denote the *set of all processes reachable from* F. The *transition system* of FCP F factorises the reachable processes along structural congruence, $\mathcal{T}(F) \stackrel{\text{df}}{=} (\mathcal{R}(F)/_{\equiv}, \hookrightarrow, \underline{F})$ where $\underline{F_1} \hookrightarrow \underline{F_2}$ if $F_1 \rightarrow F_2$.

Normal Form Assumptions. To ease the definition of the Petri net translation, we make assumptions about the shape of the specification (cf. [13] for details). These assumptions are not restrictive, as any FCP can be translated into the required form. First, we require that the sets of identifiers called (both directly and indirectly from defining equations) by different threads are disjoint [14]. We also assume that defining equations do not call themselves. This means, if $K(\tilde{f}) := S$ then S does not contain $K\lfloor\tilde{a}\rfloor$.

We assume there are artificial defining equations $K_{Init,i}(\tilde{f}_{Init,i}) := S_{Init,i}$ that are called by a virtual initialisation step. They allow us to write the initial FCP as

$$F = \nu\tilde{a}.(S_{Init,1}\sigma_1 \mid \ldots \mid S_{Init,n}\sigma_n).$$

We assume $fn\,(S_{Init,i}) = \tilde{f}_{Init,i} \subseteq \mathcal{F}$. Substitution σ_i maps $\tilde{f}_{Init,i}$ into $\tilde{a}$ and $\mathcal{P}$, $\sigma_i : \tilde{f}_{Init,i} \rightarrow \tilde{a} \cup \mathcal{P}$. We additionally assume that the $S_{Init,i}$ are choices or calls.

3 From Finite Control Processes to Safe Petri Nets

The idea of our translation is to replace restricted names by fresh public names. Indeed, the behaviour of $F = \nu\tilde{a}.(S_{Init,1}\sigma_1 \mid \ldots \mid S_{Init,n}\sigma_n)$ coincides with that of $S_{Init,1}\sigma'_1 \mid \ldots \mid S_{Init,n}\sigma'_n$ with $\sigma'_i \stackrel{\mathrm{df}}{=} \sigma_i\{\tilde{n}/\tilde{a}\}$, provided the names $\tilde{n}$ are fresh. These new names are picked from a set $\mathcal{N}$, and since for FCP specifications there is a bound on the number of restricted names in all processes reachable from F, a finite $\mathcal{N}$ suffices. But how to support name creation and deletion with a constant number of free names? The trick is to reuse the names: $n \in \mathcal{N}$ may first represent a restricted name r_1 and later a different restricted name r_2. To implement this recycling of names, we keep track of whether or not $n \in \mathcal{N}$ is currently used in the process. This can be understood as reference counting.

The translation takes the finite set of names $\mathcal{N}$ as a parameter. The rough overapproximation $|\mathcal{N}| \stackrel{\mathrm{df}}{=} |\mathcal{R}|+|\mathcal{I}|+|\mathcal{F}|$ of its cardinality is sufficient to prove the polynomiality of the translation. The rationale is that there should be enough values in $\mathcal{N}$ to replace each bound name by a unique value. A better bound on $|\mathcal{N}|$ can be obtained using static analysis, see Section 5.

The resulting PN is a composition

$$N(F) \stackrel{\mathrm{df}}{=} N_{Subst} \lhd H(N(S_{Init,1}) \parallel \ldots \parallel N(S_{Init,n})).$$

Petri net $N(S_{Init,i})$ is a finite automaton (transitions have one incoming and one outgoing arc and the initial marking has one token) that reflects the control flow of thread $S_{Init,i}$ and explicitly handles the introduction and removal of name bindings. The transitions of $N(S_{Init,i})$ are annotated with synchronisation actions and sets of commands. Transitions with complementary synchronisation actions are appropriately merged by the parallel composition $\parallel$. Hiding H then removes the original transitions. Commands are handled by the *implementation operator* $\lhd$, which connects the control flow to N_{Subst} — a net that compactly represents the substitutions in a process and implements reference counting.

3.1 Construction of N_{Subst}

The key idea is to decompose a substitution $\{a, b/x, y\}$ into $\{a/x\}$ and $\{b/y\}$. The substitution net has corresponding places $[x{=}a]$ and $[y{=}b]$ for each component that may occur in such a decomposition. Moreover, there is a second set of places $[x{\neq}n]$ and $[r_*{\neq}n]$. They implement the reference counter and keep track of whether an input, a formal parameter, or a restriction is bound to $n \in \mathcal{N}$. Note that the places for the reference counter complement the substitution places. In particular $[r_*{\neq}n]$ signals that no restricted name is bound to n. Since at most one restriction can be bound to n, this one complement place is sufficient. There are no transitions and hence no arcs. We defer the explanation of the initial marking for a moment. We have $N_{Subst} \stackrel{\mathrm{df}}{=} (P_{Subst} \cup P_{Ref}, \emptyset, \emptyset, M_0)$ where

$$P_{Subst} \stackrel{\mathrm{df}}{=} ((\mathcal{I} \cup \mathcal{F}) \times \{=\} \times \mathcal{P}) \cup ((\mathcal{I} \cup \mathcal{F} \cup \mathcal{R}) \times \{=\} \times \mathcal{N})$$
$$P_{Ref} \stackrel{\mathrm{df}}{=} (\mathcal{I} \cup \mathcal{F} \cup \{r_*\}) \times \{\neq\} \times \mathcal{N}.$$

	p_1	p_2	…	p_{n_p}	n_1	n_2	…	n_{n_n}
i_1	○$[i_1{=}p_1]$	○$[i_1{=}p_2]$	…	○$[i_1{=}p_{n_p}]$	○$[i_1{=}n_1]$	⊙$[i_1{=}n_2]$	…	○$[i_1{=}n_{n_n}]$
					⊙$[i_1{\neq}n_1]$	○$[i_1{\neq}n_2]$	…	⊙$[i_1{\neq}n_{n_n}]$
⋮	⋮	⋮		⋮	⋮	⋮		⋮
i_{n_i}	○$[i_{n_i}{=}p_1]$	○$[i_{n_i}{=}p_2]$	…	○$[i_{n_i}{=}p_{n_p}]$	○$[i_{n_i}{=}n_1]$	○$[i_{n_i}{=}n_2]$	…	○$[i_{n_i}{=}n_{n_n}]$
					⊙$[i_{n_i}{\neq}n_1]$	⊙$[i_{n_i}{\neq}n_2]$	…	⊙$[i_{n_i}{\neq}n_{n_n}]$
f_1	○$[f_1{=}p_1]$	○$[f_1{=}p_2]$	…	○$[f_1{=}p_{n_p}]$	⊙$[f_1{=}n_1]$	○$[f_1{=}n_2]$	…	○$[f_1{=}n_{n_n}]$
					○$[f_1{\neq}n_1]$	⊙$[f_1{\neq}n_2]$	…	⊙$[f_1{\neq}n_{n_n}]$
⋮	⋮	⋮		⋮	⋮	⋮		⋮
f_{n_f}	○$[f_{n_f}{=}p_1]$	○$[f_{n_f}{=}p_2]$	…	○$[f_{n_f}{=}p_{n_p}]$	○$[f_{n_f}{=}n_1]$	○$[f_{n_f}{=}n_2]$	…	○$[f_{n_f}{=}n_{n_n}]$
					⊙$[f_{n_f}{\neq}n_1]$	⊙$[f_{n_f}{\neq}n_2]$	…	⊙$[f_{n_f}{\neq}n_{n_n}]$
r_1	restricted names are never mapped to public ones, so no places here				○$[r_1{=}n_1]$	○$[r_1{=}n_2]$	…	○$[r_1{=}n_{n_n}]$
⋮					⋮	⋮		⋮
r_{n_r}					○$[r_{n_r}{=}n_1]$	○$[r_{n_r}{=}n_2]$	…	○$[r_{n_r}{=}n_{n_n}]$
					⊙$[r_*{\neq}n_1]$	⊙$[r_*{\neq}n_2]$	…	⊙$[r_*{\neq}n_{n_n}]$

Fig. 1. Illustration of N_{Subst} with a substitution marking that corresponds to $\sigma : \{i_1, f_1\} \to \tilde{a} \cup \mathcal{P}$ where $\sigma(i_1) = a_1$ and $\sigma(f_1) = a_2$ with $a_1 \neq a_2$. The marking represents a_1 by n_2 and a_2 by n_1.

Substitution Markings and Correspondence. A marking M of N_{Subst} is called a *substitution marking* if it satisfies the following constraints:

$$M([r_*{\neq}n]) + \sum_{r \in \mathcal{R}} M([r{=}n]) = 1 \quad \sum_{a \in \mathcal{P} \cup \mathcal{N}} M([x{=}a]) \leq 1 \quad M([x{=}n]) + M([x{\neq}n]) = 1.$$

The first equation holds for every $n \in \mathcal{N}$ and states that at most one restricted name is bound to n, and there is a token on $[r_*{\neq}n]$ iff there is no such binding. The second inequality states that every name $x \in \mathcal{I} \cup \mathcal{F} \cup \mathcal{R}$ is bound to at most one $a \in \mathcal{P} \cup \mathcal{N}$. The reference counter has to keep track of whether a name $x \in \mathcal{I} \cup \mathcal{F}$ maps to a fresh name $n \in \mathcal{N}$, which motivates the third equation.

Consider now a substitution $\sigma : (\mathcal{I}' \cup \mathcal{F}' \to \mathcal{P} \cup \tilde{a}) \cup (\mathcal{R}' \to \tilde{a})$ with domain $\mathcal{I}' \subseteq \mathcal{I}$, $\mathcal{F}' \subseteq \mathcal{F}$, $\mathcal{R}' \subseteq \mathcal{R}$, codomain $\mathcal{P}$ and some set of names $\tilde{a}$, and where the second component $\mathcal{R} \to \tilde{a}$ is injective. A substitution marking M of N_{Subst} is said to *correspond to* σ if the following hold:

- For all $x \in \mathcal{I} \cup \mathcal{F} \cup \mathcal{R} \setminus dom(\sigma)$ and $a \in \mathcal{N} \cup \mathcal{P}$, $M([x{=}a]) = 0$.
- For all $x \in dom(\sigma)$ with $\sigma(x) \in \mathcal{P}$, $M([x{=}\sigma(x)]) = 1$.
- For all $x \in dom(\sigma)$ with $\sigma(x) \in \tilde{a}$, there is $n \in \mathcal{N}$ s.t. $M([x{=}n]) = 1$.
- The choice of n preserves the equality of names as required by σ, i.e. for all $x, y \in dom(\sigma)$ with $\sigma(x), \sigma(y) \in \tilde{a}$ and all $n \in \mathcal{N}$, we have
$$\sigma(x) = \sigma(y) \quad \text{iff} \quad M([x{=}n]) = M([y{=}n]).$$

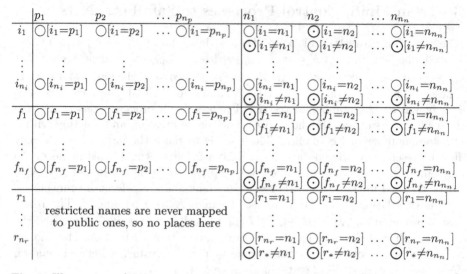

Recall that we translate the specification $F = \nu\tilde{a}.(S_{Init,1}\sigma_1 \mid \ldots \mid S_{Init,n}\sigma_n)$. As *initial marking* of N_{Subst}, we fix some substitution marking that corresponds to $\sigma_1 \cup \ldots \cup \sigma_n$. As we shall see, every choice of fresh names $\tilde{n}$ for $\tilde{a}$ indeed yields bisimilar behaviour. Note that **(NC)** ensures that the union of substitutions is again a function. Fig. 1 illustrates N_{Subst} and the concepts of substitution markings and correspondence.

3.2 Construction of $N(S_{Init})$

Petri net $N(S_{Init})$ reflects the control flow of thread S_{Init}. To synchronise send and receive prefixes in different threads, we annotate its transitions with labels from $\mathcal{L} \stackrel{\text{df}}{=} \{\tau, \mathit{send}(a,b), \mathit{rec}(a,b) \mid a,b \in \mathcal{P} \cup \mathcal{N}\}$. To capture the effect that reactions have on substitutions, transitions also carry a set of commands from

$$\mathcal{C} \stackrel{\text{df}}{=} \{\mathit{map}(x,b), \mathit{unmap}(x,b), \mathit{test}([x=b]) \mid x \in \mathcal{I} \cup \mathcal{F} \cup \mathcal{R} \text{ and } b \in \mathcal{P} \cup \mathcal{N}\}.$$

These commands maintain the name binding in the overall net. Formally, a *control flow net* is a tuple (P,T,F,M_0,l,c) where (P,T,F,M_0) is a Petri net and $l : T \to \mathcal{L}$ and $c : T \to \mathbb{P}(\mathcal{C})$ are the labellings.

Since S_{Init} is a sequential process, transitions in $N(S_{Init})$ will always have a single input and and a single output place. This allows us to understand $N(S_{Init})$ as a finite automaton, and hence define it implicitly via a new labelled transition system for S_{Init}. Recall that $\mathcal{S}$ is the set of sequential processes. We extend them by sequences of names: $\mathcal{S} \times (\mathcal{I} \cup \mathcal{F} \cup \mathcal{R})^*$. These lists will carry the names that have been forgotten and should be eventually unmapped in N_{Subst}. Among such extended processes, we then define the labelled transition relation

$$\twoheadrightarrow \subseteq (\mathcal{S} \times (\mathcal{I} \cup \mathcal{F} \cup \mathcal{R})^*) \times \mathcal{L} \times \mathbb{P}(\mathcal{C}) \times (\mathcal{S} \times (\mathcal{I} \cup \mathcal{F} \cup \mathcal{R})^*).$$

Each transition carries a label and a set of commands, and will yield a Petri net transition. We have the following transitions among extended processes.

For restrictions $\nu r.S$, we allocate a fresh name. Since we can select any name that is not in use, such a transition exists for every $n \in \mathcal{N}$:

$$(\nu r.S, \lambda) \xrightarrow[\{map(r,n)\}]{\tau} (S, \lambda).$$

Fig. 2 depicts the transition, together with the implementation of mapping defined below.

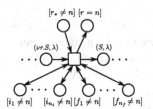

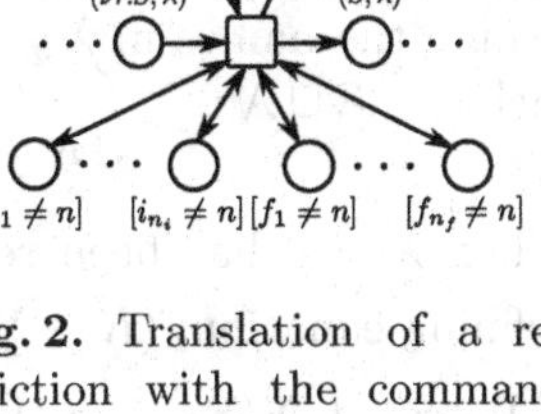

Fig. 2. Translation of a restriction with the command $map(r,n)$ implemented

Silent actions yield an unlabelled transition as expected. Communications are more subtle. Consider $\overline{x}\langle y\rangle.S + \sum_{i\in I} \pi_i.S_i$ that sends y on channel x. Via appropriate tests, we find the names a and b that x and y are bound to. These names then determine the transition label. So for all $a, b \in \mathcal{P} \cup \mathcal{N}$, we have

$$(\overline{x}\langle y\rangle.S + \textstyle\sum_{i\in I} \pi_i.S_i, \lambda) \xrightarrow[\{test([x=a]),test([y=b])\}]{send(a,b)} (S, \lambda \cdot \lambda'),$$

where $\lambda' = \mathit{fn}\,(\overline{x}\langle y\rangle.S + \sum_{i\in I} \pi_i.S_i) \setminus \mathit{fn}\,(S)$. This means λ' contains the names that were free in the choice process but have been forgotten in S. With an

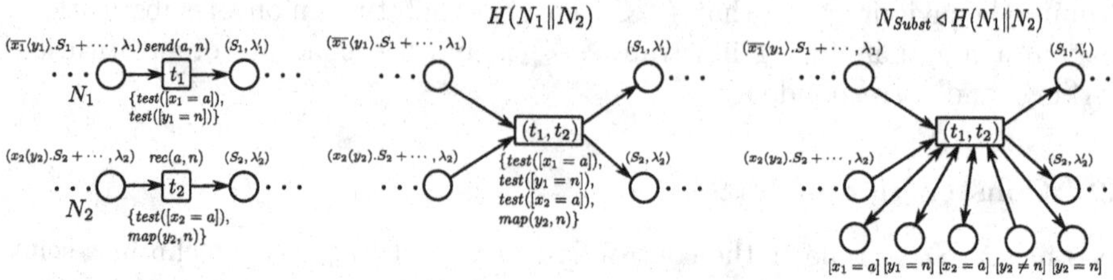

Fig. 3. Translation of communication (left), parallel composition and hiding (center), and implementation of the commands (right)

ordering on $\mathcal{P} \cup \mathcal{N}$, we can understand this set as a sequence. A receive action in $x(y).S + \sum_{i \in I} \pi_i.S_i$ is handled like a send, but introduces a new binding. For all $a, b \in \mathcal{P} \cup \mathcal{N}$, we have

$$(x(y).S + \textstyle\sum_{i \in I} \pi_i.S_i, \lambda) \xrightarrow[\{test([x=a]), map(y,b)\}]{rec(a,b)} (S, \lambda \cdot \lambda').$$

Sequence λ' again contains the names that are no longer in use. There are similar transitions for the remaining prefixes π_i with $i \in I$. Fig. 3(left) illustrates the transitions for send and receive actions.

For a call to an identifier $K\lfloor x_1, \ldots, x_n \rfloor$ with $K(f_1, \ldots, f_n) := S$, the idea is to iteratively update the substitution, by binding the formal parameters to the factual ones and then unmapping the names in λ (which will include the factual parameters). Note that no equation calls itself by our assumption from Sect. 2, which ensures that we do not accidentally unmap the just mapped formal parameters. The following transitions are created for each $a \in \mathcal{P} \cup \mathcal{N}$:

$$(K\lfloor x_1, \ldots, x_m \rfloor, \lambda) \xrightarrow[\{test([x_m=a]), map(f_m,a)\}]{\tau} (K\lfloor x_1, \ldots, x_{m-1} \rfloor, \lambda'),$$

where $\lambda' \stackrel{\text{df}}{=} \lambda$ if $x_m \in \lambda$ and $\lambda' \stackrel{\text{df}}{=} \lambda \cdot x_m$ otherwise. This case distinction ensures we unmap a name precisely once. When all parameters have been handled, we unmap the names in $\lambda \neq \varepsilon$. To this end, we create the following transitions for each $a \in \mathcal{P} \cup \mathcal{N}$:

$$(K\lfloor - \rfloor, x \cdot \lambda) \xrightarrow[\{unmap(x,a)\}]{\tau} (K\lfloor - \rfloor, \lambda).$$

When $\lambda = \varepsilon$ has been reached, we transfer the control to the body S of the defining equation: $(K\lfloor - \rfloor, \varepsilon) \xrightarrow[\emptyset]{\tau} (S, \varepsilon)$.

Petri net $N(S_{Init})$ is the restriction of $(\mathcal{S} \times (\mathcal{I} \cup \mathcal{F} \cup \mathcal{R})^*, \twoheadrightarrow)$ to the extended processes that are reachable from (S_{Init}, ε) via $\twoheadrightarrow$, and the total size of all nets $N(S_{Init,i})$ is linear in the size of the FCP specification. The initial marking puts one token on place (S_{Init}, ε) and leaves the remaining places unmarked.

3.3 Operations on Nets

Parallel Composition $\|$**.** Parallel composition of labelled nets is classical in Petri net theory. The variant we use is inspired by [2]. The parallel composition

$N_1 \parallel N_2$ forms the disjoint union of N_1 and N_2, and then synchronises the transitions t_1 in N_1 that are labelled by $l_1(t_1) = \mathit{send}(a,b)$ (resp. $\mathit{rec}(a,b)$) with the transitions t_2 in N_2 that are labelled by $l_2(t_2) = \mathit{rec}(a,b)$ (resp. $\mathit{send}(a,b)$). The result is a new transition (t_1,t_2) without a label, which carries the union of the commands for t_1 and t_2. Note that a labelled transition that has been used for synchronisation in $N_1 \parallel N_2$ is still available for further synchronisations with N_3. This in particular implies that $\parallel$ is associative and commutative.

Hiding H**.** The *hiding operator* removes from a labelled PN N all transitions t with $l(t) \neq \tau$. Since $H(N)$ contains only τ-labelled transitions, we can omit the labelling function from the result. The combination of parallel composition and hiding is illustrated in Fig. 3(center).

Implementation Operation $\lhd$**.** Consider the two Petri nets $N_1 = N_{\mathit{Subst}} = (P_1, \emptyset, \emptyset, M_{0,1})$ and $N_2 = H(N(S_{\mathit{Init},1}) \parallel \ldots \parallel N(S_{\mathit{Init},n})) = (P_2, T, F_2, M_{0,2}, c)$ defined so far. The implementation operation

$$N_1 \lhd N_2 \stackrel{\mathrm{df}}{=} (P_1 \cup P_2, T, F_2 \cup F, M_{0,1} \cup M_{0,2}).$$

yields a standard Petri net without labelling. Its purpose is to implement the commands carried by the transitions of N_2 by adding arcs between the two nets. We fix a transition $t \in T$ and a command $c \in c(t)$, and define the arcs that have to be added between t and some places of N_1 to implement c. We do the case analysis for the possible types of c:

$\mathit{test}([x{=}b])$ We add a loop to place $[x{=}b]$: $([x{=}b], t), (t, [x{=}b]) \in F$.

$\mathit{map}(x,p), \mathit{map}(x,n), \mathit{map}(r,n)$ A map command differentiates according to whether the first component is an input or a formal parameter $x \in \mathcal{I} \cup \mathcal{F}$, or whether it is a restricted name $r \in \mathcal{R}$. If x is assigned a public name, $\mathit{map}(x,p) \in c(t)$ with $p \in \mathcal{P}$, we just add a token to the substitution net, $(t, [x{=}p]) \in F$. If x is assigned some $n \in \mathcal{N}$, $\mathit{map}(x,n) \in c(t)$, we additionally remove the token from the reference counter: $(t, [x{=}n]), ([x{\neq}n], t) \in F$. To represent the restricted name $r \in \mathcal{R}$ by a name $n \in \mathcal{N}$, we first check that no other name is currently mapped to n using the reference counter for n. In case n is currently unused, we introduce the binding $[r{=}n]$ to the substitution net: $([r_*{\neq}n], t), (t, [r{=}n]) \in F$ and $\{([x{\neq}n], t), (t, [x{\neq}n]) \mid x \in \mathcal{I} \cup \mathcal{F}\} \subseteq F$.

$\mathit{unmap}(x,p), \mathit{unmap}(x,n), \mathit{unmap}(r,n)$ An unmap command removes the binding of $x \in \mathcal{I} \cup \mathcal{F}$: $([x{=}p/n], t) \in F$; moreover, in case of $n \in \mathcal{N}$, it updates the reference counter: $(t, [x{\neq}n]) \in F$. When we remove the binding of $r \in \mathcal{R}$ to $n \in \mathcal{N}$, we update $[r_*{\neq}n]$ in the reference counter: $([r{=}n], t), (t, [r_*{\neq}n]) \in F$.

Fig. 2 illustrates the implementation of mapping for a restriction, $\mathit{map}(r,n)$. Tests and mapping of an input name are shown in Fig. 3(right).

3.4 Size of the Translation

The size of the PN generated by our translation is dominated by the number of transitions modelling communication — in fact they determine the degree of the polynomial giving the asymptotic worst-case size of the PN. In the worst case, the numbers of sending and receiving actions are $O(\|F\|)$ and almost all pairs of send/receive actions can synchronise; thus the total number of such synchronisations is $O(\|F\|^2)$. Recall that for a pair of actions $\overline{x_1}\langle y_1\rangle$ and $x_2(y_2)$, a separate transition is generated for each $a, b \in \mathcal{P} \cup \mathcal{N}$. In the worst case $\mathcal{P} \cup \mathcal{N} = O(\|F\|)$, and thus the total number of transitions implementing communication, as well as the size of the resulting PN, are $O(\|F\|^4)$. However, the 'communication splitting' optimisation described in Sect. 5 reduces this size down to $O(\|F\|^3)$.

4 Correctness of the Translation

To show the correctness of the proposed translation we relate F and $N(F)$ by a suitable form of bisimulation. The problem is that $N(F)$ may perform several steps to mimic one transition of F. The reason is that changes to substitutions (as induced e.g. by $\nu r.S$) are handled by transitions in $N(F)$ whereas F uses structural congruence. To obtain a clean relationship between the models, we restrict the transition system of $N(F)$ to so-called stable markings and race free transition sequences between them. We show below that this restriction is insignificant, as any transition sequence is equivalent to some race free one.

Marking M of $N(F) = N_{Subst} \triangleleft H(N(S_{Init,1}) \parallel \ldots \parallel N(S_{Init,n}))$ is called *stable* if, in every control flow net $N(S_{Init,i})$, it marks a place (S, λ) where S either is a choice or a call to a process identifier with full parameter list. We denote by $\mathcal{R}_{Stbl}(N(F))$ the set of stable markings that are reachable in $N(F)$. A transition sequence $M \rightarrow^+ M'$ between stable markings $M, M' \in \mathcal{R}_{Stbl}(N(F))$ is *race free* if it corresponds to an identifier call $(K\lfloor\tilde{a}\rfloor, \lambda) \twoheadrightarrow^+ (S, \lambda')$ with $K(\tilde{f}) := \nu\tilde{r}.S$, to a silent action, or to the communication of two threads. We denote the fact that there is such a race free transition sequence by $M \Rightarrow M'$. The *stable transition system of* $N(F)$ is now

$$\mathcal{T}_{Stbl}(N(F)) \stackrel{\text{df}}{=} (\mathcal{R}_{Stbl}(N(F)), \Rightarrow, M_0).$$

Here, M_0 is the initial marking of $N(F)$. By the assumption on $S_{Init,i}$ from Sect. 2, the marking is stable.

Theorem 1. *The transition system of F and the stable transition system of $N(F)$ are bisimilar, $\mathcal{T}(F) \sim \mathcal{T}_{Stbl}(N(F))$, via the bisimulation $\mathcal{B}$ defined below.*

To define the bisimulation relation, we use the fact that every process reachable from F is structurally congruent to a process

$$\nu\tilde{a}.(S_1\sigma_1 \mid \ldots \mid S_n\sigma_n).$$

Here, S_i is a choice or an identifier call that has been derived from S with $K(\tilde{f}) := S$. Derived means $(S, \varepsilon) \twoheadrightarrow^+ (S_i, \lambda_i)$ so that no intermediary process is a call to a process identifier. As second requirement, we have

$$\sigma_i : fn(S_i) \cup \lambda_i \rightarrow \tilde{a} \cup \mathcal{P}.$$

This means the domain of σ_i are the free names in S_i together with the names λ_i that have already been forgotten. The two sets are disjoint, $fn(S_i) \cap \lambda_i = \emptyset$. The above process actually is in standard form [15], but makes additional assumptions about the shape of threads and the domain of substitutions.

We define $\mathcal{B} \subseteq \mathcal{R}(F)/_{\equiv} \times \mathcal{R}_{Stbl}(N(F))$ to contain $(\underline{G}, M_1 \cup M_2) \in \mathcal{B}$ if there is a process $\nu\tilde{a}.(S_1\sigma_1 \mid \ldots \mid S_n\sigma_n) \equiv G$ as above so that the following hold:

- marking M_1 of N_{Subst} corresponds to $\sigma_1 \cup \ldots \cup \sigma_n$; and
- for the control flow marking, we have $M_2(S_i, \lambda_i) = 1$ for all $i \in \{1, \ldots, n\}$.

To relate $\mathcal{T}(F)$ and the full transition system $\mathcal{T}(N(F))$, consider a transition sequence $M_1 \to^+ M_2$ between stable markings $M_1, M_2 \in \mathcal{R}(N(F))$ that need not be race free. It can be shown that the transitions can be rearranged to a race free sequence $M_1 \Rightarrow^+ M_2$ [13]. With the above bisimilarity, this race free transition sequence is mimicked by a sequence of π-calculus transitions. In the reverse direction, a single process transition is still mimicked by a sequence of Petri net transitions (that happens to be race free).

Theorem 2. *The transition systems of F and $N(F)$ are weakly bisimilar, $\mathcal{T}(F) \approx \mathcal{T}(N(F))$, taking $\mathcal{B}$ defined above as a weak bisimulation.*

These results allow one to model check temporal properties defined for F using its Petri net representation $N(F)$. Moreover, [13] explains how to check process reachability using $N(F)$.

5 Optimisation of the Translation

We briefly describe a number of optimisations of the proposed translation of FCPs to safe PNs. They can significantly reduce the size of the resulting PN and increase the efficiency of subsequent model checking. More details can be found in [13].

Communication Splitting. The size of the translation is dominated by the number of transitions modelling communication. One can significantly reduce this number by modelling the synchronisation between $\overline{x_1}\langle y_1\rangle$ and $x_2(y_2)$ not by a single atomic step but by a pair of steps. The first step checks that $\sigma(x_1) = \sigma(x_2)$; it is not executable if the corresponding values are different. The second step maps y_2 to $\sigma(y_1)$. This reduces the number of communication transitions, and thus the size of the PN, from $O(\|F\|^4)$ down to $O(\|F\|^3)$. A generalisation of this idea yields a polynomial translation for polyadic π-calculus, see Sect. 6.

Abstractions of Names. In N_{Subst} (see Fig. 1), each name is represented by a separate row of places. However, it is often the case that some names can never be simultaneously active, and so can share the same row of places.

Better Overapproximations for Name Domains. By *domain* of a name we refer to an overapproximation of the set of values from $\mathcal{P} \cup \mathcal{N}$ that it can take. While the overapproximation used in the translation is sufficient to guarantee its polynomiality, its quality can be substantially improved by static analysis, resulting in a much smaller PN. In particular, the number of synchronisations between communication actions can be significantly reduced; furthermore, the number of transitions for passing parameters in calls and the number of places in N_{Subst} can also decrease substantially.

Better Overapproximation for $|\mathcal{N}|$. The cardinality of $\mathcal{N}$ is an important parameter of the translation. A better approximation can make the translation more amenable to model checking. In fact, an overapproximation of the number of names that can be simultaneously active can be taken as $|\mathcal{N}|$.

Sharing Subnets for Unmapping Names. When we call $K\lfloor\tilde{a}\rfloor$, some names have to be unmapped in the substitution. The subnet for unmapping a particular name can be shared by all points where such unmapping is necessary. This reduces the size of the resulting PN. The optimisation is especially effective when name abstractions are used.

Using Symmetries. The translation introduces a number of symmetries in the resulting PN, as (i) the values in $\mathcal{N}$ (and thus the corresponding columns of the substitution, see Fig. 1) are interchangeable, and (ii) when an FCP is translated to the assumed form, some definitions of process identifiers are replicated. Hence, it is desirable to exploit these symmetries during model checking.

6 Extensions

Match and Mismatch. The match and mismatch operators are a common extension of π-calculus. Intuitively, the process $[x = y].S$ behaves as S if $x = y$ and does nothing otherwise, and the process $[x \neq y].S$ behaves as S if $x \neq y$ and does nothing otherwise. To handle these operators, we extend the construction of $N(S_{Init})$ with the following transitions. For each $a \in \mathcal{P} \cup \mathcal{N}$, we have

$$([x = y].S, \lambda) \xrightarrow[\{test([x=a]),\ test([y=a])\}]{\tau} (S, \lambda) \qquad ([x \neq y].S, \lambda) \xrightarrow[\{test([x=a]),\ test([y\neq a])\}]{\tau} (S, \lambda).$$

For the latter rule, new places $[x{\neq}a]$ complementing $[x{=}a]$ have to be introduced in the substitution net (some of these places already exist).

In the presence of match/mismatch, the relationship between the FCP and its PN translation is more subtle: the latter simulates the former only in a non-deterministic sense, i.e. some executions of the PN are considered invalid and do not correspond to any executions of the original FCP, in particular, false deadlocks could be introduced. For example, in $[x = y].[u = v].S$ the first guard can be true while the second is false, in which case the resulting PN will get stuck between the guards. This does not happen in the original π-calculus process. Nevertheless, such invalid executions can easily be distinguished from valid ones, and so the resulting PN is still suitable for model checking.

Polyadic π-Calculus. Polyadic communication exchanges multiple names in a single reaction. Intuitively, a sending prefix $\overline{a}\langle x_1 \ldots x_n\rangle$ (with $n \in \mathbb{N}$) and a receiving prefix $b(y_1 \ldots y_n)$ (with all y_i different) can synchronise iff $a = b$, and after synchronisation each y_i gets the value of x_i.

A polynomial translation of this extension generalises the 'communication splitting' idea described in Sect. 5: we perform polyadic communication in stages, where at the first step one checks that $\sigma(a) = \sigma(b)$, and the subsequent steps map, one-by-one, y_i to $\sigma(x_i)$ in N_{Subst}.

7 Experimental Results

To demonstrate the practicality of our approach, we implemented the proposed translation of FCPs to safe PNs in the tool FCP2PN and tested the translation on a number of benchmarks.[1]

We briefly describe the case studies; see [13] for more details. The *NESS (Newcastle E-Learning Support System)* series of benchmarks [8] models an electronic coursework submission system scaled by the number of students. The *DNESS* models are refined versions of *NESS*. The *CS* (m,n) benchmarks model a client-server architecture with one server, n clients, and the server spawning m sessions that handle the clients' requests. The *GSM* benchmark is the well-known specification of the handover procedure in the GSM Public Land Mobile Network. We use the standard π-calculus model with one mobile station, two base stations, and one mobile switching center presented in [17]. We also studied a variant of this benchmark with the sender process modified by dropping a restriction, i.e. it keeps sending the same message instead of generating a new one every time. Since the content of the message is not important, this change is inconsequential from the modelling point of view, but it significantly reduces the size of the resulting PN, as the modified FCP contains no restriction operators and so $\mathcal{N} = \emptyset$. The *PHONES* benchmark is a classical example taken from [15].

The experimental results are given in Table 1, with the columns showing (from left to right): name of the case study († indicates deadlocks), sizes of the original FCP and its normal form (see Sect. 2), cardinality of $\mathcal{N}$ determined by static analysis, number of places and transitions in the resulting safe PN, and deadlock checking time.

Table 1. Experimental results

Problem	Process size FCP	nfFCP	$\lvert\mathcal{N}\rvert$	Safe PN $\lvert P\rvert$	$\lvert T\rvert$	Dlck [sec]
NESS (04)	110	110	0	137	145	0.02
NESS (05)†	137	137	0	196	246	0.09
NESS (06)	164	164	0	265	385	0.16
NESS (07)†	191	191	0	344	568	0.45
DNESS (06)	118	118	0	157	103	0.02
DNESS (08)	157	157	0	241	169	0.05
DNESS (10)	196	196	0	341	251	0.13
DNESS (12)	235	235	0	457	349	2.27
DNESS (14)	274	274	0	589	463	1.71

Problem	Process size FCP	nfFCP	$\lvert\mathcal{N}\rvert$	Safe PN $\lvert P\rvert$	$\lvert T\rvert$	Dlck [sec]
CS (2,1)	45	54	7	138	149	1.01
CS (2,2)	48	68	10	243	320	0.16
CS (3,2)	51	80	11	284	431	1.28
CS (3,3)	54	94	14	428	728	3.67
CS (4,4)	60	120	18	663	1368	11.73
CS (5,5)	66	146	22	948	2288	46.61
GSM	175	231	12	636	901	4.39
GSM'	174	230	0	355	503	3.09
PHONES	157	157	0	131	94	0.01

[1] The tool and benchmarks are available from `http://homepages.cs.ncl.ac.uk/victor.khomenko/tools/fcp2pn`

The experiments were conducted on a PC with an Intel Core 2 Quad Q9400 2.66 GHz (quad-core) processor (a single core was used) and 4G RAM. The deadlock checking was performed with the LoLA tool,[2] configured to assume the safeness of the PN (`CAPACITY 1`), use the stubborn sets and symmetry reductions (`STUBBORN`, `SYMMETRY`), compress states using P-invariants (`PREDUCTION`), use a light-weight data structure for states (`SMALLSTATE`), and check for deadlocks (`DEADLOCK`). The FCP to PN translation times were negligible (< 0.1 sec) in all cases and so are not reported.

The experiments indicate that the sizes of the PNs grow moderately with the sizes of the FCPs, and the PNs are suitable for efficient model checking.

8 Conclusions

We developed a polynomial translation from finite control processes (an important fragment of π-calculus) to safe low-level Petri nets. To our knowledge, this is the first such translation. Furthermore, there is a close correspondence between the control flow of the π-calculus specification and the resulting PN, and the latter is suitable for practical model checking. The translation has been implemented in a tool FCP2PN, and the experimental results are encouraging.

We have also proposed a number of optimisations allowing one to reduce the size of the resulting PN, as well as a number of extensions, in particular the match/mismatch operators and polyadic π-calculus.

In future work we plan to further improve the translation by a more thorough static analysis, and to incorporate the translation into a verification tool-chain.

Acknowledgements. The authors would like to thank Ivan Poliakov for his help in producing the experimental results. This research was supported by the EPSRC grant EP/G037809/1 (VERDAD).

References

1. Amadio, R., Meyssonnier, C.: On decidability of the control reachability problem in the asynchronous π-calculus. Nord. J. Comp. 9(1), 70–101 (2002)
2. Best, E., Devillers, R., Koutny, M.: Petri Net Algebra. Monographs in Theoretical Computer Science. An EATCS Series. Springer (2001)
3. Busi, N., Gorrieri, R.: Distributed semantics for the π-calculus based on Petri nets with inhibitor arcs. J. Log. Alg. Prog. 78(1), 138–162 (2009)
4. Dam, M.: Model checking mobile processes. Inf. Comp. 129(1), 35–51 (1996)
5. Devillers, R., Klaudel, H., Koutny, M.: A compositional Petri net translation of general π-calculus terms. For. Asp. Comp. 20(4-5), 429–450 (2008)
6. Esparza, J.: Decidability and Complexity of Petri Net Problems—An Introduction. In: Reisig, W., Rozenberg, G. (eds.) APN 1998. LNCS, vol. 1491, pp. 374–428. Springer, Heidelberg (1998)

[2] Available from `http://service-technology.org/tools/lola`

7. Ferrari, G.-L., Gnesi, S., Montanari, U., Pistore, M.: A model-checking verification environment for mobile processes. ACM Trans. Softw. Eng. Methodol. 12(4), 440–473 (2003)
8. Khomenko, V., Koutny, M., Niaouris, A.: Applying Petri net unfoldings for verification of mobile systems. In: Proc. of MOCA, Bericht FBI-HH-B-267/06, pp. 161–178. University of Hamburg (2006)
9. Khomenko, V., Meyer, R.: Checking π-calculus structural congruence is graph isomorphism complete. In: Proc. of ACSD, pp. 70–79. IEEE Computer Society Press (2009)
10. Meyer, R.: On Boundedness in Depth in the π-Calculus. In: Ausiello, G., Karhumäki, J., Mauri, G., Ong, L. (eds.) IFIP TCS 2008. IFIP, vol. 273, pp. 477–489. Springer, Boston (2008)
11. Meyer, R.: A theory of structural stationarity in the π-calculus. Acta Inf. 46(2), 87–137 (2009)
12. Meyer, R., Gorrieri, R.: On the Relationship between π-Calculus and Finite Place/Transition Petri Nets. In: Bravetti, M., Zavattaro, G. (eds.) CONCUR 2009. LNCS, vol. 5710, pp. 463–480. Springer, Heidelberg (2009)
13. Meyer, R., Khomenko, V., Hüchting, R.: A polynomial translation of π-calculus (FCP) to safe Petri nets. Technical Report CS-TR-1323, Newcastle Univ. (2012)
14. Meyer, R., Khomenko, V., Strazny, T.: A practical approach to verification of mobile systems using net unfoldings. Fundam. Inf. 94, 439–471 (2009)
15. Milner, R.: Communicating and Mobile Systems: the π-Calculus. CUP (1999)
16. Montanari, U., Pistore, M.: Checking Bisimilarity for Finitary π-Calculus. In: Lee, I., Smolka, S.A. (eds.) CONCUR 1995. LNCS, vol. 962, pp. 42–56. Springer, Heidelberg (1995)
17. Orava, F., Parrow, J.: An algebraic verification of a mobile network. For. Asp. Comp. 4(6), 497–543 (1992)
18. Peschanski, F., Klaudel, H., Devillers, R.: A Petri Net Interpretation of Open Reconfigurable Systems. In: Kristensen, L.M., Petrucci, L. (eds.) PETRI NETS 2011. LNCS, vol. 6709, pp. 208–227. Springer, Heidelberg (2011)
19. Pistore, M.: History Dependent Automata. PhD thesis, Dipartimento di Informatica, Università di Pisa (1999)
20. Sangiorgi, D., Walker, D.: The π-calculus: a Theory of Mobile Processes. CUP (2001)
21. Victor, B., Moller, F.: The Mobility Workbench: A Tool for the π-Calculus. In: Dill, D.L. (ed.) CAV 1994. LNCS, vol. 818, pp. 428–440. Springer, Heidelberg (1994)

Algebraic Structure of Combined Traces

Łukasz Mikulski

Faculty of Mathematics and Computer Science
Nicolaus Copernicus University
Toruń, Chopina 12/18, Poland
frodo@mat.umk.pl

Abstract. Traces – and their extension called combined traces (comtraces) – are two formal models used in the analysis and verification of concurrent systems. Both models are based on concepts originating in the theory of formal languages, and they are able to capture the notions of causality and simultaneity of atomic actions which take place during the process of a system's operation. The aim of this paper is a transfer to the domain of comtraces and developing of some fundamental notions, which proved to be successful in the theory of traces. In particular, we introduce and then apply the lexicographical canonical form of comtraces, as well as the representation of a comtrace utilising its linear projections to binary action subalphabets. We also provide two algorithms related to the new notions. Using them, one can solve, in an efficient way, the problem of step sequence equivalence in the context of comtraces. One may view our results as a first step towards the development of infinite combined traces, as well as recognisable languages of combined traces.

Introduction

The dynamic behaviours of concurrent systems are usually described as sequences of atomic actions of such system, which leads to its formal language semantics. Using this simple approach we cannot express some phenomena, e.g, concurrency and causality, that are crucial in the process of understanding and analysing concurrent behaviours of a system. In case of a particular operational model, one can consider extending the sequential description by adding some information about the relevant properties of behaviours. One can do it by considering sequences of steps of actions and by adding some causal dependencies between actions. A well known approach that helps to capture concurrency and causality of a system are traces [1,8].

Consider, for example, the elementary net system with inhibitor arcs [13] in Example 1(a). We have four actions, a, b, c and d, which may be executed in the initial marking, and two actions, e and f, which need a previous history of computation to be enabled. Let us focus on action e. To enable this action we need to execute actions a and c. We can execute them together or in any order. To capture the concurrent behaviour of this computation we need to identify two sequences of executions – ace and cae. Using step semantics, which is not

M. Koutny and I. Ulidowski (Eds.): CONCUR 2012, LNCS 7454, pp. 456–470, 2012.

necessary in this case, we add also step sequence $(ac)(e)$ as another possible execution. Traces are sufficient to deal with such behaviours.

The situation is more complex in case of action f. Now we need three tokens in the pre-set of the considered action, hence actions b, c and d should be executed before the action f. Because of the presence of inhibitors, there is only one way to execute them sequentially, they should be executed in the order $bcdf$. Note that $bdcf$ or $dcbf$ are not correct sequences of execution. There are, however, other possibilities to execute the four actions in the step semantics. For instance all three actions may be executed simultaneously as a step (b,c,d). This gives $(bcd)(f)$ as our allowed sequence of steps. Another step sequences are $(b)(cd)(f)$ and $(bc)(d)(f)$. It is important that action d has to be executed not later than action c, and action c has to be executed not later than action b. In this case traces are still applicable, but they lose some important behavioural information.

Another case is depicted in Example 1(b). The upper part of the net is identical to the first case. Here, however, there is a single action g that waits for tokens in all four middle places. In other words, whole tuple (a,b,c,d) has to be executed before action g. It is easy to see that because of inhibitors there is no valid sequential execution of the four actions. After executing one of these action, one of the remaining becomes disallowed. The only possible execution is the step sequence $(abcd)(f)$.

Example 1. Two elementary net systems with inhibitor arcs.

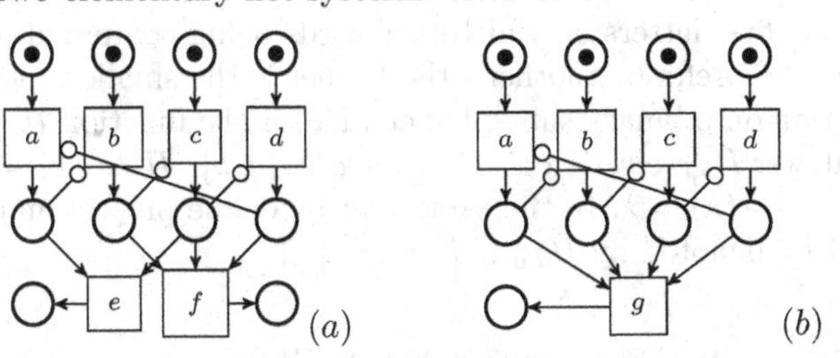

In this paper, we are concerned with the understanding of the algebraic inner structure of the combined traces (see [6]). We start by recalling some standard notions about formal languages, traces and comtraces. In particular, we give the definition of a lexicographical order on step sequences. We then recall the Foata canonical form of a comtrace that turns out to be maximal with respect to their order, and propose another canonical representative - the lexicographical canonical form. In the following sections, we propose an algebraic representation of a comtrace based on projections onto sequential subalphabets, and give a nondeterministic procedure that allows to reconstruct step sequences of the original comtrace. We also give two strategies of determining such reconstruction, each of them leading to a proper canonical form of a comtrace. In the next section we introduce and discuss this specific subclasses of comtraces – the trace-like comtraces, and weakly simultaneous comtraces. The elements of these subclasses are fully described by one rather than two relations which brings them closer to the classical notion of a trace. We link them with the general comtraces by using the notions of indivisible steps and expansion of the alphabet. In the final section, we describe some natural applications of the algebraic properties developed in this paper, and sketch the directions for further research. Proofs of all the results can be found in [9].

1 Preliminaries

Throughout the paper we use the standard notions of the formal language theory. In particular, by an *alphabet* we mean a nonempty finite set Σ, the elements of which are called *(atomic) actions*. Finite sequences over Σ are called *words*. The set of all finite words, including the empty word λ, is denoted by Σ^*.

Let $w = a_1 \ldots a_n$ and $v = b_1 \ldots b_m$ be two words. Then $w \circ v = wv = a_1 \ldots a_n b_1 \ldots b_m$ is the concatenation of w and v. The alphabet $alph(w)$ of w is the set of all the actions occurring within w, and $\#_a(w)$ is the number of occurrences of an action a within w. By $|w|$ we denote the length of word w. More generally, for an object X, whenever the notion of size is dear from the contexts, we denote its size by $|X|$.

Let $w = a_1 \ldots a_n$ be a word. We use the notions of a prefix and a suffix of the word w. For any $k \leq n$, the *k-suffix* of w, denoted by suff_k, is a word $a_k \ldots a_n$. Similarly, the *k-prefix* of w, denoted by pref_k, is the word $a_1 \ldots a_k$.

We assume that the alphabet Σ is given together with a total order $\leq$, called lexicographical order and extend it to the level of words. Such an order is inherited from the first letters on which two words being compared differ. In case that one word is a prefix of another - the former is the smaller one.

The projection onto binary subalphabet $\{a, b\}$ is the function $\Pi_{a,b} : \Sigma^* \to \Sigma^*$ defined as follows: $\Pi_{a,b}(cw) = c\Pi_{a,b}(w)$ for $c \in \{a, b\}$, $\Pi_{a,b}(cw) = \Pi_{a,b}(w)$ for $c \notin \{a, b\}$, and $\Pi_{a,b}(\lambda) = \lambda$. In the same way we define projection onto a unary subalphabet $\{a\}$, denoted by $\Pi_{a,a} : \Sigma^* \to \Sigma^*$.

1.1 Elementary Net Systems with Inhibitor Arcs

In this paper we introduce some algebraic properties of combined traces which are the abstract model that describes causal relationships between executed actions of a concurrent system. The underlying structure, which was a motivation to define combined traces, are elementary net systems with inhibitor arcs.

Formally, the *elementary net system with inhibitor arcs* (or $ENI - system$) is a tuple $N = (P, T, F, I, M_0)$, where P and T are two disjoint and finite sets of *places* and *transitions (actions)* respectively. Two other elements, $F \subseteq (P \times T) \cup (T \times P)$ and $I \subseteq P \times T$ are two relations, called *flow relation* and *inhibition relation*. These relations describe possible dynamic behaviours of a net, which are manifested by executing sets of enabled transitions called *steps*. Such an execution leads from one set of places (called *marking*) to another. The initial marking $M_0 \in P^{\{0,1\}}$, from which the action of a system begins, is the last element of the tuple N.

Given an ENI-system $N = (P, T, F, I, M_0)$ and $x \in P \cup T$, the *pre-set* of x, denoted by ${}^\bullet x$, is defined as ${}^\bullet x = \{y | (y, x) \in F\}$, while the *post-set* of x, denoted by $x^\bullet$, is defined as $x^\bullet = \{y|(x,y) \in F\}$. We also use the notion ${}^\bullet x^\bullet$ for the union of the post-set and pre-set of x, calling it the *set of neighbouring places/transitions*. Moreover, if $x \in T$, the *inh-set* of x, denoted by ${}^\circ x$, is defined by ${}^\circ x = \{y|(y,x) \in I\}$. The dot notations are lifted in the usual way to the sets of elements. Graphically, the places are drawn as circles, transitions as rectangles, elements of flow relation as arcs, and elements of inhibition relation as arcs with small circles as arrowheads. Marked places are depicted by drawing small dot called *token* inside.

We say that a step $S = \{t_1, t_2, \ldots, t_n\}$ is *enabled* in marking M if and only if ${}^\bullet S \subseteq M$, $S^\bullet \cap M = \varnothing$ and ${}^\circ S \cap M = \varnothing$. The *execution* of the step S leads from the marking M to the new marking $M' = M \setminus {}^\bullet S \cup S^\bullet$.

An ENI-system with empty inhibition relation, often considered under the sequential rather than step semantics, is called an *elementary net system* (or *EN – system*).

Example 2. Consider a system $N = (P, T, F, I, M_0)$ depicted below.

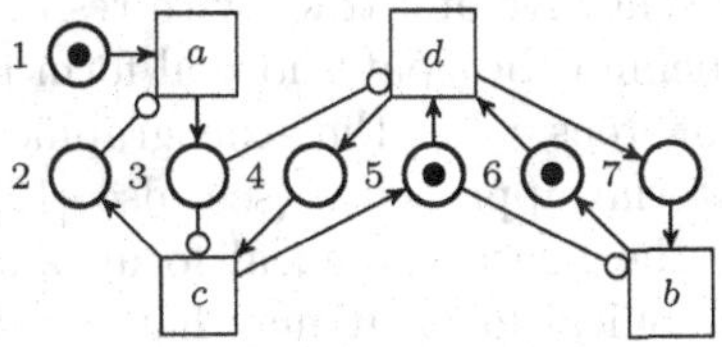

In the initial marking, three steps are enabled – (a), (d) and (ad). Note that after executing transition d, transition a remains enabled, however, after executing transition a there is a token in place 3 and transition d is no more enabled.

1.2 Traces

In this section we recall well-known notion of traces (see [4,8]). Traces are an abstract model describing causal relationships between executed actions in, for example EN-systems. They capture independence, hence the possibility to be executed in any order (and also together) for some actions. Structurally, pairs of actions with disjoint sets of neighbouring places are in the independence relation.

A *concurrent alphabet* is a pair $\Psi = (\Sigma, dep)$, where Σ is an alphabet and $dep \subseteq \Sigma \times \Sigma$ is a reflexive and symmetric *dependence* relation. The corresponding *independence* relation is given by $ind = (\Sigma \times \Sigma) \setminus dep$.

A concurrent alphabet Ψ defines an equivalence relation $\equiv_\Psi$ identifying words which differ only by the ordering of independent actions. Two words, $w, v \in \Sigma^*$, satisfy $w \equiv_\Psi v$ if there exists a finite sequence of commutations of adjacent independent actions transforming w into v. More precisely, $\equiv_\Psi$ is a binary relation over Σ^* which is the reflexive and transitive closure of the relation $\sim_\Psi$ such that $w \sim_\Psi v$ if there are $u, z \in \Sigma^*$ and $(a,b) \in ind$ satisfying $w = uabz$ and $v = ubaz$.

Equivalence classes of $\equiv_\Psi$ are called *(Mazurkiewicz) traces* (see [4,8,10]), and the trace containing a given word w is denoted by $[w]$. The set of all traces over Ψ is denoted by $\Sigma^*/_{\equiv_\Psi}$, and the pair $(\Sigma^*/_{\equiv_\Psi}, \circ)$ is a (trace) monoid, where

$\tau \circ \tau' = [w \circ w']$, for any words $w \in \tau$ and $w' \in \tau'$, is the concatenation operation for traces. Note that trace concatenation is well-defined as $[w \circ w'] = [v \circ v']$, for all $w, v \in \tau$ and $w', v' \in \tau'$. Similarly, for every trace $\tau = [w]$ and every action $a \in \Sigma$, we can define $alph(\tau) = alph(w)$ and $\#_a(\tau) = \#_a(w)$.

Projections onto unary binary dependent subalphabets (i.e. $\{a, b\}$ such that $(a, b) \in dep$) are invariants for traces. Moreover, two words $u, w \in \Sigma^*$ are in relation $\equiv_\Psi$ if and only if $\forall_{(a,b)\in dep}\ \Pi_{a,b}(u) = \Pi_{a,b}(w)$. Following [10], we define the *projection representation* of a trace τ as a function $\Pi_\tau : dep \to \Sigma^*$, where $\Pi_\tau(a, b) = \Pi_{a,b}(\tau)$.

A word $w \in \Sigma^*$ is in *Foata canonical form* (see [3]) w.r.t. the dependence relation *dep* and a lexicographical order $\leq$ on Σ, if $w = w_1 \dots w_n$ $(n \geq 0)$, where each w_i is a nonempty word such that $alph(w_i)$ is pairwise independent and w_i minimal w.r.t. lexicographical order $\leq$ among $[w_i]$, and for each $i > 1$ and a occurring in w_i, there is b occurring in w_{i-1} such that $(a, b) \in dep$.

Another canonical form of a trace that one may consider is the *lexicographical canonical form* (see also [3]). It is based only on the lexicographical order and is defined as the least representative of a trace with respect to the lexicographical ordering. The intuition behind the Foata normal form is that it groups actions into maximally concurrent steps, while the lexicographical canonical form is very useful in some combinatorial approaches (see also [12]). Each trace contains exactly one sequence in the Foata canonical form, and exactly one sequence in the lexicographical canonical form. It may happen that the two versions of canonical form coincide.

1.3 Comtraces

Whereas traces are good to describe the concurrent behaviour of EN-systems, they are not sufficient to capture the behaviour of systems with inhibitor arcs.

A *comtrace alphabet* is a triple $\Theta = (\Sigma, sim, ser)$, where Σ is an alphabet and $ser \subseteq sim \subseteq \Sigma \times \Sigma$ are two relations, respectively called *serialisability* and *simultaneity*; it is assumed that *sim* is irreflexive and symmetric. Intuitively, if $(a, b) \in sim$ then a and b may occur simultaneously, whereas $(a, b) \in ser$ means that in such a case a may also occur before b (with both executions being equivalent). The set of all (potential) steps over Θ, or *step alphabet*, is then defined as the set $\mathbb{S}$ comprising all nonempty sets of actions $A \subseteq \Sigma$ such that $(a, b) \in sim$, for all distinct $a, b \in A$. To avoid confusion with the well-established operation of concatenating sets in formal languages theory, we follow Diekert ([3]) and denote a step containing actions a and b by (ab) rather then $\{a, b\}$, etc. Finite sequences in $\mathbb{S}^*$, including the empty one (λ), are called *step sequences.*

We now lift a number of notions and notations introduced for words to the level of step sequences. In what follows, $\Theta = (\Sigma, sim, ser)$ is a *fixed* comtrace alphabet. Let $w = A_1 \dots A_n$ and $v = B_1 \dots B_m$ be two step sequences. Then $w \circ v = wv = A_1 \dots A_n B_1 \dots B_m$ is the concatenation of w and v. The alphabet $alph(w)$ of w comprises all action occurring within w, and $\#_a(w)$ is the number of occurrences of an action a within w.

The *comtrace congruence* over Θ, denoted by $\equiv_\Theta$, is the reflexive, symmetric and transitive closure of the relation $\sim_\Theta \subseteq \mathbb{S}^* \times \mathbb{S}^*$ such that $w \sim_\Theta v$ if there are $u, z \in \mathbb{S}^*$ and $A, B, C \in \mathbb{S}$ satisfying $w = uAz$, $v = uBCz$, $A = B \cup C$ and $B \times C \subseteq ser$. Note that $B \cap C = \varnothing$ as ser is irreflexive.

Equivalence classes of the relation $\equiv_\Theta$ are called *comtraces* (see [5]), and the comtrace containing a given step sequence w is denoted by $[w]$. The set of all comtraces is denoted by $\mathbb{S}^*/_\equiv$, and the pair $(\mathbb{S}^*/_\equiv, \circ)$ is a (comtrace) monoid, where $\tau \circ \tau' = [w \circ w']$, for any step sequences $w \in \tau$ and $w' \in \tau'$. Comtrace concatenation is well-defined as $[w \circ w'] = [v \circ v']$, for all $w, v \in \tau$ and $w', v' \in \tau'$. A comtrace τ is a prefix of a comtrace τ' if there is a comtrace τ'' such that $\tau \circ \tau'' = \tau'$. As in the case of traces, for every comtrace τ and every $a \in \Sigma$, we can define $alph(\tau) = alph(w)$ and $\#_a(\tau) = \#_a(w)$, where w is any step sequence belonging to τ.

Next, we give the canonical form of a comtrace which essentially captures a greedy, maximally concurrent, execution of the actions occurring in the comtrace conforming to the simultaneity and serialisability relations. A step sequence $w = A_1 \ldots A_n \in \mathbb{S}^*$ is in *Foata canonical form* if, for each $i \leq n$, whenever $Av \equiv_\Theta A_i \ldots A_k$ for some $A \in \mathbb{S}$ and $v \in \mathbb{S}^*$, then $A \subseteq A_i$. This canonical form of a comtrace are widely described in [7]. One can see that all suffixes of step sequence in Foata canonical form are also in Foata canonical form, and that each comtrace comprises a unique step sequence in Foata normal form. Note that an alternative (equivalent) definition of normal form requires that, for every $i < k$, there is no $\varnothing \neq A \subseteq A_{i+1}$ such that $A_i \times A \subseteq ser$ and $A \times (A_{i+1} \setminus A) \subseteq ser$.

1.4 Relations between Actions

In our discussion, we use a number of relations capturing semantically meaningful relationships between individual actions (see also [11]):

- Dependence $dep = (\Sigma \times \Sigma) \setminus sim$, and independence $ind = ser \cap ser^{-1}$.
  Both relations have their counterparts in trace theory, and we denote them in the same way. If two actions are dependent then they never occur in a common step. Two actions are independent if they can be executed in any order as well as simultaneously (as $ser \subseteq sim$).
- Semi-independence $sin = sim \setminus ser$.
  In contrast to the situation found in traces, dependence and independence do not describe all possible relationships between individual actions in comtraces. The remaining ones are called, due to the possibility of occurring together without being fully independent, semi-independent actions. Semi-independent actions may be further divided into symmetric and antisymmetric parts:
  - Strong simultaneity $ssm = sim \setminus (ser \cup ser^{-1}) = sin \setminus ser^{-1}$.
    If two actions are strongly simultaneous then may occur simultaneously but cannot be serialised at all.
  - Weak dependence $wdp = ser^{-1} \setminus ser = sin \setminus sin^{-1}$.
    Two actions are weakly dependent if they can be serialised only in one way.

Similarly to the case of simultaneity and serialisability [6], each of these relations can be described semantically by specific relationships between pre-sets, post-sets and inh-sets of pairs of actions. The following table gives a straightforward description of the above five relations for ENI-systems.

simultaneity	$(a,b) \in sim$	${}^\bullet a^\bullet \cap {}^\bullet b^\bullet = \varnothing \wedge ({}^\circ a \cap {}^\bullet b) \cup ({}^\circ b \cap {}^\bullet a) = \varnothing$
serialisability	$(a,b) \in ser$	$(a,b) \in sim \wedge a^\bullet \cap {}^\bullet b = \varnothing$
dependence	$(a,b) \in dep$	${}^\bullet a^\bullet \cap {}^\bullet b^\bullet \neq \varnothing \vee ({}^\circ a \cap {}^\bullet b) \cup ({}^\circ b \cap {}^\bullet a) \neq \varnothing$
independence	$(a,b) \in ind$	$(a,b) \notin dep \wedge ({}^\circ a \cap b^\bullet) \cup ({}^\circ b \cap a^\bullet) = \varnothing$
semi-independence	$(a,b) \in sin$	$(a,b) \notin dep \wedge ({}^\circ b \cap a^\bullet) \neq \varnothing$
strong simultaneity	$(a,b) \in ssm$	$(a,b) \notin dep \wedge ({}^\circ b \cap a^\bullet) \neq \varnothing \wedge ({}^\circ a \cap b^\bullet) \neq \varnothing$
weak dependence	$(a,b) \in wdp$	$(a,b) \notin dep \wedge ({}^\circ b \cap a^\bullet) \neq \varnothing \wedge ({}^\circ a \cap b^\bullet) = \varnothing$

Example 3. Consider a comtrace alphabet Θ for ENI-system from Example 2. The simultaneity and serialisability relations are given by:

sim :
a
b
d
c
ser :
a
b
d
c

Then the five derived relations on actions are as follows:

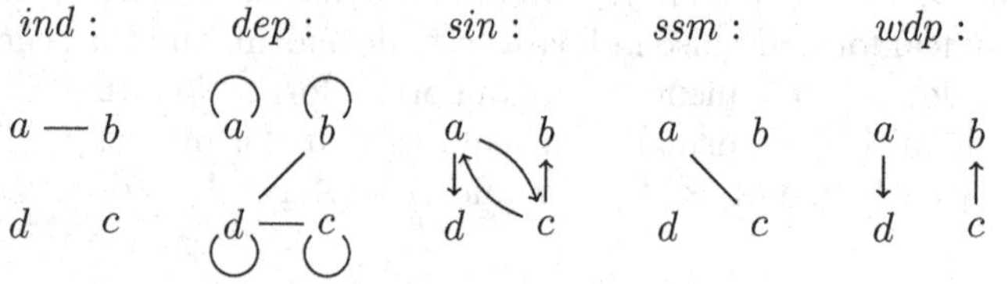
ind :
dep :
sin :
ssm :
wdp :
a
b
d
c

We also have $\tau = [w] = [v] = [u]$, where:

$w = (d)(ab)(d), \quad v = (d)(a)(b)(d), \quad u = (ad)(b)(d).$

Moreover, u is a step sequence in Foata canonical form. □

2 Lexicographical Canonical Form

Let $(\Sigma, \leq)$ be a total order on actions. Using the order $\leq$ we define $min(A)$, the minimal representative of a step $\varnothing \neq A \in \mathbb{S}$ as the minimal action in A with respect to $\leq$. Note that $min(\varnothing)$ is not defined.

We extend the order on actions to the case of steps (sets of actions). Let $A, B \in \mathbb{S}$ be two steps. If the size of A is smaller then the size of B then $A \widehat{\leq} B$. If the sizes are equal, $A \widehat{\leq} B$ if and only if $A = B$ or $A \neq B$ and $min(A \setminus B) \leq min(B \setminus A)$. In this way, $(\mathbb{S}, \widehat{\leq})$ is a totally ordered set.

Using the order $\widehat{\leq}$ we can define *lexicographical order* on step sequences in the usual way. The *lexicographical canonical form* of a comtrace τ, denoted by $minlex(\tau)$, is the least (with respect to the lexicographical order) step sequence contained in the comtrace. Note that, in contrast to the Foata canonical normal form, the lexicographical canonical form captures one of the most sequential executions of a comtrace. Hence the two canonical forms lie on the opposite sides of the concurrent/sequential spectrum of behaviours. Note that the step sequence v from Example 3 is in lexicographical canonical form.

Theorem 4. *For a given comtrace τ, its Foata normal form is the $\widehat{\lesssim}$-greatest, and lexicographical normal form is the $\widehat{\lesssim}$-least, step sequence contained in τ.*

2.1 Indivisible Steps and Sequences

The structure and semantics of relations *sim* and *ser* mean that some actions have to appear simultaneously in every step sequence contained in a comtrace (in other word, they cannot be separated according to the comtrace congruence). A very good example of such actions are those in the *ssm* relation. The strong simultaneity, however, does not exhaust all situations when actions are "glued" together in the permanent manner. In this section, we discuss this phenomenon in depth.

Let us consider a step $A \in \mathbb{S}$ and a relation $\equiv_A \subseteq A \times A$, such that, for all $a, b \in A$, we have $a \equiv_A b$ if and only if $(a, b) \in sin^* \wedge (b, a) \in sin^*$. Intuitively, the relation $\equiv_A$ joins actions that can be executed simultaneously, but cannot be executed in a sequential way (see Example 6).

Lemma 5. *For every $A \in \mathbb{S}$, $\equiv_A$ is an equivalence relation.*

We say that a step $A \in \mathbb{S}$ is *indivisible* if and only if $\forall_{a,b \in A}\ a \equiv_A b$. The set of all indivisible steps is denoted by $\widehat{\mathbb{S}}$. By $indiv(\tau)$ we denote the set of all step sequences contained in a comtrace τ and built with indivisible steps only. Intuitively, we can treat the indivisible step sequences belonging to $indiv(\tau)$ as classical sequences over the alphabet $\widehat{\mathbb{S}}$. Hence we define two complementary relations over this alphabet, the independence relation $\widehat{ind}$ and the dependence relation $\widehat{dep}$. We say that two indivisible steps A and B are *independent* if $A \times B \subseteq ind = ser \cap ser^{-1}$; otherwise two indivisible steps are *dependent*.

Example 6. Let us recall the comtrace alphabet from Example 3 and relations *sim* and *sin*, which are crucial in determining indivisible steps. The set of all possible steps is $\mathbb{S} = \{(a), (b), (c), (d), (ab), (ac), (ad), (bc), (abc)\}$, while the set of all indivisible steps is $\widehat{\mathbb{S}} = \{(a), (b), (c), (d), (ac)\}$ Note that step $A = (abc)$ is divided by the relation $\equiv_A$ into two indivisible steps $B = (b)$ and $C = (ac)$ and step B occurs not later than step C, while step $D = (ab)$ is divided by the relation $\equiv_D$ into two, completely independent, indivisible steps (a) and (b).

Moreover, only two sequences of indivisible steps are in the trace τ, defined in Example 3. These two sequences are $v = (d)(a)(b)(d)$ and $v' = (d)(b)(a)(d)$. □

Lemma 7. *Let $A \in \mathbb{S} \setminus \widehat{\mathbb{S}}$ be a step that is not indivisible. Then there exist two steps B and C such that $A \sim_\Theta BC$. Moreover, $A/_{\equiv_A} = B/_{\equiv_B} \cup C/_{\equiv_C}$.*

Proposition 8. *All steps contained in the lexicographical normal form of a comtrace are indivisible ($minlex(\tau) \in indiv(\tau)$).*

Theorem 9. *Let τ be a comtrace. The set $indiv(\tau)$ is a trace over the concurrent alphabet $(\widehat{\mathbb{S}}, \widehat{dep})$.*

As an immediate corollary of the above facts, we can observe that

Corollary 10. *There is a one to one correspondence between the comtraces over* $\Theta = (\Sigma, sim, ser)$ *and traces over* $\Phi = (\widehat{\mathbb{S}, dep})$ *given by the construction of the set of indivisible steps and dependence relation on them.*

$$\tau \text{ over } \Theta \longleftrightarrow indiv(\tau) \longleftrightarrow \tau' \text{ over } \Phi$$

One can think about using the above correspondence to apply the methods of enumerating all traces of a given size [12] to enumerate comtraces of a given size.

3 Projection Representation of Comtraces

In the trace theory employing projections onto the cliques of the graph of dependence relation (see also [14]) turned out to be a very useful tool. We now extend this notion, in the case of the binary and unary cliques only (see also [10]), to define the projection representation of comtraces. In the case of traces, we have only two kinds of relationships between actions. As independent actions may be executed in any order (or together in case of step semantics) one can focus on the order implied by the dependence relation.

In the case of comtraces, the situation is more complicated. However, once more we can ignore independent actions and store information about the other three types of relations (dependency, weak dependency and strong simultaneity). Once more, it is sufficient to store the information in the form of sequences. In the case of strong simultaneity, however, we need to add a special symbol $\perp$ that separates the situations of sequential and simultaneous execution of pairs of actions being considered.

Let $a, b \in \Sigma$ and $(a, b) \notin ind$ (possibly $a = b$). For each such pair we define the projection function $\Pi_{a,b} : \mathbb{S}^* \to (\Sigma \cup \{\perp\})^*$ as follows. First, for a step $A \in \mathbb{S}$ we have

$$\Pi_{a,b}(A) = \Pi_{b,a}(A) = \begin{cases} \lambda & \text{if } \{a,b\} \cap A = \varnothing \\ a & \text{if } a \in A \wedge b \notin A \\ ba & \text{if } \{a,b\} \subseteq A \wedge (a,b) \in wdp \\ \perp & \text{if } \{a,b\} \subseteq A \wedge (a,b) \in ssm \end{cases}$$

Note that in this way we have $\Pi_{a,a}(A) = \lambda$ if $a \notin A$ and $\Pi_{a,a}(A) = a$ if $a \in A$.

Then, for a step sequence $w = A_1 A_2 \ldots A_n$ we have $\Pi_{a,b}(w) = \Pi_{a,b}(A_1) \circ \Pi_{a,b}(A_2) \circ \ldots \circ \Pi_{a,b}(A_n)$.

Theorem 11. *Let* w, u *be step sequences over comtrace alphabet* $\Theta = (\mathbb{S}, sim, ser)$*. Then* $w \equiv_\Theta u \Leftrightarrow \forall_{(a,b) \notin ind}\ \Pi_{a,b}(w) = \Pi_{a,b}(u)$.

The projection representation of a comtrace τ is a function $\Pi_\tau : (\Sigma \times \Sigma) \setminus ind \to (\Sigma \cup \{\perp\})^*$, given by $\Pi_\tau(a, b) = \Pi_{a,b}(\tau)$. Moreover, any function $\Pi : (\Sigma \times \Sigma) \setminus ind \to (\Sigma \cup \{\perp\})^*$ is called the *projection set.* Clearly, not every projection set is a projection representation of a comtrace. In the next section, we give a procedure that decides whether a given projection set is a projection representation of a comtrace. Moreover, if the answer is positive, the procedure computes such a comtrace.

First, however, we provide the algorithm computing projection representation of a comtrace. This algorithm comes directly from the definition. However, it is important to discuss the data structures which might be used by this algorithm. At the beginning, let us consider the input. We get a comtrace alphabet Θ which consists of the alphabet Σ of size k and two relations, *sim* and *ser*, of size at most k^2 each. We also get a step sequence w which steps consist of n occurrences of atomic actions (elements of Σ) all together. As a result, we obtain the set of at most k^2 sequences (projections onto specified subalphabets).

We process the step sequence w step by step, which means that the algorithm is online, and after consuming a step we get a result for a proper prefix of w. The processing of a single step is done according to the definition of projections onto the pairs in specified relation. It is worth carrying out some preprocessing and, for every action, compute the list of all subalphabets in which it may occur. By storing, for every computed projection, the number of the step when it was lately updated, we avoid problems with the special cases of relations *wdp* and *ssm* (in these cases two rather than one action may be added to one sequence while processing a single step).

Proposition 12. *The procedure of computing Π_τ from a step sequence $w \in \tau$ has the time and memory complexities of $O(nk)$.*

Theorem 13. *Testing comtrace equivalence can be done in the time complexity of $O(nk)$.*

3.1 Reconstructing Step Sequence from Projection Function

The idea of constructing a step sequence from a projection set is based on revealing the first possible step whose projection representation would form a set of prefixes of the given projection set. At first, we identify the set of all possible elements of such a step. We do it in two stages. We identify the set of conditionally possible actions, i.e. those actions whose first occurrences are the first (or in particular situations the second) letters in all projections, where they could appear. Note that we treat the special symbol $\perp$ as a pair of proper letters, so its occurrence means that both letter might be conditionally possible. After this identification, we remove actions that cannot satisfy some of the necessary conditions. These conditions are related to the cases when the considered action appears as the second letter in some sequences connected with the weak dependence relation or are verified positively because of the special symbol $\perp$.

As a result of the first stage, we obtain the set of all actions that may appear in the first step of the constructed sequence. The second stage consist of dividing this set into indivisible steps and combining those indivisible steps into one of the allowed steps. The result is obtained by taking advantage of the weak dependence relation inside the set of indivisible steps. It is similar to ideas behind the proof of Lemma 7. Let us look into the details of the proposed procedure.

Let Π be a projection set. We say that an action $a \in \Sigma$ is *conditionally possible* for projection function Π if and only if for all $b \in \Sigma$ the following implications are satisfied:

- $(a, b) \in dep \Rightarrow pref_1(\Pi(a, b)) = a$
- $(b, a) \in wdp \Rightarrow pref_1(\Pi(a, b)) = a$
- $(a, b) \in wdp \Rightarrow pref_1(\Pi(a, b)) = a \vee pref_2(\Pi(a, b)) = ba$
- $(a, b) \in ssm \Rightarrow pref_1(\Pi(a, b)) = a \vee pref_1(\Pi(a, b)) = \perp$

We denote all conditionally possible actions as *cpa* and define the relation $cnd \subseteq \Sigma \times \Sigma$, which describes the conditions that must be satisfied. Only in situations where $(a, b) \in wdp \wedge pref_2(\Pi(a, b)) = ba$ or $(a, b) \in ssm \wedge pref_1(\Pi(a, b)) = \perp$ we say that the existence of action b in the constructed step is the necessary condition for the presence of action a in this step, which is denoted by $(a, b) \in cnd$.

We exclude conditionally possible actions with impossible to satisfy conditions to form a set of possible actions. Any action $a \in \Sigma$ that is not conditionally possible in Π is *impossible* in Π. Moreover, any action a conditionally possible under impossible condition (i.e. $(a, b) \in cnd$ and b is impossible) is also impossible. Formally, the set of impossible actions for the projection function Π is the smallest set imp that satisfies the following conditions:

$$\circ \Sigma \setminus cpa \subseteq imp \qquad\qquad \circ b \in imp \wedge (a, b) \in cnd \Rightarrow a \in imp$$

By $M(\Pi)$ we denote the set of actions which are not impossible (which means that they are possible) for projection set Π. In the set of $M(\Pi)/_{\equiv_{M(\Pi)}}$ of all possible and indivisible steps we distinguish the *allowed subsets*. We say that $X \subseteq M(\Pi)/_{\equiv_{M(\Pi)}}$ is allowed if and only if for every $B \in X$ and every action $b \in B$ we have $(b, a) \in sin^* \Rightarrow [a]_{\equiv_{M(\Pi)}} \in X$. Finally, by the *allowed step* we mean the union of elements of any allowed subset.

We can extract from Π any step that is the union of indivisible steps contained in $M(\Pi)/_{\equiv_{M(\Pi)}}$. Such an extraction $extr : ((\Sigma \times \Sigma \setminus ind)^* \to (\Sigma \cup \perp)^*) \times \mathbb{S} \to ((\Sigma \times \Sigma \setminus ind)^* \to (\Sigma \cup \perp)^*)$ is done in the following way:

$$extr(\Pi, B)(a, b) = \begin{cases} \Pi(a, b) & if\ |\{a, b\} \cap B| = 0 \\ suff_2(\Pi(a, b)) & if\ |\{a, b\} \cap B| = 1 \\ suff_2(\Pi(a, b)) & if\ |\{a, b\} \cap B| = 2 \wedge (a, b) \in ssm \\ suff_3(\Pi(a, b)) & if\ |\{a, b\} \cap B| = 2 \wedge (a, b) \in wdp \cup wdp^{-1} \end{cases}$$

Example 14. Let us consider the comtrace τ from Example 3.

The projection representation of the comtrace τ (omitting projections to the unary subalphabets and multiplications of projections to the same pairs in opposite order):

$$\Pi_\tau(b, d) = dbd \quad \Pi_\tau(c, d) = dd \quad \Pi_\tau(a, c) = a \quad \Pi_\tau(b, c) = b \quad \Pi_\tau(d, a) = da$$

The set of conditionally possible actions for Π_τ is $\{a, d\}$, while $(a, d) \in cnd$. Every conditionally possible action is also possible, so $M(\Pi_\tau) = \{a, d\}$. It gives the set of two indivisible steps (a) and (d) and, finally, two steps that may appear as the first step of constructed sequence: (d) and (ad). □

Theorem 15. *Let Π_τ be the projection representation of a comtrace τ, and $M(\Pi)$ be a maximal possible step of Π_τ. For every allowed set $B \in \mathbb{S}$, we have*

$$\tau = B \circ \sigma, \text{ where } \Pi_\sigma = extr(\Pi_\tau, B).$$

By suitably using the extraction function we can compute any representative of a comtrace τ. In particular, similarly to the case of normal forms, we can do this using a maximal or minimal strategy. In the maximal strategy, we always take the whole set $M(\Pi)$ and, as a result, we obtain the Foata canonical form of the original comtrace. In the minimal strategy, we take the least in sense of order $\widehat{\leq}$ union of the allowed step obtained from allowed subset $M(\Pi)/\equiv_{M(\Pi)}$ and obtain the lexicographical canonical form.

The algorithm reconstructing a step sequence from a projection representation of a comtrace follows the notions defined above. From the technical point of view, some concrete solutions of data structures are worth noticing. Whole algorithm can be divided into parts. In each part we compute a set of allowed steps, choose one, and extract it from the projection set. The procedure repeats until projection set or computed set of allowed steps is empty. In the first case, it returns a step sequence consisting of n occurrences of actions. In the second case, algorithm returns that an input is not a projection representation of a comtrace.

A single part starts from computing the set of conditionally possible actions and the relation describing the conditions. A good idea is to preprocess for every atomic action a list of pointers which helps to browse only the projections related to this action. Doing so, we can check conditional possibility in the time linearly dependent on the size of alphabet, denoted by k. Simultaneously, we build the directed graph of conditions. In the time linearly dependent on the number of arcs in this graph, we remove from the set of conditionally possible actions all impossible ones (browsing, using DFS, all paths which begins in vertices which are not conditionally possible).

In the next phase, we compute a vertices induced subgraph of *sin* relation that contains all possible actions, and once more using DFS, we compute a graph of its strongly connected components (called *condensation graph* [2]). The condensation graph is an acyclic directed graph. We choose an arbitrary union of filters of the condensation graph. All actions contained in the elements of this union forms allowed step. To obtain a Foata canonical form, we take the maximal union of the filters by choosing the whole condensation graph. Whereas, if we wish to obtain the lexicographical normal form, we should choose the $\widehat{\leq}$-smallest allowed step. To compute it, we may consider only the maximal elements of provided condensation graph.

In the last phase, we need to extract the chosen allowed step. We do it according to the definition of extraction operation. During this phase, we can once more use the precomputed lists of pointers.

Proposition 16. *Projection set Π is a projection representation of a comtrace if and only if the described procedure ends with an empty projection set.*

Theorem 17. *The procedure of computing canonical forms from a projection representation of a comtrace has the time complexity of $O(nk^2)$.*

4 Special Subclasses of Comtraces

4.1 Traces as a Subclass of Comtraces

In Section 1 we defined EN-systems as a special case of ENI-systems without inhibitors and with the sequential semantics. We also introduced traces as a model of the causal behaviour of EN-systems. In this section, we show what kind of comtraces are directly related to systems without inhibitors. We start with a simple operation that helps to change step semantics into sequential semantics.

Let $A \in \mathbb{S}$ be a step and $\leq$ be a total order on actions. We define the *lexicographical linearization* of step A as

$$lex(A) = \begin{cases} \lambda & \text{for } A = \varnothing \\ min(A)lex(A \setminus min(A)) & \text{for } A \neq \varnothing. \end{cases}$$

We extend the operation lex to step sequence in the usual way, i.e. $lex(A_1A_2 \dots A_n) = lex(A_1)lex(A_2)\dots lex(A_n)$.

The comtrace alphabet $\Theta = (\Sigma, sim, ser)$ with the empty relation sin is called *trace-like comtrace alphabet.* Moreover, comtraces over this alphabet are called *trace-like comtraces.* Such comtraces behave exactly like traces with the step semantics. We can equip them with a sequential semantics by applying lex operator or by using only indivisible steps. Later in this section we discuss some properties of this subclass.

Proposition 18. *Let $\tau \in \mathbb{S}^*$ be a trace-like comtrace and $w \in indiv(\tau)$. Then each step of w is a singleton.*

Corollary 19. *Let $\Theta = (\Sigma, sim, ser)$ be a trace-like comtrace alphabet. The number of all indivisible steps in $\widehat{\mathbb{S}}$ is equal to $|\Sigma|$.*

Using Theorem 9 and Lemma 19 we can associate an alphabet of indivisible steps $\widehat{\mathbb{S}}$ with Σ and trace-like comtrace τ over a comtrace alphabet $\Theta = (\Sigma, sim, ser)$ with a trace σ over the concurrent alphabet $\Phi = (\Sigma, \widehat{dep})$. We say that such a trace σ is a *trace representation* of a trace-like comtrace τ. Note that since the relation sin is empty, $\widehat{dep} = dep$.

Theorem 20. *Let τ be a trace-like comtrace and σ be its trace representation. Then $\Pi_\tau = \Pi_\sigma$.*

Theorem 21. *Let $\tau \in \mathbb{S}^*$ be a trace-like comtrace and σ be its trace representation. Then the linearizations of the Foata and the lexicographical canonical forms of τ are equal to the Foata and the lexicographical canonical forms of σ, respectively.*

4.2 Weakly Simultaneous Comtraces

Taking into account Vogler's ST-traces and structures for modelling causality and start precedences [15], we can make further investigation into the properties of comtraces connected with the indivisible steps. To obtain structures similar to those considered by Vogler, we should forbid execution of indivisible steps which are not singletons. Such a restriction gives a model that is applicable to the case of elementary nets with read arcs, but it is not expressible in terms of comtraces. Instead of such a semantic restriction, we introduce another structural simplification that provides weakly simultaneous comtraces and gives a method of transforming an arbitrary comtrace alphabet to one satisfying new constraints. The price is the possibility of an exponential growth of the size of the alphabet.

Let $\Theta = (\Sigma, sim, ser)$ be the comtrace alphabet, $\mathbb{S}$ the set of all potential steps and $\widehat{\mathbb{S}}$ the set of all indivisible steps over this alphabet. For each $A \in \mathbb{S}$, we give $\widehat{A} \subseteq \widehat{\mathbb{S}}$ in the following way. The indivisible set $B \in \widehat{\mathbb{S}}$ is an element of $\widehat{A}$ if and only if the elements of B are permanently glued together inside step A, which means that $\forall_{b_1,b_2 \in B}\, b_1 \equiv_A b_2$ and $\forall_{a \in A \setminus B} b \in B \Rightarrow a \not\equiv_A b$.

In this way, with every step sequence $w = A_1 A_2 \ldots A_n$ over the concurrent alphabet $\Theta = (\Sigma, sim, ser)$, we can associate a step sequence $\widehat{w} = \widehat{A_1}\widehat{A_2}\ldots\widehat{A_n}$ over the alphabet $\widehat{\Theta} = (\widehat{\mathbb{S}}, \widehat{sim}, \widehat{ser})$, where $(\widehat{A}, \widehat{B}) \in \widehat{sim}$ if and only if $A \times B \subseteq sim$ and $(\widehat{A}, \widehat{B}) \in \widehat{ser}$ if and only if $A \times B \subseteq ser$. The main advantage of such a comtrace alphabet is that if $(\widehat{A}, \widehat{B}) \in \widehat{sim}$ then $(\widehat{A}, \widehat{B}) \in \widehat{ser} \cup \widehat{ser}^{-1}$, in other words $\widehat{ssm} = \varnothing$.

Every comtrace over comtrace alphabet that satisfies the above condition is called a *weakly simultaneous comtrace*. In this new subclass of comtraces we can omit, as implied by serialisability, the simultaneity relation. To restrict some behaviours which are not possible in the case of ST-traces, we should limit the graphs of *wdp* relation to acyclic. Comtraces with such a restriction cannot, however, describe all behaviours covered by ST-traces.

5 Summary and Future Work

In this paper we presented some algebraic aspects of combined traces. Similar algebraic tools were successfully used in the study of the Mazurkiewicz traces, a simpler model for capturing and analysing concurrent behaviours.

In particular, we defined lexicographical canonical form of a comtrace and its projection representation. We gave two simple algorithms which generate these representations from arbitrary step sequence. Those algorithms seem to have a potential to provide a base for the development of solutions to some natural problems related to the comtrace theory. In particular, one can use them to design efficient methods of the enumeration of all the representatives of a fixed comtrace, and the enumeration of all comtraces of a given size.

Another interesting direction of further studies would be the notion of recognisable and rational languages of combined traces. The projection representation seems to be a good start point in this area; in particular, if one recalls Zielonka's asynchronous automata [16] for traces. Finally, the projection representation may find an application in another important aspect of combined trace theory. A fair strategy of reconstructing step sequences from a projection set might be useful as a starting point in the theory of infinite combined traces.

Acknowledgments. I would like to thank the anonymous reviewers for their comments and suggestions. The study is cofounded by the European Union from resources of the European Social Fund. Project PO KL „Information technologies: Research and their interdisciplinary applications", Agreement UDA-POKL.04.01.01-00-051/10-00.

References

1. Cartier, P., Foata, D.: Problèmes Combinatoires de Commutation et Réarrangements. LNM, vol. 85. Springer, Berlin (1969)
2. Deo, N.: Graph theory with applications to engineering and computer science. Prentice-Hall (1974)
3. Diekert, V., Métivier, Y.: Partial commutation and traces. In: Handbook of Formal Languages, vol. 3, pp. 457–533. Springer (1997)
4. Diekert, V., Rozenberg, G. (eds.): The Book of Traces. World Scientific, Singapore (1995)
5. Janicki, R., Klein, J., Koutny, M.: Quotient monoids and concurrent behaviours. In: Martín-Vide, C. (ed.) Scientific Applications of Language Methods, ch. 6, pp. 313–386. Imperial College Press, London (2011)
6. Janicki, R., Koutny, M.: Semantics of inhibitor nets. Information and Computation 123(1), 1–16 (1995)
7. Janicki, R., Le, D.T.M.: Modelling concurrency with comtraces and generalized comtraces. Information and Computation 209(11), 1355–1389 (2011)
8. Mazurkiewicz, A.: Concurrent program schemes and their interpretations. Daimi report pb-78, Aarhus University (1977)
9. Mikulski, Ł.: `http://www.mat.umk.pl/~frodo/ASCT-appendix.pdf`
10. Mikulski, Ł.: Projection representation of Mazurkiewicz traces. Fundamenta Informaticae 85, 399–408 (2008)
11. Mikulski, Ł., Koutny, M.: Hasse diagrams of combined traces. Technical report cs-tr-1301, Newcastle University (2011)
12. Mikulski, Ł., Piątkowski, M., Smyczyński, S.: Algorithmics of posets generated by words over partially commutative alphabets. In: Holub, J., Žďárek, J. (eds.) Proceedings of the Prague Stringology Conference 2011, pp. 209–219. Czech Technical University in Prague, Czech Republic (2011)
13. Rozenberg, G., Engelfriet, J.: Elementary Net Systems. In: Reisig, W., Rozenberg, G. (eds.) APN 1998. LNCS, vol. 1491, pp. 12–121. Springer, Heidelberg (1998)
14. Shields, M.W.: Concurrent machines. The Computer Journal 28(5), 449–465 (1985)
15. Vogler, W.: Partial order semantics and read arcs. Theoretical Computer Science 286(1), 33–63 (2002)
16. Zielonka, W.: Asynchronous automata [4]. In: Diekert, V., Rozenberg, G. (eds.) The Book of Traces, ch. 7, pp. 205–247. World Scientific, Singapore (1995)

Verification of Petri Nets with Read Arcs

César Rodríguez and Stefan Schwoon

LSV (ENS Cachan & CNRS & INRIA), France

Abstract. Recent work studied the unfolding construction for contextual nets, i.e. nets with read arcs. Such unfoldings are more concise and can usually be constructed more efficiently than for Petri nets. However, concrete verification algorithms exploiting these advantages were lacking so far. We address this question and propose SAT-based verification algorithms for deadlock and reachability of contextual nets. Moreover, we study optimizations of the SAT encoding and report on experiments.

1 Introduction

Petri nets are a well-known model for concurrent systems. McMillan [17] introduced unfoldings as a tool for verifying properties of such nets. Roughly speaking, the unfolding of a net N is an acyclic net bisimilar to N. McMillan showed that for bounded nets one can use a finite prefix $\mathcal{P}$ of the unfolding to check certain properties of N, e.g. reachability of markings or deadlock-freeness; McMillan himself proposed a deadlock-checking algorithm based on this idea.

The interest of unfoldings lies in the fact that, while $\mathcal{P}$ is in general larger than N, it is smaller than the full reachability graph. Moreover, deadlock or reachability checking are NP-complete for $\mathcal{P}$ but PSPACE-complete for N. Thus, the unfolding technique represents a time/space tradeoff for verifying Petri nets. This tradeoff is particularly attractive when testing multiple properties of the same net because $\mathcal{P}$ needs to be constructed only once.

The publication of [17] triggered a large body of research. To name a few items, the necessary size of $\mathcal{P}$ has been reduced [9], efficient tools for generating $\mathcal{P}$ have been implemented [16,24], and unfoldings-based verification algorithms have been developed [7,10,11,14,18]. An extensive survey can be found in [8].

Recently, unfoldings of *contextual* nets (c-nets) have been studied, i.e. nets with *read arcs* that check for the presence of tokens without consuming them. Their unfoldings can be exponentially more compact than for Petri nets. It is thus natural to base verification on unfoldings of c-nets rather than Petri nets.

Previous work on c-net unfoldings has concentrated on their *construction*: [2] gave an abstract algorithm, and [1,22] provided efficient construction methods. However, concrete verification algorithms making use of them are still missing. In this paper, we aim to close this gap. Our contributions are twofold: we investigate SAT-encodings of unfoldings, and we extend them to c-nets.

Concerning the first point, recall that given a finite complete prefix $\mathcal{P}$ of a bounded Petri net N, deciding deadlock-freeness, reachability, or coverability on N is NP-complete. Thus, previous works consisted in reductions to different

M. Koutny and I. Ulidowski (Eds.): CONCUR 2012, LNCS 7454, pp. 471–485, 2012.

NP-complete problems: McMillan [17] employed a branch-and-bound technique, Heljanko [11] a stable-models encoding, and Melzer and Römer [18] used mixed integer linear programming, later improved by Khomenko and Koutny [14, 15]. The technique used by Esparza and Schröter [10] is an ad-hoc algorithm based on additional information obtained while computing the unfolding.

The previous decade has seen the emergence of powerful SAT solvers. It is natural to profit from these advances and reduce to SAT instead; all the more so because unfoldings are 1-safe nets, so the marking of a place naturally translates to a boolean variable. Indeed, SAT solving has already been proposed for the similar problem of model-checking merged processes [13], and [8] gives an explicit SAT encoding for Petri net unfoldings. However, we are not aware of a publicly available tool that uses this idea. We examine the performance of the encoding and propose some optimizations.

Our principal contribution consists in extending the techniques for deadlock checking and reachability to unfoldings of c-nets. Thus, we intend to leverage their advantages w.r.t. ordinary unfoldings, i.e. faster construction and smaller size. It is worth noting that the smaller size of c-net unfoldings does not automatically translate to an easier SAT problem, for the following reasons: First, the presence of read arcs may cause so-called *cycles of asymmetric conflict*. Thus, a SAT encoding requires acyclicity constraints, which are not necessary for conventional unfoldings. Secondly, an event in a c-net unfolding can occur in multiple different execution contexts, called *histories*, and the constructions proposed in [1,2,22] require to annotate events with potentially many such histories. In contrast, every event in a Petri net unfolding has only one history. Some verification algorithms for Petri nets rely on this fact and do not easily adapt to c-nets. We propose solutions for both problems. Our encoding does not refer to the histories at all, and the effect of the acyclicty constraints can be palliated by several strategies. We add that the SAT-encoding for c-net unfoldings was already briefly sketched in [25], but without considering these problems.

To our knowledge, this is the first paper proposing practical verification algorithms using unfoldings of c-nets. These algorithms are provided as an add-on to the tool CUNF, which is freely available [20]. The tool is more efficient than previous approaches when applied to Petri net unfoldings, and even more efficient than that when used on c-net unfoldings.

The paper is structured as follows: In Section 2, we recall notation and previous results. In Section 3 we explain how unfoldings can be used to check for deadlock and reachability, and in Section 4, we discuss the reduction of the problem to SAT. We report on experiments in Section 5 and conclude in Section 6. A longer version of this paper is available at [21].

2 Basic Notions

In this section, we establish our basic definitions and recall previous results. Due to space constraints, this section is quite concise (see [2, 22] for background).

2.1 Contextual Nets

A *contextual net* (c-net) is a tuple $N = \langle P, T, F, C, m_0 \rangle$, where P and T are disjoint sets of *places* and *transitions*, $F \subseteq (P \times T) \cup (T \times P)$ is the *flow relation*, $C \subseteq P \times T$ is the *context relation* and $m_0 \colon P \to \mathbb{N}$ is the *initial marking*. A pair $(p, t) \in C$ is called *read arc*. A *Petri net* is a c-net without read arcs. N is called *finite* if P and T are finite sets. Fig. 1 (a) depicts a c-net. Read arcs are drawn as undirected lines, here between p and C.

For $x \in P \cup T$, let ${}^\bullet x := \{ y \in P \cup T \mid (y, x) \in F \}$ the *preset* of x and $x^\bullet := \{ y \in P \cup T \mid (x, y) \in F \}$ the *postset* of x. The *context* of a place p is defined as $\underline{p} := \{ t \in T \mid (p, t) \in C \}$, and the context of a transition t as $\underline{t} := \{ p \in P \mid (p, t) \in C \}$. These notions extend to sets in the usual fashion.

A function $m \colon P \to \mathbb{N}$ is called *marking* of N. A transition t is *enabled* at m if $m(p) \geq 1$ for all all $p \in \underline{t} \cup {}^\bullet t$. Such, t can *fire*, leading to marking m', where $m'(p) = m(p) - |\{p\} \cap {}^\bullet t| + |\{p\} \cap t^\bullet|$ for all $p \in P$. We say that some marking m is *reachable* if it can be obtained by a finite sequence of firings starting at m_0. A marking m is *deadlocked* if it does not enable any transition.

N is called *k-bounded* if $m(p) \leq k$ for all reachable m and $p \in P$, and *safe* if it is 1-bounded. For safe nets, we treat markings as sets of places carrying tokens.

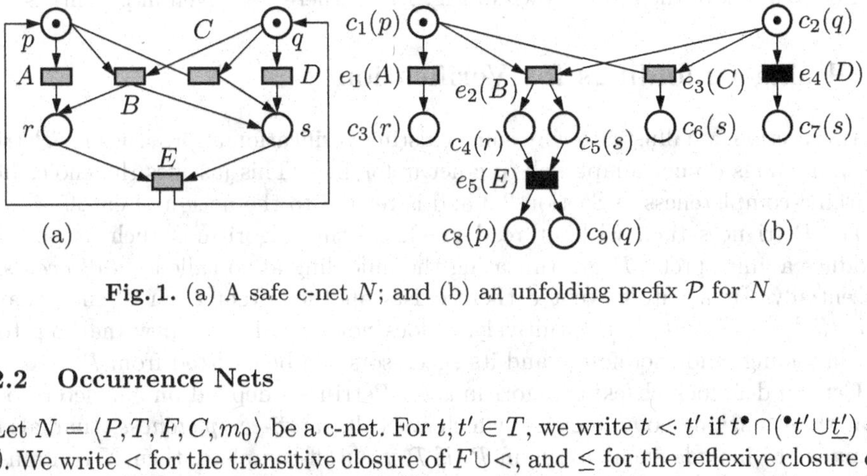

Fig. 1. (a) A safe c-net N; and (b) an unfolding prefix $\mathcal{P}$ for N

2.2 Occurrence Nets

Let $N = \langle P, T, F, C, m_0 \rangle$ be a c-net. For $t, t' \in T$, we write $t \lessdot t'$ if $t^\bullet \cap ({}^\bullet t' \cup \underline{t'}) \neq \emptyset$. We write $<$ for the transitive closure of $F \cup \lessdot$, and $\leq$ for the reflexive closure of $<$. For $x \in P \cup T$, we write $[x]$ for the set of *causes* of x, defined as $\{ t \in T \mid t \leq x \}$. A set $X \subseteq T$ is *causally closed* if $[t] \subseteq X$ for all $t \in X$.

Two transitions t, t' are in *symmetric conflict*, denoted $t \# t'$, iff ${}^\bullet t \cap {}^\bullet t' \neq \emptyset$, and in *asymmetric conflict*, written $t \nearrow t'$, iff (i) $t \lessdot t'$, or (ii) $\underline{t} \cap {}^\bullet t' \neq \emptyset$, or (iii) $t \neq t'$ and $t \# t'$. In case (ii) we also write $t \nearrow\!\!\!\nearrow t'$. For a set of events $X \subseteq T$, we write $\nearrow_X$ to denote the relation $\nearrow \cap (X \times X)$.

A c-net $O = \langle B, E, G, D, \widehat{m_0} \rangle$ is called an *occurrence net* iff (i) O is safe and for any $b \in B$, we have $|{}^\bullet b| \leq 1$; (ii) $<$ is a strict partial order for O; (iii) for all $e \in E$, $[e]$ is finite and $\nearrow_{[e]}$ acyclic; (iv) $\widehat{m_0} = \{ b \in B \mid {}^\bullet b = \emptyset \}$.

Let O be such an occurrence net. As per tradition, we call the elements of B *conditions*, and those of E *events*. A *configuration* of O is a finite, causally closed set of events $\mathcal{C}$ such that $\nearrow_{\mathcal{C}}$ is acyclic. $\mathit{Conf}(O)$ denotes the set of all such configurations. For a configuration $\mathcal{C}$, let $\mathit{cut}(\mathcal{C}) := (\widehat{m}_0 \cup \mathcal{C}^{\bullet}) \setminus {}^{\bullet}\mathcal{C}$.

A *prefix* of O is a net $\mathcal{P} = \langle B', E', G', D', \widehat{m}_0 \rangle$ such that $E' \subseteq E$ is causally closed, $B' = \widehat{m}_0 \cup (E')^{\bullet}$, and G', D' are the restrictions of G, D to $(B' \cup E')$.

2.3 Unfoldings

Let $N = \langle P, T, F, C, m_0 \rangle$ be a bounded c-net. It is possible [2,22] to produce an occurrence net $\mathcal{U}_N = \langle B, E, G, D, \widehat{m}_0 \rangle$, called the *unfolding* of N and equipped with a mapping $f \colon (B \cup E) \to (P \cup T)$, that has the following properties:

- f maps conditions to places and events to transitions. We extend f to sets, multisets, and sequences in the usual way; f applied to a marking of $\mathcal{U}_N$ (a set) will yield a marking of N (a multiset).
- $\mathcal{U}_N$ is an acyclic version of N, i.e. the firing sequences and reachable markings of $\mathcal{U}_N$, modulo the mapping f, are exactly the same as in N.

In general, $\mathcal{U}_N$ is infinite, but one can generate a finite prefix $\mathcal{P}$ of it that is *marking-complete*, meaning that any marking m is reachable in N iff there exists a marking $\widehat{m}$ reachable in $\mathcal{P}$ with $f(\widehat{m}) = m$. Fig. 1 (b) depicts a marking-complete prefix of the c-net shown in Fig. 1 (a), where f is given in parentheses.

3 Using Unfoldings for Verification

In this section, we illustrate why some existing verification approaches for Petri net unfoldings do not adapt well to c-net unfoldings. This justifies the choice of marking-completeness in Section 2.3 and is related to the notion of cutoff.

For Petri nets (i.e., without read arcs), existing algorithms such as [9,17] produce a finite prefix $\mathcal{P}$ by truncating the unfolding at so-called *cutoff events*. Essentially, for a cutoff event e there exists another event e' in $\mathcal{P}$ such that $f(\mathit{cut}([e])) = f(\mathit{cut}([e']))$. Intuitively, e does not contribute a new marking to the unfolding, and therefore e and its successors can be omitted from $\mathcal{P}$.

Certain deadlock-checking algorithms for Petri nets depend on a stricter notion than marking-completeness, which we call *cutoff-completeness*, that also demands to include such cutoffs in $\mathcal{P}$. If $\mathcal{P}$ is cutoff-complete, then N contains a deadlock iff $\mathcal{P}$ contains a cutoff-free configuration $\mathcal{C}$ such that $\mathit{cut}(\mathcal{C})$ is deadlocked in $\mathcal{P}$. This reduction is directly employed in [14,18] and indirectly in [17].

Seeing as the algorithm in [14] performs very well, it would be tempting to adapt this reduction to c-nets. However, we provide an example showing that this reduction is problematic for c-nets. First, recall that the unfolding construction for c-nets given in [1,2,22] lifts the notion of cutoff to event-history pairs. Here, a configuration H is called *history* of an event e if $e' (\nearrow_H)^* e$ for all $e' \in H$. In this case $\langle e, H \rangle$ is called *extended event*, and in analogy to Petri nets, some extended events will be marked as cutoffs when another extended event $\langle e', H' \rangle$ exists such that $f(\mathit{cut}(H)) = f(\mathit{cut}(H'))$. An event may have multiple histories, some of which are cutoffs while others are not.

The net shown in Fig. 1 (a) is free of deadlocks. An unfolding prefix $\mathcal{P}$ is shown in Fig. 1 (b), the mapping f is given in parentheses. Event e_1 has two histories: $H_1 = \{e_1\}$ and $H_2 = \{e_3, e_1\}$. The unfolding algorithm will make $\langle e_1, H_2\rangle$ a cutoff but not $\langle e_1, H_1\rangle$; indeed H_2 leads to the same marking $\{r, s\}$ as $\langle e_2, \{e_2\}\rangle$[1]. An event is shown in black if all its histories are cutoffs.

The prefix in Fig. 1 (b) is marking-complete and also cutoff-complete, when the latter notion is lifted to enriched events. Under this assumption the above-given reduction of the deadlock-checking problem is still valid.

Consider the marking $m' = \{c_3, c_6\}$, which is deadlocked in $\mathcal{P}$. The configuration leading to m' has a cutoff (namely, $\langle e_1, H_2\rangle$), so m' cannot be interpreted as representing a deadlock of N – indeed $f(m') = \{r, s\}$ enables transition E in N. However, as this example demonstrates, *checking* whether a given configuration is cutoff-free requires to reason about histories and not just about events. This is undesirable because forbidding certain histories would result in a rather more complex SAT formula. We therefore use another solution that is completely event-based and requires only marking-completeness:

Remark 1. Let N be a bounded c-net and $\mathcal{P}$ a marking-complete prefix for N. Then N contains a deadlock iff $\mathcal{P}$ has a reachable marking m' such that $f(m')$ is deadlocked. Moreover, m is reachable in N iff $\mathcal{P}$ has a reachable marking m' such that $f(m') = m$.

In the following, we assume that every event in a marking-complete prefix has at least one non-cutoff history; the unfolding tool CUNF [20] can be instructed to remove the others at no extra cost.

4 SAT-Encodings of C-Nets

The SAT problem is as follows: given a formula ϕ of propositional logic, find whether there exists a satisfying assignment that makes ϕ true. SAT solving has taken a quantum leap during the last decade, and many efficient solvers for this problem exist. Here, we encode the deadlock-checking and reachability problem for c-nets in SAT, based on Remark 1. For Petri nets, such an encoding was given in [8]; we generalize it to c-nets and enrich it with optimizations. Notice that most constraints that we give translate directly into CNF.

For the rest of this section, let $N = \langle P, T, F, C, m_0\rangle$ be a finite safe c-net and $\mathcal{P} = \langle B, E, G, D, \widehat{m}_0\rangle$ a finite marking-complete prefix of N. We first construct a propositional formula $\phi_{\mathcal{P}}^{\text{dead}}$ that is unsatisfiable iff N is deadlock-free. Section 4.4 explains the modifications needed to implement reachability checking, and Section 4.5 explains how the encoding can be generalized to bounded nets.

The formula $\phi_{\mathcal{P}}^{\text{dead}}$ is defined over variables e for $e \in E$ and p for $p \in P$ as:

$$\phi_{\mathcal{P}}^{\text{dead}} := \phi_{\mathcal{P}}^{\text{causal}} \wedge \phi_{\mathcal{P}}^{\text{sym}} \wedge \phi_{\mathcal{P}}^{\text{asym}} \wedge \phi_{\mathcal{P}}^{\text{mark}} \wedge \phi_{\mathcal{P}}^{\text{dis}}$$

[1] It is not important to understand why the unfolding construction prefers to declare $\langle e_1, H_2\rangle$ a cutoff rather than $\langle e_2, \{e_2\}\rangle$, and our point is independent of this choice; what matters is that some events may have cutoff and non-cutoff histories.

The first three constraints enforce that any satisfying assignment represents a configuration C, and $\phi_{\mathcal{P}}^{\text{mark}}$ defines the marking $m := f(cut(C))$, which $\phi_{\mathcal{P}}^{\text{dis}}$ verifies to be deadlocked.

Recall that a configuration is a causally closed set of events free of loops in the $\nearrow$ relation. Subformulae $\phi_{\mathcal{P}}^{\text{causal}}$ and $\phi_{\mathcal{P}}^{\text{sym}}$ request C to be a causally closed set of events that has no pair of events in symmetric conflict:

$$\phi_{\mathcal{P}}^{\text{causal}} := \bigwedge_{\substack{e \in E \\ e' \in {}^\bullet({}^\bullet e \cup \underline{e})}} (\mathsf{e} \to \mathsf{e}') \qquad\qquad \phi_{\mathcal{P}}^{\text{sym}} := \bigwedge_{c \in C} \text{AMO}(c^\bullet),$$

where $\text{AMO}(\mathsf{x}_1, \ldots, \mathsf{x}_n)$ is satisfied iff *at most one* of $\mathsf{x}_1, \ldots, \mathsf{x}_n$ is satisfied(see Section 5.1). $\phi_{\mathcal{P}}^{\text{asym}}$ ensures that C is free of $\nearrow$-cycles; the details come in Section 4.1. $\phi_{\mathcal{P}}^{\text{mark}}$ characterizes supersets of the marking m reached by C:

$$\phi_{\mathcal{P}}^{\text{mark}} := \bigwedge_{\substack{c \in B \\ p = f(c) \\ \{e\} = {}^\bullet c}} \Big(\big(\mathsf{e} \wedge \bigwedge_{e' \in c^\bullet} \neg \mathsf{e}' \big) \to \mathsf{p} \Big)$$

Finally, $\phi_{\mathcal{P}}^{\text{dis}}$ ensures that m is indeed deadlocked in N:

$$\phi_{\mathcal{P}}^{\text{dis}} := \bigwedge_{t \in T} \bigvee_{p \in {}^\bullet t \cup \underline{t}} \neg \mathsf{p}$$

Notice that a variable p may be true even if $p \notin m$. However, such an assignment can only serve to *hide* a deadlock, so this encoding is safe.

4.1 Asymmetric Conflict Loops

We now explain $\phi_{\mathcal{P}}^{\text{asym}}$, which ensures that $\nearrow_C$ is acyclic (for convenience, we equate a relation with a directed graph in the natural way). Symmetric conflicts form cycles of length 2 in $\nearrow$ and are efficiently handled by the AMO constraints of $\phi_{\mathcal{P}}^{\text{sym}}$. In a Petri net, these are the only cycles that can occur. However, in a c-net there may also be cycles in the relation $R := \lessdot \cup \nearrow\!\!\!\nearrow$. We show now that they occur naturally in well-known examples:

Consider Fig. 2, which shows the beginning of an unfolding of Dekker's mutual-exclusion algorithm [19] (only some events of interest are shown). In the beginning, both processes indicate their interest to enter the critical section by raising their flag (events e_1, f_1). They then check whether the flag of the other process is low (events e_2, f_2) and if so, proceed (e_3) and possibly repeat (e_4, e_5). If both processes want to enter the critical section (f_2'), some arbitration happens (not displayed). Two conflict cycles in this example are $e_1 \lessdot e_2 \nearrow\!\!\!\nearrow f_1 \lessdot f_2 \nearrow\!\!\!\nearrow e_1$ and $f_1 \lessdot f_2' \nearrow\!\!\!\nearrow e_3 \lessdot e_4 \lessdot e_5 \nearrow\!\!\!\nearrow f_1$.

Several encodings have been proposed in the literature for acyclicity constraints, including transitive closure and ranks (see, e.g., [4]). In the ranking method, one introduces for each event e additional boolean variables that represent an integer up to r (the so-called *rank* of e), where r is a large enough number. Then, for each pair $(e, f) \in R$, one introduces a clause $(\mathsf{e} \wedge \mathsf{f}) \to [\![\mathsf{e} < \mathsf{f}]\!]$, where $[\![\mathsf{e} < \mathsf{f}]\!]$ is an additional variable that, if true, forces the rank of e to be less than the rank of f. Naturally, this clause is only necessary if e and f are in the same strongly connected component (SCC) of R.

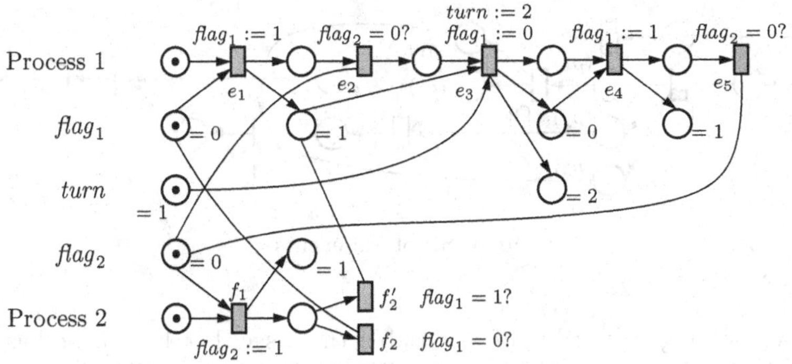

Fig. 2. Partial unfolding of Dekker's algorithm algorithm with asymmetric cycles

A lower bound for r is the length of the longest chain in $\nearrow$ that does not contain a cycle; however, finding the latter is itself an NP-complete problem. A simple upper bound for r is the size of the largest SCC of R. To further reduce this upper bound, one can exploit the fact that $\mathcal{C}$ is causally closed and that every cycle in R contains at least two edges stemming from $\nearrow\!\!\!\nearrow$. Consider the relation $R' := \{\, (e,g) \mid \exists f,h : e \nearrow\!\!\!\nearrow f \leq g \nearrow\!\!\!\nearrow h \,\}$. One can easily see that any causally closed set of events contains a cycle in R iff it contains a cycle in R', so r can be bounded by the largest SCC of R' instead.

On the other hand, R' may actually contain more pairs than R, and computing R' may take quadratic time in $|E|$. So instead, we reduce the size of R by a less drastic method that can run in linear time: An event e is eliminated from R by fusing its incoming and outgoing edges in R only if (i) e is not the source of a $\nearrow\!\!\!\nearrow$-edge and (ii) fusing the edges and eliminating e will not increase the number of edges in R.

Fig. 2 demonstrates another important point. The figure contains two different cycles, both of which contain f_1. Thus, all events in Fig. 2 belong to the same SCC in R. Indeed, we observe in our experiments that the SCCs of R tend to be large, often composed of thousands of events, but consist of many short, interlocking cycles. This suggests that an upper bound for r better than the size of R, even after reduction, may still be feasible. We therefore suggest another trick: first, check for deadlock while omitting $\phi_{\mathcal{P}}^{\mathrm{asym}}$ from $\phi_{\mathcal{P}}^{\mathrm{dead}}$ altogether. This may result in false positives, i.e. a set of events leading to a deadlocked marking that is not actually reachable because it contains a cycle in $\nearrow$. If the SAT solver comes up with such a spurious deadlock, repeat with $\phi_{\mathcal{P}}^{\mathrm{asym}}$ properly included. The experiments concerning these points are discussed in Section 5.1.

4.2 Reduction of Stubborn Events

In this section, we discuss an optimization that palliates a problem of SAT checkers. Consider the occurrence net shown in Fig. 3. If event e_1 fires, then nothing can prevent e_2, e_3, e_4, and e_5 from firing. Thus, any configuration leading to a deadlock must either contain all five events or none of them. However, e_1 is not guaranteed to fire due to the white event that consumes from its context.

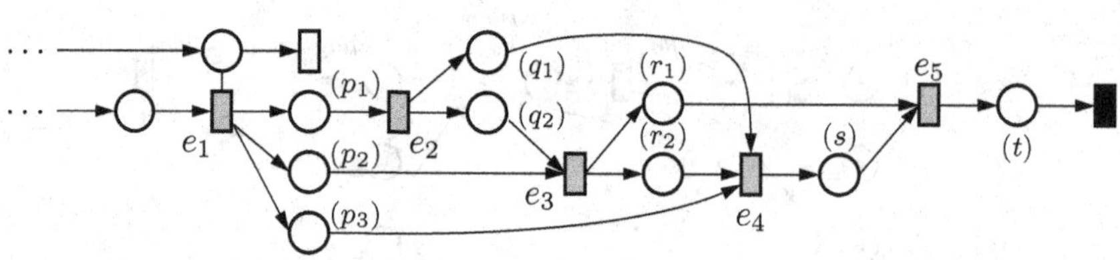

Fig. 3. Stubborn events

In SAT solving, the value of a variable that is either known or has been tentatively decided is *propagated* to simplify other clauses [6]. Thus, in the SAT encoding for Fig. 3 (see [21] for more details), a SAT solver can immediately decide that no deadlock configuration may contain e_5 when the black event is a cutoff. This propagation is handled very efficiently by modern solvers, and there is no gain in emulating this behaviour while generating the SAT encoding.

However, unit propagation in our encoding is not able to detect that e_3 and e_4 are logical implications of e_1. Even when a solver tentatively sets e_1 to true, unit propagation only infers that e_2 must also be true, but not e_3 or e_4. It takes another decision, e.g. for e_3 or e_4, to derive a contradiction and, depending on the solver, possibly multiple steps to decide that e_1 must necessarily be false.

On the other hand, such information is easy to detect on the unfolding structure, and we shall modify the proposed SAT encoding in these cases. Let us call *stubborn* any event e satisfying $({}^\bullet e \cup \underline{e})^\bullet = \{e\}$. Intuitively, once all events preceding e have fired, then firing e is unavoidable to find a deadlock. In Fig. 3, events e_2, e_3, e_4, e_5 are all stubborn.

Indeed, consider any deadlocked configuration $\mathcal{C}$ of $\mathcal{P}$, and let e be any stubborn event verifying ${}^\bullet({}^\bullet e \cup \underline{e}) \subseteq \mathcal{C}$. Then either e is in C or it is enabled at $cut(\mathcal{C})$, since $\mathcal{C}$ contains all events preceding e. But the latter is not possible because $\mathcal{C}$ is a deadlock, so e must be in C, which proves that $e \in C$ iff ${}^\bullet({}^\bullet e \cup \underline{e}) \subseteq \mathcal{C}$ (the other direction follows from the fact that $\mathcal{C}$ is causally closed).

This suggests that we could substitute every occurrence of e by a conjunction of the variables associated to the predecessors of e. We denote by E_s the set of stubborn events, and define inductively the set of *predecessors* of any event e as $pred(e) := {}^\bullet({}^\bullet e \cup \underline{e}) \setminus E_s \cup \bigcup_{e' \in {}^\bullet({}^\bullet e \cup \underline{e}) \cap E_s} pred(e')$.

Proposition 1. *If e is stubborn, then any deadlocked configuration $\mathcal{C}$ of $\mathcal{P}$ verifies that $e \in \mathcal{C}$ iff $pred(e) \subseteq \mathcal{C}$.*

Corollary 1. $\phi_{\mathcal{P}}^{dead} \equiv \phi_{\mathcal{P}}^{dead} \wedge \bigwedge_{e \in E_s} (\mathsf{e} \leftrightarrow \bigwedge_{e' \in pred(e)} \mathsf{e}')$

Corollary 1 can be exploited to modify $\phi_{\mathcal{P}}^{\text{dead}}$ in two ways: for every stubborn event e, (i) add a clause $\bigwedge_{e' \in pred(e)} \mathsf{e}' \rightarrow \mathsf{e}$, or (ii) substitute e by $\bigwedge_{e' \in pred(e)} \mathsf{e}'$. In our experiments, we chose method (ii), which eliminates the stubborn events from the encoding altogether. The resulting formula, after an initial unit propagation phase by the SAT solver, allows to immediately derive $\neg \mathsf{e}_1$. We note that in certain cases, this can increase the formula by a quadratic factor, see [21].

We briefly explain the changes to $\phi^{\text{dead}}_{\mathcal{P}}$ motivated by method (ii): $\phi^{\text{sym}}_{\mathcal{P}}$ is not affected because no stubborn event appears in any symmetric conflict, and neither is $\phi^{\text{dis}}_{\mathcal{P}}$. In $\phi^{\text{causal}}_{\mathcal{P}}$, however, clauses $\mathsf{e} \to \mathsf{e}'$ will be replaced by $\mathsf{e} \to \mathsf{e}''$ for every $e'' \in \mathit{pred}(e)$. In a clause $\left(\mathsf{e} \wedge \bigwedge_{e' \in c^\bullet} \neg \mathsf{e}'\right) \to \mathsf{p}$ of $\phi^{\text{mark}}_{\mathcal{P}}$, we need to replace e by a conjunction over $\mathit{pred}(e)$. In principle, the same needs to be done for e'. However, if $|c^\bullet| \geq 2$, then no event in $c^\bullet$ is stubborn, and nothing changes; but if $c^\bullet = \{e'\}$ is a singleton, and e' is stubborn, then the clause is split into $|\mathit{pred}(e')|$ different clauses. For $\phi^{\text{asym}}_{\mathcal{P}}$, in a clause of the form $\mathsf{e} \wedge \mathsf{f} \to [\![\mathsf{e} < \mathsf{f}]\!]$, both e and f are replaced by conjunctions, if applicable; thus, the formula will still require ranks for e and f even if e or f are not present.

We remark that stubborn events are also treated specially in the stable-models encoding of [11]. While stable models are similar to SAT, the treatment in [11] is simpler; its analogue in propositional logic would not eliminate stubborn events from the formula nor allow to directly conclude that e_1 cannot be fired.

4.3 Additional Simplification

We briefly mention some possible simplifications of the formula. First, for a place p, if $p^\bullet \cup \underline{p} = \emptyset$, then p does not appear in $\phi^{\text{dis}}_{\mathcal{P}}$ and can be omitted from $\phi^{\text{mark}}_{\mathcal{P}}$.

Secondly, for two conditions c, d, if $c^\bullet \subseteq d^\bullet$, then $\text{AMO}(c^\bullet)$ is implied by $\text{AMO}(d^\bullet)$ and can be omitted from $\phi^{\text{sym}}_{\mathcal{P}}$. Similarly, for two transition t, u where ${}^\bullet t \subseteq {}^\bullet u$, disabledness of t implies disabledness of u, so u can be omitted from $\phi^{\text{dis}}_{\mathcal{P}}$. We return to this point in Section 5.1.

4.4 Reachability and Coverability

The SAT encoding can be easily modified to check reachability or coverability of a marking. For simplicity, the formulas given here are not directly in CNF.

For coverability, we want to check whether N has a reachable marking m such that $P_M \subseteq m$, where $P_M \subseteq P$. This requires the following modifications: $\phi^{\text{mark}}_{\mathcal{P}}$ still has the same intention but the sense of the implication is reversed; if a variable p is true we need to ensure that indeed some condition labelled by p is marked in $\mathcal{C}$. We introduce additional variables c for some conditions c:

$$\phi^{\text{mark}}_{\mathcal{P}} := \bigwedge_{p \in P_M} \left(\mathsf{p} \to \bigvee_{f(c)=p} \mathsf{c}\right) \;\wedge\; \bigwedge_{f(c) \in P_M} \left(\mathsf{c} \to \left(\bigwedge_{e \in {}^\bullet c} \mathsf{e} \wedge \bigwedge_{e \in c^\bullet} \neg \mathsf{e}\right)\right)$$

Moreover, $\phi^{\text{dis}}_{\mathcal{P}}$ specifies reachability of P_M: $\phi^{\text{dis}}_{\mathcal{P}} := \bigwedge_{p \in P_M} \mathsf{p}$

For reachability, we want to check whether a given marking m is reachable. Then, the variables representing the places must contain the exact marking reached by the event, which is achieved by replacing the one-sided implications of $\phi^{\text{mark}}_{\mathcal{P}}$ by equivalences. Moreover, $\phi^{\text{dis}}_{\mathcal{P}}$ needs to be changed to $\bigwedge_{p \in m} \mathsf{p} \wedge \bigwedge_{p \notin m} \neg \mathsf{p}$.

4.5 Bounded Nets

We briefly sketch an extension to k-bounded nets. For deadlock checking, actually no modifications are needed because we require the preset and context of each transition to be a set. This is in the tradition of [1, 2, 22], where it helps to ease the presentation. However, if presets and contexts could be general multisets, then, for $p \in P$, one could replace the variable p by variables p^i, where $1 \le i \le k$, with the meaning "p carries at least i tokens". Then one would modify $\phi_{\mathcal{P}}^{\text{mark}}$ to make p^i true if at least i conditions with label p are marked in $\mathcal{C}$, and $\phi_{\mathcal{P}}^{\text{dis}}$ requires that for each transition t there exists some $p \in {}^\bullet t \cup \underline{t}$ such that p^i is false, where i is the number of tokens in p required by t. The extension for reachability is analogous, modulo the sense of the implication (cf. Section 4.4).

5 Experimental Evaluation

In this section, we evaluate the SAT-based reduction proposed in Section 4. For this, we wrote a program that reads an unfolding prefix $\mathcal{P}$ generated by CUNF [20] and outputs the associated formula $\phi_{\mathcal{P}}^{\text{dead}}$ in DIMACS CNF format. As a SAT solver, we used the well-known tool MINISAT [6].

In Section 5.1, we first report on the effect of certain encoding variants and optimizations like those in Sections 4.1 to 4.3. In Section 5.2, we then compare against other unfolding-based methods, and we evaluate the effect of using c-nets rather than Petri nets. We concentrate on the aspect of deadlock checking; as pointed out in Section 4.4, the encoding for reachability is very similar.

5.1 Optimizations

Section 4 proposed several optimizations of the encoding. We now empirically evaluate their impact on the solving time. We employed as benchmarks the same set of safe nets that has previously been used in other papers of the literature on Petri net unfoldings, e.g. [11, 12, 22, 23]. For each Petri net N in the set, we obtained a c-net N' by substituting pairs of arcs (p, t) and (t, p) in N by read arcs; we thus have a set of Petri nets and an alternative set of c-nets.

Stubborn Event Elimination and Subset Reduction. Over the set of Petri nets shown in Table 2, we found that removal of stubborn events reduces the accumulated SAT solving time by 27%. When applied together with the subset optimization from Section 4.3, this grows to 30%. For c-nets, we measured a 14% reduction when stubborn events are removed from the encoding *without* acyclicity constraints but only a 6% reduction if additionally the subset optimizations are applied. Experiments over the encoding *with* acyclicity were similar.

This suggest that removal of stubborn events has a positive impact on performance, while subset optimization has very limited, even negative impact. For the following, we applied only the stubborn event optimization.

AMO Constraint. The constraint $\text{AMO}(\mathsf{x}_1, \ldots, \mathsf{x}_n)$ in $\phi_{\mathcal{P}}^{\text{sym}}$ can be trivially encoded by $\bigwedge_{1 \le i < j \le n} (\neg \mathsf{x}_\mathsf{i} \vee \neg \mathsf{x}_\mathsf{j})$. However, this *pairwise encoding* is quadratic, and the SAT performance suffered for examples with large conflict sets.

A survey of better encodings can be found in [3]. Our tool uses a *k-tree* encoding, that introduces $\mathcal{O}(n)$ additional variables and adds $\mathcal{O}(n)$ clauses, see [21]. We observed an overall improvement when replacing the pairwise with the k-tree encoding. The accumulated SAT solving time on our benchmarks under values of $k = 2,\ldots,8$ was minimal for $k = 4$. Experiments over c-nets on the encoding suggested $k = 4$ as a good candidate, as well. We therefore used 4-tree encodings in $\phi_{\mathcal{P}}^{\text{sym}}$ for the following experiments.

Acyclicity Checking. Section 4.1 explained that $\phi_{\mathcal{P}}^{\text{asym}}$ encodes cycle-freeness of configuration $\mathcal{C}$ w.r.t. the relation $R = \lessdot \cup \nearrow$. We investigated three encodings suggested in [4]: transitive closure, unary ranks, and binary ranks. The latter clearly outperformed the others. In the binary rank encoding, every event is associated with a rank, i.e. an integer up to some bound r, that is represented by $\lceil \log_2 r \rceil$ boolean variables. Constraints of the form $[\![\mathrm{e} < \mathrm{f}]\!]$ ensure that the rank of event e is less than the rank of event f if $(e, f) \in R$. If n is the number of events in $\mathcal{P}$, the resulting SAT encoding is of size $\mathcal{O}(n^2 \log n)$.

Moreover, Section 4.1 proposed a method to reduce the size of R. Table 1 shows the size of the direct asymmetric conflict relation before and after this reduction for some c-nets unfoldings with at least one cycle in R. More precisely, we show the size of the largest SCC (in most examples there is in fact only one non-trivial SCC). In average, the method proposed eliminates 66% of the nodes and 26% of the edges, seeming thus to be more effective at reducing the number of nodes rather than the number of edges, wich in turn becomes a reduction in the number of variables rather than the number of clauses of the encoding.

Table 1. Reduction of the asymmetric-conflict relation

Net	Before reduction Nodes	Before reduction Edges	After reduction Nodes	After reduction Edges	Ratio after/before Nodes	Ratio after/before Edges
`bds_1.sync`	192	271	27	52	0.14	0.19
`byzagr4_1b`	3197	64501	2348	61088	0.73	0.95
`q_1.sync`	189	4095	126	4032	0.67	0.98
`bds_1.fsa`	66	89	9	16	0.14	0.18
`dme11`	8745	44968	4918	40301	0.56	0.90
`rw_2w1r`	1766	8877	915	7447	0.52	0.84

However, in some examples, the remaining SCCs are still rather large, on the order of tens of thousands of events, and in these cases $\phi_{\mathcal{P}}^{\text{asym}}$ negatively impacts the running time. We therefore implemented a two-stage approach, in which the first stage simply omits $\phi_{\mathcal{P}}^{\text{asym}}$ from the formula. Only when this first stage yields a false positive, a second stage with $\phi_{\mathcal{P}}^{\text{asym}}$ is used to obtain a definitive result. This approach was very successful: in over 100 different nets from various sources that we tried, only 2 (small) nets yielded a false positive. The experiments presented in the following use this two-stage approach.

SAT-Solver Settings. MiniSat allows to change aspects of the SAT-solving algorithm, such as decision variables, default polarity etc. We attempted to tweak these settings in order to exploit knowledge about the problem domain, but without obtaining significant improvements. More details are given in [21].

5.2 Comparisons

In [15], Khomenko and Koutny compared three versions of their deadlock checking method, implemented in the tool CLP, against the methods by McMillan [17], Melzer and Römer [18], and Heljanko [11]. In their benchmarks, the first version of their algorithm[2] outperformed the other methods on almost all examples. We experimentally confirmed this conclusion. Moreover, we learnt of an unpublished SAT-based tool by Khomenko which is said to be slower than CLP.[3] We therefore compare our technique with the first method of CLP.[4]

We discuss two families of examples: a standard suite of benchmarks known from the unfolding literature (see Section 5.1), and another family encoding networks of logic gates. The first family does not specifically exploit the features of c-nets; here the savings are not dramatic but still significant. In the second family, c-nets lead to large time savings.

Table 2 presents the results on the aforementioned standard suite. We used Mole [24] to produce finite complete prefixes of the Petri nets and Cunf [20] to do the same for c-nets.[5] The running times for Mole and Cunf are given in the respective columns, the number of events and conditions of the two prefixes is indicated in the columns $|E|$ and $|B|$. For Petri nets, we also give the running times of CLP, and the running time of MiniSat in our encoding on the Petri net. For c-nets we provide the running times of MiniSat with the settings discussed in Section 5.1. Times are given in seconds and represent averages over 10 runs.

We do not provide the translation times to generate linear equation systems (for CLP) or SAT formulas (for MiniSat). Those times would not be very representative since both translators are suboptimal; our own translator to SAT is in a preliminary stage. Also, there is no reason to suspect that the translation times for the linear equations of [15] and SAT, when optimized, would be very different, and we expect such optimized times to be fractions of a second.

Compared to CLP, SAT checking performs well over Petri nets, solving the problems twice as fast on aggregate. Concerning the comparison of SAT checking between Petri nets and c-nets, we obtain another advantage of 13% for deadlock verification. More significantly, the time for generating c-net unfoldings is 30% less than for Petri nets. This advantage is not huge, but recall that these benchmarks are already favourable examples for Petri net unfoldings and

---

[2] Column *std* in Tables 1 and 2 in [15].

[3] According to the author, V. Khomenko.

[4] All experiments have been performed using Cunf v1.4, Mole v1.0.6, both compiled with gcc 4.4.5, version 301 of CLP, and MiniSat v2.2.0. Our machine has twelve 64bit Intel Xeon CPUs, running at 2.67GHz, 50GB RAM and executes Linux 2.6.32-5.

[5] The running times of Mole and Cunf are comparable on Petri nets, but Mole produces prefixes in a format suitable for CLP.

Table 2. Comparison of deadlock-checking methods; the Res(ult) is L(ive) or D(ead)

		Petri net unfolding					c-net unfolding			
		MOLE			CLP	SAT	CUNF			SAT
Net	Res.	Time	$\|E\|$	$\|B\|$	Time	Time	Time	$\|E\|$	$\|B\|$	Time
bds_1.sync	L	0.58	12900	37306	0.04	0.01	0.14	1830	2771	<0.01
byzagr4_1b	L	3.71	14724	42276	0.53	0.26	3.25	8044	17603	0.19
dme11	L	6.56	9185	31186	0.60	0.28	10.86	9185	16710	0.25
dpd_7.sync	L	1.21	10354	29939	0.10	0.18	1.09	10354	21359	0.02
ftp_1.sync	L	45.37	91730	275099	1.13	0.38	26.85	50928	96617	0.05
furnace_4	L	37.44	114477	264823	1.29	0.19	19.11	94413	147438	0.12
rw_12.sync	L	3.95	98361	295152	0.08	0.02	3.96	98361	196796	0.02
rw_1w3r	L	0.30	15432	28207	0.11	0.22	0.36	14521	24174	0.40
rw_2w1r	L	0.22	9363	18575	0.04	0.34	0.32	9363	15304	0.58
elevator_4	D	2.58	16856	47743	0.24	0.03	1.51	16856	28593	0.06
key_4	D	1.68	69600	139206	0.07	0.08	2.07	4754	7862	<0.01
mmgt_4.fsa	D	1.16	46902	92940	0.02	0.04	1.17	46902	92076	0.05
q_1.sync	D	1.76	10716	30087	<0.01	0.02	1.54	10716	20567	0.01
$\sum$		106.52			4.25	2.05	72.23			1.75

were not specifically designed to exploit the advantages of c-nets. The two-stage approach was essential for performance: while the acyclic constraints had a big impact only on a few examples (notably byzagr4_1b,dme,rw*), that effect would have more than nullified the advantage of faster unfolding times.

We now present a class of nets in which read arcs have natural advantages: the encoding of asynchronous circuits of logic gates as Petri nets, one of the motivations originally mentioned by McMillan [17]. In this encoding, the signals, i.e. the inputs and outputs of each gate, are modelled with two places for indicating whether the signal is high (1) or low (0). The outputs change as a function of *reading* the inputs. Fig. 4 (a) shows an AND-gate and its encoding as a c-net fragment.

To illustrate the benefits that c-nets enjoy here, we discuss a simple experiment. We consider a grid of $n := k \times k$ AND-gates, shown in Fig. 4 (b) for $k = 3$. The inputs for the AND-gates are at the left and top of the figure, and outputs propagate to the right and towards the bottom. Inputs may switch freely between high and low. We encoded such grids into c-nets; additionally, we replaced read arcs with arrow loops to obtain equivalent Petri nets (so called *plain encodings*). We then used CUNF to construct complete unfolding prefixes of the c-nets and their plain encodings, and observed that signal changes may be propagated to the bottom right in many different orders, which are distinguished by Petri-net unfoldings but not by c-net unfoldings. Hence, unfoldings of the plain nets were of exponential size in n, while the contextual ones were linear. Moreover, CUNF built the latter ones in time $\mathcal{O}(n^3)$, see Fig. 4 (c). The verification method for c-nets herein presented allows to profit from the reduced unfolding time.

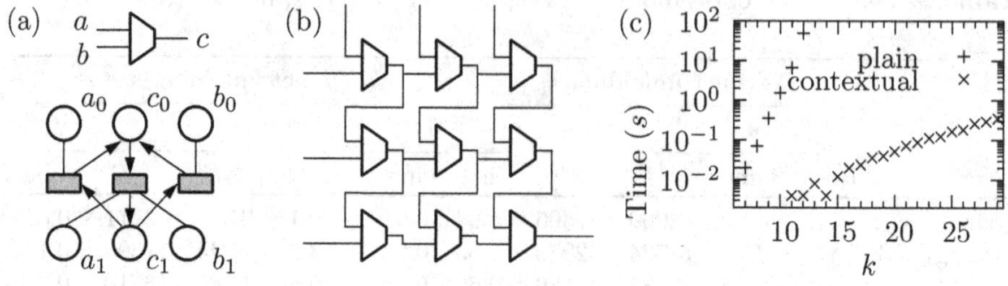

Fig. 4. (a) Encoding of a logical AND-gate; (b) grid of AND-gates; (c) unfolding times

6 Conclusions

We presented verification algorithms based on c-net unfoldings. The twofold advantages over previous work are the overall performance of the SAT encoding, and that c-nets allow to profit from faster unfolding procedures and/or faster verification on the resulting unfolding prefixes. The latter result was not a foregone conclusion due to the richer structure of c-net unfoldings, in particular the presence of cycles and histories.

We studied optimizations of the encoding, concentrating on optimizations on the net level, while leaving optimizations on the logical level to the SAT solver.

An interesting future direction of work would be to extend the verification algorithms to a richer set of properties. E.g., LTL model-checking for Petri nets has been investigated in [7], but the trace logics investigated by Diekert and Gastin [5] and others seem like another natural choice.

Acknowledgements. The authors would like to thank Keijo Heljanko, Victor Khomenko, Paolo Baldan, and the referees for helpful hints and discussions.

References

1. Baldan, P., Bruni, A., Corradini, A., König, B., Schwoon, S.: On the Computation of McMillan's Prefix for Contextual Nets and Graph Grammars. In: Ehrig, H., Rensink, A., Rozenberg, G., Schürr, A. (eds.) ICGT 2010. LNCS, vol. 6372, pp. 91–106. Springer, Heidelberg (2010)
2. Baldan, P., Corradini, A., König, B., Schwoon, S.: McMillan's Complete Prefix for Contextual Nets. In: Jensen, K., van der Aalst, W.M.P., Billington, J. (eds.) ToPNoC 1. LNCS, vol. 5100, pp. 199–220. Springer, Heidelberg (2008)
3. Chen, J.: A new SAT encoding of the at-most-one constraint. In: Proc. Constraint Modelling and Reformulation (2010)
4. Codish, M., Genaim, S., Stuckey, P.J.: A declarative encoding of telecommunications feature subscription in SAT. In: Proc. PPDP, pp. 255–266. ACM (2009)
5. Diekert, V., Gastin, P.: From local to global temporal logics over Mazurkiewicz traces. Theoretical Computer Science 356(1-2), 126–135 (2006)
6. Eén, N., Sörensson, N.: An Extensible SAT-solver. In: Giunchiglia, E., Tacchella, A. (eds.) SAT 2003. LNCS, vol. 2919, pp. 502–518. Springer, Heidelberg (2004)

7. Esparza, J., Heljanko, K.: Implementing LTL Model Checking with Net Unfoldings. In: Dwyer, M.B. (ed.) SPIN 2001. LNCS, vol. 2057, pp. 37–56. Springer, Heidelberg (2001)
8. Esparza, J., Heljanko, K.: Unfoldings - A Partial-Order Approach to Model Checking. EATCS Monographs in Theoretical Computer Science. Springer (2008)
9. Esparza, J., Römer, S., Vogler, W.: An improvement of McMillan's unfolding algorithm. Formal Methods in System Design 20, 285–310 (2002)
10. Esparza, J., Schröter, C.: Unfolding based algorithms for the reachability problem. Fund. Inf. 47(3-4), 231–245 (2001)
11. Heljanko, K.: Using logic programs with stable model semantics to solve deadlock and reachability problems for 1-safe Petri nets. Fund. Inf. 37(3), 247–268 (1999)
12. Khomenko, V.: Model Checking Based on Prefixes of Petri Net Unfoldings. Ph.D. thesis, School of Computing Science, Newcastle University (2003)
13. Khomenko, V., Kondratyev, A., Koutny, M., Vogler, W.: Merged processes – a new condensed representation of Petri net behaviour. Act. Inf. 43(5), 307–330 (2006)
14. Khomenko, V., Koutny, M.: LP Deadlock Checking Using Partial Order Dependencies. In: Palamidessi, C. (ed.) CONCUR 2000. LNCS, vol. 1877, pp. 410–425. Springer, Heidelberg (2000)
15. Khomenko, V., Koutny, M.: Verification of bounded Petri nets using integer programming. Formal Methods in System Design 30(2), 143–176 (2007)
16. Khomenko, V.: PUNF, `homepages.cs.ncl.ac.uk/victor.khomenko/tools/punf/`
17. McMillan, K.L.: Using Unfoldings to avoid the State Explosion Problem in the Verification of Asynchronous Circuits. In: Probst, D.K., von Bochmann, G. (eds.) CAV 1992. LNCS, vol. 663, pp. 164–177. Springer, Heidelberg (1993)
18. Melzer, S., Römer, S.: Deadlock Checking using Net Unfoldings. In: Grumberg, O. (ed.) CAV 1997. LNCS, vol. 1254, pp. 352–363. Springer, Heidelberg (1997)
19. Raynal, M.: Algorithms for Mutual Exclusion. MIT Press (1986)
20. Rodríguez, C.: CUNF, `http://www.lsv.ens-cachan.fr/~rodriguez/tools/cunf/`
21. Rodríguez, C., Schwoon, S.: Verification of Petri Nets with Read Arcs. Tech. Rep. LSV-12-12, LSV, ENS de Cachan (2012)
22. Rodríguez, C., Schwoon, S., Baldan, P.: Efficient Contextual Unfolding. In: Katoen, J.-P., König, B. (eds.) CONCUR 2011. LNCS, vol. 6901, pp. 342–357. Springer, Heidelberg (2011)
23. Schröter, C.: Halbordnungs- und Reduktionstechniken für die automatische Verifikation von verteilten Systemen. Ph.D. thesis, Universität Stuttgart (2006)
24. Schwoon, S.: MOLE, `http://www.lsv.ens-cachan.fr/~schwoon/tools/mole/`
25. Schwoon, S., Rodríguez, C.: Construction and SAT-Based Verification of Contextual Unfoldings. In: Holzer, M. (ed.) DCFS 2011. LNCS, vol. 6808, pp. 34–42. Springer, Heidelberg (2011)

Efficient Checking of Link-Reversal-Based Concurrent Systems

Matthias Függer[1,*] and Josef Widder[2,**]

[1] TU Wien, Embedded Computing Systems Group
[2] TU Wien, Formal Methods in Systems Engineering Group

Abstract. Link reversal is an algorithmic method with various applications. Originally proposed by Gafni and Bertsekas in 1981 for routing in radio networks, it has been later applied also to solve concurrency related problems as mutual exclusion, resource allocation, and leader election. For resource allocation, conflicts can be represented by conflict graphs, and link reversal algorithms work on these graphs to resolve conflicts. In this paper we establish that executions of link reversal algorithms on large graphs are similar (a notion which we make precise in the paper) to executions on smaller graphs. This similarity then allows to verify linear time temporal properties of large systems, by verifying a smaller one.

1 Introduction

Model checking has been applied successfully to finite state hardware and software systems. Application of these techniques to concurrent systems that involve a possibly unbounded number of processes is still a major research question. In a seminal paper, Emerson and Namjoshi [12] showed that the problem is undecidable even in quite simple settings. Despite this discouraging result, Emerson and Namjoshi studied systems where verification is possible. In particular, they considered systems consisting of an arbitrary number of concurrent processes, where processes are organized in a logical ring and a token that circulates in the ring is used to coordinate special actions. They showed that verifying certain correctness properties of such systems of any size can be reduced to verifying small systems of that kind. The token circulation scheme ensures that certain actions of processes are scheduled in a strict round-robin fashion. Later, Clarke *et al.* [9] generalized the work of Emerson and Namjoshi by replacing the round-robin schedule by a more relaxed fairness assumption in which in each infinite run, each process receives the token infinitely often, while the frequency at which the token visits processes may vary between the processes.

While the techniques developed in [12] and [9] allow efficient verification, the results are limited to single token-based concurrent systems. The basic idea

* Supported by projects P21694 and P20529 of the Austrian Science Fund (FWF).
** Supported in part by the Austrian National Research Network S11403-N23 (RiSE) of the Austrian Science Fund (FWF), by the Vienna Science and Technology Fund (WWTF) grant PROSEED, and by NSF grant 0964696.

M. Koutny and I. Ulidowski (Eds.): CONCUR 2012, LNCS 7454, pp. 486–499, 2012.

behind structuring concurrent applications using a token is that the current holder of the token is privileged, and thus allowed to enter its critical section. Thus, tokens are a means to resolve conflicts over shared resources. However, the systems considered in [12] or [9] are based on the assumption that at each time at most one process may be privileged, which implicitly means that in both systems the (conservative) assumption is made that all processes are in conflict with all other processes. This assumption is usually overly pessimistic. Moreover, it drastically restricts the degree of concurrency in a system, as at each time at most one process may be scheduled to execute critical code, which basically boils down to serializing concurrent actions. Link reversal algorithms have been used to get rid of these limitations [6,3], thus allowing to model systems with multiple tokens.

Substantial amount of literature is devoted to link-reversal algorithms (cf. [18] for an overview). Link reversal algorithms work on directed graphs, where to each node a process is associated. A process that is a *sink*, that is, all its incident links are incoming, reverses some of its incident links to be no longer a sink. Algorithms differ in which links are reversed. In this paper we will first focus on the *full reversal* (FR) algorithm in which always *all* incident links are reversed, and will then briefly discuss possible generalizations to the algorithm LR by using a recently introduced formalism [8].

The application of link-reversal algorithms ranges from routing and other problems in wireless networks [16,15,5] to resource allocation in concurrent systems [6,3]. While in the routing problem, the communication graph is the underlying graph on which the algorithms work, in resource allocation, one considers the conflict graph: Let G be a *conflict graph*, that is, a directed graph, whose underlying non-directed graph is connected. If two processes have a conflict—for instance, access a common shared resource—there is a link between the two processes in G. If a link points from i to j, then process j is currently preferred to i. If a node is a sink, it is preferred with respect to all nodes it has a conflict with. As two neighbors cannot be sinks at the same time, a process associated to a sink may thus safely enter the critical section. Upon leaving the critical section it has to reverse the direction of some incident links.

This approach allows high degrees of concurrency in that processes that do not have a conflict may be in their critical sections at the same time. (Obviously, there may be multiple sinks in a directed graph.) Note that in the case where all processes have conflicts with all processes, this leads to a complete conflict graph in which there is (at most) one sink; link reversal thus generalizes the (round-robin) token based approach.

Link reversal algorithms determine the order in which processes take steps, that is, the *schedule*. These schedules induce executions of a transition system or Kripke structure for which temporal logic formulas can be verified. We are interested in linear time temporal logic properties that consider only some of the processes in a system.

Contributions. After recalling the FR algorithm and giving basic definitions, we provide preliminary analysis of FR executions in Section 2. Apart from providing a result on how steps of processes change the conflict graph, we explain how systems can be composed to ensure liveness and fairness. In Section 3, we define the model checking problem we are interested in, and will recall an important theorem that relates model checking of properties in the temporal logic LTL \ X to stutter equivalence of traces. We can therefore concentrate on stutter equivalence of FR executions in the following. In Section 4, we characterize properties of conflict graphs which imply stutter equivalence of FR executions from these graphs. This analysis eventually leads to our major result in Corollary 1, which provides us with a tool to construct small conflict graphs that allow to verify properties of larger ones. For instance, properties that consider only two processes can be verified by considering just a chain graph. In Section 4 we give some examples. After discussing possible generalizations to other link reversal algorithms in Section 5, we close with conclusions that can be drawn from our results, for instance, concerning cut-off sizes.

2 The Full Reversal Algorithm

As mentioned above, the underlying structure of full reversal (FR) is a directed graph. The FR algorithm [13], consists of the following rule which can be applied by any node i that is a sink:

FR: All the links incident on i are reversed.

Note that the FR rule neither changes the set of nodes of the graph nor its undirected support. Let $G_0 = \langle V, E\rangle$ be a conflict graph, i.e., a directed graph whose underlying non-directed graph is connected, with the set of nodes V and the set of links E. An *FR execution* from G_0 is an infinite sequence G_0, S_1, ..., G_{t-1}, S_t, ... of alternating directed graphs and sets of nodes satisfying that for each $t \geq 1$, (i) if there is a sink in G_{t-1}, then S_t is a nonempty subset of the sinks in G_{t-1}, and $S_t = \emptyset$ otherwise, and (ii) G_t is obtained from G_{t-1} by requiring each node i in S_t to apply the FR rule. A sequence of subsets of V, $S = S_1, S_2, \dots$ is called a *schedule*, and a schedule satisfying (i) and (ii) for initial graph G_0 is called an FR schedule from G_0. If i is in S_t, we say i *takes a step at iteration* t in schedule S. For a given schedule S and a node i, let $W_i(t)$ be the *work of* i by t, that is, the number of iterations $t' \leq t$ in which $i \in S_{t'}$. Formally, $W_i(t) = |\{t' \colon 1 \leq t' \leq t \wedge i \in S_{t'}\}|$. Initially, $W_i(0) = 0$ for all nodes i.

2.1 Basic Properties of FR-Based Schedules

We start by introducing some notation. In the following, let $G = \langle V, E\rangle$ be an *acyclic* conflict graph. A *chain* is a sequence $i_0, \dots, i_k$ of nodes in G, such that either (i_m, i_{m+1}) is in E or (i_{m+1}, i_m) is in E, for $0 \leq m < k$, where k is called the *length* of a chain c, denoted by len(c). A *circuit* is a chain with $i_0 = i_k$ and length greater than 0. A chain is *simple* if its nodes are pairwise distinct, except for the first and last node which may be equal. Let $C^s(i, j)$ be the set of simple chains of nonzero length that start at i and end at j. A *path* is a chain $i_0, \dots, i_k$

such that (i_m, i_{m+1}) is in E, for $0 \leq m < k$. The quantity $r_G(c)$, is the number of links in c that are directed "to the right." More formally, if $c = i_0, \ldots, i_k$ is a chain in the graph G, $r_G(c) = |\{(i_m, i_{m+1}) \in E\colon 0 \leq m < k\}|$. Clearly, $r_G(c) = \text{len}(c)$ if and only if c is a path. As the FR algorithm only changes the direction of the links, but not the undirected support of the graph, we observe that for any FR schedule from a graph G_0, c is a chain in G_t if and only if c is a chain in G_{t+1}.

Let $\Sigma(G_0)$ be the *set of schedules*, and let $\Sigma_{FR}(G_0) \subseteq \Sigma(G_0)$ be the *set of FR schedules* from initial graph G_0. We obtain the following invariant of chains within FR executions:

Proposition 1. *Let $G_0, S_1, \ldots, G_t, S_{t+1}, G_{t+1}, \ldots$ be an FR execution. For any two nodes i and j in V, and any chain c in $C^s(i,j)$:*

(1) $r_{G_{t+1}}(c) = r_{G_t}(c)$, if $S_{t+1} \setminus \{i,j\} = S_{t+1}$,
(2) $r_{G_{t+1}}(c) = r_{G_t}(c) + 1$, if $i \in S_{t+1}$ and $j \notin S_{t+1}$,
(3) $r_{G_{t+1}}(c) = r_{G_t}(c) - 1$, if $i \notin S_{t+1}$ and $j \in S_{t+1}$, and
(4) $r_{G_{t+1}}(c) = r_{G_t}(c)$, otherwise, that is, if $\{i,j\} \subseteq S_{t+1}$.

Proof. Let the chain $c = i_0, \ldots, i_\ell$.

(1) Nodes that do not belong to c and take steps, or nodes that do not take steps have no influence on $r(c)$. As neither i nor j take a step at iteration $t+1$, we only have to consider nodes k with two distinct incoming links relative to c. These nodes reverse the directions of both links relative to c. As both links are reversed, the numbers of links pointing to left and right in c, respectively, remain unchanged, which proves (1).

(2) Consider the case where $i = i_0$ takes a step at iteration $t+1$, but j does not. As i_0 takes a step, it is a sink in G_t and therefore (i_0, i_1) is not a link of G_t. Therefore i_1 is not a sink in G_t, and $i_1 \notin S_{t+1}$. Letting c' be the subchain $i_1, \ldots, i_\ell$ of c, we may therefore apply case (1) to c' and obtain

$$r_{G_{t+1}}(c') = r_{G_t}(c'). \tag{i}$$

As i_0 reverses all links in iteration $t+1$, (i_0, i_1) is a link G_{t+1}. As (i_0, i_1) is not a link of G_t, letting $c'' = i_0, i_1$ we obtain

$$r_{G_{t+1}}(c'') = r_{G_t}(c'') + 1. \tag{ii}$$

As c is the concatenation of the chains c'' and c', we obtain from (i) and (ii) that $r_{G_{t+1}}(c) = r_{G_{t+1}}(c'') + r_{G_{t+1}}(c') = r_{G_t}(c'') + 1 + r_{G_t}(c') = r_{G_t}(c) + 1$. The proposition follows in this case, and (3) can be proven analogously.

Similar arguments can be used for (4): Since (1) can be applied to $i_1, \ldots, i_{\ell-1}$, the number of right links stays constant in this subchain. As i and j take steps, the first link (i_1, i_0) and the last link $(i_{\ell-1}, i_\ell)$ in G_t are reversed in G_{t+1}. These two reversal cancel each other out, and (4) follows. □

For a graph G we define $R_G(i,j) = \min\{r_G(c) \mid c \in C^s(i,j)\}$. For the cases of Proposition 1 we thus observe, that in cases (1) and (4) $R_{G_{t+1}}(i,j) = R_{G_t}(i,j)$, in case (2) $R_{G_{t+1}}(i,j) = R_{G_t}(i,j) + 1$, and in case (3) $R_{G_{t+1}}(i,j) = R_{G_t}(i,j) - 1$. By repeated application of Proposition 1 we thus obtain:

Proposition 2. *If* $G_0, S_1, \ldots, G_t, S_{t+1}, G_{t+1}, \ldots$ *is an FR execution from* G_0*, then for any two nodes* i *and* j *in* V*, and any* $t \geq 0$*:*

$$R_{G_t}(i,j) = R_{G_0}(i,j) + W_i(t) - W_j(t).$$

Proposition 3. *Let* $G_0, S_1, \ldots, G_t, S_{t+1}, G_{t+1}, \ldots$ *be an FR execution from* G_0*. For any* $t > 0$*, if* $j \in S_t$ *and* $i \in V$*, then*

$$W_j(t-1) - W_i(t-1) < R_{G_0}(i,j).$$

Proof. As $j \in S_t$, node j is a sink in G_{t-1}. It follows that at least the last link in each chain ending at j is directed towards j and therefore $R_{G_{t-1}}(i,j) > 0$.

From Proposition 2 follows that

$$R_{G_{t-1}}(i,j) = R_{G_0}(i,j) + W_i(t-1) - W_j(t-1). \qquad \text{(i)}$$

Now, assume by ways of contradiction that $W_j(t-1) - W_i(t-1) \geq R_{G_0}(i,j)$, that is,

$$0 \leq -R_{G_0}(i,j) + W_j(t-1) - W_i(t-1). \qquad \text{(ii)}$$

Adding (i) and (ii), we obtain that $R_{G_{t-1}}(i,j) \leq 0$ which provides the required contradiction. □

2.2 Ensuring Liveness and Fairness

Emerson and Namjoshi [12], restricted the systems by requiring that processes are organized in a directed ring. In the link reversal approach processes can be organized in different ways. Two important properties of schedules that should be met by possible organizations are liveness and fairness: An FR schedule S from graph G_0 is called *live* if there is no $t' \geq 1$ such that $S_t = \emptyset$ for all $t \geq t'$. It is further called *fair* if each node in V takes an infinite number of steps in S. If the difference on the number of times processes are scheduled is bounded, we say a system ensures *strong fairness.*

To see when FR ensures liveness, we first observe that any acyclic conflict graph always contain at least one sink. Further, as in FR always all links incident to a sink are reversed, it is easy to see that FR maintains acyclicity. (This is a well known fact already used in [13]; a proof based on invariants is given in [8].) Hence, FR ensures that starting from an initial acyclic graph, all following graphs are acyclic, and thus contain at least one sink. For our purposes we obtain:

Proposition 4. *All FR schedules from an acyclic conflict graph are live.*

We next show that any FR schedule is not only fair but even provides stronger fairness guarantees:

Proposition 5. *Let* G_0 *be an acyclic conflict graph. All FR schedules from* G_0 *ensure strong-fairness: for any two nodes* i *and* j*, and any iteration* $t \geq 1$*,*

$$W_i(t) - W_j(t) \leq R_{G_0}(j,i).$$

Proof. Assume by means of contradiction that there is an FR execution from G_0 and an iteration $t \geq 1$ such that $W_i(t) - W_j(t) > R_{G_0}(j,i)$. Application of Proposition 2 yields, $R_{G_t}(j,i) = R_{G_0}(j,i) - (W_i(t) - W_j(t)) < 0$; a contradiction to $R_{G_t}(j,i)$ being by definition non-negative. The proposition follows. □

Since $R_{G_0}(j,i)$ is bounded by the diameter of the graph G_0, one immediately obtains that $|W_i(t) - W_j(t)|$ is at most the diameter of G_0 for all $t \geq 0$. We thus conclude that from a composability viewpoint, composition of FR instances without violating liveness and (strong) fairness requires just checking whether the resulting graph is acyclic and is therefore not significantly more complex than the composition of rings treated by Emerson and Namjoshi [12].

3 Checking FR Scheduled Systems

We assume that each node i in V is equipped with a deterministic finite state machine on i's *local state* s_i, where s_i can attain values from state space $\sigma(i)$. The *global state* is defined to be a tuple of local states $s = (s_i)_{i \in V}$. In the following we denote by $I = \{i_j \colon 1 \leq j \leq |I|\}$ a nonempty subset of V. If s is a global state, then we denote by $s|I$ the projection of the global state s to I, that is, $s|I = (s_i)_{i \in I}$. We assume for simplicity that nodes change their local state, according to their state machine, only when scheduled. Thus given an initial global state $s^0 = (s_i^0)_{i \in V}$, a schedule S from $\Sigma(G_0)$ induces an *execution* from s^0, that is, an infinite sequence $s^0, s^1, \ldots$ of global states. From the initial global states and $\Sigma(G_0)$ one can define a transition system. Let AP be a set of atomic propositions, and λ_I be a function $\lambda_I \colon \sigma(i_1) \times \sigma(i_2) \times \cdots \times \sigma(i_{|I|}) \rightarrow 2^{AP}$. Then, λ is defined to be a labeling function for global states such that $\lambda(s) = \lambda_I(s|I)$. Fixing AP and λ, the transition system then defines a Kripke structure, which we denote by $M_{G_0|I}$. The Kripke structure then defines a set of sequences of atomic propositions, called *traces*. The model checking problem is whether $M_{G_0|I}$ is a model for some temporal logic formula φ over the atomic propositions AP, denoted by $M_{G_0|I} \models \varphi$.

Note that in an FR execution where $I \cap S_t = \emptyset$, $\lambda_I(s^{t-1}|I) = \lambda_I(s^t|I)$ and thus $\lambda(s^{t-1}) = \lambda(s^t)$. This behavior is called stuttering. In the following we shall use well established results regarding stutter equivalence to show how to efficiently verify FR scheduled systems. We need some more preliminaries. Stutter equivalence of two traces τ_1 and τ_2 is defined as follows: From a trace τ, the stutter free trace $\bar{\tau}$ is obtained by removing all successive repetitions. Then two traces are stutter equivalent if $\bar{\tau}_1 = \bar{\tau}_2$.

For each schedule $S = S_1, S_2, \ldots$ from $\Sigma(G_0)$ and each nonempty subset I of V, we define $S \mid I$ to be the infinite sequence $S_1 \cap I, S_2 \cap I, \ldots$ called the projection of S to I. Further for an infinite sequence S of subsets of V, denote by $Co(S)$ the *condensed sequence of* S, that is obtained from S by removing all empty sets. We observe that if for two schedules S and S', $Co(S \mid I) = Co(S' \mid I)$ then the traces defined by S and S' are stutter equivalent.

In this paper we consider model checking against linear temporal logic formulas. More precisely, we consider the linear temporal logic without the "next time" operator LTL \ X. For this temporal logic, there exists the following theorem, whose proof is given, for instance, in [2, page 534].

Theorem 1. *For any two infinite traces τ_1 and τ_2 over atomic propositions AP, and for any LTL\ X formula φ over AP, if τ_1 and τ_2 are stutter equivalent, then $\tau_1 \models \varphi$ if and only if $\tau_2 \models \varphi$.*

In the following we are therefore interested in stutter equivalence of schedules, and consequently stutter equivalence between the traces of the Kripke structures. In particular, we will show that the set of all condensed FR schedules from some conflict graph is equal to the set of all condensed FR schedules from a considerably simpler and smaller "reduced" graph.

4 Equivalence of FR Schedules

In this section we will develop our central result in Corollary 1, that can be found at the end of this section. It considers two graphs G_0 and G'_0, where the set of nodes U is contained in both graphs. We show that if certain properties of the directions on links along chains connecting nodes in U are satisfied in both, then $M_{G_0|U} \models \varphi$ if and only if $M_{G'_0|U} \models \varphi$. Then, we will show that the corollary gives us a tool to construct a small graph satisfying the same temporal logic formulas as a large graph.

We start by analyzing the relationship between schedules of FR executions, and initial link directions. We say a conflict graph G_0 is *U-oriented*, where U is a nonempty subset of nodes in G_0, if there exists a path from each node in G_0 to a node in U.

Proposition 6. *Let G be an acyclic conflict graph and U a nonempty subset of nodes in G. If only nodes in U are sinks in G, then G is U-oriented.*

Proof. Assume that only nodes in U are sinks. Choose an arbitrary node i_0 in G. In case i_0 is in U, there exists a path from i_0 to a node in U, namely the empty path, and we are done. Otherwise, i_0 is not a sink in G. Thus there exists a node i_1 such that (i_0, i_1) is a link in G. Again, either i_1 in U in which case there exists a path from i_0 to a node in U, or i_1 is not a sink. By repeated application of the above arguments, we obtain a sequence of nodes $i_0, i_1, \ldots$ whose nodes are pairwise distinct because G is acyclic. As V is finite, one eventually ends up in a node in U. Since the finite sequence is a path in G and its last node is in U, the proposition follows. □

Using Proposition 6, we shall next establish the relation between FR executions from a graph G_0, and the direction of links on chains connecting two nodes in G_0. Intuitively, node i may take a step before node j if and only if on each chain connecting j and i, at least one link is directed towards i.

Proposition 7. *Let G_0 be an acyclic conflict graph. For any two disjoint subsets I and J of V, where I is nonempty, the following statements are equivalent:*

(A) *There exists an FR execution from G_0 such that all nodes in I take their first step at the same iteration $t \geq 1$, and no node in J takes a step before or at iteration t.*

(B) *For all nodes $i \in I$ and $j \in I \cup J$, $R_{G_0}(j,i) > 0$.*

Proof. To show that Statement (A) implies (B), let $G_0, S_1, G_1, \ldots$ be an FR execution from G_0, where all nodes in I take their first step at iteration t, and no node in J takes a step before or at iteration t. Then, all nodes i in I are sinks in G_{t-1}. Thus all chains ending at i have at least one link directed towards i and for all i in I and j in $I \cup J$, $R_{G_{t-1}}(j,i) > 0$. Proposition 2 yields

$$R_{G_0}(j,i) + W_j(t-1) - W_i(t-1) = R_{G_{t-1}}(j,i) > 0.$$

From $W_i(t-1) = W_j(t-1) = 0$, one finally obtains $R_{G_0}(j,i) > 0$.

To show that Statement (B) implies (A), let $G_0, S_1, G_1, \ldots, S_{t-1}, G_{t-1}$, with $t-1 \geq 0$, be a (finite) prefix of an FR execution from G_0, where for all t', $1 \leq t' \leq t-1$, no node in $I \cup J$ takes a step at iteration t', and only nodes in $I \cup J$ are sinks in G_{t-1}. Such a prefix must exist as otherwise in all FR executions from G_0, where nodes $I \cup J$ do not take steps, there exists a node u in $V \backslash (I \cup J)$ that takes an infinite number of steps, which contradicts strong-fairness of Proposition 5. Proposition 6 further yields that G_{t-1} is $(I \cup J)$-oriented.

To show that Statement (A) follows, it is thus sufficient to show that all nodes in I are sinks in G_{t-1}: Assume by means of contradiction that there is a node i in I that is not a sink in G_{t-1}. Then there exists a neighbor u of i, such that, (i,u) is a link in G_{t-1}. Since G_{t-1} is $(I \cup J)$-oriented, there must be a path from u to some j' in $I \cup J$. Thus there is a path from i to j'. It follows that $R_{G_{t-1}}(j',i) = 0$. Further, by Proposition 2, $R_{G_0}(j',i) + W_{j'}(t-1) - W_i(t-1) = R_{G_{t-1}}(j',i)$. Because $W_{j'}(t-1) = W_i(t-1) = 0$, it holds that $R_{G_0}(j',i) = 0$, a contradiction to Statement (B). □

For a nonempty set of nodes $U \subseteq V$, Proposition 7 allows to determine whether there exist FR schedules S from initial graph G_0 such that the condensed schedule $Co(S \mid U)$ starts with a set $I \subseteq U$. For example, in case $U = \{i,j\}$, there exists a condensed schedule $Co(S \mid U)$ that starts with $\{i,j\}$ if and only if $R_{G_0}(i,j) > 0$ and $R_{G_0}(j,i) > 0$.

Repeated application of Propositions 2 and 7, finally allows us to determine the set of all possible condensed schedules $Co(S \mid U)$, where S is an FR schedule from G_0 and $U \subseteq V$. This set is called the *set of U-condensed FR schedules from G_0*.

Theorem 2. *Let G_0 be an acyclic conflict graph, U a nonempty subset of its nodes, and $S = S_1, S_2, \ldots$ a schedule of nodes in U. The following statements are equivalent:*

(A) *Schedule S is a U-condensed FR schedule from G_0.*

(B) *For all $t \geq 1$, (B.i) S_t is nonempty, and (B.ii) for each node i in S_t, and each j in U, $W_i(t-1) - W_j(t-1) < R_{G_0}(j,i)$.*

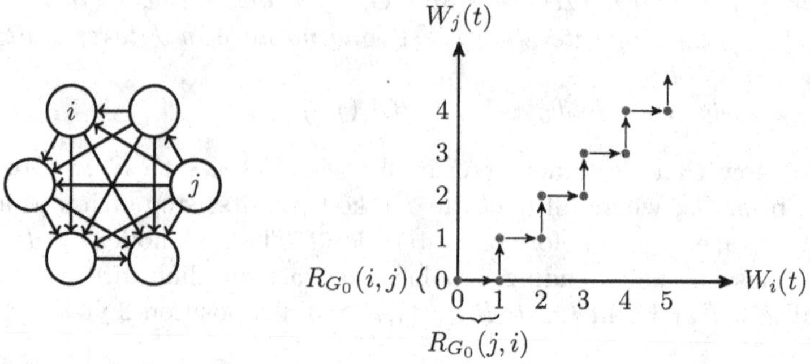

Fig. 1. Complete conflict graph G_0 and set of $\{i, j\}$-condensed FR schedules from G_0

Proof. To show that Statement (A) implies (B), first observe that (B.i) immediately follows from liveness and fairness of FR schedules from acyclic conflict graphs. Further, (B.ii) follows from Proposition 3.

To show that Statement (B) implies (A), we prove by induction on $t \geq 1$, that for all $t \geq 1$ there exists an FR schedule S' from initial graph G_0 such that $Co(S' \mid U)$ has a prefix of length t equal to $S_1, S_2, \ldots, S_t$. From this it follows that $Co(S' \mid U) = S$, and thus (A) holds.

Induction basis ($t = 1$). Let $I = S_1$ and $J = U$. For all $i \in I$ and $j \in J$ follows from our assumption that $R_{G_0}(j, i) > W_i(0) - W_j(0)$. As $W_i(0) = W_j(0) = 0$, it follows that $R_{G_0}(j, i) > 0$. Therefore, we may apply Proposition 7 with initial graph G_0, in order to obtain that there exists an FR schedule S' from initial graph G_0 such that schedule $Co(S' \mid U)$ starts with $I = S_1$.

Inductive step ($t - 1 \to t$). Assume that there is an FR schedule S' such that $Co(S' \mid U)$ has a prefix of length $t - 1$ equal to $S_1, S_2, \ldots, S_{t-1}$. Letting $I = S_t$ and $J = U$, we obtain from Proposition 2 that for all i in I and j in J,

$$R_{G_{t-1}}(j, i) = R_{G_0}(j, i) - (W_i(t-1) - W_j(t-1)) > 0 \ . \tag{1}$$

Application of Proposition 7 with G_{t-1} as initial graph, and the sets I and J as defined above, together with Equation (1) yields that there exists an FR schedule S' from initial graph G_0 such that schedule $Co(S' \mid U)$ starts with $S_1, S_2, \ldots, S_t$. The theorem follows. □

Figures 1 and 2 show examples of condensed schedules as characterized by Theorem 2. Figure 1 depicts a complete conflict graph and Figure 2 a chain conflict graph, respectively, together with a graphical representation of the set of all $\{i, j\}$-condensed FR schedules from the respective graphs: Hereby a schedule is represented by a path in the infinite lattice. For example the (only) path in Figure 1 corresponds to the (only) $\{i, j\}$-condensed FR schedule $\{i\}, \{j\}, \{i\}, \ldots$ from the complete conflict graph.

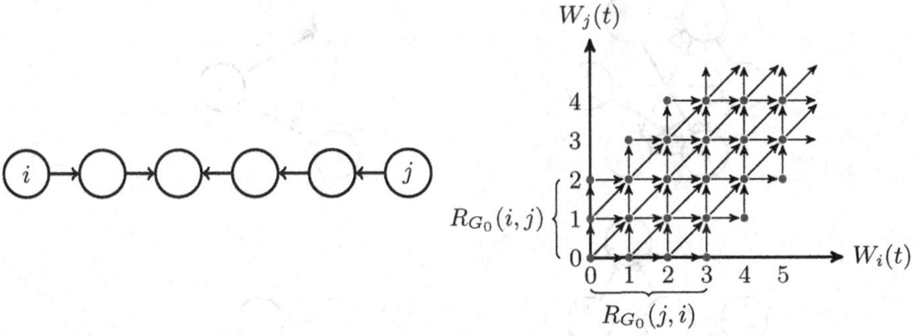

Fig. 2. Chain conflict graph G_0 and set of $\{i,j\}$-condensed FR schedules from G_0

From the understanding of FR schedules we obtained from Theorem 2, we are now in the position to state the main theorem of this paper. It is an exact characterization of all conflict graphs G_0 for which the set of U-condensed FR schedules from G_0 is the same.

Theorem 3. *Let $G_0 = \langle V, E\rangle$ and $G'_0 = \langle V', E'\rangle$ be acyclic conflict graphs and let $U \subseteq V \cap V'$ be nonempty. If for all i and j in U, $R_{G_0}(i,j) = R_{G'_0}(i,j)$, then the set of U-condensed FR schedules from G_0 is identical to the set of U-condensed FR schedules from G'_0.*

Proof. According to Theorem 2, the set of U-condensed FR schedules from G_0 is the set of schedules satisfying that for all $t \geq 1$ (i) S_t is nonempty, and (ii) for each node i in $S_t \subseteq U$, and each node j in U, $W_i(t-1) - W_j(t-1) < R_{G_0}(j,i)$. This condition depends on G_0 only by the value of $R_{G_0}(j,i)$, for any i and j in U. As by our assumption, $R_{G_0}(i,j) = R_{G'_0}(i,j)$, for all i and j in U, the theorem follows. □

Combination of Theorem 3 and Theorem 1 thus allows us to check properties on executions induced by an FR schedule from the simple reduced graph of the original graph G_0:

Corollary 1. *Let $G_0 = \langle V, E\rangle$ and $G'_0 = \langle V', E'\rangle$ be acyclic conflict graphs and let $U \subseteq V \cap V'$ be nonempty. Further let φ be a LTL $\setminus$ X formula over AP. If, for all nodes i and j in U, $R_{G_0}(i,j) = R_{G'_0}(i,j)$, then $M_{G_0|U} \models \varphi$ if and only if $M_{G'_0|U} \models \varphi$.*

Corollary 1 provides us with a way to construct from G_0 simpler graphs G'_0 that allow to verify the same properties. We just have to ensure that $R_{G_0}(i,j) = R_{G'_0}(i,j)$. Interestingly there exists a very simple graph in the case U comprises of two distinct nodes i and j of G_0, only: We denote by $Red_{ij}(G_0)$ a *reduced graph of* G_0. It is a chain graph that starts with node i, ends with node j, and has $R_{G_0}(j,i)$ links pointing towards i and $R_{G_0}(i,j)$ links pointing towards j in it. Then, the set of $\{i,j\}$-condensed FR schedules from G_0 is identical to the set of $\{i,j\}$-condensed FR schedules from $Red_{ij}(G_0)$.

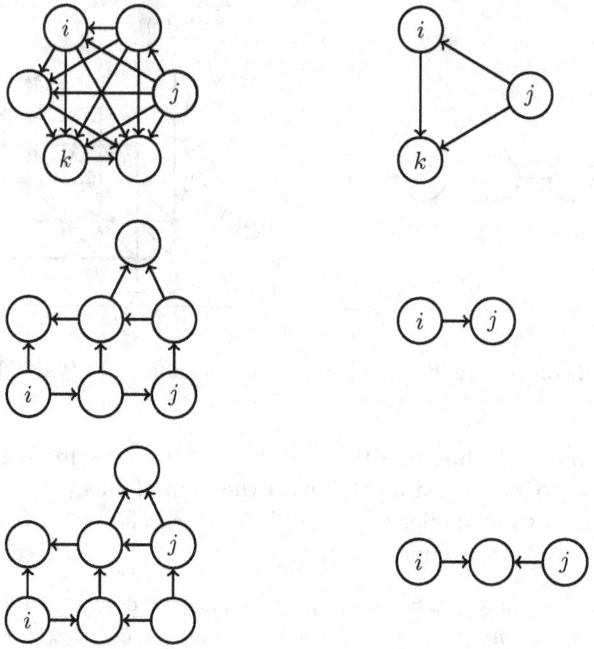

Fig. 3. Conflict graphs (on the left) and their small reduced graphs (on the right)

One can easily generalize graph $Red_{ij}(G_0)$ to the case where U is an arbitrary nonempty subset of nodes in G_0: For each pair i, j of nodes in U, there is a chain in $Red_U(G_0)$ that starts with node i, ends with node j, and has $R_{G_0}(j, i)$ links pointing towards i and $R_{G_0}(i, j)$ links pointing towards j in it. Any two such chains have distinct nodes except possibly for the first or last node. Figure 3 shows some examples of how small reduced graphs can be constructed from conflict graphs G_0.

5 Generalizing FR

Recently, Charron-Bost *et al.* [8] introduced a new formalism called LR that generalizes FR and another link reversal algorithm introduced by Gafni and Bertsekas [13] called partial reversal (PR). In PR only those links are reversed that have not been reversed since the last time a node was a sink.

The LR algorithm works on directed graphs whose links are labeled with $\mathbb{0}$ or $\mathbb{1}$. Each node i can apply the following (mutually exclusive) rules if it is a sink:

R1: If at least one link incident on i is labeled $\mathbb{0}$, then all the links incident on node i that are labeled with $\mathbb{0}$ are reversed, the other incident links are not reversed, and the labels on all the incident links are flipped.

R2: If all the links incident on node i are labeled $\mathbb{1}$, then all the links incident on i are reversed, but none of their labels is changed.

This approach generalizes FR and PR via different initial link labelings: if the links are all initially labeled with $\mathbb{1}$, links remain labeled with $\mathbb{1}$ and a sink can execute R2 only. The generated executions are FR executions. Otherwise, if all links are initially labeled with $\mathbb{0}$, then certain nodes may apply R1. One can show that the generated executions are PR executions. Non-uniform labelings may lead to executions different from FR and PR.

Ensuring Liveness and Fairness. We have discussed above that composing two graphs without violating liveness and fairness in the FR case requires just to ensure acyclicity of the resulting initial graph. In the general LR case liveness and fairness do not follow from the initial graph being acyclic. However, in [8] we introduced a simple property (AC) on graphs that guarantees both liveness and fairness of LR schedules from graphs where (AC) is satisfied. It was shown in [7] that checking the (AC) condition for a graph can be reduced to checking the acyclicity of a transformed graph and can thus be achieved efficiently. Moreover, in [8] we discussed a specialization of (AC) that can be easily implemented: for each node, all incoming labels are locally uniformly labeled (either by $\mathbb{0}$ or $\mathbb{1}$). Finding working initial labelings can thus be done efficiently.

For composition purposes, note that joining two graph components A and B can be done by connecting nodes in A with nodes in B. If all links are directed from A to B and labeled with $\mathbb{1}$, (AC) is satisfied if (AC) is satisfied in A and B.

Hence, from a composability viewpoint the more general link reversal approach is not significantly more complex than FR.

Checking LR scheduled systems. We have recently shown [7] that any LR execution from a labeled conflict graph G_0 is equivalent to an FR execution from a (non labeled) transformed conflict graph G_0^{FR}: For each node i in G_0, there is either one node i' or two nodes i'_0 and i'_1 in graph G_0^{FR}. Node i' respectively nodes i'_0 and i'_1 are called the corresponding nodes of i. Whether there are one or two corresponding nodes of i depends on the labels and directions of links incident on i only. In [7], we have shown that there is a bijection from the set of LR schedules from G_0 to the set of FR schedule from G_0^{FR} such that, node i takes a step at iteration t in the LR execution if and only if one of the corresponding nodes of i takes a step at iteration t in the FR execution.

Consequently, we can apply Corollary 1 to conflict graph G_0^{FR}, which easily generalizes our approach to LR. Note, that since G_0^{FR} has at most twice the nodes of G_0, this approach is still efficient.

6 Discussions

We recalled the link reversal approach for scheduling concurrent systems, and presented new results regarding the verification of systems based on this approach. The work is closely related to parameterized model checking [1,4,14,17,10,11] where one tries to verify properties of systems of any size. In this context, Emerson and Namjoshi [12] and Clarke *et al.* [9] presented constant size cut-offs — that is, graphs consisting of two to five nodes — for restricted classes of temporal logic formulas. They proved for token-based systems that if some temporal logic formula can be verified for the cut-off graphs, then they hold for systems of any size. One important property of the restricted classes of temporal logic is that their satisfiability has to be independent of the system size. This is why usually the "next time" operator has to be forbidden.

For link-reversal-based systems, one consequence of our Corollary 1 is that system size cannot be determined by our logic: For each graph G_0, all nodes i and j in U, one can easily create a graph G'_0 containing more nodes (for instance by appending a chain of arbitrary length to one node), that still satisfies $R_{G_0}(i,j) = R_{G'_0}(i,j)$. With this respect, the correctness of some systems of arbitrary size follows from the correctness of systems that are scheduled according to our reduced graphs.

With respect to cut-off sizes, assume each node i's state machine can represent — for some constant C — a counter c_i, for $0 \leq c_i < C$. Upon each step of node i the counter c_i is increased by one. One can then define a constant D, satisfying $D < C$, and a labeling function that maps the global states satisfying $c_i - c_j \leq D$ to some atomic proposition p. Consider the problem of verifying the property $\varphi \equiv \mathbf{G}p$, which means that p is always satisfied. Proposition 5 shows that the difference of the work done by two nodes $W_i(t) - W_j(t)$ is bounded by the diameter, from which follows that any graph with diameter at most D satisfies φ, while it is easy to construct a graph with a diameter greater than D that violates φ. We conclude, that there cannot be a constant size cut-off for link-reversal-based systems even if one wants to verify properties that depend on two processes only. This is in sharp contrasts to the results on single token-based systems mentioned above.

Acknowledgments. We are grateful to Igor Konnov for valuable discussions and comments on earlier versions of the paper.

References

1. Apt, K.R., Kozen, D.: Limits for automatic verification of finite-state concurrent systems. Inf. Process. Lett. 22(6), 307–309 (1986)
2. Baier, C., Katoen, J.-P.: Principles of model checking. MIT Press (2008)
3. Barbosa, V.C., Gafni, E.: Concurrency in heavily loaded neighborhood-constrained systems. ACM Trans. Program. Lang. Syst. 11(4), 562–584 (1989)
4. Browne, M.C., Clarke, E.M., Grumberg, O.: Reasoning about networks with many identical finite state processes. Inf. Comput. 81(1), 13–31 (1989)
5. Busch, C., Surapaneni, S., Tirthapura, S.: Analysis of link reversal routing algorithms for mobile ad hoc networks. In: Proceedings of the 15th ACM Symposium on Parallelism in Algorithms and Architectures (SPAA), pp. 210–219 (2003)
6. Mani Chandy, K., Misra, J.: The drinking philosopher's problem. ACM Transactions on Programming Languages and Systems 6(4), 632–646 (1984)
7. Charron-Bost, B., Függer, M., Welch, J.L., Widder, J.: Partial is Full. In: Kosowski, A., Yamashita, M. (eds.) SIROCCO 2011. LNCS, vol. 6796, pp. 113–124. Springer, Heidelberg (2011)

8. Charron-Bost, B., Gaillard, A., Welch, J.L., Widder, J.: Routing without ordering. In: Proceedings of the 21st ACM Symposium on Parallelism in Algorithms and Architectures (SPAA), pp. 145–153 (2009)
9. Clarke, E., Talupur, M., Touili, T., Veith, H.: Verification by Network Decomposition. In: Gardner, P., Yoshida, N. (eds.) CONCUR 2004. LNCS, vol. 3170, pp. 276–291. Springer, Heidelberg (2004)
10. Allen, E., Emerson, V.K.: Reducing Model Checking of the Many to the Few. In: McAllester, D. (ed.) CADE 2000. LNCS, vol. 1831, pp. 236–254. Springer, Heidelberg (2000)
11. Emerson, E.A., Kahlon, V.: Parameterized Model Checking of Ring-Based Message Passing Systems. In: Marcinkowski, J., Tarlecki, A. (eds.) CSL 2004. LNCS, vol. 3210, pp. 325–339. Springer, Heidelberg (2004)
12. Allen Emerson, E., Namjoshi, K.S.: Reasoning about rings. In: 22nd ACM SIGPLAN-SIGACT Symposium on Principles of Programming Languages (POPL), pp. 85–94 (1995)
13. Gafni, E., Bertsekas, D.P.: Distributed algorithms for generating loop-free routes in networks with frequently changing topology. IEEE Transactions on Communications 29(1), 11–18 (1981)
14. German, S.M., Sistla, A.P.: Reasoning about systems with many processes. J. ACM 39(3), 675–735 (1992)
15. Malpani, N., Welch, J.L., Vaidya, N.: Leader election algorithms for mobile ad hoc networks. In: Proceedings of the 4th International Workshop on Discrete Algorithms and Methods for Mobile Computing and Communication (2000)
16. Park, V.D., Scott Corson, M.: A highly adaptive distributed routing algorithm for mobile wireless networks. In: 16th Conference on Computer Communications (Infocom), pp. 1405–1413 (April 1997)
17. Pnueli, A., Xu, J., Zuck, L.D.: Liveness with $(0, 1, \infty)$-Counter Abstraction. In: Brinksma, E., Larsen, K.G. (eds.) CAV 2002. LNCS, vol. 2404, pp. 107–122. Springer, Heidelberg (2002)
18. Welch, J.L., Walter, J.E.: Link Reversal Algorithms. Synthesis Lectures on Distributed Computing Theory. Morgan & Claypool Publishers (2011)

Efficient Coverability Analysis by Proof Minimization*

Alexander Kaiser[1], Daniel Kroening[1], and Thomas Wahl[2]

[1] University of Oxford, United Kingdom
[2] Northeastern University, Boston, United States

Abstract. We consider multi-threaded programs with an unbounded number of threads executing a finite-state, non-recursive procedure. Safety properties of such programs can be checked via reduction to the *coverability problem* for *well-structured transition systems* (WSTS). In this paper, we present a novel, sound and complete yet empirically much improved solution to this problem. The key idea to achieve a compact search structure is to track *uncoverability* only for *minimal* uncoverable elements, even if these elements are not part of the original coverability query. To this end, our algorithm examines elements in the downward closure of elements backward-reachable from the initial queries. A downside is that the algorithm may unnecessarily explore elements that turn out coverable and thus fail to contribute to the proof minimization. We counter this effect using a forward search engine that simultaneously generates (a subset of all) coverable elements, e.g., a generalized Karp-Miller procedure. We demonstrate in extensive experiments on C programs that our approach targeting minimal uncoverability proofs outperforms existing techniques by orders of magnitude.

1 Introduction

In anticipation of the prominent role concurrency is predicted to play in future software, popular systems languages like C and Java readily embrace support for multiple threads of execution. Communication among threads is naturally enabled via shared variables, mutexes, but also via non-blocking sleep/wake-up mechanisms. The correct use of these communication mechanisms is largely up to the user. The inevitable frustration caused by attempts to find and reproduce concurrency bugs through conventional program testing strongly encourages the use of automated formal techniques.

In this paper, we consider finite-state, non-recursive procedures executed by an *unspecified* number of threads. This scenario is highly relevant in practice. For example, the number of processes concurrently requesting I/O services in an operating system environment cannot be determined a priori. For settings like this, we are interested in detecting, or proving the absence of, assertion failures, mutual-exclusion violations, etc.

Despite the arbitrary number of threads, problems of this kind have long been known to be decidable [2], for instance by reduction to the *coverability problem* for the rich class of *well-structured transition systems* (WSTS) [23,16]. "Coverability" of an erroneous configuration of threads (e.g., violating mutual exclusion) is tantamount to the existence of a reachable program state exhibiting such an error.

* This research is supported by the EPSRC project EP/G026254/1 and ERC project 280053.

M. Koutny and I. Ulidowski (Eds.): CONCUR 2012, LNCS 7454, pp. 500–515, 2012.

While decidable, checking coverability for WSTS incurs a high computational cost. For example, for the subclass of *vector addition systems* the problem was shown to be EXPSPACE-complete [6]. Extensions such as *transfer transitions*, which allow several threads to change their local state simultaneously and are essential to model broadcast primitives and predicate abstractions of broadcast-free programs [10,9], render the problem Ackermann-hard [33]. The significance of the coverability problem both as a theoretical challenge, as well as in practical concurrent program verification, has led to a flurry of related activity in recent years [29,2,21,20,3,25]. The most general solution to the coverability problem was presented in a paper by Abdulla et al. [2], which backward-explores states starting from the target state.

In this paper, we introduce a new, sound and complete solution to the coverability problem in WSTS. In contrast to existing techniques, our method relies on sequences of many inexpensive uncoverability proofs that build upon one another. We compute such proofs by searching the downward-closure of states encountered during backward exploration from the target state for smallest uncoverable members. Elements encountered during that search that are not currently known to be coverable give rise to "uncoverability candidates". If a candidate proves uncoverable, so are all elements in its upward closure, which in the end contributes to the decision for the target state. Otherwise, the coverable candidate is retained to prevent it from being expanded again.

The downside of such a "speculative exploration" is that *coverable* exploration candidates mean wasted effort. This effort can, however, be largely reduced using a simultaneously running forward search engine that labels states as coverable and thus prevents them from being explored in the (futile) hope of finding an uncoverability proof. The key is that such a forward engine acts only as a "catalyst": it affects the speed of the overall algorithm, not its result. Thus, we can use incomplete procedures such as generalizations of the (forward-directed) Karp-Miller algorithm [26,11,14].

To summarize, this work makes the following contributions:

- We present a novel approach to coverability checking in WSTS that combines forward propagation of underapproximations with backward propagation of overapproximations.
- We provide an implementation (publicly available; see Section 5) that accepts Petri nets with transfer arcs, and an extension to verifying C programs with unbounded thread counts in a predicate abstraction-based CEGAR loop [4,7]. Our algorithm outperforms the best known coverability approach by orders of magnitude, enabling the analysis of programs which are out of scope of the previous technology. The experiments also reveal that our approach is able to guide the search far more effectively than existing structural invariant heuristics [13,8].

These improvements are possible thanks to the compactness of the uncoverability proofs generated during exploration. On our C benchmarks, we observe reductions of up to 95% in the proof size.

2 System Model and Problem Definition

Our algorithms operate on *well-structured transition systems* (WSTS) [16]. A WSTS is a transition system equipped with a well-quasi-ordering $\succeq$ on its states that satisfies the following monotonicity property: for all states u, u', r, if u' is a successor of u and $r \succeq u$, then there exists a successor r' of r such that $r' \succeq u'$. In other words, $\succeq$ is a simulation relation for the transition system. A state q is *coverable* if there exists a reachable state v such that $v \succeq q$; the definition of "reachable (with respect to a set of initial states)" is standard.

Let now $(M, \succeq)$ be a WSTS. We denote by Cover the *coverability set*, consisting of all states covered by some reachable state. The *coverability problem* is: given a state $q \in V$, determine whether q is coverable.

Thread Transition Systems. We give an example of a class of WSTS called *thread transition system* (TTS) that are motivated by the task of verifying multi-threaded asynchronous software. A TTS is a machine model that gives rise to transition systems equal in expressiveness to Petri nets [25,28]. We use TTS in examples throughout this paper.

Let S and L be finite sets of *shared* and *local* states, respectively. The elements of $T = S \times L$ are called *thread states*. Formally, a *thread transition system* (TTS) is a pair (T, Δ), where $\Delta \subseteq T \times T$ models thread transitions. Let $V = \cup_{n=0}^{\infty}(S \times L^n)$. The elements of V are called *states*; we write them in the form $(s \,|\, l_1, \ldots, l_n)$. A TTS gives rise to a transition system $M = (V, \rightarrowtail)$ with

$$(s \,|\, l_1, \ldots, l_n) \rightarrowtail (s' \,|\, l'_1, \ldots, l'_n)$$

exactly if, for some $i \in \{1, \ldots, n\}$, $(s, l_i, s', l'_i) \in \Delta$ and for all $j \neq i$, $l_j = l'_j$. That is, transitions may affect the shared state, and the local state of exactly one thread in local state l.

Given sets $I_s \subseteq S$ and $I_l \subseteq L$ of initial shared and local states, respectively, we define the set of initial states to be $I = I_s \times (\cup_{n=0}^{\infty} I_l^n)$. An *execution* of transition system M is a finite or infinite sequence of states in V whose adjacent states are related by $\rightarrowtail$; the first state must be initial. A state is *reachable* if it appears in some execution.

To show that M is a WSTS, let the *covers* relation $\succeq$ over V be defined as follows:

$$(s \,|\, l_1, \ldots, l_n) \succeq (s' \,|\, l'_1, \ldots, l'_n)$$

whenever $s = s'$ and $\langle l_1, \ldots, l_n \rangle \supseteq \langle l'_1, \ldots, l'_{n'} \rangle$, where $\langle x \rangle$ denotes the *multiset* with the elements from x. Let further $v \succ v'$ whenever $v \succeq v'$ and $v \neq v'$. If $0 \in S$ and $0, 1, 2 \in L$, then for example $(0 \,|\, 0, 2, 0, 1) \succeq (0 \,|\, 2, 0)$, but $(0 \,|\, 0, 2, 0, 1) \not\succeq (0 \,|\, 0, 2, 0, 0)$. Relation $\succeq$ is neither symmetric nor anti-symmetric: states that cover each other are identical *up to permutations of the threads* and thus form a classical thread symmetry equivalence class. Relation $\succeq$ is thus a quasi-order, and in fact a *well-quasi-order* (wqo) on V: any infinite sequence $v_1, v_2, \ldots$ of elements from V contains an increasing pair $v_i \preceq v_j$ with $i < j$. It is easy to see that $(M, \succeq)$ fulfills the definition of a WSTS.

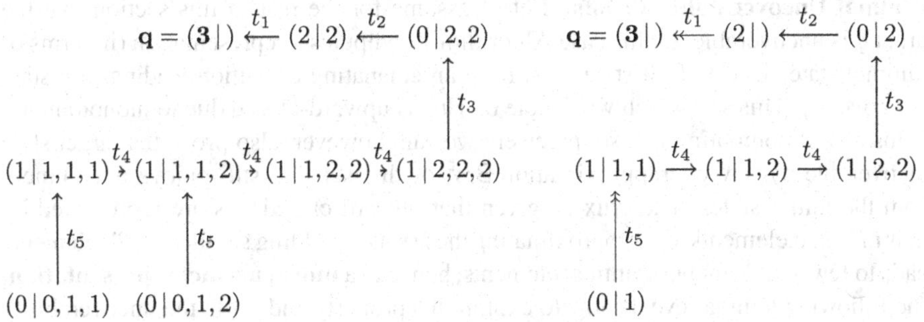

Fig. 1. Standard and minimal uncoverability proof for target q. Arrows $\rightarrow$ visualize covering predecessor relations, subscripted by the inducing thread transition; note that $p \rightarrow w$ implies $p \in \mathsf{CPre}(w)$. Arrows $p \twoheadrightarrow w$ indicate that there exists some $v \in \mathsf{CPre}(w)$ such that $v \succ p$.

3 Compact Backward Reachable Sets

We introduce some basic definitions and sketch the idea underlying our approach. A set $P \subseteq V$ of states is *upward-closed* if, for any $v \in P$ and any v', $v' \succeq v$ implies $v' \in P$. We write $\uparrow P$ for the *upward closure* of P, i.e., the least upward-closed set that contains P, and $\min P$ for the set of minimal elements of P, i.e., the least subset M of P such that $\uparrow P = \uparrow M$. Every upward-closed set is representable by its minimal elements, of which only a finite number exists due to the wqo properties of $\preceq$. The term and symbol *downward-closed* and $\downarrow P$ are defined analogously.

Let the *covering predecessors* of a state $v \in V$, denoted by $\mathsf{CPre}(v)$, be all the minimal states that have a successor covering v:

$$\mathsf{CPre}(v) = \min\{p \in V \mid \exists v' \in V : p \rightarrowtail v' \wedge v' \succeq v\}\,.$$

Note that for TTS a state $(s \mid \ldots) \in \mathsf{CPre}(v)$ involves an additional thread if no thread in v is responsible for the transition to shared state s (we will see an example later on).

Backward Reachability. Algorithm 1 shows a refined version of the classical backward search for WSTS [2,1]. Input is a target state $q \in V$. The algorithm maintains a set $U \subseteq V$ with *vertices* that are labeled and identified with encountered states, and a *work set* $W \subseteq U$ of yet unprocessed vertices.

Algorithm 1. $\mathsf{Bc}(q \in V)$

$W := \{q\}$; $U := \{q\}$
while $\exists w \in W : w \in \min(U)$ **do**
  $W := W \setminus \{w\}$
  for all $p \in \mathsf{CPre}(w) : p \notin \uparrow U$ **do**
    if $p \in I$ **then**
      return "$q \in \mathsf{Cover}$"
    $W := W \cup \{p\}$; $U := U \cup \{p\}$
return "$q \notin \mathsf{Cover}$"

The algorithm performs an iterative search over covering predecessors starting from q. It terminates either by finding an execution leading to a state that covers q, or when no minimal and unprocessed vertex remains (this eventually happens since $\succeq$ is a wqo), thus proving the uncoverability of the target state.

Minimal Uncoverability Proofs. Let us assume for the rest of this section that the target q is uncoverable. In this case Algorithm 1 computes a representation (in terms of minimal states in U) of all states that have an emanating execution leading to a state that covers q. This set, which we denote by Brs, is upward-closed due to monotonicity.

Instead of computing this set precisely we can, however, also prove the target state uncoverable by any overapproximation $\mathsf{Brs}^\sharp$ of this set that still enjoys disjointness from the initial states. The crux is, given that upward-closed sets are represented by their minimal elements, overapproximating these sets by adding smaller ("$\preceq$") elements leads to fewer and smaller minimal elements, hence to a **more succinct representation**. The following lemma reveals how to exploit this property and settle the uncoverability more efficiently.

Lemma 1. *Let v and v' be two states such that $v' \preceq v$. Then for all $m \in \mathsf{CPre}(v)$ there exists $m' \in \mathsf{CPre}(v')$ such that $m' \preceq m$.*

The proof of Lemma 1 is straightforward. Applied to Algorithm 1 this property generalizes to paths of arbitrary length through the search: the smaller the covering predecessors we examine in Line 4, the shorter the paths we need to explore.

Definition 2. *An **uncoverability proof** for an element q is an upward-closed set of states $\mathsf{Brs}^\sharp$ such that $q \in \mathsf{Brs}^\sharp$, $\mathsf{Brs}^\sharp \supseteq \mathsf{CPre}(\mathsf{Brs}^\sharp)$, and $\mathsf{Brs}^\sharp \cap I = \emptyset$. An uncoverability proof $\mathsf{Brs}^\sharp$ for q is **minimal** if $\min \mathsf{Brs}^\sharp \subseteq \min(V \setminus \mathsf{Cover})$, and every upward-closed subset $X \subset \mathsf{Brs}^\sharp$ is not an uncoverability proof for q.*

Minimal uncoverability proofs thus consist solely of smallest uncoverable states and cannot be reduced by removing the upward-closure of some of its minimal states. Note that multiple minimal uncoverability proofs may exist.

Bearing Lemma 1 in mind, we observe that minimal uncoverability proofs are an interesting means for proving the uncoverability of target q, as they minimize the maximum length of paths Algorithm 1 needs to traverse.

Example. To illustrate this idea, let us consider the TTS with shared and local states $0, \ldots, 3$ and thread transitions $t_1 = (2,2,3,0)$, $t_2 = (0,2,2,0)$, $t_3 = (1,2,0,0)$, $t_4 = (1,1,1,2)$, and $t_5 = (0,0,1,1)$; the initial shared and local state sets are $I_s = I_l = \{0\}$. Assume we wish to check whether shared state 3 can be reached, i.e., the target is $(3\,|\,)$. Figure 1 (left) depicts the minimal states of the corresponding set Brs computed by Algorithm 1. If we search, however, the downward-closure of encountered states for smallest uncoverable members, we obtain the minimal uncoverability proof shown on the right: the covering predecessors $(2\,|\,2)$ and $(0\,|\,0,1,2)$ give rise to candidate $(2\,|\,)$ and $(0\,|\,1)$, respectively. Comparing both uncoverability proofs, we observe reductions in various dimensions: the number of minimal states drops from 9 to 7, the longest traversed path from 7 to 6, and the maximum thread count from 3 to 2. □

In Section 5 we present experimental evidence that show the potential for compressing the proof size along these dimensions in practice: for our concurrent C program benchmarks we observed **reductions by 95%, 67%, and 50%**, respectively. This potential is the key for the efficiency of our approach.

4 Minimal Uncoverability Proof Algorithm

In this section, we develop our approach to compute minimal uncoverability proofs. An obstacle is the determination of "helpful" candidates. We begin by illustrating it on the TTS from the previous example; we omit non-minimal states for sake of brevity.

Example. Again, we start from target $(3\,|\,)$. However, before exploring covering predecessors, we check whether a helpful candidate for a smaller state exists. Since this is not the case (no smaller state exists), we proceed as usual and obtain predecessor $(2\,|\,2)$ which gives rise to candidate $(2\,|\,)$. If we find a path showing $(2\,|\,)$ coverable, we will withdraw the candidate and proceed with the former state as usual. From $(2\,|\,)$ we encounter predecessor $(0\,|\,2)$; although $(0\,|\,2)$ strictly covers $(0\,|\,)$, we do not create a corresponding candidate as it is initial. However, for its predecessor $(1\,|\,2,2)$ in turn we do so, and create candidate $(1\,|\,)$. Further exploring this state we obtain path $(0\,|\,0) \to (1\,|\,)$, proving the candidate's coverability. We withdraw the candidate and mark the downward-closure of all states along the execution as coverable, so that these elements are not expanded again. With path $(0\,|\,0) \to (1\,|\,1) \to (1\,|\,2)$ the next candidate proof attempt also fails. From the original predecessor $(1\,|\,2,2)$ we arrive at $(1\,|\,1,2)$, of which we can rule out the existence of smaller uncoverable states from the collected coverability results; the same holds for the next predecessor $(1\,|\,1,1)$. We finally arrive at predecessor $(0\,|\,0,1)$ and create the candidate $(0\,|\,1)$. Since no new (w.r.t. $\uparrow$) predecessor exists, we terminate with the tree shown in Figure 1 on the right. □

4.1 Backward-Constructed Minimal Proofs

In addition to the data structures used by Algorithm 1, namely a set $U \subseteq V$ with vertices that are labeled and identified with encountered states, and a work set $W \subseteq U$ of unprocessed vertices, our algorithm maintains

i) a set E storing (directed) *edges* between vertices, $E \subseteq U \times U$;
ii) a mapping ζ *associating* each vertex with a unique vertex, $\zeta\colon U \to U$;
iii) a downward-closed set D storing collected *coverability results*, $D \subseteq V$.

As already indicated in Figure 1, we write $u \to r$ for $(u, r) \in E$, and $\to^*$ for the reflexive transitive closure of $\to$. We call a vertex $u \in U$ *candidate vertex* if $\zeta(u) = u$, and *predecessor vertex* otherwise. A *path* of (U, E) is a finite sequence of vertices from U whose adjacent vertices are related by $\to$; the *last* state must be a candidate vertex. The mapping ζ (extended to sets X by $\zeta(X) = \{\zeta(x)|x \in X\}$) clusters the vertices into $|\,\zeta(U)|$ *partitions*, one per candidate vertex (vertices that are associated with that candidate vertex). The set D stores states that were shown to be coverable.

The algorithm takes a target q as input and ensures at all times that restricting the partitioned graph (U, E, ζ) to any equivalence class of vertices with the same associated candidate vertex, say u, forms a tree with u as root, and all other vertices being predecessor vertices. Each tree represents an attempt to prove the corresponding candidate (as done by Algorithm 1 for input u). Edges and the mapping ζ enable the withdrawal of unhelpful candidates in a way that preserves parts of their partition that are shared with remaining candidates.

Fig. 2. Effect of routine Backtrack in the presence of candidate vertices s, r and t, each with a single primed predecessor vertex in their partition; the partition of candidate vertex r we wish to remove is highlighted, and the single conflicting edge is marked with "∘" (left). After the call, the partition of r is removed and its former predecessor vertex r' is associated with s (right).

The algorithm consists of three routines: Enlarge creates a new candidate vertex, Backtrack removes partitions of candidates, and Mcov is the main routine.

Enlargement Routine. The Enlarge routine takes a candidate u we wish to add as input. If u is a new vertex ($u \notin U$), it is inserted in the work and vertex set. In all cases, the graph is repartitioned by adjusting ζ and associating every vertex in the set

$$\Lambda(u) = \{r \in U | u = r \vee (r \to^* u \wedge \zeta(r) = \zeta(u))\}$$

with u. This repartitioning (observe $u \in \Lambda(u)$) ensures that $r \in \Lambda(u)$ now entails $\zeta(r) = u$. The graph thus contains the new candidate vertex u, with a partition in the shape of a tree.

Backtracking Routine. The purpose of the Backtrack routine, shown in Algorithm 2, is to remove unhelpful candidate vertices $P \subseteq \zeta(U)$ and their partitions. An obstacle is that paths $u \to^* r \notin P$ to remaining candidate vertices may have segments in partitions that will be removed (paths can traverse multiple partitions). To ensure soundness, we need to preserve them.

Algorithm 2. Backtrack($P \subseteq \zeta(U)$)

1: **while** $\exists (r, s) \in E : (r, s)$ is P-confl. **do**
2:     **for all** $t \in \Lambda(r)$ **do**
3:         $\zeta(t) := \zeta(s)$
4: **for all** $r \in U : \zeta(r) \in P$ **do**
5:     $W := W \setminus \{r\}$; $U := U \setminus \{r\}$
6:     **for all** $(t, r) \in E$ **do**
7:         $E := E \setminus \{(t, r)\}$

Definition 3. *Consider a set P of candidate vertices. An edge $(r, s) \in E$ is called P-**conflicting** if $\zeta(r) \in P$ and $\zeta(s) \notin P$.*

Hence, P-conflicting edges induce segments of the above kind. To preserve them, we exhaustively resolve conflicts in a first step (Lines 1–3): for a conflicting edge, say $r \to s$, we do this by reassociating vertices in $\Lambda(r)$ to $\zeta(s)$.

Once all conflicts are resolved and thus $r \to s$ and $\zeta(r) \in P$ entails $\zeta(s) \in P$, remaining vertices and edges of partitions in P are removed in Lines 4–7. Figure 2 sketches both steps.

Main Routine. We introduce some terminology:

Algorithm 3. Minimal Uncoverability Proof Algorithm: $\mathsf{Mcov}(q \in V)$

1: $W := \{q\}$; $U := \{q\}$; $D := I$; $E := \emptyset$; $\zeta : q \mapsto q$
2: **select** $n \in \min C(q)$; $\mathsf{Enlarge}(n)$ // create candidate vertex
3: **while** $\exists w \in W : w \in \min(U)$ **do**
4: $\quad W := W \setminus \{w\}$
5: $\quad$ **for all** $p \in \mathsf{CPre}(w)$: p is $\zeta(w)$-minimal **do**
6: $\quad\quad$ **if** $p \notin D$ **then**
7: $\quad\quad\quad E := E \cup \{(p, w)\}$
8: $\quad\quad\quad$ **if** $p \notin U$ **then**
9: $\quad\quad\quad\quad W := W \cup \{p\}$; $U := U \cup \{p\}$; $\zeta(p) := w$ // add covering predecessor
10: $\quad\quad\quad\quad$ **select** $n \in \min C(p)$; $\mathsf{Enlarge}(n)$ // create candidate vertex
11: $\quad\quad$ **else if** $q \notin \downarrow p$ **then**
12: $\quad\quad\quad D := D \cup \downarrow p$ // mark coverable states
13: $\quad\quad\quad \mathsf{Backtrack}(\zeta(\downarrow p))$ // call backtrack routine
14: $\quad\quad\quad$ **while** $\exists u \in \min(U) \cap \uparrow P$ **do**
15: $\quad\quad\quad\quad$ **select** $n \in \min C(u)$; $\mathsf{Enlarge}(n)$
16: $\quad\quad\quad$ **break** // skip forward to next iteration of **while**
17: $\quad\quad$ **else**
18: $\quad\quad\quad$ **return** "$q \in$ Cover"
19: **return** "$q \notin$ Cover"

Definition 4. *Let $v \in V$, and $u \in \zeta(U)$. State v is **u-minimal** if $v \not\succeq u$ and for all $s, s' \in U$ such that $s \to s'$ and $\zeta(s') = u$, we have $v \not\succeq s$.*

That is, state v is u-minimal if it covers neither the candidate vertex u nor any predecessor vertex in u's partition (observe that a predecessor vertex may yet belong to a partition other than $\zeta(u)$).

Definition 5. *Let $P \subseteq V$. P is **lower successor-closed** if, for any $p \in P$ and any v, $(p \to v \vee p \succeq v)$ entails $v \in P$.*

That is, a lower successor-closed set is both "successor-closed" (where successors are formed according to $\to$) and downward-closed. We write $\downarrow v$ for the least lower successor-closed set containing v. This set is obtained by closing $\{v\}$ under $\to$ successors and downward until fixpoint. The point of this definition is that, if v is coverable, so is every vertex in $\downarrow v$: coverability itself is closed under $\to$ successors and downward.

Algorithm 3 shows the main routine, Mcov, of our approach. The algorithm works as follows. Initially W and U contain one candidate vertex (target q), D is the set of initial states, the set E of edges is empty, and ζ associates q to itself (Line 1). If target q gives rise to a candidate we create a minimal candidate vertex (Line 2). The set of potential candidates $C(p) \subseteq V$ is given by

$$C(p) = \{v \in V | v \prec p \text{ and } v \notin D\}.$$

The set contains all the states that are strictly covered by p but not yet marked coverable. If $p = (0\,|\,0,0,1)$, and $D = \{(0\,|\,), (0\,|\,0), (0\,|\,1)\}$, then for example $C(p) = \{(0\,|\,0,1), (0\,|\,0,0)\}$. We tacitly assume that Line 2 has no side-effect if $C(p) = \emptyset$.

The algorithm now picks and removes a minimal and unprocessed vertex w from the work set, or returns "$q \notin$ Cover" (Line 19) if no such vertex remains. In the former case, the **for** loop in Line 5 steps through all covering predecessors p of w that are $\zeta(w)$-minimal and processes them as follows:

Lines 6–10 If p is not currently known to be coverable, then the graph is expanded. If p is a new vertex ($p \notin U$, Line 8), then we ensure that p will be processed when it turns minimal among the vertices by adding it as predecessor vertex to w's partition. Finally, we call the Enlarge routine to create new minimal candidate vertices.

Lines 11–16 If p is found to be coverable but not q, we add $\downarrow p$ (which is coverable as well) to D and invoke the Backtrack routine to remove partitions of coverable candidate vertices. Since this may remove candidate vertices of remaining predecessor vertices, we have to ensure that their downward-closure is further searched for minimal, yet helpful candidates. We therefore create new minimal candidate vertices (Lines 14–15). Again, we tacitly assume that Line 15 has no side-effect if $C(p) = \emptyset$. Then, the **break** instruction skips forward to the next iteration of the **while** loop. As a consequence of backtracking, unprocessed vertices that were previously *not* minimal may now be.

Lines 17–18 Otherwise we return "$q \in$ Cover", since the coverability of target q has been settled (in the affirmative).

Example. We continue with the example from the beginning of this section. In this case routine Enlarge is called four times: predecessor vertices $(2\,|\,2)$, $(1\,|\,2,2)$, and $(0\,|\,0,1)$ give rise to candidates $(2\,|\,)$, $(1\,|\,)$ (and after its removal to $(1\,|\,2)$), and $(0\,|\,1)$, respectively. Routine Backtrack is called once after candidate vertices $(1\,|\,2)$ and $(1\,|\,2,2)$ turn out unhelpful. The mapping ζ shown in Figure 1 on the right has three partitions, one for each of the candidate vertices $(3\,|\,)$, $(2\,|\,)$, and $(0\,|\,1)$. The collected coverability results are $D = \downarrow\{(0\,|\,0),(1\,|\,1),(1\,|\,2)\}$, and the mapping ζ is: $\zeta(u) = (2\,|\,)$ if $u \in \{(0\,|\,2),(1\,|\,2,2),(1\,|\,1,2),(1\,|\,1,1)\}$, and $\zeta(u) = u$ if $u \in \{(3\,|\,),(2\,|\,),(0\,|\,1)\}$. □

Due to the finiteness of downward closures (we create a finite number of candidate vertices) the algorithm eventually terminates. Completeness follows from that of Algorithm 1, and the fact that we only remove conflicting edges during backtracking. When Mcov terminates for an uncoverable target q, the remaining minimal nodes represent an uncoverability proof for q: $\mathsf{Brs}^\sharp = \uparrow U$ (cmp. Definition 2).

In its current form Algorithm 3 computes uncoverability proofs with the property $\min \mathsf{Brs}^\sharp \subseteq \min(V \setminus \mathsf{Cover})$, but not necessarily minimal ones. This is attributed to two factors. First, if a covering predecessor gives rise to a candidate and we later remove this predecessor, then a created uncoverability candidate may turn irrelevant for the coverability of target q. Second, when we add a candidate vertex that is incomparable to existing candidate vertices, this may still turn some of the latter irrelevant as well. In order to obtain truly minimal uncoverability proofs, we remove candidate vertices that are no longer needed during calls to Backtrack, and after every call to Enlarge.

4.2 Balancing the Search via Supplementary Coverability Results

If candidates are chosen unwisely, the search may incur extra work to identify and eliminate the coverable elements. To reduce this overhead, we have to prevent unhelpful candidates from being created. In its current form, Algorithm 3 does so by incorporating collected coverability results when it creates a new candidate. These coverability results may also, however, come from any external source, which we call a *coverability oracle*. A coverability oracle *a*) needs to report states that are provably coverable and should thus reasonably search in a *forward direction*; *b*) is not required to find *all* coverable states: creating some unhelpful candidates does not harm the search. This flexibility allows us to use any underapproximating forward-directed search: a standard or random reachability analysis works just as well as generalizations of the Karp-Miller procedure to broadcast synchronization [11], which are known not to guarantee termination for WSTS.

We finally remark: since detecting coverable elements is one of the main goals of Algorithm 3, the coverability results reported by the coverability oracle directly benefit the algorithm itself. The coverability oracle and Algorithm 3 run in parallel and synchronize via the set D: the coverability oracle populates this set while maintaining $D \subseteq \mathsf{Cover}$. Receiving such updates, Algorithm 3 terminates if $q \in D$, or otherwise invokes the Backtrack routine on now known-to-be-coverable candidate vertices in regular intervals to restore the invariant $D \cap U = \emptyset$.

5 Experimental Evaluation

In this section, we evaluate our algorithms on 21 concurrent C programs. The programs feature a diverse set of communication primitives, such as shared variables, mutexes, condition variables and broadcasts. For each benchmark, we consider verification of a safety property, specified via an assertion. The C programs, ranging from 40 to 1000 lines of code, are:

1–4 broadcast-based code from FreeBSD, NetBSD and Solaris that is related to RDMA ZFS file system support and interface/system monitoring;
5–9 programs using several basic language features and the pthread library;
10–12 programs using multiple locks to control access to a shared resource;
13,14 blocking and non-blocking pseudo-random number generators [31,10];
15 a program used in [17] to illustrate thread-modular model checking [24];
16,17 lock-based and lock-free stack described in [31], supporting concurrent pushes and pops (adapted from an IBM implementation) [10];
18,19 a Linux driver skeleton and a Mozilla vulnerability fix [27,24];
20,21 algorithms to establish mutual exclusion [24].

We implemented our Mcov routine (Algorithm 3) for TTSs and transfer Petri nets in our tool BREACH, equipped with a generalization of the Karp-Miller procedure (GKM) as coverability oracle; our tool (we used v1.0) and all benchmarks are available online at www.cprover.org/bfc. The oracle reports coverability results to a data pool our Mcov routine taps into at regular intervals; both run in parallel. In order to measure the impact

Table 1. Comparison of classical coverability approaches to our MCOV algorithm; buggy benchmarks in **bold**, run times in seconds, or **TO** (**MO**) in case the time (memory) limit is hit

C Programs	Final TTS		Classical approaches			Our new approach			
			GKM	BC		MCOV		MCOV/GKM	
id/Name	$\lvert T\rvert$	$\lvert\Delta\rvert$	*Time*	*Iter.*	*Time*	*Iter.*	*Time*	*Iter.*	*Time*
1/BSD-ABDD	82	288	**MO**	23476	19.1	328	0.1	184	0.0
2/BSD-RDMA-ADDR	101	304	1.6	12479	7.6	295	0.1	146	0.0
3/NETBSD-SYSMON-PWR	291	704	**MO**	–	**TO**	124	0.1	126	0.0
4/SOLARIS-SPACE-MAP	539	992	**MO**	10348	5.8	3412	2.2	2834	1.0
5/**BS-LOOP**	11616	20485	0.1	1483	1.5	1049	1.1	–	0.1
6/COND	280	1045	0.0	809	0.2	4660	88.4	–	0.0
7/FUNCTION-POINTER	9216	746770	**MO**	–	**TO**	–	**TO**	23139	592.0
8/S-LOOP	516	2813	0.0	3567	1.5	1567	1.4	–	0.5
9/PTHREAD	17920	135300	**MO**	–	**TO**	70841	1521.0	51265	189.7
10/DOUBLE-LOCK1	34880	233025	**MO**	–	**TO**	–	**MO**	90488	1146.5
11/DOUBLE-LOCK2	17216	114752	**MO**	–	**TO**	–	**MO**	46012	285.9
12/DOUBLE-LOCK3	3264	19250	**MO**	–	**TO**	24161	75.8	9514	14.5
13/PRNG (NON-BL.)	142	954	**MO**	191	0.0	4791	6.9	64	0.0
14/PRNG	788	5650	**MO**	–	**TO**	–	**TO**	9168	33.9
15/SPIN2003	188	984	0.0	6436	1.7	699	0.2	–	0.1
16/STACK (NON-BL.)	352	2550	**MO**	34046	133.7	18603	128.6	8249	12.5
17/STACK	648	3626	**MO**	35500	38.7	7616	20.2	2723	2.3
18/**BOOP**	7488	25929	0.0	1446	7.8	10776	361.1	–	0.1
19/MOZILLA-VUL.-FIXED	1648	8050	0.0	77053	84.2	3723	4.3	–	1.7
20/PETERSON	2048	8988	0.0	22951	15.5	2373	2.3	–	1.2
21/SZYMANSKI	8448	35896	0.1	–	**TO**	9597	35.8	–	11.0

of our new approach, the oracle can be deactivated, turning BREACH into the refined version of the classical backward search (Algorithm 1). Due to efficiency limitations of the underlying data structures, we do not add candidate vertices that involve two threads or more (which we found to be a good trade-off between efficiency and proof minimization). To apply BREACH to the C programs, we extended the abstract language interface of the C software model checker SATABS to TTS. SATABS implements the CEGAR loop based on a symmetry-aware predicate-abstraction technique [10], and handles function calls by inlining. All experiments are performed on a 3GHz Intel Xeon machine with 20 GB memory, running 64-bit Linux, with a timeout of 30 minutes.

Evaluation. Table 1 presents results for various configurations of our implementation. Columns on the left show the benchmark id and name, and the total number of thread states and transitions emerged in the last, and always most expensive, CEGAR iteration. Remaining columns show details for:

GKM: Our coverability oracle (stand-alone);
BC: Refined version of the classical backward algorithm (Algorithm 1);
MCOV: Our MCOV algorithm (Algorithm 3);
MCOV/GKM: The MCOV algorithm equipped with the coverability oracle GKM.

For each approach we show the total model checking run time, and in addition for backward-directed algorithms the number of iterations.

The results demonstrate that our new approach outperforms the classical algorithms: MCOV/GKM solves *all* 21 programs, and MCOV 17 instances, compared to 13 and 9 for the classical backward algorithm and the coverability oracle, respectively. Comparing the results for BC and MCOV clearly shows that the uncoverability proofs the latter

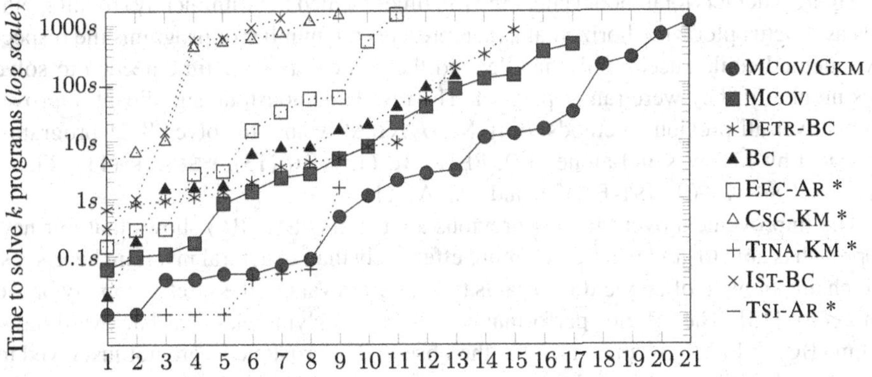

Fig. 3. Cactus plot on the 21 multi-threaded C programs comparing our Mcov and Mcov/Gkm approaches to various existing ones; due to broadcasts, the limit for tools marked with * is $k = 17$

generates are much smaller. This is reflected by a strict decrease of the iteration count in 17 cases. In the majority of cases, this improvement manifests in the running time: Mcov outperforms Bc on 13 programs (often significantly), compared to 4 the other way around. Furthermore, the results for Mcov/Gkm show that the coverability oracle can substantially reduce the cost of unhelpful candidates, showing their synergies (observe that running Gkm and Bc stand-alone in parallel is not helpful). As a result, the positive effect is amplified: compared to Bc, the iteration count strictly decreases on *all* programs.

To measure the difference between standard and minimal uncoverability proofs, we removed the bound on candidate vertices (in return for longer runtimes). In this setup, we observed the following reductions (averaged): the the longest traversed path drops from 28 to 14 (-50%), the threads included in the proof from 6 to 2 (-67%), and the proof size in terms of minimal states from 22518 to 1222 (-95%). While the classical backward-approach includes up to eight threads in a proof, our approach always generates minimal uncoverability proofs which involve no more than *two threads*. With the bound on candidate vertices mentioned above and used for Table 1, the reductions are only marginally smaller (e.g., the previous thread number increases by one).

Comparison. There exist a number of other approaches to the coverability problem. We compare to the following tools (all available online):

Ist-Bc: Classical backward search using interval sharing-trees (v1.0.3) [18];
Petr-Bc: Refined backward search with structural invariants (v0.1) [29,30];
Tina-Km: Karp-Miller procedure (v3.0.0) [5];
Csc-Km: Refined Karp-Miller procedure using interval sharing-trees (v0.1) [22];
Eec-Ar: Pure forward algorithm with enumerative refinement (v1.0.3) [21];
Tsi-Ar: Variant of [21] using backward underapprox. for refinement (v1.0.3) [19].

Only Ist-Bc and Petr-Bc support broadcast primitives. In order to allow for a meaningful comparison, we translated abstract TTS templates generated by SatAbs into (transfer) Petri nets and replaced the model checker back-end.

Figure 3 depicts total model checking run times (scaled logarithmically) for all methods as "cactus plot": the horizontal axis represents the number of programs the respective method could successfully handle, and the vertical axis the time needed to solve this number if they were ran in parallel. The results demonstrate significant improvements over all previous methods: only MCOV/GKM is able to solve all 21 programs, followed by MCOV stand-alone (17), PETR-BC (15), BC (13), EEC-AR (11), TINA-KM and CSC-KM (9), IST-BC (7), and TSI-AR (1).

The improvement over the best previous approach (PETR-BC) shows that our new approach is able to guide the search more effectively than structural invariant heuristics, which are know to often yield invariants that are irrelevant to the safety property or too imprecise [15]. The inferior performance of our underlying classical backward algorithm (BC) to PETR-BC indicates that the observed improvements are not just owed to clever implementation, but rather the result of our novel approach.

6 Related Work

Algorithmic solutions to coverability analysis were first proposed for *vector addition systems* in a landmark paper by Karp and Miller [26]. The solution constructs a pseudo-reachability tree by forward exploration and replaces newly discovered states that are strictly greater than predecessors by their limit. It has a non-primitive recursive worst-case complexity [32]. The purpose there was mainly to show decidability of the coverability problem for VASes and the equivalent Petri nets. The technique is implemented in the tool TINA-KM [5]. It cannot be extended to broadcast primitives [12]. An improvements of this procedure that computes minimal coverability sets is [22].

To afford more flexibility in modeling parametrized programs, various algorithms were later proposed for WSTS, originally in a pure backward fashion [2], which was implemented in the tools IST-BC and PETR-BC [29], later as forward exploration [14,34]. The paradigm presented in [21] (and implemented in the tool EEC-AR) is also a pure forward algorithm; it constructs abstractions of increasing precision. In contrast to the paradigm of EEC-AR, the implementation itself does not support broadcasts. Other approaches are the backward and forward unfolding algorithms from [3] and [25].

Solutions combining forward and backward exploration are rare; we are only aware of the methods described in [15] and [19]. The authors of [15] propose to use a CSC-KM-like approach to compute overapproximations of the coverability set, which are then used in a *subsequent* backward exploration to prune the search space. Our experimental results demonstrate, however, that this approach cannot cope with programs of the sizes we consider. In [19], the authors combine overapproximations computed in a forward fashion, which are refined by using backward underapproximations; the approach is implemented in the tool TSI-AR. On an abstract level, our algorithm can be seen as the dual of this approach. To the best of our knowledge, our approach is the first to combine forward propagation of *under*approximations with backward propagation of *over*approximations to the coverability problem in WSTS.

7 Conclusion

We introduced a new approach to the coverability problem in WSTS. The novelty of our algorithm is the way it proves uncoverable instances via a sequence of many inexpensive uncoverability proofs. Our algorithm can be used to check assertion failures, mutual exclusion violations and many other properties for parametrized programs communicating via mutexes, shared variables or common concurrency primitives such as broadcasts.

We demonstrated in extensive experiments on large benchmarks, generated by the software model checker SATABS from C programs, that our algorithm outperforms the best known coverability approach by orders of magnitude, enabling the verification of programs which are out of scope of the previous technology. The experiments also reveal that our approach is able to guide the search far more effectively than existing structural invariant heuristics [13,8]. We conclude from our experiments that programs tend to feature minimal uncoverability proofs with fewer and smaller minimal elements compared to those targeted by existing methods.

The ideas we have presented, supported by the simplicity of their implementation, are naturally applicable to coverability methods in general. We believe, for example, that while our method outperforms techniques based on structural net invariants, even more practical benefit is achievable by combining these strategies.

Acknowledgments. We wish to thank Michael Tautschnig for assistance with SATABS, and Pierre Ganty, Leopold Haller, Philipp Rümmer and Emelie Vollmer for their insightful comments on earlier drafts of this work.

References

1. Abdulla, P.A.: Well (and better) quasi-ordered transition systems. Bulletin of Symbolic Logic 16(4) (2010)
2. Abdulla, P.A., Cerans, K., Jonsson, B., Yih-Kuen, T.: General decidability theorems of infinite-state systems. In: Logic in Computer Science, LICS (1996)
3. Abdulla, P.A., Iyer, S.P., Nylén, A.: SAT-solving the coverability problem for Petri nets. Formal Methods in System Design, FMSD (2004)
4. Ball, T., Rajamani, S.: The SLAM project: debugging system software via static analysis. In: Principles of Programming Languages, POPL (2002)
5. Berthomieu, B., Vernadat, F.: The Tina tool, release 2.9.6, LAAS/CNRS (November 2009), http://homepages.laas.fr/bernard/tina/
6. Cardoza, E., Lipton, R.J., Meyer, A.R.: Exponential space complete problems for Petri nets and commutative semigroups: Preliminary report. In: STOC, pp. 50–54 (1976)
7. Clarke, E., Kroning, D., Sharygina, N., Yorav, K.: SATABS: SAT-Based Predicate Abstraction for ANSI-C. In: Halbwachs, N., Zuck, L.D. (eds.) TACAS 2005. LNCS, vol. 3440, pp. 570–574. Springer, Heidelberg (2005)
8. Delzanno, G., Raskin, J.-F., Van Begin, L.: Attacking Symbolic State Explosion. In: Berry, G., Comon, H., Finkel, A. (eds.) CAV 2001. LNCS, vol. 2102, pp. 298–310. Springer, Heidelberg (2001)

9. Delzanno, G., Raskin, J.-F., Van Begin, L.: Towards the Automated Verification of Multi-threaded Java Programs. In: Katoen, J.-P., Stevens, P. (eds.) TACAS 2002. LNCS, vol. 2280, pp. 173–187. Springer, Heidelberg (2002)
10. Donaldson, A., Kaiser, A., Kroening, D., Wahl, T.: Symmetry-Aware Predicate Abstraction for Shared-Variable Concurrent Programs. In: Gopalakrishnan, G., Qadeer, S. (eds.) CAV 2011. LNCS, vol. 6806, pp. 356–371. Springer, Heidelberg (2011)
11. Emerson, A., Namjoshi, K.K.: On model checking for non-deterministic infinite-state systems. In: Logic in Computer Science (LICS), pp. 70–80 (1998)
12. Esparza, J., Finkel, A., Mayr, R.: On the verification of broadcast protocols. In: Logic in Computer Science, LICS (1999)
13. Esparza, J., Melzer, S.: Verification of safety properties using integer programming: Beyond the state equation. Formal Methods in System Design, FMSD (2000)
14. Finkel, A., Goubault-Larrecq, J.: Forward Analysis for WSTS, Part II: Complete WSTS. In: Albers, S., Marchetti-Spaccamela, A., Matias, Y., Nikoletseas, S., Thomas, W. (eds.) ICALP 2009. LNCS, vol. 5556, pp. 188–199. Springer, Heidelberg (2009)
15. Finkel, A., Raskin, J.-F., Samuelides, M., Begin, L.V.: Monotonic extensions of Petri nets: Forward and backward search revisited. ENTCS (2002)
16. Finkel, A., Schnoebelen, P.: Well-structured transition systems everywhere! Theoretical Computer Science, TCS (2001)
17. Flanagan, C., Qadeer, S.: Thread-Modular Model Checking. In: Ball, T., Rajamani, S.K. (eds.) SPIN 2003. LNCS, vol. 2648, pp. 213–224. Springer, Heidelberg (2003)
18. Ganty, P., Meuter, C., Delzanno, G., Kalyon, G., Raskin, J.-F., Van Begin, L.: Symbolic data structure for sets of k-uples. Technical report, Université Libre de Bruxelles (2007)
19. Ganty, P., Raskin, J.-F., Van Begin, L.: A Complete Abstract Interpretation Framework for Coverability Properties of WSTS. In: Emerson, E.A., Namjoshi, K.S. (eds.) VMCAI 2006. LNCS, vol. 3855, pp. 49–64. Springer, Heidelberg (2005)
20. Ganty, P., Raskin, J.-F., Van Begin, L.: From Many Places to Few: Automatic Abstraction Refinement for Petri Nets. In: Kleijn, J., Yakovlev, A. (eds.) ICATPN 2007. LNCS, vol. 4546, pp. 124–143. Springer, Heidelberg (2007)
21. Geeraerts, G., Raskin, J.-F., Begin, L.V.: Expand, enlarge and check: New algorithms for the coverability problem of WSTS. JCSS (2006)
22. Geeraerts, G., Raskin, J.-F., Van Begin, L.: On the Efficient Computation of the Minimal Coverability Set for Petri Nets. In: Namjoshi, K.S., Yoneda, T., Higashino, T., Okamura, Y. (eds.) ATVA 2007. LNCS, vol. 4762, pp. 98–113. Springer, Heidelberg (2007)
23. German, S., Sistla, P.: Reasoning about systems with many processes. Journal of the ACM, JACM (1992)
24. Gupta, A., Popeea, C., Rybalchenko, A.: Threader: A Constraint-Based Verifier for Multi-threaded Programs. In: Gopalakrishnan, G., Qadeer, S. (eds.) CAV 2011. LNCS, vol. 6806, pp. 412–417. Springer, Heidelberg (2011)
25. Kaiser, A., Kroening, D., Wahl, T.: Dynamic Cutoff Detection in Parameterized Concurrent Programs. In: Touili, T., Cook, B., Jackson, P. (eds.) CAV 2010. LNCS, vol. 6174, pp. 645–659. Springer, Heidelberg (2010)
26. Karp, R.M., Miller, R.E.: Parallel program schemata. J. Comput. Syst. Sci. 3(2), 147–195 (1969)
27. Lu, S., Park, S., Seo, E., Zhou, Y.: Learning from mistakes: a comprehensive study on real world concurrency bug characteristics. In: Architectural Support for Programming Languages and Operating Systems, ASPLOS (2008)
28. Malkis, A., Podelski, A., Rybalchenko, A.: Thread-Modular Verification Is Cartesian Abstract Interpretation. In: Barkaoui, K., Cavalcanti, A., Cerone, A. (eds.) ICTAC 2006. LNCS, vol. 4281, pp. 183–197. Springer, Heidelberg (2006)

29. Meyer, R., Strazny, T.: Petruchio: From Dynamic Networks to Nets. In: Touili, T., Cook, B., Jackson, P. (eds.) CAV 2010. LNCS, vol. 6174, pp. 175–179. Springer, Heidelberg (2010)
30. Meyer, R., Strazny, T.: An algorithmic framework for coverability in well-structured systems. In: Application of Concurrency to System Design, ACSD (2012)
31. Peierls, T., Goetz, B., Bloch, J., Bowbeer, J., Lea, D., Holmes, D.: Java Concurrency in Practice. Addison-Wesley Professional (2005)
32. Rackoff, C.: The covering and boundedness problems for vector addition systems. Theoretical Computer Science, TCS (1978)
33. Schnoebelen, P.: Revisiting Ackermann-Hardness for Lossy Counter Machines and Reset Petri Nets. In: Hliněný, P., Kučera, A. (eds.) MFCS 2010. LNCS, vol. 6281, pp. 616–628. Springer, Heidelberg (2010)
34. Zufferey, D., Wies, T., Henzinger, T.A.: Ideal Abstractions for Well-Structured Transition Systems. In: Kuncak, V., Rybalchenko, A. (eds.) VMCAI 2012. LNCS, vol. 7148, pp. 445–460. Springer, Heidelberg (2012)

A Framework for Formally Verifying Software Transactional Memory Algorithms

Mohsen Lesani[1], Victor Luchangco[2], and Mark Moir[2]

[1] University of California, Los Angeles, USA
lesani@ucla.edu
[2] Oracle Labs, Burlington, MA, USA
{victor.luchangco,mark.moir}@oracle.com

Abstract. We present a framework for verifying transactional memory (TM) algorithms. Specifications and algorithms are specified using I/O automata, enabling hierarchical proofs that the algorithms implement the specifications. We have used this framework to develop what we believe is the first fully formal machine-checked verification of a practical TM algorithm: the NOrec algorithm of Dalessandro, Spear and Scott.

Our framework is available for others to use and extend. New proofs can leverage existing ones, eliminating significant work and complexity.

1 Introduction

As multicore computing becomes ubiquitous, it is increasingly important to support effective concurrent programming for a wide range of programmers. *Transactional memory* (TM) [9] allows programmers to specify a sequence of operations on shared objects that should be executed as a transaction that appears to be applied without interference from concurrent transactions, and without concurrent transactions observing partial results of the sequence. Programmers do not specify *how* these guarantees are made; this is a responsibility of the system. TM aims to deliver to shared memory programmers the benefits that transactions provide to database programmers.

We present a framework for specifying the guarantees that a TM system must provide (i.e., the TM specification), modeling TM implementations, and verifying that the implementations provide the specified guarantees. Our framework is based on I/O automata and simulation proof techniques [11,12], which support hierarchical proofs by modeling both specifications and implementations as automata and proving simulation relations between these automata. The hierarchical proof approach allows a proof for one TM algorithm to leverage parts of the hierarchy constructed for other TM algorithms, thus significantly improving productivity. The framework is formalized in the PVS language [14,16].

Using this framework, we have achieved the first fully formal machine-checked verification of a practical TM algorithm, the NOrec algorithm [3]. As described in [10], we have also recently used the framework to clarify relationships between the TMS1, TMS2, and opacity correctness conditions (see Section 2.1). The primary

M. Koutny and I. Ulidowski (Eds.): CONCUR 2012, LNCS 7454, pp. 516–530, 2012.

goal of this paper is to give readers a concrete understanding of the nature of our framework and proofs, and to make the framework more approachable. Readers interested in more detail can contact us to obtain the framework and explore our proofs interactively using PVS.

Section 2 presents background on TM correctness conditions and algorithms, particularly the NOrec algorithm we have verified. Section 3 contains background on I/O automata and simulation proof techniques. Section 4 describes our framework, and Section 5 shares lessons we have learned that have made it significantly easier to construct and reuse proofs. We briefly summarize related work in Section 6, and conclude in Section 7.

2 Transactional Memory

A *transactional memory system* supports one or more shared objects, typically a memory object consisting of a set of locations, each of which supports read and write operations. A sequence of operations on such objects can be executed as a transaction. To guarantee that transactions appear not to interleave with each other, a transaction may sometimes *abort* so that it appears not to execute at all. Transactions that successfully complete are said to *commit*.

2.1 Specifications

Verifying a TM implementation requires a precise specification of what it means for it to be correct. No single TM correctness condition is universally accepted, and indeed, different conditions are appropriate for different contexts. We have recently studied this problem for TM algorithms intended to support transactional language features in languages such as C and C++ [5]. To avoid fatal errors such as divide-by-zero in this context, transactions—even those that ultimately abort—must observe behavior that is consistent with some execution in which all transactions that commit do so instantaneously [5,8]. Traditional correctness conditions for transactions in database systems—such as *serializability* [15]—do not ensure this.

In [5], we defined a general condition TMS1 and a more restrictive condition TMS2. TMS1 aims to allow all implementations that provide reasonable behavior for the intended context, and as a result is somewhat abstract. TMS2 is more restrictive, but is closer to the intuition behind many practical TM algorithms. Briefly, TMS2 requires a writing transaction to append a new state to a sequence of memory states during its commit operation, while a read-only transaction is allowed to read from any state that was the last state in that sequence at some point during the execution of the transaction. We proved in [5] that TMS2 implements TMS1, and we have recently proved the same result again using our framework, specifically by proving that TMS2 implements opacity [8], and opacity implements TMS1, thereby clarifying the relationships between these conditions and confirming our conjecture [5]. This result implies that, in order to prove that an algorithm satisfies the TMS1 condition, it suffices to prove that it satisfies TMS2. This is the approach we have taken for our NOrec proof.

2.2 The NOrec Algorithm

NOrec [3] significantly reduces low-contention overhead as compared to previous TM algorithms such as TL2 [4] by eliminating *ownership records*, which hold TM metadata that is used when an associated location is accessed. NOrec achieves this by using a sequence lock (seqlock) that is acquired by every transaction that successfully writes any shared location. The seqlock is implemented by a counter that is incremented upon acquisition and release: the lock is free when the counter's value is even; it is held by the transaction that most recently incremented it when the value is odd. Although this lock limits scalability, it is held only while a transaction is committing, and NOrec's low overhead makes it attractive in low-to-moderate contention workloads.

Briefly, NOrec works as follows: When a transaction begins, it checks that the seqlock is free, and records a "snapshot" of the lock value. (Whenever a transaction discovers the seqlock is held by some other transaction, it waits until the lock is released before continuing.) To write a shared location, a transaction records the location and the value to be written to it in a private *write set*. These changes are written to the shared locations only when the transaction commits.

A transaction records values it reads in its private *read set*. After reading a location l, a transaction checks that the lock value has not changed since the transaction's most recent snapshot. If the lock value has changed, then the transaction revalidates its read set by updating its snapshot of the lock and checking that every object in its read set has the previously recorded value (aborting if not), before reading location l again and checking that the lock value has not changed again. This process is repeated until the transaction aborts or the read set validation and subsequent rereading of l is successful; in the latter case, the value read from l is stored in the transaction's read set and returned to the transaction.

To commit, a transaction attempts to acquire the lock while ensuring that its value has not changed since the transaction's most recent snapshot. (If it has, the transaction revalidates its reads and refreshes its snapshot as described above before attempting again to acquire the lock.) After acquiring the lock, the transaction performs the writes recorded in its writeset and then releases the lock by incrementing its value once more. Because no transaction reads any location while the lock is held, the writes performed by a transaction while it is committing appear atomic to all other transactions.

3 Theory Background

In Sections 3.1 and 3.2, we briefly summarize the standard I/O automata theory and simulation proof techniques upon which our framework is built. We have not only formalized this theoretical foundation in PVS, but also verified within the framework the theorems from the literature that we have used.

3.1 Automata

We use simplified[1] *input/output automata* (IOAs) [11] to express TM correctness conditions and to model TM algorithms. An automaton A is a labeled transition system that consists of: a set *states*(A) of states, with a nonempty subset *start*(A) $\subseteq$ *states*(A) of start states; a nonempty set *acts*(A) of actions, partitioned into *external* and *internal* actions; and a transition relation *trans*(A) $\subseteq$ *states*(A) $\times$ *acts*(A) $\times$ *states*(A).We describe the states using a collection of *variables*, and the transition relation using a *precondition* (a predicate on states) and an *effect* (a set of assignments to variables) for each action.

An *execution fragment* of A is a sequence $s_0 a_1 s_1 \ldots$ of alternating states and actions of A such that $(s_{k-1}, a_k, s_k) \in trans(A)$ for all $k > 0$; a finite sequence must end with a state. An *execution* is an execution fragment with $s_0 \in start(A)$. A state is *reachable* if it appears in some execution. An *invariant* is a predicate that is true for all reachable states; it is typically proved by induction on the length of an execution.

The subsequence of external actions in an execution fragment is called its *trace*, and represents its externally visible *behavior*. The traces of an automaton A are the traces of its executions; we denote the set of such traces by *traces*(A). These traces therefore represent the behavior that the automaton can exhibit.

We can interpret an automaton as a specification and as an implementation. For an "abstract" automaton A, interpreted as a specification, and a "concrete" automaton C, interpreted as an implementation, C *implements* A iff *traces*(C) $\subseteq$ *traces*(A): every behavior of the implementation is allowed by the specification.

This dual interpretation of automata enables *hierarchical proofs*: If automaton C implements another automaton B, and B implements automaton A, then C also implements A. When proving that one automaton implements another, it is often helpful to introduce "intermediate" automata to break the proof into more manageable pieces. These intermediate automata may represent classes of implementations that share common approaches and ideas, allowing proofs of implementations in the class to reuse properties already proved for the class, as discussed further in Section 4.2.

3.2 Simulation Proofs

One way to prove that C implements A is to use a *simulation relation* [12], which establishes a correspondence (not necessarily 1-1) between *states*(C) and *states*(A) such that for each step in any execution of C, there is a finite execution fragment of A with the same trace whose first and last states correspond to the pre- and post-states of the step, and execution fragments for successive steps can be "pasted together" into a single execution of A.

A *forward simulation* from C to A, for example, requires that every start state of C correspond to some start state of A, and that, for every step of an

[1] Our automata are simplified because we have not yet needed to explicitly compose automata and we have concentrated only on safety properties. We anticipate adding support for composition soon as it is needed for our ongoing work.

execution of C and every state of A corresponding to the prestate, there is a corresponding execution fragment of A that starts from that state and has the same external action, if any, as the step of C. Thus, given a forward simulation from C to A, and an execution of C, we can construct an execution of A with the same trace by starting from a corresponding start state and extending the execution with a corresponding execution fragment for each successive step of C. This implies that every trace of C is a trace of A.

Lemma 1. *If there is a forward simulation from C to A then C implements A.*

A forward simulation that is a function on the states of C is a *refinement*.

Sometimes, a forward simulation cannot prove that C implements A because knowledge of the future is needed in order to choose an appropriate execution fragment for a step of an execution of C. In such cases, *backward simulations* can be used. The conditions for a backward simulation are similar to those for forward simulations, but they allow an abstract execution to be constructed by working backwards from the last state of a (finite) execution of C, thus allowing use of knowledge of the future.

4 A Framework for Verifying TM Implementations

Our framework uses the PVS system [14,16], which supports a specification language based on typed higher-order logic, and tools for working in this language, including an interactive theorem prover that provides inference rules and decision procedures that are used in proofs. User guidance for a theorem can be saved and rerun for repeatable verification and can also be edited and applied to other theorems. Users can combine inference rules into high-level "strategies" that simplify proofs and promote reuse.

The foundation of our framework is a set of PVS theories that describe automata and simulations, as well as definitions and lemmas that facilitate reasoning about them. These foundational concepts are not TM-specific.

Our framework further comprises specific automata specifying TM correctness conditions (such as TMS2) and implementations (such as NOrec). We use several automata modeling specifications and implementations in varying levels of detail to construct hierarchical proofs that, for example, a detailed model of the NOrec algorithm correctly implements the TMS2 condition. All our proofs have been checked by the PVS prover. This section overviews our framework.

4.1 Foundations: Automata and Simulations

It is convenient, when defining an automaton in PVS, to have a single type that encompasses all its actions. In standard I/O automata theory, a simulation between two automata requires them to have the same external actions. This implies that all the actions of all automata in a proof hierarchy must be of the same type. Changes to this type—to add internal actions for a new automaton, for example—affect all automata in that proof hierarchy, triggering obligations to reverify every lemma and invariant, even those unrelated to the changes. This was a problem in some of our previous proofs, and is unacceptable in the context of developing a framework that includes many automata.

We address this problem by splitting an automaton into a *basic* automaton, which specifies its states, actions and transitions (`Automaton` theory in Figure 1), and a *view*, which maps its external actions to external *events* (`View` theory in Figure 2). Only the events need to be shared among automata.

To define a basic automaton, we define a type for states (usually a record type with components for modeling shared variables, private variables, control states, etc.), a type for actions, a predicate over the states to identify initial states, and a predicate that specifies the legal steps of the automaton. We then import the `Automaton` theory, shown in Figure 1, instantiating it with these elements.

The `Automaton` theory defines key properties of a basic automaton, such as its finite execution fragments, and what it means for a state to be reachable and for a state predicate to be an invariant of the automaton. We also prove several lemmas (not shown) that help us manipulate executions and prove invariants. For example, we use the following lemma to prove invariants by induction:

```
invariantInduction: LEMMA
  FORALL (p: pred[State]):
    (FORALL s: start(s) IMPLIES p(s))
    AND
    (FORALL s0, a, s1:
       reachable(s0) AND reachable(s1) AND p(s0) AND trans(s0,a,s1)
           IMPLIES p(s1))
    IMPLIES invariant(p)
```

(Although `reachable(s1)` is redundant—it is implied by `reachable(s0)` and `trans(s0,a,s1)`—we include it for convenience, as it allows us to apply already-established invariants to the poststate `s1` without proving each time that the poststate is reachable.)

The `View` theory (Figure 2) is parameterized by types for events and actions, a predicate identifying external actions, and a map from those actions to events, which we call a *view*. This theory defines the trace of a sequence of actions to be the subsequence of those actions that are external, mapped to events by the specified view. The `AutomatonWithView` theory (Figure 2) puts together a basic automaton and a view to define an automaton and its set of traces.

Views allow us to use different types for the actions of different automata, while retaining the ability to express that an external action of one automaton is "equal to" an external action of another, by mapping each to the same event. When views are 1-1 mappings, as they are in all our work to date, there is a straightforward isomorphism between automata in the standard theory and our "automata with views".

Views also add flexibility in modeling algorithms and specifications because multiple external actions of an automaton can be mapped to the same event. For example, when the actions of an automaton are deterministic (i.e., the post-state of a transition is uniquely determined by the prestate and the action), we

```
Automaton[State, Action: TYPE+,
          start: nonempty_pred[State],
          trans: pred[[State,Action,State]]]: THEORY
BEGIN

Step: TYPE = [State, Action, State]

IMPORTING finseq_props[State]

FiniteStepSeq: TYPE = [# actions: finseq[Action],
                         states: { ss: nonempty_finseq[State] |
                                   ss`length = actions`length + 1 }
                       #]
stepseq: VAR FiniteStepSeq

length(stepseq): nat = stepseq`actions`length

first(stepseq): State = first(stepseq`states)

last(stepseq): State = last(stepseq`states)

steps(stepseq): finseq[Step] =
  (# length := stepseq`actions`length,
     seq := LAMBDA (n: below[stepseq`actions`length]):
              (stepseq`states(n), stepseq`actions(n), stepseq`states(n+1))
   #)

finiteExecFrag(stepseq): bool =
  FORALL (n: below[length(stepseq)]): trans(steps(stepseq)(n))

finiteExecution(stepseq): bool =
  finiteExecFrag(stepseq) AND start(first(stepseq))

reachable(s: State): INDUCTIVE bool =
  start(s) OR (EXISTS (s0: State, a: Action): reachable(s0) AND trans(s0,a,s))

invariant(p: pred[State]): bool = FORALL (s: State): reachable(s) IMPLIES p(s)

END Automaton
```

Fig. 1. Definitions in `Automaton.pvs`

can specify the effect of actions with a function, which has various advantages, especially for automated theorem provers. For internal actions that are nondeterministic, we can create a variant of the automaton in which such actions have additional parameters, so that each parameterized action is deterministic. However, we cannot add parameters to a nondeterministic external action in standard I/O automata theory because doing so would change the externally visible behavior. Using automata with views, we can map each parameterized action to the same event as the original action.

The `Simulations` theory (not shown) takes as parameters the components for two automata, the events type that they share, and views mapping their

```
View[Event, Action: TYPE+,
     external: pred[Action],
     view: [(external) -> Event]]: THEORY
BEGIN

IMPORTING filter_props[Action]

trace(acts: finseq[Action]): finseq[Event] =
  map[(external),Event](view)(filter(external)(acts))

END View

AutomatonWithView[Event, State, Action: TYPE+,
                  start: nonempty_pred[State],
                  trans: pred[[State,Action,State]],
                  external: pred[Action],
                  view: [(external) -> Event]]: THEORY
BEGIN

IMPORTING Automaton[State, Action, start, trans]
IMPORTING View[Event, Action, external, view]

trace(stepseq: FiniteStepSeq): finseq[Event] = trace(stepseq`actions)

finiteTrace(eventseq: finseq[Event]): bool =
  EXISTS (fexec: (finiteExecution)): trace(fexec) = eventseq

END AutomatonWithView
```

Fig. 2. View and AutomatonWithView theories

respective external actions to events. It defines forward simulations and refinements, and also proves some lemmas (not shown). For example, the equivalent of Lemma 1 in our context states that the existence of a forward simulation implies finite trace inclusion between the two automata (R is universally quantified, and CA and AA are aliases for the two automata that are created by instantiating the AutomatonWithView theory with their components):

```
forwardSimulationImpliesFiniteTraceInclusion: LEMMA
  forwardSimulation(R) IMPLIES subset?(finiteTraces(CA), finiteTraces(AA))
```

Thus, one can prove that one automaton implements another by instantiating the Simulations theory with these automata, specifying a relation between their states, and proving that the relation satisfies the definition of a forward simulation. Similar definitions and lemmas are included for refinements. In addition to standard refinements, we define "simple refinements", in which each step of the concrete automaton corresponds to at most one abstract action. When it holds, this condition is more convenient to use as it avoids the need to specify and manipulate execution fragments.

In separate PVS theories (not shown), we also define backward simulations and *history mappings* [12], and prove similar lemmas about them. A history mapping between two automata is equivalent to a forward simulation from the first to the second and a refinement from the second to the first, showing that the automata are equivalent. We provide a rule for proving history mappings that requires less work than proving the two properties separately.

Our framework further comprises a set of PVS *strategies*, which help us to automate and hide parts of proofs. For example, by structuring our automata consistently, we can write strategies that automatically perform the mundane "unpacking" of definitions, thus making it easier to both construct and read proofs. We do not discuss our strategies further in this paper, but they is documented in the release notes of our framework.

4.2 TM-Specific Automata Included in the Framework

We define a number of TM-specific automata using the foundations described above. These automata, and the relationships we have proved between them, are depicted in Figure 3. The `TMS2` automaton produces exactly the set of traces allowed by the TMS2 condition presented in [5].

To prove that NOrec implements TMS2, we construct a hierarchical proof using several intermediate automata, each modeling a successively more detailed version of NOrec. In the simplest version, `NOrecAtomicCommitValidate`, the reading of shared objects (including checking that the global sequence lock is not held), validating a transaction, and committing a transaction (including writing all the changes in its write set) are each done in a single atomic step. No lock is needed in this version, because the lock is held only while a transaction is committing, which occurs in a single step in this automaton.

In `NOrecDerived`, validation and committing are no longer atomic, but reading a shared object and checking the global sequence number still is. `NOrec` models an abstract version of the NOrec algorithm, in which each step accesses at most one shared variable. Together, the proofs between these automata (Figure 3) verify an abstract version of NOrec that is consistent with synchronization support in real systems. However, we go one step further.

The `NOrecPaperPseudocode` automaton is a straightforward encoding of the pseudocode in [3], explicitly modeling details such as the control flow presented in [3]. For example, we explicitly use program counter values like begin2, corresponding to line 2 of the Begin procedure (Listing 3 in [3]), and validate6start and validate6iter, corresponding respectively to line 6 just before initializing the loop and just before executing the body of the loop beginning on line 6 of the Validate procedure (Listing 2 in [3]).

If the code for the NOrec algorithm were refactored without fundamentally changing it, we could verify the new version simply by repeating this last step for a different automaton encoding the new pseudocode, thus effectively reusing all of the more substantial proofs above the `NOrec` automaton in the hierarchy.

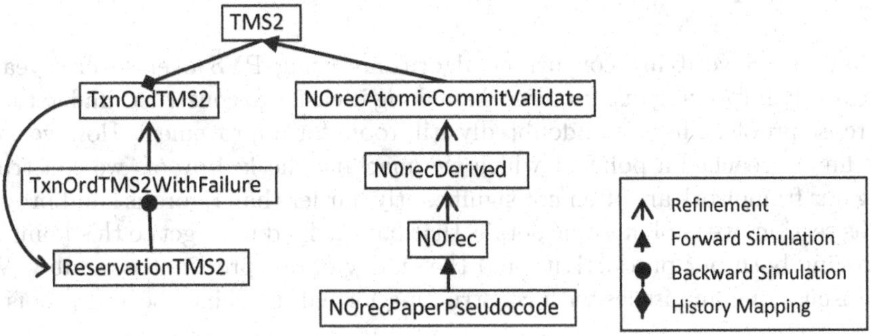

Fig. 3. Relationships between TM-specific automata in our framework. Direction of history map arrows indicates the forward simulation.

Some TM algorithms cannot be proved to implement TMS2 by a forward simulation. For example, in TL2 [4], a transaction "validates" the reads it has performed using a technique that ensures that its reads were consistent at the *beginning* of the validation process, but only determines that the validation was successful later. Thus, the transaction must take effect *before* it is known to have committed successfully. Exploiting such "knowledge of the future" in a simulation proof requires a backward simulation. Verifying a backward simulation can be challenging because it requires reasoning about extending an execution backwards from a poststate to a prestate.

To facilitate verification of such algorithms, we provide an alternate formulation of the TMS2 correctness condition as an automaton `ReservationTMS2`, in which a writing transaction "reserves" a place in the order of (writing) transactions before it knows whether its commit will succeed. This way, algorithms such as TL2 can be verified via a forward simulation to `ReservationTMS2`, reserving a transaction's place at the beginning of validation.

To prove that `ReservationTMS2` captures the TMS2 correctness condition, we show that it both implements and is implemented by `TMS2`. To do this, we introduce intermediate automata `TxnOrdTMS2` and `TxnOrdTMS2WithFailures`. `TxnOrdTMS2` is just like `TMS2` except that it records the initial state of the memory and a sequence of committed writer transactions (in the order that they commit) instead of the sequence of memory states that those transactions write. `TxnOrdTMS2WithFailures` is similar except that the sequence of transactions may include transactions that abort rather than commit. It is easy to verify that there are refinement mappings from `TxnOrdTMS2WithFailures` to `TxnOrdTMS2`, and from `TxnOrdTMS2` to `ReservationTMS2`, and a history mapping from `TMS2` to `TxnOrdTMS2`. A backward simulation is necessary only to show that `ReservationTMS2` implements `TxnOrdTMS2WithFailures`.

5 Our Experience

We have been verifying concurrent algorithms using PVS over several years, successively improving our framework, making it easier to construct, understand, and reuse proofs. There is undoubtedly still room for improvement. However, we have finally reached a point at which the machine-checked proofs we construct using our framework are often not significantly harder than rigorous hand proofs. In this section, we explain some details that have helped us to get to this point by improving both our productivity and the clarity of our proofs considerably. We also discuss ongoing issues with constructing formal, machine-checked proofs.

5.1 Reasons Why Proofs Are Easier Than Before

We are able to construct proofs more quickly and easily than before in part due to our increased facility with using PVS, particularly with its dependent type system and its inductive inference rules, in part due to improvements in our libraries defining the basic theory on automata and simulations, and in part due to our development of the libraries on basic data structures, particularly finite sequences. Although the concepts embodied in the `Automaton`, `View` and `AutomatonWithView` theories are essentially the same as those in the corresponding `Automata` theory of our earlier verification work, several factors have made our recent verifications significantly simpler.

First, changes in the way we represent sequences significantly simplified our proofs. In previous work, envisaging a framework that would evolve to also support progress proofs, we defined a type that could represent both finite and infinite sequences by using partial functions subject to a dependent typing condition to preclude "gaps" in the sequence. (PVS provides finite and infinite sequences, but not both in the same type.) While not conceptually difficult, the way PVS represents partial functions requires frequent conversions to distinguish values in the range of the function from "undefined"; this was a tedious and error-prone distraction in our previous work. It made proof sequents difficult to read, and generated many proof obligations due to type-checking conditions. It became clear that this was not worthwhile.

Thus far we have only done safety proofs for which finite sequences are sufficient. Therefore, our current framework uses only finite sequences, which has greatly simplified our proofs, both for writing and for reading, as well as allowing us to use the built-in definitions and lemmas in PVS. (Nonetheless, we did need to define some functionality on finite sequences, such as truncation, mapping a function over a sequence's elements, etc., as well as many lemmas to help us reason about sequences.) When we need sequences that can be either finite or infinite in future work, we plan to define a type whose elements can be either a finite sequence or an infinite sequence, using the built-in PVS theories for each, and to prove metatheorems to avoid duplication of proofs where possible.

Using the 'o' infix operator (defined in the PVS prelude of built-in theories) has also improved the readability of proof sequents.

Finally, PVS auto-rewrite rules can be included in a theory definition, so that they are automatically applied when the theory is imported, or they can be explicitly enabled in a proof script when needed. The latter option imposes more work on the user, but avoids spending time on applying the rules when they are not needed, and also prevents confusion that can arise when they are applied unexpectedly. We have chosen the latter option.

5.2 Using Our Framework to Verify the NOrec Algorithm

Unlike our previous verification efforts, we did not first write out a careful hand proof for NOrec and then attempt to translate it into PVS. Rather, we informally reasoned at a high level about why NOrec is correct, and tried to construct the formal proof guided by this informal reasoning and our past experience with simulation proofs. In particular, as described in the previous section, we defined an "intermediate" automaton that collapsed several steps of the NOrec algorithm into single atomic steps, and then successively refined that automaton until it had the granularity of the actual NOrec algorithm.

We were pleased to find that this approach worked quite well, and that using PVS to verify NOrec was not significantly more difficult than we estimate a similarly careful hand proof would have been. Indeed, in some respects, it was easier because when we discovered and corrected a mistake in a definition or lemma, we could rerun our earlier proofs and examine only those, if any, that no longer succeeded. Correcting those proofs was typically straightforward.

One exception was that, after proving that `NOrecAtomicCommitValidate` implements `TMS2`, we defined a variant that refines the validation operation but still treats commit as a single atomic operation, and proved that it implements `NOrecAtomicCommitValidate`. However, when we attempted to refine this automaton further so that the commit operation was no longer atomic, we found that it was difficult to prove that this automaton implemented the version with the atomic commit, and that it was easier to prove that it implemented `NOrecAtomicCommitValidate` directly. This problem was with our proof approach, and would have occurred in a hand proof as well.

Another exception was in the proof that `NOrecPaperPseudocode` implements `NOrec` (the abstract NOrec algorithm, in which some "local" actions happen atomically together with an action that accesses shared state), which was much more difficult than we expected: it required great care to correctly express the state correspondence (i.e., the forward simulation). Again, this problem would exist for a hand proof as well, but hand proofs are rarely done to that level of detail, and indeed, we had not initially intended to do so in our verification.

While working on our proofs, we discovered several small mistakes we had made in specifying the automata involved. Because we had done all the proofs with PVS, we could simply rerun them after fixing the mistakes, thereby identifying within minutes which proofs had been broken by the fixes. Of course we had to construct proofs to address the cases missed due to the fixed mistakes, but otherwise proofs were typically broken in straightforward and predictable ways, and could be quickly and easily repaired.

5.3 Formal Proofs Are Still Harder Than Typical Hand Proofs

Machine-checked PVS proofs are still harder to write than hand proofs. First, there is the difficulty of specifying automata and related properties in the PVS language. In a hand proof, we use whatever notation and mathematical definitions are most convenient. However, a formal language is more limited. For example, the `Automaton` theory (Figure 1) defines an execution fragment using a sequence of actions and a sequence of states that is exactly one longer than the sequence of actions, rather than as an alternating sequence of states and actions, which is more natural but would require a common supertype for actions and states that would pollute our proofs with many inconvenient conversions.

Second, in PVS, we need to prove that our definitions are type-correct, even for cases that are never used. For example, the `effect` function we use to determine the poststate of a transition must be well defined even when the precondition does not hold, even though its value in that case is unimportant. To address this, we define the poststate to be an arbitrary state in case the precondition does not hold, requiring extra steps in every proof that deals with the `effect` function. This issue is mitigated by the use of automated strategies. This kind of problem seems to be inherent in formal machine-checked proofs. Although annoying, such issues are usually manageable once one becomes familiar with PVS.

Third, "obvious" facts that would usually be used implicitly in a hand proof must be proved and cited. Associativity of concatenation is an example. Developing and verifying richer theories that assert these obvious facts and using auto-rewrite rules to avoid the need to cite them explicitly helps.

Fourth, we prove results about automata and simulations only when we need them. This disrupts our work when it happens, but will happen less as our framework matures. For example, in proving that `NOrecPaperPseudocode` implements `NOrec`, we needed an invariant of `NOrec` that would be somewhat involved to prove. However, we had already proved (an abstract version of) this invariant for `NOrecAtomicCommitValidate`, and refinements from `NOrec` to `NOrecDerived`, and from `NOrecDerived` to `NOrecAtomicCommitValidate`.

Rather than proving the invariant directly, we proved two new "metatheorems" for this purpose: one shows that the composition of two refinements is a refinement, and the other allows us to derive an invariant of one automaton from an invariant of another automaton and a refinement from the first automaton to the second. This approach has several advantages: (1) There is no need to replicate the proof. (2) The proof in the abstract automaton is simpler than the direct proof in `NOrec` would have been because the abstract automaton is simpler than `NOrec`. (3) We can use these metatheorems in future proofs.

6 Related Work

Cohen et al. [1] verified small instances of some simple TM algorithms directly using a model checker. This approach cannot verify larger instances, especially for more complex algorithms, and is limited to finite instances regardless. Others have attempted to overcome these limitations using more complex techniques.

Guerraoui et al. [7] showed that TM algorithms satisfying certain structural properties can be verifed by model checking small instances of them. To our knowledge, these structural properties have not been formally verified for any TM algorithm, so this work does not yield fully machine checked proofs. Emmi et al. [6] used techniques to automatically generate and check parameterized invariants. However, limitations of their approach forced them to use abstract models that assume away complex concurrency-related aspects of the practical TM algorithms considered. Overall, while model checking approaches can be valuable for testing hypotheses and finding bugs, we do not believe that they will be sufficient to fully verify practical TM algorithms any time soon.

Cohen et al. [2] used PVS to verify another simple TM algorithm. Like us, they used PVS to model algorithms and specifications, and used the PVS theorem prover to verify that a TM algorithm satisfies the specification. While this work is similar in spirit to ours, there are two notable differences. First, we have used correctness conditions that ensure aborted transactions cannot observe inconsistent behavior, which is critical in some contexts (see Section 2). Other than [7], all other work mentioned above use specifications that do not constrain the behavior of aborted transactions. Second, in contrast to the other work mentioned above, we have have modeled a practical TM algorithm in faithful detail, and have proved it correct in a hierarchical manner that can be leveraged to significantly reduce the effort required to verify other TM algorithms.

Finally, other frameworks exist for specifying and verifying relationships between I/O automata in PVS, analogous to the non-TM-specific foundations of our framework. To our knowledge, the most mature of these is TAME [13]. However TAME is not generally available, so we developed our own framework so that we could make it available for others to use and extend.

7 Concluding Remarks

We have built a framework for formally verifying transactional memory (TM) algorithms using the PVS theorem prover. To demonstrate its utility, we have used it to complete what we believe is the first fully formal, machine-checked correctness proof of a practical TM algorithm (NOrec). Our framework is available so that others may use and extend it, for example to verify other TM algorithms.

We continue to improve our framework, and we plan to extend it with proofs of additional TM algorithms. We are particularly interested in verifying an algorithm—such as TL2 [4]—that requires a backward simulation to prove that it implements TMS2. As discussed in Section 4.2, we expect to be able to prove that TL2 implements TMS2 by proving that it implements `ReservationTMS2`, thus avoiding the need for a backward simulation.

Acknowledgments. We thank Sam Owre for PVS assistance, Andy Lewis for machines, and Simon Doherty for contributions to earlier versions of our framework.

References

1. Cohen, A., O'Leary, J., Pnueli, A., Tuttle, M., Zuck, L.: Verifying correctness of transactional memories. In: FMCAD 2007: Proceedings of Formal Methods in Computer Aided Design, pp. 37–44 (2007)
2. Cohen, A., Pnueli, A., Zuck, L.D.: Mechanical Verification of Transactional Memories with Non-transactional Memory Accesses. In: Gupta, A., Malik, S. (eds.) CAV 2008. LNCS, vol. 5123, pp. 121–134. Springer, Heidelberg (2008)
3. Dalessandro, L., Spear, M., Scott, M.: NOrec: Streamlining STM by abolishing ownership records. In: PPoPP 2010: Proceedings of the 15th ACM SIGPLAN Symposium on Principles and Practice of Parallel Programming (January 2010)
4. Dice, D., Shalev, O., Shavit, N.: Transactional locking II. In: International Symposium on Distributed Computing, pp. 194–208 (2006)
5. Doherty, S., Groves, L., Luchangco, V., Moir, M.: Towards formally specifying and verifying transactional memory. Formal Aspects of Computing (2012), `http://labs.oracle.com/projects/scalable/pubs/Doherty-FAC-2012.pdf`
6. Emmi, M., Majumdar, R., Manevich, R.: Parameterized verification of transactional memories. In: Proceedings of the 2010 ACM SIGPLAN Conference on Programming Language Design and Implementation, PLDI 2010, pp. 134–145. ACM, New York (2010)
7. Guerraoui, R., Henzinger, T., Jobstmann, B., Singh, V.: Model checking transactional memories. In: PLDI 2008: Proceedings of the 2008 ACM SIGPLAN Conference on Programming Language Design and Implementation, pp. 372–382 (2008)
8. Guerraoui, R., Kapalka, M.: On the correctness of transactional memory. In: PPoPP 2008: Proceedings of the 13th ACM SIGPLAN Symposium on Principles and Practice of Parallel Programming, pp. 175–184 (2008)
9. Herlihy, M., Moss, J.E.B.: Transactional memory: Architectural support for lock-free data structures. In: Proceedings of the 20th Annual International Symposium on Computer Architecture (1993)
10. Lesani, M., Luchangco, V., Moir, M.: Putting opacity in its place (May 2012), `http://labs.oracle.com/projects/scalable/pubs/OpacityInPlace.pdf`
11. Lynch, N., Tuttle, M.: Hierarchical correctness proofs for distributed algorithms. In: Proceedings of the Sixth Annual ACM Symposium on Principles of Distributed Computing, pp. 137–151 (August 1987)
12. Lynch, N., Vaandrager, F.: Forward and backward simulations, I: Untimed systems. Information and Computation 121(2), 214–233 (1995)
13. Mitra, S., Archer, M.: PVS strategies for proving abstraction properties of automata. Electron. Notes Theor. Comput. Sci. 125(2), 45–65 (2005)
14. Owre, S., Shankar, N., Rushby, J.: PVS: A Prototype Verification System. In: Kapur, D. (ed.) CADE 1992. LNCS, vol. 607, pp. 748–752. Springer, Heidelberg (1992)
15. Papadimitriou, C.: The serializability of concurrent database updates. J. ACM 26, 631–653 (1979)
16. The PVS Specification and Verification System, `http://pvs.csl.sri.com/`

Propositional Dynamic Logic with Converse and Repeat for Message-Passing Systems

Roy Mennicke

Institut für Theoretische Informatik, Technische Universität Ilmenau, Germany

Abstract. The model checking problem for propositional dynamic logic (PDL) over message sequence charts (MSCs) and communicating finite state machines (CFMs) asks, given a channel bound B, a PDL formula φ and a CFM $\mathcal{C}$, whether every existentially B-bounded MSC M accepted by $\mathcal{C}$ satisfies φ. Recently, it was shown that this problem is PSPACE-complete. In the present work, we consider CRPDL over MSCs which is PDL equipped with the operators converse and repeat. The former enables one to walk back and forth within an MSC using a single path expression whereas the latter allows to express that a path expression can be repeated infinitely often. To solve the model checking problem for this logic, we define global message sequence chart automata (gMSCAs) which are multi-way alternating parity automata walking on MSCs. By exploiting a new concept called concatenation states, we are able to inductively construct, for every CRPDL formula φ, a finite set of gMSCAs $\mathfrak{G}$ such that the set of models of φ equals the union of the languages of the gMSCAs from $\mathfrak{G}$. As a result, we obtain that the model checking problem for CRPDL and CFMs is still in PSPACE.

1 Introduction

Automatic verification is the process of translating a computer system to a mathematical model, formulating a requirements specification in a formal language, and automatically checking the obtained model against this specification. In the past, finite automata, Kripke structures, and Büchi automata turned out to be suitable formalisms to model the behavior of complex non-parallel systems. Two of the most common specification languages are the temporal logics LTL and CTL. After deciding on a modeling and a specification formalism, automatic verification melts down to the *model checking problem*: Given a model $\mathcal{A}$ with behavior $L(\mathcal{A})$ and a specification φ representing the expected behavior $L(\varphi)$, does $L(\mathcal{A}) \subseteq L(\varphi)$ hold?

Distributed systems exchanging messages can be modeled by communicating finite-state machines (CFMs). A CFM consists of a finite number of finite automata communicating using order-preserving channels. Each run of such a machine can be understood as a message sequence chart (MSC). The latter is an established ITU standard and comes with a formal definition as well as a convenient graphical notation. In a simplified model, an MSC can be considered as a labeled partial order consisting of send and receive events which are

M. Koutny and I. Ulidowski (Eds.): CONCUR 2012, LNCS 7454, pp. 531–546, 2012.

assigned to unique processes. Each such process has a minimal element and its events are linearly ordered. For each send event there exists a matching receive event and vice versa. Unfortunately, the model checking problem for CFMs is undecidable even for very simple temporal logics – this is a direct consequence of the undecidability of the emptiness problem for CFMs. One solution to this problem is to establish a bound B on the number of messages pending on a channel. The bounded model checking problem of CFMs then reads like that: given a channel bound B, a specification φ and a CFM $\mathcal{C}$, does every existentially B-bounded MSC M accepted by $\mathcal{C}$ satisfy φ? An existentially B-bounded MSC is an MSC which admits an execution with B-bounded channels. Using this approach several results for different temporal logics were obtained in [12,7,6,1].

In [1], a bidirectional propositional dynamic logic (PDL) was proposed for the automatic verification of distributed systems modeled by CFMs. This logic was originally introduced by Fischer and Ladner [3] for Kripke structures and allows to express fundamental properties in an easy and intuitive manner. PDL for MSCs is closed under negation, it is a proper fragment of the existential monadic second-order logic (EMSO), and the logic TLC^{-} considered by Peled [14] is a fragment of it. PDL distinguishes between local and global formulas. The former ones are evaluated at a specific event of an MSC whereas the latter are Boolean combinations of local formulas quantifying existentially over all events of an MSC. Consider for example the local formula $\alpha = p!q \wedge \neg \langle \mathsf{proc}^* \rangle\, p?q$. An event satisfies α if it is a send event of a message from process p to q which is not followed by a reply message from q to p. The global formula $\mathsf{E}\alpha$ expresses that there exists such an event v.

By a rather involved translation of PDL formulas into CFMs, Bollig, Kuske, and Meinecke demonstrated in [1] that the bounded model checking problem for CFMs and PDL can be decided in polynomial space. However, by means of this approach, Bollig et al. were not able to support the popular converse operator. The latter, introduced in [15], is an extension of PDL which allows to walk back and forth within an MSC using a single path expression of PDL. For example one can specify a path expression $(\mathsf{proc}^{-1}; \mathsf{msg})^*$ describing "zigzag-like" paths going back on a process and traversing a send event in an alternating manner. It is an open question whether PDL formulas enriched with the converse operator can be translated into CFMs. Bollig et al. only managed to provide an operator which enables path expressions to either walk backward or forward.

In the present work, we consider CRPDL over MSCs which is PDL equipped with the operators converse ($\_^{-1}$) and repeat ($\_^{\omega}$) [16]. The latter allows to express that a path expression can be repeated infinitely often. For example, an event v on process p satisfies $\langle \mathsf{proc} \rangle^{\omega}$ if there are infinitely many events on p succeeding v. We are able to demonstrate that the bounded model checking problem of CFMs and CRPDL is in PSPACE and therefore generalize the model checking result from [1]. In order to obtain this result, we define multi-way alternating parity automata over MSCs which we call MSCAs. MSCAs are started at specific events of an MSC and accept sets of pointed MSCs which are pairs of an MSC M and an event v of M. Using a game theoretic approach, it can be shown that MSCAs are closed under complementation. We effectively demonstrate that every local formula α of CRPDL can be translated into an MSCA linear in the size of α. We also define global MSCAs (gMSCAs) consisting of an MSCA $\mathcal{M}_p$ for every process p. If there exists an accepting run of every MSCA $\mathcal{M}_p$ on the process p beginning in the minimal event of p, then the gMSCA accepts the whole MSC. For every global formula φ, we can construct a finite set of gMSCAs $\mathfrak{G}$ such that the set of models of φ equals the union of the languages of the gMSCAs from $\mathfrak{G}$.

In the literature, one can basically find two types of approaches to turn a temporal formula into a Büchi automaton. On the one hand, Vardi and others [17,5] transformed LTL formulas into alternating automata in one single step and, afterwards, these alternating automata were translated into Büchi automata. On the other hand, there were performed inductive constructions which lead to a Büchi automaton without the need for an intermediate step [10,4,1]. In the present work, we combine these two approaches, i.e., for a given CRPDL formula, we inductively construct an alternating automaton which is later translated into a Büchi automaton. In this process, we utilize a new concept called concatenation states. These special states allow the concatenation of MSCAs. For example, if $\mathcal{M}$ is the MSCA obtained for the formula $\langle \mathsf{proc} \rangle\, \mathsf{tt}$, then we can concatenate two copies of $\mathcal{M}$ to obtain an automaton for the formula $\langle \mathsf{proc}; \mathsf{proc} \rangle\, \mathsf{tt}$.

We proceed as follows. In Sect. 2, we define MSCs, CRPDL, and (global) MSCAs, give introductory examples, and prove several closure properties of (global) MSCAs. In Sect. 3, we construct, for every local CRPDL formula α, an MSCA which precisely accepts the models of α. In Sect. 4, we effectively show that, for every global CRPDL formula φ, the set of models of φ is a union of gMSCAs languages. In Sect. 5, we prove that the bounded model checking problem for CRPDL and CFMs is PSPACE-complete.

2 Preliminaries

We fix a finite set $\mathcal{P} = \{1, 2, \ldots, |\mathcal{P}|\}$ of processes. Let $\mathsf{Ch} = \{(p,q) \in \mathcal{P}^2 \mid p \neq q\}$ denote the set of *communication channels.* For all $p \in \mathcal{P}$, we define a local alphabet $\Sigma_p = \{p!q, p?q \mid q \in \mathcal{P} \setminus \{p\}\}$ which we use in the following way. An event labeled by $p!q$ marks the send event of a message from process p to process q whereas $p?q$ is the label of a receive event of a message sent from q to p. We set $\Sigma = \bigcup_{p \in \mathcal{P}} \Sigma_p$. Since $\mathcal{P}$ is finite, the local alphabets Σ_p and Σ are also finite. For every natural number $n \geq 1$, we set $[n] = \{1, 2, \ldots, n\}$.

2.1 Message Sequence Charts

Let $\mathbb{D}$ be a finite set of labels. A $(\Sigma, \mathbb{D})$*-labeled partial order* is a quadruple $(V, \leq, \lambda, \eta)$ where $(V, \leq)$ is a partially ordered set, $\lambda : V \to \Sigma$ is a total mapping, and $\eta : V \times V \dashrightarrow \mathbb{D} \cup \{\mathsf{id}\}$ is a partial mapping with $\eta(v,v) = \mathsf{id}$ for all $v \in V$. For $v \in V$ with $\lambda(v) \in \{p!q, p?q\}$, let $P(v) = p$ denote the process that v is located at. Furthermore, we set $V_p = P^{-1}(p)$. The elements of V are called *events.*

We fix the set $\mathbb{D} = \{\mathsf{proc}, \mathsf{proc}^{-1}, \mathsf{msg}, \mathsf{msg}^{-1}\}$ of labels which we will use for our definition of message sequence charts. The idea is the following: A message sequence chart is a special $(\Sigma, \mathbb{D})$-labeled partial order $(V, \leq, \lambda, \eta)$. If we have $\eta(v, v') = \mathsf{proc}$ for $v, v' \in V$, then v' is the director successor event of v on process $P(v)$. Provided that $\eta(v, v') = \mathsf{proc}^{-1}$, v' is the direct predecessor event of v on process $P(v)$. In contrast, if $\eta(v, v') = \mathsf{msg}$, then v' is the receive event corresponding to the send event v. The label msg^{-1} is to be understood similarly.

More precisely, a *message sequence chart (MSC)* is a $(\Sigma, \mathbb{D})$-labeled partial order $M = (V, \leq, \lambda, \eta)$ where

- $\leq$ is the reflexive, transitive closure of $\{(v, v') \in V^2 \mid \eta(v, v') \in \{\mathsf{proc}, \mathsf{msg}\}\}$,
- $\{v' \in V \mid v' \leq v\}$ is finite for any $v \in V$,
- V_p is non-empty and linearly ordered by $\leq$ for any $p \in \mathcal{P}$,
- $|\lambda^{-1}(p!q)| = |\lambda^{-1}(q?p)|$ for any $(p, q) \in \mathsf{Ch}$, and
- for all $v, v' \in V$,

$$\eta(v, v') = \begin{cases} \mathsf{proc} & \text{if } P(v) = P(v'),\ v < v' \text{ and, for any } t \in V \text{ with} \\ & \qquad P(v) = P(t) \text{ and } v \leq t < v', \text{ we have } v = t \\ \mathsf{proc}^{-1} & \text{if } \eta(v', v) = \mathsf{proc} \\ \mathsf{msg} & \text{if there exists } (p, q) \in \mathsf{Ch} \text{ with } \lambda(v) = p!q,\ \lambda(v') = q?p, \\ & \qquad |\{t \mid \lambda(t) = p!q, t \leq v\}| = |\{t \mid \lambda(t) = q?p, t \leq v'\}| \\ \mathsf{msg}^{-1} & \text{if } \eta(v', v) = \mathsf{msg} \\ \mathsf{id} & \text{if } v = v' \\ \text{undef.} & \text{otherwise} \end{cases}$$

If $v \in V$, then (M, v) is a *pointed MSC*. Note that we decided to use the mapping η and the labels $\mathsf{proc}, \mathsf{msg}, \ldots$ instead of binary relations over $V \times V$ for technical reasons.

A message sequence chart can be depicted by drawing the processes from $\mathcal{P}$ as top-down time axes. Events can then be visualized by dots on these vertical lines and messages between events can be illustrated by arrows pointing from the send events to the receive events.

Example 1. Figure 1 shows a finite MSC over the set of processes $\mathcal{P} = \{1, 2, 3\}$.

2.2 Propositional Dynamic Logic with Converse and Repeat

We extend PDL for MSCs, which was proposed in [1], by the popular converse and repeat operators. The former operator, introduced in [15], allows to walk back and forth within an MSC using a single path expression of PDL, i.e., we can have a mixed use of proc, proc^{-1}, msg, and msg^{-1}. The repeat operator [16], which we denote by $\_^{\omega}$, allows to express that a path expression can be repeated infinitely often.

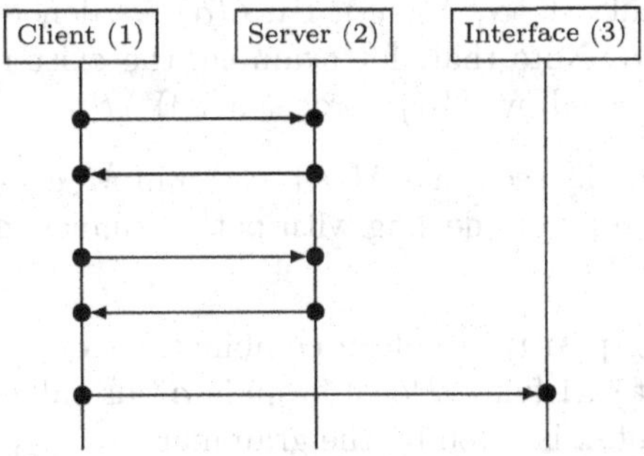

Fig. 1. An example MSC

Path expressions π and *local formulas* α of CRPDL are defined by the following grammar, where σ ranges over the alphabet Σ:

$$\pi ::= \mathsf{proc} \mid \mathsf{proc}^{-1} \mid \mathsf{msg} \mid \mathsf{msg}^{-1} \mid \{\alpha\} \mid \pi;\pi \mid \pi+\pi \mid \pi^* \quad \text{and}$$
$$\alpha ::= \sigma \mid \neg\alpha \mid \langle\pi\rangle\,\alpha \mid \langle\pi\rangle^\omega$$

Local formulas are evaluated at individual events of an MSC. If $M = (V, \leq, \lambda, \eta)$, $v \in V$, and $D \in \mathbb{D}$, then the semantics of local formulas are

$$\begin{aligned}
M, v \models \sigma &\iff \lambda(v) = \sigma \text{ for } \sigma \in \Sigma\\
M, v \models \neg\alpha &\iff M, v \not\models \alpha\\
M, v \models \langle D\rangle\,\alpha &\iff \text{there exists } v' \text{ with } \eta(v, v') = D \text{ and } M, v' \models \alpha\\
M, v \models \langle\{\alpha\}\rangle\,\beta &\iff M, v \models \alpha \text{ and } M, v \models \beta\\
M, v \models \langle\pi_1 + \pi_2\rangle\,\alpha &\iff M, v \models \langle\pi_1\rangle\,\alpha \text{ or } M, v \models \langle\pi_2\rangle\,\alpha\\
M, v \models \langle\pi_1;\pi_2\rangle\,\alpha &\iff M, v \models \langle\pi_1\rangle\,\langle\pi_2\rangle\,\alpha\\
M, v \models \langle\pi^*\rangle\,\alpha &\iff \text{there exists an } n \geq 0 \text{ with } M, v \models (\langle\pi\rangle)^n\alpha\\
M, v \models \langle\pi\rangle^\omega &\iff \text{there exist infinitely many events } v_0, v_1, \ldots \text{ such that}\\
&\qquad\quad v_0 = v \text{ and } v_{i+1} \in R(v_i, \pi) \text{ for all } i \geq 0
\end{aligned}$$

where, for all events v and path expressions π, $R(v, \pi)$ denotes the set of events which can be reached from v using a path described by π. Formally, we define $R(v, \pi)$ inductively as follows, where $D \in \mathbb{D}$:

$$R(v, D) = \begin{cases} \{v'\} & \text{if } \eta(v, v') = D \\ \emptyset & \text{otherwise} \end{cases} \qquad R(v, \pi_1;\pi_2) = \bigcup_{v' \in R(v,\pi_1)} R(v', \pi_2)$$

$$R(v, \pi_1 + \pi_2) = R(v, \pi_1) \cup R(v, \pi_2)$$

$$R(v, \{\alpha\}) = \begin{cases} \{v\} & \text{if } M, v \models \alpha \\ \emptyset & \text{otherwise} \end{cases} \qquad R(v, \pi^*) = \{v\} \cup \bigcup_{n\geq 1} R(v, \pi^n)$$

Formulas of the form $\langle\pi\rangle\,\alpha$ are called *path formulas*. We set $\mathsf{tt} = \sigma \vee \neg\sigma$ for some $\sigma \in \Sigma$. Furthermore, we use $\alpha_1 \wedge \alpha_2$ as an abbreviation for $\langle\{\alpha_1\}\rangle\,\alpha_2$ and write

$\alpha_1 \vee \alpha_2$ for the formula $\neg(\neg\alpha_1 \wedge \neg\alpha_2)$. By $L(\alpha)$ we denote the set of pointed MSCs which satisfy α. Note that, for example, the existential until construct $\alpha \mathsf{EU} \beta$ [9] can be expressed by $\langle((\{\alpha\}; (\mathsf{proc} + \mathsf{msg}))^*\rangle\, \beta$.

Remark 2. It can be easily seen that $M, v \models \langle\pi\rangle\, \alpha$ iff $M, v \models \langle\pi; \{\alpha\}\rangle\, \mathsf{tt}$. Because of this fact, every time we are dealing with path formulas in the future, we will assume that $\alpha = \mathsf{tt}$.

Global formulas φ are positive Boolean combinations of properties of the form "there exists an event satisfying a local formula α" or "all events satisfy a local formula α". Their syntax is given by the grammar

$$\varphi ::= \mathsf{E}\alpha \mid \mathsf{A}\alpha \mid \varphi \vee \varphi \mid \varphi \wedge \varphi$$

where α ranges over the set of local formulas. Their semantics is as follows:

$$\begin{aligned} M \models \mathsf{E}\alpha &\iff \text{there exists } v \in V \text{ with } M, v \models \alpha \\ M \models \mathsf{A}\alpha &\iff M, v \models \alpha \text{ for all } v \in V \\ M \models \varphi_1 \vee \varphi_2 &\iff M \models \varphi_1 \text{ or } M \models \varphi_2 \\ M \models \varphi_1 \wedge \varphi_2 &\iff M \models \varphi_1 \text{ and } M \models \varphi_2 \end{aligned}$$

Note that even though there are no negation operators allowed in global formulas, the expressible properties are still closed under negation. This is because conjunction and disjunction operators as well as existential and universal quantification are available. By $L(\varphi)$, we denote the set of MSCs M with $M \models \varphi$. We define the *size* $s(\alpha)$ of a local formula α to be the length of the string α. Let $s(\varphi)$ for a global formula φ be defined analogously.

Example 3 ([1]). For all $p \in \mathcal{P}$, we define $\alpha_p = \bigvee_{q \in \mathcal{P}, q \neq p}(p!q \vee p?q)$. We have $M, v \models \alpha_p$ iff $P(v) = p$ for every pointed MSC (M, v). From every event v which satisfies the local formula $\beta_p = \langle\mathsf{proc}^*; \mathsf{msg}; \mathsf{proc}^*; \mathsf{msg}\rangle\, \alpha_p$, process p can be reached with exactly two messages. If M is the MSC from Fig. 1, then $M, v \models \beta_3$ iff v is an event from process 2. The global formula $\varphi_p = \mathsf{A}\beta_p$ states that this holds for every event of an MSC.

Example 4. Let α_p be the formula from Example 3. If $M = (V, \leq, \lambda, \eta)$ is an MSC, then $M \models \mathsf{E} \bigwedge_{p \in \mathcal{P}}(\langle(\mathsf{proc} + \mathsf{msg} + \mathsf{proc}^{-1} + \mathsf{msg}^{-1})^*\rangle\, \alpha_p)$ iff the graph $(V, \mathsf{proc} \cup \mathsf{msg} \cup \mathsf{proc}^{-1} \cup \mathsf{msg}^{-1})$ is connected.

Now let $\pi_p = ((\mathsf{proc} + \mathsf{msg})^*; \{\alpha_p\})$ for every $p \in \mathcal{P}$. Imagine that M is an MSC which models the circulation of a single token granting access to a shared resource. Then $M \models \mathsf{E}\, \langle\pi_1; \pi_2; \ldots; \pi_{|\mathcal{P}|}\rangle^\omega$ iff no process ever gets excluded from using the shared resource.

2.3 Message Sequence Chart Automata (MSCAs)

In this section, we give the definition of (global) MSCAs which basically are multi-way alternating parity automata walking forth and back on the process and message edges of MSCs. First of all, we define labeled trees which will serve as a basis for our definition of the runs of an MSCA.

A *tree* is a directed, cycle-free graph (C, E) with the set of nodes C and the set of edges E such that there exists exactly one node with no incoming edges (which is called *root*) and all other nodes have exactly one incoming edge. Let S be an arbitrary set, $M = (V, \leq, \lambda, \eta)$ be an MSC, and $v \in V$. An *S-labeled tree over* (M, v) is a five-tuple $\rho = (C, E, r, \mu, \nu)$ where

- (C, E) is a tree with root r,
- $\mu : C \to S$ is a labeling function,
- $\nu : C \to V$ is a positioning function with $\nu(r) = v$,
- $\mu(y_1) \neq \mu(y_2)$ or $\nu(y_1) \neq \nu(y_2)$ for all $(x, y_1), (x, y_2) \in E$ with $y_1 \neq y_2$, and
- $\eta(\nu(x), \nu(y))$ is defined for all $(x, y) \in E$.

The elements of C are called *configurations*. If x is a configuration from C, then we denote by $E_\rho(x) = \{y \in C \mid (x, y) \in E\}$ the set of the direct successor configurations of x in ρ. A *path* in ρ of length $n \in \mathbb{N} \cup \{\omega\}$ is a sequence $x_1 x_2 x_3 \ldots \in C^n$ such that $x_{i+1} \in E_\rho(x_i)$ for all $1 \leq i < n$. It is a *branch of* ρ if $x_1 = r$ and $E_\rho(x_n) = \emptyset$ (provided that $n \in \mathbb{N}$). For convenience, we identify μ with its natural extension, i.e., $\mu(x_1 x_2 x_3 \ldots) = \mu(x_1)\mu(x_2)\mu(x_3) \ldots \in S^* \cup S^\omega$. We define $\mathsf{tr}_\rho : C \to S \times \Sigma \times 2^{(\mathbb{D} \cup \{\mathsf{id}\}) \times S}$ to be the function which maps every $x \in C$ to the triple $(\mu(x), \lambda(\nu(x)), A)$ where $A = \{(\eta(x, x'), \mu(x')) \mid x' \in E_\rho(x)\}$.

A *message sequence chart automaton (MSCA)* is a quadruple $\mathcal{M} = (S, \Delta, \iota, c)$ where

- S is a finite set of states,
- $\Delta \subseteq S \times \Sigma \times (2^{(\mathbb{D} \cup \{\mathsf{id}\}) \times S} \setminus \emptyset)$ is a transition relation,
- $\iota \in S$ is an initial state, and
- $c : S \to \{0, 1, \ldots, m-1\}$ is a ranking function with $m \in \mathbb{N}$.

The *size* $s(\mathcal{M})$ of $\mathcal{M}$ is $|S|$. An element $\tau = (s, \sigma, \{(D_1, s_1), \ldots, (D_n, s_n)\})$ of Δ is called a *transition*. It can be interpreted in the following way: Let us assume that $\mathcal{M}$ is in state $s \in S$ at an event $v \in V$. If it performs the transition τ, then it changes from the state s into the states $s_1, s_2, \ldots, s_n$, i.e., the run splits. For every $i \in [n]$ with $D_i = \mathsf{proc}^{-1}$ ($D_i = \mathsf{proc}$), the automaton moves to the event of the current process preceding (succeeding) the event v and changes into state s_i. In contrast, if we have $D_i = \mathsf{msg}$ ($D_i = \mathsf{msg}^{-1}$), the automaton moves from the send (receive) event v to the matching receive (send) event and changes into state s_i. For every $i \in [n]$ with $(D_i, s_i) \in \{\mathsf{id}\} \times S$, the automaton goes into state s_i without moving away from v.

By $\mathsf{mov}(\tau)$ we denote the set $\{(D_1, s_1), \ldots, (D_n, s_n)\}$ of *movements* of τ. We sometimes write (s, σ, D, s') as an abbreviation for a transition $(s, \sigma, \{(D, s')\})$ which does not use the alternation mechanism. For convenience, we define

$$\Delta_{s,\sigma} = \{\tau \in \Delta \mid \tau = (s, \sigma, \mathsf{mov}(\tau))\} .$$

Let $M = (V, \leq, \lambda, \eta)$ be an MSC. The MSCA $\mathcal{M}$ is *stuck* at an event $v \in V$ in the state $s \in S$ if for every transition $\tau \in \Delta_{s,\lambda(v)}$ there exists a movement

$(D,s') \in \mathsf{mov}(\tau)$ such that there exists no event $v' \in V$ with $\eta(v,v') = D$. If ρ is an S-labeled tree over the pointed MSC (M,v), then ρ is a *run* of $\mathcal{M}$ on (M,v) if $\mu(r) = \iota$ and, for all $x \in C$, the *run condition* is fulfilled, i.e.,

- if $E_\rho(x) \neq \emptyset$, then there exists a transition $\tau \in \Delta$ with $\tau = \mathsf{tr}_\rho(x)$, and
- if $E_\rho(x) = \emptyset$, then $\mathcal{M}$ is stuck at the event $\nu(x)$ in state $\mu(x)$.

Let $(s_i)_{i\geq 1} \in S^* \cup S^\omega$ be a sequence of states. By $\mathsf{inf}((s_i)_{i\geq 1})$, we denote the set of states occurring infinitely often in $(s_i)_{i\geq 1}$. If $(s_i)_{i\geq 1}$ is finite, then it is *accepting* if it ends in a state s whose rank $c(s)$ is even. If it is infinite, it is accepting if the minimum of the ranks of all states occurring infinitely often is even, i.e., $\min\{c(s) \mid s \in \mathsf{inf}((s_i)_{i\geq 1})\}$ is even. If ρ is a run of $\mathcal{M}$, and β is a branch of ρ, then β is *accepting* if its label $\mu(\beta)$ is accepting. A run ρ of $\mathcal{M}$ is *accepting* if every branch of ρ is accepting. By $L(\mathcal{M})$, we denote the set of pointed MSCs (M,v) for which there exists an accepting run of $\mathcal{M}$. Furthermore, $L_p(\mathcal{M})$ is the set of MSCs M with $(M,v) \in L(\mathcal{M})$ where v is the minimal element from V_p with respect to $\leq$.

Example 5. Let $p \in \mathcal{P}$. Consider the MSCA $\mathcal{M}_p = (\{s_1,s_2,s_3\},\Delta,s_1,c)$ where $c(s_1) = c(s_2) = 1$, $c(s_3) = 0$, and Δ is the smallest set such that, for all $\sigma \in \Sigma$ and $q \in \mathcal{P} \setminus \{p\}$, we have:

$$(s_1,\sigma,\mathsf{proc},s_1),(s_1,\sigma,\mathsf{msg},s_2),(s_2,\sigma,\mathsf{proc},s_2),(s_2,q!p,\mathsf{id},s_3) \in \Delta$$

For every pointed MSC (M,v), we have $(M,v) \in L(\mathcal{M}_p)$ iff $M,v \models \beta_p$ where β_p is the formula from Example 3.

Now, consider the new MSCA $\mathcal{M}'_p = (\{s_1,s_2,s_3,s_4,s_5\},\Delta \cup \Delta',s_4,c')$ where $c'(s_1) = c'(s_2) = 1$, $c'(s_3) = 0$, $c'(s_4) = 1$, $c'(s_5) = 0$, and Δ' contains only the transitions $(s_4,\sigma,\{(\mathsf{id},s_5),(\mathsf{id},s_1)\})$ and $(s_5,\sigma,\mathsf{proc},s_4)$ for all $\sigma \in \Sigma$. Then (M,v) is accepted by $\mathcal{M}'_p$ iff $M,v' \models \alpha_p$ for all $v' \geq v$ with $P(v') = P(v)$.

A *global MSCA* (gMSCA) is a tuple $\mathcal{G} = (\mathcal{M}_1,\ldots,\mathcal{M}_{|\mathcal{P}|})$, where, for all $p \in \mathcal{P}$, $\mathcal{M}_p$ is an MSCA. The language of $\mathcal{G}$ is defined by $L(\mathcal{G}) = \bigcap_{p\in\mathcal{P}} L_p(\mathcal{M}_p)$ and its size $s(\mathcal{G})$ is $\sum_{p\in\mathcal{P}} s(\mathcal{M}_p)$. If $\mathfrak{G}$ is a set of global MSCAs, then we define $L(\mathfrak{G}) = \bigcup_{\mathcal{G}\in\mathfrak{G}} L(\mathcal{G})$.

Example 6. Let $p \in \mathcal{P}$ and $\mathcal{G} = (\mathcal{M}'_p,\mathcal{M}'_p,\ldots,\mathcal{M}'_p)$ be a gMSCA where $\mathcal{M}'_p$ is the MSCA from Example 5. We have $M \in L(\mathcal{G})$ if and only if $M \models \varphi_p$ where φ_p is the global formula from Example 3.

2.4 Closure Properties of (Global) MSCAs

In this section, we prove several closure properties of (global) MSCAs which are need for our constructions of automata from CRPDL formulas. First of all, we effectively show that MSCAs are closed under union and intersection. Let $\mathcal{M}_i = (S_i,\Delta_i,\iota_i,c_i)$ be an MSCA for every $i \in [2]$, $S = S_1 \uplus S_2 \uplus \{\iota\}$ and $c : S \to \mathbb{N}$ such that $c(\iota) = 1$ and $c(s) = c_i(s)$ for all $s \in S_i$ and $i \in [2]$. By

$\mathcal{M}_1 \oplus \mathcal{M}_2$ we denote the MSCA $\mathcal{M}_\oplus = (S, \Delta_\oplus, \iota, c)$ whereas $\mathcal{M}_1 \otimes \mathcal{M}_2$ denotes the MSCA $\mathcal{M}_\otimes = (S, \Delta_\otimes, \iota, c)$ where

$$\Delta_\oplus = \Delta_1 \cup \Delta_2 \cup \{(\iota, \sigma, \mathsf{id}, \iota') \mid \iota' \in \{\iota_1, \iota_2\}, \sigma \in \Sigma\}$$
$$\Delta_\otimes = \Delta_1 \cup \Delta_2 \cup \{(\iota, \sigma, \{(\mathsf{id}, \iota_1), (\mathsf{id}, \iota_2)\}) \mid \sigma \in \Sigma\}$$

Informally speaking, $\mathcal{M}_\oplus$ non-deterministically decides to either run a copy of $\mathcal{M}_1$ or $\mathcal{M}_2$. In contrast, $\mathcal{M}_\otimes$ runs copies of $\mathcal{M}_1$ and $\mathcal{M}_2$ in parallel. It can be easily shown that the following holds:

Lemma 7. *$L(\mathcal{M}_\oplus) = L(\mathcal{M}_1) \cup L(\mathcal{M}_2)$ and $L(\mathcal{M}_\otimes) = L(\mathcal{M}_1) \cap L(\mathcal{M}_2)$.*

Now, we effectively demonstrate that the complement of an MSCA language is again an MSCA language. Let $\mathcal{M} = (S, \Delta, \iota, c)$ be an MSCA. Its *dual MSCA* $\mathcal{M}^\#$ is the MSCA $(S, \Delta^\#, \iota, c^\#)$ where

- $c^\#(s) = c(s) + 1$ for all $s \in S$ and,
- for all $\tau^\# = (s, \sigma, \mathsf{mov}(\tau^*)) \in S \times \Sigma \times (2^{(\mathbb{D}\cup\{\mathsf{id}\})\times S} \setminus \emptyset)$, we have $\tau^\# \in \Delta^\#$ if and only if $\mathsf{mov}(\tau) \cap \mathsf{mov}(\tau^\#) \neq \emptyset$ for all transitions $\tau \in \Delta_{s,\sigma}$.

If (M, v) is a pointed MSC, ρ is a run of $\mathcal{M}$ on (M, v), and $\rho^\#$ is a run of $\mathcal{M}^\#$ on (M, v), then one can observe that ρ contains a branch $x_1x_2x_3\ldots$ and $\rho^\#$ contains a branch $x'_1x'_2x'_3\ldots$ such that $\mu(x_1x_2x_3\ldots) = \mu(x'_1x'_2x'_3\ldots)$, i.e. they are labeled by the same sequence of states. Because of our definition of $c^\#$, a state $s \in S$ has an even rank in $\mathcal{M}$ iff it has an odd rank in $\mathcal{M}^\#$. As a consequence, $x_1x_2x_3\ldots$ is accepting in $\mathcal{M}$ iff $x'_1x'_2x'_3\ldots$ is not accepting in $\mathcal{M}^\#$.

In [11], a proof was presented showing that parity games enjoy memoryless determinacy, i.e., that at any game position one of the two players has a memoryless winning strategy. Using this result, the ideas presented in [13], and the above observation, the following theorem can be proved:

Theorem 8. *If $\mathcal{M}$ is an MSCA and (M, v) is a pointed MSC, then*

$$(M, v) \in L(\mathcal{M}) \iff (M, v) \notin L(\mathcal{M}^\#)\,.$$

Finally, we effectively show that global MSCAs are closed under intersection. If $\mathcal{G} = (\mathcal{M}_1, \ldots, \mathcal{M}_{|\mathcal{P}|})$ and $\mathcal{G}' = (\mathcal{M}'_1, \ldots, \mathcal{M}'_{|\mathcal{P}|})$ are two gMSCAs, then we denote by $\mathcal{G} \otimes \mathcal{G}'$ the gMSCA $(\mathcal{M}_1 \otimes \mathcal{M}'_1, \mathcal{M}_2 \otimes \mathcal{M}'_2, \ldots, \mathcal{M}_{|\mathcal{P}|} \otimes \mathcal{M}'_{|\mathcal{P}|})$.

Lemma 9. *$L(\mathcal{G} \otimes \mathcal{G}') = L(\mathcal{G}) \cap L(\mathcal{G}')$*

3 Translation of Local CRPDL Formulas

In this section, we effectively show that, for every local CRPDL formula α, the set of models of α is the language of an MSCA whose size is linear in α. In fact, we inductively define a computable function $\mathcal{M}_\_$ mapping from the set of all local formulas to the set of all MSCAs such that, for all local formulas α, we have $L(\alpha) = L(\mathcal{M}_\alpha)$. If α is a local formula, then we distinguish the following cases:

- Case $\alpha = \sigma$: We define $\mathcal{M}_\sigma = (\{\iota, s\}, \Delta, \iota, c)$ where $(\iota, \sigma, \mathsf{id}, s)$ is the only transition from Δ, $c(\iota) = 1$, and $c(s) = 0$.
- Case $\alpha = \neg\beta$: We define $\mathcal{M}_{\neg\beta}$ to be the dual automaton of $\mathcal{M}_\beta$.
- Case $\alpha = \langle D\rangle\,\mathsf{tt}$ with $D \in \mathbb{D} \cup \{\mathsf{id}\}$: We define $\mathcal{M}_{\langle D\rangle\mathsf{tt}} = (\{\iota, s_{\langle D\rangle\mathsf{tt}}\}, \Delta, \iota, c)$ where $c(\iota) = 1$, $c(s_{\langle D\rangle\mathsf{tt}}) = 0$, and $\Delta = \{(\iota, \sigma, D, s_{\langle D\rangle\mathsf{tt}}) \mid \sigma \in \Sigma\}$.
Note that the state $s_{\langle D\rangle\mathsf{tt}}$ is a so called concatenation state. We will use this type of states to "concatenate" MSCAs in order to obtain MSCAs which correspond to more complex formulas. For example, we can concatenate two copies of $\mathcal{M}_{\langle\mathsf{proc}\rangle\mathsf{tt}}$ to obtain a new automaton for the formula $\langle\mathsf{proc};\mathsf{proc}\rangle\,\mathsf{tt}$. Let (M, v) be a pointed MSC. If we start a copy of $\mathcal{M}_{\langle\mathsf{proc}\rangle\mathsf{tt}}$ on an event v, then it will reach the event v' with $\eta(v, v') = \mathsf{proc}$ in state $s_{\langle D\rangle\mathsf{tt}}$ iff $(M, v) \models \langle\mathsf{proc}\rangle\,\mathsf{tt}$. Since $s_{\langle D\rangle\mathsf{tt}}$ is our concatenation state, we start a second copy of $\mathcal{M}_{\langle\mathsf{proc}\rangle\mathsf{tt}}$. The latter will reach the event v'' with $\eta(v', v'') = \mathsf{proc}$ iff $M, v \models \langle\mathsf{proc};\mathsf{proc}\rangle\,\mathsf{tt}$.
- Case $\alpha = \langle\pi_1;\pi_2\rangle\,\mathsf{tt}$: If $\mathcal{M}_{\langle\pi_i\rangle\mathsf{tt}} = (S_i, \Delta_i, \iota_i, c_i)$ for $i \in [2]$, then we define
$$\mathcal{M}_{\langle\pi_1;\pi_2\rangle\mathsf{tt}} = (S, \Delta_1 \cup \Delta_2 \cup \Delta_3, \iota_1, c)$$
where $S = S_1 \uplus S_2$, $c(s) = (c_1 \cup c_2)(s)$ if $s \in S \setminus \{s_{\langle\pi_1\rangle\mathsf{tt}}\}$, $c(s_{\langle\pi_1\rangle\mathsf{tt}}) = 1$, and $\Delta_3 = \{(s_{\langle\pi_1\rangle\mathsf{tt}}, \sigma, \mathsf{id}, \iota_2) \mid \sigma \in \Sigma\}$. Furthermore, we set $s_{\langle\pi_1;\pi_2\rangle\mathsf{tt}} = s_{\langle\pi_2\rangle\mathsf{tt}}$.
The automaton $\mathcal{M}_{\langle\pi_1;\pi_2\rangle\mathsf{tt}}$ is the concatenation of the MSCAs $\mathcal{M}_{\langle\pi_1\rangle\mathsf{tt}}$ and $\mathcal{M}_{\langle\pi_2\rangle\mathsf{tt}}$. Intuitively, $\mathcal{M}_{\langle\pi_1;\pi_2\rangle\mathsf{tt}}$ starts a copy of $\mathcal{M}_{\langle\pi_1\rangle\mathsf{tt}}$ and, when this copy changes into its concatenation state, the automaton $\mathcal{M}_{\langle\pi_1;\pi_2\rangle\mathsf{tt}}$ starts a copy of the MSCA $\mathcal{M}_{\langle\pi_2\rangle\mathsf{tt}}$.
- Case $\alpha = \langle\{\beta\}\rangle\,\mathsf{tt}$: We define $\mathcal{M}_{\langle\{\beta\}\rangle\mathsf{tt}} = \mathcal{M}_\beta \otimes \mathcal{M}_{\langle\mathsf{id}\rangle\mathsf{tt}}$ and $s_{\langle\{\beta\}\rangle\mathsf{tt}} = s_{\langle\mathsf{id}\rangle\mathsf{tt}}$.
Intuitively, the MSCA $\mathcal{M}_{\langle\{\beta\}\rangle\mathsf{tt}}$ starts $\mathcal{M}_\beta$ to test whether $M, v \models \beta$ holds and, at the same time, changes into its concatenation state.
- Case $\alpha = \langle\pi_1 + \pi_2\rangle\,\mathsf{tt}$: If $\mathcal{M}_{\langle\pi_1\rangle\mathsf{tt}} \oplus \mathcal{M}_{\langle\pi_2\rangle\mathsf{tt}} = (S, \Delta', \iota, c')$, then we define
$$\mathcal{M}_{\langle\pi_1+\pi_2\rangle\mathsf{tt}} = (S \uplus \{s_{\langle\pi_1+\pi_2\rangle\mathsf{tt}}\}, \Delta \cup \Delta', \iota, c)$$
where c and c' coincide on $S \setminus \{s_{\langle\pi_1\rangle\mathsf{tt}}, s_{\langle\pi_2\rangle\mathsf{tt}}\}$, $c(s) = 1$ if $s \in \{s_{\langle\pi_1\rangle\mathsf{tt}}, s_{\langle\pi_2\rangle\mathsf{tt}}\}$, $c(s_{\langle\pi_1+\pi_2\rangle\mathsf{tt}}) = 0$, and $\Delta = \{(s_{\langle\pi_i\rangle\mathsf{tt}}, \sigma, \mathsf{id}, s_{\langle\pi_1+\pi_2\rangle\mathsf{tt}}) \mid \sigma \in \Sigma, i \in [2]\}$.
- Case $\alpha = \langle\pi^*\rangle\,\mathsf{tt}$: If $\mathcal{M}_{\langle\pi\rangle\mathsf{tt}} = (S', \Delta', \iota', c')$, then we set $\mathcal{M}_{\langle\pi^*\rangle\mathsf{tt}} = (S, \Delta, \iota, c)$ where $S = S' \uplus \{\iota, s_{\langle\pi^*\rangle\mathsf{tt}}\}$, c and c' coincide on $S' \setminus \{s_{\langle\pi\rangle\mathsf{tt}}\}$, $c'(s) = 1$ if $s \in \{\iota, s_{\langle\pi\rangle\mathsf{tt}}\}$, $c'(s_{\langle\pi^*\rangle\mathsf{tt}}) = 0$, $\Delta = \Delta' \cup \Delta_1 \cup \Delta_2$,
$$\Delta_1 = \{(s_{\langle\pi\rangle\mathsf{tt}}, \sigma, \mathsf{id}, \iota) \mid \sigma \in \Sigma\},$$
$$\Delta_2 = \{(\iota, \sigma, \mathsf{id}, \iota'), (\iota, \sigma, \mathsf{id}, s_{\langle\pi^*\rangle\mathsf{tt}}) \mid \sigma \in \Sigma\},$$
Intuitively, the MSCA $\mathcal{M}_{\langle\pi^*\rangle\mathsf{tt}}$ executes a copy of the automaton $\mathcal{M}_{\langle\pi\rangle\mathsf{tt}}$ and, every time this copy changes into its concatenation state $s_{\langle\pi\rangle\mathsf{tt}}$, the MSCA $\mathcal{M}_{\langle\pi^*\rangle\mathsf{tt}}$ nondeterministically decides whether it restarts this copy again or changes into its concatenation state.

– Case $\alpha = \langle\pi\rangle^\omega$: If $\mathcal{M}_{\langle\pi\rangle\mathrm{tt}} = (S, \Delta', \iota, c)$, then we set $\mathcal{M}_{\langle\pi\rangle^\omega} = (S, \Delta \cup \Delta', \iota, c)$ where $\Delta = \{(s_{\langle\pi\rangle\mathrm{tt}}, \sigma, \mathsf{id}, \iota) \mid \sigma \in \Sigma\}$.

Theorem 10. *If α is a local formula, then $M, v \models \alpha$ iff $(M, v) \in L(\mathcal{M}_\alpha)$ for all pointed MSCs (M, v). The size of $\mathcal{M}_\alpha$ is linear in the size of α.*

4 Translation of Global CRPDL Formulas

In this section, we effectively demonstrate that, for every global CRPDL formula φ, the set of models of φ is a union of gMSCA languages. More precisely, we inductively define a computable function $\mathfrak{G}_{\_}$ mapping from the set of all global formulas to the power set of all gMSCAs such that, for all global formulas φ, we have $L(\varphi) = L(\mathfrak{G}_\varphi)$. If φ is a global formula, we distinguish the following cases:

– Case $\varphi = \mathsf{E}\alpha$: If $\mathcal{M}_\alpha = (S, \Delta', \iota', c')$, then we set $\mathcal{M} = (S \uplus \{\iota\}, \Delta' \cup \Delta, \iota, c)$ where $c(s) = c'(s)$ for all $s \in S$, $c(\iota) = 1$, and

$$\Delta = \{(\iota, \sigma, \mathsf{proc}, \iota), (\iota, \sigma, \mathsf{id}, \iota') \mid \sigma \in \Sigma\}.$$

Intuitively, the automaton $\mathcal{M}$ moves forward on a process finitely many times. At some event $v \in V$, it nondeterministically decides to start the automaton $\mathcal{M}_\alpha$ to check if $(M, v) \models \alpha$ holds.
Now, for every $p \in \mathcal{P}$, we define $\mathcal{G}_p = (\mathcal{M}_1, \ldots, \mathcal{M}_{|\mathcal{P}|})$ where $\mathcal{M}_p = \mathcal{M}$ and $\mathcal{M}_q = \mathcal{M}_{\mathrm{tt}}$ for all $q \in \mathcal{P} \setminus \{p\}$. Note that $\mathcal{M}_{\mathrm{tt}}$ accepts the language of all MSCs. Finally, we let $\mathfrak{G}_{\mathsf{E}\alpha} = \{\mathcal{G}_p \mid p \in \mathcal{P}\}$.

– Case $\varphi = \mathsf{A}\alpha$: If $\mathcal{M}_\alpha = (S, \Delta', \iota', c')$, we set $\mathcal{M} = (S \uplus \{\iota_1, \iota_2\}, \Delta' \cup \Delta, \iota_1, c)$ where $c(s) = c'(s)$ for all $s \in S$, $c(\iota_1) = 1$, $c(\iota_2) = 0$, and

$$\Delta = \{(\iota_1, \sigma, \{(\mathsf{id}, \iota_2), (\mathsf{id}, \iota')\}) \mid \sigma \in \Sigma\} \cup \{(\iota_2, \sigma, \mathsf{proc}, \iota_1) \mid \sigma \in \Sigma\}.$$

Informally speaking, the automaton $\mathcal{M}$ moves forward on a certain process and checks, for every event $v \in V$ of this process, if $(M, v) \models \alpha$ holds.
We define $\mathfrak{G}_{\mathsf{A}\alpha} = \{(\mathcal{M}_1, \ldots, \mathcal{M}_{|\mathcal{P}|})\}$ where $\mathcal{M}_p = \mathcal{M}$ for all $p \in \mathcal{P}$.

– Case $\varphi = \varphi_1 \wedge \varphi_2$: We let $\mathfrak{G}_{\varphi_1 \wedge \varphi_2} = \{\mathcal{G}_1 \otimes \mathcal{G}_2 \mid \mathcal{G}_1 \in \mathfrak{G}_{\varphi_1}, \mathcal{G}_2 \in \mathfrak{G}_{\varphi_2}\}$.

– Case $\varphi = \varphi_1 \vee \varphi_2$: We define $\mathfrak{G}_{\varphi_1 \vee \varphi_2} = \mathfrak{G}_{\varphi_1} \cup \mathfrak{G}_{\varphi_2}$.

Theorem 11. *If φ is a global CRPDL formula, then $M \in L(\mathfrak{G}_\varphi)$ iff $M \models \varphi$ for every MSC M. The size of every gMSCA from $\mathfrak{G}_\varphi$ is linear in the size of φ.*

5 Model Checking

A CFM, which is well suited to model the behaviour of a distributed system, consists of a finite number of finite automata communicating using order-preserving channels. To be more precise, we recapitulate the definition of CFMs from [1]. A *communicating finite-state machine* (*CFM*) is a structure $\mathcal{C} = (H, (\mathcal{T}_p)_{p \in \mathcal{P}}, F)$ where

- H is a finite set of *message contents*,
- for every $p \in \mathcal{P}$, $\mathcal{T}_p = (S_p, \to_p, \iota_p)$ is a finite labeled transition system over the alphabet $\Sigma_p \times H$ (i.e., $\to_p \subseteq S_p \times \Sigma_p \times H \times S_p$) with initial state $\iota_p \in S_p$,
- $F \subseteq \prod_{p \in \mathcal{P}} S_p$ is a set of global final states.

Let $\mathcal{C}$ be a CFM and $M = (V, \leq, \lambda, \eta)$ be an MSC. A *run* of $\mathcal{C}$ on M is a pair (ζ, χ) of mappings $\zeta : V \to \bigcup_{p \in \mathcal{P}} S_p$ and $\chi : V \to H$ such that, for all $v, v' \in V$,

- $\chi(v) = \chi(v')$ if $\eta(v, v') = \mathsf{msg}$,
- $(\zeta(v'), \lambda(v), \chi(v), \zeta(v)) \in \to_{P(v)}$ if $\eta(v', v) = \mathsf{proc}$, and $(\iota_p, \lambda(v), \chi(v), \zeta(v)) \in \to_{P(v)}$ otherwise.

Let $\mathsf{cofin}_\zeta(p) = \{s \in S_p \mid \forall v \in V_p \exists v' \in V_p : v \leq v' \wedge \zeta(v') = s\}$. The run (ζ, χ) is *accepting* if there is some $(s_p)_{p \in \mathcal{P}} \in F$ such that $s_p \in \mathsf{cofin}_\zeta(p)$ for all $p \in \mathcal{P}$. The *language* of $\mathcal{C}$ is the set $L(\mathcal{C})$ of all MSCs M for which there exists an accepting run.

We strive for an algorithm that decides, given a global CRPDL formula φ and a CFM $\mathcal{C}$, whether $L(\mathcal{C}) \subseteq L(\varphi)$ holds. Unfortunately, this problem is undecidable – this is a direct consequence of the undecidability of the emptiness problem for CFMs. However, if one only considers existentially B-bounded MSCs [14,12,7,6] from $L(\mathcal{C})$, then the problem becomes decidable. Intuitively, an MSC M is *existentially B-bounded* if its events can be scheduled in such a way that at every moment no communication channel contains more than B pending messages. The rest of this section prepares the proof of our main theorem which is stated below. The proof itself can be found on page 544.

Theorem 12. *The following problem is PSPACE-complete:*
Input: $B \in \mathbb{N}$ (given in unary), CFM $\mathcal{C}$, and a global CRPDL formula φ.
Question: Is there an existentially B-bounded MSC $M \in L(\mathcal{C})$ with $M \models \varphi$?

5.1 Definitions

A *word* is a $(\Sigma, \{\mathsf{next}, \mathsf{prev}\})$-labeled partial order $W = (V, \leq, \lambda, \eta)$ such that $\leq$ is a linear order, $\{v' \in V \mid v' \leq v\}$ is finite for any $v \in V$, and

$$\eta(v,u) = \begin{cases} \mathsf{next} & \text{if } v < u \text{ and, for any } t \in V,\ v < t \leq u \text{ implies } t = u \\ \mathsf{prev} & \text{if } \eta(u,v) = \mathsf{next} \\ \mathsf{id} & \text{if } v = u \\ \text{undef.} & \text{otherwise} \end{cases}$$

Note that we define words to be labeled linear orders as this allows us a uniform definition of automata over MSCs and words, respectively. If $M = (V, \leq, \lambda, \eta)$ is an MSC, then a *linearization* of M is a word $W = (V, \preceq, \lambda, \eta')$ where $\preceq \supseteq \leq$ and η' is the mapping naturally arising from the linear ordering $\preceq$. The word W is *B-bounded* if we have

$$0 \leq |\{v' \mid v' \leq v, \lambda(v') = p!q\}| - |\{v' \mid v' \leq v, \lambda(v') = q?p\}| \leq B\,,$$

for every $v \in V$ and $(p,q) \in \mathsf{Ch}$. An MSC M is *existentially B-bounded* if there exists a B-bounded linearization of M, i.e., if it allows for an execution with B-bounded channels.

A *two-way alternating word automaton* (2AWA) $\mathcal{W} = (S, \Delta, \iota, c)$ is an automaton running on words which is defined analogously to MSCAs. By $L(\mathcal{W})$, we denote the set of words $W = (V, \leq, \lambda, \eta)$ for which there exists an accepting run of $\mathcal{W}$ on (W, v) where v is the minimal element from V with respect to $\leq$. If $\mathcal{W}_1$ and $\mathcal{W}_2$ are 2AWAs, then the automata $\mathcal{W}_1 \oplus \mathcal{W}_2$ and $\mathcal{W}_1 \otimes \mathcal{W}_2$ are defined analogously to the ones from Sect. 2.4.

Now, let us fix a bound $B \in \mathbb{N}$ and the alphabet $\Gamma = \Sigma \times \{0, 1, \ldots, B-1\}$. If $W = (V, \leq, \lambda, \eta)$ is a B-bounded word over Σ, then we associate with W the unique B-bounded word $W_\Gamma = (V, \leq, \lambda', \eta)$ over Γ where, for every $v \in V$, we have $\lambda'(v) = (\lambda(v), i)$ and $i = |\{v' \in V \mid v' \preceq v, \lambda(v) = \lambda(v')\}| \bmod B$, i.e., the second component counts events labeled by the same action modulo B. In W_Γ, we are able to quickly locate matching send and receive events. For example, if v is a send event of W_Γ labeled by $(p!q, i)$, we just need to move to the smallest event $v' \in V$ (with respect to $\leq$) with $v \leq v'$ and $\lambda(v') = (q?p, i)$.

5.2 Translation of Global MSCAs to 2AWAs

We can construct, from a global MSCA $\mathcal{G}$, a 2AWA $\mathcal{W}_\mathcal{G}$ that accepts exactly the set of words W_Γ where W is a B-bounded linearization of an MSC from $L(\mathcal{G})$. For the sake of clarity, we do not elaborate on the details of the construction of $\mathcal{W}_\mathcal{G}$ but rather present the underlying ideas. At the beginning, each run of $\mathcal{W}_\mathcal{G}$ splits into $|\mathcal{P}|$ configurations which are the starting points of the simulations of the MSCAs of which the gMSCA $\mathcal{G}$ is consisting.

Let $M = (V, \leq, \lambda, \eta)$ be an MSC and $W = (V, \preceq, \lambda, \eta')$ be a B-bounded linearization of M. If $v, v' \in V$ with $\eta(v, v') = \mathsf{proc}$, then an MSCA is capable of directly moving to v'. In general, this cannot be accomplished by a 2AWA since there may exist events $v'' \in V$ with $v \prec v'' \prec v'$. Hence, we need to address this issue in our construction of $\mathcal{W}_\mathcal{G}$. The idea is to introduce transitions which allow the 2AWA to move forward on W_Γ and skip non-relevant events until it reaches the event v'. Note that we have to analogously deal with proc^{-1}, msg, and msg^{-1} transitions of MSCAs.

In the 2AWA $\mathcal{W}_\mathcal{G}$, we use a state of the form (s, p, next) to remember that we are searching for the next event on process p in the next-direction. In contrast, a state of the form $(s, p!q, i, \mathsf{prev})$ means that we are looking for the nearest send event $p!q$ indexed by i in the prev-direction. The first component is always used to remember the state from which we need to continue the simulation of the MSCA after finding the correct event.

Assuming that we reached the event v we were looking for, we simulate a transition τ of the MSCA in the following manner: If $(\mathsf{proc}, s) \in \mathsf{mov}(\tau)$, then we change into the state (s, p, next) and move along the next-direction. If $(\mathsf{proc}^{-1}, s) \in \mathsf{mov}(\tau)$, then we act analogously in the prev-direction. If we have $(\mathsf{msg}, s) \in \mathsf{mov}(\tau)$ and $\lambda(v) = (p!q, i)$, then we change into $(s, q?p, i, \mathsf{next})$ and move along the next-direction. If $(\mathsf{msg}^{-1}, s) \in \mathsf{mov}(\tau)$, then we proceed similarly in the prev-direction.

Theorem 13. *Let $\mathcal{G}$ be a gMSCA, M be an MSC, and W some B-bounded linearization of M. We have $M \in L(\mathcal{G})$ iff $W_\Gamma \in L(\mathcal{W}_\mathcal{G})$. The size of $\mathcal{W}_\mathcal{G}$ is polynomial in B and the size of $\mathcal{G}$.*

Proof (Sketch). If ρ is a successful run of $\mathcal{W}_\mathcal{G}$, then ρ can be pruned and decomposed in such a way that we obtain accepting runs of the MSCAs of which $\mathcal{G}$ is consisting. Basically, we only have to remove those configurations from ρ in which $\mathcal{W}_\mathcal{G}$ is searching for the events at which it needs to simulate MSCAs of $\mathcal{G}$. The converse can be shown analogously. This time one needs to pad and combine the accepting runs of the MSCAs of $\mathcal{G}$ in order to obtain a successful run of $\mathcal{W}_\mathcal{G}$.

We are now able to prove our main theorem:

Proof (of Theorem 12). The global formula φ is a positive Boolean combination of global formulas $\varphi_1, \ldots, \varphi_n$ where, for every $i \in [n]$, φ_i is of the form $\mathsf{A}\alpha_i$ or $\mathsf{E}\alpha_i$ for some local formula α_i. For every $i \in [n]$, we can, by Theorem 11, construct a finite set of gMSCAs $\mathfrak{G}_i$ such that $L(\varphi_i) = L(\mathfrak{G}_i)$ and $\mathfrak{G}_i$ is linear in the size of φ_i. By Theorem 13, we can construct, for every $i \in [n]$, a 2AWA $\mathcal{W}_i$ such that, for all MSCs M and B-bounded linearizations W of M, we have $M \in L(\mathfrak{G}_i)$ iff $W_\Gamma \in L(\mathcal{W}_i)$. The automaton $\mathcal{W}_i$ is polynomial in B and the size of $\mathfrak{G}_i$. By combining the automata $\mathcal{W}_1, \ldots, \mathcal{W}_n$ using the operators $\oplus$ and $\otimes$ according to the construction of φ, we can build a 2AWA $\mathcal{W}_\varphi$ such that, for all MSCs M and B-bounded linearizations W of M, we have $W_\Gamma \in L(\mathcal{W}_\varphi)$ iff $M \in L(\varphi)$. The 2AWA $\mathcal{W}_\varphi$ is again polynomial in B and the size of φ. Using the alternation elimination scheme from [2], we can transform $\mathcal{W}_\varphi$ into a Büchi automaton $\mathcal{A}_\varphi$ exponential in the number of states and the maximal rank of $\mathcal{W}_\varphi$. Without loss of generality, we can assume that the rank of the 2AWA $\mathcal{W}_\varphi$ is linear in its number of states. Hence, the number of states of $\mathcal{A}_\varphi$ is exponential in B and φ.

In [1], it was shown that one can construct a Büchi automaton $\mathcal{A}_\mathcal{C}$ from $\mathcal{C}$ which recognizes exactly the set of all B-bounded linearizations of the MSCs from $L(\mathcal{C})$. It consists of $O(n)$ states where n is the maximal number of local states a finite automaton of $\mathcal{C}$ has. Therefore, one can construct a Büchi automaton recognizing the intersection of $L(\mathcal{A}_\mathcal{C})$ and $L(\mathcal{A}_\varphi)$ whose number of states is exponential in the size of the input. Hence, the model checking problem can be decided in polynomial space. The hardness result follows from the PSPACE-hardness of LTL model checking. □

Remark 14. The model checking problem for CRPDL and high-level message sequence charts (HMSCs) asks, given an HMSC $\mathcal{H}$ and a global CRPDL formula φ, is there an MSC $M \in L(\mathcal{H})$ with $M \models \varphi$. Using techniques from [1] and the ideas from the proof of Theorem 12, it can be shown that this problem is also PSPACE-complete.

6 Open Questions

It needs to be investigated whether PDL is a proper fragment of CRPDL and if CRPDL and global MSCAs are expressively equivalent. Furthermore, we would like to know about the expressive power of CRPDL and gMSCAs in comparison with EMSO. Another open question is whether the bounded model checking problem of CFMs and CRPDL enriched with the intersection operator [8,1] is still in PSPACE.

Acknowledgements. The author likes to express his sincere thanks to his doctoral adviser Dietrich Kuske for his guidance and valuable advice. Furthermore, he is grateful to Benedikt Bollig for comments leading to a considerable technical simplification. The author also thanks the anonymous referees for their detailed reviews and helpful remarks.

References

1. Bollig, B., Kuske, D., Meinecke, I.: Propositional Dynamic Logic for Message-Passing Systems. In: Arvind, V., Prasad, S. (eds.) FSTTCS 2007. LNCS, vol. 4855, pp. 303–315. Springer, Heidelberg (2007)
2. Dax, C., Klaedtke, F.: Alternation Elimination by Complementation (Extended Abstract). In: Cervesato, I., Veith, H., Voronkov, A. (eds.) LPAR 2008. LNCS (LNAI), vol. 5330, pp. 214–229. Springer, Heidelberg (2008)
3. Fischer, M.J., Ladner, R.E.: Propositional dynamic logic of regular programs. J. Comput. Syst. Sci. 18(2), 194–211 (1979)
4. Gastin, P., Kuske, D.: Satisfiability and Model Checking for MSO-Definable Temporal Logics Are in PSPACE. In: Amadio, R.M., Lugiez, D. (eds.) CONCUR 2003. LNCS, vol. 2761, pp. 222–236. Springer, Heidelberg (2003)
5. Gastin, P., Oddoux, D.: LTL with Past and Two-Way Very-Weak Alternating Automata. In: Rovan, B., Vojtáš, P. (eds.) MFCS 2003. LNCS, vol. 2747, pp. 439–448. Springer, Heidelberg (2003)
6. Genest, B., Kuske, D., Muscholl, A.: A Kleene theorem and model checking algorithms for existentially bounded communicating automata. Inf. Comput. 204(6), 920–956 (2006)
7. Genest, B., Muscholl, A., Seidl, H., Zeitoun, M.: Infinite-State High-Level MSCs: Model-Checking and Realizability. In: Widmayer, P., Triguero, F., Morales, R., Hennessy, M., Eidenbenz, S., Conejo, R. (eds.) ICALP 2002. LNCS, vol. 2380, pp. 657–668. Springer, Heidelberg (2002)
8. Harel, D., Kozen, D., Tiuryn, J.: Dynamic Logic. MIT Press (2000)
9. Katz, S., Peled, D.: Interleaving set temporal logic. Theor. Comput. Sci. 75(3), 263–287 (1990)
10. Kesten, Y., Pnueli, A., Raviv, L.-o.: Algorithmic Verification of Linear Temporal Logic Specifications. In: Larsen, K.G., Skyum, S., Winskel, G. (eds.) ICALP 1998. LNCS, vol. 1443, pp. 1–16. Springer, Heidelberg (1998)
11. Küsters, R.: Memoryless Determinacy of Parity Games. In: Grädel, E., Thomas, W., Wilke, T. (eds.) Automata, Logics, and Infinite Games. LNCS, vol. 2500, pp. 95–106. Springer, Heidelberg (2002)

12. Madhusudan, P., Meenakshi, B.: Beyond Message Sequence Graphs. In: Hariharan, R., Mukund, M., Vinay, V. (eds.) FSTTCS 2001. LNCS, vol. 2245, pp. 256–267. Springer, Heidelberg (2001)
13. Muller, D.E., Schupp, P.E.: Alternating automata on infinite trees. Theor. Comput. Sci. 54, 267–276 (1987)
14. Peled, D.: Specification and verification of message sequence charts. In: FORTE. FIP Conference Proceedings, vol. 183, pp. 139–154. Kluwer (2000)
15. Pratt, V.R.: Semantical considerations on floyd-hoare logic. In: FOCS, pp. 109–121. IEEE (1976)
16. Streett, R.S.: Propositional dynamic logic of looping and converse. In: STOC, pp. 375–383. ACM (1981)
17. Vardi, M.Y.: Alternating Automata and Program Verification. In: van Leeuwen, J. (ed.) Computer Science Today. LNCS, vol. 1000, pp. 471–485. Springer, Heidelberg (1995)

MSO Decidability of Multi-Pushdown Systems via Split-Width*

Aiswarya Cyriac[1], Paul Gastin[1], and K. Narayan Kumar[2]

[1] LSV, ENS Cachan, CNRS & INRIA, France
{cyriac,gastin}@lsv.ens-cachan.fr
[2] Chennai Mathematical Institute, India
kumar@cmi.ac.in

Abstract. Multi-threaded programs with recursion are naturally modeled as multi-pushdown systems. The behaviors are represented as multiply nested words (MNWs), which are words enriched with additional binary relations for each stack matching a push operation with the corresponding pop operation. Any MNW can be decomposed by two basic and natural operations: shuffle of two sequences of factors and merge of consecutive factors of a sequence. We say that the split-width of a MNW is k if it admits a decomposition where the number of factors in each sequence is at most k. The MSO theory of MNWs with split-width k is decidable. We introduce two very general classes of MNWs that strictly generalize known decidable classes and prove their MSO decidability via their split-width and obtain comparable or better bounds of tree-width of known classes.

1 Introduction

Multi-pushdown systems (MPDS) — finite state systems with several stacks — are natural abstractions of concurrent programs. Verification of multi-pushdown systems is undecidable in general. However concurrency is indispensable for many critical systems. Hence, several behavioral restrictions have been proposed and employed for their under-approximate verification [10,13,16,17,19].

The first behavioral restriction shown to have a decidable reachability problem was bounded context switching [19] in which the control can switch from one stack to another only a fixed number of times [13,16,17]. This was followed by ordered MPDS where the stacks have a priority ordering between them [2,3], and a stack could pop only when all higher priority stacks are empty. Another restriction is allowing only a fixed number of phases [12], where in one phase only one stack was allowed to return. Later bounded scope MPDS [14], where there are at most k context switches between any push and the corresponding pop, were also shown to have a decidable emptiness. In [18], Madhusudan and Parlato give a unified proof of decidability of emptiness of all but the last, by showing that these restrictions impose bounds on the *tree-width* of the underlying runs.

* Supported by LIA InForMel, and DIGITEO LoCoReP.

M. Koutny and I. Ulidowski (Eds.): CONCUR 2012, LNCS 7454, pp. 547–561, 2012.

As more general classes are desirable in the under-approximate verification, we propose a bigger and natural class of MPDS which is a generalization of ordered and scope bounded MPDS. We freely allow pops of both kinds in this restriction. This can be thought of as the fair runs which comply to the following scheduling policy. There is no restriction on pushes. But the corresponding pop a) has to be within fixed number of context switches from then (analogous to time-out) or b) if a) fails, then all such events will be ordered on a priority basis (assuming a total order on the priorities of different stacks). This class is called scope bounded or ordered return (SBO) in the paper. Thus under-approximate verification wrt. SBO is a kind of fair model checking, in which at least those runs which comply to the fair scheduling policy can be verified against some specification. A similar generalization can be thought of when the ordering policy is replaced by a bounded phase restriction. These two general classes are shown to be decidable. Note that, however, a joint generalization of ordered and phase bounded yields undecidablity.

The decidability proofs for the above classes are done by showing that these classes have bounded split-width. The behaviors of a multi-pushdown system as a graph are called multiply-nested words (MNWs). These are words enriched with additional binary relations matching a push on a stack with the corresponding pop. Split-width is a measure on MNWs which is comparable to tree-width (or *clique-width*) [7,11]. This, particularly since the latter was used in [18], calls for a comparison of split-width to tree-width.

Split-width has a simpler definition. It is defined in terms of two basic and natural operations — *shuffle* of two sequences of factors and *merge* of consecutive factors in a sequence. Thus split-width is easier to handle as these are well-tuned for MNW's, where as tree-width is defined for general graphs. This gives easier and simpler proofs.

Bound on split-width can be translated (up to a constant factor) to bound on tree-width (or clique-width). MNWs with split-width at most k have tree-width at most $2k-1$ and clique-width at most $2k+1$. For the other direction, MNWs with clique-width at most k have split-width at most $2k$. Thus we do not yet know whether we have an "equivalence" between split-width and tree-width (or clique-width).

Even though the class of bounded split-width MNWs is not known to be MSO definable, they enjoy a decidable MSO theory. Furthermore, split-width is general enough to capture all classes of MNWs with a decidable MSO theory, thanks to the translation from clique-width to split-width.

Thus split-width should be seen as a complementary approach which gives more insight into the structure of the MNWs which have bounded tree-width (or clique-width). The advantages of split-width are reflected in the fact that it helped in improving bounds for tree-width of known classes, and lifting up proofs from different classes to get proofs for joint generalizations.

To summarize, the contributions of this paper are manyfold. On one hand it introduces more general classes of MNWs for more accurate under-approximate verification of MPDS. It introduces the notion of split-width, a measure of complexity of MNWs, which is easier than, yet as general as tree-width or clique-width. It significantly improves the known bounds on tree-width for ordered MPDS and scope bounded MPDS.

The paper is organized as follows. Section 2 recalls some preliminary notions. Section 3 gives the definition of split-width and compares it to tree-width and clique-width. It also shows the MSO decidability of bounded split-width. In Section 4 various decidable classes of MNWs are formally defined, and proof of their decidability is given by showing a bound on split-width of these classes. Some proofs are omitted due to lack of space. These can be found in [9].

2 Preliminaries

$\mathbb{N}$ denotes the set of natural numbers. For $n \in \mathbb{N}$, by $[n]$ we denote the set $\{1, \ldots, n\}$. Let S be a set. For a binary relation $\mathcal{R} \subseteq S \times S$, we define *support* of $\mathcal{R}$, denoted $\mathsf{supp}(\mathcal{R})$, to be $\{x \in S \mid$ there is some $y \in S$ such that $(x, y) \in \mathcal{R}$ or $(y, x) \in \mathcal{R}\}$.

Multi-Pushdown Systems (MPDS). are finite state systems with a finite number of stacks. A transition may push onto a stack (push transitions), pop from a stack (pop transitions) or leave the stacks untouched. However, in one transition a MPDS can touch at most one stack. Moreover the push transitions and pop transitions are disjoint. Let Σ be the finite alphabet and $s \in \mathbb{N}$ be the number of stacks. We fix the finite alphabet Σ and the set of stacks $[s]$ for the rest of this paper. The behaviors of a multi-pushdown system are represented as multiply-nested words (MNWs).

Multiply-Nested Words (MNWs). A multiply-nested word (MNW) w over Σ is a structure $w = (\mathsf{dom}(w), \lambda, \lessdot, \curvearrowright^1, \ldots, \curvearrowright^s)$ where

- $\mathsf{dom}(w)$ is the set of positions
- $\lambda : \mathsf{dom}(w) \mapsto \Sigma$ is the node labeling function
- $\lessdot$ is the successor relation of a total order on $\mathsf{dom}(w)$. We denote this total order by $<$. That is, $< = \lessdot^+$.
- For each $i \in [s]$, $\curvearrowright^i \subseteq <$ is a binary relation such that
  1. For $i \neq j$, $\mathsf{supp}(\curvearrowright^i) \cap \mathsf{supp}(\curvearrowright^j) = \emptyset$
  2. For all $i \in [s]$, $x \curvearrowright^i y \implies (\forall z\, (x \curvearrowright^i z \implies z = y) \land (z \curvearrowright^i y \rightarrow z = x))$
  3. For all $i \in [s]$, there do not exist $x < x' < y < y'$ such that $x \curvearrowright^i y$ and $x' \curvearrowright^i y'$

We may think of this structure as a graph whose vertices are labelled by the function λ and edges are labelled using the symbols $\Gamma = \{\lessdot, \curvearrowright^1, \curvearrowright^2, \ldots, \curvearrowright^s)\}$. We refer to the edges labelled by $\lessdot$ as *linear edges* and those labelled by $\curvearrowright^i$ as *nesting edges*. If $s = 1$, a MNW is simply called a *nested word* in the literature [1].

MSO over MNWs. We assume that we have an infinite supply of first-order variables $x, y, \ldots$ and second-order variables $X, Y, \ldots$. First order variables vary over positions of an MNW while second order variables vary over subsets of positions. The syntax of the monadic second order logic over MNWs is as follows:

$$\varphi ::= a(x) \mid x \in X \mid x \curvearrowright^{i} y \mid x < y \mid x = y \mid \varphi_1 \vee \varphi_2 \mid \neg\varphi \mid \exists x.\varphi \mid \exists X.\varphi$$

where $a \in \Sigma$ and $i \in [s]$. We assume familiarity with logic and hence omit the obvious semantics associated with this logic.

Remark 1. The language of a Multi-pushdown system as a set of MNWs can be described in MSO.

3 Split-Width of MNWs

Given a MNW $w = (\mathsf{dom}(w), \lambda, \lessdot, \curvearrowright^{1}, \ldots, \curvearrowright^{s})$, an *m-split of w* is a structure $\overline{w} = (\mathsf{dom}(w), \lambda, \rightarrow, \dashrightarrow, \curvearrowright^{1}, \ldots, \curvearrowright^{s})$ where $\rightarrow \cap \dashrightarrow\ = \emptyset$, $\rightarrow \cup \dashrightarrow\ = \lessdot$ and $|\dashrightarrow| = m - 1$. The intuition is that the $\dashrightarrow$-edges are *missing* and these missing edges divide the linear order into m linear components (though there may be nesting edges connecting these different components).

A *split multiply nested word (SMNW)* is an m-split $\overline{w}$ of some MNW w for some m. We say that $\overline{w}$ is an m-SMNW. The entire multiply nested word is always a 1-SMNW. Notice that SMNWs continue to have the well nesting property for each $\curvearrowright^{i}$ w.r.t. the linear order generated by $\rightarrow \cup \dashrightarrow$.

Let $\overline{u} = (\mathsf{dom}(u), \lambda_u, \rightarrow_u, \dashrightarrow_u, \curvearrowright^{1}_u, \ldots, \curvearrowright^{s}_u)$ be an m-SMNW and let $\overline{v} = (\mathsf{dom}(v), \lambda_v, \rightarrow_v, \dashrightarrow_v, \curvearrowright^{1}_v, \ldots, \curvearrowright^{s}_v)$ be an n-SMNW. The *shuffle* of $\overline{u}$ and $\overline{v}$, denoted $\overline{u} \sqcup\!\sqcup \overline{v}$ is a set of $(m+n)$-SMNWs. A $(m+n)$-SMNW $\overline{w} = (\mathsf{dom}(w), \lambda_w, \rightarrow_w, \dashrightarrow_w, \curvearrowright^{1}_w, \ldots, \curvearrowright^{s}_w) \in \overline{u} \sqcup\!\sqcup \overline{v}$ if and only if:

- $\mathsf{dom}(w) = \mathsf{dom}(u) \uplus \mathsf{dom}(v)$
- $\lambda_w = \lambda_u \uplus \lambda_v$
- $\rightarrow_w = (\rightarrow_u \cup \rightarrow_v)$
- $\curvearrowright^{i}_w = \curvearrowright^{i}_u \cup \curvearrowright^{i}_v$

Note that, by explicitly stating that $\overline{w}$ is an $(m+n)$-SMNW, we have ensured that the nesting edges in $\overline{w}$ are well nested w.r.t. the linear order generated by $\dashrightarrow_w \cup \rightarrow_w$. Note also that, $\dashrightarrow_w \not\supseteq \dashrightarrow_u \cup \dashrightarrow_v$. In fact, by alternately choosing components from $\overline{u}$ and $\overline{v}$, we can have $\dashrightarrow_w \cap (\dashrightarrow_u \cup \dashrightarrow_v) = \emptyset$.

Let $\overline{u} = (\mathsf{dom}(u), \lambda_u, \rightarrow_u, \dashrightarrow_u, \curvearrowright^{1}_u, \ldots, \curvearrowright^{s}_u)$ be an m-SMNW. The *merge* of $\overline{u}$, denoted $\mathsf{merge}(\overline{u})$, is a set of n-SMNWs for $1 \leq n < m$, obtained by replacing some $\dashrightarrow$ by $\rightarrow$ in $\overline{u}$.

Let $k \geq 2$. We define the class k-BS (for *k-bounded splits*) to be the smallest set of SMNWs closed under the following operations

- $a \in k$-BS. That is, a single node labelled a is in k-BS.
- $a \overset{i}{\dashrightarrow} b \in k$-BS. That is, two nodes labelled a and b, connected by a $\curvearrowright^{i}$-edge is in k-BS.

- if $\overline{u}$ is an m-SMNW in k-BS, $\overline{v}$ is an n-SMNW in k-BS and if $m+n \leq k$, then $\overline{u} \sqcup\!\sqcup \overline{v} \subseteq k$-$\mathsf{BS}$.
- if $\overline{u}$ is in k-BS, then $\mathsf{merge}(\overline{u}) \subseteq k$-$\mathsf{BS}$

For any SMNW $\overline{w}$, if $\overline{w} \in k$-BS we say that the *split-width* of $\overline{w}$ is at most k.

3.1 Split-Width, Tree-Width and Clique-Width of MNWs

Split-width compares well to the usual measures of graph complexity: *tree-width* and *clique-width* [5,11,20]. This relation is stated in the following theorem:

Theorem 2. *1. The tree-width of a MNW of split-width k is at most $2k-1$.*
2. The clique-width of a MNW with split-width k is at most $2k+1$.
3. The split-width of a MNW with clique-width k is at most $2k$.

It is known that any class of graphs with tree-width bounded by k has clique-width bounded by $2^{k-1}-1$ [8]. However, Item 2 gives a better bound on clique-width. We give only the proof of Item 1 in this paper. The proof of the other two items can be found in [9].

We use the algebraic characterization of tree-width as in [4]. For this we define a syntax for generating graphs.[1] Let C be a finite set of colors. Then C-expressions are given by:

$$e ::= x \mid x \mathrel{\mathsf{E}} y \mid e_1 \parallel e_2 \mid \mathsf{rnm}_{x\leftrightarrow y}(e) \mid \mathsf{fg}_x(e)$$

where $x, y \in C$ and E is an edge relation. In particular for nested words $x \rightarrow y$, $x \curvearrowright^{i} y$ are C-expressions. Each expression defines an edge labelled graph (up to isomorphism) as described below:

- The expression x denotes the graph with a single vertex colored x.
- The expression $x \mathrel{\mathsf{E}} y$ denotes the graph with two vertices colored x and y and these vertices are connected by an edge E.
- The expression $e_1 \parallel e_2$ (parallel composition) denotes the disjoint union of the graphs defined by the expressions e_1 and e_2, where the nodes with the same labels are fused.
- The expression $\mathsf{rnm}_{x\leftrightarrow y}(e)$ (renaming) denotes the graph obtained by recoloring the vertices colored x and y in the graph denoted by e with y and x.
- The expression $\mathsf{fg}_x(e)$ (forget color) denotes the graph obtained by removing the color of the vertices colored x in the graph denoted by e.

Notice that there can be at most one vertex colored x for each color x, since the parallel composition fuses nodes with the same color. Also once the color of a vertex is forgotten, that vertex cannot be colored later. Notice that we have ignored the node labels in this definition, as these are not the most interesting. However, one could easily include them.

The tree-width of a graph is at most $|C|-1$ if there is a C-expression denoting it [4]. Using this we will now prove Item 1 of Theorem 2.

[1] This is F_C^{HR} in [4].

Proof (of Item 1 of Theorem 2). There are at most k components in any SMNW of split-width at most k. We use $2k$ colors of the form b_i, e_i for $1 \leq i \leq k$. That is we fix $C = \{b_1, e_1, \ldots, b_k, e_k\}$. We maintain the invariant INV1: *Color the first node and the last node of factor i by b_i and e_i respectively. If a factor has only one node, its color is b_i.* We show how to obtain a SMNW of split-width at most k using C-expressions inductively. The base cases are the basic splits: The expression for an internal node is b_1, and that for a nesting edge on stack i is $b_1 \curvearrowright^i b_2$.

For $w \in u \sqcup\!\sqcup v$: We identify the index in w of each factor in u and v. Then we do a sequence of renamings in u and v such that each node gets its intended label in w. This is followed by a simple parallel composition. Note that this parallel composition does not result in the fusion of any nodes, as the colors are disjoint. For example, consider $w = (n_1, n_2 n_3, n_4, n_5)$ and $u = (n_1, n_5)$ and $v = (n_2 n_3, n_4)$. Since u and v satisfies the invariant INV1, n_1 and n_2 are colored b_1; n_5 and n_4 are colored b_2; and n_3 is colored e_1. Let e_u, e_v denote the expressions for u and v respectively. Then $e_w = (\mathsf{rnm}_{b_2 \leftrightarrow b_4}(e_u)) \parallel (\mathsf{rnm}_{b_1 \leftrightarrow b_2}(\mathsf{rnm}_{e_1 \leftrightarrow e_2}(\mathsf{rnm}_{b_2 \leftrightarrow b_3}(e_v))))$.

For $w \in \mathsf{merge}(u)$: If w contains a linear edge from factor i in u to factor $i+1$ in u, we do a parallel composition with $(e_i \to b_{i+1})$ (If the factor i is singleton, we do a parallel composition with $(b_i \to b_{i+1})$). The graph $(e_i \to b_{i+1})$ is represented by $\mathsf{rnm}_{b_1 \leftrightarrow e_i}(\mathsf{rnm}_{b_2 \leftrightarrow b_{i+1}}(b_1 \to b_2))$. We do this for each linear edge added in w. Finally, in order to maintain the invariant INV1, we do a sequence of forgets and renamings. □

A theorem by Courcelle [6] says that if MSO is decidable for a class $\mathcal{C}$ of graphs with bounded degree, then $\mathcal{C}$ has bounded clique-width. This theorem, along with Item 3, says that any class of MNWs with decidable MSO theory indeed has bounded split-width.

Corollary 3. *Let $\mathcal{C}$ be a class of MNWs. If $\mathcal{C}$ has a decidable MSO theory, then $\mathcal{C}$ has bounded split-width.*

3.2 MSO is Decidable over Bounded Split-Width MNWs

An MSO definable class with bounded tree-width (or clique-width) has a decidable MSO theory. However, we do not know whether the class of k-BS MNWs is MSO-definable. Thus Theorem 2 does not imply MSO decidability for k-BS MNWs. Nevertheless, we have the following theorem:

Theorem 4. *Let $k \in \mathbb{N}$. The class of MNWs with split-width at most k has a decidable MSO theory.*

The proof is via a tree interpretation along the lines of the proof of MSO decidability over bounded clique-width graphs [7,11]. Let $\overline{w}$ be a SMNW in k-BS. By definition, the proof of the membership of $\overline{w}$ in k-BS is a tree whose nodes are labelled by elements of k-BS and whose degree is bounded by 2 such that

1. the root is labelled by $\overline{w}$.
2. leaves are labelled by atomic SMNWs.

3. if an internal node labelled $\overline{u}$ has only one child labelled $\overline{v}$ then $\overline{u} \in \mathsf{merge}(\overline{v})$.
4. if an internal node labelled $\overline{u}$ has two children labelled $\overline{x}$ and $\overline{y}$ then $\overline{u} \in \overline{x} \sqcup\!\sqcup \overline{y}$.

We abstract such a proof as a finitely labelled tree, called a proof tree. We can show that the set of valid proof-trees (of membership of SMNWs in k-BS) is accepted by a tree automaton of size exponential in k and s. Then we give a translation from any MSO formula Φ over MNWs to an "equivalent" formula Φ' over proof-trees. The detailed proof is given in [9] where this technique is extended to also show

Theorem 5. *Given a MPDS $\mathcal{M}$ and an integer k, we can construct a tree automaton $\mathcal{A}$ over the proof trees for k-BS, such that $\mathcal{A}$ accepts all the valid proof trees of MNWs in k-BS which have an accepting run in $\mathcal{M}$. The size of $\mathcal{A}$ is exponential in k and the number of stacks s, but is polynomial (with exponent $\mathcal{O}(k)$) in the number of states of $\mathcal{M}$.*

The above theorem allows us to derive several corollaries. *Emptiness checking* of a multi-pushdown system restricted to bounded split-width behaviors is EXPTIME. In fact, this allows *MSO-model checking* of a MPDS restricted to k-BS. Given a multi-pushdown system $\mathcal{M}$, an integer k and an MSO formula φ over MNWs, it decidable to check whether all MNWs of split-width at most k generated by $\mathcal{M}$ satisfy φ in time non-elementary in $|\varphi|$, exponential in k and the number of stack s, and polynomial in the number of states of $\mathcal{M}$. *Inclusion checking* of two MPDS wrt. k-BS is 2EXPTIME. As the set of all valid proof trees is recognizable, *universality checking* of a MPDS wrt. k-BS is also 2EXPTIME.

4 Classes of MNWs

Let w be a MNW. A *factor* u of w is defined to be a sequence of consecutive positions of w. We say that a position $x \in \mathsf{dom}(u)$ is an *i-pending call* in u if there exists $y \in \mathsf{dom}(w) \setminus \mathsf{dom}(u)$ such that $x \curvearrowright^i y$. Similarly, x is an *i-pending return* in u if there exists $y \in \mathsf{dom}(w) \setminus \mathsf{dom}(u)$ such that $y \curvearrowright^i x$. We say that u is complete for i if there are no i-pending calls or i-pending returns in u. This notion is lifted naturally to sequences of factors as well. A *context* is a set of consecutive positions which involves at most one stack.

We recall the definitions of three classes of MNWs for which MSO theory is known to be decidable and follow it with definitions of two new classes we propose.

Bounded Scope MNWs. [14] We fix a parameter $m \in \mathbb{N}$. We say that a MNW is m-scope bounded if for all nesting edges, there are *no* more than m different contexts between its source and target.

Bounded Phase MNWs. [12] A *phase* is a factor of a MNW in which at most one stack is allowed to return. We fix a parameter $p \in \mathbb{N}$. We say that a MNW is p-phase bounded if it can be partitioned into p phases.

Ordered MNWs. [2,3] Let $[s]$ be the set of stacks with the natural ordering on them. We say that a MNW is ordered if for all stacks $i \in [s]$, there are no pending calls of any stack $j > i$ at the target of a $\curvearrowright^i$ edge. In other words, if there are many pending calls at any instant, the pending calls of the highest stack will return first, then the second highest and so on. This means that, when stack i is returning, all stacks higher than i are empty.

Scope Bounded or Ordered Returns MNWs (SBO). Let $[s]$ be the set of stacks with the natural ordering on them. We fix a parameter $m \in \mathbb{N}$. Given a MNW and the parameter m, we classify the nesting edges into *long* and *short*. A nesting edge is long if there are more than m different contexts between its source and target. It is short otherwise. We say that a MNW is SBO MNW if for all stacks $i \in [s]$, there are no pending long nesting edges of any stack $j > i$ at the target of a long nesting edge of i. In other words, if there are many pending long nesting edges at any instant, the pending long nesting edges of the highest stack will return first, then the second highest and so on. That is to say that, with respect to the long nesting edges, a SBO MNW behaves exactly like an ordered MNW.

Scope or Phase Bounded Returns MNWs (SPB). Given a MNW and the parameters m and p, as in the case of SBO we classify the nesting edges into *long* and *short* (wrt. the parameter m). We say that a MNW is (m, p)-SPB if it can be partitioned into p phases wrt. the long returns.

Proposition 6. *The classes Bounded Scope, Bounded Phase, Ordered,* SBO, SPB *are MSO definable.*

Proof. All the returns of a MNW have to satisfy certain conditions to belong to a class. These conditions are easily MSO-definable. □

All the above classes have bounded split-width.

Theorem 7. *1. m-Bounded scope MNWs have split-width at most $m + 2$.*
2. p-Bounded phase MNWs have split-width at most 2^p.
3. Ordered MNWs have split-width at most 2^s.
4. m-SBO have split-width at most $2^s(2m + 1)$.
5. (m, p)-SPB have split-width at most $2^p(2m + 1))$.

The proof is given in Section 4.1 below.

Theorem 4 along with Proposition 6 and Theorem 7 gives us the MSO decidability of the classes defined in Section 4:

Corollary 8. *The classes Bounded Scope, Bounded Phase, Ordered,* SBO, SPB *have a decidable MSO theory.*

Theorem 2 along with Theorem 7 gives us new bounds of tree-width of the different classes of MNWs. We improve the $s2^{s-1}$ bound on tree-width of ordered MNWs obtained in [18] to 2^{s+1}. We also improve the $2ms$ bound on tree-width for bounded scope MNWs obtained in [15] to $2(m + 2)$.

Corollary 9. *1. m-Bounded scope MNWs have tree-width at most* $2(m+2)$.
2. p-Bounded phase MNWs have tree-width at most 2^{p+1}.
3. Ordered MNWs have tree-width at most 2^{s+1}.
*4. m-*SBO *have tree-width at most* $2^{s+1}(2m+1)$.
5. (m,p)-SPB *have tree-width at most* $2^{p+1}(2m+1)$.

4.1 Bounded Split-Width

Proof of Bounded Split-Width of Bounded Scope MNWs. Our idea is to split the first $m-1$ contexts of a bounded scope MNW into different components.

We write w_i to denote the ith component of a SMNW $\overline{w}$. Given an m-scope bounded MNW w, we repeatedly decompose it using the shuffle and merge operations till we are left with atomic SMNWs, ensuring that we stay within $(m+2)$-BS in this process. We maintain the invariant INV2: *All but the last component of the SMNWs are single contexts.* To begin, observe that any m-scope bounded MNW w is the merge of a SMNW $\overline{w}$ with at most m components, where the first $m-1$ components are the first $m-1$ contexts of w. We continue by applying the following rules:

1. If some component w_i is a complete MNW, let $\overline{v} = w_i$ and $\overline{u}$ be $\overline{w}$ without w_i. Clearly $\overline{w} \in \overline{u} \sqcup \overline{v}$.
2. If some component w_i has a non trivial prefix or suffix which is a complete MNW, we split w_i into $u_i v_i$ (both nonempty) such that one of them, say v_i is a complete MNW. Let $\overline{v}$ be v_i and $\overline{u}$ be $\overline{w}$ without v_i. Clearly $\overline{w} \in \mathsf{merge}(\overline{u} \sqcup \overline{v})$.
3. If there is a $\curvearrowright^i$-edge e whose source, labelled a, is the first node or last node of w_k and whose target, labelled b, is the first node or last node of w_ℓ, then $\overline{w} \in \mathsf{merge}(\overline{u} \sqcup)$ where $\overline{u}$ is $\overline{w}$ without the edge e and its source and target nodes.
4. If the last component is w_j with $j < m$ and has more than one context, then we split the first context of the last component into a separate component. Repeated application of this rule yields as many components (but at most m) as possible.

Observe that if the invariant holds for $\overline{w}$ then the same holds for the two SMNWs obtained by the application of any of these four rules, thus the invariant INV2 is maintained. Observe that the rules preserve another invariant INV3: *If there is a position x in ith component and a position y in jth component, then there are at least $|i-j|+1$ different contexts between x and y in the original MNW we started with.*

We will now argue that the above operations decompose the SMNW to base cases. Suppose, for the sake of contradiction, that a non-atomic SMNW $\overline{u}$ is obtained by the above operations from $\overline{w}$ and none of the above operations are applicable.

If for any stack there is a pending return in the first $m-1$ components, consider the first pending return which is in w_j. Let the corresponding call be in

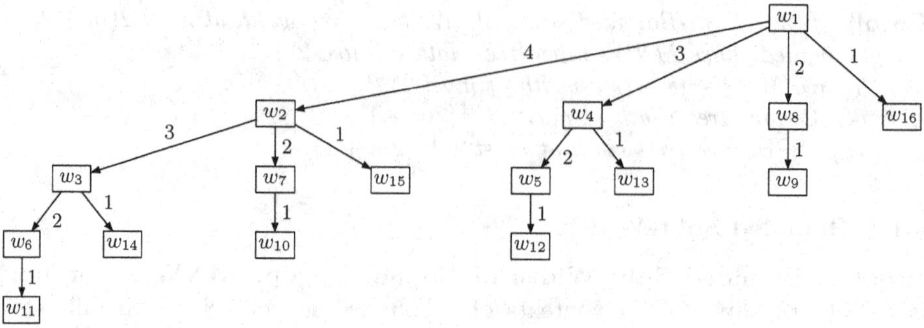

Fig. 1. A binomial tree of rank 5

w_i $(i < j)$. Since we are not in case 2, the component w_i, which is single context, ends with this pending call and similarly w_j begins with this pending return, making case 3 applicable. Thus we may assume that in $\overline{w}$ there are no pending returns in any of the first $m - 1$ components, and there are m components if the last component has at least two contexts. Since the first $m - 1$ components cannot be complete MNWs (case 1 is not applicable) they must involve pending calls. Since they do not have complete MNWs as prefixes or suffices and are single context, each of them must begin and end with pending calls with the corresponding returns in w_m.

Claim: The first node of w_m necessarily has to be a pending return of the stack of w_1. The claim holds since a) the first context of w_m belong to the same stack as that of w_1 and also contains the pending returns called in w_1 (Otherwise there are more than m contexts switches between the first pending call and its corresponding return, thanks to invariant INV3). b) w_m cannot have a complete MNW as a prefix, as case 4 was not applicable. This makes case 3 applicable, contradicting the assumption that none of the above cases are applicable.

Notice that, just before any merge, the SMNW contains at most $m + 2$ components. □

Proof of Bounded Split-Width of Ordered MNWs. We show that any ordered MNW admits a decomposition in which the SMNWs have at most 2^s components. For that, we restrict the number of components of each SMNW to 2^{s-1} before any shuffle operation. A shuffle is followed by a few merge operations so that the bound of 2^{s-1} is maintained before the next shuffle.

The (2^{s-1})-SMNWs we obtain in the decomposition have some nice properties which let us embed them in a binomial tree of size 2^{s-1}. Each node in the binomial tree is a single component of the SMNW. The structure of the binomial tree is given in Figure 1 and is defined below.

A binomial tree is an edge labelled tree where each node has a rank. A node of rank i will have $i-1$ outgoing edges labelled with $i-1, \ldots, 1$, and the j-child (child along the edge labeled j) will be a node of rank j. The rank of a binomial tree is the rank of its root. A binomial tree with rank k has height $k-1$ and has 2^{k-1} nodes. We identify a node by the path to that node from the root. In the figure, root is identified by ε, the leftmost node by 4321 and the rightmost node by 1. The i-child of node x is xi. Note that the rank as well as the labels along any path from the root to a leaf are decreasing.

We say that a SMNW $\overline{w}$ has a *k-binomial embedding* if every component w_i of the SMNW can be assigned a node $\mathsf{node}(i)$ of a binomial tree of rank k such that no two components are assigned to the same node. We will shortly show that a SMNW $\overline{w}$ obtained from the decomposition of an ordered MNW has an s-binomial embedding, satisfying the following properties. We denote the s-binomial embedding of $\overline{w}$ by W. If $\mathsf{node}(i) = x$ under W, then we denote w_i by W_x in the following.

P1 There is a $\curvearrowright^i$ edge from a component w_k to another component w_l only if $\mathsf{node}(l)$ is the i-child of $\mathsf{node}(k)$.
P2 Let x be a node of rank i. All the returns in W_x are on a stack which is at least i.

If $s = 4$, and $\overline{w}$ has 16 nonempty components, a binomial embedding satisfying the above properties may assign nodes of the binomial tree to components as shown in Figure 1. One can verify that it is in fact the only possible binomial embedding satisfying the stack policy and the ordering policy.

Any ordered MNW w is a 1-SMNW. The binomial tree embedding embeds this only component at its leftmost child (node with id $(s-1)(s-2)\cdots 1$). That is, $\overline{w} = w = W_{(s-1)(s-2)\cdots 1}$. Clearly it satisfies the properties P1 and P2.

We show the decomposition by induction. Let $\overline{w}$ be a SMNW with a s-binomial embedding satisfying the properties P1 and P2. We do the following case splittings in a greedy manner (we will go to a case only if it is not possible to match any of the previous cases).

1. If there is a nesting edge $\curvearrowright^i$ whose source, labeled a, is the first or the last position of w_k and whose target, labeled b, is the first or the last position of w_l, then $\overline{w} \in \mathsf{merge}(\overline{u} \sqcup)$ where $\overline{u}$ is $\overline{w}$ without the nesting edge and its source and target nodes. Clearly $\overline{u}$ has a s-binomial embedding inherited from that of $\overline{w}$, satisfying properties P1 and P2.
2. If some w_i is of the form $u_i v_i$ where v_i is complete (there are no pending calls or returns in v_i) and u_i and v_i are nonempty, then $\overline{w} \in \mathsf{merge}(\overline{u} \sqcup \overline{v})$ where $\overline{u}$ is $\overline{w}$ minus v_i and $\overline{v}$ is v_i. Also, $\overline{u}$ has a binomial embedding U inherited from $\overline{w}$ and $\overline{v}$ has a binomial embedding V which embeds its only component at its leftmost child. We have a symmetric dual case when u_i is complete. Note that $\overline{u}$ and U as well as $\overline{v}$ and V satisfies the properties P1 and P2.
3. If W has two nonempty nodes x and y both containing no pending returns: Wlog. let y be of smaller rank if the ranks are different. Due to property P1, we can conclude that the subtree rooted at y is disconnected from the rest. $\overline{v}$ is obtained by projecting $\overline{w}$ to those components whose embedding is in the subtree rooted at y and $\overline{u}$ is $\overline{w}$ without $\overline{v}$. Let U be a binomial embedding identical to W on the subtree rooted at y and empty elsewhere, and V be identical to W everywhere, except on the subtree rooted at y where it is empty. Clearly $\overline{w} \in \overline{u} \sqcup \overline{v}$. Moreover, $\overline{u}$ and U as well as $\overline{v}$ and V satisfies the properties P1 and P2.

4. This splitting in this case is depicted in Figure 2. Let x be a non-empty node such that W_x is of the form $U_x V_x$ where U_x and V_x are non-empty, and V_x does not have any pending return. We will split its children W_{xi} as $W_{xi} = V_{xi}U_{xi}$ such that all pending returns of U_{xi} are called in U_x and those of V_{xi} are called in V_x and there are no nesting edges between U_{xi} and V_{xi}. For this we can take U_{xi} to be the shortest suffix containing all the pending returns from U_x. Note that U_x is a prefix and U_{xi} is a suffix. This is because among all the nesting edges between W_x and W_{xi} (all of them belong to stack i, thanks to property P1), the first pending call will be returned last and the last pending call will be returned first. All the pending returns of U_{xi} should be called in U_x or V_{xi}. Since U_{xi} starts with a pending return of stack i whose call is in U_x , there are no pending returns of stack i in U_{xi} which is called in V_{xi}. Since the ordering policy on stacks is followed, there cannot be any pending returns of stack $j > i$ in U_{xi} which is called in V_{xi}. Due to property P2, there cannot be any returns of stacks $j < i$ in U_{xi}. Thus we can split its children W_{xi} as $W_{xi} = V_{xi}U_{xi}$. SImilarly, we split recursively all nodes in the subtree of x. For all y, $W_{xy} \in \mathsf{merge}(U_{xy} \sqcup\!\sqcup V_{xy})$ (In fact $W_{xy} = U_{xy}V_{xy}$ if $|y|$ is even, $W_{xy} = V_{xy}U_{xy}$ otherwise. For the nodes y which are not split by the above procedure, let $U_y = W_y$ and $V_y = \varepsilon$. Clearly $\overline{w} \in \mathsf{merge}(\overline{u} \sqcup\!\sqcup \overline{v})$ where $\overline{u}, \overline{v}$ are such that U and V are the binomial embeddings of $\overline{u}$ and $\overline{v}$. Once again, $\overline{u}$ and U as well as $\overline{v}$ and V satisfies the properties P1 and P2.

In fact if root of W (node ε) is non empty, then one of the above cases apply. We argue why. Let $w_1 = W_\varepsilon \neq \varepsilon$. If w_1 starts with an internal action, then it is a base case or case 2 or case 3 applies. If w_1 starts with a call to stack $j < s$, thanks to property P2, it is either a base case or case 1 or case 2 or case 3 is applicable. If it is a call to stack s, either case 1 or case 2 or case 4 is applicable.
5. From the above remark, the only remaining case is when root is empty. Let xi be the nonempty node of W with the highest rank (which is i). If W_{xi} does not contain any returns of stack i then we shift node xi to x followed by a shift of nodes xiy to xy. It can be verified that shifting of the nodes gives a binomial embedding satisfying the properties P1 and P2 . Hence we can safely assume that W is a binomial embedding and xi is the nonempty node of W with highest rank and that it contains a return of stack i. Consider the first return of stack i. We split W_{xi} into $W'_x W'_{xi}$ such that W'_{xi} is the shortest suffix containing all the returns of stack i. This will result in the splitting of the children of W_{xi} which are attached to W'_x or W'_{xi} similar to that in case 4. One can verify that $\overline{w'} \in \mathsf{merge}(\overline{w'})$. Once again $\overline{w}$ and its binomial embedding W' satisfies the properties P1 and P2. The splitting in this case is illustrated in Figure 3.

Notice that in each of the above cases, the length of the SMNW decreases, or the number of components increases (it is bounded by 2^{s-1}). Thus by induction, the proof follows. □

Proof of Bounded Split-Width of Bounded Phase. The proof for this case is very similar to that of Ordered MNWs. We will only mention the main differences from that of ordered. For the sake of easiness, we will identify the

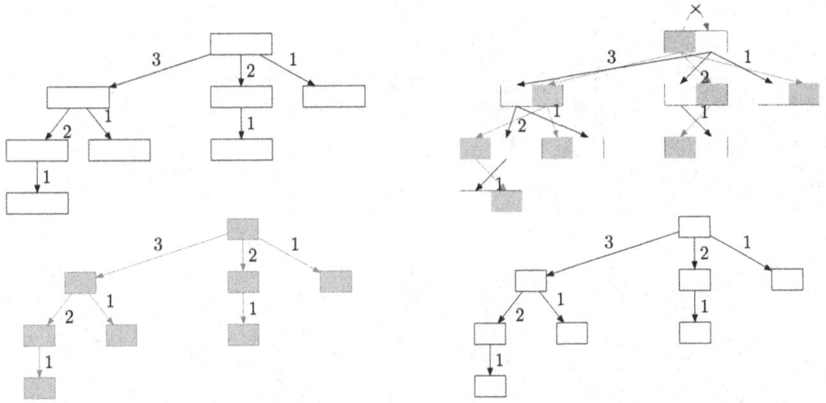

Fig. 2. Splitting of a binomial tree in case 4. Note the left/right alternation of gray (denotes U) and white (denotes V) parts along levels. This is needed since the stacks impose LIFO policy.

phases in the decreasing order. That is, the first phase is called phase_p, second phase is called phase_{p-1} and so on and the last phase is called phase_1.

As in the case of ordered MNWs, our SMNWs $\overline{w}$ will have a p-binomial embedding W satisfying the properties P1' and P2':

P1' There is a $\curvearrowright$edge from a component w_k to a component w_l only if $\mathsf{node}(l)$ is the i-child of $\mathsf{node}(k)$ and the return is in phase_i.

P2' If rank of x is i, then all the returns in W_x are in phase_j where $j \geq i$.

For the inductive decomposition, all the cases remain the same except for case 5. Let W_{xi} be the nonempty node of W with highest rank and assume that it contains at least one return from phase_i. We split W_{xi} into $W'_x W'_{xi}$ such that W'_{xi} is the shortest suffix containing all the returns of phase_i. The figures for ordered MNWs explains the splits for bounded phase as well, except that the edge labels of the binomial tree indicates the phase number of its children rather than the stack to which it belong. The bound follows. □

Proof of Bounded Split-Width of SBO and SPB. The proof for this case is a joint generalization of the proof of bounded scope MNWs and that of ordered (resp. bounded phase) MNWs. We first split according to the long nesting edges and obtain a binomial embedding. In order to handle the short edges, we separate the outermost m contexts of this component so that a decomposition similar to that for bounded scope goes through. Thus we have a binomial tree embedding where instead of having a single component in a node of the binomial tree, we have $2m+1$ components. The details can be found in [9].

5 Discussion and Perspectives

We have introduced and studied a new metric on MNWs called split-width and its relationship with clique-width and tree-width. Using split-width as a tool,

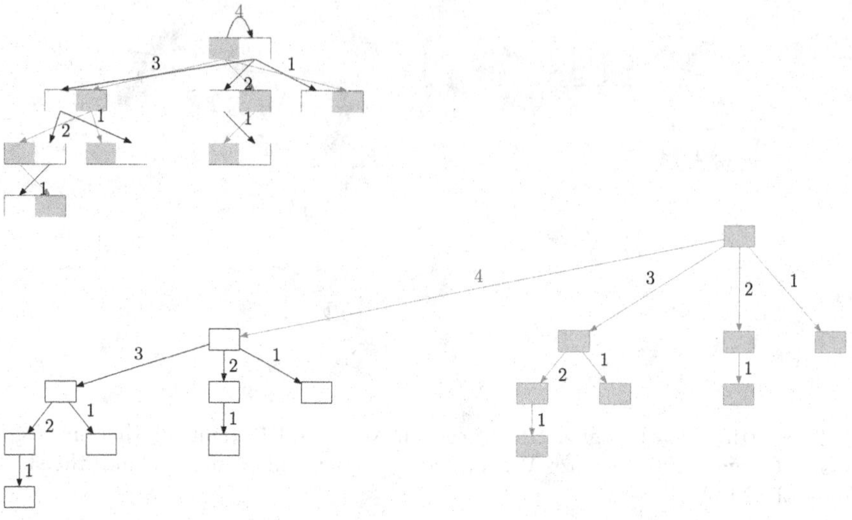

Fig. 3. Splitting of a binomial tree in case 5

decidability of MSO for several existing as well as new classes of MPDS have been shown. We can even extend the decidable classes further.

An *i-pending-call-context* of a MNW w is a factor u of w in which there are no j-pending calls for $j \neq i$. A *pending-call-context* is an i-pending-call-context for some i.

The proof of bounded scope goes through to show that the same split-width bound of $m + 2$ holds for a generalization of bounded scope. The generalization allows at most m pending-call-contexts at every return. The classes SBO and SPB could be generalized further to replace bounded scope constraint on short returns by the generalization. These generalizations are MSO definable and the split-width remains unchanged.

A next step is to bridge the gap in the translations between split-width and tree-width (or clique-width). Is it possible to obtain a linear translation from tree-width to split-width? Is it possible to close the gap in the back and forth translations between split-width and tree-width (or clique-width)? In other words, is split-width another characterization of tree-width (or clique-width) of MNWs?

Another interesting question is whether MPDS with k bounded split-width restriction are closed under complementation. That is, given a MPDS $\mathcal{M}$ and k, is there another MPDS $\mathcal{M}'$ such that for all k-bounded split-width MNWS w, w is accepted by $\mathcal{M}$ if and only if w is not accepted by $\mathcal{M}'$?

It is interesting to know whether one could employ temporal logics instead of MSO for model checking MPDS wrt. k-split-width-bounded runs, and get a reasonable complexity.

Another important direction is to find notions similar to split-width for other domains like message sequence charts, data words etc.

References

1. Alur, R., Madhusudan, P.: Adding nesting structure to words. J. ACM 56(3) (2009)
2. Atig, M.F., Bollig, B., Habermehl, P.: Emptiness of Multi-pushdown Automata Is 2ETIME-Complete. In: Ito, M., Toyama, M. (eds.) DLT 2008. LNCS, vol. 5257, pp. 121–133. Springer, Heidelberg (2008)
3. Breveglieri, L., Cherubini, A., Citrini, C., Crespi-Reghizzi, S.: Multi-pushdown languages and grammars. Int. J. Found. Comput. Sci. 7(3), 253–292 (1996)
4. Courcelle, B.: Graph grammars, monadic second-order logic and the theory of graph minors. In: Graph Structure Theory. Contemporary Mathematics, vol. 147, pp. 565–590. American Mathematical Society (1993)
5. Courcelle, B.: The expression of graph properties and graph transformations in monadic second-order logic. In: Rozenberg, G. (ed.) Handbook of Graph Grammars, pp. 313–400. World Scientific (1997)
6. Courcelle, B.: The monadic second-order logic of graphs xv: On a conjecture by D. Seese. Journal of Applied Logic 8, 1–40 (2006)
7. Courcelle, B., Engelfriet, J., Rozenberg, G.: Handle-rewriting hypergraph grammars. J. Comput. Syst. Sci. 46(2), 218–270 (1993)
8. Courcelle, B., Olariu, S.: Upper bounds to the clique width of graphs. Discrete Applied Mathematics 101(1-3), 77–114 (2000)
9. Cyriac, A., Gastin, P., Narayan Kumar, K.: MSO decidability of multi-pushdown systems via split-width. Research Report LSV-12-11, Laboratoire Spécification et Vérification, ENS Cachan, France (June 2012)
10. Heußner, A., Leroux, J., Muscholl, A., Sutre, G.: Reachability Analysis of Communicating Pushdown Systems. In: Ong, L. (ed.) FOSSACS 2010. LNCS, vol. 6014, pp. 267–281. Springer, Heidelberg (2010)
11. Kreutzer, S.: Algorithmic meta-theorems. CoRR, abs/0902.3616 (2009)
12. La Torre, S., Madhusudan, P., Parlato, G.: A robust class of context-sensitive languages. In: LICS 2007, pp. 161–170. IEEE Computer Society (2007)
13. La Torre, S., Madhusudan, P., Parlato, G.: Context-Bounded Analysis of Concurrent Queue Systems. In: Ramakrishnan, C.R., Rehof, J. (eds.) TACAS 2008. LNCS, vol. 4963, pp. 299–314. Springer, Heidelberg (2008)
14. La Torre, S., Napoli, M.: Reachability of Multistack Pushdown Systems with Scope-Bounded Matching Relations. In: Katoen, J.-P., König, B. (eds.) CONCUR 2011. LNCS, vol. 6901, pp. 203–218. Springer, Heidelberg (2011)
15. La Torre, S., Parlato, G.: Scope-bounded multistack pushdown systems: fixed-point, sequentialization, and tree-width. Technical report, University of Southampton (February 2012)
16. Lal, A., Reps, T.W.: Reducing concurrent analysis under a context bound to sequential analysis. Formal Methods in System Design 35(1), 73–97 (2009)
17. Lal, A., Touili, T., Kidd, N., Reps, T.: Interprocedural Analysis of Concurrent Programs Under a Context Bound. In: Ramakrishnan, C.R., Rehof, J. (eds.) TACAS 2008. LNCS, vol. 4963, pp. 282–298. Springer, Heidelberg (2008)
18. Madhusudan, P., Parlato, G.: The tree width of auxiliary storage. In: Ball, T., Sagiv, M. (eds.) POPL 2011, pp. 283–294. ACM (2011)
19. Qadeer, S., Rehof, J.: Context-Bounded Model Checking of Concurrent Software. In: Halbwachs, N., Zuck, L.D. (eds.) TACAS 2005. LNCS, vol. 3440, pp. 93–107. Springer, Heidelberg (2005)
20. Seese, D.: The structure of models of decidable monadic theories of graphs. Ann. Pure Appl. Logic 53(2), 169–195 (1991)

Decidability Problems for Actor Systems

Frank S. de Boer[1], Mahdi M. Jaghoori[1], Cosimo Laneve[2], and Gianluigi Zavattaro[2]

[1] CWI, Amsterdam, The Netherlands
[2] University of Bologna, INRIA Focus Research Team, Bologna, Italy
{f.s.de.boer,jaghoori}@cwi.nl, {laneve,zavattar}@cs.unibo.it

Abstract. We introduce a nominal actor-based language and study its expressive power. We have identified the presence/absence of fields as a relevant feature: the dynamic creation of names in combination with fields gives rise to Turing completeness. On the other hand, restricting to stateless actors gives rise to systems for which properties such as termination are decidable. Such decidability result holds in actors with states when the number of actors is finite and the state is read-only.

1 Introduction

Since their introduction in [13], actor languages have evolved as a powerful computational model for defining distributed and concurrent systems [2,3]. Languages based on actors have been also designed for modelling embedded systems [16,17], wireless sensor networks [7], multi-core programming [15], and web services [5,6]. The underlying concurrent model of actor languages also forms the basis of the programming languages Erlang [4] and Scala [12] that have recently gained in popularity, in part due to their support for scalable concurrency.

In actor languages [2,13], actors use a queue for storing the invocations to their methods in a FIFO manner. The queued invocations are processed sequentially by executing the corresponding method bodies. The encapsulated memory of an actor is represented by a finite number of *fields* that can be read and set by its methods and as such exist throughout its life time.

In this paper we introduce a nominal actor-based language and study its expressive power. This language, besides dynamic creation of actors, also supports the dynamic creation of variable names that can be stored in fields and communicated in method calls. As such our nominal actor-based language gives rise to unboundedness in (1) internal queues of the actors, (2) dynamic actor creation/activation and (3) dynamic creation of variable names.

Statelessness has recently been adopted as a basic principle of service oriented computing, in particular by RESTful services. Such services are designed to be stateless, and contextual information should be added to messages, so a service can customize replies simply by looking at the received request messages. In service oriented computing read-only fields (which are initialized upon activation) are used to provide configuration/deployment information that distinguishes the distinct instances of the same service. We have identified the presence/absence

M. Koutny and I. Ulidowski (Eds.): CONCUR 2012, LNCS 7454, pp. 562–577, 2012.

of fields as a relevant feature of our language: (1) and (3) in combination with fields gives rise to a Turing complete calculus. On the other hand, restricting to stateless actors gives rise to systems for which properties such as termination are decidable. In order to preserve this decidability result to actors with states we have to restrict the number of actors to be finite and the state to be read-only.

More specifically, we model systems consisting of finitely many actors with read-only fields as a well-structured transition system [10] – henceforth the decidability of termination. Further, we show that a termination and process reachability preserving abstraction of systems of unboundedly many stateless actors (i.e., actors without fields) is also an instance of well-structured transition system. It turns out that, in the context of unbounded actor creation, this restriction to stateless actors is necessary by a reduction to the halting problem for 2 Counter Machines.

To the best of our knowledge, the technique we use to establish the decidability results for the above languages is original since (*i*) these systems respectively admit the creation of unboundedly many variables and of unboundedly many variables and actor names; (*ii*) actors in general are sensitive to the identity of names because of the presence of a name-match operator. In particular, in the case of finitely many actors with read-only fields, we define an equivalence on process instances in terms of renamings of the variables that *generate the same partition*. This equivalence allows us to compute an upper bound to the instances of method bodies, which is the basic argument for the model being a well-structured transition system. In case of systems with unboundedly many stateless actors, the reasonable extensions of this equivalence on process instances have been unsuccessful because of the required abstraction of the identity of actor names. Therefore we decided to apply our arguments to an abstract operational model where messages may be enqueued in every actor of the same class. The above equivalence can be successfully used in this model, thus yielding again the upper bounds for the number of method body instances. Further, the abstract model still provides enough information to derive decidable properties of the language.

Related Works. There exist a vast body of related work on decidability of infinite-state systems (see [1]) that however does not address the specific characteristics of the pure asynchronous mechanism of queued and dequeued method calls in actor-based languages. It is interesting to observe that the most expressive known fragment of the pi-calculus for which interesting verification problems are still decidable is the depth-bounded fragment [18]. In [20] the theory of well-structured transition systems is applied to prove the decidability of coverability problems for bounded depth pi-calculus. Our nominal actor language also features the creation and communication of new names. In our decidable fragments however, differently from the depth-bounded pi-calculus fragment, we do not restrict the creation and communication of names. For instance, in the queue of an actor we might have unboundedly many messages (representing process continuations) where each message shares one name with the previous message in the queue. Recent work on actor-based language focusses on deadlock analysis:

In [11], a technique for the deadlock analysis has been introduced for a version of Featherweight Java which features asynchronous method invocations and a synchronization mechanism based on futures variables. The approach followed in [9] for detecting deadlock in an actor-like subset of Creol [14] is based on suitable over-approximations.

Disclaimer. Due to space limitations, proofs have been removed; they are in [8].

2 The Language Actor

Four disjoint infinite sets of names are used: *actor classes*, ranged over C, D, $\cdots$, *method names*, ranged over m, m', n, n', $\cdots$, *field names*, ranged over f, g, $\cdots$, and *variables*, ranged over x, y, z, $\cdots$. For notational convenience, we use $\widetilde{x}$ when we refer to a list of variables $x_1, \ldots, x_n$ (and similarly for other kinds of terms).

The syntax of the language Actor uses *expressions* E and *processes* P defined by the rules

$$
\begin{array}{lcl}
E & ::= & \mathtt{f} \;\mid\; x \;\mid\; \mathtt{new}\ \mathtt{C}(\widetilde{E}) \\
P & ::= & \mathtt{0} \;\mid\; (\mathtt{f} \hookleftarrow E)\mathtt{.}P \;\mid\; \mathtt{let}\ x = E\ \mathtt{in}\ P \;\mid\; x\,\mathtt{!}\,m(\widetilde{E})\mathtt{.}P \;\mid \\
 & & [E = E]P\mathtt{;}P \;\mid\; P + P
\end{array}
$$

An expression E either denotes a value stored in a field f, or a variable x, or a new actor of class C with fields initialized to the values of $\widetilde{E}$. A process may be either the terminated one 0, or a field update $(\mathtt{f} \hookleftarrow E)\mathtt{.}P$, or the assignment $\mathtt{let}\ x = E\ \mathtt{in}\ P$ of a value to a variable, or an invocation $x\,\mathtt{!}\,m(\widetilde{E})\mathtt{.}P$ of a method m of the actor x with arguments $\widetilde{E}$, or a check $[E = E']P\mathtt{;}P'$ of the identity of expressions with positive and negative continuations, or, finally a nondeterministic process $P + P'$. We never write the tailing 0 in processes; for example $(\mathtt{f} \hookleftarrow x)\mathtt{.0}$ will be always shortened into $(\mathtt{f} \hookleftarrow x)$. We will also shorten $[E = E']P\mathtt{;0}$ into $[E = E']P$.

The operation $\mathtt{let}\ x = E\ \mathtt{in}\ P$ is a binder of the occurrences of the variable x in the process P that are not already bound by a nested let operation of x; the occurrences of x in E are *free*. Let *free*(P) be the set of variables of P that are not bound. As usual, the substitution operation $P[{}^{y}/_{x}]$ returns the process P where the free occurrences of x are replaced by y.

A *program* is a *main process* P and a finite set of *actor class definitions* $\mathtt{C}.m(\widetilde{x}) = P_{\mathtt{C},m}$, where $P_{\mathtt{C},m}$ may contain the special variable *this* (which can be seen as an implicit formal parameter of each method). In the following we restrict to programs that are

1. *unambiguous*, namely, every pair C, m has at most one definition;
2. *correct*, namely, let *fields*$(\cdot)$ be a map that associates a tuple of field names to every actor class. Then, (i) in every expression $\mathtt{new}\ \mathtt{C}(\widetilde{E})$, the length of the tuples $\widetilde{E}$ and *fields*(C) are the same; (ii) in every definition $\mathtt{C}.m(\widetilde{x}) = P_{\mathtt{C},m}$, the field names occurring in $P_{\mathtt{C},m}$ are in the tuple *fields*(C).

In this paper, we abstract from types and type-correctness because we are only interested in expressive power issues. However, it is straightforward to equip the above language with a type discipline.

The operational semantics. The operational semantics of the language `Actor` will use an infinite set of *actor names*, ranged over A, B, $\cdots$. This set is partitioned by the actor classes in such a way that every partition retains infinitely many actor names. We write $A \in \mathtt{C}$ to say that A belongs to the partition of C. In the following, the (*run-time*) expressions will also include actor names and, with an abuse of notation, this estended set of expressions will be ranged over by E. The set of terms that are variables or actor names, called *values*, will be addressed by U, V, $\cdots$.

The semantics is defined in terms of a *transition relation* $\mathtt{S} \longrightarrow \mathtt{S}'$, where S, S′, called *configurations*, are sets of terms $A \triangleright (P, \varphi, q)$ with A being an actor name, φ, the *state* of A, being a map from *fields*(C) to values, where $A \in \mathtt{C}$, and q being a queue of terms $m(\widetilde{U})$. The empty queue will be denoted with ε. Configurations contain at most one $A \triangleright (P, \varphi, q)$ for each actor name A.

The operational semantics of `Actor` is defined in Table 1, where the *evaluation function* $E \overset{\varphi}{\rightsquigarrow} U \;;\; \mathtt{S}$ is used. This function takes an expression E and a store φ and returns a value U and a possibly empty configuration S of terms $A \triangleright (\mathtt{0}, \varphi, \varepsilon)$. These terms represent actors created during the evaluation – the names A are *fresh* – and φ records the initial values of the fields of A. The auxiliary function *fresh*$(\cdot)$ used in the evaluation function takes a class actor and returns an actor name of that class that is fresh. The same auxiliary function is used in rule (INST) on a tuple of variables. In this case it returns a tuple of the same length of variables that are fresh. For notational convenience, we always omit the standard curly brackets in the set notation and we use "," both to separate elements inside sequences and for set union (the actual meaning is made clear by the context).

Given a program, with main process P, the initial configuration is $\aleph \triangleright (P, \varnothing, \varepsilon)$, where $\aleph$ is a name of the *root*, an actor of a class without fields and methods. We assume that the class of $\aleph$ does not belong to the classes of the program. Note that the root actor is guaranteed to terminate because its queue remains empty (no method invocation may be enqueued) and the main process (as any other one) terminates.

We finally remark that transition systems of the language `Actor` are *not finitely branching* because of the choice of actor names (in the evaluation of `new C`) and the choice of fresh variables (in the instantiation of the bodies of methods). For example, if $\mathtt{C}.m() = [x = x]P$ then $A \triangleright (\mathtt{0}, \varnothing, m()) \longrightarrow A \triangleright ([z = z]P, \varnothing, m())$ for every z. Additionally, every configuration $A \triangleright ([z = z]P, \varnothing, m())$ transits to $A \triangleright (P, \varnothing, m())$. Said otherwise, the sets $Succ(\mathtt{S}) = \{\mathtt{S}' \in \mathcal{S} \mid \mathtt{S} \longrightarrow \mathtt{S}'\}$, called the *successor configurations* of S, and $Pred(\mathtt{S}) = \{\mathtt{S}' \in \mathcal{S} \mid \mathtt{S}' \longrightarrow \mathtt{S}\}$, called the *predecessor configurations* of S, are not finite, in general.

Relevant sublanguages. We will consider the following fragments of `Actor` whose relevance has been already discussed in the Introduction:

Table 1. The operational semantics of the language `Actor`

The *evaluation relation* $E \overset{\mathcal{S}}{\rightsquigarrow} U \,;\, \mathtt{S}$:

$$U \overset{\mathcal{S}}{\rightsquigarrow} U \,;\, \varnothing \qquad \mathtt{f} \overset{\mathcal{S}}{\rightsquigarrow} \varphi(\mathtt{f}) \,;\, \varnothing \qquad \frac{\widetilde{E} \overset{\mathcal{S}}{\rightsquigarrow} \widetilde{U} \,;\, \mathtt{S} \quad \widetilde{\mathtt{f}} = \mathit{fields}(\mathtt{C}) \quad A = \mathit{fresh}(\mathtt{C})}{\mathtt{new}\ \mathtt{C}(\widetilde{E}) \overset{\mathcal{S}}{\rightsquigarrow} A \,;\, A \triangleright (\mathtt{0}, [\widetilde{\mathtt{f}} \mapsto \widetilde{U}], \varepsilon), \mathtt{S}}$$

$$\frac{E_i \overset{\mathcal{S}}{\rightsquigarrow} U_i \,;\, \mathtt{S}_i, \quad \text{for} \quad i \in 1..n}{E_1, \cdots, E_n \overset{\mathcal{S}}{\rightsquigarrow} U_1, \cdots, U_n \,;\, \mathtt{S}_1, \cdots, \mathtt{S}_n}$$

The *transition relation* $\mathtt{S} \longrightarrow \mathtt{S}'$:

(UPD)

$$\frac{E \overset{\mathcal{S}}{\rightsquigarrow} U \,;\, \mathtt{S}}{A \triangleright ((\mathtt{f} \leftarrow E).P, \varphi, q) \longrightarrow A \triangleright (P, \varphi[\mathtt{f} \leftarrow U], q), \mathtt{S}}$$

(LET)

$$\frac{E \overset{\mathcal{S}}{\rightsquigarrow} U \,;\, \mathtt{S}}{A \triangleright (\mathtt{let}\ x = E\ \mathtt{in}\ P, \varphi, q) \longrightarrow A \triangleright (P[{}^{U}/_{x}], \varphi, q), \mathtt{S}}$$

(INVK-S)

$$\frac{\widetilde{E} \overset{\mathcal{S}}{\rightsquigarrow} \widetilde{U} \,;\, \mathtt{S}}{A \triangleright (A\,!\,m(\widetilde{E}).P, \varphi, q) \longrightarrow A \triangleright (P, \varphi, q \cdot m(\widetilde{U})), \mathtt{S}}$$

(INVK)

$$\frac{\widetilde{E} \overset{\mathcal{S}}{\rightsquigarrow} \widetilde{U} \,;\, \mathtt{S}}{A \triangleright (A'\,!\,m(\widetilde{E}).P, \varphi, q), A' \triangleright (P', \varphi', q') \longrightarrow A \triangleright (P, \varphi, q), A' \triangleright (P', \varphi', q' \cdot m(\widetilde{U})), \mathtt{S}}$$

(INST)

$$\frac{A \in \mathtt{C} \quad \mathtt{C}.m(\widetilde{x}) = P \quad \widetilde{y} = \mathit{free}(P) \setminus \widetilde{x} \quad \widetilde{y'} = \mathit{fresh}(\widetilde{y})}{A \triangleright (\mathtt{0}, \varphi, m(\widetilde{U}) \cdot q) \longrightarrow A \triangleright (P[{}^{A}/_{\mathit{this}}][{}^{\widetilde{y'}}/_{\widetilde{y}}][{}^{\widetilde{U}}/_{\widetilde{x}}], \varphi, q)}$$

(MATCH)

$$\frac{E, E' \overset{\mathcal{S}}{\rightsquigarrow} U, U \,;\, \mathtt{S}}{A \triangleright ([E = E']P; Q, \varphi, q) \longrightarrow A \triangleright (P, \varphi, q), \mathtt{S}}$$

(MMATCH)

$$\frac{E, E' \overset{\mathcal{S}}{\rightsquigarrow} U, V \,;\, \mathtt{S} \quad U \neq V}{A \triangleright ([E = E']P; Q, \varphi, q) \longrightarrow A \triangleright (Q, \varphi, q), \mathtt{S}}$$

(PLUS-L)

$$\frac{A \triangleright (P, q), \mathtt{S} \longrightarrow \mathtt{S}'}{A \triangleright (P + Q, q), \mathtt{S} \longrightarrow \mathtt{S}'}$$

(PLUS-R)

$$\frac{A \triangleright (P, q), \mathtt{S} \longrightarrow \mathtt{S}'}{A \triangleright (Q + P, q), \mathtt{S} \longrightarrow \mathtt{S}'}$$

(CONTEXT)

$$\frac{\mathtt{S} \longrightarrow \mathtt{S}'}{\mathtt{S}, \mathtt{S}'' \longrightarrow \mathtt{S}', \mathtt{S}''}$$

- $\texttt{Actor}_{\texttt{ba}}$ is the sublanguage where the `new` expression only occurs in the main process (the number of actor names that it is possible to create is bounded).
- $\texttt{Actor}^{\texttt{ro}}$ is the sublanguage without the field update operation ($\texttt{f} \hookleftarrow E$) (fields are read-only as they cannot be modified after the initialization).
- $\texttt{Actor}^{\texttt{ro}}_{\texttt{ba}}$ is the intersection of $\texttt{Actor}_{\texttt{ba}}$ and $\texttt{Actor}^{\texttt{ro}}$.
- $\texttt{Actor}^{\texttt{sl}}$ is the sublanguage with classes without fields (objects are stateless).

3 Undecidability Results for $\texttt{Actor}_{\texttt{ba}}$ and $\texttt{Actor}^{\texttt{ro}}$

In this section we establish the main undecidability results for the actor language in Section 2. In particular, we will prove the undecidability of *termination* and *process reachability*.

Definition 1. *An actor program* terminates *if it has no infinite computation; it* reaches a process P *if it has a computation traversing a configuration having a term* $A \rhd (P', \varphi, q)$ *with* P' *being equal to* P *up-to renaming of variables and actor names.*

Actually, in order to convey a stronger result, we consider two sublanguages: (*i*) where methods never use the `new` expression – actors may be only created by the main process –, therefore the actor names are bounded, and (*ii*) where fields cannot be updated – the fields are read-only after the initialization.

We will use a reduction technique of the halting and reachability problems in 2 Counter Machines (2CMs) [19] – a well-known Turing-complete model – to that of our actor model. A 2CM is a machine with *two registers* R_1 and R_2 holding arbitrary large natural numbers and a *program* P consisting of a finite sequence of numbered instructions of the following type:

- $j : \mathsf{Inc}(R_i)$: increments R_i and goes to the instruction $j+1$;
- $j : \mathsf{DecJump}(R_i, l)$: if the content of R_i is not zero, then decreases it by 1 and goes to the instruction $j+1$, otherwise jumps to the instruction l;
- $j : \mathsf{Halt}$: stops the computation and returns the value in the register R_1.

A state of the machine is given by a tuple (i, v_1, v_2) where i indicates the next instruction to execute (the program counter) and v_1 and v_2 are the contents of the two registers. The user has to provide the initial state of the machine. In the sequel, we consider 2CMs in which registers are initially set to zero.

3.1 The Language $\texttt{Actor}_{\texttt{ba}}$

We encode the value n stored in a register as n messages (of the same type) that are enqueued in an actor – see Figure 1. Namely, let R_1 and R_2 be two actors of class `R` and let the number of messages *item* in R_1 and R_2 be their value. The instruction Inc is implemented by inserting one *item* message in the queue of the corresponding register. In our formalism, this is done by invoking the method *item* whose execution has two possible outcomes: (i) the invocation is enqueued

$$
\begin{array}{ll}
\mathtt{R} & \texttt{// R has fields dec, ctr, loop and stop} \\
& \mathtt{R}.\mathit{item}(tt, ff) = [\mathtt{stop} = ff]\big([\mathtt{dec} = ff]\,\mathit{this}\,!\,\mathit{item}(tt, ff)\,;\,(\mathtt{dec} \hookleftarrow ff)\big) \\
& \mathtt{R}.\mathit{inc}(pc, tt, ff) = [\mathtt{stop} = ff](\mathtt{loop} \hookleftarrow ff)\,.\; \mathit{this}\,!\,\mathit{item}(tt, ff)\,.\,\mathtt{ctr}\,!\,\mathit{run}(pc, tt, ff) \\
& \mathtt{R}.\mathit{decjump}(pc, pc', tt, ff) = [\mathtt{stop} = ff](\mathtt{loop} \hookleftarrow ff)\,.\; (\mathtt{dec} \hookleftarrow tt)\,.\,\mathit{this}\,!\,\mathit{checkzero}(pc, pc', tt, ff) \\
& \mathtt{R}.\mathit{checkzero}(pc, pc', tt, ff) = [\mathtt{stop} = ff](\mathtt{loop} \hookleftarrow ff)\,.\; \big([\mathtt{dec}{=}\,tt]\mathtt{ctr}\,!\,\mathit{run}(pc', tt, ff)\,;\,\mathtt{ctr}\,!\,\mathit{run}(pc, tt, ff)\big) \\
& \mathtt{R}.\mathit{init}(tt, ff, \mathit{Ctrl}) = (\mathtt{dec} \hookleftarrow ff)\,.\,(\mathtt{ctr} \hookleftarrow \mathit{Ctrl})\,.\,(\mathtt{loop} \hookleftarrow ff)\,.\,(\mathtt{stop} \hookleftarrow ff)\,.\; \mathit{this}\,!\,\mathit{bottom}(tt, ff) \\
& \mathtt{R}.\mathit{bottom}(tt, ff) = [\mathtt{loop} = ff](\mathtt{loop} \hookleftarrow tt).\mathit{this}\,!\,\mathit{bottom}(tt, ff); (\mathtt{stop} \hookleftarrow tt) \\
\mathtt{Ctrl} & \texttt{// Ctrl has fields } \mathtt{stm}_1, \cdots, \mathtt{stm}_n \texttt{ and } \mathtt{r}_1 \texttt{ and } \mathtt{r}_2 \\
& \mathtt{Ctrl}.\mathit{run}(pc, tt, ff) = [pc = \mathtt{stm}_1][\![\mathit{Instruction\_1}]\!]_{1,\boldsymbol{t},\boldsymbol{f}} \\
& \qquad \cdots \\
& \qquad [pc = \mathtt{stm}_n][\![\mathit{Instruction\_n}]\!]_{n,\boldsymbol{t},\boldsymbol{f}} \\
& \mathtt{Ctrl}.\mathit{init}() = \mathtt{r}_1\,!\,\mathit{init}(tt, ff, \mathit{this})\,.\,\mathtt{r}_2\,!\,\mathit{init}(tt, ff, \mathit{this})\,.\; \mathit{this}\,!\,\mathit{run}(\mathtt{stm}_1, tt, ff)
\end{array}
$$

where $[\![\mathit{Instruction\_i}]\!]_{i,\boldsymbol{t},\boldsymbol{f}}$ is equal to

- $\mathtt{r}_j\,!\,\mathit{inc}(\mathtt{stm}_{i+1}, tt, ff)$ if $\mathit{Instruction\_i} = \mathsf{Inc}(R_j)$;
- $\mathtt{r}_j\,!\,\mathit{decjump}(\mathtt{stm}_{i+1}, \mathtt{stm}_k, tt, ff)$ if $\mathit{Instruction\_i} = \mathsf{DecJump}(R_j, k)$;
- $\mathsf{0}$ if $\mathit{Instruction\_i} = \mathsf{Halt}$.

The main process is

$$\mathtt{let}\ x = \mathtt{new\ Ctrl}(x_1, \cdots, x_n, \mathtt{new\ R}(\_,\_,\_,\_), \mathtt{new\ R}(\_,\_,\_,\_))\ \mathtt{in}\ x\,!\,\mathit{init}().$$

Fig. 1. Encoding a 2CM in $\mathtt{Actor_{ba}}$ ("_" denotes an irrelevant initialization parameter)

again; (ii) the invocation is discarded because we are in the presence of a residual of a DecJump operation, as described next.

In case (i), to avoid an infinite sequence of *item* dequeues and enqueues, the queue of the registers is initialized with a *bottom* message. The execution of *bottom* updates the field `loop` to *tt* (it is initialized to *ff*). This field is reset to *ff* when either *inc*, or *decjump*, or *checkzero* is executed. If the *bottom* method is executed with `loop` set to *tt*, the register becomes inactive by setting another field `stop`. This value of `stop` possibly makes the overall computation block as soon as an instruction concerning that register is performed.

In case (ii), registers have a field `dec` that is set to *tt* by a *decjump* method execution. This field means that the actual decrement of the register is delayed to the next execution of *checkzero*. Since in (ii) *item* in not enqueued, then the register is actually decremented and the field `dec` is set to *ff*. When *checkzero* will be executed, since `dec` = *ff* then the next instruction of the 2CM is simulated. On the contrary, when *checkzero* is executed with `dec` = *tt* then the decrement has not been performed (the register is 0) and the simulation jumps.

Booleans are implemented by two variables – see the method `Ctrl`.*init* – that are distributed during the invocations. With a similar machinery, in the actor class `Ctrl`, the labels of the instructions are represented by the variables $x_1, \cdots, x_n$, which are stored in the fields $\mathtt{stm}_1, \ldots, \mathtt{stm}_n$ of *Ctrl*.

Theorem 1. *Termination and process reachability are undecidable in* $\mathtt{Actor}_{\mathsf{ba}}$.

The undecidability of termination in $\mathtt{Actor}_{\mathsf{ba}}$ follows by the property that a 2CM diverges if and only if the corresponding actor program has an infinite computation. As regards process reachability, we need a smooth refinement of the encoding in Figure 1 where the Halt instruction is simulated by a specific process P' (see Definition 1).

3.2 The Language $\mathtt{Actor}^{\mathtt{ro}}$

We show that $\mathtt{Actor}^{\mathtt{ro}}$ is Turing-complete by delivering another encoding of a 2CM – see Figure 2. In this encoding the two registers are represented by two disjoint stacks of actors linked by the `next` field. The top elements of the two stacks are passed as parameters r_1 and r_2 of the *run* method of the controller. As before, this actor encodes the control of the 2CM.

The instruction Inc is implemented by pushing an element on top of the corresponding stack. This element is an actor of class `R` storing in its field the old pointer of the stack. The new pointer, *i.e.* the new actor name, is passed to the next invocation of the *run* method.

The instruction DecJump is implemented by popping the corresponding stack. In particular, the method *run* of the controller is invoked with the field `next` of the register being decreased. This pop operation is performed provided the register that is argument of *run* is different from *nil*. Otherwise a jump is performed. Note that the other top of the stack r_j $(i \neq j)$ and the next instruction to be executed are simply passed around and therefore they do not need to be stored in updatable fields.

Theorem 2. *Termination and process reachability are undecidable in* $\mathtt{Actor}^{\mathtt{ro}}$.

4 Decidability Results for $\mathtt{Actor}^{\mathtt{ro}}_{\mathsf{ba}}$

We demonstrate that programs in $\mathtt{Actor}^{\mathtt{ro}}_{\mathsf{ba}}$ are well-structured transition systems [1,10]. This will allow us to decide a number of properties, such as termination. We begin with some background on well-structured transition systems.

A reflective and transitive relation is called *quasi-ordering*. A *well-quasi-ordering* is a quasi-ordering $(X, \leq)$ such that, for every infinite sequence $x_1, x_2, x_3, \cdots$, there exist $i < j$ with $x_i \leq x_j$.

```
R                              // R has a field next
```

$$\mathtt{R}.dec_1(ctrl, r, stm) = \quad ctrl\,!\,run(\mathtt{next}, r, stm)$$

$$\mathtt{R}.dec_2(ctrl, r, stm) = \quad ctrl\,!\,run(r, \mathtt{next}, stm)$$

```
Ctrl                           // Ctrl has fields stm1, ..., stmn and nil
```

$$\mathtt{Ctrl}.run(r_1, r_2, pc) = \quad [pc = \mathtt{stm}_1][\![Instruction\_1]\!]; \\ \ldots \\ [pc = \mathtt{stm}_n][\![Instruction\_n]\!]$$

where $[\![Instruction\_i]\!]$ is equal to

- $this\,!\,run(\mathtt{new\ R}(r_1), r_2, \mathtt{stm}_{i+1})$ if $Instruction\_i = \mathsf{Inc}(R_1)$;
- $this\,!\,run(r_1, \mathtt{new\ R}(r_2), \mathtt{stm}_{i+1})$ if $Instruction\_i = \mathsf{Inc}(R_2)$;
- $[r_1 = \mathtt{nil}]this\,!\,run(r_1, r_2, \mathtt{stm}_k)\,; r_1\,!\,dec_1(this, r_2, \mathtt{stm}_{i+1})$ if $Instruction\_i = \mathsf{DecJump}(R_1, k)$;
- $[r_2 = \mathtt{nil}]this\,!\,run(r_1, r_2, \mathtt{stm}_k)\,; r_2\,!\,dec_2(this, r_1, \mathtt{stm}_{i+1})$ if $Instruction\_i = \mathsf{DecJump}(R_2, k)$;
- $\mathsf{0}$ if $Instruction\_i = \mathsf{Halt}$.

The program is invoked with $\mathtt{let}\ x = \mathtt{new\ Ctrl}(x_1, \cdots, x_n, nil)\ \mathtt{in}\ x\,!\,run(nil, nil, x_1)$.

Fig. 2. Encoding a 2CM in $\mathtt{Actor}^{\mathrm{ro}}$

Definition 2. *A* well-structured transition system *is a transition system* $(\mathcal{S}, \longrightarrow, \preceq)$ *where* $\preceq$ *is a quasi-ordering relation on states such that*

1. $\preceq$ *is a well-quasi-ordering*
2. $\preceq$ *is upward compatible with* $\longrightarrow$*, i.e., for every* $\mathrm{S}_1 \preceq \mathrm{S}_1'$ *such that* $\mathrm{S}_1 \longrightarrow \mathrm{S}_2$*, there exists* $\mathrm{S}_1' \longrightarrow^* \mathrm{S}_2'$ *such that* $\mathrm{S}_2 \preceq \mathrm{S}_2'$.

In the following we assume given an actor program with its main process and its set of actor class definitions. The first relation we convey is $\doteq$ that relates renamings of variables *that are not free in the main process* into either actor names or variables *that are not free in the main process*. Let

$$\rho \doteq \rho' \quad \stackrel{def}{=} \quad \text{for every } x, y : (i) \quad \rho(x) = \rho(y) \quad \text{if and only if} \quad \rho'(x) = \rho'(y) \\ (ii) \quad \rho(x) = \rho'(x) \quad \text{if} \quad \rho(x) \text{ or } \rho'(x) \text{ is an actor name}$$

Namely, two renamings are in the relation $\doteq$ if they identify the same variables, regardless the value they associate when such a value is a variable. For example, $[x \mapsto y, y \mapsto z] \doteq [x \mapsto x, y \mapsto z]$ and $[x \mapsto y, y \mapsto y, z \mapsto A] \doteq [x \mapsto x', y \mapsto x', z \mapsto A]$. However $[x \mapsto y, y \mapsto z] \not\doteq [x \mapsto x, y \mapsto x]$ and $[x \mapsto A] \not\doteq [x \mapsto B]$. In general, if ρ and ρ' are injective renamings that always return variables then $\rho \doteq \rho'$. The requirements of $\doteq$ are stronger for actor names: in this case the two renamings should be identical. We also notice that renamings never apply to free variables of the main process and never return free variables of the main processes. This because these variables are possibly stored in fields of actors and their renamings might change the behaviours of actors in a way that breaks the upward compatibility of the following relation $\preceq$ and $\longrightarrow$ (*c.f.* proof of Theorem 3, part **(2)**). We finally notice that the above renamings *do not change the main process* (because they do not apply to its free variables).

We denote by $P\rho$ the result of the application of ρ to P.

Next, let $\simeq$ be the least relation on terms $m(U_1, \cdots, U_n)$ and on processes such that

$$\frac{\rho \doteq \rho'}{m(\rho(x_1), \cdots, \rho(x_k)) \simeq m(\rho'(x_1), \cdots, \rho'(x_k))} \qquad \frac{\rho \doteq \rho'}{P\rho \simeq P\rho'}$$

For example, it is easy to verify that $m(x, y) \simeq m(x', y')$ and that $[x = A]y\,!\,m(x, A, y) \simeq [z = A]y'\,!\,m(z, A, y')$. On the contrary $[x = A]B\,!\,m(x, A, B) \not\simeq [z = A]y'\,!\,m(z, A, y')$. The rationale behind $\simeq$ is that we are identifying processes that "behave in similar ways", namely they enqueue "similar invocations" in the same actor queue. Method invocations $m(U_1, \cdots, U_n)$ of a given actor are identified if the processes they trigger "behave in similar ways".

Lemma 1. *Let T be either a process or a method invocation $m(U_1, \cdots, U_n)$ of a program in $\mathtt{Actor_{ba}}$ (and therefore in $\mathtt{Actor^{ro}_{ba}}$). Let $\mathcal{T} = \{T\rho_1, T\rho_2, T\rho_3, \cdots\}$ be such that $i \neq j$ implies $T\rho_i \not\simeq T\rho_j$. Then $\mathcal{T}$ is finite.*

In order to define a well-quasi ordering on states, we consider the following *embedding relation* $\leq$ on queues (except the part about $\simeq$, it is almost standard [10]):

$$\frac{\textit{there exist } i_1 < i_2 < \cdots < i_k \leq h \textit{ such that, for } j \in 1..k, \quad m_j(\widetilde{U_j}) \simeq n_{i_j}(\widetilde{V_{i_j}})}{m_1(\widetilde{U_1}) \ldots m_k(\widetilde{U_k}) \leq n_1(\widetilde{V_1}) \ldots n_h(\widetilde{V_h})}$$

Then we define the following relation on states:

$$\frac{P_i \simeq P'_i \quad \text{and} \quad q_i \leq q'_i \quad \text{for } i \in 1..\ell}{A_1 \triangleright (P_1, \varphi_1, q_1), \cdots, A_\ell \triangleright (P_\ell, \varphi_\ell, q_\ell) \ \preceq\ A_1 \triangleright (P'_1, \varphi_1, q'_1), \cdots, A_\ell \triangleright (P'_\ell, \varphi_\ell, q'_\ell)}$$

It is worth to notice that the relation $\preceq$ constraints corresponding elements $A \triangleright (P, \varphi, q)$ and $A \triangleright (P', \varphi, q')$ to have the same states. In fact these states are defined by the main process using either its free variables or the actor names that it has created.

Theorem 3. *Let $(\mathcal{S}, \longrightarrow)$ be a transition system of a program of* $\mathtt{Actor^{ro}_{ba}}$. *Then $(\mathcal{S}, \longrightarrow, \preceq)$ is a well-structured transition system.*

We notice that the well-structured transition system $(\mathcal{S}, \longrightarrow, \preceq)$ has transitive and stuttering compatibility (see [10], pp 9, 10). Additionally, $(\mathcal{S}, \longrightarrow, \preceq)$ has decidable algorithms for computing $\preceq$ and for computing the next states. Then decidability of termination follows directly from Theorems 4.6 in [10].

Theorem 4. *In* $\mathtt{Actor}^{\mathtt{ro}}_{\mathtt{ba}}$ *termination is decidable.*

As discussed in Section 2, the transition systems of the actor language are not finite branching. This is also the case for programs in $\mathtt{Actor}^{\mathtt{ro}}_{\mathtt{ba}}$ (due to the presence of fresh variables in method body instantiations). However, in this case, the sets $\mathit{Succ}(\mathtt{S})$ and $\mathit{Pred}(\mathtt{S})$ are finite if we reason up-to the well-quasi ordering relation $\preceq$.

Lemma 2. *Let* $(\mathcal{S}, \longrightarrow, \preceq)$ *be a well-structured transition system of a program in* $\mathtt{Actor}^{\mathtt{ro}}_{\mathtt{ba}}$*, and let* $\mathtt{S} \in \mathcal{S}$*. Then there is a finite set* $\mathcal{X} \subseteq \mathit{Pred}(\mathtt{S})$ *such that, for every* $\mathtt{S}' \in \mathit{Pred}(\mathtt{S})$*, there is* $\mathtt{T} \in \mathcal{X}$ *with* $\mathtt{T} \preceq \mathtt{S}'$*.* $\mathcal{X}$ *can be effectively computed.*

Lemma 2 and Theorem 4.8 in [10] allow us to decide the so-called *control-state reachability problem*: given two states $\mathtt{S}$ and $\mathtt{T}$ of a well-structured transition system with well-quasi ordering $\preceq$, decide whether there is $\mathtt{T}' \succeq \mathtt{T}$ such that $\mathtt{S} \longrightarrow^* \mathtt{T}'$.

Theorem 5. *In* $\mathtt{Actor}^{\mathtt{ro}}_{\mathtt{ba}}$ *process reachability is decidable.*

In addition to the above decidability results, the process reachability problem – see Definition 1 – is decidable in the sublanguage of the present section. In fact, in order to verify whether a configuration $A \rhd (P', \varphi, q), \mathtt{S}$ is reachable with P' equal to P up-to renaming of variables and actor names, we proceed as follows. First, consider a configuration $\mathtt{T}$ reachable after the complete execution of the main process. Therefore, in $\mathtt{T}$, every possible actor has been created (with the corresponding initialization performed). Let $\mathtt{T} = A_1 \rhd (P_1, \varphi_1, q_1), \cdots, A_\ell \rhd (P_\ell, \varphi_\ell, q_\ell)$. If this part of the computation already traverses a configuration with a term $A \rhd (P', \varphi, q)$, then the reply is positive. Otherwise, we check control-state reachability from $\mathtt{T}$ to at least one of the states in the following finite set:

$$\begin{array}{l} \mathcal{S} = \{\ A_1 \rhd (Q_1, \varphi_1, \varepsilon), \cdots, A_\ell \rhd (Q_\ell, \varphi_\ell, \varepsilon) \ \mid \\ \qquad \text{for every } 1 \leq i \leq \ell,\ Q_i \text{ is a suffix of a method definition and} \\ \qquad \text{there exists } 1 \leq j \leq \ell \text{ such that } Q_j \text{ is equal to } P \text{ up-to renaming } \} \end{array}$$

We conclude this section by observing that we have already proved the undecidability of termination in programs with finitely many actors and field updates. If we remove the constraint of finite actor names then the relation $\preceq$ is not a well-quasi ordering anymore. Consider for instance, the configuration $\mathtt{S}_n$ defined as follows:

$$\mathtt{S}_n \stackrel{def}{=} A_1 \rhd (0, \varnothing, \varepsilon), \cdots, A_n \rhd (0, \varnothing, \varepsilon)$$

The infinite sequence $\mathtt{S}_1, \mathtt{S}_2, \mathtt{S}_3, \cdots$ is such that, for every $i < j$, $\mathtt{S}_i \not\preceq \mathtt{S}_j$. This trivial counterexample seems to suggest the following patch of $\preceq$:

$$\mathtt{S} \preceq' \mathtt{T} \stackrel{def}{=} \text{there exists } \mathtt{S}' \subseteq \mathtt{T} \text{ such that } \mathtt{S} \preceq \mathtt{S}'$$

However, the infinite sequence $\mathtt{S}_2, \mathtt{S}_3, \mathtt{S}_4, \cdots$ where $\mathtt{S}_n$ is defined as

$$\begin{array}{rl} \mathtt{S}_n \stackrel{def}{=} & A_0 \rhd (0, \varnothing, m(A_{n-1}, A_1)),\ A_1 \rhd (0, \varnothing, m(A_n, A_2)), \\ & \bigcup_{i \in 2..n-1} A_i \rhd (0, \varnothing, m(A_{i-2}, A_{i+1})),\ A_n \rhd (0, \varnothing, m(A_{n-2}, A_0)) \end{array}$$

is such that, for every $i < j$, $\mathtt{S}_i \not\preceq' \mathtt{S}_j$.

5 Decidability Results for $\texttt{Actor}^{\texttt{sl}}$

We prove that in $\texttt{Actor}^{\texttt{sl}}$ termination and process reachability are decidable, too. As discussed at the end of Section 4, we have not succeeded in demonstrating these decidability results by patching the definition of $\preceq$ in Section 4. The reason is that $\texttt{Actor}^{\texttt{sl}}$ programs may produce unboundedly many actor names. Therefore, in order to compute an upper bound to the instances of method bodies, which is the basic argument for the model of Section 4 to be a well-structured transition system, we need to abstract from the identity of these names – as we have done with variables. However, in case of actor names, the abstractions we have devised all break the delivering of messages. Therefore we decided to apply our arguments to an abstraction of the operational model where the delivery of messages is inexact: it may be enqueued in every actor of the same class. Yet, this abstract model allows us to derive interesting decidability properties for the original language.

Since we need a model with inexact message deliveries, we change the operational semantics in Table 1 in order to decouple the evaluation of the body of a method from the actor name of that method. Let $\texttt{S} \longrightarrow_\alpha \texttt{S}'$ be the *abstract transition relation* defined as $\texttt{S} \longrightarrow \texttt{S}'$ in Table 1 except the two rules (INVK) and (INVK-A) for method invocation and the rule (INST) for the instantiation of method bodies, which are replaced by the following ones:

(INK-SA)
$$\frac{\widetilde{E} \overset{\varphi}{\rightsquigarrow} \widetilde{U}\ ;\ \texttt{S} \quad A, A' \in \texttt{C}}{A \rhd (A'\,!\,m(\widetilde{E})\,.\,P, \varphi, q) \longrightarrow_\alpha A \rhd (P, \varphi, q \cdot m(\widetilde{U}, A')), \texttt{S}}$$

(INVK-A)
$$\frac{\widetilde{E} \overset{\varphi}{\rightsquigarrow} \widetilde{U}\ ;\ \texttt{S} \qquad A', A'' \in \texttt{C}}{A \rhd (A'\,!\,m(\widetilde{E})\,.\,P, \varphi, q), A'' \rhd (P', \varphi', q') \longrightarrow_\alpha A \rhd (P, \varphi, q), A'' \rhd (P', \varphi', q' \cdot m(\widetilde{U}, A')), \texttt{S}}$$

(INST-A)
$$\frac{A' \in \texttt{C} \quad \texttt{C}\,.\,m(\widetilde{x}) = P \quad \widetilde{y} = \mathit{free}(P) \setminus \widetilde{x} \quad \widetilde{y}' = \mathit{fresh}(\widetilde{y})}{A \rhd (\texttt{0}, \varphi, m(\widetilde{U}, A') \cdot q) \longrightarrow_\alpha A \rhd (P[^{A'}/_{\mathit{this}}][^{\widetilde{y}'}/_{\widetilde{y}}][^{\widetilde{U}}/_{\widetilde{x}}], \varphi, q)}$$

In the abstract transition relation, an item $m(\widetilde{U})$ is added in a queue of an actor name *nondeterministically selected* among those names belonging to the same class of the target actor. The item $m(\widetilde{U})$ is enqueued with an additional argument – the actor name of the target actor. This additional argument is used when a method body is instantiated. In fact it replaces the variable *this*, thus making the execution of a body invariant regardless the actor that actually performs it.

The next proposition formalizes the correspondence between $\longrightarrow$ and $\longrightarrow_\alpha$ (for stateless programs). We first introduce few notations:

- Let $\alpha()$ be a map from "concrete" to "abstract" configurations: given a configuration $\texttt{S}$, we denote with $\alpha(\texttt{S})$ the configuration obtained from $\texttt{S}$ by replacing each of its actor $A \rhd (P, \varnothing, q)$ with $A \rhd (P, \varnothing, q')$ where q' is obtained from q by adding to each of its method invocations the parameter A.
- We use $\mathcal{M}$, $\mathcal{M}'$ to denote multisets of terms $m(\widetilde{U})$. We extend $\simeq$ to such multisets: $\mathcal{M} \simeq \mathcal{M}'$ iff there exists a bijection ρ from $\mathcal{M}$ to $\mathcal{M}'$ such that $m(\widetilde{U}) \simeq \rho(m(\widetilde{U}))$.

- Let $\mathtt{S} \xrightarrow{\mathcal{M}} \mathtt{S}'$ be the least relation such that

$$\mathtt{S} \xrightarrow{\varnothing} \mathtt{S} \qquad \frac{\mathtt{S} \xrightarrow{\mathcal{M}} \mathtt{S}' \qquad (\mathtt{S}' \longrightarrow \mathtt{S}'' \text{ proved without (INVK) or (INVK-S)})}{\mathtt{S} \xrightarrow{\mathcal{M}} \mathtt{S}''}$$

$$\frac{\mathtt{S} \xrightarrow{\mathcal{M}} A \triangleright (P, \varnothing, q), \mathtt{S}' \qquad A \triangleright (P, \varnothing, q), \mathtt{S}' \longrightarrow A \triangleright (P', \varnothing, q \cdot m(\widetilde{U})), \mathtt{S}''}{\mathtt{S} \xrightarrow{\mathcal{M} \uplus \{m(\widetilde{U}, A)\}} A \triangleright (P', \varnothing, q \cdot m(\widetilde{U})), \mathtt{S}''}$$

Namely, this transition $\mathtt{S} \xrightarrow{\mathcal{M}} \mathtt{S}'$ collects in $\mathcal{M}$ all the method invocations that have been performed during the computation $\mathtt{S} \longrightarrow \mathtt{S}'$. These method invocations are extended with the target actor name as last parameter.
- Let $\mathtt{S} \xrightarrow{\mathcal{M}}_\alpha \mathtt{S}'$ be the least relation such that

$$\mathtt{S} \xrightarrow{\varnothing}_\alpha \mathtt{S} \qquad \frac{\mathtt{S} \xrightarrow{\mathcal{M}}_\alpha \mathtt{S}' \qquad (\mathtt{S}' \rightarrow_\alpha \mathtt{S}'' \text{ proved without (INVK-A) or (INVK-SA)})}{\mathtt{S} \xrightarrow{\mathcal{M}}_\alpha \mathtt{S}''}$$

$$\frac{\mathtt{S} \xrightarrow{\mathcal{M}}_\alpha A \triangleright (P, \varnothing, q), \mathtt{S}' \qquad A \triangleright (P, \varnothing, q), \mathtt{S}' \rightarrow_\alpha A \triangleright (P', \varnothing, q \cdot m(\widetilde{U})), \mathtt{S}''}{\mathtt{S} \xrightarrow{\mathcal{M} \uplus \{m(\widetilde{U})\}}_\alpha A \triangleright (P', \varnothing, q \cdot m(\widetilde{U})), \mathtt{S}''}$$

Note that in this case the additional argument A is not explicitly added as it is already introduced as argument by the transition system $\longrightarrow_\alpha$.

Proposition 1. *Let* $\mathtt{S}$ *be a state of a transition system of a program in* $\mathtt{Actor}^{\mathtt{sl}}$*.*

- $\mathtt{S}$ terminates *in the concrete transition system if and only if* $\alpha(\mathtt{S})$ terminates *in the abstract transition system;*
- *given a process* P*, there exist* A'*,* q'*, and* $\mathtt{S}'$ *such that* $\mathtt{S} \longrightarrow^* A' \triangleright (P, \varnothing, q'), \mathtt{S}'$ *if and only if there exist* A''*,* q''*, and* $\mathtt{S}''$ *such that* $\alpha(\mathtt{S}) \longrightarrow^*_\alpha A'' \triangleright (P, \varnothing, q''), \mathtt{S}''$.

We now move to the definition of $\preceq_\alpha$, a variant of the ordering $\preceq$ defined in the previous section, such that $(\mathcal{S}, \longrightarrow_\alpha, \preceq_\alpha)$ turns out to be a well-structured transition system (for configurations of stateless programs). To this aim, we redefine the notions of Section 4. Let

- $\stackrel{\bullet}{=}_\alpha$ be the least relation such that

$$\rho \stackrel{\bullet}{=}_\alpha \rho' \quad \stackrel{def}{=} \quad \text{for every } x, y: \quad \begin{array}{l} (i)\ \rho(x) = \rho(y) \text{ if and only if } \rho'(x) = \rho'(y) \\ (ii)\ \rho(x) \in \mathtt{C} \text{ if and only if } \rho'(x) \in \mathtt{C} \end{array}$$

Differently from the definition of $\stackrel{\bullet}{=}$, $\stackrel{\bullet}{=}_\alpha$ does not care of the identity of actor names. Moreover, $\stackrel{\bullet}{=}_\alpha$ identifies two renamings that "have matching types", letting the type of variable being distinct from those of class actors.
- $\simeq_\alpha$ be the relation defined as $\simeq$ in Section 4, with $\stackrel{\bullet}{=}_\alpha$ instead of $\stackrel{\bullet}{=}$.
- $\leq_\alpha$ be the relation defined as $\leq$ in Section 4, with $\simeq_\alpha$ instead of $\simeq$.
- $\preceq_\alpha$ be the ordering:

$$\frac{A_i, A'_{j_i} \in \mathtt{C}_i \quad P_i \simeq_\alpha P'_{j_i} \quad \text{and} \quad q_i \leq q'_{j_i} \quad \text{for } i \in 1..\ell,\ 1 \leq j_1 < j_2 < \cdots < j_\ell \leq \kappa}{A_1 \rhd (P_1, \varnothing, q_1), \cdots, A_\ell \rhd (P_\ell, \varnothing, q_\ell) \preceq_\alpha A'_1 \rhd (P'_1, \varnothing, q'_1), \cdots, A'_\kappa \rhd (P'_\kappa, \varnothing, q'_\kappa)}$$

Next, we observe that Lemma 1 can be adapted to the case of unbounded actors by using $\simeq_\alpha$ instead of $\simeq$. Let T be either a process or a method invocation $m(U_1, \cdots, U_n)$ of a stateless program and let $\mathcal{T} = \{T\rho_1, T\rho_2, T\rho_3, \cdots\}$ be such that $i \neq j$ implies $T\rho_i \not\simeq_\alpha T\rho_j$. By proceeding as in the proof of Lemma 1, we prove that $\mathcal{T}$ is finite.

Theorem 6. *Let $(\mathcal{S}, \longrightarrow_\alpha)$ be the abstract transition system of a program in* $\mathtt{Actor^{sl}}$*. Then $(\mathcal{S}, \longrightarrow_\alpha, \preceq_\alpha)$ is a well-structured transition system.*

In the light of Theorem 6, it is possible to decide the termination for the abstract transition system of a stateless program. As termination is preserved by the abstract semantics (see Proposition 1) we can conclude that termination is also decidable for the concrete transition system of a stateless program.

We complete this section by demonstrating the decidability of control-state reachability for the well-structured transition system $(\mathcal{S}, \longrightarrow_\alpha, \preceq_\alpha)$ of a stateless program (see the definition after Lemma 2). The proof is similar to the one of Theorem 5, with the difference that it is needed a more sophisticated algorithm for computing the predecessors of a configuration.

Lemma 3. *Let $(\mathcal{S}, \longrightarrow_\alpha, \preceq_\alpha)$ be a well-structured transition system of a program in* $\mathtt{Actor^{sl}}$*, and let $\mathtt{S} \in \mathcal{S}$. Then there is a finite set $\mathcal{X}$ such that, for every $\mathtt{S}' \succeq_\alpha \mathtt{S}$ and $\mathtt{S}'' \in \mathit{Pred}(\mathtt{S}')$, there is $\mathtt{T} \in \mathcal{X}$ with $\mathtt{T} \preceq_\alpha \mathtt{S}''$. $\mathcal{X}$ can be effectively computed.*

It turns out that control-state reachability is decidable for the abstract transition system of $\mathtt{Actor^{sl}}$. This entails the decidability of process reachability. In fact, given a process P, the reachability of a configuration $A \rhd (P', \varphi, q), \mathtt{S}$ with P' equal to P up-to renaming of variables and actor names can be solved in the abstract transition system simply by checking the control-state reachability of at least one of the following states. Let $\mathtt{C}_1, \ldots, \mathtt{C}_n$ be the actor classes of the considered actor system and let $A_1, \cdots, A_n$ be such that $A_i \in \mathtt{C}_i$. We consider the following finite set of states:

$$\mathcal{S} = \{\ A_i \rhd (Q_i, \varnothing, \varepsilon) \mid 1 \leq i \leq n, \quad Q_i \text{ is a suffix of a method definition in the class } \mathtt{C}_i \text{ and it is equal to } P \text{ up-to renaming}\ \}$$

From the decidability of the process reachability problem for the abstract transition system we can conclude its decidability for the concrete semantics. By Proposition 1, this problem is preserved by the abstract semantics. Note that control-state reachability is not preserved by the abstract semantics. In fact, the abstract transition system is guaranteed to execute the same method invocations, but this can be done in a different order and also by different actors.

6 Conclusions

To the best of our knowledge this paper contains a first systematic study on the computational power of Actor-based languages. We have focussed on the pure asynchronous queueing and dequeuing of method calls between actors in the context of a nominal calculus which features the dynamic creation of variable names that can be passed around.

References

1. Abdulla, P.A., Cerans, K., Jonsson, B., Tsay, Y.-K.: General decidability theorems for infinite-state systems. In: LICS, pp. 313–321. IEEE (1996)
2. Agha, G.: The Structure and Semantics of Actor Languages. In: de Bakker, J.W., de Roever, W.-P., Rozenberg, G. (eds.) REX 1989. LNCS, vol. 430, pp. 1–59. Springer, Heidelberg (1990)
3. Agha, G., Mason, I., Smith, S., Talcott, C.: A foundation for actor computation. Journal of Functional Programming 7, 1–72 (1997)
4. Armstrong, J.: Erlang. Communications of ACM 53(9), 68–75 (2010)
5. Chang, P.-H., Agha, G.: Supporting reconfigurable object distribution for customized web applications. In: SAC, pp. 1286–1292 (2007)
6. Chang, P.-H., Agha, G.: Towards Context-Aware Web Applications. In: Indulska, J., Raymond, K. (eds.) DAIS 2007. LNCS, vol. 4531, pp. 239–252. Springer, Heidelberg (2007)
7. Cheong, E., Lee, E.A., Zhao, Y.: Viptos: a graphical development and simulation environment for tinyos-based wireless sensor networks. In: SenSys, pp. 302–302 (2005)
8. de Boer, F., Jaghoori, M., Laneve, C., Zavattaro, G.: Decidability Problems for Actor Systems. Technical report (2012), cs.unibo.it/~laneve
9. de Boer, F.S., Grabe, I., Steffen, M.: Termination detection for active objects. Journal of Logic and Algebraic Programming (2012)
10. Finkel, A., Schnoebelen, P.: Well-structured transition systems everywhere! Theoretical Computer Science 256, 63–92 (2001)
11. Giachino, E., Laneve, C.: Analysis of Deadlocks in Object Groups. In: Bruni, R., Dingel, J. (eds.) FMOODS/FORTE 2011. LNCS, vol. 6722, pp. 168–182. Springer, Heidelberg (2011)
12. Haller, P., Odersky, M.: Scala actors: Unifying thread-based and event-based programming. Theoretical Computer Science 410(2-3), 202–220 (2009)
13. Hewitt, C.: Procedural embedding of knowledge in planner. In: Proc. the 2nd International Joint Conference on Artificial Intelligence, pp. 167–184 (1971)
14. Johnsen, E.B., Owe, O.: An asynchronous communication model for distributed concurrent objects. Software and System Modeling 6(1), 39–58 (2007)
15. Karmani, R.K., Shali, A., Agha, G.: Actor frameworks for the jvm platform: a comparative analysis. In: PPPJ, pp. 11–20. ACM (2009)
16. Lee, E.A., Liu, X., Neuendorffer, S.: Classes and inheritance in actor-oriented design. ACM Transactions in Embedded Computing Systems 8(4) (2009)

17. Lee, E.A., Neuendorffer, S., Wirthlin, M.J.: Actor-oriented design of embedded hardware and software systems. Journal of Circuits, Systems, and Computers 12(3), 231–260 (2003)
18. Meyer, R.: On Boundedness in Depth in the pi-Calculus. In: Ausiello, G., Karhumäki, J., Mauri, G., Ong, L. (eds.) IFIP TCS 2008. IFIP, vol. 273, pp. 477–489. Springer, Boston (2008)
19. Minsky, M.: Computation: finite and infinite machines. Prentice Hall (1967)
20. Wies, T., Zufferey, D., Henzinger, T.A.: Forward Analysis of Depth-Bounded Processes. In: Ong, L. (ed.) FOSSACS 2010. LNCS, vol. 6014, pp. 94–108. Springer, Heidelberg (2010)

Author Index